Iain McKay has done a superb job collecting Proudhon's most important, provocative and influential writings in one volume, many of which have not previously appeared in English. This collection will become an indispensable source book for anyone interested in Proudhon's ideas and the origins of the socialist and anarchist movements in 19th century Europe.

—**Robert Graham**, editor of *Anarchism: A Documentary History of Libertarian Ideas, Vols 1–3*

Even Proudhon's harshest critics, including Marx, agreed that his passion for liberty and equality was inspiring, and it's time to re-evaluate his substantive work. This reader is the ideal place to begin. Iain McKay's introduction offers a sure-footed guide through the misconceptions surrounding Proudhon's thought, and the rich collection spans his years as an activist and theorist. Unlike much of the polemical argument around Proudhon, this volume will open up debate, rather than shut it down; it will let readers make up their own minds about the "father" of anarchism.

—**Mark Leier**, author of *Bakunin: The Creative Passion*

Pierre-Joseph Proudhon was a hugely influential figure in French working-class history and in the history of the French Left, as well as being widely acknowledged as the "father of anarchy," as Kropotkin once put it. Yet the precise nature of his political thought, his relation to anarchism as it came to be understood after his death and the value of his contribution have been the focus of much (often acrimonious) debate. He has over the years been accused of being eclectic, inconsistent, self-contradictory and reactionary—not to mention the reductionist Marxist criticism of being a petit bourgeois. A number of scholars in recent years have argued—as does Iain McKay in his introduction to this volume—that much of what has been said about Proudhon has been based on ignorance and received ideas, as well as questionable methodological approaches, and they have proposed a re-evaluation of his ideas. However, one of the problems hitherto for those wishing to return to the sources to see for themselves what Proudhon actually wrote has been the lack of English translations of most of his works. This anthology of Proudhon's writings, the most comprehensive yet published, is therefore extremely welcome and an important addition to the growing literature on Proudhon, and will hopefully make possible a more rigorous and fruitful engagement with this important figure.

—**David Berry**, author of *A History of the French Anarchist Movement 1917–1945*

Publisher, political prisoner, political economist, and (briefly) parliamentarian, Proudhon was a pillar of nineteenth century socialism. His insights into economic and political issues led the young Karl Marx to call him "the most consistent and wisest of socialist writers." His libertarian vision of an egalitarian society based on self-management and federalism deeply influenced Mikhail Bakunin, founder of anarchism, who called him "the master of us all." Today, Proudhon's strategy for change—the creation of an alternative economy, created from below, through co-operatives—influences movements across the world. Yet his enduring influence and importance has been shrouded by caricature and his works remain difficult to obtain. This remarkable collection thus makes a vital contribution to the task of left and labour renewal in the post-Soviet world. Iain McKay has provided, at last, the definitive English-language collection of the master's masterworks, framed by a powerful introduction and insightful notes.

—**Lucien van der Walt**, co-author of *Black Flame: The Revolutionary Class Politics of Anarchism and Syndicalism*

In the English-speaking world, Proudhon is one of the best known but least well understood anarchists, largely because the bulk of his work is not available in translation. Iain McKay's comprehensive anthology, which draws on Proudhon's correspondence as well as his published work, fills a real gap and should encourage new readers to engage with his work and appreciate both the positive contribution he has made to anarchist thinking and the enormity of his influence on the anarchist movement.

—**Ruth Kinna**, author of *Anarchism: A Beginner's Guide* and editor of *Anarchist Studies*

From Iain McKay, principal author of the standard anarchist educational resource *An Anarchist FAQ*, comes *Property is Theft! A Pierre-Joseph Proudhon Anthology*. Besides replacing Stewart Edwards's *Selected Writings* as the definitive Proudhon reader after several decades, it is clearly superior to Edwards's collection. First, instead of Edwards's unsatisfactory approach of compiling snippets of text under subject headings in a sort of Bartlett's quotations format, McKay's anthology provides complete digests of Proudhon's texts with important passages in unbroken form. Second, this collection includes a wide variety of new texts, many of them translated especially for the present effort. This new anthology may well serve as the definitive reference source for as long as *Selected Writings* did. This should be cause for excitement and eager anticipation among Proudhon enthusiasts everywhere.

—**Kevin Carson**, author of *Studies in Mutualist Political Economy*

# PROPERTY IS THEFT!

## A PIERRE-JOSEPH PROUDHON ANTHOLOGY

*Pierre-Joseph Proudhon*

# PROPERTY IS THEFT!

# A PIERRE-JOSEPH PROUDHON ANTHOLOGY

*Edited by*
*Iain McKay*

AK Press Publishing & Distribution | 2011

*Property Is Theft!*
*A Pierre-Joseph Proudhon Anthology*
Edited and Introduced by Iain McKay

Introduction and Appendix © 2011 Iain McKay

This edition © 2011 AK Press (Edinburgh, Oakland, Baltimore)

ISBN-13: 978-1-84935-024-2
Library of Congress Control Number: 2010925767

| AK Press | AK Press UK |
|---|---|
| 674-A 23rd Street | PO Box 12766 |
| Oakland, CA 94612 | Edinburgh EH8 9YE |
| USA | Scotland |
| www.akpress.org | www.akuk.com |
| akpress@akpress.org | ak@akdin.demon.co.uk |

The above addresses would be delighted to provide you with the latest AK Press
distribution catalog, which features several thousand books, pamphlets, zines,
audio and video recordings, and gear, all published or distributed by AK Press.
Alternately, visit our websites to browse the catalog and find out
the latest news from the world of anarchist publishing:
www.akpress.org | www.akuk.com
revolutionbythebook.akpress.org

Printed in Canada on 100% recycled, acid-free paper with union labor.

Cover design by John Yates | www.stealworks.com
Interior by Margaret Killjoy | www.birdsbeforethestorm.net

*I dedicate this book to my daughters.*

*May it show the importance of being bilingual!*

# CONTENTS

# INTRODUCTION
## GENERAL IDEA OF THE REVOLUTION IN THE 21ST CENTURY

*But then came Proudhon: the son of a peasant, and, by his works and instinct, a hundred times more revolutionary than all the doctrinaire and bourgeois Socialists, he equipped himself with a critical point of view, as ruthless as it was profound and penetrating, in order to destroy all their systems. Opposing liberty to authority, he boldly proclaimed himself an Anarchist by way of setting forth his ideas in contradistinction to those of the State Socialists.*
—Michael Bakunin[1]

IN 1840, TWO SHORT EXPRESSIONS, A MERE SEVEN WORDS, TRANSFORMED socialist politics forever. One, only four words long, put a name to a tendency within the working class movement: "I am an Anarchist." The other, only three words long, presented a critique and a protest against inequality which still rings: "Property is Theft!"

Their author, Pierre-Joseph Proudhon (1809–1865), was a self-educated son of a peasant family and his work, *What Is Property?*, ensured he became one of the leading socialist thinkers of the nineteenth century. From his works and activity, the libertarian[2] movement was born: that form of

---

1    *The Political Philosophy of Bakunin* (New York: Free Press, 1953), 278.

2    Sadly, it is necessary to explain what we mean by "libertarian" as this term has been appropriated by the free-market capitalist right. Socialist use of libertarian dates from 1858 when it was first used by communist-anarchist Joseph Déjacque as a synonym for anarchist for his paper *La Libertaire, Journal du Mouvement Social*. This usage became more commonplace in the 1880s and 1895 saw leading anarchists Sébastien Faure and Louise Michel publish *La Libertaire* in France (Max Nettlau,

socialism based on "the denial of Government and of Property."[3] It would be no exaggeration to state that if you do not consider property as "theft" and "despotism" and oppose it along with the state then you are not a libertarian. As George Woodcock summarised:

"*What is Property?* embraces the core of nineteenth century anarchism... all the rest of later anarchism is there, spoken or implied: the conception of a free society united by association, of workers controlling the means of production. Later Proudhon was to elaborate other aspects: the working class political struggle as a thing of its own, federalism and decentralism as a means of re-shaping society, the commune and the industrial association as the important units of human intercourse, the end of frontiers and nations. But *What is Property?...* remains the foundation on which the whole edifice of nineteenth century anarchist theory was to be constructed."[4]

Michael Bakunin, who considered the "illustrious and heroic socialist"[5] as a friend, proclaimed that "Proudhon is the master of us all."[6] For Peter Kropotkin, the leading theoretician of communist-anarchism of his day, Proudhon laid "the foundations of Anarchism"[7] and became a socialist after reading his work. Benjamin Tucker, America's foremost individualist anarchist thinker, considered Proudhon as both "the father of the Anarchistic school of socialism" and "the Anarchist *par excellence.*"[8] Alexander Herzen, leading populist thinker and father of Russian socialism, praised Proudhon's "powerful and vigorous thought" and stated his "works constitute a revolution in the history not only of

*A Short History of Anarchism* [London: Freedom Press, 1995], 75–6, 145, 162). By the end of the 19th century libertarian was used as an alternative for anarchist internationally. The right-wing appropriation of the term dates from the 1950s and, in wider society, from the 1970s. Given that property is at its root and, significantly, property always trumps liberty in that ideology, anarchists suggest a far more accurate term would be "propertarian" (See my "150 Years of Libertarian," *Freedom* 69: 23–24 [2008]). We will use the term *libertarian* in its original, correct, usage as an alternative for anti-state socialist.

3    Proudhon, *General Idea of the Revolution in the Nineteenth Century* (London: Pluto Press, 1989), 100.

4    "On Proudhon's 'What is Property?'" (*The Raven* 31 [Autumn 1995]), 21.

5    *The Basic Bakunin: Writings 1869–1871* (Buffalo, NY: Prometheus Books, 1992), Robert M. Cutler (ed.), 105.

6    Quoted in George Woodcock, *Anarchism: A History of Libertarian Ideas and Movements* (Harmondsworth: Penguin Books, 1986), 127.

7    "Modern Science and Anarchism" in *Evolution and Environment* (Montréal: Black Rose, 1995), 27.

8    *Instead of a Book: By a Man Too Busy to Write One* (New York: Haskell House Publishers, 1969), 391.

socialism but also French logic."[9] Leo Tolstoy greatly admired and was heavily influenced by Proudhon, considering his "property is theft" as "an absolute truth" which would "survive as long as humanity."[10] For leading anarcho-syndicalist thinker Rudolf Rocker, Proudhon was "one of the most intellectually gifted and certainly the most many-sided writer of whom modern socialism can boast."[11]

Historian Robert Tomes notes that Proudhon was "the greatest intellectual influence on French socialism" whose "ideas had durable influence on the working-class elite"[12] while Julian P. W. Archer considered him "the pre-eminent socialist of mid-nineteenth century France."[13] Sharif Gemie recounts that for many workers in France "Proudhon was the living symbol of working class self-emancipation."[14] His ideas "anticipated all those later movements in France which, like the revolutionary syndicalists during the late nineteenth century and the students of 1968, demanded *l'autogestion ouvrière*. Their joint demand was that the economy be controlled neither by private enterprise nor by the state (whether democratic or totalitarian), but by the producers."[15] Even Friedrich Engels had to admit that Proudhon had "a preponderating place among the French Socialists of his epoch."[16]

The aim of this anthology is to show why Proudhon influenced so many radicals and revolutionaries, and why Proudhon should be read today. His work marks the beginning of anarchism as a named socio-economic theory and the libertarian ideas Proudhon championed (such as anti-statism, anti-capitalism, self-management, possession, socialisation, communal-economic federalism, decentralisation, and so forth) are as important today as they were in the 19th century.

---

9    *My Past and Thoughts: The Memoirs of Alexander Herzen* (Berkeley, California: University of California Press, 1982), 416, 417.

10   Quoted in Jack Hayward, *After the French Revolution: Six Critics of Democracy and Nationalism* (Hemel Hempstead: Harvester Wheatsheaf, 1991), 213.

11   *Anarcho-Syndicalism: Theory and Practice* (Edinburgh/Oakland: AK Press, 2004), 4–5.

12   *The Paris Commune 1871* (Harlow/New York: Addison Wesley Longman, 1999), 91, 73.

13   *The First International in France, 1864–1872: Its Origins, Theories, and Impact* (Lanham/Oxford: University Press of America, Inc, 1997), 23.

14   *French Revolutions, 1815–1914: An Introduction* (Edinburgh: Edinburgh University Press, 1999), 196.

15   K. Steven Vincent, *Pierre-Joseph Proudhon and the Rise of French Republican Socialism* (Oxford: Oxford University Press, 1984), 165.

16   "Preface," Karl Marx, *The Poverty of Philosophy* (Amherst, NY: Prometheus Books, 1995), 9.

# PROUDHON'S IDEAS

ANARCHISM DID NOT spring ready-made from Proudhon's head in 1840. Nor, for that matter, did Proudhon's own ideas! This is to be expected: he was breaking new ground in terms of theory, creating the foundations upon which other anarchists would build.

His ideas developed and evolved as he thought through the implications of his previous insights. Certain ideas mentioned in passing in earlier works (such as workers' self-management) come to the fore later, while others (such as federalism) are discussed years after *What Is Property?*. His ideas also reflected, developed and changed with the social and political context (most notably, the 1848 revolution and its aftermath). However, "contrary to persistent legend, Proudhon was not the egregious eccentric who continually contradicted himself... Proudhon had a consistent vision of society and its need... which revolves around his desire to instil a federal arrangement of workers' associations and to instil a public regard for republican virtue."[17]

Regardless of the attempts by both the propertarian right and the authoritarian left to reduce it simply to opposition to the state, anarchism has always presented a critique of state *and* property as well as other forms of oppression.[18] All are interrelated and cannot be separated without making a mockery of libertarian analysis and history:

> *Capital*... in the political field is analogous to *government*...
> The economic idea of capitalism, the politics of government
> or of authority, and the theological idea of the Church are
> three identical ideas, linked in various ways. To attack one
> of them is equivalent to attacking all of them... What capital
> does to labour, and the State to liberty, the Church does to
> the spirit. This trinity of absolutism is as baneful in practice
> as it is in philosophy. The most effective means for oppressing
> the people would be simultaneously to enslave its body, its
> will and its reason.[19]

Proudhon's two key economic ideas are free credit and workers' associations. To quote economist John Kenneth Galbraith's excellent summary:

> Scholars have regularly assigned Proudhon a position of
> importance in the history of socialism, syndicalism and
> anarchism but not in the history of economic theory. It is

---

17    Vincent, 3–4.

18    This can be seen from Proudhon's defining work of 1840, entitled *What Is Property?* not *What Is the State?*.

19    Quoted in Nettlau, 43–44.

a distinction without merit. Two ideas of influence can be found in the modern residue of Proudhon's theories. One is the belief, perhaps the instinct, that there is a certain moral superiority in the institution of the co-operative. Or the worker-owned plant. When farmers unite to supply themselves with fertilisers, oil or other farm supplies, and consumers to provide themselves with groceries, the ideas of Proudhon are heard in praise. So also when steel workers come together to take over and run a senescent mill... And Proudhon is one among many parents of the continuing faith in monetary magic—of the belief that great reforms can be accomplished by hitherto undiscovered designs for financial or monetary innovation or manipulation.[20]

In terms of politics, his vision was one of federations of self-governing communities. He repeatedly stressed the importance of decentralisation and autonomy to ensure effective liberty for the people. "Among these liberties," Proudhon argued, "one of the most important is that of the commune." A country "by its *federations*, by municipal and provincial independence... attested its local liberties, corollary and complement of the liberty of the citizen. Without the liberty of the commune, the individual is only half free, the feudal yoke is only half broken, public right is equivocal, public integrity is comprised."[21]

He called this socio-economic vision "mutualism," a term Proudhon did not invent.[22] The workers' organisations in Lyon, where Proudhon stayed in 1843, were described as *mutuellisme* and *mutuelliste* in the 1830s. There is "close similarity between the associational ideal of Proudhon... and the program of the Lyon Mutualists" and it is "likely that Proudhon was able to articulate his positive program more coherently because of the example of the silk workers of Lyon. The socialist ideal that he championed was already being realised, to a certain extent, by such workers."[23]

In short, Proudhon "was working actively to replace capitalist statism with an anti-state socialism in which workers manage their own affairs without exploitation or subordination by a 'revolution from below.'"[24]

---

20    *A History of Economics: The Past As The Present* (London: Hamilton, 1987), 99.

21    Quoted in Vincent, 212–3.

22    Mutualism was first used by Fourier, the French utopian socialist, in 1822 while "mutualist" was coined by a follower of Robert Owen in America four years later (Arthur E. Bestor, Jr., "The Evolution of the Socialist Vocabulary," *Journal of the History of Ideas* 9:3 [1948]: 272–3). Proudhon first used the term in 1846's *System of Economic Contradictions*.

23    Vincent, 164.

24    Hayward, 191.

ON PROPERTY

Proudhon's analysis of property was seminal. The distinction he made between use rights and property rights, possession and property, laid the ground for both libertarian and Marxist communist perspectives. It also underlay his analysis of exploitation and his vision of a libertarian society. Even Marx admitted its power:

> Proudhon makes a critical investigation—the first resolute,
> ruthless, and at the same time scientific investigation—of the
> basis of political economy, private property. This is the great
> scientific advance he made, an advance which revolutionises
> political economy and for the first time makes a real science
> of political economy possible.[25]

Proudhon's critique rested on two key concepts. Firstly, property allowed the owner to exploit its user ("property is theft"[26]). Secondly, that property created authoritarian and oppressive social relationships between the two ("property is despotism"). These are interrelated, as it is the relations of oppression that property creates which allows exploitation to happen and the appropriation of our common heritage by the few gives the rest little alternative but to agree to such domination and let the owner appropriate the fruits of their labour.

Proudhon's genius and the power of his critique was that he took all the defences of, and apologies for, property and showed that, logically, they could be used to attack that institution. By treating them as absolute and universal as its apologists treated property itself, he showed that they undermined property rather than supported it.[27]

To claims that property was a natural right, he explained that the essence of such rights was their universality and that private property ensured that this right could not be extended to all. To those who argued that property was required to secure liberty, Proudhon rightly objected that "if the liberty of man is sacred, it is equally sacred in all individuals; that, if it needs property for its objective action, that is, for its life, the appropriation of material is

---

25  *Marx-Engels Collected Works*, 4: 32. Moreover: "Not only does Proudhon write in the interest of the proletarians, he is himself a proletarian, an *ouvrier*. His work is a scientific manifesto of the French proletariat" (41).

26  Louis Blanc's claim, repeated by Marx, that Proudhon took this phrase from J.P. Brissot de Warville, a Girondin during the Great French Revolution, is thoroughly debunked by Robert L. Hoffman (*Revolutionary Justice: The Social and Political Theory of P-J Proudhon* [Urbana: University of Illinois, 1969], 46–48).

27  In addition, following the best traditions of French rationalism Proudhon also tried to prove that it was contradictory (and so "impossible").

equally necessary for all."[28] To claims that labour created property, he noted that most people have no property to labour on and the product of such labour was owned by capitalists and landlords rather than the workers who created it. As for occupancy, he argued that most owners do not occupy all the property they own while those who do use and occupy it do not own it.

Proudhon showed that the defenders of property had to choose between self-interest and principle, between hypocrisy and logic. If it is right for the initial appropriation of resources to be made (by whatever preferred rationale) then, by that very same reason, it is right for others in the same and subsequent generations to abolish private property in favour of a system which respects the liberty of all rather than a few ("If the right of life is equal, the right of labour is equal, and so is the right of occupancy.") This means that "those who do not possess today are proprietors by the same title as those who do possess; but instead of inferring therefrom that property should be shared by all, I demand, in the name of general security, its entire abolition."[29]

For Proudhon, the notion that workers are free when capitalism forces them to seek employment was demonstrably false. He was well aware that in such circumstances property "violates equality by the rights of exclusion and increase, and freedom by despotism." It has "perfect identity with robbery" and the worker "has sold and surrendered his liberty" to the proprietor. Anarchy was "the absence of a master, of a sovereign" while proprietor was "synonymous" with "sovereign" for he "imposes his will as law, and suffers neither contradiction nor control." Thus "property is despotism" as "each proprietor is sovereign lord within the sphere of his property"[30] and so freedom and property were incompatible:

> The civilised labourer who bakes a loaf that he may eat a slice
> of bread, who builds a palace that he may sleep in a stable,
> who weaves rich fabrics that he may dress in rags, who pro-
> duces every thing that he may dispense with every thing,—is
> not free. His employer, not becoming his associate in the ex-
> change of salaries or services which takes place between them,
> is his enemy.[31]

Hence the pressing need, if we really seek liberty for all, to abolish property and the authoritarian social relationships it generates. With wage-workers and tenants, property is "the right to use [something] by his neighbour's labour" and so resulted in "the exploitation of man by man" for to "live as

---

28    *What Is Property?* (London: William Reeves Bookseller Ltd., 1969), 84–5.
29    *What Is Property?*, 77, 66.
30    *What Is Property?*, 251, 130, 264, 266, 259, 267.
31    *What Is Property?*, 142.

a proprietor, or to consume without producing, it is necessary, then, to live upon the labour of another."[32]

## ON EXPLOITATION

Proudhon's aim "was to rescue the working masses from capitalist exploitation."[33] However, his analysis of exploitation has been misunderstood and, in the case of Marxists, distorted. J.E. King's summary is sadly typical:

> Marx's main priority was to confront those 'utopian' social-
> ists (especially... Proudhon in France) who saw inequality of
> exchange as the *only* source of exploitation, and believed that
> the establishment of equal exchange in isolation from changes
> in production relations was sufficient in itself to eliminate
> all sources of income other than the performance of labour...
> [Marx proved that] exploitation in production was sufficient
> to explain the existence of non-wage incomes.[34]

Yet anyone familiar with Proudhon's ideas would know that he was well aware that exploitation occurred at the point of production. Like Marx, but long before him, Proudhon argued that workers produced more value than they received in wages:

> Whoever labours becomes a proprietor... And when I say pro-
> prietor, I do not mean simply (as do our hypocritical econo-
> mists) proprietor of his allowance, his salary, his wages,—I
> mean proprietor of the value he creates, and by which the
> master alone profits... *The labourer retains, even after he has
> received his wages, a natural right in the thing he has produced.*[35]

---

32  *What Is Property?*, 395, 129, 293.

33  *Selected Writings of Pierre-Joseph Proudhon* (London: MacMillan, 1969), Stewart Edwards (ed.), 80.

34  "Value and Exploitation: Some Recent Debates," *Classical and Marxian Political Economy: Essays In Honour of Ronald L. Meek* (London: Macmillan Press, 1982), Ian Bradley and Michael Howard (eds.), 180. Ironically, Marx was not above invoking unequal exchange to explain exploitation: "Capital is concentrated social force, while the workman has only to dispose of his working force. The contract between capital and labour can therefore never be struck on equitable terms, equitable even in the sense of a society which places the ownership of the material means of life and labour on one side and the vital productive energies on the opposite side" (*The First International and After: Political Writings Volume 3* [London: Penguin Books, 1992], 91).

35  *What Is Property?*, 123–4.

Property meant "another shall perform the labour while [the proprietor] receives the product." Thus the "free worker produces ten; for me, thinks the proprietor, he will produce twelve" and thus to "satisfy property, the labourer must first produce beyond his needs."[36] This is why "property is theft!"[37] Proudhon linked rising inequality to the hierarchical relationship of the capitalist workplace:

> I have shown the contractor, at the birth of industry, negotiating on equal terms with his comrades, who have since become *his workmen*. It is plain, in fact, that this original equality was bound to disappear through the advantageous position of the master and the dependence of the wage-workers.[38]

Thus unequal exchange did not explain exploitation, rather the hierarchical relationship produced by wage-labour does. This can be seen from another key aspect of Proudhon's analysis, what he termed "collective force." This was "[o]ne of the reasons Proudhon gave for rejecting 'property' [and] was to become an important motif of subsequent socialist thought," namely that "collective endeavours produced an additional value" which was "unjustly appropriated by the *proprietaire*."[39] To quote Proudhon:

> It is an economic power of which I was, I believe, the first to accentuate the importance, in my first memoir upon *Property* [in 1840]. A hundred men, uniting or combining their forces, produce, in certain cases, not a hundred times, but two hundred, three hundred, a thousand times as much. This is what I have called *collective force*. I even drew from this an argument... that it is not sufficient to pay merely the wages of a given number of workmen, in order to acquire their product legitimately; that

---

36   *What Is Property?*, 98, 184–5.

37   Compare this to Engels's explanation that the "value of the labour-power, and the value which that labour-power creates in the labour-process, are two different magnitudes" and so if "the labourer each day *costs* the owner of money the value of the product of six hours' labour" and works twelve, he "*hands over*" to the capitalist "each day the value of the product of twelve hours' labour." The difference in favour of the owner is "unpaid surplus-labour, a surplus-product." He gushes that the "solution of this problem was the most epoch-making achievement of Marx's work. It spread the clear light of day through economic domains in which socialists no less than bourgeois economists previously groped in utter darkness. Scientific socialism dates from the discovery of this solution and has been built up around it" (*Marx-Engels Collected Works* 25: 189–90).

38   *System of Economical Contradictions* (Boston: Benjamin Tucker, 1888), 202.

39   Vincent, 64–5.

they must be paid twice, thrice or ten times their wages, or an equivalent service rendered to each one of them.[40]

Proudhon's "position that property is theft locates a fundamental antagonism between producers and owners at the heart of modern society. If the direct producers are the sole source of social value which the owners of capital are expropriating, then exploitation must be the root cause of... inequality." He "located the 'power to produce without working' at the heart of the system's exploitation and difficulties very early, anticipating what Marx and Engels were later to call the appropriation of surplus value."[41]

So even a basic awareness of Proudhon's ideas would be sufficient to recognise as nonsense Marxist claims that he thought exploitation "did not occur in the labour process" and so "must come from outside of the commercial or capitalist relations, through force and fraud" or that Marx "had a very different analysis which located exploitation at the very heart of the capitalist production process."[42] Proudhon thought exploitation was inherent in wage-labour and occurred at the point of production.[43] Unsurprisingly, he sought a solution there.

## ON ASSOCIATION
Given an analysis of property that showed that it produced exploitation ("theft") and oppression ("despotism"), the question of how to end it arises. There are two options: Either abolish collective labour and return to small-scale production or find a new form of economic organisation which ensures that collective labour is neither exploited nor oppressed.

The notion that Proudhon advocated the first solution, a return to pre-capitalist forms of economy, is sadly all too common. Beginning with Marx, this notion has been vigorously propagated by Marxists with Engels in 1891 proclaiming Proudhon "the socialist of the small peasant or master craftsman."[44] The reality is different:

---

40    *General Idea of the Revolution*, 81–2.

41    John Ehrenberg, *Proudhon and His Age* (New York: Humanity Books, 1996), 56, 55.

42    Donny Gluckstein, *The Paris Commune: A Revolutionary Democracy* (London: Bookmarks, 2006), 72. Gluckstein does, implicitly, acknowledge Proudhon's real position by noting that big capitalists "could be excluded from commodity production through mutualism, or workers' co-operatives" (75). If Proudhon *really* thought that exploitation did not occur within the workplace then why did he advocate co-operatives? Why did he consistently argue for the abolition of wage labour?

43    This is *not* to suggest that Proudhon thought that exploitation *only* occurred in the workplace. Far from it! His analysis of rent and interest showed that it did, and could, occur when workers were not toiling for bosses. Usury can exist in non-capitalist economies. However, to suggest that Proudhon argued that exploitation did not happen in production is to make a travesty of his thought.

44    *The Marx-Engels Reader* (London: W.W. Norton & Co, 1978), 2nd Edition, 626.

On this issue, it is necessary to emphasise that, contrary to
the general image given in the secondary literature, Proudhon
was not hostile to large industry. Clearly, he objected to many
aspects of what these large enterprises had introduced into
society... But he was not opposed in principle to large-scale
production. What he desired was to humanise such production, to socialise it so that the worker would not be the mere
appendage to a machine. Such a humanisation of large industries would result, according to Proudhon, from the introduction of strong workers' associations. These associations would
enable the workers to determine jointly by election how the
enterprise was to be directed and operated on a day-today
basis.[45]

To quote Proudhon: "Large industry and high culture come to us by big
monopoly and big property: it is necessary in the future to make them rise
from the association."[46] He did not ignore the economic conditions around
him, including industrialisation, and noted in 1851, of a population of 36
million, 24 million were peasants and 6 million were artisans. The remaining
6 million included wage-workers for whom "workmen's associations" would
be essential as "a protest against the wage system," the "denial of the rule
of capitalists" and for "the management of large instruments of labour."[47]
Rather than seeking to turn back the clock, Proudhon was simply reflecting
and incorporating the aspirations of *all* workers in his society—an extremely
sensible position to take.[48]

This support for workers' self-management of production was raised in
1840 at the same time Proudhon proclaimed himself an anarchist. As "every
industry needs... leaders, instructors, superintendents" they "must be chosen
from the labourers by the labourers themselves, and must fulfil the conditions of eligibility" for "all accumulated capital being social property, no one
can be its exclusive proprietor."[49]

In subsequent works Proudhon expanded upon this core libertarian
position of "the complete emancipation of the workers... the abolition of

---

45   Vincent, 156.

46   Quoted in Vincent, 156.

47   *General Idea of the Revolution*, 97–8.

48   Donny Gluckstein asserts that "Proudhon wanted to return society to an earlier
     golden age" after admitting that, in 1871, "[o]lder forms of production predominat-
     ed" and conceding "the prevalence of artisans and handicraft production" in France
     (73, 69)! How you "return" to something that dominates your surroundings is not
     explained.

49   *What Is Property?*, 137, 130.

the wage worker"[50] by self-management ("In democratising us," he argued, "revolution has launched us on the path of industrial democracy"[51]). Co-operatives[52] ended the exploitation and oppression of wage-labour as "every individual employed in the association" has "an undivided share in the property of the company," "all positions are elective, and the by-laws subject to the approval of the members" and "the collective force, which is a product of the community, ceases to be a source of profit to a small number of managers and speculators: It becomes the property of all the workers."[53]

"Mutuality, reciprocity exists," Proudhon stressed, "when all the workers in an industry, instead of working for an *entrepreneur* who pays them and keeps their products, work for one another and thus collaborate in the making of a common product whose profits they share amongst themselves. Extend the principle of reciprocity as uniting the work of every group, to the Workers' Societies as units, and you have created a form of civilisation which from all points of view—political, economic and aesthetic—is radically different from all earlier civilisations." In short: "All associated and all free."[54]

Thus "the means of production should be publicly owned, production itself should be organised by workers companies."[55] As Daniel Guérin summarised:

> Proudhon and Bakunin were 'collectivists,' which is to say
> they declared themselves without equivocation in favour of
> the common exploitation, not by the State but by associated
> workers of the large-scale means of production and of the
> public services. Proudhon has been quite wrongly presented as
> an exclusive enthusiast of private property.[56]

It is important to stress that Proudhon's ideas on association as part of the solution of the social question were not invented by him. Rather, he generalised and developed what working class people were *already* doing.[57]

---

50    Quoted in Vincent, 222.

51    *Selected Writings*, 63.

52    Proudhon called these worker-managed firms various names including workers' associations, workers' companies and corporations. The latter should not be confused with modern corporations but rather referenced the producer organisations in medieval France (i.e., like a Guild in Britain).

53    *General Idea of the Revolution*, 222–3.

54    Quoted in Martin Buber, *Paths in Utopia* (London: RKP, 1949), 29–30.

55    Hayward, 201.

56    "From Proudhon to Bakunin," *The Radical Papers* (Montréal: Black Rose, 1987), Dimitrios I. Roussopoulos (ed.), 32.

57    "Associationism" was born during the waves of strikes and protests in the 1830s, with co-operatives being seen by many workers as a method of emancipation from wage labour.

As Proudhon put it in 1848, "the proof" of his mutualist ideas lay in the "current practice, revolutionary practice" of "those labour associations... which have spontaneously... been formed in Paris and Lyon."[58] These hopes were well justified as the "evidence is strong that both worker participation in management and profit sharing tend to enhance productivity and that worker-run enterprises often are more productive than their capitalist counterparts."[59]

Finally, a few words on why this fundamental position of Proudhon is not better known, indeed (at best) ignored or (at worse) denied by some commentators on his ideas. This is because state socialists like Louis Blanc advocated forms of association which Proudhon rejected as just as oppressive and exploitative as capitalism: what Proudhon termed "the principle of Association." Blanc came "under attack by Proudhon for eliminating all competition, and for fostering state centralisation of initiative and direction at the expense of local and corporative powers and intermediate associations. But the term association could also refer to the mutualist associations that Proudhon favoured, that is, those initiated and controlled from below."[60] If Blanc advocated *Association*, Proudhon supported *associations*. This is an important distinction lost on some.

## ON CREDIT

While Proudhon's views of workers' associations are often overlooked, the same cannot be said of his views on credit. For some reform of credit was all he advocated! However, for Proudhon, the socialisation and democratisation of credit was seen as one of the key means of reforming capitalism out of existence and of producing a self-employed society of artisans, farmers and co-operatives.

The Bank of the People "embodies the financial and economic aspects of modern democracy, that is, the sovereignty of the People, and of the republican motto, *Liberty, Equality, Fraternity*." Like the desired workplace associations, it also had a democratic nature with a "committee of thirty representatives" seeing "to the management of the Bank" and "chosen by the General Meeting" made up of "nominees of the general body of associates" ("elected according to industrial categories and in proportion to the number... there are in each category.")[61]

---

58   *No Gods, No Masters: An Anthology of Anarchism* (Edinburgh/Oakland: AK Press, 2005), 75.

59   David Schweickart, *Against Capitalism* (Cambridge: Cambridge University Press, 1993), 100. For a fuller discussion of co-operatives see section I.3 of *An Anarchist FAQ*, Iain McKay (ed.) (Edinburgh/Oakland: AK Press, 2008).

60   Vincent, 224–5.

61   *Selected Writings*, 75, 79.

Proudhon rightly mocked the notion that interest was a payment for abstinence[62] noting, in his exchange with the *laissez-faire* economist Frédéric Bastiat, that the capitalist lends "because he has no use for it himself, being sufficiently provided with capital without it." There is no sacrifice and so "it is society's duty to procure Gratuitous Credit for all; that, failing to do this, it will not be a society, but a conspiracy of Capitalists against Workers, a compact for purposes of robbery and murder."[63] The obvious correctness of this analysis is reflected in Keynes' admission that interest "rewards no genuine sacrifice, any more than does the rent of land. The owner of capital can obtain interest because capital is scarce, just as the owner of land can obtain rent because land is scarce. But whilst there may be intrinsic reasons for the scarcity of land, there are no intrinsic reasons for the scarcity of capital."[64]

As is clear from his exchange with Bastiat, Proudhon took care to base his arguments not on abstract ideology but on the actual practices he saw around him. He was well aware that banks issued credit and so increased the money supply in response to market demand. As such, he was an early exponent of the endogenous theory of the money supply.[65] His argument against metallic money was rooted in the fact that this legacy of the past ensured that interest remained as the supply of money, though dynamic due to credit creation, was ultimately limited by the available gold and silver deposits monopolised by capitalist banks.

In other words, Proudhon was pointing out that a money economy, one with an extensive banking and credit system, operates in a fundamentally different way than the barter economy assumed by most economics (then and now). He recognised that income from property violated the axiom that products exchanged for products. As interest rates within capitalism did not reflect any real cost and credit creation by banks violated any notion that they reflected savings, these facts suggested that interest could be eliminated as it was already an arbitrary value.

The availability of cheap credit would, Proudhon hoped, lead to the end of landlordism and capitalism. Artisans would not be crushed by interest

---

62  This mutated into a "waiting" theory although the argument is identical. The economist Alfred Marshall who popularised the change in terminology did so as the rich obviously did not abstain from anything (see section C.2.7 of *An Anarchist FAQ*).

63  *Œuvres Complètes* (Lacroix edition) 19: 197, 219.

64  *The General Theory of Employment, Interest and Money* (London: MacMillan Press, 1974), 376.

65  An endogenous money supply analysis recognises that money arises from within the economy in response to its needs rather than being determined from outside by the state or gold. So the emergence of bank notes, fractional reserve banking and credit was a spontaneous process, not planned or imposed by the state, but rather came from the profit needs of banks which, in turn, reflected the real needs of the economy. This analysis is championed by the post-Keynesian school today.

payments and so be able to survive on the market, proletarians would be able to buy their own workplaces and peasants would be able buy their land. To aid this process he also recommended that the state decree that all rent should be turned into part-payment for the property used and for public works run by workers' associations.

While these notions are generally dismissed as utopian, the reality is somewhat different. As Proudhon's ideas were shaped by the society he lived in, one where the bulk of the working class were artisans and peasants, the notion of free credit provided by mutual banks as the means of securing working class people access to the means of production was perfectly feasible. Today, economies world-wide manage to work without having money tied to specie. Proudhon's desire "to abolish the royalty of gold"[66] was no mere utopian dream—capitalism itself has done so.

Perhaps this correspondence between Proudhon's ideas on money and modern practice is not so surprising. Keynes's desire for "the euthanasia of the rentier, and, consequently, the euthanasia of the cumulative oppressive power of the capitalist to exploit the scarcity-value of capital"[67] has distinctly Proudhonian elements to it while he praised Proudhon's follower Silvio Gesell.[68] Sadly, only the economist Dudley Dillard's essay "Keynes and Proudhon"[69] addresses any overlap between the two thinkers and even this is incomplete (it fails to discuss Proudhon's ideas on co-operatives and falsely suggests that his critique of capitalism was limited to finance capital[70]). Another area of overlap was their shared concern over reducing uncertainty in the market and stabilising the economy (by the state, in the case of Keynes, by mutualist associations for Proudhon). Both, needless to say, under-estimated the power of *rentier* interests as well as their willingness to wither away.

This abolition of gold-backed money has not lead to the other reforms Proudhon had hoped for. This is unsurprising, as this policy has been implemented to keep capitalism going and not as a wider reform strategy as expounded by the Frenchman.[71] So while the banks may issue credit and

---

66   *Œuvres Complètes* 6: 90.

67   Keynes, 376.

68   Gesell produced "an anti-Marxian socialism" which the "future will learn more from" than Marx (Keynes, 355).

69   *The Journal of Economic History* 2: 1 (1942).

70   Libertarian Marxist Paul Mattick noted in passing that Keynes shared the Frenchman's "attack upon the payment of interest" and wished to see the end of the rentier. Mattick, however, acknowledged that Keynes did not subscribe to Proudhon's desire to use free credit to fund "independent producers and workers' syndicates" as a means create an economic system "without exploitation" (*Marx and Keynes: The Limits of the Mixed Economy* [London: Merlin Press, 1971], 5–6).

71   "Proudhon viewed monetary reforms in the context of the institution of producers' associations" and so he "was not promoting a simple 'bankism', but rather advancing

central banks accommodate it with non-specie money, they are still capitalist enterprises working within a capitalist environment—they have not been turned into a Bank of the *People*. Interest was not abolished nor was there a social movement, as in the 19th century, aiming to create workers' associations. Nationalisation, not socialisation, was the preferred social reform of the post-World War II years.

The notion that a mutual bank should fund investment is also hardly utopian. The stock market is not the means by which capital is actually raised within capitalism and is largely of symbolic value (the overwhelming bulk of transactions are in shares of existing firms). Small and medium sized firms are hardly inefficient because they lack equity shares. Moreover, there is good reason to think that the stock market *hinders* economic efficiency by generating a perverse set of incentives and "the signals emitted by the stock market are either irrelevant or harmful to real economic activity." As "the stock market itself counts little or nothing as a source of finance," shareholders "have no useful role." Moreover, if the experience of capitalism is anything to go by, mutual banks will also reduce the business cycle for those countries in which banks provide more outside finance than markets have "greater growth in and stability of investment over time than the market-centred ones."[72]

All of which confirms Proudhon's arguments for mutual credit and attacks on *rentiers*. There is no need for capital markets in a system based on mutual banks and networks of co-operatives. New investments would be financed partly from internal funds (i.e., retained income) and partly from external loans from mutual banks.

The standard argument against mutual credit is that it would simply generate inflation. This misunderstands the nature of money and inflation in a capitalist economy. The notion that inflation is caused simply by there being too much money chasing too few goods and that the state simply needs to stop printing money to control it was proven completely false by the Monetarist experiments of Thatcher and Reagan. Not only could the state *not* control the money supply, changes in it were *not* reflected in subsequent changes in inflation.[73]

---

this as one element in a larger social transformation" (Vincent, 172–73). As such it was misleading for Marx to suggest in 1865 that "to consider interest-bearing capital as the principal form of capital, and to wish to make of a particular application of credit—the pretended abolition of the rate of interest—to think to make that the basis of the social transformation—that was indeed a petty chandler's fantasy." Proudhon's perspective was wider than this. It is ironic, though, to read Marx admit that there was "no doubt, there is indeed evidence to show, that the development of credit... might... serve, in certain political and economic conditions, to accelerate the emancipation of the working class" (*Poverty of Philosophy*, 200–01).

72   Doug Henwood, *Wall Street: How It Works and for Whom* (London: Verso, 1998), 292, 174–5.

73   See section C.8.3 of *An Anarchist FAQ*.

In a real capitalist economy credit is offered based on an analysis of whether the bank thinks it will get it back.[74] In a mutualist economy, credit will likewise be extended to those whom the bank thinks will increase the amount of goods and services available.[75] The Bank of the People would not just print money and hand it out in the streets,[76] it would ration credit and aim to fund investment in the real economy. This would create money and lead to debt but it adds to the goods and services in the economy as well as the capacity to service that debt. Moreover, the reduction of interest to zero would ensure more people repaid their loans as servicing debt would be easier.[77]

Finally, John Ehrenberg's assertion that 1848 saw a "subtle and important shift" in Proudhon's ideas is simply untenable. He asserts that whereas Proudhon "formerly placed primary importance on the organisation of work, he was now thinking of the organisation of credit and exchange; where he had previously made an attempt to articulate the needs of the proletariat, he was now demanding help for the petty bourgeois."[78] Yet "the organisation of credit" in Proudhon's eyes did not exclude "the organisation of labour." If anything, Proudhon's arguments for workers' associations and against wage-labour became *more*, not less, pronounced! Proudhon started to discuss "the organisation of credit" more because it reflected a shift from goals to means, from critique to practical attempts to solve the social question in the revolution of 1848.

Proudhon's letter to Louis Blanc in April 1848 suggested that "the Exchange Bank is the organisation of labour's greatest asset" and allowed "the new form of society to be defined and created among the workers."[79]

---

74   In a capitalist economy, with banks seeking profits, there is a systemic pressure on them to get caught up in waves of lending euphoria during upswings. This leads to periodic episodes of financial fragility which, in turn, lead to crisis (see section C.8 of *An Anarchist FAQ*). Similarly, loans are generally made to capitalist firms and their need for profits adds an extra level of uncertainty and fragility, also provoking crisis. Such forces would be lacking in a mutualist system based on labour-income.

75   "Since money as well as other merchandise is subject to the law of proportionality, if its quantity increases and if at the same time other products do not increase in proportion, money loses it value, and nothing, in the last analysis, is added to the social wealth" (*Œuvres Completès* 5: 89).

76   To explain how the state printing money ended up in people's pockets and so caused inflation Milton Friedman, founder of Monetarism, imagined government helicopters dropping money from the skies.

77   See section G.3.6 of *An Anarchist FAQ*. A useful post-Keynesian introduction and analysis of banking and interest can be found in Hugh Stretton's *Economics: A New Introduction* (London: Pluto Press, 2000).

78   Ehrenberg, 88.

79   *Correspondance* 2: 307, 308.

Another, written two days later, reiterated this point: "To organise credit and circulation is to increase production, to determine the new shapes of industrial society."[80] His second election manifesto of 1848 argued that workers "have organised credit among themselves" and "labour associations" have grasped "spontaneously" that the "organisation of credit and organisation of labour amount to one and the same." By organising both, the workers "would soon have wrested alienated capital back again, through their organisation and competition."[81] This was reiterated in a letter to socialist Pierre Leroux in December 1849, with credit being seen as the means to form workers' associations.[82]

Moreover, the necessity to differentiate his ideas from other socialists who advocated "the organisation of labour" (such as Louis Blanc) must also have played its part in Proudhon's use of "the organisation of credit." Given his opposition to centralised state-based systems of labour organisation it made little sense to use the same expression to describe his vision of a self-managed and decentralised socialism.

### ON THE STATE

Proudhon subjected the state to withering criticism. For some, this has become the defining aspect of his theories (not to mention anarchism in general). This is false. This opposition to the state flowed naturally from the critique of property and so anarchist anti-statism cannot be abstracted from its anti-capitalism. While recognising that the state and its bureaucracy had exploitative and oppressive interests of its own, he analysed its role as an instrument of class rule:

> In a society based on the principle of inequality of conditions,
> government, whatever it is, feudal, theocratic, bourgeois,
> imperial, is reduced, in last analysis, to a system of insurance
> for the class which exploits and owns against that which is
> exploited and owns nothing.[83]

He repeatedly pointed to its function of "protecting the nobility and upper class against the lower classes."[84] This analysis was consistent throughout his political career. In 1846 he had argued that the state "finds itself inevitably enchained to capital and directed against the proletariat."[85]

---

80   *Correspondance* 6: 372.
81   *No Gods, No Masters*, 75.
82   *Correspondance* 14: 295.
83   *Œuvres Completès* 21: 121.
84   *General Idea of the Revolution*, 286.
85   *System of Economical Contradictions*, 399. Which makes a mockery of Engels' claims that Proudhon had, in 1851, appropriated, without acknowledgement, Marx's ideas

So what was the state? For Proudhon, the state was a body above society, it was "the EXTERNAL constitution of the social power" by which the people delegate "its power and sovereignty" and so "does not govern itself; now one individual, now several, by a title either elective or hereditary, are charged with governing it, with managing its affairs, with negotiating and compromising in its name." Anarchists "deny government and the State, because we affirm that which the founders of States have never believed in, the personality and autonomy of the masses." Ultimately, "the only way to organise democratic government is to abolish government."[86]

His attacks on "Direct Legislation" and "Direct Government" in *General Idea of the Revolution* refer to using elections and referenda in a centralised state on a national scale rather than decentralised communal self-government. For Proudhon democracy could not be limited to a nation as one unit periodically picking its rulers ("nothing resembles a monarchy more than a *république unitaire*"[87]). Its real meaning was much deeper: "politicians, whatever their colours, are insurmountably repelled by anarchy which they construe as disorder: as if democracy could be achieved other than by distribution of authority and as if the true meaning of the word 'democracy' was not dismissal of government."[88]

Given this analysis, it becomes unsurprising that Proudhon did not seek political power to reform society. This was confirmed when, for a period, he was elected to the National Assembly in 1848: "As soon as I set foot in the parliamentary Sinai, I ceased to be in touch with the masses; because I was absorbed by my legislative work, I entirely lost sight of the current events... One must have lived in that isolator which is called a National Assembly to realise how the men who are most completely ignorant of the state of the country are almost always those who represent it." There was "ignorance of daily facts" and "fear of the people" ("the sickness of all those who belong to authority") for "the people, for those in power, are the enemy."[89]

---

as his own. In a letter to Marx, Engels proclaimed that he was "convinced" that the Frenchman had read *The Communist Manifesto* and Marx's *The Class Struggles in France* as "our premises on the decisive historical initiative of material production, class struggle, etc., largely adopted": "A number of points were indubitably lifted from them— e.g., that a *gouvernement* is nothing but the power of one class to repress the other, and will disappear with the disappearance of the contradictions between classes" (*Marx-Engels Collected Works* 38: 434–5). In reality, Proudhon had concluded that the state was an instrument of class power long before Marxism was invented.

86 *Œuvres Completès* 19: 11, 12, 15.

87 Quoted in Vincent, 211.

88 *No Gods, No Masters*, 57.

89 Quoted in George Woodcock, *Pierre-Joseph Proudhon: A Biography* (Montréal: Black Rose, 1987), 129.

Real change must come from "outside the sphere of parliamentarism, as sterile as it is absorbing."[90] Unsurprisingly, then, the "social revolution is seriously compromised if it comes through a political revolution"[91] and "to be in politics was to wash one's hands in shit."[92]

Thus, rather than having some idealistic opposition to the state,[93] Proudhon viewed it as an instrument of class rule which could not be captured for social reform. As David Berry suggests, "repeated evidence of the willingness of supposedly progressive republican bourgeoisie to resort to violent repression of the working classes had led Proudhon, like many of his class and generation, to lose faith in politics and the state and to put the emphasis on working-class autonomy and on the question of socio-economic organisation. For Proudhon and the mutualists, the lessons of the workers' uprising of 1830 and 1848 were that the powers of the state were merely another aspect of the powers of capital, and both were to be resisted equally strongly."[94]

## ON STATE SOCIALISM

Like other libertarians, Proudhon was extremely critical of state socialist schemes which he opposed just as much as he did capitalism: "The entire animus of his opposition to what he termed 'community' was to avoid the central ownership of property and the central control of economic and social decision-making."[95]

He particularly attacked the ideas of Jacobin socialist Louis Blanc whose *Organisation of Work* argued that social ills resulted from competition and they could be solved by eliminating it. "The Government," argued Blanc, "should be regarded as the supreme director of production, and invested with great strength to accomplish its task." The government would "raise a loan" to create social workplaces, "provide" them "with Statues" which "would have the force and form of laws" and "regulate the hierarchy of workers" (after the first year "the hierarchy would be appointed on the elective principle" by the workers in the associations). Capitalists would "receive interest for their capital" while workers would keep the remaining income.

---

90   *General Idea of the Revolution*, 45–6.

91   Quoted in Woodcock, *Proudhon*, 75.

92   Quoted in Vincent, 208.

93   Cf. Marx in "Political Indifferentism" (*Marx-Engels Collected Works* 23: 392–7).

94   *A History of the French Anarchist Movement, 1917–1945* (Westport: Greenwood Press, 2002), 16.

95   Vincent, 141. Proudhon usually termed such systems community (*la communauté*) or communism and had in mind such socialists as Henri de Saint-Simon, Charles Fourier, Robert Owen, Louis Blanc and Pierre Leroux. These are usually termed, following Marx, Utopian Socialists and generally thought of socialism as being organised around (usually highly regulated and hierarchical) communities or implemented by means of the state.

They would "destroy competition" by "availing itself of competition" as their higher efficiency would force capitalist firms to become social workplaces.[96]

Proudhon objected to this scheme on many levels. Blanc appealed "to the state for its silent partnership; that is, he gets down on his knees before the capitalists and recognises the sovereignty of monopoly." As it was run by the state, the system of workshops would hardly be libertarian as "hierarchy would result from the elective principle... as in constitutional politics... Who will make the law? The government."[97] This was because of the perspective of state socialists:

> As you cannot conceive of society without hierarchy, you
> have made yourselves the apostles of authority; worshippers
> of power, you think only of strengthening it and muzzling
> liberty; your favourite maxim is that the welfare of the people
> must be achieved in spite of the people; instead of proceeding
> to social reform by the extermination of power and politics,
> you insist on a reconstruction of power and politics.[98]

Proudhon questioned whether any regime based on "from each according to their abilities, to each according to their needs" could avoid conflict due to individuals and society disagreeing over what these were. This would result in either oppression ("What difference is there then between fraternity and the wage system?") or the society's "end from lack of associates."[99] He was also doubtful that state monopolies could efficiently allocate resources.[100] Ultimately, the problem was that reform by means of the state violated basic socialist principles:

> M. Blanc is never tired of appealing to authority, and social-
> ism loudly declares itself anarchistic; M. Blanc places power
> above society, and socialism tends to subordinate it to society;
> M. Blanc makes social life descend from above, and social-
> ism maintains that it springs up and grows from below; M.
> Blanc runs after politics, and socialism is in quest of science.

---

96  *Revolution from 1789 to 1906* (New York: Harper Torchbooks, 1962), P.W. Postgate (ed.), 186–7.

97  *System of Economical Contradictions*, 313, 269.

98  *System of Economical Contradictions*, 397.

99  *General Idea of the Revolution*, 96–7.

100 "How much does [a product] sold by the [state] administration cost? How much is it worth? You can answer the first of these questions: you need only call at the first... shop you see. But you can tell me nothing about the second, because you have no standard of comparison and are forbidden to verify by experiment ... business, made into a monopoly, necessarily costs society more than it brings in" (*System of Economical Contradictions*, 232–3).

No more hypocrisy, let me say to M. Blanc: you desire neither
Catholicism nor monarchy nor nobility, but you must have
a God, a religion, a dictatorship, a censorship, a hierarchy,
distinctions, and ranks. For my part, I deny your God, your
authority, your sovereignty, your judicial State, and all your
representative mystifications.[101]

Proudhon continually stressed that state control of the means of production
was a danger to the liberty of the worker and simply the continuation of capitalism with the state as the new boss. He rejected the call of "certain utopians" that "the Government seize trade, industry and agriculture, to add them
to its attributes and to make the French nation a nation of wage-workers."[102]
Nationalisation would simply be "more wage slavery."[103]

The net result of state socialism would be "a compact democracy, seemingly rooted in dictatorship of the masses, but wherein the masses merely
have the opportunity to consolidate universal slavery in accordance with
formulas and guide-lines borrowed from the former absolutism": "Indivisibility of power"; "Voracious centralisation"; "Systematic demolition of all
individual, corporative and local thought, these being deemed sources of
discord"; and "Inquisitorial policing."[104]

Proudhon's fears on the inefficiency of state socialism and that it would be
little more than state capitalist tyranny became all too real under Leninism.
His prediction that reformist socialism would simply postpone the abolition
of exploitation indefinitely while paying capitalists interest and dividends
was also proven all too correct (as can be seen with the British Labour Party's
post-war nationalisations).

Proudhon's polemics against state socialists have often been taken to suggest that he considered his mutualism as non-socialist (this is often generalised into anarchism as well, with a contrast often being made between it and
the wider socialist movement). Occasionally (most notably in *System of Economic Contradictions*) Proudhon used the term "socialism" to solely describe
the state socialist schemes he opposed.[105] Usually, however, he described
himself as a socialist[106] and publicly embraced the Red Flag at the start of

---

101  *System of Economical Contradictions*, 263.

102  *Œuvres Completès* 6: 12.

103  *No Gods, No Masters*, 77–8.

104  *No Gods, No Masters*, 125.

105  "As critic, having sought social laws through the negation of property, I belong to
    socialist protest... In seeking to achieve practical improvements, I repudiate social-
    ism with all my strength" (Quoted in Hayward, 183).

106  "I am a socialist" (*Selected Writings*, 195). He also considered his critique of property
    as a "socialist polemic" (*Œuvres Completès* 20: 50).

the 1848 revolution,[107] considering it "the federal standard of humanity, the symbol of universal fraternity" signifying the "Abolition of the proletariat and of servitude" and "Equality of political rights: universal suffrage."[108]

Socialism, for Proudhon, was "the final term, the complete expression of the Republic."[109] So although he criticised both centralised democracy and state socialism, he still considered himself a democrat and socialist: "We are also democracy and socialism; we may at times laugh at both the names and the personnel, but what those words cover and what those people stand for belong to us also; we must be careful of them!"[110] Proudhon stated the obvious: "Modern Socialism was not founded as a sect or church; it has seen a number of different schools."[111] Like Bakunin and Kropotkin, he argued against state socialism and called for a decentralised, self-managed, federal, bottom-up socialism: anarchism.

### ON TRANSITION

While Proudhon repeatedly called himself a revolutionary and urged a "revolution from below," he also rejected violence and insurrection. While later anarchists like Bakunin and Kropotkin embraced the class struggle, including strikes, unions and revolts, Proudhon opposed such means and preferred peaceful reform: "through Political Economy we must turn the theory of Property against Property in such a way as to create... *liberty*."[112]

Unsurprisingly, as he considered the state as being dominated by capital, the "problem before the labouring classes... consists not in capturing, but in subduing both power and monopoly,—that is, in generating from the bowels of the people, from the depths of labour, a greater authority, a more potent fact, which shall envelop capital and the state and subjugate them." For, "to combat and reduce power, to put it in its proper place in society, it is of no use to change the holders of power or introduce some variation into its workings: an agricultural and industrial combination must be found by means of which power, today the ruler of society, shall become its slave."[113]

The 1848 revolution gave Proudhon the chance to implement this strategy. On May 4th he "propose[d] that a provisional committee be set up to orchestrate exchange, credit and commerce amongst the workers" and this would "liaise with similar committees" elsewhere in France. This would be "a body representative of the proletariat..., a state within the state, in opposition

107  *Œuvres Complètes* 6: 20–1.
108  *Carnets* (Paris: Marcel Riviere, 1968) 3: 289.
109  Quoted in Vincent, 189.
110  Quoted in Henri de Lubac, *The Un-Marxian Socialist: A Study of Proudhon* (New York: Octagon Books, 1978), 29–30.
111  *Selected Writings*, 177.
112  *Selected Writings*, 151.
113  *System of Economical Contradictions*, 398, 397.

to the bourgeois representatives." He urged that "a new society be founded in the centre of the old society" by the working class for "the government can do nothing for you. But you can do everything for yourselves."[114]

Proudhon also pointed to the clubs, directly democratic neighbourhood associations grouped around political tendencies, seeing them "as the beginning for a true popular democracy, sensitive to the needs of the people."[115] As Peter Henry Aman describes it, a "newspaper close to the club movement, Proudhon's *Le Représentant du Peuple*, suggested a division of labour between clubs and National Assembly... By shedding light on social questions, the daily club discussions would prepare the National Assembly's legislative debates as 'the indispensable corollary.' This flattering vision of a dual power, with clubs representing 'the poorest and most numerous parts of the population,' apparently proved seductive."[116] In 1849 Proudhon argued that clubs "had to be organised. The organisation of popular societies was the fulcrum of democracy, the corner-stone of the republican order." These were "the one institution that democratic authorities should have respected, and not just respected but also fostered and organised."[117] As Daniel Guérin summarised, "in the midst of the 1848 Revolution," Proudhon "sketched out a minimum libertarian program: progressive reduction in the power of the State, parallel development of the power of the people from below, through what he called clubs" which today we "would call councils."[118]

These organisations would be the means of exercising popular pressure and influence onto the state to force it into implementing appropriate reforms for government "can only turn into something and do the work of the revolution insofar as it will be so invited, provoked or compelled by some power outside of itself that seizes the initiative and sets things rolling."[119] This would be combined with the creation of organisations for mutual credit and production in order to create the framework by which capitalism and the state would disappear. Proudhon "believed fervently... in the salvation

---

114  *Œuvres Complètes* 17: 25.

115  Gemie, 129.

116  *Revolution and Mass Democracy: The Paris Club Movement in 1848* (Princeton: Princeton University Press, 1975), 200–1.

117  *No Gods, No Masters*, 63.

118  *Anarchism: From Theory to Practice* (New York: Monthly Review Press, 1970), 152–3. Proudhon "demanded that a network of proletarian committees—Soviets, we might say—should be constituted to fight" the National Assembly (Postgate, 205).

119  *Œuvres Complètes* 17: 28. Interestingly, given Proudhon's opposition to economic strikes, during his discussion of "legal resistance" to oppressive governments in Chapter XVIII of *Confessions of a Revolutionary* he pointed to when the plebs walked out of Rome during their struggle with the aristocratic patricians in 494 B.C. In effect a general strike, it left the patricians rulers of an empty city. He was sure that if this were repeated centralisation would soon be replaced by federalism.

of working men, by their own efforts, through economic and social action alone" and "advocated, and to a considerable extent inspired, the undercutting of this terrain [of the state] from without by means of autonomous' working-class associations."[120] He hoped that the "proletariat, gradually dejacobinised" would seek "its share not only of direct suffrage in the affairs of society but of direct action."[121]

Over a decade later Proudhon noted that in 1848 he had "called upon the state to intervene in establishing" various "major public utilities" but "once the state had completed its task of creation" then these should not be left in its hands.[122] Rather than "fatten certain contractors," the state should create "a new kind of property" by "granting the privilege of running" public utilities "to responsible companies, not of capitalists, but of *workmen.*" Municipalities and their federations would take the initiative in setting up public works but actual control would rest with workers' co-operatives for "it becomes necessary for the workers to form themselves into democratic societies, with equal conditions for all members, on pain of a relapse into feudalism."[123] As he summarised in his notebooks:

> the abolition of the State is the last term of a series, which
> consists of an incessant diminution, by political and adminis-
> trative simplification the number of public functionaries and
> to put into the care of responsible workers' societies the works
> and services confided to the state.[124]

Thus "the most decisive result of the Revolution is, after having organised labour and property, to do away with political centralisation, in a word, with the State."[125]

This may, for some, appear as a contradiction in Proudhon's ideas for, as an anarchist, he was against the state. This would be a superficial analysis as it confuses short-term reforms and long-term social transformation. Moreover, anarchism is not purely anti-state. It is also anti-capitalist and so advocating capitalist banking or the privatisation of utilities and industries would be anti-anarchist. Proudhon was *not* advocating nationalisation (or state socialism). He simply considered limited state action to create the correct environment to allow co-operatives to flourish and to run public services and utilities as being more consistent with libertarian goals than supporting wage-labour by turning

---

120  Paul Thomas, *Karl Marx and the Anarchists* (London: Routledge & Kegan Paul plc, 1985), 177–8.

121  Quoted in Hayward, 201.

122  *The Principle of Federation* (Toronto: University of Toronto Press, 1980), 46.

123  *General Idea of the Revolution*, 151, 276–7.

124  *Carnets* 3: 293.

125  *General Idea of the Revolution*, 286.

more parts of the economy over to the capitalist class.

In the grim days of the Second Empire, when the hopes and self-activity of 1848 appeared to be crushed, Proudhon suggested encouraging investors to fund co-operatives rather than capitalist companies, seeking to encourage the industrial democracy he wished to replace the industrial feudalism of capitalism by means of the institutions of capitalism itself. In return for funds, the capitalists would receive dividends until such time as the initial loan was repaid and then the company would revert into a proper co-operative (i.e., one owned as well as operated by its workers).[126] So the optimism produced by the February Revolution that drove his more obviously anarchist works that climaxed in 1851's *General Idea of the Revolution* gave way to more cautious reforms. Significantly, in the 1860s, "Proudhon's renewed interest in socialism was precipitated... by the renewed activity of workers themselves."[127]

So, in general, Proudhon placed his hopes for introducing socialism in alternative institutions created by working class people themselves and "insisted that the revolution could only come from below, through the action of the workers themselves."[128] Joining the government to achieve that goal was, for Proudhon, contradictory and unlikely to work. The state was a centralised, top-down structure and so unable to take into account the real needs of society:

> experience testifies and philosophy demonstrates... that any
> revolution, to be effective, must be spontaneous and emanate,
> not from the heads of the authorities but from the bowels of
> the people: that government is reactionary rather than revo-
> lutionary: that it could not have any expertise in revolutions,
> given that society, to which that secret is alone revealed, does
> not show itself through legislative decree but rather through
> the spontaneity of its manifestations: that, ultimately, the only
> connection between government and labour is that labour,
> in organising itself, has the abrogation of government as its
> mission.[129]

This suggested a bottom-up approach, socialism *from below* rather than a socialism imposed by the state:

> The Revolution *from above* is the intervention of power in
> everything; it is the absolutist initiative of the State, the pure

---

126  Letter to Villiaumé, 24th January 1856 (*Correspondance* 7: 8–21).

127  Vincent, 220.

128  Vincent, 157.

129  *No Gods, No Masters*, 67.

> governmentalism of... Louis Blanc. The Revolution *from above*
> is the negation of collective activity, of popular spontane-
> ity... What serious and lasting Revolution was not made *from
> below*, by the people? How did the Revolution of 1789 come
> about? How was that of February made? The Revolution *from
> above* has never been other than the oppression of the wills of
> those below.[130]

Ultimately: "No authority is compatible with the principle of mutuality, but no authority can help bring about reform. For all authority is antithetical to equality and justice."[131]

Proudhon's overarching perspective was to avoid violence and so as well as encouraging working class self-activity he also sought to persuade the capitalist class that social reform, as well as benefiting the working class, would also benefit them in terms of a general improved standard of living and freedom and so they had no reason to oppose it.[132] The bourgeoisie were not convinced and after the experience of the Second Republic his calls upon them ceased. Instead, he completely directed his hopes for reform towards the activities of working class people themselves, in their ability to act for themselves and build just and free associations and federations. This perspective was hardly new, though. As he put it in 1842's *Warning to Proprietors*:

> Workers, labourers, men of the people, whoever you may be,
> the initiative of reform is yours. It is you who will accomplish
> that synthesis of social composition which will be the master-
> piece of creation, and you alone can accomplish it.[133]

For "revolutionary power... is no longer in the government or the National Assembly, it is in you. Only the people, acting directly, without intermedi-aries, can bring about the economic revolution."[134] It was Proudhon "who first drew to the attention of the wider public of Europe the fact that social-ism would henceforward become identified, not with the plans of utopian dreamers, but with the concrete and daily struggles of the working class."[135] It is this vision which was taken up and expanded upon by subsequent gen-erations of libertarians.

---

130  Quoted in Woodcock, *Proudhon*, 143.

131  Quoted in Alan Ritter, *The Political Thought Of Pierre-Joseph Proudhon* (Princeton: Princeton University Press, 1969), 163.

132  See, for example, "Résumé de la Question Sociale" (*Œuvres Complètes* 17: 29–30)

133  Quoted in Woodcock, *Proudhon*, 64.

134  Quoted in Hayward, 186.

135  George Woodcock, *Anarchism and Anarchists: Essays* (Kingston, Ontario: Quarry Press, 1992), 150.

As he refused to suggest that socialists should take state power themselves but, instead, organise outside political structures to create a socialist society Proudhon's various schemes of social change, while reformist, were ultimately anarchistic in nature. This became clear in his final work, *The Political Capacity of the Working Classes*, where he advocated a radical separation of the working class from bourgeois institutions, urging that they should organise themselves autonomously and reject all participation in bourgeois politics.[136] Such an alliance between the proletariat, artisans and peasantry (the plural working *classes* of the title[137]) would replace the bourgeois regime with a mutualist one as the workers became increasingly conscious of themselves as a class and of their growing political capacity. This perspective "is nothing less than the dispute which would later split Marxists from anarchists, and... socialists from syndicalists."[138]

## ON MUTUALIST SOCIETY

In place of capitalism and the state, Proudhon suggested a socio-economic federal system, a decentralised federation of self-managed associations.[139]

This federation's delegates would be mandated and subject to recall by their electors: "we can follow [our deputies] step by step in their legislative acts and their votes; we shall make them transmit our arguments and our documents; we shall indicate our will to them, and when we are discontented, we will revoke them... the imperative mandate [*mandat imperatif*], permanent revocability, are the most immediate, undeniable, consequences of the electoral principle. It is the inevitable program of all democracy."[140] Moreover, the "legislative power is not distinguished from the executive power."[141]

This system would be based on free association and would reject the "unity that tends to absorb the sovereignty of the villages, cantons, and provinces, into a central authority. Leave to each its sentiments, its affections, its beliefs,

---

136  Proudhon's arguments for electoral abstention can be found in his lengthy 1864 "Letter to Workers" (*No Gods, No Masters*, 110–122).

137  "Proudhon always wished to separate the *haute bourgeoisie* from the *petite bourgeoisie*, and to reconcile the latter with salaried workers... all the works have the same fundamental message: cooperation between the proletariat and the *petite bourgeoisie* (or 'middle-class'), exclusion of the *haute bourgeoisie* of *propriétaires-capitalistes-entrepreneurs*" (Vincent, 293).

138  Vincent, 222.

139  "If political right is inherent in man and citizen, consequently if suffrage ought to be direct, the same right is inherent as well, so much the more so, for each corporation [see note 52], for each commune or city, and the suffrage in each of these groups, ought to be equally direct" (Quoted in Vincent, 219).

140  *Œuvres Completès* 6: 58. "My opinion is that the mandate should be imperative and at any moment revocable" (*Carnets* 3: 45).

141  *Œuvres Completès* 22: 125.

its languages and its customs." "The first effect of centralisation," Proudhon stressed, "is to bring about the disappearance, in the diverse localities of the country, of all types of indigenous character; while one imagines that by this means to exalt the political life among the masses, one in fact destroys it... The fusion that is to say the annihilation, of particular nationalities where citizens live and distinguish themselves, into an abstract nationality where one can neither breathe nor recognise oneself: there is unity."[142]

He based his federalism on functional groups, in both society and economy. As his discussion of "collective force" in *"Petit Catéchisme Politique"* shows,[143] Proudhon was no individualist. He was well aware that groups were greater than the sum of their parts and viewed federalism as the best means of allowing this potential to be generated and expressed. Only that could ensure a meaningful democracy (what anarchists call self-management) rather than the current system of centralised, statist, democracy in which people elect their rulers every four years. Thus "universal suffrage provides us,... in an embryonic state, with the complete system of future society. If it is reduced to the people nominating a few hundred deputies who have no initiative... social sovereignty becomes a mere fiction and the Revolution is strangled at birth."[144] By contrast, his mutualist society was fundamentally democratic:

> We have, then, not an abstract sovereignty of the people, as
> in the Constitution of 1793 and subsequent constitutions, or
> as in Rousseau's Social Contract, but an effective sovereignty
> of the working, reigning, governing masses... how could it be
> otherwise if they are in charge of the whole economic system
> including labour, capital, credit, property and wealth?[145]

Initially, Proudhon focused on economic federalism. In his *Programme révolutionnaire* of early 1848 he "had spoken of organising society into democratically controlled groups of workers and professionals. These would form a congress which would determine how to deal with those issues of a national scope beyond the competency of any one category."[146] However, three years later, in *General Idea of the Revolution*, he placed communes at the heart of his agricultural reforms as well as for public works. After 1852 he became

---

142  Quoted in Vincent, 211, 219.

143  *De La Justice dans La Révolution et dans L'Église*, 4th Study.

144  *Selected Writings*, 123.

145  *Selected Writings*, 116–7.

146  Vincent, 210. Specifically: "it is when the representative of the people will be the expression of organised labour that the people will have a true representation... Outside of that, one had nothing but deception, impotence, waste, corruption, despotism." Moreover: "The State, in a well organised society, must be reduced... to nothing" (*Œuvres Complètes* 17: 73).

more explicit, adding a geographical federalism to economic federalism. The two cannot be considered in isolation:

> Proudhon placed socioeconomic relations on as high a level (or higher) than political ones. Proudhon's... federalism... was to apply to all public dimensions of society. A just society required the autonomy of workshops *and* of communes: advancement on one level alone had little chance of success. Without political federalism, he warned, economic federalism would be politically impotent... Workers' associations would be ineffective in a political environment which encouraged meddling by the central administration. Conversely, without economic mutualism, political federalism would remain impotent and precarious... and would degenerate back into centralism. In short, it was necessary that federalism be both professional and regional, both social and political.[147]

There were three alternatives: capitalism ("monopoly and what follows"), state socialism ("exploitation by the State") or "a solution based on equality,—in other words, the organisation of labour, which involves the negation of political economy and the end of property."[148] Rejecting the first two, Proudhon favoured *socialisation*,[149] genuine common-ownership and free access of the means of production and land.[150] The "land is indispensable to our existence, consequently a common thing, consequently insusceptible of appropriation" and "all capital, whether material or mental, being the result of collective labour, is, in consequence, collective property."[151] Self-managed workers' associations would run industry. In short:

> Under the law of association, transmission of wealth does not apply to the instruments of labour, so cannot become a cause of inequality... We are socialists... under universal association, ownership of the land and of the instruments of labour is *social* ownership... We want the mines, canals, railways handed over to democratically organised workers' associations... We want these associations to be models for agriculture, industry

---

147  Vincent, 216.

148  *System of Economical Contradictions*, 253.

149  This should not be confused with *nationalisation*. See section I.3.3 of *An Anarchist FAQ*.

150  As Proudhon stressed in a letter to Pierre Leroux: "it does not follow at all... that I want to see individual ownership and non-organisation of the instruments of labour endure for all eternity. I have never penned nor uttered any such thing: and have argued the opposite a hundred times over" (*Correspondance*, 14: 293).

151  *What Is Property?*, 107, 153.

and trade, the pioneering core of that vast federation of companies and societies, joined together in the common bond of the democratic and social Republic.[152]

Against property, Proudhon argued for possession. This meant free access to the resources required to live and the inability to bar access to resources you claimed to own but did not use. Those who used a resource (land, tools, dwelling, workplace) should control both it and the product of their labour. Such possession allowed people to live and prosper and was the cornerstone of liberty. Whether on the land or in industry, Proudhon's aim was to create a society of "possessors without masters."[153]

Only self-governing producers' associations could be the basis for a society in which concentration of political, economic and social power can be avoided and individual freedom protected: "Because the right to live and to develop oneself fully is equal for all, inequality of conditions is an obstacle to the exercise of this right."[154]

So "political right had to be buttressed by economic right" for if society became "divided into two classes, one of landlords, capitalists, and entrepreneurs, the other of wage-earning proletarians" then "the political order will still be unstable." To avoid this outcome an "agro-industrial federation" was required which would "provide reciprocal security in commerce and industry" and "protect the citizens... from capitalist and financial exploitation." In this way, the agro-industrial federation "will tend to foster increasing equality... through mutualism in credit and insurance... guaranteeing the right to work and to education, and an organisation of work which allows each labourer to become a skilled worker and an artist, each wage-earner to become his own master." Mutualism recognises that "industries are sisters" and so "should therefore federate, not in order to be absorbed and confused together, but in order to guarantee mutually the conditions of common prosperity, upon which no one has exclusive claim."[155]

The empirical evidence for economic federalism is supportive of it. In negative terms, it is clear that isolated co-operatives dependent on funding from capitalist banks find it hard to survive and grow. In positive terms, it is no coincidence that the Mondragon co-operative complex in the Basque region of Spain has a credit union and mutual support networks between its co-operatives and is by far the most successful co-operative system in the world. Other successful clusters of co-operation within capitalism also have support networks.[156]

---

152  *Œuvres Complètes* 17: 188–9.

153  *What Is Property?*, 167.

154  Quoted in Ehrenberg, 48–9.

155  *Principle of Federation*, 67, 70–1, 72.

156  One argument against co-operatives is that they do not allow the diversification of risk (all the worker's eggs are placed in one basket). Ignoring the obvious point that most

Clear evidence for Proudhon's argument that all industries are related and need to support each other.

Proudhon was an early advocate of what is now termed market socialism—an economy of competing co-operatives and self-employed workers. Some incorrectly argue that market socialism is not socialist.[157] Donny Gluckstein, for instance, suggests with casual abandon that Proudhon's ideas are "easily recognisable as the precursor of neo-liberal economics today" but "were located in a different context and so took a far more radical form when adopted by the male artisan class."[158]

Such claims are premised on a basic misunderstanding, namely that markets equate to capitalism. Yet this hides the key defining feature of capitalism: wage-labour.[159] Thus capitalism is uniquely marked by wage-labour,

---

workers today do not own shares and are dependent on their job to survive, this objection can be addressed, as David Ellerman points out, by means of "the *horizontal association* or grouping of enterprises to pool their business risk. The Mondragon co-operatives are associated together in a number of regional groups that pool their profits in varying degrees. Instead of a worker diversifying his or her capital in six companies, six companies partially pool their profits in a group or federation and accomplish the same risk-reduction purpose without transferable equity capital." Thus "risk-pooling in federations of co-operatives" ensure that "transferable equity capital is not necessary to obtain risk diversification in the flow of annual worker income" (*The Democratic Worker-Owned Firm: A New Model for East and West* [Boston, Mass.: Unwin Hyman, 1990], 104).

157  Leninist David McNally talks of the "anarcho-socialist Pierre-Joseph Proudhon" and how Marx combated "Proudhonian socialism" before concluding that it was "non-socialism" because it has "wage-labour and exploitation" (*Against the Market: Political Economy, Market Socialism and the Marxist Critique* [London: Verso, 1993], 139, 169). As Justin Schwartz correctly points out, "McNally is right that even in market socialism, market forces rule workers' lives" and this is "a serious objection" however "it is not tantamount to capitalism or to wage labour" and it "does not have exploitation in Marx's sense (i.e., wrongful expropriation of surplus by non-producers)" (*The American Political Science Review* 88: 4 [1994]: 982).

158  Gluckstein, 72. Interestingly, various Marxists have suggested, but never proven, that neo-classical economics was a response to Marx. This not only ignores the earlier socialists who utilised classical economics to attack capitalism, it also ignores the awkward fact that Léon Walras, one of the founders of that economic theology, wrote a book attacking Proudhon in 1860.

159  Engels stressed that the "object of production—to produce commodities—*does not import* to the instrument the character of capital" as the "production of commodities is one of the preconditions for the existence of capital... as long as the producer sells only *what he himself* produces, he is not a capitalist; he becomes so only from the moment he makes use of his instrument *to exploit the wage labour of others*" (*Marx-Engels Collected Works* 47: 179–80). In this he was merely echoing Marx (*Capital: A Critique of Political Economy* [London: Penguin Books, 1976] 1: 270–73, 875, 949–50).

not markets (which pre-date it by centuries) and so it is possible to support markets while being a socialist. In a mutualist society, based on workers' self-management and socialisation, wage-labour would not exist. Rather workers would be seeking out democratic associations to join and, once a member, have the same rights and duties as others within it.[160] In short, as K. Steven Vincent argues, "Proudhon consistently advanced a program of industrial democracy which would return control and direction of the economy to the workers. And he envisaged such a socialist program to be possible only within the framework of a society which encouraged just social relationships and which structured itself on federal lines."[161]

It is also fair to ponder when an advocate of neo-liberal economics has ever argued that the idol of *laissez-faire* capitalism, the law of supply and demand, was a "deceitful law... suitable only for assuring the victory of the strong over the weak, of those who own property over those who own nothing"?[162] Or denounced capitalist firms because they result in the worker being "subordinated, exploited: his permanent condition is one of obedience" and so people are related as "subordinates and superiors" with "two... castes of masters and wage-workers, which is repugnant to a free and democratic society" and urged co-operatives to replace them?[163] Or suggested that we "shall never have real workingmen's associations until the government learns that public services should neither be operated by itself or handed over to private stock companies; but should be leased on contract to organised and responsible companies of workers"?[164] Nor would an ideologue of *laissez-faire* capitalism be happy with an agro-industrial federation nor would they advocate regulation of markets:

> The advocates of mutualism are as familiar as anyone with
> the laws of *supply* and *demand* and they will be careful not
> to infringe them. Detailed and frequently reviewed statistics,

---

160  As Ellerman explains, the democratic workplace "is a social community, a community of work rather than a community of residence. It is a republic, or *res publica* of the workplace. The ultimate governance rights are assigned as personal rights... to the people who work in the firm... This analysis shows how a firm can be socialised and yet remain 'private' in the sense of not being government-owned." In such an economy "the labour market would not exist" as labour would "always be the residual claimant." "There would be a job market in the sense of people looking for firms they could join but it would not be a labour market in the sense of the selling of labour in the employment contract" (76, 91).

161  Vincent, 230.

162  Quoted in Ritter, 121.

163  *General Idea of the Revolution*, 215–216.

164  Quoted in Dorothy W. Douglas, "Proudhon: A Prophet of 1848: Part II," *The American Journal of Sociology* 35: 1 (1929): 45.

precise information about needs and living standards, an
honest breakdown of cost prices... the fixing after amicable
discussion of a *maximum* and *minimum* profit margin, taking
into account the risks involved, the organising of regulating
societies; these things, roughly speaking, constitute all the
measures by which they hope to regulate the market.[165]

Finally, what neo-liberal would proclaim: "What is the capitalist? Everything! What should he be? Nothing!"?[166] Or that "I belong to the Party of
Work against the party of Capital"?[167]

In fact, Proudhon had nothing but contempt for the neo-liberals of his
time and they for him.[168] He recognised the class basis of mainstream economic ideology: "Political economy, as taught by MM. Say, Rossi, Blanqui,
Wolovski, Chevalier, etc., is only the economy of the property-owners, and
its application to society inevitably and organically gives birth to misery."[169]
In short: "The enemies of society are Economists."[170] Claims that Proudhon
was a propertarian or a supporter of neo-liberalism simply misunderstand
both capitalism and Proudhon's ideas.

Unsurprisingly, then, Bakunin wrote of Proudhon's "socialism, based on
individual and collective liberty and upon the spontaneous action of free
associations."[171] Proudhon is placed firmly into the socialist tradition due to

---

165  *Selected Writings*, 70.

166  As added to the banner of *Le Représentant du Peuple* in August 1848, joining "What
is the Producer? Nothing. What should he be? Everything!" (Quoted in Woodcock,
*Proudhon*, 136, 123).

167  Quoted in Hayward, 172.

168  "The school of Say," Proudhon argued, was "the chief focus of counter-revolution"
and "has for ten years past seemed to exist only to protect and applaud the execrable work of the monopolists of money and necessities, deepening more and more
the obscurity of a science [economics] naturally difficult and full of complications"
(*General Idea of the Revolution*, 225). All of which seems sadly too applicable today!

169  Quoted in de Lubac, 190. Not to mention their role as apologists for the system:
"Capitalistic exploitation, despised by the ancients, who certainly were better informed on this subject than we, for they saw it in its origin, was thus established:
it was reserved for our century to supply it with defenders and advocates" (*Œuvres
Complètes* 19: 236).

170  *Carnets* 3: 209. Proudhon would not have been surprised that neo-classical economics turned political economy into little more than a public relations exercise for
the *rentier* classes he criticised: capitalists, landlords and bankers. It was largely to
counter such telling criticisms of their unearned wealth that economics was limited
to mathematically expounding on unrealistic assumptions that are so blatantly self-
serving to the *status quo*.

171  *Michael Bakunin: Selected Writings* (London: Jonathan Cape, 1973), 100.

his support for workers' associations and his belief that "socialism is... the elimination of misery, the abolition of capitalism and of wage-labour, the transformation of property, the decentralisation of government, the organisation of universal suffrage, the effective and direct sovereignty of the workers, the equilibrium of economic forces, the substitution of the contractual regime for the legal regime, etc."[172] In opposition to various schemes of state socialism and communism, Proudhon argued for a decentralised and federal market socialism based on workers' self-management of production and community self-government.

# PROUDHON'S LEGACY

As WOULD BE expected of the leading French socialist of his time, Proudhon's impact continued long after his death in 1865. Most immediately was the growth of the *International Workingmen's Association* founded by his followers and the application of many of his ideas by the Paris Commune.[173] His most important contribution to politics was laying the foundations for all the subsequent schools of anarchism.

Another key legacy is his consistent vision of socialism as being rooted in workers' self-management. Dorothy W. Douglas correctly notes that "the co-operative movement... syndicalism... guild socialism... all bear traces of the kind of self-governing industrial life to which Proudhon looked forward."[174] This vision was expressed within the First International by both the mutualists and the collectivists around Bakunin. While later eclipsed by schemes of nationalisation, the bankruptcy of such "state capitalism" (to use Kropotkin's term) has re-enforced the validity of Proudhon's arguments. Indeed, as Daniel Guérin suggested, when Marxists advocate self-management they "have been reverting... unwittingly and in an unspoken way to the Proudhon school" for "anarchism, ever since Proudhon, has acted as the advocate of... self-management."[175] No other socialist thinker of his time so consistently advocated workers' self-management of production or placed it at the core of his socialism.

This is not to say that Proudhon was without flaws, for he had many. He was not consistently libertarian in his ideas, tactics and language. His personal bigotries are disgusting and few modern anarchists would tolerate

---

172  Quoted in Ehrenberg, 111.

173  There is some irony in knowing that Marx eclipsed Proudhon thanks to these two developments that were dominated by Proudhon's own followers.

174  Douglas, 54.

175  "Anarchism Reconsidered," *Anarchism: A Documentary History of Libertarian Ideas* (Montréal: Black Rose Books, 2009), Vol. 2, Robert Graham (ed.), 280.

them.[176] He made some bad decisions and occasionally ranted in his private notebooks (where the worst of his anti-Semitism was expressed). We could go on but to concentrate on these aspects of Proudhon's thought would be to paint a selective, and so false, picture of his ideas and influence. Anarchists seek Proudhon's legacy in those aspects of his ideas that are consistent with the goal of human liberation, not those when he did not rise to the ideals he so eloquently advocated. This is what we discuss here, the positive impact of a lifetime fighting for justice, equality and liberty.

### INTERNATIONAL WORKINGMEN'S ASSOCIATION

The *International Workingmen's Association* (IWMA) is usually associated with Marx. In fact, it was created by British trade unionists and "French mutualist workingmen, who in turn were direct followers of Pierre-Joseph Proudhon" ("Contrary to stubborn legend, Karl Marx was not one of its actual founders").[177] The negotiations that lead to its founding began in 1862 when the mutualists (including Henri-Louis Tolain and Eugene Varlin[178]) visited the London International Exhibition.[179]

Like Proudhon, his followers in the IWMA thought workers "should be striving for the abolition of salaried labour and capitalist enterprise" by

---

176  Namely, racism and sexism. While he did place his defence of the patriarchal family at the core of his ideas, they are in direct contradiction to his own libertarian and egalitarian ideas. In terms of racism, he sometimes reflected the less-than-enlightened assumptions and prejudices of the nineteenth century. While this does appear in his public work, such outbursts are both rare and asides (usually an extremely infrequent passing anti-Semitic remark or caricature). In short, "racism was never the basis of Proudhon's political thinking" (Gemie, 200–1) and "anti-Semitism formed no part of Proudhon's revolutionary programme" (Robert Graham, "Introduction," *General Idea of the Revolution*, xxxvi). To quote Proudhon: "There will no longer be nationality, no longer fatherland, in the political sense of the words: they will mean only places of birth. Man, of whatever race or colour he may be, is an inhabitant of the universe; citizenship is everywhere an acquired right" (*General Idea of the Revolution*, 283).

177  Woodcock, *Anarchism and Anarchists*, 75. Marx fortuitously turned up to the founding meeting in 1864 after being invited by some German socialist exiles. The IWMA did not become "Marxist" until the gerrymandered Hague Congress of 1872 approved the expulsion of Bakunin and imposed the necessity of "political action" (i.e., standing for elections to capture political power) upon the organisation. It promptly collapsed, although the libertarian sections (such as Belgium, Spain and Italy) successfully organised their own IWMA congresses until 1877.

178  According to Archer, "the philosophical structure of Tolain's address derived" from Proudhon while the "preponderance of organisers and members of the International in France were Proudhonist" (23). Varlin was "an autodidact bookbinder, labour organiser and leading Proudhonist member of the International" (Tomes, 81).

179  Woodcock, *Anarchism*, 198–9.

means of co-operatives for the "manager/employer (patron) was a superflu-ous element in the production process who was able to deny the worker just compensation for his labour merely by possessing the capital that paid for the workshop, tools, and materials."[180] The French Internationalists were "strongly hostile to centralisation. They were federalists, intent on building up working-class organisations on a local basis and then federating the lo-cal federations. The free France they looked forward to was to be a country made up of locally autonomous communes, freely federated for common purposes which required action over larger areas... In this sense they were Anarchists."[181] Thus in 1866 the International officially adopted the Red Flag as its symbol, confirming Proudhon's declaration that "the red flag represents the final revolution... The red flag is the federal standard of humanity!"[182]

Given their role in setting up the International, the mutualists dominated the agenda in its first years. According to the standard, and usually Marxist or Marxist-influenced, accounts of the International this initial domination by the mutualists was eclipsed by the rise of a collectivist current (usually identified with Marxism). This is not entirely true. Yes, the Basel Congress of 1869 saw the success of a collectivist motion which was opposed by To-lain and some of his fellow French Internationalists, but this was a debate on the specific issue of agricultural collectivisation rather than a rejection of mutualism as such:

> The endorsement of collectivism by the International at the
> Basel Congress might appear to be a rejection of the French
> position on co-operatives. Actually, it was not, for collectivism
> as it was defined by its proponents meant simply the end of
> private ownership of agricultural land. Lumped together with
> this was usually the demand for common ownership of mines
> and railways.[183]

Thus it was "not a debate over co-operative production in favour of some other model" but rather concerned its extension to agriculture. At the Ge-neva Congress of 1866 the French mutualists "persuaded the Congress to agree by unanimous vote that there was a higher goal—the suppression of 'salaried status'—which... could be done only through co-operatives." At the Lausanne Congress of 1867, the mutualists around Tolain "acknowledged the necessity of public ownership of canals, roads, and mines" and there was "unanimous accord" on public ownership of "the means of transportation

---

180  Archer, 45.

181  G.D.H. Cole, *A History Of Socialist Thought* (London: Macmillan , 1961), Vol. 2, 140.

182  Quoted in Hayward, 246. Proudhon had "predicted in March 1848 the internation-alism of the Red Flag" (Hayward, 246).

183  Archer, xxi.

and exchange of goods." This was Proudhon's position as well. The proponents of collectivisation at the Lausanne Congress wanted to "extend Tolain's ideas to all property."[184]

While the resolution on collectivisation "represents the final decisive defeat of the strict Proudhonist element which, centred in Paris, had dominated in France and had drawn the parameters of the debates at the International's congresses in the beginning,"[185] this did not automatically mean the end of Proudhonian influences in the International. After all, the main leader of the "collectivist" position was César De Paepe, a self-proclaimed Mutualist and follower of Proudhon. As such, the debate was fundamentally one between followers of Proudhon, not between mutualists and Marxists, and the 1869 resolution was consistent with Proudhon's ideas. This can be seen from the fact that resolution itself was remarkably Proudhonian in nature, with it urging the collectivisation of roads, canals, railways, mines, quarries, collieries and forests, and these to be "ceded to 'workers' companies' which would guarantee the 'mutual rights' of workers and would sell their goods or services at cost." The land would "be turned over to 'agricultural companies' (i.e., agricultural workers) with the same guarantees as those required of the 'workers' companies'"[186] De Paepe himself clarified the issue: "Collective property would belong to society as a whole, but would be conceded to associations of workers. The State would be no more than a federation of various groups of workers."[187]

Given that Proudhon had advocated workers' companies to run publicly owned industries as well as arguing the land was common property and be transferred to communes, the resolution was not the rejection of Proudhon's ideas that many assume. In fact, it can be considered a logical fusion of his arguments on land ownership and workers' associations. As Daniel Guérin notes, "in the congresses of the First International the libertarian idea of self-management prevailed over the statist concept."[188] Moreover, at the Basel Congress of 1869 "Bakunin emerged as the main champion of collectivism."[189] As Kropotkin suggested:

---

184  Archer, xxi, 69, 101. As an example of the ambiguity of words used at the time, public ownership was to be achieved by means of the state, although the "state" was defined as a "collectivity of individuals" with "no interests apart from society" (Quoted in Archer, 101).

185  Archer, 171.

186  Archer, 128.

187  Quoted in Guérin, *Anarchism*, 47. At the Brussels Congress, De Paepe had "reminded Tolain and other opponents of collective property that they were in favour of collectivising mines, railroads, and canals" (Archer, 127).

188  *Anarchism*, 47.

189  Archer, 170.

> As to his economical conceptions, Bakunin described him-
> self, in common with his Federalist comrades of the Interna-
> tional (César De Paepe, James Guillaume, Schwitzguébel), a
> 'collectivist anarchist'... a state of things in which all neces-
> saries for production are owned in common by the labour
> groups and the free communes, while the ways of retribu-
> tion of labour, communist or otherwise, would be settled by
> each group for itself.[190]

So the rise of the collectivists in the IWMA does not represent a defeat for Proudhon's ideas. Rather, it reflected their development by debates between socialists heavily influenced by the anarchist. This is obscured by the fact that Proudhon's ideas on workers' associations are not well known today. Once this is understood, it is easy to see that it was in the IWMA that Proudhon's mutualist ideas evolved into collectivist and then communist anarchism.

The main areas of change centred on means (reform versus revolution) and the need for strikes, unions and other forms of collective working class direct action and organisation rather than the goal of a federated, associated, self-managed socialist society. As G.D.H. Cole perceptively writes, Varlin "had at bottom a great deal more in common with Proudhon than with Marx" and had a "Syndicalist outlook."[191] Like Bakunin, Varlin argued that unions have "the enormous advantage of making people accustomed to group life and thus preparing them for a more extended social organisation. They accustom people not only to get along with one another and to understand one another, but also to organise themselves, to discuss, and to reason from a collective perspective." Again, like Bakunin, Varlin argued that unions also "form the natural elements of the social edifice of the future; it is they who can be easily transformed into producers associations; it is they who can make the social ingredients and the organisation of production work."[192]

Thus, by 1868 "a transition from mutualism to 'antistatist' or 'antiauthoritarian collectivism' had begun."[193] This is to be expected. Just as Proudhon developed his ideas in the face of changing circumstances and working class self-activity, so working class people influenced by his ideas developed and changed what they took from Proudhon in light of their own circumstances. However, the core ideas of anti-statism and anti-capitalism remained and so these changes must be viewed as a development of Proudhon's ideas rather than something completely new or alien to them. Thus the revolutionary anarchism which grew within the IWMA had distinct similarities to that of Proudhon's reformist kind, even if it diverges on some issues.

---

190  *Anarchism and Anarchist Communism* (London: Freedom Press, 1987), 16–7.
191  Cole, 168.
192  Quoted in Archer, 196.
193  Berry, 17.

## THE PARIS COMMUNE

By 1871, the transition from reformist mutualism to revolutionary collectivism as the predominant tendency within anarchism was near complete. Then came the Paris Commune. With its ideas on decentralised federations of communes and workers' associations, the Commune applied Proudhon's ideas on a grand scale and, in the process, inspired generations of socialists. Sadly, this revolt, Proudhon's greatest legacy, has been appropriated by Marxism thanks to Marx's passionate defence of the revolt and his and Engels's systematic downplaying of its obvious Proudhonian themes.

In reality, while many perspectives were raised in the revolt, what positive themes it expressed were taken from Proudhon as many Communards "were influenced by Proudhon's advocacy of autonomous economic organisation and decentralised self-government." Thus the Commune reflected "a distinctly French variant of socialism, strongly influenced by Proudhon and to a lesser extent by the Russian anarchist Bakunin, which advocated destroying oppressive state structures by devolving power to local democratic communities (federalism) and abolishing exploitation by decentralising economic control to workers' co-operative associations—'Its apostles are workers, its Christ was Proudhon,' proclaimed Courbet."[194]

So it is that we find the Paris section of the IWMA in 1870 arguing along very Proudhonian lines that "we must accomplish the *Democratic and Social Revolution*." The aim was "the establishment of a new social order; the elimination of classes, the abolition of employers and of the proletariat, the establishment of universal co-operation based upon equality and justice." Thus "it is necessary, citizens, to eliminate wage labour, the last form of servitude," "implement the principles of justice in social relationships" and ensure the "distribution of what is produced by labour, based upon the principles of the value of the work and a mutualist organisation of services." "Has it not always been evident," they asked, "that the art of governing peoples has been the art of exploiting them?"[195]

As Paul Avrich suggested, the "influence of Proudhon—unquestionably greater than that of Marx—was reflected in the title of 'Federals' by which the Communards were known." The Commune's "social composition... was a mixture of workers and professionals, of tradesmen and artisans... its thrust was overwhelmingly decentralist and libertarian," its ideal society was "a direct democracy of councils, clubs, and communes, an anti-authoritarian commonwealth in which workers, artisans, and peasants might live in peace and contentment, with full economic and political liberty organised from

---

194  Tomes, 84, 117–8. Gustave Courbet was one of France's most famous painters, one of the Commune's leading members and Proudhon's close friend.

195  *The Paris Commune of 1871: The View From the Left* (London: Cape, 1972), Eugene Schulkind (ed.), 68–9. The "socialism of the Commune was almost exclusively the work of individuals with close ties to the International" (Archer, 258).

below."[196] "[I]n reality," Thomas concedes, "the Commune owed precious little to Marxism and a great deal more, ironically enough, to the Proudhonists, who had proved themselves thorns in Marx's side during the first four years of the International's existence."[197]

This Proudhonian influence on the Paris Commune was expressed in two main ways: politically in the vision of a France of federated communes; economically in the vision of a socialist society based on workers' associations.

Politically, Proudhon "had stressed the commune as the fundamental unit of democratic sovereignty"[198] as well as their federation. All this was reflected in the Commune. Indeed, the "rough sketch of national organisation which the Commune had no time to develop"[199] which Marx praised but did not quote was written by a follower of Proudhon and was "strongly federalist in tone, and it has a marked proudhonian flavour."[200]

Marx also praised the Communal Council being composed of delegates who would be "at any time revocable and bound by the *mandat imperatif* (formal instructions) of his constituents" and the fact that it was a "working, not a parliamentary, body, executive and legislative at the same time" This, he averred, was "the political form at last discovered under which to work out the economical emancipation of labour."[201] Yet this was not a novel "discovery" as Proudhon had consistently raised these ideas since the 1848 revolution:

> It is up to the National Assembly, through organisation of
> its committees, to exercise executive power, just the way it
> exercises legislative power... Besides universal suffrage and as a
> consequence of universal suffrage, we want implementation of
> the binding mandate. Politicians balk at it! Which means that
> in their eyes, the people, in electing representatives, do not
> appoint mandatories but rather abjure their sovereignty! That
> is assuredly not socialism: it is not even democracy.[202]

During the Commune anarchist James Guillaume pointed out the obvious: "the Paris Revolution is federalist... in the sense given it years ago by the

---

196 *Anarchist Portraits* (Princeton: Princeton University Press, 1988), 232, 231.

197 Thomas, 194.

198 Tomes, 73.

199 *Marx-Engels Reader*, 633.

200 Vincent, 232. It "might have been written by Proudhon himself" (Woodcock, *Proudhon*, 276).

201 *Marx-Engels Reader*, 633, 632, 635.

202 *No Gods, No Masters*, 78–9. Proudhon raised similar demands in his pamphlet *Democracy* earlier that year while Bakunin had been advocating mandated and recallable delegates to federal social organisations for some time before 1871 (ibid., 181–2).

great socialist, Proudhon." It is "above all the negation of the nation and the State."[203] It is hard not to concur with K.J. Kenafick:

> the programme [the Commune] set out is... the system of Feder-
> alism, which Bakunin had been advocating for years, and which
> had first been enunciated by Proudhon. The Proudhonists...
> exercised considerable influence in the Commune. This 'political
> form' was therefore not 'at last' discovered; it had been discovered
> years ago; and now it was proven to be correct by the very fact
> that in the crisis the Paris workers adopted it... as being the form
> most suitable to express working class aspirations.[204]

Economically, the same can be said. Echoing Proudhon's calls for workers' companies, the Communards considered that "the worker-directed work-shop... very soon would become the universal mode of production."[205] A meeting of the Mechanics Union and the Association of Metal Workers ar-gued that "our economic emancipation... can only be obtained through the formation of workers' associations, which alone can transform our position from that of wage earners to that of associates." They instructed their del-egates to the Commune's Commission on Labour Organisation to aim for the "abolition of the exploitation of man by man, the last vestige of slavery" by means of the "organisation of labour in mutual associations with collec-tive and inalienable capital." A group of foundry workers wrote that it was "exploitation that we seek to abolish through the right of workers to their work and to form federated producer co-operatives. Their formation would be a great step forward... towards... the federation of peoples."[206]

Marx praised the efforts made within the Paris Commune to create co-oper-atives, so "transforming the means of production, land and capital... into mere instruments of free and associated labour." He argued "what else... would it be but... Communism?"[207] Well, it could be mutualism and Proudhon's vision of an agro-industrial federation. Had not Varlin, in March 1870, argued that co-oper-atives were "actively preparing the bases for the future society"? Had he not, like Proudhon, warned that "placing everything in the hands of a highly centralised, authoritarian state... would set up a hierarchic structure from top to bottom of the labour process"? Had he not, like Proudhon, suggested that "the only alterna-tive is for workers themselves to have the free disposition and possession of the tools of production... through co-operative association"?[208]

---

203  Schulkind (ed.), 191.
204  *Michael Bakunin and Karl Marx* (Melbourne: A. Maller, 1948), 212–3.
205  Archer, 260.
206  Schulkind (ed.), 164, 167.
207  *Marx-Engels Reader*, 635.
208  Schulkind (ed.), 63–4.

Engels in 1891 painted a picture of Proudhon being opposed to association (except for large-scale industry) and stated that "to combine all these associations in one great union" was "the direct opposite of the Proudhon doctrine" and so the Commune was its "grave."[209] Yet, as he most certainly was aware, Proudhon had publicly called for economic federation. In 1863, he termed it the "agro-industrial federation" and fifteen years earlier he had demanded an economy based on a "vast federation" of "democratically organised workers' associations"[210] so making true his 1846 statement that "to unfold the system of economical contradictions is to lay the foundations of universal association."[211]

Elsewhere, Engels argued that the "economic measures" of the Commune were driven not by "principles" but by "simple, practical needs." This meant that "the confiscation of shut-down factories and workshops and handing them over to workers' associations" had been "not at all in accordance with the spirit of Proudhonism but certainly in accordance with the spirit of German scientific socialism."[212] This seems unlikely, given Proudhon's well known and long-standing advocacy of co-operatives as well as Marx's comment in 1866 that in France the workers ("especially those in Paris") "are, without realising it[!], strongly implicated in the garbage of the past" and that the "Parisian gentlemen had their heads stuffed full of the most vacuous Proudhonist clichés."[213] Given that the *Communist Manifesto* stressed state ownership and failed to mention co-operatives, the claim that the Commune had acted in its spirit seems a tad optimistic particularly as this decision "bore the mark of the French socialist tradition, which envisaged workers' co-operative *association*, not state ownership, as the solution to 'the social question.'"[214]

The obvious influence of Proudhon in the Commune's socio-economic vision has been obscured by Marxist revisionism. These links with Proudhon are hardly surprising as "men sympathetic to Proudhon's ideas were conspicuously present" in the revolt.[215] This is not to suggest that the Paris Commune unfolded precisely as Proudhon would have wished (Bakunin and Kropotkin analysed it and drew conclusions from its failings[216]). However,

---

209 *Marx-Engels Reader*, 626.

210 *No Gods, No Masters*, 78.

211 *System of Economical Contradictions*, 132.

212 *Marx-Engels Collected Works* 23: 370.

213 *Marx-Engels Collected Works* 42: 326.

214 Tomes, 93.

215 Vincent, 232.

216 Discussion of this important issue is outside the scope of this introduction. Those interested in the anarchist analysis and critique of the Paris Commune, and of Marxist accounts of it, can consult my article "The Paris Commune, Marxism and Anarchism" (*Anarcho-Syndicalist Review* 50 [2008]).

it is clear that the Commune's vision of a federated, self-managed society and economy owes much to Proudhon's tireless advocacy of such ideas. As Bakunin suggested, Marx and Engels "proclaim[ing] that [the Commune's] programme and purpose were their own" flew "in face of the simplest logic" and was "a truly farcical change of costume."[217]

## ANARCHISM

Proudhon's lasting legacy is his contribution to anarchism. It is little wonder that he has been termed "the father of anarchism" for while anarchism has evolved since Proudhon's time it still bases itself on the themes first expounded in a systematic way by the Frenchman. Indeed, it is hard to imagine anarchism without Proudhon.

While Proudhon may not have been the first thinker to suggest a stateless and classless society, he was the first to call himself an anarchist and to influence a movement of that name. This is not to suggest that libertarian ideas and movements had not existed before Proudhon[218] nor that anarchistic ideas did not develop spontaneously after 1840 but these were not a coherent, named, articulate *theory*. While anarchism does not have to be identical to Proudhon's specific ideas and proposals, it does have to be consistent with the main thrust of his ideas—in other words, anti-state and anti-capitalism. Thus collectivist anarchism built on Proudhon, as did communist-anarchism, anarcho-syndicalism and individualist anarchism. While none of these later developments were identical to Proudhon's mutualism—each stressed different aspects of his ideas, developing some, changing others—the links and evolution remain clear.

Proudhon straddles both wings of the anarchist movement, social *and* individualist although the former took more of his vision of libertarian socialism.[219] Perhaps this division was inevitable considering Proudhon's ideas. He was, after all, an advocate of both competition and association, against both capitalism and communism, a reformist who talked constantly of revolution. Suffice to say, though, both wings considered themselves, as did Proudhon, part of the wider socialist movement and hoped to see the end of capitalism while disagreeing on how to do so and the exact nature of a free society. Whether Proudhon would have agreed with Tucker or Kropotkin is a moot point (probably not!) but he would have recognised elements of his ideas in both.

---

217  *Michael Bakunin: Selected Writings*, 261.

218  Proudhon drew on such movements and ideas, such as the mutualist ideas of the French workers, particularly those in Lyon, as well as libertarian tendencies in the Great French Revolution.

219  As such mutualism *must* be considered as one of the four main forms of social anarchism alongside collectivism, communism and syndicalism (see section A.3.2 of *An Anarchist FAQ*).

### Individualist Anarchism

Proudhon's ideas found a welcome home in North America where "his impact was greater than has been commonly supposed," with his "views given wide publicity" in "the years preceding the Civil War."[220] This makes sense, given that (like France) the USA was going through the process of industrialisation and proletarianisation with the state intervening in the economy (as it always has) to foster capitalist property rights and social relationships. Radicals in America, facing the same transformation as Proudhon's France, took up his ideas and propagated them.

While Josiah Warren had independently advocated certain ideas usually associated with Proudhon, the first study of Proudhon's work was Charles A. Dana's *Proudhon and His "Bank of the People"* in 1849 followed by William B. Greene's translations from Proudhon's *Organisation du Crédit et de la Circulation et Solution du Problème Social* in his 1850 *Mutual Banking*. Greene was president of the Massachusetts Labour Union and was active in the French-speaking section of the IWMA in Boston although, unlike Proudhon, he "championed the cause of women's rights."[221]

For Greene there was "no device of the political economists so infernal as the one which ranks labour as a commodity, varying in value according to supply and demand... To speak of labour as merchandise is treason; for such speech denies the true dignity of man... Where labour is merchandise in fact... there man is merchandise also, whether in England or South Carolina." The alternative was the "triple formula of practical mutualism": "the associated workshop" for production, the "protective union store" for consumption and "the Mutual Bank" for exchange. All three were required, for "the Associated Workshop cannot exist for a single day without the Mutual Bank and the Protective Union Store." The "Associated Workshop ought to be an organisation of personal credit. For what is its aim and purpose? Is it not the emancipation of the labourer from all dependence upon capital and capitalists?"[222]

Benjamin Tucker took up Greene's work and translated substantial material by Proudhon into English including numerous articles, *What is Property?* and volume one of *System of Economic Contradictions*. In 1881, he proclaimed that his new journal, *Liberty*, was "brought into existence as a direct consequence of the teachings of Proudhon" and "lives principally to emphasise and spread them."[223] Proudhon's maxim from the 1848 revolution that "Liberty, Not the Daughter but the Mother of Order" adorned its masthead. Like Proudhon, his aim was the "emancipation of the workingman from his present slavery to capital."[224]

---

220 Avrich, 137.
221 Avrich, 140, 139.
222 *Mutual Banking* (West Brookfield: O. S. Cooke, 1850), 49–50, 37, 34.
223 Quoted in Avrich, 141.
224 *Instead of a Book*, 323.

To achieve this, Tucker looked to Proudhon as well as the radical ideas and movements of his own country. He took Proudhon's reformism, his "occupancy and use" critique of land-ownership, elimination of interest by mutual banking, opposition to the state and defence of competition and markets. Somewhat ironically, while Tucker is often portrayed as being Proudhon's disciple he ignored many of the French anarchist's key ideas. Workers' associations and co-operative production, the agro-industrial federation, communes and their federation find no echo in Tucker, nor did Proudhon's opposition to wage-labour. Somewhat ironically it was Tucker's arch-foe in the movement, the communist-anarchist Johann Most, who echoed the French anarchist on most issues.

Other individualist anarchists were closer to Proudhon's concerns. Dyer Lum "drew from the French anarchist Proudhon... a radical critique of classical political economy and... a set of positive reforms in land tenure and banking... Proudhon paralleled the native labour reform tradition in several ways. Besides suggesting reforms in land and money, Proudhon urged producer cooperation." As with Proudhon's, a key element of "Lum's anarchism was his mutualist economics, an analysis of 'wage slavery' and a set of reforms that would 'abolish the wage system.'"[225] Other individualist anarchists joined Lum in opposing wage-labour.[226]

While individualist anarchism dominated the movement in America before and immediately after the Civil War, by the 1880s the displacement of reformist by revolutionary forms of anarchism which had occurred in Europe was repeated in America. While the repression after the Haymarket police riot in 1886 hindered this, "[b]y the turn of the century, the anarchist movement in America had become predominantly communist in orientation."[227] While individualist anarchism never totally disappeared, to this day it remains very much the minority trend in American anarchism.

### Revolutionary Anarchism

Even a cursory glance at revolutionary anarchism shows the debt it has to Proudhon. Bakunin, unsurprisingly, considered his own ideas as "Proudhonism widely developed and pushed right to these, its final consequences."[228] Proudhon's critique of property, state and capitalism, his analysis of exploitation being rooted in wage-labour, his advocacy of a

---

225  Frank H. Brooks, "Ideology, Strategy, and Organization: Dyer Lum and the American Anarchist Movement," *Labor History* 34: 1 (1993): 72, 71.

226  See section G.1.3 of *An Anarchist FAQ*. Sections G.4.1 and G.4.2 discuss the contradictions in supporting wage labour while opposing political authority and supporting "occupancy and use."

227  Paul Avrich, *Anarchist Voices: An Oral History of Anarchism in America* (Edinburgh/Oakland: AK Press, 2005), 5.

228  *Michael Bakunin: Selected Writings*, 198.

decentralised and federal system of communes and workers' associations, his support for workers' self-management of production, his call for working class autonomy and self-activity as the means of transforming society from below, all these (and more) were taken up and developed by collectivist, communist and syndicalist anarchists.

Just as Proudhon had pointed to the directly democratic clubs of the 1848 Revolution and co-operatives as key institutions of a free society, so Bakunin viewed communes and unions in the same light while, in addition to these, Kropotkin pointed to the directly democratic "sections" of the Great French Revolution. As with Proudhon, the revolutionary anarchists argued that political and social change must occur at the same time. Like Proudhon, they saw the future free society as a dual federation of social and economic organisations. For Kropotkin "*the form that the Social Revolution must take*" was "the independent Commune" and their federations along with "a parallel triumph of the people in the economic field" based on "associations of men and women who would work on the land, in the factories, in the mines, and so on" and so become "themselves the managers of production."[229] For Bakunin, "socialism is federalist" and "true federalism, the political organisation of socialism, will be attained only" when "popular grass-roots institutions" like "communes, industrial and agricultural associations" are "organised in progressive stages from the bottom up."[230] The links with Proudhon's ideas, particularly the agro-industrial federation, are all too clear.

Revolutionary anarchism bases itself on Proudhon's distinction between property and possession.[231] It shares his vision of an economy based on socialisation of the means of production, use rights and workers' association. Kropotkin's co-founder of the newspaper *Freedom*, Charlotte M. Wilson, made the link clear:

> Proudhon's famous dictum, 'Property is theft', is the key to the equally famous enigma... 'From each according to his capacities, to each according to his needs'... as long as land and capital are un-appropriated, the workers are free, and that, when these have a master, the workers also are slaves... Anarchism proposes, therefore,—1. That usufruct of instruments

---

229 "Modern Science and Anarchism," 74, 78.

230 *Bakunin on Anarchism*, 2nd edition (Montréal: Black Rose, 1980), 402.

231 As do other forms of socialism. This can be seen from libertarian communist William Morris who classed the French anarchist as "the most noteworthy figure" of a group of "Socialist thinkers who serve as a kind of link between the Utopians and the school of... scientific Socialists." As far as his critique of property went, Morris argued that in *What is Property?*, Proudhon's "position is that of a Communist pure and simple" (*Political Writings: Contributions to Justice and Commonweal 1883–1890* [Bristol: Thoemmes Press, 1994], 569–70).

of production—land included—should be free to all workers, or groups of workers. 2. That the workers should group themselves, and arrange their work as their reason and inclination prompt... 3. That the necessary connections between the various industries and branches of trade should be managed on the same voluntary principle.[232]

Revolutionary anarchism nevertheless differed from that of Proudhon in three areas.

First, its proponents rejected Proudhon's support for patriarchy in the family as being inconsistent with the libertarian principles he advocated against capitalism and the state.[233] This was an obvious self-contradiction, which anarchists have critiqued by means of the very principles Proudhon himself used to criticise the state and capitalism. Joseph Déjacque, for example, wrote a critique of Proudhon's sexist views in 1857, urging him to renounce "this gender aristocracy that would bind us to the old regime."[234] André Léo, a feminist libertarian and future Communard, pointed out the obvious contradiction in 1869: "These so-called lovers of liberty, if they are unable to take part in the direction of the state, at least they will be able to have a little monarchy for their personal use, each in his own home... Order in the family without hierarchy seems impossible to them—well then, what about in the state?"[235]

Second, they rejected Proudhon's reformism and transformed his call for a "revolution from below" into a literal support for a social revolution (insurrections, general strikes and other activities which reflect the popular understanding of "revolution"). Bakunin, while "convinced that the co-operative will be the preponderant form of social organisation in the future" and could "hardly oppose" their creation under capitalism, argued that Proudhon's hope for gradual change by means of mutual banking and the higher efficiency of workers' co-operatives was unlikely to be realised as it did "not take into account the vast advantage that the bourgeoisie enjoys against the proletariat through its monopoly on wealth, science, and secular custom, as well

---

232  *Anarchist Essays* (London: Freedom Press, 2000), 20–1.

233  While firmly supporting the patriarchal family, Proudhon also stressed that he did "not mistake the family for the model of society" as he considered it "the rudiment of royalty" while "the model of civil society is the fraternal association" (*No Gods, No Masters*, 79).

234  "On Being Human," *Anarchism: A Documentary History of Libertarian Ideas, Volume 1: From Anarchy to Anarchism (300CE-1939)* (Montréal: Black Rose Books, 2005) Robert Graham (ed.), 68–71.

235  Quoted in Carolyn J. Eichner, "'Vive La Commune!' Feminism, Socialism, and Revolutionary Revival in the Aftermath of the 1871 Paris Commune," *Journal of Women's History* 15: 2 (2003): 75.

as through the approval—overt or covert but always active—of States and through the whole organisation of modern society. The fight is too unequal for success reasonably to be expected."[236] Thus capitalism "does not fear the competition of workers' associations—neither consumers', producers', nor mutual credit associations—for the simple reason that workers' organisations, left to their own resources, will never be able to accumulate sufficiently strong aggregations of capital capable of waging an effective struggle against bourgeois capital."[237]

Having found reformism insufficient, the revolutionary anarchists stressed the need for what would now be termed a syndicalist approach to social change.[238] Rather than seeing workers co-operatives and mutual banks as the focus for social transformation, unions came to be seen as the means of both fighting capitalism and replacing it. They took Proudhon's dual-power strategy from 1848 and applied it in the labour movement with the long term aim of smashing the state and replacing it with these organs of popular power.[239]

Third, they rejected Proudhon's anti-communism and advocated distribution according to *need* rather than *deed*. That is, the extension of the critique of wage-*labour* into opposition to the wages-*system*.[240]

---

236  *The Basic Bakunin*, 153, 152.

237  *The Political Philosophy of Bakunin*, 293. Even a large co-operative sector would be unlikely to reform society. As Emma Goldman noted, after reading Proudhon's *General Idea* in the light of the Spanish Revolution, had Proudhon been accurate then, the collectivisation of the economy after the start of the civil war "should have weakened the republican government, but as a matter of fact it has not." It only gave the state "a breathing space so that they could reorganise their forces and become the dead weight of the Revolution" (*Vision on Fire* [Edinburgh/Oakland: AK Press, 2006], 275).

238  See section H.2.8 of *An Anarchist FAQ*.

239  "As early as the 1860's and 1870's, the followers of Proudhon and Bakunin in the First International were proposing the formation of workers' councils designed both as a weapon of class struggle against capitalists and as the structural basis of the future libertarian society" (Paul Avrich, *The Russian Anarchists* [Edinburgh/Oakland: AK Press, 2005], 73). Echoing Proudhon, leading syndicalist Fernand Pelloutier argued that the aim was "to constitute within the bourgeois State a veritable socialist (economic and anarchic) State" (Quoted in Jeremy Jennings, *Syndicalism in France: A Study of Ideas* [London: Macmillan, 1990], 22). The IWW's "we are building a new world in the shell of the old" has obvious similarities to Proudhon's 1848 call that "a new society be founded in the centre of the old society" (*Œuvres Complètes* 17:25).

240  Proudhon's anti-communism is well known but there are different schools of communism, just as there are different schools of socialism. As Kropotkin argued "before and in 1848, the theory [of communism] was put forward in such a shape as to fully account for Proudhon's distrust as to its effect upon liberty. The old idea of

The rationale behind this change was straightforward. As Kropotkin explained, "this system of remuneration for work done" was contradictory and unjust. Not only do deeds not correlate with needs (most obviously, children, the ill and elderly cannot be expected to work as much as others) it was also "evident that a society cannot be based on two absolutely opposed principles, two principles that contradict one another continually." How can labour-money be advocated "when we admit that houses, fields, and factories will no longer be private property, and that they will belong to the commune or the nation?" Abolition of property in the means of production cannot co-exist with property in the products of labour created by their use. This suggested that, to be consistent, anarchists must pass from mutualism and collectivism to communism, distribution according to need rather than deed.[241] Most anarchists then, and now, concurred.

Ultimately, though, Proudhon and the likes of Bakunin and Kropotkin had more in common than differences. His ideas were the foundation upon which revolutionary anarchism was built. Bakunin "reaped the harvest sown by Proudhon—the father of anarchism—filtering, enriching and surpassing it"[242] and "Proudhon's thought found a strong echo in revolutionary syndicalism."[243]

Finally, it should be noted that revolutionary anarchism developed independently from Proudhon's mutualism in at least three cases. Joseph Déjacque drew libertarian communist conclusions from Proudhon's work in the 1850s. Bakunin developed Proudhon's ideas in a similar direction after 1864 while Eugene Varlin "seems to have moved independently towards his collectivist position."[244] So while Bakunin's ideas were quickly adopted by

---

Communism was the idea of monastic communities under the severe rule of elders or of men of science for directing priests. The last vestiges of liberty and of individual energy would be destroyed, if humanity ever had to go through such a communism" (*Act for Yourselves* [London: Freedom Press, 1988], 98). This is *not* to suggest that Proudhon would have agreed with communist-anarchism (after all, he rejected Joseph Déjacque's communistic interpretation of his ideas) merely that Proudhon's opposition to *state* communism does not mean that anarchists cannot be *libertarian* communists. This was the position often taken by the American Individualist Anarchists around Tucker, with him in the lead. However, as discussed in section G.2.1 of *An Anarchist FAQ*, they also regularly admitted that voluntary communism *was* compatible with anarchism making their strident anti-communism both contradictory and needlessly sectarian.

241  *The Conquest of Bread* (Edinburgh/Oakland: AK Press, 2008), 189, 191, 188.

242  Guérin, "From Proudhon to Bakunin," 33.

243  Vincent, 232.

244  Woodcock, *Anarchism*, 239. Significantly, when Bakunin met him at the International's Basel Congress and, "once the program of the Alliance was explained to" him, Varlin said he "shared the same ideas and agreed to co-ordinate with their revolutionary plans" (Archer, 186).

working class militants familiar with Proudhon across Europe, even without him Proudhon's legacy was evolving in the direction of revolutionary collectivism in the 1860s. Indeed, it could be argued that Bakunin and his ideas became so influential in the IWMA because he was part of a general development within Internationalist circles which he simply helped.

# CONCLUSION

PROUDHON'S INFLUENCE WAS significant during the nineteenth century. Sadly, his ideas are not acknowledged as much as they should be given their impact and how they laid the basis for modern anarchism.

Anarchists, though, are not Proudhonists, Bakuninists, Kropotkinites, or whoever-ists. We reject the idea of calling ourselves after individuals. However, we can and do acknowledge the contributions of outstanding thinkers and activists, people who contribute to the commonwealth of ideas which is anarchism. Seen in this light, Proudhon (for all his faults) should be remembered as the person who laid the foundations of anarchism. His libertarian socialism, his critique of capitalism and the state, his federalism, advocacy of self-management and change from below, defined what anarchism is.

In terms of his critique of capitalism, most of it holds up well. Workers are still exploited at the point of production and this can only be stopped by abolishing wage-labour. Landlords are still parasites, interest still bleeds dry those subject to it. Capitalism has proven itself to be the efficient machine for increasing inequality by exploiting the many that Proudhon analysed. As far as his anti-statism goes, his analysis of the state as an instrument of minority class rule still rings true as does his insights that centralised structures result in rule by the few and are simply not reflexive of, nor accountable to, the public in any meaningful way. His denunciations of executive power and the *unitaire* State as a new form of royalty have been confirmed time and time again. His critique of State socialism, his prediction that it would be just another form of wage-labour with the state replacing the boss, has been more than confirmed, not to mention his fear that it would become little more than a dictatorship by a party rather than a genuine worker democracy.

While we should not slavishly copy Proudhon's ideas, we can take what is useful and, like Bakunin, Kropotkin and others, develop them further in order to inspire social change in the 21st century. His vision of a decentralised, self-managed, federal socialist society and economy has obvious relevance today. Centralised political and economic systems have been tried and failed. His continued emphasis on working class autonomy and self-emancipation, of building the new world in the heart of the old, are core libertarian principles.

Proudhon wrote that "the twentieth century will open the age of federations, or else humanity will undergo another purgatory of a thousand years."[245] The 20th century, with its centralised states, neo-liberalism and nationalistic irrationalities, reached depths of destruction and misery suggested by purgatory. We can only hope that it is the 21st century that inaugurates the libertarian age Proudhon hoped for.

Iain McKay
www.anarchistfaq.org.uk

---

245  Quoted in Hayward, 211.

# PROUDHON:
## A BIOGRAPHICAL SKETCH

PIERRE-JOSEPH PROUDHON WAS BORN ON 15TH OF JANUARY 1809 IN THE town of Besançon in Franche-Comté, a province in the east of France bordering the Jura region of Switzerland. Almost unique for his time, he was a major socialist thinker who was working class and he declared that his aim was to work "for the complete liberation of [his] brothers and comrades."[1] He lived in a period of massive social and economic change. The industrialisation of France was beginning (its full flowering came in the 1860s), he grew up surrounded by those who had taken part in the Revolution of 1789, experienced the July Revolution of 1830 and saw the birth of the French labour and socialist movements in the 1830s. All these influenced his ideas.

After a brief period at the college in Besançon he was forced to leave school before completing his baccalaureate in order to support his family. In 1828 he became a working compositor; later he rose to be a corrector for the press. The following year he met utopian socialist Charles Fourier when supervising the printing of his *Le Nouveau Monde Industriel et Sociétaire*. Having several discussions with Fourier, he later recounted that for "six whole weeks" he was "the captive of this bizarre genius."[2] While rejecting Fourier's utopian visions of perfect and regulated communities in favour of a "scientific socialism,"[3] he had a lasting influence as can be seen in many of Proudhon's works.

The turning point in Proudhon's life came when, in 1838, he was awarded a scholarship to study in Paris by the Besançon Academy. The following year saw him write the treatise *On The Utility of Sunday Observance from the Viewpoints*

---

1     Quoted in Hayward, 172.

2     Quoted in Woodcock, *Proudhon*, 13.

3     *What Is Property?*, 264. Critiques of utopianism played a large role in *System of Economic Contradictions*.

*of Public Hygiene, Morality and Civic and Family Relations.* However, 1840 saw him produce the work that ensured his lasting fame: *What is Property? An Inquiry into the Principle of Right and of Government.* This work was to encapsulate the core themes of his life's work—liberty, social justice, the iniquities of capitalist property rights, the epochal importance of socialism and his theory of anarchism. It caused a sensation and Proudhon was soon recognised as a leading light of the French, indeed international, socialist movement. It also resulted in the public prosecutor sending a recommendation to the Minister of Justice that a case be launched against him. Fortunately for Proudhon, leading economist Jérome-Adolphe Blanqui was approached by the Minister over the book's seditious nature. Blanqui had been assigned the book to review and while disagreeing with it, declared it was a philosophical work which would appeal only to "high intelligences and cultivated minds."[4] This verdict was accepted and Proudhon was spared prosecution.

*What is Property?* was quickly followed by two more works. In 1841 he wrote his *Second Memoir* on property (*Letter to M. Blanqui*) were he developed his ideas in a reply to comments made by Blanqui. His *Third Memoir* (*Warning to Proprietors*) was published in 1842 and answered criticisms by a follower of Fourier. This work was seized by the Besançon public prosecutor and Proudhon was charged with "1, Attacking Property; 2, Troubling the public peace by exciting mistrust or hatred of the citizens against one or more persons; 3, Exciting hatred and mistrust of the King's Government; 4, Outrage to the Catholic religion."[5] Proclaiming his work too hard to follow and not wishing to imprison someone due to misunderstanding their ideas, the jury refused to convict Proudhon.

His next major work was published in the following year. *On the Creation of Order in Humanity* adapted Fourier's "serial method" and was an attempt to develop a comprehensive social science premised on Fourier's anti-rationalist social theory and Auguste Comte's philosophy of history. He later admitted that this work was not successful, but it discussed a set of themes he was to return to again and again. Proudhon also moved to Lyons, serving for several years as an office manager for a water transport firm. This allowed him to travel and he frequently stayed in Paris, where Marx, Bakunin, and Herzen visited him to discuss ideas. In Lyons, he became part of the flourishing radical scene and met with its revolutionary silk-weavers who called themselves Mutualists and argued for a form of associational socialism based on producer co-operatives and credit unions. They had a significant influence on Proudhon, reflected by "his preoccupation at this period with the idea of an association of workers."[6] These influences and thoughts were publicly expressed in 1846 with the publication of the two volume *System of*

4    Quoted in Woodcock, 55.

5    Woodcock, 66.

6    Woodcock, 74.

*Economic Contradictions, or The Philosophy of Misery* in which he proclaimed his own ideas mutualism.

In October 1847 Proudhon settled in Paris again, hoping to start a newspaper. When the 1848 Revolution broke out, he helped build barricades and set the type for the first republican proclamation. A group of workers, fresh from the barricades and still armed with muskets, visited Proudhon and asked that he resume his plan to publish a newspaper. He agreed and *Le Réprésentant du Peuple* (*The Representative of the People*) was born, its masthead proclaiming "What is the producer? Nothing! What should he be? Everything!"[7] This was the first of four newspapers Proudhon edited during the revolution, all with "People" in their name and all suppressed by the state.[8]

Fearing, rightly, that the Republicans had "made a revolution without an idea"[9] Proudhon used his articles to comment on events, criticise the policies of the government and stress the need to go beyond mere political reform as this could never solve problems whose roots were primarily economic. Socioeconomic change was essential.[10] His first major works after the revolution included an analysis of its causes and meaning and a critique of (statist) democracy, subsequently published as *Solution of the Social Problem*. These were quickly followed by the *Organisation of Credit and Circulation* in which he argued that a Bank of Exchange was required to both solve the economic problems facing France and secure the end of capitalism.

However, it was the various incarnations of his newspapers that Proudhon made his greatest impact on the public and by the end of 1848 he was being read by 40,000 mostly working-class readers.[11] These articles present a libertarian, albeit reformist,[12] analysis of the revolution and how to solve its problems. This clarified his own ideas, as it forced him to present positive ideas to change society for the better, as well as enriching anarchist theory for later libertarians to build upon.

In April 1848 he stood as a candidate in the elections for the Constituent Assembly with his name appearing on the ballots in Paris, Lyon, Besançon, and Lille. He proclaimed in his election manifesto that he regarded "Property is theft!" as "the greatest truth of the century" and that "the negation of property is necessary for the abolition of misery, for the emancipation of

---

7    Woodcock, 123.

8    *La Réprésentant du Peuple* (February to August 1848); *Le Peuple* (September 1848 to June 1849); *La Voix du Peuple* (September 1849 to May 1850); *Le Peuple de 1850* (June to October 1850).

9    Quoted in Woodcock, 119.

10   "Never modest concerning his abilities, Proudhon wrote in his notebooks that the Revolution was doomed without his help" (Vincent, 169).

11   Ehrenberg, 103.

12   As Proudhon himself recognised in 1850, he was a "man of polemics, not of the barricades" (Quoted in Vincent, 169).

the proletariat."[13] Unsuccessful, he was not deterred and ran in the complementary elections held on June 4th and was duly elected.[14] He later recalled:

> When I think of everything that I have said, written and pub-
> lished over these past ten years regarding the State's role in
> society, bringing the authorities to heel and government's dis-
> qualification from revolution, I am tempted to believe that my
> election in June 1848 was the result of some incomprehension
> on the part of the people... I may have appeared momentar-
> ily to the society which I take for my judge and the authorities
> with whom I want no truck, as a formidable agitator.[15]

Following the June Days, Proudhon's paper was temporarily suppressed
when he demanded immediate economic relief for the working class and appealed directly to the National Guard for support. Viewed by conservatives
as a leading member of the left, his proposals for reform were condemned on
the floor of the assembly by Adolphe Thiers. Proudhon responded on July
31st with a three-and-a-half-hour speech that stressed "social liquidation" was
needed and that the end of property was the real meaning of the revolution.
He was defiant in the face of hecklers: "When I say WE, I identify myself
with the proletariat; when I say YOU, I identify you with the bourgeois
class."[16] Only one representative, a socialist worker from Lyons, supported
Proudhon and a motion of censure was passed (with socialists like Louis
Blanc and Pierre Leroux voting for it). Even Marx had to (grudgingly) admit
that "his attitude in the National Assembly merits nothing but praise."[17]

When *La Représentant du Peuple* was allowed to reappear in August and
"What is the capitalist? Everything! What should he be? Nothing!" was added to its masthead.[18] The repression did not dull its social criticism, with
Proudhon on fine ironic form with the searing *The Malthusians* attacking
bourgeois hypocrisy and *laissez-faire* capitalism. It was soon, however, completely suppressed, but Proudhon himself could not be prosecuted because
he enjoyed parliamentary immunity.

In October 1848, Proudhon gave a *Toast to the Revolution* at a banquet in
Paris. He spoke on the successive manifestation of justice in human life (what
he termed a "permanent revolution") before concluding that revolutionary

---

13    *Œuvres Completès*, 17: 45.

14    "Most of the votes for Proudhon were cast in working-class districts of Paris—a
fact which stands in contrast to the claims of some Marxists, who have said he was
representative only of the petite bourgeoisie" (Hoffman, 136).

15    *No Gods, No Masters*, 68.

16    Quoted in Vincent, 186.

17    *Poverty of Philosophy*, 200.

18    Woodcock, 136.

power lay not with the government, but in the people. Only the people, acting themselves, could achieve social transformation. That month also saw the launch of *Le Peuple* (*The People*) in which Proudhon argued that the creation of a strong executive elected directly by the people was monarchical and reactionary. Initially, he advocated abstaining in the Presidential election but then supported the candidacy of socialist François-Vincent Raspail. Proudhon's election manifesto was serialised in *Le Peuple* and is a succinct summation of his socio-economic ideas. Very successful, the newspaper turned from a weekly to a daily at the end of November.[19]

A few days later, Louis-Napoléon Bonaparte won the Presidential election in a surprise landslide. Proudhon had strenuously opposed Louis-Napoléon before the election and redoubled his criticism afterwards. He accurately predicted on the 22nd of December 1848 that Louis-Napoléon would produce a "monarchical restoration" and "organise the crusade of the exploiters against the exploited."[20] As well as continued journalism, Proudhon tried to create a bank of exchange, now called the *Bank of the People.* Organised in early 1849 with the participation of workers previously associated with the Luxembourg Commission, it soon had over ten thousand adherents (mostly workers) but its assets were meagre and so was essentially stillborn.

Faced with Proudhon's attacks and attempts at socialist reform, the conservative government responded by getting the assembly to lift Proudhon's immunity from prosecution. Charged with sedition, he was sentenced in March 1849 to three years in prison and fined 3,000 Francs. Proudhon liquidated his *Bank of the People*, ostensibly to prevent it from falling into the hands of the authorities, and went into hiding (although he still wrote articles for *Le Peuple*). On June 5th he was finally caught and imprisoned in Sainte-Pélagie.

During his three years in prison he founded and wrote for two newspapers (with the assistance of Alexander Herzen), wrote four books, married Euphrasie Piégard and fathered a child.[21] Two of the books written in prison became classic works of libertarian thought while his polemics with leading representatives of the statist left and *laissez-faire* right showed the weaknesses of both. Clearly, he spent his time as a political prisoner well.

The first book to appear was *Confessions of a Revolutionary* (1849), Proudhon's personal account of the 1848 revolution and its lessons. It argued that social revolution could not be achieved by means of the state, a structure incapable of being revolutionised or utilised for social transformation. He stressed how his own experiences as a politician confirmed his previous

---

19   Ehrenberg, 122.

20   Quoted in Vincent, 189.

21   He rejected a Church wedding: "When the Pope becomes a *social democrat* I will allow him to bless my marriage" (Quoted in Hayward, 207). The first of three daughters: Catherine, Marcelle and Stephanie. Sadly, Marcelle died of cholera in the summer of 1854, aged two.

arguments on the impossibility of implementing social reform from above by means of the state. Only a revolution "from below" could achieve change. Then, during the winter of 1849, Proudhon participated in two polemics in *La Voix du Peuple* (*The Voice of the People*). The first was an exchange of letters with *laissez-faire* economist Frédéric Bastiat on the justice of usury. It was subsequently published as a pamphlet entitled *Interest and Principal* (1850). The second was with Blanc and Leroux over the nature of socialism, revolution and the state, clarifying the differences between the two schools of socialism—libertarian and state.

The next book written in prison was *General Idea of the Revolution in the Nineteenth Century* (1851). This summarised Proudhon's ideas on social, economic and political transformation and was his solution to the problems and contradictions of capitalism he had raised in the 1840s, "the scientific and positive conclusion which *System of [Economic] Contradictions* was only the preamble."[22] Broken into seven studies, with a striking epilogue, it sketched his ideas both on the nature of a free socio-economic order, how to create it and the need for anarchy—self-managed social and economic associations bound by free agreements.

Just as Proudhon had warned, Louis-Napoléon seized power in a *coup d'état* on 2nd December 1851 to remain head of state. As Proudhon was already a prisoner, he avoided the repression inflicted upon the left by the new regime. He was outraged by the brutality of the army, but the lack of popular resistance to the *coup* and its subsequent approval by an overwhelming majority in a referendum profoundly disillusioned Proudhon.

The third book was published shortly after Proudhon's release from prison in July 1852. Pointing to the regime's popular support, *The Social Revolution Demonstrated by the Coup d'État of Second of December 1851* tried to make the best of a bad situation. Calling the *coup* "the act of a highway robber," he stressed that he was "opposed to dictatorship and any type of *coup d'État*" and was "repelled by dictatorship," considering it "a theocratic and barbarous institution, in every case a menace to liberty." Having "defended universal suffrage," he did "not ask that it be repressed" but rather "that it be organised, and that it lives." Although recognising Louis-Napoléon's support in the bourgeoisie, Proudhon urged him to use the mandate of the referendum to implement economic and political reforms. The choice was either "anarchy or Caesarism… there is no middle course… you are caught between the *Emperor* and the *Social Republic*!"[23] Perhaps unsurprisingly, Louis-Napoléon chose not to abolish his own power and, after another referendum, proclaimed himself Emperor on 2nd December 1852.

---

22  *Correspondance*, 3: 377.

23  *December 2, 1851: Contemporary Writings on the coup d'état of Louis Napoleon* (Garden City, N.J.; Doubleday, 1972), John B. Halsted (ed.), 253, 276, 283, 261, 307.

The fourth book, *Philosophy of Progress* (1853), was more theoretical in nature and comprised of the two lengthy letters sent from prison in 1851. While having little to do with the Revolutions of 1848 or even politics in general, it proved too much for the Imperial Censors. While not banned, the police declared that allowing publication did not guarantee that Proudhon would not be prosecuted. Finally published in Belgium, the police did ban its import into France.

French publishers consistently refused to handle his new works. His next major book, initially published anonymously, was the *Stock Exchange Speculator's Manual* (1853). Its title hid a subversive message—the abolition of wage-labour, the end of the capitalist company and the advocacy of producer and consumer associations. Originally written as a source of much needed income for his family, it took until the enlarged 3rd edition of 1856 before Proudhon put his name on it.

Then came the publication of his *magnum opus*, the massive *Justice in the Revolution and in the Church* (1858). This work is divided into twelve studies, on a host of subjects, each relating to the social origin of justice in that area. Arguing against religious claims of revelatory justice and philosophical ideas about rationalism, Proudhon argued that justice in areas of philosophy, work, the state, education, and so on, can be determined by the correspondence of social utility, conscience and historical "immanence." His conclusions range from the radical ("The land to those who cultivate it"; "Capital to those who use it"; "The product to the producer"[24]) to the conservative (patriarchy, marriage and women). The book sold exceptionally well considering it was nearly 2000 pages, but hopes for a second edition were foiled when the police seized the remaining copies and Proudhon was charged by the authorities two days after publication for attacking religion, law, morality and (ironically) the family.

To avoid jail, Proudhon and his family left in July 1858 for indefinite exile in Belgium. There, his focus turned almost exclusively to foreign affairs and in 1861 *War and Peace*[25] was published. A much misrepresented book, this work continued themes developed in *Justice* and sought to discover how war as a historical process shaped norms of social justice as well as to understand the nature and causes of war in order to end it. In the first volume Proudhon extolled the virtues of war in pre-industrial society before denouncing it as barbaric and antiquated in an age where indiscriminate killing was becoming the norm as war was increasingly industrialised. Proudhon argued that war

---

24  *Œuvres Completès*, 22: 264. These are possible because labour is "reconciled by its free nature with capital and property, from which wage-labour banished it, [and so] cannot cause a distinction of classes." This "makes society, as well as [economic] science, safe from any contradiction."

25  Pacifist thinker Leo Tolstoy was so impressed by this work he borrowed its title for his own masterpiece.

could now be ended because "the Revolution made the public conscience the only interpreter of right, the only judge of the material world and the only sovereign, which constitutes true democracy and marked the end of priesthood and militarism." Moreover, war was rooted in inequality and "whatever the officially declared reasons" it existed only "for exploitation and property" and "until the constitution of economic right, between nations as well as between individuals, war does not have any other function on earth." Given this, radical economic reform was required and "[o]nly the toiling masses are able to put an end to war, by creating economic equilibrium, which presupposes a radical revolution in ideas and morals." It concluded: "HUMANITY DOES NOT WANT ANY MORE WAR."[26]

Proudhon returned to Paris in September 1862, taking advantage of a general amnesty. This marked a renewed involvement in French politics and in 1863 he began a campaign urging the casting of blank ballots as a protest against the Second Empire. That year also saw the publication of *The Federative Principle* in which he discussed the necessity of a federal social structure as the best alternative to centralised states as well as the required economic reforms needed to maintain a just social order. An "agricultural-industrial federation" would complement and support the federation of communes and stop the degeneration of both the economic and political systems into inequality and tyranny.

In 1864, Henri Tolain published what was to become known as the *Manifesto of the Sixty*. It demanded social reforms and urged standing working class candidates in elections to achieve them. A group of workers wrote to Proudhon, asking his thoughts on this development and in a lengthy *Letter to Workers* he replied that while overjoyed by these public stirrings of the workers' movement, he was critical of their electoral stand. With his health deteriorating,[27] he composed his last work *The Political Capacity of the Working Class* to address the issues raised. His political testament, it summarised his views after 25 years of fighting for socialism. He presented a mutualist analysis of economics, federalism, association, and a host of other issues and urged workers and peasants to reject all participation in bourgeois politics in favour of creating their own self-managed organisations. By so doing, they would become conscious of themselves as a class and their ability to replace the bourgeois regime with a mutualist one based on his three great loves—freedom, equality and justice.

Proudhon died in his wife's arms on January 19th 1865 and is buried in Montparnasse cemetery, Paris.[28] Thousands followed the casket and thronged the cemetery, saying a final goodbye to one of the greatest socialist thinkers the world has ever seen.

---

26    *Œuvres Completès* 14: 327, 272, 300, 330.
27    In fact, he dictated its last chapters as he lay in bed dying.
28    Second division, near the Lenoir alley, in the tomb of the Proudhon family.

# FURTHER NOTES

## ON TERMINOLOGY

IN TERMS OF THE LANGUAGE HE USED, PROUDHON WAS BY NO MEANS CON-
sistent. Thus we have the strange sight of the first self-proclaimed anarchist
often using "anarchy" in the sense of chaos. Then there is the use of the terms
property and the state, both of which Proudhon used to describe aspects of
the current system which he opposed and the desired future he hoped for.

After 1850, Proudhon started to increasingly use the term "property"
to describe the possession he desired. This climaxed in the posthumously
published *Theory of Property*[1] in which he apparently proclaimed his whole-
hearted support for "property." Proudhon's enemies seized on this but a close
reading, as Woodcock demonstrates, finds no such thing:

> Much has been made of this essay in an attempt to show
> that it represents a retreat from Proudhon's original radical-
> ism. Fundamentally, it does not... What Proudhon does is to
> change his definition of property... he is thinking, not of the
> usurial property he condemned in his earlier works, but of
> the property that guarantees the independence of the peasant
> and artisan... Because of his changes in definition, Proudhon
> appears more conservative, but the alterations are not radical,
> since he continues to uphold the basic right of the producer
> to control his land or his workshop.[2]

---

1   This was prepared by J.A. Langlois, his old friend and follower, and others from the
    notes Proudhon had been working on during the three last years of his life. Except
    for the first chapter, it was not completed by Proudhon.

2   Woodcock, *Proudhon*, 239–40. Ironically, Proudhon recognised the confusion this
    would cause in 1841: "it is proper to call different things by different names, if

This can easily been seen when Proudhon re-iterated his opposition to ownership of land:

> I quite agree that the man who first ploughed up the land
> should receive compensation for his labour. What I cannot
> accept, regarding land, is that the work put in gives a right to
> ownership of what has been worked on.[3]

Workers' associations continued to play a key role in his theory (with workplaces becoming "little republics of workingmen"[4]). The only difference, as Stewart Edwards notes, was that "Proudhon came to consider that liberty could be guaranteed only if property ownership was not subject to any limitation save that of size."[5] Proudhon stressed that property "must be spread and consolidated... more equally." This was because he was still aware of its oppressive nature, arguing that it was "an absolutism within an absolutism," and "by nature autocratic." Its "politics could be summed up in a single word," namely "exploitation." "Simple justice," he stressed, "requires that equal division of land shall not only operate at the outset. If there is to be no abuse, it must be maintained from generation to generation."[6]

Resources were seen as being divided equally throughout a free society, which would be without concentrations and inequalities of wealth and the economic power, exploitation and oppression that they produced. The Proudhon of the 1860s was not so different from the firebrand radical of 1840. This can be seen when he wrote that his works of the 1840s contained "the mutualist and federative theory of property" in his last book, *The Political Capacity of the Working Classes*.[7]

Then there is his use of the term "state" and "government" to describe both the current centralised and top-down regime he opposed as well as the decentralised, bottom-up federation of the social organisation of the future. While these terms were used as synonyms for "social organisation" their use can only bred confusion so raising the possibility that he moved from libertarian to liberal socialism.

---

we keep the name 'property' for [individual possession], we must call [the domain of property] robbery, repine, brigandage. If, on the contrary, we reserve the name 'property' for the latter, we must designate the former by the term *possession* or some other equivalent; otherwise we should be troubled with an unpleasant synonym" (*What Is Property?*, 373).

3   *Selected Works*, 129.

4   Quoted in Douglas, 45.

5   *Selected Works*, 33.

6   *Selected Works*, 133, 141, 140, 134, 129.

7   *De la Capacité Politique des Classes Ouvrières* (Paris: Lacroix, 1868), 142.

Thus we find him discussing States within a confederation while maintaining that "the federal system is the contrary of hierarchy or administrative
and governmental centralisation" and that "a confederation is not exactly a
state... What is called federal authority, finally, is no longer a government; it
is an agency created... for the joint execution of certain functions."[8] His aim
was "to found an order of things wherein the principle of the sovereignty of
the people, of man and of the citizen, would be implemented to the letter"
and "where every member" of a society, "retaining his independence and
continuing to act as sovereign, would be self-governing." Social organisation
"would concern itself solely with collective matters; where as a consequence,
there would be certain common matters but no centralisation." He suggests
that "under the democratic constitution... the political and the economic
are... one and the same system... based upon a single principle, mutuality... and form this vast humanitarian organism of which nothing previously
could give the idea": "is this not the system of the old society turned upside
down... ?" he asks.[9] If so, then why suggest that this new "humanitarian
organism" is made up of states as well as communes and confederations?

The confusions that this would provoke are obvious and, unsurprisingly,
later anarchists have been more consistent in what they described as a state.
Not all forms of social organisation can be equated to the State and more appropriate words are needed to describe a fundamentally new form of socio-
political institution.[10]

Moreover, Proudhon saw anarchy as a long term goal and advocated appropriate means to achieve it.[11] If we remember that Proudhon sometimes
referred to anarchy as a form of government[12] we should not construe his extensive discussion of governments and governmental forms as a rejection of
anarchist ideas. Even during his most anarchistic phase in 1849 he suggested

---

8    *Principle of Federation*, 41, 40–1.

9    Graham (ed.), Vol. 1, 74–5.

10   "The anarchists soon saw... that it was rather dangerous for them to use the same
     word as the authoritarians while giving it a quite different meaning. They felt that
     a new concept called for a new word and that the use of the old term could be
     dangerously ambiguous; so they ceased to give the name 'State' to the social collec-
     tive of the future" (Guérin, *Anarchism*, 60–1). While, for some, this may appear to
     be purely a case of semantics, anarchists would reply that it just shows intellectual
     confusion to use the same name to describe things that are fundamentally organised
     in different ways and for different purposes. See section H.2.1 of *An Anarchist FAQ*.

11   As he put it in the 1860s, "centuries will pass before that ideal may be attained" but
     he wished to "grow unceasingly nearer to that end, and it is thus that I uphold the
     principle of federation" (Quoted in Woodcock, *Proudhon*, 249).

12   Anarchy is one of "four forms of government," government "of each by each" and
     the phrase "anarchic government" was not "impossible" nor "the idea absurd" (*Prin-
     ciple of Federation*, 8–9, 11).

that "as the negation of property implies that of authority, I immediately deduced from my definition this no less paradoxical corollary: that the authentic form of government is anarchy."[13] It should also be remembered that in the 1850s and 1860s Proudhon was, bar a period of exile in Belgium, writing under the watchful eyes of the censors of the Second Empire and so, perhaps, toned down some of his language as a result. Similarly, the reactionary atmosphere of the period and lack of social protest may have played their part (as can be seen from the return to radicalism shown by *The Political Capacity of the Working Classes* written in response to the stirrings of the labour movement in the early 1860s).

Then there is "democracy," a concept Proudhon eviscerated in his seminal 1848 article of the same name but later he was more than happy to proclaim that the "federative, mutualist republican sentiment" will "bring about the victory of Worker Democracy right around the world."[14] A close reading shows that his main opposition to democracy in 1848 was that it was, paradoxically, not democratic enough as it referred to the Jacobin notion that the whole nation as one body should elect a government. However, within a decentralised system it was a case of providing "a little philosophy of universal suffrage, in which I show that this great principle of democracy is a corollary of the federal principle or nothing."[15]

This changing terminology and ambiguous use of terms like government, state, property and so forth can cause problems when interpreting Proudhon. This is not to suggest that he is inconsistent or self-contradictory. In spite of changing from "possession" to "property" between 1840 and 1860 what Proudhon actually advocated was remarkably consistent.[16] This caveat should be borne in mind when reading Proudhon and these ambiguities in terminology should be taken into consideration when evaluating his ideas.

# PROUDHON AND MARX

No DISCUSSION OF Proudhon would be complete without mentioning Marx particularly as Marx's discussions of Proudhon's ideas "span almost

---

13   *No Gods, No Masters*, 46.

14   Graham (ed.), Vol. 1, 77.

15   Quoted in Woodcock, *Proudhon*, 251.

16   The peasants "desired to own the property they worked" and Proudhon was "quite content to call such ownership 'proprietary.'" Before ownership limited to what was necessary to earn a living was termed "possession" while "property" was "reserved for onerous seigniorial types of ownership. Proudhon was now perfectly happy to consider possession a form of property. There was a change in terminology, but there was no change in position" (Vincent, 195).

the entirety of his career."[17] The first public work on Marxism, *The Poverty of Philosophy*, was directed against Proudhon while jabs at him surface in *Capital, Theories of Surplus Value* and throughout his correspondence. For most Marxists (and even some anarchists) all they know of Proudhon has been gathered from Marx and Engels.

Suffice to say, the accounts of Marx and Engels are highly distorted and almost always charged with scorn.[18] This is unsurprising given that they considered Proudhon as their main theoretical competitor within the socialist movement. Indeed, at the start of the Franco-Prussian war Marx wrote that the French needed "a good hiding" and that a German victory would "shift the centre of gravity of West European labour movements from France to Germany" which would "mean the predominance of *our* theory over Proudhon's."[19]

Be that as it may, and regardless of the misrepresentations that Marx inflicted on Proudhon, it is also fair to say that he developed many of the themes he appropriated from Proudhon. ("One of Marx's most important teachers and the one who laid the foundations for his subsequent development."[20]) As Marx suggested:

> Proudhon's treatise *Qu'est-ce que la propriété?* is the criticism of political economy from the standpoint of political economy... Proudhon's treatise will therefore be scientifically superseded by a criticism of political economy, including Proudhon's conception of political economy. This work became possible only owing to the work of Proudhon himself.[21]

Marx may well have done this, but in so doing he distorted Proudhon's ideas and claimed many of his insights as his own. To set the record straight is not a call for Marx to be rejected in favour of Proudhon, it is a call for an honest appraisal of both.

The awkward fact is that many key aspects of Marxism were first suggested by Proudhon. For Benjamin Tucker "the tendency and consequences of capitalistic production... were demonstrated to the world time and time

17  Thomas, 193.

18  In response to a comment in Marx's "Political Indifferentism" on Proudhon's attitude to strikes even the editor of a collection of Marx's works had to state "[t]o give Proudhon his due, he was not so much justifying the actions of the French authorities as exposing the 'contradictions' he saw as an inevitable evil of the present social order" (*The First International*, 330).

19  *Marx-Engels Collected Works* 44: 3–4.

20  Rudolf Rocker, "Marx and Anarchism," *The Poverty of Statism* (Orkney: Cienfuegos Press, 1981), Albert Meltzer (ed.), 77.

21  *Marx-Engels Collected Works* 4: 31.

again during the twenty years preceding the publication of '*Das Kapital*'" by Proudhon, as were "the historical persistence of class struggles in successive manifestations." "Call Marx, then, the father of State socialism, if you will," Tucker argued, "but we dispute his paternity of the general principles of economy on which all schools of socialism agree."[22] Moreover "Proudhon propounded and proved [the theory of surplus value] long before Marx advanced it."[23]

Tucker had a point. It was Proudhon, not Marx, who first proclaimed the need for a "scientific socialism."[24] It was Proudhon who first located surplus value production within the workplace, recognising that the worker was hired by a capitalist who then appropriates their product in return for a less than equivalent amount of wages. Marx, a mere twenty-seven years later, agreed that "property turns out to be the right, on the part of the capitalist, to appropriate the unpaid labour of others or its product, and the impossibility, on the part of the worker, of appropriating his own product" as "the product belongs to the capitalist and not to the worker."[25] He also repeated Proudhon's analysis of "collective force," again without acknowledgement.[26] In *The Holy Family* he was more forthcoming:

> Proudhon was the first to draw attention to the fact that
> the sum of the wages of the individual workers, even if
> each individual labour be paid for completely, does not
> pay for the collective power objectified in its product, that
> therefore the worker is not paid as a part of the collective
> labour power.[27]

Marx mocked that Proudhon "might perhaps have discovered that this right [of free competition] (with capital R) exists only in the Economic Manuals written by the Brothers Ignoramus of bourgeois political economy, in which manuals are contained such pearls as this: 'Property is the fruit of labour' ('of the labour', they neglect to add, 'of others')."[28] This would be the same Proudhon who proclaimed, three decades before, that "Property is the right

---

22   *Liberty* 35 (1883): 2.
23   *Liberty* 92 (1887): 1.
24   *What Is Property?*, 264.
25   *Capital* 1: 730–1.
26   *Capital* 1: 451. Engels in one of his many introductions to *Capital* notes that "passages from economic writers are quoted in order to indicate when, where and by whom a certain proposition was for the first time clearly enunciated" (111). Clearly Marx could not bring himself to acknowledge that Proudhon had first formulated this part of his critique of capitalism.
27   *Marx-Engels Collected Works* 4: 52.
28   *The First International*, 331.

to enjoy and dispose of another's goods,—the fruit of another's labour"?[29] He also ridiculed Proudhon for the axiom that "all labour must leave a surplus" by stating he "attempts to explain this fact" in capitalist production "by reference to some mysterious natural attribute of labour." Yet Marx points to the "peculiar property" of labour that results in "the value of the labour-power" being "less than the value created by its use during that time"[30] which sounds remarkably like Proudhon's axiom.

Little wonder Rudolf Rocker argued that we find "the theory of surplus value, that grand 'scientific discovery' of which our Marxists are so proud of, in the writings of Proudhon."[31]

Comparing Proudhon's critique of property with Marx's we discover that "Communism deprives no man of the power to appropriate the products of society; all that it does is to deprive him of the power to subjugate the labour of others by means of such appropriation."[32] Which echoes Proudhon's argument that possession does not allow the appropriation of the means of life (land and workplaces) as these should be held in common.

Much the same can be said of the co-operative movement. For Marx it was "one of the transforming forces of the present society based upon class antagonism. Its great merit is to practically show, that the present pauperising, and despotic system of the *subordination of labour* to capital can be superseded by the republican and beneficent system of *the association of free and equal producers*."[33] In the 1880s, Engels suggested as a reform the putting of public works and state-owned land into the hands of workers' co-operatives rather than capitalists. Neither he nor Marx "ever doubted that, in the course of transition to a wholly communist economy, widespread use would have to be made of co-operative management as an intermediate stage" although "initially" the State "retains ownership of the means of production."[34] That these echoed earlier comments by Proudhon goes without saying.

Marx argued that credit system presents "the means for the gradual extension of co-operative enterprises on a more or less national scale" and so the "development of credit" has "the latent abolition of capital ownership contained within it." It "constitutes the form of transition to a new mode of production" and "there can be no doubt that the credit system will serve as a powerful lever in the course of transition from the capitalist mode of production to the mode of production of associated labour."[35] Proudhon would

29   *What Is Property?*, 171.
30   *Capital* 1: 1011–2, 270, 731.
31   "Marx and Anarchism," 77.
32   *Marx-Engels Reader*, 486.
33   *The First International*, 90.
34   *Marx-Engels Collected Works* 47: 239, 389.
35   *Capital: A Critique of Political Economy* (London: Penguin Books, 1981) 3: 571–72, 572, 743.

hardly have disagreed. For Marx, abolishing interest and interest-bearing capital "means the abolition of capital and of capitalist production itself."[36] For Proudhon, "reduction of interest rates to vanishing point is itself a revolutionary act, because it is destructive of capitalism."[37]

Marx asserted that "Proudhon has failed to understand" that "economic forms" and "the social relations corresponding to them" are "*transitory and historical*," thinking that "the bourgeois form of production" and "bourgeois relations" were "eternal."[38] Yet Proudhon explicitly argued that the "present form" of organising labour "is inadequate and transitory."[39] Hence the need to "organise industry, associate labourers and their functions." Association "is the annihilation of property" and this "non-appropriation of the instruments of production" would be based on "the equality of associates."[40]

Marx ignored this. He commented upon Proudhon's exchange with Bastiat many times and in all of them overlooked that Proudhon was discussing a *post*-capitalist economy. Proudhon was well aware that under capitalism "a worker, without property, without capital, without work, is hired by [the capitalist], who gives him employment and takes his product" and his wages fail to equal the price of the commodities he creates. "In mutualist society," however, "the two functions" of worker and capitalist "become equal and inseparable in the person of every worker" and so he "alone profits by his products" (and the "surplus" he creates).[41] So much for Marx's assertion that this exchange showed Proudhon "want[ed] to preserve wage-labour and thus the basis of capital."[42] As he acknowledged elsewhere, when "the direct producer" is "the possessor of his own means of production" then he is "a non-capitalist producer." This is "a form of production that does not correspond to the capitalist mode of production" even if "he produces his product as a commodity."[43]

Marx usually argued that Proudhon was "the scientific exponent of the French petty bourgeoisie, which is a real merit since the petty bourgeoisie will be an integral part of all impeding social revolutions"[44] and wrote *The Philosophy of Poverty* accordingly. Yet when it comes to Proudhon, Marx never expressed *Capital*'s clear distinction between commodity production and capitalism and presents him as advocating wage-labour. Proudhon explicitly

36    *Theories of Surplus Value*, (London: Lawrence and Wishart , 1972) 3: 472.

37    Quoted in Edward Hyams, *Pierre-Joseph Proudhon: His Revolutionary Life, Mind and Works* (London: John Murray, 1979), 188.

38    *Marx-Engels Collected Works* 38: 97, 103.

39    *System of Economical Contradictions*, 55.

40    *What Is Property?*, 310, 363, 372, 365.

41    *Œuvres Complètes* 19: 295, 305.

42    *Theories of Surplus Value* 3: 525.

43    *Capital* 3: 735, 1015.

44    *Marx-Engels Collected Works* 38: 105.

did not and argued that while interest was justified in previous societies, it was not in a mutualist one and lambasted Bastiat for refusing to envision anything other than capitalism—a refusal Marx shared in this instance. So when Marx interpreted Proudhon as defending "the productive capitalist in contrast to the lending capitalist" and argued that ending interest "in no way affects the value of the hats, but simply the distribution of the surplus-value already contained in the hats among different people"[45] he utterly missed the point. Marx did, once, vaguely recognise this:

> In order that it should be impossible for commodities and money to become capital and therefore be lent as capital *in posse* [in potential but not in actuality], they must not con-front wage-labour. If they are... not to confront it as *commodities* and *money*... labour itself is not to become a commodity... this is only possible where the workers are the owners of their means of production... Mr. Proudhon's hatters do not appear to be *capitalists* but journeymen.[46]

Precisely, Herr Marx, precisely...

So Marx, like Proudhon before him, differentiated between possession and private property and argued that co-operatives should replace capitalist firms. Both recognised that capitalism was but a transitory form of economy due to be replaced (as it replaced feudalism) with a new one based on *associated* rather than wage labour. While their specific solutions may have differed (with Proudhon aiming for a market economy consisting of artisans, farmers and co-operatives while Marx aimed, after a lengthy transition period, for centrally planned communism) their analysis of capitalism and private property were identical. Understandably, given the parallels, Marx was keen to hide them.

In terms of politics, Marx also repeated Proudhon. When Marx placed "the emancipation of the working classes must be conquered by the working classes themselves"[47] in the statues of the IWMA, the mutualist delegates must have remembered Proudhon's exhortation from 1848 that "the proletariat must emancipate itself without the help of the government."[48]

Both argued that the state was an instrument of class rule, Proudhon in 1846 and Marx a year later in reply to that work.[49] Then there is Proudhon's

---

45   *Capital* 3: 467.

46   *Theories of Surplus Value* 3: 525–6.

47   *The First International*, 82.

48   Quoted in Woodcock, *Proudhon*, 125. The expression "the emancipation of the working class is the task of the working class itself" was first used by the remarkable socialist-feminist Flora Tristan in 1843 (Mattick, 333).

49   Although Marx, unlike Proudhon, repeatedly stated that universal suffrage gave the

call for a dual-power within the state in early 1848 and support for the clubs which Marx subsequently echoed in 1850 in an address to the Communist League.[50] With the Paris Commune of 1871, this appropriation became wholesale. Marx eulogised the political vision of the Communards without once mentioning that their decentralised, bottom-up system based on federations of mandated and recallable delegates who combined executive and legislative powers had been publicly urged by Proudhon since 1848.

Not bad for someone dismissed as an advocate of "Conservative, or bourgeois, socialism"![51] Of course, all this could be just a coincidence and just a case of great minds thinking alike—with one coming to the same conclusions a few years after the other expressed them in print.

## THE POVERTY OF PHILOSOPHY

Given all this, we can see the point of Proudhon's comment, scribbled as a marginal note in his copy of Marx's *The Poverty of Philosophy*, that "what Marx's book really means is that he is sorry that everywhere *I* have thought the way *he* does, and said so before he did. Any determined reader can see that it is Marx who, having read me, regrets thinking like me. What a man!" And it is to that book which we need to turn, as no account of Proudhon's ideas would be complete without a discussion of what the Frenchman proclaimed "a tissue of vulgarity, of calumny, of falsification and of plagiarism" written by "the tapeworm of socialism."[52]

*The Poverty of Philosophy*[53] was written in reply to Proudhon's *System of Economic Contradictions*. What to make of it?

First, it must be remembered that this work is not really about Proudhon but Marx. Proudhon's fame is used to get people to read the work of an unknown radical thinker and for that thinker to expound his ideas on various subjects. Second, it is a hatchet-job of epic proportions—although as few Marxists bother to read Proudhon as Marx has pronounced judgment on him, they would not know that and so they contribute to "the perpetuation of a spiteful distortion of his thought" produced by Marx's "desire to denigrate" his "strongest competitors."[54]

While, undoubtedly, Marx makes some valid criticisms of Proudhon, the book is full of distortions. His aim was to dismiss Proudhon as being the ideologist of the petit-bourgeois[55] and he obviously thought all means

---

working class political power and so could be used to capture the state. See section H.3.10 of *An Anarchist FAQ.*

50    *Marx-Engels Reader*, 507–8.
51    *Marx-Engels Reader*, 496.
52    Quoted in Thomas, 211.
53    All quotes unless indicated otherwise are from this work.
54    Vincent, 230.
55    "He wished to soar as a man of science above the bourgeoisie and the proletarians;

were applicable to achieve that goal. So we find Marx arbitrarily arranging quotations from Proudhon's book, often out of context and even tampered with, to confirm his own views. This allows him to impute to Proudhon ideas the Frenchman did not hold (often explicitly rejects!) in order to attack him. Marx even suggests that his own opinion is the opposite of Proudhon's when, in fact, he is simply repeating the Frenchman's thoughts. He takes the Frenchman's sarcastic comments at face value, his metaphors and abstractions literally.[56] And, above all else, Marx seeks to ridicule him.[57]

Here we address a few of the many distortions Marx inflicted on Proudhon and see how his criticism has faired.[58]

Marx quotes Proudhon as stating that the economists "have very well explained the double character of value; but what they have not set out with equal clearness is its *contradictory nature*" and then goes on to state that, for Proudhon, the economists "have neither seen nor known, either the opposition or the contradiction" between use-value and exchange-value. (37–8) Marx then quotes three economists expounding on this contradiction. Except Proudhon had not suggested that economists had "neither seen nor known" this, but that they had "not set out with equal clearness" this contradiction. Presumably Marx hoped that readers would be too distracted by his witticism to notice that he had lambasted Proudhon for something he had not actually said. Nor did Proudhon "say that J-B Say was the *first* to

---

he is only the petty bourgeois, tossed about constantly between capital and labour, between political economy and communism" (137). If Marx embodied proletarian socialism, regardless of whether the proletariat knew this or not, then Proudhon must, by definition, represent another class. Given the starting assumption, what other conclusion could flow?

56    Thus we find Marx ignoring Proudhon's analysis of classes in capitalism in favour of this assertion: "What... is this Prometheus resuscitated by M. Proudhon? It is society, it is the social relations based on the antagonism of classes... Efface these relations and you have extinguished the whole of society, and your Prometheus is nothing more than a phantom" (109). It is almost redundant to note that Proudhon analysed the class nature of capitalist society in *System of Economic Contradictions*. His discussion of machinery, for example, shows that he was well aware that capitalists introduce it to increase their profits at the expense of the workers.

57    Somewhat ironically, Marx himself has suffered from being subject to the approach he inflicted on Proudhon. Just as Marx mocked Proudhon for his high-level of abstraction when the Frenchman used the notion of a consuming and producing Prometheus to illustrate some of his points, so the German has been subject to similar abuse by bourgeois economists for his high level abstractions in Volume 1 of *Capital* which they stress are unrealistic. Poetic Justice, some would say.

58    We have taken the liberty of adding footnotes to the extracts of *System of Economic Contradictions* we provide to show what Marx claimed and what Proudhon actually wrote.

recognise 'that in the division of labour the same cause which produces good engenders evil.'" (140) Rather Proudhon wrote that "Say goes so far as to recognise that in the division of labour the same cause which produces the good engenders the evil."[59] Which makes the subsequent quoting of economists showing that Say was not the first to recognise this fact misleading.

Marx repeatedly accused Proudhon of advocating ideas which he rejected in his book. We find Proudhon discussing the suggestion of an economist, M. Blanqui, who argued for "an increase of wages resulting from the co-partnership, or at least from the interest in the business, which he confers upon the labourers." Proudhon then asked: "What, then, is the value to the labourer of a participation in the profits?" He replied by providing an example of a mill, whose profit amounts to "annual dividend of twenty thousand francs." If this were divided by the number of employees and "by three hundred, the number of working days, I find an increase... of eighteen centimes, just a morsel of bread." He concluded that this would be "a poor prospect to offer the working class."[60] All of which makes this comment by Marx incredulous and misleading:

> If then, in theory, it suffices to interpret, as M. Proudhon
> does, the formula of the surplus of labour in the sense of
> equality without taking account of the actual relations of
> production, it must suffice, in practice, to make among the
> workers an equal distribution of wealth without changing
> anything in the actual conditions of production. This distri-
> bution would not assure a great degree of comfort to each of
> the participants. (109–10)

Moreover Proudhon was well aware of the actual relations of production. He indicated that with "machinery and the workshop, divine right—that is, the principle of authority—makes its entrance into political economy. Capital... Property... are, in economic language, the various names of... Power, Authority." Thus, under capitalism, the workplace has a "hierarchical organisation."[61] He was well aware of the oppressive nature of wage labour. As Proudhon argued in volume 2 of *System of Economic Contradictions*:

> Do you know what it is to be a wage-worker? It is to la-
> bour under a master, watchful for his prejudices even more
> than for his orders... It is to have no mind of your own...
> to know no stimulus save your daily bread and the fear of
> losing your job.

---

59    *System of Economical Contradictions*, 134.
60    *System of Economical Contradictions*, 145.
61    *System of Economical Contradictions*, 203–4.

> The wage-worker is a man to whom the property owner
> who hires him says: What you have to make is none of your
> business; you do not control it.[62]

Which raises the question of what Marx had in mind if not those relations *within* the workplace? Proudhon was well aware that exploitation occurred there as workers had "parted with their liberty" and "have sold their arms" to a boss who appropriated their product and "collective force."[63] To suggest that Proudhon was blind to what happened in production under capitalism is false.

Then there is the perennial Marxist assertion that Proudhon wished to return to pre-industrial forms of economy.[64] Marx suggests "[t]hose who, like Sismondi, would return to the just proportion of production, while conserving the existing bases of society, are reactionary, since, to be consistent, they must also desire to re-establish all the other conditions of past times" (73). Yet Proudhon explicitly rejected such an option, using almost the same words as Marx did.[65] Unsurprisingly, given that Proudhon argued that workers' co-operatives were essential to ensure the application of large-scale technology.

Marx then goes on to argue that either you have "just proportions of past centuries, with the means of production of our epoch, in which case you are at once a reactionary and a utopian" or "you have progress without anarchy: In which case, in order to conserve productive forces, you must abandon individual exchanges" (73). This comes from the extreme technological determinism Marx expounds:

> The social relations are intimately attached to the productive
> forces. In acquiring new productive forces men change their
> mode of production; and in changing their mode of produc-
> tion, their manner of gaining a living, they change all their
> social relations. The windmill gives you society with the feudal
> lord; the steam-mill, society with the industrial capitalist. (119)

---

62   *Œuvres Complètes* 5: 230–1. So much for the assertion by Marxist Paul Thomas that "Proudhon had no real conception of alienation in the labour process" (243).

63   *System of Economical Contradictions*, 301–2.

64   "M. Proudhon has not got beyond the ideal of the petty bourgeois. And in order to realise this ideal he thinks of nothing better than to bring us back to the companion, or at most the master, workman of the Middle Ages" (157).

65   "M. de Sismondi, like all men of patriarchal ideas, would like the division of labour, with machinery and manufactures, to be abandoned, and each family to return to the system of primitive indivision,—that is, to *each one by himself, each one for himself*, in the most literal meaning of the words. That would be to retrograde; it is impossible" (*System of Economical Contradictions*, 206).

This is nonsense, with Marx himself subsequently acknowledging that co-operatives show "[b]y deed instead of by argument" that "production on a large scale... may be carried on without the existence of a class of masters employing a class of hands."[66] In them "the opposition between capital and labour is abolished," they are "a new mode of production" which "develops and is formed naturally out of the old."[67] So the steam-mill *can* be run without the industrial capitalist, by a workers association. Which was *precisely* what Proudhon did advocate:

> it is necessary to destroy or modify the predominance of capi-tal over labour, to change the relations between employer and worker, to solve, in a word, the antinomy of division and that of machinery; it is necessary to ORGANISE LABOUR.[68]

Marx's comments were related to his dismissal of Proudhon's "constituted value" which he asserted was incompatible with an advanced economy. Commodities "produced in such proportions that they can be sold at an honest price" was "only possible in the epoch in which the means of pro-duction were limited, and in which exchange only took place within very narrow limits" (72–3). Yet Proudhon has had the last laugh for, as capitalism has developed, the market price of goods has been replaced to a large degree with administered prices. Empirical research has concluded that a significant proportion of goods have prices based on mark-up, normal cost and target rate of return pricing procedures and "the existence of stable, administered market prices implies that the markets in which they exist are not organised like auction markets or like the early retail markets and oriental bazaars" as imagined in mainstream economic ideology.[69] Proudhon's notion of an economy based on the "just price," one which reflects costs, has become *more* possible over time rather than less as Marx had asserted.

Another area where Marx's critique has proven to be lacking was his argument in favour of central planning. Given the actual experience of planned economies, it is amusing to read him suggest that "[i]f the divi-sion of labour in a modern factory, were taken as a model to be applied to an entire society, the society best organised for the production of wealth would be incontestably that which had but one single master distributing the work, according to a regulation arranged beforehand, to the various members of the community" (147). In reality, such a centralised system would be, and was, swamped by the task of gathering and processing the

---

66    *The First International*, 79.

67    *Capital* 3: 571.

68    *System of Economical Contradictions*, 244.

69    Frederic S. Lee, *Post Keynesian Price Theory* (Cambridge: Cambridge University Press, 1998), 212.

information required to plan well. Proudhon's decentralised system would be the best organised simply because it can access and communicate the necessary information to make informed decisions on what, when and how to produce goods.[70]

The core of Marx's critique rested on a massive confusion of commodity production (the market) and capitalism. Yet in 1867 he was clear that wage-labour was the necessary pre-condition for capitalism, not commodity production, as "the means of production and subsistence, while they remain the property of the immediate producer, are not capital. They only become capital under circumstances in which they serve at the same time as means of exploitation of, and domination over, the worker." When the producer owns his "conditions of labour" and "employs that labour to enrich himself instead of the capitalist" then it is an economic system "diametrically opposed" to capitalism.[71]

While Proudhon was in favour of commodity production, he was against wage-labour, that is labour as a commodity. Yet this did not stop Marx asserting that in Proudhon's system labour was "itself a commodity" (55). Marx did let that awkward fact slip into his diatribe:

> [Proudhon] has a misgiving that it is to make of the minimum wage the natural and normal price of direct labour, that it is to accept the existing state of society. So, to escape from this fatal consequence he performs a *volte-face* and pretends that labour is not a commodity, that it could not have a value... He forgets that his whole system rests on the labour commodity, on labour which is trafficked, bought and sold, exchanged for products... He forgets all. (62–3)

Or, conversely, Marx *remembers* that Proudhon's whole system rests on abolishing labour as a commodity.

In short, the future Marx, with his comments on artisan production and co-operative workplaces, shows how wrong he was in 1847 to assert against Proudhon that the "mode of exchange of products depends upon the mode of production... Individual exchange also corresponds to a determined method production, which itself corresponds to the antagonism of classes. Thus there is no individual exchange without the antagonism of classes" (84).

This is not the only area in which the Marx of 1847 is in direct contradiction to his more mature future self. Marx proclaims against Proudhon that "relative value, measured by labour-time, is fatally the formula of the modern slavery of the worker. Instead of being, as M. Proudhon would have it, the 'revolutionary theory' of the emancipation of the proletariat" (55). Come

---

70   See section I.1.2 of *An Anarchist FAQ*.
71   *Capital* 1: 938, 931.

1875, Marx-the-older proclaims in his *Critique of the Gotha Programme* the use of labour-notes in the period of transition to communism.[72]

Key aspects of Marx's later analysis of capitalism can be found in Proudhon's work. Marx mocks the suggestion that labour "is said *to have value*, not as merchandise itself, but in view of the values supposed to be contained in it potentially. The *value of labour* is a figurative expression, an anticipation of effect from cause" which "becomes a reality through its product."[73] Marx argues:

> All the reasonings of M. Proudhon confine themselves to this:
> We do not purchase labour as an instrument of immediate
> consumption. No, we buy it as an instrument of production...
> Merely as a commodity labour is worth nothing and produces
> nothing. M. Proudhon might as well have said that there are
> no commodities in existence at all, seeing that every commod-
> ity is only acquired for some use and never merely as a com-
> modity. (62)

Marx-the-older, however, argued that the "purchaser of labour-power consumes it by setting the seller of it to work" and so "becomes in actuality what previously he only was potentially," a worker who produces "a specific article."[74] Thus Proudhon "anticipated an idea that Marx was to develop as one of the key elements in the concept of *labour power*, viz. that *as a commodity*, labour produces nothing and it exists independently of and prior to the exercise of its potential to produce value as *active* labour."[75] Marx-the-older used this insight to argue that labour-power "is purchased for the production of commodities which contain more labour than [is] paid for" and so "surplus-value is nothing but objectified surplus labour."[76] In this he repeated Proudhon who argued that non-labour incomes are "but the materialisation of the aphorism, *All labour should leave an excess*." As "all value is

---

72   Discussing communism as "it *emerges* from capitalist society" Marx argued that "the individual producer... receives a certificate from society that he has furnished such-and-such an amount of labour" and "draws from the social stock of means of consumption as much as the same amount of labour cost." So ("obviously"!) "the same principle prevails as that which regulates the exchange of commodities, as far as this is exchange of equal values. Content and form are changed" as "nothing can pass to the ownership of individuals, except individual means of consumption" (*Marx-Engels Reader*, 529–30).

73   *System of Economical Contradictions*, 101.

74   *Capital* 1: 283.

75   Allen Oakley, *Marx's Critique of Political Economy: intellectual sources and evolution, 1844 to 1860* Vol. 1, (London: Routledge & Kegan Paul, 1984), 118.

76   *Capital* 1: 769, 325.

born of labour" it meant "that no wealth has its origin in privilege" and so "labour alone is the source of revenue among men."[77] Thus profit, interest and rent came from the capitalist appropriating the surplus-labour and collective force of workers:

> the worker... create[s], on top of his subsistence, a capital always greater. Under the regime of property, the surplus of labour, essentially collective, passes entirely, like the revenue, to the proprietor: now, between that disguised appropriation and the fraudulent usurpation of a communal good, where is the difference?
>
> The consequence of that usurpation is that the labourer, whose share of the collective product is constantly confiscated by the entrepreneur, is always on his uppers, while the capitalist is always in profit... and that political economy, that upholds and advocates that regime, is the theory of theft.[78]

This analysis of exploitation occurring in production feeds into Proudhon's few tantalising glimpses of his vision of a free society.[79] Thus we discover that as "all labour must leave a surplus, all wages [must] be equal to product." To achieve this, the workplace must be democratic for "[b]y virtue of the principle of collective force, workers are the equals and associates of their leaders" and to ensure "that association may be real, he who participates in it must do so" as "an active factor" with "a deliberative voice in the council" with everything "regulated in accordance with equality." These "conditions are precisely those of the organisation of labour." This requires free access and so all workers "straightway enjoy the rights and prerogatives of associates and even managers" when they join a workplace. This would ensure "equality of fortunes, voluntary and free association, universal solidarity, material comfort and luxury, and public order without prisons, courts, police, or hangmen."[80]

Needless to say, Marx ignores all this. Once acknowledged, it is incredulous to assert that Proudhon "borrows from the economists the necessity of eternal relations" and to end its troubles society has "only to eliminate all the ill-sounding terms. Let it change the language" and that such "activities

---

77    *System of Economical Contradictions*, 56–7.

78    *Œuvres Completès* 5: 246–7.

79    While Marx suggests that Proudhon's work was presenting a panacea to society's ills, it was primarily a work of critique: "We will reserve this subject [the organisation of labour] for the time when, the theory of economic contradictions being finished, we shall have found in their general equation the programme of association, which we shall then publish in contrast with the practice and conceptions of our predecessors" (*System of Economical Contradictions*, 311).

80    *System of Economical Contradictions*, 340, 411, 312, 307, 37.

form an essential part of the argument of M. Proudhon" (137, 61). In reality, Proudhon denounced "the radical vice of political economy" of "affirming as a definitive state a transitory condition—namely, the division of society into patricians and proletaires." He noted that the "period through which we are now passing" is "distinguished by a special characteristic: WAGE-LABOUR."[81] His arguments for socialisation and self-management prove that he sought to end bourgeois relations *within production*. As Marx-the-older admitted, capital's "existence" is "by no means given with the mere circulation of money and commodities." This "new epoch" in social production requires the proprietor finding "in the market" the worker "as seller of his own labour-power."[82] So "if one eliminates the capitalists, the means of production cease to be *capital*"[83] and when "the workers are themselves in possession of their respective means of production and exchange their commodities with one another" then these commodities "would not be products of capital."[84]

This is not to suggest that Marx's diatribe did not make some valid points. Far from it. Revolutionary anarchists would agree with Marx on unions being "a rampart for the workers in their struggle with the capitalists" and that "the determination of value by labour time, that is to say the formula which M. Proudhon has given us as the regenerating formula of the future, is... only the scientific expression of the economic relations of existing society" (187, 74). Such valid points should not blind us to the distortions that work contains, distortions which ultimately undermine Marx's case.

Significantly, while Marx's 1847 work has become considered by Marxists as a key document in the development of his ideas, at the time its impact was null. Proudhon remained one of Europe's foremost socialist thinkers and Marx's attack "sank into obscurity" and "by 1864 his name meant nothing to the new generation of working-class leaders" in France.[85] It is only after the eclipse of Proudhon by social democracy that it became better known. It undoubtedly helped that, unlike when it was written, few would have read Proudhon's two volumes.

Proudhon carefully read and annotated his copy of *The Poverty of Philosophy*. Sadly a family crisis followed swiftly by the outbreak of the February Revolution of 1848 stopped a reply being written. Proudhon, rightly, thought social transformation more pressing than bothering with an obscure German communist. That he never did so is one of the great lost opportunities of socialism as it would have clarified some of the issues raised by Marx and allowed Proudhon to extend his critique of state socialism to Marxism.

Finally, given how many people think Marx was extremely witty in

---

81  *System of Economical Contradictions*, 67, 198 (translation corrected).
82  *Capital* 1: 274.
83  *Theories of Surplus Value* 3: 296.
84  *Capital* 3: 276.
85  Archer, 50.

reversing the sub-title of Proudhon's book, it should be pointed out that even in this he was plagiarising Proudhon:

> Modern philosophers, after collecting and classifying their an-
> nals, have been led by the nature of their labours to deal also
> with history: then it was that they saw, not without surprise,
> that the *history of philosophy* was the same thing at bottom as
> the *philosophy of history*.[86]

All in all, it is hard not to disagree with Edward Hyams' summation: "since [*The Poverty of Philosophy*] no good Marxists have had to think about Proudhon. They have what is mother's milk to them, an *ex cathedra* judgement."[87]

# FURTHER READING

SADLY, VERY LITTLE of Proudhon's voluminous writings has been translated into English. Benjamin Tucker translated the First and Second Memoirs of *What is Property?* and volume 1 of *System of Economic Contradictions* and both are available on-line. He also translated numerous other shorter pieces. The First Memoir of *What is Property?* in a new translation is also available from Cambridge University Press. *General Idea of the Revolution in the Nine-teenth Century* was translated in 1923 by John Beverley Robinson (available on-line). The First Part and chapter one of the Second Part of *Du Principe Fédératif* was translated by Richard Vernon under the title *The Principle of Federation*. Other selections (mostly related to his Bank of Exchange, extracts from his exchange with Bastiat and a few parts of volume 2 of *System of Economic Contradictions*) have appeared in Clarence L. Swartz's *Proudhon's Solution to the Social Question*. *Selected Writings of Pierre-Joseph Proudhon* edited by Stewart Edwards has a comprehensive selection of short extracts on various subjects.

Most anthologies of anarchism have selections from Proudhon's works. George Woodcock's *The Anarchist Reader* has a few short extracts, while Daniel Guérin's essential *No Gods, No Masters: An Anthology of Anarchism* has a comprehensive section on Proudhon. Robert Graham's excellent anthology *Anarchism: A Documentary History of Libertarian Ideas, Volume 1: From Anarchy to Anarchism (300CE–1939)* has selections from Proudhon's major works.

The best introduction to Proudhon's ideas is K. Steven Vincent's *Pierre-Joseph Proudhon and the Rise of French Republican Socialism*, which

---

86   *System of Economical Contradictions*, 171.
87   Hyams, 92.

places his ideas within the context of the wider working class and socialist movements.[88] George Woodcock's *Pierre-Joseph Proudhon: A Biography* is the best available and is essential reading. Other studies include Robert L. Hoffman's *Revolutionary Justice: The Social and Political Theory of P-J Proudhon*, Alan Ritter's *The Political Thought of Pierre-Joseph Proudhon* and *Pierre-Joseph Proudhon: His Revolution Life, Mind and Works* by Edward Hyman. J. Hampden Jackson's *Marx, Proudhon and European Socialism* is a good short overview of the Proudhon's life, ideas and influence. Henri de Lubac's *The Un-Marxian Socialist: A Study of Proudhon* is more concerned about Proudhon's relationship with Christianity. *Political Economy From Below: Economic Thought in Communitarian Anarchism, 1840–1914* by Rob Knowles presents a useful extended discussion of Proudhon's economic ideas.

Shorter accounts of Proudhon and his ideas include Robert Graham's excellent introduction to the 1989 Pluto Press edition of *General Idea*. Jack Hayward has a comprehensive chapter entitled "Proudhon and Libertarian Socialism" in his *After the French Revolution: Six Critics of Democracy and Nationalism*. Martin Buber's *Paths in Utopia* contains a useful account of Proudhon's ideas. Other useful short pieces on Proudhon include George Woodcock's "Pierre-Joseph Proudhon; An Appreciation" (in the anthology *Anarchism and Anarchists*) and "On Proudhon's 'What is Property?'" (*The Raven* 31). Daniel Guérin's "From Proudhon to Bakunin" (*The Radical Papers*, Dimitrios I. Roussopoulos, ed.) is a good introduction to the links between the French Anarchist and revolutionary anarchism. Charles A. Dana's *Proudhon and his "Bank of the People"* is a contemporary (1849) account of his economic ideas.

George Woodcock's *Anarchism: A History of Libertarian Ideas and Movements* and Peter Marshall's *Demanding the Impossible: A History of Anarchism*, both have chapters on Proudhon's life and ideas. Daniel Guérin's *Anarchism: From Theory to Practice* is an excellent short introduction to anarchism which places Proudhon, with Bakunin, at its centre. Max Nettlau's *A Short History of Anarchism* should also be consulted.

For those Marxists keen to read a generally accurate and sympathetic account of Proudhon, albeit one still rooted in Marxist dogmas and dubious assumptions, then John Ehrenberg's *Proudhon and His Age* would be of interest.[89]

---

88  It is only marred by Vincent considering anarchism as being incompatible with social organisation and, as such, Proudhon's theory "conflicts with the traditional concept of anarchism" and so he was not an anarchist in the "popular meaning" (269, 234)!

89  For a short critique of Ehrenberg's Marxist assumptions, see K. Steven Vincent's review (*The American Historical Review* 102: 4 [1997]).

# ACKNOWLEDGEMENTS

I WOULD LIKE to thank Shawn Wilbur, Paul Sharkey, Ian Harvey, Martin Walker, James Bar Bowen, Nathalie Colibert, Jesse Cohn, John Duda and Barry Marshall for their kindness in translating so much. Without their work, this anthology would be impoverished. I must also thank Shawn for his suggestions and toleration in replying to a constant stream of emails asking questions, clarifications and opinions on a whole host of issues for this work. Lastly, I would like to thank Nicholas Evans and Alex Prichard for their useful comments on my introduction.

A special note of thanks for Jesse Cohn who not only helped me work out two particularly puzzling translation issues but also did a wonderful job in proof-editing the manuscript. Many of the footnotes, for example, are his work.

In addition, I would like to thank Robert Graham for providing me with the full version of Chapter XV of *The Political Capacity of the Working Classes* which had previously appeared in an edited form in volume 1 of his anthology *Anarchism: A Documentary History of Libertarian Ideas*.

Finally, I would like to thank my partner for her knowledge, experience and patience in answering my numerous questions on issues related to translating from French.

# A NOTE ON THE TEXTS

THE TEXTS ARE presented in chronological order, so that readers can get a feel for how Proudhon's ideas and ways of expressing himself changed over time. We have aimed to present newly translated material in full and have edited those which are available in English already. Any edits are indicated by bracketed ellipses and any additions are surrounded by brackets. We have tried to reproduce Proudhon's own stresses and capitalisations.

For those interested in reading the full versions of the material we present here, then please visit Shawn Wilbur's *New Proudhon Library* (www.proudhonlibrary.org). A complete translation of *The Philosophy of Progress* is there, along with other material.

This is but a small part of Proudhon's works and there are many key works, such as *Confessions of a Revolutionary* and *The Political Capacity of the Working Classes*, which should be made available to the English-speaking world in full. This anthology should hopefully show why such a task would be worthwhile. For those interested in such a project, please visit the translation project at *Collective Reason* (www.collectivereason.org).

Lastly, the material in this book will be available on-line at www.property-is-theft.org. We plan to add new translations as and when they become available as well as supplementary material on Proudhon. In addition, the site will have links to complete versions of works we have provided extracts from.

# A NOTE ON THE TRANSLATIONS

ALL THE TEXTS have been translated in British English rather than American English.

In addition, certain parts of previous translations have been corrected to bring their meaning more in line with the original French (as such consistently translating *salariat* as "wage-labour" or "wage-worker," "entrepreneur" rather than "contractor", etc.), popular usage (such as replacing Tucker's "property is robbery" with "property is theft"), or to bring them up-to-date (such as "worker" rather than "labourer"). "Workman," "working men," etc., have been changed to "worker," "workers," etc. This is because they sound antiquated, are unnecessarily gendered in English and using "workman" simply reflects the unthinking cultural sexism of translators from previous generations. In addition, it reads better and fits in with the new translations which render it as "worker." We have used the original "Commune" in the translation of *General Idea of the Revolution*, while words Tucker did not translate, like *proletaire*, have been translated.

Finally, I have revised and edited all the translations and, as a consequence, I take full responsibility for any errors that may occur in the texts.

*I.M.*

Workers, labourers, men of the people, whoever you may be, the initiative of reform is yours. It is you who will accomplish that synthesis of social composition which will be the masterpiece of creation, and you alone can accomplish it.

—Pierre-Joseph Proudhon
*What Is Property? Third Memoir*

*1840*
*Translation by Benjamin R. Tucker*

# WHAT IS PROPERTY?
## OR, AN INQUIRY INTO THE PRINCIPLE OF RIGHT AND OF GOVERNMENT

## CHAPTER I
### METHOD PURSUED IN THIS WORK—THE IDEA OF A REVOLUTION

IF I WERE ASKED TO ANSWER THE FOLLOWING QUESTION: *What is slavery?* and I should answer in one word, *It is murder*, my meaning would be understood at once. No extended argument would be required to show that the power to take from a man his thought, his will, his personality, is a power of life and death; and that to enslave a man is to kill him. Why, then, to this other question: *What is property?* may I not likewise answer, *It is theft*, without the certainty of being misunderstood; the second proposition being no other than a transformation of the first?

I undertake to discuss the vital principle of our government and our institutions, property: I am in my right. I may be mistaken in the conclusion which shall result from my investigations: I am in my right. I think best to place the last thought of my book first: still am I in my right.

Such an author teaches that property is a civil right, born of occupation and sanctioned by law; another maintains that it is a natural right, originating in labour,—and both of these doctrines, totally opposed as they may seem, are encouraged and applauded. I contend that neither labour, nor occupation, nor law, can create property; that it is an effect without a cause: am I censurable?

But murmurs arise!

*Property is theft*! That is the war-cry of '93! That is the signal of revolutions!

Reader, calm yourself: I am no agent of discord, no firebrand of sedition. I anticipate history by a few days; I disclose a truth whose development we may try in vain to arrest; I write the preamble of our future constitution. This proposition which seems to you blasphemous—*Property is theft*—would, if our prejudices allowed us to consider it, be recognised as the lightning-rod to shield us from the coming thunderbolt; but too many interests stand in the way!... Alas! philosophy will not change the course of events: destiny will fulfil itself regardless of prophecy. Besides, must not justice be done and our education be finished?

[...]

We must ascertain whether the ideas of *despotism, civil inequality* and *property*, are in harmony with the primitive notion of justice, and necessarily follow from it,—assuming various forms according to the condition, position, and relation of persons; or whether they are not rather the illegitimate result of a confusion of different things, a fatal association of ideas. And since justice deals especially with the questions of government, the condition of persons, and the possession of things, we must ascertain under what conditions, judging by universal opinion and the progress of the human mind, government is just, the condition of citizens is just, and the possession of things is just; then, striking out every thing which fails to meet these conditions, the result will at once tell us what legitimate government is, what the legitimate condition of citizens is, and what the legitimate possession of things is; and finally, as the last result of the analysis, what *justice* is.

Is the authority of man over man just?

Everybody answers, "No; the authority of man is only the authority of the law, which ought to be justice and truth." The private will counts for nothing in government, which consists, first, in discovering truth and justice in order to make the law; and, second, in superintending the execution of this law. I do not now inquire whether our constitutional form of government satisfies these conditions; whether, for example, the will of the ministry never influences the declaration and interpretation of the law; or whether our deputies, in their debates, are more intent on conquering by argument than by force of numbers: it is enough for me that my definition of a good government is allowed to be correct. This idea is exact. Yet we see that nothing seems more just to the Oriental nations than the despotism of their sovereigns; that, with the ancients and in the opinion of the philosophers themselves, slavery was just; that in the middle ages the nobles, the priests, and the bishops felt justified in holding slaves; that Louis XIV thought that he was right when he said, "The State! I am the State"; and that Napoléon deemed it a crime for the State to oppose his will. The idea of justice, then, applied to sovereignty and government, has not always been what it is today; it has gone on developing and shaping itself by degrees, until it has arrived at its present state. But has it reached its last phase? I think not: only, as the last obstacle to be overcome arises from the institution of property which we have kept intact, in order to finish the reform in government and consummate the revolution, this very institution we must attack.

Is political and civil inequality just?

Some say yes; others no. To the first I would reply that, when the people abolished all privileges of birth and caste, they did it, in all probability, because it was for their advantage; why then do they favour the privileges of fortune more than those of rank and race? Because, say they, political inequality is a result of property and without property society is impossible: thus the question just raised becomes a question of property. To the second I content myself with this remark: If you wish to enjoy political equality, abolish property; otherwise, why do you complain?

Is property just?

Everybody answers without hesitation, "Yes, property is just." I say everybody, for up to the present time no one who thoroughly understood the meaning of his words has answered no. For it is no easy thing to reply understandingly to such a question; only time and experience can furnish an answer. Now, this answer is given; it is for us to understand it. I undertake to prove it.

We are to proceed with the demonstration in the following order:

I. We dispute not at all, we refute nobody, we deny nothing; we accept as sound all the arguments alleged in favour of property, and confine ourselves to a search for its principle, in order that we may then ascertain whether this principle is faithfully expressed by property. In fact, property being defensible on no ground save that of justice, the idea, or at least the intention, of justice must of necessity underlie all the arguments that have been made in defence of property; and, as on the other hand the right of property is only exercised over those things which can be appreciated by the senses, justice, secretly objectifying itself, so to speak, must take the shape of an algebraic formula.

By this method of investigation, we soon see that every argument which has been invented in behalf of property, *whatever it may be*, always and of necessity leads to equality; that is, to the negation of property.

The first part covers two chapters: one treating of occupation, the foundation of our right; the other, of labour and talent, considered as causes of property and social inequality.

The first of these chapters will prove that the right of occupation *obstructs* property; the second that the right of labour *destroys* it.

II. Property, then, being of necessity conceived as existing only in connection with equality, it remains to find out why, in spite of this necessity of logic, equality does not exist. This new investigation also covers two chapters: in the first, considering the fact of property in itself, we inquire whether this fact is real, whether it exists, whether it is possible; for it would imply a contradiction, were these two opposite forms of society, equality and inequality, both possible. Then we discover, singularly enough, that property may indeed manifest itself accidentally; but that, as an institution and principle, it is mathematically impossible. So that the axiom of the school—*ab actu ad posse valet consecutio*: from the actual to the possible the inference is good—is given the lie as far as property is concerned.

Finally, in the last chapter, calling psychology to our aid, and probing man's nature to the bottom, we shall disclose the principle of *justice*—its formula and character; we shall state with precision the organic law of society; we shall explain the origin of property, the causes of its establishment, its long life, and its approaching death; we shall definitively establish its identity with theft. And, after having shown that these three prejudices—*the sovereignty of man, the inequality of conditions, and property*—are one and the same; that they may be taken for each other, and are reciprocally convertible,—we shall have no trouble in inferring therefrom, by the principle of contradiction, the basis of government and right. There our investigations will end, reserving the right to continue them in future works.

[...]

# CHAPTER II
## PROPERTY CONSIDERED AS A NATURAL RIGHT. OCCUPATION AND CIVIL LAW AS EFFICIENT BASES OF PROPERTY

### DEFINITIONS

THE ROMAN LAW defined property as the right to use and abuse one's own within the limits of the law—*jus utendi et abutendi re sua, guatenus juris ratio patitur*. A justification of the word *abuse* has been attempted, on the ground that it signifies, not senseless and immoral abuse, but only absolute domain. Vain distinction! invented as an excuse for property, and powerless against the frenzy of possession, which it neither prevents nor represses. The proprietor may, if he chooses, allow his crops to rot under foot, sow his field with salt, milk his cows on the sand, change his vineyard into a desert, and use his vegetable-garden as a park: do these things constitute abuse, or not? In the matter of property, use and abuse are necessarily indistinguishable.

According to the Declaration of Rights, published as a preface to the Constitution of '93, property is "the right to enjoy and dispose at will of one's goods, one's income, and the fruit of one's labour and industry."

Code Napoléon, article 544: "Property is the right to enjoy and dispose of things in the most absolute manner, provided we do not overstep the limits prescribed by the laws and regulations."

These two definitions do not differ from that of the Roman law: all give the proprietor an absolute right over a thing; and as for the restriction imposed by the code—*provided we do not overstep the limits prescribed by the laws and regulations*—its object is not to limit property, but to prevent the domain of one proprietor from interfering with that of another. That is a confirmation of the principle, not a limitation of it.

There are different kinds of property: 1. Property pure and simple, the dominant and seigniorial power over a thing; or, as they term it, *naked property*. 2. *Possession.* "Possession," says Duranton, "is a matter of fact, not of right." Toullier: "Property is a right, a legal power; possession is a fact." The tenant, the farmer, the *commandité*, the usufructuary, are possessors; the owner who lets and lends for use, the heir who is to come into possession on the death of a usufructuary, are proprietors. If I may venture the comparison: a lover is a possessor, a husband is a proprietor.[1]

This double definition of property—domain and possession—is of the highest importance; and it must be clearly understood, in order to comprehend what is to follow.

From the distinction between possession and property arise two sorts of rights: the *jus in re*, the right *in* a thing, the right by which I may reclaim the property which I have acquired, in whatever hands I find it; and the *jus ad rem*, the right *to* a thing, which gives me a claim to become a proprietor. Thus the right of the partners to a marriage over each other's person is the *jus in re*; that of two who are betrothed is only the *jus ad rem*. In the first, possession and property are united; the second includes only naked property. With me who, as a worker, have a right to the possession of the products of Nature and my own industry,—and who, as a proletarian, enjoy none of them,—it is by virtue of the *jus ad rem* that I demand admittance to the *jus in re*.

This distinction between the *jus in re* and the *jus ad rem* is the basis of the famous distinction between *possessoire* and *pétitoire*,—actual categories of jurisprudence, the whole of which is included within their vast boundaries. *Pétitoire* refers to every thing relating to property; *possessoire* to that relating to possession. In writing this memoir against property, I bring against universal society an *action pétitoire*: I prove that those who do not possess today are proprietors by the same title as those who do possess; but, instead of inferring therefrom that property should be shared by all, I demand, in the name of general security, its entire abolition. If I fail to win my case, there is nothing left for us (the proletarian class and myself) but to cut our throats: we can ask nothing more from the justice of nations; for, as the code of procedure (art. 26) tells us in its energetic style, *the plaintiff who has been non-suited in an action pétitoire, is debarred thereby from bringing an action possessoire.* If, on the contrary, I gain the case, we must then commence an *action possessoire*, that we may be reinstated in the enjoyment of the wealth of which we are deprived by property. I hope that we shall not be forced to that extremity; but these two actions cannot be prosecuted at once, such a course being prohibited by the same code of procedure.

---

1    An arresting observation in light of Proudhon's patriarchal conceptions of marriage and family. (Editor)

Before going to the heart of the question, it will not be useless to offer a few preliminary remarks.

### §1 PROPERTY AS A NATURAL RIGHT

The Declaration of Rights has placed property in its list of the natural and inalienable rights of man, four in all: *liberty, equality, property, security*. What rule did the legislators of '93 follow in compiling this list? None. They laid down principles, just as they discussed sovereignty and the laws; from a general point of view, and according to their own opinion. They did every thing in their own blind way.

If we can believe Toullier: "The absolute rights can be reduced to three: *security, liberty, property*." Equality is eliminated by the Rennes professor; why? Is it because *liberty* implies it, or because property prohibits it? On this point the author of *Droit Civil Expliqué* is silent: it has not even occurred to him that the matter is under discussion.

Nevertheless, if we compare these three or four rights with each other, we find that property bears no resemblance whatever to the others; that for the majority of citizens it exists only potentially, and as a dormant faculty without exercise; that for the others, who do enjoy it, it is susceptible of certain transactions and modifications which do not harmonise with the idea of a natural right; that, in practice, governments, tribunals, and laws do not respect it; and finally that everybody, spontaneously and with one voice, regards it as chimerical.

Liberty is inviolable. I can neither sell nor alienate my liberty; every contract, every condition of a contract, which has in view the alienation or suspension of liberty, is null: the slave, when he plants his foot upon the soil of liberty, at that moment becomes a free man. When society seizes a malefactor and deprives him of his liberty, it is a case of legitimate defence: whoever violates the social compact by the commission of a crime declares himself a public enemy; in attacking the liberty of others, he compels them to take away his own. Liberty is the original condition of man; to renounce liberty is to renounce the nature of man: after that, how could we perform the acts of man?

[...]

To sum up: liberty is an absolute right, because it is to man what impenetrability is to matter,—a sine qua non of existence; equality is an absolute right, because without equality there is no society; security is an absolute right, because in the eyes of every man his own liberty and life are as precious as another's. These three rights are absolute; that is, susceptible of neither increase nor diminution; because in society each associate receives as much as he gives,—liberty for liberty, equality for equality, security for security, body for body, soul for soul, in life and in death.

But property, in its derivative sense, and by the definitions of law, is a right outside of society; for it is clear that, if the wealth of each was social wealth, the conditions would be equal for all, and it would be a contradiction to say: *property is a man's right to dispose at will of social property*. Then if we are associated for the sake of liberty, equality, and security, we are not associated for the sake of property; then if property is a *natural* right, this natural right is not *social*, but *anti-social*. Property and society are utterly irreconcilable institutions. It is as impossible to associate two proprietors as to join two magnets by their opposite poles. Either society must perish, or it must destroy property.

If property is a natural, absolute, imprescriptible, and inalienable right, why, in all ages, has there been so much speculation as to its origin?—for this is one of its distinguishing characteristics. The origin of a natural right! Good God! who ever inquired into the origin of the rights of liberty, security, or equality? They exist by the same right that we exist; they are born with us, they live and die with us. With property it is very different, indeed. By law, property can exist without a proprietor, like a quality without a subject. It exists for the human being who as yet is not, and for the octogenarian who is no more. And yet, in spite of these wonderful prerogatives which savour of the eternal and the infinite, they have never found the origin of property; the doctors still disagree. On one point only are they in harmony: namely, that the validity of the right of property depends upon the authenticity of its origin. But this harmony is their condemnation. Why have they acknowledged the right before settling the question of origin?

[...]

## §2 OCCUPATION AS THE TITLE TO PROPERTY
[...]

The right of *occupation*, or of the *first occupant*, is that which results from the actual, physical, real possession of a thing. I occupy a piece of land; the presumption is, that I am the proprietor, until the contrary is proved. We know that originally such a right cannot be legitimate unless it is reciprocal; the jurists say as much.

Cicero compares the earth to a vast theatre: *Quemadmodum theatrum cum commune sit, recte tamen dici potest ejus esse eum locum quem quisque occuparit.*

This passage is all that ancient philosophy has to say about the origin of property.

The theatre, says Cicero, is common to all; nevertheless, the place that each one occupies is called *his own*; that is, it is a place *possessed*, not a place *appropriated*. This comparison annihilates property; moreover, it implies equality. Can I, in a theatre, occupy at the same time one place in the pit, another in the boxes, and a third in the gallery? Not unless I have three bodies, like Geryon, or can exist in different places at the same time, as is related of the magician Apollonius.

According to Cicero, no one has a right to more than he needs: such is the true interpretation of his famous axiom—*suum quidque cujusque sit*, to each one that which belongs to him—an axiom that has been strangely applied. That which belongs to each is not that which each *may* possess, but that which each *has a right* to possess. Now, what have we a right to possess? That which is required for our labour and consumption; Cicero's comparison of the earth to a theatre proves it. According to that, each one may take what place he will, may beautify and adorn it, if he can; it is allowable: but he must never allow himself to overstep the limit which separates him from another. The doctrine of Cicero leads directly to equality; for, occupation being pure toleration, if the toleration is mutual (and it cannot be otherwise) the possessions are equal.

[...]

Reid writes as follows:

"The right of property is not innate, but acquired. It is not grounded upon the constitution of man, but upon his actions. Writers on jurisprudence have explained its origin in a manner that may satisfy every man of common understanding.

"The earth is given to men in common for the purposes of life, by the bounty of Heaven. But to divide it, and appropriate one part of its produce to one, another part to another, must be the work of men who have power and understanding given them, by which every man may accommodate himself, *without hurt to any other*.

"This common right of every man to what the earth produces, before it be occupied and appropriated by others, was, by ancient moralists, very properly compared to the right which every citizen had to the public theatre, where every man that came might occupy an empty seat, and thereby acquire a right to it while the entertainment lasted; but no man had a right to dispossess another.

"The earth is a great theatre, furnished by the Almighty, with perfect wisdom and goodness, for the entertainment and employment of all mankind. Here every man has a right to accommodate himself as a spectator, and to perform his part as an actor; but without hurt to others."

Consequences of Reid's doctrine.

1. That the portion which each one appropriates may wrong no one, it must be equal to the quotient of the total amount of property to be shared, divided by the number of those who are to share it;

2. The number of places being of necessity equal at all times to that of the spectators, no spectator can occupy two places, nor can any actor play several parts;

3. Whenever a spectator comes in or goes out, the places of all contract or enlarge correspondingly: for, says Reid, "*the right of property is not innate, but acquired;*" consequently, it is not absolute; consequently, the occupancy on which it is based, being a conditional fact, cannot endow this right with a stability which it does not possess itself. This seems to have been the thought of the Edinburgh professor when he added:

"A right to life implies a right to the necessary means of life; and that justice, which forbids the taking away the life of an innocent man, forbids no less the taking from him the necessary means of life. He has the same right to defend the one as the other. To hinder another man's innocent labour, or to deprive him of the fruit of it, is an injustice of the same kind, and has the same effect as to put him in fetters or in prison, and is equally a just object of resentment."

Thus the chief of the Scotch school, without considering at all the inequality of skill or labour, posits a priori the equality of the means of labour, abandoning thereafter to each worker the care of his own person, after the eternal axiom: *whoso does well, shall fare well.*

The philosopher Reid is lacking, not in knowledge of the principle, but in courage to pursue it to its ultimate. If the right of life is equal, the right of labour is equal, and so is the right of occupancy. Would it not be criminal, were some islanders to repulse, in the name of property, the unfortunate victims of a shipwreck struggling to reach the shore? The very idea of such cruelty sickens the imagination. The proprietor, like Robinson Crusoe on his island, wards off with pike and musket the proletarian washed overboard by the wave of civilisation, and seeking to gain a foothold upon the rocks of property. "Give me work!" cries he with all his might to the proprietor: "don't drive me away, I will work for you at any price." "I do not need your services," replies the proprietor, showing the end of his pike or the barrel of his gun. "Lower my rent at least." "I need my income to live upon." "How can I pay you, when I can get no work?" "That is your business." Then the unfortunate proletarian abandons himself to the waves; or, if he attempts to land upon the shore of property, the proprietor takes aim, and kills him.

[...]

Shameful equivocation, not justified by the necessity for generalisation! The word *property* has two meanings: 1. It designates the quality which makes a thing what it is; the attribute which is peculiar to it, and especially distinguishes it. We use it in this sense when we say *the properties of the triangle or of numbers; the property of the magnet,* etc. 2. It expresses the right of absolute control over a thing by a free and intelligent being. It is used in this sense by writers on jurisprudence. Thus, in the phrase, *iron acquires the property of a magnet,* the word *property* does not convey the same idea that it does in this one: *I have acquired this magnet as my property.* To tell a poor man that he *has* property because he *has* arms and legs,—that the hunger from which he suffers, and his power to sleep in the open air are his property,—is to play upon words, and to add insult to injury.

[...]

In fact, to become a proprietor, in M. Cousin's opinion, one must take possession by occupation and labour. I maintain that the element of time must be considered also; for if the first occupants have occupied every thing, what are the new comers to do? What will become of them, having an instrument with which to work, but no material to work upon? Must they devour each other? A terrible extremity, unforeseen by philosophical prudence; for the reason that great geniuses neglect little things.

Notice also that M. Cousin says that neither occupation nor labour, taken separately, can legitimate the right of property; and that it is born only from the union of the two. This is one of M. Cousin's eclectic turns, which he, more than any one else, should take pains to avoid. Instead of proceeding by the method of analysis, comparison, elimination, and reduction (the only means of discovering the truth amid the various forms of thought and whimsical opinions), he jumbles all systems together, and then, declaring each both right and wrong, exclaims: "There you have the truth."

But, adhering to my promise, I will not refute him. I will only prove, by all the arguments with which he justifies the right of property, the principle of equality which kills it. As I have already said, my sole intent is this: to show at the bottom of all these positions that inevitable major, *equality*; hoping hereafter to show that the principle of property vitiates the very elements of economical, moral, and governmental science, thus leading it in the wrong direction.

Well, is it not true, from M. Cousin's point of view, that, if the liberty of man is sacred, it is equally sacred in all individuals; that, if it needs property for its objective action, that is, for its life, the appropriation of material is equally necessary for all; that, if I wish to be respected in my right of appropriation, I must respect others in theirs; and, consequently, that though, in the sphere of the infinite, a person's power of appropriation is limited only by himself, in the sphere of the finite this same power is limited by the mathematical relation between the number of persons and the space which they occupy? Does it not follow that if one individual cannot prevent another—his fellow-man—from appropriating an amount of material equal to his own, no more can he prevent individuals yet to come; because, while individuality passes away, universality persists, and eternal laws cannot be determined by a partial view of their manifestations? Must we not conclude, therefore, that whenever a person is born, the others must crowd closer together; and, by reciprocity of obligation, that if the new comer is afterwards to become an heir, the right of succession does not give him the right of accumulation, but only the right of choice?

I have followed M. Cousin so far as to imitate his style, and I am ashamed of it. Do we need such high-sounding terms, such sonorous phrases, to say such simple things? Man needs to labour in order to live; consequently, he needs tools to work with and materials to work upon. His need to produce constitutes his right to produce. Now, this right is guaranteed him by his fellows, with whom he makes an agreement to that effect. One hundred thousand men settle in a large country like France with no inhabitants: each man has a right to 1/100,000 of the land. If the number of possessors increases, each one's portion diminishes in consequence; so that, if the number of inhabitants rises to thirty-four million, each one will have a right only to 1/34,000,000. Now, so regulate the police system and the government, labour, exchange, inheritance, etc., that the means of labour shall be shared by all equally, and that each individual shall be free; and then society will be perfect.

[...]

## §3 CIVIL LAW AS THE FOUNDATION AND SANCTION OF PROPERTY

Pothier seems to think that property, like royalty, exists by divine right. He traces back its origin to God himself—*ab Jove principium*. He begins in this way:

"God is the absolute ruler of the universe and all that it contains: *Domini est terra et plenitudo ejus, orbis et universi qui habitant in eo.* For the human race he has created the earth and all its creatures, and has given it a control over them subordinate only to his own. 'Thou madest him to have dominion over the works of thy hands; thou hast put all things under his feet,' says the Psalmist. God accompanied this gift with these words, addressed to our first parents after the creation: 'Be fruitful, and multiply and replenish the earth,' etc."

After this magnificent introduction, who would refuse to believe the human race to be an immense family living in brotherly union, and under the protection of a venerable father? But, heavens! are brothers enemies? Are fathers unnatural, and children prodigal?

*God gave the earth to the human race*: why then have I received none? *He has put all things under my feet,*—and I have nowhere to lay my head! *Multiply*, he tells us through his interpreter, Pothier. Ah, learned Pothier! that is as easy to do as to say; but you must give moss to the bird for its nest.

"The human race having multiplied, men divided among themselves the earth and most of the things upon it; that which fell to each, from that time exclusively belonged to him. That was the origin of the right of property."

Say, rather, the right of possession. Men lived in a state of communism; whether positive or negative it matters little. Then there was no property, not even private possession. The genesis and growth of possession gradually forcing people to labour for their support, they agreed either formally or tacitly,—it makes no difference which,—that the worker should be sole proprietor of the fruit of his labour; that is, they simply declared the fact that thereafter none could live without working. It necessarily followed that, to obtain equality of products, there must be equality of labour; and that, to obtain equality of labour, there must be equality of facilities for labour. Whoever without labour got possession, by force or by strategy, of another's means of subsistence, destroyed equality, and placed himself above or outside of the law. Whoever monopolised the means of production on the ground of greater industry, also destroyed equality. Equality being then the expression of right, whoever violated it was *unjust*.

Thus, labour gives birth to private possession; the right in a thing—*jus in re*. But in what thing? Evidently *in the product*, not *in the soil*. So the Arabs have always understood it; and so, according to Caesar and Tacitus, the Germans formerly held. "The Arabs," says M. de Sismondi, "who admit a man's property in the flocks which he has raised, do not refuse the crop to him who planted the seed; but they do not see why another, his equal, should not have a right to plant in his turn. The inequality which results from the pretended right of the first occupant seems to them to be based on no principle of justice; and when all the land falls into the hands of a certain number of inhabitants, there results a monopoly in their favour against the rest of the nation, to which they do not wish to submit."

Well, they have shared the land. I admit that therefrom results a more powerful organisation of labour; and that this method of distribution, fixed and durable, is advantageous to production: but how could this division give to each a transferable right of property in a thing to which all had an inalienable right of possession? In the terms of jurisprudence, this metamorphosis from possessor to proprietor is legally impossible; it implies in the jurisdiction of the courts the union of *possessoire* and *pétitoire*; and the mutual concessions of those who share the land are nothing less than traffic in natural rights. The original cultivators of the land, who were also the original makers of the law, were not as learned as our legislators, I admit; and had they been, they could not have done worse: they did not foresee the consequences of the transformation of the right of private possession into the right of absolute property. But why have not those, who in later times have established the distinction between *jus in re* and *jus ad rem*, applied it to the principle of property itself?

Let me call the attention of the writers on jurisprudence to their own maxims.

The right of property, provided it can have a cause, can have but one—*Dominium non potest nisi ex una causa contingere*. I can possess by several titles; I can become proprietor by only one—*Non ut ex pluribus causis idem nobis deberi potest, ita ex pluribus causis idem potest nostrum esse*.[2] The field which I have cleared, which I cultivate, on which I have built my house, which supports myself, my family, and my livestock, I can possess: 1st As the original occupant; 2nd As a worker; 3rd By virtue of the social contract which assigns it to me as my share. But none of these titles confer upon me the right of property. For, if I attempt to base it upon occupancy, society can reply, "I am the original occupant." If I appeal to my labour, it will say, "It is only on that condition that you possess." If I speak of agreements, it will respond, "These agreements establish only your right of use." Such, however, are the only titles which proprietors advance. They never have been able to discover any others. Indeed, every right—it is Pothier who says it—supposes

---

2   Quoting from the collection of Roman legal writings, *Digest of Justinian*. (Editor)

a producing cause in the person who enjoys it; but in man who lives and dies, in this son of earth who passes away like a shadow, there exists, with respect to external things, only titles of possession, not one title of property. Why, then, has society recognised a right injurious to itself, where there is no producing cause? Why, in according possession, has it also conceded property? Why has the law sanctioned this abuse of power?

[…]

To satisfy the husbandman, it was sufficient to guarantee him possession of his crop; admit even that he should have been protected in his right of occupation of land, as long as he remained its cultivator. That was all that he had a right to expect; that was all that the advance of civilisation demanded. But property, property! the right of escheat [*droit d'aubaine*] over lands which one neither occupies nor cultivates,—who had authority to grant it? who pretended to have it?

[…]

The authority of the human race is of no effect as evidence in favour of the right of property, because this right, resting of necessity upon equality, contradicts its principle; the decision of the religions which have sanctioned it is of no effect, because in all ages the priest has submitted to the prince, and the gods have always spoken as the politicians desired; the social advantages, attributed to property, cannot be cited in its behalf, because they all spring from the principle of equality of possession.

What means, then, this dithyramb upon property?

"The right of property is the most important of human institutions."...

Yes; as monarchy is the most glorious.

"The original cause of man's prosperity upon earth."

Because justice was supposed to be its principle.

"Property became the legitimate end of his ambition, the hope of his existence, the shelter of his family; in a word, the corner-stone of the domestic dwelling, of communities, and of the political State."

Possession alone produced all that.

"Eternal principle—"

Property is eternal, like every negation,—

"Of all social and civil institutions."

For that reason, every institution and every law based on property will perish.

"It is a boon as precious as liberty."

For the rich proprietor.

"In fact, the cause of the cultivation of the habitable earth."

If the cultivator ceased to be a tenant, would the land be worse cared for?

"The guarantee and the morality of labour."

Under the regime of property, labour is not a condition, but a privilege.

"The application of justice."

What is justice without equality of fortunes? A balance with false weights.

"All morality,—"

A famished stomach knows no morality,—

"All public order,—"

Certainly, the preservation of property,—

"Rest on the right of property."[3]

Corner-stone of all which is, stumbling-block of all which ought to be,— such is property.

To sum up and conclude:

Not only does occupation lead to equality, it *prevents* property. For, since every man, from the fact of his existence, has the right of occupation, and, in order to live, must have material for cultivation on which he may labour; and since, on the other hand, the number of occupants varies continually with the births and deaths,—it follows that the quantity of material which each worker may claim varies with the number of occupants; consequently, that occupation is always subordinate to population. Finally, that, inasmuch as possession, in right, can never remain fixed, it is impossible, in fact, that it can ever become property.

Every occupant is, then, necessarily a possessor or usufructuary,—a function which excludes proprietorship. Now, this is the right of the usufructuary: he is responsible for the thing entrusted to him; he must use it in conformity with general utility, with a view to its preservation and development; he has no power to transform it, to diminish it, or to change its nature; he cannot so divide the usufruct that another shall perform the labour while he receives the product. In a word, the usufructuary is under the supervision of society, submitted to the condition of labour and the law of equality.

Thus is annihilated the Roman definition of property—*the right of use and abuse*—an immorality born of violence, the most monstrous pretension that the civil laws ever sanctioned. Man receives his usufruct from the hands of society, which alone is the permanent possessor. The individual passes away, society is deathless.

What a profound disgust fills my soul while discussing such simple truths! Do we doubt these things today? Will it be necessary to again take arms for their triumph? And can force, in default of reason, alone introduce them into our laws?

*All have an equal right of occupancy.*

*The amount occupied being measured, not by the will, but by the variable conditions of space and number, property cannot exist.*

This no code has ever expressed; this no constitution can admit! These are axioms which the civil law and the law of nations deny!...

But I hear the exclamations of the partisans of another system: "Labour, labour! that is the basis of property!"

---

3    Giraud, *Investigations into the Right of Property among the Romans.*

Reader, do not be deceived. This new basis of property is worse than the first, and I shall soon have to ask your pardon for having demonstrated things clearer, and refuted pretensions more unjust, than any which we have yet considered.

# CHAPTER III
## LABOUR AS THE EFFICIENT CAUSE OF THE DOMAIN OF PROPERTY

NEARLY ALL THE modern writers on jurisprudence, taking their cue from the economists, have abandoned the theory of first occupancy as a too dangerous one, and have adopted that which regards property as born of labour. In this they are deluded; they reason in a circle. To labour it is necessary to occupy, says M. Cousin.

[...]

I have asserted that the system which bases property upon labour implies, no less than that which bases it upon occupation, the equality of fortunes; and the reader must be impatient to learn how I propose to deduce this law of equality from the inequality of skill and faculties: directly his curiosity shall be satisfied. But it is proper that I should call his attention for a moment to this remarkable feature of the process; to wit, the substitution of labour for occupation as the principle of property; and that I should pass rapidly in review some of the prejudices to which proprietors are accustomed to appeal, which legislation has sanctioned, and which the system of labour completely overthrows.

Reader, were you ever present at the examination of a criminal? Have you watched his tricks, his turns, his evasions, his distinctions, his equivocations? Beaten, all his assertions overthrown, pursued like a fallow deer by the inexorable judge, tracked from hypothesis to hypothesis,—he makes a statement, he corrects it, retracts it, contradicts it, he exhausts all the tricks of dialectics, more subtle, more ingenious a thousand times than he who invented the seventy-two forms of the syllogism. So acts the proprietor when called upon to defend his right. At first he refuses to reply, he exclaims, he threatens, he defies; then, forced to accept the discussion, he arms himself with chicanery, he surrounds himself with formidable artillery,—crossing his fire, opposing one by one and all together occupation, possession, limitation, covenants, immemorial custom, and universal consent. Conquered on this ground, the proprietor, like a wounded boar, turns on his pursuers. "I have done more than occupy," he cries with terrible emotion; "I have laboured, produced, improved, transformed, *created*. This house, these fields, these trees are the work of my hands; I changed these brambles into a vineyard, and this bush into a fig-tree; and today I reap the harvest of my labours. I have enriched the soil with my sweat; I have paid those men who, had they not had the work which I gave them, would have died of hunger. No one shared with me the trouble and expense; no one shall share with me the benefits."

You have laboured, proprietor! why then do you speak of original occupancy? What, were you not sure of your right, or did you hope to deceive men, and make justice an illusion? Make haste, then, to acquaint us with your mode of defence, for the judgement will be final; and you know it to be a question of restitution.

You have laboured! but what is there in common between the labour which duty compels you to perform, and the appropriation of things in which there is a common interest? Do you not know that domain over the soil, like that over air and light, cannot be lost by prescription?

You have laboured! have you never made others labour? Why, then, have they lost in labouring for you what you have gained in not labouring for them?

You have laboured! very well; but let us see the results of your labour. We will count, weigh, and measure them. It will be the judgement of Balthasar; for I swear by balance, level, and square, that if you have appropriated another's labour in any way whatsoever, you shall restore it every stroke.

Thus, the principle of occupation is abandoned; no longer is it said, "The land belongs to him who first gets possession of it." Property, forced into its first entrenchment, repudiates its old adage; justice, ashamed, retracts her maxims, and sorrow lowers her bandage over her blushing cheeks. And it was but yesterday that this progress in social philosophy began: fifty centuries required for the extirpation of a lie! During this lamentable period, how many usurpations have been sanctioned, how many invasions glorified, how many conquests celebrated! The absent dispossessed, the poor banished, the hungry excluded by wealth, which is so ready and bold in action! Jealousies and wars, incendiarism and bloodshed, among the nations! But henceforth, thanks to the age and its spirit, it is to be admitted that the earth is not a prize to be won in a race; in the absence of any other obstacle, there is a place for everybody under the sun. Each one may harness his goat to the barn, drive his cattle to pasture, sow a corner of a field, and bake his bread by his own fireside.

But, no; each one cannot do these things. I hear it proclaimed on all sides, "Glory to labour and industry! to each according to his capacity; to each capacity according to its results!" And I see three-fourths of the human race again despoiled, the labour of a few being a scourge to the labour of the rest.

"The problem is solved," exclaims M. Hennequin. "Property, the daughter of labour, can be enjoyed at present and in the future only under the protection of the laws. It has its origin in natural law; it derives its power from civil law; and from the union of these two ideas, *labour* and *protection*, positive legislation results."...

Ah! *The problem is solved! Property is the daughter of labour!* What, then, is the right of accession, and the right of succession, and the right of donation, etc., if not the right to become a proprietor by simple occupancy? What are your laws concerning the age of majority, emancipation, guardianship, and interdiction, if not the various conditions by which he who is already a worker gains or loses the right of occupancy; that is, property?

Being unable, at this time, to enter upon a detailed discussion of the Code, I shall content myself with examining the three arguments oftenest resorted to in support of property. 1. *Appropriation*, or the formation of property by possession; 2. *The consent of mankind*; 3. *Prescription*. I shall then inquire into the effects of labour upon the relative condition of the workers and upon property.

## §1 THE LAND CANNOT BE APPROPRIATED

"It would seem that lands capable of cultivation ought to be regarded as natural wealth, since they are not of human creation, but Nature's gratuitous gift to man; but inasmuch as this wealth is not fugitive, like the air and water,—inasmuch as a field is a fixed and limited space which certain men have been able to appropriate, to the exclusion of all others who in their turn have consented to this appropriation,—the land, which was a natural and gratuitous gift, has become social wealth, for the use of which we ought to pay."—Say: *Political Economy*.

Was I wrong in saying, at the beginning of this chapter, that the economists are the very worst authorities in matters of legislation and philosophy? It is the *father* of this class of men who clearly states the question, How can the supplies of Nature, the wealth created by Providence, become private property? and who replies by so gross an equivocation that we scarcely know which the author lacks, sense or honesty. What, I ask, has the fixed and solid nature of the earth to do with the right of appropriation? I can understand that a thing *limited* and *stationary*, like the land, offers greater chances for appropriation than the water or the sunshine; that it is easier to exercise the right of domain over the soil than over the atmosphere: but we are not dealing with the difficulty of the thing, and Say confounds the right with the possibility. We do not ask why the earth has been appropriated to a greater extent than the sea and the air; we want to know by what right man has appropriated wealth *which he did not create, and which nature gave to him gratuitously*.

Say, then, did not solve the question which he asked. But if he had solved it, if the explanation which he has given us were as satisfactory as it is illogical, we should know no better than before who has a right to exact payment for the use of the soil, of this wealth which is not man's handiwork. Who is entitled to the rent of the land? The producer of the land, without doubt. Who made the land? God. Then, proprietor, retire!

But the creator of the land does not sell it: he gives it; and, in giving it, he is no respecter of persons. Why, then, are some of his children regarded as legitimate, while others are treated as bastards? If the equality of shares was an original right, why is the inequality of conditions a posthumous right?

Say gives us to understand that if the air and the water were not of a FUGITIVE nature, they would have been appropriated. Let me observe in passing that this is more than an hypothesis; it is a reality. Men have appropriated the air and the water, I will not say as often as they could, but as often as they have been allowed to.

The Portuguese, having discovered the route to India by the Cape of Good Hope, pretended to have the sole right to that route; and Grotius, consulted in regard to this matter by the Dutch who refused to recognise this right, wrote expressly for this occasion his treatise on the "Freedom of the Seas," to prove that the sea is not liable to appropriation.

The right to hunt and fish used always to be confined to lords and proprietors; today it is leased by the government and communes to whoever can pay the license-fee and the rent. To regulate hunting and fishing is an excellent idea, but to make it a subject of sale is to create a monopoly of air and water.

What is a passport? A universal recommendation of the traveller's person; a certificate of security for himself and his property. The treasury, whose nature it is to spoil the best things, has made the passport a means of espionage and a tax. Is not this a sale of the right to travel?

Finally, it is permissible neither to draw water from a spring situated in another's grounds without the permission of the proprietor, because by the right of accession the spring belongs to the possessor of the soil, if there is no other claim; nor to pass a day on his premises without paying a tax; nor to look at a court, a garden, or an orchard, without the consent of the proprietor; nor to stroll in a park or an enclosure against the owner's will: every one is allowed to shut himself up and to fence himself in. All these prohibitions are so many positive interdictions, not only of the land, but of the air and water. We who belong to the proletarian class: property excommunicates us! *Terra, et aqua, et aere, et igne interdicti sumus.*

Men could not appropriate the most fixed of all the elements without appropriating the three others; since, by French and Roman law, property in the surface carries with it property from zenith to nadir—*Cujus est solum, ejus est usque ad caelum.* Now, if the use of water, air, and fire excludes property, so does the use of the soil. This chain of reasoning seems to have been presented by M. Ch. Comte, in his *Treatise on Property,* chap. 5.

"If a man should be deprived of air for a few moments only, he would cease to exist, and a partial deprivation would cause him severe suffering; a partial or complete deprivation of food would produce like effects upon him though less suddenly; it would be the same, at least in certain climates! were he deprived of all clothing and shelter... To sustain life, then, man needs continually to appropriate many different things. But these things do not exist in like proportions. Some, such as the light of the stars, the atmosphere of the earth, the water composing the seas and oceans, exist in such large quantities that men cannot perceive any sensible increase or diminution; each one can appropriate as much as his needs require without detracting from the enjoyment of others, without causing them the least harm. Things of this sort are, so to speak, the common property of the human race; the only duty imposed upon each individual in this regard is that of infringing not at all upon the rights of others."

Let us complete the argument of M. Ch. Comte. A man who should be prohibited from walking in the highways, from resting in the fields, from taking shelter in caves, from lighting fires, from picking berries, from gathering herbs and boiling them in a bit of baked clay,—such a man could not live. Consequently the earth—like water, air, and light—is a primary object of necessity which each has a right to use freely, without infringing another's right. Why, then, is the earth appropriated? M. Ch. Comte's reply is a curious one. Say pretends that it is because it is not *fugitive*; M. Ch. Comte assures us that it is because it is not *infinite*. The land is limited in amount. Then, according to M. Ch. Comte, it ought to be appropriated. It would seem, on the contrary, that he ought to say, Then it ought not to be appropriated. For, no matter how large a quantity of air or light anyone appropriates, no one is damaged thereby; there always remains enough for all. With the soil, it is very different. Lay hold who will, or who can, of the sun's rays, the passing breeze, or the sea's billows; he has my consent, and my pardon for his bad intentions. But let any living man dare to change his right of territorial possession into the right of property, and I will declare war upon him, and wage it to the death!

M.Ch. Comte's argument disproves his position. "Among the things necessary to the preservation of life," he says, "there are some which exist in such large quantities that they are inexhaustible; others which exist in lesser quantities, and can satisfy the wants of only a certain number of persons. The former are called *common*, the latter *private*."

This reasoning is not strictly logical. Water, air, and light are *common* things, not because they are *inexhaustible*, but because they are *indispensable*; and so indispensable that for that very reason Nature has created them in quantities almost infinite, in order that their plentifulness might prevent their appropriation. Likewise the land is indispensable to our existence,— consequently a common thing, consequently unsusceptible of appropriation; but land is much scarcer than the other elements, therefore its use must be regulated, not for the profit of a few, but in the interest and for the security of all.

In a word, equality of rights is proved by equality of needs. Now, equality of rights, in the case of a commodity which is limited in amount, can be realised only by equality of possession. An agrarian law underlies M. Ch. Comte's arguments.

From whatever point we view this question of property—provided we go to the bottom of it—we reach equality. I will not insist farther on the distinction between things which can, and things which cannot, be appropriated. On this point, economists and legists talk worse than nonsense. The Civil Code, after having defined property, says nothing about susceptibility of appropriation; and if it speaks of things *which are in the market*, it always does so without enumerating or describing them. However, light is not wanting. There are some few maxims such as these: *Ad reges potestas omnium pertinet, ad singulos proprietas; Omnia rex imperio possidet, singula dominio.* Social sovereignty opposed to private property!— might not that be called a prophecy of equality, a republican oracle? Examples crowd upon us: once the possessions of the church, the estates of the crown, the fiefs of the nobility were inalienable and imprescriptible. If, instead of abolishing this privilege, the Constituent had extended it to every individual; if it had declared that the right of labour, like liberty, can never be forfeited,—at that moment the revolution would have been consummated, and we could now devote ourselves to improvement in other directions.

### §2 UNIVERSAL CONSENT NO JUSTIFICATION OF PROPERTY

In the extract from Say, quoted above, it is not clear whether the author means to base the right of property on the stationary character of the soil, or on the consent which he thinks all men have granted to this appropriation. His language is such that it may mean either of these things, or both at once; which entitles us to assume that the author intended to say, "The right of property resulting originally from the exercise of the will, the stability of the soil permitted it to be applied to the land, and universal consent has since sanctioned this application."

However that may be, can men legitimate property by mutual consent? I say, no. Such a contract, though drafted by Grotius, Montesquieu, and J.-J. Rousseau, though signed by the whole human race, would be null in the eyes of justice, and an act to enforce it would be illegal. Man can no more give up labour than liberty. Now, to recognise the right of territorial property is to give up labour, since it is to relinquish the means of labour; it is to traffic in a natural right, and divest ourselves of manhood.

But I wish that this consent, of which so much is made, had been given, either tacitly or formally. What would have been the result? Evidently, the surrenders would have been reciprocal; no right would have been abandoned without the receipt of an equivalent in exchange. We thus come back to equality again,—the sine qua non of appropriation; so that, after having justified property by universal consent, that is, by equality, we are obliged to justify the inequality of conditions by property. Never shall we extricate ourselves from this dilemma. Indeed, if, in the terms of the social compact, property has equality for its condition, at the moment when equality ceases to exist, the compact is broken and all property becomes usurpation. We gain nothing, then, by this pretended consent of mankind.

## §3 PRESCRIPTION GIVES NO TITLE TO PROPERTY

The right of property was the origin of evil on the earth, the first link in the long chain of crimes and misfortunes which the human race has endured since its birth. The delusion of prescription is the fatal charm thrown over the intellect, the death sentence breathed into the conscience, to arrest man's progress towards truth, and bolster up the worship of error.

The Code defines prescription thus: "The process of gaining and losing through the lapse of time." In applying this definition to ideas and beliefs, we may use the word *prescription* to denote the everlasting prejudice in favour of old superstitions, whatever be their object; the opposition, often furious and bloody, with which new light has always been received, and which makes the sage a martyr. Not a principle, not a discovery, not a generous thought but has met, at its entrance into the world, with a formidable barrier of preconceived opinions, seeming like a conspiracy of all old prejudices. Prescriptions against reason, prescriptions against facts, prescriptions against every truth hitherto unknown,—that is the sum and substance of the *statu quo* philosophy, the watchword of conservatives throughout the centuries.

When the evangelical reform was broached to the world, there was prescription in favour of violence, debauchery, and selfishness; when Galileo, Descartes, Pascal, and their disciples reconstructed philosophy and the sciences, there was prescription in favour of the Aristotelian philosophy; when our fathers of '89 demanded liberty and equality, there was prescription in favour of tyranny and privilege. "There always have been proprietors and there always will be": it is with this profound utterance, the final effort of selfishness dying in its last ditch, that the friends of social inequality hope to repel the attacks of their adversaries; thinking undoubtedly that ideas, like property, can be lost by prescription.

[...]

In order to confine myself to the civil prescription of which the Code speaks, I shall refrain from beginning a discussion upon this worn-out objection brought forward by proprietors; it would be too tiresome and declamatory. Everybody knows that there are rights which cannot be prescribed; and, as for those things which can be gained through the lapse of time, no one is ignorant of the fact that prescription requires certain conditions, the omission of one of which renders it null. If it is true, for example, that the proprietor's possession has been *civil, public, peaceable,* and *uninterrupted,* it is none the less true that it is not based on a just title; since the only titles which it can show— occupation and labour—prove as much for the proletarian who demands, as for the proprietor who defends. Further, this possession is *dishonest,* since it is founded on a violation of right, which prevents prescription, according to the saying of St. Paul—*Nunquam in usucapionibus juris error possessori prodest.* The violation of right lies either in the fact that the holder possesses as proprietor, while he should possess only as usufructuary; or in the fact that he has purchased a thing which no one had a right to transfer or sell.

Another reason why prescription cannot be adduced in favour of property (a reason borrowed from jurisprudence) is that the right to possess real estate is a part of a universal right which has never been totally destroyed even at the most critical periods; and the proletarian, in order to regain the power to exercise it fully, has only to prove that he has always exercised it in part.

He, for example, who has the universal right to possess, give, exchange, loan, let, sell, transform, or destroy a thing, preserves the integrity of this right by the sole act of loaning, though he has never shown his authority in any other manner. Likewise we shall see that *equality of possessions, equality of rights, liberty, will, personality*, are so many identical expressions of one and the same idea,—the *right of preservation* and *development*; in a word, the right of life, against which there can be no prescription until the human race has vanished from the face of the earth.

Finally, as to the time required for prescription, it would be superfluous to show that the right of property in general cannot be acquired by simple possession for ten, twenty, a hundred, a thousand, or one hundred thousand years; and that, so long as there exists a human head capable of understanding and combating the right of property, this right will never be prescribed. For principles of jurisprudence and axioms of reason are different from accidental and contingent facts. One man's possession can prescribe against another man's possession; but just as the possessor cannot prescribe against himself, so reason has always the faculty of change and reformation. Past error is not binding on the future. Reason is always the same eternal force. The institution of property, the work of ignorant reason, may be abrogated by a more enlightened reason. Consequently, property cannot be established by prescription. This is so certain and so true, that on it rests the maxim that in the matter of prescription a violation of right goes for nothing.

[…]

I ask, then, in the first place, how possession can become property by the lapse of time? Continue possession as long as you wish, continue it for years and for centuries, you never can give duration—which of itself creates nothing, changes nothing, modifies nothing—the power to change the usufructuary into a proprietor. Let the civil law secure against chance-comers the honest possessor who has held his position for many years,—that only confirms a right already respected; and prescription, applied in this way, simply means that possession which has continued for twenty, thirty, or a hundred years shall be retained by the occupant. But when the law declares that the lapse of time changes possessor into proprietor, it supposes that a right can be created without a producing cause; it unwarrantably alters the character of the subject; it legislates on a matter not open to legislation; it exceeds its own powers. Public order and private security ask only that possession shall be protected. Why has the law created property? Prescription was simply security for the future; why has the law made it a matter of privilege?

[…]

"Where is the man," [Grotius] says, "with so unchristian a soul that, for a trifle, he would perpetuate the trespass of a possessor, which would inevitably be the result if he did not consent to abandon his right?" By the Eternal! I am that man. Though a million proprietors should burn for it in hell, I lay the blame on them for depriving me of my portion of this world's goods. To this powerful consideration Grotius rejoins, that it is better to abandon a disputed right than to go to law, disturb the peace of nations, and stir up the flames of civil war. I accept, if you wish it, this argument, provided you indemnify me. But if this indemnity is refused me, what do I, a proletarian, care for the tranquillity and security of the rich? I care as little for *public order* as for the proprietor's safety. I ask to live a worker; otherwise I will die a warrior.

Whichever way we turn, we shall come to the conclusion that prescription is a contradiction of property; or rather that prescription and property are two forms of the same principle, but two forms which serve to correct each other; and ancient and modern jurisprudence did not make the least of its blunders in pretending to reconcile them. Indeed, if we see in the institution of property only a desire to secure to each individual his share of the soil and his right to labour; in the distinction between naked property and possession only an asylum for absentees, orphans, and all who do not know, or cannot maintain, their rights; in prescription only a means, either of defence against unjust pretensions and encroachments, or of settlement of the differences caused by the removal of possessors,—we shall recognise in these various forms of human justice the spontaneous efforts of the mind to come to the aid of the social instinct; we shall see in this protection of all rights the sentiment of equality, a constant levelling tendency. And, looking deeper, we shall find in the very exaggeration of these principles the confirmation of our doctrine; because, if equality of conditions and universal association are not soon realised, it will be owing to the obstacle thrown for the time in the way of the common sense of the people by the stupidity of legislators and judges; and also to the fact that, while society in its original state was illuminated with a flash of truth, the early speculations of its leaders could bring forth nothing but darkness.

[...]

## §4 LABOUR—THAT LABOUR HAS NO INHERENT POWER TO APPROPRIATE NATURAL WEALTH

We shall show by the maxims of political economy and law, that is, by the authorities recognised by property,—

1. That labour has no inherent power to appropriate natural wealth.

2. That, if we admit that labour has this power, we are led directly to equality of property,—whatever the kind of labour, however scarce the product, or unequal the ability of the workers.

3. That, in the order of justice, labour *destroys* property.

Following the example of our opponents, and that we may leave no obstacles in the path, let us examine the question in the strongest possible light.

M.Ch. Comte says, in his *Treatise on Property*:—

"France, considered as a nation, has a territory which is her own."

France, as an individuality, possesses a territory which she cultivates; it is not her property. Nations are related to each other as individuals are: they are commoners and workers; it is an abuse of language to call them proprietors. The right of use and abuse belongs no more to nations than to men; and the time will come when a war waged for the purpose of checking a nation in its abuse of the soil will be regarded as a holy war.

Thus, M. Ch. Comte—who undertakes to explain how property comes into existence, and who starts with the supposition that a nation is a proprietor—falls into that error known as *begging the question*; a mistake which vitiates his whole argument.

If the reader thinks it is pushing logic too far to question a nation's right of property in the territory which it possesses, I will simply remind him of the fact that at all ages the results of the fictitious right of national property have been pretensions to suzerainty, tributes, monarchical privileges, statute-labour, quotas of men and money, supplies of merchandise, etc.; ending finally in refusals to pay taxes, insurrections, wars, and depopulations.

"Scattered through this territory are extended tracts of land, which have not been converted into individual property. These lands, which consist mainly of forests, belong to the whole population, and the government, which receives the revenues, uses or ought to use them in the interest of all."

*Ought to use* is well said: a lie is avoided thereby.

"Let them be offered for sale...."

Why offered for sale? Who has a right to sell them? Even were the nation proprietor, can the generation of today dispossess the generation of tomorrow? The nation, in its function of usufructuary, possesses them; the government rules, superintends, and protects them. If it also granted lands, it could grant only their use; it has no right to sell them or transfer them in any way whatever. Not being a proprietor, how can it transmit property?

"Suppose some industrious man buys a portion, a large swamp for example. This would be no usurpation, since the public would receive the exact value through the hands of the government, and would be as rich after the sale as before."

How ridiculous! What! Because a prodigal, imprudent, incompetent official sells the State's possessions, while I, a ward of the State,—I who have neither an advisory nor a deliberative voice in the State councils,—while I am allowed to make no opposition to the sale, this sale is right and legal! The guardians of the nation waste its substance, and it has no redress! I have received, you tell me, through the hands of the government my share of the proceeds of the sale: but, in the first place, I did not wish to sell; and, had I wished to, I could not have sold. I had not the right. And then I do not see that I am benefited by the sale. My guardians have dressed up some soldiers, repaired an old fortress, erected in their pride some costly but worthless monument,—then they have exploded some fireworks and set up a greased pole! What does all that amount to in comparison with my loss?

The purchaser draws boundaries, fences himself in, and says, "This is mine; each one by himself, each one for himself." Here, then, is a piece of land upon which, henceforth, no one has a right to step, save the proprietor and his friends; which can benefit nobody, save the proprietor and his servants. Let these sales multiply, and soon the people—who have been neither able nor willing to sell, and who have received none of the proceeds of the sale—will have nowhere to rest, no place of shelter, no ground to till. They will die of hunger at the proprietor's door, on the edge of that property which was their birthright; and the proprietor, watching them die, will exclaim, "So perish idlers and vagrants!"

To reconcile us to the proprietor's usurpation, M. Ch. Comte assumes the lands to be of little value at the time of sale.

"The importance of these usurpations should not be exaggerated: they should be measured by the number of men which the occupied land would support, and by the means which it would furnish them.

"It is evident, for instance, that if a piece of land which is worth today one thousand francs was worth only five centimes when it was usurped, we really lose only the value of five centimes. A square league of earth would be hardly sufficient to support a savage in distress; today it supplies one thousand persons with the means of existence. Nine hundred and ninety-nine parts of this land is the legitimate property of the possessors; only one-thousandth of the value has been usurped."

A peasant admitted one day, at confession, that he had destroyed a document which declared him a debtor to the amount of three hundred francs. Said the father confessor,—"You must return these three hundred francs." "No," replied the peasant, "I will return a penny to pay for the paper."

M. Ch. Comte's logic resembles this peasant's honesty. The soil has not only an integrant and actual value, it has also a potential value,—a value of the future,—which depends on our ability to make it valuable, and to employ it in our work. Destroy a bill of exchange, a promissory note, an annuity deed,—as a paper you destroy almost no value at all; but with this paper you destroy your title, and, in losing your title, you deprive yourself of your goods. Destroy the land, or, what is the same thing, sell it,—you not only transfer one, two, or several crops, but you annihilate all the products that you could derive from it; you and your children and your children's children.

When M. Ch. Comte, the apostle of property and the eulogist of labour, supposes an alienation of the soil on the part of the government, we must not think that he does so without reason and for no purpose; it is a necessary part of his position. As he rejected the theory of occupancy, and as he knew, moreover, that labour could not constitute the right in the absence of a previous permission to occupy, he was obliged to connect this permission with the authority of the government, which means that property is based upon the sovereignty of the people; in other words, upon universal consent. This theory we have already considered.

To say that property is the daughter of labour, and then to give labour material on which to exercise itself, is, if I am not mistaken, to reason in a circle. Contradictions will result from it.

"A piece of land of a certain size produces food enough to supply a man for one day. If the possessor, through his labour, discovers some method of making it produce enough for two days, he doubles its value. This new value is his work, his creation: it is taken from nobody; it is his property."

I maintain that the possessor is paid for his trouble and industry in his doubled crop, but that he acquires no right to the land.—"Let the worker have the fruits of his labour."—Very good; but I do not understand that property in products carries with it property in raw material. Does the skill of the fisherman, who on the same coast can catch more fish than his fellows, make him proprietor of the fishing-grounds? Can the expertness of a hunter ever be regarded as a property-title to a game-forest? The analogy is perfect,—the industrious cultivator finds the reward of his industry in the abundancy and superiority of his crop. If he has made improvements in the soil, he has the possessor's right of preference. Never, under any circumstances, can he be allowed to claim a property-title to the soil which he cultivates, on the ground of his skill as a cultivator.

[…]

"If men succeed in fertilising land hitherto unproductive, or even death-producing, like certain swamps, they create thereby property in all its completeness."

What good does it do to magnify an expression, and play with equivocations, as if we expected to change the reality thereby? *They create property in all its completeness.* You mean that they create a productive capacity which formerly did not exist; but this capacity cannot be created without material to support it. The substance of the soil remains the same; only its qualities and modifications are changed. Man has created every thing—every thing save the material itself. Now, I maintain that this material he can only possess and use, on condition of permanent labour,—granting, for the time being, his right of property in things which he has produced.

This, then, is the first point settled: property in product, if we grant so much, does not carry with it property in the means of production; that seems to me to need no further demonstration. There is no difference between the soldier who possesses his arms, the mason who possesses the materials committed to his care, the fisherman who possesses the water, the hunter who possesses the fields and forests, and the cultivator who possesses the lands: all, if you say so, are proprietors of their products—not one is proprietor of the means of production. The right to product is exclusive—*jus in re*; the right to means is common—*jus ad rem.*

## §5 THAT LABOUR LEADS TO EQUALITY OF PROPERTY

[Let us] Admit, however, that labour gives a right of property in material.

Why is not this principle universal? Why is the benefit of this pretended law confined to a few and denied to the mass of workers? A philosopher, arguing that all animals sprang up formerly out of the earth warmed by the rays of the sun, almost like mushrooms, on being asked why the earth no longer yielded crops of that nature, replied: "Because it is old, and has lost its fertility." Has labour, once so fecund, likewise become sterile? Why does the tenant no longer acquire through his labour the land which was formerly acquired by the labour of the proprietor?

"Because," they say, "it is already appropriated." That is no answer. A farm yields fifty bushels per hectare; the skill and labour of the tenant double this product: the increase is created by the tenant. Suppose the owner, in a spirit of moderation rarely met with, does not go to the extent of absorbing this product by raising the rent, but allows the cultivator to enjoy the results of his labour; even then justice is not satisfied. The tenant, by improving the land, has imparted a new value to the property; he, therefore, has a right to a part of the property. If the farm was originally worth one hundred thousand francs, and if by the labour of the tenant its value has risen to one hundred and fifty thousand francs, the tenant, who produced this extra value, is the legitimate proprietor of one-third of the farm. M. Ch. Comte could not have pronounced this doctrine false, for it was he who said:

"Men who increase the fertility of the earth are no less useful to their fellow-men, than if they should create new land."

Why, then, is not this rule applicable to the man who improves the land, as well as to him who clears it? The labour of the former makes the land worth one; that of the latter makes it worth two: both create equal values. Why not accord to both equal property? I defy anyone to refute this argument, without again falling back on the right of first occupancy.

"But," it will be said, "even if your wish should be granted, property would not be distributed much more evenly than now. Land does not go on increasing in value for ever; after two or three seasons it attains its maximum fertility. That which is added by the agricultural art results rather from the progress of science and the diffusion of knowledge, than from the skill of the cultivator. Consequently, the addition of a few workers to the mass of proprietors would be no argument against property."

This discussion would, indeed, prove a well-nigh useless one, if our labours culminated in simply extending land-privilege and industrial monopoly; in emancipating only a few hundred workers out of the millions of proletarians. But this also is a misconception of our real thought, and does but prove the general lack of intelligence and logic.

If the worker, who adds to the value of a thing, has a right of property in it, he who maintains this value acquires the same right. For what is maintenance? It is incessant addition,—continuous creation. What is it to cultivate?

It is to give the soil its value every year; it is, by annually renewed creation, to prevent the diminution or destruction of the value of a piece of land. Admitting, then, that property is rational and legitimate,—admitting that rent is equitable and just,—I say that he who cultivates acquires property by as good a title as he who clears, or he who improves; and that every time a tenant pays his rent, he obtains a fraction of property in the land entrusted to his care, the denominator of which is equal to the proportion of rent paid. Unless you admit this, you fall into absolutism and tyranny; you recognise class privileges; you sanction slavery.

Whoever labours becomes a proprietor—this is an inevitable deduction from the acknowledged principles of political economy and jurisprudence. And when I say proprietor, I do not mean simply (as do our hypocritical economists) proprietor of his allowance, his salary, his wages,—I mean proprietor of the value which he creates, and by which the master alone profits.

As all this relates to the theory of wages and of the distribution of products,—and as this matter never has been even partially cleared up,—I ask permission to insist on it: this discussion will not be useless to the work in hand. Many persons talk of admitting working-people to a share in the products and profits; but in their minds this participation is pure benevolence: they have never shown—perhaps never suspected—that it was a natural, necessary right, inherent in labour, and inseparable from the function of producer, even in the lowest forms of his work.

This is my proposition: *the worker retains, even after he has received his wages, a natural right of property in the thing which he has produced.*

I again quote M. Ch. Comte:

"Some workers are employed in draining marshes, in cutting down trees and brushwood,—in a word, in cleaning up the soil. They increase the value, they make the amount of property larger; they are paid for the value which they add in the form of food and daily wages: it then becomes the property of the capitalist."

The price is not sufficient: the labour of the workers has created a value; now this value is their property. But they have neither sold nor exchanged it; and you, capitalist, you have not earned it. That you should have a partial right to the whole, in return for the materials that you have furnished and the provisions that you have supplied, is perfectly just. You contributed to the production, you ought to share in the enjoyment. But your right does not annihilate that of the workers, who, in spite of you, have been your colleagues in the work of production. Why do you talk of wages? The money with which you pay the wages of the workers remunerates them for only a few years of the perpetual possession which they have abandoned to you. Wages is the cost of the daily maintenance and refreshment of the worker. You are wrong in calling it the price of a sale. The worker has sold nothing; he knows neither his right, nor the extent of the concession which he has made to you, nor the meaning of the contract which you pretend to have made with him. On his side, utter ignorance; on yours, error and surprise, not to say deceit and fraud.

Let us make this clearer by another and more striking example.

No one is ignorant of the difficulties that are met with in the conversion of untilled land into arable and productive land. These difficulties are so great, that usually an isolated man would perish before he could put the soil in a condition to yield him even the most meagre living. To that end are needed the united and combined efforts of society, and all the resources of industry. M. Ch. Comte quotes on this subject numerous and well-authenticated facts, little thinking that he is amassing testimony against his own system.

Let us suppose that a colony of twenty or thirty families establishes itself in a wild district, covered with underbrush and forests; and from which, by agreement, the natives consent to withdraw. Each one of these families possesses a moderate but sufficient amount of capital, of such a nature as a colonist would be apt to choose,—animals, seeds, tools, and a little money and food. The land having been divided, each one settles himself as comfortably as possible, and begins to clear away the portion allotted to him. But after a few weeks of fatigue, such as they never before have known, of inconceivable suffering, of ruinous and almost useless labour, our colonists begin to complain of their trade; their condition seems hard to them; they curse their sad existence.

Suddenly, one of the shrewdest among them kills a pig, cures a part of the meat; and, resolved to sacrifice the rest of his provisions, goes to find his companions in misery. "Friends," he begins in a very benevolent tone, "how much trouble it costs you to do a little work and live uncomfortably! A fortnight of labour has reduced you to your last extremity!... Let us make an arrangement by which you shall all profit. I offer you provisions and wine: you shall get so much every day; we will work together, and, zounds! my friends, we will be happy and contented!"

Would it be possible for empty stomachs to resist such an invitation? The hungriest of them follow the treacherous tempter. They go to work; the charm of society, emulation, joy, and mutual assistance double their strength; the work can be seen to advance. Singing and laughing, they subdue Nature. In a short time, the soil is thoroughly changed; the mellowed earth waits only for the seed. That done, the proprietor pays his workers, who, on going away, return him their thanks, and grieve that the happy days which they have spent with him are over.

Others follow this example, always with the same success. Then, these installed, the rest disperse,—each one returns to his grubbing. But, while grubbing, it is necessary to live. While they have been clearing away for their neighbour, they have done no clearing for themselves. One year's seed-time and harvest is already gone. They had calculated that in lending their labour they could not but gain, since they would save their own provisions; and, while living better, would get still more money. False calculation! they have created for another the means wherewith to produce, and have created nothing for themselves. The difficulties of clearing remain the same; their clothing wears out, their provisions give out; soon their purse becomes empty for the profit of the individual for whom they have worked, and who alone can furnish the provisions which they need, since he alone is in a position to produce them. Then, when the poor grubber has exhausted his resources, the man with the provisions (like the wolf in the fable, who scents his victim from afar) again comes forward. One he offers to employ again by the day; from another he offers to buy at a favourable price a piece of his bad land, which is not, and never can be, of any use to him: that is, he uses the labour of one man to cultivate the field of another for his own benefit. So that at the end of twenty years, of thirty individuals originally equal in point of wealth, five or six have become proprietors of the whole district, while the rest have been philanthropically dispossessed!

In this century of bourgeoisie morality, in which I have had the honour to be born, the moral sense is so debased that I should not be at all surprised if I were asked, by many a worthy proprietor, what I see in this that is unjust and illegitimate? Debased creature! galvanised corpse! how can I expect to convince you, if you cannot tell theft when I show it to you? A man, by soft and insinuating words, discovers the secret of taxing others that he may establish himself; then, once enriched by their united efforts, he refuses, on the very conditions which he himself dictated, to advance the well-being of those who made his fortune for him: and you ask how such conduct is fraudulent! Under the pretext that he has paid his workers, that he owes them nothing more, that he has nothing to gain by putting himself at the service of others, while his own occupations claim his attention,—he refuses, I say, to aid others in getting a foothold, as he was aided in getting his own; and when, in the impotence of their isolation, these poor workers are compelled to sell their birthright, he—this ungrateful proprietor, this knavish upstart—stands ready to put the finishing touch to their deprivation and their ruin. And you think that just? Take care!

I read in your startled countenance the reproach of a guilty conscience, much more clearly than the innocent astonishment of involuntary ignorance.

"The capitalist," they say, "has paid the workers their *daily wages*." To be accurate, it must be said that the capitalist has paid as many times one day's wage as he has employed workers each day,—which is not at all the same thing. For he has paid nothing for that immense power which results from the union and harmony of workers, and the convergence and simultaneousness of their efforts. Two hundred grenadiers stood the obelisk of Luxor upon its base in a few hours; do you suppose that one man could have accomplished the same task in two hundred days? Nevertheless, on the books of the capitalist, the amount of wages paid would have been the same. Well, a desert to prepare for cultivation, a house to build, a factory to run,—all these are obelisks to erect, mountains to move. The smallest fortune, the most insignificant establishment, the setting in motion of the lowest industry, demand the concurrence of so many different kinds of labour and skill, that one man could not possibly execute the whole of them. It is astonishing that the economists never have called attention to this fact. Strike a balance, then, between the capitalist's receipts and his payments.

[...]

Consequently, when M. Ch. Comte—following out his hypothesis—shows us his capitalist acquiring one after another the products of his employees' labour, he sinks deeper and deeper into the mire; and, as his argument does not change, our reply of course remains the same.

"Other workers are employed in building: some quarry the stone, others transport it, others cut it, and still others put it in place. Each of them adds a certain value to the material which passes through his hands; and this value, the product of his labour, is his property. He sells it, as fast as he creates it, to the proprietor of the building, who pays him for it in food and wages."

*Divide et impera*—divide, and you shall command; divide, and you shall grow rich; divide, and you shall deceive men, you shall daze their minds, you shall mock at justice! Separate workers from each other, perhaps each one's daily wage exceeds the value of each individual's product; but that is not the question under consideration. A force of one thousand men working twenty days has been paid the same wages that one would be paid for working fifty-five years; but this force of one thousand has done in twenty days what a single man could not have accomplished, though he had laboured for a million centuries. Is the exchange an equitable one? Once more, no; when you have paid all the individual forces, the collective force still remains to be paid.

Consequently, there remains always a right of collective property which you have not acquired, and which you enjoy unjustly.

Admit that twenty days' wages suffice to feed, lodge, and clothe this multitude for twenty days: thrown out of employment at the end of that time, what will become of them, if, as fast as they create, they abandon their creations to the proprietors who will soon discharge them? While the proprietor, firm in his position (thanks to the aid of all the workers), dwells in security, and fears no lack of labour or bread, the worker's only dependence is upon the benevolence of this same proprietor, to whom he has sold and surrendered his liberty. If, then, the proprietor, shielding himself behind his comfort and his rights, refuses to employ the worker, how can the worker live? He has ploughed an excellent field, and cannot sow it; he has built an elegant and commodious house, and cannot live in it; he has produced all, and can enjoy nothing.

Labour leads us to equality. Every step that we take brings us nearer to it; and if workers had equal strength, diligence, and industry, clearly their fortunes would be equal also. Indeed, if, as is pretended,—and as we have admitted,—the worker is proprietor of the value which he creates, it follows:

1. That the worker should acquire at the expense of the idle proprietor;

2. That all production being necessarily collective, the worker is entitled to a share of the products and profits commensurate with his labour;

3. That all accumulated capital being social property, no one can be its exclusive proprietor.

These inferences are unavoidable; these alone would suffice to revolutionise our whole economic system, and change our institutions and our laws. Why do the very persons, who laid down this principle, now refuse to be guided by it? Why do the Says, the Comtes, the Hennequins, and others— after having said that property is born of labour—seek to fix it by occupation and prescription?

But let us leave these sophists to their contradictions and blindness. The good sense of the people will do justice to their equivocations. Let us make haste to enlighten it, and show it the true path. Equality approaches; already between it and us but a short distance intervenes: tomorrow even this distance will have been traversed.

## §6 THAT IN SOCIETY ALL WAGES ARE EQUAL

When the St. Simonians, the Fourierists, and, in general, all who in our day are connected with social economy and reform, inscribe upon their banner,—

"To each according to his capacity, to each capacity according to its results" (St. Simon);

"To each according to his capital, his labour, and his skill" (Fourier),— they mean—although they do not say so in so many words—that the products of Nature procured by labour and industry are a reward, a palm, a crown offered to all kinds of pre-eminence and superiority. They regard the land as an immense arena in which prizes are contended for,—no longer, it is true, with lances and swords, by force and by treachery; but by acquired wealth, by knowledge, talent, and by virtue itself. In a word, they mean—and everybody agrees with them—that the greatest capacity is entitled to the greatest reward; and, to use the mercantile phraseology,—which has, at least, the merit of being straightforward,—that salaries must be governed by capacity and its results.

[...]

This proposition, taken, as they say, *in sensu obvio*—in the sense usually attributed to it—is false, absurd, unjust, contradictory, hostile to liberty, friendly to tyranny, anti-social, and was unluckily framed under the express influence of the property idea.

And, first, *capital* must be crossed off the list of elements which are entitled to a reward. The Fourierists—as far as I have been able to learn from a few of their pamphlets—deny the right of occupancy, and recognise no basis of property save labour. Starting with a like premise, they would have seen— had they reasoned upon the matter—that capital is a source of production to its proprietor only by virtue of the right of occupancy, and that this production is therefore illegitimate. Indeed, if labour is the sole basis of property, I cease to be proprietor of my field as soon as I receive rent for it from another. This we have shown beyond all cavil. It is the same with all capital; so that to put capital in an enterprise, is, by the law's decision, to exchange it for an equivalent sum in products. […]

Thus, capital can be exchanged, but cannot be a source of income.
[…]

In labour, two things must be noticed and distinguished: *association* and *available material*.

In so far as workers are associated, they are equal; and it involves a contradiction to say that one should be paid more than another. […]
[…]

But every industry needs—they will add—leaders, instructors, superintendents, etc. Will these be engaged in the general task? No; since their task is to lead, instruct, and superintend. But they must be chosen from the workers by the workers themselves, and must fulfil the conditions of eligibility. It is the same with all public functions, whether of administration or instruction.

Then, article first of the universal constitution will be:

"The limited quantity of available material proves the necessity of dividing the labour among the whole number of workers. The capacity, given to all, of accomplishing a social task,—that is, an equal task,—and the impossibility of paying one worker save in the products of another, justify the equality of wages."
[…]

# CHAPTER IV
## THAT PROPERTY IS IMPOSSIBLE

THE LAST RESORT of proprietors,—the overwhelming argument whose invincible potency reassures them,—is that, in their opinion, equality of conditions is impossible. "Equality of conditions is a chimera," they cry with a knowing air; "distribute wealth equally today—tomorrow this equality will have vanished."

To this hackneyed objection, which they repeat everywhere with the most marvellous assurance, they never fail to add the following comment, as a sort *Of Glory be to the Father*: "If all men were equal, nobody would work." This anthem is sung with variations.

"If all were masters, nobody would obey."

"If nobody were rich, who would employ the poor?"

And, "If nobody were poor, who would labour for the rich?"

But let us have done with invective—we have better arguments at our command.

If I show that property itself is impossible—that it is property which is a contradiction, a chimera, a utopia; and if I show it no longer by metaphysics and jurisprudence, but by figures, equations, and calculations,—imagine the fright of the astounded proprietor! And you, reader; what do you think of the retort?

[...]

AXIOM: *Property is the Right of Increase [droit d'aubaine] claimed by the Proprietor over any thing which he has stamped as his own.*

[...]

*Observations*: Increase [*aubaine*] receives different names according to the thing by which it is yielded: if by land, *farm-rent;* if by houses and furniture, *rent;* if by life-investments, *revenue;* if by money, *interest;* if by exchange, *advantage gain, profit* (three things which must not be confounded with the wages or legitimate price of labour).

[...]

*Property is impossible, because it demands Something for Nothing.*

The discussion of this proposition covers the same ground as that of the origin of farm-rent, which is so much debated by the economists. When I read the writings of the greater part of these men, I cannot avoid a feeling of contempt mingled with anger, in view of this mass of nonsense, in which the detestable vies with the absurd. It would be a repetition of the story of the elephant in the moon, were it not for the atrocity of the consequences. To seek a rational and legitimate origin of that which is, and ever must be, only theft, extortion, and plunder—that must be the height of the proprietor's folly; the last degree of bedevilment into which minds, otherwise judicious, can be thrown by the perversity of selfishness.

"A farmer," says Say, "is a wheat manufacturer who, among other tools which serve him in modifying the material from which he makes the wheat, employs one large tool, which we call a field. If he is not the proprietor of the field, if he is only a tenant, he pays the proprietor for the productive service of this tool. The tenant is reimbursed by the purchaser, the latter by another, until the product reaches the consumer; who redeems the first payment, *plus* all the others, by means of which the product has at last come into his hands."

Let us lay aside the subsequent payments by which the product reaches the consumer, and, for the present, pay attention only to the first one of all,—the rent paid to the proprietor by the tenant. On what ground, we ask, is the proprietor entitled to this rent?

[...]

Buchanan—a commentator on Smith—regarded farm-rent as the result of a monopoly, and maintained that labour alone is productive. Consequently, he thought that, without this monopoly, products would rise in price; and he found no basis for farm-rent save in the civil law. This opinion is a corollary of that which makes the civil law the basis of property. But why has the civil law—which ought to be the written expression of justice—authorised this monopoly? Whoever says monopoly, necessarily excludes justice. Now, to say that farm-rent is a monopoly sanctioned by the law, is to say that injustice is based on justice,—a contradiction in terms.

Say answers Buchanan, that the proprietor is not a monopolist, because a monopolist "is one who does not increase the utility of the merchandise which passes through his hands."

How much does the proprietor increase the utility of his tenant's products? Has he ploughed, sowed, reaped, mowed, winnowed, weeded? These are the processes by which the tenant and his employees increase the utility of the material which they consume for the purpose of reproduction.

"The landed proprietor increases the utility of products by means of his implement, the land. This implement receives in one state, and returns in another the materials of which wheat is composed. The action of the land is a chemical process, which so modifies the material that it multiplies it by destroying it. The soil is then a producer of utility; and when it asks its pay in the form of profit, or farm rent, for its proprietor, it at the same time gives something to the consumer in exchange for the amount which the consumer pays it. It gives him a produced utility; and it is the production of this utility which warrants us in calling land productive, as well as labour."

Let us clear up this matter.

The blacksmith who manufactures for the farmer implements of husbandry, the wheelwright who makes him a cart, the mason who builds his barn, the carpenter, the basket-maker, etc.,—all of whom contribute to agricultural production by the tools which they provide,—are producers of utility; consequently, they are entitled to a part of the products.

"Undoubtedly," says Say; "but the land also is an implement whose service must be paid for, then..."

I admit that the land is an implement; but who made it? Did the proprietor? Did he—by the efficacious virtue of the right of property, by this *moral quality* infused into the soil—endow it with vigour and fertility? Exactly there lies the monopoly of the proprietor; in the fact that, though he did not make the implement, he asks pay for its use. When the Creator shall present himself and claim farm-rent, we will consider the matter with him; or even when the proprietor—his pretended representative—shall exhibit his power-of-attorney.

"The proprietor's service," adds Say, "is easy, I admit."

It is a frank confession.

"But we cannot disregard it. Without property, one farmer would contend with another for the possession of a field without a proprietor, and the field would remain uncultivated..."

Then the proprietor's business is to reconcile farmers by robbing them. O logic! O justice! O the marvellous wisdom of economists! The proprietor, if they are right, is like Perrin-Dandin[4] who, when summoned by two travellers to settle a dispute about an oyster, opened it, gobbled it, and said to them:

"The Court awards you each a shell."

Could anything worse be said of property?

Will Say tell us why the same farmers, who, if there were no proprietors, would contend with each other for possession of the soil, do not contend today with the proprietors for this possession? Obviously, because they think them legitimate possessors, and because their respect for even an imaginary right exceeds their avarice. I proved, in Chapter II, that possession is sufficient, without property, to maintain social order. Would it be more difficult, then, to reconcile possessors without masters than tenants controlled by proprietors? Would labouring men, who respect—much to their own detriment—the pretended rights of the idler, violate the natural rights of the producer and the manufacturer? What! if the husbandman forfeited his right to the land as soon as he ceased to occupy it, would he become more covetous? And would the impossibility of demanding increase [*aubaine*], of taxing another's labour, be a source of quarrels and law-suits? The economists use singular logic. But we are not yet through. Admit that the proprietor is the legitimate master of the land.

"The land is an instrument of production," they say. That is true. But when, changing the noun into an adjective, they alter the phrase, thus, "The land is a productive instrument," they make a wicked blunder.

According to Quesnay and the early economists, all production comes from the land. Smith, Ricardo, and de Tracy, on the contrary, say that labour is the sole agent of production. Say, and most of his successors, teach that BOTH land AND labour AND capital are productive. The latter constitute the eclectic school of political economy. The truth is, that NEITHER land NOR labour NOR capital is productive. Production results from the co-operation of these three equally necessary elements, which, taken separately, are equally sterile.

Political economy, indeed, treats of the production, distribution, and consumption of wealth or values. But of what values? Of the values produced by human industry; that is, of the changes made in matter by man, that he may appropriate it to his own use, and not at all of Nature's spontaneous productions. Man's labour consists in a simple laying on of hands. When he has taken that trouble, he has produced a value. Until then, the salt of the sea, the water of the springs, the grass of the fields, and the trees of the forests are to him as if they were not. The sea, without the fisherman and his line, supplies no fish. The forest, without the wood-cutter and his axe, furnishes neither fuel nor timber. The meadow, without the mower, yields neither hay nor aftermath. Nature is a vast mass of material to be cultivated and converted into products; but Nature produces nothing for

4   Perrin Dandin, a character in François Rabelais's *Third Book*. (Editor)

2

herself; in the economical sense, her products, in their relation to man, are not yet products.

Capital, tools, and machinery are likewise unproductive. The hammer and the anvil, without the blacksmith and the iron, do not forge. The mill, without the miller and the grain, does not grind, etc. Bring tools and raw material together; place a plough and some seed on fertile soil; enter a smithy, light the fire, and shut up the shop,—you will produce nothing. The following remark was made by an economist who possessed more good sense than most of his fellows: "Say credits capital with an active part unwarranted by its nature; left to itself, it is an idle tool" (J. Droz: *Political Economy*).

Finally, labour and capital together, when unfortunately combined, produce nothing. Plough a sandy desert, beat the water of the rivers, pass type through a sieve,—you will get neither wheat, nor fish, nor books. Your trouble will be as fruitless as was the immense labour of the army of Xerxes; who, as Herodotus says, with his three million soldiers, scourged the Hellespont for twenty-four hours, as a punishment for having broken and scattered the pontoon bridge which the great king had thrown across it.

Tools and capital, land and labour, considered individually and abstractly, are not, literally speaking, productive. The propriet or who asks to be rewarded for the use of a tool, or the productive power of his land, takes for granted, then, that which is radically false; namely, that capital produces by its own effort,—and, in taking pay for this imaginary product, he literally receives something for nothing.

*Objection*—But if the blacksmith, the wheelwright, all manufacturers in short, have a right to the products in return for the implements which they furnish; and if land is an implement of production,—why does not this implement entitle its proprietor, be his claim real or imaginary, to a portion of the products; as in the case of the manufacturers of ploughs and wagons?

*Reply*—Here we touch the heart of the question, the mystery of property; which we must clear up, if we would understand anything of the strange effects of the right of increase [*droit d'aubaine*].

He who manufactures or repairs the farmer's tools receives the price *once*, either at the time of delivery, or in several payments; and when this price is once paid to the manufacturer, the tools which he has delivered belong to him no more. Never does he claim double payment for the same tool, or the same job of repairs. If he annually shares in the products of the farmer, it is owing to the fact that he annually makes something for the farmer.

The proprietor, on the contrary, does not yield his implement; eternally he is paid for it, eternally he keeps it.

In fact, the rent received by the proprietor is not intended to defray the expense of maintaining and repairing the implement; this expense is charged to the borrower, and does not concern the proprietor except as he is interested in the preservation of the article. If he takes it upon himself to attend to the repairs, he takes care that the money which he expends for this purpose is repaid.

This rent does not represent the product of the implement, since of itself the implement produces nothing; we have just proved this, and we shall prove it more clearly still by its consequences.

Finally, this rent does not represent the participation of the proprietor in the production; since this participation could consist, like that of the blacksmith and the wheelwright, only in the surrender of the whole or a part of his implement, in which case he would cease to be its proprietor, which would involve a contradiction of the idea of property.

Then, between the proprietor and his tenant there is no exchange either of values or services; then, as our axiom says, farm-rent is real increase,—an extortion based solely upon fraud and violence on the one hand, and weakness and ignorance upon the other. *Products*, say the economists, *are bought only by products.* This maxim is property's condemnation. The proprietor, producing neither by his own labour nor by his implement, and receiving products in exchange for nothing, is either a parasite or a thief. Then, if property can exist only as a right, property is impossible.

· *Corollaries*—1. The republican constitution of 1793, which defined property as "the right to enjoy the fruit of one's labour," was grossly mistaken. It should have said, "Property is the right to enjoy and dispose at will of another's goods,—the fruit of another's industry and labour."

2. Every possessor of lands, houses, furniture, machinery, tools, money, etc., who lends a thing for a price exceeding the cost of repairs (the repairs being charged to the lender, and representing products which he exchanges for other products), is guilty of swindling and extortion. In short, all rent received (nominally as damages, but really as payment for a loan) is an act of property,—of theft.

*Historical comment*—The tax which a victorious nation levies upon a conquered nation is genuine farm-rent. The seigniorial rights abolished by the Revolution of 1789,—tithes, mortmain, statute-labour, etc.,—were different forms of the rights of property; and they who under the titles of nobles, seigneurs, prebendaries, etc. enjoyed these rights, were neither more nor less than proprietors. To defend property today is to condemn the Revolution.

[...]

When the ass is too heavily loaded, he lies down; man always moves on. Upon this indomitable courage, the proprietor—well knowing that it exists—bases his hopes of speculation. The free worker produces ten; for me, thinks the proprietor, he will produce twelve.

Indeed,—before consenting to the confiscation of his fields, before bidding farewell to the paternal roof,—the peasant, whose story we have just told, makes a desperate effort; he leases new land; he will sow one-third more; and, taking half of this new product for himself, he will harvest an additional sixth, and thereby pay his rent. What an evil! To add one-sixth to his production, the farmer must add, not one-sixth, but two-sixths to his labour. At such a price, he pays a farm-rent which in God's eyes he does not owe.

The landlord's example is followed by the industrialist. The former tills more land, and dispossesses his neighbours; the latter lowers the price of his merchandise, and endeavours to monopolise its manufacture and sale, and to crush out his competitors. To satisfy property, the worker must first produce beyond his needs. Then, he must produce beyond his strength [...].

[...]

If the worker receives for his labour an average of three francs per day, his employer (in order to gain anything beyond his own salary, if only interest on his capital) must sell the day's labour of his employee, in the form of merchandise, for more than three francs. The worker cannot, then, repurchase that which he has produced for his master. It is thus with all trades whatsoever. The tailor, the hatter, the cabinet-maker, the blacksmith, the tanner, the mason, the jeweller, the printer, the clerk, etc., even to the farmer and wine-grower, cannot repurchase their products; since, producing for a master who in one form or another makes a profit, they are obliged to pay more for their own labour than they get for it.

The labouring people can buy neither the cloth which they weave, nor the furniture which they manufacture, nor the metal which they forge, nor the jewels which they cut, nor the prints which they engrave. They can procure neither the wheat which they plant, nor the wine which they grow, nor the flesh of the animals which they raise. They are allowed neither to dwell in the houses which they build, nor to attend the plays which their labour supports, nor to enjoy the rest which their body requires. And why? Because the right of increase [*droit d'aubaine*] does not permit these things to be sold at the cost-price, which is all that workers can afford to pay. On the signs of those magnificent warehouses which he in his poverty admires, the worker reads in large letters: "This is thy work, and thou shalt not have it." *Sic vos non vobis!*

[...]

If the factory stops running, the manufacturer has to pay interest on his capital the same as before. He naturally tries, then, to continue production by lessening expenses. Then comes the lowering of wages; the introduction of machinery; the employment of women and children to do the work of men; bad workmen, and wretched work. They still produce, because the decreased cost creates a larger market; but they do not produce long, because, the cheapness being due to the quantity and rapidity of production, the productive power tends more than ever to outstrip consumption. It is when workers, whose wages are scarcely sufficient to support them from one day to another, are thrown out of work, that the consequences of the principle of property become most frightful. They have not been able to economise, they have made no savings, they have accumulated no capital whatever to support them even one day more. Today the factory is closed. To-morrow the people starve in the streets. Day after tomorrow they will either die in the hospital, or eat in the jail.

And still new misfortunes come to complicate this terrible situation. In consequence of the cessation of business, and the extreme cheapness of merchandise, the manufacturer finds it impossible to pay the interest on his borrowed capital; whereupon his frightened creditors hasten to withdraw their funds. Production is suspended, and labour comes to a standstill. Then people are astonished to see capital desert commerce, and throw itself upon the Stock Exchange; and I once heard M. Blanqui bitterly lamenting the blind ignorance of capitalists. The cause of this movement of capital is very simple; but for that very reason an economist could not understand it, or rather must not explain it. The cause lies solely in *competition*.

I mean by competition, not only the rivalry between two parties engaged in the same business, but the general and simultaneous effort of all kinds of business to get ahead of each other. This effort is today so strong, that the price of merchandise scarcely covers the cost of production and distribution; so that, the wages of all workers being lessened, nothing remains, not even interest for the capitalists.

The primary cause of commercial and industrial stagnations is, then, interest on capital,—that interest which the ancients with one accord branded with the name of usury, whenever it was paid for the use of money, but which they did not dare to condemn in the forms of house-rent, farm-rent, or profit: as if the nature of the thing lent could ever warrant a charge for the lending; that is, theft.

In proportion to the increase received by the capitalist will be the frequency and intensity of commercial crises,—the first being given, we always can determine the two others; and vice versa. Do you wish to know the regulator of a society? Ascertain the amount of active capital; that is, the capital bearing interest, and the legal rate of this interest. The course of events will be a series of overturns, whose number and violence will be proportional to the activity of capital.

[...]

*Property is impossible, because it is powerless against Property.*

I. By the third corollary of our axiom, interest tells against the proprietor as well as the stranger. This economic principle is universally admitted. Nothing simpler at first blush; yet, nothing more absurd, more contradictory in terms, or more absolutely impossible.

The manufacturer, it is said, pays himself the rent on his house and capital. *He pays himself*; that is, he gets paid by the public who buy his products. For, suppose the manufacturer, who seems to make this profit on his property, wishes also to make it on his merchandise, can he then pay himself one franc for that which cost him ninety centimes, and make money by the operation? No: such a transaction would transfer the merchant's money from his right hand to his left, but without any profit whatever.

Now, that which is true of a single individual trading with himself is true also of the whole business world. Form a chain of ten, fifteen, twenty producers; as many as you wish. If the producer A makes a profit out of the producer B, B's loss must, according to economic principles, be made up by C, C's by D; and so on through to Z.

But by whom will Z be paid for the loss caused him by the profit charged by A in the beginning? *By the consumer*, replies Say. Contemptible equivocation! Is this consumer any other, then, than A, B. C, D, etc., or Z? By whom will Z be paid? If he is paid by A, no one makes a profit; consequently, there is no property. If, on the contrary, Z bears the burden himself, he ceases to be a member of society; since it refuses him the right of property and profit, which it grants to the other associates.

Since, then, a nation, like universal humanity, is a vast industrial association which cannot act outside of itself, it is clear that no man can enrich himself without impoverishing another. For, in order that the right of property, the right of increase [*droit d'aubaine*], may be respected in the case of A, it must be denied to Z; thus we see how equality of rights, separated from equality of conditions, may be a truth. The iniquity of political economy in this respect is flagrant. "When I, a manufacturer, purchase the labour of a worker, I do not include his wages in the net product of my business; on the contrary, I deduct them. But the worker includes them in his net product..." (Say: *Political Economy*).

That means that all which the worker gains is *net product*; but that only that part of the manufacturer's gains is *net product*, which remains after deducting his wages. But why is the right of profit confined to the manufacturer? Why is this right, which is at bottom the right of property itself, denied to the worker? In the terms of economic science, the worker is capital. Now, all capital, beyond the cost of its maintenance and repair, must bear interest. This the proprietor takes care to get, both for his capital and for himself. Why is the worker prohibited from charging a like interest for his capital, which is himself?

Property, then, is inequality of rights; for, if it were not inequality of rights, it would be equality of goods,—in other words, it would not exist. Now, the charter guarantees to all equality of rights. Then, by the charter, property is impossible.

II. Is A, the proprietor of an estate, entitled by the fact of his proprietorship to take possession of the field belonging to B. his neighbour? "No," reply the proprietors; "but what has that to do with the right of property?" That I shall show you by a series of similar propositions.

Has C, a hatter, the right to force D, his neighbour and also a hatter, to close his shop, and cease his business? Not the least in the world.

But C wishes to make a profit of one franc on every hat, while D is content with fifty centimes. It is evident that D's moderation is injurious to C's extravagant claims. Has the latter a right to prevent D from selling? Certainly not.

Since D is at liberty to sell his hats fifty centimes cheaper than C if he chooses, C in his turn is free to reduce his price one franc. Now, D is poor, while C is rich; so that at the end of two or three years D is ruined by this intolerable competition, and C has complete control of the market. Can the proprietor D get any redress from the proprietor C? Can he bring a suit against him to recover his business and property? No; for D could have done the same thing, had he been the richer of the two.

On the same ground, the large proprietor A may say to the small proprietor B: "Sell me your field, otherwise you shall not sell your wheat,"—and that without doing him the least wrong, or giving him ground for complaint. So that A can devour B if he likes, for the very reason that A is stronger than B. Consequently, it is not the right of property which enables A and C to rob B and D, but the right of might. By the right of property, neither the two neighbours A and B, nor the two merchants C and D, could harm each other. They could neither dispossess nor destroy one another, nor gain at one another's expense. The power of invasion lies in superior strength.

But it is superior strength also which enables the manufacturer to reduce the wages of his employees, and the rich merchant and well-stocked proprietor to sell their products for what they please. The manufacturer says to the worker, "You are as free to go elsewhere with your services as I am to receive them. I offer you so much." The merchant says to the customer, "Take it or leave it; you are master of your money, as I am of my goods. I want so much." Who will yield? The weaker.

Therefore, without force, property is powerless against property, since without force it has no power to increase [*s'accroître par aubaine*]; therefore, without force, property is null and void.

[...]

# CHAPTER V
## PSYCHOLOGICAL EXPOSITION OF THE IDEA OF JUSTICE, AND A DETERMINATION OF THE PRINCIPLE OF GOVERNMENT AND OF RIGHT

PROPERTY IS IMPOSSIBLE; equality does not exist. We hate the former, and yet wish to possess it; the latter rules all our thoughts, yet we know not how to reach it. Who will explain this profound antagonism between our conscience and our will? Who will point out the causes of this pernicious error, which has become the most sacred principle of justice and society?

I am bold enough to undertake the task, and I hope to succeed.

[...]

When two or more individuals have regularly organised a society,—when the contracts have been agreed upon, drafted, and signed,—there is no difficulty about the future. Everybody knows that when two men associate—for instance—in order to fish, if one of them catches no fish, he is none the less entitled to those caught by his associate. If two merchants form a partnership, while the partnership lasts, the profits and losses are divided between them; since each produces, not for himself, but for the society: when the time of distribution arrives, it is not the producer who is considered, but the associate. That is why the slave, to whom the planter gives straw and rice; and the civilised worker, to whom the capitalist pays a salary which is always too small,— not being associated with their employers, although producing with them,— are disregarded when the product is divided. Thus, the horse who draws our coaches, and the ox who draws our carts produce with us, but are not associated with us; we take their product, but do not share it with them. The animals and workers whom we employ hold the same relation to us. Whatever we do for them, we do, not from a sense of justice, but out of pure benevolence.[5]

But is it possible that we are not all associated? Let us call to mind what was said in the last two chapters, That even though we do not want to be associated, the force of things, the necessity of consumption, the laws of production, and the mathematical principle of exchange combine to associate us. There is but a single exception to this rule,—that of the proprietor, who, producing by his right of increase [*droit d'aubaine*], is not associated with any one, and consequently is not obliged to share his product with any one; just as no one else is bound to share with him. With the exception of the proprietor, we labour for each other; we can do nothing by ourselves unaided by others, and we continually exchange products and services with each other. If these are not social acts, what are they?

Now, neither a commercial, nor an industrial, nor an agricultural association can be conceived of in the absence of equality; equality is its sine qua non. So that, in all matters which concern this association, to violate society is to violate justice and equality. Apply this principle to humanity at large.

After what has been said, I assume that the reader has sufficient insight to enable him to dispense with any aid of mine.

By this principle, the man who takes possession of a field, and says, "This field is mine," will not be unjust so long as every one else has an equal right of possession; nor will he be unjust, if, wishing to change his location, he exchanges this field for an equivalent. But if, putting another in his place, he says to him, "Work for me while I rest," he then becomes unjust, unassociated, *unequal*. He is a proprietor.

Reciprocally, the sluggard, or the rake, who, without performing any social task, enjoys like others—and often more than others—the products of

5    To perform an act of benevolence towards one's neighbour is called, in Hebrew, to do justice; in Greek, to take compassion or pity (ἐλεημοσύνη, from which is derived the French *aumone*); in Latin, to perform an act of love or charity; in French, give alms. We can trace the degradation of this principle through these various expressions: the first signifies duty; the second only sympathy; the third, affection, a matter of choice, not an obligation; the fourth, caprice.

society, should be proceeded against as a thief and a parasite. We owe it to
ourselves to give him nothing; but, since he must live, to put him under
supervision, and compel him to labour.

Sociability is the attraction felt by sentient beings for each other. Justice
is this same attraction, accompanied by thought and knowledge. But under what general concept, in what category of the understanding, is justice
placed? In the category of equal quantities. Hence, the ancient definition of
justice—*Justum aequale est, injustum inaequale*. What is it, then, to practise
justice? It is to give equal wealth to each, on condition of equal labour. It is to
act socially. Our selfishness may complain; there is no escape from evidence
and necessity.

What is the right of occupancy? It is a natural method of dividing the
earth, by reducing each worker's share as fast as new workers present themselves. This right disappears if the public interest requires it; which, being the
social interest, is also that of the occupant.

What is the right of labour? It is the right to obtain one's share of wealth
by fulfilling the required conditions. It is the right of society, the right of
equality.

Justice, which is the product of the combination of an idea and an instinct, manifests itself in man as soon as he is capable of feeling, and of
forming ideas. Consequently, it has been regarded as an innate and original
sentiment; but this opinion is logically and chronologically false. But justice,
by its composition hybrid—if I may use the term,—justice, born of emotion
and intellect combined, seems to me one of the strongest proofs of the unity
and simplicity of the ego; the organism being no more capable of producing
such a mixture by itself, than are the combined senses of hearing and sight of
forming a binary sense, half auditory and half visual.

[...]

*When property is abolished, what will be the form of society? Will it be
communism?*

[...]

Communism—the first expression of the social nature—is the first term
of social development,—the *thesis*; property, the reverse of communism, is
the second term,—the *antithesis*. When we have discovered the third term,
the *synthesis*, we shall have the required solution. Now, this synthesis necessarily results from the correction of the thesis by the antithesis. Therefore it
is necessary, by a final examination of their characteristics, to eliminate those
features which are hostile to sociability. The union of the two remainders will
give us the true form of human association.

[...]

I. I ought not to conceal the fact that property and communism have
been considered always the only possible forms of society. This deplorable
error has been the life of property. The disadvantages of communism are
so obvious that its critics never have needed to employ much eloquence to

thoroughly disgust men with it. The irreparability of the injustice which it causes, the violence which it does to attractions and repulsions, the yoke of iron which it fastens upon the will, the moral torture to which it subjects the conscience, the debilitating effect which it has upon society; and, to sum it all up, the pious and stupid uniformity which it enforces upon the free, active, reasoning, unsubmissive personality of man, have shocked common sense, and condemned communism by an irrevocable decree.

The authorities and examples cited in its favour disprove it. The communistic republic of Plato involved slavery; that of Lycurgus employed Helots, whose duty it was to produce for their masters, thus enabling the latter to devote themselves exclusively to athletic sports and to war. Even J. J. Rousseau—confounding communism and equality—has said somewhere that, without slavery, he did not think equality of conditions possible. The communities of the early Church did not last the first century out, and soon degenerated into monasteries. In those of the Jesuits of Paraguay, the condition of the blacks is said by all travellers to be as miserable as that of slaves; and it is a fact that the good Fathers were obliged to surround themselves with ditches and walls to prevent their new converts from escaping. The followers of Babeuf—guided by a lofty horror of property rather than by any definite belief—were ruined by exaggeration of their principles; the St. Simonians, lumping communism and inequality, passed away like a masquerade. The greatest danger to which society is exposed today is that of another shipwreck on this rock.

Singularly enough, systematic communism [*communauté*]—the deliberate negation of property—is conceived under the direct influence of the proprietary prejudice; and property is the basis of all communistic theories.

The members of a community, it is true, have no private property; but the community is proprietor, and proprietor not only of the goods, but of the persons and wills. In consequence of this principle of absolute property, labour, which should be only a condition imposed upon man by Nature, becomes in all communities a human commandment, and therefore odious. Passive obedience, irreconcilable with a reflecting will, is strictly enforced. Fidelity to regulations, which are always defective, however wise they may be thought, allows of no complaint. Life, talent, and all the human faculties are the property of the State, which has the right to use them as it pleases for the common good. Private associations are sternly prohibited, in spite of the likes and dislikes of different natures, because to tolerate them would be to introduce small communities within the large one, and consequently private property; the strong work for the weak, although this ought to be left to benevolence, and not enforced, advised, or enjoined; the industrious work for the lazy, although this is unjust; the clever work for the foolish, although this is absurd; and, finally, man—casting aside his personality, his spontaneity, his genius, and his affections—humbly annihilates himself at the feet of the majestic and inflexible Commune!

Communism is inequality, but not as property is. Property is the exploitation of the weak by the strong. Communism is the exploitation of the strong by the weak. In property, inequality of conditions is the result of force, under whatever name it be disguised: physical and mental force; force of events, chance, *fortune*; force of accumulated property, etc. In communism, inequality springs from placing mediocrity on a level with excellence. This damaging equation is repellent to the conscience, and causes merit to complain; for, although it may be the duty of the strong to aid the weak, they prefer to do it out of generosity,—they never will endure a comparison. Give them equal opportunities of labour, and equal wages, but never allow their jealousy to be awakened by mutual suspicion of unfaithfulness in the performance of the common task.

Communism is oppression and slavery. Man is very willing to obey the law of duty, serve his country, and oblige his friends; but he wishes to labour when he pleases, where he pleases, and as much as he pleases. He wishes to dispose of his own time, to be governed only by necessity, to choose his friendships, his recreation, and his discipline; to act from judgement, not by command; to sacrifice himself through selfishness, not through servile obligation. Communism is essentially opposed to the free exercise of our faculties, to our noblest desires, to our deepest feelings. Any plan which could be devised for reconciling it with the demands of the individual reason and will would end only in changing the thing while preserving the name. Now, if we are honest truth-seekers, we shall avoid disputes about words.

Thus, communism violates the sovereignty of the conscience, and equality: the first, by restricting spontaneity of mind and heart, and freedom of thought and action; the second, by placing labour and laziness, skill and stupidity, and even vice and virtue on an equality in point of comfort. For the rest, if property is impossible on account of the desire to accumulate, communism would soon become so through the desire to shirk.

II. Property, in its turn, violates equality by the rights of exclusion and increase, and freedom by despotism. The former effect of property having been sufficiently developed in the last three chapters, I will content myself here with establishing by a final comparison, its perfect identity with theft.

[...]

In those forms of theft which are prohibited by law, force and artifice are employed alone and undisguised; in the authorised forms, they conceal themselves within a useful product, which they use as a tool to plunder their victim.

The direct use of violence and stratagem was early and universally condemned; but no nation has yet got rid of that kind of theft which acts through talent, labour, and possession, and which is the source of all the dilemmas of casuistry and the innumerable contradictions of jurisprudence.

[...]

The second effect of property is despotism. Now, since despotism is inseparably connected with the idea of legitimate authority, in explaining the natural causes of the first, the principle of the second will appear.

What is to be the form of government in the future? I hear some of my younger readers reply: "Why, how can you ask such a question? You are a republican." "A republican! Yes; but that word specifies nothing. *Res publica;* that is, the public thing. Now, whoever is interested in public affairs—no matter under what form of government—may call himself a republican. Even kings are republicans."—

"Well! you are a democrat?"—"No."—"What! you would have a monarchy."—"No."—"A constitutionalist?"—"God forbid!"—"You are then an aristocrat?"—"Not at all."—"You want a mixed government?"—"Still less."—"What are you, then?"—"I am an anarchist."

"Oh! I understand you; you speak satirically. This is a hit at the government."—"By no means. I have just given you my serious and well-considered profession of faith. Although a firm friend of order, I am (in the full force of the term) an anarchist. Listen to me."

[...]

By means of self-instruction and the acquisition of ideas, man finally acquires the idea of *science,*—that is, of a system of knowledge in harmony with the reality of things, and inferred from observation. He searches for the science, or the system, of inanimate bodies,—the system of organic bodies, the system of the human mind, and the system of the universe: why should he not also search for the system of society? But, having reached this height, he comprehends that political truth, or the science of politics, exists quite independently of the will of sovereigns, the opinion of majorities, and popular beliefs,—that kings, ministers, magistrates, and nations, as wills, have no connection with the science, and are worthy of no consideration. He comprehends, at the same time, that, if man is born a sociable being, the authority of his father over him ceases on the day when, his mind being formed and his education finished, he becomes the associate of his father; that his true chief and his king is the demonstrated truth; that politics is a science, not a stratagem; and that the function of the legislator is reduced, in the last analysis, to the methodical search for truth.

Thus, in a given society, the authority of man over man is inversely proportional to the stage of intellectual development which that society has reached; and the probable duration of that authority can be calculated from the more or less general desire for a true government,—that is, for a scientific government. And just as the right of force and the right of artifice retreat before the steady advance of justice, and must finally be extinguished in equality, so the sovereignty of the will yields to the sovereignty of the reason, and must at last be lost in scientific socialism. Property and royalty have been crumbling to pieces ever since the world began. As man seeks justice in equality, so society seeks order in anarchy.

*Anarchy,*—the absence of a master, of a sovereign,[6]—such is the form of government to which we are every day approximating, and which our accustomed habit of taking man for our rule, and his will for law, leads us to regard as the height of disorder and the expression of chaos. The story is told, that a citizen of Paris in the seventeenth century having heard it said that in Venice there was no king, the good man could not recover from his astonishment, and nearly died from laughter at the mere mention of so ridiculous a thing. So strong is our prejudice. As long as we live, we want a chief or chiefs; and at this very moment I hold in my hand a *brochure*, whose author—a zealous communist—dreams, like a second Marat, of the dictatorship. The most advanced among us are those who wish the greatest possible number of sovereigns,—their most ardent wish is for the royalty of the National Guard. Soon, undoubtedly, some one, jealous of the citizen militia, will say, "Everybody is king." But, when he has spoken, I will say, in my turn, "Nobody is king; we are, whether we will or no, associated." Every question of domestic politics must be decided by departmental statistics; every question of foreign politics is an affair of international statistics. The science of government rightly belongs to one of the sections of the Academy of Sciences, whose permanent secretary is necessarily prime minister; and, since every citizen may address a memoir to the Academy, every citizen is a legislator. But, as the opinion of no one is of any value until its truth has been proven, no one can substitute his will for reason,—nobody is king.

All questions of legislation and politics are matters of science, not of opinion. The legislative power belongs only to the reason, methodically recognised and demonstrated. To attribute to any power whatever the right of veto or of sanction, is the last degree of tyranny. Justice and legality are two things as independent of our approval as is mathematical truth. To compel, they need only to be known; to be known, they need only to be considered and studied. What, then, is the nation, if it is not the sovereign,—if it is not the source of the legislative power?

The nation is the guardian of the law—the nation is the *executive power*. Every citizen may assert: "This is true; that is just;" but his opinion controls no one but himself. That the truth which he proclaims may become a law, it must be recognised. Now, what is it to recognise a law? It is to verify a mathematical or a metaphysical calculation; it is to repeat an experiment, to observe a phenomenon, to establish a fact. Only the nation has the right to say, "Be it known and decreed."

I confess that this is an overturning of received ideas, and that I seem to be attempting to revolutionise our political system; but I beg the reader to consider that, having begun with a paradox, I must, if I reason correctly, meet with paradoxes at every step, and must end with paradoxes. For the

---

6   The meaning ordinarily attached to the word "anarchy" is absence of principle, absence of rule; consequently, it has been regarded as synonymous with "disorder."

rest, I do not see how the liberty of citizens would be endangered by entrusting to their hands, instead of the pen of the legislator, the sword of the law. The executive power, belonging properly to the will, cannot be confided to too many proxies. That is the true sovereignty of the nation.[7]

The proprietor, the robber, the hero, the sovereign—for all these titles are synonymous—imposes his will as law, and suffers neither contradiction nor control; that is, he pretends to be the legislative and the executive power at once. Accordingly, the substitution of the scientific and true law for the royal will is accomplished only by a terrible struggle; and this constant substitution is, after property, the most potent element in history, the most prolific source of political disturbances. Examples are too numerous and too striking to require enumeration.

Now, property necessarily engenders despotism,—the government of caprice, the reign of libidinous pleasure. That is so clearly the essence of property that, to be convinced of it, one need but remember what it is, and observe what happens around him. Property is the right to *use* and *abuse*. If, then, government is economy,—if its object is production and consumption, and the distribution of labour and products,—how is government possible while property exists? And if goods are property, why should not the proprietors be kings, and despotic kings—kings in proportion to their *facultes bonitaires*? And if each proprietor is sovereign lord within the sphere of his property, absolute king throughout his own domain, how could a government of proprietors be anything but chaos and confusion?

[...]

Then, no government, no public economy, no administration, is possible, which is based upon property.

Communism seeks *equality* and *law*. Property, born of the sovereignty of the reason, and the sense of personal merit, wishes above all things *independence* and *proportionality*.

---

7  If such ideas are ever forced into the minds of the people, it will be by representative government and the tyranny of talkers. Once science, thought, and speech were characterised by the same expression [in Greek, *logos*]. To designate a thoughtful and a learned man, they said, "a man quick to speak and powerful in discourse." For a long time, speech has been abstractly distinguished from science and reason. Gradually, this abstraction is becoming realised, as the logicians say, in society; so that we have today savants of many kinds who talk but little, and *talkers* who are not even savants in the science of speech. Thus a philosopher is no longer a savant: he is a talker. Legislators and poets were once profound and sublime characters: now they are talkers. A talker is a sonorous bell, whom the least shock suffices to set in perpetual motion. With the talker, the flow of speech is always directly proportional to the poverty of thought. Talkers govern the world; they stun us, they bore us, they worry us, they suck our blood, and [they] laugh at us. As for the savants, they keep silence: if they wish to say a word, they are cut short. Let them write.

But communism, mistaking uniformity for law, and levelism for equality, becomes tyrannical and unjust. Property, by its despotism and encroachments, soon proves itself oppressive and anti-social.

The objects of communism and property are good—their results are bad. And why? Because both are exclusive, and each disregards two elements of society. Communism rejects independence and proportionality; property does not satisfy equality and law.

. Now, if we imagine a society based upon these four principles,—equality, law, independence, and proportionality,—we find:

1. That *equality*, consisting only in *equality of conditions*, that is, *of means*, and not in *equality of comfort*,—which it is the business of the workers to achieve for themselves, when provided with equal means,—in no way violates justice and equity.

2. That *law*, resulting from the knowledge of facts, and consequently based upon necessity itself, never clashes with independence.

3. That individual *independence*, or the autonomy of the private reason, originating in the difference in talents and capacities, can exist without danger within the limits of the law.

4. That *proportionality*, being admitted only in the sphere of intelligence and sentiment, and not as regards material objects, may be observed without violating justice or social equality.

This third form of society, the synthesis of communism and property, we will call *liberty*.[8]

In determining the nature of liberty, we do not unite communism and property indiscriminately; such a process would be absurd eclecticism. We search by analysis for those elements in each which are true, and in harmony with the laws of Nature and society, disregarding the rest altogether; and the result gives us an adequate expression of the natural form of human society,—in one word, liberty.

Liberty is equality, because liberty exists only in society; and in the absence of equality there is no society.

Liberty is anarchy, because it does not admit the government of the will, but only the authority of the law; that is, of necessity.

Liberty is infinite variety, because it respects all wills within the limits of the law.

Liberty is proportionality, because it allows the utmost latitude to the ambition for merit, and the emulation of glory.

[...]

I have accomplished my task; property is conquered, never again to arise. Wherever this work is read and discussed, there will be deposited the germ

---

8   *libertas, librare, libratio, libra,*—liberty, to liberate, libration, balance (pound [in French, *livre*]),—words which have a common derivation. Liberty is the balance of rights and duties. To make a man free is to balance him with others,—that is, to put him on their level.

of death to property; there, sooner or later, privilege and servitude will disappear, and the despotism of will will give place to the reign of reason. What sophisms, indeed, what prejudices (however obstinate) can stand before the simplicity of the following propositions:

I. Individual *possession*[9] is the condition of social life; five thousand years of property demonstrate it. *Property* is the suicide of society. Possession is a right; property is against right. Suppress property while maintaining possession, and, by this simple modification of the principle, you will revolutionise law, government, economy, and institutions; you will drive evil from the face of the earth.

II. All having an equal right of occupancy, possession varies with the number of possessors; property cannot establish itself.

III. The effect of labour being the same for all, property is lost in the common prosperity.

IV. All human labour being the result of collective force, all property becomes, by the same reason, collective and undivided. To speak more exactly, labour destroys property.

V. Every capacity for labour being, like every instrument of labour, an accumulated capital, and a collective property, inequality of wages and fortunes (on the ground of inequality of capacities) is, therefore, injustice and theft.

VI. The necessary conditions of commerce are the liberty of the contracting parties and the equivalence of the products exchanged. Now, value being expressed by the amount of time and outlay which each product costs, and liberty being inviolable, the wages of workers (like their rights and duties) should be equal.

VII. Products are bought only by products. Now, the condition of all exchange being equivalence of products, profit is impossible and unjust. Observe this elementary principle of economy, and pauperism, luxury, oppression, vice, crime, and hunger will disappear from our midst.

VIII. Men are associated by the physical and mathematical law of production, before they are voluntarily associated by choice. Therefore, equality of conditions is demanded by justice; that is, by strict social law: esteem, friendship, gratitude, admiration, all fall within the domain of *equitable* or *proportional* law only.

IX. Free association, liberty—whose sole function is to maintain equality in the means of production and equivalence in exchanges—is the only possible, the only just, the only true form of society.

---

9    Individual possession is no obstacle to extensive cultivation and unity of exploitation. If I have not spoken of the drawbacks arising from small estates, it is because I thought it useless to repeat what so many others have said, and what by this time all the world must know. But I am surprised that the economists, who have so clearly shown the disadvantages of spade-husbandry, have failed to see that it is caused entirely by property; above all, that they have not perceived that their plan for mobilising the soil is a first step towards the abolition of property.

X. Politics is the science of liberty. The government of man by man (under whatever name it be disguised) is oppression. Society finds its highest perfection in the union of order with anarchy.

The old civilisation has run its race; a new sun is rising, and will soon renew the face of the earth. Let the present generation perish, let the old prevaricators die in the desert! the holy earth shall not cover their bones. Young man, exasperated by the corruption of the age, and absorbed in your zeal for justice!—if your country is dear to you, and if you have the interests of humanity at heart, have the courage to espouse the cause of liberty! Cast off your old selfishness, and plunge into the rising flood of popular equality! There your regenerate soul will acquire new life and vigour; your enervated genius will recover unconquerable energy; and your heart, perhaps already withered, will be rejuvenated! Every thing will wear a different look to your illuminated vision; new sentiments will engender new ideas within you; religion, morality, poetry, art, language will appear before you in nobler and fairer forms; and thenceforth, sure of your faith, and thoughtfully enthusiastic, you will hail the dawn of universal regeneration!

And you, sad victims of an odious law!—you, whom a jesting world despoils and outrages!—you, whose labour has always been fruitless, and whose rest has been without hope,—take courage! your tears are numbered! The fathers have sown in affliction, the children shall reap in rejoicings!

O God of liberty! God of equality! Thou who didst place in my heart the sentiment of justice, before my reason could comprehend it, hear my ardent prayer! Thou hast dictated all that I have written; Thou hast shaped my thought; Thou hast directed my studies; Thou hast weaned my mind from curiosity and my heart from attachment, that I might publish Thy truth to the master and the slave. I have spoken with what force and talent Thou hast given me: it is Thine to finish the work. Thou knowest whether I seek my welfare or Thy glory, O God of liberty! Ah! perish my memory, and let humanity be free! Let me see from my obscurity the people at last instructed; let noble teachers enlighten them; let generous spirits guide them! Abridge, if possible, the time of our trial; stifle pride and avarice in equality; annihilate this love of glory which enslaves us; teach these poor children that in the bosom of liberty there are neither heroes nor great men! Inspire the powerful man, the rich man, him whose name my lips shall never pronounce in Thy presence, with a horror of his crimes; let him be the first to apply for admission to the redeemed society; let the promptness of his repentance be the ground of his forgiveness! Then, great and small, wise and foolish, rich and poor, will unite in an ineffable fraternity; and, singing in unison a new hymn, will rebuild Thy altar, O God of liberty and equality!

*Paris, April 1st, 1841*
*Translation by Benjamin R. Tucker*

# LETTER TO M. BLANQUI ON PROPERTY
## *WHAT IS PROPERTY?* SECOND MEMOIR

Monsieur,

[...]

IN ORDER TO LIVE AS A PROPRIETOR, OR TO CONSUME WITHOUT PRODUCING, IT is necessary, then, to live upon the labour of another; in other words, it is necessary to kill the worker. It is upon this principle that proprietors of those varieties of capital which are of primary necessity increase their farm-rents as fast as industry develops, much more careful of their privileges in that respect, than those economists who, in order to strengthen property, advocate a reduction of interest. But the crime is unavailing: labour and production increase; soon the proprietor will be forced to labour, and then property is lost.

The proprietor is a man who, having absolute control of an instrument of production, claims the right to enjoy the product of the instrument without using it himself. To this end he lends it; and we have just seen that from this loan the worker derives a power of exchange, which sooner or later will destroy the right of increase [*droit d'aubaine*]. In the first place, the proprietor is obliged to allow the worker a portion of the product, for without it the worker could not live. Soon the latter, through the development of his industry, finds a means of regaining the greater portion of that which he gives to the proprietor; so that at last, the objects of enjoyment increasing continually, while the income of the idler remains the same, the proprietor, having exhausted his resources, begins to think of going to work himself. Then the victory of the producer is certain. Labour commences to tip the balance towards its own side, and commerce leads to equilibrium.

Man's instinct cannot err; as, in liberty, exchange of functions leads inevitably to equality among men, so commerce—or exchange of products, which is identical with exchange of functions—is a new cause of equality. As long as the proprietor does not labour, however small his income, he enjoys a privilege; the worker's welfare may be equal to his, but equality of conditions does not exist. But as soon as the proprietor becomes a producer—since he can exchange his special product only with his tenant or his *commandité*[1]—sooner or later this tenant, this *exploited* man, if violence is not done him, will make a profit out of the proprietor, and will oblige him to restore—in the exchange of their respective products—the interest on his capital. So that, balancing one injustice by another, the contracting parties will be equal. Labour and exchange, when liberty prevails, lead, then, to equality of fortunes; mutuality of services neutralises privilege. That is why despots in all ages and countries have assumed control of commerce; they wished to prevent the labour of their subjects from becoming an obstacle to the rapacity of tyrants.

Up to this point, all takes place in the natural order; there is no premeditation, no artifice. The whole proceeding is governed by the laws of necessity alone. Proprietors and workers act only in obedience to their wants. Thus, the exercise of the right of increase [*droit d'aubaine*], the art of robbing the producer, depends—during this first period of civilisation—upon physical violence, murder, and war.

[...]

[...] In '89 and '93, the possessions of the nobility and the clergy were confiscated, the clever proletarians were enriched; and today the latter, having become aristocrats, are making us pay dearly for our fathers' robbery. What, therefore, is to be done now? It is not for us to violate right, but to restore it. Now, it would be a violation of justice to dispossess some and endow others, and then stop there. We must gradually lower the rate of interest, organise industry, associate workers and their functions, and take a census of the large fortunes, not for the purpose of granting privileges, but that we may effect their redemption by settling a life-annuity upon their proprietors. We must apply on a large scale the principle of collective production, give the State eminent domain over all capital! make each producer responsible, abolish the custom-house, and transform every profession and trade into a public function. Thereby large fortunes will vanish without confiscation or violence; individual possession will establish itself, without communism, under the inspection of the republic; and equality of conditions will no longer depend simply on the will of citizens.

[...]

---

1   Member of a limited partnership company, with shares and who is fully responsible for its debts. (Editor)

How many small proprietors and manufacturers have not been ruined by large ones through chicanery, law-suits, and competition? Strategy, violence, and usury,—such are the proprietor's methods of plundering the worker.

Thus we see property, at all ages and in all its forms, oscillating by virtue of its principle between two opposite terms—extreme division and extreme accumulation.

Property, at its first term, is almost null. Reduced to personal exploitation, it is property only potentially. At its second term, it exists in its perfection; then it is truly property.

When property is widely distributed, society thrives, progresses, grows, and rises quickly to the zenith of its power. Thus, the Jews, after leaving Babylon with Esdras and Nehemiah, soon became richer and more powerful than they had been under their kings. Sparta was in a strong and prosperous condition during the two or three centuries which followed the death of Lycurgus. The best days of Athens were those of the Persian war; Rome, whose inhabitants were divided from the beginning into two classes, the exploiters and the exploited, knew no such thing as peace.

When property is concentrated, society, abusing itself, polluted, so to speak, grows corrupt, wears itself out—how shall I express this horrible idea?—plunges into long-continued and fatal luxury.

[...]

The most exact idea of property is given us by the Roman law, faithfully followed in this particular by the ancient legists. It is the absolute, exclusive, autocratic domain of a man over a thing, a domain which begins by *usucaption*, is maintained by *possession*, and finally, by the aid of *prescription*, finds its sanction in the civil law; a domain which so identifies the man with the thing, that the proprietor can say, "He who uses my field, virtually compels me to labour for him; therefore he owes me compensation."

I pass in silence the secondary modes by which property can be acquired—*tradition, sale, exchange, inheritance*, etc.—which have nothing in common with the origin of property.

Accordingly, Pothier said *the domain of property*, and not simply *property*. And the most learned writers on jurisprudence—in imitation of the Roman praetor who recognised a *right of property* and a *right of possession*—have carefully distinguished between the *domain* and the right of *usufruct, use*, and *habitation*, which, reduced to its natural limits, is the very expression of justice; and which is, in my opinion, to supplant domanial property, and finally form the basis of all jurisprudence.

But, sir, admire the clumsiness of systems, or rather the fatality of logic! While the Roman law and all the savants inspired by it teach that property in its origin is the right of first occupancy sanctioned by law, the modern legists, dissatisfied with this brutal definition, claim that property is based upon *labour*. Immediately they infer that he who no longer labours, but makes another labour in his stead, loses his right to the earnings of the latter. It is by virtue of this principle that the serfs of the middle ages claimed a legal right to property, and consequently to the enjoyment of political rights; that the clergy were despoiled in '89 of their immense estates, and were granted a pension in exchange; that at the restoration the liberal deputies opposed the indemnity of one billion francs. "The nation," said they, "has acquired by twenty-five years of labour and possession the property which the emigrants forfeited by abandonment and long idleness: why should the nobles be treated with more favour than the priests?"[2]

All usurpations, not born of war, have been caused and supported by labour. All modern history proves this, from the end of the Roman empire down to the present day. And as if to give a sort of legal sanction to these usurpations, the doctrine of labour, subversive of property, is professed at great length in the Roman law under the name of *prescription*.

The man who cultivates, it has been said, makes the land his own; consequently, no more property. This was clearly seen by the old jurists, who have not failed to denounce this novelty; while on the other hand the young school hoots at the absurdity of the first-occupant theory. Others have presented themselves, pretending to reconcile the two opinions by uniting them. They have failed, like all the *juste-milieux* of the world, and are laughed at for their eclecticism. At present, the alarm is in the camp of the old doctrine; from all sides pour *in defences of property, studies regarding property, theories of property*, each one of which, giving the lie to the rest, inflicts a fresh wound upon property.

Consider, indeed, the inextricable embarrassments, the contradictions, the absurdities, the incredible nonsense, in which the bold defenders of property so lightly involve themselves. I choose the eclectics, because, those killed, the others cannot survive.

M. Troplong, jurist, passes for a philosopher in the eyes of the editors of *Le Droit*. I tell the gentlemen of *Le Droit* that, in the judgement of philosophers, M. Troplong is only a lawyer; and I prove my assertion.

M. Troplong is a defender of progress. "The words of the code," says he, "are fruitful sap with which the classic works of the eighteenth century

---

2   A professor of comparative legislation, M. Lerminier, has gone still farther. He has dared to say that the nation took from the clergy all their possessions, not because of *idleness*, but because of *unworthiness*. "You have civilised the world," cries this apostle of equality, speaking to the priests; "and for that reason your possessions were given you. In your hands they were at once an instrument and a reward. But you do not now deserve them, for you long since ceased to civilise any thing whatever…"

This position is quite in harmony with my principles, and I heartily applaud the indignation of M. Lerminier; but I do not know that a proprietor was ever deprived of his property because *unworthy*; and as reasonable, social, and even useful as the thing may seem, it is quite contrary to the uses and customs of property.

overflow. To wish to suppress them. ... is to violate the law of progress, and to forget that a science which moves is a science which grows."[3]

Now, the only mutable and progressive portion of law, as we have already seen, is that which concerns property. If, then, you ask what reforms are to be introduced into the right of property? M. Troplong makes no reply; what progress is to be hoped for? no reply; what is to be the destiny of property in case of universal association? no reply; what is the absolute and what the contingent, what the true and what the false, in property? no reply. M. Troplong favours quiescence and *in statu quo* in regard to property. What could be more unphilosophical in a progressive philosopher?

Nevertheless, M. Troplong has thought about these things. "There are," he says, "many weak points and antiquated ideas in the doctrines of modern authors concerning property: witness the works of MM. Toullier and Duranton." The doctrine of M. Troplong promises, then, strong points, advanced and progressive ideas. Let us see; let us examine:

"Man, placed in the presence of matter, is conscious of a power over it, which has been given to him to satisfy the needs of his being. King of inanimate or unintelligent nature, he feels that he has a right to modify it, govern it, and fit it for his use. There it is, the subject of property, which is legitimate only when exercised over things, never when over persons."

M. Troplong is so little of a philosopher, that he does not even know the import of the philosophical terms which he makes a show of using. He says of matter that it is the *subject* of property; he should have said the *object*. M. Troplong uses the language of the anatomists, who apply the term *subject* to the human matter used in their experiments.

This error of our author is repeated farther on: "Liberty, which overcomes matter, the subject of property, etc." The *subject* of property is man; its *object* is matter. But even this is but a slight mortification; directly we shall have some crucifixions.

Thus, according to the passage just quoted, it is in the conscience and personality of man that the principle of property must be sought. Is there anything new in this doctrine? Apparently it never has occurred to those who, since the days of Cicero and Aristotle, and earlier, have maintained that *things belong to the first occupant*, that occupation may be exercised by beings devoid of conscience and personality. The human personality, though it may be the principle or the subject of property, as matter is the object, is not the *condition*. Now, it is this condition which we most need to know. So far, M. Troplong tells us no more than his masters, and the figures with which he adorns his style add nothing to the old idea.

Property, then, implies three terms: The subject, the object, and the condition. There is no difficulty in regard to the first two terms. As to the third, the condition of property down to this day, for the Greek as for the

---

3   *Treatise on Prescription.*

Barbarian, has been that of first occupancy. What now would you have it, progressive doctor?

"When man lays hands for the first time upon an object without a master, he performs an act which, among individuals, is of the greatest importance. The thing thus seized and occupied participates, so to speak, in the personality of him who holds it. It becomes sacred, like himself. It is impossible to take it without doing violence to his liberty, or to remove it without rashly invading his person. Diogenes did but express this truth of intuition, when he said: 'Stand out of my light!'"

Very good! but would the prince of cynics, the very personal and very haughty Diogenes, have had the right to charge another cynic, as rent for this same place in the sunshine, a bone for twenty-four hours of possession? It is that which constitutes the proprietor; it is that which you fail to justify. In reasoning from the human personality and individuality to the right of property, you unconsciously construct a syllogism in which the conclusion includes more than the premises, contrary to the rules laid down by Aristotle. The individuality of the human person proves *individual possession*, originally called *proprietas*, in opposition to collective possession, *communio*.

It gives birth to the distinction between *thine* and *mine*, true signs of equality, not, by any means, of subordination. "From equivocation to equivocation," says M. Michelet,[4] "property would crawl to the end of the world; man could not limit it, were not he himself its limit. Where they clash, there will be its frontier." In short, individuality of being destroys the hypothesis of communism, but it does not for that reason give birth to domain, that domain by virtue of which the holder of a thing exercises over the person who takes his place a right of prestation and suzerainty, that has always been identified with property itself.

Further, that he whose legitimately acquired possession injures nobody cannot be nonsuited without flagrant injustice, is a truth, not of *intuition*, as M. Troplong says, but of *inward sensation*,[5] which has nothing to do with property.

M. Troplong admits, then, occupancy as a condition of property. In that, he is in accord with the Roman law, in accord with MM. Toullier and Duranton; but in his opinion this condition is not the only one, and it is in this particular that his doctrine goes beyond theirs.

---

4   *Origin of French Law.*

5   To honour one's parents, to be grateful to one's benefactors, to neither kill nor steal,—truths of inward sensation. To obey God rather than men, to render to each that which is his; the whole is greater than a part, a straight line is the shortest road from one point to another,—truths of intuition. All are a priori but the first are felt by the conscience, and imply only a simple act of the soul; the second are perceived by the reason, and imply comparison and relation. In short, the former are sentiments, the latter are ideas.

"But, however exclusive the right arising from sole occupancy, does it not become still more so, when man has moulded matter by his labour; when he has deposited in it a portion of himself, re-creating it by his industry, and setting upon it the seal of his intelligence and activity? Of all conquests, that is the most legitimate, for it is the price of labour.

"He who should deprive a man of the thing thus remodelled, thus humanised, would invade the man himself, and would inflict the deepest wounds upon his liberty."

I pass over the very beautiful explanations in which M. Troplong, discussing labour and industry, displays the whole wealth of his eloquence. M. Troplong is not only a philosopher, he is an orator, an artist. *He abounds with appeals to the conscience and the passions.* I might make sad work of his rhetoric, should I undertake to dissect it; but I confine myself for the present to his philosophy.

If M. Troplong had only known how to think and reflect, before abandoning the original fact of occupancy and plunging into the theory of labour, he would have asked himself: "What is it to occupy?" And he would have discovered that *occupancy* is only a generic term by which all modes of possession are expressed, seizure, station, immanence, habitation, cultivation, use, consumption, etc.; that labour, consequently, is but one of a thousand forms of occupancy. He would have understood, finally, that the right of possession which is born of labour is governed by the same general laws as that which results from the simple seizure of things. What kind of a legist is he who declaims when he ought to reason, who continually mistakes his metaphors for legal axioms, and who does not so much as know how to obtain a universal by induction, and form a category?

If labour is identical with occupancy, the only benefit which it secures to the worker is the right of individual possession of the object of his labour; if it differs from occupancy, it gives birth to a right equal only to itself, that is, a right which begins, continues, and ends, with the labour of the occupant. It is for this reason, in the words of the law, that one cannot acquire a just title to a thing by labour alone. He must also hold it for a year and a day, in order to be regarded as its possessor; and possess it twenty or thirty years, in order to become its proprietor.

These preliminaries established, M. Troplong's whole structure falls of its own weight, and the inferences, which he attempts to draw, vanish.

"Property once acquired by occupation and labour, it naturally preserves itself, not only by the same means, but also by the refusal of the holder to abdicate; for from the very fact that it has risen to the height of a right, it is its nature to perpetuate itself and to last for an indefinite period... Rights, considered from an ideal point of view, are imperishable and eternal; and time, which affects only the contingent, can no more disturb them than it can injure God himself." It is astonishing that our author, in speaking of the *ideal, time,* and *eternity,* did not work into his sentence the *divine wings* of Plato—so fashionable today in philosophical works.

With the exception of falsehood, I hate nonsense more than anything else in the world. *Property once acquired!* Good, if it is acquired; but, as it is not acquired, it cannot be preserved. *Rights are eternal!* Yes, in the sight of God, like the archetypal ideas of the Platonists. But, on the earth, rights exist only in the presence of a subject, an object, and a condition. Take away one of these three things, and rights no longer exist. Thus, individual possession ceases at the death of the subject, upon the destruction of the object, or in case of exchange or abandonment.

[...]

I had resolved to submit to a systematic criticism the semi-official defence of the right of property recently put forth by M. Wolowski, your colleague at the Conservatory. With this view, I had commenced to collect the documents necessary for each of his lectures, but, soon perceiving that the ideas of the professor were incoherent, that his arguments contradicted each other, that one affirmation was sure to be overthrown by another, and that in M. Wolowski's lucubrations the good was always mingled with the bad, and being by nature a little suspicious, it suddenly occurred to me that M. Wolowski was an advocate of equality in disguise, thrown in spite of himself into the position in which the patriarch Jacob pictures one of his sons—*inter duas clitellas*, between two stools, as the proverb says. In more parliamentary language, I saw clearly that M. Wolowski was placed between his profound convictions on the one hand and his official duties on the other, and that, in order to maintain his position, he had to assume a certain slant. Then I experienced great pain at seeing the reserve, the circumlocution, the figures, and the irony to which a professor of legislation, whose duty it is to teach dogmas with clearness and precision, was forced to resort; and I fell to cursing the society in which an honest man is not allowed to say frankly what he thinks. Never, sir, have you conceived of such torture: I seemed to be witnessing the martyrdom of a mind. I am going to give you an idea of these astonishing meetings, or rather of these scenes of sorrow.

*Monday, November* 20th, 1840. The professor declares, in brief, 1. That the right of property is not founded upon occupation, but upon the impress of man; 2. That every man has a natural and inalienable right to the use of matter.

Now, if matter can be appropriated, and if, notwithstanding, all men retain an inalienable right to the use of this matter, what is property?—and if matter can be appropriated only by labour, how long is this appropriation to continue?—questions that will confuse and confound all jurists whatsoever.

Then M. Wolowski cites his authorities. Great God! what witnesses he brings forward! First, M. Troplong, the great metaphysician, whom we have discussed; then, M. Louis Blanc, editor of the *Revue du Progres*, who came near being tried by jury for publishing his *Organisation of Labour*, and who escaped from the clutches of the public prosecutor only by a juggler's trick;[6] Corinne,—I mean Madame de Staël,—who, in an ode, making a poetical comparison of the land with the waves, of the furrow of a plough with the wake of a vessel, says "that property exists only where man has left his trace," which makes property dependent upon the solidity of the elements; Rousseau, the apostle of liberty and equality, but who, according to M. Wolowski, attacked property only *as a joke*, and in order to point a paradox; Robespierre, who prohibited a division of the land, because he regarded such a measure as a rejuvenescence of property, and who, while awaiting the definitive organisation of the republic, placed all property in the care of the people, that is, transferred the right of eminent domain from the individual to society; Babeuf, who wanted property for the nation, and communism for the citizens; M. Considérant, who favours a division of landed property into shares, that is, who wishes to render property nominal and fictitious: the whole being intermingled with jokes and witticisms (intended undoubtedly to lead people away from the *hornets' nests*) at the expense of the adversaries of the right of property!

*November 26th*. M. Wolowski supposes this objection: Land, like water, air, and light, is necessary to life, therefore it cannot be appropriated; and he replies: The importance of landed property diminishes as the power of industry increases.

Good! this importance *diminishes*, but it does not *disappear*; and this, of itself, shows landed property to be illegitimate. Here M. Wolowski pretends to think that the opponents of property refer only to property in land, while they merely take it as a term of comparison; and, in showing with wonderful clearness the absurdity of the position in which he places them, he finds a way of drawing the attention of his hearers to another subject without being false to the truth which it is his office to contradict.

"Property," says M. Wolowski, "is that which distinguishes man from the animals." That may be; but are we to regard this as a compliment or a satire?

"Mahomet," says M. Wolowski, "decreed property." And so did Genghis Khan, and Tamerlane, and all the ravagers of nations. What sort of legislators were they?

"Property has been in existence ever since the origin of the human race." Yes, and so has slavery, and despotism also; and likewise polygamy and idolatry. But what does this antiquity show?

The members of the Council of the State—M. Portalis at their head—did not raise, in their discussion of the Code, the question of the legitimacy of

---

6  In a very short article, which was read by M. Wolowski, M. Louis Blanc declares, in substance, that he is not a communist (which I easily believe); that one must be a fool to attack property (but he does not say why); and that it is very necessary to guard against confounding property with its abuses. When Voltaire overthrew Christianity, he repeatedly avowed that he had no spite against religion, but only against its abuses.

property. "Their silence," says M. Wolowski, "is a precedent in favour of this right." I may regard this reply as personally addressed to me, since the observation belongs to me. I reply, "As long as an opinion is universally admitted, the universality of belief serves of itself as argument and proof. When this same opinion is attacked, the former faith proves nothing; we must resort to reason. Ignorance, however old and pardonable it may be, never outweighs reason."

Property has its abuses, M. Wolowski confesses. "But," he says, "these abuses gradually disappear. To-day their cause is known. They all arise from a false theory of property. In principle, property is inviolable, but it can and must be checked and disciplined." Such are the conclusions of the professor.

When one thus remains in the clouds, he need not fear to equivocate. Nevertheless, I would like him to define these *abuses* of property, to show their cause, to explain this true theory from which no abuse is to spring; in short, to tell me how, without destroying property, it can be governed for the greatest good of all. "Our civil code," says M. Wolowski, in speaking of this subject, "leaves much to be desired." I think it leaves everything undone.

Finally, M. Wolowski opposes, on the one hand, the concentration of capital, and the absorption which results therefrom; and, on the other, he objects to the extreme division of the land. Now I think that I have demonstrated in my First Memoir, that large accumulation and minute division are the first two terms of an economic trinity—a *thesis* and an *antithesis*. But, while M. Wolowski says nothing of the third term, the *synthesis*, and thus leaves the inference in suspense, I have shown that this third term is *association*, which is the annihilation of property.

[...]

The ordinary resources of the law no longer sufficing, philosophy, political economy, and the framers of systems have been consulted. All the oracles appealed to have been discouraging.

The philosophers are no clearer today than at the time of the eclectic efflorescence; nevertheless, through their mystical apothems, we can distinguish the words *progress, unity, association, solidarity, fraternity,* which are certainly not reassuring to proprietors. One of these philosophers, M. Pierre Leroux, has written two large books, in which he claims to show by all religious, legislative, and philosophical systems that, since men are responsible to each other, equality of conditions is the final law of society. It is true that this philosopher admits a kind of property; but as he leaves us to imagine what property would become in presence of equality, we may boldly class him with the opponents of the right of increase [*droit d'aubaine*].

[...]

In his work on *Humanity,*[7] M. Leroux commences by positing the necessity of property: "You wish to abolish property; but do you not see that thereby you

---

7    Pierre Leroux, *De l'humanité, de son principe, et de son avenir, où se trouve exposée la vrais définition de la religion et où l'on explique le sens, la suite et l'enchaînement du mosaisme et du christianisme* (Paris: Perrotin, 1840). (Editor)

would annihilate man and even the name of man?... You wish to abolish property; but could you live without a body? I will not tell you that it is necessary to support this body;... I will tell you that this body is itself a species of property."

In order clearly to understand the doctrine of M. Leroux, it must be borne in mind that there are three necessary and primitive forms of society—communism, property, and that which today we properly call association. M. Leroux rejects in the first place communism, and combats it with all his might. Man is a personal and free being, and therefore needs a sphere of independence and individual activity. M. Leroux emphasises this in adding: "You wish neither family, nor country, nor property; therefore no more fathers, no more sons, no more brothers. Here you are, related to no being in time, and therefore without a name; here you are, alone in the midst of a billion of men who today inhabit the earth. How do you expect me to distinguish you in space in the midst of this multitude?"

If man is indistinguishable, he is nothing. Now, he can be distinguished, individualised, only through a devotion of certain things to his use—such as his body, his faculties, and the tools which he uses. "Hence," says M. Leroux, "the necessity of appropriation"; in short, property.

But property on what condition? Here M. Leroux, after having condemned communism, denounces in its turn the right of domain. His whole doctrine can be summed up in this single proposition—*Man may be made by property a slave or a despot by turns.*

That posited, if we ask M. Leroux to tell us under what system of property man will be neither a slave nor a despot, but free, just, and a citizen, M. Leroux replies in the third volume of his work on *Humanity*:

"There are three ways of destroying man's communion with his fellows and with the universe:... 1. By separating man in time; 2. by separating him in space; 3. by dividing the land, or, in general terms, the instruments of production; by attaching men to things, by subordinating man to property, by making man a proprietor."

This language, it must be confessed, savours a little too strongly of the metaphysical heights which the author frequents, and of the school of M. Cousin. Nevertheless, it can be seen, clearly enough it seems to me, that M. Leroux opposes the exclusive appropriation of the instruments of production; only he calls this non-appropriation of the instruments of production a *new method* of establishing property, while I, in accordance with all precedent, call it a destruction of property. In fact, without the appropriation of instruments, property is nothing.

"Hitherto, we have confined ourselves to pointing out and combating the despotic features of property, by considering property alone. We have failed to see that the despotism of property is a correlative of the division of the human race;... that property, instead of being organised in such a way as to facilitate the unlimited communion of man with his fellows and with the universe, has been, on the contrary, turned against this communion."

Let us translate this into commercial phraseology. In order to destroy despotism and the inequality of conditions, men must cease from competition and must associate their interests. Let master and worker, now enemies and rivals, become associates.

Now, ask any manufacturer, merchant, or capitalist, whether he would consider himself a proprietor if he were to share his revenue and profits with this mass of wage-workers whom it is proposed to make his associates.

[...]

"All the evils which afflict the human race arise from caste. The family is a blessing; the family caste (the nobility) is an evil. Country is a blessing; the country caste (supreme, domineering, conquering) is an evil; property (individual possession) is a blessing; the property caste (the domain of property of Pothier, Toullier, Troplong, etc.) is an evil."

Thus, according to M. Leroux, there is property and property,—the one good, the other bad. Now, as it is proper to call different things by different names, if we keep the name "property" for the former, we must call the latter theft, rapine, brigandage. If, on the contrary, we reserve the name "property" for the latter, we must designate the former by the term *possession*, or some other equivalent; otherwise we should be troubled with an unpleasant synonymy.

What a blessing it would be if philosophers, daring for once to say all that they think, would speak the language of ordinary mortals! Nations and rulers would derive much greater profit from their lectures, and, applying the same names to the same ideas, would come, perhaps, to understand each other. I boldly declare that, in regard to property, I hold no other opinion than that of M. Leroux; but, if I should adopt the style of the philosopher, and repeat after him, "Property is a blessing, but the property caste—the *statu quo* of property—is an evil," I should be extolled as a genius by all the bachelors who write for the reviews.[8] If, on the contrary, I prefer the classic language

---

8    M. Leroux has been highly praised in a review for having defended property. I do not know whether the industrious encyclopedist is pleased with the praise, but I know very well that in his place I should mourn for reason and for truth.

*Le National*, on the other hand, has laughed at M. Leroux and his ideas on property, charging him with *tautology* and *childishness*. *Le National* does not wish to understand. Is it necessary to remind this journal that it has no right to deride a dogmatic philosopher, because it is without a doctrine itself? From its foundation, *Le National* has been a nursery of intriguers and renegades. From time to time it takes care to warn its readers. Instead of lamenting over all its defections, the democratic sheet would do better to lay the blame on itself, and confess the shallowness of its theories. When will this organ of popular interests and the electoral reform cease to hire sceptics and spread doubt? I will wager, without going further, that M. Leon Durocher, the critic of M. Leroux, is an anonymous or pseudonymous editor of some *bourgeois*, or even aristocratic, journal.

of Rome and the civil code, and say accordingly, "Possession is a blessing, but property is theft," immediately the aforesaid bachelors raise a hue and cry against the monster, and the judge threatens me. Oh, the power of language! [...]

The economists, questioned in their turn, propose to associate capital and labour. You know, sir, what that means. If we follow out the doctrine, we soon find that it ends in an absorption of property, not by the community [*communauté*], but by a general and indissoluble *commandite*, so that the condition of the proprietor would differ from that of the worker only in receiving larger wages. This system, with some peculiar additions and embellishments, is the idea of the phalanstery. But it is clear that, if inequality of conditions is one of the attributes of property, it is not the whole of property. That which makes property a *delightful thing*, as some philosopher (I know not who) has said, is the power to dispose at will, not only of one's own goods, but of their specific nature; to use them at pleasure; to confine and enclose them; to excommunicate mankind, as M. Pierre Leroux says; in short, to make such use of them as passion, interest, or even caprice, may suggest. What is the possession of money, a share in an agricultural or industrial enterprise, or a government-bond coupon, in comparison with the infinite charm of being master of one's house and grounds, under one's vine and fig-tree? "*Beati possidentes!*" says an author quoted by M. Troplong. Seriously, can that be applied to a man of income, who has no other possession under the sun than the market, and in his pocket his money? As well maintain that a trough is a coward. A nice method of reform! They never cease to condemn the thirst for gold, and the growing individualism of the century; and yet, most inconceivable of contradictions, they prepare to turn all kinds of property into one—property in coin.

I must say something further of a theory of property lately put forth with some ado: I mean the theory of M. Considérant.

The Fourierists are not men who examine a doctrine in order to ascertain whether it conflicts with their system. On the contrary, it is their custom to exult and sing songs of triumph whenever an adversary passes without perceiving or noticing them.

These gentlemen want direct refutations, in order that, if they are beaten, they may have, at least, the selfish consolation of having been spoken of. Well, let their wish be gratified.

M. Considérant makes the most lofty pretensions to logic. His method of procedure is always that of *major, minor,* and *conclusion.* He would willingly write upon his hat, "*Argumentator in barbara.*" But M. Considérant is too intelligent and quick-witted to be a good logician, as is proved by the fact that he appears to have taken the syllogism for logic.

The syllogism, as everybody knows who is interested in philosophical curiosities, is the first and perpetual sophism of the human mind,—the favourite tool of falsehood, the stumbling-block of science, the advocate of crime.

The syllogism has produced all the evils which the fabulist so eloquently condemned, and has done nothing good or useful: it is as devoid of truth as of justice. We might apply to it these words of Scripture: "*Celui qui met en lui sa confiance, perira.*" Consequently, the best philosophers long since condemned it; so that now none but the enemies of reason wish to make the syllogism its weapon.

M. Considérant, then, has built his theory of property upon a syllogism. Would he be disposed to stake the system of Fourier upon his arguments, as I am ready to risk the whole doctrine of equality upon my refutation of that system? Such a duel would be quite in keeping with the warlike and chivalric tastes of M. Considérant, and the public would profit by it; for, one of the two adversaries falling, no more would be said about him, and there would be one grumbler less in the world.

The theory of M. Considérant has this remarkable feature, that, in attempting to satisfy at the same time the claims of both workers and proprietors, it infringes alike upon the rights of the former and the privileges of the latter. In the first place, the author lays it down as a principle: "1. That the use of the land belongs to each member of the race; that it is a natural and imprescriptible right, similar in all respects to the right to the air and the sunshine. 2. That the right to labour is equally fundamental, natural, and imprescriptible." I have shown that the recognition of this double right would be the death of property. I denounce M. Considérant to the proprietors!

But M. Considérant maintains that the right to labour creates the right of property, and this is the way he reasons:

Major Premise: "Every man legitimately possesses the thing which his labour, his skill—or, in more general terms, his action—has created."

To which M. Considérant adds, by way of comment: "Indeed, the land not having been created by man, it follows from the fundamental principle of property, that the land, being given to the race in common, can in no wise be the exclusive and legitimate property of such and such individuals, who were not the creators of this value."

If I am not mistaken, there is no one to whom this proposition, at first sight and in its entirety, does not seem utterly irrefutable. Reader, distrust the syllogism.

First, I observe that the words *legitimately possesses* signify to the author's mind is *legitimate proprietor;* otherwise the argument, being intended to prove the legitimacy of property, would have no meaning. I might here raise the question of the difference between property and possession, and call upon M. Considérant, before going further, to define the one and the other; but I pass on.

This first proposition is doubly false. 1. In that it asserts the act of *creation* to be the only basis of property. 2. In that it regards this act as sufficient in all cases to authorise the right of property.

And, in the first place, if man may be proprietor of the game which he does not create, but which he *kills;* of the fruits which he does not create, but which he gathers; of the vegetables which he does not create, but which he *plants*; of the animals which he does not create, but which he *rears*,—it is conceivable that men may in like manner become proprietors of the land which they do not create, but which they clear and fertilise. The act of creation, then, is not *necessary* to the acquisition of the right of property. I say further, that this act alone is not always sufficient, and I prove it by the second premise of M. Considérant:

Minor Premise: "Suppose that on an isolated island, on the soil of a nation, or over the whole face of the earth (the extent of the scene of action does not affect our judgement of the facts), a generation of human beings devotes itself for the first time to industry, agriculture, manufactures, etc. This generation, by its labour, intelligence, and activity, creates products, develops values which did not exist on the uncultivated land. Is it not perfectly clear that the property of this industrious generation will stand on a basis of right, if the value or wealth produced by the activity of all be distributed among the producers, according to each one's assistance in the creation of the general wealth? That is unquestionable."

That is quite questionable. For this value or wealth, *produced by the activity of all*, is by the very fact of its creation *collective* wealth, the use of which, like that of the land, may be divided, but which as property remains *undivided*. And why this undivided ownership? Because the society which creates is itself indivisible—a permanent unit, incapable of reduction to fractions. And it is this unity of society which makes the land common property, and which, as M. Considérant says, renders its use imprescriptible in the case of every individual. Suppose, indeed, that at a given time the soil should be equally divided; the very next moment this division, if it allowed the right of property, would become illegitimate. Should there be the slightest irregularity in the method of transfer, men, members of society, imprescriptible possessors of the land, might be deprived at one blow of property, possession, and the means of production. In short, property in capital is indivisible, and consequently inalienable, not necessarily when the capital is *uncreated*, but when it is *common* or *collective*.

I confirm this theory against M. Considérant, by the third term of his syllogism:

Conclusion: "The results of the labour performed by this generation are divisible into two classes, between which it is important clearly to distinguish. The first class includes the products of the soil which belong to this first generation in its usufructuary capacity, augmented, improved and refined by its labour and industry. These products consist either of objects of consumption or instruments of labour. It is clear that these products are the legitimate property of those who have created them by their activity... Second class.—Not only has this generation created the products just mentioned (objects of consumption and instruments of labour), but it has also added to the original value of the soil by cultivation, by the erection of buildings, by all the labour producing permanent results, which it has performed. This additional value evidently constitutes a product—a value created by the activity of the first generation; and if, *by any means whatever*, the ownership of this value be distributed among the members of society equitably,—that is, in proportion to the labour which each has performed,—each will legitimately possess the portion which he receives. He may then dispose of this legitimate and private property as he sees fit—exchange it, give it away, or transfer it; and no other individual, or collection of other individuals—that is, society—can lay any claim to these values."

Thus, by the distribution of collective capital, to the use of which each associate, either in his own right or in right of his authors, has an imprescriptible and undivided title, there will be in the phalanstery, as in the France of 1841, the poor and the rich; some men who, to live in luxury, have only, as Figaro says, to take the trouble to be born, and others for whom the fortune of life is but an opportunity for long-continued poverty; idlers with large incomes, and workers whose fortune is always in the future; some privileged by birth and caste, and others pariahs whose sole civil and political rights are *the right to labour, and the right to land.* For we must not be deceived; in the phalanstery every thing will be as it is today, an object of property—machines, inventions, thought, books, the products of art, of agriculture, and of industry; animals, houses, fences, vineyards, pastures, forests, fields—everything, in short, except the *uncultivated land.* Now, would you like to know what uncultivated land is worth, according to the advocates of property? "A square league hardly suffices for the support of a savage," says M. Charles Comte. Estimating the wretched subsistence of this savage at three hundred francs per year, we find that the square league necessary to his life is, relatively to him, faithfully represented by a rent of fifteen francs. In France there are twenty-eight thousand square leagues, the total rent of which, by this estimate, would be four hundred and twenty thousand francs, which, when divided among nearly thirty-four million people, would give each an *income of a centime and a quarter.* That is the new right which the great genius of Fourier has invented *in behalf of the French people*, and with which his first disciple hopes to reform the world. I denounce M. Considérant to the proletariat!

If the theory of M. Considérant would at least really guarantee this property which he cherishes so jealously, I might pardon him the flaws in his syllogism, certainly the best one he ever made in his life. But, no: that which M. Considérant takes for property is only a privilege of extra pay. In Fourier's system, neither the created capital nor the increased value of the soil are divided and appropriated in any effective manner: the instruments of labour, whether created or not, remain in the hands of the phalanx; the pretended proprietor can touch only the income. He is permitted neither to realise his share of the stock, nor to possess it exclusively, nor to administer it, whatever it be. The cashier throws him his dividend; and then, proprietor, eat the whole if you can!

The system of Fourier would not suit the proprietors, since it takes away the most delightful feature of property,—the free disposition of one's goods. It would please the communists no better, since it involves unequal conditions. It is repugnant to the friends of free association and equality, in consequence of its tendency to wipe out human character and individuality by suppressing possession, family, and country—the threefold expression of the human personality.

[...]

These considerations alone oblige me to reply to the strange and superficial conclusions of the *Journal du Peuple* (issue of October 11th, 1840), on the question of property. I leave, therefore, the journalist to address myself only to his readers. I hope that the self-love of the writer will not be offended, if, in the presence of the masses, I ignore an individual.

You say, proletarians of the *Peuple*, "For the very reason that men and things exist, there always will be men who will possess things; nothing, therefore, can destroy property."

In speaking thus, you unconsciously argue exactly after the manner of M. Cousin, who always reasons from *possession* to *property*. This coincidence, however, does not surprise me. M. Cousin is a philosopher of much mind, and you, proletarians, have still more. Certainly it is honourable, even for a philosopher, to be your companion in error.

Originally, the word *property* was synonymous with *proper* or *individual possession*. It designated each individual's special right to the use of a thing. But when this right of use, inert (if I may say so) as it was with regard to the other usufructuaries, became active and paramount—that is, when the usufructuary converted his right to personally use the thing into the right to use it by his neighbour's labour—then property changed its nature, and its idea became complex. The legists knew this very well, but instead of opposing, as they ought, this accumulation of profits, they accepted and sanctioned the whole. And as the right of farm-rent necessarily implies the right of use—in other words, as the right to cultivate land by the labour of a slave supposes one's power to cultivate it himself, according to the principle that the greater includes the less—the name property was reserved to designate this double right, and that of possession was adopted to designate the right of use.

Whence property came to be called the perfect right, the right of domain, eminent right, the heroic or *quiritary* right—in Latin, *jus perfectum, jus optimum, jus quiritarium, jus dominii*—while possession became assimilated to farm-rent.[9]

Now, that individual possession exists of right, or, better, from natural necessity, all philosophers admit, and can easily be demonstrated; but when, in imitation of M. Cousin, we assume it to be the basis of the domain of

---

9    In Roman law, *quiritary* or "free" ownership entailed absolute rights over the thing owned, as opposed to limited or *bonitary* ownership. (Editor)

property, we fall into the sophism called *sophisma amphiboliae vel ambigui-tatis*, which consists in changing the meaning by a verbal equivocation.

People often think themselves very profound, because, by the aid of expressions of extreme generality, they appear to rise to the height of absolute ideas, and thus deceive inexperienced minds; and, what is worse, this is commonly called *examining abstractions*. But the abstraction formed by the comparison of identical facts is one thing, while that which is deduced from different acceptations of the same term is quite another. The first gives the universal idea, the axiom, the law; the second indicates the order of generation of ideas. All our errors arise from the constant confusion of these two kinds of abstractions. In this particular, languages and philosophies are alike deficient. The less common an idiom is, and the more obscure its terms, the more prolific is it as a source of error: a philosopher is sophistical in proportion to his ignorance of any method of neutralising this imperfection in language. If the art of correcting the errors of speech by scientific methods is ever discovered, then philosophy will have found its criterion of certainty.

Now, then, the difference between property and possession being well established, and it being settled that the former, for the reasons which I have just given, must necessarily disappear, is it best, for the slight advantage of restoring an etymology, to retain the word *property*? My opinion is that it would be very unwise to do so, and I will tell why. I quote from the *Journal du Peuple*:

"To the legislative power belongs the right to regulate property, to prescribe the conditions of acquiring, possessing, and transmitting it... It cannot be denied that inheritance, assessment, commerce, industry, labour, and wages require the most important modifications."

You wish, proletarians, to *regulate property*; that is, you wish to destroy it and reduce it to the right of possession. For to regulate property without the consent of the proprietors is to deny the right *of domain*; to associate employees with proprietors is to destroy the *eminent* right; to suppress or even reduce farm-rent, house-rent, revenue, and increase generally, is to annihilate *perfect* property. Why, then, while labouring with such laudable enthusiasm for the establishment of equality, should you retain an expression whose equivocal meaning will always be an obstacle in the way of your success?

There you have the first reason—a wholly philosophical one—for rejecting not only the thing, but the name, property. Here now is the political, the highest reason.

Every social revolution—M. Cousin will tell you—is effected only by the realisation of an idea, either political, moral, or religious. When Alexander conquered Asia, his idea was to avenge Greek liberty against the insults of Oriental despotism; when Marius and Caesar overthrew the Roman patricians, their idea was to give bread to the people; when Christianity revolutionised the world, its idea was to emancipate mankind, and to substitute the worship of one God for the deities of Epicurus and Homer; when France rose in '89, her idea was liberty and equality before the law. There has been no true revolution, says M. Cousin, without its idea; so that where an idea does not exist, or even fails of a formal expression, revolution is impossible. There are mobs, conspirators, rioters, regicides. There are no revolutionists. Society, devoid of ideas, twists and tosses about, and dies in the midst of its fruitless labour.

Nevertheless, you all feel that a revolution is to come, and that you alone can accomplish it. What, then, is the idea which governs you, proletarians of the nineteenth century?—for really I cannot call you revolutionists. What do you think?—what do you believe?—what do you want? Be guarded in your reply. I have read faithfully your favourite journals, your most esteemed authors. I find everywhere only vain and puerile *entites*; nowhere do I discover an idea.

[...]

Forever promises! Forever oaths! Why should the people trust in tribunes, when kings perjure themselves? Alas! truth and honesty are no longer, as in the days of King John, in the mouth of princes. A whole senate has been convicted of felony, and, the interest of the governors always being, for some mysterious reason, opposed to the interest of the governed, parliaments follow each other while the nation dies of hunger. No, no! No more protectors, no more emperors, no more consuls. Better manage our affairs ourselves than through agents. Better associate our industries than beg from monopolies; and, since the republic cannot dispense with virtues, we should labour for our reform.

This, therefore, is my line of conduct. I preach emancipation to the proletarians; association to the workers; equality to the wealthy. I push forward the revolution by all means in my power—the tongue, the pen, the press, by action, and example. My life is a continual apostleship.

[...]

Paris, 2<sup>nd</sup> May 1841
*Translation by James Bar Bowen*

# LETTER TO ANTOINE GAUTHIER

My dear old friend,[1]

YOUR CRITICISMS OF ME ARE WELL DESERVED, AS I REALLY OUGHT TO KNOW what the process of printing a book entails; but a writer always thinks he has done all that is required when he finishes writing and that the printing presses should be able to work as quickly as his thoughts. Gutenberg's art has yet to reach that point. The printing of my little *Mémoire* took five weeks or more which was long enough to annoy me in the first place. At last it is completed, and now I am at the mercy of the critics. On all sides, they declare that I am immoderate: the wind blows and the sky turns black; bad times are on the way. Whatever happens, I must add that I have nothing to fear from the Authorities, which is the most important thing; as for the dogs of the Court and others, I have known them for years and I am ready for them. I am reckless and foolhardy as much as any man of the world; but when it comes to printing, you assume that I have enough good sense not to publish anything which is not well considered, even in my crazier moments. The radical reformers fulminate against me because of a few bad jokes that I have addressed to them; what do you think they'll say next year, for God's sake, when I have killed off their pet obsession! But let the storm come and let us consider, O gentle observer, the hurricane's progress. I have always thought that this will blow over; a wise man always takes a second look before attacking a man who is well equipped to fight back, particularly if he has already hit hard and hit true. You can be the judge of that.

However, my dear friend, my oldest comrade, if the fuss of factions, if a conspiracy of scribbling journalists manages to demonise me in the eyes of this enormous beast that we call the public, have I not already been compensated by being held up in the estimation of those honest, independent men

---

1    Proudhon had been an employee of MM. Gauthier Frères (publishers). (Translator)

whose opinions are not easily swayed, and in the affections of my friends? This is one thing about which I take the greatest pleasure: perhaps no man has quite as many true friends as I, and I count among them such essentially upright, moral, remarkable men of talent and ability. Given my natural ways and my slightly rustic tastes, you know how easy it is for me to console myself with the troubles of literature and of the writer's craft. When I put my pen down, it is as if I become someone else: I become once more a lazy, fun-loving fellow, a wanderer of the streets, frequenting the café and tavern, looking for a good time. Was I not created specifically to whip into shape that pack of curs who only know how to savage their own sheep while merely howling at the wolves? Invulnerable with regard to self-love, since I have no time for their flattery, and beyond reproach in my private life, what have I to fear from them? I am still only on my second act, and I didn't start writing just to take it all back later. This play will be a long one, and there are many who have yet to feel the lash of my goad.

It is always a great pleasure for me to correspond with you because I rarely receive letters quite so frank, quite so lively, quite so piquant as yours. As I read them, I recognise that healthy Franche-Comté regional style that our academics, in their ignorance and stupidity, work so hard to eliminate and corrupt. In fact, you are very similar to me. Like you, I first felt my indignation rising when I saw the hypocrisy, the baseness, the lies, the ignorance and the charlatanism of this world; and I wanted this bilious anger to feature in my writing style. I wanted, above all, to be rooted in my place of birth: loyal and honest, reasonable, biting, caustic, able to laugh and mock, lacking any sympathy for the *minus habentes*[2] who are so easily taken in by what we say. I know that I am often criticised for indulging in too much posturing and polemicising but, with a bit of reflection, one can see that it is just a tactic, a means, like any other, of making my ideas known. And what is more, there is such a preponderance of half-baked thinking, of laziness, of style over substance among the current batch of critics that it is necessary to have a chef who is willing to throw a dash of vinegar or lemon juice into the mix. As for the rest, I would expect them to do to me as I do to them: I expect nothing less. For every blow that I have struck, I haven't even been scratched back. I find that boring.

You ask me to explain my method of reconstituting society. With just a few words in reply, I will try to give you a few accurate ideas on the subject.

Since you have read my book, you must understand that it is not just a matter of imagining, of combining in our heads a system which we can subsequently present to the world; this is not how one changes the world. Only society can ameliorate itself; that is to say, it is necessary to study human nature in all its forms—in laws, in religion, dress, political economy—and

---

2   Latin for "absentminded"; here Proudhon means something like "ignorant fools." (Translator)

then, *by means of metaphysical operations*, to extract from this mass of information that which is true; to eliminate that which is corrupt, false or incomplete; and then, from the elements which remain, to form general guiding principles which can serve as *rules*. This work will take centuries to complete.

This probably looks to be a hopeless task to you: but rest assured! In every reform there are two distinct features, which are often confused the one with the other: the *transition* and the *perfection* or *completion*.

The first is the only thing that *today's* society can be expected to set in motion. And then what? How are we to carry out this transition? You will find the answer to this by combining a few passages of my second *Mémoire*: pp.10–11 deals with all forms of income and, in general, lowers the level of all revenues; p.16 deals with bank reforms; pp.28–29 looks at the issue of low-interest capital and reform of the bankers; pp.33–37, progressive abolition of customs duty; pp.179 attacks property by means of interest; pp.184 ditto, etc.

You understand that a system of progressive abolition of what I call *increase [aubaine]* (i.e. private incomes from property or renting, inflated salaries, competitive profiteering, etc.) would render the ownership of property effectively worthless since its harmfulness lies above all in the profits gleaned from interest.

At all times, this progressive abolition will only be a *negation of harm*, or perhaps, rather, a *positive reorganisation*. Nevertheless, my dear old friend, for this to be the case, I can propose the principles and the general laws, but I cannot fill in all the details on my own. That is a task which would occupy fifty Montesquieus. For my part, I will supply the axioms, I will give examples and I will supply a methodology; I will set the process in motion. It is up to everyone else to do the rest.

What I am saying is that no person on Earth is capable (as they do say of Saint-Simon and Fourier) of proposing a system which has all its pieces and details in place, meaning that all the rest of us have to do is implement it. That is the most damnable lie that can be put forward amongst men, and that is why I am so vehemently opposed to Fourierism. Social science is infinite; no single human can ever understand it all, in the same way that no one person can understand medicine, physics or mathematics. However, we can discover its *principles*, followed by its *elements*, then just one *part* of it, and it will grow from there on. In any case, what I am doing at the moment is determining the *elements* of political and legislative science.

For example, I wish to preserve the right of inheritance and I want equality. How is that going to work? This is where the question of organisation enters. This problem will be resolved in the third *Mémoire* along with many others. I am unable to recount all my ideas here, as I would need another twenty pages to do so.

Anyway, if politics and the law are *science*, you understand that the principles are likely to be extremely simple, comprehensible to the least intelligent;

but that, in order to reach solutions to certain questions of detail or of a higher level of complexity, a series of reasoning processes and inductions will be necessary which are completely analogous to the calculations by which one determines the movement of the stars. In actual fact, the description of the process of resolving the problems of social science will be one of the more interesting aspects of my third *Mémoire*, and it will serve to better prove my own good faith and the emptiness of most political *inventions*.

In brief: *abolish to the point of extinction all forms of private income*, which will be the TRANSITION. The ORGANISATION will result from the principles of the *division of labour* and from the *collective force*, combined with the maintenance of the *individuality* of man and citizen.

This might all look like hieroglyphics to you now, but this is where the enigma becomes explained; this is where the mystery resides. You will watch me begin the process and you may well say to yourself: To achieve this goal, all that is required is men and the means of study.

You have forced me to be pedantic in an informal letter answering one simple question. When I correspond with you, am I putting myself in the role of teacher? One can never fully explain oneself regarding something complicated in just a page or two because there are always details requiring clarification in order to resolve issues. The most important thing today is to look closely at Property, reconsidering domestic policy regarding *abolition* and foreign policy regarding *customs duties*. It is all there; the rest will slot into place accordingly...

Yesterday I received a charming and flattering letter from M. [Jérôme-Adolphe] Blanqui which actually makes me feel quite proud. You understand that this teacher does not accept my doctrine in the terms that I have outlined it; but, aside from the words and the humility which is his natural demeanour, he is a man of considerable learning—indeed, he's a wise man, well-loved by everybody, and the most able organiser that we have. From time to time I receive testimonies of good faith from eminent people who, without agreeing with me, say: "Keep up the good work!"

When I began this letter, I wanted to chat and banter with you; but my writer's instincts always take over. And you're partly to blame too! Why do you ask me such questions?

Farewell, then, my oldest fellow student, my comrade of the *Rosa*. I have no more time to write, but I see from your letter that *the oldest ones are still the best*.

Yours truly,

P-J PROUDHON

*Lyons, May 17th, 1846*
*Translation by Barry Marshall*

# LETTER TO KARL MARX

My Dear *Monsieur Marx*,

I WILL GLADLY AGREE TO BE ONE OF THE RECIPIENTS OF YOUR CORRESPOND-ence, the aim and organisation of which seems very useful to me.

However, I cannot promise to write to you all that much or all that often. All of my interests, combined with a natural laziness, leave me little time for engagement in epistolary efforts. I do want to take the liberty of making some criticisms, suggested to me by different parts of your letter.

First of all, although when it comes to ideas of organisation and achievement my thoughts are at this point in time more or less established, at least as far as principles go, I believe it is my duty, as it is the duty of all socialists, to keep a critical and sceptical frame of mind. In short, I am making a public profession of an almost absolute economic anti-dogmatism.

Let us seek together, if you will, for the laws of society, the manner in which these laws are manifested, the progress of our efforts to discover them. But for God's sake, after having demolished all *a priori* dogmatisms, let us not in turn dream of making our own, of indoctrinating the people. Let us not fall into the same contradiction of your countryman Martin Luther, who, having overturned Catholic theology, immediately set about founding a Protestant theology with excommunications and anathemas. For the last three centuries, Germany has been largely engaged in tearing down all that Luther built. We should not leave humanity with a similar mess as a result of our own efforts. With all my heart, I applaud your idea of bringing all opinions to light; let us show the world an example of learned and insightful tolerance, but since we are in the lead, let us not set ourselves up as leaders of a new intolerance; let us not be the apostles of a new religion, one that makes itself a religion of reason, a religion of logic. We should welcome and encourage all protestations. Let us get rid of all divisiveness, all mysticism. Let us never consider a question exhausted, and when we do get down to our last argument, let's start again if need be with wit and irony! I will join your organisation on that condition—or else not.

I also want to make a few observations on this phrase in your letter: "At the moment of action." Perhaps you are still of the mind that no reform is possible with a *coup de main*, without what we used to call a revolution, and what is in reality nothing but a jolt. That opinion—which I understand, which I excuse, which I would willingly discuss having myself held it for a long time—I must admit to you that my latest studies have made me completely abandon it. We do not need it to succeed, and as a result we do not have to promote revolutionary action as a means to achieve social reform, because that pretended method is only simply a call for force, for arbitrariness—in short, a contradiction. I have set out the problem like this: to bring back to society through an economic combination the wealth that has left society by means of a different economic combination. In other words, via political economy, to turn the theory of property against property in such a way as to bring about what you German socialists call community [*communauté*] but which I prefer to call freedom or equality. But I believe in a little while I will have the means of solving this problem. I would therefore prefer to burn property slowly with a small fire than to give it new strength by carrying out a Saint Bartholomew's Night of the Proprietors.[1]

My next book, which is at the printers, will have more to say to you.[2]

There you have it, my dear *philosopher:* that is where I stand right now. Except for me deceiving myself—and should that happen getting a rap on the knuckles from you—this is what I submit to in good faith while awaiting my revenge [*en attendant ma revanche*]. I should tell you in passing that this also seems to be the mood of the French working class. Our proletariat has a great thirst for science, which would be very poorly served if you only brought them blood to drink. In short, to my mind it would be terrible politics to talk like killers [*exterminateurs*]. The usual methods will suffice; the people do not need any exhortation for that.

I am very sorry for these petty divisions which, it seems, still exist in German socialism and which your complaints to me about M. Grun prove.[3] I am afraid that you have seen this author in a poor light. My dear Marx, I want to set things straight. Grun has found himself exiled with no money, a wife and two children, and no means of making a living except by his pen. How else do you want him to make a living if not by modern ideas? I understand your philosophical ire and I admit that the quest for the ultimate truth [*sainte parole*] of humankind should not be underhand, but I see here only misfortune and extreme necessity and I excuse the man. Oh! If we were

---

1   Saint Bartholomew's Night refers to the massacre in 1572 of thousands of Huguenot Protestants by French Catholics. (Translator)

2   A reference to Proudhon's *System of Economic Contradictions*. (Editor)

3   Marx in his letter to Proudhon warned Proudhon that Grun had poked fun at him in his book on the French socialists and that Grun had also made erroneous claims that he had tutored him. (Translator)

all millionaires, things would be easier. We would be saints and angels. It is simple, we have to live. You know that that word does not yet express the idea of a pure society—far from it. Living means buying your bread, wood, meat, paying the landlord, and, by Jove!, he who sells social ideas is no more unworthy than he who sells a sermon. I am completely unaware that Grun had made himself out to be my tutor: tutor of what? I stick to political economy, things he knows nothing about. I look on literature as a little girl's toy, and as for philosophy, I know enough to have the right to be poked fun at myself on occasion. Grun has said nothing about it to me at all. If he did say that, he was being impertinent and I am sure he apologises.

What I do know and what I do value more than what I blame for a bit of conceit is that I owe to M. Grun and his friend Ewerbeck the acquaintance I have with your own writings, my dear M. Marx, those of M. Engels and that very important book by Feuerbach. They have kindly undertaken some analysis for me in French (I unfortunately cannot read German) of the most important socialist publications, and it is because of a suggestion of theirs that I include (besides what I had done by myself) in my next book mention of the works of MM. Marx, Engels, Feuerbach, etc. Finally Grun and Ewerbeck are working to keep the sacred fire [*feu sacré*] going in the German émigrés who live in Paris, and the respect that they have for the workers they are talking to assures me of the honesty of their intentions.

I hope to see you, my dear Marx, come back from a hasty judgement made in a moment of irritation, just because you were angry when you wrote to me. Grun has indicated to me his desire to translate my latest book. He can only do this with some help. I would be obliged to you and your friends if you lent your assistance on this occasion, by contributing towards the sale of a book, which would be a great benefit to me.

If you wanted to give me assurance of your help, my dear M. Marx, I would very shortly send my proofs to M. Grun, and I think that, in spite of your personal grievances, which I do not want to judge, this conduct would honour us all.

Yours very devotedly,

Pierre-Joseph PROUDHON

1846
*Translation by Benjamin R. Tucker*

# SYSTEM OF ECONOMIC CONTRADICTIONS,
## OR, THE PHILOSOPHY OF MISERY
## VOLUME I

*Destruam et dificabo*[1]
—Deuteronomy: c. 32

# CHAPTER I
## OF THE ECONOMIC SCIENCE

[...]

I AFFIRM THE REALITY OF AN ECONOMIC SCIENCE.

[...]

But I hasten to say that I do not regard as a science the incoherent ensemble of theories to which the name political economy has been officially given for almost a hundred years, and which, in spite of the etymology of the name, is after all but the code, or immemorial routine, of property. These theories offer us only the rudiments, or first section, of economic science; and that is why, like property, they are all contradictory of each other, and half the time inapplicable. The proof of this assertion, which is, in one sense, a denial of political economy as handed down to us by Adam Smith, Ricardo, Malthus, and J-B Say, and as we have known it for half a century, will be especially developed in this treatise.

The inadequacy of political economy has at all times impressed thoughtful minds, who, too fond of their dreams for practical investigation, and

---

1    "I shall destroy and I shall build." (Editor)

confining themselves to the estimation of apparent results, have constituted from the beginning a party of opposition to the *statu quo*, and have devoted themselves to a persevering and systematic ridicule of civilisation and its customs. Property, on the other hand, the basis of all social institutions, has never lacked zealous defenders, who, proud to be called practical, have exchanged blow for blow with the traducers of political economy, and have laboured with a courageous and often skilful hand to strengthen the edifice which general prejudice and individual liberty have erected in concert. The controversy between conservatives and reformers, still pending, finds its counterpart, in the history of philosophy, in the quarrel between realists and nominalists;[2] it is almost useless to add that, on both sides, right and wrong are equal, and that the rivalry, narrowness, and intolerance of opinions have been the sole cause of the misunderstanding.

Thus two powers are contending for the government of the world, and cursing each other with the fervour of two hostile religions: political economy, or tradition; and socialism, or utopia.

[...]

Political economy tends toward the glorification of selfishness; socialism favours the exaltation of communism.

The economists, saving a few violations of their principles, for which they deem it their duty to blame governments, are optimists with regard to accomplished facts; the socialists, with regard to facts to be accomplished.

The first affirm that that which ought to be is; the second, that that which ought to be is not. Consequently, while the first are defenders of religion, authority, and the other principles contemporary with, and conservative of, property,—although their criticism, based solely on reason, deals frequent blows at their own prejudices,—the second reject authority and faith, and appeal exclusively to science,—although a certain religiosity, utterly illiberal, and an unscientific disdain for facts, are always the most obvious characteristics of their doctrines.

For the rest, neither party ever ceases to accuse the other of incapacity and sterility.

The socialists ask their opponents to account for the inequality of conditions, for those commercial debaucheries in which monopoly and competition, in monstrous union, perpetually give birth to luxury and misery; they reproach economic theories, always modelled after the past, with leaving the future hopeless; in short, they point to the regime of property as a horrible hallucination, against which humanity has protested and struggled for four thousand years.

---

2   A reference to a philosophical controversy that arose in the Middle Ages over the problem of universals (general categories or classes of things, as distinct from the individual examples or members of those classes). Realist philosophers held that universals exist in reality; the nominalists held that only individual, particular things exist in reality, and that universals are merely "names." (Editor)

The economists, on their side, defy socialists to produce a system in which property, competition, and political organisation can be dispensed with; they prove, with documents in hand, that all reformatory projects have ever been nothing but rhapsodies of fragments borrowed from the very system that socialism sneers at,—plagiarisms, in a word, of political economy, outside of which socialism is incapable of conceiving and formulating an idea.

[...]

Thus society finds itself, at its origin, divided into two great parties: the one traditional and essentially hierarchical, which, according to the object it is considering, calls itself by turns royalty or democracy, philosophy or religion, in short, property; the other socialism, which, coming to life at every crisis of civilisation, proclaims itself pre-eminently anarchical and atheistic; that is, rebellious against all authority, human and divine.

[...]

What is there, then, in political economy that is necessary and true; whither does it tend; what are its powers; what are its wishes? It is this which I propose to determine in this work. What is the value of socialism? The same investigation will answer this question also.

[...]

The question now most disputed is unquestionably that of the *organisation of labour*.

As John the Baptist preached in the desert, *Repent ye so* the socialists go about proclaiming everywhere this novelty old as the world, *Organise labour*, though never able to tell what, in their opinion, this organisation should be. However that may be, the economists have seen that this socialistic clamour was damaging their theories: it was, indeed, a rebuke to them for ignoring that which they ought first to recognise,—labour. They have replied, therefore, to the attack of their adversaries, first by maintaining that labour is organised, that there is no other organisation of labour than liberty to produce and exchange, either on one's own personal account, or in association with others,—in which case the course to be pursued has been prescribed by the civil and commercial codes. Then, as this argument served only to make them the laughing-stock of their antagonists, they assumed the offensive; and, showing that the socialists understood nothing at all themselves of this organisation that they held up as a scarecrow, they ended by saying that it was but a new socialistic chimera, a word without sense,—an absurdity. The latest writings of the economists are full of these pitiless conclusions.

Nevertheless, it is certain that the phrase *organisation of labour* contains as clear and rational a meaning as these that follow: organisation of the workshop, organisation of the army, organisation of police, organisation of charity, organisation of war. In this respect, the argument of the economists is deplorably irrational. No less certain is it that the organisation of labour cannot be a utopia and chimera; for at the moment that labour, the supreme condition of civilisation, begins to exist, it follows that it is already submitted to an organisation, such as it is, which satisfies the economists, but which the socialists think detestable.

There remains, then, relative to the proposal to organise labour formulated by socialism, this objection,—that labour is organised. Now, this is utterly untenable, since it is notorious that in labour, supply, demand, division, quantity, proportion, price, and security, nothing, absolutely nothing is regulated; on the contrary, everything is given up to the caprices of free-will; that is, to chance.

As for us, guided by the idea that we have formed of social science, we shall affirm, against the socialists and against the economists, not that labour *must be organised*, nor that it is *organised* but that it *is being organised*.

Labour, we say, is being organised: that is, the process of organisation has been going on from the beginning of the world, and will continue till the end. Political economy teaches us the primary elements of this organisation; but socialism is right in asserting that, in its present form, the organisation is inadequate and transitory; and the whole mission of science is continually to ascertain, in view of the results obtained and the phenomena in course of development, what innovations can be immediately effected.

Socialism and political economy, then, while waging a burlesque war, pursue in reality the same idea,—the organisation of labour.

But both are guilty of disloyalty to science and of mutual calumny, when on the one hand political economy, mistaking for science its scraps of theory, denies the possibility of further progress; and when socialism, abandoning tradition, aims at re-establishing society on undiscoverable bases.

[...]

Another question, no less disputed than the preceding one, is that of usury, or lending at interest.

Usury, or in other words the price of use, is the emolument, of whatever nature, which the proprietor derives from the loan of his property. *Quidquid sorti accrescit usura est*, say the theologians. Usury, the foundation of credit, was one of the first of the means which social spontaneity employed in its work of organisation, and whose analysis discloses the profound laws of civilisation. The ancient philosophers and the Fathers of the Church, who must be regarded here as the representatives of socialism in the early centuries of the Christian era, by a singular fallacy,—which arose however from the paucity of economic knowledge in their day,—allowed farm-rent and condemned interest on money, because, as they believed, money was unproductive. They distinguished consequently between the loan of things which are consumed by use—among which they included money—and the loan of things which, without being consumed, yield a product to the user.

The economists had no difficulty in showing, by generalising the idea of rent, that in the economy of society the action of capital, or its productivity, was the same whether it was consumed in wages or retained the character of an instrument; that, consequently, it was necessary either to prohibit the rent of land or to allow interest on money, since both were by the same title payment for privilege, indemnity for loan. It required more than fifteen centuries to get this idea accepted, and to reassure the consciences that had been terrified by the anathemas pronounced by Catholicism against usury. But finally the weight of evidence and the general desire favoured the usurers: they won the battle against socialism; and from this legitimation of usury society gained some immense and unquestionable advantages. Under these circumstances socialism, which had tried to generalise the law enacted by Moses for the Israelites alone, *Non foeneraberis proximo tuo, sed alieno*, was beaten by an idea which it had accepted from the economic routine,—namely, farm-rent,—elevated into the theory of the productivity of capital.

But the economists in their turn were less fortunate, when they were afterwards called upon to justify farm-rent in itself, and to establish this theory of the product of capital. It may be said that, on this point, they have lost all the advantage they had at first gained against socialism.

Undoubtedly—and I am the first to recognise it—the rent of land, like that of money and all personal and real property, is a spontaneous and universal fact, which has its source in the depths of our nature, and which soon becomes, by its natural development, one of the most potent means of organisation. I shall prove even that interest on capital is but the materialisation of the aphorism, *All labour should leave a surplus*. But in the face of this theory, or rather this fiction, of the productivity of capital, arises another thesis no less certain, which in these latter days has struck the ablest economists: it is that all value is born of labour, and is composed essentially of wages; in other words, that no wealth has its origin in privilege, or acquires any value except through work; and that, consequently, labour alone is the source of revenue among men. How, then, reconcile the theory of farm-rent or productivity of capital—a theory confirmed by universal custom, which conservative political economy is forced to accept but cannot justify—with this other theory which shows that value is normally composed of wages, and which inevitably ends, as we shall demonstrate, in an equality in society between net product and raw product?

[…]

In such a situation what is the mandate of science?

Certainly not to halt in an arbitrary, inconceivable, and impossible *juste milieu*; it is to generalise further, and discover a third principle, a fact, a superior law, which shall explain the fiction of capital and the myth of property, and reconcile them with the theory which makes labour the origin of all wealth. This is what socialism, if it wishes to proceed logically, must undertake. [...]

[…]

For example, what is profit? That which remains for the manager after he has paid all the expenses. Now, the expenses consist of the labour performed and the materials consumed; or, in fine, wages. What, then, is the wages of a worker? The least that can be given him; that is, we do not know. What should be the price of the merchandise put upon the market by the manager? The highest that he can obtain; that is, again, we do not know. Political economy prohibits the supposition that the prices of merchandise and labour can be fixed, although it admits that they can be estimated; and that for the reason, say the economists, that estimation is essentially an arbitrary operation, which never can lead to sure and certain conclusions. How, then, shall we find the relation between two unknowns which, according to political economy, cannot be determined? Thus political economy proposes insolvable problems; and yet we shall soon see that it must propose them, and that our century must solve them. That is why I said that the Academy of Moral Sciences, in offering for competition the question of the relation of profits and wages, spoke unconsciously, spoke prophetically.

But it will be said, is it not true that, if labour is in great demand and workers are scarce, wages will rise, while profits on the other hand will decrease; that if, in the press of competition, there is an excess of production, there will be a stoppage and forced sales, consequently no profit for the manager and a danger of idleness for the worker; that then the latter will offer his labour at a reduced price; that, if a machine is invented, it will first extinguish the fires of its rivals; then, a monopoly established, and the worker made dependent on the employer, profits and wages will be inversely proportional? Cannot all these causes, and others besides, be studied, ascertained, counterbalanced, etc.?

Oh, monographs, histories!—we have been saturated with them since the days of Adam Smith and J-B Say, and they are scarcely more than variations of these authors' words. But it is not thus that the question should be understood, although the Academy has given it no other meaning. The relation of profits and wages should be considered in an absolute sense, and not from the inconclusive point of view of the accidents of commerce and the division of interests: two things which must ultimately receive their interpretation. Let me explain myself.

Considering producer and consumer as a single individual, whose recompense is naturally equal to his product; then dividing this product into two parts, one which rewards the producer for his outlay, another which represents his profit, according to the axiom that all labour should leave a surplus, we have to determine the relation of one of these parts to the other. This done, it will be easy to deduce the ratio of the fortunes of these two classes of men, employers and employees, as well as account for all commercial oscillations. This will be a series of corollaries to add to the demonstration.

Now, that such a relation may exist and be estimated, there must necessarily be a law, internal or external, which governs wages and prices; and since, in the present state of things, wages and prices vary and oscillate continually, we must ask what are the general facts, the causes, which make value vary and oscillate, and within what limits this oscillation takes place.

But this very question is contrary to the accepted principles; for whoever says oscillation necessarily supposes a mean direction toward which value's centre of gravity continually tends; and when the Academy asks that we determine the oscillations of profit and wages, it asks thereby that we determine value. Now that is precisely what the gentlemen of the Academy deny: they are unwilling to admit that, if value is variable, it is for that very reason determinable; that variability is the sign and condition of determinability. They pretend that value, ever varying, can never be determined. This is like maintaining that, given the number of oscillations of a pendulum *per second*, their amplitude, and the latitude and elevation of the spot where the experiment is performed, the length of the pendulum cannot be determined because the pendulum is in motion. Such is political economy's first article of faith.

As for socialism, it does not appear to have understood the question, or to be concerned about it. Among its many organs, some simply and merely put aside the problem by substituting division for distribution,—that is, by banishing number and measure from the social organism: others relieve themselves of the embarrassment by applying universal suffrage to the wages question. It is needless to say that these platitudes find dupes by thousands and hundreds of thousands.

The condemnation of political economy has been formulated by Malthus in this famous passage:

"A man who is born into a world already possessed, if he cannot get subsistence from his parents on whom he has a just demand, and if the society do not want his labour, has no claim of *right* to the smallest portion of food, and, in fact, has no business to be where he is. At nature's mighty feast there is no vacant cover for him. She tells him to be gone, and will quickly execute her own orders..."[3]

This then is the necessary, the fatal, conclusion of political economy,—a conclusion which I shall demonstrate by evidence hitherto unknown in this field of inquiry,—Death to him who does not possess!

In order better to grasp the thought of Malthus, let us translate it into philosophical propositions by stripping it of its rhetorical gloss:

"Individual liberty, and property, which is its expression, are economical data; equality and solidarity are not.

"Under this system, each one by himself, each one for himself: labour, like all merchandise, is subject to fluctuation: hence the risks of the proletariat.

"Whoever has neither income nor wages has no right to demand anything of others: his misfortune falls on his own head; in the game of fortune, luck has been against him."

---

3   Tucker supplies a slightly different version of this passage, having translated Proudhon's quotation of Joseph Garnier's French translation of Malthus back into English. This passage, which Malthus struck from subsequent editions of his *Essay on the Principle of Population*, appears in the 1803 edition. (Editor)

From the point of view of political economy these propositions are irrefutable; and Malthus, who has formulated them with such alarming exactness, is secure against all reproach. From the point of view of the conditions of social science, these same propositions are radically false, and even contradictory.

The error of Malthus, or rather of political economy, does not consist in saying that a man who has nothing to eat must die; or in maintaining that, under the system of individual appropriation, there is no course for him who has neither labour nor income but to withdraw from life by suicide, unless he prefers to be driven from it by starvation: such is, on the one hand, the law of our existence; such is, on the other, the consequence of property; and M. Rossi has taken altogether too much trouble to justify the good sense of Malthus on this point. I suspect, indeed, that M. Rossi, in making so lengthy and loving an apology for Malthus, intended to recommend political economy in the same way that his fellow-countryman Machiavelli, in his book entitled *The Prince*, recommended despotism to the admiration of the world. In pointing out misery as the necessary condition of industrial and commercial absolutism, M. Rossi seems to say to us: There is your law, your justice, your political economy; there is property.

But Gallic simplicity does not understand artifice; and it would have been better to have said to France, in her immaculate tongue: The error of Malthus, the radical vice of political economy, consists, in general terms, in affirming as a definitive state a transitory condition,[4]—namely, the division of society into patricians and proletarians;[5] and, particularly, in saying that in an organised, and consequently interdependent [*solidaire*], society, there may be some who possess, labour, and consume, while others have neither possession, nor labour, nor bread. Finally Malthus, or political economy, reasons erroneously when seeing in the faculty of indefinite reproduction—which the human race enjoys in neither greater nor less degree than all animal and vegetable species—a permanent danger of famine; whereas it is only necessary to show the necessity, and consequently the existence, of a law of equilibrium between population and production.

In short, the theory of Malthus—and herein lies the great merit of this writer, a merit which none of his colleagues has dreamed of attributing to him—is a *reductio ad absurdum* of all political economy.

[...]

---

4   Cf. Marx's comment in *The Poverty of Philosophy* (Amherst, NY: Prometheus Books, 1995) that Proudhon "borrows from the economists the necessity of eternal relations" (137). (Editor)

5   This is a reference to Ancient Rome where the patricians were rich and powerful families who managed to secure power over plebeians. Subsequently "patrician" became a vaguer term used for aristocrats and elite bourgeoisie in many countries. (Editor)

# CHAPTER II

## OF VALUE

[...]

VALUE IS THE corner-stone of the economic edifice. The divine artist who has entrusted us with the continuation of his work has explained himself on this point to no one; but the few indications given may serve as a basis of conjecture. Value, in fact, presents two faces: one, which the economists call value in use, or intrinsic value; another, value in exchange, or of opinion. The effects which are produced by value under this double aspect, and which are very irregular so long as it is not established,—or, to use a more philosophical expression, so long as it is not constituted, are changed totally by this constitution.

[...]

The economists have very clearly shown the double character of value, but what they have not made equally plain is its contradictory nature. Here begins our criticism.

Utility is the necessary condition of exchange; but take away exchange, and utility vanishes: these two things are indissolubly connected. Where, then, is the contradiction?

Since all of us live only by labour and exchange, and grow richer as production and exchange increase, each of us produces as much useful value as possible, in order to increase by that amount his exchanges, and consequently his enjoyments. Well, the first effect, the inevitable effect, of the multiplication of values is to LOWER them: the more abundant is an article of merchandise, the more it loses in exchange and depreciates commercially. Is it not true that there is a contradiction between the necessity of labour and its results?

I adjure the reader, before rushing ahead for the explanation, to arrest his attention upon the fact.

A peasant who has harvested twenty sacks of wheat, which he with his family proposes to consume, deems himself twice as rich as if he had harvested only ten; likewise a housewife who has spun fifty yards of linen believes that she is twice as rich as if she had spun but twenty-five. Relatively to the household, both are right; looked at in their external relations, they may be utterly mistaken. If the crop of wheat is double throughout the whole country, twenty sacks will sell for less than ten would have sold for if it had been but half as great; so, under similar circumstances, fifty yards of linen will be worth less than twenty-five: so that value decreases as the production of utility increases, and a producer may arrive at poverty by continually enriching himself. And this seems unalterable, inasmuch as there is no way of escape except all the products of industry become infinite in quantity, like air and light, which is absurd. God of my reason! Jean-Jacques [Rousseau] would have said: it is not the economists who are irrational; it is political economy itself which is false to its definitions. *Mentita est iniquitas sibi.*

In the preceding examples the useful value exceeds the exchangeable value: in other cases it is less. Then the same phenomenon is produced, but in the opposite direction: the balance is in favour of the producer, while the consumer suffers. This is notably the case in seasons of scarcity, when the high price of provisions is always more or less factitious. There are also professions whose whole art consists in giving to an article of minor usefulness, which could easily be dispensed with, an exaggerated value of opinion: such, in general, are the arts of luxury. Man, through his aesthetic passion, is eager for the trifles the possession of which would highly satisfy his vanity, his innate desire for luxury, and his more noble and more respectable love of the beautiful: upon this the dealers in this class of articles speculate. To tax fancy and elegance is no less odious or absurd than to tax circulation: but such a tax is collected by a few fashionable merchants, whom general infatuation protects, and whose whole merit generally consists in warping taste and generating fickleness. Hence no one complains; and all the maledictions of opinion are reserved for the monopolists who, through genius, succeed in raising by a few cents the price of linen and bread.

It is little to have pointed out this astonishing contrast between useful value and exchangeable value, which the economists have been in the habit of regarding as very simple: it must be shown that this pretended simplicity conceals a profound mystery, which it is our duty to fathom.

[...]

Say and the economists who have succeeded him have observed that, labour being itself an object of valuation, a species of merchandise indeed like any other, to take it as the principal and efficient cause of value is to reason in a vicious circle. Therefore, they conclude, it is necessary to fall back on scarcity and opinion.

These economists, if they will allow me to say it, herein have shown themselves wonderfully careless. Labour is said *to have value*, not as merchandise itself, but in view of the values supposed to be contained in it potentially. The *value of labour* is a figurative expression, an anticipation of effect from cause.

It is a fiction by the same title as the *productivity of capital*. Labour produces, capital has value: and when, by a sort of ellipsis, we say the value of labour, we make an *enjambment* which is not at all contrary to the rules of language, but which theorists ought to guard against mistaking for a reality. Labour, like liberty, love, ambition, genius, is a thing vague and indeterminate in its nature, but qualitatively defined by its object,—that is, it becomes a reality through its product.[6] When, therefore, we say: This man's labour is

---

6   Marx (op. cit.) quotes this and then adds, without indicating the different source, the following sentences from Chapter V: "But what need of insisting? From the moment that the communist changes the name of things, *vera rerum vocabala*, he tacitly admits his powerlessness, and puts himself out of the question." Ironically,

worth five francs per day, it is as if we should say: The daily product of this man's labour is worth five francs.

Now, the effect of labour is continually to eliminate scarcity and opinion as constitutive elements of value, and, by necessary consequence, to transform natural or indefinite utilities (appropriated or not) into measurable or social utilities: whence it follows that labour is at once a war declared upon the parsimony of Nature and a permanent conspiracy against property.

[...]

It is an axiom generally admitted by the economists that all labour should leave a surplus.

I regard this proposition as universally and absolutely true; it is a corollary of the law of proportionality, which may be regarded as an epitome of the whole science of economy. But—I beg pardon of the economists—the principle that all labour should leave a surplus has no meaning in their theory, and is not susceptible of demonstration. If supply and demand alone determine value, how can we tell what is a surplus and what is a sufficiency? If neither cost, nor market price, nor wages can be mathematically determined, how is it possible to conceive of a surplus, a profit? Commercial routine has given us the idea of profit as well as the word; and, since we are equal politically, we infer that every citizen has an equal right to realise profits in his personal industry. But commercial operations are essentially irregular, and it has been proved beyond question that the profits of commerce are but an arbitrary discount forced from the consumer by the producer,—in short, a displacement, to say the least. This we should soon see, if it was possible to compare the total amount of annual losses with the amount of profits. In the thought of political economy, the principle that all labour should leave a surplus is simply the consecration of the constitutional right which all of us gained by the revolution,—the right of robbing one's neighbour.

The law of proportionality of values alone can solve this problem. I will approach the question a little farther back: its gravity warrants me in treating it with the consideration that it merits.

[...]

I have demonstrated theoretically and by facts the principle that all labour should leave a surplus; but this principle, as certain as any proposition in arithmetic, is very far from universal realisation. While, by the progress of collective industry, each individual day's labour yields a greater and greater product, and while, by necessary consequence, the worker, receiving the same wages, must grow ever richer, there exist in society classes which thrive and classes which perish; workers paid twice, thrice, a hundred times over, and workers continually out of pocket; everywhere, finally, people who enjoy and people who suffer, and, by a monstrous division of the means of

---

he also changes (again without indicating) "communist" to "economist" and mockingly inserts "(read M. Proudhon)" in the modified text (61). (Editor)

industry, individuals who consume and do not produce. The distribution of well-being follows all the movements of value, and reproduces them in misery and luxury on a frightful scale and with terrible energy. But everywhere, too, the progress of wealth—that is, the proportionality of values—is the dominant law; and when the economists combat the complaints of the socialists with the progressive increase of public wealth and the alleviations of the condition of even the most unfortunate classes, they proclaim, without suspecting it, a truth which is the condemnation of their theories.

For I entreat the economists to question themselves for a moment in the silence of their hearts, far from the prejudices which disturb them, and regardless of the employments which occupy them or which they wait for, of the interests which they serve, of the votes which they covet, of the distinctions which tickle their vanity: let them tell me whether, hitherto, they have viewed the principle that all labour should leave a surplus in connection with this series of premises and conclusions which we have elaborated, and whether they ever have understood these words to mean anything more than the right to speculate in values by manipulating supply and demand; whether it is not true that they affirm at once, on the one hand the progress of wealth and well-being, and consequently the measure of values, and on the other the arbitrariness of commercial transactions and the incommensurability of values,—the flattest of contradictions? Is it not because of this contradiction that we continually hear repeated in lectures, and read in the works on political economy, this absurd hypothesis: If the price of ALL things was doubled...? As if the price of all things was not the proportion of things, and as if we could double a proportion, a relation, a law! Finally, is it not because of the proprietary and abnormal routine upheld by political economy that every one, in commerce, industry, the arts, and the State, on the pretended ground of services rendered to society, tends continually to exaggerate his importance, and solicits rewards, subsidies, large pensions, exorbitant fees: as if the reward of every service was not determined necessarily by the sum of its expenses? Why do not the economists, if they believe, as they appear to, that the labour of each should leave a surplus, use all their influence in spreading this truth, so simple and so luminous: Each man's labour can buy only the value which it contains, and this value is proportional to the services of all other workers?[7]

[...]

---

7   Cf. Marx (op. cit.): "It is beyond doubt that M. Proudhon confounds the two measures, the measure by the labour-time necessary to the production of a commodity, and the measure by the value of labour. 'The labour of every man,' says he, 'will purchase the labour which it embodies.' Thus according to him, a certain quantity of labour embodied in a product equals in value the remuneration of the worker, that is to say, the value of labour" (59). Proudhon, in fact, is taunting the bourgeois economists as he is well aware that a workers' wages did *not* equal their product under capitalism, arguing that the capitalist appropriates both the workers' "collective power" (Chapter VI: section II) and "surplus of labour" (Chapter XI: section IV). (Editor)

# CHAPTER III
ECONOMIC EVOLUTIONS—FIRST PERIOD—THE DIVISION OF LABOUR

THE FUNDAMENTAL IDEA, the dominant category, of political economy is VALUE.

Value reaches its positive determination by a series of oscillations between supply and demand.

[...]

In society, on the contrary, as well as in the mind, so far from the idea reaching its complete realisation at a single bound, a sort of abyss separates, so to speak, the two antinomical positions, and even when these are recognised at last, we still do not see what the synthesis will be. The primitive concepts must be fertilised, so to speak, by burning controversy and passionate struggle; bloody battles will be the preliminaries of peace. At the present moment, Europe, weary of war and discussion, awaits a reconciling principle; and it is the vague perception of this situation which induces the Academy of Moral and Political Sciences to ask, "What are the general facts which govern the relations of profits to wages and determine their oscillations?" in other words, what are the most salient episodes and the most remarkable phases of the war between labour and capital?[8]

If, then, I demonstrate that political economy, with all its contradictory hypotheses and equivocal conclusions, is nothing but an organisation of privilege and misery, I shall have proved thereby that it contains by implication the promise of an organisation of labour and equality, since, as has been said, every systematic contradiction is the announcement of a composition; further, I shall have fixed the bases of this composition. Then, indeed, to unfold the system of economic contradictions is to lay the foundations of universal association; to show how the products of collective labour come out of society is to explain how it will be possible to make them return to it; to exhibit the genesis of the problems of production and distribution is to prepare the way for their solution. All these propositions are identical and equally evident.

---

8   As can be seen, Proudhon was well aware of the class nature of capitalism and the conflicts it produces. Marx, on the other hand, takes Proudhon's use of a high-level abstraction to prove one thing to mean that Proudhon ignores the reality of class society: "What then [...] is the Prometheus resuscitated by Proudhon? It is society, it is social relations based on the antagonism of classes [...] Efface these relations and you have extinguished the whole of society, and your Prometheus is nothing more than a phantom [...] If then, in theory, it suffices to interpret, as M. Proudhon does, the formula of the surplus of labour in the sense of equality without taking into account of the actual conditions of production, it must suffice, in practice, to make among the workers an equal distribution of wealth without changing anything in the actual conditions of production" (op. cit. 109–10). (Editor)

[...]

Considered in its essence, the division of labour is the way in which equality of condition and intelligence is realised. Through diversity of function, it gives rise to proportionality of products and equilibrium in exchange, and consequently opens for us the road to wealth; as also, in showing us infinity everywhere in art and Nature, it leads us to idealise our acts, and makes the creative mind—that is, divinity itself, *mentem diviniorem*—immanent and perceptible in all workers.

Division of labour, then, is the first phase of economic evolution as well as of intellectual development: our point of departure is true as regards both man and things, and the progress of our exposition is in no wise arbitrary.

But, at this solemn hour of the division of labour, tempestuous winds begin to blow upon humanity. Progress does not improve the condition of all equally and uniformly, although in the end it must include and transfigure every intelligent and industrious being. It commences by taking possession of a small number of privileged persons, who thus compose the elite of nations, while the mass continues, or even buries itself deeper, in barbarism. It is this exception of persons on the part of progress which has perpetuated the belief in the natural and providential inequality of conditions, engendered caste, and given an hierarchical form to all societies. It has not been understood that all inequality, never being more than a negation, carries in itself the proof of its illegitimacy and the announcement of its downfall: much less still has it been imagined that this same inequality proceeds accidentally from a cause the ulterior effect of which must be its entire disappearance.

Thus, the antinomy of value reappearing in the law of division, it is found that the first and most potent instrument of knowledge and wealth which Providence has placed in our hands has become for us an instrument of misery and imbecility. Here is the formula of this new law of antagonism, to which we owe the two oldest maladies of civilisation, aristocracy and the proletariat: Labour, in dividing itself according to the law which is peculiar to it, and which is the primary condition of its productivity, ends in the frustration of its own objects, and destroys itself, in other words: Division, in the absence of which there is no progress, no wealth, no equality, subordinates the worker, and renders intelligence useless, wealth harmful, and equality impossible.

All the economists, since Adam Smith, have pointed out the advantages and the inconveniences of the law of division, but at the same time insisting much more strenuously upon the first than the second, because such a course was more in harmony with their optimistic views, and not one of them ever asking how a law can have inconveniences. This is the way in which J-B Say summed up the question:

"A man who during his whole life performs but one operation, certainly acquires the power to execute it better and more readily than another; but at the same time he becomes less capable of any other occupation, whether

physical or moral; his other faculties become extinct, and there results a degeneracy in the individual man. That one has made only the eighteenth part
of a pin is a sad account to give of one's self: but let no one imagine that it
is the worker who spends his life in handling a file or a hammer that alone
degenerates in this way from the dignity of his nature; it is the same with
the man whose position leads him to exercise the most subtle faculties of
his mind... On the whole, it may be said that the separation of tasks is an
advantageous use of human forces; that it increases enormously the products
of society; but that it takes something from the capacity of each man taken
individually."[9]

What, then, after labour, is the primary cause of the multiplication of
wealth and the skill of workers? Division.

What is the primary cause of intellectual degeneracy and, as we shall
show continually, civilised misery? Division.

How does the same principle, rigorously followed to its conclusions, lead
to effects diametrically opposite? There is not an economist, either before
or since Adam Smith, who has even perceived that here is a problem to be
solved. Say goes so far as to recognise that in the division of labour the same
cause which produces the good engenders the evil;[10] then, after a few words
of pity for the victims of the separation of industries, content with having
given an impartial and faithful exhibition of the facts, he leaves the matter
there. "You know," he seems to say, "that the more we divide the workers'
tasks, the more we increase the productive power of labour; but at the same
time the more does labour, gradually reducing itself to a mechanical operation, stupefy intelligence."

In vain do we express our indignation against a theory which, creating by
labour itself an aristocracy of capacities, leads inevitably to political inequality; in vain do we protest in the name of democracy and progress that in the
future there will be no nobility, no bourgeoisie, no pariahs. The economist
replies, with the impassability of destiny: You are condemned to produce
much, and to produce cheaply; otherwise your industry will be always insignificant, your commerce will amount to nothing, and you will drag in the
rear of civilisation instead of taking the lead.—What! among us, generous
men, there are some predestined to brutishness; and the more perfect our
industry becomes, the larger will grow the number of our accursed brothers!......—Alas!..... That is the last word of the economist.

We cannot fail to recognise in the division of labour, as a general fact and
as a cause, all the characteristics of a LAW; but as this law governs two orders

---

9    *Treatise on Political Economy*.

10   Cf. Marx, *Poverty of Philosophy*: "Proudhon... say[s] that J-B Say was the *first* to rec-
     ognise 'that in the division of labour the same cause which produces good engenders
     evil'" (140). Marx then quotes numerous economists showing that Say was not the
     *first* to recognise this fact, something that Proudhon did *not* claim. (Editor)

of phenomena radically opposite and destructive of each other, it must be confessed also that this law is of a sort unknown in the exact sciences,—that it is, strange to say, a contradictory law, a counter-law, an antinomy. Let us add, in anticipation, that such appears to be the identifying feature of social economy, and consequently of philosophy.

Now, without a RECOMPOSITION of labour which shall obviate the inconveniences of division while preserving its useful effects, the contradiction inherent in the principle is irremediable. It is necessary,—following the style of the Jewish priests plotting the death of Christ,—it is necessary that the poor should perish to secure the proprietor his fortune, *expedit unum hominem pro populo mori*. I am going to demonstrate the necessity of this decree; after which, if the *parcellaire* worker[11] still retains a glimmer of intelligence, he will console himself with the thought that he dies according to the rules of political economy.

Labour, which ought to give scope to the conscience and render it more and more worthy of happiness, leading through *parcellaire* division to prostration of mind, dwarfs man in his noblest part, *minorat capitis*, and throws him back into animality. Thenceforth the fallen man labours as a brute, and consequently must be treated as a brute. This sentence of Nature and necessity society will execute.

[...]

Everywhere, then, in public service as well as free industry, things are so ordered that nine-tenths of the workers serve as beasts of burden for the other tenth: such is the inevitable effect of industrial progress and the indispensable condition of all wealth. It is important to look well at this elementary truth before talking to the people of equality, liberty, democratic institutions, and other utopias, the realisation of which involves a previous complete revolution in the relations of workers.

[...]

# CHAPTER IV
## SECOND PERIOD—MACHINERY

"I HAVE witnessed with profound regret the CONTINUANCE OF DISTRESS in the manufacturing districts of the country."

Words of Queen Victoria on the reassembling of parliament.

If there is anything of a nature to cause sovereigns to reflect, it is that, more or less impassable spectators of human calamities, they are, by the very

---

11  *Parcellaire* as in divided, fragmented, compartmentalised. In other words, labour which is subject to extensive division of labour. For example, Adam Smith's example in *The Wealth of Nations* of a worker who makes one nineteenth of a pin. (Editor)

constitution of society and the nature of their power, absolutely powerless to cure the sufferings of their subjects; they are even prohibited from paying any attention to them. Every question of labour and wages, say with one accord the economic and representative theorists, must remain outside of the attributes of power. From the height of the glorious sphere where religion has placed them, thrones, dominations, principalities, powers, and all the heavenly host view the torment of society, beyond the reach of its stress; but their power does not extend over the winds and floods. Kings can do nothing for the salvation of mortals. And, in truth, these theorists are right: the prince is established to maintain, not to revolutionise; to protect reality, not to bring about utopia. He represents one of the antagonistic principles: hence, if he were to establish harmony, he would eliminate himself, which on his part would be sovereignly unconstitutional and absurd.

But as, in spite of theories, the progress of ideas is incessantly changing the external form of institutions in such a way as to render continually necessary exactly that which the legislator neither desires nor foresees,—so that, for instance, questions of taxation become questions of distribution; those of public utility, questions of national labour and industrial organisation; those of finance, operations of credit; and those of international law, questions of customs duties and markets,—it stands as demonstrated that the prince, who, according to theory, should never interfere with things which nevertheless, without theory's foreknowledge, are daily and irresistibly becoming matters of government, is and can be henceforth, like Divinity from which he emanates, whatever may be said, only an hypothesis, a fiction.

And finally, as it is impossible that the prince and the interests which it is his mission to defend should consent to diminish and disappear before emergent principles and new rights posited, it follows that progress, after being accomplished in the mind insensibly, is realised in society by leaps, and that force, in spite of the calumny of which it is the object, is the necessary condition of reforms. Every society in which the power of insurrection is suppressed is a society dead to progress: there is no truth of history better proven.

And what I say of constitutional monarchies is equally true of representative democracies: everywhere the social compact has united power and conspired against life, it being impossible for the legislator either to see that he was working against his own ends or to proceed otherwise.

Monarchs and representatives, pitiable actors in parliamentary comedies, this in the last analysis is what you are: talismans against the future! Every year brings you the grievances of the people; and when you are asked for the remedy, your wisdom covers its face! Is it necessary to support privilege,—that is, that consecration of the right of the strongest which created you and which is changing every day? Promptly, at the slightest nod of your head, a numerous army starts up, runs to arms, and forms in line of battle. And when the people complain that, in spite of their labour and precisely because of their labour, misery devours them, when society asks you for life, you recite acts of mercy! All your energy is expended for conservatism, all your virtue vanishes in aspirations! Like the Pharisee, instead of feeding your father, you pray for him! Ah! I tell you, we possess the secret of your mission: you exist only to prevent us from living. *Nolite ergo imperare*, get you gone!

As for us, who view the mission of power from quite another standpoint, and who wish the special work of government to be precisely that of exploring the future, searching for progress, and securing for all liberty, equality, health, and wealth, we continue our task of criticism courageously, entirely sure that, when we have laid bare the cause of the evils of society, the principle of its fevers, the motive of its disturbances, we shall not lack the power to apply the remedy.

## §1 OF THE FUNCTION OF MACHINERY IN ITS RELATIONS TO LIBERTY

The introduction of machinery into industry is accomplished in opposition to the law of division, and as if to re-establish the equilibrium profoundly compromised by that law. To truly appreciate the significance of this movement and grasp its spirit, a few general considerations become necessary.

   [...]

At the end of the preceding chapter we left the worker at loggerheads with the law of division: how will this indefatigable Oedipus manage to solve this enigma?

In society the incessant appearance of machinery is the antithesis, the inverse formula, of the division of labour; it is the protest of the industrial genius against *parcellaire* and homicidal labour. What is a machine, in fact? A method of reuniting diverse particles of labour which division had separated. Every machine may be defined as a summary of several operations, a simplification of powers, a condensation of labour, a reduction of costs. In all these respects machinery is the counterpart of division. Therefore through machinery will come a restoration of the *parcellaire* worker, a decrease of toil for the worker, a fall in the price of his product, a movement in the relation of values, progress towards new discoveries, advancement of the general welfare.[12]

As the discovery of a formula gives a new power to the geometer, so the invention of a machine is an abridgement of manual labour which multiplies the power of the producer, from which it may be inferred that the antinomy of the division of labour, if not entirely destroyed, will be balanced and neutralised. No one should fail to read the lectures of M. Chevalier setting forth

12   Cf. Marx: "The division of labour in the automatic factory is characterised by [...] labour [which] has lost all specialised character. But from the moment that all special development ceases, the need of universality, the tendency towards an integral development of the individual begins to make itself felt" (op. cit., 157). (Editor)

the innumerable advantages resulting to society from the intervention of machinery; they make a striking picture to which I take pleasure in referring my reader.

Machinery, positing itself in political economy in opposition to the division of labour, represents synthesis opposing itself in the human mind to analysis; and just as in the division of labour and in machinery, as we shall soon see, political economy entire is contained, so with analysis and synthesis goes the possession of logic entire, of philosophy. The man who labours proceeds necessarily and by turns by division and the aid of tools; likewise, he who reasons performs necessarily and by turns the operations of synthesis and analysis, nothing more, absolutely nothing. And labour and reason will never get beyond this: Prometheus, like Neptune, attains in three strides the confines of the world.

[...]

Labour, then, after having distinguished capacities and arranged their equilibrium by the division of industries, completes the armament of intelligence, if I may venture to say so, by machinery. According to the testimony of history as well as according to analysis, and notwithstanding the anomalies caused by the antagonism of economic principles, intelligence differs in men, not by power, clearness, or reach, but, in the first place, by speciality, or, in the language of the schools, by qualitative determination, and, in the second place, by exercise and education. Hence, in the individual as in the collective man, intelligence is much more a faculty which comes, forms, and develops, *quae fit*, than an entity or entelechy which exists, wholly formed, prior to apprenticeship. Reason, by whatever name we call it,—genius, talent, industry,—is at the start a naked and inert potentiality, which gradually grows in size and strength, takes on colour and form, and shades itself in an infinite variety of ways. By the importance of its acquirements, by its capital, in a word, the intelligence of one individual differs and will always differ from that of another; but, being a power equal in all at the beginning, social progress must consist in rendering it, by an ever increasing perfection of methods, again equal in all at the end. Otherwise labour would remain a privilege for some and a punishment for others.

[...]

## §II MACHINERY'S CONTRADICTION—ORIGIN OF CAPITAL AND WAGE-LABOUR

From the very fact that machinery diminishes the worker's toil, it abridges and diminishes labour, the supply of which thus grows greater from day to day and the demand less. Little by little, it is true, the reduction in prices causing an increase in consumption, the proportion is restored and the worker set at work again: but as industrial improvements steadily succeed each other and continually tend to substitute mechanical operations for the labour of man, it follows that there is a constant tendency to cut off a portion of the service and consequently to eliminate workers from production. Now, it is with the economic order as with the spiritual order: outside of the church there is no salvation; outside of labour there is no subsistence. Society and nature, equally pitiless, are in accord in the execution of this new decree.

"When a new machine, or, in general, any process whatever that expedites matters," says J-B Say, "replaces any human labour already employed, some of the industrious arms, whose services are usefully supplanted, are left without work. A new machine, therefore, replaces the labour of a portion of the workers, but does not diminish the amount of production, for, if it did, it would not be adopted; it displaces revenue. But the ultimate advantage is wholly on the side of machinery, for, if abundance of product and lessening of cost lower the venal value, the consumer—that is, everybody—will benefit thereby."

Say's optimism is infidelity to logic and to facts. The question here is not simply one of a small number of accidents which have happened during thirty centuries through the introduction of one, two, or three machines; it is a question of a regular, constant, and general phenomenon. After revenue has been displaced as Say says, by one machine, it is then displaced by another, and again by another, and always by another, as long as any labour remains to be done and any exchanges remain to be effected. That is the light in which the phenomenon must be presented and considered: but thus, it must be admitted, its aspect changes singularly. The displacement of revenue, the suppression of labour and wages, is a chronic, permanent, indelible plague, a sort of cholera which now appears wearing the features of Gutenberg, now assumes those of Arkwright; here is called Jacquard, there James Watt or Marquis de Jouffroy. After carrying on its ravages for a longer or shorter time under one form, the monster takes another, and the economists, who think that he has gone, cry out: "It was nothing!" Tranquil and satisfied, provided they insist with all the weight of their dialectics on the positive side of the question, they close their eyes to its subversive side, notwithstanding which, when they are spoken to of poverty, they again begin their sermons upon the improvidence and drunkenness of workers.

In 1750,—M. Dunoyer makes the observation, and it may serve as a measure of all lucubrations of the same sort,—"in 1750 the population of the duchy of Lancaster was 300,000 souls. In 1801, thanks to the development of spinning machines, this population was 672,000 souls. In 1831 it was 1,336,000 souls. Instead of the 40,000 workers whom the cotton industry formerly employed, it now employs, since the invention of machinery, 1,500,000."

M. Dunoyer adds that at the time when the number of workers employed in this industry increased in so remarkable a manner, the price of labour rose one hundred and fifty percent. Population, then, having simply followed industrial progress, its increase has been a normal and irreproachable fact,—what do I say?—a happy fact, since it is cited to the honour and glory of the development of machinery. But suddenly M. Dunoyer executes an about-face: this multitude of spinning-machines soon being out of work, wages necessarily declined; the population which the machines had called forth found itself abandoned by the machines, at which M. Dunoyer declares: Abuse of marriage is the cause of poverty.

English commerce, in obedience to the demand of the immense body of its patrons, summons workers from all directions, and encourages marriage; as long as labour is abundant, marriage is an excellent thing, the effects of which they are fond of quoting in the interest of machinery; but, the patronage fluctuating, as soon as work and wages are not to be had, they denounce the abuse of marriage, and accuse workers of improvidence. Political economy—that is, proprietary despotism—can never be in the wrong: it must be the proletariat.

The example of printing has been cited many a time, always to sustain the optimistic view. The number of persons supported today by the manufacture of books is perhaps a thousand times larger than was that of the copyists and illuminators prior to Gutenberg's time; therefore, they conclude with a satisfied air, printing has injured nobody. An infinite number of similar facts might be cited, all of them indisputable, but not one of which would advance the question a step. Once more, no one denies that machines have contributed to the general welfare; but I affirm, in regard to this incontestable fact, that the economists fall short of the truth when they advance the absolute statement that the simplification of processes has nowhere resulted in a diminution of the number of hands employed in any industry whatever. What the economists ought to say is that machinery, like the division of labour, in the present system of social economy is at once a source of wealth and a permanent and fatal cause of misery.[13]

In 1836, in a Manchester mill, nine frames, each having three hundred and twenty-four spindles, were tended by four spinners. Afterwards the mules were doubled in length, which gave each of the nine six hundred and eighty spindles and enabled two men to tend them.

There we have the naked fact of the elimination of the worker by the machine. By a simple device three workers out of four are evicted; what matters it that fifty years later, the population of the globe having doubled and the trade of England having quadrupled, new machines will be constructed and the English manufacturers will reemploy their workers? Do the economists mean to point to the increase of population as one of the benefits of machinery? Let them renounce, then, the theory of Malthus, and stop declaiming against the excessive fecundity of marriage.

They did not stop there: soon a new mechanical improvement enabled a single worker to do the work that formerly occupied four.

---

13   Cf. Marx: "Is it necessary to speak of the *providential* and philanthropic *end* which M. Proudhon discovers in the original invention and application of machinery?" (op. cit., 152).

A new three-fourths reduction of manual work: in all, a reduction of human labour by fifteen-sixteenths.

A Bolton manufacturer writes: "The elongation of the mules of our frames permits us to employ but twenty-six spinners where we employed thirty-five in 1837."

Another decimation of workers: one out of four is a victim.

These facts are taken from the *Revue Economique* of 1842; and there is nobody who cannot point to similar ones. I have witnessed the introduction of printing machines, and I can say that I have seen with my own eyes the evil which printers have suffered thereby. During the fifteen or twenty years that the machines have been in use a portion of the workers have gone back to composition, others have abandoned their trade, and some have died of misery: thus workers are continually crowded back in consequence of industrial innovations. Twenty years ago eighty canal-boats furnished the navigation service between Beaucaire and Lyons; a score of steam-packets has displaced them all. Certainly commerce is the gainer; but what has become of the boating-population? Has it been transferred from the boats to the packets? No: it has gone where all superseded industries go,—it has vanished.

For the rest, the following documents, which I take from the same source, will give a more positive idea of the influence of industrial improvements upon the condition of the workers.

The average weekly wages, at Manchester, is ten shillings. Out of four hundred and fifty workers there are not forty who earn twenty shillings.

The author of the article is careful to remark that an Englishman consumes five times as much as a Frenchman; this, then, is as if a French worker had to live on two francs and a half a week.

*Edinburgh Review*, 1835: "To a combination of workers (who did not want to see their wages reduced) we owe the mule of Sharpe and Roberts of Manchester; and this invention has severely punished the imprudent unionists."

Punished should merit punishment. The invention of Sharpe and Roberts of Manchester was bound to result from the situation; the refusal of the workers to submit to the reduction asked of them was only its determining occasion.[14] Might not one infer, from the air of vengeance affected by the *Edinburgh Review*, that machines have a retroactive effect?

An English manufacturer: "The insubordination of our workers has given us the idea of dispensing with them. We have made and stimulated every imaginable effort of the mind to replace the service of men by tools more docile, and we have achieved our object. Machinery has delivered capital from the oppression of labour. Wherever we still employ a man, we do so only

---

14   Cf. Marx, in *Poverty of Philosophy*, that Proudhon is unaware that "strikes have regularly given rise to invention and to the application of new machinery" as "the arms which the capitalists used to defeat revolted labour" (183). (Editor)

temporarily, pending the invention for us of some means of accomplishing his work without him."

What a system is that which leads a business man to think with delight that society will soon be able to dispense with men! Machinery has delivered capital from the oppression of labour![15] That is exactly as if the cabinet should undertake to deliver the treasury from the oppression of the taxpayers. Fool! though the workers cost you something, they are your customers: what will you do with your products, when, driven away by you, they shall consume them no longer? Thus machinery, after crushing the workers, is not slow in dealing employers a counter-blow; for, if production excludes consumption, it is soon obliged to stop itself.

During the fourth quarter of 1841 four great failures, happening in an English manufacturing city, threw seventeen hundred and twenty people on the street.

These failures were caused by over-production,—that is, by an inadequate market, or the distress of the people. What a pity that machinery cannot also deliver capital from the oppression of consumers! What a misfortune that machines do not buy the fabrics which they weave! The ideal society will be reached when commerce, agriculture, and manufactures can proceed without a man upon earth!

In a Yorkshire parish for nine months the operatives have been working but two days a week.

Machines!

At Geston two factories valued at sixty thousand pounds sterling have been sold for twenty-six thousand. They produced more than they could sell.

Machines!

In 1841 the number of children under thirteen years of age engaged in manufactures diminishes, because children over thirteen take their place.

Machines! The adult worker becomes an apprentice, a child, again: this result was foreseen from the phase of the division of labour, during which we saw the quality of the worker degenerate in the ratio in which industry was perfected.

In his conclusion the journalist makes this reflection: "Since 1836 there has been a retrograde movement in the cotton industry";—that is, it no

---

15    Cf. Marx: "It is necessary to speak of the *providential* and philanthropic *end* which M. Proudhon discovers in the original invention and application of machinery? [...] [F]rom 1825 all the new inventions were the result of conflicts between the worker and the capitalist who sought at all costs to depreciate the speciality of the workman. After each new strike, however unimportant, a new machine appeared. The workman was so far from seeing in the machines a kind of rehabilitation, of *restoration* as M. Proudhon calls it, that, in the 18th century, he for a long time resisted the nascent empire of the automation" (op. cit., 152–3). Proudhon, clearly, did not ignore the use of machinery against labour. (Editor)

longer keeps up its relation with other industries: another result foreseen from the theory of the proportionality of values.

Today workers' coalitions and strikes seem to have stopped throughout England, and the economists rightly rejoice over this return to order,—let us say even to common sense. But because workers henceforth—at least I cherish the hope—will not add the misery of their voluntary periods of idleness to the misery which machines force upon them, does it follow that the situation is changed? And if there is no change in the situation, will not the future always be a deplorable copy of the past?

The economists love to rest their minds on pictures of public felicity: it is by this sign principally that they are to be recognised, and that they estimate each other. Nevertheless there are not lacking among them, on the other hand, moody and sickly imaginations, ever ready to offset accounts of growing prosperity with proofs of persistent poverty.

[…]

But it is necessary to penetrate still farther into the antinomy. Machines promised us an increase of wealth; they have kept their word, but at the same time endowing us with an increase of poverty.[16] They promised us liberty; I am going to prove that they have brought us slavery.

I have stated that the determination of value, and with it the tribulations of society, began with the division of industries, without which there could be no exchange, or wealth, or progress. The period through which we are now passing—that of machinery—is distinguished by a special characteristic: WAGE-LABOUR.

Wage-labour stems from the use of machinery,—that is, to give my thought the entire generality of expression which it calls for, from the economic fiction by which capital becomes an agent of production. Wage-labour, in short, coming after the division of labour and exchange,[17] is the necessary correlative of the theory of the reduction of costs, in whatever way this reduction may be accomplished. This genealogy is too interesting to be passed by without a few words of explanation.

The first, the simplest, the most powerful of machines is the workshop.

Division simply separates the various parts of labour, leaving each to devote himself to the speciality best suited to his tastes: the workshop groups the workers according to the relation of each part to the whole. It is the most

---

16   Cf. Marx: "the relations of production in which the bourgeoisie exists have a double character […] wealth is produced, poverty is produced also" (op. cit., 134). (Editor)

17   The section is quoted by Marx in a mutilated form: "The period through which we are passing, that of machinery, is distinguished by a special character, it is that of the *wage worker*. The wage worker is posterior to the division of labour and exchange" (op. cit., 146). Given this, it is somewhat incredulous to see Marx lecture Proudhon that "[in proportion as the bourgeoisie develops, it develops in its bosom a new proletariat, a modern proletariat" (op. cit., 133). (Editor)

elementary form of the balance of values, undiscoverable though the economists suppose this to be. Now, through the workshop, production is going
to increase, and at the same time the deficit.

Somebody discovered that, by dividing production into its various parts
and causing each to be executed by a separate worker, he would obtain a
multiplication of power, the product of which would be far superior to the
amount of labour given by the same number of workers when labour is not
divided.

Grasping the thread of this idea, he said to himself that, by forming a
permanent group of workers assorted with a view to his special purpose,
he would produce more steadily, more abundantly, and at less cost. It is
not indispensable, however, that the workers should be gathered into one
place: the existence of the workshop does not depend essentially upon such
contact. It results from the relation and proportion of the different tasks and
from the common thought directing them. In a word, concentration at one
point may offer its advantages, which are not to be neglected; but that is not
what constitutes the workshop

This, then, is the proposition which the speculator makes to those whose
collaboration he desires: I guarantee you a perpetual market for your products, if you will accept me as purchaser or middle-man. The bargain is so
clearly advantageous that the proposition cannot fail of acceptance. The
worker finds in it steady work, a fixed price, and security; the employer, on
the other hand, will find a readier sale for his goods, since, producing more
advantageously, he can lower the price; in short, his profits will be larger
because of the mass of his investments. All, even to the public and the magistrate, will congratulate the employer on having added to the social wealth
by his combinations, and will vote him a reward.

But, in the first place, whoever says reduction of expenses says reduction
of services, not, it is true, in the new shop, but for the workers at the same
trade who are left outside, as well as for many others whose accessory services
will be less needed in future. Therefore every establishment of a workshop
corresponds to an eviction of workers: this assertion, utterly contradictory
though it may appear, is as true of the workshop as of a machine.

The economists admit it: but here they repeat their eternal refrain that,
after a lapse of time, the demand for the product having increased in proportion to the reduction of price, labour in turn will come finally to be
in greater demand than ever. Undoubtedly, WITH TIME, the equilibrium
will be restored; but, I must add again, the equilibrium will be no sooner
restored at this point than it will be disturbed at another, because the spirit
of invention never stops, any more than labour. Now, what theory could
justify these perpetual hecatombs? "When we have reduced the number of
toilers," wrote Sismondi, "to a fourth or a fifth of what it is at present, we
shall need only a fourth or a fifth as many priests, physicians, etc. When we
have cut them off altogether, we shall be in a position to dispense with the

human race." And that is what really would happen if, in order to put the labour of each machine in proportion to the needs of consumption,—that is, to restore the balance of values continually destroyed,—it were not necessary to continually create new machines, open other markets, and consequently multiply services and displace other arms. So that on the one hand industry and wealth, on the other population and misery, advance, so to speak, in procession, one always dragging the other after it.

I have shown the entrepreneur, at the birth of industry, negotiating on equal terms with his comrades, who have since become his workers. It is plain, in fact, that this original equality was bound to disappear through the advantageous position of the master and the dependence of the wage-workers. In vain does the law assure to each the right of enterprise, as well as the faculty to labour alone and sell one's products directly. According to the hypothesis, this last resource is impracticable, since it was the object of the workshop to annihilate isolated labour. And as for the right to take the plough, as they say, and go at speed, it is the same in manufactures as in agriculture; to know how to work is nothing, it is necessary to arrive at the right time; the shop, as well as the land, is to the first comer. When an establishment has had the leisure to develop itself, enlarge its foundations, ballast itself with capital, and assure itself a body of patrons, what can the worker who has only his arms do against a power so superior? Hence it was not by an arbitrary act of sovereign power or by fortuitous and brutal usurpation that the guilds and masterships were established in the Middle Ages: the force of events had created them long before the edicts of kings could have given them legal consecration; and, in spite of the reform of '89, we see them re-establishing themselves under our eyes with an energy a hundred times more formidable. Abandon labour to its own tendencies, and the subjection of three-fourths of the human race is assured.

But this is not all. The machine, or the workshop, after having degraded the worker by giving him a master, completes his degeneracy by reducing him from the rank of artisan to that of unskilled labourer.

[...]

If not misery, then degradation: such is the last alternative which machinery offers to the worker. For it is with a machine as with a piece of artillery: the captain excepted, those whom it occupies are servants, slaves.

Since the establishment of large factories, a multitude of little industries have disappeared from the domestic hearth: does anyone believe that the girls who work for ten and fifteen cents have as much intelligence as their ancestors?

"After the establishment of the railway from Paris to Saint Germain," M. Dunoyer tells us, "there were established between Pecq and a multitude of places in the more or less immediate vicinity such a number of omnibus and stage lines that this establishment, contrary to all expectation, has considerably increased the employment of horses."

Contrary to all expectation! It takes an economist not to expect these things. Multiply machinery, and you increase the amount of arduous and disagreeable labour to be done: this apothegm is as certain as any of those which date from the deluge. Accuse me, if you choose, of ill-will towards the most precious invention of our century,—nothing shall prevent me from saying that the principal result of railways, after the subjection of petty industry, will be the creation of a population of degraded workers,—signalmen, sweepers, loaders, lumpers, draymen, watchmen, porters, weighers, greasers, cleaners, stokers, firemen, etc. Two thousand miles of railway will give France an additional fifty thousand serfs: it is not for such people, certainly, that M. Chevalier asks professional schools.

Perhaps it will be said that, the mass of transportation having increased in much greater proportion than the number of day-workers, the difference is to the advantage of the railway, and that, all things considered, there is progress. The observation may even be generalised and the same argument applied to all industries.

But it is precisely out of this generality of the phenomenon that springs the subjection of workers. Machinery plays the leading role in industry, man is secondary: all the genius displayed by labour tends to the degradation of the proletariat. What a glorious nation will be ours when, among forty million inhabitants, it shall count thirty-five million drudges, paper-scratchers, and flunkies!

With machinery and the workshop, divine right—that is, the principle of authority—makes its entrance into political economy. Capital, Mastership, Privilege, Monopoly, Loaning, Credit, Property, etc.,—such are, in economic language, the various names of I know not what, but which is otherwise called Power, Authority, Sovereignty, Written Law, Revelation, Religion, God in short, cause and principle of all our miseries and all our crimes, and who, the more we try to define him, the more eludes us.

Is it, then, impossible that, in the present condition of society, the workshop with its hierarchical organisation, and machinery, instead of serving exclusively the interests of the least numerous, the least industrious, and the wealthiest class, should be employed for the benefit of all?

That is what we are going to examine.

### §III OF PRESERVATIVES AGAINST THE DISASTROUS INFLUENCE OF MACHINERY

Reduction of manual labour is synonymous with lowering of price, and, consequently, with increase of exchange, since, if the consumer pays less, he will buy more.

But reduction of manual labour is synonymous also with restriction of market, since, if the producer earns less, he will buy less. And this is the course that things actually take. The concentration of forces in the workshop and the intervention of capital in production, under the name of machinery, engender at the same time overproduction and destitution; and everybody has witnessed these two scourges, more to be feared than incendiarism and plague, develop in our day on the vastest scale and with devouring intensity. Nevertheless it is impossible for us to retreat:[18] it is necessary to produce, produce always, produce cheaply; otherwise, the existence of society is compromised. The worker, who, to escape the degradation with which the principle of division threatened him, had created so many marvellous machines, now finds himself either prohibited or subjugated by his own works. Against this alternative what means are proposed?

M. de Sismondi, like all men of patriarchal ideas, would like the division of labour, with machinery and manufactures, to be abandoned, and each family to return to the system of primitive indivision,—that is, *to each one by himself, each one for himself,* in the most literal meaning of the words. That would be to retrograde; it is impossible.[19]

M. Blanqui returns to the charge with his plan of participation by the worker, and of consolidation of all industries in a joint-stock company for the benefit of the collective worker. I have shown that this plan would impair public welfare without appreciably improving the condition of the workers; and M. Blanqui himself seems to share this sentiment. How reconcile, in fact, this participation of the worker in the profits with the rights of inventors, entrepreneurs, and capitalists, of whom the first have to reimburse themselves for large outlays, as well as for their long and patient efforts; the second continually endanger the wealth they have acquired, and take upon themselves alone the chances of their enterprises, which are often very hazardous; and the third could sustain no reduction of their dividends without in some way losing their savings? How harmonise, in a word, the equality desirable to establish between workers and employers with the preponderance which cannot be taken from heads of establishments, from loaners of capital, and from inventors, and which involves so clearly their exclusive appropriation of the profits? To decree by a law the admission of all workers to a share of the profits would be to pronounce the dissolution of society: all the economists have seen this so clearly that they have finally changed into an exhortation to employers what had first occurred to them as a project. Now, as long as the wage-worker gets no profit save what may be allowed him by

---

18   Cf. Marx: "M. Proudhon has not got beyond the ideal of the petty bourgeois. And in order to realise this ideal he thinks of nothing better than to bring us back to the companion, or at most the master, workman of the Middle Ages" (op. cit., 157). (Editor)

19   Proudhon's outright rejection of returning to pre-industrial production methods did not stop Marx, nor countless Marxists, suggesting he sought a similar return to the past. Cf. Marx: "Those who, like Sismondi, would return to the just proportion of production, while conserving the existing bases of society, are reactionary, since, to be consistent, they must also desire to re-establish all the other conditions of past times" (op. cit., 73). (Editor)

the entrepreneur, it is perfectly safe to assume that eternal poverty will be his lot: it is not in the power of the holders of labour to make it otherwise.

[...]

Whatever the pace of mechanical progress; though machines should be invented a hundred times more marvellous than the mule-jenny, the knitting-machine, or the cylinder press; though forces should be discovered a hundred times more powerful than steam,—very far from freeing humanity, securing its leisure, and making the production of everything gratuitous, these things would have no other effect than to multiply labour, induce an increase of population, make the chains of serfdom heavier, render life more and more expensive, and deepen the abyss which separates the class that commands and enjoys from the class that obeys and suffers.[20]

[...]

# CHAPTER V
## THIRD PERIOD—COMPETITION

BETWEEN THE HUNDRED-HEADED hydra, division of labour, and the unconquered dragon, machinery, what will become of humanity? A prophet has said it more than two thousand years ago: Satan looks on his victim, and the fires of war are kindled, *Aspexit gentes, et dissolvit.* To save us from two scourges, famine and pestilence, Providence sends us discord.

Competition represents that philosophical era in which, a semi-understanding of the antinomies of reason having given birth to the art of sophistry, the characteristics of the false and the true were confounded, and in which, instead of doctrines, they had nothing but deceptive mental tilts. Thus the industrial movement faithfully reproduces the metaphysical movement; the history of social economy is to be found entire in the writings of the philosophers. Let us study this interesting phase, whose most striking characteristic is to take away the judgement of those who believe as well as those who protest.

### §I NECESSITY OF COMPETITION
[...]

Is it not immediately and intuitively evident that COMPETITION DESTROYS COMPETITION? Is there a theorem in geometry more certain, more peremptory, than that? How then, upon what conditions, in what

---

20   Cf. Marx: "In short, by the introduction of machinery the division of labour within society has been developed, the task of the workman within the factory has been simplified, capital has been accumulated, and man has been further dismembered" (op. cit., 153). (Editor)

196 Pierre-Joseph Proudhon

sense, can a principle which is its own denial enter into science? How can it become an organic law of society? If competition is necessary; if, as the school says, it is a postulate of production,—how does it become so devastating in its effects? And if its most certain effect is to ruin those whom it incites, how does it become useful? For the inconveniences which follow in its train, like the good which it procures, are not accidents arising from the work of man: both follow logically from the principle, and subsist by the same title and face to face.

And, in the first place, competition is as essential to labour as division, since it is division itself returning in another form, or rather, raised to its second power; division, I say, no longer, as in the first period of economic evolution, adequate to collective force, and consequently absorbing the personality of the worker in the workshop, but giving birth to liberty by making each subdivision of labour a sort of sovereignty in which man stands in all his power and independence. Competition, in a word, is liberty in division and in all the divided parts: beginning with the most comprehensive functions, it tends toward its realisation even in the inferior operations of *parcellaire* labour.

[...]

Competition is necessary to the constitution of value,—that is, to the very principle of distribution, and consequently to the advent of equality. As long as a product is supplied only by a single manufacturer, its real value remains a mystery, either through the producer's misrepresentation or through his neglect or inability to reduce the cost of production to its extreme limit. Thus the privilege of production is a real loss to society, and publicity of industry, like competition between workers, a necessity. All the utopias ever imagined or imaginable cannot escape this law.[21]

Certainly I do not care to deny that labour and wages can and should be guaranteed; I even entertain the hope that the time of such guarantee is not far off: but I maintain that a guarantee of wages is impossible without an exact knowledge of value, and that this value can be discovered only by competition, not at all by communistic institutions or by popular decree. For in this there is something more powerful than the will of the legislator and of citizens,—namely, the absolute impossibility that man should do his duty after finding himself relieved of all responsibility to himself: now, responsibility to self, in the matter of labour, necessarily implies competition with others. Ordain that, beginning January 1st, 1847, labour and wages are guaranteed to all: immediately an immense relaxation will succeed the

---

21  Cf. Marx: "It is important to insist upon this point, that what determines value is not the time in which a thing has been produced, but the minimum time in which it is susceptible of being produced, and this minimum is demonstrated by competition" (op. cit., 70–1). Proudhon clearly was aware of the need for competition to determine value. (Editor)

extreme tension to which industry is now subjected; real value will fall rapidly below nominal value; metallic money, in spite of its effigy and stamp,
will experience the fate of the assignats; the merchant will ask more and give
less; and we shall find ourselves in a still lower circle in the hell of misery in
which competition is only the third turn.

Even were I to admit, with some socialists, that the attractiveness of labour may some day serve as food for emulation without any hidden thought
of profit, of what utility could this utopia be in the phase which we are
studying? We are yet only in the third period of economic evolution, in the
third age of the constitution of labour,—that is, in a period when it is impossible for labour to be attractive. For the attractiveness of labour can result
only from a high degree of physical, moral, and intellectual development
of the worker. Now, this development itself, this education of humanity by
industry, is precisely the object of which we are in pursuit through the contradictions of social economy. How, then, could the attractiveness of labour
serve us as a principle and lever, when it is still our object and our end?

[...]

In proof of the industrial capacity of the State, and consequently of the
possibility of abolishing competition altogether, they cite the administration
of the tobacco industry. There, they [the communists] say, is no adultera-
tion, no litigation, no bankruptcy, no misery. The condition of the workers,
adequately paid, instructed, sermonised, moralised, and assured of a retiring
pension accumulated by their savings, is incomparably superior to that of the
immense majority of workers engaged in free industry.

All this may be true: for my part, I am ignorant on the subject. I know
nothing of what goes on in the administration of the tobacco factories; I
have procured no information either from the directors or the workers, and I
have no need of any. How much does the tobacco sold by the administration
cost? How much is it worth? You can answer the first of these questions: you
only need to call at the first tobacco shop you see. But you can tell me nothing about the second, because you have no standard of comparison and are
forbidden to verify by experiment the items of cost of administration, which
it is consequently impossible to accept. Therefore the tobacco business, made
into a monopoly, necessarily costs society more than it brings in; it is an
industry which, instead of subsisting by its own product, lives by subsidies,
and which consequently, far from furnishing us a model, is one of the first
abuses which reform should strike down.

And when I speak of the reform to be introduced in the production of
tobacco, I do not refer simply to the enormous tax which triples or quadru-
ples the value of this product; neither do I refer to the hierarchical organisation of its employees, some of whom by their salaries are made aristocrats as
expensive as they are useless, while others, hopeless receivers of petty wages,
are kept forever in the situation of subalterns. I do not even speak of the
privilege of the tobacco shops and the whole world of parasites which they

198 Pierre-Joseph Proudhon

support: I have particularly in view the useful labour, the labour of the workers. From the very fact that the administration's worker has no competitors and is interested neither in profit nor loss, from the fact that he is not free, in a word, his product is necessarily less, and his service too expensive. This being so, let them say that the government treats its employees well and looks out for their comfort: what wonder? Why do not people see that liberty bears the burdens of privilege, and that, if, by some impossibility, all industries were to be treated like the tobacco industry, the source of subsidies failing, the nation could no longer balance its receipts and its expenses, and the State would become a bankrupt?

[...]

Therefore competition, analysed in its principle, is an inspiration of justice; and yet we shall see that competition, in its results, is unjust.

### §II SUBVERSIVE EFFECTS OF COMPETITION, AND THE DESTRUCTION OF LIBERTY THEREBY

The kingdom of heaven suffereth violence, says the Gospel, and the violent take it by force. These words are the allegory of society. In society regulated by labour, dignity, wealth, and glory are objects of competition; they are the reward of the strong, and competition may be defined as the regime of force. The old economists did not at first perceive this contradiction: the moderns have been forced to recognise it.

"To elevate a State from the lowest degree of barbarism to the highest degree of opulence," wrote A. Smith, "but three things are necessary,—peace, moderate taxes, and a tolerable administration of justice. All the rest is brought about by the natural course of things."

On which the last translator of Smith, M. Blanqui, lets fall this gloomy comment:

"We have seen the natural course of things produce disastrous effects, and create anarchy in production, war for markets, and piracy in competition. The division of labour and the perfecting of machinery, which should realise for the great working family of the human race the conquest of a certain amount of leisure to the advantage of its dignity, have produced at many points nothing but degradation and misery..... When A. Smith wrote, liberty had not yet come with its embarrassments and its abuses, and the Glasgow professor foresaw only its blessings... Smith would have written like M. de Sismondi, if he had been a witness of the sad condition of Ireland and the manufacturing districts of England in the times in which we live."

Now then, litterateurs, statesmen, daily publicists, believers and half-believers, all you who have taken upon yourselves the mission of indoctrinating men, do you hear these words which one would take for a translation from Jeremiah? Will you tell us at last to what end you pretend to be conducting civilisation? What advice do you offer to society, to the country, in alarm?

But to whom do I speak? Ministers, journalists, sextons, and pedants! Do such people trouble themselves about the problems of social economy? Have they ever heard of competition?

[...]

Competition, with its homicidal instinct, takes away the bread of a whole class of workers, and sees in it only an improvement, a saving; it steals a secret in a cowardly manner, and glories in it as a discovery; it changes the natural zones of production to the detriment of an entire people, and pretends to have done nothing but utilise the advantages of its climate. Competition overturns all notions of equity and justice; it increases the real cost of production by needlessly multiplying the capital invested, causes by turns the dearness of products and their depreciation, corrupts the public conscience by putting chance in the place of right, and maintains terror and distrust everywhere.

But what! Without this atrocious characteristic, competition would lose its happiest effects; without the arbitrary element in exchange and the panics of the market, labour would not continually build factory against factory, and, not being maintained in such good working order, production would realise none of its marvels. After having caused evil to arise from the very utility of its principle, competition again finds a way to extract good from evil; destruction engenders utility, equilibrium is realised by agitation, and it may be said of competition, as Samson said of the lion which he had slain: *De comedente cibus exiit, et de forti dulcedo.* Is there anything, in all the spheres of human knowledge, more surprising than political economy?

Let us take care, nevertheless, not to yield to an impulse of irony, which would be on our part only unjust invective. It is characteristic of economic science to find its certainty in its contradictions, and the whole error of the economists consists in not having understood this. Nothing poorer than their criticism, nothing more saddening than their mental confusion, as soon as they touch this question of competition: one would say that they were witnesses forced by torture to confess what their conscience would like to conceal. The reader will take it kindly if I put before his eyes the arguments for laissez-passer, introducing him, so to speak, into the presence of a secret meeting of economists.

M. Dunoyer opens the discussion.

Of all the economists M. Dunoyer has most energetically embraced the positive side of competition, and consequently, as might have been expected, most ineffectually grasped the negative side. M. Dunoyer, with whom nothing can be done when what he calls principles are under discussion, is very far from believing that in matters of political economy yes and no may be true at the same moment and to the same extent; let it be said even to his credit, such a conception is the more repugnant to him because of the frankness and honesty with which he holds his doctrines. What would I not give to gain an entrance into this pure but so obstinate soul for this truth as certain to me as the existence of the sun,—that all the categories of political economy are contradictions! Instead of uselessly exhausting himself in reconciling practice and theory; instead of contenting himself with the ridiculous excuse that everything here below has its advantages and its inconveniences,—M. Dunoyer would seek the synthetic idea which solves all the antinomies, and, instead of the paradoxical conservative which he now is, he would become with us an inexorable and logical revolutionist.

"If competition is a false principle," says M. Dunoyer, "it follows that for two thousand years humanity has been pursuing the wrong road."

No, what you say does not follow, and your prejudicial remark is refuted by the very theory of progress. Humanity posits its principles by turns, and sometimes at long intervals: never does it give them up in substance, although it destroys successively their expressions and formulas. This destruction is called negation; because the general reason, ever progressive, continually denies the completeness and sufficiency of its prior ideas. Thus it is that, competition being one of the periods in the constitution of value, one of the elements of the social synthesis, it is true to say at the same time that it is indestructible in its principle, and that nevertheless in its present form it should be abolished, denied.[22] If, then, there is anyone here who is in opposition to history, it is you.

"I have several remarks to make upon the accusations of which competition has been the object. The first is that this regime, good or bad, ruinous or fruitful, does not really exist as yet; that it is established nowhere except in a partial and most incomplete manner."

This first observation has no sense. Competition kills competition, as we said at the outset; this aphorism may be taken for a definition. How, then, could competition ever be complete? Moreover, though it should be admitted that competition does not yet exist in its integrity, that would simply prove that competition does not act with all the power of elimination that there is in it; but that will not change at all its contradictory nature. What need have we to wait thirty centuries longer to find out that, the more competition develops, the more it tends to reduce the number of competitors?

"The second is that the picture drawn of it is unfaithful; and that sufficient heed is not paid to the extension which the general welfare has undergone, including even that of the labouring classes."

If some socialists fail to recognise the useful side of competition, you on your side make no mention of its pernicious effects. The testimony of your opponents coming to complete your own, competition is shown in the fullest light, and from a double falsehood we get the truth as a result. As for the

---

22  Cf. Marx: "Since competition was established in France, in the eighteenth century, as a consequence of historical needs, [Proudhon thinks] this competition must not be destroyed in the nineteenth century in consequence of other historical needs" (op. cit., 161). (Editor)

gravity of the evil, we shall see directly what to think about that.

"The third is that the evil experienced by the labouring classes is not referred to its real causes."

If there are other causes of poverty than competition, does that prevent it from contributing its share? Though only one manufacturer a year were ruined by competition, if it were admitted that this ruin is the necessary effect of the principle, competition, as a principle, would have to be rejected.

"The fourth is that the principal means proposed for obviating it would be inexpedient in the extreme."

Possibly: but from this I conclude that the inadequacy of the remedies proposed imposes a new duty upon you,—precisely that of seeking the most expedient means of preventing the evil of competition.

"The fifth, finally, is that the real remedies, in so far as it is possible to remedy the evil by legislation, would be found precisely in the regime which is accused of having produced it,—that is, in a more and more real regime of liberty and competition."

Well! I am willing. The remedy for competition, in your opinion, is to make competition universal. But, in order that competition may be universal, it is necessary to procure for all the means of competing; it is necessary to destroy or modify the predominance of capital over labour, to change the relations between employer and worker, to solve, in a word, the antinomy of division and that of machinery; it is necessary to ORGANISE LABOUR: can you give this solution?[23]

[...]

In theory we have demonstrated that competition, on its useful side, should be universal and carried to its maximum of intensity; but that, viewed on its negative side, it must be everywhere stifled, even to the last vestige. Are the economists in a position to effect this elimination? Have they foreseen the consequences, calculated the difficulties? If the answer should be affirmative, I should have the boldness to propose the following case to them for solution.

---

23  Cf. Marx: "The economic categories are only the theoretical expressions, the abstractions, of the social relations of production. M. Proudhon, as a true philosopher, taking the things inside out, sees in the real relations only the incarnations of these principles, of these categories, which sleep—M. Proudhon the philosopher tells us again—in the bosom of 'the impersonal reason of humanity.' [...] [W]hat he has not understood is that these determined social relations [...] are intimately attached to the productive forces. [...] Thus these ideas, these categories, are not more eternal than the relations which they express. They are *historical and transitory products*" (op. cit., 119). See also Proudhon's marginal comments in his copy of *The Poverty of Philosophy*: "Have I ever said that principles are anything other than the intellectual representation, not the generative cause, of facts?" (Proudhon, *Œuvres Complètes*, Rivière ed., I: 418). (Editor)

A treaty of coalition, or rather of association,—for the courts would be greatly embarrassed to define either term,—has just united in one company all the coal mines in the basin of the Loire. On complaint of the municipalities of Lyons and Saint Etienne, the ministry has appointed a commission charged with examining the character and tendencies of this frightful society. Well, I ask, what can the intervention of power, with the assistance of civil law and political economy, accomplish here?

They cry out against coalition. But can the proprietors of mines be prevented from associating, from reducing their general expenses and costs of exploitation, and from working their mines to better advantage by a more perfect understanding with each other? Shall they be ordered to begin their old war over again, and ruin themselves by increased expenses, waste, overproduction, disorder, and decreased prices? All that is absurd.

Shall they be prevented from increasing their prices so as to recover the interest on their capital? Then let them be protected themselves against any demands for increased wages on the part of the workers; let the law concerning joint-stock companies be re-enacted; let the sale of shares be prohibited; and when all these measures shall have been taken, as the capitalist-proprietors of the basin cannot justly be forced to lose capital invested under a different condition of things, let them be indemnified.

Shall a tariff be imposed upon them? That would be a law of maximum. The State would then have to put itself in the place of the exploiters; keep the accounts of their capital, interest, and office expenses; regulate the wages of the miners, the salaries of the engineers and directors, the price of the wood employed in the extraction of the coal, the expenditure for material; and, finally, determine the normal and legitimate rate of profit. All this cannot be done by ministerial decree: a law is necessary. Will the legislator dare, for the sake of a special industry, to change the public law of the French, and put power in the place of property? Then of two things one: either commerce in coals will fall into the hands of the State, or else the State must find some means of reconciling liberty and order in carrying on the mining industry, in which case the socialists will ask that what has been executed at one point be imitated at all points.

The coalition of the Loire mines has posited the social question in terms which permit no more evasion. Either competition,—that is, monopoly and what follows; or exploitation by the State,—that is, dearness of labour and continuous impoverishment; or else, in short, a solution based upon equality,—in other words, the organisation of labour, which involves the negation of political economy and the end of property.

[...]

## §III REMEDIES AGAINST COMPETITION

Can competition in labour be abolished?

It would be as well worth while to ask if personality, liberty, individual responsibility can be suppressed.

Competition, in fact, is the expression of collective activity; just as wages, considered in its highest acceptation, is the expression of the merit and demerit, in a word, the responsibility, of the worker. It is vain to declaim and revolt against these two essential forms of liberty and discipline in labour. Without a theory of wages there is no distribution, no justice; without an organisation of competition there is no social guarantee, consequently no solidarity.

The socialists have confounded two essentially distinct things when, contrasting the union of the domestic hearth with industrial competition, they have asked themselves if society could not be constituted precisely like a great family all of whose members would be bound by ties of blood, and not as a sort of coalition in which each is held back by the law of his own interests.

The family is not, if I may venture to so speak, the type, the organic molecule, of society. In the family, as M. de Bonald has very well observed, there exists but one moral being, one mind, one soul, I had almost said, with the Bible, one flesh. The family is the type and the cradle of monarchy and the patriciate: in it resides and is preserved the idea of authority and sovereignty, which is being obliterated more and more in the State. It was on the model of the family that all the ancient and feudal societies were organised, and it is precisely against this old patriarchal constitution that modern democracy protests and revolts.

The constitutive unit of society is the workshop.

Now, the workshop necessarily implies an interest as a body and private interests, a collective person and individuals. Hence a system of relations unknown in the family, among which the opposition of the collective will, represented by the *employer*, and individual wills, represented by the *wage-workers*, figures in the front rank. Then come the relations from shop to shop, from capital to capital,—in other words, competition and association. For competition and association are supported by each other; they do not exist independently; very far from excluding each other, they are not even divergent. Whoever says competition already supposes a common object; competition, then, is not egoism, and the most deplorable error of socialism consists in having regarded it as the subversion of society.

Therefore there can be no question here of destroying competition, as impossible as to destroy liberty; the problem is to find its equilibrium, I would willingly say its police. For every force, every form of spontaneity, whether individual or collective, must receive its determination: in this respect it is the same with competition as with intelligence and liberty. How, then, will competition be harmoniously determined in society?

We have heard the reply of M. Dunoyer, speaking for political economy: Competition must be determined by itself. In other words, according to M. Dunoyer and all the economists, the remedy for the inconveniences of competition is more competition; and, since political economy is the theory of property, of the absolute right of use and abuse, it is clear that political economy has no other answer to make. Now, this is as if it should be pretended that the education of liberty is effected by liberty, the instruction of the mind by the mind, the determination of value by value, all of which propositions are evidently tautological and absurd.

And, in fact, to confine ourselves to the subject under discussion, it is obvious that competition, practised for itself and with no other object than to maintain a vague and discordant independence, can end in nothing, and that its oscillations are eternal. In competition the struggling elements are capital, machinery, processes, talent, and experience,—that is, capital again; victory is assured to the heaviest battalions. If, then, competition is practised only to the advantage of private interests, and if its social effects have been neither determined by science nor reserved by the State, there will be in competition, as in democracy, a continual tendency from civil war to oligarchy, from oligarchy to despotism, and then dissolution and return to civil war, without end and without rest. That is why competition, abandoned to itself, can never arrive at its own constitution: like value, it needs a superior principle to socialise and define it. These facts are henceforth well enough established to warrant us in considering them above criticism, and to excuse us from returning to them. Political economy, so far as the police of competition is concerned, having no means but competition itself, and unable to have any other, is shown to be powerless.

It remains now to inquire what solution socialism contemplates. A single example will give the measure of its means, and will permit us to come to general conclusions regarding it.

Of all modern socialists M. Louis Blanc, perhaps, by his remarkable talent, has been most successful in calling public attention to his writings. In his *Organisation of Labour*, after having traced back the problem of association to a single point, competition, he unhesitatingly pronounces in favour of its abolition. From this we may judge to what an extent this writer, generally so cautious, is deceived as to the value of political economy and the range of socialism. On the one hand, M. Blanc, receiving his ideas ready made from I know not what source, giving everything to his century and nothing to history, rejects absolutely, in substance and in form, political economy, and deprives himself of the very materials of organisation; on the other, he attributes to tendencies revived from all past epochs, which he takes for new, a reality which they do not possess, and misconceives the nature of socialism, which is exclusively critical. M. Blanc, therefore, has given us the spectacle of a vivid imagination ready to confront an impossibility; he has believed in the divination of genius; but he must have perceived that science does not improvise itself, and that, be one's name Adolphe Boyer, Louis Blanc, or J.-J. Rousseau, provided there is nothing in experience, there is nothing in the mind.

M. Blanc begins with this declaration:

"We cannot understand those who have imagined I know not what mysterious coupling of two opposite principles. To graft association upon competition is a poor idea: it is to substitute hermaphrodites for eunuchs."

These three lines M. Blanc will always have reason to regret. They prove that, when he published the fourth edition of his book, he was as little advanced in logic as in political economy, and that he reasoned about both as a blind man would reason about colours. Hermaphrodism, in politics, consists precisely in exclusion, because exclusion always restores, in some form or other and in the same degree, the idea excluded; and M. Blanc would be greatly surprised were he to be shown, by his continual mixture in his book of the most contrary principles,—authority and right, property and communism, aristocracy and equality, labour and capital, reward and sacrifice, liberty and dictatorship, free inquiry and religious faith,—that the real hermaphrodite, the double-sexed publicist, is himself. M. Blanc, placed on the borders of democracy and socialism, one degree lower than the Republic, two degrees beneath M. Barrot, three beneath M. Thiers, is also, whatever he may say and whatever he may do, a descendant through four generations from M. Guizot, a doctrinaire.

"Certainly," cries M. Blanc, "we are not of those who anathematise the principle of authority. This principle we have a thousand times had occasion to defend against attacks as dangerous as absurd. We know that, when organised force exists nowhere in a society, despotism exists everywhere."

Thus, according to M. Blanc, the remedy for competition, or rather, the means of abolishing it, consists in the intervention of authority, in the substitution of the State for individual liberty: it is the inverse of the system of the economists.

I should dislike to have M. Blanc, whose social tendencies are well known, accuse me of making impolitic war upon him in refuting him. I do justice to M. Blanc's generous intentions; I love and I read his works, and I am especially thankful to him for the service he has rendered in revealing, in his *History of Ten Years*, the hopeless poverty of his party. But no one can consent to seem a dupe or an imbecile: now, putting personality entirely aside, what can there be in common between socialism, that universal protest, and the hotchpotch of old prejudices which make up M. Blanc's republic? M. Blanc is never tired of appealing to authority, and socialism loudly declares itself anarchistic; M. Blanc places power above society, and socialism tends to subordinate it to society; M. Blanc makes social life descend from above, and socialism maintains that it springs up and grows from below; M. Blanc runs after politics, and socialism is in quest of science. No more hypocrisy, let me say to M. Blanc: you desire neither Catholicism nor monarchy nor nobility, but you must have a God, a religion, a dictatorship, a censorship, a hierarchy, distinctions, and ranks. For my part, I deny your God, your authority, your sovereignty, your judicial State, and all your representative mystifications; I want neither Robespierre's censer nor Marat's rod; and, rather than submit to your androgynous democracy, I would support the status quo. For sixteen years your party has resisted progress and blocked opinion; for sixteen years it has shown its despotic origin by following in the wake of power at the extremity of the left centre: it is time for it to abdicate or undergo a metamorphosis. Implacable theorists of authority, what then do you propose which the government upon which you make war cannot accomplish in a fashion more tolerable than yours?

M. Blanc's SYSTEM may be summarised in three points:

1. *To give power a great force of initiative,—that is, in plain English, to make absolutism omnipotent in order to realise a utopia.*
2. *To establish public workshops, and supply them with capital, at the State's expense.*
3. *To extinguish private industry by the competition of national industry.*

And that is all.

Has M. Blanc touched the problem of value, which involves in itself alone all others? He does not even suspect its existence. Has he given a theory of distribution? No. Has he solved the antinomy of the division of labour, perpetual cause of the worker's ignorance, immorality, and poverty? No. Has he caused the contradiction of machinery and wage-labour to disappear, and reconciled the rights of association with those of liberty? On the contrary, M. Blanc consecrates this contradiction. Under the despotic protection of the State, he admits in principle the inequality of ranks and wages, adding thereto, as compensation, the ballot. Are not workers who vote their regulations and elect their leaders free? It may very likely happen that these voting workers will admit no command or difference of pay among them: then, as nothing will have been provided for the satisfaction of industrial capacities, while maintaining political equality, dissolution will penetrate into the workshop, and, in the absence of police intervention, each will return to his own affairs. These fears seem to M. Blanc neither serious nor well-founded: he awaits the test calmly, very sure that society will not go out of his way to contradict him.

[...]

To sum up:

Competition, as an economic position or phase, considered in its origin, is the necessary result of the intervention of machinery, of the establishment of the workshop, and of the theory of reduction of general costs; considered in its own significance and in its tendency, it is the mode by which collective activity manifests and exercises itself, the expression of social spontaneity, the emblem of democracy and equality, the most energetic instrument for the constitution of value, the support of association. As the essay of individual forces, it is the guarantee of their liberty, the first moment of their harmony, the form of responsibility which unites them all and makes them interdependent [*solidaires*].

But competition abandoned to itself and deprived of the direction of a superior and efficacious principle is only a vague movement, an endless oscillation of industrial power, eternally tossed about between those two equally disastrous extremes,—on the one hand, corporations and patronage, to which we have seen the workshop give birth, and, on the other, monopoly, which will be discussed in the following chapter.

Socialism, while protesting, and with reason, against this anarchical competition, has as yet proposed nothing satisfactory for its regulation, as is proved by the fact that we meet everywhere, in the utopias which have seen the light, the determination or socialisation of value abandoned to arbitrary control, and all reforms ending, now in hierarchical corporation, now in State monopoly, or the tyranny of community [*communauté*].

# CHAPTER VI
## FOURTH PERIOD—MONOPOLY

*Monopoly*, THE EXCLUSIVE commerce, exploitation, or enjoyment of a thing.

Monopoly is the natural opposite of competition. This simple observation suffices, as we have remarked, to overthrow the utopias based upon the idea of abolishing competition, as if its contrary were association and fraternity. Competition is the vital force which animates the collective being: to destroy it, if such a supposition were possible, would be to kill society.

But, the moment we admit competition as a necessity, it implies the idea of monopoly, since monopoly is, as it were, the seat of each competing individuality. Accordingly the economists have demonstrated—and M. Rossi has formally admitted it—that monopoly is the form of social possession, outside of which there is no labour, no product, no exchange, no wealth. Every landed possession is a monopoly; every industrial utopia tends to establish itself as a monopoly; and the same must be said of other functions not included in these two categories.

Monopoly in itself, then, does not carry the idea of injustice; in fact, there is something in it which, pertaining to society as well as to man, legitimates it: that is the positive side of the principle which we are about to examine.

But monopoly, like competition, becomes anti-social and disastrous: how does this happen? By abuse, reply the economists. And it is to defining and repressing the abuses of monopoly that the magistrates apply themselves; it is in denouncing them that the new school of economists glories.

We shall show that the so-called abuses of monopoly are only the effects of the development, in a negative sense, of legal monopoly; that they cannot be separated from their principle without ruining this principle; consequently, that they are inaccessible to the law, and that all repression in this direction is arbitrary and unjust. So that monopoly, the constitutive principle of society and the condition of wealth, is at the same time and in the same degree a principle of spoliation and pauperism; that, the more good it is made to produce, the more evil is received from it; that without it progress comes to a standstill, and that with it labour becomes stationary and civilisation disappears.

## §1 NECESSITY OF MONOPOLY

Thus monopoly is the inevitable end of competition, which engenders it by a continual denial of itself: this generation of monopoly is already its justification. For, since competition is inherent in society as motion is in living beings, monopoly which comes in its train, which is its object and its end, and without which competition would not have been accepted,—monopoly is and will remain legitimate as long as competition, as long as mechanical processes and industrial combinations, as long, in fact, as the division of labour and the constitution of values shall be necessities and laws.

Therefore by the single fact of its logical generation monopoly is justified. Nevertheless this justification would seem of little force and would end only in a more energetic rejection of competition than ever, if monopoly could not in turn posit itself by itself and as a principle.

In the preceding chapters we have seen that division of labour is the specification of the worker considered especially as intelligence; that the creation of machinery and the organisation of the workshop express his liberty; and that, by competition, man, or intelligent liberty, enters into action. Now, monopoly is the expression of victorious liberty, the prize of the struggle, the glorification of genius; it is the strongest stimulant of all the steps in progress taken since the beginning of the world: so true is this that, as we said just now, society, which cannot exist with it, would not have been formed without it.

Where, then, does monopoly get this singular virtue, which the etymology of the word and the vulgar aspect of the thing would never lead us to suspect?

Monopoly is at bottom simply the autocracy of man over himself: it is the dictatorial right accorded by nature to every producer of using his faculties as he pleases, of giving free play to his thought in whatever direction it prefers, of speculating, in such speciality as he may please to choose, with all the power of his resources, of disposing sovereignly of the instruments which he has created and of the capital accumulated by his economy for any enterprise the risks of which he may see fit to accept on the express condition of enjoying alone the fruits of his discovery and the profits of his venture.

This right belongs so thoroughly to the essence of liberty that to deny it is to mutilate man in his body, in his soul, and in the exercise of his faculties, and society, which progresses only by the free initiative of individuals, soon lacking explorers, finds itself arrested in its onward march.

[...]

What, then, is this reality, known to all peoples, and nevertheless still so badly defined, which is called interest or the price of a loan, and which gives rise to the fiction of the productivity of capital?

Everybody knows that an entrepreneur, when he calculates his costs of production, generally divides them into three classes: 1, the values consumed and services paid for; 2, his personal salary; 3, recovery of his capital with interest. From this last class of costs is born the distinction between entrepreneur and capitalist, although these two titles always express but one faculty, monopoly.

Thus an industrial enterprise which yields only interest on capital and nothing for net product, is an insignificant enterprise, which results only in a transformation of values without adding anything to wealth,—an enterprise, in short, which has no further reason for existence and is immediately abandoned. Why is it, then, that this interest on capital is not regarded as a sufficient supplement of net product? Why is it not itself the net product?

Here again the philosophy of the economists is wanting. To defend usury they have pretended that capital was productive, and they have changed a metaphor into a reality. The anti-proprietary socialists have had no difficulty in overturning their sophistry; and through this controversy the theory of capital has fallen into such disfavour that today, in the minds of the people, *capitalist* and *idler* are synonymous terms. Certainly it is not my intention to retract what I myself have maintained after so many others, or to rehabilitate a class of citizens which so strangely misconceives its duties: but the interests of science and of the proletariat itself oblige me to complete my first assertions and maintain true principles.

[...]

If an entrepreneur is his own capitalist, it may happen that he will content himself with a profit equal to the interest on his investment: but in that case it is certain that his industry is no longer making progress and consequently is suffering. This we see when the capitalist is distinct from the entrepreneur: for then, after the interest is paid, the manufacturer's profit is absolutely nothing; his industry becomes a perpetual peril to him, from which it is important that he should free himself as soon as possible. For as society's comfort must develop in an indefinite progression, so the law of the producer is that he should continually realise a surplus: otherwise his existence is precarious, monotonous, fatiguing. The interest due to the capitalist by the producer therefore is like the lash of the planter cracking over the head of the sleeping slave; it is the voice of progress crying: "On, on! Toil, toil!" Man's destiny pushes him to happiness: that is why it denies him rest.

[...]

I have proved, and better, I imagine, than it has ever been proved before:

That monopoly is necessary, since it is the antagonism of competition;

That it is essential to society, since without it society would never have emerged from the primeval forests and without it would rapidly go backwards;

Finally, that it is the crown of the producer, when, whether by net product or by interest on the capital which he devotes to production, it brings to the monopolist that increase of comfort which his foresight and his efforts deserve.

Shall we, then, with the economists, glorify monopoly, and consecrate it to the benefit of well-secured conservatives? I am willing, provided they in turn will admit my claims in what is to follow, as I have admitted theirs in what has preceded.

## §II THE DISASTERS IN LABOUR AND THE PERVERSION OF IDEAS CAUSED BY MONOPOLY

Like competition, monopoly implies a contradiction in its name and its definition. In fact, since consumption and production are identical things in society, and since selling is synonymous with buying, whoever says privilege of sale or exploitation necessarily says privilege of consumption and purchase: which ends in the denial of both. Hence a prohibition of consumption as well as of production laid by monopoly upon the wage-workers. Competition was civil war, monopoly is the massacre of the prisoners.

[...]

But the distressing feature in the spectacle of monopoly's effects is the sight of the unfortunate workers blaming each other for their misery and imagining that by uniting and supporting each other they will prevent the reduction of wages. "The Irish," says an observer, "have given a disastrous lesson to the working classes of Great Britain... They have taught our workers the fatal secret of confining their needs to the maintenance of animal life alone, and of contenting themselves, like savages, with the minimum of the means of subsistence sufficient to prolong life... Instructed by this fatal example, yielding partly to necessity, the working classes have lost that laudable pride which led them to furnish their houses properly and to multiply about them the decent conveniences which contribute to happiness."

I have never read anything more afflicting and more stupid. And what would you have these workers do? The Irish came: should they have been massacred? Wages were reduced: should death have been accepted in their stead? Necessity commanded, as you say yourselves. Then followed the interminable hours, disease, deformity, degradation, debasement, and all the signs of industrial slavery: all these calamities are born of monopoly and its sad predecessors,—competition, machinery, and the division of labour: and you blame the Irish!

At other times the workers blame their luck, and exhort themselves to patience: this is the counterpart of the thanks which they address to Providence, when labour is abundant and wages are sufficient.

I find in an article published by M. Leon Faucher, in the *Journal des Economistes* (September, 1845), that the English workers lost some time ago the habit of combining, which is surely a progressive step on which they are only to be congratulated, but that this improvement in the morale of the workers is due especially to their economic instruction. "It is not upon the manufacturers, cried a spinner at the meeting in Bolton, that wages depend. In periods of depression the employers, so to speak, are only the lash with which necessity is armed; and whether they will or no, they have to strike. The regulative principle is the relation of supply to demand; and the employers have not this power.... Let us act prudently, then; let us learn to be resigned to bad luck and to make the most of good luck: by seconding the progress of our industry, we shall be useful not only to ourselves, but to the entire country." (Applause.)

Very good: well-trained, model workers, these! What men these spinners must be that they should submit without complaint to *the lash of necessity*, because the regulative principle of wages is *supply and demand*! M. Leon Faucher adds with a charming simplicity: "English workers are fearless reasoners. Give them a *false principle*, and they will push it mathematically to absurdity, without stopping or getting frightened, as if they were marching to the triumph of the truth." For my part, I hope that, in spite of all the efforts of economic propagandism, French workers will never become reasoners of such power. [The notions of] *Supply and demand*, as well as [of] *the lash of necessity*, no longer have any hold on their minds. England lacked this poverty [of reasoning power]: it will not cross the channel.[24]

[...]

Monopoly, which just now seemed to us so well founded in justice, is the more unjust because it not only makes wages illusory, but deceives the worker in the very valuation of his wages by assuming in relation to him a false title, a false capacity.

M. de Sismondi, in his *Studies of Social Economy*, observes somewhere that, when a banker delivers to a merchant bank-notes in exchange for his values, far from giving credit to the merchant, he receives it, on the contrary, from him.

"This credit," adds M. de Sismondi, "is in truth so short that the merchant scarcely takes the trouble to inquire whether the banker is worthy, especially as the former asks credit instead of granting it."

So, according to M. de Sismondi, in the issue of bank paper, the functions of the merchant and the banker are inverted: the first is the creditor, and the second is the credited.

Something similar takes place between the monopolist and wage-worker.

In fact, the workers, like the merchant at the bank, ask to have their labour discounted; in right, the entrepreneur ought to furnish them bonds and security. I will explain myself.

In any exploitation, no matter of what sort, the entrepreneur cannot legitimately claim, in addition to his own personal labour, anything but the

---

24  Marx turns Proudhon's very obvious sarcasm into: "'Well and good,' cries M. Proudhon, 'these are well developed model workmen, etc., etc. The poverty we have here does not exist in England; it cannot cross the Channel.'" His claim that "M. Proudhon is so unfortunate as to take the foremen and overseers for ordinary workmen, and to urge upon them the advice not to cross the Channel" is equally misleading as is the notion that Proudhon "cordially agrees with the foremen of Bolton because they determine value by supply and demand" (op. cit., 183, 184, 185). (Editor)

IDEA: as for the EXECUTION, the result of the co-operation of numerous workers, that is an effect of collective power, with which the authors, as free in their action as the chief, can produce nothing which should go to him gratuitously. Now, the question is to ascertain whether the amount of individual wages paid by the entrepreneur is equivalent to the collective effect of which I speak: for, were it otherwise, Say's axiom, *Every product is worth what it costs*, would be violated.

"'The capitalist,' they say, 'has paid the workers their daily wages at a rate agreed upon; consequently he owes them nothing.' To be accurate, it must be said that he has paid as many times one day's wage as he has employed workers,—which is not at all the same thing. For he has paid nothing for that immense power which results from the union of workers and the convergence and harmony of their efforts; that saving of expense, secured by their formation into a workshop; that multiplication of product, foreseen, it is true, by the capitalist, but realised by free forces. Two hundred grenadiers, working under the direction of an engineer, stood the obelisk upon its base in a few hours; do you think that one man could have accomplished the same task in two hundred days? Nevertheless, on the books of the capitalist, the amount of wages is the same in both cases, because he allots to himself the benefit of the collective power. Now, of two things one: either this is usurpation on his part, or it is error" (*What is Property?*: Chapter III)

To properly exploit the mule-jenny, engineers, builders, clerks, brigades of workingmen and workingwomen of all sorts, have been needed. In the name of their liberty, of their security, of their future, and of the future of their children, these workers, on engaging to work in the mill, had to make reserves; where are the letters of credit which they have delivered to the employers? Where are the guarantees which they have received? What! Millions of men have sold their arms and parted with their liberty without knowing the import of the contract; they have engaged themselves upon the promise of continuous work and adequate reward; they have executed with their hands what the thought of the employers had conceived; they have become, by this collaboration, associates in the enterprise: and when monopoly, unable or unwilling to make further exchanges, suspends its manufacture and leaves these millions of workers without bread, they are told to be resigned! By the new processes they have lost nine days of their labour out of ten; and for reward they are pointed to the lash of necessity flourished over them! Then, if they refuse to work for lower wages, they are shown that they punish themselves. If they accept the rate offered them, they lose that noble pride, that taste for decent conveniences which constitute the happiness and dignity of the worker and entitle him to the sympathies of the rich. If they combine to secure an increase of wages, they are thrown into prison! Whereas they ought to prosecute their exploiters in the courts, on them the courts will avenge the violations of liberty of commerce! Victims of monopoly, they will suffer the penalty due to the monopolists! O justice of men, stupid courtesan, how long, under your goddess's tinsel, will you drink the blood of the slaughtered proletarian?

Monopoly has invaded everything,—land, labour, and the instruments of labour, products and the distribution of products. Political economy itself has not been able to avoid admitting it.

[...]

Finally, monopoly, by a sort of instinct of self-preservation, has perverted even the idea of association, as something that might infringe upon it, or, to speak more accurately, has not permitted its birth.

Who could hope today to define what association among men should be? The law distinguishes two species and four varieties of civil societies, and as many commercial societies, from the simple partnership to the joint-stock company. I have read the most respectable commentaries that have been written upon all these forms of association, and I declare that I have found in them but one application of the routine practices of monopoly between two or more partners who unite their capital and their efforts against everything that produces and consumes, that invents and exchanges, that lives and dies. The *sine qua non* of all these companies is capital, whose presence alone constitutes them and gives them a basis; their object is monopoly,—that is, the exclusion of all other workers and capitalists, and consequently the negation of social universality so far as persons are concerned.

Thus, according to the definition of the statute, a commercial society which should lay down as a principle the right of any stranger to become a member upon his simple request, and to straightway enjoy the rights and prerogatives of associates and even managers, would no longer be a company; the courts would officially pronounce its dissolution, its non-existence. So, again, articles of association[25] in which the contracting parties should stipulate no contribution of capital, but, while reserving to each the express right to compete with all, should confine themselves to a reciprocal guarantee of labour and wages, saying nothing of the branch of exploitation, or of capital, or of interest, or of profit and loss,—such articles would seem contradictory in their tenor, as destitute of purpose as of reason, and would be annulled by the judge on the complaint of the first rebellious associate. Agreements thus drawn up could give rise to no judicial action; people calling themselves the associates of everybody would be considered associates of nobody; treatises contemplating guarantee and competition between associates at the same time, without any mention of social capital and without any designation

---

25   The term "*acte de société*" literally means "deed of partnership." Proudhon is referring to the process of creating and joining workplaces, contrasting the forms created within capitalism (with wage-labour as management rights reflect the capital provided) to the socialised, egalitarian, and self-managed ones of mutualism (with management rights granted automatically on joining). It should also be noted that "*société*" can be translated as "society" as well as "company." (Editor)

of purpose, would pass for a work of transcendental charlatanism, whose author could readily be sent to a madhouse, provided the magistrates would consent to regard him as only a lunatic.

And yet it is proved, by the most authentic testimony which history and social economy furnish, that humanity has been thrown naked and without capital upon the earth which it cultivates; consequently that it has created and is daily creating all the wealth that exists; that monopoly is only a relative view serving to designate the grade of the worker, with certain conditions of enjoyment; and that all progress consists, while indefinitely multiplying products, in determining their proportionality,—that is, in organising labour and comfort by division, machinery, the workshop, education, and competition. On the other hand, it is evident that all the tendencies of humanity, both in its politics and in its civil laws, are towards universalisation,—that is, towards a complete transformation of the idea of the company as determined by our statutes.

Whence I conclude that articles of association which should regulate, no longer the contribution of the associates,—since each associate, according to economic theory, is supposed to possess absolutely nothing upon his entrance into the company,—but the conditions of labour and exchange, and which should allow access to all who might present themselves,—I conclude, I say, that such articles of association would contain nothing that was not rational and scientific, since they would be the very expression of progress, the organic formula of labour, and since they would reveal, so to speak, humanity to itself by giving it the rudiment of its constitution.[26]

[...]

As for the personal composition of the [joint-stock] company, it naturally divides itself into two categories,—the managers and the stockholders. The managers, very few in number, are chosen from the promoters, organisers, and patrons of the enterprise: in truth, they are the only associates. The stockholders, compared with this little government, which administers the society with full power, are a people of taxpayers who, strangers to each other, without influence and without responsibility, have nothing to do with the affair beyond their investments. They are lenders at a premium, not associates.

One can see from this how all the industries of the kingdom could be carried on by such companies, and each citizen, thanks to the facility for

---

26    Cf. Marx in *Poverty of Philosophy*: "[Proudhon's] whole system rests on the labour commodity, on labour which is trafficked, bought and sold..." (63). Proudhon repeatedly contrasts the associated (self-managed) workplaces of mutualism with capitalist firms with their "hierarchical organisation" (Chapter IV: section II) in which wage-workers toil "under a master" (Chapter XI: section III) after they "parted with their liberty" and "have sold their arms" to a boss who appropriates both the "collective power" (Chapter VI: section II) and the "surplus of labour" they create (Chapter XI: section IV).

multiplying his shares, be interested in all or most of these companies without thereby improving his condition: it might happen even that it would be more and more compromised. For, once more, the stockholder is the beast of burden, the exploitable material of the company: not for him is this company formed. In order that association may be real, he who participates in it must do so, not as a gambler, but as an active factor; he must have a deliberative voice in the council; his name must be expressed or implied in the title of the society; everything regarding him, in short, should be regulated in accordance with equality. But these conditions are precisely those of the organisation of labour, which is not taken into consideration by the code; they form the ULTERIOR object of political economy, and consequently are not to be taken for granted, but to be created, and, as such, are radically incompatible with monopoly.[27]

Socialism, in spite of its high-sounding name, has so far been no more fortunate than monopoly in the definition of society: we may even assert that, in all its plans of organisation, it has steadily shown itself in this respect a plagiarist of political economy. M. Blanc, whom I have already quoted in discussing competition, and whom we have seen by turns as a partisan of the hierarchical principle, an officious defender of inequality, preaching communism, denying with a stroke of the pen the law of contradiction because he cannot conceive it, aiming above all at power as the final sanction of his system,—M. Blanc offers us again the curious example of a socialist copying political economy without suspecting it, and turning continually in the vicious circle of proprietary routine. M. Blanc really denies the sway of capital; he even denies that capital is equal to labour in production, in which he is in accord with healthy economic theories. But he can not or does not know how to dispense with capital; he takes capital for his point of departure; he appeals to the State for its silent partnership: that is, he gets down on his knees before the capitalists and recognises the sovereignty of monopoly. Hence the singular contortions of his dialectics. I beg the reader's pardon for these eternal personalities: but since socialism, as well as political economy, is personified in a certain number of writers, I cannot do otherwise than quote its authors.

"Has or has not capital," said *La Phalange*, "in so far as it is a faculty in production, the legitimacy of the other productive faculties? If it is illegitimate, its pretensions to a share of the product are illegitimate; it must be excluded; it has no interest to receive: if, on the contrary, it is legitimate, it cannot be legitimately excluded from participation in the profits, in the increase which it has helped to create."

---

27  Possibly these paragraphs will not be clear to all without the explanation that the form of association discussed in them, called in French the *commandite*, is a jointstock company to which the shareholders simply lend their capital, without acquiring a share in the management or incurring responsibility for the results thereof. (Translator)

The question could not be stated more clearly. M. Blanc holds, on the contrary, that it is stated in a very confused manner, which means that it embarrasses him greatly, and that he is much worried to find its meaning.

In the first place, he supposes that he is asked "whether it is equitable to allow the capitalist a share of the profits of production *equal to the worker's?*" To which M. Blanc answers unhesitatingly that that would be unjust. Then follows an outburst of eloquence to establish this injustice.

Now, the phalansterian does not ask whether the share of the capitalist should or should not *be equal to the worker's*; he wishes to know simply whether *he is to have a share*. And to this M. Blanc makes no reply.

Is it meant, continues M. Blanc, that capital is *indispensable* to production, like labour itself? Here M. Blanc distinguishes: he grants that capital is indispensable, as labour is, but not to the extent that labour is.

Once again, the phalansterian does not dispute as to quantity, but as to right.

Is it meant—it is still M. Blanc who interrogates—that all capitalists are not idlers? M. Blanc, generous to capitalists who work, asks why so large a share should be given to those who do not work? A flow of eloquence as to the impersonal services of the capitalist and the *personal* services of the worker, terminated by an appeal to Providence.

For the third time, you are asked whether the participation of capital in profits is legitimate, since you admit that it is indispensable in production.

At last M. Blanc, who has understood all the time, decides to reply that, if he allows interest to capital, he does so only as a transitional measure and to ease the descent of the capitalists. For the rest, his project leading inevitably to the absorption of private capital in association, it would be folly and an abandonment of principle to do more. M. Blanc, if he had studied his subject, would have needed to say but a single phrase: I deny capital.

Thus M. Blanc,—and under his name I include the whole of socialism,—after having, by a first contradiction of the title of his book, *ORGANISATION OF LABOUR*, declared that capital was *indispensable* in production, and consequently that it should be organised and participate in profits like labour, by a second contradiction rejects capital from organisation and refuses to recognise it: by a third contradiction he who laughs at decorations and titles of nobility distributes civic crowns, rewards, and distinctions to such litterateurs inventors, and artists as shall have deserved well of the country; he allows them salaries according to their grades and dignities; all of which is the restoration of capital as really, though not with the same mathematical precision, as interest and net product: by a fourth contradiction M. Blanc establishes this new aristocracy on the principle of equality,—that is, he pretends to vote masterships to equal and free associates, privileges of idleness to workers, spoliation in short to the despoiled: by a fifth contradiction he rests this equalitarian aristocracy on the basis of a power endowed with great force,—that is, on despotism, another form of monopoly: by a sixth contradiction, after having, by his encouragements to labour and the arts, tried to proportion reward to service, like monopoly, and wages to capacity, like monopoly, he sets himself to eulogise life in common, labour and consumption in common, which does not prevent him from wishing to withdraw from the effects of common indifference, by means of national encouragements taken out of the common product, the grave and serious writers whom common readers do not care for: by a seventh contradiction.... but let us stop at seven, for we should not have finished at seventy-seven.

[...]

Thus M. Blanc asks for State aid and the establishment of national workshops; thus Fourier asked for six million francs, and his followers are still engaged today in collecting that sum; thus the communists place their hope in a revolution which shall give them authority and the treasury, and exhaust themselves in waiting for useless subscriptions. Capital and power, secondary organs in society, are always the gods whom socialism adores: if capital and power did not exist, it would invent them. Through its anxieties about power and capital, socialism has completely overlooked the meaning of its own protests: much more, it has not seen that, in involving itself, as it has done, in the economic routine, it has deprived itself of the very right to protest. It accuses society of antagonism, and through the same antagonism it goes in pursuit of reform. It asks capital for the poor workers, as if the misery of workers did not come from the competition of capitalists as well as from the factitious opposition of labour and capital; as if the question were not today precisely what it was before the creation of capital,—that is, still and always a question of equilibrium; as if, in short,—let us repeat it incessantly, let us repeat it to satiety,—the question were henceforth of something other than a synthesis of all the principles brought to light by civilisation, and as if, provided this synthesis, the idea which leads the world, were known, there would be any need of the intervention of capital and the State to make them evident.

[...]

# CHAPTER VII
## FIFTH PERIOD—POLICE, OR TAXATION

IN POSITING ITS principles humanity, as if in obedience to a sovereign order, never goes backward. Like the traveller who by oblique windings rises from the depth of the valley to the mountain-top, it follows intrepidly its zigzag road, and marches to its goal with confident step, without repentance and without pause. Arriving at the angle of monopoly, the social genius casts backward a melancholy glance, and, in a moment of profound reflection, says to itself:

"Monopoly has stripped the poor hireling of everything,—bread, clothing, home, education, liberty, and security. I will lay a tax upon the monopolist; at this price I will save him his privilege.

"Land and mines, woods and waters, the original domain of man, are forbidden to the proletarian. I will intervene in their exploitation, I will have my share of the products, and land monopoly shall be respected.

"Industry has fallen into feudalism, but I am the suzerain. The lords shall pay me tribute, and they shall keep the profit of their capital.

"Commerce levies usurious profits on the consumer. I will strew its road with toll-gates, I will stamp its checks and endorse its invoices, and it shall pass.

"Capital has overcome labour by intelligence. I will open schools, and the worker, made intelligent himself, shall become a capitalist in his turn.

"Products lack circulation, and social life is cramped. I will build roads, bridges, canals, marts, theatres, and temples, and thus furnish at one stroke work, wealth, and a market.

"The rich man lives in plenty, while the worker weeps in famine. I will establish taxes on bread, wine, meat, salt, and honey, on articles of necessity and on objects of value, and these shall supply alms for my poor.

"And I will set guards over the waters, the woods, the fields, the mines, and the roads; I will send collectors to gather the taxes and teachers to instruct the children; I will have an army to put down refractory subjects, courts to judge them, prisons to punish them, and priests to curse them. All these offices shall be given to the proletariat and paid by the monopolists.

"Such is my certain and efficacious will."[28]

We have to prove that society could neither think better nor act worse: this will be the subject of a review which, I hope, will throw new light upon the social problem.[29]

---

28  Marx summarised this as follows: "M. Proudhon talks to us of the social genius who, after having intrepidly pursued his zigzag route, 'after having marched with a firm step, without regret and without halting, and having *arrived at the angle of monopoly*, casts a melancholy and, after profound reflection, fixes imposts [taxes] on all objects of production, and creates an entire administrative organisation, on order that all employment should be delivered to the proletariat and be paid by the men of monopoly'" (op. cit., 166). (Editor)

29  Cf. Marx: "In order to get a glimpse of the manner in which M. Proudhon treats economic details, it will suffice to say that, according to him, the impost on articles of consumption must have been established with a view to equality and in order to render assistance to the proletariat." It soon becomes clear that Proudhon explicitly states that this was how state intervention was justified but in practice it was done to render assistance to the property-owning class. In others words, to quote Marx, "these imposts [taxes] serve precisely to give the bourgeoisie the means of conserving its position as the dominant class" (op. cit., 166). (Editor)

Every measure of general police, every administrative and commercial regulation, like every law of taxation, is at bottom but one of the innumerable articles of this ancient bargain, ever violated and ever renewed, between the patriciate and the proletariat. That the parties or their representatives knew nothing of it, or even that they frequently viewed their political constitutions from another standpoint, is of little consequence to us: not to the man, legislator, or prince do we look for the meaning of his acts, but to the acts themselves.

[...]

In short, the practical and avowed object of the tax is to effect upon the rich, for the benefit of the people, a proportional resumption of their capital.

Now, analysis and the facts demonstrate:

That the distributive tax [*l'impôt de répartition*], the tax upon monopoly, instead of being paid by those who possess, is paid almost entirely by those who do not possess;

That the proportional tax [*l'impôt de quotité*], separating the producer from the consumer, falls solely upon the latter, thereby taking from the capitalist no more than he would have to pay if fortunes were absolutely equal;[30]

Finally, that the army, the courts, the police, the schools, the hospitals, the almshouses, the houses of refuge and correction, public functions, religion itself, all that society creates for the protection, emancipation, and relief of the proletarian, paid for in the first place and sustained by the proletarian, is then turned against the proletarian or wasted as far as he is concerned; so that the proletariat, which at first laboured only for the class that devours it,—that of the capitalists,—must labour also for the class that flogs it,—that of the non-producers.[31]

---

30   The *impôt de repartition* (distributive tax) and *impôt de quotité* (proportional tax) were two alternative methods of taxation in France. Distributive taxation fixed the sum to be collected, then assessed the fraction of that amount that would be provided by each part of the country; proportional taxation applied to particular transactions, e.g., customs duties, sales, stock dividends, etc., so that revenue from them could only be estimated beforehand. (Editor)

31   Earlier in the *System of Economic Contradictions*, Proudhon defined non-producers as the "species of functionaries which Adam Smith has designated by the word unproductive, although he admits as much as any one the utility and even the necessity of their labour in society [...] [T]he functionaries called public [...] obtain their right to subsistence, not by the production of real utilities, but by the very state of unproductivity in which, by no fault of their own, they are kept [...] State functionaries [...] the government's employees [...] a category of services [...] which do not fall under the law of exchange, which cannot become the object of private speculation, competition, joint-stock association, or any sort of commerce, but which, theoretically regarded as performed gratuitously by all, but entrusted, by virtue of the law of division of labour, to a small number of special

These facts are henceforth so well known, and the economists—I owe them this justice—have shown them so clearly, that I shall abstain from correcting their demonstrations, which, for the rest, are no longer contradicted by anybody. What I propose to bring to light, and what the economists do not seem to have sufficiently understood, is that the condition in which the worker is placed by this new phase of social economy is susceptible of no amelioration; that, unless industrial organisation, and therefore political reform, should bring about an equality of fortunes, evil is inherent in police institutions as in the idea of charity which gave them birth; in short, that the STATE, whatever form it affects, aristocratic or theocratic, monarchical or republican, until it shall have become the obedient and submissive organ of a society of equals, will be for the people an inevitable hell,—I had almost said a deserved damnation.

[...]

The democrats, who reproach us with sacrificing the revolutionary interest (what is the revolutionary interest?) to the socialistic interest, ought really to tell us how, without making the State the sole proprietor and without decreeing the community [*communauté*] of goods and gains, they mean, by any system of taxation whatever, to relieve the people and restore to labour what capital takes from it. In vain do I rack my brains; on all questions I see power placed in the falsest situation, and the opinion of journals straying into limitless absurdity.

[...]

In 1844, at the time of the troubles in Rive-de-Gier, M. Anselme Petetin published in the *Revue Independante* two articles, full of reason and sincerity, concerning the anarchy prevailing in the conduct of the coal mines in the basin of the Loire. M. Petetin pointed out the necessity of uniting the mines and centralising their administration. The facts which he laid before the public were not unknown to power; has power troubled itself about the union of the mines and the organisation of that industry? Not at all. Power has followed the principle of free competition; it has let alone and looked on.

Since that time the mining companies have combined, not without causing some anxiety to consumers, who have seen in this combination a plot to raise the price of fuel. Will power, which has received numerous complaints upon this subject, intervene to restore competition and prevent monopoly? It cannot do it; the right of combination is identical in law with the right of association; monopoly is the basis of our society, as competition is its conquest; and, provided there is no riot, power will let alone and look on. What other course could it pursue? Can it prohibit a legally established commercial association? Can it oblige neighbours to destroy each other? Can it

men who devote themselves exclusively to them, must consequently be paid for."
(Editor)

forbid them to reduce their expenses? Can it establish a maximum? If power should do any one of these things, it would overturn the established order. Power, therefore, can take no initiative: it is instituted to defend and protect monopoly and competition at once, within the limitations of patents, licenses, land taxes, and other bonds which it has placed upon property. Apart from these limitations power has no sort of right to act in the name of society. The social right is not defined; moreover, it would be a denial of monopoly and competition. How, then, could power take up the defence of that which the law did not foresee or define, of that which is the opposite of the rights recognised by the legislator?

Consequently, when the miner, whom we must consider in the events of Rive-de-Gier as the real representative of society against the mine-owners, saw fit to resist the scheme of the monopolists by defending his wages and opposing combination to combination, power shot the miner down. And the political brawlers accused authority, saying it was partial, ferocious, sold to monopoly, etc. For my part, I declare that this way of viewing the acts of authority seems to me scarcely philosophical, and I reject it with all my energies. It is possible that they might have killed fewer people, possible also that they might have killed more: the fact to be noticed here is not the number of dead and wounded, but the repression of the workers. Those who have criticised authority would have done as it did, barring perhaps the impatience of its bayonets and the accuracy of its aim: they would have repressed, I say; they would not have been able to do anything else. And the reason, which it would be vain to try to brush aside, is that competition is legal, joint-stock association is legal, supply and demand are legal, and all the consequences which flow directly from competition, joint-stock association, and free commerce are legal, whereas workers' strikes are ILLEGAL. And it is not only the penal code which says this, but the economic system, the necessity of the established order. As long as labour is not sovereign, it must be a slave; society is possible only on this condition. That each worker individually should have the free disposition of his person and his arms may be tolerated;[32] but that the workers should undertake, by combinations, to

---

32   The new law regarding service-books [*livrets d'ouvrier*, employment records, instituted by Napoléon I, that workers were required by law to carry, policing their mobility] has confined the independence of workers within narrower limits. The democratic press has again thundered its indignation this subject against those in power, as if they had been guilty of anything more than the application of the principles of authority and property, which are those of democracy. What the Chambers have done in regard to service-books was inevitable, and should have been expected. It is as impossible for a society founded on the proprietary principle not to end in class distinctions as for a democracy to avoid despotism, for a religion to be reasonable, for fanaticism to show tolerance. This is the law of contradiction: how long will it take us to understand it?

do violence to monopoly society cannot permit.[33] Crush monopoly, and you abolish competition, and you disorganise the workshop, and you sow dissolution everywhere. Authority, in shooting down the miners, found itself in the position of Brutus placed between his paternal love and his consular duties: he had to sacrifice either his children or the republic. The alternative was horrible, I admit; but such is the spirit and letter of the social compact, such is the tenor of the charter, such is the order of Providence.

Thus the police function, instituted for the defence of the proletariat, is directed entirely against the proletariat. The proletarian is driven from the forests, from the rivers, from the mountains; even the cross-roads are forbidden him; soon he will know no road save that which leads to prison.

The advance in agriculture has made the advantage of artificial meadows and the necessity of abolishing common land generally felt. Everywhere communal lands are being cleared, let, enclosed; new advances, new wealth. But the poor day-worker, whose only patrimony is the communal land and who supports a cow and several sheep in summer by letting them feed along the roads, through the underbrush, and over the stripped fields, will lose his sole and last resource. The landed proprietor, the purchaser or farmer of the communal lands, will alone thereafter sell, with his wheat and vegetables, milk and cheese. Instead of weakening an old monopoly, they create a new one. Even the road-workers reserve for themselves the edges of the roads as a meadow belonging to them, and drive off all non-administrative cattle. What follows? That the day-worker, before abandoning his cow, lets it feed in contravention of the law, becomes a marauder, commits a thousand depredations, and is punished by fine and imprisonment: of what use to him are police and agricultural progress? Last year the mayor of Mulhouse, to prevent grape-stealing, forbade every individual not an owner of vines to travel by day or night over roads running by or through vineyards,—a charitable precaution, since it prevented even desires and regrets. But if the public highway is nothing but an accessory of private property; if the communal lands are converted into private property; if the public domain, in short, assimilated to private property, is guarded, exploited, leased, and sold like private property,—what remains for the proletarian? Of what advantage is it to him that society has left the state of war to enter the regime of police?
[…]
The farther we delve into this system of illusory compromises between monopoly and society,—that is […] between capital and labour, between

---

33  Marx selectively quotes this passage, omitting the key phrase and so utterly changes Proudhon's intention: "For workers to strike is *illegal*, and it is not only the penal code which says so, it is the economic system, it is the necessity of the established order […] That each workman should have the free disposal of his hands and of his person, that can be tolerated, but that workmen should undertake by combination to do violence to monopoly, that is what society can never permit" (op. cit., 185). (Editor)

the patriciate and the proletariat,—the more we discover that it is all fore-seen, regulated, and executed in accordance with this infernal maxim, with which Hobbes and Machiavelli, those theorists of despotism, were unac-quainted: EVERYTHING BY THE PEOPLE AND AGAINST THE PEO-PLE. While labour produces, capital, under the mask of a false fecundity, enjoys and abuses; the legislator, in offering his mediation, thought to recall the privileged class to fraternal feelings and surround the worker with guar-antees; and now he finds, by the fatal contradiction of interests, that each of these guarantees is an instrument of torture. It would require a hundred volumes, the life of ten men, and a heart of iron, to relate from this stand-point the crimes of the State towards the poor and the infinite variety of its tortures. A summary glance at the principal classes of police will be enough to enable us to estimate its spirit and economy.

[...]

To conduct this offensive and defensive war against the proletariat a pub-lic force was indispensable: the executive power grew out of the necessities of civil legislation, administration, and justice. And there again the most beautiful hopes have changed into bitter disappointments.

As legislator, as burgomaster, and as judge, the prince has set himself up as a representative of divine authority. A defender of the poor, the widow, and the orphan, he has promised to cause liberty and equality to prevail around the throne, to come to the aid of labour, and to listen to the voice of the people. And the people have thrown themselves lovingly into the arms of power; and, when experience has made them feel that power was against them, instead of blaming the institution, they have fallen to accusing the prince, ever unwilling to understand that, the prince being by nature and purpose the chief of non-producers and greatest of monopolists, it was im-possible for him, in spite of himself, to take up the cause of the people.

All criticism, whether of the form or the acts of government, ends in this essential contradiction. And when the self-styled theorists of the sovereignty of the people pretend that the remedy for the tyranny of power consists in causing it to emanate from popular suffrage, they simply turn, like the squirrel, in their cage. For, from the moment that the essential conditions of power—that is, authority, property, hierarchy—are preserved, the suffrage of the people is nothing but the consent of the people to their oppression,—which is the silliest charlatanism.

In the system of authority, whatever its origin, monarchical or democrat-ic, power is the noble organ of society; by it society lives and moves; all initia-tive emanates from it; order and perfection are wholly its work. According to the definitions of economic science, on the contrary,—definitions which harmonise with the reality of things,—power is the series of non-producers which social organisation must tend to indefinitely reduce. How, then, with the principle of authority so dear to democrats, shall the aspiration of politi-cal economy, an aspiration which is also that of the people, be realised? How shall the government, which by the hypothesis is everything, become an obedient servant, a subordinate organ? Why should the prince have received power simply to weaken it, and why should he labour, with a view to order, for his own elimination? Why should he not try rather to fortify himself, to add to his courtiers, to continually obtain new subsidies, and finally to free himself from dependence on the people, the inevitable goal of all power originating in the people?

It is said that the people, naming its legislators and through them making its will known to power, will always be in a position to arrest its invasions; that thus the people will fill at once the role of prince and that of sovereign. Such, in a word, is the utopia of democrats, the eternal mystification with which they abuse the proletariat.

But will the people make laws against power; against the principle of authority and hierarchy, which is the principle upon which society is based; against liberty and property? According to our hypothesis, this is more than impossible, it is contradictory. Then property, monopoly, competition, in-dustrial privileges, the inequality of fortunes, the preponderance of capital, hierarchical and crushing centralisation, administrative oppression, legal ab-solutism, will be preserved; and, as it is impossible for a government not to act in the direction of its principle, capital will remain as before the god of society, and the people, still exploited, still degraded, will have gained by their attempt at sovereignty only a demonstration of their powerlessness.

[...]

At least, the partisans of governmental initiative will say, you will admit that, in the accomplishment of the revolution promised by the development of antinomies, power would be a potent auxiliary. Why, then, do you oppose a reform which, putting power in the hands of the people, would second your views so well? Social reform is the object; political reform is the instru-ment: why, if you wish the end, do you reject the means?

Such is today the reasoning of the entire democratic press, which I for-give with all my heart for having at last, by this quasi-socialistic confession of faith, itself proclaimed the emptiness of its theories. It is in the name of science, then, that democracy calls for a political reform as a preliminary to social reform. But science protests against this subterfuge as an insult; science repudiates any alliance with politics, and, very far from expecting from it the slightest aid, must begin with politics its work of exclusion.

How little affinity there is between the human mind and truth! When I see the democracy, socialistic but yesterday, continually asking for capital in order to combat capital's influence; for wealth, in order to cure poverty; for the abandonment of liberty, in order to organise liberty; for the reformation of government, in order to reform society,—when I see it, I say, taking upon itself the responsibility of society, provided social questions be set aside or solved, it seems to me as if I were listening to a fortune-teller who, before answering the questions of those who consult her, begins by inquiring into their age, their condition, their family, and all the accidents of their life. Eh! miserable sorceress, if you know the future, you know who I am and what I want; why do you ask me to tell you?

Likewise I will answer the democrats: If you know the use that you should make of power, and if you know how power should be organised, you possess economic science. Now, if you possess economic science, if you have the key of its contradictions, if you are in a position to organise labour, if you have studied the laws of exchange, you have no need of the capital of the nation or of public force. From this day forth you are more potent than money, stronger than power. For, since the workers are with you, you are by that fact alone masters of production; you hold commerce, manufactures, and agriculture enchained; you have the entire social capital at your disposition; you have full control of taxation; you block the wheels of power, and you trample monopoly under foot. What other initiative, what greater authority, do you ask? What prevents you from applying your theories?

Surely not political economy, although generally followed and accredited: for, everything in political economy having a true side and a false side, your only problem is to combine the economic elements in such a way that their total shall no longer present a contradiction.

Nor is it the civil law: for that law, sanctioning economic routine solely because of its advantages and in spite of its disadvantages, is susceptible, like political economy itself, of being bent to all the exigencies of an exact synthesis, and consequently is as favourable to you as possible.

Finally, it is not power, which, the last expression of antagonism and created only to defend the law, could stand in your way only by forswearing itself.

Once more, then, what stops you?

If you possess social science, you know that the problem of association consists in organising, not only the non-producers,—in that direction, thank heaven! little remains to be done,—but also the producers, and by this organisation subjecting capital and subordinating power. Such is the war that you have to sustain: a war of labour against capital; a war of liberty against authority; a war of the producer against the non-producer; a war of equality against privilege. What you ask, to conduct the war to a successful conclusion, is precisely that which you must combat. Now, to combat and reduce power, to put it in its proper place in society, it is of no use to change the holders of power or introduce some variation into its workings: an agricultural and industrial combination must be found by means of which power, today the ruler of society, shall become its slave. Have you the secret of that combination?

But what do I say? That is precisely the thing to which you do not consent. As you cannot conceive of society without hierarchy, you have made yourselves the apostles of authority; worshippers of power, you think only of strengthening it and muzzling liberty; your favourite maxim is that the welfare of the people must be achieved in spite of the people; instead of proceeding to social reform by the extermination of power and politics, you insist on a reconstruction of power and politics. Then, by a series of contradictions which prove your sincerity, but the illusory character of which is well known to the real friends of power, the aristocrats and monarchists, your competitors, you promise us, in the name of power, economy in expenditures, an equitable assessment of taxes, protection to labour, gratuitous education, universal suffrage, and all the utopias repugnant to authority and property. Consequently power in your hands has never been anything but ruinous, and that is why you have never been able to retain it; that is why, on the Eighteenth of Brumaire, four men were sufficient to take it away from you, and why today the bourgeoisie, which is as fond of power as you are and which wants a strong power, will not restore it to you.

Thus power, the instrument of collective might, created in society to serve as a mediator between labour and privilege, finds itself inevitably enchained to capital and directed against the proletariat. No political reform can solve this contradiction, since, by the confession of the politicians themselves, such a reform would end only in increasing the energy and extending the sphere of power, and since power would know no way of touching the prerogatives of monopoly without overturning the hierarchy and dissolving society. The problem before the labouring classes, then, consists, not in capturing, but in subduing both power and monopoly,—that is, in generating from the bowels of the people, from the depths of labour, a greater authority, a more potent fact, which shall envelop capital and the State and subjugate them. [34] Every proposition of reform which does not satisfy this condition is simply one scourge more, a rod doing sentry duty, *virgem vigilantem*, as a prophet said, which threatens the proletariat.

[...]

O toiling people! disinherited, harassed, proscribed people! people whom they imprison, judge, and kill! despised people, branded people! Do you not know that there is an end, even to patience, even to devotion? Will you not cease to lend an ear to those orators of mysticism who tell you to pray and to wait, preaching salvation now through religion, now through power, and whose vehement and sonorous words captivate you? Your destiny is an enigma which neither physical force, nor courage of soul, nor the illuminations of enthusiasm, nor the exaltation of any sentiment, can solve. Those who tell you to the contrary deceive you, and all their discourses serve only to postpone the hour of your deliverance, now ready to strike. What are

---

34  Cf. Marx: "The working class will substitute, in the course of its development, for the old order of civil society and association which will exclude classes and their antagonism, and there will no longer be political power, properly speaking, since political power is simply the official form of the antagonism in civil society" (op. cit., 190). (Editor)

enthusiasm and sentiment, what is vain poesy, when confronted with necessity? To overcome necessity there is nothing but necessity itself, the last
reason of nature, the pure essence of matter and spirit.

Thus the contradiction of value, born of the necessity of free will, must
be overcome by the proportionality of value, another necessity produced by
the union of liberty and intelligence. But, in order that this victory of intelligent and free labour might produce all its consequences, it was necessary
that society should pass through a long succession of torments.

It was a necessity that labour, in order to increase its power, should be
divided; and a necessity, in consequence of this division, that the worker
should be degraded and impoverished.

It was a necessity that this original division should be reconstructed by
scientific instruments and combinations; and a necessity, in consequence of
this reconstruction, that the subordinated worker should lose, together with
his legitimate wages, even the exercise of the industry which supported him.

It was a necessity that competition then should step in to emancipate
liberty on the point of perishing; and a necessity that this deliverance should
end in a vast elimination of workers.

It was a necessity that the producer, ennobled by his art, as formerly the
warrior was by arms, should bear aloft his banner, in order that the valour of
man might be honoured in labour as in war; and a necessity that of privilege
should straightway be born the proletariat.

It was a necessity that society should then take under its protection the
conquered plebeian, a beggar without a roof; and a necessity that this protection should be converted into a new series of tortures.

We shall meet on our way still other necessities, all of which will disappear, like the others, before greater necessities, until shall come at last the
general equation, the supreme necessity, the triumphant fact, which must
establish the kingdom of labour forever.

But this solution cannot result either from surprise or from a vain compromise. It is as impossible to associate labour and capital as to produce
without labour and without capital; as impossible to establish equality by
power as to suppress power and equality and make a society without people
and without police.

There is a necessity, I repeat, of a MAJOR FORCE to invert the actual
formulas of society; a necessity that the LABOUR of the people, not their
valour nor their votes, should, by a scientific, legitimate, immortal, insurmountable combination, subject capital to the people and deliver to them
power.

*1846*
*Translators: Clarence L. Swartz (Chapters X and XIV) and Shawn P.*
*Wilbur (Chapter XI)*

# SYSTEM OF ECONOMIC CONTRADICTIONS,
## OR, THE PHILOSOPHY OF MISERY
### VOLUME II

## CHAPTER X
### SEVENTH PERIOD—CREDIT

[...]

### §I ORIGIN AND DEVELOPMENT OF THE IDEA OF CREDIT

THE POINT OF DEPARTURE OF CREDIT IS MONEY.

We have seen in chapter II how by a combination of happy circumstances, the value of gold and silver having been the first to be constituted, money became the symbol of all dubious and fluctuating values; that is to say, those not socially constituted or not officially established. It was there demonstrated how, if the value of all products were once determined and rendered highly exchangeable, acceptable, in a word, like money, in all payments, society would by that single fact arrive at the highest degree of economic development of which it is capable from the commercial point of view. Social economy would no longer be then, as it is today, in relation to exchange, in a state of simple formation; it would be in a state of perfection. Production would not be definitely organised, but exchange and circulation would, and it would suffice for the worker to produce, to produce incessantly, either in reducing his costs or in dividing his labour and discovering better processes, inventing new objects of consumption, opposing his rivals or resisting their attacks, for acquiring wealth and assuring his well being.

In the same chapter, we have pointed out the lack of intelligence of socialists in regard to money; and we have shown in going back, to the origin of this contrivance, that what we had to repress in the precious metals is not the use, but the privilege.

Indeed, in all possible societies, even communistic, there is need for a measure of exchange, otherwise either the right of the producer, or that of the consumer, is affected. Until values are generally constituted by some method of association, there is need that one certain product, selected from among all others, whose value seems to be the most authentic, the best defined, the least alterable, and which combines with this advantage durability and portability, be taken for the symbol, that is to say, both for the instrument of circulation and the standard of other values.

It is, then, inevitable that this truly privileged product should become the object of all the ambitions, the paradise in perspective of the worker, the palladium of monopoly; that, notwithstanding all warnings, this precious talisman should circulate from hand to hand, concealed from a jealous authority; that the greater part of the precious metals, serving as specie, should be thus diverted from their real use and become, in the form of money, idle capital, wealth outside of consumption; that, in this capacity as instrument of exchange, gold should be taken in its turn for an object of speculation and serve as the basis of a great commerce; that, finally, protected by public opinion, loaded with public favour, it should obtain power, and by the same stroke destroy the social fabric! The means of destroying this formidable force does not lie in the destruction of the medium—I almost said the depository; it is in generalising its principle. All these propositions are admitted as well demonstrated, and as strictly linked together, as the theorems of geometry.

Gold and silver, that is to say, the merchandise whose value was first constituted, being therefore taken as the standard of other values and as universal instruments of exchange, all commerce, all consumption, all production are dependent on them. Gold and silver, precisely because they have acquired in the highest degree the character of sociality and of justice, have become synonyms of power, of royalty, almost of divinity.

Gold and silver represent commercial life, intelligence and virtue. A chest full of specie is an arch saint, a magic urn that brings wealth, pleasure and glory to those who have the power to draw those things from it. If all the products of labour had the same exchange value as money, all the workers would enjoy the same advantages as the holders of money: everyone would have, in his ability to produce, an inexhaustible source of wealth. But the religion of money cannot be abolished, or, to better express it, the general constitution of values cannot function except by an effort of reason and of justice; until then it is inevitable that, as in polite society, the possession of money is a sure sign of wealth, the absence of money is an almost certain sign of poverty. Money being, then, the only value that bears the stamp of society, the only merchandise standard that is current in commerce, money is, according to the general view, the idol of the human species. The imagination attributing to the metal that which is the effect of the collective thought toward the metal, every one, instead of seeking well being at its true source,—that is to say, in the socialisation of all values, in the continuous creation of new monetary figures—busies himself exclusively in acquiring money, money, always money.

It was to respond to this universal demand for money, which was really but a demand for subsistence, a demand for exchange and for output, that, instead of aiming directly at the mark, a stop was made at the first term of the series, and, instead of making successively of each product a new money, the one thought was to multiply metallic money as much as possible, first by perfecting the process of its manufacture, then, by the facility of its emission, and finally by fictions. Obviously it was to mistake the principle of wealth, the character of money, the object of labour and the condition of exchange; it was a retrogression in civilisation to reconstitute value in the monarchical regime that was already beginning to change. Such is the mother idea which gave birth to the institutions of credit; and such is the fundamental prejudice, which error we need no longer demonstrate, which antagonises in their very conceptions all these institutions.

But, as we have often said, humanity, even when it yields to an imperfect idea, is not mistaken in its views. However, one sees, strange to say, that, in proceeding to the organisation of wealth by a retreat, it has operated as well, as usefully, as infallibly as possible, considering the condition of its evolutionary existence. The retrogressive organisation of credit as well as previous manifestations of economics, at the same time that it gave to industry new scope, had caused, it is true, an aggravation of poverty; but finally the social question appeared in a new light and the contradictions, better known today, give the hope of an immediate and complete solution.

Thus the ulterior object, hitherto unperceived, of credit is to constitute, with the aid and on the prototype of money, all the values still fluctuating whose immediate and avowed end is to furnish to that combination the supreme condition of order in society and of well being among the workers, by a still greater diffusion of metallic value. Money, the promoters of this new idea tell us, money is wealth; if then we can provide everybody with money, plenty of money, all will be rich: and it is by virtue of this syllogism that institutions of credit have developed everywhere.

But it is clear that, to the extent that the ulterior object of credit presents a logical, luminous and fruitful idea, conforms, in a word, to the law of progressive organisation, its immediate end, alone sought, alone desired, is full of illusion and, by its tendency toward the status quo, of perils. Since money as well as other merchandise is subject to the law of proportionality, if its quantity increases and if at the same time other products do not increase in proportion, money loses it value, and nothing, in the last analysis, is added to the social wealth; if, on the contrary, with specie production increasing everywhere, population following at the same rate, there is still no change in the respective position of the producers, in both cases, the solution required does not advance a single step. *A priori*, then, it is not true that the organisation of credit, in the terms in which it is proposed, contains the solution of the social problem.

After having related the development of and the reason for the existence of credit, we have to justify its appearance, that is to say, the rank to which it should be assigned in the category of science. It is here above all that we have to point out the lack of profundity and the incoherence of political economy.

Credit is at once the result and the contradiction of the theory of markets, since the last word, as we have seen, is the absolute freedom of trade.

I have said from the first that credit is the consequence of the theory of markets, and as such already contradictory.

At this point in this history of society, both real and fanciful, we have seen all the processes of organisation and the means of equilibrium tumble one upon the other and reproduce constantly, more arrogantly and more murderously than before, the antinomy of value. Arriving at the sixth phase of its evolution, social genius, obedient to the movement of expansion that pushes it, seeks abroad, in foreign commerce, the market, that is to say, the counterpoise which it lacks. Presently we shall see it, deceived in its hope, seek this counterpoise, this output, this guarantee of exchange that it must have at any price in domestic commerce, at home. By credit, society falls back in a manner on itself: it seems to have understood that production and consumption are for it identical and inadequate things; it is in itself, and not by indefinite ejaculations, that it ought to find the equilibrium.

[...]

Credit is the canonisation of money, the declaration of its royalty over all products whatsoever. In consequence, credit is the most formal denial of free trade, a flagrant justification on the part of the economists, of the balance of trade. Let the economists learn, then, to generalise their ideas, and let them tell us why, if it is immaterial for one nation to pay for the goods which it buys with money or with its own products, it always has need of money? How can it be that a nation which works, exhausts itself? Why is there always a demand from it for the only product that it does not consume, that is to say, money? How all the subtleties conceived up to this day for supplying the lack of money, such as bills of exchange, bank paper, paper money, do nothing but interpret and make this need more evident?

In truth, the free trade fanaticism, which today distinguishes the sect of economists, is not understandable, aside from the extraordinary efforts by which it tries to propagate the commerce of money and to multiply credit institutions.

What then, once more, is credit? It is, answers the theory, a release of engaged value, which permits the making of this same value, which before was sluggish, circulable; or, to speak a language more simple: credit is the advance made by a capitalist, against a deposit of values of difficult exchange, of the merchandise the most susceptible of being exchanged, in consequence the most precious of all money, money which holds in suspense all exchangeable values, and without which they would themselves be struck down by the interdiction; money which measures, dominates and subordinates all other products; money with which alone one discharges one's debts and frees oneself from one's obligations; money which assures nations, as well as individuals, well being and independence; money, finally, that not only is power, but liberty, equality, property, everything.

This is what the human species, by an unanimous consent, has understood; that which the economists know better than anyone, but what they never have ceased combating with a comical stubbornness, to sustain I know not what fantasy of liberalism in contradiction to their most loudly confessed principles. Credit was invented to assist labour, to bring into the hands of the worker the instrument that destroys him, money: and they proceed from there to maintain that, among manufacturing nations, the advantage of money in exchange is nothing; but that it is insignificant in balancing their accounts in merchandise or specie: that it is low prices alone that they have to consider!

But if it is true that, in international commerce, the precious metals have lost their preponderance, this means that, in international commerce, all values have reached the same degree of determination, and like money, are equally acceptable; in other words, that the law of exchange is found, and labour is organised, *among the various nations*. Then, let them formulate this law; let them explain that organisation, and, instead of talking of credit and forging new chains for the labouring class, let them teach, by an application of the principle of international equilibrium, all the manufacturers who ruin themselves because they are not exchanging, teach those workers, who die of hunger because they have no work, how their products, how the work of their hands are values which they can use for their consumption, as well as if they were bank-bills or money. What! this principle which, following the economists, rules the trade of nations, is inapplicable to private industry! How is this? Why? Some reasons, some proofs, in the name of God.

[...]

# CHAPTER XI
## EIGHTH EPOCH—PROPERTY

### §II CAUSES OF THE ESTABLISHMENT OF PROPERTY

PROPERTY OCCUPIES THE eighth place in the chain of economic contradictions; this point is the first one that we have to establish.

It is proven that the origin of property cannot be related to first-occupancy nor to labour. The first of these opinions is nothing more than a vicious cycle, in which the phenomenon is given as an explanation of the very phenomenon; the second is eminently subversive concerning property, because considering labour as supreme condition, it is impossible for property to establish itself. As for the theory that makes property go back to an act of collective will, it has the defect of remaining silent about the motivations of this will: well, these are the very motivations that we needed to know.

However, although all these theories, considered separately, always end in contradiction, it is certain that each of them possess a parcel of truth and it can be supposed that if, instead of isolating them, all three were studied in connection and synthetically, the real theory would be discovered in them, that is, the reason for the existence of property.

Yes, then, property begins, or to put it better it manifests itself by a sovereign, effective occupation, which excludes every idea of participation and community [*communauté*]; yes, again, that occupation, in its legitimate and authentic form, is nothing other than work: otherwise, how could society have consented to concede and to respect property? Yes, finally, society has desired property, and all the legislations in the world have only been made for it.

Property has been established by occupation, which is to say by labour: it is necessary to recall it often, not for the preservation of property, but for the instruction of the workers. Labour seated in power, it must produce, by the evolution of its laws, property; just as it has given rise to the separation of industries, then the hierarchy of workers, then competition, monopoly, police, etc. All these antinomies are also successive positions of labour, mileposts planted by it on the eternal route, and destined to formulate, by their synthetic joining, the true right of men. But fact is not right: property, the natural product of occupation and labour, was a principle of anticipation and invasion; thus it needed to be recognised and legitimated by society: these two elements, occupation by labour and legislative sanction, that the jurists have mistakenly separated in their commentaries, are joined together to constitute property. Now, it is a question for us of knowing the providential motives of that concession, what role it enjoys in the economic system: such will be the object of this section.

Let us prove first that in order to establish property, social consent was necessary.

As long as property is not recognised and legitimated by the State, it remains an extra-social fact; it is in the same position as the child, who is only supposed to become a member of the family, the city and the Church, by the recognition of the father, the inscription in the register of the civil state, and the ceremony of baptism. In the absence of these formalities, the child is as we believe the animals to be: it is a useless member, a base and servile soul, unworthy of consideration; it is a bastard. Thus the social recognition was necessary to property, and all property implies a primitive community. Without that recognition, property remains simple occupation, and can be contested by the first comer.

"The right to a thing," said Kant, "is the right of private use of a thing with regard to which I am in common possession (primitive or subsequent) with all other men: for that common possession is the unique condition under which I could forbid to any other possessor the private use of the thing; because without the supposition of that possession, it would be impossible to conceive how I, though not presently possessor of the thing, can be wronged by those who possess it and who use it.—My individual or unilateral will cannot oblige anyone else to forbid themselves the use of a thing, if they were not so obliged before. Thus, the use can only be forbidden by wills joined in a common possession. If it was not thus, one would need to conceive a right in a thing, as if it was an obligation towards me, and from which would be derived in the last analysis the right against every possessor of that thing: a truly absurd idea."[1]

Thus, according to Kant, the right of property, that is the legitimacy of occupation, proceeds from the consent of the State, which originally implies common possession. It cannot, said Kant, be otherwise. Thus, every time that the proprietor dares to oppose his right to the State, the State, reminding the proprietor of the convention, can always end the dispute with this ultimatum: Either recognise my sovereignty, and submit that which the public interest demands, or I will declare that your property has ceased to be placed under the safeguard of the laws, and withdraw from you my protection.

It follows from this that in the mind of the legislator the institution of property, like those of credit, commerce and monopoly, has been made with an aim of equilibrium, which first places property among the elements of organisation, and the first among the general means of constituting values. "The right to a thing..." said Kant, "is the right to private use of a thing with regard to which I am in common possession (primitive or subsequent) with all other men": by virtue of that principle, every man deprived of property can and must appeal for it to the community, guardian of the rights of all; from which it results, as one has said, that in the sight of Providence, conditions must be equal.

. This is what Kant, as well as Reid, clearly understood and expressed in the following passage: "One asks now how far does the faculty to take possession of a resource [*fonds*] extend?—As far as the faculty to have it in its power, which is as far the one who appropriates it can defend it. As if the resource said: If you cannot defend me, no more can you command me."[2]

I am not however sure whether or not this passage must be understood as applying to possession prior to property. For, Kant adds, the acquisition

---

1    *The Metaphysics of Morals*, 1.11.
2    *The Metaphysics of Morals*, 1.15. (Editor)

is only *peremptory* in society; in the state of nature, it is only *provisory.* One could then conclude from this that, in the thought of Kant, acquisition, once become peremptory by social consent, can increase indefinitely under social protection: something which could not take place in the state of nature, where the individual alone defends his property.

Whichever it is, it at least follows from the principle of Kant, that in the state of nature, acquisition extends for each family to all that which it can defend, which is to say all that it can cultivate; or better, it is equal to a fraction of the cultivatable surface divided by the number of families: since, if acquisition surpasses this quotient, it immediately encounters more enemies than defenders. Now, as in the state of nature that acquisition, thus limited, is only provisory, the State, by putting an end to the provision, has wanted to put an end to the reciprocal hostility of the acquirers, by rendering their acquisitions peremptory. Equality has thus been the secret thought, the key object of the legislator, in the constitution of property. In this system, the only reasonable thing, the only one admissible, is the property of my neighbour which is the guarantee of my property. I no longer say with the moneylender, *possideo quia possideo*; I say with the philosopher, *possideo quia possides.*[3]

We will see by what follows that equality by property is every bit as chimerical as equality by credit, monopoly, competition, or any other economic category; and that in this regard the providential genius, while gathering from property the most precious fruits and the most unexpected, has not been less deceived in his hope, and is bound to the impossible. Property contains neither more nor less truth than all the moments which preceded it in the economic evolution; like them, it contributes, in equal proportion, to the development of well-being and to the increase of misery; it is not the form of order, it must change and disappear with order. Thus the systems of the philosophers on certainty, after having enriched logic with their glimpses, resolve themselves and disappear in the conclusions of common sense.

But in the end the thought which has presided at the establishment of property has been good: thus we have to seek what justifies that establishment, how property serves wealth, and what are the positive and determinant reasons that have caused it.

First, let us recall the general character of the economic movement.

The first period aimed to inaugurate labour on the earth by the separation of industries, to bring an end to the inhospitable character of nature, to pull man out of his original poverty, and to convert his inert faculties into positive and active faculties, which will be for him so many instruments of happiness. As in the creation of the universe the infinite force was divided, so, in order to create society, the providential genius divided labour. By that division, equality beginning to manifest itself, no longer as identity in plurality, but as equivalence in variety, the social organism is constituted in

---

3    "I possess because I possess"; "I possess because you possess." (Editor)

principle, the germ has received the vivifying principle, and the collective man comes into existence.

But the division of labour supposes some generalised functions and some divided functions: from the inequality of conditions among the workers, raising some up and bringing others low; and from the first period, industrial antagonism replaces primitive community.

All the subsequent evolutions tend at once, on the one hand to bring about the equilibrium of the faculties, and on the other always to develop industry and goodwill. We have seen how, on the contrary, the providential effort led always to an equal and divergent progress of poverty and wealth, of incapacity and science. In the second period, appears the selfish and injurious division, capital and wage-labour; in the third, the evil is increased by commercial war; in the fourth, it is concentrated and generalised by monopoly; in the fifth, it receives the consecration of the State. International commerce and credit come in their turn to give a new development to the antagonism. Later, the fiction of the productivity of capital becoming, by the power of opinion, nearly a reality, a new peril threatens society, the negation of labour itself by the overflow of capital. It is in this moment, and from this extreme situation, that property rises theoretically: and such is the transition that we must understand well.

Up to the present, if one set aside the ulterior aim of economic evolution, and were to consider it only in itself, all that society does, it does alternately for and against monopoly. Monopoly has been the pivot around which the various economic elements move and circulate. However, despite the necessity of its existence, despite the efforts without number that it has made for its development, despite the authority of the universal consent that admits it, monopoly is still only provisional; it is supposed, as Kant said, to endure only as long as the occupant is able to use and defend it. This is why sometimes it ends by right at death, as in the permanent, but non-venal duties [*fonctions*]; sometimes it is reduced to a limited time, as in patents; sometimes it is lost by non-exercise, which has given rise to the theories of prescription, such as annual possession, still in use among the Arabs. At other times, monopoly is revocable at the will of the sovereign, as in the permission to build on a military field, etc. Thus monopoly is only a form without reality; the monopoly pertains to the man, but it does not include the materials: it is properly the exclusive privilege to produce and sell; it is still not the alienation of the instruments of labour, the alienation of the land. Monopoly is a type of tenant farming which only interests the man through the consideration of profit. The monopolist holds to no industry, to no instrument of labour, to no residence: he is cosmopolitan and omni-functional; it matters little to him, provided that he gains; his soul is not chained to a point on the horizon, to a particle of matter. His existence remains vague, as long as society, which has conferred on him the monopoly as a means of fortune, does not make that monopoly a necessity for his life.

Now, monopoly, so precarious by itself, exposed to all the incursions, all the trials of competition, tormented by the State, pressured by credit, not sticking at all in the heart of the monopolist; monopoly tends incessantly, under the action of agiotage, to objectify itself; so that humanity, delivered constantly to the financial storm by the general disengagement of capital, is at risk of detaching itself from even labour and to retrogress in its march.

Indeed, what was monopoly before the establishment of credit, before the reign of the bank? A privilege of *gain,* not a right of *sovereignty;* a privilege on the product, much more than a privilege on the instrument. The monopolist remained a foreigner on the land that he inhabited, but that he did not really possess; he could very well multiply his exploitations, enlarge his manufactures, join lands together: he was always a steward, rather than a master; he did not imprint his character on these things; they were not made in his image; he did not love them for themselves, but only for the values that it should render to him; in a word, he did not want monopoly as an end, but as a means.

After the development of institutions of credit, the condition of monopoly is still worse.

The producers, that it is a question of associating, have become totally incapable of association; they have lost the taste and the spirit of labour: they are gamblers. To the fanaticism for competition, they have joined the frenzies of roulette. The *bankocracy* has changed their character and their ideas. Once they lived together as masters and waged workers, vassals and suzerains: now they are no longer known as anything but borrowers and usurers, winners and losers. Labour has given way before credit; real value vanishes before fictitious value, production before speculation [*agiotage*]. Earth, capital, talent, labour even, if we somewhere still encounter labour, serves as a stake. One no longer concerns oneself with privileges, monopolies, public functions, industry; one no longer asks labour for wealth, one awaits a roll of the dice. Credit, the theory said, needs a fixed basis; and this is exactly what credit has put in motion. It rests, it added, only on some mortgages, and it makes those mortgages run. It seeks guarantees; and despite the theory that wants to see guarantees only in realities, the pledge of credit is always the man, since it is the man who puts the pledge to work, and without the man the pledge would be absolutely ineffective and null, it happens that the man no longer holds to the realities, with the guarantee of the man the pledge disappears, and credit remains that which it had vainly boasted not to be, a fiction.

Credit, in a word, by dint of releasing capital, has finishing by releasing man himself from society and from nature. In that universal idealism, man no longer keeps to the soil; he is suspended in the air by an invisible power. The land is covered with people, some basking in opulence, the others hideous from poverty, and it is possessed by no one. It no longer has anything but masters who despise it, and some serfs who hate it: for they do not cultivate it for themselves, but for a holder of coupons[4] that no one knows, that they never see, who will perhaps pass on that land without having laid eyes on it, without doubting that it is his. The holder of the land, that is the owner of the registered annuity, resembles the merchant of bric-a-brac: he has in his portfolio some smallholdings, some pastures, some rich harvests, some excellent vineyards; what does it matter to him! He is ready to give it all up for ten centimes of increase: in the evening he will part with his goods, as in the morning he had received them, without love and without regret.

Thus, by way of the fiction of the productivity of capital, credit has arrived at the fiction of wealth. The land is no longer the workshop of the human race; it is a bank, and if it were possible that this bank would not ceaselessly make new victims, forced to ask again from labour the income that it has lost gambling, and by that to sustain the reality of capital; if it were possible that bankruptcy would not come now and again to interrupt that infernal orgy, the value of the security decreasing always while the fiction would multiply its paper, real wealth would become null, and registered wealth would increase to infinity.

But society cannot retreat: it must thus redeem monopoly or risk perishing, to save the human individuality that is ready to ruin itself for the sake of a merely ideal ownership; it must, in a word, consolidate, establish monopoly. Monopoly was, so to speak, a bachelor: We desire, says society, that it be married. It was the sycophant of the land,[5] the exploiter of capital: I want it to become its lord and spouse. Monopoly stopped at the individual, from now on it will extend to the race. By it the human race only had some heroes and barons; in the future, it will have dynasties. Monopoly familised [*familisé*], man will become attached to his land, to his industry, as he is to his wife and to his children, and man and nature will be united in an eternal affection.

Credit had put society in a condition that was indeed the most detestable that one could imagine, where man could abuse the most and have the least. Now, in the view of Providence, in the destinies of humanity and of the globe, man should be animated by a spirit of conservation and love for the instrument of his works, an instrument represented in general by the land. For man it is not only a question of exploiting the land, but of cultivating it, improving and loving it: now, how could society fulfil this aim other than by changing monopoly into property, cohabitation into marriage, *propriamque*

---

4   A coupon is the amount of interest paid per year expressed as a percentage of the face value of a bond. A bond is, in finance, a debt security in which the issuer is the borrower (debtor) and the holder is the lender (creditor). (Editor)

5   Proudhon writes "Il était le courtisan de la terre." Courtesan historically referred to a courtier. However, these were often considered as insincere, skilled at flattery and intrigue, ambitious and lacking regard for the national interest and so, in French, courtesan figuratively means "sycophant." (Editor)

*dicabo,* opposing to the fiction that exhausts and soils, the reality which fortifies and ennobles?[6]

The revolution that is prepared in monopoly therefore has above all in mind the monopoly of the land: for it is to this example, it is on the model of property in land that all properties are constituted. From the conditional, temporary and lifelong, appropriation would thus become perpetual, transmissible and absolute. And in order to better defend the inviolability of property, goods would in the future be distinguished as *moveable* and *immoveable,* and laws would be made to regulate the transmission, alienation and expropriation of both.

[...]

## §III HOW PROPERTY IS CORRUPTED

By means of property, society has realised a thought that is useful, laudable, and even inevitable: I am going to prove that by obeying an invincible necessity, it has cast itself into an impossible hypothesis. I believe that I have not forgotten or diminished any of the motives which have presided over the establishment of property; I even dare say that I have given these motives a unity and an obviousness unknown until this moment. Let the reader fill in, moreover, what I may have accidentally omitted: I accept in advance all his reasons, and propose nothing to contradict him. But let him then tell me, with hand on conscience, what he finds to reply to the counterproof that I am going to make.

Doubtless the collective reason, obeying the order of destiny that prescribed it, by a series of providential institutions, to consolidate monopoly, has done its duty: its conduct is irreproachable, and I do not blame it. It is the triumph of humanity to know how to recognise what is inevitable, as the greatest effort of its virtue is to know how to submit to it. If then the collective reason, in instituting property, has followed its orders, it has earned no blame: its responsibility is covered. But that property, which society, forced and constrained, if I thus do dare to say, has unearthed, who guarantees that it will last? Not society, which has conceived it from on high, and has not been able to add to it, subtract from it, or modify it in any way. In conferring property on man, it has left to it its qualities and its defects; it has taken no precaution against its constitutive vices, or against the superior forces which could destroy it. If property in itself is corruptible, society knows nothing of it, and can do nothing about it. If property is exposed to the attacks of a more powerful principle, society can do nothing more. How, indeed, will society cure the vice proper to property, since property is the daughter of

---

6   Proudhon is alluding to the Latin phrase "conubio iungam stabili propriamque dicabo" from Virgil's epic, *The Aeneid* (4.126), in which the goddess Juno proposes to "consecrate" the passion of Dido for Aeneas through marriage, turning unstable passion into a stable bond of property. (Editor)

destiny? And how will it protect it against a higher idea, when it only subsists by means of property, and conceives of nothing above property?

Here then is the proprietary theory.

Property is of necessity providential; the collective reason has received it from God and given it to man. But if not property is corruptible by nature, or assailable by *force majeure*, society is irresponsible; and whoever, armed with that force, will present themselves to combat property, society owes them submission and obeisance.

Thus it is a question of knowing, first, if property is in itself a corruptible thing, which gives rise to destruction; in second place, if there exists somewhere, in the economic arsenal, an instrument which can defeat it.

I will treat the first question in this section; we will seek later to discover what the enemy is which threatens to devour property.

Property is the right to *use* and *abuse,* in a word, despotism. Not that the despot is presumed ever to have the intention of destroying the thing: that is not what must be understood by the right to use and abuse. Destruction for its own sake is not assumed on the part of the proprietor; one always supposes some use that he will make of his goods, and that there is for him a motive of suitability and utility. By abuse, the legislator has meant that the proprietor has the right to be mistaken in the use of his goods, without ever being subject to investigation for that poor use, without being responsible to anyone for his error. The proprietor is always supposed to act in his own best interest; and it is in order to allow him more liberty in the pursuit of that interest, that society has conferred on him the right of use and abuse of his monopoly. Up to this point, then, the domain of property is irreprehensible.

But let us recall that this domain has not been conceded solely in respect for the individual: there exist, in the account of the motives for the concession, some entirely social considerations; the contract is synallagmatic between society and man. That is so true, so admitted even by the proprietors, that every time someone comes to attack their privilege, it is in the name, and only in the name, of society that they defend it.

Now, does proprietary despotism give satisfaction to society? For if it were otherwise, reciprocity being illusory, the pact would be null, and sooner or later either property or society will perish. I reiterate then my question. Does proprietary despotism fulfil its obligation toward society? Is proprietary despotism a prudent administrator? Is it, in its essence, just, social, humane? There is the question.

And this is what I respond without fear of refutation:

If it is indubitable, from the point of view of individual liberty, that the concession of property had been necessary; from the juridical point of view, the concession of property is radically null, because it implies on the part of the concessionaire certain obligations that it is optional for him to fulfil or not fulfil. Now, by virtue of the principle that every convention founded on the accomplishment of a non-obligatory condition does not compel, the tacit contract of property, passed between the privileged and the State, to the ends that we have previously established, is clearly illusory; it is annulled by the non-reciprocity, by the injury of one of the parties. And as, with regard to property, the accomplishment of the obligation cannot be due unless the concession itself is by that alone revoked, it follows that there is a contradiction in the definition and incoherence in the pact. Let the contracting parties, after that, persist in maintaining their treaty, the force of things is charged with proving to them that they do useless work: despite the fact that they have it, the inevitability of their antagonism restores discord between them.

All the economists indicate the disadvantages for agricultural production of the parcelling of the territory. In agreement on this with the socialists, they would see with joy a joint exploitation which, operating on a large scale, applying the powerful processes of the art and making important economies on the material, would double, perhaps quadruple product. But the proprietor says, *Veto*, I do not want it. And as he is within his rights, as no one in the world knows the means of changing these rights other than by expropriation, and since expropriation is nothingness, the legislator, the economist and the proletarian recoil in fright before the unknown, and content themselves to expect nowhere near the harvests promised. The proprietor is, by character, envious of the public good: he could purge himself of this vice only by losing property.

Thus, property becomes an obstacle to labour and wealth, an obstacle to the social economy: these days, there is hardly anyone but the economists and the men of law that this astonishes. I seek a way to make it enter into their minds all at once, without commentary...

[...]

Let us suppose that the proprietor, by a chivalrous liberality, yields to the invitation of science, allows labour to improve and multiply its products. An immense good will result for the day-workers and peasants, whose fatigues, reduced by half, will still find themselves, by the lowering of the price of goods, paid double.

But the proprietor: I would be pretty silly, he says, to abandon a profit so clear! Instead of a hundred days of labour, I would not have to pay more than fifty: it is not the proletarian who would profit, but me.—But then, observe, the proletarian will be still more miserable than before, since he will be idle once more.—That does not matter to me, replies the proprietor. I exercise my right. Let the others buy well, if they can, or let them go to other parts to seek their fortune, there are thousands and millions!

Every proprietor nourishes, in his heart of hearts, this homicidal thought. And as by competition, monopoly and credit, the invasion always grows, the workers find themselves incessantly eliminated from the soil: property is the depopulation of the earth.

Thus then the revenue of the proprietor, combined with the progress of industry, changes into an abyss the pit dug beneath the feet of the worker by monopoly; the evil is aggravated by privilege. The revenue of the proprietor is no longer the patrimony of the poor,—I mean that portion of the agricultural product which remains after the costs of farming have been paid off, and which must always serve as a new material for the use of labour, according to that fine theory which shows us accumulated capital as a land unceasingly offered to production, and which, the more one works it, the more it seems to extend. The revenue has become for the proprietor the token of his lechery, the instrument of his solitary pleasures. And note that the proprietor who abuses, guilty before charity and morality, remains blameless before the law, unassailable in political economy. To eat up his income! What could be more beautiful, more noble, more legitimate? In the opinion of the common people as in that of the great, unproductive consumption is the virtue *par excellence* of the proprietor. Every trouble in society comes from this indelible selfishness.

In order to facilitate the exploitation of the soil, and put the different localities in relation, a route, a canal is necessary. Already the plan is made; one will sacrifice an edge on that side, a strip on the other; some hectares of poor terrain, and the way is open. But the proprietor cries out with his booming voice: I do not want it! And before this formidable *veto,* the would-be lender dares not go through with it. Still, in the end, the State has dared to reply: I want it! But what hesitations, what frights, what trouble, before taking that heroic resolution! What trade-offs! What trials! The people have paid dearly for this act of authority, by which the promoters were still more stunned than the proprietors. For it came to establish a precedent the consequences of which appeared incalculable!... One promised themselves that after having passed this Rubicon, the bridges were broken, and they would stay that way. To do violence to property, what could this portend! The shadow of Spartacus would have appeared less terrible.

In the depths of a naturally poor soil, chance, and then science, born of chance, discovers some treasure troves of fuel. It is a free gift of nature, deposited under the soil of the common habitation, of which each has a right to claim his share. But the proprietor arrives, the proprietor to whom the concession of the soil has been made solely with a view to cultivation. You shall not pass, he says; you will not violate my property! At this unexpected summons, great debate arises among the learned. Some say that the mine is not the same thing as the arable land, and must belong to the State; others maintain that the proprietor owns the property above and below, *cujus est soluw, ejus est usque ad inferos.* For if the proprietor, a new Cerberus posted as the guard of dark kingdoms, can put a ban on entry, the right of the State is only a fiction. It would be necessary to return to expropriation, and where would that lead? The State gives in: "Let us affirm it boldly," it says through the mouth of M. Dunoyer, supported by M. Troplong; "it is no more just and reasonable to say that the mines are the property of the nation, than it once was to claim that it was the property of the king. The mines are essentially part of the soil. It is with a perfect good sense that the common law has said that the property in what is above implies property in what is below. Where, indeed, would we make the separation?"

M. Dunoyer is troubled by very little. Who hesitates to separate the mine from the surface, just as we sometimes separate, in a succession, the ground floor from the first floor? That is what is done very well by the proprietors of the coal-mining fields in the department of the Loire, where the property in the *depths* has been nearly everywhere separated from the surface property, and transformed into a sort of circulating value like the actions of a public limited company. Who still hesitates to regard the mine as a new land for which one needs a way of clearing?... But what! Napoléon, the inventor of the *juste-milieu*, the prince of the Doctrinaires, had wanted it otherwise; the counsel of State, M. Troplong and M. Dunoyer applaud: there is nothing more to consider. A transaction has taken place under who-knows-what insignificant reservations; the proprietors have been rewarded by the imperial munificence: how have they acknowledged that favour?

I have already had more than one occasion to speak of the coalition of the mines of the Loire. I return to it for the last time. In that department, the richest in the kingdom in coal deposits, the exploitation was first conducted in the most expensive and most absurd manner. The interest of the mines, that of the consumers and of the proprietors, demanded that the extraction was made jointly: We do not want it, the proprietors have repeated for who knows how many years, and they have engaged in a horrible competition, of which the devastation of the mines has paid the first costs. Were they within their rights? So much so, that one will see the State finding it bad that they left there.

Finally the proprietors, at least the majority, managed to get along: they associated. Doubtless they have given in to reason, to motives of conservation, of good order, of general as much as private interest. From then on, the consumers would have fuel at a good price, the miners a regular labour and guaranteed wages. What thunder of acclamations in the public! What praise in the academies! What decorations for that fine devotion! We will not inquire whether the gathering is consistent with the text and to the spirit of the law, which forbids the joining of the concessions; we will only see the advantage of the union, and we will have proven that the legislator has neither wanted, nor been able to want, anything but the well-being of the people: *Salus populi suprema lex esta.*

Deception! First, it is not reason that the proprietors followed in coming together: they submitted only to force. To the extent that competition ruins them, they range themselves on the side of the victor, and accelerate by their growing mass the rout of the dissidents. Then, the association constitutes itself in a collective monopoly: the price of the merchandise increases, so much for consumption; wages are reduced, so much for labour. Then, the public complains; the legislature thinks of intervening; the heavens threaten with a bolt of lightning; the prosecution invokes article 419 of the Penal Code which forbids coalitions, but which permits every monopolist to combine, and stipulates no measure for the price of the merchandise; the administration appeals to the law of 1810 which, wishing to encourage exploitation, while dividing the concessions, is rather more favourable than opposed to unity; and the advocates prove by dissertations, writs and arguments, these that the coalition is within its rights, those that it is not. Meanwhile the consumer says: Is it just that I pay the costs of speculation [*agiotage*] and of competition? Is it just that what has been given for nothing to the proprietor in my greatest interest comes back to me at such an expense? Let one establish a tariff! We do not want it, respond the proprietors. And I defy the State to defeat their resistance other than by an act of authority, which resolves nothing; or else by an indemnity, which is to abandon all.

Property is unsocial, not only in possession, but also in production. Absolute mistress of the instruments of labour, she renders only imperfect, fraudulent, detestable products. The consumer is no longer served, he is robbed of his money.—Shouldn't you have known, one said to the rural proprietor, to wait some days to gather these fruits, to reap this wheat, dry this hay; do not put water in this milk, rinse your barrels, care more for your harvests, bite off less and do better. You are overloaded: put back a part of your inheritance.—A fool! responds the proprietor with a mocking air. Twenty badly worked acres always render more than ten which take us so much time, and will double the costs. With your system, the earth will feed more men: but what is it to me if there are more men? It is a question of my profit. As to the quality of my products, they will always be good enough for those who lack. You believe yourself skilled, my dear counsellor, and you are only a child. What's the use of being a proprietor, if one only sells what is worth carrying to market, and at a just price, at that?... I do not want it.

Well, you say, let the police do their duty!... The police! You forget that its action only begins when the evil has already been done. The police, instead of watching over production, inspects the product: after having allowed the proprietor to cultivate, harvest, manufacture without conscience, it appears to lay hands on the green fruit, spill the terrines of watered milk, the casks of adulterated beer and wine, to throw the prohibited meats into the road: all to the applause of the economists and the populace, who want property to be respected, but will not put up with trade being free. Heh! Barbarians! It is the poverty of the consumer which provokes the flow of these impurities. Why, if you cannot stop the proprietor from acting badly, do you stop the poor from living badly? Isn't it better if they have colic than if they die of hunger?

Say to that industrialist that it is a cowardly, immoral thing, to speculate on the distress of the poor, on the inexperience of children and of young girls: he simply will not understand you. Prove to him that by a reckless overproduction, by badly calculated enterprises, he compromises, along with his own fortune, the existence of his workers; that if his interests are not touched, those of so many families, grouped around him, merit consideration; that by the arbitrariness of his favours he creates around him discouragement, servility, hatred. The proprietor takes offence: Am I not the master? says he in parody of the legend; and because I am good to a few, do you claim to make of my kindness a right for all? Must I render account to those who should obey me? That home is mine; what I should do regarding the direction of my affairs, I alone am the judge of it. Are my workers my slaves? If my conditions offend them, and they find better, let them go! I will be the first to compliment them. Very excellent philanthropists, who then prevents you from labouring in the workshops? Act, give the example; instead of that delightful life that you lead by preaching virtue, set up a factory, put yourself to work. Let us see finally through you association on the earth! As for me, I reject with all my strength such a servitude. Associates! Rather bankruptcy, rather death!

[...]

A poor worker having his wife in childbirth, the midwife, in despair, must ask assistance of a physician.—I must have 200 francs, says the doctor, I won't budge.—My God! replies the worker, my household is not worth 200 francs; it will be necessary that my wife die, or else we will all go naked, the child, her and me!

That obstetrician, let God rejoice! was yet a worthy man, benevolent, melancholic and mild, member of several scientific and charitable societies: on his mantle, a bronze of Hippocrates, refusing the presents of Artaxerxes.[7] He was incapable of saddening a child, and would have sacrificed himself for his cat. His refusal did not come from hardness; that was tactical. For a physician who understands business, devotion has only a season: the clientele acquired, the reputation once made, he reserves himself for the wealthy, and, save for ceremonial occasions, he rejects the indiscreet. Where would we be, if it were necessary to heal the sick indiscriminately? Talent and reputation are precious properties, that one must make the most of, not squander.

The trait that I have just cited is one of the most benign; what horrors, if I should penetrate to the bottom of this medical matter! Let no one tell me that these are exceptions: I except everyone. I criticise property, not men. Property, in Vincent de Paul[8] as in Harpagon[9], is always monstrous; and until the service of medicine is organised, it will be for the physician as for the scientist, for the advocate as for the artist: he will be a being degraded by his own title, by the title of proprietor.

---

7   Artaxerxes I was king of the Persian Empire from 464 BC to 424 BC. After Persia had been defeated at Eurymedon, Artaxerxes began to weaken the Athenians by funding their enemies in Greece. (Editor)

8   Vincent de Paul (1581–1660) was a Catholic priest dedicated to serving the poor. He was canonised in 1737. (Editor)

9   Harpagon was the name of the miser in Molière's comedy *L'Avare* (*The Miser*). (Editor)

This is what this judge did not understand, too good a man for his time, who, yielding to the indignation of his conscience, decided one day to express public criticism of the corporation of lawyers. It was something immoral, according to him, scandalous, that the ease with which these gentlemen welcome all sorts of causes. If this blame, starting so high, had been supported and commented on by the press, it was made perhaps for the legal profession. But the honourable company could not perish by the censure, any more than property can die from a diatribe, any more than the press can die of its own venom. Besides, isn't the judiciary interdependent with the corporation of lawyers? Isn't the one, like the other, established by and for property? What would Perrin Dandin[10] become, if he were forbidden to judge? And what would we argue about, without property? The order of lawyers therefore rises; journalism, the chicanery of the pen, came to the rescue of the chicanery of words: the riot went rumbling and swelling until that imprudent magistrate, involuntary organ of the public conscience, had made an apology to sophistry, and retracted the truth that had arisen spontaneously through him.

[...]

Thus property becomes more antisocial to the extent that it is distributed on a greater number of heads. What seems necessary to soften, and to humanise property, collective privilege, is precisely what shows property in its hideousness: property divided, impersonal property, is the worst of properties. Who does not realise today that France is covered with *great companies*, more formidable, more eager for booty, than the famous bands with which the brave du Guesclin[11] delivered France!...

Be careful not to take community of property for association. The individual proprietor can still show himself accessible to mercy, justice, and shame; the proprietor-corporation is heartless, without remorse. It is a fantastic, inflexible being, freed from every passion and all love, which moves in the circle of its ideas as the millstone in its revolutions crushes grain. It is not by becoming common that property can become social: one does not relieve rabies by biting everyone. Property will end by the transformation of its principle, not by an indefinite co-participation. And that is why democracy, or system of universal property, that some men, as hard-nosed as they are blind, insist on preaching to the people, is powerless to create society.

[...]

Work, the economists repeat ceaselessly to the people; work, save, capitalise, become proprietors in your turn. As they said: Workers, you are the

---

10  Perrin Dandin is a simple citizen in François Rabelais' *Third Book*. He seats himself as a judge and passes offhand judgements in any matter of litigation. (Editor)

11  Bertrand du Guesclin (1320–80), known as the Eagle of Brittany, was a Breton knight and French military commander during the Hundred Years' War. (Editor)

recruits of property. Each of you carries in your own sack[12] the rod that serves to correct you, and that may one day serve you to correct others.[13] Raise yourself up to property by labour; and when you have the taste for human flesh, you will no longer want any other meat, and you will make up for your long abstinences.

To fall from the proletariat into property! From slavery into tyranny, which is to say, following Plato, always into slavery! What a perspective! And though it is inevitable, the condition of the slave is no more tenable. In order to advance, to free yourself from wage-labour, it is necessary to become a capitalist, to become a tyrant! It is necessary; do you understand, proletarians? Property is not a matter of choice for humanity, it is the absolute order of destiny. You will only be free after you have redeemed yourself, by subjugation to your masters, from the servitude that they have pressed upon you.[14]

One beautiful Sunday in summer, the people of the great cities leave their sombre and damp residences, and go to seek the vigorous and pure air of the country. But what has happened! There is no more countryside! The land, divided in a thousand closed cells, traversed by long galleries, the land is no longer found; the sight of the fields exists for the people of the towns only in the theatre and the museum: the birds alone contemplate the real landscape from high in the air. The proprietor, who pays very dearly for a lodge on this hacked-up earth, enjoys, selfish and solitary, some strip of turf that he calls his country: except for this corner, he is exiled from the soil like the poor. Some people can boast of never having seen the land of their birth! It is necessary to go far, into the wilderness, in order to find again that poor nature, that we violate in a brutal manner, instead of enjoying, as chaste spouses, its heavenly embraces.

Thus, property, which should make us free, makes us prisoners. What am I saying? It degrades us, by making us servants and tyrants to one another.

Do you know what it is to be a wage-worker? To work under a master, watchful [*jaloux*] of his prejudices even more than of his orders; whose dignity

12　This is an allusion to tradesmen who owned their own tools and took them in a bag or sack ("sac") when they were dismissed from employment. Hence the expression "get the sack" which is derived from the 17th century French expression "On luy a donné son sac." (Editor)

13　There is a play-on-words in Proudhon's "Chacun de vous porte dans son sac la verge qui sert à le corriger, et qui peut lui servir un jour à corriger les autre." *Corriger* as well as meaning "to correct" also means "to give a good hiding to" or "to punish." (Editor)

14　Proudhon wrote: "Vous ne serez libres qu'après vous être rachetés, par l'asservissement de vos maîtres, de la servitude qu'ils font peser sur vous." *Racheter* as well as meaning "to atone for" or "to redeem" also means "to buy" and he plays with this dual meaning. (Editor)

consists above all in demanding, *sic volo, sic jubeo*,[15] and never explaining; often you have a low opinion of him, and you mock him! Not to have any thought of your own, to study without ceasing the thought of others, to know no stimulus except your daily bread, and the fear of losing your job!

The wage-worker is a man to whom the proprietor who hires his services gives this speech: What you have to do does not concern you at all: you do not control it, you do not answer for it. Every observation is forbidden to you; there is no profit for you to hope for except from your wage, no risk to run, no blame to fear.

Thus one says to the journalist: Lend us your columns, and even, if that suits you, your administration. Here is what you have to say, and here is what you have to do. Whatever you think of our ideas, of our ends and of our means, always defend our party, emphasise our opinions. That cannot compromise you, and must not disturb you: the character of the journalist, it is anonymous. Here is, for your fee, ten thousand francs and a hundred subscriptions. What are you going to do? And the journalist, like the Jesuit, responds by sighing: *I must live!*

One says to the lawyer: This matter presents some pros and cons; there is a party whose luck I have decided to try, and for this I have need of a man of your profession. If it is not you, it will be your colleague, your rival; and there are a thousand crowns for the lawyer if I win my case, and five hundred francs if I lose it. And the lawyer bows with respect, saying to his conscience, which murmurs: *I must live!*

One says to the priest: Here is some money for three hundred masses. You don't have to worry yourself about the morality of the deceased: it is probable that he will never see God, being dead in hypocrisy, his hands full of the goods of other, and laden with the curses of the people. These are not your affairs: we pay, fire away! And the priest, raising his eyes to heaven, says: *Amen, I must live.*

One says to the purveyor of arms: We need thirty thousand rifles, ten thousand swords, a thousand quintals of shot, and a hundred barrels of powder. What we can do with it is not your concern; it is possible that all will pass to the enemy: but there will be two thousand francs of profit. That's good, responds the purveyor: each to his craft, *everyone must live!*... Make the tour of society; and after having noticed the universal absolutism, you will have recognised the universal indignity. What immorality in this system of servility [*valetage*]! What stigma in this mechanisation!

[...]

Abuse! Cry the jurists, perversity of man. It is not property that makes us envious and greedy, which makes our passions spring up, and arms with its sophisms our bad faith. It is our passions, our vices, on the contrary, which sully and corrupt property.

---

15  "Thus I wish. Thus I command." (Editor)

I would like it as well if one says to me that it is not concubinage that sullies man, but that it is man who, by his passions and vices, sullies and corrupts concubinage. But, doctors, the facts that I denounce, are they, or are they not, of the essence of property? Are they not, from the legal point of view, irreprehensible, placed in the shelter of every judiciary action? Can I remand to the judge, summon to appear before the tribunals this journalist who prostitutes his pen for money? That lawyer, that priest, who sells to iniquity, one his speech, the other his prayers? This doctor who allows the poor man to perish, if he does not submit in advance the fee demanded? This old satyr who deprives his children for a courtesan? Can I prevent a licitation[16] that will abolish the memory of my forefathers, and render their posterity without ancestors, as if it were of incestuous or adulterous stock? Can I restrain the proprietor, without compensating him beyond what he possesses, that is without wrecking society, for heeding the needs of society?...

Property, you say, is innocent of the crime of the proprietor; property is good and useful in itself: it is our passions and our vices which deprave it.

Thus, in order to save property, you distinguish it from morals! Why not distinguish it right away from society? That was precisely the reasoning of the economists. Political economy, said M. Rossi, is in itself good and useful; but it is not moral: it proceeds, setting aside all morality; it is for us not to abuse its theories, to profit from its teachings, according to the higher laws of morality. As if he said: Political economy, the economy of society is not society; the economy of society proceeds without regard to any society; it is up to us not to abuse its theories, to profit from its teachings, according to the higher laws of society! What chaos!

I not only maintain with the economists that property is neither morals nor society; but more that it is by its principle directly contrary to morals and to society, just as political economy is anti-social, because its theories are diametrically opposed to the social interest.

According to the definition, property is the right of use and abuse, which is to say the absolute, irresponsible domain of man over his person and his goods. If property ceased to be the right of abuse, it would cease to be property. I have taken my examples from the category of abusive acts permitted to the proprietor: what happens here that is not of an unimpeachable legality and propriety? Hasn't the proprietor the right to give his goods to whomever seems good to him, to leave his neighbour to burn without crying fire, to oppose himself to the public good, to squander his patrimony, to exploit and fleece the worker, to produce badly and sell badly? Can the proprietor be judicially constrained to use his property well? Can he be disturbed in the abuse? What am I saying? Isn't property, precisely because it is abusive, that which is most sacred for the legislator? Can one conceive of a property for which police would determine the use, and suppress the abuse? And is

---

16   Licitation is sale to the highest bidder. (Translator)

it not evident, finally, that if one wanted to introduce justice into property, one would destroy property; as the law, by introducing honesty into concubinage, has destroyed concubinage?

Thus, property, in principle and in essence, is immoral: that proposition is soon reached by critique. Consequently the Code, which, in determining the right of the proprietor, has not reserved those of morals, is a code of immorality; jurisprudence, that alleged science of right, which is nothing other than the collection of the proprietary rubrics, is immoral, and justice, is instituted in order protect the free and peaceful abuse of property; justice, which orders us to come to the aid against those who would oppose themselves to that abuse; which *afflicts* and *marks with infamy* whoever is so daring as to claim to mend the outrages of property, justice is infamous. If a son, supplanted in the paternal affection by an unworthy mistress, should destroy the document which disinherits and dishonours him, he would answer in front of justice. Accused, convicted, condemned, he would go to the penal colony to make honourable amends to property, while the prostitute will be sent off in possession. Where then is the immorality here? Where is the infamy? Is it not on the side of justice? Let us continue to unwind this chain, and we will soon know the whole truth that we seek. Not only is justice, instituted to protect property, itself abusive, itself immoral, infamous; but the penal sanction is infamous, the police are infamous, the executioner and the gallows, infamous, and property, which embraces that whole series, property, from which this odious lineage come, property is infamous.

Judges armed to defend it, magistrates whose zeal is a permanent threat to those accused by it, I question you. What have you seen in property which has been able in this way to subjugate your conscience and corrupt your judgement? What principle, superior without doubt to property, more worthy of your respect than property, makes it so precious to you? When its works declare it infamous, how do you proclaim it holy and sacred? What consideration, what prejudice affects you?

Is it the majestic order of human societies that you do not understand, but of which you suppose that property is the unshakeable foundation?—No, since property, as it is, is for you order itself; since first it is proven that property is by nature abusive, that is to say disorderly and anti-social.

Is it Necessity or Providence, the laws of which we do not understand, but the designs of which we adore?—No, since, according to the analysis, property being contradictory and corruptible, it is for that very reason a negation of Necessity, an injury to Providence.

Is it a superior philosophy considering human miseries from on high, and seeking by evil to obtain the good?—No, since philosophy is the agreement of reason and experience, and in the judgement of reason as in that of experience, property is condemned.

[...]

## §IV DEMONSTRATION OF THE HYPOTHESIS OF GOD BY PROPERTY

If God did not exist, there would be no proprietors: that is the conclusion of political economy.

And the conclusion of social science is this: Property is the crime of the Supreme Being. There is for man only one duty, only one religion, it is to renounce God. *Hoc est primum et maximum mandatum.*[17]

It is proven that the establishment of property among men has not been a matter of choice and philosophy: its origin, like that of royalty, like that of languages and forms of worship, is entirely spontaneous, mystical, in a word, divine. Property belongs to the great family of instinctive beliefs, which, under the mantle of religion and authority, still reigns everywhere over our over-proud species. Property, in a word, is itself a religion: it has its theology, political economy; its casuistics, jurisprudence; its mythology and its symbols, in the external forms of justice and of contracts. The historical origin of property, like that of every religion, is hidden in the shadows. Asked about itself, it responds with the fact of its existence; it explains itself with legends, and gives allegories for truths. Finally, property, like every religion once more, is subject to the law of development. Thus one sees it by turns as simple right of use and habitation, as among the Germans and the Arabs; patrimonial possession, inalienable in perpetuity, as among the Jews; feudal and emphyteutic[18] as in the Middle Ages; absolute and circulable at the will of the proprietor, pretty much as the Romans knew it, and as we have it today. But already property, come to its apogee, turns towards its decline: attacked by limited partnership, by the new laws of mortgage, by expropriation for reasons of public utility, by the innovations of the *crédit agricole*, by the new theories on rent,[19] etc., the moment approaches when it will no longer be anything but the shadow of itself.

[...]

So property, once we cease to defend it in its original brutality, and once we speak of disciplining it, of subjecting it to morals, of subordinating it to

---

17   From the Latin Bible: "Jesus said to him: Thou shalt love the Lord thy God with thy whole heart and with thy whole soul and with thy whole mind. This is the first and greatest commandment" (Matthew 22:37–38). (Editor)

18   A form of long-term lease that was an institution of Roman law (although derived from the Greek law) and found in French law. An owner of poorly cultivated land granted such leases so that a tenant would take on the task of improving the land. The tenant paid a small rent or canon for this right and the owner regained the land in its improved condition after a number of years. (Editor)

19   See [Raymond-Théodore] Troplong, *Contrat de Louage* [*Rental Contracts*], Volume I, in which he argues, alone among all the jurisconsults who are his precursors and contemporaries, and with reason, as we think, that in renting, the tenant acquires a right *in the thing*, and that the lease gives way immediately to a real and personal share.

the state, that is, of socialising it, property collapses, it perishes. It perishes, I say, because it is progressive; because its idea is incomplete and its nature is not at all final; because it is the principal moment of a series of which only the ensemble can give a true idea, in a word because it is a religion. What one looks to preserve, and what one pursues in reality under the name of property, is no longer property; it is a new form of possession, without example in the past, and that one strives to deduce from the principles or presumed motives of property, in continuation of that illusion of logic which always makes us suppose at the *origin* or the *end* a thing that must be sought *in* the thing itself, namely, its meanings and its scope.

But if property is a religion, and if, like every religion, it is progressive, it has, like every religion as well, its own specific object. Christianity and Buddhism are religions of penance, or of the education of humanity; Mohammedanism is the religion of fate; monarchy and democracy are one and the same religion, the religion of authority; philosophy itself is the religion of reason. What is this particular religion, the most persistent of the religions, which must lead all the others in its fall and yet only perishes the last, whose devotees no longer believe in it,—property?

Since property manifests itself by occupation and use, since it aims to strengthen and extend monopoly by domain and inheritance, since by means of the revenue that it accumulates without labour, and mortgages committed to without guarantees, since it is resistant to society, since its rule is sheer whim, and since it must perish by justice, property is the religion of FORCE.

[...]

Thus, according to grammar, as well as to fable and analysis, property, the religion of force, is at the same time the religion of servitude. Depending on whether it takes over at gunpoint, or whether it proceeds by exclusion and monopoly, it engenders two sorts of servitudes: the one, the ancient proletariat, result of the primitive fact of conquest or from the violent division of *Adam*, humanity, into *Cain* and *Abel*, patricians and plebeians; the other, the modern proletariat, the *working class* of the economists, caused by the development of the economic phases, which are all summed up, as one has seen, in the mortal deed of the consecration of monopoly by domain, inheritance, and revenue.

[...]

In my discussion of value, I have shown that every labour must leave a surplus; so that, supposing the consumption of the worker to remain constant, his labour should create, on top of his subsistence, an ever greater capital. Under the regime of property, the surplus of labour, essentially collective, passes entirely, like the revenue, to the proprietor: now, where is the difference between that disguised appropriation and the fraudulent usurpation of a communal good?

The consequence of that usurpation is that the worker, whose share of the collective product is constantly confiscated by the entrepreneur, is always on his uppers, while the capitalist is always in profit; that commerce, the exchange of essentially equal values, is no more than the art of buying for 3 fr. what is worth 6, and of selling of 6 fr. that which is worth 3; and that political economy, which upholds and advocates that regime, is the theory of theft, as property, the respect for which maintains a similar state of things, is the religion of force. It is just, M. Blanqui said recently to the Academy of Moral Sciences in a speech on coalitions, that labour should participate in the wealth that it produces. If then it does not participate, it is unjust; and if it is unjust, it is robbery, and the proprietors are robbers. Speak plainly then, economists!...

[...]

But if property, spontaneous and progressive, is a religion, it is, like monarchy and priesthood, of divine right. Similarly, the inequality of conditions and fortunes, poverty, is of divine right; perjury and robbery are of divine institution; the exploitation of man by man is the affirmation, I almost said the manifestation of God. The true theists are the proprietors; the defenders of property are all God-fearing men; the death sentences and torments that they call upon one another as a result of their misunderstandings of property are human sacrifices offered to the god of force. Those, on the contrary, who proclaim the imminent end of property, who, with Jesus Christ and Saint Paul, call for the abolition of property; who think about the production, consumption and distribution of wealth, are the anarchists and the atheists; and society, which advances visibly toward equality and knowledge, society is the incessant negation of God.

[...]

# CHAPTER XIV
## SUMMARY AND CONCLUSION

[...]

IF I AM not mistaken, the reader ought to be convinced at least of one thing, that social truth cannot be found either in utopia or in routine: that political economy is not the science of society, but contains, in itself, the materials of that science, in the same way that chaos before the creation contained the elements of the universe. The fact is that, to arrive at a definite organisation, which appears to be the destiny of the race on this planet, there is nothing left but to make a general equation of our contradictions.

But what will be the formula of this equation?

We already foresee that there should be a law of *exchange*, a theory of MUTUALITY, a system of guarantees which determines the old forms of our civil and commercial societies, and gives satisfaction to all the conditions of efficiency, progress and justice which the critics have pointed out; a society no longer merely conventional, but real, which makes of the subdivision of real estate a scientific instrument; that will abolish the servitude of the machines, and may prevent the coming of crises; that makes of competition a benefit, and of monopoly a pledge of security for all; which by the strength of its principles, instead of making credit of capital and protection of the State, puts capital and the State to work; which by the sincerity of exchange, creates a real solidarity among the nations; which without forbidding individual initiative, without prohibiting domestic economy, continuously restores to society the wealth which is diverted by appropriation; which by the ebb and flow of capital, assures political and industrial equality of the citizenry, and, through a vast system of public education, secures the equality of functions and the equivalence of aptitudes, by continuously raising their level; which through justice, well being and virtue, revives the human conscience, assures the harmony and the equality of the people; a society, in a word, which, being at the same time organisation and transition, escapes what has taken place, guarantees everything and compels nothing...

The theory of *mutuality*, or of *mutuum*, that is to say, the natural form of exchange, of which the most simple form is loan for consumption, is, from the point of view of the collective existence, the synthesis of the two ideas of property and of communism [*communauté*], a synthesis as old as the elements of which it is constituted, since it is nothing more than the return of society to its primitive custom, through the maze of inventions and of systems, the result of a meditation of six thousand years on the fundamental proposition that A equals A.

Everything today is making ready for this solemn restoration; everything proclaims that the reign of fiction has passed, and that society will return to the sincerity of its nature. Monopoly is inflated to world-wide proportions, but a monopoly which encompasses the world cannot remain exclusive; it must republicanise itself or be destroyed. Hypocrisy, venality, prostitution, theft, form the foundation of the public conscience; but, unless humanity learns to live upon what kills it, we must believe that justice and expiation approach....

Already socialism, feeling the error in its utopias, turns to realities and to facts, it laughs at itself in Paris, it discusses in Berlin, in Cologne, in Leipzig, in Breslau; it murmurs in England, it thunders on the other side of the ocean; it commits suicide in Poland, it tries to govern in Berne and in Lausanne. Socialism, in pervading the masses, has become entirely different: the people will not bother about the honour of schools; they ask for work, education, well being, equality; the system does not matter so much, provided that the result is obtained. But when the people want something and it is only a question of finding out how to obtain it, the discovery does not wait; prepare yourself to see the coming of the grand masquerade.

[...]

*Paris, 22ⁿᵈ (Chapter I) and 26ᵗʰ (Chapter II) March 1848*
*Translation by Nathalie Colibert (Chapter I) and Ian Harvey (Chapter II)*

# SOLUTION OF THE SOCIAL PROBLEM

## CHAPTER I
### THE REVOLUTION IN 1848

1. *The Revolution of 24ᵗʰ of February is legitimate, although it was illegal.*
2. *The Provisional Government did not understand the revolution.*
   [...]

THE REVOLUTION, ONE CANNOT DENY IT, HAS BEEN MADE BY THE RED FLAG:[1] the provisional Government, however, has decided to keep the tricolour. To explain this repudiation M. de Lamartine made speeches, *Le National* made dissertations. Red, they say, in the old days was the colour of royalty; red is the colour of the *atrocious* Bourbon, tyrant of the *Deux-Siciles*.[2] Red cannot be the colour of France.

One is not saying red is the colour of justice, [or] the colour of sovereignty. And since all men like red, would it not mean that red is the symbol

---

1   The February Revolution 1848 saw the first major use of the Red Flag by working class insurgents. (Editor)

2   The House of Bourbon was a European royal dynasty whose members ruled France from 1589 to 1792 when it was overthrown during the French Revolution. It was restored briefly in 1814 with the abdication of Napoléon and definitively in 1815 after the Battle of Waterloo. The senior line of the Bourbons was finally overthrown in the July Revolution of 1830. A cadet branch, the House of Orléans, then ruled for 18 years until it too was overthrown by the February Revolution 1848. The Bourbons held thrones in Naples & Sicily, Spain and Parma. (Editor)

of human fraternity? To deny the red flag, the crimson!—but it is the social question you are getting rid of. Every time the People, defeated by suffering, wanted to express its wishes and its complaints outside the law that kills it, it has walked under a red banner. It is true that the red flag has not gone around the world like its happy rival the tricolour. Justice, as M. de Lamartine clearly stated, did not go any further than the Champ-de-Mars.[3] It is so terrible, justice, that one would not know how to hide it enough. Poor red flag. Everyone is abandoning you! Me, I embrace you; I clutch you to my breast. Long live fraternity!

Let us keep, if you wish, the tricolour, symbol of our nationality. But remember that the red flag is the sign of a revolution that will be the last. The red flag! It is the federal standard of humanity.

[...]

# CHAPTER II
## DEMOCRACY

1. *Problem of the people's sovereignty; conditions for the solution.*
2. *Whether universal suffrage expresses the people's sovereignty.*
3. *Whether social reform must come out of political reform or political reform out of social reform; the difference between democracy and republic.*

*Listen, heavens! Earth, lend an ear! The Lord has spoken!*

Thus cried the prophets when, with sparkling eyes and foaming mouths, they announced to the liars and apostates the punishment for their crimes. Thus spoke the Church of the Middle Ages, and Earth, bowing in fear, crossed herself at the voice of the pontiff, at the pastorals of his bishops. Thus came Moses, Elijah, John the Baptist, Mohammed and Luther in turn, all the founders and reformers of religions, each new modification of the dogma proclaimed as emanating from divine authority. And still we see the human masses bowing down in the name of the Most High and submissively receiving the revealers' discipline.

---

3   The Champ de Mars in Paris ("Field of Mars," after Mars, the god of war) was originally used for military drills. During the French Revolution, it was the setting of the *Fête de la Fédération* on July 14th, 1790. It was also the setting of a massacre on July 17th, 1791, when a crowd collected to draft a petition seeking the removal of King Louis XVI. On February 25th, 1848, Lamartine gave a speech in which he declared that "I will never adopt the red flag... because the tri-colour flag has made the tour of the world, under the Republic and the Empire, with our liberties and our glories, and... the red flag has only made the tour of the Champ-de-Mars, trained through torrents of the blood of the people" (quoted in Alphonse de Lamartine, *History of the Girondists; Or, Personal Memoirs of the Patriots of the French Revolution from Unpublished Sources* (New York: Harper & Bros, 1854), xix). (Editor)

But after all, as a philosopher once said, if God has spoken, why have I not heard anything?

These words are enough to shake up the Church, cancel the Scriptures, wipe out faith and hasten the reign of the Antichrist!

I do not want, following [David] Hume's example, to prejudge the reality or possibility of a revelation: how could we make an *a priori* argument about a supernatural fact, a manifestation of the Supreme Being? For me, the question is entirely one of experiencing revelations, and I reduce the religious controversy to that one point—the authenticity of the divine word. Prove that authenticity, and I will be a Christian. Who would then dare to argue with God if he were sure that it was God who was speaking to him?

It is the same with the People as it is with divinity: *vox populi, vox Dei.*[4]

Since the world began, since human tribes started forming monarchies and republics, vacillating from one idea to another like wandering planets, mixing and combining the most diverse elements to organise themselves into societies, overturning courts and thrones as children do to a house of cards, we have seen, at each political shake-up, the leaders of the movement invoking, with varying degrees of explicitness, the sovereignty of the People.

Brutus and Caesar, Cicero and Catalina all availed themselves of popular suffrage in turn. If we must believe the partisans of the deposed system, the Charter of 1830 was the expression of national sovereignty at least as much as the Constitution of Year III, and Louis-Philippe, like Charles X, Napoléon and the Directorate, was the elected representative of the nation. Why not, if the Charter of 1830 was only an amendment to the Constitutions of Year III, Year IV and 1814?

The most advanced organ of the legitimist party would still tell us, if it dared, that the law results from the People's consent and the king's decree: *Lex fit consensu populi et constitutione regis.* The sovereignty of the nation is the first principle of both monarchists and democrats. Listen to the echo that reaches us from the North: on the one hand, there is a despotic king who invokes national traditions, that is, the will of the People expressed and confirmed over the centuries. On the other hand, there are subjects in revolt who maintain that the People no longer think what they formerly did and who ask that the People be consulted. Who then shows here a better understanding of the People? The monarchs who believe that their thinking is immutable, or the citizens who suppose them to be versatile? And when you say the contradiction is resolved by progress, meaning that the People go through various phases before arriving at the same idea, you only avoid the problem: who will decide what is progress and what is regression?

Therefore, I ask as Rousseau did: if the People have spoken, why have I heard nothing?

---

4   The voice of the people, the voice of God. (Translator)

You point out this astonishing revolution to me, a revolution in which I, too, have participated, the legitimacy of which I alone have proven, the idea I have raised. And you say to me: there is the People!

But in the first place, I have seen only a tumultuous crowd without awareness of the thought that made it act, without any comprehension of the revolution it brought about with its own hands. Then what I have called the logic of the People might well be nothing but the reason of events, all the more so because, once they are over and everyone agrees on their significance, opinions are divided again on the consequences. Now the revolution has been carried out, the People say nothing [*La révolution faite, le Peuple se tait*]! What then? Does popular sovereignty exist only for things in the past, which no longer interest us, and not at all for those in the future, which alone can be the objects of the People's decrees?

Oh, all you enemies of despotism and its corruption, anarchy and its thievery, who never cease invoking the People, you who speak frankly of the People's sovereign reason, irresistible strength and formidable voice, I command you to tell me: where and when have you heard the People? Through what mouths, in what language, do they express themselves? How is this astonishing revelation accomplished? What authentic, conclusive examples do you cite? What guarantee do you have of the sincerity of these laws you say issue from the People? What sanction of them? By what claims, by what signs, will I distinguish those whom the People have elected from the apostates who take advantage of its trust and usurp its authority? In short, how do you establish the legitimacy of the popular Word?

I believe in the existence of the People as I do in the existence of God.

I bow before their holy will; I submit to all their orders; the People's word is my law, my strength and my hope. But, following St. Paul's precept, to be worthy, my obedience must be rational, and what a misfortune for me, what ignominy, if, while believing myself to be submitting only to the People's authority, I am a despicable charlatan's plaything! How then, I beg of you, among so many rival apostles, contradictory opinions and obstinate partisans, am I to recognise the voice, the true voice, of the People?

The problem of the People's sovereignty is the fundamental problem of liberty, equality and fraternity, the first principle of social organisation. Governments and peoples have had no other goal, through all the storms of revolutions and diversions of politics, than to constitute this sovereignty. Each time they have been diverted from this goal, they have fallen into servitude and shame. With that in mind, the provisional government has convened a National Assembly named by all citizens, without distinction of wealth and capacity: universal suffrage seems to them to be the closest approach to expressing the People's sovereignty.

Thus, it is supposed first that the People can be consulted, second, that it can respond, third, that its will can be truly observed and finally, that government founded upon the manifest will of the People is the only legitimate government.

In particular, such is the pretension of DEMOCRACY, which presents itself as the form of government that best expresses the People's sovereignty.

However, if I prove that democracy is, as is the case with monarchy, only a symbol of sovereignty, that it does not answer any of the questions raised by that idea, that it cannot, for example, either establish the authenticity of the actions attributed to the People or state what society's purpose and destination are: if I prove that democracy, far from being the most perfect government, is the negation of the People's sovereignty and the origin of its ruin, it will be demonstrated, in fact and in right, that democracy is nothing more than one constitutional arbitrariness succeeding another, that it does not possess any scientific value and that it must be seen solely as a preparation for the one and indivisible republic.

It is important to clarify opinion on this point immediately and to eliminate all illusion.

I

The People, a collective being—I almost said rational being—does not speak in the material sense of the word at all. Like God, the People also has no eyes to see, no ears to hear, no mouth to speak. How do I know if the People is endowed with some sort of soul, a divinity inherent to the masses, the universal soul some philosophers suppose that sometimes moves and urges the masses on, or whether the People's reason is merely the pure idea of the most abstract, comprehensive and freest of all individual forms, as other philosophers claim: that God is merely order in the universe, an abstraction? I am not getting involved in the investigations of esoteric psychology: as a practical man, I wonder how this soul, reason, will or what have you occurs outside itself, so to speak, and makes itself known. Who can serve as its representative? Who has the right to tell others that the People speaks through him? How will I believe that he who harangues five hundred applauding individuals from atop a stepladder is the People's spokesman? How does election by the citizens, even by their unanimous vote, have the virtue of conferring that kind of privilege of serving as the People's medium? And when you show me a coterie of nine hundred dignitaries thus chosen by their fellow citizens, why should I believe that those nine hundred delegates, who do not all agree with each other, are inspired by the People's spirit? And when all is said and done, how could the laws they make obligate me?

Here is a president or a directorate, personification, symbol or fiction of national sovereignty: the first power of the state.

Here are two chambers or agencies: one in the interests of conservation and the other with the instinct for development, the second power of the state.

Here is the press, the third power of the state—eloquent, seasoned and tireless—pouring out millions of ideas in torrents each morning to swirl in millions of citizens' brains.

The executive power is action, the chambers, deliberation, and the press, opinion.

Which of these powers represents the People? Or indeed, if you say that it is all of them that represent the People, how is it that they do not all agree? Put royalty in place of the presidency, and it is the same thing: my criticisms apply equally to both monarchy and democracy.

In France there are 500 or 600 newspapers, fountains of opinion, the titles of which greatly attest to the owners' pretence that they are the interpreters of popular thought: *Le Siècle, La Réforme, La Liberté, Le Progrès, La Presse, Le Temps, L'Opinion, La Démocratie, L'Atelier, Les Ecoles, La Vérité, La France, Le Monde, Le Constitutionnel, Le National, Le Commerce, Les Débats, Le Courrier, Le Populaire, Le Peuple, La Voix du Peuple, Le Peuple Constituent, Le Représentant du Peuple,* etc., etc., etc.

With such publicity, when we are so well stocked with writers not lacking in erudition, ideas or style, I am certainly astonished that we still need representation in the form of a national assembly.

But, how can it be that, with all this, I know positively nothing about what interests the People even though it is the press's duty and mission to teach me; how can it be that, instead of shedding any light, the flood of publications increases the darkness?

I ask what is the best political constitution, the law of progress, the march of the century, the thought of the epoch, the value of opinion and the future of France and the world? Will the republic arise from the workshop, the school or the guardhouse? Is democracy at peace or war? What truth, what reform, must arise from all these revelations of the People? What is liberty?

Journalism speaks on all those questions, but it does not answer them; it knows nothing. What if I asked, for example, if the organisation of society has a definite form and what that form is? If we are finished with revolutions, or if the revolutionary movement is eternal? How, in the latter case, is that perpetual agitation reconciled with liberty, security and well-being? If all men must be equal despite their nature, or treated according to their worth, despite the motto of the republic? What must be the worker's wage, the entrepreneur's profit, the contribution to be paid to the state, the credit to be granted to citizens? How will we escape the catastrophe of poverty when the population grows faster than its livelihood? Etc., etc.

I could infinitely extend this questioning and make my questions increasingly pressing and difficult. If the press is the People's means of speaking, why does it digress instead of answering? The press is so far from possessing a positive spirit that it seems to have been expressly invented for diverting reason and killing contemplation. Ideas fall into the newspapers but do not take root: the newspapers are the cemeteries of ideas.

And what do we hear from the rostrum? And what does the government know? Not so long ago it was escaping its responsibilities by denying its own authority to make decisions. It did not exist, it claimed, to organise work and give bread to the People. For a month it has received the proletariat's demands; for a month it has been at work, and every day for a month it has had *Le Moniteur* publish the great news that it knows nothing, that it discovers nothing! The Government divides the People and arouses hatred among the classes that compose it. Organising the People and creating that sovereignty that is both liberty and harmony exceeds the Government's ability, as formerly it exceeded its jurisdiction. However, in a Government describing itself as instituted by the People's will, such remarkable ignorance is a contradiction: it is already clear that the People are no longer sovereign.

Does the People, who are sometimes said to have risen as a single man, also think, reflect, reason and form conclusions like a man? Does the People have a memory, imagination and ideas? If, in reality, the People is sovereign, it must think; if it thinks, surely it has its own way of thinking and formulating thoughts. How then does the People think? What are the forms of the popular reason? Does it categorise, use syllogisms, induction, analysis, antinomy, or analogy? It is Aristotelian or Hegelian? You must explain all that; otherwise, your respect for the People's sovereignty is only an absurd fetishism, and you might as well worship a stone.

Does the People use its experience in its meditations? Does it consider its memories, or does it endlessly produce new ideas? How does it reconcile respect for its traditions with its needs for development? How does it dispense with a worn-out hypothesis and go on to try another? What is the law of its transitions and enjambments? What motivates it, and what defines the path of its progress? Why this capriciousness, this instability? I need to know this, or the law you impose on me in the name of the People is no longer authentic, no longer law, but violence.

Does the People always think? And if not, how do you account for the intermittent character of its thoughts? If we suppose that the People can be represented, what will its representatives do during those interruptions? Do the People sometimes sleep like Jupiter in the arms of Juno? When do they dream? When are they awake? You must teach me about all these things; otherwise, because the power you exercise by delegation from the People is only interim, and the length of the interim is unknown, that power has been usurped, and you are inclined toward tyranny.

If the People think, reflect, reason (sometimes *a priori*, according to the rules of pure reason, and sometimes *a posteriori*, based on the data of experience), they run the risk of deceiving themselves. The demonstrated authenticity of the People's thought is no longer enough for me to accept that thought as law: it must also be legitimate. Who will choose among the People's ideas and fantasies? To whom will we appeal its possibly erroneous, and therefore despotic, will?

Here I present this dilemma:

If the People can err, then there are two alternatives. On the one hand, the error may seem as respectable as the truth, and the People has the right to be completely obeyed despite its error. In this case the People is a supremely immoral being because it can simultaneously think of, desire to do, and carry out evil.

On the other hand, must the People be reproached for its errors? There would then be, in certain cases, a duty for a government to resist the People! Who will tell it that it is deceiving itself? Who could set it straight and restrain it?

But what am I saying? If the People are liable to err, what becomes of its sovereignty? Isn't it obvious that the People's will must be considered no less seriously than its dreaded consequences, and isn't it the true principle of all politics, the guarantee of the security of nations, to consult the People only in order to distrust it, that all inspiration from it could hide enormous peril or success, and its will could be only suicidal thoughts?

Doubtless, you will say, the People has only a mystical existence. It only appears rarely in predestined epochs! Despite that, the People is not a phantom, and when it rises, no one can fail to recognise it. The People appeared on July 14th, 1789, and on August 10th, 1830. It was at Jemmapes and fought at Mayence and Valmy.

Why are you stopping? Why choose? Was the People absent during the 9th of Thermidor or the 18th Brumaire? Was it hiding on January 21st and December 5th? Were they not the emperor as he defeated the king? Did it not, by turns, adore and strike at Christ and Reason? Do you want to go further back? It was the People who, with its blood and guts, produced Gregory the Seventh on one day and Luther on another, who made Marius and Caesar arise after having chased off the Tarquins in a series of revolutions, who overturned the Decemviri, created the galleries to balance the consuls and, through the first example of a political shake-up, gave us the doctrinaire system. It was the People who worshiped the Caesars after it let them assassinate the Greeks!

Would you rather remain in the present? So tell me what the People are thinking today, March 25th, 1848, or rather, what it is not thinking.

Is the People thinking, with Abbé Lacordaire,[5] about making penance in sackcloth and ashes? Is it thinking that it was born out of the dust and will return to the dust, that its destiny here below is not pleasure but work and mortification? Or might it be thinking, like Saint-Simon and Fourier, that the fate of a human being is like that of a horse and that everything on earth is futile besides living well and making love?

Is the People thinking about the abolition of grants, progressive tax, national workshops, agricultural banks or paper money? Or is it not thinking instead that, amazingly, imposing unduly upon wealth kills wealth, that instead of expanding the state's jurisdiction, it should be restricted, that the

---

5   Henri Lacordaire (1802–61), together with Lamennais, was one of the leading lights
    of nineteenth-century Catholic liberalism. (Editor)

organisation of labour is only the organisation of competition and that the greatest service to be rendered to agriculture, instead of creating a special bank for it, is to sever all its relations with the bank?

Is the People for direct or [indirect] election? Is it for a representation of 900 or 450?

Is the People communist, phalansterian, neo-Christian, or utilitarian, or is not it? For, in fact, all of these are to be found within the People. Is it for Pythagoras, Morelly, Campanella or the good Icarus? For the Trinity or the Triad?[6] Isn't it the People who speaks in those rantings that say nothing, in those contradictory posters and those governmental acts conceived in a sense that goes against February 24th? Is it asking for bread and circuses or for liberty? Did it have the revolution only to renounce it soon afterwards, or does it intend to continue it?

However, if the People has, in all historical epochs, thought, expressed, wanted and done a multitude of contradictory things, if, even today, among so many opinions dividing it, it is impossible for it to choose one without repudiating another and consequently contradicting itself: what do you want me to think of the reason, morality and justice of its acts? What can I expect from its representatives? What proof of authenticity will you give me in favour of an opinion that I cannot immediately claim for an opposing one?

What astonishes me in the midst of the confusion of ideas is that faith in the People's sovereignty, far from dwindling, seems by this very confusion to reach its own climax. In this obstinate belief of the multitude in the intelligence that exists within it I already see a manifestation of the People affirming itself, like Jehovah, saying, "I AM." I cannot then deny—on the contrary—I am forced to affirm the People's sovereignty. But beyond this initial affirmation, and when it is a question of going from the subject of the thought to its object, when, in other words, it is a question of applying the criterion to the government's acts, someone tell me: where are the People?

In principle then, I admit that the People exist, that it is sovereign, that it asserts itself in the popular consciousness, but nothing yet has proven to me that it can perform an overt act of sovereignty and that an explicit revelation of the People is possible. For in view of the dominance of prejudices, contradictory ideas and interests, variable opinions, and the multitude's impulsiveness, I still wonder what establishes the authenticity and legitimacy of such a revelation, and this is what democracy cannot answer.

## II

But, the democrats observe, not without reason, that the People has never been suitably called to action. It has only been able to demonstrate its will in momentary flashes: the role it has played in history up to now has been

---

6   A reference to Catholicism and leading Saint-Simonian Pierre Leroux's philosophy. (Editor)

completely subordinate. For the People to be able to express its thoughts, it must be democratically consulted: that is, all citizens, on a non-discriminatory basis, must participate, directly or indirectly, in creating the law. However, this mode of democratic consultation has never been exercised in a sustained manner: the perpetual conspiracy of the privileged has not allowed it. Princes, nobles and priests, military men, magistrates, teachers, scholars, artists, industrialists, merchants, financiers and landowners have always succeeded in breaking up the democratic whole by changing the People's voice into the voice of a monopoly. Now that we possess the only true way of having the People speak, we will also know what constitutes the authenticity and legitimacy of its word, and all your preceding objections will vanish. The sincerity of the democratic regime will guarantee the solution for us.

I acknowledge that the crux of the problem is the People speaking and acting as one. In my opinion, the REPUBLIC is nothing else, and that is also the entire social problem. Democracy claims to resolve this problem through universal suffrage applied on the broadest scale, replacing royal authority with the authority of the multitude. That is why *Democracy* is called the government of the multitude.

Therefore, it is the theory of universal suffrage that we have to judge, or, to be more precise, it is democracy that we have to demolish as we demolished the monarchy: that transition will be the last one before attaining the Republic.

### 1. Democracy is a disguised aristocracy

According to the theory of universal suffrage, experience has proven that the middle class, which alone has exercised political rights recently, does not represent the People—far from it—along with the monarchy, it has been in constant reaction against the People.

We conclude that it belongs to the entire nation to name its representatives.

But if it is one class of men that is singled out as the *natural* elite of the People by the free development of society, the spontaneous development of the sciences, arts, industry and commerce, the necessity of institutions, the tacit consent or the well-known incapacity of the lower classes, and, finally, its own talent and wealth, what is to be expected from a representation which, having been arrived at by means of assemblies, the inclusivity, enlightenment, and freedom of which may vary, acting under the influence of local passions, class prejudices, and hatred of persons or principles, can only constitute, in the last analysis, a *simulated* representation, the product of the electoral mob's arbitrary will?

If we are to have an aristocracy of our own choosing, I would greatly prefer it to a natural aristocracy, but aristocracy for aristocracy, I prefer, with M. Guizot, that of fatality to that of arbitrary will: at least fatality does not obligate me.

Or, rather, we will only restore, by another route, the same aristocrats because for whom do you want named to represent these journeymen, these day workers, these toilers, if not their bourgeoisie? Unless you only want them to kill them!

One way or another, preponderant strength in government belongs to those with the preponderance of talent and wealth. From the very start, it has been clear that social reform will never come from political reform; on the contrary, political reform must come from social reform.

The illusion of democracy springs from the example of constitutional monarchy: attempting to organise government by representative means. Neither the revolution of July [1830] nor that of February [1848] has sufficed to illuminate this. What they always want is inequality of wealth, delegation of sovereignty and government by influential people. Instead of saying, as M. Thiers did, that *the King reigns and does not govern*, democracy says that *the People reigns and does not govern*, which is to deny the Revolution.

It was not because he was opposed to electoral reform that M. Guizot fell, taking the monarchy and throne with him, but because, in the public awareness, the constitution was worn out and not wanted any more. All of the reforms the opposition demanded prove, and I have demonstrated this, that they were attacking the Charter even more than the minister; it was something even higher than the Charter: the very constitution of the society.

Therefore, when they talk today about substituting a representative democracy for a representative monarchy, they are not doing anything besides changing the phrase "Fair Marquise, your lovely eyes make me die of love" to "Your lovely eyes, fair Marquise, dying of love make me,"[7] and we can say, as *L'Atelier* put it, that the Revolution has vanished.

But, patience! Although it may seem difficult right now to escape this governmental alternative, the discomfort will not last long. Representation has fallen at the barricades and will never get up. Constitutional democracy has gone the way of constitutional monarchy. According to Latin etymology, February is the month of burials. Social reform will lead to political reform, the intelligence of the first involving the intelligence of the second. We will have a government of the People by the People but not through a representation of the People, and we will have the Republic, I say, or we will perish a second time with democracy.

### 2. Democracy is exclusive and doctrinaire

Since, according to the democrats' ideology, the People cannot govern itself and is forced to hand itself over to representatives who govern by delegation with the right of review, it is assumed that at least the People is quite capable of being represented at least, that it can be represented faithfully. Well! This hypothesis is utterly false; there is not and never can be legitimate

---

7   This is a slight misquotation of Molière's *The Bourgeois Gentleman* (Act II; Scene IV) in which Monsieur Jourdain (the would-be "bourgeois gentilhomme" of the title) is being advised on his prose style by a "master of philosophy." (Editor)

representation of the People. All electoral systems are mechanisms for deceit: to know but one is enough to condemn them all.

Take the example of the provisional government.

When a theory is produced in the People's name, that theory and its expression must demonstrate complete irreproachability with regard to logic, justice, traditions and trends. I do not recognise the People's voice in Fourier's books any more than in *Le Père Duchêne*.[8]

The provisional government's system pretends to be universal.

But whatever we do, in any electoral system, there will always be exclusions, absences and invalidated, erroneous and unfree votes.

The hardiest innovators have not yet dared to demand suffrage for women, children, domestic servants or those with criminal records. About four-fifths of the People are not represented and are cut off from the communion with the People. Why?

You set electoral capacity at 21 years of age, but why not 20? Why not 19, 18, 17? What! One year, one day makes the elector rational? A Barra or Viala is incapable of voting discerningly while the Fouchés and Héberts vote for them![9]

You eliminate women. You have thus resolved the major problem of the inferiority of the sex. What! No exception for a Lucretia, a Cornelia, a Joan of Arc or a Charlotte Corday! A Madame Roland, a de Staël or a George Sand will find no favour before your manliness! The Jacobins welcomed women garment workers at their meetings; no one has ever said that the presence of women weakened the men's courage!

You reject the domestic servant. You say that there is no generous soul behind this sign of servitude, that no idea capable of saving the republic beats in the valet's heart! Is the race of Figaro lost? It is that man's fault, you will say: why, with so many means, is he a servant? And why are there servants?

I want to see and hear the People in their variety and multitude, all ages, sexes, conditions, virtues and miseries because all that is the People.

You claim that there would be serious trouble in keeping good discipline, the peace of the state and the tranquillity of families if women, children and domestic servants obtained the same rights as husbands, fathers and masters,

---

8   *Le Père Duchêne* ("Old Man Duchesne") was the title of a newspaper which appeared during revolutionary periods of the nineteenth century including during the Revolution of 1848. It borrowed its title from the *Père Duchesne* published by Jacques Hébert during the French Revolution. (Editor)

9   Joseph Barra (1779–1793) and Joseph Agricol Viala (1780–1793), said to have died fighting for the French Republic against the Royalists at the age of thirteen, were posthumously honoured as Revolutionary martyrs. Joseph Fouché (1759–1820) was Minister of Police during the reign of Napoléon I. Jacques-René Hébert (1757–1794), editor of the far-left *Le Père Duchesne*, was among those who helped usher in the Terror with the slogan, "hunt down the traitors." (Editor)

that, in addition, the former are adequately represented by the latter through their solidarity of interests and the familial bond.

I acknowledge that the objection is a serious one, and I do not attempt to refute it. But take care: you must, by the same reasoning, exclude the proletarians and all workers.[10] Seven-tenths of this category receive the aid of public charity: they will then vote in government jobs, salary increases and labour reductions for themselves, and they will not fail in this, I assure you, if their delegates represent them ever so little. In the National Assembly, the proletariat will be like the officials in M. Guizot's chamber, judging its own case, having power over the budget and putting nothing into it, creating a dictatorship with its appointments until, with capital exhausted by taxation and property producing nothing any longer, general bankruptcy will break apart this parliamentary begging.

And all these citizens who, because of work, sickness, travel or lack of money to go to the polls, are forced to abstain from voting: how do you count them? Will it be according to the proverb, "Who says nothing, consents"? But, consents to what? To the opinion of the majority, or indeed to that of the minority?

And those who vote only on impulse, through good nature or interest, faith in their republican committee or parish priest: what do you make of them? It is an old maxim that in all deliberations it is necessary not only to count the votes but also to weigh them. In your committees,[11] on the contrary, the vote of an Arago or Lamartine counts no more than that of a beggar.[12] Will you say that the consideration due men for their merit is acquired by the influence they exert on the electors? Then the voting is not free. It is the voice of abilities that we hear, not the People's. We might as well keep the 200–franc system.[13]

We have given the army the right to vote, which means that soldiers who do not vote as their captain votes will go to the stockade, the captain who does not vote as the colonel votes will be put under arrest and the colonel who does not vote as the government does will be destitute.

I will not discuss the material and moral impossibilities abounding in the mode of election the provisional government has adopted. It is completely devoted to the opinion that, by doubling the national representation and having the People vote by election-by-list, the provisional government

---

10   This is effectively what the Conservative dominated National Assembly did on May 31st, 1850. (Editor)

11   *Comices* were the legislative or elective formal assemblies of the people in Ancient Rome. (Editor)

12   Politicians François Arago (1786–1853) and Alphonse de Lamartine (1790–1869) were, respectively, a scientist and a poet of renown. (Editor)

13   That is, limited suffrage based on ownership of a minimum amount of property. (Editor)

wanted the citizens to choose concerning principles rather than persons precisely in the manner of the former government, which also made voters vote on the system, not on the candidates. How do we discuss the choice of 10, 20 or 25 deputies? If each citizen votes freely and is knowledgeable of his cause, how are the votes of such elections-by-list counted? How are such elections brought to a conclusion if they are serious? Evidently, it is impossible.

I repeat that I am not talking the purely material side of the issue: I keep to issues of rights. What they once obtained through venality they now tear away from impotence. They tell the electors, "Here are our friends, the friends of the republic, and there are our adversaries, who also are the adversaries of the republic—choose." The electors, who cannot appraise the candidates' abilities, vote on trust!

Instead of naming deputies for each ward, as under the fallen regime, they are now elected by department. They wanted, with this measure, to destroy the spirit of localism. How wonderful it is that the democrats are so sure of their principles!

They say that if deputies were named by ward, it would not be France that was represented but the wards. The National Assembly would no longer represent the country but would be a congress of 459 representatives.

Why then, I reply, don't you have each elector name the deputies for all of France?

It would be desirable, you answer, but impossible.

First of all, I note that any system that can be true only under impossible conditions seems to me a poor system. But, to me, the democrats here appear singularly inconsistent and perplexed by small matters. If the representatives should only represent FRANCE and not the departments, wards, cities, countryside, industry, commerce, agriculture or interests, why have they decided that there will be one deputy per 40,000 residents? Why not one for each 100,000 or 200,000? Ninety instead of nine hundred: was that not enough? In Paris, could you not end your list when the legitimists, conservatives and royalists ended theirs? Was it more difficult to vote on a list of 90 names than on a list of 15?

But who does not see that deputies thus elected apart from all special interests and groups, all considerations of place and person, supposedly representing France, represent absolutely nothing, that they are no longer representatives, but senators, and that instead of a representative democracy, we have an elective oligarchy, the middle ground between democracy and royalty?

There, citizen reader, is where I wanted to take you. From whatever perspective you consider democracy, you will always see it between two extremes, each of which is as contrary as the other to its principles, condemned to vacillating between absurdity and impossibility without ever being able to establish itself. Among a million equally arbitrary intermediate terms, the provisional government has done like M. Guizot: he preferred what appeared to him to best agree with his democratic prejudices, that is, the provisional government did not consider the representative truth, such as a government of the People by the People. I do not reproach him for it. Minds are not at the top of the republic; we have to go through democracy once again. However, transition for transition, I like the system of the provisional government as much as M. Duvergier de Hauranne's.[14] I do not believe that the choice merits a minute of examination.

### 3. Democracy is ostracism

In order for deputies to represent their constituents, they must represent all the competing ideas from the election.

But with the electoral system, deputies, so-called legislators sent by the citizens to reconcile all ideas and interests in the name of the People, only ever represent one idea and one interest; the rest are mercilessly excluded. For who makes the law in elections? Who decides the choice of deputies? The majority, one half plus one of the voices. Therefore, it follows that the half-minus-one of the voters is not represented or is represented against his own will, and that of all the opinions dividing the citizens, one alone, as long as it is an opinion held by a deputy, makes it to the legislature and therefore enters into the law, which should be the expression of the People's will but is only the expression of half of the People.

Therefore, in the theory of democracies, the problem of government is to eliminate, through the mechanism of a supposedly universal suffrage, all, minus one, of the ideas finding favour in public opinion, and to declare the majority's opinion to be sovereign.

But perhaps one might say that an idea that fails in one such electoral college might triumph in another and that therefore all ideas may be represented in the National Assembly.

Even in that case, the difficulty would merely be postponed, since the question is to know how all those divergent and antagonistic ideas will be combined and reconciled in the law.

Therefore, according to some ideas, revolution is only an accident that should not change anything in the general social order. According to some other ideas, revolution is even more social than political. How are such clearly incompatible claims satisfied? How do we give security to the bourgeoisie and guarantees to the proletariat at the same time? How will these contrary wishes, these opposing trends, be merged into a common result [résultante] under a single universal law?

Far from democracy being capable of deciding this question, all of its art and science consists in cutting it off. It uses the ballot, which is simultaneously

---

14    In *Des Principes du gouvernement représentatif et de leurs applications* (1838), Prosper Duvergier de Hauranne (1789–1881) coined the famous phrase: "The king reigns but does not govern." (Editor)

democracy's standard, balance, and criterion, to eliminate men with the popular vote and ideas with the legislative vote.

It has barely been a month since everyone was shouting about the 200 francs poll tax: What? It is one franc, one centime, that qualifies a voter?

It is always the same thing. What? One vote elects the representative, and one vote decides the law! Concerning a question on which the honour and health of the republic depend, the citizens are divided into two equal factions. Both sides bring to bear the most serious reasoning, weightiest authorities and most positive facts; the nation is in doubt, and the National Assembly is suspended. If one representative, without a substantial reason, passes from right to left and tips the balance, it is he who makes the law.

And this law, the expression of some bizarre will, is deemed the People's will! I will have to submit to it, defend it and die for it! On a parliamentary whim, I lose my most precious right; I lose my liberty! And my most sacred duty, the duty to resist tyranny by force, falls before an imbecile's sovereign vote!

Democracy is nothing but the tyranny of majorities, the most execrable tyranny of all because it is not based on the authority of a religion, nobility of blood or the prerogatives of talent and wealth: its foundation is numbers, and its mask is the People's name. Under Louis-Philippe's reign, M. de Genoude refused to pay taxes, saying that they had not been voted upon by a true national representation. It was decent of M. de Genoude to stop so short. When it chances that a more democratic majority votes in a budget, should the minority also believe that it has voted it in, too, and that it is therefore obliged to pay even though it voted against that very budget?

In the first volume of this work, I proved the legitimacy of the Revolution and the moral necessity of the Republic by demonstrating that, on February 22$^{nd}$, all opinions, all parties, whatever their disagreements, agreed on a group of reforms for which the general formula was invariably THE REPUBLIC. Democracy, with universal suffrage, destroys that justification, the only one, however, that it can provide for its arrival. It tries to make the masses and departments say that they belong to the Republic, and if they do not, democracy will resist with force! Intimidation: here is the democrats' strongest argument on the Republic! Is it now clear that neither universal suffrage nor democracy expresses the People's sovereignty?

I hope that the force of things, the inflexible reason of facts, will inspire our future National Assembly, but I would not be surprised if, formed by a government that has so little understood the revolution, the National Assembly ends up damaging the Revolution, and we will once again see the People disavow their representatives' politics through an act analogous with that of February.

### 4. Democracy is a form of absolutism

If universal suffrage, the most complete manifestation of democracy, has won so many partisans, especially among the working classes, it is because it has always been presented as an appeal to the masses' talents, abilities, good sense and morality. How often have they avoided the harmful contrasts of the speculator who becomes politically influential through plunder and the man of genius whom poverty has kept far away from the stage! What sarcasm about 200 franc capacities and the incapacities of those such as Béranger, Chateaubriand and Lamennais![15]

In the end, we are all voters; we can choose the most worthy.

We can do more; we can follow them step-by-step in their legislative acts and their votes; we will make them transmit our arguments and our documents; we will suggest our will to them, and when we are discontented, we will recall and dismiss them.

The choice of talents, the imperative mandate [*mandate impertif*], and permanent revocability are the most immediate and incontestable consequences of the electoral principle. It is the inevitable program of all democracy.

No more than constitutional monarchy, however, does democracy agree to such a deduction from its principle.

What democracy demands, like monarchy, is silent representatives who do not discuss but vote; who, when they receive their orders from the government, crush the opposition with their heavy battalions. They are passive creatures (I almost said satellites), whom the danger of a revolution does not intimidate, whose reason is not too rebellious and whose consciences do not recoil before any arbitrariness or proscription.

You will say that this is pushing the paradox to the point of slander, so we will prove the paradox then in fact and in law: it will not take too long.

Everyone has read the bulletin of the Minister of Public Education to teachers about the elections and noted this passage:

"The greatest error of our country residents is to believe that it is necessary to have an EDUCATION or wealth to be a representative.

"Most of the assembly plays the role of jury, judging with a *yes* or *no* if what the ELITE members propose is good or bad. They only need to be honest and have good sense. They do not CREATE.—Here is the fundamental principle of republican law."

The Minister then expresses the desire that primary school teachers become candidates for the National Assembly, not because they are sufficiently enlightened but because they are not: "The lower they start, the higher they will go," which, geometrically speaking, is indisputable.

If the Minister, convinced of the well-known ability of many respectable teachers, were content to point them out as hidden lights that democracy's arrival must reveal, I would applaud the bulletin, but who does not see that, in the Minister's thinking, the primary school teacher is an envious

---

15  Proudhon names several well-known political figures here: songwriter Pierre Jean de Béranger (1780–1857), Romantic poet François-René de Chateaubriand (1768–1848), and Catholic liberal Félicité Robert de Lamennais (1782–1854). (Editor)

mediocrity that has not created and will not create anything and is destined to serve the war for the rich and democratic arbitrariness with his silent votes? In that regard, I protest that candidacy, or to be more specific, that prostitution of teachers.

Furthermore, the constitutional monarchy, seeking to surround itself with a talented and wealthy aristocracy, turns to dignitaries in the same way as democracy, which is the drunkenness of that system, comprises its patrician class of those of little distinction. This is not, as one might believe, an opinion specific to the Minister; I will soon prove that it is the pure essence of democracy.

I shall cite another fact.

All the authors of public law, specifically the democrats, speak out against the imperative mandate; I say that all of them unanimously consider it impolitic, abusive, leading to the oppression of the government by the populace, offending against the dignity of the deputies, etc. The imperative mandate has been roundly declared anathema. In civil law, it would be a monstrous thing if the mandate had less authority than the representative; in politics, it is just the opposite. Here, the representatives become judges and referees of their constituents' interests. What is orthodox in a legal context is considered heretical in the field of constitutional ideas: it is one of the thousand inconsistencies of the human mind.

The length of the mandate, revocable at will under civil law, is, in policy, independent of the will of the electors. In all our constitutions, the length of the mandate has varied from one to seven years following the agreement, not of the governed citizens, but of the governing citizens.

In fact, it is indeed understood in and proven by the authors' doctrine and the ministers' bulletins that, in any type of government, the representatives belong to power, not to the populace; that is why monarchies require representatives to be capable or rich, and democracy requires them to be incapable or indigent. Both monarchy and democracy require that representatives are masters of their own votes, that is, of trafficking in and selling them, and that the mandate has a definite length of at least a year, during which the government, in agreement with the representatives, does what it pleases and gives the force of law to whatever acts it likes.

Could it be otherwise? No, and the discussion of the point of law does not require a long speech.

The fallen system could define itself as the society's government by the bourgeoisie, that is, by the aristocracy of talent and wealth. The system that they are working right now to establish—democracy—may be defined by its opposite—the society's government by the vast majority of its citizens, who have little talent and no wealth. The exceptions that may be encountered in either of those systems do nothing to this principle, neither changing nor modifying the trend. Under a representative monarchy, it is inevitable that the People will be exploited by the bourgeoisie, and under a democratic government, it is inevitable that they will be exploited by the proletariat.

But whoever wills the end wills the means.

If monarchic representation were formed of representatives with an imperative mandate revocable upon the will of the electors, the bourgeoisie would soon lose its privileges, and royalty, which personifies that monarchic representation, would be reduced to zero. At the same time, if the democratic assembly were comprised of bourgeois individuals, powerful due to their talent and the wealth devoted to their principles and instantly replaceable if they betrayed those principles, the dictatorship of the masses would fall quickly, and the proletarians would return to their proletariat.

Therefore, it is necessary for each form of government to surround itself with the stability conditions best for its particular nature: hence, M. Guizot's resistance to electoral reform, universal suffrage and [Minister of Public Education] M. Carnot's bulletin.

But because nothing that creates a division in the People can last, it is also inevitable that those forms of tyranny will perish one after the other and, remarkably, always for the same reason: the bourgeoisie's tyranny by the proletariat's misery and the proletariat's tyranny by the bourgeoisie's ruin, which is universal misery.

This was not the trend of thought on February 22$^{nd}$, 23$^{rd}$ and 24$^{th}$.

The bourgeoisie, tired of its own government's shamefulness, marched alone with cries of "Long live reform!" to the republic, and the working masses, enthusiastically repeating the cry of reform, caressing the bourgeoisie with their eyes and voices, also marched alone to the republic. The fusion of ideas and hearts was complete. The goal was the same although no one knew the route to which they were committed.

Since February 25$^{th}$, the revolution, misunderstood, has become deformed. The social that was in everyone's thoughts was made political because it is always the political that is occupied with labour in the state (under the pretext of organisation), and the demarcation line between the bourgeoisie and the People, momentarily erased, reappeared deeper and wider. Incapable of understanding the republican ideal, handed over to demagogic and mercenary routine, the provisional government is working to organise civil war and horrible misery instead of labour.

If the National Assembly does not end this despicable policy, France will soon learn through the most painful experience how much distance there is between a republic and democracy.

### 5. Democracy is materialistic and atheistic

If monarchy is the hammer that crushes the People, democracy is the axe that divides them: they concur on the death of liberty.

Universal suffrage is a kind of atomism through which legislators, who cannot make the People speak as a unit about their essence, invite citizens to

express their opinions one-by-one, *viritim*, absolutely like the Epicurean philosopher explains thought, will and intelligence as combinations of atoms. It
is political atheism in the worst meaning of the word. As if adding up some
quantity of votes could ever produce unified thought!

"It's from the clash of ideas that sparks of intelligence fly," say the elders.
It is both true and false, like all proverbs. Between the clash and the spark,
a thousand years may pass. History has only begun to reveal itself to us for
half a century; the ideas that once agitated Rome, Athens, Jerusalem and
Memphis are only just enlightening us today. The People has spoken, no
doubt, but no one has understood its words because it has been diffused in
individual voices. The light of ancient ideas had been concealed from modern society. It shone for the first time in the eyes of the Vicos, Montesquieus,
Lessings, Guizots and Thierrys and their emulators. Will we have to cut our
own throats for posterity, too?

The most certain way of making the People lie is to establish universal
suffrage. The individual vote, with regard to government, as a means of observing the national will, is exactly the same thing as a new division of land
would be in the political economy. It is the agrarian law transported from
the soil to authority.

Because the authors, the first of whom were concerned with the origin of
governments, have taught that the source of all power is national sovereignty,
it has been boldly concluded that it is best to have all citizens vote verbally,
by rump or ballot and that the majority of votes thus expressed was equal
to the People's will. They have taken us back to the practices of barbarians
who, lacking rationality, proceeded by acclamation and election. They have
taken a material symbol for the true formula of sovereignty and have told
the proletarians that when they vote, they will be free and rich, that they will
rule capital, profit and wages, that they will, as other versions of Moses have,
make thrushes and manna fall from heaven, that they will become like gods
because they will not have to work anymore or will work so little that it will
be nothing.

Whatever they do and say, universal suffrage, evidence of discord, can
only produce discord. I am ashamed for my homeland that for seventeen
years they have agitated the poor people with this miserable idea! It is why
the bourgeoisie and workers have sung the *Marseillaise* in chorus at seventy
political banquets and, after a revolution as glorious as it was legitimate, why
they have given in to a sect of doctrinaires! For six months, the deputies of
the opposition, like actors on holiday, travelled through the provinces, and
what did they bring back to us as the result of their benefit performances
upon the stage of political privilege? Agrarian politics! It is under this divisive
banner that we have claimed to preserve the initiative of progress, to march
at the forefront of nations in the conquest of liberty, to usher in harmony
around the world! Yesterday, we had pity for the Peoples who did not know
as we do how to raise themselves up to constitutional sublimity. Today, fallen

a hundred times lower, we still pity them, but we will go with a 100,000 bayonets to make them share the benefits of democratic absolutism with us. And we are the great nation! Oh, be silent! If you do not know how to do great things, or express great ideas, at least let's preserve common sense.

With 8 million or 8,000 electors, your representation with some different qualities will be worth the same.

The law, whether 900 or 90 deputies create it, sometimes more plebeian, sometimes more bourgeois, will be no better or no worse.

If I place any hope in the National Assembly, it is indeed due less to its origin and the number of its members than to events that can only advise it and the work of public reason, which will be to the National Assembly as light is to the daguerreotype.[16]

### 6. Democracy is retrograde and contradictory

In monarchy, the government's acts are the deployment of authority; in democracy, they constitute authority. The authority in monarchy that is the principle of governmental action is the goal of government in democracy. The result is that democracy is inevitably retrograde and contradictory.

Let us place ourselves at the point of departure for democracy, at the moment of universal suffrage.

All citizens are equal and independent. Their egalitarian combination is power's point of departure: it is power itself, in its highest form, in its fullness.

According to democratic principle, all citizens must participate in the formation of the law, the government of the state, the exercise of public functions, the discussion of the budget and the appointment of officials. Everyone must be consulted and give their opinions on peace and war, treaties of commerce and alliance, colonial undertakings, works of public utility, the award of compensation and the infliction of punishments. Finally, they all must pay their debt to their homeland as taxpayers, jurors, judges and soldiers.

If things could happen in this way, the democratic ideal would be attained. It would have a normal existence, developing directly in line with its principle, as do all things that live and develop. That is how the acorn becomes an oak and the embryo an animal; that is how geometry, astronomy and chemistry are the infinite development of a small number of items.

It is completely different in democracy, which, according to the authors, exists fully only at the moment of elections and in the formation of legislative

---

16   The daguerreotype was the first publicly announced photographic process, developed by Louis Daguerre. The image is exposed directly onto a mirror-polished surface of silver. The daguerreotype is a negative image, but the mirrored surface of the metal plate reflects the image and makes it appear positive in the proper light. (Editor)

power. Once that moment has passed, democracy retreats; it withdraws into itself again and begins its anti-democratic work. It becomes AUTHORITY. Authority was M. Guizot's idol as it is that of the democrats.

It is not true, in fact, that in any democracy all citizens participate in the formation of the law: that prerogative is reserved for the representatives.

It is not true that they deliberate on all public affairs, domestic and foreign: that is no longer even the representatives' privilege, but the ministers'. Citizens discuss affairs, but ministers alone deliberate on them.

It is not true that each citizen has public functions: those functions that do not produce marketable goods must be reduced as much as possible. By their nature, public functions exclude the vast majority of citizens. In ancient Greek society, each citizen held a position paid by the state treasury: in that context, the democratic ideal was achieved in Athens and Sparta. But the Greeks lived off slave labour, and war filled their treasuries: the abolition of slavery and the increasing difficulty of war have made democracy impossible in the modern nations.

It is not true that citizens participate in the nomination of officials; moreover, that participation is as impossible as the preceding one, since it would result in creating anarchy in the bad sense of the word. Power names its own subordinates, sometimes according to its own arbitrary will, sometimes according to certain conditions for appointment or promotion, the order and discipline of officials and centralisation requiring that it be thus. Article 13 of the Charter of 1830, which assigned the king *the appointment of all positions in public administration*, is customary in both democracy and monarchy. In the revolution that has just been achieved, everyone understood this to such a degree that we could believe that it was the dynasty of *Le National* that succeeded the Orléans dynasty.

Finally, it is not true that all citizens participate in justice and in war: as judges and officers, most are eliminated; as jurors and simple soldiers, all abstain as much as they can. In short, because hierarchy is government's primary condition, democracy is a chimera.

The reason that all the authors give for this merits our study. They say that the People is unable to govern itself because it does not know how, and when it does know how, it will not be able to do it. EVERYBODY CANNOT COMMAND AND GOVERN AT THE SAME TIME; authority must belong solely to some who exercise it in the name of and through the delegation of all.

According to democratic theory, due to ignorance or impotence, the People cannot govern themselves: after declaring the principle of the People's sovereignty, democracy, like monarchy, ends up declaring *the incapacity of the People*!

This is what is our democrats mean: once they are in the government, they dream only of consolidating and strengthening the authority in their hands. This is what the multitude understood when they threw themselves upon the doors of the *Hôtel de Ville*, demanding government employment, money, work, credit, bread! And there indeed is our nation, monarchist to its very marrow, idolising power, devoid of individual energy and republican initiative, accustomed to expecting everything from authority and doing nothing except through authority! When monarchy does not come to us from on high, as it did formerly, or on battlefield, as in 1800, or in the folds of a charter, as in 1814 or 1830, we proclaim it in the public square, between two barricades, in the electoral assembly or at a patriotic banquet. Drink to the People's health, and the multitude will crown you! What then? Is monarchy the end and democracy the means?

The authors can think whatever they like, but the republic is as opposed to democracy as it is to monarchy. In the republic, everyone reigns and governs; the People think and act as one person. Representatives are plenipotentiaries with the imperative mandate and are recallable at will. The law is the expression of the unanimous will: there is no other hierarchy besides the solidarity of functions, no other aristocracy besides labour's, no other initiative besides the citizens'.

Here is the republic! Here is the People's sovereignty!

## III
[...]

But democracy is the idea of the endless extension of the State; it is the combining of all agricultural operations into one agricultural operation, all industrial companies into one such company, all mercantile establishments into one such establishment and all partnerships into one. However, it is not the endless decrease of general costs, as it must be under the Republic, but the endless increase of those costs.

Thirty days of dictatorship have exposed democracy's powerlessness and uselessness. All its old memories, philanthropic prejudices, communist instincts, conflicting passions, sentimental phrases and anti-liberal tendencies have been expended in one month. It went through utopia and routine, consulted quacks and charlatans, welcomed skilful speculators, listened to the preaching of the lawyers and received the Monsignor's holy water. Yet, in everything that democracy proposed, decreed, sermonised and blustered for a month, who would dare to say that the People were recognised even once?

I will conclude by repeating my question: the People's sovereignty is the starting point of the social sciences, so how is that sovereignty established and expressed? We cannot take one step forward until we solve that problem.

Of course, I repeat it so that I am not misunderstood. I do not in any way want to deny the workers, the proletarians, the exercise of their political rights: I only maintain that the manner in which they aspire to exercise them is only a mystification. Universal suffrage is the Republic's symbol but not its reality.

Furthermore, look at the indifference with which the working masses greet that suffrage! The most that can be gotten from them is their registration to vote. While the philosophers praise universal suffrage, popular common sense mocks it!

The Republic is the organisation through which all opinions and activities remain free, the People, through the very divergence of opinions and wills, thinking and acting as a single man. In the Republic, all citizens, by doing what they want and nothing more, directly participate in the legislation and the government as they participate in the production and circulation of wealth. Therefore, all citizens are kings because they all have complete power; they reign and govern. The Republic is a positive anarchy. It is neither liberty subject to order, as in the constitutional monarchy, nor liberty imprisoned *in* order, as the provisional government understands it, but liberty delivered from all its obstacles, superstition, prejudice, sophistry, speculation and authority; it is a reciprocal, not limited, liberty; it is the liberty that is the MOTHER, not the daughter, of order.

This is the program of modern societies. May democracy be forgiven for having, so to speak, formulated it through the very spectacle of its contradictions.

*31ˢᵗ March 1848*
*Translators: Clarence L. Swartz and Jesse Cohn*

# ORGANISATION OF CREDIT AND CIRCULATION
## AND THE SOLUTION OF THE SOCIAL PROBLEM

## PROGRAMME

IT HAS BEEN PROVED THAT SOCIALIST DOCTRINES ARE POWERLESS TO RE-lieve the People in the present crisis.[1] Utopia needs for its realisation capital accumulated, credit opened, circulation established and a prosperous state. It has need of everything we now lack; and these it is powerless to create.

It has been proved that political economy, both descriptive and *routinière*, is as impotent as Socialism in the present situation. The school which is based wholly upon the principle of supply and demand would be without means or power on the day when everybody would demand and nobody would want to supply.

It has been proved, finally, that dictatorships, seizure of power, and all revolutionary expedients, are powerless against the universal economic paralysis, as moxa is without action on a corpse.

At present the field is open to other ideas, public opinion calls for them, their sway is assured. I no longer hesitate to propose that which speculative study of social economy shows me is most applicable to the situation in

---

1    The crisis was that of March 1848 which enabled Proudhon to epitomise the Social Problem and point the way out in the exact terms of the moment. (Translator)

which we find ourselves; it rests with you, citizen reader, to see in my proposition a goal for our future.

Work is at a standstill—it must be resumed. Credit is dead—it must be resuscitated.

Circulation is stopped—it must be re-established. The market is closed—it must be reopened.

Taxes never suffice—they must be abolished. Money hides itself—we must dispense with it.

Or better still, since we should express ourselves in an absolute manner, for what we are going to do today must serve for all time:

Double, triple, augment labour indefinitely, and in consequence the products of labour; Give credit so broad a base that no demand will exhaust it;

Create a market that no amount of production can supply;

Organise a full, regular circulation, which no accident can disturb.

Instead of taxes, always increasing and always insufficient, abolish all taxes; Let all merchandise become current money, and abolish the royalty of gold.

But I must point out in advance some of the prejudices which, as the result of long habit, prevent us, at this time from seeing the true cause of the evil, and from discerning the remedy. To be on the look-out for error is to be half the way along the road which leads to truth.

The first of these prejudices consists in the desire to reform everything in detail, instead of attacking the whole; in taking up difficulties one after another, and resolving them in turn in the way common sense seems to indicate: whereas economic questions, essentially contradictory in themselves and among themselves, must be solved all at once, through some dominant principle which respects all rights, ameliorates all conditions, and conciliates all interests.

Another prejudice is the one which, attributing the cause of poverty to the imperfect organisation of labour, concludes that labour should be regimented; that it is in that part of the social organism—labour—that the remedy should be applied. People will not understand that human labour and individual liberty are synonymous; that, except for fairness in exchange, the liberty of labour must be absolute; that governments exist only to protect free labour, not to regulate and to restrain it. When you speak in this way of organising labour, it is as if you propose to put a strait-jacket on liberty.

A third prejudice, resulting from the preceding one, is that which, suppressing individual initiative, would seek to obtain everything through authority. One can say that this prejudice is the leprosy of the French spirit. We ask the State for everything, we want everything from the State; we understand only one thing, that the State is the master and we are the servants. The analogy to this prejudice, in the field of economics, is that which makes gold the universal motivating force. Gold is for us the principle of production, the sinew of commerce, the substance itself of credit, the king of labour. That is why we all worship gold even as we worship authority.

It is the business of the State, I repeat, only to pronounce on the justice of economic relationships, not to determine the manifestations of liberty. Also in the matter of justice, the state has only the right to enforce the general will. A fourth prejudice, finally, and the most deplorable of all, is that which, under the pretext of harmony and fraternity, tends to destroy in society the divergence of opinion, the opposition of interests, the battle of passions, the antagonism of ideas, the competition of workers. It is nothing less than the motion and life that would be thus cut off from the social body. Therein lies the fatal error of communism.

A great effort of reflection is, however, not necessary to understand that justice, union, accord, harmony, fraternity itself, necessarily presupposes two opposites; and that, unless one falls into the absurd notion of absolute identity, that is to say, absolute nothingness, contradiction is the fundamental law, not only of society, but of the universe.

That is also the first law which I proclaim, in agreement with religion and philosophy: that is Contradiction—the universal Antagonism.

But, just as life implies contradiction, contradiction in its turn calls for justice; which leads to the second law of creation and humanity: the mutual interaction of antagonistic elements, or *Reciprocity*.

Reciprocity, in creation, is the principle of existence. In the social order, reciprocity is the principle of social reality, the formula of justice. It has for its basis the eternal antagonism of ideas, of opinions, passions, capacities, temperaments, interests. It is the condition of love itself.

*Reciprocity* can be expressed in the precept: *Do unto others as you would have them do unto you:* a precept which political economy has translated into this celebrated formula: *Products exchange for products.*

It is therefore not the *organisation of labour* which we need at this moment. The organisation of labour is the proper object of individual liberty. He who works hard, gains much. The State has nothing further to say, in this respect, to the workers. What we need, that which I call for in the name of all workers, is reciprocity, equity in exchange, the *organisation of credit*.

[...]

# THE BANK OF EXCHANGE

PUBLIC CREDIT ORGANISED, labour restored and value decreed, nothing is left but to organise circulation, in the absence of which production is impossible.

This point is the summit of the revolution.

We have driven out the last of our kings, we have cried: Down with monarchy! Long live the Republic! But you can believe me, if the doubt has come to you, there are in France, there are in all Europe only a few lesser princes. Royalty is always in existence. Royalty will subsist as long as we will not have abolished it in its most material and most abstract form—the royalty of gold.

Gold is the talisman which congeals life in society, which binds circulation, kills labour and credit, and makes slavery mutual.

We must destroy the royalty of gold; we must republicanise specie, by making every product of labour ready money.

Let no one be frightened beforehand. I by no means propose to reproduce, under a rejuvenated form, the old ideas of paper money, money of paper, assignats, bank-bills, etc., etc.; for all these palliatives have been known, tried and rejected long ago. These representatives on paper, by which men have believed themselves able to replace the absent god, are, all of them, nothing but a homage paid to metal—an adoration of metal, which has been always present to men's minds, and which has always been taken by them as the measure or evaluator of products.

[...]

Everybody knows what a bill of exchange is. The creditor requests the debtor to pay to him, or to his order, at such a place, at such a date, such a sum of money.

The promissory note is the bill of exchange inverted; the debtor promises the creditor that he will pay, etc.

"The bill of exchange," says the statute, "is drawn from one place on another. It is dated. It announces the sum to be paid; the time and place where the payment is to be made; the value to be furnished in specie, in merchandise, in account, or in other form. It is to the order of a third person, or to the order of the drawer himself. If it is by 1$^{st}$, 2$^{nd}$, 3$^{d}$, 4$^{th}$, etc., it must be so stated."

The bill of exchange supposes, therefore, *exchange*, *provision* and *acceptance*; that is to say, a value created and delivered by the drawer; the existence, in the hands of the drawee, of the funds destined to acquit the bill, and the promise on the part of the drawee, to acquit it. When the bill of exchange is clothed with all these formalities; when it represents a real service actually rendered, or merchandise delivered; when the drawer and drawee are known and solvent; when, in a word, it is clothed with all the conditions necessary to guarantee the accomplishment of the obligation, the bill of exchange is considered *good*; it circulates in the mercantile world like bank-paper, like specie. No one objects to receiving it under pretext that a bill of exchange is nothing but a piece of paper. Only—since at the end of its circulation, the bill of exchange, before being destroyed, must be changed for specie—it pays to specie a sort of seigniorial duty, called *discount*.

That which, in general, renders the bill of exchange insecure is precisely this promise of final conversion into specie; and thus the idea of metal, like a corrupting royalty, infects even the bill of exchange and takes from it its certainty.

Now, the whole problem of the circulation consists in generalising the bill of exchange; that is to say, in making of it an anonymous title, exchangeable forever, and redeemable at sight, but only in merchandise and services.

Or, to speak a language more comprehensible to financial adepts, the problem of the circulation consists in *basing* bank paper, not upon specie, nor bullion, nor immovable property, which can never produce anything but a miserable oscillation between usury and bankruptcy, between the five-franc piece and the assignat; but by basing it upon *products*.

I conceive this generalisation of the bill of exchange as follows:

A hundred thousand manufacturers, miners, merchants, commissioners, public carriers, agriculturists, etc., throughout France, unite with each other in obedience to the summons of the government and by simple authentic declaration, inserted in *Le Moniteur*, bind themselves respectively and reciprocally to adhere to the statutes of the Bank of Exchange; which shall be no other than the Bank of France itself, with its constitution and attributes modified on the following basis:

1st The Bank of France, become the Bank of Exchange, is an institution of public interest. It is placed under the guardianship of the state and is directed by delegates from all the branches of industry.

2nd Every subscriber shall have an account open at the Bank of Exchange for the discount of his business paper; and he shall be served to the same extent as he would have been under the conditions of discount in specie; that is, in the known measure of his faculties, the business he does, the positive guarantees he offers, the real credit he might reasonably have enjoyed under the old system.

3rd The discount of ordinary commercial paper, whether of drafts, orders, bills of exchange, notes on demand, will be made in bills of the Bank of Exchange, of denominations of 25, 50, 100 and 1,000 francs. Specie will be used in making change only.

4th The rate of discount will be fixed at—percent, commission included, no matter how long the paper has to run. With the Bank of Exchange all business will be finished on the spot.

5th Every subscriber binds himself to receive in all payments, from whomsoever it may be and at par, the paper of the Bank of Exchange.

6th Provisionally and by way of transition, gold and silver coin will be received in exchange for the paper of the bank, and at their nominal value.

Is this a paper currency?

I answer unhesitatingly, No! It is neither paper money, nor money of paper; it is neither government checks, nor even bank-bills; it is not of the nature of anything that has been hitherto invented to make up for the scarcity of specie. It is the bill of exchange generalised.

The essence of the bill of exchange is constituted—first, by its being drawn from one place on another; second, by its representing a real value equal to the sum it expresses; third, by the promise or obligation on the part of the drawee to pay it when it falls due.

In three words, that which constitutes the bill of exchange is *exchange, provision, acceptance.*

[...]

In the combination I propose, the paper (at once sign of credit and instrument of circulation) grows out of the best business-paper, which itself represents products delivered, and by no means merchandise unsold. This paper, I affirm, can never be refused in payment, since it is subscribed beforehand by the mass of producers.

This paper offers so much the more security and convenience, inasmuch as it may be tried on a small scale, and with as few persons as you see fit, and that without the least violence, without the least peril.

[...]

We have said before that all economic negations overlap one another and generalise themselves, especially in the negation of money considered as an emblem of value and instrument of exchange. There are few economists today who, upon reflection, do not admit the possibility of such a reform; but it is no less true that in the theory of the old political economy—the highly praised English political economy, which they strive to implant among us as they already have implanted constitutional monarchy—the idea of abolishing specie is supremely absurd, as absurd as the thought of abolishing property.

[...]

## PRODUCTS EXCHANGE FOR PRODUCTS

*Products exchange for products:* This aphorism of political economy is no longer contradicted. Socialists and economists are in accord with the fact and the law, it is common ground where theories are reconciled, and opinions unite on the same doctrine.

Exchange is direct or indirect: What must we do to make possible direct exchange, not only among three, four, six, ten or one hundred traders, but among one hundred thousand, between all producers and all consumers; simply this: centralise all the operations of commerce by means of a bank in which all the bills of exchange, drafts and sight-bills representing the bills and the invoices of merchants, will be received. Then generalise or convert these obligations into paper of equivalent value, which, in consequence, will itself be a pledge of the products or real values that these obligations represent.

Bank paper so issued would have all the qualities of first class paper.

It would not be subject to depreciation since it would be delivered only against actual values and acceptable bills of exchange, and would be based, not on manufactured products, but on products sold and delivered, for which payment would be required. There would be no danger of excessive emission, since they would be delivered only against first class commercial paper—that is to say, against promises of certain repayment.

No one would refuse it, since, by the fact of the centralisation of exchanges, all citizens would become members of the bank. The most remarkable fact to be noted in this constitution of the bank is not so much the idea in itself, an idea more simple perhaps than the one which gave birth to money, but the coincidence of the employment of specie with the regime of feudal property and with the monarchical organisation of society.

We have pointed out several times and we cannot repeat it too often: as long as the family had to live, by its own activity and like a little world in itself, on property, property has been the principle and the cornerstone of the social order.

During that period, the infrequency of exchanges, the scarcity of transactions, called exclusively for the employment of specie. The agent of circulation had to carry in itself its guarantee so as to be accepted. That was the age of gold, even as it was the age of royalty.

But when, by the multiplicity of labour, by the division of industries, by the frequency of exchanges, circulation became the principal factor in the economy of nations, individual property became, as we have said, an obstacle to collective life, and the employment of specie became nothing but the sign of privilege and of despotism, the same as the royal prerogative was the sign of corruption and of tyranny.

Therefore, society, in its development, destroys or transforms its former work. It is when we have acquired full knowledge of this law that revolutions can come peacefully.

Royalty, property, specie: this is the monarchical trinity which we have to demolish, the triple negation that sums up for us entirely the revolutionary movement begun in February.

For as we shall prove, all negation—that is to say, all reform in religion, philosophy, rights, literature, art—brings us to the negation of property, and, property abolished, we shall see what we want to put in place of property, in place of authority, in place of God.

All this having been posited, so that what follows will be better understood, we place before our readers the project, as we had planned it, of a Bank of Exchange.

[...]

The object of the Association is:

First, particularly and immediately, by the institution of the Bank of Exchange, to procure for every member of the Association, without the aid of specie, all products, whether commodities, merchandise, services or labour.

Second, ultimately, to reorganise agricultural and industrial labour by changing the condition of the producer.

The association is universal. All citizens, without exception, are invited to join. No funds are required; for membership it will suffice to sign the present by-laws, and to agree to accept, for all payments, the paper of the Bank of Exchange.

The association has no capital. Its existence is perpetual.

The Bank of Exchange is an essentially republican institution; it is a paradigmatic example of government of the People by the People. It is an active protest against any re-establishment of hierarchical and feudal principles: it is the concrete abrogation of all civil and political inequality. The privilege of gold having been abolished, all privileges disappear. Equality in exchange, necessarily resulting from the mutuality of exchange, becomes in its turn the basis of the equality of labour, of real solidarity, of personal responsibility, and of absolute liberty. The Bank of Exchange, finally, is the principle, the means and the measure of wealth, of universal and perpetual peace.

[...]

Through its influence, its knowledge, and its credit, the Bank of Exchange promotes, inspires, encourages, supports, and sponsors all agricultural, manufacturing, commercial and scientific enterprises, etc., that workers' associations may attempt, when these present sufficient guarantees of competency, morality, and success.

[...]

The Bank of Exchange is an institution of public interest; as such, it is under the State's supervision but is independent of it.

The State is a member of the same standing as all citizens. It takes no part in the management, and does not interfere directly or indirectly with its administration.

[...]

The administration of the Bank is in the hands of a Board of Directors under the supervision of a Council of Oversight.

[...]

The members of the Board are elected for five years by the General Assembly and are eligible for re-election.

[...]

Any member of the Board of Directors can be suspended from his office by the Council of Oversight and can only be reinstated by a two-third vote of the General Assembly.

## THE COUNCIL OF OVERSIGHT

The Council of Oversight shall be elected annually by the General Assembly.

It is composed, like the General Assembly itself, of delegates chosen by all branches of production and of the public service. The number of these delegates shall not at any time exceed thirty.

The State shall be represented by the Minister of Justice, who shall be chairman of the Committee by virtue of his office in the Government.

The Council of Oversight shall have the absolute right of control.

[...]

It has the right to convoke the General Assembly in extraordinary session, and to request the resignation of any or all of the members of the Board.

[...]

The General Assembly is composed of the entire membership, who shall have a right to be present and take part.

They may delegate their powers and may be represented by proxy.

When, by the adherence of all producers to the Bank of Exchange, the General Assembly will become equal and identical with the totality of citizens, it will be composed of none but the representatives of production, named by each industry, the number of which shall be in proportion to its importance.

The General Assembly, thus composed, representing the general welfare and no longer the selfish interests, will be the true representative of the people.

[...]

In our preceding articles, we proved that all methods of philosophic— and, we may add, mathematical—investigation proceed necessarily by elimination or negation that such is the revolutionary method by which society progresses, incessantly abolishing its own institutions, and securing the unlimited establishment of liberty.

According to this conception of progress, the ultimate goal of civilisation would be the one in which society exists without government, without police, and without law, the collective activity exercising itself by a kind of immanent reflection; the exploitation of the earth would take place unitedly and in perfect harmony, and the individual, following only his own inclination, would attain the maximum of wealth, of science and of virtue.

[...]

TO LABOUR IS TO PRODUCE SOMETHING OUT OF NOTHING

Man, by this proposition, becomes equal to God. Like God, he creates things out of nothing. Thrown naked upon the earth, among briers and thorns, among tigers and serpents, finding hardly enough sustenance for one person on each square league; without tools, without patterns, without supplies, without previous experience, he has had to clear, lay out, eradicate, cultivate his domain; he has embellished nature itself; he is surrounded by the unknown marvels of the ancient author of things, and has given birth to luxury where nature had given nothing but profusion. At the origin of society there was only raw material, there was no capital. It is labour that has created capital; it is the worker who is the real capitalist. Because to work means to produce something out of nothing, to consume without producing is not to exploit capital, it is to destroy capital.

Such, then, is the first principle of the new economy, a principle full of hope and of consolation for the worker without capital, but a principle full of terror for the parasite and for the tools of parasitism, who see reduced to naught their celebrated formula: *Capital, labour, talent!*

Producing something out of nothing is the first term of a marvellous equation, which in these fundamental propositions we shall see unfold and yield, as a result and conclusion—wealth.

### TO GIVE CREDIT IS TO EXCHANGE

This axiom is, like the first, the overturning and the overthrowing of all economic and phalansterian ideas.[2]

In the system of interest-bearing property, where capital, by a purely grammatical fiction, passes from the hands of the worker to those of a parasite who is for that reason called a capitalist, credit is *unilateral*, proceeding from the parasite, who possesses without producing, to the worker, who produces without possessing. Thus established, credit demands a tribute from the debtor, in exchange for the permission—which the parasite grants him—to make use of his own capital.

In the system of the Bank of Exchange, on the contrary, credit is *bilateral*: it flows from each worker and is directed to all the others in such a manner that, instead of borrowing capital bearing interest, the workers mutually pledge each other their respective products, on the sole condition of equality in exchange.

Thus, in this system of credit, every creditor or mortgagee becomes a debtor in his turn; one thing is exchanged for another. In the other system, which is that of *La Démocratie Pacifique*,[3] there is only one creditor and one debtor, and something is given in exchange for nothing. The one of the two contracting parties who gives without receiving is the worker, the one who receives without giving is the capitalist. To give and not to receive; to receive, and not to give: what could be more unreasonable or unjust? Yet this takes us back further than the Code; it goes back further than Justinian, Numa, even Moses: it is the old iniquity of Cain, the first proprietor and the first murderer. This is also why *La Démocratie Pacifique*, which according to Fourier's precepts, must make reform proceed by a *great leap [grand écart]*, is attached to the capitalist law, to the tradition of Cain. Mutuality of credit, for shame! is egoism. But non-reciprocity of credit, good!—*that* is fraternity.

### TO EXCHANGE IS TO CAPITALISE

In the old political economy, this has no meaning. In the mutualist system, nothing is more rational.

In fact, if, as we have just shown, giving credit is the same thing as exchanging; if nothing should be given for nothing; if products can be delivered

---

2    Referring to the utopian scheme of Charles Fourier, who proposed the "phalanstery" as an ideal living arrangement. (Editor)

3    *La Démocratie Pacifique* was a Fourierist journal founded by Victor Considérant, Proudhon frequently excoriates Fourierist notions of "fraternity" as naïve and incipiently authoritarian. (Editor)

only for equivalent products, and not for an authorisation to produce: the moment that direct exchange no longer encounters any obstacles, it is evident that the means for each individual worker to obtain wealth is for him to acquire the greatest possible amount of different products, in exchange for his one unvarying product.

The contrary happens when exchanges can be made only by the intervention of money, and subject to the discount profit [*bénéfice d'escompte*] of the holder of coin, like the profit [*bénéfice d'aubaine*] accruing to the holder of the tools of production. In this instance, it is clear that exchanges are infrequent and costly, because they are hampered. Conversion of the product is difficult, sales always restricted, demand always timid; capitalisation takes place only in the form of money, consequently instead of having consumption active it has frugality for its only principle, and, like frugality, it is poor and indigent.

Whether one views it from one or the other standpoint, the savings bank is a philanthropic institution, or an economic absurdity.

## A CONSUMER IS A PARTNER

This axiom is a consequence of the third paragraph—*To exchange is to capitalise*, as the latter is the consequence of the second, *Credit is exchange*. In reality, where, by the direct exchange of products, all producers are considered as creditors, the consumer becomes the sleeping partner of those who, not having any products to offer for exchange, ask either for work or for instruments of labour. "What can you offer us?" one says to the idle worker. "Some cloth, shawls, jewellery, etc.," he answers. "Very well; here are our orders: Take them to the Bank, and, on the guaranty of our signatures, you will get an advance, you will receive the means to work, to live, to cover your credit; in short, that which will enrich you."

Such is the very nature of credit.

Between the producer and the consumer, the current view places the capitalist; between product and product, it places money; between the worker and the employer, that is to say, between labour and talent, it places capital, property. What a splendid trinity! What a perfect triad! And how much does this synthesis of the three degrees outweigh the dualism of reciprocity!

[...]

The mutualist association is like nature, which is wealthy, beautiful, and luxuriant because she draws her wealth and her beauty from the creative force that is within her; in a word, because she produces everything from nothing. Nature in producing does not profit thereby.

At whose expense, upon what, would nature make a profit? On itself? To profit, for nature, would thus be synonymous with *resting, ceasing to produce*; profit would be the same thing as impoverishment.

Likewise, in the association, profit is synonymous with poverty, since to profit can signify nothing for her, but to take from herself, as in trade profit is synonymous with taking from others. Profit is therefore here synonymous with theft, and what is true of society is true of the individual, who is always less wealthy and less happy in proportion to the poverty of his fellows.

Thus, production without capital, exchange without profit—these are the two terms between which social economy oscillates, the result of which is WEALTH.

The two negations balance each other. The first shows the *debit* of the worker, the second his *credit*.

This is the principle of mutualist accounting.

How does the Bank of Exchange begin its bookkeeping? It is not with an account of *capital*, since it has no capital; nor with an account of *stock*, since it possesses nothing as yet, not even bills; nor with *cash*, since it has nothing in its till; nor with *general merchandise*, or *profits and loss*, since it has produced nothing, and before any operations it cannot lose or gain.

The Bank opens accounts by the process of *drafts and remittances*; that is to say, as soon as it begins to function, as soon as it operates, as soon as it has availed itself through the universal partnership of the special work done by circulation, receiving from some and supplying to others, the Bank retains from each transaction the price of its service, its own *wage, capital* and *profit*, three terms from now on synonymous. The greater the number of transactions it performs, the greater the number of emoluments it realises, or, in other words, profits; and since working productively is synonymous with working as cheaply as possible, the greater the reduction the Bank of Exchange makes in its discount, the more other associations, who in their own lines follow the same movement of reduction, will thrive…

Thus, by the sole fact of the inauguration of the mutualist principle and the abolition of specie, the relations of labour and capital are inverted; the principles of commerce are overthrown; the forms of society, both civil and commercial, are reversed; the rights and the duties of the members are changed, property revolutionised, accounting reformed; equity, hitherto hobbled, is reconstituted on a stable basis.

[…]

The Bank of Exchange loans on mortgages, WITHOUT INTEREST, accepting repayments in annual instalments. This signifies that through the Bank of Exchange the whole of the producers voluntarily loan to the farmer, on a mortgage of his property, the amount he needs for supplies and help and other purposes in carrying on his affairs.

In exchange for this credit, the borrower each year repays the Bank—which means all the producer-lenders—the instalment promised, so that the repayment to the creditor is as real as the credit. No longer will there be any parasitic middleman, usurping, like the State, the rights of the worker, and absorbing, like the capitalist, a part of his product.

The State, as well as specie, being excluded from this regime, credit reduces itself to a simple exchange in which one of the parties delivers his product at one time, the other remits his in various instalments, all without interest, without any other costs than those of accounting.

In this system, let the operations multiply themselves as much as they will, for, far from showing an increase of charges for the producer, like those which take place in the mortgage bank, this acceleration of business will be a sign of an increase of wealth, since credit is here nothing but exchange and since products call for products.

[...]

*Paris, 8<sup>th</sup> April 1848*
*Translation by Paul Sharkey*

# LETTER TO LOUIS BLANC

To Citizen Louis Blanc, Secretary of the Provisional Government
   Citizen,
   I am taking the liberty of sending you a copy of the first print run of my
*Solution au problème social,* as well as of the accompanying *Spécimen* relating
to circulation and credit.

   To be blunt with you, these two pamphlets contain things vexatious to
the provisional government and to yourself. I regret those things; and I have
come unsolicited, citizen, to offer you an explanation and do amends. It is
for you to determine how you must act should my declarations strike you as
heartfelt. Given the unanticipated nature of the position in which it found
itself, the provisional government made mistakes; that goes without saying.
Like everyone else, I am within my rights to point them out; but maybe it
was out of place for me to be flagging them up with quite the vehemence I
put into all my discourse. It is my misfortune that my passions are at odds
with my ideas; the light which illuminates other men burns me. Should I
happen to devise a critique of a theory, on foot of the unwitting assumption
that the author is a man after my own heart, I reason as if determination and
judgement were one and the same. And when I go astray, I get confused and
blame myself as if over some crime. No matter what I may do, there is no
way for me to alter this unfortunate frame of mind.

   If I have weighed you up correctly, citizen Blanc, the very opposite has
been the case with you. You are a man of sentiment, love and enthusiasm.
Whereas with me passions spring from the head, in your case all your ideas
seem to well up from the heart. Maybe, between the pair of us, we would
make one complete person: but until such time as we swap our respective
qualities, it is inevitable that we should not see eye to eye: and almost certain
that we are going to be enemies. Deep down, that with which I reproach you
is precisely the thing in which I am found wanting and what I envy you: in

the light of which you will overlook a number of attacks which cannot add to or subtract from your success, I am weary of warfare; I should rather have something to defend; besides, the common foe is not the government. Give me yours and I shall let you have mine. Which is the only way we can earn self-respect and render good service to the Republic. Such reciprocity sums up my entire secret formula for a solution to the social question.

Your plan to organise national workshops contains an authentic idea, one that I endorse, for all my criticisms.

Of that thought you yourself are aware: but it seems that you regard it as merely secondary, whereas, in my view, it is everything: I mean to say that by national workshops you mean core workshops, main works, so to speak, for all the workshops are owned by the nation, even though they remain and must always remain free.

Your preoccupation, therefore, is with the need to make a reality of a principle: to invest the new institution with flesh and face and then to let it develop unaided on the basis of the virtues of the idea and vigour of the principle.

Would you, citizen, make it your business to have my scheme for the organisation of loans looked at and, if appropriate, welcomed by the provisional government? In return I will make it my business to organise your workshops.

My scheme for an Exchange Bank, which lies at the heart of my *Spécimen,* is an idea that is as much yours as it is mine. It is what you were looking for and may well have had in mind in your studies of [John] Law's system; and what every economist has been questing for. By virtue of its over-arching mandate, the Exchange Bank is the organisation of labour's greatest asset.

If, after reading, your considered opinion is that I am mistaken, it only remains for me to drop my gaze, cease all publication and cease all further engagement with economic issues.

Conversely, afford my idea your protection and hand yours over to me; forgive me for saying so, citizen, but the organising of workshops is a venture beyond your remit, not because of any lack of ability on your part but because you are precluded from it by your office.

You are a member of the government; you no longer stand for a faction but represent the general interests of society. No longer are you the man of *La Réforme* nor the man of *L'Organisation du Travail;* and any initiative that seems to conflict with the interests of any class within society is off limits to you. You belong as much to the bourgeoisie as you do to the proletariat. Sponsor and encourage the emancipation of the labouring classes: teach the workers what it is they should be doing; but keep out of it yourself and do not compromise your responsibility. You are a statesman; you stand for the past as well as the future.

With this thought in mind, citizen, whilst asking your support for an idea that falls entirely within the remit of government, I place myself at your disposal for another idea which is not at all within its competence. If my services were to be accepted by you, citizen, I should ask that the items and documents already amassed by the commission be passed on to me; it should then be my honour to put before you a project relating both to the course to be followed and to the new form of society to be defined and created among the workers.

I write to you, citizen, at a time when, sensitivity having gained the upper hand in me, it restores my soul to an even keel. My overtures to you are all devotion and I hope that you will appreciate them as such. Yet, no matter my wish to be agreeable to you, allow me to add that I am above all prompted by the overriding interests of the Republic.

I am relying, citizen, upon the honour of a response. The second run of my book is ready: given the difficulties of the situation, I propose to suspend publication. To which end I need to know if, instead of writing, I might be able to make a more effective contribution to the consolidation of the Republic.

My cordial greetings, citizen

P-J PROUDHON

# LETTER TO PROFESSOR CHEVALIER

To Monsieur Michel Chevalier, Professor of Political Economy
Sir,

In your third letter on the organisation of labour, as published in yesterday's edition of [*Journal des*] *Débats,* you mention me in the same breath as Monsieur Pecqueur as head of a strange sect of communists whom you dub egalitarian communists and heirs to Babeuf: Thereby dismissing me as you do Monsieur Louis Blanc, the official labour organisation entrepreneur, and you curtly pronounce my *system* as being every bit as powerless as Monsieur Louis Blanc's in the eradication of pauperism, which is the great issue of our times.

So that I, who have so rebutted communism as to spare us the need ever again to concern ourselves with it in the future, find myself lumped in with your sweeping condemnation of the communists.

I, whose thinking bears no relation to that of Monsieur Louis Blanc and who has not once put in an appearance at the Luxembourg [Commission], find myself entombed by you in the very same grave as Monsieur Louis Blanc.

And, finally, I, who have thus far published naught but criticisms: criticisms of political economy, criticisms of socialism, communism, Fourierism, Saint-Simonianism; criticism of monarchy, democracy, property, etc., etc., must now listen to a damning verdict passed upon my *system*, when no such system has ever seen the light of day!

The day before yesterday *Le Constitutionnel* was labelling me a communist; recently the *Revue des Deux Mondes* was also depicting me as a communist; everybody—except those who read me—has me marked as a communist, on which basis, no opportunity is ever missed to denounce my *system* as false and unfeasible and inimical to freedom, subversive of society and of the family, and a number of other more or less displeasing characterisations.

I have allowed such ugliness to have the run of it out of the straightforward fear that my corrections might be construed as complaints, and if I have now determined to address myself to you, it is because I hold that it serves the general interest that I should break my silence. It would be too convenient to respond to the criticisms that have been levelled at society's institutions these past twenty years by tossing the label *communist* around, and the enemies of the February Revolution would all too soon have done with the proletariat.

So, if you please, let us drop Monsieur Louis Blanc and his utopia. Monsieur Louis Blanc is by no means the incarnation of a new social system. This, if I am not mistaken, is how the matter ought to be tackled by every well-meaning writer.

The people, and it was they that made the February Revolution, are neither Saint-Simonian, Fourierist, communist, nor Babouvist: nor even Jacobin or Girondin.

But the people has a perfect grasp on these two things: on the one hand, that politics is nothing; on the other, that political economy, as taught by Messieurs Say, Rossi, Blanqui, Wolowski, Chevalier, etc., is merely the economics of the propertied, the application of which to society inevitably and organically engenders misery.

I reckon that I have done more than anybody to establish this view. What holds economically true for the ordinary individual become false the moment one tries to extend it to society; that proposition encapsulates all my criticisms. This, for instance, is why *net* product and *gross* product, which in private industry are different things, are one and the same when it comes to the nation; why a fall in pay that spells impoverishment for the worker who suffers it becomes an increase in wealth when it applies to everyone;[1] how, from the collective point of view, the same holds true for all of the theorems of the old political economy which, let me say it again, is nothing more than household economics. Now what is that the people asks for today? The people asks, and this is the issue raised by 24 February, that, whilst respecting the freedom of the individual, in whatever guise it may show itself, we should reshape a political economy (public or social, whatever takes your fancy) that is not a lie; for attempting to explain the practices of selfishness to society is tantamount to lying to the people and to justice. The facts are there to prove that.

And what do the socialists do to satisfy this craving of the people?

---

1    Proudhon subscribed to the (false) position that wages and prices were directly proportional, meaning that a cut in wages would lead to a cut in prices. He is, therefore, arguing that while a cut in wages would be bad for the workers in question, society would benefit from the lower prices. (Editor)

Due to an error of the same sort as the economist's, they would extend to the whole of society the principle of fraternity which exists within the family, plus the principle of solidarity, which lies at the root of the civil and commercial companies defined by the Code. Hence the phalansterian utopia and the many others with which you are as conversant as I am.

Now, fraternity and solidarity within the body of society have no more in common with the domestic fraternity and solidarity of so-called collective societies than, in the people's view, the laws governing loans, production and commerce have in common with the rules of private credit, private production and private consumption.

In a work that appeared more than eighteen months ago, I have expanded upon this underlying opposition. Had the economists seen fit to register my observations, they would have been able to prevent the events of February and the social revolution might have been carried through without disaster. And had socialism, and Monsieur Louis Blanc in particular, been capable of taking the good advice offered which ran counter to their dreams, we would not, today, have the depressing spectacle the Luxembourg [Commission] offers us. But, in critiquing every opinion, I should have expected that no one would heed me; so I ask but one thing: spare me the calumny. As I see it, therefore, economists and socialists alike are chasing after an unattainable goal: the former by applying the rules of private economics to society; the latter by applying private fraternity to it. And still we have individualism, still subjectivity and contradiction.

This is something that I have been repeating without cease for the past eight years. Moreover, I have been measured in my assertions: I have not published any system, and nobody can say whether I am or am not capable of curing poverty.

However, desirous to give some notion of what the solution to the social question ought to be, as I see things, I have just published a draft for the organisation of labour and credit and so I take the liberty of addressing myself to you.

Either I am sorely mistaken or you will not discover within it any trace of communism or of Babouvism and you will see there a political economy built on different foundations than those of J-B Say and Ricardo.

Since, and it was you yourself, Monsieur who said this, since the day has come when all systems are up for discussion, you force my hand and it would be only fair of you to scrutinise this little morsel of mine. The people has gone too far to back down; it is absolutely necessary to establish one of new principles: the right of the capitalist and the workers; in short, the social question is in need of sorting out. Otherwise, expect all the horrors of civil war and all the wretchedness of agrarian law.

Sir, I genuinely regret the destitution by which you have been stricken and which has, I fear, found you unduly sensitive for a man of such lofty intellect. I might not have recommended this act of pointless rigour, especially as, being primarily an economist, you are a sceptic in matters of government. Had you candidly thrown in your lot with the Revolution, you, with those talents of yours, might have been of service to the people even whilst setting your face against innovation.

I deplore the fact that petty resentments have propelled you into the enemy camp.

I am relying upon your being accommodating enough to have this present text inserted in the most imminent edition of *Débats* and would ask you to accept assurances of my perfect esteem.

P-J PROUDHON

*20<sup>th</sup> April 1848*

*Le Représentant du Peuple*

*Translation by Paul Sharkey*

# THE SITUATION

What we had foreseen, what we had foretold has come to pass.

The revolution is bound for doctrinaire, bourgeois democracy; the provisional government, a motley crew, has just carried out a sort of a purge of itself. The personnel remain; the principles had been struck out. Serious failings have accelerated this outcome which was in any case inevitable. Let us recount them in a few lines; by way of a preamble to our profession of faith.

Victory on 24 February had hoisted three different parties into power and refreshed our ancient strifes; the Girondin or Thermidorean camp represented by *Le National*; the Montagnard camp represented by *La Réforme*; and the socialist-communist party represented by Louis Blanc.

Discounting the monarchy, those three parties covered the full spectrum of views.

So it looked as if the provisional government, precisely because of its motley composition, should have, in the eyes of France, been an expression of the reconciliation of all the ideas, all the interests. With the bourgeoisie and the proletariat linking hands over *L'Organisation du Travail* as if it were the gospel of the future, there was some credibility to the notion that the poverty problem, side-stepped by the outgoing government, was on the point of being resolved in an amiable, peaceable fashion by the incoming one.

We have just seen, and for the thousandth time, what such reconciliations, built on vague fellow feeling and not underpinned by any principle, are worth.

Yet the policy the provisional government should have followed was quite straightforward and self-evident. The problem of the proletariat posed with determination and vigour; the workers employed and fed; the bourgeois class revived; then, pending the National Assembly, the building of a republican status quo; this was what common sense, as well as high politics, required of the provisional government.

In such a situation, conserving everything amounted to advancing.

Well now, no one grasped what was so straightforward and wise, what not only had the advantage of common sense but also had the merit of profundity.

Scarcely had it received its brand new mandate to represent the Republic than the bourgeois party within the provisional government, relapsing into its old concerns, started to sound the retreat.—For its part, the revolutionary faction, carried away by the enthusiasm of its memories, and deluding itself utterly about the power of its resources and aiming, as it says, to *engage the future*, has begun to display *vigour* and exclusivity. Finally, not content with having laid out its principle, socialism has sought to move on to implementation, looking exclusively to itself for the implementation of its handiwork.

And we know what the upshot of these tensions has been. Everything that the provisional government has done has, in the view of the former bourgeoisie, proven a backward step—everything that it has undertaken in a revolutionary sense has been counter-revolutionary;—everything that it has decreed in the interests of the proletariat has run counter to the proletariat's interests.

When, thus, in sticking to the conventions of bourgeois economics, the provisional government took out a loan of 100 million; when, in order to prove the soundness of its credit, it handed 50 million over to the *rentiers*; when it raised the interest on monies deposited with the savings funds; when it put off the insurance companies, etc., etc., and I would say when faced with the socialist principle, which should have informed the law but did not inform it, the government acted contrary to its rights and its duties.

Likewise, when the provisional government set about writing the dictatorial circulars that in 1848 frightened hardly anyone except old ladies; when, without a penny or a person other than what the pleasure of the departments afforded it, it spoke to the departments as if it were an authority; when, in the middle of a France that was republican in mind and heart—albeit in defiance of the Republic—it conjured up the reaction and the counter-revolution just as it would shortly conjure up coalition; in all of these circumstances, the provisional government was acting like a sleep-walker. It has presented us with the spectacle—the only one history has to show—of statesmen acting out an old tragedy with laughable seriousness. Through its backward-looking radicalism, it has compromised future reforms: the electoral law is sufficient proof of that for me.

If we move on from the revolutionary element to the socialist element, we find a similar series of mistakes and miscalculations.

How come there was no one to tell Monsieur Blanc: You are banned from the organisation of labour, such as you understand it, not that you are lacking in ability but because our position forbids it. You see the workshop, namely individualism, as the way to tackle the problem; whereas it is only from the side of society that you can provide the solution, to wit, credit. But even in that light, there is nothing you can do: as a member of this government, you no longer represent one class within society, but the general interests of society, and are precluded from every initiative that might serve the interests of one fraction rather than another. You belong to the bourgeoisie rather than the proletariat. Sponsor and give encouragement to the emancipation of the labouring classes: do not take a hand in it yourself, do not compromise your responsibility, the responsibility of the government. Wait for some higher authority to bestow both credit and power upon you.

Across the board, the actions of the provisional government have not met with success. So protesting voices were not long in making themselves heard. The demonstrations on 16th and 17th March; multiple commissioners driven out of the departments; latterly, the 16th April revolt; all of these, mounted to the accompaniment of cries of *Long live the Republic! Long live the provisional government!*, were proof even to the least clear-sighted that France is sincerely republican, but that she would not countenance a dictatorship; that by revolution, she means reconciliation; that she rejects doctrinairism, Jacobinism and utopianism equally; but that while she has protested against each of the factions making up the revolutionary government, she retains that government as it stands, it is because she is no longer willing to endure personality issues and looks upon those who govern her as ministering to her will.

That, as we see it, is how things actually stand; the position of the provisional government is admirable and its strength beyond measure; but the difficulties to be overcome are infinite too. They can all be summed up in this formula which encapsulates its role and its rule alike: reconciling diverging interests through the generality of measures.

But just as the tree always falls in the direction in which it leans, the provisional government's tendency is presently inclining towards the anti-socialist protest of 16 April. There is plenty of encouragement along those lines and formal advice. Many people imagine, the social question having been bungled at the Luxembourg [Commission], that the social question has been dealt with; that from now on capital is spared the need to reckon with labour. Bedazzled by that notion, there is an inevitability to the provisional government's marching towards bourgeois restoration, at the price of a few gestures made to the ardour of social ideas.

That much is being hinted at already, both by the hypocritical reflections in reactionary newspapers on the difficulty, uncertainty and impossibility of a solution, and the decrees whereby the provisional government simultaneously cuts or abolishes the levies on salt, beef and beverages and introduces other taxes on servants, dogs, quality wines, rents over 800 francs, etc., etc.

The removal of the tax on salt, beef and beverages, in the current economic circumstances, is only a philanthropic exaggeration that will cost the State dearly without bettering the lot of the workers.

The introduction of extravagant taxes is a socialist fantasy that will cost the workers dearly without filling the State's coffers.

The provisional government's decrees shift poverty the way bankruptcy shifts capital; they solve nothing. Blind and ignorant, the clamour for revolution is satisfied by these decrees; but the people is bamboozled by those same decrees. In return for an apparent sacrifice, we have an actual restoration: People, you will find that out soon enough.

As for ourselves, even though we may also be as dissatisfied with 16 April as we had been by 17th March, we bow to the fait accompli. We like clear cut stances. The threefold essence of the provisional government was an encumbrance to us. We now know to whom we must speak. Doctrinaire democracy now rules and governs. We had always thought that the proletariat must emancipate itself without the help of the government: the government, since April 16th, thinks the same way.

We are in agreement with the government!...

*29<sup>th</sup> April 1848*
*Le Représentant du Peuple*
*Translation by Paul Sharkey*

# THE REACTION

THE SOCIAL QUESTION HAS BEEN PUT ON THE LONG FINGER. APRIL 16TH HAS consigned the socialist candidates to oblivion. The cause of the proletariat, denounced with such venom on the barricades in February, has just fallen at the first hurdle in the April elections. The people's enthusiasm has given way to consternation: as before, it is the bourgeoisie that is to determine the conditions of the workers. The root of all evil, and let us spell it out one last time, has been the inadequacy of the Luxembourg [Commission] and the weakness of the Interior Ministry. Let Messieurs Blanc and Ledru-Rollin forgive themselves as we have forgiven them! They have allowed France to go to ruin and sold out the proletariat. But they are low-born: and consequently they are ours. In the wake of the battle for Cannes when Varron lost the Republic's last remaining army, the Senate passed a vote of thanks to him for not having given up hope in the country. Let Messieurs Blanc and Ledru-Rollin but tell us that they have not lost hope in the emancipation of the proletariat and we stand ready to send them our congratulations. What matters now is sizing up the situation correctly.

For some time now, in the newspapers of the provisional government, doubts have existed as to the February Revolution's having thus far been, as far as its representatives are concerned, only some sort of a retrospective revisitation of the first revolution. The two parties sharing power attack and threaten each other, under the labels Girondin and Montagnard. First and foremost, they accuse each other of restoration and counter-revolution. Little by little our makeshift monitors are wakening up to their retrograde delusions. [There is] Nothing more enlightening, nothing more telling than their mutual recriminations. Should the reaction raise its head, it will be in the ranks of the government. If plots are being hatched against the government spawned by the barricades, it is in the ministerial ante-rooms. If the authorities, pulled this way and that, should, with its communist manifestos and doctrinairian inclinations, trigger a flight of capital, murder credit, unsettle the workers, desolate property; should the organisation of labour lead to the whole of France's downing tools, the blame lies with this two-faced democracy which rules and governs. All of the ground that we have covered in retreat over the past two months was covered under the aegis of memories contrary to the old republic. It is by '93 and all of its discord that we are being ruled; and as for 1848, that is still the seven-times-sealed book. What we have here is a phenomenon of social psychology that is deserving of further exploration. That phenomenon has come to pass in every revolutionary age and it is this that has raised every peril and determined catastrophes.

The democrats of '93, conjuring up a republic with their highschool memories, after devouring one another, set the revolution back by half a century. True, Robespierre could scarcely be held to blame for the ambition and venality of Mirabeau, the hesitancy of La Fayette, the weakness of Péthion, the nonchalance of Vergniaud, the vices of Danton or the fanaticism of Marat. But Robespierre was a Spartan; it was he that triggered the counter-revolution. The democrats of 1848, building the republic on their parliamentary memories, have also set the revolution back by half a century. I am not pointing the finger at their patriotism, their good intentions, their disinterestedness. The sum total of their fault is that they are only imitators; they thought themselves statesmen because they were following the old models!

So what is this queer preoccupation which, in time of revolution, bedazzles the most steadfast minds, and, when their burning aspirations carry them forward into the future, has them constantly harking back the past? How does it come about that the People, just when it is making the break with established institutions, takes another plunge and gets further immersed in tradition? Society does not repeat itself: but one would have thought it was walking backwards, like the rope-maker playing out his rope. Could it not turn its gaze in the direction in which it is going?

This is not the place for a comprehensive exploration of this difficult problem which strikes at the very depths of our nature and relates directly to the most abstract principles of metaphysics. We shall restrict ourselves to stating, in accordance to the recent works of philosophy, that the phenomenon involved has its roots in the make-up of our understanding and can be explained by the law of the sameness of opposites, a law that lies at the bottom of creation, as well as of logic. That said, let us turn back to the issue at hand.

In order to organise the future, a general rule confirmed by experience, the reformers always start out with their gaze fixed upon the past. Hence the contradiction forever discovered in their actions: hence also the immeasurable danger of revolutions.

So, on the day when the People overthrow the monarchy, they promptly replace it with a dictatorship. In which we have nothing but remembrance, a memory that goes back further than the overthrown monarchy; and a contradiction, in that absolutism is invoked as a safeguard against absolutism.

The rest was implicit. The Convention had its pro-consuls, Napoléon his prefects. The provisional government has its commissioners. In substance nothing has changed: all we have had is a change of personnel. Everyone can see today what this re-enacted comedy has cost us. The commissioners of the provisional government, precisely because they were merely memories, have flagged up the reaction; they had had their instructions from their masters.

The February Revolution was made to the strains of the *Marseillaise* and old republican anthems. More memories and yet more contradiction.

Contradiction, I say, and note this: the 1848 revolution inspired no poet. The social idea, anti-lyrical it would appear, has been obliged to unfold itself to the rhythms of the political idea. No matter what may have been said, as far as we are concerned, the epic is no more: and, trivial though it might seem, we are doomed to perform the labours, not of heroes, but of shop assistants. The princes of the new Republic will not be sword-wielders but pen-pushers. The 1848 Revolution, an economic revolution, is as bourgeois as could be. It is the workshop, the shop counter, the household, the cash-drawer, the most prosaic things in the world, the things least suited to revolutionary energy and high-flown words. How could one set down in verse or to music the worker's sharing in the profits, the partnership between labour and capital, the balance of imports against exports? Organising trade and credit, boosting production, widening markets, determining the new shapes of industrial companies—none of this involves the temperament of 1793: like it or not, we have to resign ourselves to being mere civilians.

The *Marseillaise* is suited to the idea for which it stands: it offends our most heartfelt inclinations: instead of enlightening the citizenry, it stuns them. This nonsense costs the Republic huge sums, not to mention its security. Singing of the *Marseillaise* amounts to playing into the hands of the reaction and is tantamount to a provocation.

Among the factors that accelerated the downfall of the constitutional monarchy, pride of place has to go to weariness with, and revulsion against parliamentary proceedings. Well! scarcely had disaster struck and the bodyguard of the Palais-Royal was still smouldering than France was overrun with clubs. Instead of burning itself out, the parliamentary fever spread. Instead of one tribune, we now had ten thousand of them and what tribunes! Never has such a confusion of the gift of speech been witnessed. Cobblestones from the barricades, like the stones cast by Deucalion, became orators. Everybody was talking like a Demosthenes: albeit reasoning like a [General] La Palisse. At a gathering of five hundred citizens, I witnessed the most redoubtable issues of political economy—matters of which I am certain no one in that venerable gathering understood a word—settled in five minutes, to thunderous applause. I saw the most hare-brained motions greeted by enthusiasm and puerile proposals carried unanimously. The provisional government could scarcely fail to legislate them into existence. Several received the sanction of its decrees.

Contradiction and reminiscence! Folk played at mini-parliaments, as well as at mini-workshops and mini-wars. But, workers! The clubs are not the place to do battle with property: that would be your workshops and in the marketplace. We will shortly be looking into this new strategy with you. Leave the politicking and the eloquence to the bourgeois. The rhetoric of the clubs has nothing to teach you. All this palaver is an affront to practical reason, to labour's gravitas, to the seriousness of matters, to the silence of study, to dignity of spirit. Remember that under Napoléon, a fellow who made war the symbol of labour, there was no speechifying. And clubs belong neither to our times nor to our outlook nor to our mores. This sham agitation will die away itself of boredom and desertion: if it were otherwise, the woes that it would bring you would be incalculable.

One of the first moves of the provisional government, one of its most widely applauded moves, was the implementation of universal suffrage. On the very day when that decree was issued, we wrote these same words which might well seem a paradox: "Universal suffrage is counter-revolution."

After the event, judge for yourself if we were wrong. The 1848 elections have been carried, overwhelmingly, by the priests, by the Legitimists, by the Dynastics, by the most conservative and most backward-looking elements in France. It could not have been otherwise.

So how hard could it have been to understand that within man there are two instincts, one the conservative and the other the forward-looking: that each of these two instincts only ever serves the purposes of the other, that each individual, gauging matters from the vantage point of self-interest, takes progress to be the furtherance of that interest; that such interest being at odds with the collective interest, the sum total of votes, rather than signifying general progress, is indicative of a general retreat?

We have said and we say it again: the Republic is the form of government wherein, every will retaining it freedom, the nation thinks, speaks and acts as a single man. But in order to achieve this ideal, all private interests, rather than pulling in the opposite direction to society, must work to the same end as society, which is not a possibility under universal suffrage. Universal suffrage is the materialism of the Republic. The more this arrangement is used and until such time as the economic revolution becomes an accomplished fact, the greater the retreat towards royalty, despotism and barbarism, all the more certainly if the votes are greater in number, more considered and more free. You would point the finger at the proletarian's lack of expertise and its indifference? But that is the very thing that makes a nonsense of your theory. What would you say of a father of a family who would leave it to his children freely to dispose of his belongings and then, ruined by them, would blame the inexperience of their youth? And what an argument against you the proletariat's indifference constitutes!

Because in the entire provisional government not a grain of common sense has been found, because we deluded ourselves that the dream of revolution might be sustained by strength of numbers, here we find ourselves in the middle of the bourgeois backlash! And the emancipation of the proletariat has to be put back by fifty years! We are paying a heavy price for our bedazzlement by novelists and blatherers. And, if the chief blame did not lie with ourselves, I would say that the ministers who have, in an unprincipled way and with no basis in law, misusing a temporary dictatorship, exposed the salvation of the people to the vagaries of this monstrous reckoning, should be stripped of their civic rights.

With one hand, the provisional government imposes taxes on luxuries; with the other, it puts on a show for the people, free of charge. Remembrance and contradiction. The tax on luxury reduces the work of the poor by whatever it reduces the consumption of the rich, and it reduces the State's revenue by whatever reduction it makes in the labour of the former and in the pleasures of the latter. Threefold deficit, threefold impoverishment: such is the upshot of the tax on luxury.

Free entertainments, precisely because they are free, are a trespass against labour and the people's morals: furthermore, they are a trap set for its good faith since the money which the spectator does not pay at the box-office, will be paid over to the tax collector who will pay the performers! Ruination, ruination everywhere.

One day an order issued by the prefecture of police commanded that the names of the streets and monuments be changed. The following day, a petition signed by the clubs asked that the remains of Armand Carrel and Godefroi Cavaignac be laid to rest in the Panthéon. Contradiction and plagiary!

Historic names are replaced by other historic names and men by other men: idols by other idols. But there is still the same old idolatry, the same vandalism. So who does have the right to tear down national monuments? You Père Loriquets[1] of Jacobinism, teach your voters how to fill in their ballot papers and let the Palais-Royal be called the Palais-Royal!

It has rightly been said that the backward-looking farces played out by the provisional government have cost us more in two months than the invasions back in 1814 and 1815.

So what is going to happen when we shift from farce to tragedy? The bourgeoisie is going to get irritated and will resolve to put paid to socialism. The handiwork of reaction, begun by the radical party, will be carried on in the opposite direction and with the same vigour by the bourgeois party. We have had our 21st January, our 31st May, our 9th Thermidor and we shall have our 2nd Prairial. The proletarian masses are ready to budge: and the

1   Père Jean-Nicolas Loriquet (1767–1845), a Jesuit priest whose *Histoire de France, a l'usage de la jeunesse* (1820) delicately attempted to write Napoléon Bonaparte out of French history as much as possible. (Editor)

National Guard, abetted by the army, to offer resistance. All of the actors are in their positions, all well versed in their parts. The Rommes, the Goujons, the Duquesnois, the Soubranys are ready for the sacrifice. Messieurs Ledru-Rollin, Flocon, Albert, Louis Blanc are in position. We have found our Monsieur Boissy d'Anglas[2] is standing by: he is M. de Lamartine. M. de Lamartine, his head filled with history, was initially on the side of the Mountain and, ever faithful to his tales of drama is now going over to the side of the Girondins.

The vague notion of some fresh, inevitable terror is in the air and has souls in turmoil. The workers tell themselves that the revolution needs a fresh beginning: and who can foresee how the restarted revolution will end up? The provisional government, demolishing property, with no benefit to the proletariat, through its financial laws, which the National Assembly cannot allow to stand without the country's being exposed to danger but which cannot be rescinded without provoking an uprising, looks as if it has decided to make terror inevitable.

In '93, the only cause of the terror was the resistance from an infinitesimal aristocratic minority. The existence of society, guaranteed in any case by the rich gains of the revolution and by the overall lack of solidarity, had nothing to fear from the Terror. In 1848, the supposed cause of terror would be the antagonism between two classes of citizens, one numerically stronger and the more formidable on account of its poverty, the other superior in terms of its wealth and intelligence. With both surviving thanks only to the commerce in goods and reciprocal relations, it is inevitable that in such a clash society will perish.

Let the first moves by the National Assembly expose the plans of the reaction; let a careless vote ignite the people's wrath; let there be a general recourse to arms; let the national representation be breached and then, under pressure from some other dictatorship, let movement grind to a standstill, and France will go up like a hive wreathed in flames with the choking, singed bees stinging one another to death.

So, once the government runs out of resources:

Once the nation's progress is spent;

Once the country's production and trade have petered out;

Once a famished Paris, blockaded by departments declining to send any more shipments, any more payments, finds itself cut off;

Once the workers demoralised by the politics of the clubs and by the idleness of the national workshops turn to soldiering just to survive;

Once the State has commandeered the citizenry's silver and jewellery for forwarding to the Mint;

---

2   François Antoine de Boissy d'Anglas (1756–1828), a politician who successfully steered his career in power from the Revolution of 1789 through the rise and fall of Napoléon. (Editor)

Once a million proletarians have turned against property;

Once house searches become the only means of tax-collection;

Once the peasant, for want of hard cash, takes to paying his taxes in kind;

Once commodities have become so rare that barriers are swept away and a final blow dealt to national industry;

Once famished gangs take to roaming the land and organising raids;

Once vagabondage has become the staple condition;

Once the peasant, standing guard with loaded rifle over his harvest, gives up on farming;

Once working women, broken by hunger, have all cut loose;

Once prostitution, grief, poverty have driven them to distraction;

Once troupes of women, following the flying columns of National Guards, take to marking the Republic's feast days with ghastly bacchanalia;

Once the first blood has been spilt, once the first head has fallen;

Once the abomination of disappointment has spread throughout France:

Oh, then you will know what revolution is when it is instigated by lawyers, carried out by artists and steered by novelists and poets! Once upon a time Nero was an artist, a lyric artist and playwright, an enthusiastic lover of the ideal, a worshipper of antiquity, a medal-collector, tourist, poet, orator, swashbuckler, sophist, a Don Juan, a Lovelace, a spirited, imaginative, likeable fellow brimful of life and sensual appetites. Which is what made him Nero!

Wake from your slumbers, ye Montagnards, Girondins, Feuillants, Cordeliers, Muscadins, Jansenists and Babouvists! You are but six weeks away from the events I herald. Cry: Long live the Republic! Off with the masks!—Then about-face and march!

*30<sup>th</sup> April 1848*
*Le Représentant du Peuple*
*Translation by Paul Sharkey*

# THE MYSTIFICATION OF UNIVERSAL SUFFRAGE

HOW COME THE VERY PEOPLE WHO THREE MONTHS AGO WERE CALLING whole-heartedly for universal suffrage now want no part of it?

And how come those who could not have been more apoplectic about universal suffrage three months ago dare today to take the credit for it?

The very same lack of principle and the same bad faith explain this double paradox. Some bemoan a lottery in which they have lost power; others marvel at a mechanism to which they are indebted for their privileges. What a truly splendid, moral and grand thing politics is!...

Those of us who were taking exception to this tired foolishness, universal suffrage, long before the Cormenin Law are within our rights to complain about it and take it down a peg.

Universal suffrage, we used to say, is a sort of atom theory whereby the law-maker, powerless to have the people speak in its essential unity, invites citizens to have their individual says, *viritim*,[1] just the same way as Epicurean philosophy explains thought, will and intelligence away in terms of combinations of atoms. As if the overall mind, the People's mind could ever be construed from the sum of a given number of votes!

The most reliable way of getting the People to lie is to introduce universal suffrage. Voting by head count in matters of governance as a way of gauging the will of the nation, is the precise equivalent, in terms of political economy, of a redistribution of the land. It is agrarian law transplanted onto the terrain of authority.

Because those writers who first concerned themselves with the origins of governments have taught us that all power derives from the sovereignty

---

1   Meaning "one man at a time." (Translator)

of the nation, the bold conclusion has been drawn that the best course was to have all the citizenry vote, by word of mouth, by presence or by piece of paper and that an absolute or relative majority of the wishes so expressed was equivalent to the will of the people. We have been dragged back to the practices of the barbarians who, eschewing reasoned argument, operated in terms of acclamation and election. A material symbol has been misconstrued as the actual formula for sovereignty. The dust-cloud of votes has been construed as the very essence of the people's will! ...

And then there is the miscount of votes. I take the Paris elections by way of an example.

Upwards of 400,000 citizens were entitled to vote in the Seine department, but scarcely 300,000 cast their votes.

To whom are we to ascribe the 100,000 abstainers?

Regarding them as if they did not exist, on that very basis you chalk them up to the elected candidates whereas you might with equal justification wager that, had they voted, they would have tilted the balance to the other side, or at least that they would have altered the outcome of the poll considerably.

And another paradox:

Of the 300,000 votes cast, a mere thirteen candidates claimed more than half; the twenty-one others have been returned only by relative majorities of between 104,000 and 144,000 votes.

How can those returned by a minority of the electorate purport to be the people's choice? What! There are 200,000 voters who take exception to M. Lamennais's candidacy,[2] but because they could not agree on who they wanted instead of him, M. Lamennais wins in spite of them. In the same way—and the law has anticipated this eventuality—a candidate with 298,000 votes cast against him and 2,000 for him was returned! And that deputy would claim to have been returned by universal suffrage! What a cheek!

Furthermore, if only those who framed this wonderful law known, when looking to popular suffrage expressed on a person-by-person basis, had dealt with the issue appropriately! If they had told the citizenry:

The labouring class means to have its share of all of the advantages enjoyed by the bourgeois class. Being the more numerous and poorer and thus the stronger class, that class is the master of power. Bourgeois or workers, the point is that, by common consent, they carry through a comprehensive overhaul of the economy. So you should be choosing the men best equipped in terms of their speciality, moderation and commitment to govern the interests of all.

It is beyond doubt that, had it been posed in those terms, the question put to the electors would have produced a quite different outcome.

---

2    Felicité Robert de Lamennais (1782–1854), a Catholic liberal elected to the Constituent Assembly in 1848. (Editor)

Instead of which, what has the government done?

For a start, through its declarations, its example, its decrees and its commissioners, it has raised the basis for warfare between the two castes designed to keep the people divided, the bourgeoisie and the proletariat.

In view of which the vast majority of citizens has begun to adopt a defensive stance before the redundancy of the bankrupted banker, the jobless artisan and incomeless property-owner. Everybody has become bourgeois and nobody wants to be counted as proletarian. From which point on, the ends to which the elections would be held were foreseeable.

And there's more.

All of a sudden, on April 16th, the provisional government with its lamentable pendulum swings between communist and conservative notions provoked turmoil right across the spectrum of views and once again the issue in the election was between property and community [*communauté*].

For social reform, it was a lost cause. The mass of the citizenry, who would readily have embraced it, has just pretty much rejected it under the name of communism.

Communism shunned, that is the real meaning of the 1848 elections. We no more want community of labour than we do community of women or community of children! The 260,000 votes cast for M. de Lamartine cannot have any other meaning. Or are they an embracing of the illustrious poet's theories or some epigram? Then along comes the new National Assembly with its equivocal mandate. As for ourselves, we shall see to it that our citizen representatives are reminded of the issue.

France, we shall tell them, wants no part of community: who can question that? We do not want it any more than you do.

But has that any bearing on the social question? Is railing against community enough to stamp out poverty?

Has the privilege of property been abolished?

Have the bourgeois turned into workers?

Have the workers turned into bourgeois?

Has our public debt of six billion, a budget of two billion, for it is going to be two billion, plus another twelve billion in mortgaged funds, been reduced?

Is the crisis drawing to an end?[3]

Has commerce been re-established?

Has labour been so organised that bread is assured within and without?

Are we free?

Are we equals?

Are we brothers?

---

3   France, at this time, was still in the throes of a dire economic crisis resulting from the collapse of a speculative bubble in 1847. (Editor)

Good folk who fear the dissolution of your marriage bonds, have a second look before you retreat into your shared insignificancy. If you so much as dream that you are here only to lend your backing to a negation, you have not understood your mandate. It only remains for us to act as your guiding lights. Get on with it!

4<sup>th</sup> May 1848
*Le Représentant du Peuple*
*Translation by Paul Sharkey*

# TO PATRIOTS

TOMORROW SEES THE OPENING OF THE NATIONAL ASSEMBLY.

How do the elected members from the departments come to us?

What sort of a reception will the representatives from around France get from the people of Paris?

The only answers are with distrust and scorn. I search for brothers but all I come across are plotters! Civil war is no longer in prospect: it is upon us. No longer is it feared as the ghastliest of evils: it is accepted as a necessity. In countryside and city alike, people are manufacturing powder, casting bullets and readying weapons. The leaders send out their watchwords and issue their manifestos. No matter where you go all you hear is this deadly message: We must finish it!

The bourgeois has his mind made up to have done with the proletarian, who, for his part, has his mind made up to have done with the bourgeois. The worker wants to see an end of the capitalist, the wage-earner [an end] of the entrepreneur, the departments with Paris, the peasants with the workers. In every heart anger and hatred reign; in every mouth a threat. And what is the cause of such discord? The elections.

Universal suffrage has lied to the People.

The February Revolution was made through every party opposing the outgoing government, through the general disgust with a monarchy crowned by infamy, every mind making its contribution to the idea of a reform both political and social. The February Revolution, the outcome of eighteen months of parliamentary wrangling, reformist protests, economic criticisms, inevitably resulted in a republican organisation, in a closer amalgamation of the different classes in society. People were relying, and were entitled so to do, on the new representatives being an expression of the idea of revolution: instead we have the pandemonium of all counter-revolutionary notions. The whims of an electoral majority would have events reversed: men who under a Republic would never have had the right to vote are calling for a king in the name of the Republic and by virtue of their right of suffrage!...

The signal for this backsliding came from the provisional government. The files of *Le National* are there to show that.

Such was their grasp of revolution, such their fear of the people, these amateur republicans, these gentlemen democrats, that scarcely had they arrived in power than they sent out an appeal to every mediocrity in the land. The country then sent its mediocrities. They have succeeded beyond their hopes and already they are consumed with unease. They sense that their part has been played out. Which faction does not hold them in contempt? They are so small. So tiny, so wrong-headed that even the sharpest eye cannot distinguish between despotism and the Republican. I do not even think anybody hates them; yet they have bound France's fate in chains!...

It is to you honest patriots who since February have stayed what you were even before February, it is to you that I address myself. The lives and deaths of ten million men may well hang on whatever determination you make.

Your anger is righteous, your outrage legitimate. Like you, I have wept with rage at the sight of the perfidious reaction under way, which adds cravenness to massacre. But, citizens, you will not avenge the memory of your brothers by means of bloody reprisals; passion has no place in the decision-making of a statesman. For amid the universal anarchy in which we find ourselves, in the absence of regulated authority and acknowledged principle, I can tell you this, citizens, EVERYBODY should think like a statesman.

But first reflect upon the situation in the land.

For the past seventy days, France has not worked. Do you know what it means, for a nation not to work! Imagine a man who no longer eats, no longer drinks, no longer digests: in whom the blood has stopped coursing, the heart beating, the lungs inflating, the heat throbbing; a man in whom the vital spark has petered out. That man lives no more; he is dead!

Behold the portrait of our nation!—No more work, no more production; no more commerce, no more consumption for us. Collective life goes un-renewed; taxes are not returned; the powers that be are no longer heeded; the public forces become demoralised; the bonds of society are loosened; just a few more days in this dire condition and all movement will cease and the body of the people will lapse into dissolution.

The Poland and Italy that we pledged to defend. Poland and Italy, those two sisters of France, now broken by the arms of their tormentors, in vain do they stretch out a desolated hand to us. We shall ride to the rescue neither of Italy nor of Poland.

Do you know why? We would need a hundred thousand soldiers, a hundred million francs, and we haven't a hundred thousand *centimes* with which to equip and provision an army. We couldn't even defend our own selves if a coalition of kings was to swoop upon us just as they did sixty years ago. And do you know the reason why? Because we no longer produce through toil that on which we might subsist until such time as we might have to go down fighting.

Patriots, irked by the reaction, would you murder your motherland! Would you drive a dagger into your mother?… Yet that's what you'll be doing if you revert to barricades. Another seventy years of stagnation and the game is up for the Revolution, the game is up for the people.

Have pity on France, pity on the proletariat, pity on the bourgeoisie itself, whose tortures you cannot even begin to imagine. Can you not see that it is its ruination that has it infuriated? Ruination, bankruptcy, hideous bankruptcy, followed by shame, and then impoverishment: this is what the exasperated bourgeoisie seeks by spilling the blood of the proletariat.

So are you willing, to avenge 150 of your brothers,[1] to let the angel of death roam through the entire country? The death knell of the motherland! Is this the compensation you have in mind for the relatives of the victims?…

Your policy should be no such thing, citizens. Killing men is the worst way to combat principles. The only way to score a victory over an idea is with another idea. Now, that idea is something you already carry within yourselves, just as you have it within you to make it a reality.

What! You know how to be self-reliant, you know how to get yourselves organised for a fight and you do not know how to organise yourselves for the purposes of work?

What? A hundred thousand of you would join forces for an attack on the government and you couldn't find it within yourselves, a hundred thousand of you, to join forces for an attack on privilege?

Destruction is the only thing that holds any charms for you: you lose all enthusiasm the moment creation is at stake!…

Citizens, the motherland is in danger!

I propose a provisional committee be set up to orchestrate exchange, credit and commerce between workers;

That said committee liaise with similar committees set up in the main cities of France;

That, under the aegis of these committees, a body representative of the proletariat be formed in Paris, *imperium in imperio*,[2] in opposition to the bourgeoisie's representation.

That a new society be founded in the heart of the old society;

That a labour charter be written into the agenda forthwith and its main articles set out with minimal delay;

That the groundwork for republican government be laid down and special powers delegated to the workers' representatives.

---

1    A reference to events in Rouen. Following the general election and the defeat of the popular candidate, M. E. Deschamps, a protest demonstration was brutally repressed. (Editor).

2    A "state within the state." (Editor)

Citizens, the republic has its back to the wall: the government can do nothing for you. But you can do everything for yourselves; this I swear in the presence of God and men!

Until such time as we have exhausted economic means, I will speak out against the use of violence. Let the needless bloodshed be upon the heads of the agitators!

5<sup>th</sup> May 1848
*Le Représentant du Peuple*
Translation by Paul Sharkey

# OPENING SESSION OF THE NATIONAL ASSEMBLY

THE NATIONAL ASSEMBLY HAS BEEN FORGED AGAINST A BACKDROP OF CANnon fire, drums and fanfares, wrapped up in all of war's pomp and circumstance.

In these ties when the imagination is seduced by the senses and the heart swept along by the imagination and reason overwhelmed by sentiment; when the mind believes itself infinite because it is empty, the soul's only weakness is for the blandishments of sensibility and the mirages of hope. Considered thought seems to have lost its status and judgement set aside its authority. These are the days of Lamourette kisses,[1] the times of treacherous reconciliations.

But enthusiasm soon abates; sentiment evaporates like a caress; and in place of empathetic feelings, reason returns to pose here formidable questions.

Well then, what is this National Assembly, so laboriously nurtured and so impatiently awaited and upon which so many contradictory hopes are staked going to do? Are our deputies out-and-out republicans? Are they socialists? Are they firmly resolved to overhaul the old edifice of society from top to toe? And the provisional government which has just handed its powers back to them, has it the credibility to transform these in the light of revolution?

Why not have them take an oath?

---

1    A reference to a famous episode of the French Revolution: in 1792, the Abbé Lamourette, lamenting the bitter factionalism dividing the Legislative Assembly, implored the representatives to put aside their differences and kiss one another—which they did, in a display of ostentatious fraternity that was forgotten the next day. (Editor)

Would you like to know what the National Assembly is going to do?

For a start, it will verify its powers, appoint its speaker, fill its offices, answer a speech by the crown with an address, lay blame, endorse, upbraid and recriminate! Being unable to rescind across the board, at a stroke and without exception, every one of the acts of the provisional government and turn things back to where they were on February 25th! That would be the surest, simplest, most expeditious, most rational course of action and the only useful one. But the censure coming from the National Assembly will not be so forceful.

And then the National Assembly will turn its attention to the Constitution.

It will talk about presidency, veto, accountability, separation of powers, centralisation, municipalities, etc. It may even be disposed to vote, after a reading, without debate or amendment, as one man, resoundingly and en-thusiastically for the first constitution put before it. If such a constitution is to last and if it is to be good value for the money the National Assembly could not proceed too quickly. These representatives cost twenty-five francs a day and the people are not working!

After that, the National Assembly will talk business.

That is to say, in the name of political economy, it will deal with domestic economics, the application of huckster economics to the State, the way they have been doing in England, in France and everywhere else for the past forty years. It will distribute the land in Algeria and elsewhere: it will set up agri-cultural banks; it will legislate about manufacturers' labels; it will overhaul taxation, insurance, the mines, etc., etc: it will deliver itself up to all manner of dark, entangled, scabrous and squalid speculations.—May the Republic's representatives skip over these discussions as they would over a fire! Matters of business have a deadly impact on the conscience of the deputy: think back to the railways![2]

And finally the National Assembly will turn its mind to philanthropy.

Crèches, towers, asylums, hospitals, people's convalescent homes, poor re-lief, savings funds, rewards for virtue, sponsorship for artists, model farms, prison systems, lending banks for workers, industrial, trade, business and agri-cultural schools will come in for the most respectable attentions. And to prove its entire goodwill to the people, it will even advance Monsieur Considérant four million and a plot of land for an experimental phalanstery. How happy it would be if only the Republic could rid itself of socialism at that price!

But the social question!—you will say—The real social question! Might it be in the minds of the revolution's representatives to dodge the issue? What have a phalanstery and the social question got to do with each other?

---

2   This refers to a scandal typical of the corruption of Louis-Philippe's reign when it was discovered that all the members of the majority, including a number of minis-ters, had been shareholders in the very railway companies the legislators had award-ed construction contracts to. (Editor)

The social question!

My advice to you is to write if off from the outset. The social question is not going to make it on to the agenda of the National Assembly.

And is that assembly likely to stare privilege in the face?

Has it the strength and the calibre to lay hands on that sacred cow?

Has it the gumption to do away with the last remnant of royalty, the mere abolition of which will make dynasties impossible, namely, the royalty of gold?

Is the National Assembly likely to pronounce a death sentence upon the old society?

Might it, in the wake of its immense political, economic and philanthropic undertakings, grasp that social reform spells the abolition of politics? That political economy is the very opposite of domestic economics? That philanthropy is a corollary of poverty?

No, the National Assembly can do nothing, seeks nothing and knows nothing!

It can only turn into something and do the work of the revolution insofar as it will be so invited, provoked or compelled by some power outside of itself that seizes the initiative and sets things rolling.

A legislative assembly lays down statutes about things: it does not bring them about. In other words, the organisation of labour must not emanate from the powers that be; it ought to be SPONTANEOUS. Which is why we are repeating here the proposal that we put yesterday:

"That a provisional committee be set up to orchestrate exchange, credit and commerce between workers;

"That said committee liaise with similar committees set up in the main cities of France.

"That, under the aegis of these committees, a body representative of the proletariat be formed in Paris, *imperium in imperio*, in opposition to the bourgeoisie's representation.

"That a new society be founded in the heart of the old society.

"That a labour charter be written into the agenda forthwith and its main articles set out with minimal delay.

"That the groundwork for republican government be laid down and special powers delegated to the workers' representatives."

That is the only way that we are going to be able to stand firm against the reaction: and to ensure the wellbeing of the Republic and the emancipation of the proletariat.

9<sup>th</sup> May 1848
*Le Représentant du Peuple*
*Translation by Barry Marshall*

# OUTLINE OF THE SOCIAL QUESTION
## METHOD OF SOLUTION—EQUIVALENCE OF THE POLITICAL QUESTION AND THE SOCIAL QUESTION

PRIVILEGE PROTECTS ITSELF TO THE DEATH. IT THREATENS US FROM THE north and south, east and west. It demands revenge on us from the four points of the compass. We cried like prophets that there is a time for mercy and there will be a time for punishment.

It is marvellous, Messieurs: having looked for war, we are going to have it tough and decisive. Let privilege defend itself if it can; it is the only way it has of beating our resolve. We will be the first to congratulate it. But it cannot hope to intimidate us: to us its bayonets are no more deadly than its words. Let it be fully understood: we are going to go after privilege, no matter what it calls itself, whether respectable, traditional or holy, until it has been wiped out. While the National Assembly meets, we without ideas, without a plan, like a well without water, are going to lose time to politicking. We shall organise draining and mining underneath the citadel of property. Work will go fast; success is assured.

Long ago, gladiators who went to fight in the Colosseum, paused before the emperor's box and said to him with a poignant and terrible heroism, "Caesar, those who are about to die, salute you, *Morituri te salutant!*" Times have changed: the roles are now reversed. Labour has beaten capital. As the victorious gladiator, we can say today, while raising the sword before the

Queen of the World:[1] *morituram saluto*: Property, I salute you! You will die by my hands!

But what am I saying? What use are threats from now on? We should change our language. It makes no sense to frighten the man of property. The day when the abolition of property begins, the day when individual right is supplanted by social right, this will be the day when everyone salutes, bourgeois *and* proletarian. What the worker gains in revolution because of the poverty he shakes off, the bourgeois gains in proportion to the property he abandons. In exchange for liberty, equality, security and wealth, the first gives up his poverty, the second his despotism. Thus, after a universal negation, when we agree to an increase in the freedom, guarantees and well-being of everyone, it would be absurd to sow terror. The privileged, instead of loading their guns, will back down, and we should listen peacefully. If we keep to our principles, they will immediately find that our aims *are* peaceable. We are going to talk to them in terms of facts and figures. But we must first of all talk to them about values.

---

1   A reference to a famous *pensée* of Blaise Pascal: "Force and not opinion is the queen of the world; but it is opinion that uses the force." ("La force est la reine du monde, et non pas l'opinion; mais l'opinion est celle qui use de la force.") (Translator)

14th May 1848
*Le Représentant du Peuple*
*Translation by Paul Sharkey*

# FOREIGN AFFAIRS

OUR DIPLOMACY IS MINDLESS, OUR FOREIGN POLICY UNPRINCIPLED, AIMLESS and bereft of resources. Our statesmen supposedly as incapable of arriving at a decision as they are of prompting one. Amid the host of international law issues thrown up, they supposedly could not tell where France's interests lie nor of what those interests consist: what the latest revolution contributed to and imposed upon the European system. Even as they cannot understand the people, they have nothing to say to the people. And saddest of all, even if they were in a position to define the new righteousness, they are devoid of the wherewithal to defend it. France's word counts for nothing in the counsels of Europe and her broken sword is feared by none.

What, I ask, do either the cant of enthusiasm or flights of eloquence count for, faced with the material gravity of events! What matter to us the talent of a Lamartine when what we need is—let me dare state it—the positivism of a Talleyrand? And that great slogan *Liberty, Equality, Fraternity*… please, I beseech you, wring a diplomatic solution out of that!

Are you or are you not within your rights to insist of Austria that she withdraw her troops from Italy and give up on her claims to suzerainty there? What case, what arguments can you come up with!… It is not enough to say: We are fond of Italy; Italy is France's sister; Italy must be free even as we are free. All of that, if I may say so, is mysticism and mysticism of the worst sort, for it is revolutionary mysticism, just as the corruption of the finest things is the foulest of corruptions.—Let me ask in respect of the Italian question, what is your principle, your entitlement, your interest—in short, your motives? And once you have spelled out your motives, let me ask: what are your means? No longwindedness: facts, reasons, names. The former government was unwilling to intervene in Italy: how come what was tolerable yesterday is no longer such today? And if you cannot countenance it, are you in any position to prevent it?…

I know, I know, the February Revolution has altered every policy: civil law, public law, international law now rest upon brand new principles. In order to intervene in Italy, it tickles you to say that Italy is our ally: how so? What makes an alliance? How, in what way, in relation to what actual, short-term, specific purpose has the fact of an insurrection turned us into the allies of a people?

And, returning to the question posed earlier, what, in political terms, is the rule governing alliances?

According to some, our natural ally is England: according to others, Germany. Why not Russia? Why not Spain, Piedmont, Switzerland, Belgium who revolve around us like a crown of satellites? Ultimately, who are our natural allies? What is a natural ally? And as for those peoples who are no natural allies of ours, what are they to us? Foreigners! Which is tantamount to saying enemies! So our natural enemies are all those peoples who are not our natural allies! What confusion! What discord! Back in 1840 M. de Lamartine foretold that only the East could provide us with the key to the European problem: well! What does the mysterious and fabled East reveal to M. de Lamartine today?

The matter of international alliances has never departed from the norm. Princely whims, dynastic agreements, the ambition and vanity of government heads, the fanaticism of opinion, the obsessions of the masses, these are what govern the policies of nations. Diplomacy is one of the forms of anarchic commerce, thieving and counterfeit: questions of style aside, it is the same charlatanism, the same narrow-mindedness, the same hypocrisy, the same bad faith.

Imagine a grocer from the Rue Saint-Martin writing to his counterpart in Marseilles:

"The shipment of your crates of soap is running twenty four hours behind schedule (they were to have been delivered by an agreed date). I have withheld a third of the load (amounting to 300 francs).

"I am leaving you your rice, coffee and sugar on account, having noted a shortfall in terms of quantities (and having no further use for them).

"I will not fill your order because my custom is to ask for a 4 percent discount on all my orders, which you have failed to afford me with this shipment (which was not the issue).

"I will take receipt of your oil, but under 10 percent subsidy (particularly as, since I placed the order, this commodity has fallen by 10 percent)."

That just about sums up the entire spirit behind our diplomacy. Translate that into the poetic prose of M. de Lamartine or into M. Guizot's philosophical style and you will have yourself a master-piece of a diplomat.

Are we to have peace? Are we to have war?—That question is unanswerable, being unfathomable and shrouded in mystery as far as our statesmen are concerned.

Peace? Peace is impossible for it lacks roots and guarantees. Peace is like credit: if it is to last, it needs mortgages [*hypothèques*], not hypotheses [*hypothèses*]; it cries out for commitments not castles in Spain. Peace is not a matter of convenience and temperament: of all human affairs, it is the most substantial and as a result is absolutely insistent upon *de facto* and *de jure* reasoning, actual and positive factors.

So where are our commitments to peace with Europe? By what shared ideas, inclinations and interests are we bound to her? What over-riding obligation between the powers of Europe has taken the place of the 1815 pact?[2] Our peace is more fragile than a spider's web. I would like to believe that the outgoing government had a large hand in this destruction of the factors for peace. It was the old king's policy to exploit confusion and disorder. But Monsieur Guizot's handiwork must be repaired: so what are his successors' ideas on that score? Do they reckon they have greatly advanced alliance with Prussia, Germany and Italy, just because they have pointed them out to us—in a painting—shaking hands?

War? As unfeasible for us as peace.

Making war is not only a matter of being able to marshal the manpower, horses, munitions and money—which we do not have: war, like peace, cries out for principles, motives, some idea, some interest. Otherwise, war is immoral and before long turns into defeat through a loss of morale. Back in '93, our forefathers knew why they were making war and they won: but could we say why we would be making war? The idea, the motive, the interest may well be there: the deed and the righteousness may well be there: but what are they? Let them be spelled out, let them be made public. I scour opinion and leaf through the government records, but instead of motives and instead of a serious, real interest, all I find is our troubled thoughts and despair at the situation.

In my view, similarities between our revolutions, comparable governments and appetites, or national points of honour upon are not grounds enough for declaring a people our ally and embarking upon a propaganda war for its benefit. These are matters of opinion to be taken into account: but they are not grounds. Why, in terms of our interest, the French interest, present, positive and short-term, should we back Italy against Austria or Poland against Russia? What business is it of ours? What is our interest in these conflicts between foreign peoples? What have we to gain from it? What have we to lose by it? For think on this: if our only interest is empathy; if the only ground we can devise for our intervention is the hollow sentiment of equality and human brotherhood, we have no genuine interest at stake and our intervention is unjust. For my own part, I believe, and I make no bones about this, that the ruination of Polish nationhood and the curtailment of freedom in Italy jeopardise France's most positive interest. But before making a move,

---

2    The treaties signed after the second and final defeat of Napoléon Bonaparte. (Editor)

that interest needs to be highlighted, brought into full view and made the subject matter of all your manifestos. Now there is nothing in the government's record to make that interest known, the interest without which any armed intervention by us in the affairs of Europe would be labelled in advance as immoral and inevitably followed by a shameful defeat. Are we, then, gratuitously going to act out the part of civilisation's Don Quixotes for the satisfaction of a few humanitarian utopians?

So, in the complete absence of principles, in our present utter ignorance of our own interests, further peace and war are equally unfeasible and pose an equal danger to us.

In this truly absurd peace, bereft of principles, ideas, likelihood of survival, prospect of durability, a nonsense in all respects; in this pained wait for what events may bring, France, unsure of herself, melts into her inertia like an icicle in the July sunshine. WE are dying of a slow fever; no longer productive; no longer exchanging; frittering away our capital on contraband; another few months of this lethargy and we will be at each other's throats. Are we to throw ourselves at the foreigner as a means of escape from starvation?

As for war, until such time as a principle married to a great interest comes along to invest it with the morality it lacks, it can only culminate—no matter how its battalions may fare—in a dismal outcome. If we win, it resurrects military government as a solution to the social question: if we lose, it draws restoration down upon us along with the foreigner. Will we prove to have erected our barricades for the benefit of some Napoléon II or Henri V?...

Meanwhile, Poland sacrificed screams for vengeance: Italy is ridden over roughshod by her torturers; the king of Piedmont falters, the Pope shies away, the emperor of Austria schemes, the king of Prussia strikes bargains, England casts the net of her merchandise across Europe and France looks on! America and Great Britain make off with what is left of our produce at knock-down prices and stock up for years to come: unemployment and the obligatory imports that follow from it deliver the coup de grace to our industry. On every front, freedom goes under, there thanks to war and here to strike!

In order to put paid to this lamentable situation, the old revolutionary routine has decided to do... what? ... hold a demonstration in favour of Poland!

A demonstration! And what is that demonstration going to prove? What are its programme, its idea, its methodology, its formula, its solution going to be? What is it going to teach representatives? What firm conviction, what belief will it inject into their souls?

Patriots, let me tell it to you a second time: circumstances have turned every last one of you into a statesman. You are forbidden to talk like mindless humanitarians or to behave like brainless clubmen.

But back to principles.

To make war, as well as to preserve the peace, one must have *reasons*.

The reasons you shall know from their *means*.

What are the means of war? What are the means of peace?

Wealth, capital.

Now, capital is forged through labour:

Labour, divided and compartmentalised as it is in the economy of modern societies is built upon commerce.

Commerce requires mutual lending.

Organise commerce by means of mutual lending and you will have your labour and your capital: you will have the instruments of peace and war.

You will be invincible in peace; you will have nothing to fear from external competition or from stagnation at home, for competition organised on the principle of reciprocity opens in yourselves an infinite market; thus your production becomes infinite, your capitalisation infinite.

You will be invincible in war: 1$^{st}$ in terms of resources, because your capital; being formed through collective commerce rather than individual savings as at present, and commerce being forever expanding, there will be no end to your wealth. And 2$^{nd}$ in terms of principles, because by organising commerce at home by means of mutual lending and equality of exchange, you are thereby resolving the matter of international trade and, through that solution, conjuring up a positive interest in foreign affairs, just as you are conjuring up a positive interest abroad in your own.

And once all States, caught up by your example and impelled by necessity which is mightier than artillery and protocols have organised commerce at home and thereby followed your example and conjured up freedom and equality between their citizens: when, through such organising, they will, as you have, become unassailable at home, invincible in peace and in war, then the ALLIANCE will be world-wide and peace will be incorruptible and war impossible.

6<sup>th</sup> July 1848
*Le Représentant du Peuple*
*Translation by Martin Walker*

# TO THE EDITOR-IN-CHIEF OF *LE REPRÉSENTANT DU PEUPLE*

M. Editor,

IN YESTERDAY'S EDITION OF YOUR PAPER, AMONG MANY EXCELLENT THINGS, I read some unfortunate words with which it is impossible for me to agree.

In response to the *Journal des Débats*, you say:

"And do not make believe that we are trying to *excuse* the insurrection; on the contrary, we declare that insurrection *guilty* because it did not have legitimate motives, because, etc. Therefore, the government did its duty in *suppressing the insurrection immediately and roughly*. But, while *condemning* the insurgents, we do not want to be unjust, etc."

Such words, M. Editor, exceed the amount of blame that I believe it is possible to attribute to the events of June 23<sup>rd</sup>, 24<sup>th</sup>, 25<sup>th</sup> and 26<sup>th</sup>.

Insurrections are like homicides in that, depending on the circumstances, they can be legitimate or criminal, but they also may be neither, that is, they may be excusable, legally speaking.

Homicide committed in war for the defence of the homeland is a legitimate act that even honours the perpetrator.

Homicide committed for the purpose of personal revenge or greed is a crime that the law punishes with death.

Homicide that results following a provocation, in the case of legitimate defence, etc., is excusable. Neither the law nor morality approves it; they do not prosecute it but pardon it.

It is thus that I judge the recent events.

Was the cause of the insurrection, in which so many citizens were victims in some way, a flagrant violation of the republican principle on the part of the government or the National Assembly? No. Therefore, that insurrection, without a sufficient reason to justify it, was not legitimate. Here is a first point.

Was it the result of foreign instigations conducted with a monarchic purpose and directed against the republic? In that case, the insurrection would have been a crime, an attack against which it would have been necessary to appeal to legal prosecution. However, we do not know yet that such was the true character of this regrettable collision.

But, if the revolt of June 23<sup>rd</sup>–26<sup>th</sup> suddenly arose like an accident out of misery; if the struggle, sustained for four unfortunate days, was merely an explosion of desperation; if the prosecution proves that, despite widespread gold, despite monarchic hiring, the vast majority of the insurgents was comprised of workers demoralised by unemployment, wild with hunger, their hopes crushed, frustrated, wrongly or rightly, against power; if it were true, finally, that the government, the National Assembly itself, at first mistaken about the real meaning of the riot, had brought to a head with a fateful policy the exasperation of these people whose rallying cry was *"Bread or lead!"* Oh, then it would have been acknowledged that the civil war that had just bloodied the cradle of the republic had been a dreadful misfortune, but that, thank heavens, no one was guilty, and there were only victims.

Four months of unemployment suddenly became a *casus belli*,[1] into an insurrection against the government of the republic: here, in a few words, is the whole truth about those dismal days. Nonetheless, whatever was said, whatever self-seeking and merciless aspersion are still spread every day, the working class's generosity and high morals did not perish in the fratricide. The insurgents' destitution, the prisoners' misery and the respect for property, which, if we should believe numerous reports, was not always as great on the side of the repression as on that of the rioters, are there to attest to it.

The English proletariat lives nobly on the poor tax. German labourers, loaded with money and old clothes, are not embarrassed to beg, from workshop to workshop, for *viaticum*,[2] passing fancies. The Spanish do more, like Lazarillo[3] they ask for *charity* at the point of their guns. The French worker

---

1   A Latin expression meaning the justification for an act of war. (Editor)

2   *Viaticum* is a Latin word meaning "provisions for a journey." Within the Catholic Church, it means the communion given to a person who is dying or who faces the possibility of death. (Editor)

3   *The Life of Lazarillo de Tormes and of His Fortunes and Adversities* is an anonymous Spanish novella noted for of its heretical content and criticism of the Church and Aristocracy. It is credited with founding a literary genre, the picaresque novel (so called from the Spanish pícaro meaning "rogue" or "rascal") whose hero's adventures expose injustice while amusing the reader. (Editor)

asks for work, and if instead of work, you offer him alms, he rises up and shoots at you. I like the French worker best, and I boast that I belong to this proud race impervious to dishonour.

Please, M. Editor, do not spread salt and vinegar on open wounds; do not convey hopelessness into those gloomy consciences, the madness of which has been regrettable, but that are not criminal, after all. Let us have pity on these poor wounded people who hide and die in the straw in the throes of gangrene, cared for by hungry children and wives crazy with misery. Tomorrow, Thursday, will be a day of public mourning dedicated to the funerals of the insurrection's VICTIMS. Let us not hesitate to include in our regrets, under this common name of the victims, those who died for the defence of order and those who fell while battling misery. If the law was on one side of the barricades, it was also on the other side. The horrible carnage that we witnessed resembled those ancient tragedies in which duty and the law are opposed and which the gods share. Let us cry for our brothers from the national guard. Let us cry for our insurgent brothers and condemn no one. Let us hope that justice, once enlightened about the facts that preceded, accompanied and followed the insurrection, will relax the severity of the law and that the deportation decree, from then on without object or morality, will be revoked.

With my fraternal greetings,

P-J PROUDHON

*8<sup>th</sup> July 1848*
*Le Représentant du Peuple*
*Translation by Martin Walker*

# JULY FIFTEENTH

THE END OF THE QUARTER! TIME'S UP! HOW ARE WE GOING TO PAY OUR RENT?...[1]
For five months now we have been doing nothing: we have received nothing, delivered nothing, sold nothing! Industry has bottomed out! Commerce bottomed out! Credit bottomed out! Labour bottomed out!...

No more work, no more money, no more resources! The rental payment is due; the pawnbrokers' stockrooms are all stuffed full; the family silver, the wives' jewels, the husband's watch, the finest linen, it's all been pawned off! How else could we pay our rent?! How shall we manage to live!...

May the authors of pitiless decrees; may the great politicians who have resumed the execrable tradition of Saint-Merri and Transnonain;[2] may those who said that it was better instead of coming to a peaceful agreement to massacre ten thousand citizens for the sake of the National Assembly's dignity;[3] may these *decent* republicans, as they call themselves, who came to the Republic as perjurers, who serve it as perjurers, and who will leave it as perjurers: may all of them respond to the despairing lament of the bourgeoisie, if they can!

Go ahead, now, you errant national guards, go and ask your would-be conservatives for work, credit, bread! What they have to offer you, yourselves, your wives and your children, is blood and corpses!...

---

1   This was when quarter day fell, the traditional day for settling bills and paying rents. (Editor)

2   Reference to state repression of two popular revolts in Paris under the Monarchy, the first on 5–6 June 1832 with the last of the insurgents fighting heroically around the cloisters of Saint-Merri (at least 150 killed) and the second on 14 April 1834 with a massacre in the Rue Transnonain. (Editor)

3   A reference to the bloody repression of the barricades raised on June 23<sup>rd</sup> to protest the disbanding of the National Workshops by the government. (Editor)

And what does it mean to them? Won't they be ministers in a fortnight?...

It's no longer a matter of saving the proletariat: the proletariat no longer exists, it's been thrown to the dogs. But the bourgeoisie must be saved: the petite bourgeoisie from hunger, the middle-bourgeoisie from ruin, the haute bourgeoisie from its own infernal selfishness. Today the bourgeoisie faces the same question as did the proletariat on the June 23rd.

We shall not fail our principles. The force of destiny, the greatest of ancient divinities, inflexible Nemesis, has made out of these principles an absolute order for the good of the people.

When the State, surprised by a revolution whose true character it neglected to recognise at once, found itself incapable of paying off the floating debt and redeeming the Treasury bonds and savings books, what did it do? It took recourse to a consolidation: it converted into annuities the treasury bonds and savings accounts that it could not pay out. The national Assembly is discussing the two decrees concerning this operation this very day. That is to say that the State, as an insolvent debtor, demands release from a part of the debt and credit for the surplus. Nobody found this wrong; necessity made it into a law.

When the Bank of France found itself unable to meet all the claims for repayment of its notes and for one moment saw itself teetering over the abyss of bankruptcy, what did it do then? It obtained a decree that gave its papers forced currency, which is to say that instead of giving credit to the citizens it demanded credit from them. Nobody complained of the decree which saved the bank: the public good and necessity made it into a law.

It is no longer only the State or the Bank of France that are incapable of honouring their engagements: it is the whole class of tenants all over France.

Would it be unjust for the tenants to receive the following from their landlords: 1st a postponement of payment; 2nd a reduction of the rent to be paid?

I will dare to maintain that it is not only not unjust but a matter of public necessity.

The cessation of commerce and industry, being caused by an event equivalent to *force majeure*, has placed us all, tenants and proprietors, in exceptional circumstances, which are by the way provided for and explained in treatises of jurisprudence.

We have produced nothing, we owe nothing.

For the 400,000 tenants with their domicile in the Department of the Seine there are fewer than 20,000 proprietors, one to twenty.

When the State reduces its debt and suspends payments; when the Bank ceases to redeem its notes; when the merchant, the factory-owner and the industrialist no longer dispose of their products and find no takers for their services, would the owners of houses be right to demand payment of rent as in ordinary times? Should not the Revolution and its consequences be borne equally by all? And if the general stagnation of business joins the universal depreciation of assets, is it not evident that the tenants have a right to a reduction of the amount of the rent and not merely a postponement of payment?...

Is that communism or simply just and equitable?

And if the proprietor dared to complain that he was being bankrupted, would we not be right to reply to him that it is not us, the tenants, who bankrupt him but the force of circumstances? ...Well, what is true for the tenant is by the same reckoning true for the farmer. The farmer can't sell his foodstuffs any more, or only at a throwaway price. Wheat is at 10 francs per hectolitre and wine at 3 centimes a litre. The costs of producing the wheat and the wine are not covered by the price of sale. How then could the farmer pay the landlord and discharge his debt? Is it his fault if the Revolution has come to interrupt all transactions?...

If, finally, the landlords cannot in all fairness refuse first of all a postponement of payment and secondly a reduction of the leases in favour of the tenants and farmers; if the State by stabilising the floating debt, giving forced currency to the notes of the Bank of France, slapping a tax on debts secured by mortgages and raising the rate for rights of transfer for large inheritances has given the first signal of this universal reduction—or, to put it better, of this reciprocity of credit—then why should lenders to the state,[4] who have hitherto received their money most promptly, remain the only ones to be thus privileged? Would they be hard done by to be asked in their turn for the credit of a fraction of their income in the name of the taxpayers, tenants, farmers and proprietors?

But if all the citizens mutually give one another credit of some kind: the house proprietor giving a part of the due rent, the landowner a part of the annual farm rent, the mortgage creditor a part of his interest, the lender to the State a fraction of his income; then isn't it obvious that this mutuality is equivalent to a kind of credit organisation, and that if this road were taken quite resolutely it would result in an immediate resumption of both labour and business?...

Let the national guard that has devoted itself to public order in these miserable times reflect upon this: what we are proposing to it in these few lines is for its own benefit.

We therefore summon all the tenants and farmers to come to an agreement and present a strongly reasoned petition to the national Assembly, a petition which is not a supplication but a command.

The substance of this petition, phrased in the form of a decree so that the national Assembly would merely have to give it its sanction, would be the following:

---

4    The term "les rentiers de l'État" refers to finance capitalists who are owners of government bonds and other lenders to the State and the interest payments they receive in return for owning such government debt. (Editor)

"In view of the urgency and imminent danger,

"Considering that the public good is the supreme law;

"Considering that land rent is a free privilege that society can revoke;

"Considering it is a right of the State to regulate the rates of interest and the revenues of capital investments;

"Considering that the interests of the State, the farmers, tenants and borrowers on securities or mortgages are identical and interdependent;

"Considering that the only way of escaping the present danger, of reviving labour, of saving the family and property is by means of a vast operation of reciprocal credit,

"The national Assembly decrees:

"1st Article—To be applicable from July 15th, 1848 until July 15th, 1851: all the proprietors of houses will reduce the rent due on their properties by a third, whereof a sixth will accrue to the tenant and a sixth to the State.

"2nd Article—To be applicable from the same date for the same period of time: all the landowners will reduce the rent due on their properties by a third, whereof a sixth will accrue to the farmer and a sixth to the State.

"3rd Article—To be applicable for the same period of time: all mortgagees will reduce the interest due to them by a third, whereof a sixth will accrue to the debtor and a sixth to the State.

"4th Article—The farmers, tenants and debtors who desire to take advantage of the reduction offered by the decree on the price of housing and farm rents will be obliged to make the amount of their leases known to the tax collectors of their cantons, who will be charged with establishing the extent of the reductions.

"The deduction of one third of their obligations and contractual rents will be made by the farmers, tenants and debtors at the end of each rental period and the sixth due to the State will be paid in by them at their local tax office.

"5th Article—Independently of the above-mentioned reduction the payment of rents or obligations falling due at any time from July 15th to October 15th, 1848 is postponed for three months and will then be paid off in four instalments on the due dates following January 15th,1849.

"6th Article—The rent payments for farm leases and house tenancy, as well as mortgage payments subject to the reduction stipulated above, are deferred until 15th July 1851.

"7th Article—The lenders to the state will have their payments reduced by a third every quarter from July 15th, 1848 until 15th July, 1851.

"8th Article—The land tax of 45 centimes and the tax on mortgage loans are abolished.

"The tax payable on drinks will be reduced by three quarters and standardised in a single form.

"9th Article—The State, by means of the sums accruing to it during the three years from July 15th, 1848 to July 15th, 1851 as a result of the reductions made in the rents and interest deriving from farms, house-letting, mortgage loans and public funds, sums which will amount to several hundred thousand francs, will be assigned the task of reorganising the public credit system, insurance, circulation, transport and mines."

Nothing is easier, national guards, than for you to save your fortune, to put your business affairs back on their feet and to ensure the well-being of your families and the emancipation of the workers: it is only necessary to establish a tax on the revenue immediately by getting all the farmers, tenants and debtors interested in it. So you national guards must make these proposals to the national Assembly in order to find out very quickly who are your friends and your enemies.

*31ˢᵗ July 1848*
*Translation by Paul Sharkey*

# ADDRESS TO THE CONSTITUENT NATIONAL ASSEMBLY

**CITIZEN PROUDHON:** CITIZEN REPRESENTATIVES, YOU ARE IMPATIENT, not so much to give me a hearing, as to have done with it. For the past twenty years socialism has been exciting the people. Socialism made the February Revolution: your parliamentary squabbles would not have stirred the masses. Socialism featured in every act of the revolution: in March 17ᵗʰ, April 16ᵗʰ, and May 15ᵗʰ. Socialism held court at the Luxembourg [Palace] whilst politicking was going on at the *Hôtel de Ville*. The National Workshops have been a caricature of socialism: but, having been none of its making, they have brought no dishonour upon it. It was socialism that served as the rallying flag of the recent uprising; those who laid the groundwork for it and those who exploit it needed that great cause if they were to draw in the worker. It is socialism that you would have done with, by forcing it to give an account of itself in this forum. I would like to have done with it myself. And since you have guaranteed me freedom of speech, it will be no job of mine or of anybody else to put paid to socialism or anything else. (*Prolonged mumbling*)

With all due attention I have listened to the comments of the Finance Committee regarding the motion I had the honour of putting to you; then, with all the diligence I could muster, I pored over the report that you heard on Wednesday last and I declare that, having read it, I reckon I have more justification than ever for pressing for my motion to be passed [...]

The intention was, in riding roughshod over me, to ride roughshod over socialism at a stroke, which is to say, ride roughshod over the protests coming from the proletariat and, in so doing, to take another stride down the path of reaction. (*Go for it!—Hear! Hear!—Let loose!*)

Understand this: socialism's strength does not lie in the success of a single individual. But since a financial motion has been turned into a partisan issue, I am not about to shy away from the wider debate. It will be proven today that there are financial bigwigs who, through their ineptitude over the past twenty years, have been the cause of our ruination. Thanks to the Finance Committee, the argument is not between Citizen Thiers and me; it is between labour and privilege [...]

Citizen Representatives, the motion put before you is nothing less—and bear this in mind—than the February Revolution: and what you are about to do for one you will be doing for the other. You know nothing of my proposal, any more than you do of the Revolution (*Objections*), whether it be its principle, its purpose or its means. The Finance Committee which, given its brief, should have familiarised you with these, has not told you a single thing about them. Its entire suspicion about my motion was that it was a touch revolutionary. Does the Finance Committee welcome revolutionary thinking? Does it see the February Revolution as anything other than a surprise, a lamentable mishap? As for myself, I am one of those who do take that revolution seriously and who have pledged to see it through. So you will forgive me, citizens, if, in order to explain my motion, I take a rather loftier view of matters. Besides, in my prefatory remarks I will be extremely brief. In '93, if memory serves, just when the Republic was facing the direst threats, a tax of one third was slapped on income. I am not about to tell you how that tax was arrived at, how it was greeted or how it worked out. What I would like to point out to you, and this is the only thing that matters right now, is that in '93 property paid its dues to the revolution. Back then, when it was a life-or-death issue, property—and this was a rare event—made a sacrifice to public safety; and this has gone down in memory as one of the most horrific sacrifices since time began. Since then, in the fifty six intervening years, property, by which I mean net income, has made nil contribution to public affairs. *(Denials and laughter)* Save your laughter for later.

Tax established on the basis of proportionality, the only possible basis for it, has been a burden entirely borne by labour. Labour alone—let me say it again deliberately by way of an invitation to any who might contradict me— labour alone has paid tax just as it alone produces wealth. Along came the 1848 Revolution. Its dangers, its anguish, albeit of a different nature, have not been any less than those back in '93. So the point is to find out whether property, whether net income, insofar as it is special and separate from gross product, is willing to do ANYTHING for the Revolution! In '93, the revolution was fighting against despotism and against the foreigner. In 1848, the revolution's enemies are poverty, the division of the people into two sorts, the haves and the have-nots. The purpose of the February Revolution has, at different times, been variously described, as the *eradication of poverty*, the *organisation of labour*, the *reconciliation of labour and capital*, the *emancipation of the proletariat*, and, most recently, as the *right to work* or the *guarantee of work*. This formula of the right to work or guarantee of work is the one you embraced in your draft Constitution, Articles 2, 7 and 132 and which, I have no doubt, you will uphold. (*Noises off*)

So, accepting this encapsulation of the crux of the revolution as *the right to work*, I come directly to my motion and I wonder: of what does this *right to work* consist *and how can it possibly be achieved?* [...]

Work could be guaranteed if the market for production were without limits: that was my first argument. I do not think that that anyone will contradict me on that score. If labour, collectively speaking, was continually in greater demand than supply, then plainly there would be a guarantee of work; it would not require promises from the State; it would not compromise freedom, nor order. Thus far, no difficulty. So what is it that stops us from ensuring such an outcome? The power to consume, in society and in the individual alike, is infinite; and if the greatest of fortunes is never enough for a man who knows how to live, how might consumption stand in a country where love of comfort, an appetite for luxury and refinement of manners are taken to the lengths they have been among ourselves and if the ability to consume was bestowed upon this land in proportion with its needs? Is it not a plain fact that if, instead of a meagre product of 10 billion, which brings each of us a mere 75 centimes a day, we had the wherewithal to spend 100 billion, or 7.50 francs per day per head, we would do so? (*Shuffling*) I am not saying that we are in a position so to do right now; but I am saying that we have it in us to spend them. (*Laughter*)

So, at bottom, what is lacking is not the will to consume and thus the market; it is merely that consumption is ill served. There is something thwarting it, something vetoing it. The shops are bulging with goods yet the people go naked; trade is stagnant and the people's life is all deprivation! We being as we are, we all want comfort first and then luxury; we produce, insofar as we have it in us to do, whatsoever we have to in order to satisfy our desires; the wealth is out there waiting for us, yet we stay poor! How to explain this mystery? What thwarts consumption and which, as a necessary consequence, vetoes work, is the fact that the circulation of products is hobbled. And the circulation of products is hobbled:

1. By the exclusive use of gold and silver as instruments of exchange.

2. By the interest rate or levy that must be paid for access to them.

3. By the analogy that has been drawn between all capital and instruments of production, notably the land, and the instrument of circulation, cash, in the sense that, on every side, levies have been imposed upon the instruments of labour as upon money, rendering them, as far as their idle holders are concerned, essentially inert bodies that generate interest.

4. Finally, by the fascination with gold and the ravages of monopoly, the impact of which is that instead of producing for the purposes of enjoyment and thus consuming in proportion with his labours, the individual produces for the purpose of amassing either gold, or capital and, by means of such

348 Pierre-Joseph Proudhon

accumulation, claiming exemption from toil, the right to live without producing and to exploit the toilers [...]

The people, stealing a march on the economists on this score, is beginning to grasp this: the working class has analysed the secret power stymieing circulation, closing markets and inevitably leading to stagnation and strikes. In the proletariat's eyes, savings and retirement funds are modern society's equivalent of *devil-take-the-hindmost*. The financiers know nothing of this, or, if they know, feign ignorance; their privilege being at stake here. So, as I see it, the issue does not boil down to establishing some impossible community [*communauté*] or decreeing an illiberal and premature equality; it consists of doing away with the charges of all sorts by which production, circulation and consumption are burdened, an abolition which I sum up by the more technical and more financial formula of *Free Credit*. (*Sundry interjections*)

Free credit is the translation into the language of economics of those two words enshrined in the draft Constitution, *guaranteed work*. Now, the interest on money being the cornerstone of privilege and the regulator of all usury, by which I mean all income from capital, so it is by means of progressively whittling away the interest upon money that we must arrive at free credit and abolition of the taxes that hobble circulation and which artificially generate poverty. Which is what we will shortly be achieving by setting up a National Bank whose capital might be raised, and here I am following the usual reckonings of finance, to 1 or 2 billion, and which might ensure discount and commission in the desired conditions, but without interest, since there is an implicit contradiction in a society's profiteering from itself. So let us have our National Bank, let us organise public loans and, unless we want to cling to and forever perpetuate privilege and poverty, it is plain that with that bank we will have, setting administration and office costs aside, discount for nothing, loans for nothing and, finally, housing and land usage for nothing. (*General and prolonged hilarity*)

And once we reach that point (*further laughter*) the principle activating the businessman and the industrialist having changed, love of comfort and effective enjoyment having replaced ambition and greed as the spurs to toil and the fetishisation of gold having been overtaken by the realities of life, savings giving way to mutuality and with capital formation achieved by means of capital exchange *per se*, consumption will be relieved of all burdens, as will the faculty of enjoyment. (*Lengthy interruption. Laughter and sundry exclamations*)

So I concede and I have not the slightest difficulty in making this declaration: I concede and affirm that the guarantee of work is incompatible with retention of the established levies and charges on circulation and the instruments of labour and with property's seigneurial rights. (*Exclamations*)

Those who claim otherwise may describe themselves as phalansterians, Girondins or Montagnards; they may be very honest folk and excellent citizens—but they are certainly not socialists; I will go further, they are no republicans. (*Further exclamations*)

In the same way that political equality is incompatible with monarchy or aristocracy, so equilibrium in circulation and exchange, and parity between production and consumption—in other words, guaranteed work—cannot be reconciled with the royalty of cash or the aristocracy of capital. And since these two sets of ideas are essentially interdependent, we are forced to conclude again that property or net income which owes its existence entirely to servitude, is an impossibility in a Republic; and that only one of two things can happen: either property will overrule the Republic or the Republic will overrule property. (*Laughter. Ripples of agitation*)

It is a matter of regret to me, Citizens, that what I am saying should cause you to laugh so, because what I am saying here will be the death of you. (*Oh! Oh!—Fresh laughter*)

[...]

Let me say it again: the February Revolution has no other meaning. (*Whispering*) Progressively doing away with all these seigneurial rights which are a burden upon labour, a hindrance to circulation and a block to outlay and doing so in the quickest possible order; then, and as a necessary follow-up, whipping up an insatiable demand, opening up a bottomless market and basing the guarantee of work on indestructible foundations; that, without delving too deeply into the new forms of a society thus constructed, is how I see the chances of immediately and practically resolving the social question. That is what I call, improperly maybe, abolishing property. For, and bear this in mind, here we have no expropriation, no bankruptcies, no agrarian law, no community, no State meddling and no trespass against inheritance or family (*Gales of laughter*); only the annihilation of net income by means of the competition from the National Bank which is to say, freedom, naught but freedom. (*Interruptions*) [...]

Citizen Representatives, you have just heard my declaration of faith. It was needed in order to have you grasp the sense of my motion and the report that has been read to you made that all the more indispensable. I have been accused of disguising my intentions, or not daring to state here what I have set down in print in pamphlet and newspaper over the past ten years. You are my witnesses here today as to whether I am dissembling, whether I am afraid to spell out my beliefs and wishes in the presence of France. Yes, I seek the abolition of property in the sense of which I have just been speaking; and that is why, in an article denounced in this forum, I penned this phrase: *Property income is an unearned privilege, and one that it behooves society to revoke.*[1] But as I have

---

1  Proudhon uses the term *rente*. This can be translated as annuity—i.e., income from a capital investment paid in a series of regular payments. As he opposed all forms of non-labour income (rent, profit, interest, etc.) and so refers to all forms of revenue generated by ownship. (Editor)

pointed out to you, the repeal of that privilege might be abrupt and violent, in short, effected in such a way as a reasonable person might say was a tribute to anger, but it might equally be phased in and peaceably done. As a representative of the people and therefore mindful of my obligation to husband every interest, I call upon you here today to order such repeal to be carried out with whatever slowness of pace and arrangements the vested interests might wish for and with all of the assurances of security that the propertied might insist upon. (*Sniggering*)

And it is for the purpose of tending to the ways and means of such repeal and not at all with an eye to immediate effect that I move that a special tax be temporarily introduced, a tax upon income, by means of which the nation would weather the crisis and toilers and masters revert to the position they occupied prior to the revolution; depreciated property would recover its value; and public loans would be introduced upon a fresh footing.

Here then is […] the meaning behind my motion:

1. To spell out the import and purpose of the February Revolution to property and to the bourgeois class.

2. To serve notice upon property of the intention to proceed with the remaking of society and, in the interim, to invite it to contribute towards the revolutionary endeavour; the propertied to be held answerable for the consequences of their refusal, with nothing excluded. (*Loud interruption*)

**SEVERAL MEMBERS:** What! With nothing excluded? Explain yourself!

**CITIZEN DUPIN (representing the Nièvre):** How plain can he be? *Your money or your life*!

**NUMEROUS VOICES:** Mister Speaker, have the member explain himself!

**CITIZEN SPEAKER:** The member has heard the question; I invite him to explain himself.

**CITIZEN PROUDHON:** Reserves go hand in glove with responsibility. The meaning is ..

**SEVERAL MEMBERS:** We got your meaning!

**CITIZEN PROUDHON:** The meaning is that, in the event of a refusal, we would ourselves proceed with the liquidation without you. (*Angry rumblings*)

**NUMEROUS VOICES:** Who, you? And who might you be? (*Excitement*)

**CITIZEN ERNEST DE GIRARDIN:** Are you talking about the guillotine? (*Murmurs.—Several challenges are made to the speaker from several quarters*)

**CITIZEN SPEAKER:** I call upon all present to be silent. The speaker has the floor so that he may explain his thinking.

**CITIZEN PROUDHON:** When I used those pronouns *you* and *we*, it was self-evident that at that point I was identifying *myself* with the proletariat and identifying *you* with the bourgeois class. (*Further eruptions*)

**CITIZEN SAINT-PRIEST:** But that is social warfare!

**A MEMBER:** June 23rd holds the floor!

**SEVERAL VOICES:** Let him speak! Listen! Listen!

**CITIZEN PROUDHON** (*resuming*): My purpose in setting out the means I have was to show you that my motion also conserves the interests of property, which is so crucial to the very object of the revolution. The most irksome part of my motion is that, in terms of outcome, it can never fail; nothing like it has ever been seen in the world of finance; and, above all, it is not a translation nor a borrowing from the English. No one has dared to retort that a levy on income is unfair; they would be contradicted by the masters of the science, the secret vow of taxation and the example of England; they would have public opinion lined up against them [...]

This is the first time since a vote on taxation became a parliamentary prerogative that a levy has been accused of being *an act of piracy*! A levy on income *piracy*? What are we then to call a levy on labour? *Murder*? [...]

One has only to spell the thing out to prove to any person of good faith that such property which has so laughably been turned into the cornerstone of family and civilisation, hangs by a single thread which will not take long to snap, even though some might still wish to uphold it. The appointment of a National Bank is tantamount to killing off property at a single stroke, without argument or bandying words.

**A VOICE:** There you have it, death without further ado!

**ANOTHER VOICE:** Publish this speech in *Le Moniteur*! Haul its author away to Charenton![2]

---

2    Charenton was a lunatic asylum, founded in 1645 by the Frères de la Charité in Charenton-Saint-Maurice, now Saint-Maurice, Val-de-Marne, France. (Editor)

*10th August 1848*
*Le Représentant du Peuple*
*Translation by Benjamin Tucker*

# THE MALTHUSIANS

DR. MALTHUS, AN ECONOMIST, AN ENGLISHMAN, ONCE WROTE THE FOLLOW-ing words:

"A man who is born into a world already possessed, if he cannot get subsistence from his parents on whom he has a just demand, and if the society do not want his labour, has no claim of *right* to the smallest portion of food, and, in fact, has no business to be where he is. At nature's mighty feast there is no vacant cover for him. She tells him to be gone, and will quickly execute her own orders…"[1]

As a consequence of this great principle, Malthus recommends, with the most terrible threats, every man who has neither labour nor income upon which to live to take himself away, or at any rate to have no more children. A family,—that is, love,—like bread, is forbidden such a man by Malthus.

Dr. Malthus was, while living, a minister of the Holy Gospel, a mild-mannered philanthropist, a good husband, a good father, a good citizen, believing in God as firmly as any man in France. He died (heaven grant him peace) in 1834. It may be said that he was the first, without doubt, to reduce to absurdity all political economy, and state the great revolutionary question, the question between labour and capital. With us, whose faith in Providence still lives, in spite of the century's indifference, it is proverbial—and herein consists the difference between the English and ourselves—that "everybody must live." And our people, in saying this, think themselves as truly Christian, as conservative of good morals and the family, as the late Malthus.

---

1    Tucker supplies a slightly different version of this passage, having translated Proudhon's quotation of Joseph Garnier's French translation of Malthus back into English. This passage, which Malthus struck from subsequent editions of his *Essay on the Principle of Population*, appears in the 1803 edition. (Editor)

Now, what the people say in France, the economists deny; the lawyers and the litterateurs deny; the Church, which pretends to be Christian, and also Gallican, denies; the press denies; the large proprietors deny; the government which endeavours to represent them, denies.

The press, the government, the Church, literature, economy, wealth—everything in France has become English; everything is Malthusian. It is in the name of God and his holy providence, in the name of morality, in the name of the sacred interests of the family, that they maintain that there is not room in the country for all the children of the country, and that they warn our women to be less prolific. In France, in spite of the desire of the people, in spite of the national belief, eating and drinking are regarded as privileges, labour a privilege, family a privilege, country a privilege.

M. Antony Thouret said recently that property, without which there is neither country, nor family, nor labour, nor morality, would be irreproachable as soon as it should cease to be a privilege; a clear statement of the fact that, to abolish all the privileges which, so to speak, exclude a portion of the people from the law, from humanity, we must abolish, first of all, the fundamental privilege, and change the constitution of property.

M. A. Thouret, in saying that, agreed with us and with the people. The State, the press, political economy, do not view the matter in that light; they agree in the hope that property, without which, as M. Thouret says, there is no labour, no family, no Republic, may remain what it always has been—a privilege.

All that has been done, said, and printed today and for the last twenty years, has been done, said, and printed in consequence of the theory of Malthus.

The theory of Malthus is the theory of political murder; of murder from motives of philanthropy and for love of God. There are too many people in the world; that is the first article of faith of all those who, at present, in the name of the people, reign and govern. It is for this reason that they use their best efforts to diminish the population. Those who best acquit themselves of this duty, who practice with piety, courage, and fraternity the maxims of Malthus, are good citizens, religious men, those who protest against such conduct are anarchists, socialists, atheists.

That the February Revolution was the result of this protest constitutes its inexpiable crime. Consequently, it shall be taught its business, this Revolution which promised that all should live. The original, indelible stain on this Republic is that the people have pronounced it anti-Malthusian. That is why the Republic is so especially obnoxious to those who were, and would become again, the toadies and accomplices of kings—*grand eaters of men*, as Cato called them. They would make monarchy of your Republic; they would devour its children.

There lies the whole secret of the sufferings, the agitations, and the contradictions of our country.

The economists are the first among us, by an inconceivable blasphemy, to establish as a providential dogma the theory of Malthus. I do not reproach them; neither do I abuse them. On this point the economists act in good faith and from the best intentions in the world. They would like nothing better than to make the human race happy; but they cannot conceive how, without some sort of an organisation of homicide, a balance between population and production can exist.

Ask the Academy of Moral Sciences. One of its most honourable members, whose name I will not call—though he is proud of his opinions, as every honest man should be—being the prefect of I know not which department, saw fit one day, in a proclamation, to advise those within his province to have thenceforth fewer children by their wives. Great was the scandal among the priests and gossips, who looked upon this academic morality as the morality of swine! The *savant* of whom I speak was none the less, like all his fellows, a zealous defender of the family and of morality; but, he observed with Malthus, at the banquet of Nature there is not room for all.

M. Thiers, also a member of the Academy of Moral Sciences, lately told the committee on finance that, if he were minister, he would confine himself to *courageously and stoically passing through the crisis,* devoting himself to the expenses of his budget, enforcing a respect for order, and carefully guarding against every financial innovation, every socialistic idea—especially such as the right to labour—as well as every revolutionary expedient. And the whole committee applauded him.

In giving this declaration of the celebrated historian and statesman, I have no desire to accuse his intentions. In the present state of the public mind, I should succeed only in serving the ambition of M. Thiers, if he has any left. What I wish to call attention to is that M. Thiers, in expressing himself in this wise, testified, perhaps unconsciously, to his faith in Malthus.

Mark this well, I pray you. There are two million, four million men who will die of misery and hunger, if some means be not found of giving them work. This is a great misfortune, surely, and we are the first to lament it, the Malthusians tell you; but what is to be done? It is better that four million men should die than that privilege should be compromised; it is not the fault of capital, if labour is idle; at the banquet of credit there is not room for all.

They are courageous, they are stoical, these statesmen of the school of Malthus, when it is a matter of sacrificing workers by the millions. Thou hast killed the poor man, said the prophet Elias to the king of Israel, and then thou hast taken away his inheritance. *Occidisti et possedisti.*[2] To-day we must reverse the phrase, and say to those who possess and govern: You have the privilege of labour, the privilege of credit, the privilege of property, as M. Thouret says; and it is because you do not wish to be deprived of these privileges, that you shed the blood of the poor like water: *Possedisti et occidisti!*

---

2    1 Kings 21:19. (Editor)

And the people, under the pressure of bayonets, are being eaten slowly; they die without a sigh or a murmur; the sacrifice is effected in silence. Courage, workers! sustain each other: Providence will finally conquer fate. Courage! the condition of your fathers, the soldiers of the republic, at the sieges of Genes and Mayence, was even worse than yours.

M. Leon Faucher, in contending that journals should be forced to furnish securities and in favouring the maintenance of taxes on the press, reasoned also after the manner of Malthus. The serious journal, said he, the journal that deserves consideration and esteem, is that which is established on a capital of from four to five hundred thousand francs. The journalist who has only his pen is like the worker who has only his arms. If he can find no market for his services or get no credit with which to carry on his enterprise, it is a sign that public opinion is against him; he has not the least right to address the country: at the banquet of public life there is not room for all.

Listen to Lacordaire, that light of the Church, that chosen vessel of Catholicism.[3] He will tell you that socialism is antichrist. And why is socialism antichrist? Because socialism is the enemy of Malthus, whereas Catholicism, by a final transformation, has become Malthusian.

The gospel tells us, cries the priest, that there will always be poor people, *Pauperes semper habebitis vobsicum*,[4] and that property, consequently in so far as it is a privilege and makes poor people, is sacred. Poverty is necessary to the exercise of evangelical charity; at the banquet of this world here below there cannot be room for all.

He feigns ignorance, the infidel, of the fact that *poverty*, in Biblical language, signified every sort of affliction and pain, not hard times and the condition of the proletarian. And how could he who went up and down Judea crying, *Woe to the rich!* be understood differently? In the thought of Jesus Christ, woe to the rich means woe to the Malthusians.

If Christ were living today, he would say to Lacordaire and his companions: "You are of the race of those who, in all ages, have shed the blood of the just, from Abel unto Zacharias. Your law is not my law; your God is not my God!..." And the Lacordaires would crucify Christ as a seditious person and an atheist

Almost the whole of journalism is infected with the same ideas. Let *Le National*, for example, tell us whether it has not always believed, whether it does not still believe, that pauperism is a permanent element of civilisation; that the enslavement of one portion of humanity is necessary to the glory of another; that those who maintain the contrary are dangerous dreamers who deserve to be shot; that such is the basis of the State. For, if this be not the

---

3   Abbé Henri Lacordaire (1802–1861), who, together with Lamennais, was one of the
    leading lights of nineteenth-century Catholic liberalism. (Editor)

4   Loose quotation of the Latin version of the famous phrase repeated, with variations,
    in Matthew 26:11, Mark 14:7, John 12:8. (Editor)

secret thought of *Le National*, if *Le National* sincerely and resolutely desires the emancipation of workers, why these anathemas against, why this anger with, the genuine socialists—those who, for ten and twenty years, have demanded this emancipation?

Further, let the Bohemian of literature, today the myrmidons of Journalism, paid slanderers, courtiers of the privileged classes, eulogists of all the vices, parasites living upon other parasites, who prate so much of God only to dissemble their materialism, of the family only to conceal their adulteries, and whom we shall see, out of disgust for marriage, caressing monkeys when Malthusian women fail—let these, I say, publish their economic creed, in order that the people may know them.

*Faites des filles, nous les aimons*—beget girls, we love them—sing these wretches, parodying the poet. But abstain from begetting boys; at the banquet of sensualism there is not room for all.

The government was inspired by Malthus when, having a hundred thousand workers at its disposal, to whom it gave gratuitous support, it refused to employ them at useful labour, and when, after the civil war, it asked that a law be passed for their transportation. With the expenses of the pretended national workshops, with the costs of war, lawsuits, imprisonment, and transportation, it might have given the insurgents six months income, and thus changed our whole economic system. But labour is a monopoly; the government does not wish revolutionary industry to compete with privileged industry; at the workbench of the nation there is not room for all.

Large industrial establishments ruin small ones; that is the law of capital, that is Malthus.

Wholesale trade gradually swallows the retail; again Malthus.

Large estates encroach upon and consolidate the smallest possessions: still Malthus.

Soon one half of the people will say to the other:

The earth and its products are my property.

Industry and its products are my property.

Commerce and transportation are my property.

The State is my property.

You who possess nether reserve nor property, who hold no public offices and whose labour is useless to us, TAKE YOURSELVES AWAY! You have really no business on the earth; beneath the sunshine of the Republic there is not room for all.

Who will tell me that the right to labour and to live is not the whole of the Revolution?

Who will tell me that the principle of Malthus is not the whole of the Counter-Revolution?

And it is for having published such things as these—for having exposed the evil boldly and sought the remedy in good faith, that speech has been forbidden me by the government, the government that represents the Revolution!

That is why I have been deluged with the slanders, treacheries, cowardice, hypocrisy, outrages, desertions, and failings of all those who hate or love the people! That is why I have been given over; for a whole month, to the mercy of the jackals of the press and the screech-owls of the platform! Never was a man, either in the past or in the present, the object of so much execration as I have become, for the simple reason that I wage war upon cannibals.

To slander one who could not reply was to shoot a prisoner. Malthusian carnivora, I discover you there! Go on, then; we have more than one account to settle yet. And, if calumny is not sufficient for you, use iron and lead. You may kill me; no one can avoid his fate, and I am at your discretion. But you shall not conquer me; you shall never persuade the people, while I live and hold a pen, that, with the exception of yourselves, there is one too many on the earth. I swear it before the people and in the name of the Republic!

17th October 1848
*Le Peuple*
Translation by Shawn P. Wilbur

# TOAST TO THE REVOLUTION

*Citizens,*

WHEN OUR FRIENDS OF THE DEMOCRATIC REPUBLIC, APPREHENSIVE OF OUR ideas and our inclinations, cry out against the descriptive term *socialist* which we add to that of *democrat*, of what do they reproach us?—They reproach us for not being revolutionaries.

Let us see then if they or we are in the tradition; whether they or we have the true revolutionary practice.

And when our adversaries of the middle class, concerned for their privileges, pour upon us calumny and insult, what is the pretext of their charges? It is that we want to totally destroy property, the family, and civilisation.

Let us see then again whether we or our adversaries better deserve the title of conservatives.

Revolutions are the successive manifestation of justice in human history.—It is for this reason that all revolutions have their origins in a previous revolution.

Whoever talks about revolution necessarily talks about *progress*, but just as necessarily about *conservation*. From this it follows that revolution is always in history and that, strictly speaking, there are not several revolutions, but only one permanent revolution.

The revolution, eighteen centuries ago, called itself the gospel, the Good News. Its fundamental dogma was the *Unity of God;* its motto, *the equality of all men before God*. Ancient slavery rested on the antagonism and inequality of gods, which represented the relative inferiority of races, in the state of war. Christianity created the rights of peoples, the brotherhood of nations; it abolished simultaneously idolatry and slavery.

Certainly no one denies today that the Christians, revolutionaries who fought by testimony and by martyrdom, were men of progress. They were also conservatives.

The polytheist initiation, after civilising the first humans, after converting these men of the woods, *sylvestres homine*, as the poet says, into men of the towns, became itself, through sensualism and privilege, a principle of corruption and enslavement. Humanity was lost, when it was saved by the Christ, who received for that glorious mission the double title of *Saviour* and *Redeemer*, or as we put it in our political language, conservative and revolutionary.

That was the character of the first and greatest of revolutions. It renewed the world, and in renewing it conserved it.

But, supernatural and spiritual as it was, that revolution nevertheless only expressed the more material side of justice, the enfranchisement of bodies and the abolition of slavery. Established on faith, it left thought enslaved; it was not sufficient for the emancipation of man, who is body and spirit, matter and intelligence. It called for another revolution. A thousand years after the coming of Christ, a new upheaval began, within the religion the first revolution founded, a prelude to new progress. Scholasticism carried within it, along with the authority of the Church and the scripture, the authority of reason! In about the 16th century, the revolution burst out.

The revolution, in that epoch, without abandoning its first given, took another name, which was already celebrated. It called itself philosophy. Its dogma was *the liberty of reason*, and its motto, which follows from that, was *the equality of all before reason*.

Here then is man declared inviolable and free in his double essence, as soul and as body. Was this progress? Who but a tyrant could deny it? Was it an act of conservation? The question does not even merit a response.

The destiny of man, a wise man once said, is to contemplate the works of God. Having known God in his heart, by faith, the time had come for man to know Him with his reason. The Gospel had been for man like a primary education; now grown to adulthood, he needed a higher teaching, lest he stagnate in idiocy and the servitude that follows it.

In this way, the likes of Galileo, Arnaud de Bresce, Giordano Bruno, Descartes, Luther—all that elite of thinkers, wise men and artists, who shone in the 15th, 16th and 17th centuries as great revolutionaries—were at the same time the conservatives of society, the heralds of civilisation. They continued, in opposition to the representatives of Christ, the movement started by Christ, and for it suffered no lack of persecution and martyrdom!

Here was the second great revolution, the second great manifestation of justice. It too renewed the world—and saved it.

But philosophy, adding its conquests to those of the Gospel, did not fulfil the program of that eternal justice. Liberty, called forth from the heart of God by Christ, was still only individual: it had to be established in the tribunal. Conscience was needed to make it pass into law.

About the middle of the last century then a new development commenced and, as the first revolution had been religious and the second philosophical, the third revolution was political. It called itself the social contract.

It took for its dogma *the sovereignty of the people*: it was the counterpart of the Christian dogma of *the unity of god*.

Its motto was *equality before the law*, the corollary of those which it had previously inscribed on its flag: equality before God and equality before reason.

Thus, with each revolution, liberty appeared to us always as the instrument of justice, with equality as its criterion. The third term—the aim of justice, the goal it always pursues, the end it approaches—is brotherhood.

Never let us lose sight of this order of revolutionary development. History testifies that brotherhood, supreme end of revolutions, does not impose itself. It has as conditions first liberty, then equality. It is as if it just said to us all: Men, be free; citizens, become equal; brothers, embrace one another.

Who dares deny that the revolution undertaken sixty years ago by our fathers, and of which the heroic memory makes our hearts beat with such force that we almost forget our own sense of duty—who denies, I ask, that that revolution was a progress? Nobody. Very well, then. But was it not both progressive and conservative? Could society have survived with its time-worn despotism, its degraded nobility, its corrupt clergy, with its egotistical and undisciplined parliament, so given to intrigue, with a people in rags, a race which can be exploited at will?

Is it necessary to blot out the sun, in order to make the case? The revolution of '89 was the salvation of humanity; it is for that reason that it deserves the title of revolution.

But, citizens, if our fathers have done much for liberty and fraternity, and have even more profoundly opened up the road of brotherhood, they have left it to us to do even more.

Justice did not speak its last word in '89, and who knows when it will speak it?

Are we not witnesses, our generation of 1848, to a corruption worse than that of the worst days of history, to a misery comparable to that of feudal times, an oppression of spirit and of conscience, and a degradation of all human faculties, which exceeds all that was seen in the epochs of most dreadful cruelty? Of what use are the conquests of the past, of religion and philosophy, and the constitutions and codes, when in virtue of the same rights that are guaranteed to us by those constitutions and codes, we find ourselves dispossessed of nature, excommunicated from the human species? What is politics, when we lack bread, when even the work which might give bread is taken from us? What to us is the freedom to go or to become, the liberty to think or not to think, the guarantees of the law, and the spectacles of the marvels of civilisation? What is the meagre education which is given to us, when by the withdrawal of all those objects on which we might practice human activity, we are ourselves plunged into an absolute void; when to the appeal of our senses, our hearts, and our reason, the universe and civilisation reply: *Néant!* Nothing!

Citizens, I swear it by Christ and by our fathers! Justice has sounded its fourth hour, and misfortune to those who have not heard the call!

—Revolution of 1848, what do you call yourself?

—I am the *right to work!*

—What is your flag?

—*Association!*

—And your motto?

—*Equality before fortune!*

—Where are you taking us?

—*To Brotherhood!*

—A Toast to you, Revolution! I will serve you as I have served God, as I have served Philosophy and Liberty, with all my heart, with all my soul, with all my intelligence and my courage, and will have no other sovereign and ruler than you!

Thus the revolution, having been by turns religious, philosophical and political, has become economic. And like all its predecessors it brings us nothing less than a contradiction of the past, a sort of reversal of the established order! Without this complete reversal of principles and beliefs, there is no revolution; there is only mystification. Let us continue to interrogate history, citizens.

Within the empire of polytheism, slavery had established and perpetuated itself in the name of what principle? In the name of religion.—Christ appeared, and slavery was abolished, precisely in the name of religion.

Christianity, in its turn, made reason subject to faith; philosophy reversed that order, and subordinated faith to reason.

Feudalism, in the name of politics, controlled everything, subjecting the worker to the bourgeois, the bourgeois to the noble, the noble to the king, the king to the priest, and the priest to a dead letter.—In the name of politics again, '89 subjected everyone to the law, and recognised among men only citizens.

Today labour is at the discretion of capital. Well, then! The revolution tells you to change that order. It is time for capital to recognise the predominance of labour, for the tool to put itself at the disposition of the worker.

Such is this revolution, which has suffered sarcasm, calumny and persecution, just like any other. But, like the others, the Revolution of 1848 becomes more fertile by the blood of its martyrs. *Sanguis martyrun, semen christianorum!* exclaimed one of the greatest revolutionaries of times past, the indomitable Tertullien. Blood of republicans, seed of republicans.

Who does not dare to acknowledge this faith, sealed with the blood of our brothers, is not a revolutionary. The failure is an infidelity. He who dissembles regarding it is a renegade. To separate the Republic from socialism is to wilfully confuse the freedom of mind and spirit with the slavery of the senses, the exercise of political rights with the deprivation of civil rights. It is contradictory, absurd.

Here, citizens, is the genealogy of social ideas: are we, or are we not, in the revolutionary tradition? It is a question of knowing if at present we are also engaged in revolutionary practice, if, like our fathers, we will be at once men of conservation and of progress, because it is only by this double title that we will be men of revolution.

We have the revolutionary principle, the revolutionary dogma, the revolutionary motto. What is it that we lack in order to accomplish the work entrusted to our hands by Providence? One thing only: revolutionary practice!

But what is that practice which distinguishes the epochs of revolution from ordinary times?

What constitutes revolutionary practice is that it no longer proceeds by technicality and diversity, or by imprescriptible transitions, but by simplifications and enjambments. It passes over, in broad equations, those middle terms which suggest the spirit of routine, whose application should normally have been made during the former time, but that the selfishness of the privilege or the inertia of the governments pushed back.

These great equitations of principles, these enormous shifts in mores, they also have their laws, not at all arbitrary, no more left to chance than the practice of revolutions.

But what, in the end, is that practice?

Suppose that the statesmen we have seen in power since February 24th, these short-sighted politicians of small means, of narrow and meticulous routines, had been in the place of the apostles. I ask you, citizens, what would they have done?

They would have fallen into agreement with the innovators of the individual conferences, in secret consultations, that the plurality of gods was an absurdity. They would have said, like Cicero, that it is inconceivable that two augurs could look at one another without laughter; they would have condemned slavery very philosophically, and in a deep voice.

But they would have cried out against the bold propaganda which, denying the gods and all that society has sanctified, raised against it superstition and all the interests; they would have trusted in good policy, rather than tackling the old beliefs, and interpreting them; they would have knelt before Mercury the thief, before impudent Venus and incestuous Jupiter. They would have talked with respect and esteem of the Floralia and the Bacchanalia. They would have made a philosophy of polytheism, retold the history of the gods, renewed the personnel of the temples, published the prices of sacrifices and public ceremonies, according, as far as it was in them, reason and morality to the impure traditions of their fathers, by dint of attention, kindness and human respect; instead of saving the world, they would have caused it to perish.

There was, in the first centuries of the Christian era, a sect, a party powerful in genius and eloquence, which, in the face of the Christian revolution, undertook to continue the idolatry in the form of a moderate and progressive republic; they were the Neo-Platonists, to whom Apollonius of Tyana and the Emperor Julian attached themselves. It is in this fashion that we have seen with our own eyes certain preachers attempt the renovation of Catholicism, by interpreting its symbols from the point of view of modern ideas.

A vain attempt! Christian preaching, which is to say revolutionary practice, swept away all the gods and their hypocritical admirers; and Julian, the greatest politician and most beautiful spirit of his time, bears in the histories the name of *apostate*, for having been madly opposed to evangelical justice.

Let us cite one more example.

Let us suppose that in '89, the prudent counsellors of despotism, the well-advised spirits of the nobility, the tolerant clergy, the wise men of the middle class, the most patient of the people—let us suppose, I say, that this elite of citizens, with the most upright vision and the most philanthropic views, but convinced of the dangers of abrupt innovations, had agreed to manage, following the rules of high policy, the transition from despotism to liberty. What would they have done?

They would have passed, after long discussion and mature deliberation, letting at least ten years elapse between each article, the promised charter; they would have negotiated with the pope, and with all manner of submissiveness, the civil constitution of the clergy; they would have negotiated with the convents, by amicable agreement, the repurchase of their goods; they would have opened an investigation into the value of feudal rights, and on the compensation to be accorded to the lords; they would have sought compensation to the privileged for the rights accorded to the people. They would have made the work of a thousand years what revolutionary practice might accomplish overnight.

All of this is not just empty talk: there was no lack of men in '89 willing to connect themselves to this false wisdom of revolution. The first of all was Louis XVI, who was as revolutionary at heart and in theory as anyone, but who did not understand that the revolution must also be practised. Louis XVI set himself to haggle and quibble over everything, so much and so well, that the revolution, growing impatient, swept him away!

Here then is what I mean, today, by revolutionary practice.

The February Revolution proclaimed the *right to work*, the predominance of labour over capital.

On the basis of that principle, I say that before overriding all reforms, we have to occupy ourselves with a generalising institution, which expresses, on all the points of social economy, the subordination of capital to labour; which, in lieu of making, as it has been, the capitalist the sponsor of the worker, makes the worker the arbiter and commander of the capitalist, an institution which changes the relation between the two great economic powers, labour and property, and from which follows, consequently, all other reforms.

Will it then be revolutionary to propose an agricultural bank serving, as always, the monopolisers of money; there to create a certified loan office, monument to stagnation and unemployment; elsewhere, to found an asylum, a pawn-shop, a hospital, a nursery, a penitentiary, or a prison, to increase pauperism by multiplying its sources?

Will it be a work of Revolution to finance a few million, sometimes a company of tailors, sometimes of masons; to reduce the tax on drink and increase it on properties; to convert obligations into losses; to vote seeds and pick-axes for twelve thousand colonists leaving for Algeria, or to subsidise a trial phalanstery?

Will it be the word or deed of a revolutionary to argue for four months whether the people will work or will not, if capital hides or if it flees the country, if it awaits confidence or if it is confidence that awaits it, if there will be separation of powers or only of functions, if the president will be the superior, the subordinate or the equal of the national assembly, if the first who will fill this role will be the nephew of the emperor or the son of the king, or if it would not be better, for that plum job, to have a soldier or a poet; if the new sovereign will be named by the people or by the representatives, if the outgoing ministry of *reaction* merits more confidence than the ministry of *conciliation* now coming in, if the Republic will be blue, white, red, or tricolour?

Will it be revolutionary, when it is a question of returning to labour the fictive production of capital, to declare the net revenue inviolable, rather than to seize it by a progressive tax; when it is necessary to organise equality in the acquisition of goods, to lay the blame on the mode of transmission; when 25,000 tradesmen implore a legal settlement, to answer them by bankruptcy; when property no longer receives rent or farm rent, to refuse it further credit; when the country demands the centralisation of the banks, to deliver that credit to a financial oligarchy which only knows how to make a void in circulation and to maintain the crisis, while waiting for the discouragement of the people to bring back confidence?

Citizens, I accuse no one.

I know that to all except for us social democrats, who have envisioned and prepared for it, the February Revolution has been a surprise; and if it is difficult for the old constitutionals to pass in so short a time from the monarchical faith to republican conviction, it is still more so for the politicians of the other century to comprehend anything of the practice of the new Revolution. Other times have other ideas. The great manoeuvres of '93, good for the time, do not suit us now any more than the parliamentary tactics of the last thirty years; and if we want to abort the revolution, you have no surer means than to take up again these errors.

Citizens, you are still only a minority in this country. But already the revolutionary flood grows with the speed of the idea, with the majesty of the ocean. Again, some of that patience that made your success, and the triumph of the Revolution is assured. You have proven, since June, by your discipline, that you are politicians. From now on you will prove, by your acts, that you are organisers. The government will be enough, I hope, with the National Assembly, to maintain the republican form: such at least is my conviction. But the revolutionary power, the power of conservation and of progress, is no longer today in the hands of the government; it is not in the National Assembly: it is in you. The people alone, acting upon themselves without intermediary, can achieve the economic Revolution begun in February. The people alone can save civilisation and advance humanity!

*no date (No 2)*
*Le Peuple*
*Translation by Barry Marshall*

# THE CONSTITUTION AND THE PRESIDENCY

SINCE *Le Représentant du Peuple* CEASED TO APPEAR 70 DAYS AGO,[1] ONLY two facts have been accomplished: one in the social world and another in the political world. It will not take long to recount, just a few lines will suffice for us to relate the chain of events from August 21st to October 31st.

The first of these facts is the invasion of social ideas across all points of the civilised world. The idea of economic revolution is gaining ground throughout the land, [including] into our least advanced departments. In the more despotic states abroad, it spreads with the speed of a forest fire. All the ideas of the day before [the revolution], alleged political, are forced to bow in front of the social idea and borrow its flag to still be something.

The social revolution, inaugurated in Paris on the 25th of February, baptised in blood in the funeral days of June, the revolution of labour and capital is unstoppable from now on—in both France and the rest of Europe. The revolution had been slanderously portrayed to the population as a ruination of liberty and the destruction of the family, but now, enlightened by discussion, by the slander itself, they welcome the social revolution as the guarantor of freedom and the saviour of the family. Seeing the triumphant march of this idea, we can predict that it will not need armed struggle [to succeed]; social revolution will soon only have to present itself, along with the mass of its partisans, in order to command respect and establish itself officially in all its authority.

Only a few more weeks of suffering, workers, and you will have changed the face of the Earth more quickly than the Christian religion.

---

1   Proudhon's paper was suppressed by the state in August 1848 due to its continued criticism of the government's repressive and reactionary policies. (Editor)

The second thing to discuss is the vote on the constitution.

On October 23$^{rd}$, the National Assembly ended its consultation, the least of which concerned the new constitutional act. This act will re-establish, in four articles:

1. The right to work.
2. Universal suffrage.
3. Separation of powers.
4. The option to amend the constitution itself.

The *right to work*, rejected after long debates while discussing Article 8, has been reproduced in more or less explicit terms in Article 13.

Indeed, what is this but the *right to assistance*, recognised by the constitution in all cases where work is found to be lacking, but unemployment benefit? And what else is the promise of job creation by credit institutions, by the organisation of public workshops, if not the guarantee of work within the scope of human capability, of social capabilities?

As for *universal suffrage*, it does not say much other than declare it. It organises nothing. Universal suffrage, applied as one has just done, and we have seen and know from experience, is an excellent institution to talk down to the people, not to know what they think but what one wants of them. With universal suffrage, defined as it is in the constitution, the people will vote by turns for monarchy and republics, religion and atheism, freedom and servitude, equality and privilege. This is how the patriotic mean to run everything!

The *separation of powers* is a hangover from what we call POLITICS, something that is only the eternal deception of liberty. It is the division of what is, moreover, more radically indivisible, of that whose division implies contradiction, the *will* of the sovereign. In society, as in man, functions are diverse but the will is essentially one: the National Assembly is not arranged in this way. The fear of despotism has thrown it into antagonism, into chaos.

But after having sown division into the state and confusion into universal suffrage, the National Assembly had to make the best of all this by reserving for itself the right to *amend* the constitution. Thanks to this ability, we are from now on able to realise all social, political and legislative reforms, without conflict or catastrophe.

The constitution voted upon, what remained was to determine the time of its implementation. This is what has made the National Assembly fix the election of the President for the 10$^{th}$ of December. Such is what pre-occupies all opinions and weighs on all minds right now, what is the cause of all intrigue, what seems to keep alive the breathlessness of the Revolution: the PRESIDENCY!

Official candidates are posing in front of the nation and in open parliament. The others more modestly in the narrow shadows of the bourgeoisie, leading families and the people.

The names doing the rounds right now are those of citizens: Louis-Napoléon Bonaparte, son of Louis Bonaparte and nephew of the emperor;

Napoléon Bonaparte, son of Jerome Bonaparte, nephew of the emperor. And why not Pierre-Napoléon Bonaparte, son of Lucien Bonaparte and nephew of the emperor?

General Cavaignac: head of the executive.

General Bugeaud: conqueror of Isly.

De Lamartine: member of the provisional government.

Ledru-Rollin: member of the provisional government.

Dufaure: Minister of the Interior.

Molé: president of the council under Louis-Phillipe.

Thiers: president of the council under Louis-Phillipe.

We do not need to speak of Messrs. the Duke of Chambord and the Prince Joinville, as their candidatures are declared unconstitutional by law.

Prince Louis-Napoléon Bonaparte presents, as his qualification for his candidacy, HIS NAME. We would have preferred that he presented something else; but since his NAME is enough for him, we declare, as for us, that logically and politically there is no reason to occupy oneself with this candidate. Reason and the Constitution both oppose that the heritage of a name could ever become, in France, an hereditary entitlement to a function in the Republic.

The second of the Bonapartes offers an even more remote resemblance to his uncle. Nevertheless of all the qualities to recommend him to the electorate, the greater is still his name, the name of NAPOLÉON.

When it comes to Pierre-Napoléon Bonaparte, we can say of him that, just as the son of Louis is the ambitious one in the family, and the son of Jérome is the diplomat, so Pierre is their Hercules. Thus it is all back to the imperial heritage. Is this what makes a president?

General Cavaignac cannot count on the support of the working class. To be sure one does not accuse him, but the June Days Uprising inspired hatred for him, being to him what the massacre of the Champs de Mars was to Bailly and Lafayette. Let the bourgeoisie unite to elect Cavaignac: they owe him a debt of gratitude.

Marshal Bugeaud is in the same position as Cavaignac regarding the people. To the laurels of the Battle of Isly in Morocco, he adds the cypress of Transnonain.[2] His candidacy is only of interest to the bourgeoisie, to whom, in its intemperance of language, the Marshal promised long ago, if he is elected, he will be the *rue* of the socialists.

M. de Lamartine is like the daughter of Rhampsinith,[3] who used her father's stone-built treasure store to lure each of her lovers. M. de Lamartine, if one renders justice to his innumerable contradictions, will be elected unanimously.

---

2    Rue Transnonain was the scene of a massacre of workers in 1830. (Translator)

3    *"la fille de Rampsinith"*: Rhampsinith was an Egyptian prince mentioned by Herodotus who had a great stone tower built to store his treasures. Rhampsinitus is the ancient Greek name for Rameses III. (Translator)

M. Ledru-Rollin must by his progressive spirit always be at the head of the most advanced opinions. He is the candidate designated for the extreme left and for the party of socialism.

M. Dufaure is the man of the decent people, who, making cheap parties and systems, requires above all a man of the State who works and who is honest. It was said of M. Dufaure that he was a minister of *transition*; he will be an irremovable minister when it is understood that history is a perpetual transition. We are still not revolutionary enough for that.

M. Molé is not canvassing for himself. He is canvassing for M. de Joinville, in other words, really for M. Thiers! We have lost the right to speak of him. We leave it for our readers to make up their own minds about this character.

And now, democratic republicans and socialists, who shall we choose from all these candidates? Do we even have a candidate? Must we vote? Should we abstain? On the one hand, the country has been keen to move on from this stop-gap; on the other hand, the parties are itching to be counted. Everyone wants to move forward. The *status quo* merely aggravates the nation. What should be our attitude?

This is for us the key question. We do not hesitate to reply and prove that:

The Presidency is the violation of revolutionary principles.

The Presidency is royalty.

The Presidency is the subordination of labour to capital.

The Presidency is the hood winking of the people.

The Presidency is the counter-revolution.

The Presidency is financial feudalism.

The Presidency is the conflict of power.

The Presidency is civil war.

We conclude that people should abstain, so that the National Assembly itself will be forced to name the president. Because if the presidency is named by the Assembly he is merely the organ of the Assembly, the head of the ministry formed by it. This will return us to the concept of the indivisibility of power.

And as it is to be supposed that the majority of the people, carried along by monarchical intrigues and reactionaries, will *not* abstain, it is necessary that the minority, using the right given to them under Article 109 of the Constitution, petition the National Assembly, demanding the Constitution be immediately revised and the part relating to the presidency removed.

This is how we think the people should respond to the question posed by the National Assembly.

In a future issue, we will further examine this imposing question.

8<sup>th</sup>−15<sup>th</sup> *November 1848*
*Le Peuple*
*Translation by Paul Sharkey*

# ELECTION MANIFESTO OF *LE PEUPLE*

THE CENTRAL ELECTORAL COMMITTEE, COMPRISING DELEGATES FROM THE fourteen Seine *arrondissements* and designed to make preparation for the election of the president of the Republic, has just concluded its operations.

Citizen Raspail, the people's representative, has been selected unanimously as the candidate of the democratic and social republican party.[1]

The central committee is to publish its circular to electors without delay.

As for ourselves, who have associated ourselves intellectually and emotionally with that candidature, who, in that context, have seen fit, in defence of the dignity of our views, to stand apart from other, less advanced factions of the democracy, we consider it our duty here to recall what our principles are: that being the best way of justifying our conduct.

Our *principles*!

Throughout history, men who have sought popular endorsement in order to succeed to power have abused the masses with alleged declarations of principle which, in essence, have never been anything other than declarations of PROMISES!

Throughout history, the ambitious and scheming have, in more or less pompous language, promised the people:

*Liberty, equality, fraternity;*
Work, family, property and progress;
Credit, education, association, order and peace;

---

1  François-Vincent Raspail (1794–1878) was a French chemist, naturalist, physiologist, and socialist politician. Stood as the Socialist candidate in the Presidential elections of 10<sup>th</sup> December 1848 but came in fourth (with 0.49% of the vote). (Editor)

Participation in government, equitable distribution of taxes, honest and inexpensive administration, fair courts, movement towards equality of income, liberation of the proletariat and eradication of poverty!

So much have they promised that, coming after them, it has to be confessed, there is nothing left to be promised.

But then again, what have they delivered? It is for the people to answer: Nothing!...

The true friends of the people must henceforth adopt a different tack. What the people expects of its candidates, what it asks of them, is not promises now, but PRACTICALITIES.

It is upon these practicalities that they suggest men should be judged: and it is upon such that we ask that we be judged.

As socialist-democrats, we belong, in truth, to no sect, no school. Or, rather, if we were obliged to come up with a description of ourselves, we should say that we are of the *critical* school. For us, socialism is not a system: it is, quite simply, a protest. We believe, though, that from socialist works is dedicated a series of principles and ideas at odds with economic convention, and which have been absorbed into popular belief: which is why we call ourselves socialists. Professing socialism while embracing nothing of socialism, as the more artful do, would be tantamount to mocking the people and abusing its credulousness... Being a republican is not the last word: it is not the last word to acknowledge that the Republic ought to be surrounded by social institutions: it is not enough to inscribe upon one's banner, *Democratic and social Republic*: one must plainly point out the difference between the old society and the new: one has to spell out the positive product of socialism: and wherein and why the February Revolution, which is the expression thereof, is a social revolution.

For a start, let us recall socialism's underlying dogma, its pure dogma.

The objective of socialism is liberation of the proletariat and eradication of poverty, which is to say, effective equality of circumstances between men. In the absence of equality, there will always be poverty, always be a proletariat.

Socialism, which is egalitarian above all else, is thus the democratic formula par excellence. Should less honest politicians be mealy-mouthed about admitting it, we respect their reservations: but they ought to know that, in our view, they are no democrats.

Now, what can be the origin of this inequality?

As we see it, that origin has been brought to light by a whole series of socialist criticisms, particularly since Jean-Jacques [Rousseau]: that origin is the realisation within society of this triple abstraction: *capital, labour, talent*.

It is because society has divided itself into three categories of citizen corresponding to the three terms in that formula—that is, because of the formation of a class of capitalists or proprietors, another class of workers, and a third of talents—that caste distinctions have always been arrived at, and one half of the human race enslaved to the other.

Wheresoever an attempt has been made to separate these three things—capital, labour and talent—effectively and organically, the worker has wound up enslaved: he has been described, in turn as slave, serf, pariah, plebeian and proletarian: and the capitalist has proved the exploiter: he may go variously by the name of patrician or noble, proprietor or bourgeois: the man of talent has been a parasite, an agent of corruption and servitude: at first he was the priest, then he was the cleric, and today the public functionary, all manner of competence and monopoly.

The underlying dogma of socialism thus consists of reducing the aristocratic formula of *capital-labour-talent* into the simpler formula of LABOUR!... in order to make every citizen simultaneously, equally and to the same extent capitalist, worker, and expert or artist.

In reality as in economic science, *producer* and *consumer* are always one and the same person, merely considered from two different viewpoints. Why should the same not be true of capitalist and worker? of worker and artist? Separate these qualities in the organisation of society and inexorably you create castes, inequality and misery: amalgamate them, on the other hand, and in every individual you have equality, you have the Republic. And that is how in the political order, all these distinctions between governors and governed, administrators and administered, public functionaries and tax-payers, etc., must some day be erased. Each citizen must, through the spread of the social idea, become all: for, if he be not all, he is not free: he suffers oppression and exploitation somewhere.

So, by what MEANS is this great amalgamation to be brought to pass?

The means is indicated by the affliction itself. And, first of all, let us try to define that affliction better, if possible.

Since the organic *origin* of the proletariat and of poverty is located in the division of society into two classes: one that works and does not own; the other that owns but does not work; and, consequently, consumes without producing; it follows that the affliction by which society is beset consists of this singular fiction according to which capital is, of itself, productive: whereas labour, of itself, is not. In fact, for all things to be equal in this hypothesis of the separation of labour and capital, then, because the capitalist profits by his capital without working, so the worker should profit from his labour, in the absence of capital. Now, that is not the case. So, in the current system, equality, liberty and fraternity are impossible: and thus, poverty and proletariat are the inevitable consequence of property as presently constituted.

Anyone knowing this but not confessing it is lying equally to bourgeoisie and to proletariat. Anyone courting the people's votes but keeping this from it is neither a socialist nor a democrat.

We say again:

The productivity of capital, which Christianity has condemned under the name of USURY, is the true cause of poverty, the true origin of the

374 Pierre-Joseph Proudhon

proletariat, the eternal obstacle to establishment of the Republic. No equivocation, no mumbo-jumbo, no sleight of hand! Let those who profess to be socialist democrats join us in signing this profession of faith: let them join our company: then, and then only, will we acknowledge them as brothers, as true friends of the people, and will we associate ourselves with their every act.

And now, what is the means whereby this affliction can be eradicated, this usury terminated? Is it to be an attack upon *net* product, seizure of revenue? Is it to be, while professing utmost regard for property, the ravishing of property by means of taxation, as it is acquired through work and enshrined by law?

It is on this count above all that the true friends of the people stand apart from those whose only wish is to command the people: it is on this count that true socialists part company with their treacherous imitators.

The means of destroying usury, is not, let us repeat, the confiscation of usury: it is by countering principle with principle, in short, by *organising credit*.

As far as socialism is concerned, the organisation of credit does not mean lending at interest, since that would still be an acknowledgement of capital's suzerainty: it is, rather, organising the workers' mutual solidarity, introducing their mutual guarantees, in accordance with that common economic principle that *anything that has an exchange value is susceptible to becoming an article of exchange* and can, in consequence, furnish the basis for credit.

Just as the banker lends money to the businessman who pays him interest upon the loan:

Or the estate-owner lends his land to the peasant who pays him a rent for it:

Or the house-owner lets his tenant have lodgings in return for payment of rent:

Or the merchant lets his goods go to the customer who pays on the instalment plan:

So the worker lends his labour to the employer who pays him by the week or by the month. Every one of us vouchsafes something on credit: do we not speak of *selling on credit, working on credit, drinking, eating on credit*?

Thus labour can make an advance of itself, and can be as much the creditor as capital can.

Furthermore, two or more workers can advance one another their respective products, and, if they were to come to an arrangement regarding permanent transactions of this sort, they would have organised credit among themselves.

This is what those labour associations are to be admired for having grasped which have spontaneously, without prompting and without capital been formed in Paris and in Lyon, and which, merely by liaising with one another and making loans to one another, have organised labour as we said. So that, organisation of credit and organisation of labour amount to one and the same. It is no school and no theoretician that is saying this: the proof of it, rather, lies in current practice, revolutionary practice. Thus application of one principle leads the people towards discovery of another, and one solution arrived at always opens doors to another.

If it were to come about that the workers were to come to some arrangement throughout the Republic and organise themselves along similar lines, it is obvious that, as masters of labour, constantly generating fresh capital through work, they would soon have wrested alienated capital back again, through their organisation and competition: they would attract to their side, to start with, small property, small traders and small industries: then large-scale property and large industries: then the very biggest ventures, mines, canals and railways: they would become the masters of it all, through the successive affiliation of producers and the liquidation of property without the proprietors' being despoiled or indemnified.

Organising labour and credit along these lines would build an alliance between agriculture and industry which, at the present time, are instantly at loggerheads with each other. For who is there but industry to extend loans to the farmer? And what market is agriculture going to have but industry?

Such is the undertaking upon which the people has spontaneously embarked before our very eyes, an undertaking that it prosecutes with admirable vigour, weathering all difficulties and the most frightful privations. And we ought not to weary of saying that this movement was initiated, not by the leaders of schools, and that the primary instigation came not from the State but from the people. We are merely its spokesmen here. Our creed, the democratic and social creed, is not a utopia any more: it is a fact. This is not our doctrine that we are preaching: these are the people's ideas that we have taken up as themes for our explorations. Those who sneer at them, who prattle to us of association and Republic and yet do not dare to acknowledge the true socialists, the true republicans as their brothers are not of our ilk.

Committed to this idea these ten years past, we have not waited for the people to triumph before lining up on its side; it didn't take Christ's resurrection to persuade us of the divinity of his mission.

Should the government, the National Assembly, the bourgeoisie itself sponsor and assist us in the accomplishment of our undertaking, we will be grateful for that. But let none try to distract us from what we regard as the people's true interests: let none try to deceive us with the empty sham of reforms. We are too clear-sighted to fall for that again, and we know more of the workings of the world than the politicians who regale us with their admonitions.

We should be delighted if the State were to contribute through its budgetary provisions to the emancipation of the workers: We would look only with mistrust upon what is termed State organisation of credit, which is, as we see it, merely the latest form of man's exploitation of his fellow-man. We repudiate State credit, because the State, in debt to the tune of eight billion, does not possess a centime that it could advance by way of a loan: because its finances rest solely upon fiat money [*papier à cours forcé*[2]]: because fiat money necessarily entails depreciation, and depreciation always hits the worker rather than the proprietor: because as associated workers or workers in the process of association, we need neither the State nor fiat money to organise of our exchanges: because, in the end, credit from the State is always credit from capital, not credit from labour, and still monarchy rather than democracy.

Under the arrangement suggested to us and which we reject with all of the vigour of our convictions, the State, in the awarding of credit, first has to secure capital. For such capital, it must look to property, by way of taxation. So we still have this reversion to principle when the point is to destroy it: we have displacement of wealth, when we ought to have its creation: we have withdrawal of property, after it has been declared by the constitution to be inviolable. Let others of less advanced and less suspect ideas, meticulous in their morals, support such ideas, and we will not question their tactics. But we, who wage war, not upon the rich but upon principles: we, whom the counter-revolution never wearies of vilifying, we have to be more demanding. We are socialists, not despoilers.

We do not want progressive taxation, because progressive taxation is the validation of *net* product and we wish to do away with *net* product, through association: because, if progressive taxation fails to divest the rich man of all his wealth, it is merely a concession made to the proletariat, a sort of ransom for the right of usury, in short, a trick: and if it seizes all income, it amounts to confiscation of property, to expropriation without prior indemnification and is of no public use.

So let those who claim to be primarily politicians invoke progressive taxation by way of a reprisal against property, a punishment for bourgeois selfishness: we respect their intentions and if it should ever happen that they get the chance to implement their principles, we will bow to the justice of God.[3] As far as we representatives of those who have lost everything to the rule of capital are concerned, progressive taxation, precisely because it is an enforced restitution, is off-limits to us: we will never propose it to the people. We are socialists, men of reconciliation and progress: we seek neither reaction nor agrarian law.

We do not want levies upon State revenues, because such a levy is, like progressive taxation in the case of *rentiers*, mere confiscation, and in the case of the people, mere sleight of hand, trickery. We believe that the State is entitled to repay its debts, and thus to borrow at the lowest rates of interest: we

---

2    *Cours forcé* (forced rate/price) refers to inconvertible money, which is legal tender by government declaration and not backed by, nor convertible into, gold or silver. (Editor)

3    As in "The voice of the people is the voice of God" ("Vox populi, vox dei"). (Editor)

do not think that it is licit for it, under cover of taxation, to default upon its commitments. We are socialists, not bankrupters.

We do not want taxes upon inheritance, because such a tax is likewise merely a retreat from property, and, property being a constitutional right acknowledged universally, the wishes of the majority must be respected with regard to it: because that would be a trespass against the family: because, in order to emancipate the proletariat, we need not indulge in such fresh hypocrisy. Under the law of association, transmission of wealth does not apply to the instruments of labour, so cannot become a cause of inequality. So, let the assets of the deceased proprietor pass to his most distant and often his most impoverished relative. We are socialists, not stealers of inheritances.

We do not seek taxes upon luxury items, because that would be to strike a blow against the luxury industries: because luxury items are the very badge of progress: because, with labour in the ascendant and capital subordinated, luxury must extend to each and every citizen. Why, having encouraged property, would we retaliate against proprietors for their pleasures? We are socialists, not begrudgers.

Taxation represents the contribution made by each worker towards the costs of the community: the natural basis for taxation, therefore, is the *product*. A few centimes in every hundred added to the purchase price of everything that circulates or is consumed. As to the land and capital, these can only be taxed to the extent that they are appropriated: direct taxation being nothing but the price of the tolerance shown to the proprietor. Then again, since, under universal association, ownership of the land and of the instruments of labour is *social* ownership, it follows that direct taxation must be little by little done away with, like the veneration of privilege, the badge of feudalism and usury. This is the very opposite of what the neophytes of social democracy propose to us.

At the moment, the costs of tax collection stand at over 50 million.— Under association, as conceived of and implemented by the people, such costs can and must be whittled down to virtually nothing. What have the new socialists, those official but rather dull-witted champions of property, to say to that?

Customs tariffs, which is to say, protection for the nation's labours, sets the country back twenty six million. People would enjoy both free exchange and equal exchange. Labour would be protected by the simple fact that it could be exchanged only against labour: such protection would not cost a thing. It is not a mere *overhaul* of customs tariffs that socialism asks for, as do its young friends: it is their utter abolition.

We do not want expropriation by the State of the mines, canals and railways: it is still monarchical, still wage-labour. We want the mines, canals, railways handed over to democratically organised workers' associations operating under State supervision, in conditions laid down by the State, and under their own responsibility. We want these associations to be models for agriculture, industry and trade, the pioneering core of that vast federation of companies and societies woven into the common cloth of the democratic and social Republic.

We do not want the government of man by man any more than the exploitation of man by man: have those who are so quick to seize upon the socialist formula given it any thought?

We want savings in State expenditure, just as we want the worker to enjoy the full range of the rights of man and the citizen, the attributes of capital and of talent. For which reason we ask for certain things that socialism suggests, and which men who purport to be particularly political fail to understand.

Politics tends to lead to specialisation and indefinite proliferation of jobs: socialism tends to amalgamate them all.

Thus we believe that virtually the totality of public works can and should be carried out by the army; that such participation in public works is the primary duty that the republican youth owes to its homeland; that, as a result, the army budget and the public works budget duplicate each other. That represents a saving of more than 100 million; politics overlooks that.

There is talk of trades education. We believe that agricultural training comes in the form of agriculture; the school for arts, crafts and manufacture is the workshop; the school for commerce is the counting-house; the mining school is the mine; the navigation school the navy; the administration school the civil service, etc.

The apprentice is as necessary to the job as the journeyman: why put him to one side in a school? We want the same education for everybody: what good are schools which the people sees as only schools for aristocrats and which represent a double drain upon our finances? Organise association, and by the same token, every workshop becoming a school, every worker becomes a master, every student an apprentice. Elite figures are turned out as well and better by the workshop as by the study hall.

Likewise in government.

It is not enough to say that one is opposed to the presidency unless one also does away with ministries, the eternal focus of political ambition. It is up to the National Assembly, through organisation of its committees, to exercise executive power, just the way it exercises legislative power through its joint deliberations and votes. Ministers, under-secretaries of State, departmental heads, etc., duplicate the work of the representatives, whose idle, dissipated life, given over to scheming and ambition, is a continual source of troubles for the administration, of bad laws for society and of needless expense for the State.

Let our young recruits get this straight in their heads: socialism is the contrary of governmentalism. For us, that is a precept as old as the adage: *There can be no familiarity between master and servant.*

Besides universal suffrage and as a consequence of universal suffrage, we want implementation of the imperative mandate [*mandat impératif*]. Politicians balk at it! Which means that in their eyes, the people, in electing representatives, does not appoint mandatories but rather abjure their sovereignty!... That is assuredly not socialism: it is not even democracy.

We seek unbounded freedom for man and the citizen, along as he respects the liberty of others:

Freedom of association;

Freedom of assembly;

Freedom of religion;

Freedom of the press;

Freedom of thought and of speech;

Freedom of labour, trade and industry;

Freedom of education;

In short, absolute freedom.

Now, among these freedoms, there is still one that the old politics will not countenance, which makes a nonsense of all the rest! Will they tell us once and for all if they want freedom on condition or unconditional freedom?

We want the family: where is there anyone who respects it more than we do?... But we do not mistake the family for the model of society. Defenders of monarchy have taught us that monarchies were made in the image of the family. The family is the *patriarchal* or dynastic element, the rudiment of royalty: the model of civil society is the fraternal association.

We want property, but property restored to its proper limits, that is to say, free disposition of the fruits of labour, property MINUS USURY!... Of that we need say no more. Those who know us get our meaning.

Such, in substance, is our profession of faith. The *Declaration* by the deputies of the Mountain leaves us duty-bound to reproduce it so that a judgement may be made as to whether, by not welcoming the honourable M. Ledru-Rollin's candidacy on the say-so of friends, we are letting down the democratic and social cause, or whether it is the authors of that *Declaration* who are lagging behind in socialism.

We acknowledge the inclinations of the young Mountain, we applaud its efforts and take note of its onward march. Today, it is the Mountain that comes to the prophet: politics is evolving into socialism; just a few steps more and all the shades of republicanism will be indistinguishable.

But even though it may say the opposite, and doubtless believes it, the Mountain is only socialist in intention. The people has read its *Declaration* and will read our own *Manifesto*. Let it compare and judge. Let it say if, in the light of this document, as lightweight in ideas as it is compromising of us in terms of its politics, we should cover our tracks and fold up our tents.

The Mountain, which is, for all its ambition, only slightly or not at all socialist, is still only slightly or not at all revolutionary, for all its fervour. Its political deeds and ideas alike are the proof of that.

Was it revolutionary in September, in the elections?

Was it revolutionary in June?

Was it revolutionary in April?

Was it revolutionary during the proceedings in the Luxembourg?

We were every bit as much as it was, and more than it was, in February.

The Mountain bemoans the fact that we are not *politicians*!

To which our retort is that the Mountain is sorely mistaken if it imagines that politics amounts to anything in the absence of socialism. Socialism is politics defined in its aims and in its means. Prior to this, politics has been mere deftness. In short, socialism is the thing, politics the man. From which it follows that socialism can manage very well without politics, whereas politics cannot dispense with socialism. We see the evidence of that in the profound mediocrity of the political deeds that have come to pass, not just over the last nine months, we should say, but over the past eighteen years!...

And now to this miserable question of the Presidency.

Assuredly, it is a serious business knowing on the one hand whether the people should vote or abstain: and, on the other, under what colours, under what profession of faith the election would proceed. And as far as the candidate goes, ours was the first.

Democratic and social opinion had to be directly consulted: the Mountain has acted alone.

It publishes its *Declaration* the way Louis XVIII did the charter he granted, without consulting anyone.

It puts up a candidate in Paris and in the departments without a word of warning.

Then, once the election committee has been formed, it walks up and tells it: Things are too far advanced, and to withdraw would be impossible! No divisiveness! The Mountain simultaneously rams the vote, the programme and the candidate down our throats. As if to say to us: You have come thus far, but you will go no further. To borrow an expression that has become parliamentary language, it has leapfrogged socialism to its own advantage!

We shall not dwell upon the personality issue. It is a matter of regret for us that a politician (and we are using that term here without the least irony) such as the honourable M. Ledru-Rollin should have played into the hands of clumsy friends. He already had our personal sympathies and preferences. The bullying approach and hurtful mistrust of his entourage, however, have pushed us into the opposition...

Besides, it is our belief that this division, far from decreasing the strength of the democratic and social camp, will increase it. As things presently stand, no candidate could attract all the votes: between the old-style socialist democracy and tomorrow's the disagreements still run too deep.

The central electoral committee has decided unanimously to support citizen RASPAIL in his candidacy for the presidency.

Raspail, returned by 66,000 Parisian and 35,000 Lyonnnais votes;

Raspail, the socialist democrat;

Raspail, the implacable exposer of political mythologies;

Raspail, whose work in the field of healing has elevated him to the ranks of the benefactors of mankind.

In lending our backing to this candidature, we do not, as the honourable Monsieur Ledru-Rollin had written somewhere, intend to endow the Republic with a possible CHIEF: far from it. We accept Raspail as a living protest against the very idea of the Presidency! We offer him to the people's suffrage, not because he is or believes himself possible, but because he is impossible: because with him, presidency, the mirror-image of royalty, would be impossible.

Nor do we mean, in calling for votes for Raspail, to issue a challenge to the bourgeoisie which fears this great citizen. Our primary intention is reconciliation and peace. We are socialists, not muddleheads.

We back Raspail's candidacy, so as to focus the eyes of the country all the more strongly upon this idea, that henceforth, under the banner of the Republic, there are but two parties in France, the party of labour and the party of capital.

It will not be through any fault of ours if the last remaining vestige of this ancient division is not soon erased.

*31ˢᵗ January 1849*
*Translation by Clarence L. Swartz ("Declaration" and "Formation of the Company") and Ian Harvey ("Report of the Luxembourg Delegate and Workers' Corporation Commission")*

# BANK OF THE PEOPLE

## DECLARATION

I SWEAR BEFORE GOD AND MAN, UPON THE GOSPEL AND ON THE CONSTITUtion, that I have never held nor professed any other principles of reform than those laid down in the present treatise, and that I ask nothing more, nothing less, than the free and peaceful application of these principles, and their logical, legal and legitimate consequences.

I declare that in my innermost thought, these principles and the results which flow from them, are the whole of Socialism, and that beyond is nothing but utopia and chimeras.

I vow that in these principles, and in all the doctrine to which they serve as a basis, nothing—absolutely nothing—can be found opposed to the family, to liberty, or to public order.

The Bank of the People is but the financial formula, the translation into economic language, of the principle of modern democracy, the sovereignty of the People, and of the Republican motto, *Liberty, Equality, Fraternity*.

I protest that in criticising property, or rather the whole mass of institutions of which property is the pivot, I have never intended either to attack individual rights, based upon existing laws, or to contest the legitimacy of acquired possessions, or to demand an arbitrary division of goods, or to place any obstacle to the free and regular acquisition, by sale and exchange, of property, or even to forbid or suppress, by sovereign degree, ground rent and interest on capital.

I think that all these manifestations of human activity should remain free and voluntary for all: I ask for them no modifications, restrictions or suppressions, other than those which result naturally and of necessity from the universalisation of the principle of reciprocity which I propose.

What I say of property, I say of every political and religious institution as well. My sole aim, in passing through the crucible of criticism the different parts of the social structure, has been to discover, by a long and laborious analysis, yet higher principles, whereof the algebraic formula is announced in this treatise.

This is my testament in life and in death: he only may doubt its sincerity who can lie when on his death-bed.

If I am mistaken, the good sense of the public will soon dispose of my theories: there will be nothing left for me but to disappear from the revolutionary arena, after having asked pardon from society and from my brothers for the annoyance which I may have caused to their minds, of which I am, after all, the first victim.

But if, after being discredited by general good sense and experience, I should seek again some day to excite the feelings and arouse false hopes by other means or by new suggestions, I would invoke upon myself thenceforth the scorn of honest people and the maledictions of the human race.

P. J. PROUDHON

# FORMATION OF THE COMPANY

[...]

*Article 2.* THE object of this Company is to organise credit democratically:

1. By procuring for everyone the use of the land, of buildings, machines, instruments of labour, capital, products and services of every kind, at the lowest price, and under the best possible conditions;
2. By facilitating for all the disposal of their products and the employment of their labour, under the most advantageous conditions.

[...]

*Article 9.* The Company holds the following principles: That all raw materials are furnished to man by nature gratuitously.

That therefore, in the economic order, all products come from *labour*, and reciprocally, that all *capital* is unproductive.

That as every transaction of credit may be regarded as an exchange, the provision of capital and the discount of notes cannot and should not give rise to any interest.

In consequence, the Bank of the People could and should operate without capital; as it has for its *base* the essential gratuity of credit and of exchange; for its *object*, the circulation of values, not their production; for its *methods*, the reciprocal agreement of producers and consumers.

This end will be attained when the entire body of producers and consumers shall have become supporters of the by-laws of the Company.

[...]

*Article 28.* [...]

The Bank of the People, while favouring workers' associations, maintains the freedom of commerce and emulative competition as the principle of all progress and the guaranty of good quality and low price of products.

[...]

*Article 51.* Advances thus made by the Bank are not made as a joint stock company, and cannot be at all likened to redemption of shares of stock; they are, like advances on Consignments of merchandise, and like opening of accounts on real estate, simple discount transactions, and compose the proper function of the Bank.

*Article 52.* For this purpose there is to be established at once in the office of the Bank of the People, a special division under the name of General Syndicate of Production and Consumption.

It will be directed by Citizen Andre-Louis-Jules Lechevalier, Ex-Secretary of the West India Company. The powers of the Syndicate are for the present as follows:

1. To receive the declarations of manufacturers and dealers who desire to place themselves in relations with the supporters of the Bank of the People and to enjoy the custom of the Company, and who therefore wish to give information as to their names, occupations, addresses, their special products or services, the qualities and prices of their merchandise, and the amount of their remittances and deliveries;

2. To receive the requests of consumers, and to make sure of the chances of success for new enterprises by exact investigation of the demand;

3. To publish a bulletin of commerce, agriculture, and industry, containing, together with the Bank's reports and the market quotations, all announcements and notices, such as demands for and offers of labour, demands for and offers of merchandise, reductions of prices, information of manufacturers and dealers newly admitted into the Company; this bulletin to be inserted in the newspaper, *Le Peuple*, which is appointed by these presents the official organ of the Bank of the People, in its relations with its shareholders, its supporters and the public;

4. To solicit the support of producers whose products and services are needed by the Company, and, in case of their refusal, to start, among the members, competing establishments in similar lines;

5. To begin a record of general, comparative and detailed statistics of commerce, industry and agriculture; in a word, to obtain, by every possible means, the extension and strengthening of the Company.

[...]

## ORGANISATION AND ADMINISTRATION OF THE BANK

[...]

*Article 63.* As soon as circumstances permit, the present Company will be changed into a joint-stock company, as this form will enable it to realise, in accordance with the desire of its founders, the triple principle, 1$^{st}$, of election; 2$^{nd}$, the division and independence of its functions; 3$^{rd}$, the individual responsibility of each employee.

[...]

*Article 66.* The General Manager may be dismissed [...]

His dismissal involves by law the revocation of all powers that he may have granted to his Assistant Managers.

[...]

## THE COUNCIL OF OVERSIGHT

*Article 70.* A council of thirty delegates will be created to supervise the administration, and to represent the sleeping partners in their relations to it.

They will be chosen by the General Assembly from among the shareholders or supporters in the various branches of production and of public service.

*Article 71.* The Council of Oversight will be renewed by thirds from year to year.

Departing members for the first two years will be selected by lot. A departing member may be re-elected.

In case of vacancy in the course of the year, the Council will fill it temporarily.

*Article 72.* The Council of Oversight will meet at least once a month, at such time and place as it may think fit. Its functions are:
1. To see that the by-laws are observed;
2. To have submitted to it, as often as it may think proper but at least once every three months, a statement of accounts by the General Manager;
3. To verify the accounts presented by him, and to make report thereon to the General Assembly;
4. To represent the shareholders, whether as plaintiff or as defendant, in all differences with the General Manager;
5. To call special meetings of the General Assembly when it thinks proper;
6. To declare that it opposes or does not oppose propositions for sale, alienation or hypothecation which may be made by the General

Manager; to provide judiciously for the replacement of the General Manager in case of death, resignation or dismissal, until the General Assembly shall have named another manager.

Each of its members, moreover, has the right to examine the books and documents of the Company whenever he may choose to do so.

The Council of Oversight may delegate three of its members for a year, who shall be particularly charged with examining as often as possible, the books, the cash, and all the transactions of the administration.

Compensation for loss of time may be granted to the delegates, of which the amount shall be determined by the General Assembly.

[...]

## THE GENERAL ASSEMBLY

*Article 74.* The General Assembly shall be composed of one thousand delegates at most, named by the whole body of members and supporters;

*Article 75.* The election of delegates shall be made by industrial classes, and proportionally to the number of members and supporters in each class.

The bulletin of the Bank will announce before the elections the number of delegates to be named by each profession and locality.

*Article 76.* The Annual Meeting of the General Assembly shall take place regularly in the first month of each year.

[...]

The General Assembly, composed as above described, represents the whole body of shareholders and supporters.

[...]

*Article 78.* Decisions shall be made by a majority of votes of members present, whatever their number.

*Article 79.* In addition to the Annual General Assembly, there may be special General Assemblies, summoned either by the management, or by the Council of Oversight.

[...]

*Article 81.* The objects of the General Assembly shall be:
1. To receive the accounts and reports of the management, and to approve them if possible, after having heard the advice of the Council of Oversight;
2. To amend, if necessary, the by-laws, upon the motion of the Manager or of his delegates, all constitutional powers for that purpose being granted to him;

3. To deliberate upon all questions submitted to it, nevertheless without interfering with the management;
4. To decide upon any increase in the capital, and to order the issue of additional shares in connection therewith;
5. To order the recall of the Manager, upon the motion of the Council of Oversight;
6. To appoint another Manager if necessary;
7. To appoint the members of the Council of Oversight and to provide every year for replacing them;
8. To determine the rate of discount for the coming year;
9. To point out the general needs of the Company, and the means of satisfying them.

[...]

# REPORT OF THE LUXEMBOURG DELEGATE AND WORKERS' CORPORATION COMMISSION

To SET THIS presentation in order, we will start by dealing with the mechanism of those various institutions by supposing their complete and definitive organisation; then we will present the various modifications intended to harmonise the institutions with the current special organisation from the start so that they operate in a practical way.

Each of the two parts of this presentation will therefore be divided into three distinct chapters:

- The Bank of the People;
- The Syndicate of Production;
- The Syndicate of Consumption.

Let us begin with an overview of all of these establishments.

All of you know that any bank is nothing other than a mechanism of circulation. Therefore, the three institutions above can be summarised with three words:

- Circulation;
- Production;
- Consumption.

That is, these are all of the social functions anticipated within their three economic aspects.

In fact, production and consumption may be considered the two poles of the social organisation that circulation is intended to balance, and from that perspective, circulation becomes the crucial cog.

We will begin this presentation with the Bank of the People, which is the circulation organisation.

# PART ONE

## CHAPTER I
### The Bank of the People

As you know, citizens, first under the name of the *Exchange Bank* and then of the *Bank of the People*, citizen Proudhon has tried to constitute an institution of circulation that can be for the People what the Bank of France is for the bankers.

Our friend's proposed goal has been to steal away the masses of workers from capital's exploitation. Therefore, he has had to try to lower capital's interest so that it only represents the indispensable fees for Bank of the People administration, that is, compensation to its employees for their labour, plus the cost of the risks inherent in any operation of that type, risks such as the prime rate decreasing due to the increased number of Bank members. Once those conditions are met, credit becomes free.

[...]

### *The bank's internal organisation*

The main establishment of the bank will be in Paris. In each neighbourhood, it will have a counter, and in each commune it will have a correspondent bank. Its internal organisation in both Paris and the department is based on the three principles:

1. Election;
2. The division and independence of employees;
3. The individual responsibility of each employee.

## CHAPTER II
### Overview of Contemplated Syndicates of Production or Consumption

Among the members of the commission responsible for developing the Bank of the People project is citizen Jules Lechevalier, a mutual friend, whom you all know, and whose great deal of work as a socialist has earned him a justly deserved position. We are indebted to him for the idea of establishing the two unions that we are going to discuss with you; the development of the organisation, as will be presented to you in the follow-up to this work, is under his special direction.

Just as Proudhon had organised circulation in his bank project, Jules Lechevalier asked himself if, to complete that work, it was essential for him to create two major controls by organising production, on the one hand, and consumption, on the other, so that the production and distribution of products could function as economically as possible and the social transformation would be facilitated by the gradual elimination of parasitic functions in production and consumption, just as the Bank of the People operates in relation to circulation.

In the name of those unions, he first designed two large corporations responsible for centralising production and consumption operations so that all the various retail operations, which came to the Bank of the People as the major circulation agent, had to first go through one of those two corporations, which, independent from the bank, also provided it with guarantees inherent to business itself, the bank coming from the community of those same businesses represented as a body by both of those large corporations, which vouch for all operations they send to the bank; furthermore, the relationships between those two corporations had to go through the Bank of the People, which was for them, as for all the business they centralised, the major and sole circulation element.

First, we have to present to you the fundamental idea on which a large part of the development work we must begin will operate.

Up until now, various economists have only understood two things as capital:

1. Raw materials appropriated for use;
2. Accumulated labour, represented by those same materials implemented.

But with regard to the human race, the great creator of all wealth: although those who exploited labour considered it as income, they did not consider the accumulated individual talent, which was the source of that income, as capital. However, in the land of slaves where the race of humans is so truly appropriated that it is designated as *real property*, humans are considered as capital on which all circulation operations, known as bank operations, take place as they do with properties (movable and immovable), which constitute what we in Europe call capital.

Therefore, let's examine if humans under the conditions of freedom lose the very thing that pertains to them, their virtue of being capital, that is, they will be able to conduct operations on themselves to their own benefit, operations that, in the state of slavery, the master conducted on them to their detriment.

The only objection that could be made is that humans in a state of slavery are a constant source of labour because that labour is forced, but in the state of freedom, with the ability to voluntarily cease to produce, they do not present the same degree of solvency as they do in the first state.

How specious that objection is, and the facts victoriously answer it: on the soil of the United States, the least encumbered soil of all civilisations, slavery is disappearing overnight due to the competition of free labour.

If we now compare humans considered from this new perspective with the dead material believed until now to be the only capital, we find that humans have the double property of being able to value and strengthen themselves in an even more effective manner through mutual life insurance.

Therefore, an average partnership of approximately 500 francs each, or 18 billion for all the French people together, will then be completely guaranteed by the living capital on which that partnership will have been made because all of the workers, by only taking as a base the effective creation of wealth in the current regime of atomisation, represent a capital of between 169 tand259 billion if we consider France's revenue to be between 8.5 and 12 billion.

Let's now move on to a specific examination of each of these institutions.

### General syndicate of production

This syndicate's active membership will be comprised of proper delegates from the various production branches. Its responsibilities will be:

1. To create the free and democratic corporation as the absolute and definitive system for all workers, regardless of their present social condition: already organised in associations, still belonging to the employers or working in isolation from each other; it must also give rise to the organisation of associations.
2. To put the workers in a position of liquidity, that is, to make themselves and their work tools available.

Workers' advances depend on these bases:

1. Each producer's prior availability;
2. Workers' reciprocal financing for means of production;
3. Reciprocal financing of food supplies for workshops and labour;
4. Centralisation of manufacturers' relations on all products;
5. Control of products;
6. Co-operation in the distribution of labour and therefore of unemployment among the various workshops with the goal of improving the balance between production and consumption;
7. Co-operation in the liquidation of obsolete industries in favour of new ones;
8. Provision of the general costs of industrial development and compensation for industrial displacements due to the use of new processes;
9. Reimbursement of inventors;
10. Solicitation of inventions and improvements;
11. Establishment of a common fund for reciprocal compensation to be awarded to various industries;
12. Establishment of mutual insurance of all the corporations against all disaster subject to valuation;
13. Negotiation and guarantee of each special corporation's loans vis-à-vis the Bank of the People, it being agreed that the only coverage will be the fair valuation of the worker's life in capital and current circulation on the labour force's obligations;
14. Organisation of apprenticeship, so that:
    1. Children can always find a place to pursue their vocations;
    2. There is no glut of workers in a corporation;

3. Apprentices, through reimbursement agreements their parents contract for them, can receive the necessary credit for food when their work does not cover its expense;

4. All corporations that need apprentices can have them at will.

15. Determination of each corporation's relationship with the general union with regard to its sharing of expenses for apprentices connected with the corporation and the means for reimbursing those expenses;

16. Determination of benefit conditions and mutual services in case of illness, accident or disability; the union provides for these by means of its reserve fund and a contribution from all the workers to the general fund. It will negotiate the conditions under which it shall interact with all corporations with regard to union members;

17. Organisation of a central pension fund, the deposits into which will be produced through the corporations' contributions; this central fund in concert or in participation with the corporations will contribute to the workers' pensions;

18. Search for a method of meshing work to avoid inherent unemployment in certain industries and the counterbalancing of the fatal influence that the extended division of work produces on workers.

## CHAPTER III
### General Syndicate of Consumption and Its Responsibilities

The Syndicate of Consumption is responsible for storing raw materials and manufactured products, as well as for ensuring flow.

It will credit workers with raw materials and make all advances on manufactured product consignments.

Therefore, it will provide raw materials to all industries from seeds to precious metals and ensure a regular supply. It will provide for all preparations, productions and services necessary for the needs of life.

### *Product distribution service*

The Syndicate of Consumption will be a general supply and commission business.

In that regard, it will have combined buildings constructed from a perspective of safety, economy and the distribution of forces for all social needs and services.

It will have bakeries, butcher shops, fruit shops, grocery stores, etc. established—in short, establishments in all branches of industry involved in people's direct consumption.

It will store all raw materials and receive them on consignment.

There will be general warehousing for all raw materials with limited consumption and special warehousing for those with significant consumption.

It will open credits and reach agreements with the Syndicate of Production and various corporations for supplies connected with various production workshops.

It will make advances to the Syndicate of Production on manufactured products deposited with it or consigned for sale.

In all centres, it will directly organise raw material warehouses and merchandise bazaars or initiate relations with already existing local establishments of that nature.

Concurrently with the Syndicate of Production, it will exert its control on product quality and prices.

It will deliver products and raw materials to the best market in return for circulating bonds and cash.

To connect the syndicates in a more unified manner with the Bank of the People, a division will be formed within the bank under the title of *central bureau of supply and demand* to receive all offers and requests and forward them to the proper syndicates so as to prevent procedural problems on the part of the public, which need not be familiar with the organisations' internal details, such as going to one of the syndicates for operations that are the domain of another syndicate. As we have seen above, this would be especially likely because the industries concerned with manufacturing products appropriate for personal use are under the aegis of the Syndicate of Consumption even though they are production work.

[...]

In 1789, despotism had its fortress; it was the Bastille. In one of its days of sublime rage, the People razed it to the ground, and on its site, that evening, one could read the inscription, so beautiful in its simplicity: *Here is where we danced.*

In 1849, financial feudalism has its fortress: it is the Bank of France. A clever engineer has come to tell us that this fortress, which all thought impregnable, is not so. Let us have courage, then, and the temple of usury, no longer seeing the product of our sweat flow into its coffers, deserted by its priests, will collapse, taking the old world with it.

*October 1849*
*Translation by James Bar Bowen (Chapters III and XXI), Martin Walker*
*(Chapters VI and XVIII), Ian Harvey (Chapter X), and Paul Sharkey*
*(Chapter XVII)*

# CONFESSIONS OF A REVOLUTIONARY
## TO SERVE AS A HISTORY OF THE FEBRUARY REVOLUTION

# CHAPTER III
## NATURE AND GOAL OF GOVERNMENT

HOLY SCRIPTURE SAYS THAT DIVISION INTO FACTIONS OR PARTIES IS INEVITA-
ble, *oportet enim hæreses esse*![1] "How terrible is this concept of the '*inevitable*'!" exclaimed Bossuet in a profound moment of clarity, without actually
daring to seek out a reason for this inevitability.

A small amount of reflection soon shows us the principle and the significance of the division into parties: but more important is to understand their
means and their ends.

All men are equal and free: society, by nature and design, is thus autonomous and, in other words, ungovernable. The sphere of activity of
each citizen being determined by the natural division of labour and by the
choice that he makes as to the work he will do, the said functions combine
in such a way as to produce a harmonious effect, order resulting from the
free actions of everyone: there is no need for government. Whoever lays

---

1    The Biblical Latin quote is from St. Paul's first letter to the Corinthians 11:19 and
     means "it is inevitable that there will be heresies." (Translator)

his hand on me to govern me is a usurper and a tyrant: I declare him my enemy.

However, the physiology of society does not immediately conform to this egalitarian organisation: the idea of Providence, one of the first to appear in society, rejects it. Equality among us comes through a succession of tyrannies and governments under which Liberty continually battles with absolutism, as Israël with Jehovah. Equality is therefore repeatedly born out of inequality; Liberty takes government as its point of departure.

When the first men gathered at the edge of the forests in order to found society, they did not say (like shareholders in a limited partnership): "Let us organise our rights and our responsibilities so as to produce for each and every person the greatest amount of well-being, thus bringing into existence both equality and independence." Such reasoning was beyond the capabilities of the first men, and contradicts what scholars have been able to discover. Indeed, theirs was a completely different concept: "Let us constitute among ourselves an *authority* to watch over and govern us!" *Constituamos super nos regem!* And that was exactly what was meant by our compatriots when they gave their votes to Louis Bonaparte on 10ᵗʰ December 1848. The voice of the people is the voice of power, with the expectation that it will become the voice of Liberty. Additionally, all authority is divine right: *omnis potestas a deo*, as St. Paul said.[2]

Authority is therefore the first social idea to have been devised by humanity.

And the second was to work immediately for the abolition of authority, each person wanting it to serve as the guarantor of their own liberty against the liberty of others: this was the inevitable result and is the inevitable function of a division into Parties.

Authority was scarcely inaugurated in the world when it became the object of universal conflict. Authority, Government, Power, State—these words all signify the same thing; each one of these embodies the means to exploit and oppress others. Absolutists, Doctrinaires, Demagogues and Socialists always turn their gaze towards authority like a magnet to a pole.

As a result of this, there rises the aphorism from the Radical Party[3] that the Doctrinaires and Absolutists of course do not disavow: *The social revolution is the end; the political revolution* (i.e. the transfer of authority) *is the means.* What this means is: "Give us the power of life and death over you, the

---

2    "All authority comes from God." (Translator)

3    Under the July Monarchy (1830–1848) the law forbade parties to define themselves as "Republican" and so "Radical" was used as an alternative. The radicals considered themselves as the heirs of the Jacobins from the Great Revolution. They advocated universal suffrage within a centralised and indivisible republic, freedom of the press, right of assembly, and so on as a vehicle of social progress. Alexandre Ledru-Rollin and Louis Blanc were part of its left-wing. (Editor)

people, and your possessions, and we will give you liberty." Kings and priests have been repeating this for the last six thousand years.

And thus government and the Parties are reciprocally, one to the other, Cause, End and Means. They exist for one another; their destiny is shared: it is to call daily on the people to emancipate themselves; it is to energetically solicit their support by suppressing their powers of discrimination; it is to shape their minds and push them in the direction of progress by prejudice, by restrictions, by a calculated resistance to all their ideas, to all their needs. You will not do this; you will abstain from that: the government, irrespective of which party happens to hold power, has never known how to say anything else. Prohibition, since Eden, has been the school of the human race. However, once Man has reached the age of majority, government and parties must disappear. This conclusion is reached by the same rigorous logic, using the same sense of inevitability by which socialism has emerged out of absolutism, philosophy out of religion, and even by which equality emerges out of inequality.

If one seeks, by means of philosophical analysis, to understand authority, its principles, its forms, its effects, one soon recognises that the constitution of authority, both spiritual and temporal, is nothing other than a preparatory organism, essentially parasitic and corruptible, incapable itself of creating anything else, such is its form, such is the idea that it represents, namely tyranny and misery. Philosophy affirms, in consequence, and contrary to faith, that the constitution of an authority over the people is only a transitional establishment; that power is not in any way a conclusion of science but a product of spontaneity, itself disappearing as soon as it develops a sense of itself; that, far from growing and strengthening in time, as the rival parties who besiege it assume, it has to reduce itself indefinitely and become absorbed into the industrial organisation; that, in consequence, it should not be placed *above* but *under* society; and in turning the aphorism of the Radicals around, it concludes: *The political revolution,* (i.e., the abolition of authority among men) *is the end; the social revolution is the means.*

And this is why, adds the philosopher, that all the Parties, without exception, and to the extent that they affect power, are all varieties of absolutism, and this is, therefore, why there will no be liberty for citizens, no order in society, no union among workers until the renunciation of authority has replaced the current faith in authority within the political catechism.

*No more parties;*

*No more authority;*

*Absolute liberty for man and citizen.*

In three short phrases, I have summed up my expression of political faith.

It is in this spirit of governmental negation that I once said to a man of rare intelligence, but who had the weakness to want to become a minister:

"Work with us for the demolition of government! Become a revolutionary for the transformation of Europe and the world, and remain a journalist" (*Représentant du Peuple,* June 5th, 1848).

The response I received was:

"There are two ways to be a revolutionary: *from above*, which is revolution by initiative, by intelligence, by progress, by ideas; and *from below*, which is revolution by insurrection, by force, by despair, on the streets.

"I am and always have been a revolutionary *from above*; I am not and never have been a revolutionary *from below*.

"So don't ever expect me to work together with anyone for the demolition of any government; my spirit refuses to act thus. I follow a single political thought and idea: to improve the government" (*La Presse*, June 6th, 1848).

In this distinction of *from above* and *from below*, there is a great deal of bluster but little truth. M. de Girardin, explaining his thoughts in this way, believes himself to have expressed an idea which is as new as it is profound; but he has simply reproduced the eternal illusion of the Demagogues who, believing, with the help of power, that they are advancing their revolutions, are in fact merely serving to undermine them. Let us have a closer look at the thoughts of M. de Girardin.

This ingenious publicist has decided to call revolution by initiative, by intelligence, by progress and ideas the revolution *from above*; he has decided to call revolution by means of insurrection and despair the revolution *from below*. However, exactly the opposite is true.

*From above*, in the thinking of the writer I am quoting, evidently signifies power; *from below* signifies the people. On the one hand we have the actions of government; on the other, the initiative of the masses.

It is a question then of identifying which of these initiatives, that of the government or that of the people, is the most intelligent, the most progressive, the most peaceful.

Nevertheless, revolution from above is (and I will explain why later) inevitably revolution according to the whims of the Prince, the arbitrary judgement of a minister, the fumblings of an Assembly or the violence of a club: it is a revolution of dictatorship and despotism.

And that is revolution as practised by Louis XIV, Napoléon, Charles X; and it was thus that Messrs. Guizot, Louis Blanc and Léon Faucher sought to act. The Whites, The Blues, The Reds are all in agreement on this!

Revolution on the initiative of the masses is a revolution by the concerted action of the citizens, by the experience of the workers, by the progress and diffusion of enlightenment, revolution by the means of liberty. Condorcet, Turgot, Robespierre all sought a revolution from below, from true democracy. One of the men who created revolution the most and governed the least was Saint Louis.[4]

---

4    Louis IX (1214–70) was King of France from 1226 until his death. He established the Parliament of Paris which gradually acquired the habit of refusing to register legislation with which it disagreed until the king held a *lit de justice* or sent a *lettre de cachet* to force them to act. He was the only king of France to be canonised (in 1297 by Pope Boniface VIII). (Editor)

France at the time of Saint Louis ran itself; it produced, as a vine produces buds, its lords and its vassals; when the king published his famous resolution, it was simply a formalisation of the public will.

Socialism gave in fully to the illusion of radicalism; the saintly Plato, more than 2000 years ago was a tragic example of this. Saint-Simon, Fourier, Owen, Cabet, Louis Blanc, all believers in the organisation of labour by the State, by Capital, by whatever authority, appealed, like M. de Girardin to revolution *from above*. Instead of teaching the people how to organise themselves, by calling on their experience and their reasoning, they demanded Power. In what way, then, do they differentiate themselves from despots? They are also utopians, like all despots: as one despot steps down, another fills his shoes!

The conclusion is that government can never be revolutionary quite simply because it is government. Society alone, the masses armed with their intelligence, can create revolution; society alone is able to deploy all its spontaneity, to analyse and explain the mystery of its destiny and its origin, to change its faith and its philosophy, because it alone is capable of fighting against its originator and bearing its fruit. Governments are God's scourge, established to *discipline* the world: do you really expect them to destroy themselves, to create freedom, to make revolution?

They cannot act otherwise. All revolutions since the coronation of the first king up until the Declaration of the Rights of Man were achieved by the spontaneity of the people: governments have always hindered, always suppressed, always beaten back; they have never created revolution. Their role is not to create change but to control it. And anyway, what is repugnant is that even if they possessed revolutionary science, social science, they could not apply it because they would have been unable to do so, they would not have the right. It would be necessary for them first of all to lay out their science before the people in order to obtain the consent of the citizens: which is to ignore the nature of authority and of power.

The facts here confirm the theory. The nations which have the most freedom are those where power holds the least sway, where its role is most restrained: one only needs to cite the United States of America, Switzerland, England and Holland. On the other hand, witness that the most subservient nations are those where power is best organised and strongest. And yet we continue to complain that we are not governed enough, and we demand strong government, always stronger government!

The Church said in times past, speaking like a tender mother: "All for the people, but all by the priests."

The Monarchy came after the Church: "All for the people, but all by the Prince."

The Doctrinaires: "All for the people, but all by the Bourgeoisie."

The Radicals changed the formula, but failed to change the principle: "All for the people, but all by the State."

It is always the same governmentalism, the same communism.

Who then is going to finally conclude; "All for the people, all by the people, including the government"? All for the people: agriculture, commerce, industry, philosophy, religion, police, etc. All by the people: government and religion, as well as agriculture and commerce.

Democracy is the abolition of all means to power, both spiritual and temporal, legislative, executive, judicial, and proprietary. It is not the Bible, without doubt, that reveals this to us: it is the logic of societies; it is the inevitable outcome of revolutionary acts; it is all of modern philosophy.

Following M. de Lamartine, and in accordance with M. de Genoude, it is government's responsibility to say: *I want.* The country has only to reply: *I consent.*

And the experience of centuries tells the people that the best government is that which manages best to render itself powerless. Do we need parasites in order to work or priests in order to speak to God? We do not need elected persons to govern us either.

The exploitation of man by man, someone once said, is theft. Well, government of man by man is slavery; and all positive religion, right up to the dogma of papal infallibility, is surely nothing other than the adoration of man by man, in other words, idolatry.

Absolutism, founded simultaneously on the power of the Church, the State and their collective stored wealth, has multiplied, like a web, the chains on humanity. As a result of the exploitation of man by man, as a result of government of man by man, we now have:

The judgement of man by man;

The condemnation of man by man;

And, to finish the sequence, the punishment of man by man!

These religious, political and judicial institutions, of which we are so proud, which we have come to respect, which we are obliged to obey, right up until they wither and fall like fruit falling in its season, are the instruments of our apprenticeship, visible signs of the government of Instinct over humanity, the weakened but not disfigured remains of the bloody customs that bear witness to our darkest human age. Cannibalism disappeared a long time ago, not without constant resistance from those who held power, in conjunction with their atrocious practices: it still exists within the spirit of our institutions, and, by way of example, I point to the Eucharistic Sacrament[5] and to the Penal Code.

Philosophical reason rejects this barbaric symbolism; it proscribes these exaggerated forms of *human respect.* And it did not intend, [as] with the Radicals and the Doctrinaires, that one can proceed to this reform by means of legislative authority; it does not admit that anyone has the right to attempt to work for the best interests of the people in spite of the people, that

---

5    Also called Holy Communion, this is a Christian sacrament or ordinance, generally considered to be a commemoration of the Last Supper. (Editor)

it is acceptable to set a nation free even if it wants to be governed. Philosophy only puts its faith in reforms which have come out of the free will of societies: the only revolutions that it admits are those which proceed on the initiative of the masses; it denies, in the most absolute manner, the revolutionary competence of governments.

To sum up:

If you do not question faith, the fragmentation of society looks like the terrible result of the original fall of man. It is what Greek mythology explained through the fable of the warriors born from the teeth of serpents that went on to kill one another after their birth. God, according to the myth, left the government of humanity in the hands of warring parties, such that discord established its reign on Earth, and that Man learned, under perpetual tyranny, to look constantly back to a bygone age.

According to this reasoning, governments and parties are merely the inevitable implementers of the fundamental concepts of society, a realisation of the abstractions, a metaphysical pantomime whose meaning is liberty.

I have made my profession of faith. You are familiar with the personalities who, in this summing up of my political life, are obliged to play the principal parts; you know what the subject of my presentation is going to be: please consider well what I am now going to describe to you.

# CHAPTER VI
## 24 FEBRUARY: PROVISIONAL GOVERNMENT

SOMEWHERE I SAID that society is a *metaphysics in action*, a sort of logic that plays itself out on a grand scale.[6] What the general study of history and the profounder study of political economy had revealed to me was rendered palpable by the experience of the events that took place in the course of two years.

Every government establishes itself in contradiction of the one that preceded it: that is its reason for evolving as it does and the justification for its existence. The July government was in opposition to the claims of legitimacy; legitimacy was in opposition to the Empire; the latter was in opposition to the Directory, which was established by the hate directed against the Convention, which was itself convoked to do away with the badly reformed monarchy of Louis XVI.

According to this law of evolution Louis Philippe's government, unexpectedly overthrown, in turn required its contrary. On the 24th of February the failure of capital took place; on the 25th the government of *labour*

---

6   *System of Economic Contradictions*, Chapter 1: "economic science is to me the objective form and realisation of metaphysics; it is metaphysics in action..." (Editor)

was inaugurated.[7] The provisional government's decree guaranteeing the right to work was in effect the birth of February's republic. Good God! Were six thousand years of revolutionary arguments necessary to lead us to this conclusion?...

Again the theory of antinomies was confirmed by experience: perhaps those who deny that any role is played by philosophy in the vicissitudes of human affairs and ascribe everything to an invisible power will finally tell us why reason explains all, even error and crime, while faith alone explains nothing?

The fact that the government of workers succeeded that of capitalists was not only logical but just. Capital, which had set itself up as the principle and goal of social institutions, had not been able to sustain itself; the proof was supplied that far from being the principle, it is the *product*, and that property is no more the driving and shaping force of society than divine right or the sword. After having corrupted everything capitalist theory had even put capital itself at risk.

In this respect the facts were flagrantly obvious; their witness spoke loud and clear. At the time of the February Revolution commerce and industry, which had been suffering for some years, were in a sad state of stagnation, agriculture was deeply in debt, workshops were out of work, the shops had a superfluity of goods but no turnover, the finances of the State were in just as desperate a condition as those of private individuals. In spite of the periodic growth of the budget, which from 1830 to 1848 had risen progressively from one hundred thousand to one and a half million, the upper and lower houses of parliament had discerned a deficit amounting to 800 million according to some and to others one billion; in this general increase of costs the pay of the officials alone represented an annual sum of 65 million. The *bankocrats*, who in 1830 had made a revolution in the name of interest and promised a *cheap* government while affecting the title of economists much more than that of politicians, these philosophers of *debit* and *credit* spent half as much again as the government of legitimacy and once as much again as the imperial government, without being able to balance receipts and expenses.

So the proof was definite: it wasn't *capital*, interest, usury, parasitism and monopoly which the legislator of 1830 had meant to say, it was *labour*. Certainly the pretended principle of the July revolution was just as incapable of producing *Order* as it was of producing *Liberty*; it was necessary to go higher up, i.e. lower down, it was necessary to go down to the proletariat, down to nothingness. The February Revolution was therefore logically and justly termed the revolution of the workers. How could the bourgeoisie of '89, of '99, of 1814 and 1830, this bourgeoisie that had passed through the

7   A reference to the Provisional Government created by the February Revolution having state socialists Louis Blanc and Albert within it and that decreed the "right to work" and the creation of National Workshops for the unemployed. (Editor)

descending chain of governmental forms from catholicism and feudalism down to capital, which only desired to produce and exchange goods, which only attained power through work and the economy, how could it see any danger to its own interests in the republic of labour?

In this way the February Revolution imposed itself on people's minds with both *de facto* and legal authority. The bourgeoisie, vanquished as it was, I do not say by the people—thank the Lord, there had been no conflict between the bourgeoisie and the people in February—but conquered *by itself*, confessed its defeat. Though taken aback by the unexpected turn of events and disquieted by the spirit and tendencies of the Republic, it did agree that certainly constitutional monarchy had had its day and that it was necessary to reform the government from top to bottom. Thus it resigned itself to supporting the new establishment with its approval and even its capital resources. Had it not, by its opposition and impatience, in fact stimulated the emergence of the very regime that became a material obstacle to its commerce, its industry and its well-being?... It is also true that the emergence of the Republic experienced even fewer contradictions than that of Louis-Philippe, since everyone had begun to grasp the meaning of the times and revolutions!

At this point I would like to claim my readers' full attention, for if we do not learn a lesson from all this it is useless to continue bothering ourselves with public affairs. Let the nations blunder on: each of us should buy a rifle, a dagger, pistols—and barricade his door. Society is but a vain utopia: man's natural state, the legal state, is war.

The government of work!... Ah! That would be a government with initiative, no doubt, a government of progress and intelligence!... But what is the government of work? Can labour turn into government? Can labour govern or be governed? What do labour and power have in common?

Nobody had foreseen such a question; no matter. Seduced by their prejudice in favour of government, the people had nothing more urgent to do but straight away form a new government. Power having fallen into their labouring hands, they made haste to pass it over to a certain number of men of their choice, whom they charged with founding the Republic and resolving the social problem, that of the proletariat, at the same time as the political problem.—We give you three months, they told them, and still sublimely naive, still tenderly heroic, they added: *We have to endure three months of misery in the service of the Republic!* Neither classical antiquity nor the revolution of '92 had anything comparable to this cry from the very innards of the people of February.

The men chosen by the people and installed at the Town Hall were called the *Provisional Government*, which one must translate as the government without any idea or goal. Those who had been impatiently observing the development of socialist ideas for 18 years and repeating in every possible register: *The social revolution is the end, the political revolution is the means,* were, God knows, embarrassed when, once in the possession of the means, they had to achieve the goal and get down to the task at hand. They thought about it, I do not doubt, and soon they had to recognise what M. Thiers revealed somewhat later, what President Sauzet had said before him, namely that the government was not made in order to give the worker work and that the surest way for them was to continue the status quo of Louis-Philippe and resist any innovation, as long as the people would not impose it on authority.

Yet they did not lack intelligence, these conspirators for thirty years who had combated every despotism, criticised every minister and written the history of every revolution; every one of them had a socio-political theory in his briefcase. They asked for nothing better than to take the initiative, any initiative, these adventurers of progress; their advisors did not fail them either. How then did they remain for three months without producing the tiniest act of reform, without advancing the revolution by a single step forward? How, after having guaranteed the right to work by decree, did they seem, during all the time they were on the job, to be occupied solely with the means of not fulfilling their promise? Why not the tiniest attempt at effecting agricultural or industrial organisation? Why did they deprive themselves of the one decisive argument against utopia, i.e. experience?...

How? Why? Do I have to say it? Do I, a socialist, have to justify the Provisional Government? It is, you see, because they were the government; it is because in the question of revolution any initiative conflicts with the State, just as labour conflicts with capital; it is because the government and labour are incompatible like reason and faith.[8] That is the key to all the things that have taken place in France and Europe since February and which might well go on taking place for a long time yet.

Here is the place to expose the juridical reason for the revolutionary incapacity of all governments.

What makes the government immobilistic, conservative, resistant to any initiative, let us even say counter-revolutionary, is that a revolution is an *organic* thing, a matter of *creation*, while governmental power is mechanical, a matter of enforcement [*d'exécution*]. I will explain.

I do not call the laws *organic*, since they are purely conventional things touching the most general elements of administration and power like municipal and departmental laws, the law concerning recruitment, the law concerning public education, etc. The word *organic* used in this sense is an abuse of language and M. Odilon Barrot was quite right to say that such laws have nothing at all organic about them. This supposed organism, invented by Bonaparte, is nothing but governmental machinery. By *organic* I understand what goes to make up the inmost and secular

---

8    Vide *General Idea of the Revolution in the Nineteenth Century*, in which the contradiction between the political regime and the economic regime is demonstrated.— Paris, Garnier frères, 1851. (Note to the 1851 edition)

constitution of society, above any political system or constitution of the state.

We say, for example, that marriage is an organic thing. It is up to the legislative power to take the initiative in any law governing the relations of public or domestic interest and order which are occasioned by conjugal society: it does not have a brief to modify the essence of that society. Is marriage an institution of absolute or doubtful morality, a progressive or decadent institution? One may dispute this point as much as one will: no government or assembly of legislators will ever have the right to take the initiative in this. It is for the spontaneous development of customs and morals, for general civilisation, for what I call human Providence to modify what can be modified, to introduce reforms which time alone can reveal. And that is, to mention it in passing, what has prevented the establishment of divorce in France. After long and serious discussions and after the experience of several years the legislator had to recognise that a question of such delicacy and gravity was not within his remit, that the time had passed when divorce could have become part of our institutions without any danger for the family and without offending public morals, and that in wishing to cut this knot the government risked degrading precisely what it wanted to ennoble.[9]

Nobody will suspect me of superstitious weakness and religious prejudices of any sort, yet I will say that religion, like marriage, is not a matter of statutory procedure [*réglementaire*] and pure discipline but an organic affair and consequently immune to the direct action of State power. Part of the function of the ancient legislative, at least that is my opinion, by virtue of the distinction of the spiritual and the temporal customary for a long time in the Gallican Church, was to regulate the temporal affairs of the clergy and redefine episcopal districts, but I deny that the National Assembly had the right to close the churches. I recognise the power of the communal authority and the Jacobin society to establish a new cult even less when I consider that the steps taken in this direction could only end in strengthening the old one. Religion was an organic thing in France when the Revolution burst on the scene; it is true that by means of the progress of philosophy it was then possible to proclaim the right to abstain from it, and that one may now in fact

---

9   On the question of divorce the best solution is still that of the Church. In principle the Church does not accept that a marriage contracted in a regular way may be dissolved, but through a casuistical fiction it declares that in certain cases the marriage does not actually exist or has ceased to exist. Clandestinity, impotence, crime that entails civil death, erroneous identification of person(s), etc., are for the Church, like death itself, so many occasions for dissolving the marriage. Perhaps it might be possible to equally satisfy the needs of society, the requirements of morality and the respect due to families by perfecting this theory without going as far as divorce, by means of which the marriage contract is really no more than a contract of concubinage.

predict the imminent extinction or transformation of Catholicism, but there was no authority at that time to abolish it. The Concordat of 1802[10] was not at all, whatever some may have said, simply a matter of consular reaction; it was a simple reparation demanded by the vast majority of the people following the vain parades of Hébert and Robespierre.—I still believe, correspondingly, that it was right for the parliament of 1830 to assure all faiths of their right to freedom, respect and incomes, but I would not agree that it was permissible, in maintaining the monarchical principle, for it to state that the Catholic religion was nothing but a majority religion. Certainly I would not today give my support to a revision, in the sense that I have suggested, of Article 7 of the Constitution of 1848: what has been done, whatever it may have cost, is done, and I consider it irrevocable. One could do better and more for the emancipation of human consciousness; but I would not have voted for article 6 of the Charter of 1830.

These examples suffice to explain my thought. A revolution is an explosion of organic force, an evolution of society expressing what was already within it; it is only legitimate if it is spontaneous, peaceful and traditional. There is equal tyranny in repressing it as in doing violence to it.

The organisation of labour which the provisional government was instructed to take steps to carry out after the events of February affected property first of all, and then the institution of marriage and the family; the terms it was expressed in even implied an abolition (or redemption, if that term is preferred) of property. The socialists who opinionatedly insist on denying it after all the study devoted to the matter, or who deplore that other socialists have said this, have not even the sad excuse of ignorance; they are quite simply speaking in bad faith.

Before acting or deliberating on the matter the provisional government should have made a preliminary distinction of the *organic question* from the *executive question,* in other words, what was the field of competence of governmental power and what was not. Then, having made this distinction, its sole duty and its sole right was to invite the citizens themselves to produce, by the full exercise of their liberty, the new facts which it, the government, would then later be called upon either to exercise some control over or give a direction to in case of need.

---

10  The Concordat of 1801 was an agreement between Napoléon Bonaparte and Pope Pius VII that re-established the Roman Catholic Church in France and ended the breach caused by the church reforms of the French Revolution. The Roman Catholic faith was acknowledged as the religion of the majority of the French people but was not proclaimed as the established religion of the state. Napoléon gained the right to nominate bishops, but their offices were conferred by the pope. The state paid the clergy. To implement the concordat Napoléon issued in 1802 the so-called Organic Articles; these restated the traditional liberties of the Gallican church including resistance to papal authority. (Editor)

It is probable that the provisional government was not led by such lofty considerations; it is even to be supposed that such scruples would never had held it back. It only desired to revolutionise, but it did not know how to go about it. It was a mixture of conservatives, doctrinaire thinkers, Jacobins, socialists, each talking a different language. It would have been a miracle, considering what trouble they had agreeing on the slightest point regarding policy, if they had succeeded in reaching an understanding about something like a revolution. It was the discord reigning in the government camp, much more than the prudence of the generals, that preserved the country from the utopias of the provisional government: the disagreements that agitated it were its substitute for philosophy.

The mistake of the provisional government, its great mistake, was not to have been unable to build; it was to have been unable to demolish.

For instance, it would have been necessary to abolish the oppressive laws concerning individual freedom, put a stop to the scandal of arbitrary arrests, fix the limits of prevention... All they thought of was to defend the prerogatives of the magistracy, and the citizens' liberty was more than ever at the arbitrary mercy of the public prosecutor. It pleases the high police to convert a restaurant into a mousetrap; two hundred citizens gathered for a dinner are torn from their wives and children, beaten, thrown in prison, accused of conspiracy and then released after the investigative magistrate, who does not know himself what the police is accusing them of, has convinced himself at length that there is no charge to press against them.

It would have been necessary to disarm the powers that be, discharge half of the army, abolish military conscription, organise a citizens' army, remove the troops from the capital, and declare that the executive power could never under any circumstance and under any pretext dissolve and disarm the national guard.—Instead of that, the government busied itself with the formation of those twenty-four mobile battalions concerning whose utility and patriotism we were later, in June, instructed. As they were suspicious of the national guard they were far from declaring it inviolable: the successors to the provisional government have also not neglected to dissolve it.

It would have been necessary to guarantee the freedom of assembly, first by abolishing the law of 1790 and all such laws which might carry ambiguous implications, then by organising the political clubs around the representatives of the people, giving them entrance into parliamentary life. The organisation of popular societies was the pivot of democracy, the cornerstone of republican order. In place of organisation the provisional government had nothing to offer the clubs but tolerance and espionage, in the expectation that public indifference and the forces of reaction would cause them to vanish.

It would have been necessary to rip the nails and teeth off state power and hand over the government's public force to the citizens, not only in order to prevent the government from taking steps against liberty but to deprive

408 Pierre-Joseph Proudhon

governmental útopias of their last hope. Did they not prove the power of the State against the enterprises of minorities on the 16th of April and the 15th of May? Well, there would have been neither a 16th of April nor a 15th of May if the government, with its power of irresistible force, had not been an irresistible temptation to the impatience of democrats.

Everything was done in a topsy-turvy manner on the day after the February Revolution. The government wanted to do what was not within its rights to do, and for that purpose it preserved and indeed even augmented the power which it had taken from the July monarchy. It failed to do what it should have done, and for that purpose the revolution was repressed on the 17th of March, in the name of power, by those very persons who appeared to be the most energetic representatives of that revolution. Instead of rendering to the people its fecundity of initiative by subordinating power to its will, they attempted by means of power to resolve those problems on the subject of which time had not yet illuminated the masses; in order to ensure the so-called revolution, they performed a vanishing trick on liberty! Nothing appeared to be an option to these reformers in the way of what had been seen in the great revolutionary epochs: no impulses from below, no indication of popular opinion, not a single principle or discovery which might have received the people's sanction. And they alarmed the rational attitude of this same people by decrees which they themselves condemned. Being unable to justify them by any principles they pretended to excuse these decrees in the name of necessity! It was no longer, as it had been only recently, the antagonism of liberty and power; it was the infernal mock-marriage of the two.

Reread history, then, and you will see how revolutions emerge and are effected.

Before Luther, Descartes and the Encyclopédists, the State, that faithful expression of society, hands over heretics and philosophers to the executioners. Jan Hus, the precursor of Protestantism, is burned at Constance by the secular arm of the state after being condemned by the Council. But little by little rational thought insinuates itself into the hearts of the masses: soon the State pardons the innovators, it takes them as guides and consecrates their right. The Revolution of '89 derives from the same source: it was already formed in public opinion when it was declared by State power. In a totally different context of ideas, when has the State ever bothered about canals and railways? When has it wanted to have a steam-powered navy? Only after a multitude of experimental attempts and the publicly recognised success of the first entrepreneurs.

It has been the privilege of our epoch to attempt a revolution by the means of State power, something never seen heretofore, and then to have it rejected by the nation. Socialism existed and had been propagating itself for 18 years under the protection of the Charter, which recognised the *right of all French people to publish their opinions and have them printed*. When they dragged socialism to power the demagogues of February possessed the secret of stirring up intolerance of it and of causing it and even its ideas to be suppressed. It was they who by their fatal reversal of principles caused the antagonism between the bourgeoisie and the people to break out, an antagonism which had not manifested itself at all during the three days of 1848 or those of 1830, an antagonism which did not derive from the revolutionary idea and which was to result in the bloodiest catastrophe and the most ridiculous debacle.

While the provisional government, bereft of the genius of revolutions, separating itself both from the bourgeoisie and from the people at the same time, lost days and weeks in sterile and tentative actions, in agitations and circulars, a governmental socialism of God knows what sort caused heated public debate, put on dictatorial airs and,—something that amazes anybody who has not studied the mechanics of these contradictions,—itself gave the signal for resistance, in contravention of its own theory.

# CHAPTER X
### 23–26 JUNE: THE CAVAIGNAC REACTION

IF, HOWEVER, YOU persist in telling me, the provisional government had been comprised of more homogenous elements and more energetic men, if Barbès and Blanqui had been able to agree instead of opposing each other, if the elections had taken place a month sooner, if the socialists had hidden their theories for a while, if, if, if, etc.: you assert that things would have happened in a completely different way. The provisional government would have achieved the revolution in fifteen days. The national assembly, completely comprised of republicans, would have united and developed its work. We would not have had a March 17th, April 16th or May 15th, and you, clever historian, would not be so clever for theorising power's impotence and the government's revolutionary incapacity.

Let us think about this then, and since facts abound, let us cite them. March 17th, April 16th and May 15th have not convinced you, so I am going to tell you a story that will cause you to reflect, but before that, let us learn a little about what history is.

There are two ways of studying history: one I will call the *providential* method and the other one the *philosophical* method.

The first method is related to the cause of events, in which a superior will, God, that is, directs the course of things from on high, or a human will momentarily placed in a way to act on events through its free will, like God. This method does not exclude absolutely any design or systematic premeditation in history, but it has nothing of the necessary and could be revoked any time its author wants; it depends entirely on the determination of dignitaries and God's sovereign will. Furthermore, according to the theologians,

God could have created an infinite number of worlds that are different from the current one, and providence could have directed the course of events of infinity in other ways. If, for example, Alexander the Great, instead of dying at the age of 32, had lived until he was 60, if Caesar had been defeated at Pharsala, if Constantine had not gone to establish himself in Byzantium, if Charlemagne had not founded and consolidated the temporal power of the popes, if the Bastille had not been taken on July 14th or a detachment of grenadiers had chased the people's representatives away from the *Jeu de Paume*[11] as Bonaparte's did in St. Cloud,[12] isn't it true, the providential historian asks, that civilisation could have gone in another direction, that Catholicism would not have the same character and that Henry V or Louis XVII would be king?

We see that the basis of this theory is nothing other than chance. What the believer calls *providence* the sceptic calls *luck*: it is one and the same. Fieschi and Alibaud, believing that regicide hastened the triumph of democracy, and Bossuet, relating universal history to the establishment of the Roman apostolic Catholic Church, were from the same school. Based on historical science, there is no difference between absolute Pyrrhonism[13] and the deepest superstition. This policy of the last reign, without a system despite its pompous verbiage and unstable expedient politics, is really worth no more than Gregory VII's, a routine followed like Catholicism, its development profoundly blind, not knowing where it is going.

The philosophical method, while recognising that particular facts have nothing to do with fate, that they may vary infinitely, depending on whose wills produce them, consider them, however, as dependent on general laws inherent in nature and humanity. Those laws are the eternal and invariable idea of history: as for the facts they reveal, they are the arbitrary side of history, like the written characters that describe speech and the terms that express ideas. They could be changed indefinitely without the immanent thought they contain suffering as a result.

---

11  The Tennis Court Oath (*serment du Jeu de Paume*) was a pivotal event of the French Revolution. The meeting of the Estates-General of 20 June 1789 saw the members of the Third Estate and a few members of the First Estate pledge to continue to meet until a constitution had been written, despite royal prohibition. It was both revolutionary act and an assertion that political authority derived from the people rather than from the monarch. (Editor)

12  The Château de Saint-Cloud was the site of the *coup d'état* led by Napoléon Bonaparte that overthrew the French Directory in 1799. (Editor)

13  The sceptical philosophy of Pyrrho, a Greek philosopher, who asserted that since all perceptions tend to be faulty, the wise man will consider the external circumstances of life to be unimportant and thus preserve tranquillity. In short, extreme or absolute scepticism. (Editor)

Therefore, to respond to the objection made to me, the provisional government could have been comprised of other men, Louis Blanc could have stayed, Barbès and Blanqui could have avoided complicating such an already complex situation with their rival influence, and the majority of the national assembly could have been more democratic: all this, I say, and many more things as well could have been possible, and events would have been completely different from those we have seen: this is the accidental, the *contingent* side of history.

But given the series of revolutions in which the modern world is engaged, a series that itself results from the conditions of the human mind, as well as a prejudice everyone simultaneously accepts and opposes, according to which it is the constituted authority of the nation [that is] to take the initiative of reform and direct the movement, I say that the events that had to be deduced from it, whatever they were, fortunate or unfortunate, could only have been the expression of the fatal struggle between tradition and the Revolution.

All the incidents we have seen since February take their meaning from this double fact: on one hand, an economic and social revolution that, I dare say, is urgently is called for following the twenty previous political, philosophical and religious revolutions, and on the other hand, faith in power that instantly falsifies the Revolution by giving it an absurd and anti-liberal face. Once again, the February Revolution could have had a different plot, different actors, roles or *themes*. The show, instead of being a tragedy, could have been merely a melodrama, but the meaning and morality of the play would have remained the same.

According to this philosophical conception of history, the general facts are classified and produced in succession with a deductive rigour that nothing in the positive sciences surpasses, and as it is possible for reason to articulate their philosophy, so is it possible for human prudence to direct their course. In the providential theory, on the contrary, history is no more than a fictional imbroglio without principle, reason or purpose, an argument for superstition as it is for atheism and an outrage against the mind and conscience.

What maintains faith in providence is the involuntary confusion of the laws of society with the accidents that comprise its staging. The vulgar perceive a certain logic in the general facts and relate the detailing facts to the same source, neither the purpose nor necessity of which they discover, because, in fact, that necessity does not exist, and they conclude that a providential will completely settles the smallest and greatest matters, *the contingent and the necessary* alike, and as the Schoolmen say,[14] all that is simply a contradiction. For us, providence in history is the same thing as supernatural revelation in philosophy, arbitrariness in government and abuse in property.

We are going to see in the event that I have to describe that, while democracy, on the one hand, and the conservative party, on the other, obey

---

14    The Scholastic theologians and philosophers of the middle ages. (Editor)

the same passions, striving with equal ardour to exert pressure favourable to their ideas on events, history unfolds following its own laws with syllogistic precision.

The provisional government had guaranteed the right to work in the most formal manner. It had made that guarantee in accordance with its claimed initiative, and the people accepted it as such. Both parties had made the commitment in good faith: how many people in France on February 24th, even among the most virulent adversaries of socialism, would have believed it impossible that a state as highly organised as ours, as abundantly equipped with resources, could ensure work for a few hundred thousand workers? The matter seemed so easy, so simple; conviction in this regard was so general that the most resistant to the new order of things were happy to end the revolution on that note. Furthermore, there was nothing to haggle over: the people were master, and when, after toiling all day in the heat, they only demanded more work as payment for their sovereignty, the people could rightly pass for the most just of kings and the most moderate of conquerors.

Three months had been given to the provisional government to honour its obligation. The three months elapsed, and the work did not come. The demonstration of May 15th created some disorder in relations, so the bill the people had issued to the government was renewed, but the deadline approached, and nothing led the people to believe it would be paid.

—"Give us work yourselves," the workers told the government, "if the entrepreneurs cannot restart their production."

To this proposal from the workers, the government responded with a triple estoppel:

—"We do not have any money and therefore cannot guarantee wages for you;"

"We only make your products for ourselves and would not know to whom we could sell them. "

"And even if we could sell them, that would not help us at all because, due to our competition, free industry would be stopped and would send us back its workers."

—"In that case, take over all industry, transportation and even agriculture, and take the workers back."

—"We cannot do it," replied the government. "Such a plan would be community and universal, absolute servitude against which the vast majority of the citizens protest. They proved it on March 17th, April 16th and May 15th and by sending us an assembly comprised of nine-tenths of the partisans of free competition, free trade and free and independent property. What do you want us to do against the will of 35 million citizens opposed to your will, oh unfortunate workers, you who saved us from dictatorship on March 17th?"

—"Give us credit then; advance us capital, and organise state sponsorship."

—"You have no security to offer us," observed the government. "And as we have told you, everyone knows that we do not have any money."

—"You told us, 'It is up to the state to give credit, not to receive it!' and we have not forgotten it. Create paper money; we accept it in advance and will pass it onto others."

—*"Fiat money! Assignats!"* the government responded despondently. "We can force payment, but we cannot force sales. Your paper money will fall after three months of depreciation, and your misery will be worse."

—"Then the February Revolution means nothing!" the workers told each other with concern. "Do we have to die again for having made it?"

The provisional government, not being able to organise work, give credit or conduct the rest of the routine business of all governments, had hoped that, with time and order, it would bring back confidence, that work would re-establish itself, that in the meantime it would suffice to offer the working masses, who could not be abandoned to their distress, a food subsidy.

Such was the thought behind the *national workshops*, a humane and well-intended but amazingly impotent idea. It was painful, perhaps dangerous, to rudely tell these men who had believed for a moment in their coming emancipation to return to their worksites and solicit their bosses' benevolence again: this was seen as treason toward the people, and until May 15th, although they were not the government, the people were king. But on the other hand, the provisional government soon perceived that the economic renovation necessary to satisfy the people was not the business of the state; it had sensed that the nation detested this revolutionary method. It increasingly felt that what had been proposed to it in the name of the *organisation of work* and that had been believed to be so easy was forbidden to it. Not seeing any way out of this labyrinth, it waited while doing its best to restart business and feed unemployed workers, for which no one could surely accuse it of committing a crime.

But here again, the government deluded itself with the most fatal illusion.

The doctrinaire party, rallying to the absolutist party, spoke aloud after the May 15th debacle. It ruled the government and the assembly and, from the podium and through its newspapers, gave France its slogan, republican if you like, but conservative above all. Meanwhile, the democrats, because they were tightening [government] power, were in the process of losing it themselves, and the doctrinaires, pushed on by the Jesuits, were preparing to snatch it back. They could not allow the favourable opportunity to escape them.

The government's opponents then claimed that the re-establishment of order and, consequently, the return of confidence, were incompatible with the existence of the national workshops, that if we seriously wanted to revive labour, it was necessary to start by dissolving those workshops. Therefore, the government found itself doubly trapped within a circle, cornered by the impossibilities that had sprung up, whether they wanted to procure work for the workers or only give them credit, whether they wanted to send them home or to feed them for a time.

The reaction proved to be especially intractable because it thought, not without reason, that the national workshops, then including more than 100,000 men, were the road to socialism, and that once this army was dispersed, we would have a healthy market and democracy, while the executive commission perhaps thought that it could put an end to the republic before discussing the constitution. They were in a strong position: they decided to follow their luck and profit from it. These men, so sensitive towards the bankrupt with regard to their annuities, were ready to violate the promise the provisional government made in the country's name, to make the workers with guaranteed work bankrupt, and, as needed, to impose that bankruptcy by force.

The situation was as follows:

As the price of the February Revolution and in view of their opinion on the quality of [those in] power, the provisional government and the people had agreed that the people would waive their sovereignty and that the government, in taking power, would commit to guaranteeing work in less than three months.

Because the execution of the agreement was impossible, the national assembly refused to agree to it.

Either a transaction would take place or, if the two parties were stubborn, there would be a catastrophe.

To one party, humanity, respect for sworn belief and concern for peace, and to the other party, the republic's financial trouble, the difficulties of the issue, and the demonstrated incompetence of power, demanded that they reach a compromise. This is what was understood by the partisans of the national workshops, represented by their delegates, but above all, by their new director, Lalanne, and by the minister of public works, Trélat, who, in these deplorable days, conducted himself as a man of courage and did his duty.

Because this part of the facts on the June insurrection has remained highly obscure up until now, the *Report of the Inquest*[15] on the June events not bothering to mention it although it reveals the cause of those bloody days, I will go into a few details. The people have to know what enemies they had to make and how revolutions are evaded; the bourgeoisie also have to know how their terrors are exploited and what schemers use their feelings of loyal moderation in their detestable politics. M. Lalanne himself provided me with the main information. On this occasion, he displayed a kindness for which I cannot thank him enough here.

The executive commission had just formed a ministry. On May 12th, Trélat was called to public works, the department responsible for the national workshops. He immediately saw the dangers of the situation and started

---

15   Referring to the findings of a government commission, published as *Rapport de la commission d'enquête sur l'insurrection qui a éclaté dans la journée du 23 juin et sur les événements du 15 mai* (Paris: Imprimerie de l'Assemblée Nationale, 1848). (Editor.)

looking for the means to ward it off. On the 17th, despite the problems of the 15th, he instituted a commission that he charged with reporting on the national workshops and proposing a solution. The next day, the 18th, this commission met and deliberated for the entire day without stopping. The report was drafted the following night, read to the commission on the morning of the 19th, discussed and decreed in this second session, copied and immediately delivered to the minister. After hearing it read, Trélat declared that he adopted all its conclusions and ordered that it be printed, and by the 20th at two o'clock, the national treasury had produced 1,200 copies intended for the national assembly and the main administrations. Distribution had to take place that same day.

Suddenly, the order was given to stop distribution: the executive commission had decided that not one copy must leave the minister's office, fearing that the conclusions of the Report, in which certain principles were expressed, including the right to work, would face violent opposition in the national assembly. Since May 15th, hostile emotions had started to arise: there was no reason to provide a pretext for them to explode. While only daring could have saved it, the executive commission gave in to fear: the time for its withdrawal had come.

Impeded right from the start on the prudent yet radical path of reform to which he was committed, the minister was not disheartened. At least he tried to eradicate the most glaring abuses among those that the commission had indicated to him, but he only received unfulfilled promises from the young director who had presided over the creation of the national workshops from the start. It was said that an evil spirit fought to simultaneously aggravate the illness and hinder the cure. A few days were lost in useless efforts. Trélat wanted to overcome the inertia that he encountered, give more authority to his orders and surround himself with more intelligence in order to reconstitute the commission with experienced administrators who represented various ministerial departments. That commission met on May 26th, presided over by the minister. It called the director and soon recognised that it could expect nothing from him. He was replaced the same day.

From this time on, the *National Workshops Commission* modified, extended or restricted each proposal of the first report. It was first concerned with reforming abuses. It reduced the offices that had grown excessively, replaced day labour with work by the job, organised, with the help of the municipal authorities, some control, and, from the start, recognised that out of 120,000 registered names 25,000 had to be deleted for double or triple entries. But all of these measures were pure repression. It was not enough to gradually reduce the cadres of this large army without providing work for those it had dismissed. The commission sensed this, and it was its unending preoccupation.

It successively presented to the minister special proposals designed to reassure workers about the intentions of power. Encouragement to workers' associations, Algerian colonisation on a grand scale, a law on industrial tribunals [*prud'hommes*] and the organisation of a pension and assistance system: this is what it proposed to do in response to the working classes' legitimate demands. Export premiums, wage advances, direct orders and a guarantee on certain manufactured objects were the measures that it indicated in favour of merchants and industrialists. The bourgeoisie and the workers shared the commission's solicitude equally as if the commission considered their interests as one. It did not separate them in its encouragement or credit projects. It valued the total expenditure to be distributed among the various ministerial departments at 200 million francs but was convinced that this was a productive expense, an apparent cost, not an actual one, much less burdensome for the country than the consequences of more unemployment.

Trélat completely adopted these views. In fact, it was no longer an issue of communism, egalitarian organisation or the state's universal grip on work and property. It was simply returning to the status quo, of re-entering the rut out of which the February shake-up had pushed us. Trélat vainly tried to introduce these ideas into national assembly commissions. They objected to the poverty of the treasury but did not want to see that it was a question of saving the treasury itself by returning its exhausted receipts to it through a large distribution of credit. They feigned not to understand that the sacrifices made to labour benefited the workers even less than the employers and that, after all, the bourgeoisie was still the party most interested in this tutelary resumption of work.—"200 million francs to hire an army of 100,000 men?!" cried the calculating Baron Charles Dupin, as if 100,000 men in the national workshops were not a minimal fraction of the then-unemployed working class. Ah! If, instead of workers, it were an issue of a railroad company!—"200 million! Is that expensive? It would be a shame to admit that, to keep the public peace, it was necessary to pay each of our 100,000 workers a bonus of 2,000 francs, to which we never would have agreed. At most, we could, by pronouncing immediate dissolution, give each worker three months salary (100 francs), 10 million in all, which is far from 200. With this advance, the workers would no doubt withdraw in satisfaction."

"And in three months?" asked Director Lalanne.

But it was really an issue of reasoning! Cries were raised against any project intended to manage transitions. They wanted NONE OF THAT. They said it very quietly at first, and then they cautiously contented themselves with raising deaf opposition to the government's acts. Soon afterwards, they got braver and decided to run the risk of a terrible struggle. The voice incessantly repeating that they would have *none of it*, which could be heard behind the doors of national assembly offices, troubled and exasperated the masses. However, the workers, already far enough past the time when they were assigned to a three month term with the agricultural-industrial organisation, all agreed to return to their employers, the only guarantee given to them being the new law on industrial tribunals [*prud'hommes*], voted in on then-minister of commerce Flocon's initiative.

Some work! Some useful work! Such were the cries of the united and unanimous voices of 800 workers raised throughout the month of June.

"Yes!" cried Trélat, in one of the finest inspirations the French podium has had: "the national assembly must decree work just as the convention decreed victory before!" This noble language brought a smile to the Malthusians' lips. In agreement with the minister, Director Lalanne vainly tried to announce that we were reaching a catastrophic point to a national assembly commission on June 18th and a labour committee on the 20th. Their ears remained closed to the truth, their eyes shut to the light. The spell was cast! Dissolution was decided and would be carried out at all costs. At the June 23rd session, citizen de Falloux came to read the report, which concluded with the immediate dismissal of the workers, in return for an unemployment benefit of three million francs, or about 30 francs per worker! Thirty francs for trampling on the revolution! Thirty francs for monopoly's ransom! Thirty francs in exchange for an eternity of misery! It was like the 30 pieces of silver Judas was paid for the blood of Jesus Christ! In response to the offer, the workers took to the barricades.

I said that it was up to the partisans of the national workshops to reach a peaceful conclusion. As a loyal historian, I am going to give the other side of the story so that the reader knows what each side's intentions and responsibility were in this dismal drama.

All my documents are taken from *Le Moniteur*.

In a hurry to terminate [the matter], the government, through a ministerial decision, at first offered workers between the ages of 17 and 25 the alternative of joining the army or, if they refused, of being excluded from the national workshops—starvation or slavery: that is how the doctrinaires intended to proceed with dissolving the national workshops.

On June 21st, the executive commission gave orders for the enlistment to begin right away. *Le Moniteur* reported:

"*The public and the workers themselves will see with pleasure that, through this measure, we are finally approaching a solution to this serious question.* The national workshops were an unavoidable necessity for some time: now *they are an obstacle* to the re-establishment of industry and work. Therefore, it is important, *in the most urgent interest of the workers themselves*, that the workshops are dissolved, and we are convinced that the workers will understand this painlessly, thanks to the common sense and intelligent patriotism that they have so often demonstrated."

On June 22nd, the government informed the workers that, according to the legislation, enlistment could only be contracted at age 18 but that, to facilitate the dissolution of the national workshops, a draft decree before the national assembly at that time *lowered the minimum age for voluntary enlistment to 17.*

The age of apprenticeship became the age of conscription! What touching concern! What a commentary on Malthus' theory!

While the executive commission attended to this urgent concern and the workers committee buried itself in investigations, reports, discussions and projects, the Jesuitical reaction harassed the minister of public works and terrified the national assembly on the communist consequences of the repurchase of the railroads, that it was clear that the hand of the state prepared to seize free labour and property. M. de Montalembert, with the most treacherous opportunism, quoted the following passage from the newspaper *La République* written under the influence of the prevailing theory of governmental initiative:

"We will not try to avoid the problem; nothing is gained by trickery with businessmen... *Yes, it is an issue of your property and of your society in which it acts.* Yes, it is about substituting legitimate property for usurped property, the association of all members of the human family in the political city, for the city of wolves against wolves which is the cause of your sorrows. Yes, the return of the public domain of transportation to the State, which you have dispossessed, is the first link in the chain of social questions that the Revolution of 1848 holds within the folds of its virile robe."[16]

But, honest Jesuit, take for the execution and exploitation of the railroads any system you like, provided that the country is not robbed, that transportation is conducted at a low price, that the workers work; and leave the *République* behind with the *Gazette* and the *Constitutionnel*!

But it was in the June 23rd session, where each speech, each sentence arising from the podium made you hear the boom of the cannons and rumble of the gunfire and where it was necessary to follow the plot of the Jesuitical coalition.

The session began with a military bulletin. The speaker informed the National Assembly that the republican guard, marching with the national guard, had just removed two Rue Planche-Mibray barricades and that line troops had fired several volleys on the boulevards.

After that communiqué, citizen Bineau asked for the floor for a motion of procedure. The day before, after the session, the minister of public works had presented a six million franc request for credit for work to be performed on the railroad between Châlon and Lyon around Collongé. In both Lyons and Paris, there were many workers demanding work, and the best the minister could do was use them on that line, the production of which

16   At the June 22nd session of the National Assembly, deputy Charles de Montalembert (1810–1870) had read this passage aloud as evidence of the danger that nationalising the railroads would set a socialistic precedent. He was careful to point out that this very passage from *La République* had been "reproduced with praise in another journal, *Le Représentant du Peuple*, directed, if I am not mistaken, by one of our most celebrated colleagues, the honourable M. Proudhon." (Editor.)

was permanently stopped. However, citizen Bineau objected that the credit could not be granted because the repurchase law had not been voted in yet, and it would not be acceptable to start the work before allocating the credit.

Trélat exclaimed that he could not understand such an opposition because, if repurchase were not voted in, then the company would have to reimburse the amount for the work, and therefore nothing prevented the workers from doing it. However, the discussion of the credit proposal was postponed upon finance minister Duclerc's motion.

The incident then dropped, minister of commerce and agriculture Flocon went to the podium. He spoke about the seriousness of the events and said that the government was ready. Flocon, no doubt believing that the insurgent masses could be held back by casting the insurrection in a dishonourable light, *loudly declared*, he said, *so that he could be heard outside,* that the agitators' only flag was disorder and that there was more than one hidden pretender behind them, supported by foreign interests. Therefore, he begged all good republicans to distance themselves from the cause of despotism.

This unfortunate ploy only managed to inflame the national guards without appeasing the workers and made the repression more merciless.

Once the struggle began, there was no retreating. M. de Falloux chose this moment to deposit the national workshop dissolution report on the podium, the workers being aware of that report's conclusions for two days, as we have seen. We can say that in this way he lit the fuse setting off the June explosion. Citizen Raynal vainly opposed the reading of the report: "I do not believe," he cried, "that this is the right time to read it," but shouts of "Read it! Read it!" arose on all sides.

So M. de Falloux read the report.

Corbon observed that the workers committee, while agreeing with the dissolution, had recognised that it must only be started after the workers were given the guarantees to which they were entitled, and that the committee had prepared a decree for that purpose, the provisions of which the committee announced. The decree was retracted.

Here, the discussion was interrupted by a new communiqué from the president on the battle exploits going on outside. It announced that gunfire had started on the boulevards, that barricades were going up in the city and that a working-class woman was wounded in the shoulder. All of Paris was up in arms!

Upon these words, the irrepressible Créton asked for the floor to declare the *urgency* of the following proposal:

"As soon as possible, the executive commission will file a detailed report of all the receipts and expenses occurring in the 127 days between February 24th and June 1st, 1848."

This was the process conducted in the provisional government and the executive commission. While it was forced to dissolve the national workshops, the only support it still had, and to please its enemies, shot its own soldiers in the streets, and all of its members risked their lives on the barricades, it was betrayed at the witness box, and its accounts were demanded. The men of God did not waste any time: providence protected them. Urgency was deemed appropriate.

Then the discussion of the railroad repurchase was taken back up. Citizen Jobez had the floor:

"Whatever the seriousness of the circumstances, I believe that this discussion must go through the phases that it would have followed at a calm and peaceful time. A committed partisan of state execution of major public works, I am here to oppose the repurchase plan presented to you and to support the conclusions of your finance commission."

Now why would this young representative, the most decent and moderate of all the republicans of the future, change his opinion so dramatically?

Ah! Because the government had made it known that it was counting on the adoption of the railroad repurchase plan to give the workers useful work and, by taking that resource from the government, they trapped the revolution between a rock and a hard place. The workers demanded work, but Jobez, who agreed with Bineau, said that there was none. Jobez continued:

"Since the national assembly meeting, every time we talk about the national workshops, you answer us with the railroad repurchase. And when we say that without that purchase, you have 311 million francs worth of work to be performed, all or part of which the national workshops could conduct, you tell us to give you the repurchase law. The arguments are always the same, and by a singular coincidence, it turns out that the national workshop inventory requested since the national assembly meeting has not yet been accomplished and that all the work that was selected is on Paris' doorstep."

Pure distraction. It was not an issue of work that the government had to perform (it has work for several billion) but rather of the sums that it could apply to it. However, it believed that the railroad repurchase law before it could procure more money and, above all, more credit, and so that law was eminently favourable to the occupation of the the workers.

On March 17th, the people requested that the provisional government pull back the troops, but that could not be obtained. On June 23rd, the reaction imposed the dispersion of the national workshops on the executive commission: that is, the dispersion of the people, which was granted right away. That rapprochement is revealing.

Citizen Jobez had barely come down from the podium when the minister of war, General Cavaignac, took it to provide new information on the insurrection. The rioters were chased away from the Saint Denis and Saint Martin suburbs and no longer occupied the Saint Jacques and Saint Antoine neighbourhoods. The national guard, the roving guard, the republican guard and finally the line troops (because all the forces at power's disposal were united against the people) were enlivened with the finest spirit.

Thus, the National Assembly paid the provisional government's debt with gunfire! Well! I wonder who were guiltier, the insurgents of March, April and

May or the June provocateurs, those who solicited the government for work or those who made it expend 2,500,000 cartridges to refuse that work.

But could there have been the cannons against the innocent if there had not been the reinforcement of slander? At the same time that General Cavaignac explained his strategic provisions to the national assembly, the mayor of Paris, A. Marrast, wrote the following circular to the municipalities of 12 wards. You could call it an edict of Diocletian:[17]

"Paris, June 23, 1848, 3 p.m.

"Citizen Mayor

"Since this morning, you have witnessed the attempted efforts of *a small number of troublemakers* to alarm the public as much as possible.

"The enemies of the republic wear many masks. They exploit all misfortune and all difficulties produced by events."—(Who then exploited the difficulty if it were not the same people who pretended to complain about it the most?)—"Foreign agents join with them, provoke them and *pay* them. It is not only civil war that they would like to foment among us, but looting and social disorder. They are preparing the very ruin of France, and we can guess for what purpose.

"Paris is the main seat of these infamous intrigues, but it will not become the capital of disorder. The national guard, which is the chief guardian of the public peace *and property*, indeed understands that it must, above all, act in *its own interests, to its own credit* and honour. If it gives way, it would be giving up the entire country to all dangers, *exposing families and property to the most terrifying calamities.*

"Garrison troops are armed, numerous and perfectly disposed. The national guard is in its quarters along the streets. Authority and the national guard will each do its duty."

The Senate's proclamation was even more furious. I will quote only a few of their words:

"They are not demanding the republic! It has already been proclaimed."

"Universal suffrage? It is completely accepted and practiced!"

"What do they want then? We already know: they want anarchy, arson and looting!"

Was a plot ever carried out with more implacable perseverance? Were famine and civil war ever exploited with more villainous skill? But they would be mistaken if they believed that I accuse all these men of wanting the

---

17  Gaius Aurelius Valerius Diocletianus (244–311), commonly known as Diocletian, was a Roman Emperor. He issued a series of edicts rescinding the legal rights of Christians and demanding that they comply with traditional religious practices. The Diocletianic Persecution was the last and most severe persecution of Christians in the Roman Empire. The edicts were unsuccessful and strengthened the resolve of the Christians. Diocletian also issued an imperial edict fixing a maximum price for provisions and other articles of commerce, and a maximum rate of wages. (Editor)

misery and massacre of 100,000 of their brothers for the interests of a clique. In all of this, there is only one collective thought that develops with all the more furious energy, the less the awareness that each of them who expresses it has of his fateful role, and insofar as, while exercising his right of initiative, he cannot take responsibility for his words. Individuals are capable of clemency, but parties are merciless. There was a great spirit of conciliation among the partisans of the national workshops: they were organised and had men speaking in their name and answering for them, Trélat and Lalanne. The reactionary party, left to its own fanatical instincts, did not want to listen to anything, since it was not represented and acted without answering for its actions. In a political struggle, do you want to murder your adversary without incurring the ignominy of the crime? No deliberation and the secret ballot.

After Cavaignac, Garnier-Pagès, lost soul, his voice full of sobs, took the reactionary elation to its height. "We have to finish them!" he shouted (Yes! Yes!): "We have to finish with the agitators!" (Yes! Yes! Bravo! Bravo!)

Citizen Bonjean proposed that a commission be named to march with the national guard and troops "and die if necessary leading them for the defence of order!" The motion was greeted with delight.

Mauguin asked that the Assembly be permanently constituted. That was adopted. Reports circulated, and news from the battlefield became increasingly serious. Considérant proposed writing a proclamation to the workers to reassure them about their fate and end the fratricidal war, but the parties were merciless. They wanted no reconciliation and did not even allow the author of the proposal to read it. It was withdrawn by the preliminary question. That—"Our duty is to remain unshaken in our position," the stoic Baze responded, "without deliberating with the mob, without coming to any terms with them whatsoever by discussing a proclamation."

Caussidières' blood was boiling. He was incensed.—"I demand," he shouted, "that some of the deputies, accompanied by a member of the executive commission, go into the heart of the insurrection and make a proclamation by torchlight." The Montagnard's words were greeted with cries:— "Order! You are talking like one of the rioters! M. President, suspend the session!" Minister Duclerc, who would soon fall to the blows of the reaction, called the proposal foolish.

Baune agreed with Caussidière. There were more cries of "Suspend the session!"

Upon the new details General Cavaignac provided, Lagrange tried bringing it up again, but there were cries of "Suspend the session!" from every direction. Finally, the outcome approached, and the word of the intrigue was revealed. Pascal Duprat proposed that Paris be declared under a state of siege and all powers granted to General Cavaignac.

—"I am opposed to dictatorship!" shouted Larabit.

Tréveneuc: "All of the national guard is asking for a state of siege."

Langlois: "It is what the people want."

Bastide: "Hurry up. In an hour, the *Hôtel-de-Ville* will be taken."

Germain Sarrut: "In the name of memories of 1832,[18] we protest against the state of siege" (Cries of "Order!")

Quentin Bauchart and others wanted to add an additional article to Pascal Duprat's proposal as follows: "The executive commission is ceasing its functions immediately."—"This is a grievance," finance minister Duclerc responded disdainfully.

Finally, they announced that the executive commission, which for twenty-four hours had been running from barricade to barricade on behalf of the "*decent*" and "*moderate*" and making them fire on their own troops, not waiting for them to depose it, resigned its duties. Now it was up to the sabre to do the rest: the curtain fell on the fourth act of the February Revolution.

"Oh, toiling people! Disinherited, harassed and outcast people! People whom they imprison, judge and kill! Scorned and dishonoured people! Will you not stop lending an ear to these orators of mysticism who, instead of calling upon your initiative, ceaselessly talk to you about heaven and the state, promising salvation soon through religion and government, and whose vehement and hollow words captivate you?

"Power, the instrument of collective might, created in society as a mediator between labour and capital, finds itself inevitably chained to capital and directed against the proletariat. No political reform can solve this contradiction because, according to the confession of the politicians themselves, such a reform would only result in increasing power's energy and scope, and, without overturning hierarchy and dissolving society, power could not affect the prerogatives of monopoly. The problem before the working classes then is not to conquer but to overcome at the same time power and monopoly, which means creating, out of the people's guts and labour's profundity, a greater authority, a more powerful fact, that surrounds and subjugates capital and the state. Every proposed reform that does not satisfy this condition is simply one more scourge, a rod on sentry duty, *virgam vigilantem*, as a prophet said, which threatens the proletariat."[19]

These lines, written in 1845, are the prophecy of the events that we have seen take place in 1848 and 1849. It is by stubbornly wanting revolution through power and social reform through political reform that the February Revolution was postponed, and the cause of the proletariat and nationalities was lost by all of Europe.[20]

---

18  Reference to state repression of a popular revolt in Paris under the Monarchy on 5–6 June 1832 with at least 150 killed. (Editor)

19  Proudhon, *System of Economic Contradictions or the Philosophy of Poverty*, 1846.

20  Five months after the June days, a cabal formed within the party of so-called decent and moderate Republicans tried to place upon General Cavaignac the sole responsibility for the civil war. If, they argued, the General, heeding the warnings and entreaties of the Executive Committee, had called more troops than he had been asked to, and earlier, and if he had launched his soldiers against the barricades from the first day instead of

allowing the insurgency to develop freely, events would have taken place differently, and Paris would not have been delivered, for four days, into the horrors of civil war.

It was quietly concluded that the riot had been favoured, the massacre prepared, organised, by General Cavaignac, in connivance with MM. Senard and Marrast, in order for the three of them to capture the government and form a triumvirate.

These rumours gave rise, on November 25th, 1848, to a solemn discussion in the Constituent Assembly, which, on the motion of Dupont (from the Eure district), declared that General Cavaignac had deserved well of his country. But the blow had been struck; the extreme left, which should have been on its guard against such gossip in view of the circumstances in which the charges had been made, the memory of the facts, and the loyalty with which General Cavaignac returned his powers, received them greedily, and General Cavaignac, whose explanations were not as conclusive as could have been expected, since in his position any recrimination was forbidden, General Cavaignac, victor of June, remained the scapegoat.

We, with no coterie interests, no personal grievances, animated by no rivalries or ambition, we can tell the truth.

Yes, there was provocation, machination, conspiracy against the Republic, in June 1848: the facts we have recounted, all of which are genuine, prove it. The national workshops were the pretext, the dissolution of these workshops was the signal.

But in this plot, everyone's hands were dirty, directly or indirectly, with or without premeditation: First, the Legitimists, the Orleanists, the Bonapartists, whose orators led the Assembly and opinion while their agents inflamed the riot; secondly, the Republican moderates, including MM. Arago, Garnier-Pages, Duclerc, Pagnerre, etc., all of whom played an active role in the repression; and finally, the Mountain, whose inertia in these deplorable times has earned them history's harshest reprimand.

Without doubt, General Cavaignac had his share in the intrigues within the Assembly, within and under the Executive Committee. But to make him the leader of the conspiracy, and moreover out of ambition—he, who only thought to get rid of the competition of Louis Bonaparte while he could—that would be to gratuitously attribute to him *before* the fact notions of ascendancy that he did not even conceive *afterward*.

General Cavaignac was the tool of an anonymous and virtually leaderless reaction against the socialist Republic that had formed out of the hostility of some, the inertia of others, and the fear and madness of all. As to the General's strategic arrangements, so strongly criticised, I will say, without setting myself up as judge, that it does not belong to the *reds* to criticize; that to reproach Cavaignac for having lacked energy and speed in suppressing the riot is to join, from another point of view, in provocation, in approving the recall of the troops which the People protested against: Finally, if the non-bloody victories of General Changarnier on January 29th and June 13th, 1849 appear to cast doubt on General Cavaignac's abilities, then one must not place such value on the strength and courage of the rebels in June 1848. To acknowledge the strength of General Cavaignac, we end up slandering the insurgency and pouring contempt on all the great days of popular action, from July 14th, 1789 to February 1848.

Combatants of June, the principle of your defeat is in the February 25th decree! They abused you, those who made, in the name of power, a promise that power could not keep. The defeat of power, that is to say, the reabsorption of power by the people through the separate centralisation of political and social functions; the defeat of capital through the mutual guarantee of circulation and credit: that is what the politics of democracy had to be. Is that so difficult to understand?

In March, April and May, instead of organising yourselves for work and freedom by benefiting from the political advantages the February victory gave you, you ran to the government and asked from it what you alone could give yourselves and set the revolution back three steps. In June, victims of a despicable lack of faith, you had the misfortune of giving in to indignation and anger: you threw yourselves into the trap set six weeks before. Your error was in demanding that power fulfil a promise it could not keep: your mistake was fighting against the representatives of the nation and the government of the republic. Without a doubt, your enemies did not collect the fruit of their intrigue; without a doubt, your martyrdom made you grow: you are a hundred times stronger today than you were in the first stage of siege, and you can attribute your later successes to the justice of your cause. But it must be acknowledged that, because victory could not give you anything more than what you already possessed, the power of planning production and markets yourselves, your victory was lost beforehand. You were the soldiers of the republic, the soldiers of order and freedom. Never accuse the entirety of the largest portion of the people of treason; do not hold on to any resentment for your deceived brothers who fought you. Only those who seduced you with disastrous utopias should beat their breasts: as for those who, in these days of mourning, only had enough intelligence to exploit your misery, I hope that they never abuse enough of their temporary power to call down too many just reprisals on their heads.

For me, the memory of the days of June will be forever remorseful in my heart. I state it with sadness: until the 25th, I had predicted nothing, known nothing and guessed nothing. Elected fifteen days before as a representative of the people, I entered the national assembly with the shyness of the child and the ardour of a neophyte. Always in attendance from nine o'clock in the morning at the office and committee meetings, I only left the assembly at night, exhausted with fatigue and disgust. Since I first set foot on this parliamentary Sinai, I ceased to be in contact with the masses: by absorbing myself in my legislative work, I had completely lost view of current affairs. I knew nothing about the national workshop situation, government policy or the intrigues going on within the assembly. One has to experience this isolation called a national assembly to understand how the men who are the most completely ignorant of the state of a country are nearly always those who represent it. I set about reading everything that the distribution office provided to representatives: proposals, reports, brochures and even *Le Moniteur* and the law bulletin. Most of my colleagues on the left and the extreme left were in the same state of mental perplexity and ignorance of daily reality. We only talked about the national workshops with a kind of dread: because the fear of the people is the evil of all those who belong to authority: for power, the people are the enemy. Every day, we voted on new subsidies for the national workshops while trembling before the incompetence of power and with our own powerlessness.

What a disastrous apprenticeship! The effect of this representative waste I had to experience was that I had no intelligence of anything. On the 23rd, when Flocon declared from the podium that the movement was being directed by political factions and supported from abroad, I let myself accept that baseless ministerial story, and on the 24th, I again asked if the real reason for the insurrection was the dissolution of the national workshops!!! No, M. Senard, I was not a coward in June, the insult you threw at me before the assembly. Like you and many others, I was an imbecile. I was lacking in my duties as a representative due to a parliamentary stupor. I was there to see, but I did not see. I was there to sound the alarm, but I did not cry out! I was like the dog that does not bark in the presence of the enemy. As an elected representative of working people, a journalist of the proletariat, I was not supposed to leave the masses without direction and advice: 100,000 regimented men deserved my concern. They were worth more than my dejection in your offices. Since then, I have done what I can to repair my irreparable error. I have not always been fortunate. I have often been mistaken: my conscience no longer reproaches me for anything.

# CHAPTER XIV
## 4 NOVEMBER: THE CONSTITUTION

ON 4TH NOVEMBER 1848 the complete Constitution was voted on. There were 769 Representatives present at the session: 739 voted for and 30 against. Of these 30 votes against the motion, 16 were democrat-socialists and 14 legitimists. M. Odilon Barrot, current head of the ministry, abstained.

On the very day of the vote I found it necessary to have a letter published in *Le Moniteur* explaining the motives that had determined my position. Here is that letter:

"Sir,
"The national Assembly has just proclaimed the Constitution to prolonged cries of: *Long Live the Republic!*
"I took part in my colleagues' exaltation of the Republic; I put a blue ticket in the urn against the Constitution. I could not have seen my way to abstaining in such solemn

circumstances, after four months of discussion; I would find it incomprehensible, after my vote, not to be permitted to explain myself.

"I did not vote against the Constitution in a vain spirit of opposition or as a form of revolutionary agitation, because the Constitution contained things I wished to eliminate or did not contain others that I wished to put in it. If reasons like that could predominate in a representative's mind then there would never be any votes on any laws at all.

"I voted against the Constitution because it is a Constitution. The essence of a constitution—I mean a political constitution, there cannot be any question here of any other sort—is the division of sovereignty, in other words the separation into two powers, legislative and executive. That is the principle and the essence of any political constitution; outside that there is no constitution in the present sense of the word, there is only a sovereign authority, making its laws and implementing them by means of its committees and ministers.[21]

"We are not at all accustomed to such an organisation of sovereignty; in my opinion, republican government is just that and nothing else.

"I therefore find that in a republic a constitution is a perfectly useless thing; I think that the interim system we had for the previous eight months could very well have been rendered definitive with a little more regularity and a little less respect for monarchical traditions; I am convinced that the Constitution, the first act of which will be to create a presidency, with all its prerogatives, ambitions and culpable hopes, will imperil rather than guarantee liberty.

> "My fraternal regards.
> "P-J PROUDHON
> "*Representative for the Seine.*
> "Paris, 4th November 1848"

For myself as legislator this letter sufficed: the reporter owes his readers more ample explanations. We are so infatuated by power, we were so effectively monarchised, we love to be governed so much, that we cannot conceive of

---

21   This phrase is sloppy. I should have written: Outside that there is no Constitution in the present sense of the word; there is only one of these two things: a monarchical or an oligarchical dictatorship, making its laws and implementing them by means of its ministers; or a mass of free citizens, negotiating on the question of their interests, either individually or in councils, carrying out all the tasks of labour and society without any intermediaries.

the possibility of living in liberty. We consider ourselves democrats because we have abolished hereditary royalty four times: some who have gone as far as rejecting elective presidency, only to invest all the powers in a Convention directed by a committee of public safety, imagine they have arrived at radicalism's Pillars of Hercules.[22] But we do not see that in holding on so obstinately to this fixed idea of Government we are all, inasmuch as we engage in war to be able to exercise power, only a kind of absolutists!

What is a *political* constitution?

Can a society survive without a *political* constitution?

These are the questions that I propose to resolve, perhaps in fewer words than others might need to pose them. The ideas I am going to present are as old as democracy, as simple as universal suffrage; my only merit will consist in systematising them by putting a little coherence and order into them. They will still appear to be but a vision, one more utopia, even to democrats, of whom the majority, taking their right hand for their left, have never known how to develop anything but dictatorship from the sovereignty of the people.

### §I[23]

In every society I find the distinction between two kinds of constitution, one of which I call the SOCIAL constitution and the other the *political* constitution; the first, native to humanity, liberal, necessary, the development of which consists above all in weakening and gradually eliminating the second, [which is] essentially factitious, restrictive and transitory.

The social constitution is nothing but the equilibrium of interests founded upon free CONTRACT and the organisation of ECONOMIC FORCES, which are in general: *Labour, Division of Labour, Collective Force, Competition, Commerce, Money, Machines, Credit, Property, Equality in transactions, Reciprocity of guarantees,* etc.

The political constitution has AUTHORITY as its principle. Its forms are: Class Distinctions, Separation of Powers, Administrative Centralisation, Judicial Hierarchy, Representation of Sovereignty by Election, etc. It was first thought up and then gradually developed in the interests of order and for lack of social constitution, the principles and rules of which were only discovered later after long experience and are still the subject of socialist controversies.

These two constitutions are, it is easy to see, of utterly different and even incompatible natures: but, as it is the destiny of the political constitution

---

22  In classical mythology, the Pillars of Hercules marked the westward bounds of the known world. (Editor)

23  This chapter, very obscure in the earliest editions, has been completely rewritten and argued according to the principles developed in the *General Idea of the Revolution in the Nineteenth Century*.

incessantly to provoke and produce the social constitution, there is always something of the latter slipping into and landing in the former, which very soon, rendered unsatisfactory, appearing contradictory and odious, finds itself propelled from concession to concession towards its final abolition.

It is from this point of view that we are going to take a closer look at the general theory of political constitutions, reserving the study of the social constitution for another time.

In the beginning the political idea is vague and undefined, reducible to the notion of Authority. In ancient times, when the legislator always speaks in the name of God, Authority is immense and constitutional regulation more or less non-existent. There is nothing in all of the Pentateuch[24] even vaguely resembling a *separation of powers,* all the more such laws as are considered organic, having the purpose of defining the attribution of those powers and bringing the system into play. Moses had no idea whatsoever of a primary, so-called *legislative* power, or of a second, the *executive,* or a third, the bastard of the two others called the *judicial order.* The *conflicts of attributions* and *jurisdictions* had never revealed to him the necessity of a *State Council;* even less had political disputes, the inevitable result of the constitutional mechanism, made him feel the importance of a *High Court.* The constitutional idea had remained a closed book to the Prophet; not until four centuries of popular resistance to the Law had passed did this idea appear for the first time in Israel, and that was specifically to justify the election of the first king. Mosaic[25] government had been found weak and it was felt to be desirable to fortify it: this amounted to a revolution. For the first time the constitutional idea manifested itself in its true character, the separation of powers. At that time, as at the time of Philippe-le-Bel[26] and Bonifacius VIII[27], they could only know two of these, the *spiritual* and the *temporal.* The distinction is easy to grasp: at the side of the Pontiff appeared the King. This did not go without protest, or to speak the language of the period, without a menacing revelation by the priesthood.

"Here is what will be the royal statute," the constitution of government, Samuel said when the people's delegates came to summon him to anoint a king for them. Take note of this: it is the preacher who is responsible for the king's investiture; among all people, even when the priesthood is rebelled against, all power is of divine right. "He will take your sons and make them

---

24  The name of the first five books of the Old Testament. (Editor)

25  The body of juridical, moral, and ceremonial institutions, laws and decisions based on the last four books of the Pentateuch, and ascribed by Christian and Hebrew tradition to Moses. (Editor)

26  Philip IV of France (1268–1314) reigned as King of France from 1285 until his death. Nicknamed the Fair (*le Bel*) because of his handsome appearance. (Editor)

27  Pope Boniface VIII (1235–1303) had feuds with Dante, who placed him in a circle of Hell in his *Commedia*, and King Philip IV of France. (Editor)

conscripts and your daughters to be perfumers and cooks and bakers. And when he has attained power he will impose taxes on persons, houses, furniture, lands, wine, salt, meat, commodities, etc, in order to maintain his soldiers and pay his servants and mistresses."

"And you yourselves shall become his servants."[28]

It is in these terms that Samuel, the successor to Moses, presented the future political constitution; and all our political commentators, from the Abbé Sieyès to M. de Cormenin, agree with him. But how could an anticipated criticism outweigh the necessity of the moment? The priesthood had served order badly, it was eliminated; this was justice. If the new government proved to be treacherous or incompetent it would be treated in the same way, and so on, until liberty and well-being were achieved, but one would never go backwards: that is the argument of all revolutions. In any case, far from being frightened off by the preacher's sinister warnings, the appetites of the day, corresponding to the needs of the epoch, would rather be all the more thrillingly excited by them. Was not the political constitution, that is royalty, first of all in fact taxation, entailing honours and sinecures? Was it not monopoly, revenues, great property, leading to the exploitation of man by man, the proletariat? Wasn't it in the last analysis *liberty within order*, in the words of Louis Blanc, liberty surrounded by pikes and arrows, and thus the omnipotence of the soldier? All the world wanted it: the Phoenicians, the English of the day, had enjoyed it for some time already; why should the Jewish people, which called itself the Messiah of nations, like all the rest of us, French, Polish, Hungarians or Cossacks—for it seems to be a mania—have remained behind its neighbours, we vainly cry? Truly, there is nothing new under the sun, not even constitutionalism, Christomania and Anglomania.

The great domain of political constitutions is, as I say in my letter to *Le Moniteur*, mainly the *separation of powers*, that is to say the distinction of the two natures—no more, no less—in government, *spiritual nature* and *temporal nature*, or, which comes to the same thing, *legislative nature* and *executive nature*, as in Jesus Christ, both God and man together: it is amazing how we always find theology at the basis of our politics.

But, you will say, does the people not know how to do without this mechanism? Does not the people, which after all established both royal families and priesthoods, know how to dispense with the two of them for its government instead of maintaining them both together? And supposing that for its religious duties and the protection of its interests it actually needs a double Authority, what need is there to further subdivide the temporal one? What is the good of a constitution? What can be the use of this distinction of two powers, with their prerogatives, their conflicts, their ambitions and all their perils? Isn't it enough to have an Assembly which as the expression of national needs makes the laws and implements them by means of the ministers which it chooses from its members?

---

28  See Samuel 8:11–17. (Editor)

It was M. Valette (from the Jura) who, among others, spoke in this manner at the Assembly of 1848.

It is this question that reveals the fatal logic which leads peoples and determines revolutions.

Man is destined to live in society. This society can only exist in two ways: either by the organisation of economic forces and the equilibrium of interests or by the institution of an authority which, in the absence of industrial organisation, serves as arbiter, checks and protects. This latter manner of conceiving and realising order in society is what is called the State or Government. Its essential attribute, the condition of its effectiveness, is *centralisation*.

The Government able to define itself as the centralisation of the nation's forces—whatever they are—will be absolute if the centre is a single one; it will be constitutional or liberal, if there is a double centre. The separation of powers has no other meaning. While it is pointless in a small State, where the citizens' assembly can intervene in public affairs on a day to day basis, it is indispensable in a nation of several million men who are forced by their great number to delegate their powers to representatives. It thus becomes a guarantee of public liberties.

Imagine all the powers concentrated in a single assembly: you will only have augmented the threats to liberty by taking away from it its last sureties. Government by assembly is just as dangerous as that by a despot, without even the personal responsibility of the latter. Experience even proves that the despotism of assemblies is a hundred times worse than the autocracy of a single person, for the reason that a collective is impervious to those considerations of humanity, moderation, respect for others' opinions, etc. that govern individuals. If therefore the unity of powers, i.e. the absence of a political constitution, has no other effect but to absorb the powers of a responsible president into the powers of an irresponsible majority, the conditions of government otherwise remaining the same, what progress has been made? Would it not be better to divide authority, make one of the powers the controller of the other, giving the executive the liberty of action while the legislative controls it as a counter-weight? Thus, we either get the separation of powers or the absolutism of power: the dilemma is inevitable.

Democracy has never produced a convincing response to this argument. Without a doubt, as the critics have well observed, the division of authority into two powers is the source of all the conflicts which have been tormenting our country for the last sixty years and pushing it to revolution more than despotism itself managed to. But this does not destroy the fundamental objection that without the separation of powers there can only be absolutist government, and that suppressing that division within the Republic is in effect establishing dictatorship in perpetuity.

The democratic Republic, the Republic without distinction of powers, has also never seemed to unprejudiced minds to be anything but a contradiction in terms, a veritable retraction of liberty. And I confess that for my part—given the hypothesis of a centralisation in which all social powers converge in a single centre, the sovereign initiator and ruler—I very much prefer separate and responsible presidential government controlled by an assembly to the absolute and irresponsible government by assembly alone, and government by a constitutional royalty to government by elective presidency. Whatever the type of Government that is to be divided, monarchy or senate, the separation of powers is the first step towards a social constitution.

This is therefore the basic pattern according to which society, ignorant of the constitution that might be appropriate to it, has hitherto sought to create within itself for the purpose of maintaining order:

First of all a centralisation of all its forces, both material and moral, political and economic, in a word, royalty, a government;

Secondly, to escape the inconvenient aspects of this absolutism, a central duality or plurality, which is to say, the separation and opposition of powers.

Given this last point, for political theoreticians the problem has been to constitute the separate powers in such a way that they could never either be fused or enter into conflict, and to find a way for society to be aided and not repressed by them in the manifestation of its wishes and the development of its interests.

It is this triple problem which all ancient and modern constitutions have endeavoured to solve, and which has represented a stumbling block for them all. The Constitution of 1848 succumbed to it as did the others.

The Constitution of 1848, an imitation of the Charter of 1830, is basically socialist but has a political or see-saw form. On its socialist side it promises instruction, credit, work, assistance; it creates universal suffrage and submits to progress: these are new principles not recognised by ancient legislators and which the constitutive Assembly added to the *Creed*. In its political form its object is to maintain order and peace while guaranteeing the exercise of ancient rights.

Now the Constitution of 1848, just like its predecessors, is incapable of actually keeping any of its promises, whether they be political or social; and, if the people were to take it too seriously, I venture to say that the government would find itself faced daily by the choice between a 24th of February or a 26th of June.

The reason for this inability is, as we will see, partly because the socialist prescriptions introduced into the Constitution are incompatible with the political allocations; the other aspect is that the tendency of government is always, whatever happens, to take centralisation to its logical conclusion, by which I mean to say: to reconcile the constitutional powers in absolutism.

One cannot accuse the parties of these contradictions: they are the natural product of both ideas and time. Governmentalism has always existed; it was in the majority in the Assembly, it was unthinkable for anyone to wish to abolish it. As to Socialism, it had been around in people's minds long before the Constitutive Assembly was convoked and the February Revolution took place;

even without any actual representatives it just had to be officially proclaimed owing to the need of the epoch and in consequence of the revolution. And if Louis-Philippe had remained on the throne, the same movement, which came into being through his fall, would have done so under his rule.

Three elements form the socialist part of the new pact:

1. The *declaration of rights and duties*, including the *right to assistance* in place of and as compensation for the RIGHT TO WORK.
2. The idea of *progress*, the origin of Article 111, which established the perpetual power of improvement for the country.
3. *Universal suffrage*, the still unnoticed but inevitable effect of which will be to change the public law utterly by suppressing government.

It is my view that these elements, in which it is necessary to see an incomplete and disguised expression of the social constitution, are by themselves incompatible with any form of governmentalism, and that furthermore when powers have been separated such declarations will inevitably become for them a perpetual occasion of division and conflict. The result of this is not only the fact that the powers are unable to fulfil the duties imposed on them by the Constitution but that thanks to those very duties they cannot fail to enter into conflict and, if that occurs, one or the other or both will provoke civil war.

As facts are the best demonstration of ideas, let us take the *right to assistance* as an example.

Who does not see at once that the right to assistance, guaranteed by the government as a *substitute for work*, it is the same thing as the right to work travestied by an appeal to selfishness? The right to assistance was granted in HATRED of the right to work; it is as if it were paying off a debt or paying ransom for a property that the Government regards itself as obliged to reorganise public charity. Now, for anybody with a sense of logic or law and who knows the way in which obligations between people are carried out, it is evident that the right to assistance, equally odious to those who receive it and those who dispense it, cannot become part of the institutions of a society, at least in this form, and therefore cannot be the object of a mandate given by the sovereign People to the government.

I am not talking of the problems of implementation, which are almost insurmountable.—Is assistance the same as charity? No. Charity cannot be organised or be the subject of a contract, it has no place in a legal system, it is animated solely by conscience. Assistance, when it is covered by the law and is the subject of an administrative or judicial action, recognised as a right by the Constitution, is something different from charity: it is *unemployment compensation*. But if the right to assistance is a compensation, what will be the minimum of compensation rendered as assistance? Will it be 25, 50, 75 centimes? Will it be the same as the minimum wage?...What will be the maximum? Which individuals will have a right to receive assistance? What will be the payment according to age, sex, profession, infirmities, domicile? Will conditions be set for the needy? Will they for example be obliged to live in special lodgings and prescribed localities—in the country more than in towns? We are falling into the regime of prisons [*maisons de force*]: assistance, or dole becomes a monstrous thing, compensation for lack of liberty. That is not all: who will bankroll the assistance—the proprietors? 200 million won't be enough; new taxes will therefore have to be created, proprietors will have to be burdened to subsidise the proletariat. Will there be a system of making deductions from salaries? Well, then it is no longer the State or the proprietors and capitalists who render assistance but the workers who assist one another mutually: the working-man who has work pays for the one who hasn't, the good pays for the bad, the thrifty for the wasteful and the dissolute. In all these cases assistance becomes a pension for misconduct, a give-away for laziness: it is the supporting pillar of beggary, the providence of poverty. Pauperism thus becomes a constitutional matter; it is a social function, a profession hallowed by law, paid, encouraged, multiplied. The poverty tax is an argument for disorder against savings accounts, pension funds, *tontines*[29] etc. While you inject moral fibre into the people by means of savings and credit institutions, you demoralise them by means of assistance. Once more: I do not wish to stir up controversy in such delicate questions, where abuse is always mixed with the good and useful, where justice is only preferential treatment. I would like to know what can be the action of power in an institution functioning on the twin principles of envy and hate? An institution that confirms, maintains and sanctifies the antagonism of the two castes and seems to figure in the Declaration of Rights and Duties as the stepping stones to a social war?

Evidently the right to assistance, as with the right to work, is not within the field of competence of the government. These two principles, affirmed by universal conscience, are part of a completely distinct order of ideas, incompatible with the political order whose base is authority and whose sanction is force. It may be, and for my part I affirm this, that the rights to work, assistance, property etc. can be realised within another Constitution; but that Constitution has nothing in common with the one that rules us at present; it is diametrically opposed to it and completely antagonistic.

I myself unintentionally contributed to the exclusion of the right to work from the Constitution—and I do not regret sparing my colleagues, as well as my country, this new lie—by a response I made to M. Thiers in the finance committee. *Let me have the right to work*, I said to him, *and you are welcome to the right to property.* By that I wished to indicate that as work incessantly

---

29  A tontine is a scheme for raising capital that combines features of a group annuity and a lottery. Each investor then receives annual dividends on his capital. As each investor dies, his or her share is reallocated among the surviving investors. This process continues until only one investor survives. (Editor)

modifies property and consequently the Constitution and the exercise of authority, the guarantee of work would be the signal for a complete reform of the institutions. However, my remark was not taken as such but as a menace to property, and I was not in the mood for explaining myself. The conservatives immediately vowed that work would be protected but not guaranteed, which from their point of view appeared fair just because they did not guarantee property itself any more than work. They thought they were working wonders and employing the ultimate tactical finesse by passing, *in the absence of work*, THE RIGHT TO ASSISTANCE, a nonsense instead of an impossibility. Could I not have said to these blind men: *Oh well! Let me have the right to assistance and you are welcome to the right to work?...* Then, hating the right to assistance, which had become as risky for all thinking persons as the right to work, it would have been necessary to fall back on another guarantee, or not grant anything at all, which was impossible. And as I could have reproduced the same argument every time in response to everything proposed by conservative philanthropy, on and on, *ad infinitum*, as social guarantees are after all nothing but the reverse of political guarantees, if I had wanted to I could have relied on making the conservatives reject everything including the very idea of the constitution, simply by pressing for those political guarantees.

It is the same with all the political and economic elements that society is founded on as with the right to work and the right to assistance: all can be replaced by one another, because they are incessantly converting and transforming themselves into one another, because they are just as correlative as they are contradictory.

*Grant me education free of charge* [*gratuité de l'enseignement*], I said on another occasion, *and you are welcome to freedom of teaching* [*liberté de l'enseignement*].[30]

In the same way I could also have said: Give me the right to credit and I'll let you have the right to work and the right to assistance in one go.

Give me the equal treatment of all religions and I'll let you have a State religion.

Give me the power of revision and I'll obey the Constitution for ever and ever.

Give me the perpetual exercise of universal suffrage and I accept all the results of universal suffrage in advance.

Give me the liberty of the press and I will, being more tough-minded than you who prohibit the discussion of principles, permit you to discuss even the principle of liberty itself.

Society, which is an essentially intelligible affair, is completely based on these oppositions, synonymies or equivalencies which all interpenetrate one

---

30  The phrase "freedom of teaching" (*liberté de l'enseignement*), in French political debates around 1848, meant preserving the role of the Church in schooling, as against demands for the establishment of a government monopoly on schools, which then would be lay institutions. (Editor)

another, and the system of which is infinite. And the solution of the social problem consists in representing the different terms of the problem in such a way that they no longer appear to *contradict* one another, as they do at first in the very early epochs of social formation, but to be mutually deduced from one another: so that for instance the right to work, the right to credit, the right to assistance, all these rights, which are impossible to realise by taking the Government way, can be deduced from a primary transaction which is both outside and higher than the political system, as would be the Constitution of property, the equilibrium of values, the mutual guarantee of exchange, etc.; instead of awaiting the initiative of the public authority, it would actually make that authority subservient to itself.

It is our ignorance of these transformations, together with our republican negligence, that makes us blind to our means and makes us always desire to inscribe promises into the text of our constitutions and add them to the catalogue of our laws, promises which it is not in the power of any government to fulfil, which are antipathetic to it, however it is organised, whether as an absolute government, a constitutional government, or a republican government.

To put it concisely: is it your sole wish to produce political acts in society, to organise wars against foreign nations, to assure the supremacy of an aristocracy and the subordination of the working class domestically, to maintain privilege against the proletariat's efforts to emancipate itself? The governmental system will suffice, with or without the separation of powers. It was invented for this purpose and has never served any other end. The separation of powers, which you propose as *the primary condition of a free government*, is nothing but a way of allowing the favoured classes of society to participate in the government's revenues.

But if on the contrary you wish to guarantee the following to all, together with legitimately acquired property: work, assistance, exchange, credit, education, cheap goods, the freedom of opinion, the right to publish, the equality of means? In a word, only the system of economic forces can satisfy you. But far from this system being something that may be established by way of authority and grafted on to the political constitution, so to speak, it is actually the negation of authority. Its principle is neither force nor number: it is a transaction, a contract.

To vote for the Constitution of 1848, therefore, in which social guarantees are regarded as something emanating from authority, was to place the social constitution beneath the political constitution, the producer's rights after the rights of the citizen; it was to abjure socialism and disown the Revolution.

Neither Article 1 of the Preamble, positing the principle of *progress*, nor Article 13, expressing the right to assistance, nor Article 24, establishing *universal suffrage*, were able to compel me to support it: these three principles were subordinated by the Constitution to the political system, despite their lofty socialist and anti-governmental drift, and it was the facts no less than logic which were to prove very soon that progress, the right to assistance and universal suffrage were to fare in the same way at the hands of the new power as the right to work had at the hands of the constituent assembly.

Progress! But it is evident that in the question of economic ideas the State is essentially stationary.

To organise work, credit or assistance is to affirm the social constitution. Now, the social constitution subordinates and even disavows the political constitution: how should the Government take the initiative in such progress? Progress, for the Government, is the opposite of what it must be for the worker; it is also true, and the whole of history proves it, that far from progressing the Government tends to regress. Where would you like it to go, indeed, with its constitutive principle of the separation of powers? To an ever greater division? That would mean its downfall. From the point of view of political constitutions the four-year presidency and the unity of national representation are far from being a step forward but rather already a sign of the system's degeneration. The true formula of the constitutional regime is the Charter of 1830, just as the perfection of government is absolute power. Do you really want to return to the July monarchy or regress to Louis XIV?—for it is only in this sense that power can progress. Let those who haven't had enough of that speak up!

Universal suffrage! But how could I have taken that into account, given a Constitution which had arrogated to itself the prerogative of not only using it to create a lie but even of restricting it? By establishing electoral indignities the Constitution opened the door to [the law of] May 31st; and as for the veracity of universal suffrage and the authenticity of its decisions, what link can there be between the elastic product of a ballot and popular thinking, which is synthetic and indivisible? How could universal suffrage manage to manifest popular thinking—the real thought of the people—when that people is divided, by the inequality of wealth and by classes subordinated to one another, voting in servility or hate; when this same people, held on a leash by power, is not able to make its thought heard on any subject despite its sovereignty; when the exercise of its rights is confined to choosing its bosses and its charlatans every three or four years; when its reason, being fashioned according to the antagonism of ideas and interests, can only go from one contradiction to the other; when its good faith is at the mercy of a telegraphic dispatch, of an unforeseen event, of a captious question; when instead of inspecting its conscience its memories are evoked; when owing to the division of parties it can only avoid one danger by leaping into another, and is forced to lie to its conscience by the threat of losing its security? Society was immobilised by the 200 franc rule[31]: a poet personified it in the

---

31  A reference to the property qualification for voting under the July Monarchy which restricted suffrage to a small number of wealthy Frenchmen. This was abolished by the February Revolution until universal male suffrage was effectively eliminated by the law of 31st May 1850. (Editor)

god Terminus. Since the establishment of universal suffrage it has been spinning—on the spot. Before that it was rotting away in its lethargy; now it
suffers from vertigo. So, let us be more advanced, richer and more liberated
when we have made a million pirouettes?...

So if now the government, as it was made by the Constitution of 1848,
cannot guarantee work, credit, assistance, education, progress, the sincerity of universal suffrage, nothing of what constitutes the social state, how
could it guarantee the political state? How should it guarantee order? What
a singular matter!—this political reform, which was intended to give us
social reform, appears to us as a perpetual anomaly, from whichever side
you take it.

The government is not only in conflict with itself through the separation of its powers, it is so with society through the incompatibility of
its functions. Without the distinction of legislative and executive the
government offers liberty no guarantees; without a declaration of social
rights it is nothing but the force given to wealth to use as disciplinary
action against poverty. But with the separation of powers you open the
door to conflicts, corruption, coalitions, rifts, competitions; with the
declaration of rights you create a final result of categorical refusal for all
its decisions and acts: whatever you do the Constitution, which is intended to reconcile all, can only organise discord. At the bottom of your
so-called social pact is civil war.

Is it possible to find a way out of this labyrinth, and to pass from the
political constitution to the social constitution without doing somer-
saults? I venture to answer in the affirmative. But I warn the reader that
this will not come to pass by a transaction, an eclecticism, the sacrifice
of an idea or any adjustment of forces and counterweights; it will be by
elevating all the constitutional and social principles presently struggling
with one another to their highest potency: centralisation and separation,
universal suffrage and government, work and credit, liberty and order. At
first sight it seems that this method must increase antagonism: its effect
will however be to make it disappear. Except that we will no longer have
this distinction of political constitution and social constitution at all:
government and society will be identified and indiscernible from each
other.

### §II[32]

I have said that the vice of any constitution, political or social, what creates

---

32  In my book *General Idea of the Revolution in the Nineteenth Century* I offered, to-
    gether with the principles and forms of the economic constitution, a solution to the
    problem of the annihilation of the government by means of social liquidation and
    the organisation of industrial forces. What I wished to demonstrate in this section
    was that the principles of centralisation and separation which constitute the political

conflicts and antagonism in society, is on the one hand—to confine myself
to the only question I wish to examine at present—the fact that the separation of powers, or to put it better, of functions, is badly done and incomplete; on the other, the fact that centralisation is insufficient, since it does not
respect the law of specialism to a sufficient degree. It follows that collective
power is almost nowhere in action, nor is thought, or universal suffrage, exercised. It is necessary to push the separation, when it is hardly begun, as far
as possible, centralising every power separately; to organise universal suffrage
in its plenitude according to individual nature and kind and give the people
the energy and activity that it lacks.

This is the principle: to demonstrate it and explain the social mechanism
I now only have to provide arguments, for which a few examples will suffice.
Here, as in the natural sciences, the practice is the theory; exact observation
of the fact is science itself.

For many centuries the *spiritual* power has been separated to a varying
extent from the *temporal* power.

I will observe in passing that the political principle of the separation of
powers, or functions, is the same as the economic principle of the separation
of industries or division of labour: at which point the identity of the political
constitution and the social constitution are already dawning upon us.

I will furthermore remark on the fact that the more reality and fecundity
a function, industrial or otherwise, contains within itself, the more it grows,
realises itself and becomes productive by means of separation and centralisation, so that a function's maximum potency corresponds to its highest degree
of division and convergence, its minimum to the lowest degree of the same.
Lack of division and lack of potency are synonymous terms here. Separation
and centralisation, that is the double criterion by means of which one may
recognise whether a function is real or fictitious.

Now, not only have the temporal and spiritual powers together with the
majority of political functions in no way been distinguished and grouped
according to the laws of economy, but we shall see that these powers and
functions are very far from being strengthened by the principles of organisation claimed to be suitable for them, but are on the contrary wasted away
and annihilated by this very organisation, to the extent that what is supposed
theoretically to give life to authority is exactly what kills it.

First of all, there would thus be a complete separation between the spiritual and the temporal if the latter not only refrained from interfering in

---

mechanism both lead, when pushed to their extreme consequences, to the absolute
suppression of the State. In a word, while in the *General Idea* I showed the economic
constitution producing itself out of many parts and replacing the political constitution by eliminating it, in the *Confessions* I confine myself to showing the political
constitution transforming itself into the economic one.—It is always the same equation obtained by different procedures.

the celebration of the mysteries, the administering of the sacraments and the government of church parishes, etc., but also did not intervene in the matter of the nomination of bishops. There would subsequently be greater centralisation and therefore more regular government if the people in each parish had the right to choose its priests and succursalists[33] or even not take any at all; if the preachers in each diocese elected their bishop, if the bishops' assembly or a primate of the Gauls sorted out all their religious affairs, the teaching of theology and questions of religious service by themselves. By this separation the clergy would cease to be in the hands of political power and thus no longer an instrument of tyranny towards the people; it would no longer retain the secret hope of recapturing political supremacy; and by this application of universal suffrage the ecclesiastical government, centralised in itself, receiving its inspirations from the people and not from the government or the Pope, would be in constant harmony with the needs of society and the moral and intellectual state of its citizens.

For it means nothing for the centralisation of a country that the church ministers, the agents of power as of every other social function, are answerable to a centre, if the centre itself is not answerable to the people but is placed above the people and independent of it. In that case centralisation is no longer centralisation; it is despotism.

Where the sovereignty of the people is taken as a dogma, political centralisation means nothing else than the people itself being centralised as a political force: to take away central agency from the people's direct action is to deny it sovereignty and give it tyranny instead of centralisation. The suffrage of subordinates is the point of departure of all central administration.

Instead of this democratic, rational system what do we see? The Government, it is true, does not intervene in matters of religious practice, it does not teach the catechism, it does not give instruction at the seminary. But it does choose the bishops, who only find their centre at Rome in the person of the Pope without agreeing among themselves and without any superiors. The bishops choose the priests and succursalists, sending them into the parishes without the slightest participation of popular suffrage, often in fact in spite of the people's wishes. This all amounts to the Church and the State, interlocked, if sometimes at war with each other, forming a kind of offensive and defensive league apart from the people, united against its liberty and initiative. Their concerted government weighs heavily on the nation instead of serving it. It is pointless for me to enumerate the consequences of this order of affairs: they immediately spring to everybody's mind.

In order to achieve organic truth, political, economic or social, it is therefore necessary—for in this all is one:—first to abolish the existing constitutional amalgamation by taking the appointment of bishops away from

---

33  Heads of a succursal parish (mission church). They were not canonically parish priests (*curés*) and received no remuneration from the State. (Editor)

the State and finally separating the spiritual from the temporal;—second to centralise the Church in itself by a system of graduated elections;—third to put the suffrage of the citizens at the basis of ecclesiastical power as with all the other powers of the State.

In this system what is meant by GOVERNMENT today is nothing but *administration;* the whole of France is centralised, as far as ecclesiastical functions are concerned; the country governs itself solely by means of its electoral initiative, as much in questions of salvation as in secular matters; it is no longer governed. Whether established religion will have to be maintained or suppressed is not the question at the moment. If it survives it will be by the energy intrinsic to it; if it dies out it will be for lack of vitality: in either case its destiny, whatever that might be, will be the expression of the people's sovereignty, manifested by absolute separation and regular centralisation of functions, in other terms, by the organisation of universal suffrage in religious matters. And one already foresees that if it were possible to organise the whole country for temporal matters in the way we have indicated for its spiritual organisation, then the most perfect order and the most vigorous centralisation would exist without there being anything of what we call constituted authority, otherwise known as Government, which is nothing but a simulacrum of centralisation.

Another example:

At one time there was considered to be a third power, beyond the legislative and the executive, the *judicial* power. The Constitution of 1848, following those of 1830 and 1814, only speaks of the *judicial order.*

Whether order, power or function, here I find, as with the Church, a further example of the preponderance of the State, this time under the pretext of centralisation and, consequently, a new inroad on the sovereignty of the people.

Judicial functions, by their different specialities, their hierarchy, their convergence in a single ministry, manifest an unequivocal tendency to separation and centralisation.

But they are not at all answerable to judicially liable persons; they are all at the disposition of the executive power, appointed every four years by the people with irremovable spheres of duties, and are subordinate, not to the country by election but to the government—of president or prince. The result is that the liable persons are brought before their supposedly natural judges like the parishioners to their priests, meaning that the people belongs to the judiciary as by inheritance, that the litigant belongs to the judge and not the judge to the litigant.

Apply universal suffrage and election by degrees to judicial functions as to ecclesiastical functions, suppress irremovability, which is the loss of the electoral right; divest the State of all action or influence upon the judicial order and ensure that this order, being centralised in itself and separate, is only answerable to the people: and then you will first of all have robbed power of its most potent instrument of tyranny, having made justice a principle of liberty as much as of order. And, if you do not suppose that the people, from which must emanate all powers by virtue of universal suffrage, is in contradiction of itself by not wanting in justice what it wants in religion, you are assured that the separation of power cannot engender any conflict and can safely posit that henceforth separation and equilibrium are in principle synonyms.

In this way the people have the final say on the church and justice by means of a genuine separation of powers and centralisation; the functionaries of the two orders are directly or indirectly answerable to them, and the people do not obey but command, are not governed but govern.

But the consequences of effective separation and centralisation do not stop there. There are in society artificial functions, as we have said, which primitive barbarism suggested and made necessary but which civilisation tends to cause to disappear, first by the practice of liberty and then by the progress of separation itself. Religious observance and the courts are of this number.

If opinion in the matter of faith is truly free; if by the effect of this liberty all religions, either existing ones or those yet to emerge, are declared equal before the law; if every citizen is consequently permitted to vote for the ministers and contributions to the cost of his own religion without being forced to contribute to the maintenance of the others: then it follows first that as everyone is the judge in the last resort concerning a matter lacking in rational certainty and positive sanction, the unity or centralisation of a church is rendered impossible, all the more so because the divergence of professions of faith will become greater; second that the importance of religious opinions will be weakened and the authority of the churches diminished by the same mechanism that was supposed to increase them; third and finally, that the ecclesiastical function, being incompatible with universal suffrage and the laws of social organisation, will gradually fall into disuse so that the church personnel will sooner or later be reduced to zero.

In a word, while the separation of industries is the condition of their equilibrium and the cause of wealth, religious liberty is the ruin of religion with respect to its power and social function: what more could one wish for? Faced with society, the Church does not exist.

The same must happen with justice, too. The election of judges by the People every five or ten years is not the final consequence of the principle: it will have to be recognised that in every court case the litigant or the accused has the right to choose his judges. What am I saying here? It is that one must avow with Plato that the true judge for every man is his own conscience, which leads in the long run to replacing the regime of courts and laws by the regime of personal obligations and contracts, that is to say, to the suppression of the judicial system ...

In this way, once the hypothesis of absolute Government is dismissed, and it cannot but be treated thus, the governmental principle, as with religion and justice, through the development of its own laws, the separation of faculties and their centralisation, ends up by negating itself: it is a contradictory idea.

I now pass to another order of things, *the institution of the military*.

Is it not true that the army is the Government's own province and that it belongs much less to the country than to the State, whatever constitutional fictions might suggest? Once upon a time the staff of the army was part of the *royal household*; under the empire the gathering of the elite army corps bore the name of *imperial guard*, young and old. It is the Government that takes 80,000 recruits annually, not the country that gives them; it is Power that in the interests of its personal policy and to make its will respected appoints the leadership and orders troop movements at the same time as it disarms the national guards, not the nation which arming spontaneously for its defence avails itself of the public force, of its purest blood. There again the social order is compromised, and why? On the one hand because military centralisation not answerable to the people is nothing but pure despotism, on the other because the ministry of war, however independent it may be of the other ministries, is nevertheless still a prerogative of the executive Power, which only recognises one head, the President.

The people have a confused instinct for this anomaly when on the occasion of every revolution they insist on the removal of the troops, when they demand a law pertaining to military recruitment and the organisation of the national guard and the army. And the authors of the Constitution foresaw the danger when they wrote in article 50: *The president of the Republic has the armed forces at his disposal without ever being able to command them in person.* What prudent legislators, indeed! And what, one may inquire, does it signify that he does not command them in person if they are at his disposal, if he can send them where he will, to Rome or to Mogador?—if it is he who gives the orders, who appoints the different ranks of officers, who bestows the military crosses and pensions?—and if there are generals who command for him?

It is the right of the citizens to appoint the hierarchy of their military chiefs, the simple soldiers and national guards appointing the lower ranks of officers, the officers appointing their superiors.

Organised in this way the army retains its civic feelings; it is then no longer a nation within the nation, a fatherland within the fatherland, a sort of travelling colony in which the citizen as a naturalised soldier learns to fight against his own country. It is the nation itself, centralised in its strength and youth quite independently of Power, which like any magistrate of the judicial order or of the police can call for the public force in the name of the law, though that force is not at its disposal and cannot be commanded by it. As for the eventuality of war, the army only owes its obedience to the representatives of the nation and the military chiefs appointed by them.

Does it follow that I regard the military as a natural institution inherent to society and in which I only find one fault that endangers liberty, i.e.

that of a defective organisation? That would be to suppose me to have a very mediocre understanding of the Revolution. I have endeavoured to show how the People has to organise its military in such a way as to simultaneously guarantee its defence and its liberties, while waiting for the nations to agree to terminate the armed peace, since they are the only ones competent to judge the opportunity of general disarmament. But who does not see that the same applies to war as to justice and religion and that the only sure means of abolishing it, after the conciliation of international interests, would be to organise the military as I have just indicated—and as prescribed by the principles of '93—while depriving the Government of its power to wage war against the wishes of the nation?

I will continue.

At all times societies have felt it necessary to protect their trade and industry against foreign imports: the power or function that protects indigenous labour in every country, guaranteeing it the national market, is the Customs.

I do not wish to give any impression here of prejudging the morality or immorality, the utility or disutility of the Customs: I shall take it as society offers it to me and confine myself to examining it from the point of view of the constitution of powers. Later, when we pass from political and social questions to the purely economic question, we shall seek to find a solution to the problem of the balance of commerce that is appropriate to it and see whether indigenous production can be protected without the cost of law and surveillance, in a word, without the Customs.

The Customs is by virtue of the fact of its existence a centralised function: its very origin, like its form of action, excludes any idea of piecemeal structure. But how is it that this function, which is within the special competence of merchants and industrialists and should by rights be exclusively the concern of the authority of the chambers of commerce, is still a dependency of the State?

For the protection of its industry France maintains an army of more than 40,000 customs officials, all armed with rifles and sabres, costing the nation a sum of 26 million francs per annum. This army has a double mission: to pursue smugglers and to collect a tax of 100 to 110 million francs on imported and exported goods.

Now, who can know better than industry itself what need it has of being protected, what duties must be levied, which products merit premiums and encouragements? And as to the actual service provided by Customs, is it not evident that it is up to the interested parties to calculate its expense and not the job of Power to make it a source of emoluments for its creatures, for example by making the legislation on differential tariffs a source of revenue for its extravagances?

As long as the administration of Customs remains in the hands of government authority, the protectionist system, which by the way I do not judge *per se*, is bound to be defective; it will be lacking in sincerity and justice; the tariffs imposed by Customs will be extortionate, and smuggling can only be seen, in the words of the honourable M. Blanqui, as both a right and a duty.

Besides the ministries of the *Cults* [established religions], of *Justice*, of *War*, of international trade or of *Customs*, the government has accumulated others, such as the ministry of *Agriculture and Commerce*, the ministry of *Public Works*, the ministry of *Public Education* and above all, to juggle all of them, the ministry of *Finance*! Our supposed separation of powers is only the accumulation of powers, our centralisation is only an absorption.

Does it not appear to you that the farmers, already organised as they are in their confederations and associations, could well operate their centralisation and manage their general interests without passing through the hands of the State? And that the merchants, producers, manufacturers and industrialists of all kinds, with their completely open associations in the chambers of commerce, might equally, without the aid of Power, without having to await their salvation from its tender mercies or their ruin from its inexperience, organise a central administration themselves and at their own expense, debate their affairs in the general assembly, correspond with the other administrations and take all useful decisions without the signature of the president of the republic, and then entrust one of theirs, chosen by his peers to be the minister, with the execution of their wishes?

And that the public works, which concern everybody, whether in agriculture, industry, trade, the departments or the communes, should be distributed forthwith among the local and central administrations with an interest in them and no longer form a separate corporation which—as with the army, Customs, Excise Office, etc.—is completely under the control of the State with its own hierarchy, privileges and ministry, all with the purpose of permitting the State to traffic in mines, canals, railways, play the stock market, speculate on shares, hand over building projects of 99 years' duration to friends' companies, award works on roads, bridges, ports, sea walls, drillings, tunnels, locks, dredgings etc., etc., to a legion of entrepreneurs, speculators, usurers, corrupters and swindlers who live off the public wealth, the exploitation of artisans and workers, and the follies of the State?

Does it not seem to you that national education would be just as well UNIVERSALISED, administered and ruled; the primary and secondary school teachers, headmasters and inspectors just as well chosen; the study syllabuses just as perfectly in harmony with interests, customs and morals— if town or other local councils were authorised to appoint schoolteachers while the University only had to hand out diplomas to them; if in both public education and a military career periods of service on the lower echelons were required for promotion to the higher levels; if every grand university dignitary had had to pass through the positions of primary teacher and class monitor? Do you believe that this system, perfectly democratic, would damage school discipline, educational morality, the dignity of teaching or the security of families?

And, since money is the nerve of any administration: it is necessary that the budget is made for the country and not the country for the budget and that a tax must be freely voted for by the representatives of the people every year; this is the basic and inalienable right of the nation whether under a monarchy or under the Republic. Since both expenses and receipts must be consented to by the country before being authorised by the government, is it not clear that the consequence of this financial initiative, which has been formally recognised as pertaining to the citizens by all our constitutions, would be that the ministry of finance—all this fiscal organisation, in a word—should belong to the nation and not to its prince; that in fact it is directly answerable to those who pay the budget, not those who eat it; that there would be far less abuse in the management of the public treasury, less squandering of funds, fewer deficits, if the State had no more control of the public finances than of the churches, of justice, of the army, of customs, of public works or of public education, etc.?

Without a doubt, in the case of Agriculture, Trade, Industry, Public Works, Education and Finance, separation will not end in annihilation, in the way that we have attempted to show it will in the case of the Churches, Justice, War and Customs. In this connection one might believe that with the development of economic forces compensating—and more—the suppression of political powers, the principle of authority will gain on the one hand what it has lost on the other, and that the governmental idea will be strengthened instead of disappearing.

But who does not see that the Government that has just come to an end with the extinction of its powers meets that end in this case in the fact of their absolute independence as much as in the mode of their centralisation, the principle of which is no longer authority but contract?

What makes for centralisation in both despotic and representative States is authority, hereditary or elective, which emanating from the King, President or directory descends on the country and absorbs all its powers. But what makes for centralisation in a society of free men, associating with different groups according to the nature of their industries or their interests and by whom neither collective nor individual sovereignty is ever abdicated or delegated, is the contract. The principle, you see, has changed: from this point on the economy is no longer the same; the organism, deriving from another law, has been turned upside down. Instead of resulting, as was hitherto the case, from the agglomeration and confiscation of forces by a so-called representative of the people, social unity is the product of the free support of the citizens. In fact and in law the Government has ceased to exist as a result of universal suffrage.[34]

---

34  See *General Idea of the Revolution in the Nineteenth Century* for how these diverse categories of services are constituted wholly apart from any governmental form by means of economic organisation.

I shall not accumulate any more examples here. After what has preceded it is easy to continue the series and see the difference between centralisation and despotism, between the separation of social functions and the separation of those two abstractions that have been rather unphilosophically named the *legislative power* and the *executive power*—in the end between administration and government. Do you believe, I say, that with this truly democratic regime, with its unity *at the bottom* and its separation *at the top*, the reverse of what now exists in all our constitutions, there would not be more severity concerning expenditure, more exactitude in the services, more responsibility for the functionaries, more benevolence on the part of administrations towards the citizens, and less servility, less *esprit de corps*, fewer conflicts, in a word, fewer disorders? Do you believe that reforms would then appear quite so difficult; that the influence of authority would corrupt the judgement of the citizens; that corruption would serve as the basis of morals, and that being a hundred times less governed we would not be a thousand times better run as a country?

It used to be believed that in order to create national unity it was necessary to concentrate all public powers in the hands of a single authority; then, as it soon became apparent that in proceeding thus one only created despotism, it was believed possible to remedy this inconvenience by means of the dualism of powers, as if in order to prevent the government's war against the people there were no other means than organising the war of the government against the government!

For a nation to be manifested in its unity it is necessary, I repeat, that this nation be centralised in its religion, centralised in its justice, centralised in its military force, centralised in its agriculture, its industry and commerce, centralised in its finances, centralised in all its functions and powers, in a word; it is necessary that centralisation be effected from the bottom to the top, from the circumference to the centre, and that all functions be independent and govern themselves independently.

Do you then want to make this purely economic and invisible unity more apparent to the senses by means of a special organ or by an Assembly; to preserve the image of the superannuated government for love of your traditions?

Group these different administrations by their leading representatives: you will then have your council of ministers, your *executive power*, which might then very well do without a State Council.

Above all that now raise a grand jury, legislature or national assembly, directly appointed by the whole country and charged, not with appointing the ministers—they will be invested in their roles by their specific electoral bodies—but with verifying the accounts, passing laws, fixing the budget, settling the differences between the administrations, all this after having heard the conclusions of the public ministry, or ministry of the interior, to which the whole government will then be reduced: and you have a centralisation which is all the stronger for your multiplying the number of centres of power, a responsibility all the more real for the separation between powers being more clean-cut: you will have a constitution which is at the same time political and social.

There, the government, the State, power—whatever name you choose to give it—brought back within its just limits, which are not to *legislate* nor to *execute*, nor even to *fight* or *judge*, but as commissioner to witness: the sermons, if there are any sermons, the debates in tribunals and parliamentary discussions, if there are any tribunals and a parliament; to supervise the generals and armies, if circumstances make it necessary to keep the armies and generals; to remind people of the meaning of the laws and warn of the contradictions involved, to see to the execution of those laws and prosecute any breaches: there, I say, government is nothing other than the head teacher of society, the sentinel of the people. Or rather, government no longer exists, since by the progress of their separation and centralisation the powers formerly gathered together by the government have all either disappeared or escaped the latter's initiative: *anarchy* has given birth to order. There at last you have the liberty of the citizens, the truth of institutions, the sincerity of universal suffrage, the integrity of the administration, the impartiality of justice, the patriotism of bayonets, the submission of parties, the impotence of sects, the convergence of wills. Your society is organised, living, progressive; it thinks, speaks, acts like a man, precisely because it is no longer represented by a man, because it no longer recognises personal authority, because in it, as in any organised and living being, as in Pascal's infinity, the centre is everywhere, the circumference nowhere.[35]

It is to this anti-governmental constitution that we are invincibly led by our democratic traditions, our revolutionary tendencies, our need for centralisation and unity, out love of liberty and equality, and the purely economic, if very badly applied, principle of all our constitutions. And it is this I would have gladly explained to the Constituent Assembly, if that Assembly, so impatient of commonplaces, had been capable of listening to something other than commonplaces; if, in its blind prejudice against any new idea, in its unfair provocations with the socialists, it had not had the empty words to say to them: I defy you to try to convince me!

But it is with assemblies as with nations: they only learn from misfortune. We have not suffered enough, we have not been sufficiently chastised for our monarchical servility and governmental fanaticism for us to come to love liberty and order so soon. Everything within us still conspires with the exploitation of man by man, the government of man by man.

---

35  A reference to the *Pensées* of philosopher and mathematician Blaise Pascal (1623–1662): "Nature is an infinite sphere of which the centre is everywhere and the circumference nowhere." (Editor)

Louis Blanc is in need of a strong power to do what he calls the *good*, which is the application of his system, and to keep down *the bad*, which is everything that opposes that system.

M. Léon Faucher is in need of a strong and pitiless power to contain the republicans and exterminate the socialists, to the glory of English political economy and Malthus.

MM. Thiers and Guizot are in need of a quasi-absolute power which enables them to exercise their great talents as tightrope walkers. What kind of nation is it from which a man of genius would be forced to exile himself for lack of men to govern, a parliamentary opposition to combat and intrigues to pursue with all the governments?

MM. de Falloux and Montalembert are in need of a power divine that every knee would bow to, every head incline to, every conscience prostrate itself to, in order that kings might no longer be any more than the gendarmes of the Pope, the vicar of God on earth.

M. Barrot is in need of a double power, legislative and executive, in order that there might be eternal contradiction in parliament and society never have any other end, in this life and the other, but to witness constitutional representations.

Ah! vain servile race that we are! We who pay 1,800 million francs a year for the follies of our governors and our own shame; who maintain 500,000 soldiers to machine-gun our children; who vote for fortresses for our tyrants so that they may keep us under perpetual siege; who invite nations to become independent only to abandon them to their despots; who wage war on our neighbours and allies, today for the vengeance of a preacher, yesterday for the pleasure of a courtesan; who have no esteem for any but our flatterers, no respect but for our parasites, no love but for our prostitutes, no hate but for our workers and our poor; once a race of heroes, now of hypocrites and sycophants: if it is true that we are the Christ of the nations, might we soon quaff the chalice of our iniquities to the dregs, or, if we have definitely abdicated liberty, serve by dint of distress and squalor as an eternal example to cowardly peoples and perjurers!

# CHAPTER XVII
## 29 JANUARY 1849: BARROT-FALLOUX REACTION. DESTRUCTION OF THE GOVERNMENT

THE FUNERAL SERVICES for the powers that be got underway, with Louis Bonaparte presiding. This supreme transition was crucial if the way was to be prepared for the advent of the democratic, social republic. The situation in place prior to then and the events that followed December 10th, which are still being played out with inexorable logic, will demonstrate as much to us.

By plumping for royalty in 1830 and founding constitutional rule, the governments of the Thiers, Guizots and Talleyrands had, deliberately and of their own volition, laid down the principle of a further revolution. Like a grub instinctively sensitive to approaching metamorphosis, it had woven its own winding-sheet. By endowing itself after a nine month crisis with a president, a shadow of a king, it had uttered its *Consummatum est*[36] and, before breathing its last, placed its final wishes on record.

The corruption of power had been the doing of the constitutional monarchy; the presidency's mission is to lead the mourning for the authorities. Just as Cavaignac had been, and as Ledru-Rollin had been, Louis Bonaparte is merely an executor of that intent. Louis Philippe poured his poison into the old society: Louis Bonaparte escorted it to the burial ground. I will parade this lugubrious procession in front of you anon.

Take a close look at France: she is spent, done for. Life has retreated into itself: where the heart should be we have only the metallic chill of interests; where the thought should be, we have a torrent of opinions all contradicting one another and holding each other in check. A vermin-riddled corpse, one might say. You speak of freedom, honour, fatherland? France is dead: Rome, Italy, Hungary, Poland and the Rhineland kneel all around the coffin and recite the *De Profundis*![37] What once was the power and the glory of the French nation—monarchy and republic, Church and parliament, bourgeoisie and nobility, military glory, the sciences, letters, the fine arts—all of it is no more: everything has been mown down like a harvest, and tossed into the revolutionary mash. Take care not to detain this work of decomposition: don't go mixing the living vermilion liquid with mud and sediment. That would be tantamount to killing Lazarus in the tomb a second time.

For nearly twenty years now our death has been in the making and we have occasionally thought our metamorphosis approaching its end! Nothing happened but this was interpreted by us as a sign of resurrection: the slightest sound reaching our ears rang like the trump of the Last Judgement. Yet year followed year and the big day never came. It was like the Middle Ages and their intoxicated millenarians. Poland, Belgium, Switzerland, Ancona, the Quadruple Alliance, the right to search, secret societies, infernal machines, parliamentary coalitions: then came Beirut, Krakow, Pritchard, the Spanish marriages, the Russian loan; then scarcity, electoral reform, the Sonderbund and, overlaying them all, corruption!...[38] Then, finally, the February Revolu-

---

36  The last words of Jesus on the cross, from the Latin Vulgate of the New Testament, John 19:30: "It is finished." (Editor)

37  Psalm 130 (*De profundis clamavi ad te, Domine*: "Out of the depths have I cried unto thee, O Lord"). (Editor)

38  Proudhon rapidly references a series of events marking the period of Louis-Philippe's reign:
    *Poland... Krakow*: Despite popular sympathy for the Polish revolts of 1830–1831, France did not come to Poland's aid.

tion, a spectacle in twelve scenes, universal suffrage, the reaction and, once again, as ever, corruption! So many occasions to make our mark if we had any sort of a heart still beating, if we were a people! Sometimes, we tried to struggle to our feet ... but the chill of death pinned us in our coffin. We have thrown away our final flames on pitchers and glasses: toasts from the dynastics, the democrats, the socialists were our only share in the history of France from July 1847 through to September 1849.

We did not cease to show, and myself first and foremost, that the government of Louis Bonaparte was unjust! The way we used to do with Louis-Philippe. The government of December 10th? It is only there to seal up the burial chamber, let me tell you; let it perform its pall-bearer's function. Following the ghastly, unparalleled handiwork of the July monarchy, the presidency's duty is to lay you out in your charnel-house. Thanks to power,

---

*Belgium... Ancona:* In 1831, France intervened on behalf of Belgium against the Netherlands, and sent troops to occupy Ancona, Italy in 1832.

*The Quadruple Alliance... Beirut:* In 1840, a Quadruple Alliance was formed between Britain, Russia, Austria, and Prussia to assist Turkey in opposing Muhammad Ali's claim to rule of Egypt and Syria; Ali resisted this pressure on the assumption that the French would act as his allies, but Louis-Philippe decided not to support him, and the British proceeded to military action against Ali, beginning by invading Beirut.

*The right to search:* The right to stop and search ships suspected of illegal trafficking in slaves on the high seas, an issue of contention between France and Britain, was the subject of a treaty signed in 1845.

*Secret societies, infernal machines:* Under Louis-Philippe's reign, secret societies were organised by a variety of political factions, from Bonapartists to Republicans; one of the latter, the *Société des Droits de l'Homme*, was the target of repressive laws proclaimed by Louis-Philippe in 1834, leading to an unsuccessful 1835 assassination attempt employing a "*machine infernale*" (a special gun with twenty-five barrels).

*Parliamentary coalitions:* Between 1832 and 1840, a series of "coalitions" were formed in the course of machinations over political power.

*Pritchard:* In 1844, British consul George Pritchard was expelled by a French admiral in the course of a dispute over control of Tahiti.

*The Spanish marriages:* In 1846, Louis-Philippe's son, Antoine d'Orléans, was married to Luisa Fernanda, heiress-presumptive to the Spanish crown.

*The Russian loan... scarcity:* During the economic crisis of 1847–1848, Russia made a 50 million franc loan to France in the form of a purchase of bonds, allowing France to buy grain from Russia.

*Electoral reform:* under Louis-Philippe, suffrage was slightly expanded, but in ways that tended to benefit the bourgeoisie.

*Switzerland... the Sonderbund*: In 1845, seven Conservative cantons created the Sonderbund, so provoking a civil war two years later. (Editor)

Louis-Philippe was society's wrecker: Louis Bonaparte will be the destroyer of what Louis-Philippe had missed, authority. The circumstances attending his election, the place he occupies in the revolutionary series, the policy his elders have foisted upon him, the use he has been induced to make of his authority, the prospects opened up in front of him: all nudging him and hurrying him forwards. It is Revolution itself that has taught Louis Bonaparte a lesson. Did not he, like Louis-Philippe, yoke together the Jesuit and the doctrinairian, only to have each of them bring disgrace upon the other? Did he not state, in his inaugural address, that he would carry on with the policies of Cavaignac, the regicide's son? ... I tell you truthfully: the role of the President of the Republic was written in the book of fate: his calling is to de-moralise the authorities the way Carrier[39] stripped the morality out of torture.

Once this situation was understood, the course that socialism had to follow was all set out. It had merely to press for demolition of the authorities, acting, so to speak, in concert with the authorities and favouring, by means of calculated opposition, the handiwork of Louis Bonaparte. Adopting those tactics, with divine Providence and human Providence in agreement, nothing would stand in our path. The misgivings that had made socialism doubtful prior to December 10th about alliance with the Mountain were banished: that alliance now became entirely profitable, wholly beneficial. Louis Bonaparte elected by an overwhelming majority, the reaction which he had made so formidable, any hope of re-capturing power was banished for a long time from the eyes of the Montagnards, committed by their programme and compelled to go where it might please us to lead them.

That left two things still undone: firstly, have the political question subsumed into the social question by simultaneously mounting a frontal assault on the capitalist principle and the authority principle: secondly, by having the latter follow through with all of the consequences of its latest formula, in other words, rendering the presidency as much help as we could muster in its suicidal undertaking.

In this way, the old society was plucked from its foundations; Jacobinism turned into pure socialism; democracy became more liberal, more philosophical, more real; socialism itself emerged from its mythological envelopment and made its stand, as if on two pillars, on the double repudiation of usury and of power. From which point onwards the social system wriggled

---

39   Jean-Baptiste Carrier (1756–94) was a French Revolutionary, known for his cruelty to his enemies, especially to clergy. Carrier was sent, early in October 1793, to Nantes by the National Convention to suppress an anti-revolutionary revolt where he invented a variety of extremely torturous means of killing. This gained Carrier a reputation for wanton cruelty. He was recalled by the National Convention, took part in the attack on Robespierre on the 9th Thermidor, and was brought before the Revolutionary Tribunal on the 11th. He was guillotined on 16 November 1794. (Editor)

free of the mists of utopias; society became conscious of itself; and, under the aegis of the popular genius, freedom blossomed without contradiction.

At the same time, power was peaceably moving towards its doom. The Freedom that had once ushered it in now spread the shroud over it; socialism's triumph lay in giving it, as the people naively say, a glorious death.[40]

Alongside capital and power, however, there was a third power that seemed to have been asleep for the past sixty years, its death throes threatening to be altogether more dreadful: namely, the Church.

*Capital*, whose mirror-image in the political sphere is *Government*, has a synonym in the religious context, to wit, *Catholicism*. The economic notion of capital, the political notion of government or authority, the theological notion of the Church, these three notions are identical and completely interchangeable: an attack upon one is an attack upon the others, as all the philosophers today know fine well. What capital does to labour and the State to freedom, the Church in turn does to understanding. This trinity of absolutism is deadly, in its practice as well as in its philosophy. In order to oppress the people effectively, they must be clapped in irons in their bodies, their will and their reason. So if socialism wanted to manifest itself completely and positively, stripped of all mysticism, there was but one thing for it to do: to set the idea of this trilogy in intellectual circulation. And the occasion could scarcely have been more propitious.

As if they saw eye to eye with us, the leaders of Catholicism had come voluntarily to abide by the determination of revolutionary dialectics. They had sided with the Holy Alliance against nationality, with governments against subjects, with capital against labour. In Rome, there was an out-and-out contest between theocracy and revolution; and as if to render the socialist proof all the more spectacular, Louis Bonaparte's government was loudly espousing the Pope's cause in the name of Catholic interests.[41] Now we had merely to highlight this triple form of social slavery, this conspiracy of altar, throne and strong-box, for it to be readily understood. Even as the reaction was denouncing our atheism, which certainly did not cause us much in the way of discomfort, we were, every morning, recounting some episode from the Holy League and, without harangue or argument, the people were being de-monarchised and de-Catholicised.

---

40  It has been just two years since these pages were written. Today, none can deny that the author's predictions have been faithfully fulfilled.

41  The Roman Republic was declared on February 9th, 1849, when the government of the Papal States was overthrown by a republican revolution led by Giuseppe Mazzini. President Louis Napoléon sent troops to restore the Pope and on April 25th some eight to ten thousand French troops landed near Rome. After a siege in June, a truce was negotiated on July 1st and the French Army entered Rome on July 3rd, re-establishing the Pope's temporal power. The expedition was commanded by Charles Nicolas Victor Oudinot. (Editor)

From December 10th on, this was the battle plan spelled out by *Le Peuple* and broadly adhered to by the newspapers of the social democracy; and, dare I say it? if said plan has not yet reaped all the success one might expect it to deliver, it has already brought forth imperishable results: and the rest is only a matter of time.

Capital will never regain its whip hand; its secret has been exposed. Let it hold its last orgy: tomorrow it must burn atop the pyre of its treasures, as did Sardanapalus.[42]

The powers that be are done for in France, doomed to acting out on a daily basis and for the sake of self-protection, the most terrifying plot that socialism might devise for their destruction.

Catholicism has not waited for its mask to be torn away: the skeleton beneath the shroud stands exposed. The Christian world cries for vengeance against Church and Pope. The Oudinot expedition has delivered the *coup de grace* to the papacy; spurred on by the Jesuits, the doctrinaires, whose every thought was of how to destroy Jacobinism by attacking it in one of its heartlands, have done socialism's job for it. Pius IX is the throne of St. Peter brought low. Now, with the papacy demolished, Catholicism has nothing to recommend it: *The serpent having died, its venom dies also.*

When partisan fury, when men of God ignorant of the concerns of philosophy are doing things so well, it is highly imprudent and bordering upon criminal to hinder them in their endeavours. It only remained for us to explain the meaning of things as the short-sightedness of our enemies brought them to light; to highlight the logic, I nearly said the loyalty, with which the Louis Bonaparte government was tearing out its own entrails; to endorse and indeed sing the praises of the eloquent arguments mounted by the Barrot-Falloux-Faucher ministry, or, (and this amounted to precisely the same thing), denounce them so that such friends might find therein a ready source of further arguments for persistence.

From before February I had foreseen what was happening. No one was ever better prepared for a cold-blooded fight. But such is the fervour in political arguments that even the wisest are carried away by passion. When reason alone would have been enough to make me the victor, I threw myself into the fray with something akin to rage. The unfair attacks to which I had been subjected by a number of men drawn from the Mountain party had wounded me: the election of Louis Bonaparte, which I held was an affront to the republican party, weighed heavily upon me. I was like the people under the lash of tyranny, rearing up and roaring against its masters. Rather than

---

42  According to the Greek writer Ctesias of Cnidus, Sardanapalus was the last king of Assyria. It is not sure whether he existed or not; Ctesias presented a character who was a debauchee, living a live of sloth and luxury who was, at the last, forced ineffectually to take up arms, and who avoided capture by suicide, dying in the flames that consumed his palace. (Editor)

assuaging my enthusiasm, the truth and justice of our cause served only to heighten it; so true is it that the men who rely so heavily upon their understanding are often the very ones whose passions are the most untameable. I have immersed myself in study; I have numbed my soul with meditations; I have merely succeeded in inflaming my irascibility all the more. Having recently recovered from a serious illness, I declared war on the President of the Republic. I marched out to do battle with the lion when I was not even a gadfly.

I freely admit it, now that I have the chance to gauge the facts better: such immoderate aggression on my part towards the head of state was unfair.

From the very first day he took office, the presidential government, faithful to the orders it had received from on high, paved the way for the extinction of the authority principle by stirring up conflict between the powers that be. Could I have asked for anything better than Monsieur Odilon Barrot's summing-up to the Constituent Assembly and the famous Rateau proposal?[43] So how come the very confirmation of my forecasts made me lose my calm? What was the point of all this invective spewed at a man when, as an instrument of fate, after all is said and done, he deserved to be applauded for his diligence?

I knew only too well that by its very nature government is counter-revolutionary: it either resists, oppresses, or corrupts or wrecks. Government knows nothing else, can do nothing else and will never seek anything else. Put a St. Vincent de Paul in power and he will turn into a Guizot or a Talleyrand. Look no further back than February and the provisional government: General Cavaignac and all those republicans and all those socialists who had a hand in affairs, were they not acting, some on behalf of dictatorship and some in the service of the reaction? How could Louis Bonaparte not have followed in their footsteps? Was it through any fault of his own? Were his intentions not pure? Were his thoughts, insofar as they were known, not at loggerheads with his politics? So why the vehement accusation which amounted to nothing short of a condemnation of fate? The blame that I was heaping on Louis Bonaparte was nonsensical: and in accusing him of reaction I myself was, in my keenness to thwart him, reactionary.

I was also not unaware—who ever knew it better than I did?—that if the President of the Republic, as specifically outlined in twenty-one articles of the Constitution, was merely the agent and subordinate of the Assembly and, under the principle of separation of powers, he was its equal and, inevitably, its antagonist. So it was impossible for the government to have been free of jurisdictional squabbling and rival prerogatives—mutual trespasses and accusations

---

43  Rateau was an obscure representative in the National Assembly who brought the motion for a no-confidence vote against the Barrot Ministry on January 6th, 1849. Proponents of the motion argued that dissolution of government was essential to restore the economy and consolidate order. (Editor)

resulting in the imminent breakdown of authority. The Rateau proposition, or anything of that sort, was bound to result from this constitutional dualism, as infallibly as the spark springs from the impact of the stone on the steel. Add that Louis Bonaparte, a mediocre philosopher, (not that I hold that against him), was being advised by the Jesuits and the doctrinaires, the worst reasoners and the most despicable politicians the world has ever seen; that in addition, due to the injustice of his position, he was personally answerable for a policy on which he had only to sign off; answerable for constitutional conflicts for which he became the whipping-boy; answerable for the silliness and noxious passions of advisors foisted upon him by the coalition of his electors!

When I think of the wretchedness of this head of state I am tempted to weep for him and I count my own imprisonment a blessing. Was there ever a man more frightfully sacrificed? The man in the street marvelled at such unprecedented elevation: I see it only as the posthumous penalty for an ambition that is in the grave but which social justice still pursues, although the people, with their short memory span, have long since forgotten it. As if the nephew should pay the penalty for the iniquities of the uncle. Louis Bonaparte, I am afraid, will prove to be merely yet another martyr to governmental fanaticism; he will be brought down as his monarch predecessors were brought down, or else he will become a companion in misfortune to the democrats who paved the way for him—Louis Blanc and Ledru-Rollin, Blanqui and Barbès. For he, no more and no less than all of them, stands for the authority principle: and whether he wishes, on his own account, to hasten or to fend off the revolution, the task will be too much for him and he will perish. You poor victim! Even as I was celebrating your efforts, I should have been pleading your case, making excuses for you, maybe even defending you, but I could spare you naught but insult and sarcasm: I behaved badly.

Had I the slightest faith in supernatural callings, I would say that one of two things must be true: that Louis Bonaparte has been summoned to the presidency of the Republic to redeem the French people from enslavement to the power restored and consolidated by the Emperor: or in order to expiate the Emperor's despotism. Actually, there are two courses open to Louis Bonaparte: one which, by means of popular initiative and an organic fellowship of interests, leads directly to equality and peace, this being the course favoured by the socialist analysis and revolutionary history; and the other which, from a position of power, will inevitably lead him to catastrophe, this being the course of usurpation, surreptitious or brazen, to which the man elected on 10 December is to all appearances committed. Was it necessary for us to see him flounder like the rest and refuse all chance to turn back?... Put it to the man himself: as for me, I have nothing more left to tell you. I am too great a foe to hazard advice: it is enough for me to open your eyes to our country's future, reflected in her past as if in a mirror. He that lives will see!

Thus, prior to December 10th, the odds were a thousand to one that the president of the Republic, whoever he might turn out to be, would make his stand on the terrain of government, and therefore on reactionary ground. By as early as the 23rd, Louis Bonaparte was confirming that sinister prediction by pledging fealty to the Constitution. He would, he stated, be following Cavaignac's policy, and, in a gesture of alliance, he shook hands with his rival. What a revelation it was for the general when, from the very lips of Louis Bonaparte, he heard it stated that his government's record had been merely a paving of the way for absolutism! How he must have rued his dismal indulgence of the *decent, moderate* folk who had so unworthily betrayed him! And how he must have groaned not to have offered the amnesty that he was no doubt holding back as a token of reconciliation, for the day when he would come into his own! *Do what you must, come what may!* This feudal maxim was worthy of a republican.

Matters of controversy quickly cropped up and the government's suicide began. Coming in the wake of the summing-up by the prime minister, the Rateau proposal exposed these frictions. Irreconcilable differences between the authorities did not need thirty whole days to come to light: similarly, the people's mutual and instinctive hatred of the government and the government's of the people were more intensely manifested. The events of January 29th, when the government and the democrats could be found accusing each other of conspiracy and taking to the streets ready to do battle, were probably sheer panic, the upshot of their mistrust of each other: what was plainest about this adventure was the fact that there was war brewing between the democracy and the President, just as it had been once upon a time between the opposition and Louis-Philippe.

*Le Peuple* stood out in the fray. Our early Parisian editions read like indictments. Harking back to his first profession, one minister, Monsieur Léon Faucher, was polite enough to answer back: his insertions in *Le Moniteur*, remarked upon by the republican press, triggered a tidal wave of anger and pity. By himself, this liverish creature, whom Heaven has made even uglier than his caricature and who suffers from a singular obsession with actually being worse than his reputation, did more damage to the authorities he represented than all the democrat and socialist diatribes. Yes, had the Mountain held its patience and Monsieur Léon Faucher held on to his ministerial office for another three months, the street-urchins of Paris might have dispatched Louis Bonaparte back to the fortress of Ham[44] and his ministers to Charenton.[45] But no such success awaited journalistic malice: the social question could not be decanted by this ridiculous bickering; which speaks volumes for it.

---

44  A castle which was turned into a state prison. It had many famous prisoners, the last of whom was Louis-Napoléon who escaped after six years by adopting the identity of a painter, Badinguet. Later, his opponents would often refer to him disparagingly as Badinguet. (Editor)

45  Charenton was a lunatic asylum, founded in 1645 by the Frères de la Charité in Charenton-Saint-Maurice, now Saint-Maurice, Val-de-Marne, France. (Editor)

Having become, thanks to the lawmaker's determination and the selfishness of his advisors, the agent in charge of a policy of reaction and rancour, within three months Louis Bonaparte had frittered away the greater part of the strength with which the December elections had endowed him. Compromised by O. Barrot, committed to a liberticidal expedition by M. de Falloux, disgraced by Léon Faucher, the government under its new President caved in beyond recovery. Belief in the powers that be and respect for authority perished in the people's hearts. What sort of power is it that is wholly reliant upon the point of a bayonet? Kings and princes no longer have any belief in it themselves: their interests as capitalists take precedence over their dignity as sovereigns. It is not their crowns that they fear for these days: it is their assets! No longer do they protest, as Louis XVIII did while exiled in Mittau, against the actions of democracy; they do insist upon their revenues from it. Trying out monarchy in France when everybody, title-holders included, now regards it only as a civil list matter, is akin to twisting the knife in a corpse.

There is no victory but brings its toll of dead or wounded. The battle fought out on January 29th between the legislative authorities and the presidential prerogatives earned me three years in prison. This being the sort of decorations and pensions that the democratic social Republic promises its soldiers. Not that I am complaining; As the holy Scripture says *He who seeks danger will perish*; and *War is war*. I cannot resist pointing out, however, the profound wisdom with which the legislator, alert to the vindictiveness of parties, has afforded them, in the shape of the jury institution, an honest means of decimating one another, and reintroduced ostracism into our laws to cater for their hatreds.

In attacking Louis Bonaparte, I had thought that I was in perfect conformity with justice. The only offence with which I can be charged, if indeed I have committed any, was having offended the President of the Republic. Now, the President of the Republic being, like any other magistrate, answerable: the prerogatives of the royal personage, as determined by the law of 1819, being non-applicable in his case, I could only have been dragged before the courts on a complaint from the President I had supposedly offended and not on a specific charge from the public prosecutor who had no remit to meddle in a dispute between private individuals. So it was not so much a political charge that I was facing, as straightforward insult or defamation of the person. On which count I had nothing to fear. I had not attacked Louis Bonaparte in his private life; I had spoken simply of his performance in office. Later, during the debate on the recent press law, it was plainly the feeling that, under a special ordinance, the pursuit of offences committed in print against the President should be handed over to the public prosecution office.

But this hurdle, which seemed insurmountable to me as a scrupulous logician, was a mere bagatelle to the legal hair-splitters. To my extreme surprise, I found myself accused in connection with a pamphlet dealing exclusively with the President of the Republic:

First: Of inciting hatred against the government;

Second: Of incitement of civil war.

Third: Of attacking the Constitution and property!

Had it pleased Monsieur Meynard de Franc to charge me also, in relation to an article in *Le Peuple* about Louis Bonaparte, with the crimes of infanticide, rape or counterfeiting currency, he could have: the charge would have stood; and there was no reason for me not to have been also and just as judiciously convicted. Acting on its honour and its conscience, before God and before men, by a majority of 8 to 4, the jury found me guilty on all counts and I got my three years. You may ask, frank readers, how honour and conscience can possibly be ascribed to the arbitrariness of such a charge. Here is the key to the puzzle which will help you resolve all problems of the sort.

"The law"—states the Criminal Prosecution Code, Article 342—"does not require of jurymen an account of the *means* whereby they have been persuaded: it prescribes them no *rules* whereby they are bound to gauge the fullness and sufficiency of evidence. It does not tell them: *You will hold as true every fact to which such-and-such a number of witness may attest.* Any more than it tells them: *You are not to regard as sufficiently established any evidence that may not be made up of such-and-such a record, such-and-such components, such-and-such a number of witnesses and such-and-such particulars.* It puts only this single question which encapsulates the entire extent of their obligations: *Is it your heartfelt conviction?*"

Now do you understand? Jurymen are told: In your heart of hearts, is it your conviction that citizen P-J Proudhon, here present, is a danger to the state, a hindrance to the Jesuits, a menace to your capital and your property? It counts for little whether or not an actual crime has occurred; that the public prosecutor has offered no evidence to substantiate his charge; that the rationale he uses bears no relationship to the crimes and offences imputed to the accused. The law does not ask you for an accounting of the means whereby you have been persuaded: it lays down no rules for your judgement. And when the aforementioned Proudhon might show you—as he is well capable of doing—that the facts cited in the charge sheet are contested and travesties; when he establishes, on the basis of evidence and testimonials, that he has done the very opposite of that of which he stands accused, and that it is Louis-Bonaparte himself who, in the indicted articles, is attacking the constitution, inciting the citizenry to civil war, demolishing the Church and the government, you are not required to pay any heed to these things. You are familiar with the accused: you have heard tell of his teachings: he is out, they say, for nothing less than robbing capital of its revenue by making it compete with credit, as well as to demolish the government by organising universal suffrage. The law poses only this question to you; it encapsulates the whole and all of your obligations: *Do you have a heartfelt conviction regarding this man?*'

In civil proceedings, the judge is required to justify his determinations. He has to review the facts, the evidence, the testimony, the legal texts and the jurisprudence: then he shows his reasoning, his induction and sets out his principles and conclusions. In short, the essential part of any judgement is the *elaboration of the rationale*.

Criminal proceedings are a different matter: the jury is spared the requirement to explain its finding. It is tested only on its heartfelt conviction. It speaks instinctively, intuitively, as do women and animals in whom, it has always been believed, divinity resides:—*What did Aristides ever do to you?* one Athenian asked the rural juryman about to black-ball that illustrious outlaw.—*He annoys me*—the upright, free man answered—*in that I am forever hearing him dubbed "THE JUST MAN"!* So much for heartfelt conviction!

I have no reason to speak ill of my judges: they have merely abided by the spirit of their imperfect institution. Besides, as my friend Langlois says, who was at the time appearing on his own account in front of a Versailles jury, one of these days this jinx must fall upon my head. But whereas I was keen enough to be judged, convicted and maybe even jailed, I had at least made myself the heartfelt pledge that it would be for a heavyweight cause, the Bank of the People, for instance. Providence which is on my trail has not found me worthy enough to suffer for truth's sake.

Long live the democratic and social Republic!

# CHAPTER XVIII
## 21 MARCH: THE LAW ON THE CLUBS; LEGAL RESISTANCE

It was thus, by the election of December 10th and the formation of the Barrot-Faucher-Falloux ministry, that the forces of reaction made new progress. The government had passed from tomorrow's republicans into the hands of the doctrinaires. One step more, one more manifestation of unintelligent democracy, and we would fall into the hands of Jesuits. Then the blows administered by its own theologians, now becoming the continuators of the Revolution, will lead to the downfall of the principle of authority.

Everything is interdependent in the forward march of societies, everything serves the progress of revolutions. And when, poor reasoners that we are, we believe all is lost because of one of those blunders committed by our own blind politics, all is saved. Reaction pushes us onwards just as much as action, resistance is movement. The President of the Republic, whose historical significance is to dissolve the principle of authority among us, did not need to address the Montagnards to accomplish his work of death. According to the laws of revolutionary dialectics, which lead both governments and societies without them being aware of it, that would have been a retrograde movement on the part of Louis Bonaparte. From February on, the axis of the world having shifted, progress was being made though there seemed to be regression. We have just observed M. Odilon Barrot attack the *Constitution* in the name of the constitution itself by increasing the conflict between the separate powers: we are going to see M. Léon Faucher, the instigator of the events of January 29th, attack the *Institutions* by the law on the clubs. After the institutions it will be the turn of the *Principles*, and after the principles, the *Classes* of society. It is in this way that power reaches its own end: it cannot live either with the Constitution or the institutions, neither with principles nor with human beings. The auto-demolition of power forms a predetermined series of special acts, a sort of analytical operation which we shall see Louis Bonaparte's government execute with a rigour and precision which are entirely peculiar to our nation. The French people is the most logical of all.

Certainly, after the February Revolution made in the name of the right of assembly, that right which citizens have to discuss the interests of the nation among themselves and solemnly express their opinion on the acts committed by the power of government; after, I say, this striking affirmation of popular initiative, if there were one institution that a democratic government was duty-bound to respect, nay, not merely to respect but to develop, to organise up to the point at which it would have made it the most potent means of order and peace, then it was the clubs. I say clubs, as I would say assemblies, popular societies, public meeting-rooms, colleges, academies, congresses, electoral committees, etc; in a word, associations and meetings of all kinds and varieties. The name is immaterial. Under the name of clubs, or any other you please to use, it is a matter of the organisation of universal suffrage in all its forms, of the very structure of Democracy itself.

The provisional government had been content with placing the clubs under surveillance: it prided itself on its tolerance. Tolerance! That was already a declaration of hostility and a denial of its own principle. After tolerance, intolerance was bound to come. Cavaignac gave the signal; the ill-tempered Léon Faucher, finding his predecessor's work insufficient, undertook to complete it. He proposed a Bill which purely and simply declared the prohibition of the clubs.

To prohibit the clubs, to suppress the right of assembly, to forbid citizens to meet in a number exceeding twenty persons for any reason except by the permission and at the pleasure of the authorities: this is to declare that power is all, that it alone owns progress, intelligence, ideas; that democracy is only a word, and the true constitution of society is the system of solitary confinement; and that it was absolutely necessary for the peace of the world and the order of civilisation that one of the two things should perish, namely either the initiative of the citizens or that of the State; either liberty or the government. M. Léon Faucher's project did not contain anything but this dilemma, essentially.

When M. Odilon Barrot raised his hand against the Holy Ark of the government by fomenting the conflict of the separate powers, we responded to his thought by holding the sword of Damocles, presidential responsibility, over Louis Bonaparte's head. M. Léon Faucher had it in for institutions: the best thing to do was to oppose a legal institution to him, namely legal resistance.

One recalls that famous session of March 21st in which M. Crémieux, the *rapporteur*[46], declared in the name of the Committee appointed to examine the Bill on the clubs that the Constitution was violated by this Bill and that consequently the Committee would cease to participate in the debate. It is well-known that following this declaration nearly two hundred members of the constitutive Assembly left the debating chamber and immediately met in the Old Chamber to TAKE COUNSEL. This was nothing less than the beginning of a demonstration similar to that of June 13th, the first measure of constitutional resistance. But the proximity to February was too great, and we should admire the prudence of the representatives: afraid of weakening authority, they preferred to tolerate a violation rather than make a revolution. Thanks to a parliamentary compromise the demonstration by the minority had no consequences. The very next day, however, *Le Peuple* completed the opposition's line of thought by calling upon all citizens to immediately offer resistance if the Assembly passed the bill.

As the question of legal resistance is of the highest seriousness, it being a part of republican law which is revived every day by the arbitrary nature of power and of the parliamentary majority, and because many people confuse it with the right to insurrection recognised by the Declaration of 1793, I am going to give a short account of its true principles before accounting for the political course followed by the *People* in this situation.

What is the right to insurrection?

How is one to understand the concept of legal resistance?

In which cases may one or the other apply?

If it were possible that the government were truly concerned with order, if it respected liberty and sought less to impose arbitrary decisions, it would make haste to deal with these questions officially and not leave the job to a journalist. But the government hates all questions of legality above all things and hushes them up as much as it can. What occupies it most is to persecute authors, printers, newspaper sellers, peddlers, bill-posters: it reserves its instructions and circulars for them.

---

46  Adolphe Crémieux (1796–1880), a moderate republican, was appointed Minister of Justice after the February Revolution. Elected to the National Assembly in April, Crémieux retained the justice portfolio and was sent as part of a parliamentary delegation to explain the decision to abolish the national workshops to national guard units in June. He acted as *rapporteur* for numerous committees, i.e., he made reports on various questions which he then read to those committees. (Translator)

I will observe first of all that the rights of insurrection and resistance belong to the period of subordination and antagonism: they fall into disuse when liberty is practised. In a democracy organised on the basis of the popular initiative originating in multiple locations with no superior authority the exercise of such rights would have no grounds for taking place at all. By the establishment of universal suffrage the Constitution of 1790 had already invalidated, while implicitly recognising, the right to insurrection. Imperial despotism, the Charters of 1814 and 1830, the 200 franc poll tax suppressing the intervention of the masses in public affairs, all these re-established it. The February Revolution had once more abolished it, at the same time as the death penalty: the monstrous doctrine of the omnipotence of parliamentary majorities which the government would like to impose restores it again.

After all, it is not, to tell the truth, a principle of democratic and social institutions that we are discussing here: it is a principle of absolute and constitutional monarchy, an idea born of privilege. Socialism repudiates the right to insurrection and legal resistance: its theory has no need of such sanctions. However, forced to defend itself on the terrain where the Constitution challenges it, it borrows the right from absolutists and doctrinaire politicians, authors or instigators of that Constitution, and uses it against them in the manner of an *argumentum ad hominem*, to use the scholastic expression.

The right to insurrection is that by virtue of which a people can claim its liberty, either against the tyranny of a despot or against the privileges of an aristocracy, without a previous denunciation as warning, and by force of arms.

It may happen, and hitherto this has been the almost constant state of the majority of nations, that an immense, scattered people, disarmed and betrayed, finds itself at the mercy of a few thousand enforcers under the orders of a despot. In this state, insurrection is fully justified and has no rules but those of prudence and opportunity. The insurrections of July 14th and August 10th were of this nature. There was a chance that Malet's conspiracy in 1812 could have provoked an insurrection which would have been equally legitimate. The insurrection of July 1830, in which the country sided with the parliamentary majority against a king who violated a pact, was irreproachable. That of 1848, in which the majority of the country rose against the parliamentary majority to claim the right to vote, was all the more rational for having as its object the abolition of the right to insurrection by re-establishing universal suffrage.

So when the Convention, after having organised the primary assemblies and re-consecrated universal suffrage, wrote the right to insurrection into the Constitution of the Year II, it was creating retrospective legislation, to be exact; it took out a guarantee against a danger which no longer existed in principle. The Constituent Assembly of 1848 acted in the same way when, having declared *direct and universal suffrage* in Article 24, in Article 110 it adds that it *entrusts the Constitution and the rights that it preserves to the guardianship and the patriotism of all the French.* In principle, let me repeat, universal suffrage abolishes the right to insurrection: in practice, the antagonism of the separate powers and the absolutism of majorities can cause it to be reborn. How and in what cases is precisely what must yet be determined.

The right of insurrection has a particular characteristic, viz. that it presupposes a people oppressed by a despot, a third estate by an aristocracy, the greater number by the lesser. That is the principle, apart from which the right of insurrection vanishes at the same time as the conflicts of opinions and interests. The social union effectively takes on a different character inasmuch as the practice of universal suffrage becomes more widespread and propagates itself, while economic forces tend toward equilibrium; the empire of minorities is succeeded by that of majorities, which latter is itself succeeded by that of universality, that is absolute liberty, which excludes any idea of conflict.

There is, however, one case when the right of insurrection might be legitimately invoked by a minority against a majority: that would be in a transitional society when the majority wishes to abolish universal suffrage, or at least limit its application, in order to perpetuate its despotism. In that case, I maintain, the minority has the right to resist oppression, even by force.

Universal suffrage is basically the mode by which the majority and the minority manifest themselves; it is this from which the majority draws its right at the same time as its very existence, which implies that if universal suffrage were suppressed any minority might stake its claim to be the majority without fear of contradiction and consequently call for an insurrection. That is what legitimises the *thirty-year-old* conspiracy which we have seen certain members of the provisional government boast of from their parliamentary platform. From 1814 to 1848 universal suffrage did not exist, so the legitimacy of the government could always be doubted, and experience has proven twice over, essentially, that outside of universal suffrage this legitimacy of the government is null and void.

In a word, notwithstanding any vote to the contrary by the people or its representatives, the tacit or manifest consent by the people to the abolition of universal suffrage cannot be presumed.[47]

---

47  This was written more than 6 months before the Law of May 31st, 1850 which deprived more than 300,000 citizens of their right to vote and replaced universal suffrage by limited suffrage. At the time of the passing of that law I was at Doullens, where the administration had sent me for an article about the April elections. It was not due to my colleagues on the *Voix du Peuple* that the democrats did not put into practice the principles developed in my *Confessions*. The police made sure of that by suppressing the newspaper; and the People, more wisely, I admit, understood that it was better for the defence of its rights to allow the powers that be to lose their way

Such is the jurisprudence, if I may put it like that, of the right of insurrection according to our imperfect constitutions and our revolutionary traditions. What is most worth retaining of all that is the fact that as the progress of democracy advances this terrible right abolishes itself, and one may assert that unless a restoration of absolutist ideas were to take place, which has in fact become impossible, the time of conspiracies and revolts has passed.

We now come to legal resistance.

We have said that the right of insurrection cannot be allowed to pertain to a minority against a majority in a country where universal suffrage has begun to develop. However arbitrary the decisions of that majority may be and however flagrant the violation of the pact may appear, a majority can always deny that there is a violation as such, which reduces the difference to a simple question of perspective and consequently offers no pretext for revolt. Even if the minority invoked certain rights *prior* or *superior* to the Constitution that it claims the majority has overlooked, it would be easy for the latter to invoke in its turn other prior or superior rights like the public safety by virtue of which it could legitimise its will. This would be so effective that it would always be necessary to arrive at a definitive solution by voting, to appeal to the law of number. So let us admit this proposition as proven: between the minority and the majority of the citizens as constitutionally manifested by universal suffrage, an armed conflict is illegitimate.

A minority cannot be permitted to be at the mercy of a majority, however: justice, which is the negation of force, demands that the minority have its guarantees. For it may occur as a result of political passions and the opposition of interests that the minority reacts to an action of the ruling majority by claiming that the Constitution has been violated, which the majority denies; when the people are called upon as a final arbiter of this disagreement, being the supreme judge in these matters, the majority of the citizens joins the majority of representatives with uncompromising egoism in deliberately treading underfoot both truth and justice, though they are precisely the ones who should defend them according to the Constitution. The minority, overtly oppressed, is then no longer a party in political and parliamentary opposition but a proscribed party, a whole class of citizens thus being placed outside the law. Such a situation is shameful, is suicide, is the destruction of all social bonds. Yet insurrection in the terms of the Constitution is forbidden: what can the minority do in this extreme case?

When the law is audaciously violated; when a fraction of the people is outlawed by society; when the passionate impetus of a party has come to the point of saying: *We will never give in*; when there are two nations in the nation, one of them weaker and oppressed, the other, more numerous, which oppresses:

---

through their own violation of the pact rather than offer them the opportunity for a useless massacre and perhaps even a victory. This wise conduct was entirely to the benefit of the Revolution and forever closed the possibility of a return to Jacobinism.

if the division is admitted on both sides, my opinion is that the minority has the right to consummate this division by declaring it. The social bond being broken, the minority is freed from any political agreement with the majority: this is expressed by the refusal to obey those in power, to pay one's taxes, to do one's military service etc. A refusal motivated in this way has been called *legal resistance* by journalists because the government has gone beyond the bounds of law, and the citizens remind it of that fact by refusing to obey it.

The law on clubs, the police intervention in electoral meetings, the bombardment of Rome, all of these violated the Constitution and outlawed the democratic party, so to speak, thus motivating the application of the principle of legal resistance, inasmuch as the democratic party was in the minority in the country; if this party gained a majority and then the government persisted the right of insurrection would follow.

With ministers like the one who pretended that the cry of *Long live the democratic and social Republic!*—which sums up the whole Constitution—is unconstitutional and seditious, or the other who denounced the democratic socialists as criminals and looters, or a third one who actually had them prosecuted, judged and condemned as such, with a government that understood by the word *order* nothing but the extermination of republican opinion, and which, not daring to openly attack the Revolution in Paris, went to Rome in order to suppress it, which declared war ON IDEAS, which said aloud: No concessions!—which repeated at every instant, as on June 23rd, *There must be an end to this!*—the situation was clear, there was nothing to be misunderstood. Open persecution was declared on social democracy, we were denounced in terms of contempt and hate, singled out for public condemnation by the authorities, as was not concealed by the minister responsible for the Bill in question. This may be judged by the following description reported at the time by *La Presse*, words that I would like to see inscribed on a bronze tablet to the eternal shame of the one who was its hero:

"There is but one thing more difficult to describe than the treatment inflicted on M. Furet, and that is the letter that was written by M. Léon Faucher when he was the domestic minister to his colleague the Minister of the Navy on the question of the discipline to which the insurgents of June were to be subjected. It was not merely a question of recommending that there should be no distinction made between them and the convicts condemned for murder and theft, no, the refinement of repression was extended to the point of refusing those convicted in June the consolation of being shackled to their fellows and ordering that every insurgent be chained to a murderer or thief! Fortunately, the ministry of the interior's temporary directive having been entrusted to M. Lacrosse, very different orders were in fact issued."

M. Léon Faucher is one of those characters whom one only encounters once every four thousand years. To find his match you have to go back to the mythical period and the Homeric brigand who caused his victims to die by attaching them to corpses. Well! This is the man who, on January 29th, *for the love of order!*—which translated means *for hatred of the revolution*, invited the national guard to massacre the socialists; who on March 21st presented the brutal law which failed to bring about the overthrow of those in power; who on May 11th lied in a telegram in order to suppress the national representation of republican candidates;[48] who, thrown out by the ministry and taking curative showers to calm his fever, still accused his successor of undue moderation towards democrats; who of late agitated among the departments, inciting them to rise against the Constitution in the name of order... I will stop here: I would need a book to tell of all the evil that the passage of this fanatic to the ministry has done to the country much more than to socialism. Visit the prisons; have them show you the registers of custody; question the detainees; ask the lawyers; check the secret and apparent reasons for convictions; and then count the number of unfortunates arbitrarily arrested, kept in preventive custody for months at a time, led with a chain round their necks from police station to police station, condemned on the most futile pretexts, all because they were socialists. Then count those who were really guilty of crimes and whose penalties were increased in severity because they were suspected of socialism, because socialism had become an aggravating circumstance for the judges, because it was the intention of the authorities to categorise socialists as criminals: and then you will tell me whether a party counting more than a third of the nation—the elections of May 13th justify that claim—might well consider itself unjustly persecuted, whether the Bill concerning the clubs knowingly violated the Constitution, whether Léon Faucher's law was not a declaration of social war?

As for me, I thought it was our duty immediately to organise—not an insurrection, for we were a minority against a majority, one party against a coalition of parties—but legal resistance to whatever extent that concept might provide for.

I have no intention at this moment to repeat a proposal which remained fruitless. From June 13th on, circumstances have changed; and if I have just given an account of the means that I proposed to employ at that time, it is because, such is at least my fervent hope, the occasion for employing those means has passed, never to return. The Revolution, in its rapid course, can make nothing of this rusty horseshoe of legal resistance any more, so now I can summarise the theory without endangering the public peace. I fought a good, hard war against the government of Louis Bonaparte; more than once, perhaps, things would have turned out differently if I had been believed. But

---

48   Just before elections, Faucher sent a telegram to the rural prefects describing the republican representatives who had opposed the military action in Rome as "*agitateurs*" who were "ready to mount the barricades and bring back the days of June," listing their names, apparently so that voters could be warned against re-electing them. The Constituent Assembly censured Faucher so harshly in response that he was forced to resign on May 14th. (Editor)

in the socialist army of Grouchy and Bourmont[49] there were incompetents and traitors: and it is just because in my opinion taking recourse to legal resistance would be a mistake in the light of the present complications of politics, almost a crime against the Revolution in fact, that I protest against the abuse that could be committed in its name at the same time as I recall here the formalities appropriate to a measure of this kind.

The means were not new. They were the same ones that MM. Guizot, Thiers and their kind were preparing to employ in 1830 before the legitimist reaction precipitated events which led to their more complete and prompt victory. But if the idea was old its execution was extremely simple and reliable.

The Mountain had to proclaim legal resistance to the tribune, at first in a commentary form. The democratic press subsequently made it the text of its instructions to the people for one month. The representatives wrote about it to their electorate: everywhere the government was enjoined not to continue on its reactionary course. If those in power persisted in their course despite the warnings that had been given them, committees were formed to block the government in an airtight manner; the citizens and local boroughs agreed to refuse to accept taxation; all governmental rights to financial awards, state control, navigation, registration etc; military service; obedience to the authorities—all at the same time. Public opinion was fomented until resistance spontaneously exploded into life everywhere without any signal. The motivation of the resistance was simple and clear: the law on clubs, the Rome expedition and judicial persecutions were part of a war on the Republic: was it the republicans' duty to furnish money and soldiers for this purpose?...

Can you imagine what an organised resistance could have been like in the 37,000 communes of France? The democratic party represented more than a third of the nation: just try to find *garnisaires* and *gendarmes* prepared to constrain three million people to make their contributions! The peasants, whatever their political opinion, would no sooner have heard about refusing to pay taxes than they would have declared themselves in favour and started by just not paying any more; their hate of the salt tax, the drinks tax and the 45 cent tax was a sure guarantee of their dispositions. Something would have happened in town and country that happens in banks, stock exchanges and all the financial and commercial world at the moment of political crises: in the uncertainty surrounding events, and in order not to be duped, everyone postpones his payments as long as he can. Would the government have wished to have implemented strict measures? Any prosecutions would only

---

49  Grouchy and Bourmont were two military commanders under Napoléon during the battle of Waterloo. Grouchy was sent to pursue part of the retreating Prussian army and despite hearing the cannon sound from nearby Waterloo, he decided to obey his orders and engage the one Prussian Corps in Wavre. The troops committed to this battle could have turned the tide at Waterloo. Bourment was a royalist who betrayed Napoléon by handing the campaign plans to the Prussians. (Editor)

have fanned the fire. At a single stroke, without any conflict, without bloodshed, our very complicated taxation system would have been overturned and changed from top to bottom as a matter of necessity; military conscription would have been abolished, the system reformed and the credit institutions conquered. The people being called upon to vote on taxes itself, socialism by means of this minority resolution would have become a law of necessity and part of the practice of the State.

One only needs very little knowledge of the people and of governmental machinery to understand what an irresistible force such a system of opposition would have had, if solemnly announced and energetically maintained, especially after the elections of May 13th. The democratic party was alone in finding it mean-spirited, impracticable, impossible. They spoke of furniture being seized and auctioned off, peasants terrified by the government debt collectors! The most advanced and furiously revolutionary papers were amazed by this *inconceivable policy*, this *procureur* tactic, as they claimed. They trembled at the idea of exposing the people to a collective billeting of *garnisaires*! The most benevolent ones still found the resolution imprudent, hazardous and above all anti-governmental. If the people, they said, refused to pay its taxes once, it would never pay them again and government would become impossible! If the citizens are taught to split themselves up, if the history of the Roman people on the Sacred Mount[50] is repeated by way of a parliamentary conflict, very soon the departments and provinces will separate from one another: centralisation will be attacked on all sides, we will fall into federalism: there will be no more Authority! It is always the government which preoccupies the Jacobins. They need a government and with it a budget, secret funds, as many as possible. In short, the counter-revolution was admirably defended by the organs of the revolution: the Jacobins, who detested the Gironde so much because it opposed centralised despotism in the name of local liberties, spoke in favour of doctrinaire politicians. *Le Peuple* got five years in prison and a fine of 10,000 francs for its initiative and *Le Constitutionnel*, laughing up its sleeve, only had to keep quiet.

What a lesson for me! What a pitiable downfall! How badly I had judged my contemporaries, conservatives and friends of *order* to the core! How little I knew of our so-called revolutionaries, really power-mongers and intriguers whose understanding of the Republic founded in 1792 was limited to Robespierre's Committee of Public Safety and his police force! And these

---

50 Ancient Rome was marked by increasing inequality and internal political struggle between the aristocratic patricians and the common people ("plebs"). Many of the latter were imprisoned or enslaved when they could not repay their debts. In 494 B.C. the plebs simply walked out of the city to the Sacred Mount leaving the patricians rulers of an empty city. The patricians had no choice but to negotiate and so the tribunes of the plebs were founded to protect the people against oppression. (Editor)

were the *reds* who enraged Léon Faucher! These were the so-called terrorists that Louis Bonaparte's government made such a bogey-man of! What calumny!

Parties are like societies, like man himself. When they get old they return to childhood. The history of Jacobinism, from the 25th of February 1848 to the 13th of June 1849, is nothing but a succession of mistakes. But I have to make another admission, however painful it is to my self-esteem. The Revolution was better served by the incapacity of its agents than by the decisive steps that I proposed. From the 13th of June on we had finished with parties and with government: that is preferable to re-establishing the Montagnards in the place of the doctrinaires and the Jesuits. The power of events leaves us nothing more to do. *Il mondo va de se!*[51]

# CHAPTER XXI
## 8 JULY 1849: CONCLUSION

AND NOW, DEAR reader, whatever your opinion may be, if the facts that I have told you are true and you do not have the means to refute them; if the importance that I have assigned to them is correct, and if it has been sufficient, in order to assure you of this, to relate them to their causes and compare these to one another; if, in the final analysis, their development proved both predictable and ultimately fatal (two terms, which, when applied to humanity, mean exactly the same thing); and if, in order to state the inevitability of this evolution, you only had to observe it as it unfolded from its very source, namely the Reason of humanity itself: if, and I urge you so to do, you permit yourself to believe your eyes, your memory, your judgement, just judge for yourself where the February Revolution has taken us.

The July Monarchy, having carried out the dissolution of all the old principles, left itself a double task to achieve. These were, on the one side, the dissolution of the Parties as a result of the dissolution of ideas; and on the other, the bankruptcy of power, reduced through the successive elimination of all its principles to the worthless corpse of authority, to the blunt instrument of force.

On June 13th, 1849, Jacobinism was the first to fall, itself having been resurrected in 1830 with the reappearance of a monarchy and then only managing to revive the revolutionary idea of 1789. This last expression of governmental democracy or demagogy, agitator without cause, ambitious without intelligence, violent without heroism, not even having four people to call upon nor a system to implement, then perished from consumption and inanity as had dogmatism, its precursor and antagonist.

---

51   Italian: "The world runs itself." (Editor)

In the same way, Socialism, mystical, theogonical and transcendental, vanished like a ghost, relinquishing its place to traditional, practicable, positive social philosophy. The day when Louis Blanc demanded his Ministry of Progress[52] and proposed to shake up and uproot the whole country, when Considérant managed to solicit an advance of four million francs and an extensive acreage upon which to build his model community, when Cabet, on abandoning France as an accursed land, thus abandoning his school and his memory to his slanderers, left for the United States to (if I may avail myself of the expression) drop his babies; on this day, judgement was passed on this governmental, phalansterian and icarian Utopia; it admitted its guilt.

Along with Socialism, Absolutism lies also on the verge of disappearing. Forced right back into a final corner by its own indefatigable contradictions, Absolutism has betrayed itself: it has revealed to the world every aspect of its hatred for liberty. Forced to revert back to tradition, as Socialism is forced to rush headlong into Utopianism, it absents itself from the present, removing itself from any sense of historical or social truth.

There are no longer any parties in French society endowed with any kind of vital force; and until new principles, springing from the inexhaustible sources of human practice, other interests, other mores, a new philosophy, transforming the old world without breaking with it, and regenerating it, have opened Opinion to new solutions; there no such parties shall be left among us. In the absence of the first idea, the diversity of opinions that would unfold from that idea is impossible.

For this very same reason there no longer exists a Government, and there never will be one. Since it creates nothing in the real world which is not as a result of something else, neither does it defend a principle nor an idea which has not been already expressed: a Government that has neither opinion nor a Party to represent expresses nothing, is nothing.

The men we see still carrying the old Party banners, who solicit and galvanise power, who tug at the Revolution's strings from both Left and Right are not even alive: they are dead. They neither govern nor represent opposition to the government: they celebrate, by means of a symbolic dance, their own funerals.

The Socialists, not daring to seize power when power was at its most audacious, lost three months involving themselves in Club intrigues, in gossip from factions and sects, in chaotic demonstrations; later, they tried to give themselves official consecration by having the "right to work" inscribed

---

52   Blanc wrote: "The logic of history demands the creation of a Ministry of Progress, having as its special purpose the energising of the Revolution, the opening of the road that leads to dazzling horizons." This proposal, which would have given him a budget to control, was rejected, and instead Blanc was given his place on the Luxembourg Commission. (Editor)

on the Constitution, without demonstrating any means by which to guarantee it; they, not knowing what to do with themselves, continue to press for ridiculous and untrustworthy schemes: the Socialists, don't they have designs on governing the world? They are dead; they have swallowed their tongues (as a French peasant would say!) Let them sleep their sleep, as they wait for a scientific answer, which is not and never has been theirs, to call them.

And the Democratic-Governmentalist Jacobins having spent eighteen years conspiring among themselves, with no concept of a single aspect of social economy, then exerted control for four months during the dictatorship[53] and failed to harvest any more fruit than a succession of reactionary actions, followed by a terrible civil war; they, at the last moment, speaking always of liberty, continue to dream of dictatorship: would it also be unfair to speak of them as dead, and to claim that their tomb has already been sealed? When the people have rebuilt a philosophy and a faith, when society knows whence it has emerged and where it is heading, what it is capable of and what it wants, only then will these demagogues be able to return, not to govern the people, but to re-ignite their passion.

The Doctrinaires are dead too: the men of the insipid *juste-milieu*, the partisans of the so-called constitutional regime, breathed their last at the session on October 20th, after having, at the one on April 16th, made a Republican Assembly decree the institution of a doctrinaire Papacy. Do you think we would let them govern us again? They have already revealed themselves. In politics no less than in philosophy, there are more than two ways to achieve a genuine eclecticism: the Charter of 1830 and the Acts of Government of Louis Bonaparte have managed to extinguish the potential creativity of the *juste-milieu*.

The Absolutist Party, first in logic, first in history, won't be far behind all the others in expiring amid convulsions of blood-spattered agony and liberticide. In the wake of the victories of Radetzki, of Oudinot, of Haynau,[54] the principle of authority, both spiritually and temporally, is destroyed. It is no longer by means of government that Absolutism is imposed: it is by means of murder. What looms over Europe now is nothing but the shadow of tyranny: soon the sunshine of Liberty will rise, only to set when humankind's time is over. Like Christ eighteen centuries ago, Liberty triumphs: it reigns, it governs. Its name is on everyone's lips and thus in everyone's heart. As for Absolutism, in order that it will not rise again, it is no longer sufficient to silence its advocates; it is necessary instead, as Montalembert wanted, to

---

53  The period between the February Revolution and the election of the Constituent Assembly in May. As the provisional government was not elected, many commentators at the time referred to it as a dictatorship as a result. (Editor)

54  Radetzki and Haynau were Austrian Generals who crushed popular revolutions in Italy in 1848–49 while Oudinot led the French destruction of the revolutionary republic in Rome in 1849. (Editor)

conduct a war of ideas. Losing the souls along with the bodies—essentially the function of the expedition of Rome, and thus also the function of ecclesiastical government—there came a realisation, too late for their common salvation, that it was also necessary to incorporate an element of secularism.

It is this confusion of Parties, this death of power that Louis Bonaparte revealed to us; and like the Chief priest among the Jews, Louis Bonaparte was prophetic: "*France has elected me,*" he said, "*because I don't belong to any Party!*" Yes, France elected him because it did not want anyone to govern any more. A man consists of a body and a soul; similarly, a government consists of a Party and a principle: however, now there are neither Parties nor principles. That is what has become of Government.

This is what the people denounced in February when, unifying two denominations in a single one, they ordered, under their sovereign authority, the fusion of two Parties which expressed in a far better way both the ideology and the practice of the revolution, thus naming the Republic *democratic and social*.

However, if, according to the will of the people, all shades of democracy and all schools of socialism were to disappear and to become unified as one, similarly absolutism and constitutionalism would equally disappear and become one. This is what the democratic socialist organs were telling us when they said that there were only two parties left in France, the Party of Labour and the Party of Capital; and this definition was accepted immediately by the two reactionary parties, and it acted as the watchword for the elections of May 13th.

The London exiles acted on the same idea when they made known their intention never to convene before the High Court. On June 13th, one of the great revolutionary stages was reached. Power fell in tandem with the last remaining Party with any life left in it: what was the point in giving an account to the New France of the demonstrations that had taken place in another era? The London Declaration[55] represented the resignation of the Jacobin Party: shadows fought shadows for a shadow of authority. Thus Ledru-Rollin and his friends perfectly understood the meaning of their presence at the trials of Versailles. Let us be wary, Republicans, of agitating retrospectively and thus creating a Counter-Revolution!

And, since I am accounting here for my every smallest utterance, I reaffirm that it is the same idea, the same necessity for social and political transformation that has informed my conduct since the last elections.

I declined the candidacy which was offered to me because the list upon which my name was inscribed no longer made any sense in the situation; the

---

55  André Louis Jules Lechevalier (1800–50) was an economist and journalist, an ardent follower of Victor Considérant. He was arrested and convicted for taking part in the demonstration on June 13th, 1849. Anticipating this, Lechevalier fled to London in July 1849 and wrote his *Déclaration* in October. (Editor)

spirit which had caused this list to be drawn up tended to perpetuate the old classifications, whereas it was necessary to oppose these; since the political routine, of which the people have been dupes and victims for sixty years, had committed a slow suicide on June 13th, I did not want to be the one to revive it.

In conjunction with my fellow prisoners, I proposed another list which, moving away from all consideration of personality, taking no account of nuances of opinion, faithful to the politics of fusion proclaimed by the people themselves after the February events, better expressed (in my opinion) the thoughts of Republican France and the needs of the movement. Published on the Tuesday, the list could have rallied all the democratic forces, had it been wished. It was criticised for arriving too late. The demagogic tail was wagging again; and my opinions and advice were currently out of fashion. Under instruction to withdraw *my* list—I say mine because it was attributed to me even though I was only its editor—with the express purpose, it was said, of not dividing the voice of the *party*, I refused. I no longer recognised the *party*; I did not even want it to continue to exist. My conduct in relation to the *party* was, on this occasion, the same as on December 10th. I protested against the general mistaken principle in the hope that the state of decay was not universal and in the hope that SOCIALIST DEMOCRACY, in opening up its ranks, could become, in a significant way, the party of LIBERTY.

No, I did not want to further the ambitions of those who, from February 25th, 1848 to June 13th, 1849, had continually sacrificed the Revolution to their own selfish passions; those who constantly misunderstood its character; those who were the first to react against it; those who, in taking up the reins of government themselves, ended up, like the men of 1793, forgetting about such matters as liberty and the people.

I did not want to assist either the prolongation of power by the Parties nor the Parties by power. With this in mind, the result of the demonstration of June 13th, as outrageous as it appeared to me with regard to the Constitution and liberty, served the Revolution only too well, such that, by July 8th, all I wanted was to overturn this result.

I refused to work for the restoration of the monarchy, seeing in the monarchy fertile ground for the re-emergence of Jacobinism. My readers must be enlightened enough about the progress of societies to know that an idea never advances alone, and that opposites often arise simultaneously.

I never consented to making myself the instrument of a coterie which, despite managing on May 13th, June 13th and July 8th, with certain amount of compromise, to rally all of the republican strands under the democratic socialist banner and thus becoming the embodiment of the nation, preferred to remain a faction; and furthermore, treating its candidates as machines, its allies as dupes, its egoism as its yardstick, when the leadership declared victory to its representatives, impatient of the law and mistrustful of their patriotism, it instructed them once more to descend to street level and to commit suicide.

As for the rest, I confess that, to the extent that one knows me and one wishes to save me from future pointless slander, I have never been much of a flexible character, and neither have I an easy-going nature and personality; never have I been one to submit to an occult power nor to work for the profit of my gainsayers, nor to devote myself to that which I despise, nor to bow down before the dogmatism of a dozen fanatics, nor, having been blessed with a sense of reasoned thinking, to become the blind instrument of a school of thought which I mistrust and which only shows its true colours under examination from the upholders of the law.

I belong to the Party of Labour against the Party of Capital; and I have laboured all my life. Now, let it be remembered: of all the parasites I know, the worst type is still the revolutionary parasite.

I wish neither to Govern nor to be *Governed*! Let those who, at the time of the elections of July 8th accused me of *ambition*, of *pride*, of *indiscipline*, of *venality*, of *treason*, search their own hearts. When I so vigorously attacked the Government's response, when I solicited the initiative of the people, when I proposed a refusal to pay a tax, when I wanted to establish democratic socialism within the law and according to the constitution, was it not perhaps against their ambition, their pride, their governmental spirit, their economic utopias that I was waging war?

Now, enough of regrets, enough of failures! We have established a slate clean of Parties and of Government. The story is reaching its climax: if the people only open their eyes, they can be free.

No power, divine or human, could stop the Revolution. What remains for us to do now is simply to declare this before the Old Order, thus strengthening support for the sacred cause. The people are propaganda enough. Our task, as publicists, is to protect the revolution from the dangers with which its path is littered, it is to guide it according to its eternal principle.

The dangers which threaten the revolution are as follows:

*The dangers presented by power*—Power, as embodied by those same people who accuse the new spirit of materialism, is nothing more than a word. Take away its bayonets and you will see what I mean. Let us take care to prevent a soul from re-inhabiting this corpse, possessed as it is by a diabolical spirit. Let us keep away from the vampire that still thirsts for our blood. May an exorcism by organised universal suffrage return it to its grave forever.

*The dangers presented by the parties*—All of the parties trailed far behind the revolutionary idea; all of them betrayed the people by implementing dictatorship; all showed themselves to be resistant to liberty and progress. Let us not resuscitate them only so that they can revive their in-fighting. Let us not try to convince the people that it would be possible to guarantee work, well-being and liberty if only the Government were to pass from this person here to that person there; the Right, having crushed the Left, is in turn crushed by the Left. As Power is the instrument and citadel of tyranny, so are Parties its lifeblood and intelligence.

*The dangers presented by the reaction*—I have fought throughout my life against many ideas: this was my right. I have never and will never simply react against an idea for its own sake. Philosophy and history prove that it is a thousand times easier, more human, more just, to change ideas than to repress them. I will remain, whatever happens, faithful to that wisdom. The Jesuits, the Janissaries of Catholicism, today the oppressors of everybody, will fall when it pleases God: I will not react to Catholicism. After the Jesuits, the governmental and communitarian demagogy[56] may give to the world, if the world permits it, one last representation of authority: I will help its emergence from the chaos into what it will become; I will work to repair its ruins; I will not react to communism.

The principle of the Revolution, let us remind ourselves, is Liberty.

Liberty! By which we mean: first, political emancipation by means of universal suffrage, by the independent centralisation of social functions, by the continuous and unceasing revision of the Constitution; second, industrial emancipation by the mutual guarantee of credit and markets.

In other words:

No more government of man by man by means of accumulated power:

No more exploitation of man by man by means of accumulated capital.

Liberty! This is the first and last word of social philosophy. Isn't it strange that, after all the oscillations and back-tracking along the unreliable and complicated road of revolutions, we should end up discovering that the remedy for all the miseries, the solution to all the problems, consists of giving a freer passage to liberty, removing the barricades which have been set in its path by public and proprietary Authority?

But no matter! This is how humanity always reaches an understanding and implementation of its ideas.

Socialism appears: it evokes the fables of antiquity, the legends of uncivilised people, all the reveries of the philosophers and thinkers. It presents itself as a pantheistic, metamorphic, epicurean trinity; it speaks of the body of Christ, of planetary generations, of unisexual love, of phanerogamy, of omnigamy, of communal child-rearing, of a gastrosophical regime, of industrial harmony, of analogies among plants and animals. It shocks and outrages everybody. What then does it want? What exactly is it? Nothing. It is the *product* that wants to become Money; it is the *Government* that wants to become Administration! And that is the only reform it offers!

What our generation lacks is not a Mirabeau nor a Robespierre, nor a Bonaparte: what it lacks is a Voltaire. We know nothing of how to understand our world with an independent and irreverent interpretation. We are slaves to our opinions and our interests and, in taking ourselves too seriously, we are rendered stupid. Science, of which the most precious fruit is its unceasing contribution to liberty and thought, becomes for us a form of

---

56   *Communautaire*, advocates of centralised and regimented socialism (or "community"). (Editor)

pedantry; instead of emancipating intelligence, it stupefies it. In sum, with regard to that which we love and that which we hate, we have lost the ability to laugh at others and they at us: in losing our spirit, we have lost our liberty.

Liberty produces everything in the world, and I mean everything; even that which it then comes to destroy, be it religions, governments, nobility, property...

In the same way that Reason, its sister, has yet to construct a system, it is still working to extend and refashion it; thus liberty tends to ceaselessly modify its earlier creations, to emancipate itself from the organs it has created and to create new ones from which it, in turn, will detach itself, as with the previous ones, regarding them with the same pity and dislike with which it regards those which it has already replaced.

Liberty, like Reason, only exists and manifests itself through the continued reinvention of its own works; its downfall is its own narcissism. This is why irony has always been the mark of liberal and philosophical genius, the seal of the human spirit, the irresistible instrument of progress. Unchanging peoples are peoples without joy; a member of a society that knows how to laugh is a thousand times closer to rationality and liberty than the praying anchorite[57] or the quibbling philosopher.

Irony, you are true liberty! You are what saves me from ambition to power, from servitude to parties, from respect for routine, from scientific pedantry, from the worship of great men, from the mystification of politics, from the fanaticism of reformers, from the superstition of this great universe and from the adoration of myself. You revealed yourself to the Wise One on the Throne when he cried out, in view of the world in which he was regarded as a demi-god: *Vanity of Vanities!* You were the familiar-demon of the Philosopher when he unmasked, at a single stroke, both the dogmatist and the sophist, the hypocrite and the atheist, the epicurean and the cynic. You consoled the Righteous One in his final hours as he prayed on the cross for his torturers: *Father, forgive them, for they know not what they do!*

Sweet Irony! You alone are pure, chaste and discreet. You give grace to the beauty and piquancy of love; you inspire charity through tolerance; you dispel murderous prejudice; you teach modesty to women, bravery to warriors, prudence to statesmen. You appease, with your smile, conflict and civil wars; you bring peace between brothers; you heal the fanatic and the sectarian. You are the Mistress of Truth; you serve to protect genius; and what of virtue? That, O Goddess, is you too!

Come, my sovereign: pour upon my citizens a ray of your light; ignite in their souls a spark of your spirit: allow this, my confession to resonate with them such that this inevitable revolution may accomplish its full potential in a spirit of serenity and joy.

Sainte-Pélagie, October 1849

---

57  A person who has retired into seclusion for religious reasons. (Editor)

3rd December, 1849
*La Voix du Peuple*
*Translation by Benjamin R. Tucker*

# RESISTANCE TO THE REVOLUTION:
## LOUIS BLANC AND PIERRE LEROUX

[…]

THE FEBRUARY REVOLUTION RAISED TWO LEADING QUESTIONS: ONE ECO-
nomic, the question of labour and property; the other political, the question
of government or the State.

On the first of these questions the socialistic democracy is substantially
in accord. They admit that it is not a question of the seizure and division
of property, or even of its repurchase. Neither is it a question of dishonour-
ably levying additional taxes on the wealthy and property-holding classes,
which, while violating the principle of property recognised in the constitution, would serve only to overturn the general economy and aggravate the
situation of the proletariat. The economic reform consists, on the one hand,
in opening usurious credit to competition and thereby causing capital to
lose its income,—in other words, in identifying, in every citizen to the same
degree, the capacity of the worker and that of the capitalist; on the other
hand, in abolishing the whole system of existing taxes, which fall only on the
worker and the poor man, and replacing them all by a single tax on capital,
as an insurance premium.

By these two great reforms social economy is reconstructed from top to
bottom, commercial and industrial relations are inverted, and the profits,
now assured to the capitalist, return to the worker. Competition, now anarchical and subversive, becomes emulative and fruitful; markets no longer being wanting, the worker and employer, intimately connected, have nothing
more to fear from stagnation or suspension. A new order is established upon
the old institutions abolished or regenerated.

On this point the revolutionary course is laid out; the meaning of the movement is known. Whatever modification may appear in practice, the reform will be effected according to these principles and on these bases; the Revolution has no other issue. The economic problem, then, may be considered solved.

It is far from being the same with the political problem,—that is, with the disposal to be made in the future, of government and the State. On this point the question is not even stated; it has not been recognised by the public conscience and the intelligence of the masses. The economic Revolution being accomplished, as we have just seen, can government, the State, continue to exist? Ought it to continue to exist? This no one, either in democracy or out of it, dares to call in question; and yet it is the problem which, if we would escape new catastrophes, must next be solved.

We affirm, then, and as yet we are alone in affirming, that with the economic Revolution, no longer in dispute, the State must entirely disappear; that this disappearance of the State is the necessary consequence of the organisation of credit and the reform of taxation; that, as an effect of this double innovation government becomes first useless and then impossible; that in this respect it is in the same category with feudal property, lending at interest, absolute and constitutional monarchy, judicial institutions, etc., all of which have served in the education of liberty, but which fall and vanish when liberty has arrived at its fullness. Others, on the contrary, in the front ranks of whom we distinguish Louis Blanc and Pierre Leroux, maintain that, after the economic revolution, it is necessary to continue the State, but in an organised form, furnishing, however, as yet no principle or plan for its organisation. For them the political question, instead of being annihilated by identification with the economic question always subsists, they favour an extension of the prerogatives of the State, of power, of authority, of government. They change names only; for example, instead of *master-State* they say *servant-State,* as if a change of words sufficed to transform things! Above this system of government, about which nothing is known, hovers a system of religion whose dogma is equally unknown, whose ritual is unknown, whose object, on earth and in heaven, is unknown.

This, then is the question which at present divides the socialistic democracy, now in accord, or nearly so, on other matters: Must the State continue to exist after the question of labour and capital shall be practically solved? In other words, shall we always have, as we have had hitherto, a political constitution apart from the social constitution?

We reply in the negative. We maintain that, capital and labour once identified, society exists by itself, and has no further need of government. We are, therefore, as we have more than once announced, *anarchists. Anarchy* is the condition of existence of adult society, as hierarchy is the condition of primitive society. There is a continual progress in human society from hierarchy to anarchy.

Louis Blanc and Pierre Leroux affirm the contrary. In addition to their capacity of *socialists* they retain that of *politicians*; they are men of government and authority, statesmen.

To settle the difference, we have, then, to consider the State, no longer from the point of view of the old society, which naturally and necessarily produced it, and which approaches its end, but from the point of view of the new society, which is, or must be, the result of the two fundamental and correlative reforms of credit and taxation.

Now if we prove that, from this last point of view, the State, considered in its nature, rests on a thoroughly false hypothesis; that, in the second place, considered in its object, the State finds no excuse for its existence save in a second hypothesis, equally false; that, finally, considered in the reasons for its continuance, the State again can appeal only to an hypothesis as false as the two others,—these three points cleared up, the question will be settled, the State will be regarded as a superfluous, and consequently harmful and impossible, thing; government will be a contradiction.

Let us proceed at once with the analysis:—

# I.
## OF THE NATURE OF THE STATE

"What is the State?" asks Louis Blanc.

And he replies:

"The State, under monarchical rule, is the power of one man, the tyranny of a single individual.

"The State, under oligarchical rule, is the power of a small number of men, the tyranny of a few.

"The State, under aristocratic rule, is the power of a class, the tyranny of many.

"The State, under anarchical rule, is the power of the first comer who happens to be the most intelligent and the strongest; it is the tyranny of chaos.

"The State, under democratic rule, is the power of all the people, served by their elect, it is the reign of liberty."

Of the twenty-five or thirty thousand readers of Louis Blanc, perhaps there are not ten to whom this definition of the State did not seem conclusive, and who do not repeat, after the master: The State is the power of one, of a few, of many, of all, or of the first comer, according as the word State is prefaced by one of these other adjectives,—*monarchical, oligarchical, aristocratic, democratic,* or *anarchical.* The delegates of the Luxembourg [Commission]—who think themselves robbed, it seems, when anyone allows himself to hold an opinion different from theirs on the meaning and tendencies of the February Revolution—in a letter that has been made public, have done me the honour to inform me that they regard Louis Blanc's answer as quite triumphant, and that I can say nothing in reply. It would seem that none of the citizen-delegates ever have studied Greek. Otherwise, they would have seen that their master and friend, Louis Blanc, instead of defining the State, has only translated into French the Greek words *monos*, one; *aligoï*, a few; *aristoï*, the great; *démos*, the people; and the privative *a*, which means no. It is by the use of these qualifying terms that Aristotle has distinguished the various forms of the State, which is designated by the word *archê*, authority, government, State. We ask pardon of our readers, but it is not our fault if the political science of the Luxembourg [Commission] does not go beyond etymology.

And mark the artifice! Louis Blanc, in his translation, only had to use the word tyranny four times, *tyranny of one, tyranny of many,* etc., and to avoid it once, *power of the people, served by their elect,* to win applause. Every state save the democratic, according to Louis Blanc, is *tyranny*. Anarchy especially receives a peculiar treatment; *it is the power of the first comer who happens to be the most intelligent and the strongest;* it is the *tyranny of chaos*. What a monster must be this *first comer,* who, first comer that he is, nevertheless happens to be *the most intelligent and the strongest,* and who exercises his *tyranny in chaos!* After that who could prefer *anarchy* to this charming government of all the people, served so well, as we know, by their elect? How overwhelming it is, to be sure! at the first blow we find ourselves flat on the ground. O rhetorician! thank God for having created for your express benefit, in the nineteenth century, such stupidity as that of your so-called delegates of the working classes; otherwise you would have perished under a storm of hisses the first time you touched a pen.

What is the State? This question must be answered. The list of the various forms of the State, which Louis Blanc, after Aristotle, has prepared, has taught us nothing. As for Pierre Leroux, it is not worthwhile to interrogate him; he would tell us that the question is inconsiderate; that the State has always existed; that it always will exist,—the final reason of conservatives and old women.

The State is the external constitution of the social power.

By this external constitution of its power and sovereignty, the people does not govern itself; now one individual, now several, by a title either elective or hereditary, are charged with governing it, with managing its affairs, with negotiating and compromising in its name; in a word, with performing all the acts of a father of a family, a guardian, a manager, or a proxy, furnished with a general, absolute, and irrevocable power of attorney.

This external constitution of the collective power, to which the Greeks gave the name *archê*, sovereignty, authority, government, rests then on this hypothesis: that a people, that the collective being which we call society, cannot govern itself, think, act, express itself, unaided, like beings endowed with individual personality; that, to do these things, it must be represented by one or more individuals, who, by any title whatever, are regarded as custodians of the will of the people, and its agents. According to this hypothesis, it is impossible for the collective power, which belongs essentially to the mass, to express itself and act directly, without the mediation of organs expressly established and, so to speak, posted ad hoc. It seems, we say,—and this is the explanation of the constitution of the State in all its varieties and forms,— that the collective being, society, existing only in the mind, cannot make itself felt save through monarchical incarnation, aristocratic usurpation, or democratic mandate; consequently, that all special and personal manifestation is forbidden it.

Now it is precisely this conception of the collective being, of its life, its action, its unity, its individuality, its personality,—for society is a person, understand! just as entire humanity is a person,—it is this conception of the collective human being that we deny today; and it is for that reason that we deny the State also, that we deny government, that we exclude from society, when economically revolutionised, every constitution of the popular power, either without or within the mass, by hereditary royalty, feudal institution, or democratic delegation.

We affirm, on the contrary, that the people, that society, that the mass, can and ought to govern itself by itself; to think, act, rise and halt, like a man; to manifest itself, in fine, in its physical, intellectual, and moral individuality, without the aid of all these spokesmen, who formerly were despots, who now are aristocrats, who from time to time have been pretended delegates, fawners on or servants of the crowd, and whom we call plainly and simply popular agitators, *demagogues*.

In short:

We deny government and the State, because we affirm that which the founders of States have never believed in, the personality and autonomy of the masses.

We affirm further that every constitution of the State has no other object than to lead society to this condition of autonomy; that the different forms of the State, from absolute monarchy to representative *democracy*, are all only middle terms, illogical and unstable positions, serving one after another as transitions or steps to liberty, and forming the rounds of the political ladder upon which societies mount to self-consciousness and self-possession.

We affirm, finally, that this *anarchy*, which expresses, as we now see, the highest degree of liberty and order at which humanity can arrive, is the true formula of the Republic, the goal towards with the February Revolution urges us; so that between the Republic and the government, between universal suffrage and the State, there is a contradiction.

These systematic affirmations we establish in two ways: first, by the historical and negative method, demonstrating that no establishment of authority, no organisation of the collective force from without, is henceforth possible for us. This demonstration we commenced in the *Confessions of a*

*Revolutionary*, in reciting the fall of all the governments which have succeeded one another in France for sixty years, discovering the cause of their abolition, and in the last place signalising the exhaustion and death of authority in the corrupted reign of Louis Philippe, in the inert dictatorship of the provisional government, and in the insignificant presidency of General Cavaignac and Louis Bonaparte.

We prove our thesis, in the second place, by explaining how, through the economic reform, through industrial solidarity and the organisation of universal suffrage, the people passes from spontaneity to reflection and consciousness; acts, no longer from impulse and enthusiasm, but with design; maintains itself without masters and servants, without delegates as without aristocrats, absolutely as would an individual. Thus, the conception of person, the idea of the *me*, becomes extended and generalised; as there is an individual person or *me*, so there is a collective person or *me*; in the one case as in the other will, actions, soul, spirit, life, unknown in their principle, inconceivable in their essence, result from the animating and vital fact of organisation. The psychology of nations and of humanity, like the psychology of man, becomes a possible science. It was this demonstration that we referred to in our publications on circulation and credit as well as in the fourteenth chapter of the manifesto of *La Voix du Peuple* relative to the Constitution.

So, when Louis Blanc and Pierre Leroux assume the position of defenders of the State,—that is, of the external constitution of the public power,—they only reproduce, in a varied form peculiar to themselves which they have not yet made known, that old fiction of representative government, whose integral formula, whose completest expression, is still the constitutional monarchy. Did we, then, accomplish the February Revolution in order to attain this retrogressive contradiction?

It seems to us—what do you say, readers?—that the question begins to exhibit itself in a somewhat clearer light; that the weak-minded, after what we have just said, will be able to form an idea of the State; that they will understand how republicans can inquire if it is indispensable, after an economic revolution which changes all social relations, to maintain, to please the vanity of pretended statesmen, and at a cost of two billion per annum, this parasitic organ called government. And the honourable delegates of the Luxembourg [Commission], who, being seated in the arm-chairs of the peerage, therefore think themselves politicians, and claim so courageously an exclusive understanding of the Revolution, doubtless will fear no longer that we, in our capacity of the *most intelligent* and the *strongest*, after having abolished government, as useless and too costly, may establish the tyranny of chaos. We deny the State and the government; we affirm in the same breath the autonomy of the people and its majority. How can we be upholders of tyranny, aspirants for the ministry, competitors of Louis Blanc and Pierre Leroux?

In truth, we do not understand the logic of our adversaries. They accept a principle without troubling themselves about its consequences; they approve, for example, the equality of taxation which the tax on capital realises; they adopt popular, mutual, and gratuitous credit, for all these terms are synonymous; they cheer at the dethronement of capital and the emancipation of labour; then, when it remains to draw the anti-governmental conclusions from these premises, they protest, they continue to talk of politics and government, without inquiring whether government is compatible with industrial liberty and equality; whether there is a possibility of a political science, when there is a necessity for an economic science! Property they attack without scruple, in spite of its venerable antiquity; but they bow before power like church-wardens before the holy sacrament. Government is to them the necessary and immutable *a priori*, the principle of principles, the eternal *archeus*.

Certainly, we do not offer our affirmations as proofs; we know, as well as anyone, on what conditions a proposition is demonstrated. We only say that, before proceeding to a new constitution of the State, we must inquire whether, in view of the economic reforms which the Revolution imposes upon us, the State itself should not be abolished; whether this end of political institutions does not result from the meaning and bearing of economic reform. We ask whether, in fact, after the explosion of February, after the establishment of universal suffrage, the declaration of the omnipotence of the masses, and the henceforth inevitable subordination of power to the popular will, any government whatever is still possible, whether a government would not be placed perpetually in the alternative either of submissively following the blind and contradictory injunctions of the multitude, or of intentionally deceiving it, as the provisional government has done, as demagogues in all ages have done. We ask, at least, which of the various attributes of the State should be retained and strengthened, which abolished. For, should we find, as may still be expected, that, of all the present attributes of the State, not one can survive the economic reform, it would be quite necessary to admit, on the strength of this negative demonstration, that in the new condition of society, the State is nothing, can be nothing; in short, that the only way to organise democratic government is to abolish government.

Instead of this positive, practical, realistic analysis of the revolutionary movement, what course do our pretended apostles take? They go to consult Lycurgus, Plato, Orpheus, and all the mythological oracles; they interrogate the ancient legends; they appeal to remotest antiquity for the solution of problems exclusively modern, and then give us for answer the whimsical illuminations of their brains.

Once more: is this the science of society and of the Revolution which must, at first sight, solve all problems; a science essentially practical and immediately applicable; a science eminently traditional doubtless, but above all thoroughly progressive, in which progress takes place through the systematic negation of tradition itself?

# II.
## OF THE END OR OBJECT OF THE STATE

WE HAVE JUST seen that the idea of the State, considered in its nature, rests entirely on an hypothesis which is at least doubtful,—that of the impersonality and the physical, intellectual, and moral inertia of the masses. We shall now prove that this same idea of the State, considered in its object, rests on another hypothesis, still more improbable than the first,—that of the permanence of antagonism in humanity, an hypothesis which is itself a consequence of the primitive dogma of the fall or of original sin.

We continue to quote *Le Nouveau Monde*:

"What would happen," asks Louis Blanc, "if we should leave the most intelligent or the strongest to place obstacles in the way of the development of the faculties of one who is less strong or less intelligent? Liberty would be destroyed.

"How to prevent this crime? By interposing between oppressor and oppressed the whole power of the people.

"If James oppresses Peter, shall the thirty-four million men of whom French society is composed run all at once to protect Peter, to maintain liberty? To pretend such a thing would be buffoonery.

"How then shall society intervene?

"*Through those whom it has chosen to* REPRESENT *it for this purpose.*

"But these REPRESENTATIVES of society, these servants of the people, who are they? The State.

"Then the State is only society itself, acting as society, to prevent—what?—oppression; to maintain—what?—liberty."

That is clear. The State is a REPRESENTATION of society, externally organised to protect the weak against the strong; in other words, to preserve peace between disputants and maintain order. Louis Blanc has not gone far, as we see, to find the object of the State. It can be traced from Grotius, Justinian, Cicero, etc., in all the authors who ever have written on public right. It is the Orphic tradition related by Horace:—

> Sylvestres homines sacer interpresque deorum.
> Cædibus et victu fœdo deterruit Orpheus,
> Dictus ob hoc lenire tigres rabidosque leones,
> Dictus et Amphion, Thebanæ conditor arcis,
> Saxa movere sono testudinis, et prece blanda
> Ducere quo vellet....[1]

---

1   "The divine Orpheus, the interpreter of the gods, called men from the depths of the forests and filled them with a horror of murder and of human flesh. Consequently it was said of him that he tamed lions and tigers, as later it was said of Amphion, founder of Thebes, that he moved the stones by the sound of his lyre, and led them whither he wished by the charm of his prayer." (Translator)

Socialism, we know, does not require with certain people great efforts of the imagination. They imitate, flatly enough, the old mythologies; they copy Catholicism, while declaiming against it; they ape power, which they lust after; then they shout with all their strength: Liberty, Equality, Fraternity; and the circle is complete. One passes for a revelator, a reformer, a democratic and social restorer, one is named as a candidate for the ministry of progress,—nay, even for the dictatorship of the Republic!

So, by the confession of Louis Blanc, power is born of barbarism; its organisation bears witness to a state of ferocity and violence among primitive men,—an effect of the utter absence of commerce and industry. To this savagism the State had to put an end by opposing to the force of each individual a superior force capable, in the absence of any other argument, of restraining his will. The constitution of the State supposes, then, as we have just said, a profound social antagonism, *homo homini lupus*. Louis Blanc himself says this when, after having divided men into the strong and the weak, disputing with each other like wild beasts for their food, he interposes between them, as a mediator, the State.

Then the State would be useless; the State would lack an object as well as a motive; the State would have to take itself away,—if there should come a day when, from any cause whatever, society should contain neither strong nor weak,—that is, when the inequality of physical and intellectual powers could not be a cause of robbery and oppression, independently of the protection, more fictitious than real by the way, of the State.

Now, this is precisely the thesis that we maintain today.

The power that tempers morals, that gradually substitutes the rule of right for the rule of force, that establishes security, that creates step by step liberty and equality, is, in a much higher degree than religion and the State, labour; first, the labour of commerce and industry; next, science, which spiritualises it; in the last analysis, art, its immortal flower. Religion by its promises and its threats, the State by its tribunals and its armies, gave to the sentiment of justice, which was too weak among primitive men, the only sanction intelligible to savage minds. For us, whom industry, science, literature and art have corrupted, as Jean-Jacques [Rousseau] said, this sanction lies elsewhere; we find it in the division of property, in the machinery of industry, in the growth of luxury, in the overruling desire for well-being,— a desire which imposes upon all a necessity of labour. After the barbarism of the early ages, after the price of caste and the feudal constitution of primitive society, a last element of slavery still remained,—capital. Capital having lost its way, the worker—that is, the merchant, the mechanic, the farmer, the *savant*, the artist—no longer needs protection; his protection is his talent, his knowledge is his industry. After the dethronement of capital, the continuance of the State, far from protecting liberty, can only compromise liberty.

He has a sorry idea of the human race—of its essence, its perfectibility, its destiny—he who conceives it as an agglomeration of individuals necessarily exposed, by the inequality of physical and intellectual forces, to the constant danger of reciprocal spoliation or the tyranny of a few. Such an idea is a proof of the most retrogressive philosophy; it belongs to those days of barbarism when the absence of the true elements of social order left to the genius of the legislator no method of action save that of force; when the supremacy of a pacifying and avenging power appeared to all as the just consequence of a previous degradation and an original stain. To give our whole thought, we regard political and judicial institutions as the esoteric and concrete formula of the myth of the fall, the mystery of redemption, and the sacrament of penitence. It is curious to see pretended socialists, enemies or rivals of Church and State, copying all that they blaspheme,—the representative system in politics, the dogma of the fall in religion.

Since they talk so much of doctrine, we frankly declare that such is not ours.

In our view, the moral condition of society is modified and ameliorated at the same rate as its economic condition. The morality of a wild, ignorant, and idle people is one thing; that of an industrious and artistic people another: consequently, the social guarantees that prevail among the former are quite different from those that prevail among the latter. In a society transformed, almost unconsciously, by its economic development, there is no longer either *strong* or *weak*; there are only workers whose faculties and means incessantly tend, through industrial solidarity and the guarantee of circulation, to become equalised. In vain, to assure the right and the duty of each, does the imagination go back to that idea of authority and government which attests the profound despair of souls long terrified by the police and the priesthood: the simplest examination of the attributes of the State suffices to demonstrate that, if inequality of fortunes, oppression, robbery, and misery are not our eternal inheritance, the first leprosy to be eradicated, after capitalistic exploitation, the first plague to be wiped out, is the State.

See, in fact, budget in hand, what the State is.

The State is the army. Reformer, do you need an army to defend you? If so, your idea of public security is Cæsar's and Napoléon's. You are not a republican; you are a despot.

The State is the police; city police, rural police, police of the waters and forests. Reformer, do you need police? Then your idea of order is Fouché's, Gisquet's, Carussidière's, and M. Carlier's.[2] You are not a democrat, you are a spy.

---

2    Joseph Fouché (1759–1820), Minister of Police for the Emperor Napoléon, and several Prefects of Police: Henri Gisquet (1792–1866), Marc Caussidière (1808–1861), and Pierre Carlier (1794–1858). (Editor)

The State is the whole judicial system; justices of the peace, tribunals of first instance, courts of appeal, court of cassation, high court, tribunals of experts, commercial tribunals, council of prefects, State council, councils of war. Reformer, do you need all this judiciary? Then your idea of justice is M. Baroche's, M. Dupin's, and Perrin Dandin's.[3] You are not a socialist; you are a red-tapist.

The State is the treasury, the budget. Reformer, you do not desire the abolition of taxation? Then your idea of public wealth is M. Thiers's who thinks that the largest budgets are the best. You are not an organiser of labour; you are an exciseman.

The State is the custom-house. Reformer, do you need, for the protection of national labour, differential duties and toll-houses? Then your idea of commerce and circulation is M. Fould's and M. Rothschild's.[4] You are not an apostle of fraternity; you are a Jew.[5]

The State is the public debt, the mint, the sinking fund, the savings-banks, etc. Reformer, are these the foundation of your science? Then your idea of social economy is that of MM. Humann, Lacave-Laplagne, Garnier-Pagès, Passy, Duclerc, and the *Man with Forty Crowns*. You are a Turcaret.[6]

The State—but we must stop. There is nothing, absolutely nothing, in the State, from the top of the hierarchy to its foot, which is not an abuse to be reformed, a parasite to be exterminated, an instrument of tyranny to be destroyed. And you talk to us of maintaining the State, of extending the functions or the State, of increasing the power of the State! Go to, you are not a revolutionist; for the true revolutionist is essentially a simplifier and a liberal. You are a mystifier, a juggler; you are a marplot.

---

3   Pierre Jules Baroche (1802–1870), Republican turned right-wing statesman after 1848, later Minister of Justice; André Dupin (1783–1865), politician and procureur-général; Perrin Dandin, a character from Rabelais notable for passing arbitrary judgements. (Editor)

4   Achille Fould (1800–1867) and Jakob Mayer Rothschild (1792–1868), both Jewish citizens of France, were financiers. (Editor)

5   One of the rare occurrences when Proudhon's personal bigotries surfaced in his public writings. (Editor)

6   Georges Humann (1780–1842), a financier, was also Minister of Finance; Jean Lacave-Laplagne (1795–1849) was a politician and financial minister; Louis-Antoine Garnier-Pagès (1803–1878) was made Minister of Finance in 1848; Hippolyte Philibert Passy (1793–1880) was an economist and politician active on financial matters; Charles Duclerc (1812–1888) succeeded Garnier-Pagès as Minister of Finance. *The Man With Forty Crowns* (*L'Homme aux quarante écus*) is a satire by Voltaire (1768), while Turcaret, a greedy money-man, is the protagonist of Alain-René Lesage's satirical play, *Le Financier* (1709). (Editor)

# III.
## OF AN ULTERIOR DESTINY OF THE STATE

THERE ARISES IN favour of the State a last hypothesis. The fact that the State, say the pseudo-democrats, hitherto has performed only a *rôle* of parasitism and tyranny is no reason for denying it a nobler and more humane destiny. The State is destined to become the principal organ of production, consumption, and circulation; the initiator of liberty and equality.

For liberty and equality are the State.

Credit is the State.

Commerce, agriculture, and manufactures are the State.

Canals, railroads, mines, insurance companies, as well as tobacco-shops and post-offices, are the State.

Public education is the State.

The State, in fine, dropping its negative attributes to clothe itself with positive ones, must change from the oppressor, parasite, and conservative it ever has been into an organiser, producer, and servant. That would be feudalism regenerated, the hierarchy of industrial associations, organised and graded according to a potent formula, the secret of which Pierre Leroux still hides from our sight.

Thus, the organisers of the State suppose—for in all this they only go from supposition to supposition—that the State can change its nature, turn itself around, so to speak; from Satan become an archangel; and, after having lived for centuries by blood and slaughter like a wild beast, feed upon plants with the deer, and give suck to the lambs. Such is the teaching of Louis Blanc and Pierre Leroux; such, as we said long ago, is the whole secret of socialism.

"We love the tutelary, generous, devoted government, taking as its motto those profound words of the gospel, 'Whosoever of you will be the chiefest, shall be the servant of all'; and we hate the deprived, corrupting, oppressive government, making the people its prey. We admire it representing the generous and living portion of humanity; we abhor it when it represents the cadaverous portion. We revolt against the insolence, usurpation, and robbery involved in the idea of the master-State; and we applaud that which is touching, fruitful, and noble in the idea of the servant-State. Or better: there is a belief which we hold a thousand times dearer than life,—our belief in the approaching and final TRANSFORMATION of power. *That is the triumphant passage from the old world to the new.* All the governments of Europe rest today on the idea of the master-State; but they are dancing desperately the dance of the dead."—*Le Nouveau Monde*, November 16th, 1849.

Pierre Leroux is a thorough believer in these ideas. What he wishes, what he teaches, and what he calls for is a regeneration of the State,—he has not told us yet whereby and by whom this regeneration should be effected,—just as he wishes and calls for a regeneration of Christianity without, as yet, having stated his dogma and given his *credo*.

We believe, in opposition to Pierre Leroux and Louis Blanc, that the theory of the tutelary, generous, devoted, productive, initiative, organising, liberal and progressive State is a utopia, a pure illusion of their intellectual vision. Pierre Leroux and Louis Blanc seem to us like a man who, standing above a mirror and seeing his image reversed, should pretend that this image must become a reality some day and replace (pardon us the expression) his *natural person*.

This is what separates us from these two men, whose talents and services, whatever they may say, we have never dreamed of denying, but whose stubborn hallucination we deplore. We do not believe in the servant-State: to us it is a flat contradiction.

*Servant* and *master*, when applied to the State, are synonymous terms; just as *more* and *less*, when applied to equality, are identical terms. The proprietor, by interest on capital, demands *more* than equality; communism, by the formula, *to each according to his needs*, allows *less* than equality: always inequality; and that is why we are neither a communist nor a proprietor. Likewise, whoever says *master-State* says usurpation of the public power; whoever says *servant-State* says delegation of the public power: always an alienation of this power, always a power, always an external, arbitrary authority instead of the immanent, inalienable, untransferable authority of citizens; always *more* or *less* than liberty. It is for this reason that we are opposed to the State.

Further, to leave metaphysics and return to the field of experience, here is what we have to say to Louis Blanc and Pierre Leroux.

You pretend and affirm that the State, that the government, can, and ought to be, wholly changed in its principle, in its essence, in its action, in its relations with citizens, as well as in its results that thus the State, a bankrupt and a counterfeiter, should be the sole source of credit; that for so many centuries an enemy of knowledge, and at the present moment still hostile to primary instruction and the liberty of the press, it is its business to officially provide for the instruction of citizens; that, after having left commerce, industry, agriculture, and all the machinery of wealth to develop themselves without its aid, often even in spite of its resistance, it belongs to it to take the initiative in the whole field of labour as in the world of ideas, that, in fine, the eternal enemy of liberty, it yet ought not to leave liberty to itself, but to create and direct liberty. It is this marvellous transformation of the State that constitutes, in your opinion, the present Revolution.

There lies upon you, then, the twofold obligation: first, of establishing the truth of your hypothesis by showing its traditional legitimacy, exhibiting its historical titles, and developing its philosophy; in the second place, of applying it in practice.

Now, it appears already that both theory and practice, in your hypothesis, formally contradict the idea itself, and the facts of the past, and the most authentic tendencies of humanity.

Your theory, we say, involves a contradiction in its terms, since it pretends to make liberty a creation of the State, while the State, on the contrary, is to be a creation of liberty. In fact, if the State imposes itself upon my will, the State is master; I am not free; the theory is undermined.

It contradicts the facts of the past, since it is certain, as you yourselves admit, that everything that has been produced within the sphere of human activity of a positive, good, and beautiful character, was the product of liberty exclusively, acting independently of the State, and almost always in opposition to the State; which leads directly to this proposition, which ruins your system, that liberty is sufficient unto itself and does not need the State.

Finally, your theory contradicts the manifest tendencies of civilisation; since, instead of continually adding to individual liberty and dignity by making every human soul, according to Kant's precept, a pattern of entire humanity, one face of the collective soul, you subordinate the private person to the public person; you submit the individual to the group; you absorb the citizen in the State.

It is for you to remove all these contradictions by a principle superior to liberty and to the State. We, who simply deny the State; who, resolutely following the line of liberty, remain faithful to the revolutionary practice,—it is not for us to demonstrate to you the falsity of your hypothesis; we await your proofs. The *master-State* is lost; you are with us in admitting it. As for the *servant-State*, we do not know what it may be; we distrust it as supreme hypocrisy. The *servant-State* seems to us quite the same thing as a servant-mistress; we do not wish it; with our present light, we prefer to espouse Liberty in legitimate marriage. Explain, then, if you can, why, after having demolished the State through love of this adored liberty, we must now, in consequence of the same love, return to the State. Until you have solved this problem, we shall continue to protest against all government, all authority, all power; we shall maintain, through all and against all, the prerogative of liberty. We shall say to you: Liberty is, for us, a thing gained; now, you know the rule of law: *Melior est conditio possidentis*. Produce your titles to the reorganisation of government; otherwise, no government!

To sum up:

The State is the *external* constitution of the social power.

The constitution supposes, in principle, that society is a creature of the mind, destitute of spontaneity, providence, unity, needing for its action to be fictitiously represented by one or more elected or hereditary commissioners: an hypothesis the falsity of which the economic development of society and the organisation of universal suffrage agree in demonstrating.

The constitution of the State supposes further, as to its object, that antagonism or a state of war is the essential and irrevocable condition of humanity, a condition which necessitates, between the *weak* and the *strong*, the intervention of a coercive power to put an end to their struggles by universal oppression. We maintain that, in this respect, the mission of the State is ended; that, by the division of labour, industrial solidarity, the desire for well-being, and the equal distribution of capital and taxation, liberty and justice obtain surer guarantees than any that ever were afforded them by religion and the State.

As for utilitarian transformation of the State, we consider it as a utopia contradicted at once by governmental tradition, and the revolutionary tendency, and the spirit of the henceforth admitted economic reforms. In any case, we say that to liberty alone it would belong to reorganise power, which is equivalent at present to the complete exclusion of power.

As a result, either no social revolution, or no more government; such is our solution to the political problem.

[...]

*14ᵗʰ December 1849*
*Translation by Paul Sharkey*

# LETTER TO PIERRE LEROUX

My dear Pierre Leroux,

I REALLY MUST FORGIVE YOU YOUR INCESSANT ACCUSATIONS, FOR YOU DO NOT
know me and do not engage in debate.

For a start, you haven't read me, so you have a cheek attacking me; next,
I think you need telling and everything that you have written over the past
month is there to prove it: you have absolutely no method. As a result of
rehashing your empty formulae, wallowing in your sterile imaginings and
focusing your thoughts upon some world beyond the senses, you have rendered yourself incapable of grasping other people's thinking; the upshot being that, all unbeknownst to yourself, your criticisms amount, I am sorry to
say, to unrelenting demonisation.

On the basis of a few snatches of text quarried from my books and utterly
misconstrued, you have cast me as an adversary of your own devising—anti-
democratic, anti-socialist, counter-revolutionary, Malthusian and atheistic.
This is the imaginary creature to which you address your arguments, without in the least bothering if the man you depict thus to proletarians fits the
description. Sometimes you credit me with saying things that I never said,
or you credit me with conclusions diametrically opposed to my actual ones;
at other times, you take the trouble to lecture me on what no one living in
this century could honestly be ignorant of; all in order to banish me benignly
from the democratic and social community.

Meanwhile, the well-intentioned readers who follow you, and the malicious ones—and of the latter sort there is no shortage—pick up on your
accusations, passing comment on them, inflating them and exploiting them.
So much so that, ultimately and thanks to you, today I find myself the Satan
of socialism, just as, as year ago, I was the Satan of property. Socialism's main

business at this point in time is to demolish Proudhon, or so one of your disciples, Madame Pauline Roland,[1] is telling all who are prepared to listen. How much more clear-sighted socialism will be, won't it?, once this renegade Proudhon has been cast down; whereupon Pierre Leroux's tittle-tattle merchants, eaten up by hypochondria, will take their seats among the denizens of the Assembly of representatives of the People!

So, my dear Pierre Leroux, would you care to see this controversy brought to an end? The crucial thing is that the debate be kept on track, that, in each particular, we deal first with one issue and then with the next, rather than rant about them all, and then some, as you do in every one of your articles; without this, our exchanges will inevitably become a laughing-stock for the Malthusians and scandalise the proletarians. As for myself, I will freely confess to you that I find it impossible to keep up such a polemic, squandering my time and my paper on relentlessly clarifying facts, reconstructing texts, clearing up your misunderstandings, rebutting your whimsy and translating your high-falutin' style into common parlance.

Thus you take me to task for having made a distinction between the labour question and the question of the State, two questions which are, at bottom, identical and susceptible to one and the same solution.

If you were as eager to acknowledge the common ground between your thoughts and mine as you are to highlight where they differ, you wouldn't have had any difficulty persuading yourself that, when it comes to the questions of labour and the State, as well as on a host of other matters, our two outlooks have no reason to feel jealous of each other. When I state, say, that the capitalist principle and the monarchist or governmental principle are one and the same principle; that the abolition of the exploitation of man by man and the abolition of the government of man by man are one and the same formula; when, taking up arms against communism and absolutism alike, those two kindred faces of the authority principle, I point out that, if the family was the building block of feudal society, the workshop is the building block of the new society; it must be as plain as day that I, like you, look upon the political question and the economic question as one and the same. What you upbraid me for not knowing on this score is your own sheer ignorance of my thinking and, what is worse, it is a waste of time.

But does it follow from the fact that the labour question and the State question resolve each other and are, fundamentally, one and the same issue, that no distinction should be made between them and that each does not deserve its own resolution? Does it follow from these two questions being, in principle, identical, that we must arrive at a particular mode of organising

<hr>

1  Pauline Roland (1805–1852), a Saint-Simonian socialist, feminist, and associate of Leroux, also wrote a column for Proudhon's *Le Représentant du peuple*, but was later to write a critique of Proudhon's antifeminism, *La femme a-t-elle le droit à la liberté?* (*Does Woman Have the Right to Liberty?*, 1851). (Editor)

the State rather than the State being subsumed by labour? Neither of those conclusions holds water. Social questions are like problems of geometry; they may be resolved in different ways, depending on how they are approached. It is even useful and vital that these differing solutions be devised so that, in adding further dimensions to theory, they may add to the sum of science.

And as to the State, since, despite this multi-faceted character, the ultimate conclusion is that the question of its organisation is bound up with that of the organisation of labour, we may, we must, further conclude that a time will come when, labour having organised itself, in accordance with its own law, and having no further need of law-maker or sovereign, the workshop will banish government. As I argue and into which we shall look, my dear philosopher, whenever, paying rather more heed to the other fellow's ideas and being a little less sensitive about your own, you may deign to enter into a serious debate about one or other of these two things, about which you are forever prattling without actually saying anything: Association and the State.

The government question and the labour question being identical, you rightly remark that such identity is articulated in the following terms: *The Question of the organisation of Society*.

Now, read through chapter one of *Contradictions Économiques* and you will find it formally spelled out that it is incorrect to say that labour is organised or that it is not; that it is *forever* self-organising; that society is an ongoing striving for organisation; that such organisation is at one and the same time the principle, the life and the purpose of society. So, my dear Pierre Leroux, be so kind as to think me somewhat less of an ignoramus and above all less of a sophist than I may seem to your frightened imagination: it will lay to rest three quarters of our quarrel.

There can be nothing easier than justifying the orthodoxy of this proposition as penned by me and upon which you seize so contemptuously and irrationally: "The February Revolution has posed two crucial questions: one economic, namely, the question of labour and property; and the other political, to wit, the question of government and the State." I merely needed to issue a reminder of the message implicit in all my words, that politics and political economy are one and the same science, the former being the more personal, arbitrary or subjective; the latter more substantial and positive. However, that interpretation of the February Revolution strikes you as *dry* and *narrow*: it lacks that certain something beyond the government and economics of societies, without which any idea looks satanic to you and every proposition fit for the pyre. That certain something is the sense of the divine, the theological and religious sense. Topped off with a quotation from some homily by Monsieur de Lamartine, and one of your usual commentaries on God, religion, the head of Christ, the Convention and the Republic.

At a time of your choosing, my dear Pierre Leroux, I shall give you such a sermon on God, his Spirit and his Word, as will draw tears from socialism's blue-stockings and their concierges; I can play that instrument every bit as deftly as you and Monsieur de Lamartine. But permit me not to throw theology into the pot with Political Economy, or, as the proverb has it, serve up *God with plums*. Such abuse of religiosity is one of the mystifications of our age and one that it behoves socialism to purge from its literature and press. Talking religion to men when the task in hand is to lay the foundations of social, mathematical and objective science amounts to a muddying of minds; and to perpetrating against the People the very same crime as the notorious Mazarin[2] was accused of having committed against the person of the young Louis XIV.

What is your God?

What is your religion, your ritual, your dogma?

What is the meaning of this constant invocation of Christ and Church?

You do not know the first thing about these things; you cannot see a single drop of them in your own thinking and all this other-worldly lyricism is nothing but a cover for the wretchedness of your alleged faith and the nullity of your means. You only prattle so much about God, of whom you, the anti-Christian, know nothing, to spare yourself the need to talk about matters here below, *non ut aliquid dicatur sed ne taciturn.*[3]

Yes, I tell you, the February Revolution (and I am sticking to my formula precisely on account of its concrete simplicity and its very materiality), the February Revolution has posed two questions; one political and the other economic. The first is the question of government and freedom; the second that of labour and capital. I defy you to express bigger issues in fewer words. So leave the Supreme Being to heaven and religion to conscience, to the household, a matter for the mother of the family and her offspring.

Let me add—and there is nothing in me to validate your entertaining doubts, the way you do, about my feelings on this score—that once those two major issues have been resolved, the republican catch-cry, *Liberty, Equality, Fraternity*, is a reality. If this is what you refer to as *God's kingdom on earth*, let me say to you, indeed, that I have no quarrel with that. It is a real comfort to me to find out at last that the kingdom of God is the kingdom of liberty, equality and fraternity. But could you not express yourself in everyday language?

You have me saying, and I really do not know where you could have found this, that *ownership of the instruments of labour must forever stay vested in the individual and remain unorganised.* These words are set in italics, as if

2   Jules Mazarin (1602–1661) was an Italian cardinal who served as the chief minister of France from 1642 until his death, first under King Louis XIII and then Louis XIV. As the latter was only five years old when he became King, Mazarin functioned essentially as the co-ruler of France alongside the queen. (Editor)

3   A slight misquotation of St. Augustine's *De Trinitate*: "Dictum est tamen tres personae, non ut aliquid diceretur, sed ne taceretur" ("We shall speak of [God as having] three persons, not in order to say anything, but in order not to be silent"). (Editor)

you had lifted them from somewhere in my books. And then, on the back of this alleged quotation, you set about answering me that society, or the State that stands for it, has the right to *buy back* all property assets, that it has a duty to pursue such *buy backs* and that it will do so.[4]

But it does not follow at all from my speaking on the basis of socialism in order to reject the buy back of such assets as nonsensical, illegitimate and poisonous that I want to see individual ownership and non-organisation of the instruments of labour endure for all eternity. I have never penned nor uttered any such thing: and have argued the opposite a hundred times over. I make no distinction, as you do, between real ownership and phoney ownership: from the lofty heights of righteousness and human destiny, I deny all kinds of proprietary domain. I deny it, precisely because I believe in an order wherein the instruments of labour will cease to be appropriated and instead become shared; where the whole earth will be depersonalised; where, all functions having become interdependent [*solidaires*], the unity and personhood of society will be articulated alongside the personality of the individual. True, were I not familiar with the candour of your soul, I should think, dear Pierre Leroux, that such misrepresentation of my meaning and my words were done on purpose.

But how is such solidarity of possession and labour to be achieved? How are we to make a reality of such personhood of society, which must result from the disappropriation, or de-personalising of things?

That plainly is the issue, the big question of the revolution.

Together with Louis Blanc, you make noises about *association* and *buy back*: but association, such as it must emerge from fresh reforms, is as much a mystery as religion, and all the attempts at association made by the workers before our very eyes and more or less modelling themselves on the forms of companies defined by our civil and commercial codes, can only be deemed transitory. In short, we know nothing about association. But, besides its requiring the acquiescence of all property-owners, by all the citizenry—which is an impossibility—buying back assets is a notion of mathematical nonsensicality. What is the State supposed to use to pay for assets? Why, assets. An across-the-board buyback amounts to universal expropriation without public utility and without compensation. Yet your sense of caution, Pierre Leroux, has no misgivings about being compromised by fostering such claptrap!

There is a more straightforward, more effective and infinitely less onerous and less risky way of transferring ownership, of achieving Liberty, Equality and Fraternity: that way is, as I have indicated many times, to put an end to

4   The French word translated here as "buy back" and "buyback," *rachat*, can also have a theological dimension, as in the English words *redeem* and *redemption*: the phrase "redeemed by the blood of Jesus Christ," in French, is "rachat par le sang de Jésus-Christ." (Editor)

capital's role in production by the democratic organisation of credit and a simplification of taxation.[5]

Capital having been divested of its power of usury, economic solidarity is gradually created, and with it, an equality of wealth.

Next comes the spontaneous, popular formation of groups, workshops or workers' associations;

Finally, the last to be conjured and formed is the over-arching group, comprising the nation in its entirety, what you term the State because you invest it in a representative body outside of society, but which, to me, is no longer the State.

That, dear philosopher, is how I see the Revolution going; this is how we should shift from Liberty to Equality and thence to Fraternity. Which is why I so forcefully insist upon the importance of economic reform, a reform that I have given this makeshift designation: *Free credit*.

And that too we might have scrutinised methodically, and have thrashed out item by item, had you but once managed to stand back from your amorous ecstasies and turn your attention to the sordid practice of loans and discounts. But you deemed it more purposeful, more urgent to have it out and repeat everywhere that I am a foe of Socialism, a foe of Democracy, a foe of Revolution, a hidden disciple of Malthus, determined to preserve *bourgeoisism* and *proprietarism*.

Hang on, Pierre Leroux: do I need to tell you what I think of your role and mine in this mammoth drama of the nineteenth century? I am the thresher of the February Revolution: the proletarians who are listening to us will be the millers and the bakers and you, with your triad,[6] and the rest with their tub-thumping claptrap, all of you are merely pastry cooks.

Yours, etc.,

P-J PROUDHON

---

5   The term Proudhon uses, *la productivité du capital*, is literally "the productivity of capital" but such a literal translation unfortunately implies that he simply wishes to end returns to capital. Rather, he wants to achieve production without the mediation of capital and the chosen translation reflects this. (Editor)

6   In Leroux's philosophy the fundamental principle was that of what he called the "triad"—a triplicity which he finds to pervade all things, which in God is "power, intelligence and love," in man "sensation, sentiment and knowledge." In society, he pointed to the division of the human race into three great classes, philosophers, artists and industrial chiefs, to be paid according to their capacity, labour, and capital. (Editor)

*28th December 1849*
*La Voix du Peuple*
*Translation by Paul Sharkey*

# IN CONNECTION WITH LOUIS BLANC:
## THE PRESENT USE AND FUTURE POSSIBILITY OF THE STATE

THERE IS SOMETHING ODD ABOUT THE FATE OF THE WRITER OF THESE LINES. No matter how little he may be tempted to take pride in an all but unprecedented situation, he would be compelled to believe that, just at the moment, everybody, excepting only himself, has taken leave of their senses; or that he himself, through some inexplicable freak, has gone mad, albeit a madness of the most erudite, considered, thought out, conscientious, philosophical sort and (in terms of its principle, its purpose, its deductions) the sort that conforms most closely to pure science and common sense.

But God forbid that we should mentally entertain this presumptuous alternative: and would do better to investigate whether the contradiction currently existing between public belief and the views we hold might not be the effect of some sort of misunderstanding. Every idea delivered into this world for the very first time, even though it may be derived from the universal consciousness, is a deduction from previous tradition and, at the moment it first appears, is nonetheless regarded, by the one who articulates it, as his own personal creation and for that reason he assumes sole responsibility for it. At which point the notion appears to sit outside of the general belief and is dubbed a *paradox*. But in next to no time that paradox is acknowledged; little by little common sense overtakes it. The idea is absorbed into the public mind which then grants it credibility and leave to circulate. There is not one of us who has not witnessed such a shift in public consciousness at least once in our lives. So might we not, today, be witnessing just such a shift?

What have we been saying since February? What has *La Voix du Peuple*, founded to carry on the work of its older siblings, *Le Peuple* and *Le Représent- ant du Peuple*, been saying for the last three months?[1]

That the Revolution in the nineteenth century has a dual purpose:

1. In economic terms, it seeks the utter subordination of capital to la- bour, the assimilation of worker and capitalist, through democratisation of credit, the abolition of interest, and the reduction of all dealings relating to the instruments of labour and products to equal and honest exchange. In this sense, we were the first to point out and remark that henceforth there are but two parties in France: the party of labour and the party of capital.

2. In political terms, the object of the Revolution is to absorb the State into society, which is to say, to put paid to all authority and do away with the entire machinery of government through the abolition of taxes, simpli- fication of administration, and the separate centralisation of each and every class of function, or, to put this another way, the organisation of universal suffrage. In which regard we say that now there are but two parties in France: the party of freedom and the party of government.

There, summed up in two articles, you have our declaration of social and political faith.

Yes, the future requires that the worker aspect and the capitalist or pro- prietor aspect of every producer be made equal and clear. Just as in a bygone age the serf was bound to the land, so today, by an inversion of relationships, capital should be bound to the worker. There you have the most positive pledge and most authentic tendency of the Revolution. Socialism and de- mocracy are of like mind with us on this count.

Yes, freedom and authority must be equal in every citizen: otherwise, there would be no equality and equality would be compromised; and the sovereignty of the people, vested in a small number of representatives, would be a fiction. Here again we have the pledge as well as the irrepressible and irresistible tendency of the Revolution, even though opinion has yet to wake up entirely to the way in which this parity between freedom and authority is to be established. In this respect, let the bourgeoisie look to tradition: let it cast its mind back to its own long exertions against despotism, its deep-seated hatred of government; let those who were the first on February 22nd to bellow *Long live Reform!* and who, even before Ledru-Rollin himself, laid the first foundation stone of universal suffrage, let them answer for us: let them say whether we have truth on our side!

Now, this double pledge, this trend, detected and acknowledged, is what we are still affirming! What is the loftier and definitive conclusion we afford the Revolution?

That between labour and liberty, like capital and government, there is a kinship and identification: so that instead of four parties such as we had in

---

1    All three of these papers were suppressed by the state, as was its next incarnation *Le Peuple de 1850*. (Editor)

the land but recently, placing us in turn in the economic point of view and in the political point of view, there are really only two: the party of labour or liberty and the party of capital or government. And these two propositions—*abolition of man's exploitation of his fellow-man and abolition of the man's government of his fellow-man*—amount to one and the same proposition; that finally the revolutionary IDEA, despite the dualism in its formula, is one and indivisible, as is the Republic itself: universal suffrage implying negation of capital's preponderance and equality of wealth, just as equality of wealth and the abolition of interest are implicit in negation of government.

We need not spell out the identity of these ideas for any logical mind to acknowledge and embrace it; it represents the point of transition between the capitalist, governmental age which is nearing its end and the era of freedom and equality which is just beginning. And, so to speak, history's apogee and the humanitarian equator.

Our entire opposition, our polemic, our revolutionary science flows from this fact: just as, further along, all philosophical advancement, every manifestation of religion—should society still need to manifest itself in this manner—will flow from it. With all of our might we are striving for, on the one hand, the abolition of interest and for lending to be free and, on the other, the obliteration of government. *La Voix du Peuple* has no other reason for its existence.

Now, this is what has befallen us.

As a result of one of those contradictions so frequent during times of great intellectual endeavour, it turns out that at present the labouring class, that which resists capital, and for whose benefit the Revolution is primarily made, is unwittingly sliding, due to a communism in its thinking and thanks above all to the ineptitude of its leaders, into the preservation of authority: the old monarchist instinct is still around, in the form of Dictatorship, Convention or whatever, to delude the people; whereas the middle class, or bourgeoisie, eternally hostile to authority, having baptised itself the liberal party, is tilting, as a consequence of its economic routine and the servility of its interests, towards perpetuation of capitalist and proprietary exploitation.

So that we who, in the name of the Revolution and of the principle invoked by every single one of the parties who stand for it, are also and simultaneously striving for the abolition of capital and of the State, at a time when we should be rallying every opinion, find ourselves at odds with each of them, and upbraided and opposed by all of the very people whose cause we serve! Politics! If you want to get surely to power then refrain from being in the right against everybody.

And so the Revolution that the middle class and the proletariat, by virtue of their shared ideas and needs, seemed to be competing to accomplish, has been stopped in its tracks by the short-sighted, illogical parting of the ways between their views and their interests. Since February 26th, when it looked as if everyone was agreed upon giving it a formidable forward thrust, the Revolution has been faced with the entire nation split into two antagonistic camps—those who, with Messieurs Dunoyer, Frédéric Bastiat, etc., following in the footsteps of J-B Say, were ready to surrender the State, were championing capital; and the rest, who, together with the provisional government, Louis Blanc, Pierre Leroux and the entire democratic and utopian tradition, were bent on turning the State into the creator of freedom and order.

For, and we can say this without fear of misquotation and calumny, it was in all seriousness that Pierre Leroux, who rejects man's governance of his fellow man, or so he assures us, nevertheless craves, in the name of the Triad and the consent of *each one*, to establish over *all* the sovereignty of *THE FEW*. The draft for a Triadic Constitution published by Pierre Leroux, which we will some day make time to examine, reeks of its author's governmental tendencies. And it was also with the utmost seriousness that Louis Blanc, for all his celebrated dictum about going "from the *master-State* to the *servant-State*," wants an authority formed, as all authorities are, through delegation by the citizenry; a State that is the organ and representative of society: in short, a government that may be to the people as the head is to the body, which is to say, master and sovereign.

This is the contradiction which we are striving with all the vigour of our consciousness and all the might of our reason to banish. Whilst the political thinking by which the middle class is prompted and the economic rationale pursued by the people should, through mutual complementation, resolve into one and the same notion that would thus encapsulate the Revolution's past and its future and reconcile those two classes, these two ideas are at war with each other and by virtue of their clash, stopping movement and jeopardising public safety.

And this also lies at the root of the recriminations that our polemic has sparked every time that, contrary to one of the half-baked ideas competing for influence, it falls to us to expand upon one of the great principles of February. On our right we find the old liberalism, inimical to the authorities, but protective of interest and exclusive property; on our left, the governmentalist democrats, inimical, like us, to man's exploitation of his fellow man, but full to the brim with faith in dictatorship and the omnipotence of the State; and in the centre ground stands absolutism, its banners emblazoned with the two faces of the counter-revolution; and, bringing up the rear, the moderates whose phoney wisdom is always ready to compromise with all shades of opinion.

Each party ascribing its own contradictions to us, we are simultaneously accused by the democratic socialists of treason; by the liberal economists, of frivolity; by the moderates, of exaggeration. The first take us to task for preaching individualism after having opposed property. They tell us: you see only one term in the republican equation of *Liberty, Equality, Fraternity*; this AN-ARCHY of yours is Monsieur Dupin's *every man for himself, each to his own*; what you attack under the name of government is the core idea of the age, association.

The economists, in turn, ask us how it is that, rejecting State initiative, we could nonetheless look to the initiative of the people; they contend that putting society in the place of government through the organisation of the free interplay of wills and interests, still amounts to going around in the same circles and to opposing freedom.

The moderates acknowledge the correctness of our reasoning: they give their blessing to our principles; but they refuse to follow us all the way to our conclusions. Following a principle through to its every consequence is, they say, tantamount to sacrificing truth on the altar of logic, venturing beyond the target one wishes to reach and going astray through exaggeration.

As for the absolutists, they are, of all our adversaries, the ones who best understand us. They level no charges against us and do not slander us; they take the line that we are playing into their hands by making our *reductio ad absurdum* of all of the notions shared by pubic opinion, democracy, constitutional monarchy, economism, socialism and philosophism; and, bedazzled by their illusions, they gravely wait for us to be converted and repent our errors. However, the situation must become clear and this already too long-lived error must come to its end.

Who, then, is contradicting himself, us, or the governmental socialists whose noxious tendencies we have been denouncing these past twenty months and whose every defeat we have foretold? Us, or the liberal economists whose errors we have been refuting these past ten years? Us, or the pig-headed doctrinaires whom we are forever telling that their alleged moderation is nothing but impotence and arbitrariness? Who is it that needs to win his adversary over—we who have kept to the broad thoroughfares of progress all the way, or the supporters of absolutism, as rigid as milestones, at the furthest extremity of the horizon?

All doubts will be dispelled and the public spared many a discussion if, just the same way as we agree in acknowledging, on the one hand, the bourgeoisie's liberal inclinations and, on the other, the proletariat's egalitarian tendencies, we might yet agree that they are one and the same.

Is it true that socialism, an expression of the proletariat, is at war for all eternity against capital, indeed, against property?—Yes.

Is it a fact that liberalism, an expression of the middle class, has, since time immemorial, been resisting the factiousness of government, the ventures of the authorities, the prerogatives of the State?—Again, yes.

Those two points made, what say we?

That what, in politics, goes under the name of *Authority* is analogous to and synonymous with what is termed, in political economy, *Property*; that these two notions overlap one with the other and are identical.

That an attack upon one is an attack upon the other.

That the one is incomprehensible without the other, and *vice versa*.

That if you do away with the former, you still have to do away with the latter, and *vice versa*.

That where capital is stripped of all interest, government is rendered useless and impossible; and, on the other hand, capital, in the absence of a government to support it, cloak it with its prerogatives and guarantee it the exercise of its privileges must, of necessity, remain unproductive and all usury unfeasible.

Finally, that Socialism and Liberalism are the two halves of the wholesale opposition that Liberty has, ever since the world began, mounted against the principle of AUTHORITY as articulated through property and through the State.

Are we wrong now, are we being frivolous, disloyal to our cause and treacherous to our principles when we champion this grand, magnificent conclusion? Is it our fault if the proletariat and the middle class, divided right now by the selfishness of their respective tendencies, are, in essence, of one mind on principles as well as on aims and on means?

And just because self-styled revolutionaries, capitalising upon hatred, service this factious antagonism for the benefit of their own despicable ambitions, are we supposed to stay silent about our ideas, the same ideas as February? Should we cravenly shy away from the risk of calumny and unpopularity?

But, they tell us, you are forever mistaking civilisation's *trends* for its *laws* and this is where you go astray: that is the origins of the contradictions, inconsistencies and exaggerations of which the entire people accuses you.

Thus one socialist says, it is correct, and we were delighted to welcome this truth, that capital and products should circulate free of charge and that use of the instruments of labour should be guaranteed for all at no cost other than what covers the costs of depreciation. This, indeed, is one of the laws of society: and you yourself have demonstrated it mathematically. But, by the same token, it is not true that society can and should dispense with government. In the absence of government, in the absence of the State, who would then extend loans to the worker, organise commerce and ensure that everyone gets education and work?

But, responds an economist from the liberal school, that is the very opposite of what is true. The abolition of governments is what societies dream about; and the elicitation of order by means of the boundless spread of freedom is their law. As for reducing interest, the phenomenon of social economics should be seen as a mere tendency rather than as a principle of amelioration. Rent on capital dwindles as capital proliferates; this is a fact. But it is nonsensical to claim that interest ever falls to zero; in that case who would be willing to make loans? Who would save? Who would work? Discard your political and egalitarian mirages, therefore, socialist, and follow freedom's banner: the banner of 1789 and 1830!

THE SOCIALIST: You do not want a social Revolution! You support usury! You actually advocate man's exploitation of his fellow man! There is enough intelligence, initiative and patriotism within the people for it to be able to complete the Revolution on its own. It will be able to do without a suspect alliance: it will never tag along behind the bourgeoisie.

THE ECONOMIST: Liberty is indebted to the bourgeois for all its gains; it is to it that the labouring class is beholden for the welfare and the rights that it enjoys, Thus far, it is this valiant and disciplined bourgeoisie that has, all unaided, shouldered the burden of Revolution: it will never allow itself to be overtaken, nor dragged along. It will never be carried along in the wake of the proletariat.

Now, now, citizens. If you cannot see eye to eye with one another, then at least try to see eye to eye with common sense. How can you fail to see that every *tendency* points to a law? That tendency is law itself, not in the form of a latency, but in the form of action? Aristotle used to teach that the first cause of motion is the intelligible heavens, by which he meant pure Idea, Reason, Law. Thus what we describe in bodies as *attraction*, or in man as *love* or *passion*, is in society, *tendency* or *progress*; in organised creatures, *life*; in the universe, *destiny*. All of which is nothing more than a manifestation of the Idea, the Law, the Intelligible Heavens, commanding the creature, nurturing it, shaping it and magnetically commanding obedience...

But let us put psychology, ontology and metaphysics to one side. Let us turn to facts and evidence. For as long as the proletariat and the bourgeoisie, in their mutual suspicion, hold each other in check, the Revolution, instead of growing peaceably, will do so in fits and starts; and at every step society will be in danger of a general dislocation. Let us show them both, therefore, that their principle is one and the same, their tendency one and the same and their pride one and the same: that whatever the one might do in the pursuit of its own interests would amount to a realisation of the wishes of the other, just as the victory of the one over the other would spell the suicide of them both.

Odd, is it not, that, in order to break through universal ostracism, we should now need to effect a universal reconciliation?

*1850*
*Translation by Benjamin R. Tucker*

# INTEREST AND PRINCIPAL
## DISCUSSION BETWEEN M. PROUDHON AND M. BASTIAT ON INTEREST ON CAPITAL

## FIRST LETTER
### 19ᵀᴴ NOVEMBER 1849

THE OBJECT OF THE FEBRUARY REVOLUTION, POLITICALLY AND ECONOMI-
cally, is the realisation of absolute liberty for the man and the citizen.

The formula of this Revolution, in the political sphere, is the organisation
of Universal Suffrage, or the absorption of the State in Society; in the economic sphere it is the organisation of circulation and credit, or the absorption of the function of the Capitalist in that of the Worker.

Undoubtedly this formula alone does not convey a complete idea of the
movement: it is only its starting-point, its *aphorism*. But it serves to show us
the Revolution as it really is today; it authorises us, consequently, to say that
the Revolution is and can be nothing else.

[...]

"The extreme eagerness," says M. Bastiat,[1] "with which the French populace have engaged in the investigation of economic problems and the incredible indifference of the privileged classes with respect to these questions
constitutes one of the most characteristic features of our epoch. While the
older journals, the organs and mirrors of the upper classes, confine themselves to the discussion of the turbulent and fruitless questions of partisan

---

1    This exchange originally appeared in Proudhon's *La Voix du Peuple* before being
     published as a book. (Editor)

politics, the papers devoted to the interests of the working classes are incessantly agitating the more fundamental questions of Socialism."

Well, we say to M. Bastiat:

You yourself, unconsciously, are an example of this *incredible indifference* with which the members of the privileged classes study social problems; and, economist of the first rank though you consider yourself, you know nothing whatever about the present state of this question of Capital and Interest, which you have undertaken to defend. Behind the times, in ideas as well as facts, you talk exactly like a Capitalist of the ante-Revolutionary era. The socialism which for ten years has protested against Capital and Interest is wholly unknown to you; you have not read its literature; for, if you have, how happens it that, in trying to refute it, you pass by all its arguments in silence?

Truly, to hear you reason against the Socialism of today, one would take you for an Epimenides suddenly awaking from an eighty years' sleep. Is it really to us that you address your patriarchal dissertations? Is it the *proletarian* of 1849 that you are seeking to convince? Begin, then, by studying his ideas; familiarise yourself with his present doctrines; reply to the arguments, be they sound or otherwise, which govern him, and refrain from bringing forward your own, which he has known from time immemorial. Doubtless it will surprise you to hear it said that you, a member of the Academy of Moral and Political Sciences, when you speak of Capital and Interest, do not touch the question! Nevertheless, that is what we undertake today to prove. Afterwards we will discuss the question itself, if you desire it.

We deny, in the first place—and this you already know—we deny, with Christianity and the Bible, the legitimacy, *per se*, of Lending at Interest. We deny it, with Judaism and Paganism, with all the philosophers and law-givers of antiquity. For you will observe this primary fact, which is important as well as primary: Usury no sooner appeared in the world than it was denied. Law-givers and moralists have not ceased to oppose it, and if they have not achieved its extinction, they have, at least, succeeded to a certain extent in clipping its claws, in fixing a *limit*, a legal rate of Interest.

This, then, is our first proposition, the only one, it seems, which you have heard stated: Everything which, in returning a loan, is given in excess of the loan is Usury, Spoliation. *Quodcumque sorti accedit, Usura est.*[2]

But that which you do not know, and which, perhaps, you will marvel at, is that this fundamental denial of Interest does not destroy, in our view, the principle—the right, if you will—which gives birth to Interest, and which has enabled it to continue to this day in spite of its condemnation by secular and ecclesiastical authority. So that the real problem before us is not to ascertain whether Usury, *per se*, is illegitimate (in this respect we are of the

---

2   From St. Ambrose's *De Tobia*: "that which exceeds the principal in a loan is usury." (Editor)

opinion of the Church), nor whether it has an excuse for its existence (on this point we agree with the economists). The problem is to devise a means of suppressing the abuse without violating the Right—a means, in a word, of *reconciling this contradiction.*

Let us, if possible, put this a little more clearly.

On the one hand, it is very true, as you have unquestionably established, that a Loan is a *service.* And as every service has a *value,* and, in consequence, is entitled by its nature to a reward, it follows that a Loan ought to have its *price,* or, to use the technical phrase, ought to *bear Interest.*

But it is also true, and this truth is consistent with the preceding one, that he who lends, under the ordinary conditions of the professional lender, does not *deprive* himself, as you phrase it, of the capital which he lends. He lends it, on the contrary, precisely because the loan is not a deprivation to him; he lends it because he has no use for it himself, being sufficiently provided with capital without it; he lends it, finally, because he neither intends nor is able to make it valuable to him personally, because, if he should keep it in his own hands, this capital, sterile by nature, would remain sterile, whereas, by its loan and the resulting interest, it yields a profit which enables the Capitalist to live without working. Now, to live without working is, in political as well as moral economy, a contradictory proposition, an impossible thing.

The proprietor who possesses two estates, one at Tours, and the other at Orleans, and who is obliged to fix his residence on the one which he uses, and consequently to abandon his residence on the other, can this proprietor claim that he deprives himself of anything, because he is not, like God, ubiquitous in action and presence? As well say that we who live in Paris are deprived of a residence in New York! Confess, then, that the privation of the capitalist is akin to that of the master who has lost his slave, to that of the prince expelled by his subjects, to that of the robber who, wishing to break into a house, finds the dogs on the watch and the inmates at the windows.

Now, in the presence of this affirmation and this negation diametrically opposed to each other, both supported by arguments of equal validity, but which, though not harmonising, cannot destroy each other, what course shall we take?

You persist in your affirmation, and say: "You do not wish to pay me Interest? Very well! I do not wish to lend you my Capital. Try working without Capital." On the other hand, we persist in our negation, and say: "We will not pay you Interest, because Interest, in social economy, is a premium on idleness, the primary cause of misery and the inequality of wealth." Neither of us is willing to yield, we come to a stand-still.

This, then, is the point at which Socialism takes up the question. On the one hand, the commutative justice of Interest; on the other, the organic impossibility, the immorality of Interest; and, to tell you the truth at once, Socialism aims to convert neither party—the Church, which denies Interest, nor the political economy, which supports it—especially as it is convinced that both are right. Let us see, now, how it analyses the problem, and what it proposes, in its turn, that is superior to the arguments of the old money-lenders, too vitally *interested* to be worthy of belief, and to the ineffectual denunciations uttered by the Fathers of the Church.

Since the theory of Usury has finally prevailed in Christian as well as in Pagan countries; since the hypothesis, or fiction, of the productivity of Capital has become a practical fact among nations—let us accept this economic fiction as we have accepted for thirty-three years the constitutional fiction, and let us see what it results in when carried to its ultimate conclusion. Instead of simply rejecting the idea, as the Church has done—a futile policy—let us make from it a historical and philosophical deduction; and, since the word is more in fashion than ever, let us trace the revolution.

Moreover, this idea must correspond to some reality; it must indicate some necessity of the mercantile spirit; else nations never would have sacrificed to it their dearest and most sacred beliefs.

See, then, how Socialism, entirely convinced of the inadequacy of the economic theory as well as of the ecclesiastical doctrine, treats in its turn the question of Usury.

First, it observes that the principle of the productivity of Capital is no respecter of persons, grants no privileges; it applies to every capitalist, regardless of rank or dignity. That which is legitimate for Peter is legitimate for Paul; both have the same right to Usury as well as to Labour. When, then, I go back to the example which you have used, when you lend me, at Interest, the plane which you have made for smoothing your planks, if, in my turn, I lend you the saw which I have made for cutting up my lumber, I also shall be entitled to Interest.

The right of Capital is alike for all; all, in the proportion that they lend and borrow, ought to receive and pay Interest. Such is the first consequence of your theory, which would not be a theory, were not the right which it establishes universal and reciprocal; this is self-evident.

Let us suppose, then, that of all the Capital that I use, whether in the form of machinery or of raw material, half is lent to me by you; suppose also that of all the capital used by you half is lent to you by me; it is clear that the interests which we must pay will offset each other; and, if equal amounts of capital are advanced, the interests cancelling each other, the balance will be zero.

In society, it is true, things do not go on precisely in this way: The mutual loans of producers are far from equal; consequently, the interests that they have to pay are no nearer so; hence, the inequality of conditions and fortunes.

But the question is to ascertain whether this equilibrium in the loaning of Capital, Labour, and Skill, and, consequently, equality of income for all citizens, perfectly admissible in theory, is capable of realisation in practice; whether this realisation is in accordance with the tendencies of society;

whether, finally and unquestionably, it is not the inevitable result of the theory of Usury itself.

Now, this is what Socialism affirms, now that it has arrived at an understanding of itself, the Socialism which no longer distinguishes itself from Economic Science, studied at once in the light of its accumulated experience and in the power of its deductions. In fact, what does the history of Civilisation, the history of Political Economy, tell us concerning this great question of Interest?

It tells us that the mutual loaning of Capital, material, or immaterial, tends more and more towards equilibrium, owing to the various causes enumerated below, which the most conservative economists cannot dispute:

*First*—The division of Labour, or the separation of Industries, which, infinitely multiplying both tools and raw material, multiplies in the same proportion the loans of Capital.

*Second*—The accumulation of Capital, an accumulation which results from diversity of Industries, producing between capitalists a competition similar to that between merchants, and, consequently, effecting gradually a lowering of the rent of capital, a reduction of the rate of Interest.

*Third*—The continually increasing power of circulation which Capital acquires through the use of Specie and Bills of Exchange.

*Fourth*—Finally, public security.

Such are the general causes which, for centuries, have developed among producers a reciprocity of loans tending more and more to equilibrium and consequently to a more and more even balance of Interests, to a continual diminution of the price of Capital.

These facts cannot be denied; you yourself admit them; only you mistake their principle and purport, by giving Capital the credit for the progress made in the domain of Industry and Wealth, whereas this progress is caused not by *Capital*, but by the CIRCULATION of Capital.

The facts being thus analysed and classified, Socialism asks whether, in order to bring about this equilibrium of Credit and Income, it is not possible to act directly, not on Capital, remember, but on Circulation; whether it is not possible so to organise this Circulation as to inaugurate, at one blow, between Capitalists and Producers (two classes now hostile, but theoretically identical) equivalence of loans, or, in other words, equality of fortunes.

To this question Socialism again replies: Yes, it is possible, and in several ways.

Suppose, in the first place, to confine ourselves to the present conditions of Credit, the operations of which are carried on mainly through the intervention of Specie—suppose that all the Producers in the Republic, numbering more than ten million, tax themselves, each one, to the amount of only one percent of their Capital. This Tax of one percent upon the total amount of the Capital of the country, both real and personal, would amount to more than a THOUSAND MILLION francs.

Suppose that by means of this tax a bank be founded, in competition with the Bank (mis-called) of France, discounting and giving credit on mortgages at the rate of one-half of one percent.

It is evident, in the first place, that the rate of discount on commercial paper, the rate of loans on mortgages, the dividend of invested capital, etc., being one-half of one percent, the cash capital in the hand of all usurers and money-lenders would be immediately struck with absolute sterility; Interest would be zero, and Credit gratuitous.

If Commercial Credit and that based on mortgages—in other words, if Money Capital, the capital whose exclusive function is to circulate—was gratuitous, House Capital would soon become so; in reality, houses no longer would be Capital; they would be merchandise, quoted in the market like brandy and cheese, and rented or sold—terms which would then be synonymous—at cost.

If houses, like money, were gratuitous—that is to say, if use was paid for as an exchange, and not as a loan—land would not be slow in becoming gratuitous also; that is, farm-rent, instead of being rent paid to a non-cultivating proprietor, would be the compensation for the difference between the products of superior and inferior soils; or, better, there no longer would exist, in reality, either tenants or proprietors; there would be only husbandmen and wine-growers, just as there are joiners and machinists.

Do you wish another proof of the possibility of making all Capital gratuitous by the development of economic institutions?

Suppose that instead of our system of taxes, so complex, so burdensome, so annoying, which we have inherited from the feudal nobility, a single tax should be established, not on production, circulation, consumption, habitation, etc., but, in accordance with the demands of Justice and the dictates of Economic Science, on the net capital falling to each individual. The Capitalist, losing by taxation as much as or more than he gains by Rent and Interest, would be obliged either to use his property himself or to sell it; economic equilibrium again would be established by this simple and moreover inevitable intervention of the treasury department.

Such is, substantially, Socialism's theory of Capital and Interest.

Not only do we affirm, in accordance with this theory (which, by the way, we hold in common with the economists) and on the strength of our belief in industrial development, that such is the tendency and the import of lending at Interest; we even prove, by the destructive results of economy as it is, and by a demonstration of the causes of poverty, that this tendency is necessary, and the annihilation of Usury inevitable.

In fact, Rent, reward of Capital, Interest on Money, in one word, Usury, constituting, as has been said, an integral part of the price of products, and this Usury not being the same for all, it follows that the price of products, composed as it is of Wages and Interest, cannot be paid by those who have only their Wages, and no Interest to pay it with; so that, by the existence of Usury, Labour is condemned to idleness and Capital to bankruptcy.

This argument, one of that class which mathematicians call the *reductio ad absurdum*, showing the organic impossibility of lending at Interest, has been repeated a hundred times by Socialism. Why do not the economists notice it?

Do you really wish to refute the ideas of Socialism on the question of Interest? Listen, then, to the questions which you must answer:

1. Is it true that, though the loaning of Capital, when viewed objectively, is a *service* which has its value, and which consequently should be paid for, this loaning, when viewed subjectively, does not involve an actual sacrifice on the part of the Capitalist; and consequently that it does not establish the right to set a price on it?

2. Is it true that Usury, to be unobjectionable, must be equal; that the tendency of Society is towards this equalisation; so that Usury will be entirely legitimate only when it has become equal for all,— that is, non-existent?

3. Is it true that a National Bank, giving Credit and Discount *gratis*, is a possible institution?

4. Is it true that the effects of the gratuity of Credit and Discount, as well as that of Taxation when simplified and restored to its true form, would be the abolition of Rent of Real Estate, as well as of Interest on Money?

5. Is it true that the old system is a contradiction and a mathematical impossibility?

6. Is it true that Political Economy, after having, for several thousand years, opposed the view of Usury held by theology, philosophy, and legislation, comes, by the application of its own principles, to the same conclusion?

7. Is it true, finally, that Usury has been, as a providential institution, simply an instrument of equality and progress, just as, in the Political sphere, absolute monarchy was an instrument of liberty and progress, and as, in the Judicial sphere, the boiling-water test, the duel, and the rack were, in their turn, instruments of conviction and progress?

These are the points that our opponents are bound to examine before charging us with scientific and intellectual weakness; these, Monsieur Bastiat, are the points on which your future arguments must turn, if you wish them to produce a definite result. The question is stated clearly and categorically: permit us to believe that, after having examined it, you will perceive that there is something in the Socialism of the nineteenth century that is beyond the reach of your antiquated Political Economy.

P-J PROUDHON

# SECOND LETTER

3RD DECEMBER 1849

[...]

WHAT! YOU UNDERTAKE to refute and convince me, and then, instead of grappling with my system hand to hand, you offer me yours! In replying to me, you begin by demanding that I shall agree with you concerning that which I positively deny! Really, would I not be justified in saying to you from this moment: Keep your theory of Lending at Interest, since it suits you, and leave me my theory of Gratuitous Lending, which I find more advantageous, more moral, more useful, and much more practical? Instead of discussing, as we had hoped, we must resort to mutual slander and recrimination. *A l'avantage!*

That, sir, is how the discussion would end, if your theory, unfortunately for itself, was not compelled, in order to maintain itself, to overthrow mine. That is what I shall have the honour of proving to you, in following your letter point by point.

[...]

You ask: Is Interest on Capital legitimate, *yes* or *no*? Reply to that, without antinomy and without antithesis.

I reply: Let us DISTINGUISH, if you please. Yes, Interest on Capital might once have been considered legitimate; no, it can no longer be considered so. Does this also seem to you ambiguous and equivocal? I will try to disperse all the clouds.

Absolute monarchy was legitimate once; it was one of the conditions of political development. Later it ceased to be legitimate, because it had become an obstacle to progress. It was the same with constitutional monarchy, which, in 1789 and even in 1830, was the only political form suited to our country; today it would occasion disturbance and decline.

Polygamy was legitimate once; it was the first step away from Communistic promiscuity. It is condemned today as contrary to the dignity of woman; we punish it with the galleys.

The judicial combat, the boiling-water test, the rack itself,—read M. Rossi—had also their kind of legitimacy. They were the earliest forms of administering justice. We repudiate them now, and any magistrate who should employ them would be guilty of a crime.

Under St. Louis the arts and trades were feudalised, organised into corporations, and armed with privileges. This regulation was useful and legitimate; it aimed to establish, in opposition to the feudality of the Landlords and the Nobility, the feudality of Labour. It has since been abandoned, and rightly; since '89 industry has been free.

I repeat then,—and, on my honour, I think I speak clearly,—yes, Lending at Interest was once legitimate, when the democratic centralisation of credit and circulation was impossible; it is so no longer, now that this centralisation has become a necessity of the age, consequently a duty of society and a right of the citizen. That is why I raise my voice against Usury; I say that society owes me Credit and Discount without Interest: Interest I call THEFT.

[...]

Now, asks the philosopher, why is a thing, true today, false tomorrow? Can Truth thus change? Is not Truth Truth? Must we believe that it is only a whim, an appearance, a prejudice? Is there, finally, or is there not, a cause for this change? Above the Truth which changes, may there exist, perchance, a Truth which does not change, an absolute, immutable Truth?

In a word, Philosophy does not stop with the fact as experience and history reveal it; it seeks its explanation.

Well, Philosophy has found, or, if you prefer, it thinks it has found, that this change in social institutions, this transformation which they undergo after a certain number of centuries, arises from the fact that the ideas of which they are the expression are possessed in and of themselves of a sort of evolutionary power, a principle of perpetual mobility, resulting from their contradictory nature.

Thus it is with Interest on Capital, legitimate when a loan was a service rendered by citizen to citizen, but which ceases to be so when society has acquired the power to organise credit gratuitously for everybody. This Interest, I say, is contradictory in its nature, in that, on the one hand, the service rendered by the lender is entitled to remuneration, and that, on the other, all Wages suppose either a production or a sacrifice, which is not the case with a Loan. The revolution which is effected in the legitimacy of Lending originates there. That is how Socialism states the question; that, therefore, is the ground on which the defenders of the old regime must take their stand.

To confine oneself to tradition, to limit oneself to saying a loan is a service rendered which ought, therefore, to be compensated, without entering into the considerations which tend to annihilate Interest, is not to reply. Socialism, with redoubled energy, protests, and says: I have nothing to do with your service,—service for you, but robbery for me,—as long as it is possible for society to furnish me with the same advantages which you offer me, and that without reward. To impose on me such a service in spite of myself, by refusing to organise the circulation of Capital, is to make me submit to an unjust discount, is to rob me.

Thus your whole argument in favour of Interest consists in confounding epochs,—I mean to say, in confounding that which is legitimate in lending with that which is not,—whereas I, on the contrary, carefully distinguish between them. I will proceed to make this intelligible to you by an analysis of your letter.

I take up your arguments one by one. In my first reply I made the observation that he who lends does not *deprive* himself of his Capital. You reply: What does it matter, if he has created his Capital for the express purpose of lending it?

In saying that you betray your own cause. You acquiesce, by those words, in my *antithesis*, which consists in saying: The hidden reason why lending

518   Pierre-Joseph Proudhon

at interest, legitimate yesterday, is no longer so today, is because lending, in itself, does not involve privation. I note this confession.

But you cling to the intention: What does it matter, you say, if the lender has created his Capital for the express purpose of lending it?

To which I reply: And what do I care, indeed, for your intention, if I have really no need of your service, if the pretended service which you wish to do me becomes necessary only through the ill-will and incapacity of society?

Your Credit resembles that which the pirate gives to his captive, when he gives him his liberty in return for a ransom. I protest against your credit at five percent, because society is able and ought to give it to me at zero percent; and, if it refuses to do so, I accuse it, as well as you, of robbery; I say that it is an accomplice, an abettor, an organiser of robbery.

Comparing a loan to a *sale*, you say: Your argument is as valid against the latter as against the former, for the hatter who sells hats does not *deprive* himself.

No, for he receives for his hats—at least he is reputed to receive for them—their exact value immediately, neither *more* nor *less*. But the Capitalist lender not only is not deprived, since he recovers his Capital intact, but he receives more than his Capital, more than he contributes to the exchange; he receives in addition to his Capital an Interest which represents no positive product on his part. Now, a service which costs no Labour to him who renders it is a service which may become gratuitous: this you have already told us yourself.

After having recognised the *non-privation* attendant upon a loan, you admit further "that *it is not theoretically impossible that Interest*, which today constitutes an integral part of the price of commodities, *may become the same for all*, and thereby be *abolished*." "But," you add, "for this other things are needed than a new bank. Let Socialism endow all men with equal activity, skill, honesty, economy, foresight, needs, desires, virtues, vices, and chances even, and then it will have succeeded."

So that you enter upon the question only to immediately avoid it. Socialism, at the point which it has now reached, justly claims that it is by means of a reform in banking and taxation that we can arrive at this balance of interests. Instead of passing over, as you do, this claim of Socialism, stop here and refute it: you will thereby demolish all the utopias of the world.

For Socialism affirms—and without this affirmation Socialism could not exist, it would be a nonentity—that it is not by endowing all men with equal "activity, skill, honesty, economy, foresight, needs, desires, virtues, vices, and chances even" that we shall succeed in balancing interest and equalising incomes; it maintains that we must, on the contrary, begin by centralising Credit and abolishing Interest, in order to equalise faculties, needs, and chances. Let there be no more robbers among us, and we shall be all virtuous, all happy! That is Socialism's creed. I feel the keenest regret in telling you of it, but really your acquaintance with Socialism is so slight that you run against it without seeing it.

You persist in attributing to Capital all social progress in the domain of wealth, while I, for my part, attribute it to Circulation; and you say that here I mistake the cause for the effect.

[...]

I repeat: The problem of Socialism is to make [...] Interest on Capital [...] equal for all producers, and consequently nugatory. We maintain that this is possible; that, if this is possible, it is society's duty to procure Gratuitous Credit for all; that, failing to do this, it will not be a society, but a conspiracy of capitalists against workers, a pact of plunder and murder.

[...]

We say: The economic system based on the fiction of the productivity of Capital, justifiable once, is henceforth illegitimate. Its inefficacy and malfeasance have been exposed; it is the cause of all existing misery, the present mainstay of that old fiction of representative government which is the last form of tyranny among men.

I will not detain myself with the purely religious considerations with which your letter closes. Religion, allow me to say, has nothing to do with Political Economy. A real science is sufficient unto itself; otherwise, it cannot exist. If Political Economy needs the sanction of Religion to make up for the inadequacy of its theories, and if, in its turn, Religion, as an excuse for the barrenness of its dogmas, pleads the exigencies of Political Economy, the result will be that Political Economy and Religion, instead of mutually sustaining each other, will accuse each other, and both will perish.

Begin, then, by doing justice, and liberty, fraternity, and wealth will increase; even the happiness of another life will be only the surer. Is the inequality of Capitalist Income, yes or no, the primary cause of the physical, moral, and intellectual misery which today afflicts society? Is it necessary to equalise the income of all men, to make the circulation of Capital gratuitous by assimilating it to the exchange of Products, and to destroy Interest? That is what Socialism asks, and it must have an answer.

Socialism, in its most positive conclusions, furnishes the solution in the democratic centralisation and gratuity of Credit, combined with a single tax, to replace all other taxes, and to be levied on Capital.

Let this solution be verified; let its application be tried. That is the only way to refute Socialism; except that is done, we shall shout louder than ever our war-cry: *Property is Theft!*

P-J PROUDHON

# THIRD LETTER
## 17ᵀᴴ DECEMBER 1849

SIR, WE DO not advance in our discussion, and the fault lies entirely with you. By your persistent refusal to place yourself upon the ground to which I summon you, and your determination to draw me upon yours, you deny me that right to an examination which belongs to every innovator; you fail in the duty which the appearance of new ideas imposes on all economists, the natural defenders of tradition and established customs; in fact, you violate ordinary charity by compelling me to attack what I recognised, in a certain sense, as irreproachable and legitimate.

[...]

Is it possible, yes or no, to abolish Interest on Money, Rent of Land and Houses, the Product of Capital, by simplifying Taxation, on the one hand, and, on the other, by organising a Bank of Circulation and Credit in the name and on the account of the people? This, in my opinion, is the way in which the question before us should be stated. Love of Humanity, Truth, and Harmony is a law to us both. What has the nation been doing since February, what has the Constituent Assembly been doing, what is the Legislature doing today, if not seeking means to improve the condition of the worker without alarming legitimate interests and invalidating the right of the proprietors? Let us see, then, if the Gratuity of Credit might, perchance, be one of these means.

Such were my words; I ventured to believe that they would be understood. Instead of replying to them, as I hoped, you retrench yourself behind your old evasion. To this question: *To prove that the Gratuity of Credit is a possible, easy, and practical thing—is that not to prove that that Interest on Credit is henceforth an illegitimate thing?* you reply, reversing the phrase: "To prove that Interest has been, legitimate, just, useful, beneficent, indestructible—is that not to prove that Gratuity of Credit is an illusion?" You reason precisely as the stage-lines did in regard to rail-ways.

See them, indeed, parading their grievances before the public, which is forsaking them for their competitors: Are not the wagon and the *malbrouck*[3] useful, legitimate, beneficent, and indestructible institutions? Do we not, in transporting your persons and products, render you a service? Has not this service a value? Ought not every value to be paid for? In transporting products at twenty-five centimes per ton and kilometre, though the locomotive does the same work, it is true, for ten centimes, are we robbers? Is not Commerce perpetually and universally extended by wagons, beasts of burden, and navigation by sail or oar? Of what importance, then, to us are steam, and atmospheric pressure, and electricity? To prove the reality and

---

3   A "malbrouck" was a kind of crude cart used by seventeenth-century Belgian farmers. (Editor)

legitimacy of the four-wheeled vehicle,—is that not to prove that the invention of railways is a chimera?

This, sir, is where your argument leads to. Your last letter, like the preceding ones, from beginning to end means nothing else. To preserve for Capital the interest, which I refuse it, you reply by the previous question; you oppose to my novel idea your old routine; you protest against railroads and steam-engines. I should be sorry to say anything to wound you; but truly, sir, it seems to me that I should be justified, at this moment, in stopping here and turning my back upon you.

But I will not do it: I wish to give you satisfaction to the last, by showing you how, to use your own words, *the remuneration of Capital passes from legitimacy to illegitimacy*, and how Gratuity of Credit is the final result of the practice of Usury. This discussion, in itself, is not an unimportant one; I will try to make it a peaceful one.

The reason why Interest of Capital, excusable and even just in the infancy of social economy, becomes, as industrial institutions develop, real spoliation and robbery, is because it has no other principle, no other *raison d'être*, than those of necessity and force. Necessity explains the unreasonableness of the lender; force causes the resignation of the borrower. But, in proportion as in human relationships, necessity gives way to liberty, and force is succeeded by right, the Capitalist loses his excuse, and the worker's claim against the proprietor becomes good.

In the beginning the land is undivided; each family lives by hunting, fishing, gathering or grazing; industry is entirely domestic, and agriculture, so to speak, nomadic. There is no commerce, neither is there property.

Later, tribes consolidating, the formation of nations commences; caste appears, the child of war and patriarchism. Property establishes itself little by little; but, by heroic law, the master, though he does not cultivate his land himself, makes use of his slaves for that purpose, as at a later period the nobleman does his serfs. Farm-rent does not yet exist; revenue, which indicates this relation, is unknown.

At this period Commerce consists mainly in barter. If Gold and Silver appear in transactions, it is rather as Merchandise than as a Circulating Medium and Unit of Value: they are weighed, not counted. Exchange, the consequent Profit, lending at Interest, sleeping-partnership, all the operations of a well-developed Commerce which are performed by means of Money, are unknown. These primitive customs are retained for a long time in agricultural districts. My mother, a simple peasant, told me that, previous to '89, she was employed in the winter at spinning hemp, receiving, as wages for six weeks' work, besides her board, a pair of wooden shoes and a loaf of rye bread.

We must look to Foreign Commerce to find the origin of lending at Interest. The *contrat a la grosse*, a variety, or rather a separate part, of the *contrat de pacotille*, was its original form, just as the farm-lease or cattle-lease was the counterpart of sleeping-partnership.

What is the *contrat de pacotille*? A contract by which a manufacturer and ship-master agree to put into a common fund, for purposes of Foreign Commerce, the former a certain quantity of merchandise which he undertakes to procure, the latter his labour as a navigator, the *Profit* resulting from the sale to be divided equally between them, or according to a proportion to be agreed upon, and the risks and damages to be charged to the firm.

Is the profit thus anticipated, however large it may be, legitimate?

*We cannot call it into question.*

Profit, at this early period of commercial relations, represents only the uncertainty which prevails among exchanging parties concerning the value of their respective products; it is an advantage which exists more in the imagination than in reality, and which is not uncommonly claimed with equal reason by both parties to a transaction. How many pounds of tin is an ounce of gold worth? What is the relation between the price of Tyrian purple and that of sable fur? No one knows; no one can tell. The Phoenician who, for a pack of furs, gives ten palms of his cloth, congratulates himself upon his bargain; so also, on his side, does the Northern hunter, proud of his red cloak. And such is still the practice of Europeans in dealing with Australian savages, who are happy to give a pig for an axe, a hen for a nail or a piece of glass.

The incommensurability of values, such is the original source of commercial profits. Gold and Silver then enter into traffic, first as merchandise, and then, soon after, by virtue of the facility with which they can be exchanged, as terms of comparison, as money. In both cases the Gold and Silver bear profit in exchange, in the first place by the very fact of exchange, next for the risk incurred. Insurance appears here as the twin brother of the *contrat a la grosse*; the premium stipulated for the first being the correlative of and identical with the share of the profit agreed upon in the second.

This *share* of the profit, which expresses the participation of the Capitalist or manufacturer who invests his products or his Capital (the same thing) in commerce, has received the Latin name of *inter-esse*, that is, participation, *Interest*.

At this time, then, and under the conditions which I have just stated, who could brand Interest as fraudulent? Interest is the *alea*, the gain obtained in operations of chance; it is the speculative profit of commerce, a profit which is irreproachable until the comparison of values furnishes the correlative ideas of *dearness*, *cheapness*, proportion, PRICE. The same analogy, the same identity, which Political Economy has always and rightly pointed out between Interest on money and Rent of Land, exists at the beginning of commercial relations between this same Interest and commercial profit: at bottom, exchange is the common form, the starting-point of all these transactions.

You see, sir, that the energy with which I oppose Capital does not prevent me from doing justice to the original good faith of its operations. I never trifle with the truth. I told you that there was a true, honest, legitimate side to

Lending at Interest; I have just shown it in a way which seems to me a better one than yours, in that it sacrifices nothing to selfishness and detracts nothing from charity. It was the impossibility of appraising commodities with any degree of exactness that made Interest legitimate in the beginning, just as, later, it is the passion for the precious metals which sustains it. Lending at Interest must have had a positive and necessary basis in order to develop and spread as it has; if not, we must condemn, with the theologians, all humanity, which, for my part, I profess to consider infallible and holy.

But who does not see already that the merchant's profit ought to decrease as fast as the risks incurred and the arbitrary method of estimating values disappear, so that finally it may be only the just price of the service rendered by him, the wages of his labour? Who does not see with equal clearness that Interest ought to disappear with the risks which Capital runs and the privation which Capital endures: so that if repayment is guaranteed by the debtor, and the labour of the creditor is zero, Interest must become zero?

[...]

I said before that in ancient times the Landed Proprietor, when neither he nor his family farmed his land, as was the case among the Romans in the early days of the Republic, cultivated it through his slaves: such was the general practice of Patrician families. Then slavery and the soil were chained together; the farmer was called *adscrpitus glebæ*, joined to the land; property in men and things was undivided. The price of a farm depended (1) upon its area and quality of its soil, (2) upon the quantity of stock, and (3) upon the number of slaves.

When the Emancipation of the Slave was proclaimed, the proprietor lost the man and kept the land; just as today, in freeing the blacks, we leave the master his property in land and stock. Nevertheless, from the standpoint of ancient law as well as of natural and Christian right, man, born to labour, cannot dispense with the implements of Labour; the principle of Emancipation involved an agrarian law which guarantees them to him and protects him in their use: otherwise, this pretended Emancipation was only an act of hateful cruelty, an infamous deception, and if, as Moses said, interest, or the yearly income from Capital, reimburses Capital, might it not be said that Servitude reimburses Property? The theologians and the law-givers of the time did not understand this, and by an irreconcilable contradiction, which still exists, they continued to rail at Usury, but gave absolution to Rent.

The result was that the emancipated slave, and, a few centuries later, the enfranchised serf, without means of existence, was obliged to become a tenant and pay tribute. The master grew still richer. I will furnish you, he says, with land; you shall furnish the labour; and we will divide the products. It was a reproduction on the farm of the ways and customs of business. I will lend you ten talents, said the moneyed man to the worker; you shall use them; and then either we will divide the profits, or else, as long as you keep my money, you shall pay me a twentieth; or, if you prefer, at the expiration of the loan, you shall return double the amount originally received. From this sprang Ground-Rent, unknown to the Russians and the Arabs. The exploitation of man by man, thanks to this transformation, passed into the form of law: Usury, condemned in the form of lending at interest, tolerated in the *contrat a la grosse*, was extolled in the form of Farm-Rent. From that moment commercial and industrial progress served to make it only more and more customary. This was necessary in order to exhibit all the varieties of Slavery and Robbery, and to establish the true law of Human Liberty.

Once engaged in this practice of *inter-esse*, so strangely understood, so improperly applied, Society began to revolve in the circle of its miseries. Then it was that inequality of conditions seemed a law of civilisation, and evil a necessity of our nature.

[...]

Again: The productivity of Capital being the immediate and sole cause of the inequality of wealth, and the continual accumulation of Capital in a few hands, it must be admitted, in spite of the progress of knowledge, in spite of Christian revelation and the extension of public liberty, that society is naturally and necessarily divided into two classes—a class of exploiting capitalists and a class of exploited workers.

Again: the aforesaid class of Capitalists, having all tools and products at its absolute disposal through lending capital at Interest, has the right, when, it sees fit, to bring Labour and Circulation to a stand-still, as was done two years ago, at the risk of people's lives; to change the natural course of things, as is the case in the Papal States, where the arable land has been used, from time immemorial, for the convenience of proprietors, as common pasture land, and where the people live upon the charity and curiosity of foreigners; to say to a body of citizens: *There are too many of you on the earth; at the banquet of life there is no place for you*, as did the Countess of Strafford, when she expelled from her estate seventeen thousand peasants at once, and as the French Government did last year, when it transported to Algeria four thousand families of useless mouths.

I now ask you the following question: If the partiality for gold and the fatality of the institution of money excuses and justifies the Capitalist, does it not also establish for the worker this system of brute force, only distinguishable from ancient slavery by its subtler and more villainous hypocrisy?

FORCE, sir—that is the first and last word of a Society organised upon the principle of Interest, and which, for three thousand years, struggled against Interest. You establish this yourself, without reserve or scruple, when you admit, with me, that the Capitalist *does not deprive himself*, and with J-B Say, that his function is to do *nothing*; and when you put into his mouth this insolent language, which every human conscience condemns:

"I impose nothing on you in spite of yourself. If you do not admit that a loan is a service, abstain from borrowing, as I do from lending. But if *Society* offers you these *advantages* without *reward*, deal directly with it, for its terms are much easier; and as for *organising the circulation of capital*, as you call upon me to do, if you mean thereby that you should have the use of my capital *gratis* through the mediation of Society, I have just the same objection to this indirect method of procedure that induced me to refuse you a direct and gratuitous loan."

Have a care, sir; the people are only too ready to believe that it is solely for love of its privileges that the Capitalist class, now dominant, opposes the organisation of Credit which they clamour for; and the day when the ill-will of that class shall be positively proven, its last excuse will vanish in the people's eyes, and their vengeance will know no bounds.

[...]

P-J PROUDHON

# FOURTH LETTER
31ST DECEMBER 1849

YOU HAVE DECEIVED me.

I expected from you a serious discussion. Your letters are but a series of insipid mystifications. If you had made a compact with me to obscure the question and to prevent our debate from coming to a definitive conclusion, by embarrassing it with incidents, digressions, trifles, and quibbles, you could have taken no other course.

Now what are we after, if you please? To ascertain whether Interest of Money ought, or ought not, to be abolished. I have told you myself that there is the pivot of Socialism, the mainspring of the Revolution.

[...]

Did you ever, in your life, hear of the Bank of France? Do me the favour to visit it some day; it is not far from the Institute. There you will find M. d'Argout, who knows more about Capital and Interest than you and all the economists of Guillaumin.[4] The Bank of France is an association of capitalists, formed fifty years ago, at the solicitation of the State and by a privilege granted by the State, for the purpose of levying usury upon the whole of France.

From its beginning it has not ceased to grow: the February Revolution, by joining with it the Departmental Banks, made it the first power in the Republic. The principle on which this association was formed is yours precisely. They said: We have obtained our Capital by our labour or by that of our fathers. Why then, in return for making it an aid to general circulation and

---

4    Antoine Maurice Apollinaire d'Argout (1782–1858), centre-right politician and manager of the Banque de France; Gilbert-Urbain Guillaumin (1801–1864), liberal economist, later publisher of Bastiat's *Œuvres complètes* (1862). (Editor)

for devoting it to the service of our country, should we not draw a legitimate salary, since the landlord derives an income from his land; since the builder derives an income from his houses; since the merchant gets a profit on his goods over and above his running expenses; since the worker who lays our floors includes in the price of his day's work a charge for the use of his tools which certainly more than covers the amount which they cost him?

There could be, as you see, no more plausible argument. It is the argument which has always, and with reason, been opposed to the Church when she has condemned Interest as distinct from Rent; it is the argument which you fall back on in every one of your letters.

Now, do you know where the stockholders of the Bank of France, all of whom, including M. d'Argout, I regard as very honest people, have been led by this seductive reasoning?—To robbery; yes, sir, to the most unmistakable, shameless, detestable robbery; for it is this robbery alone which, since February, has suspended Labour, hindered business, caused the people to die of cholera, hunger and cold, and which, with the secret intention of restoring the monarchy, is breathing despair among the working classes.

It is right here that I propose to how you how Interest passes from legitimacy to illegitimacy, and, what will surprise you still more, how paid Credit, the moment that it ceases to rob, the moment that it claims only the price which legitimately belongs to it, becomes gratuitous Credit.

What is the Capital of the Bank of France? According to the last inventory, ninety million.

What is the legal rate of discount, agreed upon between the Bank and the State?—Four percent a year.

Then the legal and legitimate annual income of the Bank of France, the just price of its services, is, for a capital of ninety million, at four percent a year, three million six hundred thousand francs.

Three million six hundred thousand francs,—that is the amount, according to the fiction of the productivity of Capital, which the commerce of France owes annually to the Bank of France as reward for its Capital, which is ninety million.

Under these conditions, the shares of the Bank of France are like so many pieces of real estate yielding a regular income of forty francs each: issued at one thousand francs, they are worth one thousand francs.

Now, do you know what follows?

Consult the same inventory: you will find that these same shares are quoted at two thousand four hundred francs, instead of one thousand. Last week they were two thousand four hundred and forty-five; and if the amount of commercial effects in the portfolio should increase a little, they would go up to two thousand five hundred or three thousand francs; which means that the capital of the bank, instead of yielding four percent, the legal and conventional rate, yields eight, ten, and twelve percent.

Has the capital of the bank, then, been doubled or tripled? This, indeed, is what should have happened, according to the theory announced in your third and fourth propositions,—namely, that *Interest decreases in proportion as Capital increases, but in such a way that the total income of the Capitalist is enlarged.*

But such is not the case at all. The capital of the bank has remained the same, ninety million. Only the company, by means of its privilege and with the aid of its financial machinery, has discovered a method of doing as much business with its capital of ninety million as if it had four hundred and fifty million, or five times as much.

Do you ask how that can be? This is the method; it is very simple, and I can explain it; it is precisely one of those which the *Bank of the People* proposes to use in the annihilation of Interest.

To avoid the transfer of specie and the troublesome handling or coin, the Bank of France issues bills of credit, called *bank notes*, which represent the specie lying in its vaults. These are the notes which it ordinarily issues to its customers in return for the drafts and bills of exchange which they bring to it, and the redemption of which, secured by drawers and drawees alike, it undertakes the task of procuring,

The bank paper has thus a double security: the coin in the vault and the commercial paper in the portfolio. This double deposit is such good security that business men prefer bank notes to specie, and every one is as anxious to know the condition of the bank as that of his own money-drawer.

It is even thought, in theory, that in this way the Bank of France might dispense with Capital altogether and discount paper without specie: indeed, the commercial paper which it discounts, and against which it issues its notes, being certain of redemption at the appointed time either in Silver or in Bank-Notes, the holders of Bank-Notes would only have to dismiss the desire to covert them into coin to enable all transactions to be effected by paper alone. Then the circulating medium would be based, not on the credit of the Bank whose Capital would thus be set free, but on the Public Credit, through the general acceptance of the notes.

In practice the facts do not harmonise exactly with the theory. Never have we seen bank-paper wholly substituted for specie; there is only a *tendency* in this direction. Now, see what results from this tendency.

The Bank, relying with perfect security upon the Public Credit, sure moreover of its debts, does not limit its discounts to the amount of its metallic reserve, but always issues more notes than it has Specie; which shows that sometimes, instead of getting real value and making an actual exchange, it only transfers debts, without using any Capital. That which here takes the place of the Capital of the Bank is, I repeat, established custom, commercial confidence, in a word, the Public Credit.

It seems, therefore, that the rate of discount ought to decrease in proportion to the amount of notes issued in excess of the Capital; that if, for example, the Capital of the Bank is ninety million, and its circulation one hundred and twelve million, the fictitious capital being one-fourth of the real Capital, the rate of discount should decrease from four to three percent. What could be fairer than that, pray? Is not the Public Credit Public Property? Is not the surplus issue of the Bank secured by the mutual obligations of citizens? Does not the acceptance of this paper, which has no metallic basis, rest entirely upon their confidence in each other? Is it not this very confidence which makes the paper pass? What has the Capital of the Bank done? What does it secure?

You can already see from this simple outline how false your third proposition is, which makes a decrease of Interest involve a corresponding increase of Capital. Nothing is falser than this proposition: the theory and practice of all Banks proves, on the contrary, that a Bank may easily get four percent on its Capital while its rate of discount is only three percent: we shall see presently that the rate may go much lower.

Why, then, does not the Bank, which, with ninety million in Capital, issues, as we suppose, one hundred and twelve million in notes, and which consequently operates, by the aid of the Public Credit, just as if its Capital had increased from ninety millions to one hundred and twelve,—why, I ask, does it not reduce its rate of Discount in a like proportion? Why this four percent Interest received by the Bank as a reward for Capital not its own? Can you give me a reason which will justify this extra one percent on one hundred and twelve million? For my part, sir, "I call a cat a cat, and Rolet a rascal,"[5] and I say quite plainly that the bank ROBS.

[...]

It is a point admitted in theory that exchange of products can be carried on very well without Specie; you admit it yourself, and all the economists know it. Now, the proof of this theory lies precisely in the fact that it is carried out under our very eyes. The Circulation of Bills of credit replacing gradually the metallic currency; paper being preferred to coin; the public choosing to pay their debts in Specie rather than in Bank Notes; and the Bank being constantly persuaded, either by the needs of the State which borrows from it, or by those of commerce which comes *en masse* to get its paper discounted, or by any other cause, to make new issues frequently,—the result is that Gold and Silver go out of circulation, and are absorbed by the Bank, thus continually increasing its reserve and making its power to multiply its Notes literally unlimited.

[...]

A decree of the National Assembly, having for its object the redemption of the stock of the Bank of France, and the conversion of this Bank into a central Bank, in which all French citizens should be silent partners, would

---

5    A well-known line from Boileau's *Satires*, roughly equivalent to "telling it like it is." (Editor)

be only an announcement of the already accomplished fact of the absorption of this association by the nation.

[...]

You must see, sir, how far short of the accuracy of Euclid's your propositions fall. It is not true—and the facts just cited prove beyond a doubt that it is not—that the decrease of Interest is proportional to the increase of Capital. Between the *Price* of Merchandise and *Interest* of Capital there is not the least analogy; the laws governing their fluctuations are not the same; and all your dinning of the last six weeks in relation to Capital and Interest has been utterly devoid of sense. The universal custom of banks and the common sense of the people give you the lie on all these points in a most humiliating manner.

[...]

If, then, Interest, after having fallen, in the case of Money, to three-fourths of one percent,—that is, to zero, inasmuch as three-fourths of one percent represents only the service of the bank,—should fall to zero in the case of merchandise also, by analogy of principles and facts it would soon fall to zero in the case of real estate: rent would disappear in becoming one with liquidation. Do you think, sir, that that would prevent people from living in houses and cultivating land?

If, thanks to this radical reform in the machinery of circulation, Labour was compelled to pay to Capital only as much Interest as would be a just reward for the service rendered by the Capitalist, Specie and Real Estate being deprived of their reproductive properties and valued only as products,—as things that can be consumed and replaced,—the favour with which Specie and Capital are now looked upon would be wholly transferred to products; each individual, instead of restricting his consumption, would strive only to increase it. Whereas, at present, thanks to the restriction laid upon consumable products by Interest, the means of consumption are always very much limited, then, on the contrary, Production would be insufficient: Labour would then be secure in fact as well as in right.

The labouring class, gaining at one stroke the five thousand million, or thereabouts, now taken in the form of Interest from the ten thousand which it produces, plus five thousand millions which this same Interest deprives it of by destroying the demand for Labour, plus five thousand million which the parasites, cut off from a living, would then be compelled to produce, the national production would be doubled and the welfare of the worker increased four-fold. And you, sir, whom the worship of Interest does not prevent from lifting your thoughts to another world,—what say you to this improvement of affairs here below? Do you see now that it is not the multiplication of Capital which decreases Interest, but on the contrary, that the decrease of Interest multiplies Capital?

[...]

P-J PROUDHON

# FIFTH LETTER
### 21ST JANUARY 1850

[...]

FROM THE STANDPOINT of private interests, Capital indicates a relation of exchange, preceded by a reciprocal valuation. It is Product judicially appraised, so to speak, by two responsible judges, the seller and the buyer, and pronounced, in consequence of this appraisal, an instrument of reproduction. From the standpoint of Society Capital and Product are indistinguishable. *Products exchange for Products* and *Capital exchanges for Capital* are two perfectly synonymous propositions. What could be simpler, clearer, more positive, more scientific, indeed, than that?

I therefore call Capital, *every settled value, whether in Land, machinery, merchandise, provisions, or Money, serving, or capable of serving, in production.*

Common language confirms this definition. Capital is said to be *free* when the product, whatever it may be, having been simply appraised by the parties, can be regarded as realised, or immediately realisable, that is, converted into such other product as may be desired: in this case the form that Capital most readily assumes is that of money. Capital is said to be *engaged*, on the contrary, when the value that constitutes it is employed definitively in production: in this case it assumes all possible forms.

Custom also sustains me. In every enterprise which is started, the entrepreneur, who, instead of money, employs in his business machinery or raw material, begins by estimating it relatively to himself, his risks, and his dangers; and this estimation, one-sided so to speak, *constitutes his Capital,* or his investment in business: it is the first thing which he makes account of.

We know what Capital is; we must now draw the consequences of our conception so far as Interest is concerned. The explanation will be a little long perhaps, but the reasoning employed will be very simple.

Products exchange for products, says J-B Say; or, in other words, Capital exchanges for Capital; or yet again, Capital exchanges for products, and vice versa: that is the bare fact.

The requisite condition, the *sine qua non*, of this exchange, that which is in fact its essence and its law, is the antagonistic and reciprocal valuation of products. Deprive exchange of the idea of price, and exchange disappears. There is transposition; there is no transaction, no exchange. Product, without price, is a nonentity: as long as it has not received, by the process of buying and selling, its authenticated value, it is regarded as of no effect, it is null. That is the intelligible fact.

Every one gives and receives, according to J-B Say's formula announcing the material fact; but according to the idea of Capital which we have just obtained by our analysis, every one ought to give and receive an equal value. An unequal exchange is a contradiction; universal consent has pronounced it a fraud and a robbery.

Now, from this primary fact that producers continually stand to each other in the relation of exchanging parties, that they are to each other, by turns and all at once, producers and consumers, workers and capitalists; and from the precisely equal valuation which constitutes exchange, it follows that the accounts of all producers and consumers ought to balance each other; that society, viewed from the standpoint of economic science, is nothing else than this general equilibrium of products, services, wages, consumptions, and fortunes; that, in the absence of this equilibrium, political economy is but a meaningless word, and public order, the well-being of workers, and the security of capitalists and proprietors, a utopia.

Now, this equilibrium, from which must spring a unity of interests and social harmony, today does not exist; it is disturbed by diverse causes, which in my opinion may be easily destroyed, and in the front rank of which I place Usury, Interest, Rent. There are, as I have so often said, errors and mis-management in the book-keeping, false entries upon the ledgers, of society. Thence arises the wrongfully-acquired luxury of some, the increasing misery of others; for this reason we have in modern society an inequality of fortunes and all sorts of revolutionary agitation. I shall furnish you, sir, by commercial accounts, with the proof and the counter-proof.

Let us first establish the facts. products exchange for products, or to speak more accurately, values exchange for values: such is the law.

But this exchange is not always made, as we say, on the spot; both parties do not always transfer the objects exchanged at the same time; often, and indeed usually, there is an interval between the two deliveries. Now, strange things happen during this interval, things which disturb the equilibrium and falsify the balance. You shall see to what I refer.

It so happens that one party to the exchange has no product which the other needs, or, which amounts to the same thing, the latter, who is quite willing to sell, wishes to refrain from buying. He intends to receive the price of his goods; but he wishes, for the present at least, to accept nothing in exchange. In both cases, the exchanging parties avail themselves of an in-termediate commodity, which in commerce plays the part of a go-between, always acceptable and always accepted, and which is known as Money. And as money, sought for by everybody, is scarce with everybody, the purchaser obtains it from a banker by giving him his note and paying a premium larger or smaller, which is called *discount*. Discount is made up of two things: a *Commission*, which is the reward for the service rendered by the banker, and *Interest*. We will now tell what *Interest* is.

It so happens that the buyer has neither product nor money to give in exchange for the product or capital of which he is in need; but he offers to pay at the end of a certain time in one or more instalments. The two cases mentioned above were *cash* sales; in this case *credit* is given. Here, then, the buyer having the advantage of the seller, the inequality is compensated for by causing the product sold to bear Interest until the time of payment. It was this compensatory Interest, the primal origin of Usury, that I referred to in one of my former letters as the agent which compels repayment. It lasts as long as credit; it is the reward of credit; but its especial object, remember, is *the abridgement of the duration of credit.* Such is the meaning, the legitimate significance, of Interest.

It often occurs—and this is the extremity in which Workers are usually placed—that Capital is absolutely indispensable to the producer, and that yet there is no probability that the latter, for a long time to come, will be able by his labour or his economy, still less by the money at his disposal, to gather together an equivalent, in a word, to repay. He needs twenty, thirty, fifty years, and sometimes a century; and the Capitalist or proprietor is unwilling to allow him so long a time. How is this difficulty avoided?

Here begins usurious speculation. A moment ago we saw Interest imposed upon the debtor as an indemnity for credit and a means of hastening repayment: now we shall see Interest taken for itself, Usury for Usury, like war for war or art for art. By a formal, legal, and authentic contract, sanctioned by all jurisprudence, all legislation, and all religions, the borrower binds himself to the lender to pay him, *to the end of time*, Interest on his Capital, land, furniture, or money; he gives himself, body and soul, himself and his heirs, to the Capitalist, and becomes his tributary *advitam æternam.* That is what is termed *the settlement of an annuity*, and, in certain cases, *emphyteusis.* By this sort of contract the object passes into the possession of the borrower, who can never be disposed of it; who uses it as if he were its purchaser and proprietor; but who is bound forever to pay a revenue—an endless liquidation, as it were. Such was the economic origin of the feudal system.

But now the thing is managed better.

Emphyteusis and the settlement of annuities are today, almost everywhere, obsolete. It was found that placing Product or Capital at perpetual interest was altogether too favourable to the Capitalist: the need of an improvement in the system was felt.

Capital and Real Estate are no longer placed at permanent rental, except with the State: they are LEASED—that is, lent—always at Interest, but for a limited period. This new kind of Usury is called *rent* or *farm-rent.*

Do you understand, sir, what lending at Interest (rent or farm-rent) for a limited period is? In emphyteusis and the settlement of annuities, of which I have just spoken, though the rent was perpetual, the Capital was surrendered for all time: between the payment and the enjoyment there was still a kind of equality. Here, however, Capital never ceases to belong to him who lends it and who may demand the restoration whenever he chooses. So that the Capitalist does not exchange Capital for Capital, Product for Product: he gives up nothing, keeps all, does no work, and lives upon his rents, his Interest, and his Usury in greater luxury than one thousand, ten thousand, or even a hundred thousand workers combined can enjoy by their production.

In this system of lending at Interest—farm-rent or rent—with the power to demand at pleasure the restitution of the sum lent, and to expel the farmer or the tenant, the Capitalist has invented something vaster than space, more lasting than time. There is no infinity equal to that of the Usury paid by tenants, that Usury which is as much worse than the perpetuity of rent as the latter is worse than the cash and Credit systems of payment. He who borrows at Interest for a limited period pays, pays again, pays continually, and he does not enjoy that for which he pays; he has only a glimpse of it, possesses only its shadow. Must it not have been this kind of Usurer which the theologian took for his model when fashioning his god, that atrocious god who exacts eternal payment from the sinner, and never releases him from his debt? Always, forever!

Well, I say that all exchanges of products and Capital can be effected by Cash payment;

That consequently the banker's discount should be just enough to defray the expenses of the bank and pay for the metal unproductively employed of which the money is made;

And therefore that all interest, rent, or farm-rent is simply a refusal to redeem, a robbery of the borrower or the tenant, and the original cause of all the miseries and upheavals of society.

In my last letter I proved to you, taking the Bank of France as an illustration, that it was an easy and a practical thing to organise equality in exchange, or the gratuitous circulation of Capital and products. You were able to see, in this conclusive and decisive fact, only a special instance of monopoly, having nothing to do with the theory of Interest. What have I to do, you ask with an air of *nonchalance*, with the Bank of France and its privileges? I am discussing Interest of Capital.—As if, after landed and commercial credit had been universally organised on a basis of one-half of one percent, Interest could exist anywhere!

I will show you now, by the bookkeeper's method, that this special payment which always comes in between the two deliveries in an exchange; this tax imposed on circulation; this duty levied on the conversion of products into values and of values into Capital; this Interest, in short; or, to call it by its own name, this commercial go-between (*interesse*), which you so obstinately defend—is the identical grand forger which, in order to appropriate, fraudulently and without labour, products that it does not create and services that it never renders, falsifies accounts, enters surcharges and suppositions upon the books, destroys the equilibrium of trade, carries disorder into business, and inevitably brings all nations to despair and misery.

[...]

In this system the production, circulation, and consumption of wealth is effected by the co-operation of two distinct and separate classes of citizens,—the Proprietors, Capitalists, and Entrepreneurs on the one hand, and the Wage-Workers on the other. These two classes, although bitterly hostile to each other, together constitute a close organisation which acts in itself, on itself, and by itself.

[...]

The Money converted into Merchandise, the Proprietor-Capitalist-Entrepreneur A now has to perform the inverse operation, and convert his Merchandise into Money. This conversion implies a Profit (Premium, Interest, etc.), since, by the hypothesis and according to the theory of Interest, Land and Houses, Capital, and the guaranty and judgement of the Entrepreneur are not to be obtained *gratis*. Admit, then, the Profit to be ten percent, according to ordinary Commercial Custom.

B, a worker, without property, without capital, without work, is hired by A, who gives him employment and takes his product. [...]

But B lives on his wages,—that is, with the money given him by A, proprietor-capitalist-entrepreneur, he procures from said A all the articles needed for his (B's) consumption, articles which are invoiced to him [...] at an advance of ten percent on the cost price. [...]

All the other workers being in the same circumstances as B, their accounts show, each, the same result. The reproduction of each of these accounts is not necessary to a clear comprehension of the fact which I desire to bring out,—namely, the absence of equilibrium in general circulation in consequence of the exactions of Capital [...] we may be convinced that misery and the proletariat are not the effects of accidental causes only, such as floods, wars, and epidemics, but that they spring also from an organic cause, inherent in the constitution of society.

[...]

We are compelled, then, to admit that Credit, under the system of Interest, inevitably results in the spoliation of the worker, and, as a corrective no less inevitable, in the bankruptcy of the entrepreneur, the ruin of the Capitalist-proprietor. Interest is like a two-edged sword: whichever way it strikes, it kills.

I have just shown you what the condition of things is under the regime of Interest. Let us now see what it would be under the regime of gratuity.

[...]

Under the regime of gratuitous credit, A no longer lends his raw material, his tools, his capital, in a word; neither does he give them away; he sells them. When he has received the price he is stripped of his rights over his Capital; he can no longer compel the payment of Interest upon it through all eternity and beyond.

[...]

In a Capitalist Society the worker, never being able to repurchase his product at the price at which he sells it, is constantly running behind, which compels him to continually decrease its production: whereby life is forbidden and the supply of capital and even of the means of subsistence is cut off.

In a Mutualist Society, on the contrary, the worker, exchanging without reserve product for product and value for value, paying only a trifling discount which is amply recompensed by the surplus which his labour leaves him at the end of the year, alone profits by his products: whereby he is enabled to produce a limitless amount, and society to increase to an indefinite extent its life and wealth.

Do you say that such a revolution in economic relations would be, after all, only a transfer of misery; that, instead of the poverty of the wage-worker, who cannot repurchase his own product, and who grows the poorer the more he works, we shall have the misery of the proprietor-capitalist-entrepreneur, who will be compelled to encroach upon his capital and thus to gradually destroy, not only the material of products, but machinery itself?

But who does not see that if, as is inevitable under the Gratuitous System, the two functions of *Wage-Worker* on the one hand, and of *Proprietor-Capitalist-Entrepreneur* on the other, become equal and inseparable in the person of every worker, A's deficit as a Capitalist is immediately covered by his profit as a worker; so that, while on the one hand by the annihilation of Interest the sum of the *products* of Labour is increased indefinitely, on the other, by the facility of circulation, these products are incessantly converted into VALUES and the values into CAPITAL?

Let every one, then, instead of charging spoliation upon Socialism, make out his own account; let every one make an inventory of his wealth and his industry, of the amount which he gains as a Capitalist-Proprietor, and that which he can obtain as a worker,—and either I am greatly mistaken, or else out of the ten million citizens enrolled upon the electoral lists there will not be found two hundred thousand—one in fifty—for whose interest it is to sustain the Usurious system and oppose Gratuitous Credit. Once again, whoever gains more by his labour, his skill, his industry, and his knowledge than by his Capital is directly and especially interested in the most immediate and complete abolition of Usury; he, I say, whether he knows it or not, is pre-eminently a partisan of the *democratic and social republic*; he is, in the broadest and most conservative acceptation of the term, a REVOLUTIONIST. What then? Must it be true, because Malthus, with a handful of pedants at his heels, has said so and has wished it to be so, that ten million workers, with their wives and children, ought forever to support two hundred thousand parasites, and that it is in order to protect this exploitation of man by man that the State exists, that it makes use of an armed force of five hundred thousand soldiers and one million officeholders, and that we pay to it two thousand million in taxes?

But why do I need, after all that has been said in the course of this discussion, to keep up longer this purely artificial distinction between *Wage-Workers and Capitalist-Proprietors*? The time has come to put an end to all class antagonism, and to interest everybody, even the Proprietors and Capitalists themselves, in the abolition of Rent and Interest. The Revolution, having assured its triumph through Justice, may, without losing its dignity, address itself to personal interests.

[...]

In what you have just read is involved, as you will not deny, a complete revolution, not only political and economic, but also, as must be much more obvious to you as well as to myself, scientific. It is for you to decide whether you accept, on your own behalf and on behalf of your co-religionists, the conclusion which clearly results from this whole discussion,—namely, that neither you, Monsieur Bastiat, nor anyone of your school, understands Political Economy. I am, etc.,

P-J PROUDHON

# SIXTH LETTER
## 11ᵀᴴ FEBRUARY 1850

MONSIEUR BASTIAT, YOUR last letter justifies all my anticipations. I knew so well what it would contain that, even before I had received *La Voix du Peuple* of February 4ᵗʰ, I had written three-fourths of the reply which you are now to read, and to which I have only to add the finishing touches.

You are sincere, Monsieur Bastiat; on that you leave no room for doubt; I have acknowledged it before, and have no desire to retract my words. But it is very necessary for me to tell you that your intellect slumbers, or rather that it has never seen the light: I shall have the honour to demonstrate this fact to you by summing up our controversy. I hope that the sort of psychological consultation at which you are to be present, and of which your own mind is to be the subject, may be to you the beginning of that intellectual education without which a man, whatever dignity of character may distinguish him and whatever talents he may display, is not, and never will be, anything but a *speaking animal*, to use Aristotle's words.

[...]

But I was dealing with a man whose intellect is hermetically sealed, and to whom logic is as nought. It is in vain that I exclaim to you: Interest is legitimate under certain conditions independent of the will of the Capitalist; not under certain others, the establishment of which depends today upon society: and is for this reason that Interest, excusable in the Lender, is, from the standpoint of Society, a spoliation. You hear nothing, you comprehend nothing, you do not even listen to my reply. You lack the first faculty of intelligence—perception.

[...]

The Bank of France, I said, is the living proof of my assertion oft-repeated during the last six weeks,—namely, that interest was once necessary and legitimate, but that today society is able, and ought, to abolish it.

It is proved, indeed, by comparing the capital of the Bank with its metallic reserve, that while paying to its stockholders interest on the said capital at four percent., it can give credit and discount at one percent., and still realise fine profits. It can, it ought; until it does, it robs. By refusing to do so, it keeps the interest, rent, and farm-rent, which ought to come down everywhere to one percent at most, up to three, four, five, six, seven, eight, ten, twelve, and fifteen percent. It causes the people to pay annually to the unproductive classes more than six thousand million in gratuities and extras, and, where they might produce annually a value of twenty thousand million, it prevents them from producing more than ten thousand. Then, either you must justify the Bank of France, or, if you cannot, if you dare not, you must admit that the institution of interest is only a transitional institution, which must disappear in a higher state of society.

That, sir, is what I said to you, and in terms sufficiently sharp, one would think, to provoke on your part, in the absence of perception, comparison, and memory concerning the wholly historical question which up to that time I had submitted to you, that simple and purely intuitive act of the mind which it performs when it find itself in the presence of a fact, and required to answer *yes* or *no*,—I mean a judgement. You had only to reply in a word, *it is*, or *it is not*, and the operation was finished.

*It is*: that is to say, yes, the Bank of France can without wronging its stockholders or injuring itself, reduce its rate of discount to one percent; it can then, through the competition which this decrease would create, lower the rent of all Capital, including its own, to less than one percent. And since this movement of reduction, once commenced, would never stop, it can, if it will, make Interest disappear entirely. Then paid Credit, if it takes only what belongs to it, leads directly to Gratuitous Credit; then Interest is only a relic of ignorance and barbarism; then Usury and Rent, in an organised democracy, are illegitimate.

*It is not*: that is to say, no, it is not true that the Bank of France, its weekly balance-sheet to the contrary notwithstanding, has a capital of ninety million and a metallic reserve of four hundred and sixty million; it is not true that this enormous reserve is the result of the substitution of bank paper for specie in commercial circulation, etc., etc. In that case I should have referred you to M. d'Argout, who is suited for such a discussion.

Should we ever have believed it, if you had not caused us to see it? To this categorical, palpable fact of the Bank of France, you replied neither *yes* nor *no*. You did not even question the identity which exists between the fact submitted to your judgement and your theory of interest. You did not perceive the synonymy of these two propositions: Yes, the Bank of France can give Credit at one percent., then my theory is false;—no, the Bank of France cannot give Credit at one percent., then my theory is true.

Your reply, indubitable monument of an intellect which the Holy Word never illuminated, was this: that you were not dealing with the Bank of France, but with capital; that you did not defend the privilege of the Bank, but only the legitimacy of Interest; that you were in favour of the liberty of banks, as well as the liberty of lending; that if it were possible for the Bank of France to give Credit and Discount for nothing, you would not try to prevent it; that you confined yourself to the one assertion that the idea of Capital supposes and necessarily implies that of Interest; that the first never exists without the second, though the second sometimes exists without the first, etc.

So, you are as powerless to judge as to perceive, compare, and remember. You are lacking in that judicial conscience which, in the presence of two facts, either identical or incompatible, decides: Yes, they are identical; no, they are not identical. Undoubtedly, since you are a thinking being, you have intuitions, illuminations, revelations; I do not undertake to say, for my part, what does go on within your brain. But surely you do not reason, you do not reflect. What sort of a man are you, Monsieur Bastiat? Are you a man at all?

[...]

However, without examining it closely, you accept my definition of Capital as a good one; you say that it is all that the discussion requires. You thereby tacitly admit that *Capital* and *Product* are, in Society, synonymous terms; that, consequently, every transaction involving credit resolves itself, in the absence of fraud, into an exchange: two things which you at first denied, and which I would congratulate you on having understood at last, could I by any possibility believe that you attach the same meaning to my words that I do. What, indeed, could be more productive of good results than this analysis: Since value is only a proportion, and since all products are necessarily proportional to each other, it follows that from the social standpoint products are always values and settled values: as far as society is concerned, there is no difference between Capital and Product. The difference is wholly confined to individuals: it arises from their inability to express in exact numbers the relative value of products, and their efforts to arrive at an approximation. For—do not forget it—the mysterious law of exchange, the absolute rule which governs transactions,—a law not written but intuitively recognised, a rule not conventional but natural,—is to make our private acts conform as far as possible to social laws.

Now,—and this is what causes my doubts,—this definition of Capital, so profound and so clear, which you see fit to accept; this identity of Capital and Product, of Credit and Exchange,—totally destroys, sir, your theory of Interest, though you do not suspect it in the least! Indeed, from the moment you admit that the formula of J-B Say, *products exchange for products*, is synonymous with this one, *Capital exchanges for Capital*; that the definition of Capital accepted by you is only an expression of this synonymy; that everything tends, in society, to bring commercial transactions more and more into conformity with this law,—from that moment it is evident, *a priori*, that the day must come when transactions involving loans, rent, farm-rent, Interest, and the like, will be abolished and converted into exchanges; and that thus the lending of Capital becoming simply an exchange of Capital, and all business being conducted on a cash basis, Interest will disappear. Defining Capital thus, the idea of Usury involves a contradiction.

[…]

**M. BASTIAT.**—"Time is precious. Time is money, say the English. Time is the stuff of which life is made, says *le Bonhomme Richard*.

"To give credit is to grant time.

"To sacrifice one's time to another is to sacrifice a precious thing: such a sacrifice cannot be gratuitous."

**MYSELF.**—There would never be such a sacrifice. I have already told you, and I repeat it, that, in the matter of credit, the case of the need of time is the difficulty of procuring money; that this difficulty is chiefly due to the Interest demanded by the hikers of money; so that if Interest were zero, the duration of credit would also be zero. Now, the Bank of France, under the conditions laid upon it by the public since the February Revolution, can reduce its Interest nearly to zero: is it you or I that reasons in a circle?

**M. BASTIAT.**—"Ah! yes …. it seems to me …. I think I understand at last what you mean. The public has renounced, in the bank's favour, its claim to the Interest on the three hundred and eighty-two million in notes which circulate on its sole guaranty. You ask whether there is no way of enabling the public to reap the benefit of this Interest, or, which amounts to the same thing, of organising a National Bank which shall receive no Interest. If I am not mistaken, it was the observation of this phenomenon that suggested to you your scheme. Ricardo devised a plan less radical, but similar, and I find in Say these remarkable lines:

"'This ingenious idea leaves only one question unanswered. Who shall get the interest on this large sum placed in circulation? Shall the Government? In its hands it would be only a means of increasing abuses, such as sinecures, Parliamentary corruption, police spies, and standing armies. Shall a financial company, like the Bank of England or the Bank of France? But why make a present to a financial company already rich of the Interest *paid by the public individually*? …… Such are the questions which this subject involves. Perhaps they can be answered. Perhaps there is some way to render highly *profitable* to the public the economy which would result; but I am not called upon here to develop this new order of ideas.'"

**MYSELF.**—Sir, your J-B Say, with all his genius, is a fool. The question is already answered: the people, who own the funds; the people, who are here the sole Capitalists, the sole furnishers of security, the true proprietors; the people, who alone should profit by the Interest,—the people, I say, ought not to pay Interest. Is there anything in the world simpler and fairer than that?

So you admit, on the authority of Ricardo and J-B Say, that there is *a way of enabling the public*—I quote your own words—*to reap the benefit of the interest which it pays to the Bank*, and this way is to organise a National Bank, which shall give credit at zero percent?

**M. BASTIAT.**—No, not that; God forbid! I admit, it is true, that the Bank ought not to profit by the interest paid by the public on capital belonging to the public; I confess further that there is a way of enabling the public to profit by said interest. But I deny that this way is the one which you recommend,—namely, the organisation of a National Bank; I say and affirm that this way is the *liberty of banks*!

"Liberty of banks! Liberty of credit! Oh! why, Monsieur Proudhon, have not your brilliant powers of persuasion been devoted to these objects?"

I spare the reader your peroration, in which you deplore my obduracy and adjure me, with a comical gravity, to substitute for my formula, *Gratuity of Credit*, yours, *Liberty of Credit*, as if Credit could be freer than when it costs nothing! Not a drop of blood in my body—mark it well!—rebels against the liberty of Credit: in the matter of banking, as in the matter of education, Liberty is my supreme law. But I say that, until the liberty of banks and the competition of bankers allows the public to reap the benefit of the Interest which it pays them, it would be well, useful, constitutional, and quite in accordance with republican economy, to establish, in the midst of the other banks and in competition with them, a National Bank giving credit temporarily at one or one-half of one percent, at the risk of what might happen. Do you object to changing the Bank of France, by reimbursing its stockholders, into this National Bank that I propose? Then, let the bank of France make restitution of the three hundred and eighty-two million specie which belong to the public, and of which it is the only holder. With three hundred and eighty-two million we might very easily organise a bank (what think you?), and the largest in the world. In what respect, then, would this bank, formed by the association of the whole people, not be free? Do that alone, and when you have belled this revolutionary act, when you have thus decreed the first act of the Democratic and Social Republic, I will undertake to deduce for you the consequences of this grand innovation. You shall then know what my system is.

As for you, Monsieur Bastiat, who, an economist, mock at metaphysics, of which Political Economy is but the concrete expression; who, a member of the Institute, are unacquainted even with the philosophy of your century; who, the author of a work entitled *Economic Harmonies* probably in opposition to my *Economic Contradictions*, have no conception of the harmonies of history, and see in progress only a desolating fatalism; who, an advocate of Capital and Interest, are utterly ignorant of the principles of commercial bookkeeping; who, conceiving finally, through the circumlocutions of a bewildered imagination and on the authority of your authors more than from your own profound conviction, that it is possible to organise, with the pubic funds, a Bank giving Credit without Interest, continue nevertheless to protest, in the name of *Liberty of Credit*, against GRATUITY OF CRED-IT—you are undoubtedly a good and worthy citizen, an honest economist, a conscientious writer, a loyal representative, a faithful Republican, a true friend of the people: but your last words entitle me to tell you, Monsieur Bastiat, that, scientifically, YOU ARE A DEAD MAN.[6]

P-J PROUDHON

---

6   It should be noted that Bastiat died of tuberculosis by the end of the year. (Editor)

1851
*Translation by John Beverly Robinson*

# GENERAL IDEA OF THE REVOLUTION IN THE NINETEENTH CENTURY

IN EVERY REVOLUTIONARY HISTORY THREE THINGS ARE TO BE OBSERVED:

The preceding state of affairs, which the revolution aims at overthrowing, and which becomes counter-revolution through its desire to maintain its existence.

The various parties which take different views of the revolution, according to their prejudices and interests, yet are compelled to embrace it and to use it for their advantage.

The revolution itself, which constitutes the solution.

The parliamentary, philosophical, and dramatic history of the Revolution of 1848 can already furnish material for volumes. I shall confine myself to discussing disinterestedly certain questions which may illuminate our present knowledge. What I shall say will suffice, I hope, to explain the progress of the Revolution of the Nineteenth Century, and to enable us to conjecture its future.

[...]

## FIRST STUDY
### REACTION CAUSES REVOLUTION

[...]

I SHALL ENDEAVOUR to show, by what is passing before our eyes, that just as the instinct for conservatism is inherent in every social institution, the need for revolution is equally irresistible; that every political party may become by turns revolutionary and reactionary; that these two terms, reaction and revolution, correlatives of each other and mutually implying each other, are both essential to Humanity, notwithstanding the conflicts between them: so that, in order to avoid the rocks which menace society on the right and on the left, the only course is for reaction to continually change places with revolution; just the reverse of what the present Legislature boasts of having done. To add to grievances, and, if I may use the comparison, to bottle up revolutionary force by repression, is to condemn oneself to clearing in one bound the distance that prudence counsels us to pass over gradually, and to substitute progress by leaps and jerks for a continuous advance.

[...]

Before the battle of June,[1] the Revolution was hardly aware of itself; it was but a vague aspiration among the working classes toward a less unhappy condition. Such complaints have been heard at every period; if it was a mistake to despise them, it was unnecessary to fear them.

Thanks to the persecution which it has suffered, the Revolution of today is fully conscious of itself. It can tell its purpose: it is in the way to define itself, to explain itself. It knows its principles, its means, its aim; it possesses its method and its criterion. In order to understand itself, it has needed only to follow the connection of ideas of its different adversaries. At this moment it is discarding the erroneous doctrines which obscured it: free and brilliant, you are about to see it take possession of the masses, and drive them toward the future with irresistible inspiration.

The Revolution, at the point at which we have arrived, is completed in thought, and needs only to be put into execution. It is too late to give vent to the mine: if the power which has come back into your hands should change its policy toward the Revolution, it would obtain no result, unless it changed its principles at the same time. The Revolution, I have just told you, has grown its teeth: the Reaction has been only a fit of teething sickness for it. It must have solid food: a few fragments of liberty, a few concessions to the interests which it represents, will only serve to increase its hunger. The Revolution means to exist, and to exist, for it, is to reign.

Are you willing then to serve this great cause; to devote yourselves, heart and soul, to the Revolution?

You may, for there is still time, again become the chiefs and regulators of the movement, save your country from a serious crisis, emancipate the lower classes without turmoil, make yourselves the arbiters of Europe, decide the destiny of civilisation and of humanity.

I know well that such is your fervent desire; but I do not speak of desire, I want acts; pledges.

---

1    A reference to the insurrection which broke out in June 1848 after the newly elected conservative government closed down the National Workshops. (Editor)

Pledges for the Revolution, not harangues; plans for economic reconstruction, not governmental theories: that is what the lower classes want and expect from you. Government! Ah! we shall still have enough of it, and to spare. Know well that there is nothing more counter-revolutionary than the Government. Whatever liberalism it pretends, whatever name it assumes, the Revolution repudiates it: its fate is to be absorbed in the industrial organisation.

Speak then, for once, straightforwardly, Jacobins, Girondists,

ists, Terrorists, Indulgents, who have all deserved equal blame, and all need equal pardon. Fortune again favouring you, which course will you follow? The question is not what you would have done in a former exigency: the question is what you are going to do now, when the conditions are no longer the same.

Will you support the Revolution: yes or no?

# SECOND STUDY
## IS THERE SUFFICIENT REASON FOR REVOLUTION IN THE NINETEENTH CENTURY?

### 1. LAW OF *TENDENCY* IN SOCIETY—THE REVOLUTION OF 1789 HAS DONE ONLY HALF ITS WORK

A REVOLUTION IS an act of sovereign justice, in the order of moral facts, springing out of the necessity of things, and in consequence carrying with it its own justification; and which it is a crime for the statesman to oppose it. That is the proposition which we have established in our first study.

Now the question is to discover whether the idea which stands out as the formula of the revolution is not chimerical; whether its object is real; whether a fancy or popular exaggeration is not mistaken for a serious and just protest. The second proposition therefore which we have to examine is the following:

*Is there today sufficient reason in society for revolution?*

For if this reason does not exist, if we are fighting for an imaginary cause, if the people are complaining because, as they say, they are too well off, the duty of the magistrate would be simply to undeceive the multitude, whom we have often seen aroused without cause, as the echo responds to one who calls.

In a word, is the occasion for revolution presented at the moment, by the nature of things, by the connection of facts, by the working of institutions, by the advance in needs, by the order of Providence?

[…]

The question which we have taken for the text of this study—*Is there sufficient reason for a revolution in the nineteenth century?*—Resolves itself into the following: *What is the tendency of society in our day?*

Hence, but a few pages will suffice to support the answer which I do not hesitate to point out now. Society, as far as it has been able to develop freely for half a century, under the distractions of '89–93, the paternalism of the Empire and the guarantees of 1814, 1830, and 1848, is on a road radically and increasingly wrong.

[...]

## 2. CHAOS OF ECONOMIC FORCES. TENDENCY OF SOCIETY TOWARD POVERTY

I call certain principles of action *economic forces*, such as the Division of Labour, Competition, Collective Force, Exchange, Credit, Property, etc., which are to Labour and to Wealth what the distinction of classes, the representative system, monarchical heredity, administrative centralisation, the judicial hierarchy, etc., are to the State.

If these forces are held in equilibrium, subject to the laws which are proper to them, and which do not depend in any way upon the arbitrary will of man, Labour can be organised, and comfort for all guaranteed. If, on the other hand, they are left without direction and without counterpoise, Labour is in a condition of chaos; the useful effects of the economic forces is mingled with an equal quantity of injurious effects; the deficit balances the profit; Society, in so far as it is the theatre, the agent, or the subject of production, circulation, and consumption, is in a condition of increasing suffering.

Up to now, it does not appear that order in a society can be conceived except under one of these two forms, the political and the industrial; between which, moreover, there is fundamental contradiction.

The chaos of industrial forces, the struggle which they maintain with the government system, which is the only obstacle to their organisation, and which they cannot reconcile themselves with nor merge themselves in, is the real, profound cause of the unrest which disturbs French society, and which was aggravated during the second half of the reign of Louis Philippe.

[...]

I shall limit myself to recalling very briefly some of the most general facts, in order to give the reader a glimpse of this order of forces and phenomena, which has been hidden from all eyes until now, and which alone can put an end to the governmental drama.

Everybody has heard of the *division of labour*.

It consists of the distribution of the manual labor of a given industry in such a manner that each person performs always the same operation, or a small number of operations, so that the product, instead of being the integral product of one worker, is the joint product of a large number.

According to Adam Smith, who first demonstrated this law scientifically, and all the other economists, the division of labour is the most powerful lever of modern industry. To it principally must be attributed the superiority of civilised peoples to savage peoples. Without division of labour, the use of machines would not have gone beyond the most ancient and most common utensils: the miracles of machinery and of steam would never have been revealed to us; progress would have been closed to society; the French Revolution itself, lacking an outlet, would have been but a sterile revolt; it could have accomplished nothing. But, on the other hand, by division of labour, the product of labour mounts to tenfold, a hundredfold, political economy rises to the height of a philosophy, the intellectual level of nations is continually raised. The first thing that should attract the attention of the legislator is the separation of industrial functions—the division of labour—in a society founded upon hatred of the feudal and warlike order, and destined in consequence to organise itself for work and peace.

It was not done thus. This economic force was left to all the overturns caused by chance and by interest. The division of labour, becoming always more minute, and remaining without counterpoise, the worker has been given over to a more and more degrading subjection to machinery. That is the effect of the division of labour when it is applied as practised in our days, not only to make industry incomparably more productive, but at the same time to deprive the worker, in mind and body, of all the wealth which it creates for the capitalist and the speculator. Here is how an observer, who is not suspected of sympathy with labour, M. de Tocqueville, sums up on this grave subject:

"In proportion to the more complete application of the principle of the division of labour, the worker becomes weaker, more limited and more dependent."

J-B Say has already said:

"A man, whose whole life is devoted to the execution of a single operation, will most assuredly acquire the faculty of executing it better and quicker than others; but he will, at the same time, be rendered less fit for every other occupation, corporeal or intellectual; his other faculties will be gradually blunted or extinguished; and the man, as an individual, will degenerate in consequence. To have never done anything but make the eighteenth part of a pin, is a sorry account for a human being to give of his existence… On the whole, we may conclude, that division of labour is a skilful mode of employing human agency, that it consequently multiplies the productions of society; in other words, the powers and the enjoyments of mankind; but that it in some degree degrades the faculties of man in his individual capacity."[2]

All the economists are in accord as to this fact, one of the most serious which the science has to announce; and, if they do not insist upon it with the vehemence which they habitually use in their polemics, it must be said,

---

2    This is C. R. Prinsep's translation of J-B Say's *Treatise on Political Economy*, 6th ed. (Editor)

to the shame of the human mind, that it is because they cannot believe that this perversion of the greatest of economic forces can be avoided.

So the greater the division of labour and the power of machines, the less the intelligence and manual skill of the worker. But the more the value of the worker falls and the demand for labour diminishes, the lower are wages and the greater is poverty. And it is not a few hundreds of men but millions, who are the victims of this economic perturbation.

[...]

Philanthropic conservatives, admirers of ancient customs, charge the industrial system with this anomaly. They want to go back to the feudal-farming period. I say that it is not industry that is at fault, but economic chaos: I maintain that the principle has been distorted, that there is disorganisation of forces, and that to this we must attribute the fatal tendency with which society is carried away.

Another example.

*Competition*, next to the division of labour, is one of the most powerful factors of industry; and at the same time one of the most valuable guarantees. Partly for the sake of it, the first revolution was brought about. The workers' associations, established at Paris some years since, have recently given it a new sanction by establishing among themselves piece work, and abandoning, after their experience of it, the absurd idea of the equality of wages. Competition is moreover the law of the market, the spice of the trade, the salt of labour. To suppress competition is to suppress liberty itself; it is to begin the restoration of the old order from below, in replacing labour by the rule of favouritism and abuse, of which '89 rid us.

Yet competition, lacking legal forms and superior regulating intelligence, has been perverted in turn, like the division of labour. In it, as in the latter, there is perversion of principle, chaos and a tendency toward evil. This will appear beyond doubt if we remember that of the thirty-six million souls who compose the French nation, at least ten million are wage workers, to whom competition is forbidden, for whom there is nothing but to struggle among themselves for their meagre stipend.

Thus that competition, which, as thought in '89, should be a general right, is today a matter of exceptional privilege: only they whose capital permits them to become heads of business concerns may exercise their competitive rights.

The result is that competition, as Rossi, Blanqui, and a host of others have recognised, instead of democratising industry, aiding the worker, guaranteeing the honesty of trade, has ended in building up a mercantile and land aristocracy, a thousand times more rapacious than the old aristocracy of the nobility. Through competition all the profits of production go to capital; the consumer, without suspecting the frauds of commerce, is fleeced by the speculator, and the condition of the workers is made more and more precarious. Speaking of this, Eugene Buret says: "I assert that the working class is turned over, body and soul, to the sweet will of industry." And elsewhere he says: "The most trifling speculation may change the price of bread one cent a pound, which means $124,100,000 for thirty-six million people."

It was recently seen how little free competition could do for the people, and how illusory it is as a guaranty with us at present, when the Prefect of Police, yielding to the general demand, authorised the sale of meat at auction. Nothing less than all the energy the people could muster, aided by governmental power, could overcome the monopoly of the butchers.

Accuse human nature, say the economists, do not accuse competition. Very well, I will not accuse competition: I will only remark that human nature does not remedy one evil by another, and ask how it has mistaken its path. What? Competition ought to make us more and more equal and free; and instead it subordinates us one to the other, and makes the worker more and more a slave! This is a perversion of the principle, a forgetfulness of the law. These are not mere accidents; they are a whole system of misfortunes.

[...]

It is not only that our present society, though having forsaken its principles, tends continually to impoverish the producer, to subordinate labour to capital—contradiction in itself—but that it tends also to make of workers a race of helots, inferior to the caste of free men as of old; and it tends to erect into a political and social dogma the enslavement of the working class and the necessity of its poverty.

[...]

### 3. ANOMALY OF GOVERNMENT. TENDENCY TOWARD TYRANNY AND CORRUPTION

It is by contrast with error that truth impresses itself upon the understanding. In place of liberty and industrial equality, the Revolution has left us a legacy of authority and political subordination. The State, growing more powerful every day, and endowed with prerogatives and privileges without end, has undertaken to do for our happiness what we might have expected from a very different source. How has it acquitted itself of its task? What part has the government played during the last fifty years, regardless of the particular form of its organisation? What has been its tendency? That is now the question.

Up to 1848, statesmen, whether belonging to the ministry or the opposition, whose influence directed public sentiment and governmental action, did not seem to have been aware of the mistaken course of society in what especially concerns the labouring classes. Most of them indeed made it a merit and a duty to busy themselves in the amelioration of the workers' lot. One would cry out for teachers; another would talk against the premature and immoral employment of children in manufactories. This one would demand the lowering of duties upon salt, beverages and meat; that one called out for the complete abolition of town and custom house tariffs. In the lofty regions of power there was a general impulse toward economic and social questions. Not a soul saw that, in the present state of our institutions, such reforms were but innocent chimeras; that, in order to bring them about, nothing less than a new creation was necessary; in other words, a revolution.

Since the abdication of Louis Philippe, on the 24th of February, the governmental set, participants in privilege, have changed their opinion. The policy of oppression and impoverishment which they formerly followed without knowing it, I had almost said in spite of themselves, has been accepted by many of them, this time with full knowledge.

[...]

What does the system demand?

That the capitalistic feudalism shall be maintained in the enjoyment of its rights; that the preponderance of capital over labour shall be increased; that the parasite class shall be reinforced, if possible, by providing for it everywhere hangers-on, through the aid of public functions, and as recruits if necessary, and that large properties shall be gradually re-established, and the proprietors ennobled—did not Louis Philippe, toward the end of his reign, devote himself to conferring titles of nobility?—that thus, by indirect ways, certain services, which the official list of offices cannot satisfy, shall be recompensed; finally, that everything shall be attached to the supreme patronage of the State—charities, recompenses, pensions, awards, concessions, exploitations, authorisations, positions, titles, privileges, ministerial offices, stock companies, municipal administrations, etc., etc.

This is the reason for that venality whereof the scandals under the last reign so surprised us; but at which the public conscience would have been less astonished, if the mystery had been explained. This too is the ulterior aim of that centralisation which, under pretext of the general interest, exerts pressure upon local interests, by selling to the last and highest bidder the justice which they claim.

Understand clearly that corruption is the soul of centralisation. There is not a monarchy nor a democracy that is free from it. Government is unchangeable in its spirit and essence; if it takes a hand in public economy, it is to establish, by favour or by force, what accident tends to bring about. [...]

[...]

Even charitable institutions serve the ends of those in authority marvellously well.

Charity is the strongest chain by which privilege and the Government, bound to protect them, holds down the lower classes. With charity, sweeter to the heart of men, more intelligible to the poor man than the abstruse laws of political economy, one may dispense with justice. Benefactors abound in the catalogue of saints; not one law dispenser is found there. The Government, like the Church, places fraternity far above justice. [Be a] good friend of the poor as much as you like, but it hates calculators. In connection with the discussion on pawnbrokers, the *Journal des Debats* recalled that there would in time be hospitals everywhere. Loan offices, it added, showed the same progress; each commune wanted one for itself, and would soon obtain it. I cannot conceive the indignation of the whole list of bourgeois delegates against the two honourable socialists who proposed to establish a loan office in each county immediately. Never was there a proposition more worthy of the favour of the *Debats*. The establishment for loans upon wages, even if the loan were gratuitous, is the antechamber of the hospital. And what is the hospital? The temple of Poverty.

Through these three ministries, that of agriculture and commerce, that of public works, and that of the interior, through the taxes of consumption and through the custom house, the Government keeps its hand on all that comes and goes, all that is produced and consumed, on all the business of individuals, communes and departments; it maintains the tendency of society toward the impoverishment of the masses, the subordinating of the workers, and the always growing preponderance of parasite offices. Through the police, it watches the enemies of the system; through the courts, it condemns and represses them; through the army it crushes them; through public institutions it distributes, in such proportions as suit it, knowledge and ignorance; through the Church it puts to sleep any protest in the hearts of men; through the finances it defrays the cost of this vast conspiracy at the expense of workers.

[...]

Thus, in 1851 as in 1788, and from analogous causes, there is in society a pronounced tendency towards poverty. Now, as then, the wrong of which the labouring class complains is not the effect of a temporary or accidental cause, it is that of a systematic diversion of the social forces.

[...]

The crash of '89–91 left no organic principle, no working structure, after having abolished, together with the monarchy, the last remains of feudalism, proclaimed equality before the law and for taxation, freedom of the press and of worship, and interested the people, as much as it could, by the sale of national property. It has not redeemed one of its promises. When the Revolution proclaimed liberty of the people, the subordination of power to the country, it set up two incompatible things, society and government; and it is this incompatibility which has been the cause or the pretext of this overwhelming, liberty-destroying concentration, called CENTRALISATION, which the parliamentary democracy admires and praises, because it is its nature to tend toward despotism.

[...]

The Republic had Society to establish: it thought only of establishing Government. Centralisation continually fortifying itself, while Society had no institution to oppose to it, through the exaggeration of political ideas and the total absence of social ideas, matters reached a point where Society and Government could not live together, the condition of existence of the latter being to subordinate and subjugate the former.

Therefore, while the problem propounded in '89 seemed to be officially solved, at the bottom there was change only in the governmental metaphysics—what Napoléon called *ideology*. Liberty, equality, progress, with all their oratorical consequences, are written in the text of the constitutions and the laws; there is no vestige of them in the institutions. The ancient hierarchy of classes has been replaced by an ignoble feudalism, based on mercantile and industrial usury; by a chaos of interests, an antagonism of principles, a degradation of law: the abuses have changed the face which they bore before '89, to assume a different form of organisation; they have diminished neither in number nor gravity. On account of our being engrossed with politics, we have lost sight of social economy. It was in this way that the democratic party itself, the heir of the first Revolution, came to attempting to reform Society by establishing the initiative of the State, to create institutions by the prolific virtue of Power, in a word, to correct an abuse by an abuse.

All minds being bewitched with politics, Society turns in a circle of mistakes, driving capital to a still more crushing agglomeration, the State to an extension of its prerogatives that is more and more tyrannical, the labouring class to an irreparable decline, physically, morally and intellectually.

[...]

In place of this governmental, feudal and military rule, imitated from that of the former kings, the new edifice of industrial institutions must be built; in place of this materialist centralisation which absorbs all the political power, we must create the intellectual and liberal centralisation of economic forces. Labour, commerce, credit, education, property, public morals, philosophy, art, everything in fact require it of us.

I conclude:

There is sufficient cause for a revolution in the nineteenth century.

# THIRD STUDY
## THE PRINCIPLE OF ASSOCIATION

[...]

I BEGIN WITH the principle of Association.

If I wanted merely to flatter the lower classes, the recipe would not be difficult. Instead of a criticism of the social principle, I should deliver a panegyric of workers' societies, I should exalt their virtues, their constancy, their sacrifices, their spirit of benevolence, their marvellous intelligence; I should herald their triumphs. What could I not say on this subject, dear to all democratic hearts? Do not the workers' societies at this moment serve as the cradle for the social revolution, as the early Christian communities served as the cradle of Catholicity? Are they not always the open school, both theoretical and practical, where the worker learns the science of the production and distribution of wealth, where he studies, without masters and without books, by his own experience solely, the laws of that industrial organisation, which was the ultimate aim of the Revolution of '89, but of which our greatest and most famous revolutionists caught only a glimpse? What a topic for me, for the manifestation of a facile sympathy, which is not the less disinterested, in that it is always sincere! With what pride do I recall that I too wanted to found an association, more than that, the central agency and circulating organ of workers' associations! And how I cursed that Government, which, with an expenditure of 300 million, could not find a cent which it could use for the benefit of poor workers...!

I have better than that to offer to associations. I am convinced that at this moment they would give much for an idea, and it is ideas that I am bringing them. I should decline their approval, if I could obtain it only by flattery. If those of their members who may read these pages will but deign to remember that, in treating of association, it is a principle, even less than that, a hypothesis, that I discuss: it is not this or that enterprise, for which, in spite of its name, association is in nowise responsible, and of which the success in point of fact, does not depend upon association. I speak of Association in general, not of associations, whatever they may be.

I have always regarded Association in general—fraternity—as a doubtful arrangement, which, the same as pleasure, love, and many other things, concealed more evil than good under a most seductive aspect. It is perhaps the effect of the temperament which nature has given me, that I distrust fraternity as much as I do passion. I have seen few men who were proud of either. Especially when Association is presented as a universal institution, the principle, means and end of the Revolution, does it appear to me to hide a secret intention of robbery and despotism. I see in it the inspiration of the governmental system, which was restored in '91, strengthened in '93, perfected in 1804, erected into a dogma and system from 1814 to 1830, and reproduced in these latter days, under the name of *direct government*, with an impulse which shows how far delusion of mind has gone with us.

Let us apply the criterion.

What does society want today?

That its tendency toward sin and poverty should become a movement toward comfort and virtue.

What is needed to bring about this change?

The reestablishment of the equilibrium of forces.

Is Association the equilibrium of forces?

No.

Is Association even a force?

No.

What, then, is Association?

A *dogma*.

Association is so much a dogma, in the eyes of those who propose it as a revolutionary expedient, something finished, complete, absolute, unchangeable, that all they who have taken up this Utopia have ended, without exception, in a SYSTEM. In illuminating with their fixed idea the different parts of the social body, they were bound to end, and in fact they did end, by reconstructing society upon an imaginary plan, much like the astronomer, who, from respect for his calculations, made over the system of the universe.

Thus the Saint Simonian school, going beyond the idea of its founder, produced a system: Fourier produced a system; Owen, a system; Cabet, a system; Pierre Leroux, a system; Louis Blanc, a system; as Babeuf, Morelly, Thomas More, Campanella, Plato, and others before them, who, each starting from a single principle, produced systems. And all these systems, antagonistic among themselves, are equally opposed to progress. Let humanity perish sooner than the principle! that is the motto of the Utopians, as of the fanatics of all ages.

Socialism, under such interpreters, became a religion which might have passed, five or six hundred years ago, as an advance upon Catholicism, but which in the nineteenth century is as little revolutionary as possible.

No, Association is not a directing principle, any more than an industrial force. Association, by itself, has no organic or productive power, nothing which, like the division of labour, competition, etc., makes the worker stronger and quicker, diminishes the cost of production, draws a greater value from materials, or which, like the administrative hierarchy, shows a desire for harmony and order.

[...]

The union of forces, which must not be confounded with association, as we shall shortly see, is equally with labour and exchange, a producer of wealth. It is an economic power of which I was, I believe, the first to accentuate the importance, in my first memoir upon *Property*. A hundred men, uniting or combining their forces, produce, in certain cases, not a hundred times, but two hundred, three hundred, a thousand times as much. This is what I have called *collective force*. I even drew from this an argument, which, like so many others, remains unanswered, against certain forms of appropriation: that it is not sufficient to pay merely the wages of a given number of workers, in order to acquire their product legitimately; that they must be paid twice, thrice or ten times their wages, or an equivalent service rendered to each one of them.

Collective force, in its bare metaphysical aspect, is another principle which is not less a producer of wealth. Moreover its application is found in every case in which individual effort, no matter how often repeated, would be ineffective. Nevertheless, no law commands its application. It is remarkable that the utopian socialists have never thought of boasting of it. It is because collective force is an impersonal act, while association is a voluntary agreement: there may be points wherein they meet, but they are not identical.

[...]

The question remains whether Association is one of these essentially immaterial [economic] forces [such as competition, division of labour, property, etc.,], which by their action become productive of utility and a source of prosperity; for it is evident that only on this condition can this principle of association—I make no distinction of schools—be advanced as the solution of the problem of the proletariat.

In a word, is Association an economic power? For twenty years now it has been heralded and its virtues set forth. How is it that no one has demonstrated its efficacy? Can it be that the efficacy of Association is more difficult to demonstrate than that of commerce, credit, or the division of labour?

For my part, I answer categorically: No. Association is not an economic force. It is in its nature sterile, even injurious, since it places fetters on the liberty of the worker. The authors who have advocated utopian fraternities, by which so many are still attracted, have attributed, without reason or proof, a virtue and efficacy to the *social contract*, which belongs only to collective force, the division of labour, or to exchange. The public has not perceived the confusion; hence the experiments of societies with constitutions, their varying fortunes, and the uncertainty of opinion.

When an industrial or commercial society aims at setting to work one of the great economic forces, or at carrying on a business, of which the nature requires that it should remain undivided, such as a monopoly, or an established line of trade, the society formed for this object may result successfully, but it does so not by virtue of its principle, but by virtue of its methods. So true is this that whenever the same result can be obtained without it, the preference is to dispense with association. Association is a bond which is naturally opposed to liberty, and to which nobody consents to submit, unless it furnishes sufficient indemnification; so that, to all utopian socialists, one may oppose this practical rule: Never, except in spite of himself, and because he cannot do otherwise, does man associate.

Let us make a distinction between the *principle* of association, and the infinitely variable *methods*, of which a society makes use when affected by external circumstances foreign to its nature; among which I place in the first rank the economic forces. The *principle* is one which would defeat the enterprise, unless another motive were found: the *methods* are what permit one to merge himself in it, in the hope of obtaining wealth by a sacrifice of independence.

[…]

The formula of association then is as follows; it is thus enunciated by Louis Blanc:

> *From each according to his ability.*
> *To each according to his needs.*

The Code, in its different definitions of civil and commercial society, is in accord with the orator of the Luxembourg [Commission]: any derogation from this principle is a return to individualism.

556 Pierre-Joseph Proudhon

Thus explained by Socialists and jurists, can Association be generalised and become the universal higher law, the public civil law of a whole nation?

Such is the question proposed by the different social schools, and all unanimously answer it in the affirmative while varying their modes of application.

My answer is: No, the contract of association, under whatever form, can never become a universal rule, because, being by its nature unproductive and harassing, applicable only to quite special conditions, its inconveniences growing much more rapidly than its benefits, it is equally opposed to the advantageous use of labour, and to the liberty of the worker. Whence I conclude that a single association can never include all the workers in one industry, nor all industrial corporations, nor, *a fortiori*, a nation of 36 million men; therefore that the principle of association does not offer the required solution.

I may add that association is not only not an economic force, but that it is applicable only under special conditions, depending on the methods. It is easy to verify this second proposition by the facts, and thence to determine the part played by association in the nineteenth century.

[...]

Association formed without any outside economic consideration, or any leading interest, association for its own sake, as an act of devotion, a family tie, as it were, is an act of pure religion, a supernatural bond, without real value, a myth.

[...]

But if association is not a productive force, if on the contrary it imposes onerous conditions, from which labour naturally seeks to free itself, it is clear that association can no longer be considered an organic law; that, far from assuring equilibrium, it would tend rather to destroy harmony, by imposing upon all general obligation, instead of justice, instead of individual responsibility. Association therefore cannot be maintained from the point of view of right, and as a scientific factor; but only as a sentiment, a mystic principle, a divine institution.

Nevertheless the champions, despite everything, of association, feeling how sterile is their principle, how opposed to liberty, how little therefore it can be accepted as the sovereign formula of the Revolution, are making the most incredible efforts to sustain this will-o'-the-wisp of fraternity. Louis Blanc has gone so far as to reverse the republic motto, as if he wanted to revolutionise the revolution. He no longer says, as everybody else says, and according to tradition, *Liberty, Equality, Fraternity;* he says *Equality, Fraternity, Liberty!* We begin with Equality nowadays; we must take equality for our first term; upon it we must build the new structure of the Revolution. As for Liberty, that is deduced from Fraternity. Louis Blanc promises liberty after association, as the priests promise paradise after death.

I leave to you to guess what kind of socialism it will be which plays thus with transpositions of words.

Equality! I had always thought that it was the natural fruit of Liberty, which has no need of theory nor of constraint. I had thought, I say, that from the organisation of economic forces, the division of labour, competition, credit, reciprocity, above all, education, that Equality would be born. Louis Blanc has changed all that. A new Sganarelle, he puts Equality on the left, Liberty on the Right, Fraternity between them, like Jesus Christ between the two thieves. We cease to be free, as nature made us, in order to become equal, which only labour can make us, as a preliminary, by State order; after which we become more or less free, according to the convenience of the Government.

> *From each according to his capacity;*
> *To each according to his needs.*

Equality demands this, according to Louis Blanc.

[...]

Who then shall determine the capacity? who shall be the judge of the needs?

You say that my capacity is 100: I maintain that it is only 90. You add that my needs are 90: I affirm that they are 100. There is a difference between us of twenty upon needs and capacity. It is, in other words, the well-known debate between *demand* and *supply*. Who shall judge between the society and me?

If the society persists, despite my protests, I resign from it, and that is all there is to it. The society comes to an end from lack of associates.

If, having recourse to force, the society undertakes to compel me; if it demands from me sacrifice and devotion, I say to it: Hypocrite! you promised to deliver me from being plundered by capital and power; and now, in the name of equality and fraternity, in your turn, you plunder me. Formerly, in order to rob me, they exaggerated my capacity and minimised my needs. They said that products cost me so little, that I needed so little to live! You are doing the same thing. What difference is there then between fraternity and wage-labour?

It is one of two things: either association is compulsory, and in that case it is slavery; or it is voluntary, and then we ask what guaranty the society will have that the member will work according to his capacity and what guaranty the member will have that the association will reward him according to his needs? Is it not evident that such a discussion can have but one solution— that the product and the need be regarded as correlated expressions, which leads us to the rule of liberty, pure and simple?

Reflect a moment. Association is not an economic force; it is only a bond of conscience, obligatory before that inward tribunal, and of no effect, or rather of an injurious effect, in relation to labour and wealth. And it is not by the aid of a more or less skilful argument that I prove it: it is the re- sult of industrial practice since the origin of associations. Posterity will not understand how, in a century of innovation, writers, reputed to be the first to understanding social matters, should have made so much noise about a principle which is entirely subjective, and which has been explored to its foundations by all the generations of the globe. In a population of 36 million, there are 24 million occupied with agriculture. These you can never associate. What use would it be? To work the soil requires no social mapping-out; and the soul of the peasant is averse to association. The peasant, remember, applauded the repression of June 1848, because he saw in it an act of liberty against communism.

Out of the 12 million remaining, at least 6 million, composed of mechanics, artisans, employers, functionaries, for whom association is without object, without profit, without attraction, would prefer to remain free.

There are then 6 million souls, composing in part the wage-working class, whom their present condition might interest in workers' associations, without closer examination, and upon the strength of promises. I venture to say in advance to these six million persons, fathers, mothers, children, old men, that they will hasten to free themselves from their voluntary yoke, if the Revolution should fail to furnish them with more serious, more real reasons for associating themselves than those which they fancy they perceive, of which I have demonstrated the emptiness.

Association has indeed its use in the economy of nations. The workers' associations are indeed called upon to play an important part in the near future; and are full of hope both as a protest against wage-labour, and as an affirmation of *reciprocity*. This part will consist chiefly in the management of large instruments of labour, and in the carrying out of certain large undertakings, which require at once minute division of functions, together with great united efficiency; and which would be so many schools for the labouring class if association, or better, participation, were introduced. Such undertakings, among others, are railroads.

But Association, by itself, does not solve the revolutionary problem. Far from that, it presents itself as a problem, the solution of which implies that the associates enjoy all their independence, while preserving all the advantages of union; which means that the best association is one into which, thanks to a better organisation, liberty enters most and devotion least.

It is for this reason that workers' associations, which have now almost changed their character as to the principles which guide them, should be judged, not by the more or less successful results which they obtain, but only according to their silent tendency to assert and establish the social republic. Whether the workers know it or not, the importance of their work lies not in the petty interests of their company but in the negation of the capitalist regime, [both] stock-market speculator [*agioteur*] and governmental, which the first revolution left undisturbed. Later, with the political lie, mercantile chaos and financial feudality overcome, the companies of workers, abandoning luxury goods and toys, will have to take over the great departments of industry, which are their natural prerogative.

[...]

# FOURTH STUDY
## THE PRINCIPLE OF AUTHORITY

[...]

SOME TWELVE YEARS ago, well I may recall it, while busying myself with researches into the foundations of society, having in view not at all political eventualities, impossible then to have foreseen, but solely for the greater glory of philosophy, I was the first to cast into the world a denial which has since obtained great renown, the denial of Government and of Property. Others before myself, to seem original, humorous, or seeking a paradox, had denied those two principles; not one had made this denial the subject of a serious, earnest criticism. One of our most good-natured journalists, M. Pelletan, undertaking my defence one day, *motu proprio*, made this singular statement to his readers, that, in attacking sometimes property, sometimes power, sometimes something else, I was firing a gun into the air, to attract toward myself the attention of empty-heads. M. Pelletan was too good indeed, and I cannot be too much obliged to him for his kindness: he must have taken me for a literary person.

It is time that the public should know that, in philosophy, in politics, in theology, in history, negation is the preliminary requirement to affirmation. All progress begins by abolishing something; every reform rests upon denunciation of some abuse; each new idea is based upon the proved insufficiency of the old idea. Thus Christianity, in denying the plurality of the gods, in becoming atheistic, from the pagan point of view, asserted the unity of God, and from this unity deduced its whole theology. Thus Luther, in denying the authority of the Church, asserted the authority of reason, and laid the first stone of modern philosophy. Thus our fathers, the revolutionaries of '89, in denying the sufficiency of feudal rule, asserted, without understanding it, the necessity of some different system, which it is the mission of our age to explain. Thus, finally, I myself, having demonstrated afresh, under the eyes of my readers, the illegitimacy and powerlessness of government as a principle of order, will cause to arise from this negation a productive, affirmative idea, which must lead to a new form of civilisation.

[...]

Priority in philosophical conceptions is not less an object of emulation than priority in industrial inventions, with lofty minds which know their value and seek the glory of their discovery, although they can be neither sold nor patented. In the domain of pure thought, as well as in that of mechanical improvement applied to the arts, there are rivalries, imitations, I had almost said counterfeits, were it not that I fear, by the use of so strong a term, to asperse an honourable ambition, which attests the superiority of the present generation. The idea of *Anarchy* had this fortune. The denial of government having been renewed since the February Revolution with new ardour and some success, certain men of note in the democratic and socialistic party, whom the idea of *Anarchy* filled with disquietude, thought that they might appropriate the arguments directed against government, and upon these arguments, which were essentially negative, might restore the very principle which was at stake, under a new name, and with a few modifications. Without intending it, without suspecting it, these honourable citizens took the position of counter-revolutionaries, since a counterfeit, for after all this word expresses my idea better than any other, a counterfeit, in political and social affairs, is really counter-revolution. I shall prove it immediately. That is what these restorations of authority really are, that have been undertaken recently in competition with *anarchy*, and that have occupied public attention under the names of *Direct Legislation, Direct Government*, of which the authors or editors are, in the first place, Messrs. Rittinghausen and Considérant, and afterwards, M. Ledru-Rollin.

According to Messrs. Considérant and Rittinghausen, the first idea of direct government came from Germany; as for M. Ledru-Rollin, he only claims it, and with reservations, for our first revolution; this idea being found at length in the Constitution of '93, and in the Social Contract.

It must be understood, that if I intervene in my turn in the discussion, it is not to claim a priority which I reject with all my power in the terms in which the question has been put. *Direct Government* and *Direct Legislation* seem to me the two biggest blunders in the annals of politics and of philosophy. How is it that M. Rittinghausen, who understands German philosophy to the bottom; how is it that M. Considérant, who ten or fifteen years ago wrote a pamphlet, under the title, *Breaking-up of Politics in France*; how is it that M. Ledru-Rollin, who, when he subscribed to the Constitution of '93, made such generous and futile efforts to make direct government practicable, and to reduce it within the bounds of common sense; how is it, I ask, that these gentlemen have not understood that the very arguments which they use against *indirect* government, have no force that does not apply equally against *direct* government; that their criticism is admissible only when made absolute; and that, in stopping half-way, they have fallen into the most pitiful inconsequence? Above all, how is it that they have not seen that their pretended direct government is nothing but the reduction to absurdity of the governmental idea; to the extent that, if through the progress of ideas and the complexity of interests, society is forced to abjure every kind of government, it will be just because direct government, the only form of government that seems to be rational, liberal, equal, is nevertheless impossible?

Meanwhile comes along M. de Girardin, aspiring, no doubt, to have a share in the invention, or at least, in the completion, who proposed this

formula: *Abolition of Authority through the Simplification of Government.*
What was M. de Girardin doing with this foolish business? Such a mind,
so resourceful, can never be restrained! You are too quick, M. de Girardin,
to accomplish anything. Authority is to Government what the thought is to
the word, the idea to the fact, the soul to the body. Authority is government
in principle, as government is authority in practice. To abolish either, if it is
a real abolition, is to abolish both. By the same token, to preserve one or the
other, if the preservation is effective, is to keep both.

    [...]

    The prejudice in favour of government having sunk into our deepest con-
sciousness, stamping even reason in its mould, every other conception has
been for a long time rendered impossible, and the boldest thinkers could but
say that Government was no doubt a scourge, a chastisement for humanity;
but that it was a necessary evil!

    That is why, up to our own days, the most emancipating revolutions and
all the eruptions of liberty have always ended in a reiteration of faith in and
submission to power; why all revolutions have served only to re-establish tyranny: I make no exception of the Constitution of '93, any more than that of
1848, the two most advanced expressions nevertheless of French democracy.

    What has maintained this mental predisposition and made its fascina-
tion invincible for so long a time, is that, through the supposed analogy
between Society and the family, Government has always presented itself
to the mind as the natural organ of justice, the protector of the weak, the
preserver of the peace. By the attribution to it of provident care and of full
guaranty, Government took root in the hearts, as well as in the minds of
men; it formed a part of the universal soul, it was the faith, the intimate,
invincible superstition of the citizens! If this confidence weakened, they said
of Government, as they said of Religion and Property, it is not the institution which is bad, but the abuse of it; it is not the king who is wicked but
his ministers; *Ah, if the king knew!*

    Thus to the hierarchical and absolutist view of a governing authority,
is added an ideal which appeals to the soul, and conspires incessantly
against the desire for equality and independence. The people at each
revolution think to reform the faults of their government according to
the inspiration of their hearts; but they are deceived by their own ideas.
While they think that they will secure Power in their own interest, they
really have it always against them: in place of a protector, they give themselves a tyrant.

    Experience, in fact, shows that everywhere and always Government, how-
ever much it may have been for the people at its origin, has placed itself on
the side of the richest and most educated class against the more numerous
and poorer class; it has little by little become narrow and exclusive; and, instead of maintaining liberty and equality among all, it works persistently to
destroy them, by virtue of its natural inclination towards privilege.

We have shown in a previous study how since 1789, the revolution having founded nothing, society, as M. Collard expressed it, having been reduced to dust, the distribution of wealth left to chance, Government, whose task it is to protect property as well as person, found itself in fact established for the rich against the poor. Who does not see now that this anomaly, which then it was thought proper to embody in the political constitution of our country, is common to all governments? At no epoch is property found to depend on labour exclusively; at no epoch has work been guaranteed by the equilibrium of economic forces: in this matter, the civilisation of the nineteenth century is not any more advanced than that of the Middle Ages. Authority, in defending rights, however established, has always been for riches against misfortune: the history of governments is the martyrology of the proletariat.

[...]

What really is the *Social Contract?* An agreement of the citizen with the government? No, that would mean but the continuation of the same idea. The social contract is an agreement of man with man; an agreement from which must result what we call society. In this, the notion of *commutative justice*, first brought forward by the primitive fact of exchange, and defined by the Roman law, is substituted for that of *distributive justice*, dismissed without appeal by republican criticism. Translate these words, *contract, commutative justice*, which are the language of the law, into the language of business, and you have *Commerce*, that is to say, in its highest significance, the act by which man and man declare themselves essentially producers, and abdicate all pretension to govern each other.

*Commutative justice*, the *reign of contract*, the *industrial* or *economic system*, such are the different synonyms for the idea which by its accession must do away with the old systems of *distributive justice*, the *reign of law*, or in more concrete terms, *feudal, governmental*, or *military* rule. The future hope of humanity lies in this substitution.

But before this revolution of doctrine can be formulated, before it can be comprehended, before it can take possession of the peoples who alone can put it into practice, what fruitless debates! what weary inactivity of ideas! what a time for agitators and sophists! From the controversy of Jurieu with Bossuet, to the publication of Rousseau's *Social Contract* almost a century elapsed; and when the latter appeared, it was not to assert the idea, but to stifle it.

Rousseau, whose authority has ruled us for almost a century, understood nothing of the social contract. To him, most of all, must be ascribed the great relapse of '93, expiated already by fifty-seven years of fruitless disorder, and which certain minds more ardent than wise wish us still to regard as a sacred tradition.

The idea of contract excludes that of government: M. Ledru-Rollin, who is a lawyer, and whose attention I call to this point, ought to know it. What characterises the contract is agreement for equal exchange; and it is by virtue of this agreement that liberty and well being increase; while by the establishment of authority, both of these necessarily diminish. This will be evident if we reflect that contract is the act whereby two or several individuals agree to organise among themselves, for a definite purpose and time, that industrial power which we have called *exchange*; and in consequence have obligated themselves to each other, and reciprocally guaranteed a certain amount of services, products, advantages, duties, etc., which they are in a position to obtain and give to each other; recognising that they are otherwise perfectly independent, whether for consumption or production.

Between contracting parties there is necessarily for each one a real personal interest; it implies that a man bargains with the aim of securing his liberty and his revenue at the same time, without any possible loss.[3] Between governing and governed, on the contrary, no matter how the system of representation or of delegation of the governmental function is arranged, there is *necessarily* alienation of a part of the liberty and of the means of the citizen [...]

The contract therefore is essentially reciprocal: it imposes no obligation upon the parties, except that which results from their personal promise of reciprocal delivery: it is not subject to any external authority: it alone forms the law between the parties: it awaits their initiative for its execution.

But if such is the contract in its most general acceptation, and in daily practice; what will be the Social Contract, which is relied upon to bind together all the members of a nation into one and the same interest?

The Social Contract is the supreme act by which each citizen pledges to the association his love, his intelligence, his work, his services, his goods, in return for the affection, ideas, labour, products, services and goods of his fellows; the measure of the right of each being determined by the importance of his contributions, and the recovery that can be demanded in proportion to his deliveries.

Thus the social contract should include all citizens, with their interests and relations.—If a single man were excluded from the contract, if a single one of the interests upon which the members of the nation, intelligent, industrious, and sensible beings, are called upon to bargain, were omitted, the contract would be more or less relative or special, it would not be social.

The social contract should increase the well-being and liberty of every citizen.—If any one-sided conditions should slip in; if one part of the citizens should find themselves, by the contract, subordinated and exploited by the others, it would no longer be a contract; it would be a fraud, against which annulment might at any time be invoked justly.

The social contract should be freely discussed, individually accepted, signed with their own hands, by all the participants. If the discussion of it

---

3    I have taken the liberty to change two words in this passage, as a literal rendering would make nonsense of it. There must be some error in the text. (Translator)

were forbidden, cut short or juggled, if consent were obtained by fraud; if signature were made in blank, by proxy, or without reading the document and the preliminary explanation; or even if, like the military oath, consent were a matter of course and compulsory; the social contract would then be no more than a conspiracy against the liberty and well-being of the most ignorant, the weakest and the most numerous, a systematic spoliation, against which every means of resistance, and even of reprisal, would be a right and a duty.

We may add that the social contract of which we are now speaking has nothing in common with the contract of association by which, as we have shown in a previous study, the contracting party gives up a portion of his liberty, and submits to an annoying, often dangerous, obligation, in the more or less well-founded hope of a benefit. The social contract is of the nature of a contract of exchange: not only does it leave the party free, it adds to his liberty; not only does it leave him all his goods, it adds to his property; it prescribes no labour; it bears only upon exchange: all these being points which are not found in the contract of association, which is even antagonistic to it.

Such should be the social contract, according to the definitions of the law and universal practice. Is it necessary now to say that, out of the multitude of relations which the social pact is called upon to define and regulate, Rousseau saw only the political relations; that is to say, he suppressed the fundamental points of the contract, and dwelt only upon those that are secondary? Is it necessary to say that Rousseau understood and respected not one of these essential, indispensable conditions,—the absolute liberty of the party, his personal, direct part, his signature given with full understanding, and the share of liberty and prosperity which he should experience?

For him, the social contract is neither an act of reciprocity, nor an act of association. Rousseau takes care not to enter into such considerations. It is an act of appointment of arbiters, chosen by the citizens, without any preliminary agreement, for all cases of contest, quarrel, fraud or violence, which can happen in the relations which they may subsequently form among themselves, the said arbiters being clothed with sufficient force to put their decisions into execution, and to collect their salaries.

Of a real, true contract, on whatsoever subject, there is no vestige in Rousseau's book. To give an exact idea of his theory, I cannot do better than compare it with a commercial agreement, in which the names of the parties, the nature and value of the goods, products and services involved, the conditions of quality, delivery, price, reimbursement, everything in fact which constitutes the material of contracts, is omitted, and nothing is mentioned but penalties and jurisdictions.

Indeed, Citizen of Geneva, you talk well. But before holding forth about the sovereign and the prince, about the policeman and the judge, tell me first what is my share of the bargain? What? You expect me to sign an agreement in virtue of which I may be prosecuted for a thousand transgressions, by municipal, rural, river and forest police, handed over to tribunals, judged, condemned for damage, cheating, swindling, theft, bankruptcy, robbery, disobedience to the laws of the State, offence to public morals, vagabond-age,—and in this agreement I find not a word of either my rights or my obligations, I find only penalties!

But every penalty no doubt presupposes a duty, and every duty corre-sponds to a right. Where then in your agreement are my rights and duties? What have I promised to my fellow citizens? What have they promised to me? Show it to me, for without that, your penalties are but excesses of power, your law-controlled State a flagrant usurpation, your police, your judgement and your executions so many abuses. You who have so well denied prop-erty, who have impeached so eloquently the inequality of conditions among men, what dignity, what heritage, have you for me in your republic, that you should claim the right to judge me, to imprison me, to take my life and honour? Perfidious declaimer, have you inveighed so loudly against exploit-ers and tyrants, only to deliver me to them without defence?

Rousseau defined the social contract thus:

"To find a form of association which defends and protects, with the whole power of the community, the person and goods of each associate; and by which each one, uniting himself to all, obeys only himself and remains as free as before."

Yes, these are indeed the conditions of the social pact, as far as concerns *the protection and defence of goods and persons*. But as for the mode of acquisi-tion and transmission, as to labour, exchange, value and price of products, as to education, as to the multitude of relations which, whether he wishes it or not, places man in perpetual association with his fellows, Rousseau says not a word; his theory is perfectly meaningless. Who does not see that without some definition of rights and duties, the sanction which follows is absolutely null; who does not see that where there are no stipulations, there can be no infractions, nor, in consequence, any criminals; and, to conclude with philosophical rigor, that a society which after having provoked revolt, punishes and kills by virtue of such authority, itself commits assassination with premeditation and by treachery.

Rousseau is so far from desiring that any mention should be made in the social contract of the principles and laws which rule the fortunes of na-tions and of individuals, that, in his demagogue's programme, as well as in his Treatise on Education, he starts with the false, thievish, murderous supposition that only the individual is good, that society depraves him, that man therefore should refrain as much as possible from all relations with his fellows; and that all we have to do in this world below, while remaining in complete isolation, is to form among ourselves a mutual insurance society, for the protection of our persons and property; that all the rest, that is to say, economic matters, really the only matters of importance, should be left to the chance of birth or speculation, and submitted, in case of litigation, to the arbitration of elected officers, who should determine according to rules laid down by themselves, or by the light of natural equity. In a word, the social contract, according to Rousseau, is nothing but the offensive and defensive alliance of those who possess, against those who do not possess; and the only part played by the citizen is to pay the police, for which he is assessed in proportion to his fortune, and the risk to which he is exposed from general pauperism.

It is this contract of hatred, this monument of incurable misanthropy, this coalition of the barons of property, commerce and industry against the disinherited lower class, this oath of social war indeed, which Rousseau calls *Social Contract*, with a presumption which I should call that of a scoundrel, if I believed in the genius of the man.

But if the *virtuous and sensitive* Jean-Jacques had taken for his aim the perpetuation of the discord among men, could he have done better than to offer them, as their contract of union, this charter of their eternal antagonism? Watch him at work: you will find in his theory of government the same spirit that inspired his theory of education. As the tutor, so the statesman. The pedagogue preaches isolation, the publicist sows dissension.

After having laid down as a principle that the people are the only sovereign, that they can be represented only by themselves, that the law should be the expression of the will of all, and other magnificent commonplaces, after the way of demagogues, Rousseau quietly abandons and discards this principle. In the first place, he substitutes the will of the majority for the general, collective, indivisible will; then, under the pretext that it is not possible for a whole nation to be occupied from morning till night with public affairs, he gets back, by the way of elections, to the nomination of representatives or proxies, who shall do the law-making in the name of the people, and whose decrees shall have the force of laws. Instead of a direct, personal transaction where his interests are involved, the citizen has nothing left but the power of choosing his rulers by a plurality vote. That done, Rousseau rests easy. Tyranny, claiming divine right, had become odious; he reorganises it and makes it respectable, by making it proceed from the people, so he says. Instead of a universal, complete agreement, which would assure the rights of all, provide for the needs of all, and guard against all difficulties, which all must understand, consent to and sign, he gives us, what? That which today we call *direct government*, a recipe by which, even in the absence of all royalty, aristocracy, priesthood, the abstract *collectivity* of the people can still be used for maintaining the parasitism of the minority and the oppression of the greater number. It is, in a word, the legalisation of social chaos by a clever fraud, the consecration of poverty, based on the sovereignty of the people. Moreover there is not a word about labour, nor property, nor industrial forces; all of which it is the very object of a Social Contract to organise. Rousseau does not know what economics means. His programme speaks of political rights only; it does not mention economic rights.

It is Rousseau who teaches us that the people, a collective being, has no unitary existence; that it is an abstract personality, a moral individuality, incapable by itself of thinking, acting, or moving; which means that general reason is not superior to individual reason, and, in consequence, that he who has the most developed individual reason best represents general reason. A false proposition, which leads directly to despotism.

It is Rousseau who teaches us by aphorisms the whole of this liberty-destroying theory, making his deductions from this first error.

That popular or direct government results essentially from the *yielding up* of liberty that each one must make for the advantage of all.

That *the separation of powers is the first condition of government*.

That in a well-ordered Republic no association or special meeting of citizens can be permitted, because it would be a State within a State, a government within a government.

That a sovereign is one thing, a prince is another.

That the first by no means excludes the second; so that the most direct government may well exist with a hereditary monarchy, as was seen under Louis Philippe, and as some people would like to see again.

That as the sovereign, that is to say, the People, is a fictitious being, an ideal person, a mere conception of the mind, it has, as its natural and visible representative, the prince, who is the more valuable because he is one.

That the Government is not within a society, but *outside* of it.

That according to all these considerations, which are linked together in Rousseau like the theorems of geometry, a real democracy has never existed, and never will exist, seeing that in a democracy it is the greater number that should lay down the law and exercise the power, while it is contrary to the order of nature that the greater number should govern and the less be governed.

That direct government is impracticable, above all in a country like France, because, before everything else, it would be necessary to equalise fortunes, and equality of fortunes is impossible.

That besides, on account of the impossibility of maintaining equal conditions, direct government is of all the most unstable, the most perilous, the most fruitful of catastrophes and civil wars.

That as the ancient democracies could not maintain themselves, despite the powerful aid of slavery, it would be vain to attempt to establish this form of government among ourselves.

That democracy is made for gods, not for men.

After having trifled with his readers thus for a long time, after having drawn up the Code of Capitalist and Mercantile Tyranny, under the deceptive title of *Social Contract*, the Genevese charlatan deduces the necessity of a lower class, of the subordination of labour, of a dictatorship and of the Inquisition.

It appears to be the advantage of literary people that style should take the place of reason and morality.

[...]

The idea of contract, in opposition to that of government, which was the outcome of the Reformation, passed through the seventeenth and eighteenth centuries, without being noticed by a single publicist, nor observed by a single revolutionary. On the other hand, all that was most illustrious in the Church, in philosophy, in politics, conspired to oppose it. Rousseau, Siéyès, Robespierre, M. Guizot, all that school of parliamentarians, bore the banner of the opposition. At last one man, perceiving the disregard of the leading principle, brought again to the light the new and fruitful idea: unfortunately the practical side of his doctrines deceived his own disciples: they could not see that the producer is the negation of the ruler, that organisation is incompatible with authority; and thus for thirty years the principle was lost to sight. Finally, it took hold of public opinion, through the loudness of protest; but then, *O vanas hominum mentes, o pectora coeca!*[4] opposition brings about revolution! The idea of Anarchy had hardly been implanted in the mind of the people when it found so-called gardeners who watered it with their calumnies, fertilised it with their misrepresentations, warmed it in the hothouse of their hatred, supported it by their stupid opposition. Today, thanks to them, it has borne the anti-governmental idea, the idea of Labour, the idea of Contract, which is growing, mounting, seizing with its tendrils the workers' societies, and soon, like the grain of mustard seed of the Gospel, it will form a great tree, with branches which cover the earth.

The sovereignty of Reason having been substituted for that of Revolution,

The notion of Contract succeeding that of Government,

Historic evolution leading Humanity inevitably to a new system,

Economic criticism having shown that political institutions must be lost in industrial organisation,

We may conclude without fear that the revolutionary formula cannot be *Direct Legislation*, nor *Direct Government*, nor *Simplified Government*, that it is NO GOVERNMENT.

Neither monarchy, nor aristocracy, nor even democracy itself, in so far as it may imply any government at all, even though acting in the name of the people, and calling itself the people. No authority, no government, not even popular, that is the Revolution.

Direct legislation, direct government, simplified government, are ancient lies, which they try in vain to rejuvenate. Direct or indirect, simple or complex, governing the people will always be swindling the people. It is always man giving orders to man, the fiction which makes an end to liberty; brute force which cuts questions short, in the place of justice, which alone can answer them; obstinate ambition, which makes a stepping stone of devotion and credulity.

---

4   "Oh, dim minds! Oh, dull hearts of men!" (Translator) A slight misquotation of
    Lucretius, *De Rerum Natura* (*On the Nature of Things*), 2.14: "o miseras hominum
    mentes, o pectora cæca!" (Oh, miserable minds, oh, blind hearts!). (Editor)

[...]

But absolute power, in its simplest expression, is odious to reason and to liberty: the feeling of the people is always aroused against it: following feeling, revolt makes its protest heard. Then the principle of authority is forced to retire: it retires step by step, by a series of concessions, each one more insufficient than the other, of which the last, pure democracy, or direct government, ends in the impossible and the absurd. The first term of the series then being *Absolutism*, the last fateful term is *Anarchy*, in every sense.

We are about to pass in review, one after the other, the principal terms of this great evolution.

Humanity asks its masters: Whence these pretensions of yours to reign over me and govern me?

They answer: Because society cannot dispense with order: because in a society it is necessary there should be some who obey and labour, while others give orders and directions: because, individual faculties being unequal, interests opposite, passions antagonistic, the advantage of one opposed to the general advantage, some authority is needed which shall assign the boundaries of rights and duties, some arbiter who will cut short conflicts, some public force which will put into execution the judgements of the sovereign. The power of the State is just this discretionary authority, this arbiter who renders to each what is his, this force which assures that the peace shall be respected. Government, in a word, is the principle and guaranty of social order: that is what both nature and common sense tell us.

This explanation has been repeated since the origin of societies. It is the same at all epochs, and in the mouth of all powers. You will find the identical, invariably, in the books of Malthusian economists, in Opposition newspapers, and in the professions of faith of Republicans. There is no difference among them, except in the proportion of the concessions to liberty that they propose to make, in derogation of the principle of authority:—illusory concessions, which add to the forms of government called moderate, constitutional, democratic, etc., a flavouring of hypocrisy, of which the taste renders them only the more contemptible.

Thus Government, in its unmodified nature, presents itself as the absolute, necessary, *sine qua non* condition of order. For that reason it always aspires toward absolutism, under all disguises; in fact, according to the principle, the stronger the Government, the nearer order approaches perfection. These two notions then, government and order, are in the relation to each other of cause of effect: the cause is *Government*, the effect is *Order*. It is thus that primitive societies have reasoned. We have already remarked upon this subject, that, from what such societies could conceive of human destiny, it was impossible that they should have reasoned otherwise.

But this reasoning is none the less false, and the conclusion is quite inadmissible, because, according to the logical classification of ideas, the relation of government to order is not that of cause to effect, as statesmen pretend, it is that of a particular to a general. ORDER is the genus: *Government* is the species. In other words, there are many ways of conceiving order; but who has proved to us that order in a society is what its masters choose to call it?

On the one hand is alleged the natural inequality of faculties, whence is deduced that of conditions; on the other, the impossibility of uniting the divergence of interests and of harmonising opinions.

But in this antagonism there is at most but a problem to be solved, it should not be a pretext for tyranny. Inequality of faculties! divergence of interests! Well, sovereigns, with your crowns, robes and fasces, that is precisely what is meant by the social question; and you think to solve it with club and bayonet! Saint Simon was quite right in regarding the words *government* and *military* as synonyms. Government cause order in society? It is like Alexander untying the Gordian knot with his sword!

Who then, shepherds of the public, authorises you to think that the problem of opposition of interests and inequality of faculties cannot be solved; that the distinction of classes necessarily springs from it; and that, in order to maintain this natural and providential distinction, force is necessary and legitimate? I affirm, on the contrary, and all they whom the world calls Utopians, because they oppose your tyranny, affirm, with me, that the solution can be found. Some believe that they have found it in community [*communauté*], others in association, yet others in the industrial series. For my part, I say that it is found in the *organisation of economic forces*, under the supreme law of CONTRACT. Who can assure you that none of these hypotheses is true?

The advance of labour and of ideas sets this liberal theory, through my lips, against your governmental theory, which has no basis but your ignorance, no principle but a sophism, no method but force, no object but the robbery of humanity.

To find a form of transaction which, in drawing together the divergence of interests, in identifying individual advantage, in effacing the inequality of nature by that of education, solves all political and economical contradictions; under which each individual will be both producer and consumer as synonymous, both citizen and prince, ruler and ruled; under which his liberty steadily increases, with no need of giving up any part of it; under which his material prosperity grows indefinitely, without his experiencing any loss through the act either of society or of his fellow citizens, either in his property, or in his work, or in his recompense, or in his relations of interest, of opinion, or of attachment among his fellows.

What, do these conditions seem to you impossible to satisfy? Does it seem to you impossible to imagine anything more inextricable than the social contract, when you think of the frightful number of relations that it must regulate—something like squaring the circle, or finding perpetual motion? That is the reason why, wearied of the struggle, you fall back upon absolutism and force.

Consider, moreover, that if the social contract can be solved between two producers,—and who doubts terms?—it can as well be solved among millions, as it relates always to a similar engagement; and that that the number of signatures adds nothing to it, while making it more and more effective. Your plea of inability then does not exist, it is ridiculous, and you are left without excuse.

However that may be, listen, men of power, to the words of the Producer, the proletarian, the slave, of him whom you expect to force to work for you: I demand neither the goods nor the money of anybody; and I am not disposed to allow the fruit of my labour to become the prey of another. I, also, want order, as much as they who are continually upsetting it by their alleged government; but I want it as the result of my free choice, a condition for my labour, a law of my reason. I will not submit to it coming from the will of another, and imposing sacrifice and servitude upon me as preliminary conditions.

[...]

But what do I say? Laws for one who thinks for himself, and who ought to answer only for his own actions; laws for one who wants to be free, and feels himself worthy of liberty? I am ready to bargain, but I want no laws. I recognise none of them: I protest against every order which it may please some power, from pretended necessity, to impose upon my free will. Laws! We know what they are, and what they are worth! Spider webs for the rich and powerful, steel chains for the weak and poor, fishing nets in the hands of the Government.

[...]

One the 25<sup>th</sup> of February, 1848, a handful of Democrats, after having driven out the monarchy, proclaimed the Republic at Paris. They took counsel with themselves only for this step: they did not wait until the people had pronounced upon it, in their primary meetings. The support of the citizens was boldly presumed by them. I believe upon my soul and conscience, that they did well: I believe that they acted in the fullness of their right, although they were to the rest of the people as one to one thousand. And, because I was convinced of the justice of their work, I did not hesitate to associate myself therewith: the Republic, in my opinion, being but the cancellation of a lease between the People and the Government. *Adversus hostem aeterna auctoritas esto*[5] says the Law of the Twelve Tables. Against Power the right to reclaim cannot lapse; usurpation is meaningless.

Nevertheless, from the point of view of the sovereignty of numbers, of the imperative mandate, and of universal suffrage, which are more or less accepted by us, these citizens committed an act of usurpation, a criminal attack against public faith and the law of nations. By what right did they without a mandate, they, whom the People had not elected, they who were

---

5  "Against the enemy the right of defence is inalienable." (Translator)

only an imperceptible minority in the mass of citizens; by what right, I ask, did they rush upon the Tuileries like a band of pirates, abolish the Monarchy and proclaim the Republic?

*The Republic is above universal suffrage!* we said in the elections of 1850; and this was repeated afterwards from the tribune, amid acclamations, by a man not suspected of anarchical opinions, General Cavaignac. If this is true the morality of the February Revolution is vindicated; but what can we say of those who, while proclaiming the Republic, saw in it nothing but the exercise of universal suffrage, the establishment of a new form of government? The governmental principle admitted, it was for the People to pronounce upon the form; and who can say that the People would have voted in favour of the Republic, if they had been appealed to?

On the 10th of December, 1848, the People were consulted upon the choice of their first magistrate, and they named Louis Bonaparte, by a majority of five and a half million, out of seven and a half million voters. In choosing this candidate, the People, in their turn, took counsel only with their own inclinations: they took no account of the predictions and opinions of Republicans. For my part, I disapproved this election for the same reasons that led me to support the proclamation of the Republic. And, because I disapproved of it, I have since opposed, as far as in me lay, the government of the People's Choice.

Nevertheless from the point of view of universal suffrage, of the imperative mandate, and of the sovereignty of numbers, I ought to believe, that Louis Bonaparte expresses the ideas, the needs and the tendencies of the nation: I ought to accept his policy as the policy of the People. Even if it were opposed to the Constitution, the mere fact that the Constitution did not emanate directly from the People, while the President was the personification of the majority of votes, his policy should be held as approved, inspired and encouraged by the sovereign People. They who went to the Conservatory on the 13th of June, 1848, were but factionaries. Who gave them the right to suppose that the People, at the end of six months, would discard their President? Louis Bonaparte presented himself under the auspices of his uncle;[6] everybody knows what that means.

Do you still talk about the People? I mean the People as it show itself in mass meetings, at the ballot box; the People, which they did not dare to consult about the Republic in February; the People, which on the 16th of April and in the days of June, declared itself by an immense majority against Socialism; the People, which elected Louis Bonaparte, because it adored Napoléon Bonaparte; the People, which elected the Constituent Assembly, and afterwards the Legislative Assembly; the People, which did not rise on the 13th of June; the People, which did not protest on the 31st of May; the People which signed petitions for revision and petitions against revision. Is

---

6   Napoléon Bonaparte. (Editor)

this the People which will be enlightened from above, its representatives, inspired by its wisdom, be rendered thereby infallible, when it comes to picking out the most virtuous and most capable, and of deciding upon the organisation of Labour, of Credit, of Property and of Power itself?

[...]

At present we are a quasi-democratic Republic: all the citizens are permitted, every third or fourth year, to elect, first, the Legislative Power, second, the Executive Power. The duration of this participation in the Government for the popular collectivity is brief; forty-eight hours at the most for each election. For this reason the correlative of the Government remains nearly the same as before, almost the whole Country. The President and the Representatives, once elected, are the masters; all the rest obey. They are *subjects*, to be *governed* and to be taxed, without surcease.

[...]

# FIFTH STUDY
## SOCIAL LIQUIDATION

THE PRECEDING STUDIES, as much upon contemporaneous society as upon the reforms which it suggests, have taught us several things which it is well to recount here summarily.

The fall of the July monarchy and the proclamation of the Republic were the signal for a social revolution.

This Revolution, at first not understood, little by little became defined, determined and settled, under the influence of the very same Reaction which was displayed against it, from the first days of the Provisional Government.

This Revolution consists in substituting the economic, or industrial, system, for the governmental, feudal and military system, in the same way that the present system was substituted, by a previous revolution, for a theocratic or sacerdotal system.

By an industrial system, we understand, not a form of government, in which men devoted to agriculture and industry, entrepreneurs, proprietors, workers, become in their turn a dominant caste, as were formerly the nobility and clergy, but a constitution of society having for its basis the organisation of economic forces, in place of the hierarchy of political powers.

And to explain that this organisation must result from the nature of things, that there is nothing arbitrary about it, that it finds its law in established practice, we have said that, in order to bring it about, the question was of one thing only: To change the course of things, the tendency of society.

Passing then to the examination of the chief ideas that offer themselves as principles for guidance, and that serve as banners to parties, we have recognised:

That the principle of association, invoked by most *Schools*, is an essentially sterile principle; that it is neither an industrial force nor an economic law; that it would involve both government and obedience, two words which the Revolution bars.

That the political principle revived recently, under the names of *direct legislation, direct government*, etc., is but a false application of the principle of authority, whereof the sphere is in the family, but which cannot legitimately be extended to the commune or the nation.

At the same time we have established:

That in place of the idea of association, there was a tendency to substitute in the workers' societies a new idea, *reciprocity*, in which we have seen both an economic force and a law.

That to the idea of government there was opposed, even in the political tradition itself, the idea of *contract*, the only moral bond which free and equal beings can accept.

Thus we come to recognise the essential factors of the Revolution.

Its cause: the economic chaos which the Revolution of 1789 left after it.

Its occasion: a progressive, systematic poverty, of which the government finds itself, willy-nilly, the promoter and supporter.

Its organic principle: reciprocity; in law terms, contract.

Its aim: the guaranty of work and wages, and thence the indefinite increase of wealth and of liberty.

Its parties, which we divide into two groups: the Socialist schools, which invoke the principle of Association; and the democratic factions, which are still devoted to the principles of centralisation and of the State.

Finally, its adversaries, the capitalistic, theological usurious, governmental, partisans of the status quo, all those indeed who live less by labour than by prejudice and privilege.

To deduce the organising principle of the Revolution, the idea at once economic and legal of *reciprocity* and of *contract*, taking account of the difficulties and opposition which this deduction must encounter, whether on the part of revolutionary sects, parties or societies, or from the reactionaries and defenders of the status quo; to expound the totality of these reforms and new institutions, wherein labour finds its guaranty, property its limit, commerce its balance, and government its farewell; that is to tell, from the intellectual point of view, the story of the Revolution.

[…]

After these preliminaries, we have now three things to do:

1st. To cut short the disorganising *tendency* which the old revolution bequeathed to us, and to proceed, with the aid of the new principle, to the dissolution of established interests.—Thus the Constituent Assembly proceeded on the night of the 4th of August 1789.

2nd. To organise, always with the aid of the new principle, the economic forces, and to lay down the law of property.

3rd. To dissolve, submerge, and cause to disappear the political or governmental system in the economic system, by reducing, simplifying, decentralising and suppressing, one after another, all the wheels of this great machine, which is called the Government or the State.

[...]

Suppose, I say, that the People, once enlightened as to their true interests, declare their will, not to reform government, but to revolutionise society: in that case, without prejudice to a better plan, without pretending that the steps herein pointed out are at all absolute, or incapable of all sorts of modifications, this is how I conceive the Representatives of the People might carry out their mandate.

[...]

Let us take up this great question of property, the source of such intolerable pretensions, and of such ridiculous fears. The Revolution has two things to accomplish about property, its dissolution and its reconstitution. I shall address myself first to its dissolution, and begin with buildings.

[...]

This understood, let us suppose that the City of Paris resuming the abandoned project of Workers' Settlements, should reopen the campaign against the cost of dwellings; should buy houses that were for sale at the lowest price, contract with building workers companies for repairing them and keeping them in repair, then lease them, according to the rules of competition and equal exchange. After a while the City of Paris would own most of the houses of which it is composed, and would have all its citizens for tenants.

In this as always, the tendency is noticeable and significant: the right is incontestable. If after the taking of the Bastille, the City of Paris had set aside for such acquisition the sums which it has spent on public festivals, royal coronations, and celebrations of the births of princes, it would already have paid for several hundred million worth of property. Let the Country be the judge: let it decide in how many years it intends to revolutionise this first class of properties: what it resolves, I shall hold to be wisely resolved and I accept in advance.

While waiting, permit me to formulate a scheme.

The right of property, so honourable in its origin, when that origin is none other than labour, has become in Paris, and in most cities, an improper and immoral instrument of speculation in the dwelling places of citizens. Speculation in bread and food of prime necessity is punished as a misdemeanour, sometimes as a crime: is it more permissible to speculate in the habitations of the People? Our consciences, selfish, lazy, blind, most of all in matters that touch our pockets, have not yet noticed this similarity: all the more reason that the Revolution should denounce it. If the trumpet of the last judgement should resound in our ears, which of us at that moment would refuse to make this confession? Let us make it then, for I vow the last hour is approaching for the ancient abuse. It is too late to talk of purgatory, of gradual penitence, of progressive reform. Eternity awaits you. There is no middle ground between heaven and hell. We must take the leap.

I propose to manage the dissolution of rentals in the same manner as that of the Bank, of the public debt, and of private debts and obligations:

"From the date of the decree which shall be passed by future representatives, all payments made as rental shall be carried over to the account of the purchase of the property, at a price estimated at twenty times the annual rental.

"Every such payment shall purchase for the tenant a proportional undivided share in the house he lives in, and in all buildings erected for rental, and serving as a habitation for citizens.

"The property thus paid for shall pass under the control of the communal administration, which shall take a first mortgage upon it, in the name of all the tenants, and shall guarantee them all a domicile, in perpetuity, at the cost price of the building.

"Communes may bargain with owners for the purchase and immediate payment for rented buildings.

"In such case, in order that the present generation may enjoy the benefit of reduction in rental, the said communes may arrange for an immediate diminution of the rental of the houses for which they have negotiated, in such manner that complete payment may be made within thirty years.

"For repairs, management, and upkeep of buildings, as well as for new constructions, the communes shall deal with bricklayers companies or building workers' associations, according to the rules and principles of the new social contract.

"Proprietors who occupy their own houses shall retain property therein, as long as suits their interests."

Let the Country enter upon this course, and the safety of the People is assured. A guaranty stronger than all laws, all electoral combinations, all popular sanctions, will assure lodging to the workers forever, and render a return to speculation of rents impossible. Neither government, nor legislation, nor code is needed, a simple agreement among citizens suffices, with the execution of it confided to the commune: the producer is housed by a simple business transaction; something which neither kings nor dictator will ever accomplish.

[...]

Through the land the plundering of man began, and in the land it has rooted its foundations. The land is the fortress of the modern capitalist, as it was the citadel of feudalism, and of the ancient patriciate. Finally, it is the land which gives authority to the governmental principle, an ever-renewed strength, whenever the popular Hercules overthrows the giant.

To-day the stronghold, attacked upon all the secret points of its bastions, is about to fall before us, as fell, at the sound of Joshua's trumpets, the walls of Jericho. The machine which is able to overthrow the ramparts has been found; it is not my invention; it has been invented by property itself.

Everybody has heard of the land banks that have been in use for a long time among the land owners of Poland, Scotland, and Prussia, of which French proprietors and farm owners are demanding so insistently the introduction into our own country. In a previous article, speaking of the liquidation of mortgage secured debts, I had occasion to recall the attempts made by several honourable conservatives in the National Assembly to endow France with this beneficent institution. I showed, in connection therewith, how the land bank might become an instrument of revolution with regard to debts and interest. I am about to show how it may be the same with regard to landed property.

The special characteristic of the land bank, after the low price and the facility of its credit, is the *reimbursement for annuities*.

Suppose that the proprietors, no longer waiting for the Government to act, but taking their affairs into their own hands, follow the example of the workers' associations, and get together to found a Bank by subscription, or mutual guaranty.

[...]

The farmer or peasant can then pay for the land that he cultivates in twenty-five, thirty, thirty-four or forty years, if the owner will agree to it: he can pay for it in twenty, eighteen, or fifteen years, if he can buy it by the system of annuities. What then prevents the peasant from becoming everywhere the owner of the soil, and freeing himself from farm rent?

What prevents him is that the owner demands to be paid in cash; and that if cash is not forthcoming, he *lets* the land; that is to say, he requires payment in perpetuity.

In that case, you will say, why does not the tenant borrow?

Ah! that is because the loan of money on mortgage agrees exactly with farm rent. The interest required for this kind of loan serves not in the least to extinguish the debt, and is even higher than the farm rent. The peasant therefore finds himself enclosed in a circle: he must cultivate to eternity, but never possess. If he borrows, he gives himself a second master, double interest, double slavery. There is no way of escape without the aid of a fairy.

Well, the fairy exists: it remains only for us to test the virtue of her wand: the fairy is the land bank.

[...]

This will be as if the cultivator had to pay rent for 15, 20 or 30 years, in order to become the owner of property worth $2,000. Thus the farm rent is not perpetual: it is annually charged off the price: it gives a title to the property. And as the price of real estate cannot be raised indefinitely, since it is only the capitalisation of twenty, thirty or forty fold of the part of the product which is in excess of the cost of working the land, it is evident that the peasant cannot fail to obtain the property. With the Land Bank the farmer is released; it is the proprietor who is caught. Do you understand now why the conservatives of the Constituent Assembly were unwilling to permit a Land Bank?

Thus what we call farm rent, left to us by Roman tyranny and feudal usurpation, hangs only by a thread, the organisation of a bank, demanded even by property itself. It has been demonstrated that the land tends to return to the hands that cultivate it, and that farm rent, like house rent, like the interest of mortgages, is but an improper speculation, which shows the disorder and anomaly of the present economic system.

Whatever may be the conditions of this Bank, which will come into existence on the day when those who need it desire it; whatever be the rate of charge for its services, however small its issues, it can be calculated in how many years the soil will be delivered from the parasitism which sucks it dry, while strangling the cultivator.

And when once the revolutionary machine shall have released the soil, and agriculture shall have become free, feudal exploitation can never re-establish itself. Property may then be sold, bought, circulated, divided or united, anything; the ball and chain of the old serfdom will never be dragged again; property will have lost its fundamental vices, it will be transfigured. It will no longer be the same thing. Still, let us continue to call it by its ancient name, so dear to the heart of man, so agreeable to the ear of the peasant, *property*.

[...]

I propose to decree:

"Every payment of rent for the use of real estate shall give title to the farmer for a share of the real estate, and shall be a lien upon it.

"When the property has been entirely paid for, it shall revert immediately to the commune, which shall take the place of the former proprietor, and shall share the fee-simple and the economic rent with the farmer.

"Communes may bargain directly with owners who wish to do so for the repurchase of rentals and the immediate purchase of the properties.

"In that case, provision shall be made for the supervision of the communes, for the installation of cultivators, and for the fixing of the boundaries of possessions, taking care to make up by an increase in quantity for any deficiency in the quality of the land, and to proportion the rent to the product.

"As soon as all landed property shall have been completely paid for, all the communes of the Republic shall come to an understanding for equalising among them the quality of tracts of land, as well as accidents of culture. The part of the rent to which they are entitled upon their respective territories shall serve for compensation and for general insurance.

"Beginning with the same date, the former proprietors who have held their title by working their properties themselves, shall be placed on the same footing as the new, subjected to the same rights; in such a manner that the chance of locality or of succession may favour no one, and that the conditions of culture shall be equal for all.

"The tax on land shall be abolished.

"The rural police are placed under the control of the municipal councils."
[...]

A general liquidation is the obligatory preliminary of every revolution. After sixty years of mercantile and economic chaos, a second night of the 4th of August is indispensable. We are still masters of the situation, and free to proceed with all the prudence, all the moderation, that we may think advisable: later, our fate may not depend upon our free choice.

I have proved at length that in the aspirations of the Country, in the ideas that are current among capitalists and proprietors, as well as among peasants and workers, everything tends toward this liquidation: co-operative associations, accumulation of coin at the Bank, discount houses, credit notes, land banks, workers' villages, right to value of improvements, etc., etc. I have analysed and deduced these ideas, and I have found at the bottom of them always the principle of reciprocity and contract, never that of government. Finally, I have shown how liquidation could, on each point, be made to work as rapidly as might be desired; and if I have pronounced myself in favour of the easiest and quickest way, it was not, as might be supposed, because I held extreme opinions, but because I was convinced that this method is the wisest, the most just, the most conservative, the most advantageous to all interested, debtors, creditors, house owners, tenants, land proprietors and tenant farmers.

[...]

# SIXTH STUDY
## ORGANISATION OF ECONOMIC FORCES

ROUSSEAU SAID TRULY: No one should obey a law to which he has not consented; and M. Rittinghausen too was right when he proved that in consequence the law should emanate directly from the sovereign, without the intermediary of representatives.

But it was in the application that both these writers failed. With suffrage, or the universal vote, it is evident that the law is neither direct nor personal, any more than collective. The law of the majority is not my law, it is the law of force; hence the government based upon it is not my government; it is government by force.

That I may remain free; that I may not have to submit to any law but my own, and that I may govern myself, the authority of the suffrage must be renounced: we must give up the vote, as well as representation and monarchy. In a word, everything in the government of society which rests on the divine must be suppressed, and the whole rebuilt upon the human idea of CONTRACT.

When I agree with one or more of my fellow citizens for any object whatever, it is clear that my own will is my law; it is I myself, who, in fulfilling my obligation, am my own government.

Therefore if I could make a contract with all, as I can with some; if all could renew it among themselves, if each group of citizens, as a commune, canton, department, corporation, company, etc., formed by a like contract, and considered as a moral person, could thereafter, and always by a similar contract, agree with every and all other groups, it would be the same as if my own will were multiplied to infinity. I should be sure that the law thus made on all questions in the Republic, from millions of different initiatives, would never be anything but my law; and if this new order of things were called government, it would be my government.

Thus the principle of contract, far more than that of authority, would bring about the union of producers, centralise their forces, and assure the unity and solidarity of their interests.

The *system of contracts*, substituted for the *system of laws*, would constitute the true government of the man and of the citizen; the true sovereignty of the People, the REPUBLIC.

For the contract is Liberty, the first term of the republican motto: we have demonstrated this superabundantly in our studies on the principle of authority and on social liquidation. I am not free when I depend upon another for my work, my wages, or the measure of my rights and duties; whether that other be called the Majority or Society. No more am I free, either in my sovereignty or in my action, when I am compelled by another to revise my law, were that other the most skilful and most just of arbiters. I am no more at all free when I am forced to give myself a representative to govern me, even if he were my most devoted servant.

The Contract is Equality, in its profound and spiritual essence.—Does this man believe himself my equal; does he not take the attitude of my master and exploiter, who demands from me more than it suits me to furnish, and has no intention of returning it to me; who says that I am incapable of making my own law, and expects me to submit to his?

The contract is Fraternity, because it identifies all interests, unifies all divergences, resolves all contradictions, and in consequence, give wings to the feelings of goodwill and kindness, which are crushed by economic chaos, the government of representatives, alien law.

The contract, finally, is order, since it is the organisation of economic forces, instead of the alienation of liberties, the sacrifice of rights, the subordination of wills.

Let us give an idea of this organism; after liquidation, reconstruction; after the thesis and antithesis, the synthesis.

## 1. CREDIT

The organisation of credit is three-quarters done by the winding up of the privileged and usurious banks, and their conversion into a National Bank of circulation and loan, at ½, ¼, or ⅛ percent. It remains only to establish branches of the Bank, wherever necessary, and to gradually retire specie from circulation, depriving gold and silver of their privilege as money.

As for *personal credit*, it is not for the National Bank to have to do with it; it is with the workers companies, and the farming and industrial societies, that personal credit should be exercised.

### 2. PROPERTY

I have shown above how property, repurchased by the house rent or ground rent, would come back to the tenant farmer and house tenant. It remains for me to show, especially in relation to property in land, the organising power of the principle which we have invoked to bring about this conversion.

All the Socialists, Saint Simon, Fourier, Owen, Cabet, Louis Blanc, the Chartists, have conceived agricultural organisation in two ways.

Either the farmer is simply a worker associate of a large workshop of culture, which is the Commune, the Phalanstery.

Or each cultivator becomes a tenant of the State, which is the only proprietor, the only landlord; all land having been taken by it. In this case, the ground rent becomes part of the taxes, and may replace them entirely.

The first of these two systems is governmental and Communist at the same time: through this double principle it has no chance of success. It is a utopian conception still-born. The Phalansterians will talk for a good while yet of their model community: the Communists are not ready to give up their rural fraternity. They may have this consolation. If the idea of a farming association or of cultivation by the government were ever brought forward as a serious proposal during the Revolution, supposing that a government could still exist in a revolution directed chiefly against itself, the chances of insurrection would be laid before the peasant. There would be the menace of tyranny for him, even from those who called themselves Socialists.

The second system seems more liberal: it leaves the cultivator his own master in his work, subjects him to no orders, imposes upon him no rules. In comparison with the present lot of farmers, it is probable that, with the greater length of leases and moderation of rents, the establishment of this system would encounter little opposition in the country. I admit, for my part, that I hesitated for a long time over this idea, which grants some liberty, and which I could reproach with no injustice.

Nevertheless I have never been completely satisfied with it. I find in it always a character of governmental autocracy which is disagreeable to me: I see in it a barrier to liberty of transactions and of inheritances; the free disposition of the soil taken away from him who cultivates it; and this precious sovereignty, this *eminent domain*, as the lawyers say, forbidden to the citizen, and reserved for that fictitious being, without intelligence, without passion, without morality, that we call the State. By this arrangement, the occupant has less to do with the soil than before; the clod of earth seems to stand up and say to him: You are only a slave of the taxes; I do not know you!

But why should the rural worker, the most ancient, the most noble of all, be thus discrowned? The peasant loves the land with a love without limit; as Michelet poetically says: he does not want a tenancy, a concubinage; he wants a marriage.

It is asserted that mankind, as a race, has an anterior, imprescriptible, inalienable right to the soil. It is thence deduced, as by the Physiocrats formerly, that the commune or the State should share in the economic rent. It is said that this economic rent should be taken in taxes. And from all this results the enfeoffment of the land by perpetual, unchangeable tenancy; and, what is more serious, the non-circulation, the immobility, of a whole class of capital, the largest in volume, and the most valuable, through its security.

This doctrine appears to me fatal; opposed to all the teachings of science, and of dangerous tenancy.

1. What is called *economic rent* in agriculture has no other cause than the inequality in the quality of the land: without this inequality there would be no economic rent, since there would be no means of comparison. Therefore if anybody has a claim on account of this inequality, it is not the State, but the other land workers who hold inferior land. That is why in our scheme for liquidation we stipulated that every variety of cultivation should pay a proportional contribution, destined to accomplish a balancing of returns among farm workers, and an assurance of products.

2. The industrial occupations, in favour of which the ground rent seems to be reserved, have no more right to it than the State, for the reason that they do not exist apart from agricultural work and independently of it: they are a subdivision of it. The farm worker cultivates and harvests for all: the artisan, the merchant, the manufacturer, work for the farm worker. As soon as the dealer has received the price of his merchandise, he is paid his share of the economic rent, as well as of the gross product of the soil; his account is settled. To make the farm worker only pay the taxes, under the pretext that they are economic rent, would be to exempt other industries from taxation, to their profit, and to permit them to receive the whole of the rent, without reciprocity on their part.

[...]

### 3. DIVISION OF LABOUR, COLLECTIVE FORCES, MACHINES, WORKERS COMPANIES

In France, two-thirds of the inhabitants are interested in land owning; and even this proportion must increase. Next to credit, which controls everything, it is the greatest of our economic forces; through it, therefore, we must proceed to the revolutionary organisation in the second place.

Agricultural labour, resting on this basis, appears in its natural dignity. Of all occupations it is the most noble, the most healthful, from the point of view of morals and health, and as intellectual exercise, the most encyclopaedic. From all these considerations, agricultural labour is the one which least requires the societary form; we may say even more strongly, which most energetically rejects it. Never have peasants been seen to form a society for the cultivation of their fields; never will they be seen to do so. The only relations of unity and solidarity which can exist among farm workers, the only centralisation of which rural industry is susceptible, is that which we have pointed out which results from compensation for economic rent, mutual insurance, and, most of all, from abolishing rent, which makes accumulation of land, parcelling out of the soil, serfdom of the peasant, dissipation of inheritances, forever impossible.

It is otherwise with certain industries, which require the combined employment of a large number of workers, a vast array of machines and hands, and, to make use of a technical expression, a great division of labour, and in consequence a high concentration of power. In such cases, worker is necessarily subordinate to worker, man dependent on man. The producer is no longer, as in the fields, a sovereign and free father of a family; it is a collectivity. Railroads, mines, factories, are examples.

In such cases, it is one of two things; either the worker, necessarily a piece-worker, will be simply the employee of the proprietor-capitalist-entrepreneur; or he will participate in the chances of loss or gain of the establishment, he will have a voice in the council, in a word, he will become an associate.

In the first case the worker is subordinated, exploited: his permanent condition is one of obedience and poverty. In the second case he resumes his dignity as a man and citizen, he may aspire to comfort, he forms a part of the producing organisation, of which he was before but the slave; as, in the town, he forms a part of the sovereign power, of which he was before but the subject.

Thus we need not hesitate, for we have no choice. In cases in which production requires great division of labour, and a considerable collective force, it is necessary to form an ASSOCIATION among the workers in this industry; because without that, they would remain related as subordinates and superiors, and there would ensue two industrial castes of masters and wage-workers, which is repugnant to a free and democratic society.

Such therefore is the rule that we must lay down, if we wish to conduct the Revolution intelligently.

Every industry, operation or enterprise, which by its nature requires the employment of a large number of workers of different specialities, is destined to become a society or a company of workers.

That is why I said one day, in February or March 1849, at a meeting of patriots, that I rejected equally the construction and management of railroads by companies of capitalists and by the State. In my opinion, railroads are in the field of workers' companies, which are different from the present commercial companies, as they must be independent of the State. A railroad, a mine, a factory, a ship, are to the workers who use them what a hive is to

584 Pierre-Joseph Proudhon

the bees, at once their tool and their home, their country, their territory, their property. It is surprising that they who so zealously maintain the principle of association should have failed to see that such was its normal application.

But where the product can be obtained by the action of an individual or a family, without the co-operation of special abilities, there is no opportunity for association. Association not being called for by the nature of the work, cannot be profitable nor of long continuance: I have given the reasons elsewhere.

When I speak of either *collective force* or of an extreme division of labour, as a necessary condition for association, it must be understood from a practical point of view, rather than in a rigorous logical or mathematical sense. Liberty of association being unrestricted, it is evident that if the peasants think well to associate, they will associate, independently of the considerations against it; on the other hand, it is not less clear that if one must live up to the rigorous definitions of science, the conclusion would be that all workers must associate, inasmuch as collective force and division of labour exist everywhere, to however slight a degree.

[...]

The capitalist, you will cry, alone runs the risk of the enterprise [...] Could the capitalists alone work a mine or run a railroad? Could one man alone carry on a factory, sail a ship, play a tragedy, build the Pantheon or the Column of July? Can anybody do such things as these, even if he has all the capital necessary? And the one who is called *the employer*, is he anything more than a leader or captain?

It is in such cases, perfectly defined, that association, due to the immorality, tyranny and theft suffered, seems to me absolutely necessary and right. The industry to be carried on, the work to be accomplished, are the common and undivided property of all those who take part therein: the granting of franchises for mines and railroads to companies of stockholders, who plunder the bodies and souls of the wage-workers, is a betrayal of power, a violation of the rights of the public, an outrage upon human dignity and personality.

[...]

Thus the outline of the Revolution begins to display itself: already its aspect is grandiose.

On the one hand, the peasants, at last masters of the soil which they cultivate, and in which they desire to take root. Their enormous, unconquerable mass, aroused by a common guaranty, united by the same interests, assures forever the triumph of the democracy, and the permanence of *Contract*.

On the other hand there are myriads of small manufacturers, dealers, artisans, the volunteers of commerce and industry, working in isolation or in small groups, the most migratory of beings; who prefer their complete independence to the sovereignty of the soil; sure of having a country wherever they can find work.

Finally appear the workers companies, regular armies of the revolution, in which the worker, like the soldier in the battalion, manoeuvres with the precision of his machines; in which thousands of wills, intelligent and proud, submit themselves to a superior will, as the hands controlled by them engender, by their concerted action, a collective force greater than even their number.

The cultivator had been bent under feudal servitude through rent and mortgages. He is freed by the land bank, and, above all, by the right of the user to the property. The land, vast in extent and in depth, becomes the basis of equality.

In the same way the wage-worker of the great industries had been crushed into a condition worse than that of the slave by the loss of the advantage of collective force. But by the recognition of his right to the profit from this force, of which he is the producer, he resumes his dignity, he regains comfort; the great industries, terrible engines of aristocracy and pauperism, become, in their turn, one of the principal organs of liberty and public prosperity.

[...]

Let us then lay down the principles of the agreement which must constitute this new revolutionary power.

Large-scale industry may be likened to a new land, discovered, or suddenly created out of the air, by the social genius; to which society sends a colony to take possession of it and to work it, for the advantage of all.

This colony will be ruled by a double contract, that which gives it title, establishes its property, and fixes its rights and obligations toward the mother-country; and the contract which unites the different members among themselves, and determines their rights and duties.

Toward Society, of which it is a creation and a dependence, this workers company promises to furnish always the products and services which are asked of it, at a price nearly as possible that of cost, and to give the public the advantage of all desirable betterments and improvements.

To this end, the workers company abjures all combinations, submits itself to the law of competition, and holds its books and records at the disposition of Society, which, upon its part, reserves the power of dissolving the workers company, as the sanction of its right of control.

Toward the individuals and families whose labour is the subject of the association, the company makes the following rules:

That every individual employed in the association, whether man, woman, child, old man, head of department, assistant head, worker or apprentice, has an undivided share in the property of the company;

That he has the right to fill any position, of any grade, in the company, according to the suitability of sex, age, skill, and length of employment;

That his education, instruction, and apprenticeship should therefore be so directed that, while permitting him to do his share of unpleasant and disagreeable tasks, they may also give variety of work and knowledge, and may assure him, from the period of maturity, an encyclopaedic aptitude and a sufficient income;

That all positions are elective, and the by-laws subject to the approval of the members;

That pay is to be proportional to the nature of the position, the importance of the talents, and the extent of responsibility;

That each member shall participate in the gains and in the losses of the company, in proportion to his services;

That each member is free to leave the company, upon settling his account, and paying what he may owe; and reciprocally, the company may take in new members at any time.

These general principles are enough to explain the spirit and scope of this institution, that has no precedent and no model. They furnish the solution of two important problems of social economy, that of *collective force*, and that of the division of labour.

By participation in losses and gains, by the graded scale of pay, and the successive promotion to all grades and positions, the collective force, which is a product of the community, ceases to be a source of profit to a small number of managers and speculators: it becomes the property of all the workers. At the same time, by a broad education, by the obligation of apprenticeship, and by the co-operation of all who take part in the collective work, the division of labour can no longer be a cause of degradation for the worker: it is, on the contrary, the means of his education and the pledge of his security.

[...]

## 4. CONSTITUTION OF VALUE. ORGANISATION OF LOW PRICES

If commerce or exchange, carried on after a fashion, is already, by its inherit merit, a producer of wealth; if, for this reason, it has been practised always and by all the nations of the globe; if, in consequence, we must consider it as an economic force; it is not the less true, and it springs from the very notion of exchange, that commerce ought to be so much the more profitable if sales and purchases are made at the lowest and most just price; that is to say, if the products that are exchanged can be furnished in greater abundance and in more exact proportion.

Scarcity of product, in other words, the high price of merchandise, is an evil in commerce: the imperfect relations, that is to say, the arbitrary prices, the anomalous values, are another evil.

To deliver commerce from these two diseases that eat into and devour it, would be to increase the productivity of commerce, and consequently the prosperity of society.

At all times speculation has taken advantage of these two scourges of commerce, scarcity of product and arbitrary value, in order to exaggerate them, and bring pressure upon the unhappy people. Always also the public conscience has rebelled against the exactions of mercantilism, and struggled to restore the equilibrium. We all know of the desperate war waged by Turgot against the monopolisers of grain, who were supported by the courts and by precedent; we can also remember the less fortunate efforts of the Convention, and its laws establishing maximum prices. In our own day, the tax on bread, the abolition of the slaughter house privilege, the railroad rate scale, and those of ministerial offices, etc., etc., are so many attempts in the same direction.

It must always be remembered with shame that certain economists have nevertheless aspired to erect into a law this mercantile disorder and commercial disturbance. They see in it a principle as sacred as that of the family or of labour. The school of Say, sold out to English and native capitalism, the chief focus of counter-revolution next to the Jesuits, has for ten years past seemed to exist only to protect and applaud the execrable work of the monopolists of money and necessaries, deepening more and more the obscurity of a science naturally difficult and full of complications. These apostles of materialism were made to work in with the eternal executioners of conscience: after the events of February, they signed an agreement with the Jesuits, a compact of hypocrisy and a bargain with starvation. Let the reaction which unites them hasten to cause them to retrace their steps, and let them get to cover quickly, for I warn them that if the Revolution spares men, it will not spare deeds.

No doubt Value, the expression of liberty, and growing out of the personality of the worker, is of all human things the most reluctant to submit to formulas. Therein lies the excuse of the misleading routine arguments of the economists. Thus the disciples of Malthus and Say, who oppose with all their might any intervention of the State in matters commercial or industrial, do not fail to avail themselves at times of this seemingly liberal attitude, and to show themselves more revolutionary than the Revolution. More than one honest searcher has been deceived thereby: they have not seen that this inaction of Power in economic matters was the foundation of government. What need should we have of a political organisation, if Power once permitted us to enjoy economic order?

[...]

When, by the liquidation of debts, the organisation of credit, the deprivation of the power of increase of money, the limitation of property, the establishment of workers companies and the use of a just price, the tendency to raising of prices shall have been definitely replaced by a tendency to lower them, and the fluctuations of the market by a normal commercial rate; when general consent shall have brought this great about-face of the sphere of trade, then Value, at once the most ideal and most real of things, may be said to have been constituted, and will express at any moment, for every kind of product, the true relation of Labour and Wealth, while preserving its mobility through the eternal progress of industry.

The constitution of Value solves the problem of competition and that of the rights of Invention; as the organisation of workers companies solves that of collective force and of the division of labour. I can merely indicate at this moment these consequences of the main theorem; their development would take too much space in a philosophical review of the Revolution.

### 5. FOREIGN COMMERCE. BALANCE OF IMPORTS AND EXPORTS

By the suppression of custom houses, the Revolution, according to theory, and regardless of all military and diplomatic influences, will spread from France abroad, extend over Europe, and afterwards over the world.

To suppress our custom houses is in truth to organise foreign trade as we have organised domestic trade; it is to place the countries with which we trade on even terms with ourselves in our trade legislation; it is to introduce among them the constitution of Value and of Property; it is, in a word, to establish the solidarity of the Revolution between the French People and the rest of the human race, by making the new social compact common to all nations through the power of Exchange.

[...]

From what we have said in connection with social liquidation, as well as in connection with the constitution of property, the organisation of workers companies and the guaranty of low prices, it follows that if the charge for loans at the Bank should diminish, if the interest on the public debt and upon private obligations were proportionally reduced, if thereupon house rent and ground rent were lowered in like proportion, if a tabulation were made of values and properties, etc., etc., the cost price of all sorts of products would decrease notably, and in consequence the tariff might be lowered to the advantage of all.

That would be a step in general progress such as has never yet been seen, because a government is incapable of bringing it about.

If this general movement, as I have more than once observed, should only make a beginning, if the tariff, driven by credit, should move on this line however little, the ancient order of things in all that concerns our foreign relations would be suddenly changed, and international economics would enter upon the road to revolution.

[...]

As for me, I, who oppose the free traders because they favour interest, while they demand the abolition of tariffs,—I should favour lowering the tariff from the moment that interest fell; and if interest were done away with, or even lowered to ¼ or ½ percent., I should be in favour of free trade.

I believe in free trade, even without reciprocity, as a consequence of the abolition of interest, not otherwise [...]

[...]

# SEVENTH STUDY
## ABSORPTION OF GOVERNMENT BY THE ECONOMIC ORGANISM
[...]

GOVERNMENT [...] HAS for its dogmas:

1. The original perversity of human nature;
2. The inevitable inequality of fortunes;
3. The permanency of quarrels and wars;
4. The irremediability of poverty.

Whence it is deduced:

5. The necessity of government, of obedience, of resignation, and of faith.

These principles admitted, as they still are, almost universally, the forms of authority are already settled. They are:

a. The division of the people into classes or castes, subordinate to one another; graduated to form a pyramid, at the top of which appears, like the Divinity upon his altar, like the king upon his throne, AUTHORITY;
b. Administrative centralisation;
c. Judicial hierarchy;
d. Police;
e. Worship.

Add to the above, in countries in which the democratic principle has become preponderant:

f. The separation of powers;
g. The intervention of the People in the Government, by vote for representatives;
h. The innumerable varieties of electoral systems, from the Convocation by Estates, which prevailed in the Middle Ages, down to universal and direct suffrage;
i. The duality of legislative chambers;
j. Voting upon laws, and consent to taxes by the representatives of the nation;
k. The rule of majorities.

Such is broadly the plan of construction of Power, independently of the modifications which each of its component party may receive; as, for example, the central Power, which may be in turn monarchical, aristocratic or democratic; which once furnished publicists with a ground for classification, according to superficial character.

It will be observed that the governmental system tends to become more and more complicated without becoming on that account more efficient or more moral, and without offering any more guarantees to person or property. This complication springs first from legislation, which is always incomplete and insufficient; in the second place, from the multiplicity of functionaries; but most of all, from the compromise between the two antagonistic elements, the executive initiative and popular consent. It has been left for our epoch to establish unmistakably that this bargaining, which the progress of centuries renders inevitable is the surest index of corruption, of decadence, and of the approaching dissolution of Authority.

What is the aim of this organisation?

To maintain *order* in society, by consecrating and sanctifying obedience of the citizen to the State, subordination of the poor and to the rich, of the common people to the upper class, of the worker to the parasite, of the layman to the priest, of the bourgeois to the soldier.

As far back as the memory of humanity extends, it is found to have been organised on the above system, which constitutes the political, ecclesiastical or governmental order. Every effort to give Power a more liberal appearance, more tolerant, more social, has invariably failed; such efforts have been even more fruitless when they tried to give the People a larger share in Government; as if the words, Sovereignty and People, which they endeavoured to yoke together, were as naturally antagonistic as these other two words, Liberty and Despotism.

Humanity has had to live, and civilisation to develop, for six thousand years, under this inexorable system, of which the first term is *Despair* and the last *Death*. What secret power has sustained it? What force has enabled it to survive? What principles, what ideas, renewed the blood that flowed forth under the poniard of authority, ecclesiastical and secular?

This mystery is now explained.

Beneath the governmental machinery, in the shadow of political institutions, out of the sight of statesmen and priests, society is producing its own organism, slowly and silently; and constructing a new order, the expression of its vitality and autonomy, and the denial of the old politics, as well as of the old religion.

This organisation, which is as essential to society as it is incompatible with the present system, has the following principles:

1. The indefinite perfectibility of the individual and of the race;
2. The honourableness of work;
3. The equality of fortunes;
4. The identity of interests;
5. The end of antagonisms;
6. The universality of comfort;
7. The sovereignty of reason;
8. The absolute liberty of the man and of the citizen.

I mention below its principal forms of activity:

a. Division of labour, through which classification of the People by INDUSTRIES replaces classification by *caste*;

b.   Collective power, the principle of WORKERS COMPANIES, in place of *armies*;
c.   Commerce, the concrete form of CONTRACT, which takes the place of *Law*;
d.   Equality in exchange;
e.   Competition;
f.   Credit, which turns upon INTERESTS, as the governmental hierarchy turns upon *Obedience*;
g.   The equilibrium of values and of properties.

The old system, standing on Authority and Faith, was essentially based on *Divine Right*. The principle of the sovereignty of the People, introduced later, did not change its nature; and it is a mistake today, in the face of the conclusions of science, to maintain a distinction which does not touch underlying principles, between absolute monarchy and constitutional monarchy, or between the latter and the democratic republic. The sovereignty of the People has been, is I may say so, for a century past, but a skirmishing line for Liberty. It was either an error, or a clever scheme of our fathers to make the sovereign people in the image of the king-man: as the Revolution becomes better understood, this mythology vanishes, all traces of government disappear and follow the principle of government itself to dissolution.

[...]

This absolute incompatibility of the two systems, so often proved, still does not convince writers who, while admitting the dangers of authority, nevertheless hold to it, as the sole means of maintaining order, and see nothing beside it but empty desolation. Like the sick man in the comedy, who is told that the first thing he must do is to discharge his doctors, if he wants to get well, they persist in asking how can a man get along without a doctor, or a society without a government. They will make the government as republican, as benevolent, as equal as possible; they will set up all possible guarantees against it; they will belittle it, almost attack it, in support of the majesty of the citizens. They tell us: You are the government! You shall govern yourselves, without president, without representatives, without delegates. But to live without government, to abolish all authority, absolutely and unreservedly, to set up pure *anarchy*, seems to them ridiculous and inconceivable, a plot against the Republic and against the nation. What will these people who talk of abolishing government put in place of it? they ask.

We have no trouble in answering.

It is industrial organisation that we will put in place of government, as we have just shown.

In place of laws, we will put contracts.—No more laws voted by a majority, nor even unanimously; each citizen, each commune or corporation, makes its own.

In place of political powers, we will put economic forces.

In place of the ancient classes of nobles, burghers, and peasants, or of bourgeoisie and proletariat, we will put the general titles and special departments of industry: Agriculture, Manufacture, Commerce, etc.

In place of public force, we will put collective force.

In place of standing armies, we will put industrial associations.

In place of police, we will put identity of interests.

In place of political centralisation, we will put economic centralisation.

Do you see now how there can be order without functionaries, a profound and wholly intellectual unity?

You, who cannot conceive of unity without a whole apparatus of legislators, prosecutors, attorneys-general, custom house officers, policemen, you have never known what real unity is! What you call unity and centralisation is nothing but perpetual chaos, serving as a basis for endless tyranny; it is the advancing of the chaotic condition of social forces as an argument for despotism—a despotism which is really the cause of the chaos.

Well, in our turn, let us ask, what need have we of government when we have made an agreement? Does not the National Bank, with its various branches, achieve centralisation and unity? Does not the agreement among farm workers for compensation, marketing, and reimbursement for farm properties create unity? From another point of view, do not the industrial associations for carrying on the large-scale industries bring about unity? And the constitution of value, that contract of contracts, as we have called it, is not that the most perfect and indissoluble unity?

And if we must show you an example in our own history in order to convince you, does not that fairest monument of the Convention, the system of weights and measures, form, for fifty years past, the corner-stone of that economic unity which is destined to replace political unity?

Never ask again then what we will put in place of government, nor what will become of society without government, for I assure you that in the future it will be easier to conceive of society without government, than of society with government.

[...]

The People is a collective entity.

They who have exploited the People from time immemorial still hold it in servitude, stand upon this collectivity of its nature, and deduce from this its legal incapacity, which requires their personal control. We, on the contrary, from that collectivity of the People, draw proof that it is completely and perfectly capable, that it can do anything, and needs no one to restrain it. The only question is how to give full play to its powers.

[...]

The judiciary too has gone. What is Justice? Mutual guarantees; that which for two hundred years we have called the Social Contract. Every man who has signed this contract is fit to be a judge: justice for all; authority for none. As for procedure, the shortest is the best. Down with tribunals and jurisdictions!

Last came administration, accompanied by the police. Our decision was taken quickly. Since the People is multiple and unity of interest constitutes its collectivity, centralisation comes about through this unity; there is no need of centralisers. Let each household, each factory, each association, each municipality, each district, attend to its own police, and administer carefully its own affairs, and the nation will be policed and administered. What need have we to be watched and ruled, and to pay, year in and year out, 25 million? Let us abolish prefects, commissioners, and policemen too.

The next question is of schools. This time there is no idea of suppression, but only of converting a political institution into an economic one. If we preserve the methods of teaching now in use, why should we need the intervention of the State?

A community needs a teacher. It chooses one at its pleasure, young or old, married or single, a graduate of the Normal School or self-taught, with or without a diploma. The only thing that is essential is that the said teacher should suit the fathers of families, and that they should be free to entrust their children to them or not. In this, as in other matters, it is essential that the transaction should be a free contract and subject to competition; something that is impossible under a system of inequality, favouritism, and university monopoly, or that of a coalition of Church and State.

As for the so-called higher education, I do not see how the protection of the State is needed, any more than in the former case. Is it not the spontaneous result, the natural focus of lower instruction? Why should not lower instruction be centralised in each district, in each province, and a portion of the funds destined for it be applied to the support of higher schools that are thought necessary, of which the teaching staff should be chosen from that of the lower schools. Every soldier, it is said, carries a marshal's baton in his knapsack. If that is not true, it ought to be. Why should not every teacher bear in his diploma the title of university professor? Why, after the example of what is done in workers companies, as the teacher is responsible to the Academic Council, should not the Academic Council be appointed by the teachers?

Thus even with the present system of instruction, the university centralisation in a democratic society is an attack upon paternal authority, and a confiscation of the rights of the teacher.

But let us go to the bottom of the matter. Governmental centralisation in public instruction is impossible in the industrial system, for the decisive reason that *instruction* is inseparable from *apprenticeship*, and scientific education is inseparable from professional education. So that the teacher, the professor, when he is not himself the foreman, is before everything the man of the association of the agricultural or industrial group which employs him. As the child is the pledge, pignus, between the parents, so the school becomes the bond between the industrial associations and families: it is unfitting that it should be divorced from the workshop, and, under the plea of perfecting it, should be subjected to external power.

To separate teaching from apprenticeship, as is done today, and, what is still more objectionable, to distinguish between professional education and the real, serious, daily, useful practice of the profession, is to reproduce in another form the separation of powers and the distinction of classes, the two most powerful instruments of governmental tyranny and the subjection of the workers.

Let the working class think of this.

If the school of mines is anything else than the actual work in the mines, accompanied by the studies suitable for the mining industry, the school will have for its object, to make, not miners, but chiefs of miners, aristocrats.

If the school of arts and crafts is anything but the art or craft taught, its aim will soon be to make, not artisans, but directors of artisans, aristocrats.

If the school of commerce is anything but the store, the counting house, it will not be used to make traders, but captains of industry, aristocrats.

If the naval school is anything but actual service on board ship, including even the service of the cabin boy, it will serve only as a means of marking two classes, sailors and officers.

Thus we see things go under our system of political oppression and industrial chaos. Our schools, when they are not establishments of luxury or pretexts for sinecures, are seminaries of aristocracy. It was not for the People that the Polytechnic, the Normal School, the military school at St. Cyr, the School of Law, were founded; it was to support, strengthen, and fortify the distinction between classes, in order to complete and make irrevocable the split between the working class and the upper class.

In a real democracy, in which each member should have instruction, both ordinary and advanced, under his control in his home, this superiority from schooling would not exist. It is contradictory to the principle of society. But when education is merged in apprenticeship; when it consists, as for theory, in the classification of ideas; as for practice, in the specialisation of work; when it becomes at once a matter of training the mind and of application to practical affairs in the workshop and in the house, it cannot any longer depend upon the State: it is incompatible with government. Let there be in the Republic a central bureau of education, another of manufactures and arts, as there is now an Academy of Sciences and an Office of Longitude. I see no objection. But again, what need for authority? Why such an intermediary between the student and the schoolroom, between the shop and the apprentice, when it is not admitted between the worker and the employer?

The three bureaus, of Public Works, of Agriculture and Commerce, and of Finance, will all disappear in the economic organism.

The first is impossible, for two reasons: 1st, the initiative of communes and departments as to works that operate within their jurisdiction; 2nd, the initiative of the workers companies as to carrying the works out.

Unless democracy is a fraud, and the sovereignty of the People a joke, it must be admitted that each citizen in the sphere of his industry, each municipal, district or provincial council within its own territory, is the only natural and legitimate representative of the Sovereign, and that therefore each locality should act directly and by itself in administering the interests which it includes, and should exercise full sovereignty in relation to them. The People is nothing but the organic union of wills that are individually free, that can and should voluntarily work together, but abdicate never. Such a union must be sought in the harmony of their interests, not in an artificial centralisation, which, far from expressing the collective will, expresses only the antagonisms of individual wills.

The direct, sovereign initiative of localities, in arranging for public works that belong to them, is a consequence of the democratic principle and the free contract: their subordination to the State is an invention of '93, and a return to feudalism. [...]

I may add that, contrary as is the supremacy of the State to democratic principles in the matter of public works, it is also incompatible with the rights of workers created by the Revolution.

We have already had occasion to show, especially in connection with the establishment of a National Bank and the formation of workers companies, that in the economic order labour subordinated to itself both talent and capital. This the more, because that under the operation, sometimes simultaneous, sometimes independent, of the division of labour and of collective power, it becomes necessary for the workers to form themselves into democratic societies, with equal conditions for all members, on pain of a relapse into feudalism. Among the industries which demand this form of organisation, we have already mentioned railroads. We may add to these the construction and support of roads, bridges and harbours, and the work of afforestation, clearing, drainage, etc., in a word, all that we are in the habit of considering in the domain of the State.

If it becomes thenceforth impossible to regard as mere mercenaries the workers who are closely or distantly connected with the associations for buildings, for waters and forests, for mines; if we are to be forced to see this low mob as sovereign societies; how can we maintain the hierarchical relations of the minister to the heads of departments, of heads of departments to engineers, and of engineers to workers; how, in short, preserve the supremacy of the State?

The workers, much elated by the use of the political rights conferred upon them, will desire to exercise them in their fullness. Associating themselves, they will first choose leaders, engineers, architects, accountants; then they will bargain directly, as one power with another, with municipal and district authorities for the execution of public works. Far from submitting to the State, they will themselves be the State; that is to say, in all that concerns their industrial speciality, they will be the direct, active representative of the

Sovereign. Let them set up an administration, open credit, give pledges, and the Country will find in them a guaranty superior to the State; for they will be responsible at least for their own acts, while the State is responsible for nothing.

[...]

After the Revolution has been accomplished at home will it also be accomplished abroad?

Who can doubt it? The Revolution would be vain if it were not contagious: it would perish, even in France, if it failed to become universal. Everybody is convinced of that. The least enthusiastic spirits do not believe it necessary for revolutionary France to interfere among other nations by force of arms: it will be enough for her to support, by her example and her encouragement, any effort of the people of foreign nations to follow her example.

What then is the Revolution, completed abroad as well as at home?

Capitalist and landlord exploitation stopped everywhere, wage-labour abolished, equal and just exchange guaranteed, value constituted, cheapness assured, the principle of protection changed, and the markets of the world opened to the producers of all nations; consequently the barrier struck down, the ancient law of nations replaced by commercial agreements; police, judiciary administration, everywhere committed to the hands of the workers; the economic organisation replacing the governmental and military system in the colonies as well as in the metropolises; finally, the free and universal commingling of races under the law of contract only: that is the Revolution.

Is it possible that in this state of affairs, in which all interests, agricultural, financial and industrial, are identical and interwoven, in which the governmental protectorate has nothing to do, either at home or abroad, is it possible that the nations will continue to form distinct political bodies, that they will hold themselves separate, when their producers and consumers are mingled, that they will still maintain diplomacy, to settle claims, to determine prerogatives, to arrange differences, to exchange guarantees, to sign treaties, etc., without any object?

To ask such a question is to answer it. It needs no demonstration; only some explanations from the point of view of nationalities.

Let us recall the principle. The reason for the institution of government, as we have said, is the economic chaos. When the Revolution has regulated this chaos, and organised the industrial forces, there is no further pretext for political centralisation; it is absorbed in industrial solidarity, a solidarity which is based upon general reason, and of which we may say, as Pascal said of the universe, that *its centre is everywhere, its circumference nowhere*.

When the institution of government has been abolished, and replaced by the economic organisation, the problem of the universal Revolution is solved. The dream of Napoléon is realised, and the chimera of the Dean of St. Peter's[7] becomes a necessity.

It is the governments who, pretending to establish order among men, arrange them forthwith in hostile camps, and as their only occupation is to produce servitude at home, their art lies in maintaining war abroad, war in fact or war in prospect.

The oppression of peoples and their mutual hatred are two correlative, inseparable facts, which reproduce each other, and which cannot come to an end except simultaneously, by the destruction of their common cause, government.

[...]

If then science, and no longer religion or authority, is taken in every land as the rule of society, the sovereign arbiter of interests, government becoming void, all the legislation of the universe will be in harmony. There will no longer be nationality, no longer fatherland, in the political sense of the words: they will mean only places of birth. Whatever a man's race or colour, he is really a native of the universe; he has citizen's rights everywhere. As in a limited territory the municipality represents the Republic, and wields its authority, each nation on the globe represents humanity, and acts for it within the boundaries assigned by Nature. Harmony reigns, without diplomacy and without council, among the nations: nothing henceforward can disturb it.

[...]

# EPILOGUE

[...]

WHEN SOCIETY HAS turned from within to without, all relations are overturned. Yesterday we were walking with our heads downwards; today we hold them erect, without any interruption to our life. Without losing our personality, we change our existence. Such is the nineteenth century Revolution.

The fundamental, decisive idea of this Revolution is it not this: NO MORE AUTHORITY, neither in the Church, nor in the State, nor in land, nor in money?

No more Authority! That means something we have never seen, something we have never understood; the harmony of the interest of one with the interest of all; the identity of collective sovereignty and individual sovereignty.

No more Authority! That means debts paid, servitude abolished, mortgages lifted, rents reimbursed, the expense of worship, justice, and the State suppressed; free credit, equal exchange, free association, regulated value, education, work, property, domicile, low price, guaranteed: no more

---

7   Charles Irénée Castel, abbé de Saint-Pierre (1658–1743), radical thinker, author of *Projet de paix perpétuelle* (1713). (Editor)

antagonism, no more war, no more centralisation, no more governments, no more priests. Is not that Society emerged from its shell and walking upright?

No more Authority! That is to say further: free contract in place of arbitrary law; voluntary transactions in place of the control of the State; equitable and reciprocal justice in place of sovereign and distributive justice; rational instead of revealed morals; equilibrium of forces instead of equilibrium of powers; economic unity in place of political centralisation. Once more, I ask, is not this what I may venture to call a complete reversal, a turn-over, a Revolution?

[...]

O, personality of man! Can it be that for sixty centuries you have grovelled in this abjection? You call yourself holy and sacred, but you are only the prostitute, the unwearied and unpaid prostitute, of your servants, of your monks, and of your soldiers. You know it, and you permit it. To be GOVERNED is to be kept in sight, inspected, spied upon, directed, law-driven, numbered, enrolled, indoctrinated, preached at, controlled, estimated, valued, censured, commanded, by creatures who have neither the right, nor the wisdom, nor the virtue to do so.... To be GOVERNED is to be at every operation, at every transaction, noted, registered, enrolled, taxed, stamped, measured, numbered, assessed, licensed, authorised, admonished, forbidden, reformed, corrected, punished. It is, under the pretext of public utility, and in the name of the general interest, to be placed under contribution, trained, ransomed, exploited, monopolised, extorted, squeezed, mystified, robbed; then, at the slightest resistance, the first word of complaint, to be repressed, fined, despised, harassed, tracked, abused, clubbed, disarmed, choked, imprisoned, judged, condemned, shot, deported, sacrificed, sold, betrayed; and, to crown all, mocked, ridiculed, outraged, dishonoured. That is government; that is its justice; that is its morality. And to think that there are democrats among us who pretend that there is any good in government; Socialists who support this ignominy, in the name of Liberty, Equality, and Fraternity; proletarians who proclaim their candidacy for the Presidency of the Republic! Hypocrisy! ...

[...]

Political economy is in fact the queen and ruler of this age, although its mercenaries are unwilling to admit it. It is political economy which directs everything, without appearing to do so. If Louis Bonaparte fails in his demand for prorogation, *business* is the cause. If the Constitution is not revised, it is the Stock Exchange which forbids. If the law of the 31$^{st}$ of May is revoked, or at least profoundly modified, it is commerce that has demanded it. If the Republic is invincible, it is because the *interests* protect it. If the peasant, of the earth from of old, embraces the Revolution, it is because the earth, his adored mistress, summons him. If we do not rest on Sunday, it is because industrial and mercantile influences are opposed to it ....

[...]

But you, Republicans of the old school, to whom the desire for advance is not lacking, and respect for authority is the only restraint, can you not for once give rein to your instincts? [...] Forward then, cowards! You have half your body on the brink already. You have said: The Republic is above Universal Suffrage. If you understand the formula, you will not avoid the commentary:

THE REVOLUTION IS ABOVE THE REPUBLIC.

# LETTER TO VILLIAUMÉ

To Monsieur Villiaumé:

MY DEAR VILLIAUMÉ, IT IS BEYOND MY ABILITY TO OFFER YOU THE EXPLA-nations you wish with the extensiveness, precision and rigorous princi-ples you might want me to furnish; that would require thoroughgoing, difficult and protracted effort from which more pressing concerns pre-clude me at the moment, no matter how eager I may be to accommodate you.

Please be content, therefore, with the following few pages and allow me to count on your intelligence and our being good friends to ensure that you will not credit me with views that I do not hold or impute to me conse-quences that are repugnant to my theories.

Here, then, is what I think your impartial criticism should be reminded of:

From 1839 to 1852 my studies had entirely to do with controversy, which is to say that I confined myself to seeking out the essence and value of *ideas per se*, their import and implications, where they led and where they did not lead; in short, I strove to achieve a full and complete grasp of principles, institutions and systems.

So there was much that I denied, in that I found that in almost every particular and place theories were not compatible with their own component parts, institutions not in harmony with their object or purpose, or writers sufficiently informed, independent and logical.

I found that this seemingly peaceable, normal, self-assured society was at the mercy of disorder and antagonism; that it was as bereft of economic sci-ence as of morality; and that this was equally applicable to parties, schools, utopias and systems.

So I embarked, or embarked afresh, on the work of general acknowledge-ment of phenomena, ideas and institutions, eschewing all partisanship and with logic itself my sole criterion.

Such work has not always been understood, the blame for which is surely mine. With regard to matters relating essentially to morality and justice, it has not always been possible for me to remain philosophically cold-blooded and indifferent, especially when dealing with self-serving, dishonest nay-sayers. Consequently I have been taken for a pamphleteer when all I ever wanted to be was a critic; an agitator when I was merely asking for justice; a hate-fuelled partisan when my vehemence was meant solely to rebut unfounded claims; and finally, as a two-faced writer because I was as quick to point out contradiction in those who believed themselves friends of mine as I was in my adversaries.

The upshot of this protracted discussion, this impassioned analysis, has proved highly illuminating for me in my belief that I had stumbled upon what I was looking for, to wit: the true meaning and determination of things *per se*, with traditions, institutions, theories and enshrined conventional beliefs and practices discounted; but this was not meant for the public which only ever read snatches of me and was forever wondering where I was going and what I was after.

Thus, whereas it seems to me that economic and social science can be tackled seriously, thanks to the work of classification I have done, and that I might try my hand at constructing them, the public, which has not kept abreast of my thought processes, finds that I had rendered the darkness denser and heaped up doubt where hitherto there was at least the advantage of being able to breathe and live in utter safety and confidence.

And this is where I find myself after thirteen or fourteen years of criticism or, if you will, of negation. I am embarking upon my POSITIVE study, establishing what they call scientific truth or, in more common parlance, having spent the first half of my career on *demolition*, I am right now engaged in *rebuilding*.[1]

Keep that in mind, dear friend, if you wish to be fair with me and not condemn me wrongly any more than you would sing my praises without good reason. Whilst I would never claim to be the equal of a learned man like Cuvier,[2] I can nevertheless confess to you with some pride that I, in my explorations of economics, was doing something akin to what that great naturalist had done with his fossils. To me the social realm seemed to be in that chaotic state that Cuvier had discerned in the underground world; and so I seized on ideas, institutions and phenomena, in a search for meaning, definition, law, relationships, analogies, etc., labelling my exhibits until such

---

1    Cf. the epigraph to the *System of Economic Contradictions*: "*Destruam et ædificabo*": "I shall destroy and I shall build." (Editor)

2    Georges Frédéric Cuvier (1769–1832), famed naturalist and zoologist, had proposed sweeping renovations of Linnaeus' system for classifying organisms in *Le Règne Animal Distribué d'après son Organisation, pour Servir de Base à l'Histoire Naturelle des Animaux et d'Introduction à l'Anatomie Comparée* (1817). (Editor)

time as I might be able to piece together the whole picture, just as Cuvier had reconstructed the skeleton of the dinothere or some other antediluvian beast.

Did I succeed? Did I go astray? Have I made any discoveries? These are questions for posterity to answer. What I can state is that this is what I did, or at any rate what I meant to do.

And now we come to examples:

1. You ask me what I mean by this proposition: *Property is theft*, and then, how could I, having uttered that proposition, have spoken out equally forcefully against *communism*?

In light of the foregoing explanatory remarks, you will appreciate that your question may serve a double purpose for me: you are either asking me what I was trying to say as an investigator, classifier or critic; or else you want to know what my view ultimately is of the role of property in human society.

On the first count, namely, what I intended to affirm with this phrase, as shocking as it is emphatic, that property is theft, let me answer that I stand by the conclusions of my 1840 *Memoire* and my definition as such. I hold that the principle of property (note that I am talking here about the principle, not the practice and intent) is very substantially the same as or closely approximates to what the morality of nations has so properly condemned and scourged under the designation *theft*; that in this respect, there is no real difference between good and evil; that here we have one of those pairs of terms, like fornication and marriage, between which there is no difference, physically or psychologically speaking, so that if the one is tolerated and even blessed whilst the other is upbraided and abhorred, this is for reasons that it is not appropriate to examine here.

Note that it is not my meaning that fornication should be applauded and marriage abolished: I am most decidedly for the latter and opposed to the former, and the same applies to property and theft.

At this point, I would have to go into long and serious consideration of the usefulness of disclosing such secrets to the public, on the steadfastness of my support for my definition, depicting it on occasion as a war cry against an entire class of citizens. It is up to you to fill in here whatever I refrain from saying. For my part, it is enough that I reiterate to you that, as a critic and classifier of ideas, I abide by my 1840 definition and do not intend to depart from it in any way.

So it only remains to be discovered how I reckon that the principle of *property*, being the same as the principle of *theft*, can become an element of order in society, a force or faculty of our economy.

Here, my dear Villiaumé, my affirmation, pure and unadorned will absolutely have to suffice. To explain myself, I would need to broach the most formidable and difficult issues of concern to the human mind; the distinction between good and evil, justice, freedom, religion, etc. Then I would have to offer you a description of the great machine that goes by the name of society, a description modelled, not upon some abstraction out of my imagination, but upon any society whatsoever; for *society* is society; despite the superficial differences, it is everywhere, always and of necessity identical and adequate to itself, just the way the human body is the human body, whether the skin covering it be white, red or black.

You will appreciate that such an exposition is utterly out of the question for me. All that I can state is that in any situation, in any society, property remains what I said it was: that this is the condition upon which it fulfils its role and has its effect; that to try to correct it is to destroy it; besides, if the disastrous effects of theft have disappeared from what is called property (as they must if theft is to cease being theft and become, if I may say so, *legitimate* or property), this results from the intrusion of another power which changes with the evil character of the principle and endows it with a contrasting virtue.

In short, in the imperfect arrangement of our society, badly controlled by freedom, justice, etc., property frequently, indeed habitually, manifests the effects of out-and-out theft; it is, so to speak, in the state of nature; whereas in a properly regulated society, it steps up from this state of raw nature to the state of a civilised, lawful nature, without thereby ceasing to be itself, pretty much as education raises an individual from a condition of savagery to a civilised state, without his thereby ceasing to be himself, without his actually renouncing his race and his temperament.

All of which, my dear friend, must strike you as oddly paradoxical: but, as you know, everything in science starts out as paradox. Despite the changes that property has undergone already, we still only know it through pagan law (*jus quiritum*) and canon law, which add up to the same thing: both depend on force when they do not reply on mystery. Now, force and mystery, faith and sword, are not valid arguments in philosophy.

2. What I am saying about property goes for other principles of action too, the criticism of which has made less of an impact, although they play no smaller part in society. Among these are, for instance, the *division of labour, monopoly, competition, government* and *community* [*communauté*].

There is not one of these principles which, analysed in itself, is not radically and essentially harmful either to the worker or to the individual or to society, and which is not therefore in some degree deserving of the anathema slapped on property.

And since, in the current state of affairs, there is nothing to stop the random spread of these principles, it is not unreasonable that they should come in for criticism, sometimes from the economists, sometimes from the moralists, and sometimes from the philanthropists or liberals. However, the fact is that they should be looked upon as forces or faculties inherent in the make-up of society and equally liable to extinction, either through exclusion or abandonment.

The best comparison I could draw to property and the principles I am talking about would be with the seven deadly sins: pride, avarice, envy, gluttony, sloth, wrath and laziness. None will rush to their defence, certainly, and Christianity has turned them into the seven demons from Hell. Now the fact is that, in proper psychological terms, the human soul only survives on a diet of these notorious *sins* or fundamental passions; that the entire craft of the moralist consists not of tearing them down or rooting them out but of educating them so as to draw from them the actual virtues that best distinguish man from the animals; dignity, ambition, taste, love, sensuality and courage. I make no mention of laziness or inertia which represent the absence of vitality and death outright.

Between vice and virtue, there is no essential difference; the making of either of them is in the seasoning, the handling, the purpose, the intent, the degree, a host of things.

Likewise, in terms of principle, there is no difference between property and theft; what makes the one just and the other infamous is the *conditions* that accompany them, the circumstances that condition them.

It must be admitted, my dear friend, that these days we are far removed from such a view of matters and that, in our stubborn attachment to tradition, Christian, feudal prejudices, are, instead, wholly disposed to regard property as something sacrosanct and entirely right, good and virtuous, the way we turn virtue into an inspiration from heaven, government into divine right, and authority into absolute law.

In a society in which property, government and all the things I have been talking about, notions that are far from true, are embraced, it is inevitable that frightening abuses will crop up, a ghastly tyranny of which no revolution can ever quite rid us; first and foremost, we must set our thinking to rights and bring things back to their rightful definitions.

3. *Socialism*

In my *Contradictions* I also held the Socialists and the Economists up to ridicule, you say; after 1848, I embraced Socialism. This shift bothers you and you ask for an explanation.

Any word in a language is susceptible to widely differing and occasionally even contradictory uses.

By *Socialism* do you mean that philosophy which teaches the theory of society or social science? This is the *Socialism* to which I subscribe.

Do we mean, not so much the philosophy or the science as the school, the sect, the faction that embraces that science, believes it feasible and quests after it? I am of such a mind. It was in this regard that *Le Peuple* and *Le Représentant du Peuple* in 1848 were both mouthpieces of Socialism.

Even today, I loudly proclaim my Socialism and am more than ever a believer in its success.

But in economic discussions, as it happens, *Socialism* is the name given to that theory which has a tendency to sacrifice the rights of the individual to the rights of society, just as *Individualism* is employed for the theory that tends to sacrifice society to the individual. In this instance, I reject *Socialism* just as I reject *Individualism*; in which I am merely following the example of Pierre Leroux who, whilst declaring himself a Socialist, as I did myself, in 1848, nevertheless in his writings opposed Socialism and asserted the prerogatives of the individual.

### 4. *The Bank of the People or Free Credit*

Here I can do no better than refer you to the articles published by Monsieur Darimon in *La Presse*.[3] The notion of a lending institution organised under the supervision of the State and operating, not for the benefit of some privileged company of investors, but for the benefit of the nation and at the lowest possible rates of interest, is by now such a commonplace as to have been absorbed into the public consciousness; which, day by day, is suggesting fresh means of implementation and regarding which there is no need for me to devise any system of my own.

Such was the challenge, the opposition, the misrepresentation encountered by the core idea that I could and had to affirm and support what was then termed the Programme of the Bank of the People.

Now that opinion has moved on, now that there are twenty solutions offered for the same problem, that implementation now awaits only the initiative of a few hundred producers or the go-ahead from the government; now that the only cause of hesitancy derives from the series of privileges which will be smashed and scattered once this new principle becomes a fact, I have no further reason to fret about what is to become of the idea, let alone to cast around for some special formula.

The idea is in the public domain, as are the ideas of freedom and equality which can never be banished; the choosing of a formula is a matter for general consensus, just as it is up to each individual theorist to tinker with it.

### 5. *Management of Public Utilities.*

As you say, there are three ways in which public utilities can be operated; by the State, like the mail today; by capitalist companies, as all the railways are at present; or, finally, by *workers' associations.*

This third model being the only one that has not been put to the test, it is still somewhat shrouded in an obscurity that I shall strive to dispel.

As with the Bank, there are a number of possible approaches, especially where the raising of capital is concerned.

I shall confine myself to just one of these.

I imagine that back in 1840 when the government awarded the concession to the Northern Railways, in the belief that enterprise was beneath itself, it may have been minded both to do private capital a favour and to offer labour a partnership; which, it seems to me, it could easily have done.

The Company would have been comprised not only of the investors supplying the working capital but of the *share-holders* and the *workers.*

---

3    Louis-Alfred Darimon (1819–1902), writer and editor for *La Presse* and Proudhon's *Le Peuple*. (Editor)

Operating profits split between the workers and the share-holders according to a specific ratio.

The portion of the profits allotted to the workers and then shared around them according to their function, rank, etc., etc.

Workers represented on the Steering Council by half or one third of the members of said Council.

Management, entrusted to a single director or to several, belonging to the "worker" category (i.e. engineers, architects, consultants, etc.).

When the franchise runs out, the Company, having discharged its obligations in terms of interest and dividends payable to its share-holders, reduces its charges accordingly and then becomes a wholly worker-owned venture.

Against this new backdrop, the Company still has to look to the maintenance of the rolling stock, the replacement of vehicles, track relaying and repairs, etc.—The nation owns the railways, the premises, all the equipment and accoutrements which the Company is under an obligation to hand over in good condition on expiry of each franchise, following an audit by arbitrators.

In principle, the State's share-holding is acknowledged... in respect of all the improvements and cost reductions that can be made to operations. That State share-holding will help, on a yearly basis, to determine the reductions to fares to be made, if any.

The State is a full partner on the Council of Oversight and Steering Council, independently of its acknowledged general oversight of any limited liability company under the law.

It is not the purpose of such State meddling to hobble the freedom of the association nor to make it subject to civil service opinion or authority, but merely to watch over the economic and social education of the working class, the nurturing of its ideas, the prudence of its advice, the direction of its morals and to ensure compliance with the principles of freedom and equality upon which the institution is built.

In principle, all of the workforce of the concern are associates, which is to say, participants. However, given the instability of service and the seasonability of work, the Company shall have the option of taking into service, as the need arises, however many wage-earners circumstances may dictate.

Steps are to be taken with regard to anything relating to training, further training and the welfare of the workers; schools, libraries, baths, retirement funds, etc., etc.

In this regard it should primarily be practical experience that provides the insights which theory can never furnish before the event.

Meanwhile, I will admit that I cannot imagine that it could be equally easy to turn over a rail franchise to a company of workers, most of them ignorant, I mean, but appropriately represented and advised, as to a company of share-holders with no interest in anything but their returns and who leave the handling of their interests to presumptuous and often disloyal managers.

There you have it, my dear Villiaumé, what I can tell you; your understanding of these matters is too great for you not to appreciate that in such matters, there is no scope for improvisation and that protracted research is often required before a solution can be found that might be spelled out in barely a single sentence.

Our concern above all else should be with *Right*, until such time as we may get to grips with the implementation of it and I dare to believe that worker association, where matters of public utility are concerned, comes closest to *Right*. Under this arrangement public services, national ownership, workers' rights are all underpinned by guarantee; where will you find such advantages in the present day?

Forgive me, my dear friend, for not being able to offer a better response to your challenges; I am firm in my belief in the truth, and I will vigorously defend it against every falsehood that is identifiable as such by its relation to contradiction, oppression and privilege; but I am not one to flatter myself that I always have it in my possession.

Yours,

P-J PROUDHON

*1857*
*Translation by Ian Harvey*

# STOCK EXCHANGE
# SPECULATOR'S MANUAL
## 4TH EDITION

## PREFACE

[...]

THE AGRICULTURAL AND industrial order, that primary and profound foundation on which rests the social structure, is in full revolution.

Is it a declining nation, disappearing society or superior civilisation that is beginning? The reader will decide. What is certain at least is that a transformation, which I am not examining here, for freedom or servitude, the supremacy of work or the superiority of privilege, is on the agenda. It is the decisive general fact standing out at the top of our industrial inventory.

[...]

The prediction has now been borne out. Industrial anarchy has produced its just consequences; faith in old ideas has also been shaken, and public honesty has disappeared. I challenge anyone to say that he believes otherwise. Therefore, industrial feudalism exists, uniting all the vices of anarchy and subordination, all the corruptions of hypocrisy and scepticism:

A system of anarchic competition and legal coalition;

A system government concessions and State monopolies;

A system of corporations, partnerships, masters and guild-masters;

A system of national debts and popular loans;

A system of capital exploiting labour;

A system of commercial seesawing and stock market banditry;

A system of sublimation of securities and mobilisation of property;

A system in which an increasingly impoverished present consumes the future.

Then, what the prophets of the social transformation themselves did not expect: industrial feudalism is no more solid than industrial anarchy was; like the latter, the former is only another crisis that must pass:

*"Sic erat instabilis tellus, innabilis unda"*[1]

In fact, history has demonstrated that anarchy or feudalism is always due to a lack of balance, to antagonism and social war, for which, in the current state of mind, only a remedy through a more powerful concentration can be imagined, a third period that we will name without any malignant purpose: the industrial empire.

[...]

In closing, toward and against us, the revolution began in 1789, based on economic and social balance, that is, law, freedom, equality, honour, peace, progress, internal joy and all civil and domestic virtues. I am not referring to the government or politics but the industrial republic.

[...]

# FINAL CONSIDERATIONS

[...]

HOWEVER, THE REVOLUTIONARY spirit is always there keeping watch: ancient feudalism, as well, although it crushed the rights of many, was called a revolution in the sense of equality; the same with the new feudalism, subordinating labour and deciding on capitalist exploitation for the benefit of a caste of parasites, is called in its turn a revolution in the sense of sharing, which we have named "liquidation."

In short, according to the law of historic antinomies, an industrial democracy must follow industrial feudalism: that arises from the opposition of terms, as the day follows the night.

[...]

Such is the problem to be resolved in favour of the middle class: we can guess through this discussion that the problem is the same one for which the lower class in turn has claimed the solution.[2]

---

1   From Ovid's description of primordial chaos in *Metamorphoses*, Book I: "Thus air was void of light, and earth unstable." (Translator)

2   Proudhon at this time divided French society into three classes: bourgeoisie, middle class and wage-workers, or lower class. The *petit-bourgeoisie* was middle class, *not* middle-income wage-workers (as the term is usually applied today). In other words, artisans and peasants who worked the tools and land they owned. The bourgeoisie, in contrast, lived off their property by getting others to work or use it in return for profits, interest and rent. While this is a somewhat different terminology than used

By lower class, we mean the one that it is not only distinguished by labour, which also distinguishes, even to a greater degree, the middle class, but the wage-workers. Under good conditions, the condition of wage-workers may be considered as more advantageous with regard to freedom of the heart and mind and, up to a certain point, to the well-being of the individual and the family, but under the general conditions of the workers due to the insecurity of commerce and businesses, the progress of machinery, the depreciation of the labour force and the stupefaction of fragmented work, wage-worker has become synonymous with servitude and poverty. For the wage-earning class, the poorest and most numerous, as poor as it is numerous, reform is always reduced to these three terms:

Guarantee of labour;

Low cost of living;

Higher education in the industrial order as in the scientific and literary orders, therefore a growing participation of workers in the advantages and prerogatives of employers, which means a merging of the classes through the equality of aptitudes and methods.

[...]

### 3. INDUSTRIAL DEMOCRACY: FINANCING OF LABOUR BY LABOUR OR UNIVERSAL MUTUALITY; END OF THE CRISIS

Except for the temperament of outlaws of the Mountain, whose temperament had been hardened by exile to such a degree that it could no longer be shaken, the Empire's strength was based on the fact that neither dynasty, fusion,[3] Church or Republic dared step forward as its successor.

The first thing that the successor would have to do would be to declare all payments suspended and then call, in lieu of parliament, a creditors' assembly in order to obtain a liquidation arrangement. Such a job could not be assigned to a Bourbon, an Orléans or even a Lamartine or General Cavaignac. Who among them would want to return at that price? It would be worse than returning, like Louis XVIII, for whom it was the only way to return, in foreign wagons. Only a Union of *Public Safety* would be strong enough to undertake such a financial redistribution: where are the Carnots, Cambons, Prieurs and Barrères who would comprise it?[4] Those of us for whom that

---

beforehand, Proudhon's position had not changed. He still desired co-operation between the middle class (*la petit-bourgeoisie*) and the working class (*le salariat*) to transform the latter into the former by abolishing the landlords and capitalists (*la bourgeoisie*). (Editor)

3    "Fusion" refers to an alliance between the rival Orléanist and Legitimist political factions. See the Glossary entry for "July Revolution." (Editor)

4    Lazare Carnot (1753–1823), Pierre Joseph Cambon (1756–1820), Pierre-Louis Prieur (1756–1827), and Bertrand Barère (1755–1841), members of the Committee of Public Safety that oversaw the Reign of Terror after the French Revolution

type of solution would not be satisfactory because it guarantees nothing, who moreover do not believe ourselves genius enough to solve problems posed in contradictory terms, we will confine ourselves, after noting the progress of the new revolution, to presenting its definitive formula according to the most significant symptoms at the present time.

## I. Workers' associations

The thought that first inspired them was naïve and unfortunately illusory. Freeing labour from its employers, workers were to form associations among themselves in order to enjoy the supposedly enormous profits and prerogatives reserved up until then for the heads of companies. They ignored the fact that in most if not all of the industries the workers' groups occupied—those in which, above all, spontaneous association seemed to be immediately practical—the profits, when they existed, were enough for one person but nothing when divided among multitudes. In a large factory, the redistribution of the owner's profits to the wage-workers he employs would not increase wages varying from 0.5 to 1.5 francs by 10%, and so would only bring slight relief to the workers' destitution. Thus it is in all occupations considered together: the owner's net income, which we must usually consider as the fruit of his specific business deals and compensation for his risks, is not what causes the workers' misery; therefore, the demand for that *net profit* will not relieve it. Of the 4 billion that labour must pay each year to maintain the feudal regime, the net income, received in the form of dividends and interest, does not reach 100 million, so the assumed cause-and-effect relationship between net income and pauperism is not there.

Workers' associations, founded on hatred of the employers, on a notion of substitution, were all too quick to make such an assumption. Other miscalculations, the result of inexperience and prejudice, of carrying out ideas of centralisation, community [*communauté*], hierarchy, supremacy and parliamentary politics, quickly sowed division and discouragement. All the abuses of corporations, owned by anonymous stockholders, were repeated on a larger scale in those so-called fraternal companies. They had dreamed of cornering every industry, rendering "free" companies void and dead, replacing the bourgeoisie with the proletariat once and for all. The better to emancipate the People, they intended to exclude from the circle of workers' communities those who had until then been the representatives of freedom! That error was long in yielding consequences. Of the several hundred workers' associations that existed in Paris in 1850–1851, there are barely 20 left. They owe their salvation solely to the abandonment of the utopian ideas of 1848 and the recognition of the true principles of social economy. In this regard, those associations merit study all the more because the phenomenon of their existence reveals a positive element of financial and industrial speculation.

(1793–1795). (Editor)

The problem for the workers' associations, outside of which they fall back fatally into the limbo of religious brotherhoods, is divided into two related questions:

1. In the competition of forces and in their combination, is there a productive potentiality that could produce financially substantial results so that workers could use it to amass the capital they are lacking and to transform themselves from wage-workers to participants?

In other words, can labour, like capital, finance businesses by itself?

2. Can the ownership and management of companies, instead of remaining individual as it has always usually been, perhaps gradually become collective to the point of providing the working classes, on the one hand, with a decisive guarantee of emancipation, and on the other hand, providing civilised nations with a revolution in the relationship between labour and capital, definitively replacing the interests of the State with justice in the political order?

The workers' entire future depends on the answer to these questions. If the answers are affirmative, a new world opens up to humanity; if they are negative, the proletariat will know it. As God and the Church advise, there is no hope for them in this base world: *Lasciate ogni speranza!*[5]

First, we understand that the solution to the problem will not come from an enthusiastic multitude only obeying its instincts and in whom a long oppression has killed intelligence. Immediate initiators are necessary here from the working masses, people from among their midst who have received from the civilisation of which they bear the burden a sum of knowledge and have learned enough in the exploiters' schools to now do without the exploiters. There are only a few such initiators with one foot in civilisation and the other in barbarism, even in the most industrially advanced nations, such as France and England. What is worse is that those elite workers, precisely due to their ambiguous nature, are generally, with regard to their less-educated co-workers, the least welcome, if not the most averse of all people. With barbarism on the one side and pride on the other, it seems that the working class, with all its categories, conspires against its own freedom.

"When," says an English economist, "the uneducated English workmen are released from the bonds of iron discipline in which they have been restrained by their employers in England, and are treated with the urbanity and friendly feeling which the more educated workmen on the Continent expect and receive from their employers, they, the English workmen, completely lose their balance: they do not understand their position, and after a certain time become totally unmanageable and useless. This result of observation is borne out by experience in England itself. As soon as any idea of equality enters the mind of an uneducated English workingman, his head is

5    From the words marking the entrance to Hell in Dante's *Inferno*: "Lasciate ogni speranza, voi ch'entrate" ("Abandon hope, all ye who enter here"). (Translator)

turned by it. When he ceases to be servile, he becomes insolent" (J. Stuart Mill, *Principles of Political Economy with some of their Applications to Social Philosophy*, I.7.5).

This weakness, which is no longer rare among French workers and is worsened even further by an excessive mobility of character, constitutes in the present state of society, in which the proletariat can expect nothing except from itself, the greatest obstacle to its liberation.

It is a question then, and that is where all the difficulty lies, of forming a union of workers with a certain dose of morality and intelligence, able to conceive of socio-economic laws and firmly desiring to follow them to the exclusion of all the fantasies and hallucinations of the time: in short, with regard to the question we have just asked, it is a matter of amassing not financial capital [*un masse de capitaux*] but human capital [*un fonds d'hommes*].

Once those initiators are found, a number of workers, or, to put it better, collaborators, must be gathered around each of them, destined to become, in each category of work, a model society, a true embryonic rebirth.

We ask if this group possesses in itself a particular productive force.

*Labour*, as we said in our INTRODUCTION, is a productive force, the first of all and the most powerful; *Capital* is another one, *Commerce* another and *Speculation* one more. We can add *Property*, *Credit*, *Competition*, etc. to that list. In Economy, everything that is an action or principle of action is a productive force. That said, apart from the labour of each individual worker and the Capital that they serve and are exploited by, is the *Group* of workers, like *Division of Labour*, also a force? Can this force stand in place of Capital and do without its protection?

The facts, more eloquent in their spontaneity than theories, are going to respond.

We have visited workers' associations. We have followed their situation since their origin up until December 31st, 1853, and from 1853 until 1856; we have studied their internal discipline and principles, more or less clearly expressed in their articles, which govern everything. We believe we have pleased the public by publishing the details you are about to read on the transformation gathering steam in the industrial economy beyond the formulas of the Code and legal predictions.

All these associations are founded on the following bases:

1.   Unlimited ability to ceaselessly admit new partners or members; consequently, there is a perpetuity and infinite multitude of companies, the constitution of which is universalist in nature.

2.   Labour's progressive formation of capital; in other words, labour's partnership with labour, so that the workers themselves manufacture for each other, according to their specialities, the tools and furnishings they respectively need, or by means of levies on the price of sales and services or monthly deductions from wages.

3. Participation of all partners in the management of the company and its profits within the limits and proportions determined by the company's constitution.
4. Piecework and proportional wages.
5. Constant company recruitment among workers to be employed as auxiliaries.
6. Retirement and relief fund based on a wage and profit levy.

To these fundamental conditions, which we can view as the common law of the associations, it would be suitable to soon add the following, which, as we have remarked several times, are the necessary complement to the system:

7. Progressive education of apprentices.
8. Mutual guarantee of work, that is, supply, consumption and adequate market among the various associations.
9. Publication of writings.

Such is, in its essence, the fundamental law of Workers' Companies: we leave aside the details of practices specific to each of them. Furthermore, of course, the principles we have just described are not written in the duly authenticated articles of the associations. Our commercial legislation and the courts in charge of interpreting that legislation would not tolerate the perpetuity, universality, declaration of the absence of capital, participation of worker-partners in the administration and profits or mutualism of the associations. The new business members had to comply with received legal practices, but they understood the implications of what is impermissible to say and acted accordingly. We see what these workers, without advice and resources, have drawn from that and what they can continue to acquire.

It is impossible for us to go into the details here of the operations and inventories of each association as we did in the second edition of this Manual.

It is enough for us to recall and state that the corporate funds in all of these companies started at zero, as did civilisation's; in a few years, they increased, depending on the importance of the industry and the number of partners, to 20,000, 30,000, 50,000 and 60,000 francs. Since 1853, this progress has been sustained, and the company funds of the Companies today also have a reserve and relief fund formed with a levy on profits. Any idea of communism has now been abandoned, and equal well-being has been subject to equality or equivalence of services with the equality of guarantees as the fulcrum.

As a corollary, workers are persuaded that the fortune of the Associations is much less in their extension than in their mutuality: experience has taught them that the association, if it is a liberal one free from any personal dependency, domestic solidarity or administrative exploitation one can imagine, still requires some education on the part of its subjects. *We are not born associates,* one of them told us; *We become them.* Is that not a translation of the famous expression: *Homo homini aut deus aut lupus?*[6]

[...]

Moreover, all of them [the workers' companies] were riddled with adversity, lack of work and poverty, plagued by parliamentary politics, discord, rivalries, defections and treasons. They paid the price for inexperience, charlatanism, infatuation and bad faith. The human mind needs time to define its principles, and as long as they are undefined, the conscience is open to problems and iniquity. Some companies' managers, once they were introduced to the business world, withdrew from the associations to establish themselves as employers and bourgeoisie; furthermore, there are the associates who, from the moment of the first inventory, claimed and left with their rightful share of the proceeds. It is true that long reflection is as repugnant to the modern proletariat as it was to the ancient slave and that the most difficult task of the associations is not to form themselves and survive but to civilise their associates. Similar details, interesting above all from a psychological perspective, on the history of the workers' associations, could not be included in this pamphlet, in which there is only room for the issue of the financial results and the economic power of those associations at the very most.

We now continue and conclude.

Workers' Associations are the locus of a new principle and model of production that must replace present-day corporations, in which we do not know who is the more shamefully exploited, the workers or the shareholders.

The principle that prevailed there, in place of that of employers and employees, after a trial entry into communism, is participation, that is, the MUTUALITY of services supplementing the force of division and the force of collectivity.

There is mutuality, in fact, when in an industry, all the workers, instead of working for an owner who pays them and keeps their product, work for one another and thereby contribute to a common product from which they share the profit.

However, extend the principle of mutuality that unites the workers of each group to all the Workers' Associations as a unit, and you will have created a form of civilisation that, from all points of view—political, economic, aesthetic—differs completely from previous civilisations, that can no longer return to feudalism or imperialism, with all possible guarantees of freedom, fair advertising, an impenetrable system of insurance against theft, fraud, misappropriation, parasitism, nepotism, monopoly, speculation, exorbitant rent, living expenses, transportation and credit; against overproduction, stagnation, gluts, unemployment, disease, and poverty, with no need for *charity* because it will provide us instead, everywhere and always, with our right.

Then, no more anticipated achievements, the bounty hunt, subsidies to be shared among ministers, procurers, lawyers and administrators; no more

---

6   Erasmus: "Man is to man either a god or a wolf." (Translator)

hush money paid by suppliers and disloyal managers; no more stock market killings, feats of accumulation and *latifundia*. The inequality of conditions and fortunes will have disappeared, returned to its basic expression that lies in the differences blind Nature creates among workers, which education and the division of labour, etc., must continually decrease.

Probity, honour and morals have fled the bourgeois world as they fled the feudal world before the revolution. They will only be encountered there.

Certainly, there is a great leap between a few hundred workers forming companies and the economic reconstitution of a nation of 36 million. Furthermore, we do not expect such a reform solely from the expansion of those associations. What is important is that the idea works, that it has been demonstrated by experience; law arises in practice as in theory.

We already know that our French example is bearing fruit abroad: corporations of workers in England have decided that, in the future, instead of spending their funds on useless strikes, they will use them to create companies based on the Parisian model. The final shock, that aforementioned inevitable liquidation, has been coming for more than eight years: it will be easier to organise work throughout the country than it has been, since 1848, to form the first 20 workers' groups in Paris.

### II. Consumers' associations

The goal of these associations, such as the *Ménagère*, is to resolve the special problem of industry-industry relations and therefore Association-Association relations. They are primarily due to bourgeois initiative. Their existence proves that if, in 1848 as always, popular instinct understands ideas in their synthesis, the average intellect, with some training, will address itself first of all and with remarkable nimbleness of intelligence to the heart of the question.

Although the internal administration of these purely commercial Companies did not present the same problems as those of the Workers' Associations, they had the valuable merit, in an era of revolutionary agitation, of appearing as a conciliation of interests. It was a step toward that fusion of employers and employees that the utopians denounced as treason toward the People and the radicals as an instant banishment of democracy.

The combination in question was less, in fact, a Company than a coalition through which a certain number of consumers guarantee a business establishment a steady clientele and constant market in return for a reduction on the current prices of products. The businesses' profits, which, due to random luck, were higher than those of the industry in general, permitted a significant reduction of prices and corresponding improvement in the position of consumers. The consequence, more or less rapid, for such establishments has been to gradually guarantee to each consumer, based on his consumption, the labour he needs in the same manner as that consumer guarantees a market to the merchant. All consumption presupposes production: those two terms are correlative and adequate to one another.

We believe that there was reason for optimistic speculation: unfortunately, this exceeds the ordinary reach of workers, whose unmanageability is so difficult to overcome, and who do not provide the bourgeoisie with immediate enough advantages for them to resign themselves to the effort, advances, and possible sacrifices required at the beginning. However, Consumers' Associations have started to multiply in the county seats of the departments thanks to the sponsorship of some bourgeois who have thus given their fellow citizens co-operative bakeries, butcher shops and grocery stores. The police closed several of them following December 2$^{nd}$: we cannot report on the status of this movement today.

1858

*Translation by Shawn P. Wilbur (Programme) and Jesse Cohn (Fourth Study: Little Political Catechism)*

# JUSTICE IN THE REVOLUTION AND IN THE CHURCH

## PROGRAMME

### §I: THE COMING OF THE PEOPLE TO PHILOSOPHY

AT THE BEGINNING OF A NEW WORK, WE MUST EXPLAIN OUR TITLE AND OUR design.

Ever since humanity entered the period of civilisation, for as long as anyone remembers, the people, said Paul Louis Courier, have *prayed* and *paid*.

They pray for their princes, for their magistrates, for their exploiters and parasites;

They pray, like Jesus Christ, for their executioners;

They pray for the very ones who should by rights pray for them.

Then they pay those for whom they pray;

They pay the government, the courts, the police, the church, the nobility, the crown, the revenue, the proprietor and the *garnisaire*, I meant the soldier;

They pay for every move they make, pay to come and to go, to buy and to sell, to eat, drink and breathe, to warm themselves in the sun, to be born and to die;

They even pay for the permission to work;

And they pray to heaven to give them enough, by blessing their labour, to always pay more.

The people have never done anything but pray and pay: we believe that the time has come to make them philosophise.

The people cannot live in scepticism, after the example of the gentlemen of the Institute and of the beautiful souls of the city and the court. Indifference is unhealthy for them; they reject libertinage; they hasten to flee from that corruption which invades from on high. Besides, what they ask for themselves, they want for everyone, and make no exception for anyone. They have never claimed, for example, that the bourgeoisie must have a religion, that religion is necessary for the regulars at the Bourse, for the bohemians of the magazines and the theatres, or for that innumerable multitude living from prostitution and intrigue; but that, as for them, their robust consciences have no need of God. The people want neither to dupe nor to be duped any longer: what they call for today is a positive law, based in reason and justice, which imposes itself on all, and which nobody is allowed to mock.

Would a reform of the old religion be enough to respond to this wish of the people? No. The people have realised that religion had not been legal tender for a long time among the upper classes, while they continued to believe in it; that, even in the temples, it had lost all credit and all prestige; that it counts for absolutely nothing in politics and business; finally, that the separation of faith and law has become an axiom of government everywhere. The tolerance of the State now covers religion, which is precisely the opposite of what had taken place in the past. Thus the people have followed the movement inaugurated by their leaders; it is wary of the spiritual, and it no longer wants a religion which has been made an instrument of servitude by clerical and anticlerical Machiavellianism. Whose fault is that?

But are the people capable of philosophy?

Without hesitation we answer: Yes, as well as reading, writing and arithmetic; as well as understanding the catechism and practising a craft. We even go as far as to think philosophy can be found in its entirety in that essential part of public education, the trade: a matter of attention and habit. Primary instruction requires three years, apprenticeship three more, for a total of six years: when philosophy, the popularisation of which has become a necessity of the first order in our times, must be taken by the plebeian, in addition to the six years of primary and professional instruction to which he is condemned, an hour per week for six more years, would that be a reason to deny the philosophical capacity of the people?

The people are philosophical, because they are as weary of praying as of paying. They have had enough of the pharisee and the publican; and all it desires, and the point we have reached, is to know how to direct its ideas, and to free itself from this world of tolls and paternosters. It is to this end that we have resolved, with some friends, to consecrate our forces, certain as we are that, if sometimes this philosophy of the people spreads a bit too much from our pen, the truth, once known, will not lack abbreviators.

## §II: THE DEFINITION OF PHILOSOPHY

Philosophy is composed of a certain number of questions that have been regarded at all times as the fundamental problems of the human mind, and that for that reason have been declared inaccessible to the common people. Philosophy, it was said, is the science of the universal, the science of principles, the science of causes; this is why we can speak of universal science, the science of things visible and invisible, the science of God, of man and of the world, *Philosophia est scientia Dei, hominis et mundi.*[1]

We believe that the questions which philosophy occupies itself are all questions of common sense; we believe all the more that, far from constituting a universal science, these questions only deal with the very conditions of knowledge. Before we think of becoming erudite, it is necessary to begin by being philosophical. Is that so much to boast of?

Thus the first and most important question, for all of philosophy, is to know what philosophy is, what it wants, and above all what it can do. What does all this come down to? The reader will judge.

Philosophy, following the etymological signification of the word, the constant practice of thinkers, the most certain results of their labours, and the best-accredited definitions, is *the Search for*, and, insofar as it is possible, *the Discovery of the reason of things.*

It has required much time and effort by the seekers, to come to that conclusion, which it seems the first comer would have found, if he had only followed common sense, and which everyone will definitely understand.

It follows that philosophy is not science, but the preliminary to science. Isn't it rational to conclude, as we just did, that education, instead of ending with philosophy, must begin with it? What we call the *philosophy of history*,

---

1   The French word "science," here as elsewhere, is sometimes best translated by the same word in English, and at other points may be better translated as "knowledge." As Raymond Williams notes, the narrowing of the term "science" from meaning nearly any kind of systematic or comprehensive knowledge to meaning primarily the specific kinds of knowledge produced by the methods of the natural sciences took place in the English language, between the 17th and 19th centuries, to an extent that it never did in Romance languages; accordingly, "this causes considerable problems in contemporary translation, notably from French" (see *Keywords: A Vocabulary of Culture and Society* [New York: Oxford University Press, 1985], 279). Proudhon's understanding of what renders knowledge *scientifique* or *positive* owes something, it is true, to Auguste Comte's "positivism," with its ambition to found an experimentally verifiable, materialist "science of society" on grounds as certain as those of physics; it also owes something to the idealism of Immanuel Kant and the relativism of Giambattista Vico. At times, then, rendering *la science* and even *scientifique* by their English cognates may have the effect of making Proudhon seem to be laying claim to a kind of knowledge that is more objective and physics-like than what he intends. (Editor)

or the *philosophy of the sciences*, is only an ambitious way to designate science itself, that is to say, that which is most detailed, most generalised in our knowledge, scientists by profession liking to stick to the pure and simple description of facts, without seeking their reason. As the reason of things is discovered, it assumes its place in science, and the scientist follows the philosopher.

Let us examine our definition more closely.

The word *thing*, one of the most general in the language, must be understood here to refer, not only to external objects, in opposition to persons, but to all that which, in the man himself, both physical and moral, can furnish material for observation: sentiments and ideas, virtue and vice, beauty and ugliness, joy and suffering, speculations, errors, sympathies, antipathies, glory and decadence, misery and felicity. Every manifestation of the human subject, in a word, all that passes in his soul, his understanding and his reason, as well as in his body; everything that effects him, either as an individual or in society, or which emanates from him, becoming thus an object of philosophy, is considered, with regard to the philosopher, a thing.

By *reason* we mean the how and why of things, as opposed to their *nature*, which is impenetrable. Thus, in each thing, the philosopher will note the beginning, duration and end; the size, the shape, the weight, the composition, the constitution, the organisation, the properties, the power, the faculties; the increase, the diminution, the evolutions, series, proportions, relations and transformations; the habits, variations, *maxima, minima* and means; the attractions, appetites, accompaniments, influences, analogies; in short all that can serve to name known the phenomenality of things and their laws. He will abstain from all investigation, and from any conclusion, on the very nature or *en soi* of things, for example on *matter, mind, life, force, cause, substance, space* or *time*, considered in themselves, and setting aside their appearances or phenomena.

Thus, by its definition, philosophy declares that there is a side in things which is accessible to it, which is their reason, and another side about which it can know absolutely nothing, which is their *nature:* can one show at once more sincerity and more prudence? And what would be better for the people than this modesty?... Philosophy, by its own testimony, is the search for, and, if possible, the discovery of the reason of things; it is not the search for, and still less the discovery of their nature: we will not complain about this distinction. What would a nature be without a reason or appearances? And if the latter were known, who would dare to say that the former was to be missed?

*To render account,* in three words, of that which occurs inside, that he observes or carries out outside, of which his senses and his consciousness give testimony, and the reason of which his mind can penetrate: that, for man, is what it is to philosophise, and all that which allows itself to be grasped by the eyes and the mind is matter for philosophy. As for the intimate nature of things, that *je ne sais quoi* of which metaphysics cannot stop talking, and which it imagines or conceives after having set aside the phenomenality of things as well as their reason, if that residue is not a pure *nothing*, we do not know what to make of it; it interests neither our sensibility nor our intelligence, and it does not even have anything in it to excite our curiosity.

Well, now. In what way is all that outside the range of the common people? Just as we are, do we not incessantly, and without knowing it, make philosophy, as the good M. Jourdain made prose? Who is the man who, in the affairs of the world, concerns himself with anything but that which interests his mind, his heart or his senses? To make ourselves consummate philosophers, it is only a question of making ourselves more sensitive to what we do, feel and say: is that so difficult? As for the contemplative, those who wanted to see beyond the reason of things and to philosophise on their very nature, they have ended by putting themselves outside nature and reason; they are the lunatics of philosophy.

## §III: ON THE QUALITY OF THE PHILOSOPHICAL MIND

But here is a rather different affair! It is a question of knowing if philosophy, of which it was first said that the people were incapable, will not, by its very practice, create inequality among men. What can we conclude from our definition?

Since philosophy is the search for, and, so far as it is possible, the discovery of the reason of things, it is clear that, in order to philosophise well, the first and most necessary condition is to is to observe things carefully; to consider them successively in all their parts and all their aspects, without permitting oneself a notion of the ensemble before being certain of the details. This is the precept of Bacon and Descartes, the two fathers of modern philosophy. Couldn't one say that in expounding it, they thought especially of the people? Philosophy is all in the observation, internal and external: there is no exception to that rule.

The philosopher, the man who seeks, who still does not know, can be compared to a navigator charged with making a map of an island, and who, in order to carry out his mission, being unable to take a photograph of the country from high in the atmosphere, is obliged to follow with attention, and to record one after another on paper, with exactitude, all the sinuosities and crevices of the coast. The circumnavigation completed, and the summary of observations finished, the geographer would have obtained as faithful a representation as possible of the island, in its parts and in the ensemble, which he never could have done, if, holding himself at a distance, he had been limited to drawing perspectives and landscapes.

The philosopher can also be compared to a traveller who, after having traversed in all directions a vast plain, having recognised and visited the woods, the fields, the meadows, the vineyards, the habitations, etc., would then climb a mountain. As he made his ascent, the objects would pass again before his eyes in a general panorama, which would make him understand that of which the inspection of the details had only given him an incomplete idea.

Thus, he must stick close to the facts and constantly refer to them, divide his material, make complete counts and exact description. He must go from simple notions to the most comprehensive formulas, testing his views of the ensemble and the glimpsed details against one another. Finally, where immediate observation becomes impossible, to show himself sober in his conjectures, circumspect with regard to probabilities, to challenge analogies, and to judge only self-consciously, and always with reserve, distant things by those near, the invisible by the visible.—Under these conditions, would it be too much to say that the practical man is closer to the truth, less subject to illusion and to error than the speculative one? Regular contact with things preserves him from fantasy and vain systems: if the *practitioner* shines little from invention, he also courts less risk of making a mistake, and rarely loses by waiting. *He who works, prays*, says an old proverb. Can we not also say: He who works, in so far as he pays attention to his work, philosophises?

It is only by following this scrupulous and slowly rising method of observation, that the philosopher could flatter himself to have reached the summit of philosophy, science, the condition of which is double, certainty and synthesis. These words should frighten no one: here again the most transcendent philosophy contains nothing outside the abilities and reach of the people.

Indeed, a man may have seen more of things than is common among his fellows; he may have viewed them in more detail and more closely; he can thus consider them from a higher level and in a larger ensemble: this question of quantity, which has no influence on the quality of the knowledge, adds nothing to the certainty, and consequently does not increase the value of the mind. This is of extreme importance for the determination of personal right, constitutive of society: allow me to clarify my thought with some examples.

2 multiplied by 2 equals 4: this is, for everyone, a perfect certainty. But how much is 27 multiplied by 23? Here, more than one innocent will hesitate, and if he has not learned to calculate by figures, it will take a long time to find the solution, let alone dare to respond. Thus I take up the pen, and making the multiplication, I respond that the product demanded is 621. Now, knowing so easily the product of 27 times 23, and being able with the same promptitude and sureness to make the multiplication of all the possible numbers by all the possible numbers, I am clearly more knowledgeable that the one whose arithmetic capacity will stop at the elementary operation 2 x 2 = 4. Does this make me more certain? Not at all. The quantity of knowledge, I repeat, adds nothing to the philosophical quality of the knowing: it is by virtue of that principle, and another just like in that we will speak of below, that French law, coming out of the Revolution of '89, has declared us all equal before the law. Between two citizens, between two men, there can be

inequality of acquired knowledge, of effective labour, of services rendered; there is no inequality of the quality of reason: such is, in France, the foundation of personal right, and such is the basis of our democracy. The old regime did not reason in the same way: is it clear now that philosophy is the legacy of the people?

It is the same for the comprehensive power of the mind.

2 multiplied by two produces 4, and 2 added to 2 also gives 4: on one side the product, on the other the sum are equal. However little the innocent to whom one makes the remark reflects on it, he will realise that addition and multiplication, although they begin from two different points of view and proceed in two different manners, resolve themselves, in this particular case, in an identical operation. By making a new effort, he will comprehend as well that 2 minus 4 or 4 divided by 2, it always remains 2, as subtraction and division still resolve, in this particular case, into one single and same operation. All this will interest, and perhaps astonish him: he will have, in the measure from 2 to 4, a synthetic view of things. But the arithmetician knows much more, and his synthesis is incomparably more comprehensive. He knows that whenever one operates on numbers larger than 2, the results can no longer be the same; that multiplication is an abbreviated addition, and division an abbreviated subtraction as well; that more, subtraction is the opposite of addition, and division the opposite of multiplication; in summary, that all these operations, and others more difficult which are deduced from them, come down to the art of composing and decomposing the series of numbers. Does this give him the right to believe himself superior to the other, in nature and dignity? Certainly not: the only difference is that one has learned more than the other; but reason is the same for both of them, and this is why the legislator, at once a revolutionary and a philosopher, has decided that he will take no account of persons. It is for this reason, finally, that modern civilisation tends invincibly to democracy: where philosophy reigns, where as a consequence the identity of philosophical reason is recognised, the distinction of classes, like the hierarchy of church and State, is impossible.

We can make analogous arguments about all of the genres of knowledge, and we will always arrive at that decisive conclusion, that, for whoever *knows*, certainty is of the same quality and degree, despite the extent of the knowledge; just as, for whoever grasps the relation of several objects or ideas, the synthesis is of the same quality and form, despite the multitude relations grasped. In no case will there be room to distinguish between the reason of the people and the reason of the philosopher.

### §IV: THE ORIGIN OF IDEAS

Here is the great temptation, I should say the great conspiracy of the philosophers; here is also their chastisement.

This principle so luminous, so simple, that in order to know the reason of things, it is necessary to have seen them, has not always been accepted (can you believe it?) in philosophy. Without speaking of those, in so great a number, aspired to sound the nature of things, one encounters profound geniuses who have asked if the human mind, so subtle and so vast, could not, by a concentrated meditation on itself; come to that intelligence of the reason of things, which is only, after all, the intelligence of the laws of the mind; if the man who thinks had such a need, in order to learn, to consult a nature which does not think; if a soul created in the image of God, the sovereign organiser, did not possess, by virtue of its divine origin, and prior to its communication with the world, the ideas of things, and if it truly needed the control of phenomena in order to recognise ideas, that is, eternal exemplars. I think, thus I know, *cogito, ergo cognosco* such is the principle of these arch-spiritualist philosophers. Never has a brain which came from the ranks of the people conceived of a chimera like that. Some, interpreting in their own way the hyper-physical dogma of creation, go so far as to pretend that external realities are products of pure thought, and the world an expression of mind, so that it would be enough to have the full possession of the Idea, innate it our soul, but more or less obscured, in order, without further information, to possess the reason and grasp the very nature of the universe!

That manner of philosophising, which would dispense with all observation and experience, if it had been justified by the least success, would be, we must admit, very attractive and could not be more convenient. The philosopher would no longer be that laboured explorer, winning the bread of his soul by the sweat of his brow, always exposed to error by the omission of the least detail, reaching only a limited comprehension, obtaining often, instead of certainty, only probabilities, and sometimes ending in doubt, after having lived through an affliction of mind. He would be a clairvoyant, a miracle-worker [*thaumaturge*], a rival to the Divinity, directing thought as a sovereign, to say nothing of creative power, and reading fluently the mysteries of Heaven, Earth and Humanity, at home with the divine thought. Ambition, as one sees, is never lacking among the philosophers.

Where does this titanic presumption come from?

From the start we have sensed, in a confused manner, what philosophical observation later clarified, that, in the formation of ideas, the perception of phenomena does not render reason by itself; that the understanding, by the constitution which is proper to it, plays a role; that the soul is not exclusively passive in its conceptions, but that in receiving the images or impressions from outside it, it reacts to them and derives ideas from them; so that, for half if not for all, the extrication of ideas, or the discovery of the truth in things, is the work of the mind.

Thus, it was said, we find in the soul, like the moulds of ideas, archetypal ideas, prior to all observation of phenomena: what were these ideas? Can we recognise them, among the multitude of those, more or less empirical, that the understanding imprints with its own stamp? How to distinguish the patrimony of the mind from its acquisitions? If something in knowledge properly belongs to it, then why no everything? Wouldn't we be justified in supposing that if the mind, possessing the innate principles of things, advanced in knowledge only with the aid of arduous observation, this was due to the heterogeneous union of the soul and the body, a union in which the ethereal substance, offended by the material, had lost the greater part of its knowledge and acuity, retaining only a memory of the fundamental principles that had formed its framework and its property?... Others attributed the darkening of the intelligence to original sin. Man, for having wanted to eat, against the express order of God, the fruit of science, would be, according to them, blinded. All the rest convince themselves that with a good mental discipline and the help of the Spirit of light, one could restore the human soul to the enjoyment of its high and immortal prerogatives, make it produce science without any imbibition of experience, by the energy of his nature alone, and by virtue of the axiom already cited: I am the child of God; I think, therefore I know...

What was at the bottom of all that? A diabolical thought of domination: for one must not be mistaken, privilege of knowledge and pride of genius are the most implacable enemies of equality. Now one thing is known: human knowledge is not enriched by the slightest scrap of a fact or idea by this exclusively spiritual practice. Nothing has served: neither metaphysics nor dialectics, nor the theory of the absolute, nor revelation, nor possession, nor ecstasy, nor magnetism, nor magic, nor theurgy, nor catalepsy, nor ventriloquy, nor the philosopher's stone, nor table-turning. All that we know, we have invariably learned, and the mystics, the illuminati, the somnambulists, even the spirits with which they speak, have learned in their turn by the known means, that is, observation, experience, reflection, calculation, analysis and synthesis: God, doubtless, jealous of his work, wanting to maintain the decree that he had entered, namely, that we would see nothing with the eyes of the mind except by the intermediary of the eyes of the body, and that all that we claim to perceive by other means would be an error and a mystification of the devil. There is no occult knowledge, no transcendent philosophy, no privileged soul, no divinatory genius, no *medium* between infinite wisdom and the common sense of mortals. Sorcery and magic, once pursued by parliaments, are dispelled by the flame of experimental philosophy; the science of the heavens had only begun to exist on the day when the Copernicuses, the Galileos and the Newtons bid an eternal *adieu* to astrology. The metaphysics of the ideal taught nothing to Fichte, Schelling and Hegel:[2] when these men, whose philosophy is rightly honoured, imagined they had deduced *a priori*, they had only, without knowing it, synthesised

---

2    Johann Gottlieb Fichte (1762–1814), Friedrich Wilhelm Joseph Schelling (1775–1854), and G. W. F. Hegel (1770–1831), German idealist philosophers who argued that truth is to be attained not through observation of the external, natural world but through the mind's own independent activity. (Editor)

experience. By philosophising more highly than their predecessors, they have enlarged the scope of science: the absolute, by itself, has produced nothing; translated into a court of law, it has been jeered at as a con. In moral philosophy, mysticism, quietism and asceticism have led to the most disgusting turpitudes. Christ himself, the Word made flesh, had taught nothing new to the conscience; and the entirety of theology, patiently studied, is found, in the last instance, convicted by its own testimony as nothing other than a phantasmagoria of the human soul, of its operations and its powers, liberty, justice, love, science and progress.

Like it or not, we must keep to the common method, profess in our hearts and with our mouths the democracy of intelligence; and since it is a question in that moment of the origin and the formation of our ideas, to ask the reason of ideas, as with everything else, from observation and analysis.

## §v: THAT METAPHYSICS IS WITHIN THE PROVINCE OF PRIMARY INSTRUCTION

The definition of philosophy implies by its terms: 1) someone who seeks, observes, analyses, synthesises and discovers, which we call the *Subject* or *Self;* 2) something which is observed, analysed, the reason of which we seek, and which we call the *Object* or *Non-Self.*

The first—the observer, subject, *self,* or mind—is active; the second—the thing observed, object, *non-self,* or phenomenon—is passive. Let us not frighten ourselves with words: this means that the one is the artisan of the idea, and that the other furnishes the material. There is no statue without the sculptor: this is very simple, is it not? But neither is there a statue without the marble: this is also clear. Now, it is thus for ideas. Suppress one or the other of these two principles, the subject or the object, and no idea will be formed; thought will no longer be possible. Philosophy vanishes. Suppress the sculptor or the block of marble, and you will have no statue. Every artistic or industrial production is like this. Take away the worker, and you will remain eternally with your raw materials; take away the materials from the worker and ask him to produce something by his thought alone, and he will think you are mocking him.

However, in this competition, or this opposition, of the subject and object, of the mind and things, we want to know in a more precise manner what is the role of each; in what consists the action of the mind, and what are the natures of the materials he puts to work.

The mind or *self* is, or at least it acts as if it is, prone to affirm itself as a simple and indivisible nature, consequently as if it is more penetrating and less penetrable, more active and less corruptible, more quick and less subject to change. Things, on the contrary, appear extended and composite, consequently divisible, successive, variable, penetrable, subject to dissolution, susceptible to a greater or lesser degree in all their qualities and properties.

What seems at first inexplicable is how the mind, put in relation with external objects by the intermediary of the senses, perceives a nature so different from itself. Can the simple see the composite? That implies a contradiction. On reflection, however, we recognise this it is precisely that difference of nature which renders objects perceptible to the mind, and subjects them to it. For it sees them, remark it well, not in their substance, which it cannot conceive as other than simple (atomistic), after its own example, and which consequently escapes it; it sees them in their composition and their differences. The intuition of the mind, its action on objects, comes thus from two causes: by its acuity, it divides them and differentiates them infinitely; then, by its simplicity, it restores all these diversities to unity. What the mind sees in things is their differences, species, series and groups, in a word their reason, and it is because it is mind, because it is simple in its essence, that is sees all that. What the mind cannot discover is the nature or the *in itself* of things, because that nature, laid bare of its differences, of its unity of composition, etc., becomes then like the mind itself, something simple, amorphous, unapproachable and invisible.

The consequence of all this is easy to grasp. The mind put in the presence of things, the *self* in communication with the *non-self,* receives impressions and images from it; it grasps differences, variations, analogies, groups, genera, species: all that is the fruit of its first perception. But the mind does not stop there; and the representation of things would not be complete in its thought, it would lack basis and perspective, if the mind did not add something more of its own.

Witnessing, then, that infinite diversity of things, such a diversity that each thing seems to denounce itself as having been capable of being something completely different than it is, the mind, which feels itself to be something singular, in opposition to things, conceives of the *One,* the *Identical,* the *Immutable,* which is nowhere to be found;

In observing the contingency of phenomena, the mind conceives of the *Necessary,* which it cannot find anywhere either: it would be fortunate if it did not dare to worship it under the name of Destiny!

In taking the comparative dimensions of objects and establishing their limits, it conceives of *Infinity,* which is no more real;

In following, in its consciousness, the revolutions of time, and measuring the duration of existences, it conceives the *Eternal,* which cannot be said of any person or any thing;

In recognising the mutual independence of creatures, it conceives of itself as superior to the creatures, and affirms it *Free Will* and its *Sovereignty,* of which nothing can yet give it the model;

In seeing movement, it conceives of *Inertia,* a hypothesis without reality;—in calculating speed, it conceives of force, which it never grasps;

In noting the action of being on one another, it conceives of *Cause,* in the analysis of which it only grasps a contradiction;

In comparing the faculties of some to the faculties of others, it conceives of *Life, Intelligence* and *Soul;* and by opposition, *Matter, Death* and *Nothingness:* abstractions or fictions? it does not know;

In classing and grouping creatures according to their genera and species, it conceives the *Universal*, superior to every collectivity;

In calculating the relations of things, it conceives of *Law*, the notion of which immediately gives it that of an *Order of the world*, although there has been struggle everywhere, and consequently as much disorder as order;

Finally, in condemning, according to the purity of its essence, all that appears to it out of proportion, small, mean, monstrous, discordant and deformed, it conceives the *Beautiful* and the *Sublime*, in a word the *Ideal*, which it is condemned to follow always, without ever enjoying it.

All these conceptions of the mind, famous in the School[3] under the name of the *categories*, are indispensable for the understanding of things; reasoning is impossible without them. At the same time, they do not result from sensation, since, as we see, they exceed the sensation, the perceived image, by the same distance that separates the finite from the infinite. What they take from sensation are the various perspectives that have served to form them antithetically; the perspective of diversity, the perspective of contingency, the perspective of the limit, etc. However, the categories or conceptions of reason all merge with one another; they are adequate to one another and imply each other mutually, since all are invariably related, not to things, but to the essence of the mind, which is single and incorruptible…

The formation of the categories or ideas, conceived by the mind apart from experience but on the occasion of experience, their collection and classification, forms what we call *metaphysics*. It is entirely in grammar, and its teaching belongs to the schoolmasters.

From the manner in which the categories form, and from their usage in language and in the sciences, it results that, as analytic or synthetic signs, they are the condition *sine qua non* of speech and of knowledge, that they form the instrumentation of intelligence, but that by themselves they are sterile, and consequently that metaphysics, excluding all positivism by its nature and purpose, can never become a science.

All science is essentially metaphysical, since every science generalises and distinguishes. Every man who knows, however little he knows, every man who speaks, provided that he understands, is a metaphysician; just as every man who seeks the reason of things is a philosopher. Metaphysics is the first thing that infants and savages think: we could even say that in the mind of every man, metaphysics is present in inverse proportion to science.

Thus, by what fanaticism of abstraction can a man call himself exclusively a metaphysician, and how, in a knowledgeable and positive century, do professors of pure philosophy still exist, these people who teach the young to philosophise apart from all science, all art, all literature and all industry, people, in a word, making a trade, the most conscientiously in the world, of selling the absolute?

---

3   A reference to the Scholastic philosophers of the Middle Ages. (Editor)

Those who should once understand the theory of the formation of ideas, and who will carefully take into account these three capital points: 1) the intervention of two agents, the subject and the object, in the formation of knowledge; 2) the difference in their roles, resulting from the difference in their natures; 3) the distinction of ideas into two species, sensory [*sensible*] ideas given immediately by objects, and extra-sensory or metaphysical ideas, resulting from the action of the mind solicited by the contemplation of the outside; that one, we say, can boast of having taken the most difficult step of philosophy. He is freed from fatalism and from superstition. He knows that all his ideas are necessarily posterior to the experience of things, metaphysical ideas as well as sensory ideas; he will remain unshakeably and forever convinced that, just as adoration, prophecy, the gift of tongues and of miracles, somnambulism, idealism, whether subjective, objective or absolute, and all the practices of the *great work* of alchemy, has never produced for indigent humanity an ounce of bread, has created neither shoes, not hats, nor shirts; so it will not have added an *iota* to knowledge. And he will conclude with the great philosopher Martin, in [Voltaire's] *Candide*: "We must cultivate our garden." The garden of the philosopher is the spectacle of the Universe. Verify unceasingly your observations; put your ideas in order; take care in your analyses, your recapitulations, your conclusions; be sober in your conjectures and hypotheses; mistrust probabilities[4] and above all authorities; do not believe the word of any soul who lives, and use the ideal as a means of scientific construction and control, but do not worship it. Those who, all times, have claimed to detach science from all empiricism and to raise the edifice of philosophy on metaphysical ideas alone, have only succeeded in making themselves plagiarists of ancient theology. Their counterfeits have fallen on their own heads; their transcendentalism has brought to ruin the supernatural in which the people have at all times believed, and they have managed to lose what they wanted to save. Remember, finally, that there is no more innate or revealed science than there are innate privileges or wealth fallen from heaven; and that, as all well-being must be obtained by labour, or be theft, so all knowledge must be the fruit of study, or be false.

## §VI: THAT PHILOSOPHY MUST BE ESSENTIALLY PRACTICAL

We would be gravely mistaken if we imagined that philosophy, because it has been defined as the *Search for the reason of things*, has no other end than to make us discover that reason, and that its object is exclusively speculative. Already, by showing that these conditions are those of common sense, its certainty the same for all, its highest conceptions of the same form and

---

4   A reference to the Catholic doctrine of "probabilism," which dictated that the believer should defer to authority (ostensibly the source of the most "probable" truth) in any matter of uncertainty. See Proudhon's attack on probabilism in *De la Justice*, 7th Study, Chapter III. (Editor)

quality as its most elementary propositions, we have had occasion to recall its eminently positive character, its egalitarian spirit as well as its democratic and anti-mystical tendencies. It is philosophy, we have said, that made the French Revolution by deducing from its own pure essence the principle of civil and political equality. We have subsequently confirmed that premise by uprooting all pretensions to transcendence, and proving that *de facto* and *de jure* there is nothing for the mind apart from observation, consequently nothing which ordinary mortals can claim by virtue of simple good sense.

Logic, which is to say philosophy itself, demands more.

In ordinary life, which is that of the immense majority and which forms three-quarters of philosophy, the knowledge of things has value only insofar as it is useful; and nature, our great schoolmistress, has been of the opinion, in giving intelligence as the light of our actions and the instrument of our felicity.

Philosophy, in a word, is essentially utilitarian, no matter what has been said: to make of it an exercise of pure curiosity is to sacrifice it. In that regard, universal testimony has judged without appeal. The people, eminently practical, asked what all that philosophy would serve, and the way to make use of it: and as one responded to them, with Schelling, that philosophy exists by itself and for itself, that it would be an injury to its dignity if one sought a use for it, the people have mocked the philosophers, and everyone has done as the people. Philosophy for philosophy's sake is a thought which would never enter a sane mind. A similar pretension might appear excusable among philosophers who seek the reason of things in the inanity of genius, or among the illuminated in communication with the spirits. But since it has been proven that all that transcendence is but a hollow gourd, and that the philosopher has been declared subject to common sense, the servant, like everyone else, of practical and empirical reason, it is imperative that philosophy should humanise itself, and that it should be *democratic and social*, or else never amount to anything. Now, what is more utilitarian than democracy?

Religion, which certainly had a very different birth than democracy, did not take it so high with our poor humanity. It has made itself all things to all people; it has been given to us, by grace from on high, to raise us from sin and misery, to teach us our duties and our rights, to give us a rule of conduct, to enlighten us on our origin and our destiny, and to prepare for us an eternal happiness. Religion responded, in its own way, to all the questions that our consciences and our hearts could address to it. It gave us rules for the conduct of our interests; it did not even disdain to explicate for us the beginnings of the world, the principle of things, the epoch of the creation, the age of the human race, etc. It only left outside its teaching, and did not deliver to our arguments, the things of which the knowledge was not of an immediate usefulness to our moral perfection and to our eternal salvation.

Will philosophy do less than religion? It has taken it upon itself to destroy these venerable beliefs; could it have had in us any other mission than to fill the void?

To pose the question in this way is to answer it. No, philosophy cannot be reduced to a kaleidoscope of the mind without practical application; its purpose is to serve us, and if the critique of religion that it allows is fair, the service that falls on to it close to us, in the place of religion, is determined in advance by that very critique. To the old dogma philosophy must substitute a new doctrine, with the only difference the first was of faith and was imposed by authority, while the second must be of science, and impose itself by demonstration.

Under the empire of religion, man found everything simple by relating it to the word of God; on the strength of that guarantee, it rested in full security. Now that, thanks to philosophical reason, the supposed divine word has become doubtful, and the celestial guarantee itself subject to caution, what remains, except that man finds in himself the rule of his actions and the guarantee of his judgements? This is what the ancient philosophers had understood very well, and that they sought so long, under the name of criterion of certainty.

Thus the aim of philosophy is to teach man to think for himself, to reason methodically, to make exact ideas of thing, to formulate truth in regular judgements, all in order to direct his life, to merit by his conduct the esteem of his fellows and himself, and to insure, along with the peace of the heart, the well-being of the body and the security of the mind.

The criterion of philosophy, deduced from its practical utility, is thus in some sense double: relative to the reason of things, that it is important for us to understand such as it is in itself, and relative to our proper reason, which is the law of our perfection and our happiness.

A principle of guarantee for our ideas;

A rule for our actions;

As a consequence of this double criterion and of the accord of our practical and speculative reason, a synthesis of all our knowledge and a sufficient idea of the economy of the world and of our destiny: this is what philosophy must accomplish.

But where do we find the criterion? As much as philosophy has shown itself powerless to discovery the smallest truth with the aid of metaphysical notions alone, so much it has up to the present been unsuccessful in establishing a principle that, serving all at once as critical instrument and rule of action, would also provide the blueprint for the scientific and social edifice, and would later show us the system of the universe.

In that which concerns the rule of judgement, we have been served, lacking an authentic instrument, and we continue to be served by different principles, chosen arbitrarily from among the axioms that we suppose most capable of responding to the wants of philosophy. Such is, for example, the principle of *contradiction,* by virtue of which yes and no cannot be affirmed simultaneously, and from the same point of view, for a single thing. It is the principle which rules mathematics. But that principle, which at first appears so sure, when we work with definite quantities, has been judged insufficient with regard to the sophists who claim that all is true and all is false, as much in the ontological as in the moral order, since, in the fundamental questions, on which depend the certainty of all the others, one can affirm simultaneously, with an equal probability, the yes and the no... The absence of a higher principle, embracing all the content of the mind, appears to make itself felt up to the highest mathematics, the style, the definitions and the theories of which have been justly criticised, though one cannot, in fact, contest the results. Wearied of struggle, we have thought to say, after Descartes, that the guarantee of our judgements is *self-evidence*. And what is it that makes that a thing appear self-evident?...

In that which concerns the rule of actions, the philosophers have not even taken the trouble to test anything. All have returned, by some detour, to the religious idea, as if philosophy and theology had exactly this in common, that *the fear of God is the beginning of wisdom*. It has even been said, and it is repeated every day, that a little philosophy leads away from religion, but that a lot of philosophy leads back to it, from which it is necessary to conclude that it is not truly the philosopher's problem. If some adventurers in free thought have abandoned the beaten path, they have lost themselves in the mires of egoism.

Finally, as to the unity of the sciences, the distress is still more noticeable. Each philosopher has built his system, leaving it to critique to show that that system was a work of marquetry. It is thus that, according to Thales, water is the principle of all things; according to others, it is fire or air; according to Democritus, it is the atoms.[5] Philosophy, like language, is materialist in its beginnings: but that is not where the danger lies; it will only go too far in the ideal. Later, indeed, one has invoked by turns, as the principle of things, love, numbers and the idea; and philosophy, from abstraction to abstraction, has ended by burning what it first worshiped, adoring the spirit that it had only glimpsed, and falling into a hopeless superstition. It is thus that eclecticism was born, the meaning of which is that there is not a unitary constitution, neither for the world, nor for thought, and that consequently there are only specific, relative certainties, between which the wise must know how to choose, giving, according to the circumstances, satisfaction to all the principles, but not allowing themselves to be mastered by any of them, and reserving always freedom of judgement. Eclecticism, which has been so criticised in our days, has not yet received its true definition: it is polytheism.

In this moment, it is with philosophy as with the public conscience: both are demoralised. Eclecticism in philosophy, just like the doctrinaire position in politics, *laissez faire, laissez passer* in economics, and free love in the family, is the negation of unity, death.

However, an unresolved problem must not be considered an insoluble

---

5    Thales of Miletus (ca. 624–546 BCE) and Democritus of Thrace (ca. 460–370 BCE) are pre-Socratic Greek philosophers. (Editor)

problem: it is even permitted to believe that we have come closer to the solution the longer we have searched for it. Also, the lack of success of philosophy on these capital questions of the certainty of ideas, of the rule of morals, and of the architectonic of science, has not prevented it from arriving at theories of which growing generality and rigorous logic seem a sure pledge of triumph. Why, indeed, if man has the certainty of his existence, would he not have at the same time certainty of his observations? Descartes' proposition—*I think, therefore I am,*—implies that consequence. Why, if the intelligence of man is capable of connecting two ideas, of forming a dyad, a triad, a tetrad, a series, finally, and if each series leads to his self, why, we ask, will he not aspire to construct the system of the world? He must advance: everything invites us. If philosophy is abandoned, it is the end of the human race.

### §VII: THE CHARACTER THAT MUST BE PRESENTED BY THE GUARANTEE OF OUR JUDGEMENTS AND THE RULE OF OUR ACTIONS—CONVERSION FROM SPECULATIVE TO PRACTICAL REASON: DETERMINATION OF THE CRITERION

Before passing on, will you allow me to make the observation that there is no artisan who is not in a perfect state to understand what philosophy proposes, since there is not one who, in the exercise of his profession, does not make use of several means of justification, measure, evaluation and control? The worker has, to direct him in his labours, the yardstick, the scale, the square, the rule, the plumb, the level, the compass, standards, specimens, guides, a touchstone, etc. Seemingly, there is no worker who cannot say the purpose of his work, the ensemble of needs or ideas to which it is attached, what its application must be, what its conditions and qualities are, and consequently its importance in the general economy.

Now, what the artisan does within his speciality, the philosopher seeks to do for the universality of things: his criterion, consequently, must be much more elementary, since it must be applied to all; his synthesis much broader, since it must embrace all.

What then is the yardstick to which we must relate all our observations, according to which we will judge, *a priori*, the harmony or discord of things, not only of the rational and the irrational, the beautiful and the ugly, but, what is more serious and which concerns us directly, the good and the evil, the true and the false? In the second place, on what basis, according to what plan, in view of what end, will we raise the edifice of our knowledge, so that we can say what Leibniz said of the world of which it must be the expression, that it is the best, the most faithful, the most perfect possible?[6]

---

6    Gottfried Wilhelm von Leibniz (1646–1716) had famously written, in his *Essais de théodicée* (1710), that "God has chosen the best of all possible worlds" (*Theodicy: Essays on the Goodness of God, the Freedom of Man, and the Origin of Evil.*, trans. E.

The day when philosophy will have responded to these two questions, philosophy, we do not say that it will be done, since, either as observation or investigation, or as acquired science, it has no limits; but it will be completely organised, it will know what it wants, where it tends, what its guarantees are, what its mission is in humanity and in the presence of the universe.

Let us backtrack a little.

From the definition of philosophy that we have given and the analysis that we have made from observation, it results for us, 1) that the idea comes to us originally, concurrently and *ex aequo*,[7] from two sources, one subjective, which is the Self, subject or mind, the other objective, which designates objects, the non-self or things; 2) that as a consequence of that double origin philosophy bears on *relations*, already by the definition, and on nothing else; 3) finally, that every relation, analysed into its elements, is, like the observation which furnishes it, essentially dualistic, which is also indicated by the etymology of the word *rapport* or *relation*, returns from one point to another, from one fact, one idea, one group, etc., to another.

It follows from this that the instrument of critique we are looking for is of necessity dualistic or binary: it could not be triadic, since there would be below it simpler elements than it, ideas that it could not explain, and since, moreover, it is easy to convince oneself that every triad, trinity or ternary is only the abridgement of two dyads, obtained by the identification or confusion of two of their terms.[8]

---

M. Huggard, [La Salle, IL: Open Court Publishing Co., 1990], 168). (Editor)

7   "on an equal footing." (Editor)

8   The trinity of the Alexandrians [early Christian theologians] was only a superstitious idea; that of the Christians is a mystery. The ternary facts, borrowed from nature, are from pure empiricism, to which is opposed, in much greater numbers, binary facts, quaternary, etc. The famous division of nature into three kingdoms [i.e., animal, vegetable, and mineral: Linnaeus' *Regnum Animale*, *Regnum Vegetabile*, and *Regnum Lapideum*] is incomplete: above the *animal* kingdom, in which are manifested sensibility, life, the affections, instinct, and to a certain degree intelligence, we must add the *spiritual* kingdom, of which humanity alone is the subject, and which is distinguished by manifestations unknown in the preceding kingdom, speech, religion, justice, logic, metaphysics, poetry and art, industry, science, exchange, war, politics and progress. The Hegelian formula is only a triad by the good pleasure or the error of the master, who counts three terms where there truly exists only two, and who has not seen that the antinomy does not resolve itself, but that it indicates an oscillation or antagonism susceptible only to equilibrium. By this point of view alone, the system of Hegel would be entirely remade. It is the same for the syllogism, in which there is also two propositions, which are equated by the relation of like terms, rather as in arithmetic proportions.

Every MAN is *mortal*, and *Pierre* is a MAN; thus, etc.

It is useless to express the conclusion here; it is enough to correctly write the premises. To take the triad for a formula of logic, a law of nature and reason, especially for

The principle of certainty can no longer be simplistic, as if it emanates exclusively from the self or the non-self; since, as we have seen, the subject, without an object to stimulate it, does not even think; and the object, without the faculty of the mind to divide, to differentiate and return diversity to unity, would only send itself unintelligible images. Metaphysical ideas themselves cannot serve as principle for philosophy, although they presuppose realistic apperceptions. The reason is that such ideas, obtained by the opposition of the self to the non-self, reflecting its simplistic nature, are extra-phenomenal, and by themselves contain no positive truth, although they are indispensable to the formation of every idea and the construction of every science.

Let us hold then as certain, and let us attach ourselves strongly to that idea, that what the philosophers sought under the name of the criterion of certainty and which must serve in the construction of science cannot be a simplistic or metaphysical notion; that it is no longer a sensory image, representative of a pure reality, since that would be to exclude the mind from its own domain, and to make it accomplish its work without putting itself into it; that it cannot be, finally, a ternary or quaternary formula, or one of a higher number, since that would be to take the series in the place of its element.

This principle must be at once subjective and objective, formal and real, intelligible and sensory, to indicate a relation of the self to the non-self, and consequently must be dualistic, like philosophical observation itself.

However, between the self and the non-self, and *vice versa*, there is an infinity of relations are possible. Among so many relations furnished to us by philosophical observation, which will we choose to serve as standard and yardstick to the others? Which will form the first basis of our knowledge, the point of departure for our civilisation, the pivot of our social constitution? For it is a question of nothing more or less than that.

To this point we have considered the self and what we call the non-self as two antithetical natures, the one spiritual, simple, active, and thinking, the other material, composite and consequently divisible, inert or passive, and non-thinking, serving simply as a target, occasion and matter for the meditations of the self. In order to not juggle too many ideas at once, we are carried to the observation of that elementary fact, intelligible even to the children to whom one teaches the grammar of Lhomond, namely, that philosophical observation implies two terms or actors, the one which observes, the other which is observed. It is the relation of active to passive, such as is shown by the conjugation of the verb in every language.

---

the archetype of judgement and the organic principle of society, is to deny analysis, to deliver philosophy to mysticism, and democracy to imbecility. It appears there, besides, by the fruits. The only thing that one can attribute to trinitarian influence is the ancient division of society by castes, *clergy, nobility, commoners*, an antihuman division, against which the Revolution was made.

But the passive does not exclude the reciprocal. What we have said of the role of the self and of the non-self in the formation of the idea by no means proves that the one that observes cannot be observed itself, and precisely by the object that it observed. Locke said, and no one has known how to respond to him: How do we know if the non-self is necessarily non-thinking?... In every case, we know, and cannot doubt, that our observations bear very often on selves like our own, but who, in this case and in so many that furnish us with the facts, observations, and impressions on which our mind then acts, are considered by us as non-selves. In love, for example, there are also two agents, one who loves, the other who is loved; this does not prevent us from reversing the proposition and saying that the person who loves is loved by the one that she loves, and that the one who is loved loves the one by whom she is loved. It is even only under these conditions that love exists in its fullness. Who, then, once more, would guarantee that we alone have thought, and that, when we describe this plant, when we analyse that rock, there is not in them something that looks at us?

One says to me that this implies a contradiction. Why?... As thought can only result from an organic centralisation; as, thus, while I look at my hand, I am quite sure that my hand does not look at me, because my hand is only a part of the organism that produces thought in me, which includes all of my parts; so it is the same in plants and rocks, which are, like the hairs and the bones of my body, parts of the great organism (which perhaps thinks, if it does not sleep, though we know nothing of it), but which by themselves do not think.

There we are. The analogies of existence induce us to suppose that, as there is in the organised being a common *sensorium*, an interdependent life, an intelligence in the service of all the members of which it is the resultant and which all express it; just as there is in nature a universal life, a soul of the world, which, if it is not acted on from outside, in the manner of our own, because there is no outside for it and because everything is in it, acts within, on itself, contrary to ours, and which is manifested by creating, as a mollusc creates its shell, that great organism of which we ourselves make part, poor individual *selves* that we are!

This is only an induction, doubtless, a hypothesis, a utopia, that I do not intend to offer for more than it is worth. If I cannot swear that the world, that alleged non-self, does not think, then I can no more swear that it thinks: that would surpass my means of observation. All that I can say is that mind is prodigiously expended in this non-self, and that I am not the only self who admires it.

Here, then, is what my conclusion will be.

Instead of seeking the law of my philosophy in a relation between myself, which I consider as the summit of being, and that which is the most inferior in creation and that I take to be non-thinking, I will seek

that law in a relation between myself and another self which is not
me, between man and man. For I know that every man, my fellow, is
the organic manifestation of a mind, is a self; I judge equally that animals, endowed with sensibility, instinct, even intelligence, although to
a lesser degree, are also selves, of a lesser dignity, it is true, and placed
at a lower degree on the scale, but created according to the same plan;
and as I no more know of a manifest demarcation between the animals
and the plants, or between those and the minerals, I ask myself if the
inorganic beings are not still minds which sleep, selves in the embryonic state, or at least the members of a self of which I ignore the life
and operations?

Supposed every being thus to be both self and non-self, what can I do
better, in this ontological ambiguity, than to take for the point of departure
of my philosophy the relation, not of me to myself, in the manner of Fichte,[9]
as if I wanted to make the equation of my mind, simple, indivisible, incomprehensible being; but of myself to another which is my equal and is not me,
which constitutes a dualism no longer metaphysical or antinomic, but a real
duality, living and sovereign?

By acting thus I do not court the risk of doing injury or grief to anyone; I have more the advantage, in descending from Humanity towards
things, of never losing sight of the legitimate ensemble; finally, whatever
the difference of natures which makes the object of my exploration, I am
so much less exposed to being mistaken, that in the last analysis every
being which is not equal to me, is dominated by me, makes a part of
me, or else belongs to other selves like me, so that the law which governs
the *subjects* between them is rationally presumed to govern the *objects* as
well, since apart from that the subordination of the ones to the others
would be impossible, and there would be contradiction between Nature
and Humanity.

Let us further observe that by that unassailable transaction, philosophy
becomes entirely practical instead of speculative, or to put it better, the two
points of view merge: the rule of my actions and the guarantee of my judgements is identical.

What now is that ruling Idea, at once objective and subjective, real and
formal, of nature and humanity, of speculation and sentiment, of logic and
art, of politics and economics; practical reason and pure reason, which govern at once the world of creation and the world of philosophy, and which
both are constructed; the idea finally which, dualistic by its formula, excludes nonetheless all anteriority and all superiority, and embraces in its synthesis the real and the ideal?

It is the idea of *Right*, Justice.

---

9   Fichte's *Wissenschaftslehre* (*Science of Knowledge*, 1794) emphasised the "Ego" as the
    necessary foundation of knowledge. (Editor)

## §VIII: JUSTICE, THE UNIVERSAL REASON OF THINGS— SCIENCE AND CONSCIENCE

The people, in their laborious existence, even more than the philosophers in their speculations, have need of a guide: they need, we have said, a guide for their reason, a rule for their conscience, a superior point of view from which they may embrace their knowledge and their destiny. All this they found in religion.

God, the eternal Word, had created man from clay and had animated him with his breath; God had taught how to him to speak; God had imprinted in his heart the ideas of the infinite, the eternal, the Just and the ideal; God had taught him religion, worship, and the mysteries; God had delivered to him the elements of all sciences by revealing the history of creation to him, making the animals appear before him and inviting him to name them, showing him the common origin of all peoples and the cause of their dispersion. It was God who had imposed on man the law of labour, created and sanctified the family, founded society, and separated the States, which he governed by his providence. God, finally, living and seeing, principle and goal, all-powerful, just and truthful, guaranteed man's faith, and promised, after a time of trials on this earth, to reward him for his piety with a limitless happiness.

Philosophy, which is the search for the reason of things, lost God in the process of seeking God's reason; at the same time, a dispersion took hold of knowledge, doubt gripped men's souls, and they became unable to think of anything but the origin of man and his final end. But this state of anguish could only be momentary: under better conditions, reason will render us what revelation had given us; and although this legitimate hope has not yet been fulfilled, we can judge, by a simple outline of the state of human knowledge, as to its conditions and its totality, as to how close it may be to that fulfilment. Is it so bad, after all, that something has always been lacking in our knowledge? Isn't it enough for our security, for our dignity, that we see our intellectual wealth increase indefinitely?

It thus is a question of assuring ourselves that Justice, the principle and the source of which we will from now on locate within ourselves, fulfils, as a critical and organic principle, the object of philosophy, and that consequently it can replace religion for us, to our advantage. Deprived of the support of heaven, man remains himself. Like Medea, he will say: "Myself, myself alone, and is that not enough?"[10] Philosophy is for the affirmative:

---

10   Medea, in Greek mythology, is a sorceress who wreaks a cruel revenge on her treacherous husband, Jason, a story retold by the playwrights Euripedes and Corneille. Proudhon is quoting loosely from Corneille's *Medée*, Act I, Scene iv. David Hume references this same passage in his *Enquiry Concerning the Principles of Morals*: "The confident of Medea in the tragedy recommends caution and submission; and enumerating all of the distresses of that unfortunate heroine, asks her, what she has to support her against her numerous and implacable enemies. 'Myself,' replies she; 'myself, I say, and it is enough'" (7.7). (Editor)

it awaits the certainty of its principles, the justification of its hopes. Let us see now.

Since philosophy is the search for the reason of things, by including under the word things all the manifestations of the human being, and since, according to this definition, any search for the nature or the in-itself of things, for their substance and materiality, just as for any kind of absolute, is excluded from philosophy, it readily follows that the principle of certainty, the archetypal idea to which all our knowledge must be referred, must be, above all, a rational principle, that which is most frankly rational, that which is most eminently intelligible, that which is least a thing, if one can put it thus.

The idea of Justice satisfies this first condition. Its most apparent character is to express a relationship that is all the more rational, one might say, to the extent that it is formed voluntarily, in full knowledge of the cause, by two reasonable beings, two persons. Justice is synallagmatic: it produces not merely the impression of the not-self upon the self and the action of the one upon the other, but an exchange between two selves who know one another as they each know themselves, and who swear, on their mutually guaranteed honour, an alliance in perpetuity. One will not find, in all the encyclopaedia of knowledge, an idea of this stature.

But it is not enough for Justice to be the relation of two wills: it would not fulfil its office if it were that alone. It is equally necessary that it be reality and ideality; moreover, that it should preserve, with the power of synthesis that we have just recognised in it, a character of sufficient primordiality to serve simultaneously as the summit of the philosophical pyramid and as the principle of all knowledge. Again, Justice combines these advantages: it is the point of transition between the sensory and the intelligible, the real and the ideal, the concepts of metaphysics and the perceptions of experience.[11]

It would be, indeed, a narrow understanding of Justice to imagine that it intervenes only in the fabrication of laws, that it has a place only in national assemblies and courts. Undoubtedly it is under this aspect of political sovereignty that it enters our thought and dominates mankind. But this Justice, with respect to which, in our relationship with our neighbours, we are especially preoccupied with enforcement, imposes itself with no less authority on

---

11   Kant endeavoured to show that there were *a priori* synthetic judgements, although that implied a contradiction to some extent, and he was right to think so, since without an *a priori* synthetic judgement, the unity of philosophical construction is impossible. Hegel, on the contrary, argued that such judgements do not exist, and all his philosophy, understood in good faith, is nothing but the analysis and then the reconstruction of a synthesis that is necessarily conceived *a priori*. What, then, is this synthesis that Kant affirms and does not find, that Hegel denies and demonstrates? It is nothing other than Justice, at once the most complete concept and the most paramount, that Hegel calls sometimes the Idea, sometimes the Spirit or the Absolute.

642  Pierre-Joseph Proudhon

the understanding and the imagination than it does on the conscience; its formula governs the whole world, and everywhere, if it is allowed to express itself in this way, it preaches to us by precept and example.

Justice thus takes various names, according to the faculties to which it is addressed. Within the order of the conscience, the highest of all, it is JUSTICE properly speaking, ruler our *rights* and our *duties*; in the order of intelligence, logic, mathematics, etc, it is *equality* or *equation*; in the sphere of imagination, it is called ideal; in nature, it is balance. Justice is essential to each one of these categories of ideas or facts under a particular name and as an *indispensable* condition; to man alone, a complex being, whose spirit embraces in its unity the acts of freedom and the operations of intelligence, the things of nature and creations of the ideal, impose themselves syntheti-cally with an authority that is always the same; and therefore the individual who, in his relationships to his fellows, neglects the laws of nature or mind, lacks Justice.

A man asks: why? Because human society, different from the animal com-munities, is established on a constantly changing totality of synallagmatic relationships, and because, without speech, the determination of these re-lationships, and consequently legislation and Justice, would be impossible. Therefore, the solemn formula of speech is the sermon, the imprecation and the anathema; the liar is everywhere considered infamous, and among civi-lised people, the man who respects himself, according to the precept of the Gospel, eschews swearing: he gives his word. How many centuries will pass before we abolish this feudal shame, the legal oath?... It is through the influ-ence of the same juridical sentiment and its dualistic formula that language tends to become more and more adequate to the idea, and that one notices there these innumerable dual forms (rhymes, parallelisms, agreements in kind, number and case, distiches, oppositions, antonymies, etc), which make grammar a system of couples, I would say almost transactions.

Man reasons, and his logic is only a development of his grammar, of which it retains the copulative paces: however, as it occupies itself less with form than content, it more closely approaches Justice, of which it is, if you will allow me this expression, the secretary. Tell me, is it by chance that what is in grammar only a phrase, becomes in logic a judgement? And if grammar is the preparation for logic, is it less true to say that logic, having for its goal to teach us how to write the judgements of Justice correctly, is the prepara-tion for jurisprudence?

At the same time as he receives impressions and images of external ob-jects, man, we have said, ascends, by virtue of the identity of his thought, to those higher concepts that are called transcendental, because they exceed the range of the senses, or metaphysical, as if they were a revelation of su-pernatural things. Here, once again, the dualism of Justice appears. While Kant, after having made the enumeration of his categories, distributed them into four groups, each one formed of a thesis and of an antithesis, balanced by a synthesis; Hegel, following this example, built his entire philosophy on a system of antinomies that produce one another, while being mistaken as to the role and value of the synthesis, revealed to us that great law which dominated his entire critique, namely that Justice, a pure concept as much as it is a fact of experience, is the muse of metaphysics.

It was Plato, if I am not mistaken, who said that the beautiful is the splendour of the truth. This definition may please the artist, who asks only to be impressed; it is not enough for the philosopher, who wants to feel and to understand at the same time. It is certain that the ideal is a transcendent conception of reason, which elevates art, like religion and Justice, above real things and simple utility. But how is this idea of beauty formed in us? By what transition does our spirit rise from the imperfect and miserable aspects of reality to this divine contemplation of the ideal? It is an artist who teaches it to us: through Justice. The goal of art, said Raphael, is to render things, not absolutely such as nature presents them to us, but such as it should have made them, and such as we discover, in studying nature, that nature tends to make them without ever arriving at it. Being, reduced to its pure and just form, without excess or defect, without violence or softness: that is art. Anytime being, in its reality, approximates its idea in some thing, it becomes beautiful, it sparkles, and, without exceeding its limitations, it takes on the character of the infinite. Justness in form and expression, Justice in social life: the law is always the same. It is thereby that the man of genius and the man of property glorify themselves; this is the secret of the mysterious bond that links art with morality.

Shall we speak of politics and its balances? Of political economy, of the endless division of functions, the balance of values, the relation of supply to demand, trade and its balance? Just as the concept of accuracy, i.e. of Justice applied to the shape of things, is the transition between the real and the ideal, so the notion of value is at once subjective and objective, and all of Justice is the transition between the world of nature and the world of society. Will we say, finally, that war, excessive, is only one investigation, through the struggle of forces, of Justice?... But what good is it to insist on things that it is enough to name in order to see at once appear the principle which governs them and constitutes them, right? It is by his conscience, much more than by his understanding and his imagination, that man embraces God, the Universe and Humanity; it is that conscience, for any statement, which creates in him reason, of which even the name, according to etymology, means nothing but the justification of the fact by its causes, its circumstances, its medium, its elements, its time, its end, in word its idea, always Justice.

Each one knows what satisfaction seizes the soul upon the clear apperception of a truth, upon the regular conclusion of a reasoning, the demonstrated certainty of an hypothesis. There is something emotional in this pleasure caused by the possession of truth, which is not pure intelligence, which is not impassioned, and that one can compare only with the joy of the triumph gained by virtue over vice. One also knows what heated controversy can exist between men of the most peaceful character with regard to questions in which their interests are by no means engaged. In all of this, I repeat, we can sense an element of will intricately mixed with the operations of understanding, and which, in my opinion, is nothing other than Justice intervening in the philosopher's investigation and rejoicing in his success. Just so, the pure form or beauty, exact knowledge or truth, is still Justice.

Conscience and science would thus be, at base, identical. What gives the sanction to the one is the other. What makes us exclaim, in a tone of satisfied pride or rather of satisfied conscience: It is obvious, is that the obviousness is not only in us an act of judgement, but an act of the conscience, a kind of stop in the last resort which defies the lie: It is obvious!

The separation of science and conscience, like that of logic and right, is only a scholastic abstraction. In our soul, things do not occur thus: the certainty of knowledge is something more intimate to us, more emotional, more vital, than the logicians and the psychologists say. Also, as one said of the good man, that he could be eloquent, *vir bonus dicendi peritus*,[12] because he had a conscience, *pectus est quod disertos facit*,[13] one could also say that the wise man is incompatible with the dishonest man, and that which science builds in us is the conscience.

Assured, by justice, as to his science and his conscience, finding in his own heart the reason of the Universe and the reason of himself, what more does man require? And what could the heavens and the powers of the skies offer to him?...

Need I add that, as the quality of the philosophical spirit is the same in all men, and as they do not differ between them, from this point of view, except by the sum of their knowledge, so the conscience in all is also of equal quality: they differ, in this regard, only by the development of their moral sense and the sum of their virtues?

It is by virtue of this second principle that the Revolution, which declared all citizens, because of the equivalence of their judgement, to be equal before the law, wanted further to make them all legislators and dispensers of justice: voters, jurors, judges, referees, experts, members of the communal assembly and the provincial council, representatives of the people, guardians of the nation; it wanted to give them all the right to publish their opinions, to discuss the acts and to control the accounts of the government, to criticise the laws and to pursue their reform.

Democracy of the intelligence and democracy of the conscience: such are the two great principles of philosophy, the two articles of faith of the Revolution.

---

12  "the good and well-spoken man": a definition of the ideal orator attributed to the Roman politician, Cato the Elder. (Editor)

13  A quotation from the Roman rhetorician Quintillian: "The heart is what makes one eloquent." (Editor)

Let us summarise this section.

Since philosophy is essentially dualistic, since in its language and its reasoning the ideas of sensory things incessantly call upon metaphysical ideas and vice versa; and since, in addition, among the objects of its study are included, often mixed and confused, things of nature and humanity, of speculation, of morals and art, it follows that the critical principle of philosophy, dualist and synthetic in its form, empirical and idealist by virtue of its double origin, must be capable of being applied, with equal suitability, to all the categories of knowledge.

However, the idea of Justice is the only one which meets these conditions: it is thus Justice which we will take for universal and absolute criterion of certainty. The proposal of Descartes, I think, therefore I am, is not certain because it is obvious, which does not mean anything; it is obvious because its two terms are adequate, i.e. equal before the justice of the understanding, confirmed by the judgement of the conscience; and every obvious proposition is found in the same case.

That is not all. With the criterion of certainty, one needs for philosophy a principle in virtue of which it co-ordinates its materials, and which, in construction without end of knowledge, does not enable him any more to be mislaid.

Once again, the idea of Justice answers this wish. Indeed, Justice, or best reason, right reason, as it was formerly said, being all at the same time paramount and understanding with the supreme degree, is with itself its principle, its measurement and its end, so that for the philosopher, the critical principle and the organic or teleological principle is the same one. From which it follows that the last word of philosophy, its constant goal, is to realise, by the synthesis of knowledge, the agreement between man and nature, that is to say, as Fourier called it, universal Harmony. There is nothing beyond that.

## §IX: SUPREMACY OF JUSTICE

Philosophy defined;

Its dualism established;

Its levelling spirit and its democratic tendency demonstrated;

The formation of ideas, perceptions and concepts explained;

The criterion having been found, the goal indicated, the synthetic formula given, man's purpose determined;

One can say, in a sense, that philosophy is finished.

It is finished, since it can present itself before the multitude and say to it: I am JUSTICE, *Ego sum qui sum;*[14] it is I who shall draw you forth from misery and servitude. There is nothing more but to fill the cadres, which is the business of the professors and the scholars.

---

14   Exodus 3:14: "I am that I am." (Editor)

Indeed, what is this Justice, if not the sovereign essence that Humanity from time immemorial adored under the name of God; what philosophy has not ceased to seek its turn under various names: the Idea of Plato and Hegel, the Absolute of Fichte, the pure and practical Reason of Kant, the [French] Revolution's *Rights of Man and of the Citizen*? Since the beginning of the world, hasn't human religious and philosophical thought constantly revolved on this pivot?

It would not be difficult to bring back to this programme all the theories—religious, philosophical, aesthetic, and moral—which since the beginning of the world have occupied the human spirit. We will exempt ourselves of this work. The people do not have time to give to such vast, wild imaginings. All that they ask, is that we summarise for them this new faith in a way that catches them, that enables them to take it seriously, and to make of it at this moment a force and a weapon.

We have found ways to make astronomy accessible to the children, without making them pass through the deserts of higher mathematics; we, formerly, had found good means to make all the substance of the religion—history, dogmas, liturgy, scriptures—penetrate into the mind of the people, without for that obliging them to become theologians. Why, today, should we not teach them philosophy and Justice in the same way, without imposing any other condition on them than to make use of their good sense?

We will thus say to the People:

Justice is simultaneously, for any reasonable being, the principle and form of thought, the guarantee of the judgement, the code of conduct, the goal of knowledge and the end of existence. It is feeling and concept, manifestation and law, idea and action; it is universal life, spirit, and reason. Just as, in nature, *all converges, all conspires, all consents*, according to the old expression, in the same way, in a word, all the world tends to harmony and balance; in society, likewise, all is subordinated to Justice, all serves it, all is done by its command, according to its measure and for its sake; it is upon its foundation that the edifice of interests is constructed, and, to this end, that of knowledge: while at the same time, it is in itself subordinate to nothing, recognising no authority beyond itself, serving as an instrument to no power, not even to freedom. It is, of all our ideas, the most understandable, the most present, and the most fertile; of our feelings, the only one that men honour without reserve, and the most indestructible. The ignoramus perceives it as fully as does the wise man, and, to defend it, becomes instantly as subtle as the doctors, as courageous as the heroes. Before the glare of right, mathematical certainty fades. So it is that the construction of Justice is the great enterprise of mankind, the most masterly of sciences, the work of the collective spontaneity much more than of the genius of legislators, and an unending task.

This, O People, is why Justice is severe, and does not suffer mocking remarks. All knees bend before it, and all heads are bowed. It alone allows, tolerates, forbids or permits: it would cease to be, if it required, on behalf of that which it is, any permission, authorisation, or tolerance. Any obstacle is an insult to it, and every man is called to arms to overcome it. Quite different is religion, which could not prolong its life except by making itself tolerant, which could not continue to exist without tolerance. It is enough to say that its role is done with. Justice, on the contrary, is fundamental and unconditioned; it suffers no opposition, it admits of no competition, neither in the conscience, nor in the mind; and whoever sacrifices it, even to the Idea, or even to Love, is excluded from the communion of mankind. No peace with iniquity, O democrats: may that be the motto of your peace and your war cry.—But, the last of the Christians will say to us, your Justice is the reign of God that the Gospel prescribes us from seeking in any thing, *Quærite primum regnum Dei et justitiam ejus*; it is the sacrifice which God prefers, *Sacrificate sacrificium justitiæ*. How, then, can you not welcome our God, and how can you reject his religion?[15]

It is because you yourselves, oh inconsistent worshippers, believe in Justice even more than you do in your God. You affirm his word, not because it is divine, but because your spirit finds it true; you follow its precepts, not because God is the author, but because they seem to you right. Theology wishes in vain to reverse this order, to give sovereignty to God and to subordinate Justice to him: the intimate sense protests, and, in popular teaching, in prayer, it is Justice that serves as witness to Divinity and the pledge of religion. Justice is the supreme God, it is the living God, God the Almighty, the only God who dares be intolerant with respect to those who blaspheme against him, beneath which are nothing but pure idealities and assumptions. Pray to your God, Christians, the law permits it; but be sure that you do not prefer him to Justice, if you would not be treated as conspirators and corrupters.

What man, now, in the presence of this great principle of Justice, would not have the right to call himself a philosopher? It would be a return immediately to the antique spirit of caste, to disavow the progress of twenty-five centuries, to hold, like the senate of old Rome, that the patrician alone has the privilege of the legal formulas and the sacred things, and that in the presence of fulgurating Jupiter the slave does not have the right to call himself religious. All the relations of men with one another are governed by Justice; all natural laws derive from that by which the beings, and the elements that compose them, are or tend to be balanced: all the formulas of reason are

---

15  From the Latin Bible: "Quærite primum regnum Dei et justitiam ejus, et cetera omnia adjicientur vobis" ("But seek ye first the kingdom of God, and his righteousness; and all these things shall be added unto you") (Matthew 6:33); "Sacrificate sacrificium justitiæ et fidite in Domino multi dicunt quis ostendit nobis bonum" ("Offer the sacrifices of righteousness, and put your trust in the Lord") (Psalms 4:5). (Editor)

reduced to the equation or series of equations. Logic, the art of right reasoning, can be defined, like chemistry since Lavoisier, as the art of maintaining balance. Whoever commits an error or a sin, one says, has *faltered*, he has *stumbled*, he has *lost his balance*. Under a thousand different expressions, language unceasingly reproduces the same idea. Do we not recognise, by this sign, the existence of a popular philosophy, which is nothing other than the philosophy of right, a philosophy that comes simultaneously from reason and from nature? And this is not, at bottom, the same philosophy taught, in his barbaric language, by that philosopher who has never been equalled by any other, the immortal Kant, when he demanded from practical reason, from that which he called its categorical imperative, the supreme guarantee of speculative reason, and when he acknowledged with frankness that nothing was certain beyond right and duty?

## §X: CONDITIONS FOR A PHILOSOPHICAL PROPAGANDA

It is when religions pass away, when monarchies fail, when the politics of exploitation, in order to preserve itself, is reduced to proscribing the worker and the idea, and when the republic, everywhere on the agenda, seeks its formula; at the hour when the old convictions are dilapidated, when consciences are routed, when opinion is abandoned, when the multitude of egoisms shouts Every man for himself! that the moment arrives for an attempt at social restoration by means of a new propaganda.

1. Let us not fear to repeat: Justice, under various names, controls the world, nature and humanity, science and conscience, logic and morals, political economy, history, literature and art. Justice is what is most primitive in the human heart, most fundamental in society, most sacred among the nations, and what the masses demand today with the greatest ardour. It is the essence of the religions at the same time as it is the form of reason, the secret object of faith, and the beginning, the middle, and the end of knowledge. What could possibly be more universal, stronger, more complete than Justice, Justice with respect to which any superiority would imply contradiction?

Now, the people possess Justice within themselves; they have preserved it better than their masters and their priests; it is stronger among them than among the savants who teach it, the lawyers who discuss it, and the judges who apply it. The people, finally, in their native intuition and their respect for right, are more advanced than their superiors; they are lacking, as they say themselves when speaking of the intelligent animals, only speech. It is speech which we want to give to the people.

Thus, we who know how to speak and write, we have but one thing to do, in order to preach to the people and to philosophise in the name of the Justice, which is to inspire ourselves with the feelings of our audience, and to take them for our arbiter. If the philosophy that we attempt to explicate is insufficient, they will tell us so; if we go astray in our controversies, if we are mistaken in our conclusions, they will inform us; if something better is offered them, they will take it. The people, in that which concerns Justice, are not, strictly speaking, disciples, much less neophytes. The idea is within them: all they need to be initiated into, like the Roman plebes of former times, is the expressions for it. All that we ask of them is that they should have faith in themselves and take note of the facts and the laws: our ministry goes no further. We are the counsellors of the people, not their initiators.

2. This first advantage entails another, no less precious: while presenting ourselves simply as missionaries of right, we need neither to prevail upon any authority, divine or human, nor to pose as geniuses, martyrs or saints. Modesty, frankness, zeal, above all, good sense—nothing more is required of us. The truths we carry are not ours; they were not revealed to us from on high by grace of the Holy Ghost, and we have no copyright or proprietary patent over them. These truths are shared by everyone; they are inscribed within every soul, and we are not called on, as a proof of our veracity, to support them with prophecies and miracles. Speak to the slave of liberty, to the proletarian of his rights, to the worker of his salary: all will understand you, and if they see there a chance of success, they will not ask themselves in the name of whom or what you speak to them. In matters of justice, nature has made everyone competent, because it has given us all the same faculty and the same interest. This is why we can fail in our teaching without ever compromising our cause, and why no difference of opinion can lead to a schism amongst us. The same zeal for Justice that has divided us on a point of doctrine will reconcile us sooner or later. No authority, no priesthood, no churches. All of us who affirm right are in our belief necessarily orthodox, consequently eternally united. Heresy in Justice is a nonsense. Oh! If the apostles of Christ had been able to hold to this teaching! If the Gnostics had dared return to it! If Arius, Pelagius, Manès, Wyclef, Jan Huss and Luther had been strong enough to understand it!...[16] But it was written that the popular Word would have for its precursor the Word of God: how blessed are both!

3. But, one says, the people are incapable of a course of study; the abstraction of ideas, the monotony of science repels them. With them, one must always concretise, personalise and dramatise, employ *ethos* and *pathos*,[17] constantly change object and tone. Constrained by imagination and passion, realist by temperament, they voluntarily follow the empirics, tribunes and charlatans. The fervour is not sustained; at every instant, it falls back into the materialism of interests. This proves one thing: the philosopher, having been fully instructed in theory, who devotes himself to teaching the masses, must be, in his lectures to the people, a practical demonstrator above

16  Proudhon refers to a long line of Christian heretics. (Editor.)

17  In classical rhetoric, appeals to *ethos* (character) and *pathos* (emotion) are alternative modes of persuasion when appeals to *logos* (reason) are insufficient. (Editor)

all. In this respect, at any rate, he will not be an innovator. Isn't the identity of the fact and the law, of the content and the form, the constant subject of the tribunes? Does jurisprudence, in its schools and its books, proceed other than by formulas and examples?

Moreover, in teaching Justice, why should we deprive ourselves of these two powerful levers, passion and interest? Has Justice any other end than to ensure the public happiness against the incursions of egoism? Does it not have poverty for its sanction? Yes, we know that the people feel themselves to be highly interested in Justice, and no one takes their material interests more seriously than we do. If it is a point on which we propose to return constantly, it is that all crimes and misdemeanours, all corporate privilege, all that is arbitrary in government, is for the people an immediate cause of pauperism and sorrow.

This is why, as missionaries for democracy, having to combat the most detestable passions, and cowardly and obstinate egoism, we never intend to make the mistake of arousing popular indignation by the vehemence of our discourse. Justice is demonstrated by sentiment as well as by logic. The penal code of despotism calls this to incite the citizens to hate one another, to mistrust and hate the government. Shall we be the dupes of a hypocritical legislation, of which the sole end is to paralyse consciences in order to assure, under a false appearance of moderation, the impunity of the most guilty parties?

Man's life is brief: the people can receive but rare and rapid lessons. What purpose do they serve if we do not render those lessons as positive as existence; if we do not put men and things in play; if, in order to seize minds, we do not give impetus to imaginations and hearts? Shall we scruple, in speaking of Justice, to be of our time, and will we not merit what is said of us by the false apostles, if, as our adversaries wish, we reduce it to a pure abstraction?

It is in the contemporaneity of facts that one must show the people, as in a mirror, the permanence of ideas. The history of religion, the Church tells us, is an uninterrupted stream of miracles. But the faithful has no need, in order to be convinced of the truth of his belief, of having seen them all; it suffices that he contemplates this Church, the establishment of which, according to the doctors, is itself the greatest of miracles. Thus it is with Justice. The history of its manifestations, of its developments, of its constitutions, of its theories, encompasses the lives of many hundreds of men. Happily, the people have nothing to do with this burden. In order to sustain their faith in Justice, it suffices for one to show it, by striking examples, Justice oppressed and then revenged, crime triumphant and then punished; it suffices that they hear the protestations of generous souls in eras of unhappiness, and that they feel that this Revolution so calumniated, which for three millennia has pushed the working masses toward liberty, is Justice.

4. But what order to follow in this teaching? What is especially painful in the study of sciences is the yoke of the methods, the length of the

preliminaries, the sequence of propositions, the accuracy of the transitions, the rigor of the analyses; it is this obligation never to pass on to a new subject, before that which precedes it on the staircase of method is exhausted. Thus, before approaching the study of philosophy, the student requires six or seven years of grammar, languages, humanities, and history; logic, metaphysics, psychology, then come morals, not to mention mathematics, physics, natural history, etc. These studies having been completed, if the poor student has obtained his diplomas, he may begin studying law, which takes at least three years. It is in these conditions that the young man, rich enough to have them as his pastime, becomes legist, lawyer, Justice of the Peace, or substitute for the imperial prosecutor.

The people, undoubtedly, cannot traverse this entire succession; if philosophy can be acquired only under such conditions, it is condemned without reprieve. Either democracy is only a word, and there is not, outside of the language of the Church, apart from feudality and of divine right, communion between men; or it is necessary here to change approaches. I want to say that, in agreement with popular reason, it is necessary to abandon the analytical and deductive method, glory of the School, and to replace it with a universalist and synthetic method, more in touch with the reason of the masses, which sees everything concretely and synthetically. I will explain.

Since everything, in nature and in society, pivots on Justice, since it is centre, base, and summit, substance and form of every fact as well as any idea, it is obvious, *a priori*, that everything can be reduced directly to Justice, consequently that the true philosophical method consists in breaking all these patterns. In that sphere of the universal where we are going to move, and of which the centre is called Justice, harmony, equilibrium, balance, equality, all the graduations and specifications of school vanish. Little matter that we take our point of departure at such a meridian or such a parallel, at the equator or at the pole; that we begin with political economy rather than logic, with aesthetic or moral philosophy rather than counting and grammar. For the same reason, it matters little to us to change the subject as many times as we please, and as it pleases us; for us, there can result from it neither confusion nor mix-ups. It is always the higher reason of things that we seek, that is to say the direct relation of each things with Justice, which does not undermine in any way classifications of school, and does not compromise any of his faculties.

To philosophise about this and that, in the manner of Socrates, will thus be then, except for the adjustments demanded by the circumstances, the approach to follow in a philosophico-juridical education destined for the people.—A method of this sort, one will say, is no method at all.—Perhaps: with regard to science, rigor of method is a sign of mistrust of mind, arising from its weakness. If we should address ourselves to superior intelligences, it is the method of Socrates that they prefer, and universal reason itself, if it could speak, would not proceed otherwise. Now nothing resembles universal reason more, as to form, than the reason of the people; in treating it thus, we do not flatter it, but serve it.

### §XI: LAW OF PROGRESS: SOCIAL DESTINATION

An objection is posed.—If the centre or pivot of philosophy, namely Justice, is, like that of being, invariable and fixed, the system of things, which, in fact and in right, rests on that centre, must also be defined in itself, and consequently fixed in its ensemble and tending to immutability. Leibniz regarded this world as the best possible; he should have said, in virtue of the law of equilibrium that presides over it, that it is the only possible one. One can thus conceive of creation, at least in its thought, as being completed, the universal order being realised in a final manner: then, as the world would no longer have a reason to exist, since it would have reached its perfection, all would return to the universal repose. This is the secret thought of the religions: The end of things, they say, is for the Creator, just as for the creature, the consummation of glory. But strip away the mythology: underneath this unutterable glory, one finds immobility, death, nothingness. The world, drawn from nothing, i.e. inorganic immobility, amorphous, dark, returns, under the terms of its law of balance, to immobility; and our justification is nothing other than the work of our annihilation. Justice, balance, order, perfection, is petrifaction. Movement, life, thought, are bad things; the ideal, the absolute, the Just, which we must continually work to realise, is plenitude, immobility, non-being. It follows that, for the intelligent, moral and free being, happiness is to be found in death, in the quiet of the tomb. Such is the Buddhist dogma, expressed by this apothem: It is better to sit than stand, to sleep than to sit, and to be dead than to sleep. Such is also the conclusion to which one of the late philosophers of Germany arrived; and it is difficult to deny that any philosophy of the absolute, just as any religion, leads to the same result. But common sense is repelled by this theory: it judges that life, action, thought are good; morality itself is repelled by it, since it gives us constantly to work, to learn, and to undertake, in a word, to do the very things that, according to our final destiny, we should regard as bad. How to escape from this contradiction?

We believe that, as the space in which the worlds whirl about is infinite; time infinite; matter, hurled into infinite space, also infinite; consequently, the power of nature and the capacity for movement infinite: in the same way, without the principle and the law of the universe changing, creation is virtually infinite, in its extent, its duration and its forms. Under this condition of infinity, that inevitably falls on creation, the assumption of a completion, of a final consummation, is contradictory. The universe does not tend to an opposition to progress; its movement is perpetual, because the universe itself is infinite. The law of balance which presides over it does not lead it to uniformity, to an immobilism; it assures, on the contrary, eternal renewal by the economy of forces, which are infinite.

But if such is the true constitution of the universe, it must be admitted that such is also that of Humanity. We are not heading for any ideal perfection, for a final state that we might reach in a moment by crossing, through death, the gap that separates us from it. We are carried, along with the rest of the universe, in a ceaseless metamorphosis, which is all the more surely and gloriously achieved as we develop more in intelligence and morality. Progress thus remains the law of our heart, not in the sense only that, by the perfection of ourselves, we must approach unceasingly absolute Justice and the ideal; but in the sense that Humanity renewing itself and developing without end, like creation itself, the ideal of Justice and beauty which we have to carry out always changes and always increases.

Thus, the contemplation of the infinite, which led us to quietism, is precisely what cures us of it: we are participants in universal, eternal life; and the more we can reflect the image of it in our own life, through action and Justice, the happier we are. The small number of days which is allotted to us has nothing to do with this: our perpetuity is in the perpetuity of our race, which in turn is linked to the perpetuity of the Universe. Even if the very globe upon which we live, which we presently know with some scientific certainty to have had a beginning, should crumble beneath our feet and disperse in space, we should see in this dissolution merely a local metamorphosis, which, changing nothing with respect to the universal organism, could not cause us despair, and consequently would not affect our happiness in any way. If the joy of the father of a family on his deathbed is in the survival of his children, why shouldn't it be the same for our terrestrial humanity, the day when it will feel life become exhausted in its soil and consequently in its veins? After us, other worlds!... Would this idea be beyond the reach of the simple, or too low for the philosophers?

Thus determined in its nature, its conditions, its principle and its object, philosophy gives us, in its own manner, the word of our destiny.

What is philosophy?

Philosophy is the search, and, as far as the strength of the human mind permits, the discovery of the reason of things. Philosophy is thus defined as opposed to theology, which would be defined, we dare say, as the knowledge of the first cause, the inmost nature, and the final end of things.

Who created the universe?

Theology answers boldly, without understanding the meaning of its proposition: It is God. Philosophy, on the contrary, says: The universe, such as it appears to the eyes and the reason, being infinite, exists for all eternity. In it, life and spirit are permanent and indefectible; justice is the law that governs all its metamorphoses. Why should the world have a beginning? Why an end? Reason sees no need of it, and repudiates it.

What is God?

God, says theology, is the author, the creator, the preserver, the destroyer, and the sovereign lord of all things.

God, says metaphysics, auxiliary and interpreter of theology, is the infinite, absolute, necessary and universal being, which serves the universe as its substratum and hides behind its phenomena. This being is essentially one, consequently possibly personal, intelligent and free; moreover, because of its infinity, it is perfect and holy.

God, philosophy says finally, is, from the ontological point of view, a conception of the human mind, the reality of which it is impossible to deny or affirm authentically;—from the point of view of humanity, a fantastic representation of the human soul raised to the infinite.

Why was man created and put on the earth?

To know God, says theology, to love him, serve him, and by this means, to acquire eternal life.

Philosophy, pruning the mystical data from theology, answers simply: To carry out Justice, to exterminate evil, to contribute by the good administration of his sphere to the harmonious evolution of the worlds, and by this means, to obtain the greatest sum of glory and happiness, in his body and his soul.

We will continue this questionnaire. The catechism, with its mythology and its mysteries, served, for eighteen centuries, as a basis for the instruction of the people. Today, children no longer want it. Would philosophy, concrete and positive, arriving at its moment, prove less popular than the catechism has ever been?

[...]

# LITTLE POLITICAL CATECHISM

### INSTRUCTION I
Of the Social Power, Considered in Itself

**Question:**—ANY MANIFESTATION ATTESTS to a reality; what constitutes the reality of social power?

**Answer:**—The collective force.

**Q.**—What do you mean by the collective force?

**A.**—Any being, and by that I mean only what exists, what is a reality, not a phantom, a pure idea, possesses in itself, to whatever degree, the faculty or property, as soon as it finds itself in the presence of other beings, of being able to attract and be attracted, to repulse and be repulsed, to move, to act, to think, to PRODUCE, at the very least to resist, by its inertia, influences from the outside.

This faculty or property, one calls *force*.

Thus force is inherent, immanent in being: it is its essential attribute, and what alone testifies to its reality. Take away gravity, and we are no longer assured of the existence of bodies.

Now, it is not only individuals that are endowed with force; collectivities also have theirs.

To speak here only of human collectivities, let us suppose that the individuals, in such numbers as one might wish, in whatever manner and to whatever end, group their forces: the resultant of these agglomerated forces, which must not be confused with their sum, constitutes the force or power of the group.

**Q.**—Give examples of this force.

**A.**—A workshop, formed of workers whose labour converges towards the same goal, which is to obtain such-and-such a product, has, as a workshop or collectivity, a power that belongs to it: the proof of this is that the product of these individuals thus grouped is quite superior to what would have been the sum of their particular products if they had worked separately. Likewise, the crew of a ship, a limited partnership, an academy, an orchestra, an army, etc., all these collectivities, more or less skilfully organised, contain power, a power which is synthetic and consequently specific to the group, superior in quality and energy to the sum of the elementary forces which compose it.

As for the rest, the beings to which we accord individuality do not enjoy it by any title other than that of the collective beings: they are always groups formed according to a law of relation and in which force, proportional to the arrangement at least as much as to the mass, is the principle of unity.

From which one concludes, contrary to the old metaphysics:

1st, That any manifestation of power being the product of a group or an organisation, the intensity and quality of this power, as well as its form, sound, savour, solidity, etc., can serve for the observation and classification of beings; 2nd, that consequently, collective force being a fact as positive as individual force, the first perfectly distinct from the second, collective beings are as much realities as individual ones are.

**Q.**—How does the collective force, an ontological, mechanical, industrial phenomenon, become a political power?

**A.**—To begin with, any human group—family, workshop, battalion—can be regarded as a social embryo; consequently the force which is in it can, to a certain extent, form the basis for political power.

But in general it is not from the group such as we have just conceived it that the city, the State, is born. The State results from the unification of several groups different in nature and purpose, each one formed for the exercise of a specific function and the creation of a particular product, then joined under a common law and in an identical interest. It is a collectivity of a higher order, in which each group, taken itself for individual, contributes to developing a new force, which will be even greater to the extent that the associated functions will be more numerous, their harmony more perfect, and the service of the forces, on behalf of the citizens, more complete.

In short, that which produces power in society and comprises the reality of this society itself is the same thing that produces force in bodies, organised as well as unorganised, and that constitutes their reality, namely the relation of the parts. Imagine a society in which all relations between individuals had suddenly ceased, in which each would provide for his own subsistence in absolute isolation: whatever amity existed between these men, whatever their proximity, their multitude would no longer form an organism, it would lose all reality and all force. Like a body whose molecules have lost the relation that determines their cohesion, at the least shock, it would collapse into dust.

**Q.**—In the industrial group, the collective force can be perceived without difficulty: the increase in production shows it. But in the political group, by what signs can one recognise it? In what respect is it distinct from the force of ordinary groups? What is its special product, and what are the nature of its effects?

**A.**—From time immemorial, the vulgar believed to see the social power in the deployment of military forces, in the construction of monuments, the completion of works of public utility. But it is clear, according to what has just been said, that all of these things, whatever their size, are effects of the ordinary collective force: it does not matter whether the productive groups, being maintained at the expense of the State, are loyal to the prince, or whether they work for themselves. It is not there that we must seek the manifestations of the social power.

The active groups which make the city differing from one another in organisation, as well as in their idea and object, the relation that links them is no longer really a relation of co-operation but a relation of commutation. The character of the social force will thus be primarily commutative; it will be no less real.

**Q.**—Demonstrate by examples.

**A.**—MONEY. In theory and in result, products are exchanged for products. In fact, this exchange, the most significant function of society, which sets in motion values of so many billions of francs, so many thousands of kilogrammes in weight, would not take place without this common denominator, at the same time a product and a sign, which one calls money. In France, the sum of circulating cash is, if one can believe it, approximately two billion francs, or 10 million kilogrammes of silver, or 645,161 kilogrammes of gold. From the point of view of the goods that this instrument makes move, and by supposing all business [is] transacted in cash, one can say that this quantity of currency represents the driving force of several million horses. Is it the metal of which currency is made which has this extraordinary force? No: it is in the public reciprocity of which currency is the sign and the pledge.

THE BILL OF EXCHANGE. Money, in spite of this marvellous power that the relation of commutation of the producing groups gives it, is still not enough for the mass of transactions. One had to compensate for this by a clever combination, the theory of which is as well known as is the theory of money. The annual production of the country being 12 billion, one can, without exaggeration, carry the sum of the exchanges which this production implies to four times as much, that is to say, 48 billion. If the business were transacted in cash, one would need a quantity of currency of at least half that, if not equal to it: so that the use of the bill of exchanges actually acts as would a score of a billion francs, in gold or silver specie. From whence does this power come? From the relation of commutation which links the members of the society, groups and individuals.

THE BANK. The discount of bills of exchange is a service for which particular banks are made to pay a rather high price, but for which the Bank of France, which has the privilege to issue bearer orders and to make them universally accepted, only charges a fee two thirds lower. And it is proven that these fees could be reduced further by nine tenths. A new degree of economy is obtained, consequently a new force is created, by virtue of social relations.

For whoever says a saving in expenses, says, in all things, a reduction in inert force or dead weight, and consequently an increase in vital force.

RENT. Three causes contribute to the production of rent: land, labour, and society. Let us disregard land initially. As for labour, we know how, by the division of industries and the formation of the working group, one increases the level of production even while the number of individuals remains the same; this is indeed the collective force of which we spoke above. But the advantage of this division is not limited to that. The more the groups, in multiplying, multiply the relations of commutation in society, the more the number of useful objects and their very utility increase. However, the increase in utility that results from the relations of the groups in equal amounts of territory and an unchanged quantity of actual service, what is this other than rent? Therefore, the creation of wealth, the creation of force.

GENERAL SECURITY. In an antagonistic population, such as existed in the Middle Ages, it is in vain that the Church tries to make its threats heard, the courts to brandish their instruments of torture, the kings and their roughneck soldiers to make their lances ring on the flagstones of their barracks; there is no safety. The earth is covered with keeps and fortresses; everyone is armed and shut in; pillage and war are the order of the day.

One blames this disorder on the barbarism of the times, and one is right to do so. But what is barbarism, or rather, what produces it? The incoherence of the industrial groups, their small numbers, and the isolation in which they act, after the example of the agricultural groups. Here, therefore, the relation of functions, the solidarity of interests that this creates, the feeling for this solidarity that the producers acquire, the new consciousness that results from it, make for more law and order than do the army, the police force, and religion. Where can a power more real and more sublime be found?

These examples suffice to explain what, in itself, is the power to which the social community gives rise. It is by exploiting this power, converted into taxes, that the princes then acquire gendarmes and all the apparatus of coercion which serves to fortify them against the attacks of their rivals, often against the wish of the populations themselves.

**Q.**—This changes all the generally accepted ideas on the origin of power, on its nature, its organisation and its exercise. How can one believe that such ideas could be established everywhere, if truly one must hold them to be false?

**A.**—The opinion of ancient peoples on the nature and the origin of social power is a testimony of its reality. Power is immanent to society just as attraction is to matter, as is Justice to the heart of man. This immanence of power in society follows from the very concept of society, since it is impossible that the units, atoms, monads,[18] molecules, or people, being agglomerated, should not maintain relations with one another, forming a collectivity from which a force springs. From there it follows that power in society, like gravity in bodies, life in animals, Justice in the conscience, is a thing *sui generis* [i.e., in a class all its own], real and objective, the negation of which, given the fact of society, would imply a contradiction.

By its power, the first and most substantial of all its attributes, the social being thus testifies to its reality and life; it is posited, it is created, on the same basis and under the same conditions of existence as other beings.

This is what the first people felt, although they expressed it in a mystical form, when they traced the origin of social power to the gods, from whom their dynasties were descended. Their naive reason, surer than their senses, refused to admit that society, the State, the power that is manifested in them, were only abstractions, although these things remained invisible.

And it is what the philosophers did not see, when they gave birth to the State from the free will of man, or more accurately the abdication of his freedom, thus destroying by their dialectic what religion had taken such care to establish.

---

18  Leibniz's *Monadologie* (1714) had proposed that the material universe is composed of infinitesimally small (hence effectively immaterial) particles, which he named "monads," from a Greek root meaning "alone," since each of these particles would be incapable of receiving any influence from outside itself. Each monad, however, Leibniz held to be immediately in relation with every other monad by virtue of a "pre-established harmony" that made each monad a "living mirror" of all the others (78, 56). Proudhon rejects the "pre-established harmony" thesis, but later in *Justice* suggests that Leibniz's philosophy might serve as a useful analogy for his own concept of the centreless, horizontal federation: whereas "the monadology was for Leibniz merely a hypothesis," Proudhon remarks, for us, "it is a question of making it a fact." (Translator)

**Q.**—An essential condition of power is its unity. How will this unity be assured if the formative groups remain equal, if none obtains preponderance over the others? However, if this preponderance is granted, we return to the old system: for what then shall serve to return power to the community?

**A.**—The diversity of functions in society entails divergence or plurality in power no more than it entails the diversity of the final product. Power is one by nature, or it is nothing: far from creating it, any competition or prepotency, either of a member, or as a fraction of society, would only serve to abolish it. Does electricity cease to be a single thing in the battery because this battery is composed of several elements? All the same the quality of the social power varies, its intensity rises or drops, according to the number and diversity of the groups: as for its unity, it remains immutable.

**Q.**—Any force presupposes direction: who directs the social power?

**A.**—Everyone, which is to say no one. Since political power results from the relation of many forces, reason dictates immediately that these forces must balance one another so as to form a regular and harmonic whole. Justice intervenes in its turn to declare, as it did in relation to general economy, that this balance of power, in conformity with right, required by right, obliges every conscience. It is thus to Justice that the direction of power belongs; so that order in the collective being, like health, the will, etc, in the animal, is not the product of any particular initiative: it results from the organisation.

**Q.**—And what guarantees that Justice will be observed?

**A.**—The same which guarantees to us that the merchant will obey the coin, the public faith, the certainty of reciprocity: in a word, Justice.—Justice is for intelligent and free beings the supreme cause of their determinations. It has need only to be explained and understood to be affirmed by everyone and to act. It exists, or the universe is only a phantom and humanity a monster.

**Q.**—Then doesn't social power, to whatever degree, itself imply Justice?

**A.**—No: just like property, competition, and all the economic forces, all the collective forces, power is, by nature, a stranger to right; it is force. Let us say however that, since force is an attribute of any reality, and any force being able to increase indefinitely by association, consciousness acquires all the more energy in men and the respect of Justice all the more certainty in so far as the social group is more numerous and better formed: this is why in a civilised society, however corrupt or servile it may be, there is always more Justice than in a barbarian society.

**Q.**—What is to be understood by the division of powers?

**A.**—It is the very unity of power, considered in the diversity of the groups which form it. If the observer is placed in the centre of the bundle, and from there traverses the series of the groups, the power appears to him divided; if he looks at it as the resultant of the forces in relation, he sees its unity. Any true separation is impossible. It is thus that the assumption of two independent powers, each having their share of the world, such as *spiritual* power and *temporal* power appear today, is against the nature of things, a utopia, a nonsense.

**Q.**—What is the proper object of the social power?

**A.**—It results from its definition: it is to add unceasingly to the power of man, his wealth and his well-being, by a higher production of force.

**Q.**—Who benefits from the social power, and generally from any collective force?

**A.**—All those which contributed to form it, in proportion to their contribution.

**Q.**—What is the limit of power?

**A.**—Power, by nature and destination, has no limits other than those of the group that it represents, those of the interests and the ideas that it must serve.

However, by the limit of power, or powers, or, to be more precise, of the action of power, we mean that which is determined by the groups and sub-groups of which it is the general expression. Since each of these groups and sub-groups, indeed, up to the last term of the social series that is the individual, represents the social power with respect to the others, in terms of its function, it follows that the limitation of power, or rather, its distribution, regularly accomplished under the law of Justice, is nothing other than the formula for an increase in freedom itself.

**Q.**—What differentiation do you make between politics and economics?

**A.**—At base, they are two different ways of naming the same thing. One does not imagine that men need, for their freedom and their well-being, anything but force; for the sincerity of their relations, anything but Justice. Economy presupposes these two conditions: what more could politics yield?

Under current conditions, politics is the equivocal and risky art of making order in a society in which all laws of economy are ignored, all balance destroyed, every freedom compromised, every conscience warped, all collective force converted into a monopoly.

### INSTRUCTION II
#### Of the Appropriation of the Collective Forces, and the Corruption of the Social Power

**Q.**—Is it possible that a phenomenon as considerable as that of the collective force, which changes the face of ontology, which almost touches physics, could have been concealed for so many centuries from the attention of the philosophers? How, in relation to something that interests them so closely, did the public reason, on the one hand, and personal interest, on the other, let themselves be misled for such a long time?

**A.**—Nothing comes except with the passage of time, in science as in nature. All starts with the infinitely small, with a seed, initially invisible, which develops little by little, toward the infinite. Thus, the persistence of error is proportional to the size of the truths. Thus, one is thus not surprised if the social power, inaccessible to the senses in spite of its reality, seemed to the first men an emanation of the divine Being, for this reason the worthy object of their religion. As little as they knew how to realise it through analysis, they had a keener sense of it, quite different in this respect from the philosophers who, arriving later, made of the State a restriction on the freedom of citizens, a mandate of their whim, a nothingness. Even today, the economists have barely identified the collective force. After two thousand years of political mysticism, we have had two thousand years of nihilism: one could not use another word for the theories which have held sway since Aristotle.

**Q.**—What was the consequence of this delay in knowledge of the collective Being for peoples and States?

**A.**—The appropriation of all collective forces and the corruption of social power; in less severe terms, an arbitrary economy and an artificial constitution of the public power.

**Q.**—Explain yourself on these two headings.

**A.**—By the constitution of the family, the father is naturally invested with the ownership and direction of the force issuing from the family group. This force soon increases from the work of slaves and mercenaries, the number of which it contributes to increase. The family becomes a tribe: the father, preserving his dignity, sees the power he has grow proportionately. It is the starting point, the type of all such appropriations. Everywhere where a group of men is formed, or a power of community, there is formed a patriciate, a seigniory.

Several families, several societies, together, form a city: the presence of a superior force is felt at once, the object of the ambition of all. Who will become its agent, its recipient, its organ? Usually, it will be that of the chiefs who hold sway over the most children, parents, allies, clients, slaves, employees, beasts of burden, capital, land—in a word, those who have at their disposal the greatest force of collectivity. It is a natural law that the greater force absorbs and assimilates the smaller forces, and that domestic power becomes a title of political power, and only the strong may compete for the crown. One knows what became of the dynasty of Saul, founded by Samuel in contempt of this law, and the difficulty of King John, called Lack-Land, in gaining the throne of England. He never would have triumphed over the resistance of the barons without the charter that he granted to them, which became the foundation of English freedoms. In our own history, when the mayor of the palace, e.g., Pépin de Herstal[19] or Hugues le Blanc[20], became more powerful in men and fiefs than the king, he was made king, in spite of the ecclesiastical consecration that protected the suzerain. In 1848, when Louis Napoléon was elected president of the Republic, the people of the countryside believed him to possess a fortune of twenty billion.

Furthermore, the alienation of the collective force, in addition to having been the result of ignorance, appears to have been a means of preparing races. To make the primitive man, the savage, fit for social life, a long trituration of bodies and souls must have been necessary. The education of humanity being accomplished by a kind of mutual instruction, the law of things dictated that the instructors enjoy certain prerogatives. In the future, equality will consist in the ability of each to exercise mastery in turn just as each in turn will have undergone discipline.

**Q.**—What you say aptly demonstrates how the great social dispossession was consummated, how inequality and misery became the cancer of civilisation. But how to explain this resignation of the consciences, this submission of wills, which for such a long period has been disturbed only by a few revolts by slaves, fanatics, proletarians?

**A.**—The old religion of power would, up to a certain point, rationalise the fact. One subjected oneself to power because one saw it as coming from the gods, i.e., because it was worshipped. But this religion is lost: dynastic legitimacy, *droit du seigneur*,[21] and divine right are no longer anything but odious words, displaced by the proud principle of popular sovereignty. However, the phenomenon persists: men nowadays appear no more reluctant to subject themselves to the authority and the exploitation of a single man than were their fathers formerly. Obvious proof of the vanity of the theological and metaphysical theories, the principles of which can either perish or survive without the facts that they are supposed to cause or prevent ever ceasing to occur.

On this sad subject, over which misanthropy and scepticism prevail, the banal excuses for so many treasons and cowardices, the theory of collective

---

19   Pippin of Herstal (635–714) was the Mayor of the Palace of Austrasia from 680 to his death and of Neustria and Burgundy from 687 to 695. He was also the first mayor of the palace to reign as Duke and Prince of the Franks, by far overshadowing the Merovingian Kings. (Editor)

20   Hugh the White (d. 956) was duke of the Franks and count of Paris. As the most powerful man in the kingdom of France (West Francia) during the reign of Louis IV d'Outremer and the early years of King Lothar, he refused the opportunity to become King twice, preferring to work from behind the throne. (Editor)

21   "the lord's right": referring to certain privileges enjoyed by feudal landlords over their serfs such as rights of hunting, taxation, and farming. (Editor)

force provides a peremptory answer that radically confirms the morality of the masses, while leaving the oppressors and their accomplices to their infamy.

Through the grouping of individual forces, and through the relation of the groups, the whole nation forms one body: it is a real being, of a higher order, whose movement implicates the existence and fortune of everyone. The individual is immersed in society; he emerges from this great power, from which he would separate only to fall into nothingness. Indeed, as great as the appropriation of the collective forces may be, however intense may be the tyranny, it is obvious that a share of the social benefit always remains to the mass, and that in the end, it is better for each to remain in the group than to leave it.

It is thus not actually the exploiter, it is not the tyrant, whom the workers and the citizens follow: seduction and terror enter little into their submission. It is the social power that they respect, a power ill-defined in their thinking, but outside of which they sense that they cannot subsist; a power whose prince, whoever it may be, may show them its seal and see them tremble to break with it by a revolt.

For this reason any usurper of the public power never fails to cover his crime with the pretext of the public safety, to call himself the father of the fatherland, restorer of the nation, as if the social force drew its existence from him, while in fact he is only an effigy for it, a stamp, and, so to speak, a commercial brand. And he will fall, with the same ease with which he was established, the moment his presence appears to threaten the great interest that he claimed to defend: there, in last analysis, is the cause of the fall of all governments.

**Q.**—Social power having been constituted as a princedom, appropriated by a dynasty or exploited by a caste, what becomes of its relations with the nation?

**A.**—These relations are completely inverted. In the natural order, power is born from society, it is the resultant of all the particular forces grouped for labour, defence, and Justice. According to the empirical conception suggested by the alienation of power, it is, on the contrary, society which is born naked from it; it is the generator, the creator, the author; he is higher than it: so that the prince, instead of being the simple agent of the republic as truth wants it, is made sovereign by the republic, and, like God, the dispenser of justice.

The consequence is that the prince, occupied with his personal domination, instead of ensuring and developing the social power, creates for himself, through the army, the police force and the tax, a particular force, able to resist any attack from the interior and to compel the nation to obedience at need: it is this princely force which will be called from now on power. Napoléon III, like Napoléon I, says *my army, my fleet, my ministers, my prefects, my government*; and he is right to say this, because none belong to the nation any longer; on the contrary, all are against the nation.

Q.—How, then, is Justice to be conceived?

A.—As an emanation of power, that which is the very negation of Justice. Indeed, under the normal condition of society, Justice dominates power, the balance and distribution of which it makes a law. Under the dynastic mode, power dominates Justice, which becomes an attribute, a function of authority. From whence the subordination of Justice to *raison d'État*, the last word of the old politics, judgement of all the governments which follow it, and that Christianity, by adding the *reason of salvation* [*raison du salut*] to it, did not sanctify it at all. Princes and priests quarrel over the exercise of power: neither one nor the other are worthy of it, because they all ignore the supremacy of right.

Q.—How, in this system of usurpation, are the relations of citizens determined as to persons, services, and goods?

A.—Such is Justice before power, such will it be in the nation: i.e., Justice being seen as an emanation of force, as much human as divine, force becomes, in sum, the measure of right, and society, instead of resting on the balance of forces, has inequality for its principle, i.e., the negation of order.

Q.—After all that, what must the social and political organisation be?

A.—It is easy to render an account of it. The collective forces having been appropriated, public power having been converted into an inheritance, individuals and families, already unequal by the chance of nature, having become more so by civilisation, society is constituted as a hierarchy. This is what was expressed by the dynastic religion and the oath of fidelity to the imperial person. In this system, it is by principle that Justice, or what is called by this name, always weighs on the side of the superior against the inferior: which, under the appearance of an inescapable autocracy, is instability itself.

And, sad to say, all the world is complicit here with the prince: the spirit of equality which Justice creates in man was neutralised or destroyed by the contrary prejudice, which renders invincible the alienation of all collective force.

Q.—How, in this travesty of Justice, society, and power, is unity preserved?

A.—The nature of things implies that unity should result from the balance of forces, made compulsory by Justice, which thus becomes the true sovereign, and which, in this capacity, educates all the participants in public power. Today, unity consists in the absorption of any faculty, any interest, any initiative by the person of the prince: it is social death. And as society can neither die nor do without unity, antagonism is established between society and power, until the catastrophe arrives.

**Q.**—In this state of affairs, the diminution of power from time immemorial seemed a guarantee for society: of what does such a reduction consist, and for what can it serve?

**A.**—Apart from what the prince has by way of inheritance or private domain, apart from the command of the armies, the collection of taxes and the appointment of civil servants, the principle is that he hands over the surplus, lands, mines, cultures, industries, transportation, banks, trade, education, to the whims, to the absolute disposition, to the unrestrained competition or immoral coalition of the privileged class. What enters into the province of economy is supposed not to concern him at all; it must not be interfered with. What one calls the limit of power, in a word, is the surrender of the true social force to a feudal caste, which is decorated with the name of civil liberties: an absurd transaction that no government can support, and that will before long serve as a new leavening agent for the revolution. Today, in France, the emperor is master of all: but by the same token, he has always put himself in danger of losing everything: thus time shall tell, one way or another.

**Q.**—Thus conditioned, power is without an object.

**A.**—No: the object of power is precisely then to maintain this system of contradictions, in the absence of Justice and as an inverted image of Justice.

**Q.**—Give the synonymy of power.

**A.**—The artificial constitution of power having deteriorated its concept, language was to feel the effects: here, as everywhere, words are the key to history.

Regarded as the inheritance of the prince, as his establishment, his profession, his trade, the social power was called the *State*. Like the common people, the king said: my State, or my Estates, for my domain, my establishment.—The Revolution, transporting from the prince to the country the property of power, preserved this word, today synonymous with the *res publica*, the republic.

As the personnel of power is supposed to govern the nation and to govern its destinies, one gives to this personnel and to power itself the name of *government*, an expression as false as it is ambitious. In theory, society is ungovernable; it obeys only Justice, on pain of death. In fact, the so-called governments, liberal and absolute, with their arsenal of laws, decrees, edicts, statutes, plebiscites, payments, ordinances, never controlled anyone or anything. Living a completely instinctive life, acting at the pleasure of invincible necessities, under the pressure of prejudices and circumstances which they do not understand, generally being pushed by the current of society which from time to time breaks them, they can hardly, by their own initiative, accomplish anything other than disorder. And the proof of it is that all end miserably.

Finally, if one considers in power this eminent dignity that makes it higher than any individual, any community, one calls it *sovereign*: a dangerous
expression, from which it is to be wished that democracy will guard itself in
the future. Whatever the power of the collective being, it does not constitute
for that reason, in comparison with the citizen, a sovereignty: it would make
almost as much sense to say that a machine in which a hundred thousand
spindles turn is the sovereign of the hundred thousand spinners it represents.
As we have said, Justice alone commands and governs, the Justice that creates
power by making the balance of power obligatory for all. Between power and
the individual, there is thus nothing but right, and all sovereignty is denied;
sovereignty is the denial of Justice, it is religion.

### INSTRUCTION III
Of the Forms of Government and Their Evolution During the
Pagan-Christian Period

**Q.**—Would the history of nations and the revolutions of States then present
nothing but the play of economic forces, at times contrary and conflictual,
according to the views of the prince, the egoism of the great, and the prejudices of the people, sometimes favoured and harmonised according to right?

**A.**—It is so: let us add only that the arbitrary must have its period, Justice
always bringing society back to balance, having sooner or later to triumph
definitively over *subversive influences*.

**Q.**—For this long period, which one could, in a sense, call revolutionary,
since the State continually goes from one revolution to another, what are the
forms of power?

**A.**—According to whether the government is supposed to belong to only
one, several, or all, one calls it monarchy, aristocracy or democracy. A compromise also often takes place between these elements, and a mixed government results from it, which one supposes for that reason to be more solid,
and which is no more sustainable than the others.

In another sense, one calls the *forms* of government the conditions to which
the existence of power is subjected. Thus, the Charter of 1830, having fixed
the principles of public law, defines in some chapters the forms of government,
i.e. that which concerns the king, the Chambers, the ministers, the legal order.

The idea of consecrating the conditions of power in writing is an old one:
the Jews attributed their constitution to God, who would have given it to
Moses under the name of *Berith*,[22] alliance, pact, charter or testament.

These constitutions all rest on the preconceived idea that since society
does not progress by itself, having in itself neither potentiality nor harmony,
power as well as direction coming to it from on high via a dynasty, a Church,

---

22  Hebrew for "Covenant," *berith* is a central concept of the Hebrew Scriptures and is
the term used for the relationship between God and his people. (Editor)

or a senate, one could not be too prudent in the organisation of power, in the choice of the prince, in the election of the senators, in legislative and administrative formalities, in jurisdiction, etc.

**Q.**—Which of these governmental forms deserves preference?

**A.**—None: other than the extent to which they partake of the nature of things and express the genius of the people, their defects are the same; this is why history shows them supplanting one another continuously, without society being able to find stability anywhere.

The consecration of the principle of inequality by the lack of balance in economic transactions;

The appropriation of collective forces;

The establishment of a factitious power in place of the real power of society;

The abolition of Justice by *raison d'État*;

Direction given over to the prince's whim, if the State is monarchical, and, on any other assumption, to party cabals;

The continual tendency to the absorption of society by the State:

That, for the duration of the preparatory period, is the basis on which the political order is constituted, whatever name it takes and whatever pretended guarantee it gives.

**Q.**—But democracy means the restoration of the nation to the ownership and enjoyment of its own forces: why does it appear that you condemn this form of government as much as the others?

**A.**—As long as democracy is not elevated to the true conception of power, it cannot be, as it has not been so far, anything other than a lie, a shameful transition of brief duration, sometimes from aristocracy to monarchy, sometimes from monarchy to aristocracy. The Revolution held onto this word as a promise [*une pierre d'attente*]; some seventy years hence, we have made of it a broken promise [*une pierre de scandale*].

**Q.**—Thus, short of a revolution in ideas, is all political stability, all social morality, all freedom or happiness impossible for man and the citizen?

**A.**—It is not only history that reveals this to be true, nor Justice and equality, which demonstrate it as their inevitable sanction; it is economic science at its most elementary, positive, and real that proves it. The collective forces having been appropriated, the social power having been corrupted and alienated, the government oscillates from demagogy to despotism and from despotism to demagogy, sowing ruin and multiplying catastrophes, in almost regular periods.

**Q.**—Is there nothing more to be gathered, for the philosopher, from this study of the formation, growth, and decline of the old States?

**A.**—They were, in their very inorganism, the revelation of a new State, and something like an embryogenesis of the Revolution. What progress, indeed, what idea do we not owe to them?

The development of the economic forces, among the first rank of which the collective forces are to be found;

The discovery of the social power in the relation of all these forces;

The rationality of forms of government, varying according to race, soil, climate, industry, the relative importance of the constituent elements serving to mark the political centre of gravity in each country;

The idea of universal solidarity or humanitarian force, sometimes emerging from the struggle of States, sometimes from their agreement;

The idea of a balance of economic and social forces, attempted in the name of a balance of powers;

The development of right, the highest expression of man and society;

A greater understanding of history, to resume the perspective of this physiology of the collective being; so many centuries of a civilisation that was seemingly negative, because it was the enemy of equality, becoming centuries of affirmation, demonstrating the genesis and equilibrium of forces:

Here are what philosophical thought discovers underneath the revolutions and cataclysms; here, for the constitution of the order to come, the fruit of so many sorrows and disappointments.

**Q.**—It is perpetual peace which you announce after so many others. But do you not think that war, having its principle in the unsoundable abysses of the human heart, the war that all religions commend, that nothing is enough to engage, like the duel, is incoercible, indestructible?

**A.**—War, in the person of which the Christian worships the judgement of God, which some so-called rationalists attribute to the ambition of princes and popular passions, is caused by the imbalance of economic forces and the insufficiency of the statutory, civil, public and popular law that serves as a rule. Any nation in which economic balance is violated, the forces of production constituted as a monopoly, and public authority given over to the discretion of exploiters is, *ipso facto*, a nation at war with the remainder of mankind. The very principle of monopolisation and inequality that presided over its political and economic constitution pushes it to the monopolisation, *per fas et nefas*,[23] of all the globe's wealth, to the subjugation of all peoples: no truth in the world is better established. Let balance be established, let Justice arrive, and all war is impossible. There is no more force to sustain it; it would imply an action of nothingness upon reality, a contradiction.

**Q.**—You explain everything by collective forces, by their diversity and inequality, by their alienation, by the conflict to which this alienation gives

---

23   Roughly, "by fair means or foul." (Editor)

rise, by their imperceptible but ultimately victorious tendency, via the influence of an indefectible Justice, to equilibrium. What share of influence over human events do you attribute to the initiative of heads of State, to their councils, their geniuses, their virtues, and their crimes? What part, in a word, is played by free will?

**A.**—It is a priest who said that man acts and God disposes. Man is the absolute power, inexperienced, blind man, to whom is promised empire over the earth; God is the social legislation that directs this untamed will without its knowledge, enlightening it little by little, and finally recreating it in its own likeness. Human action in history is thus, initially, force, spontaneity, combat; then recognition of the law that it enacts, and that is nothing other than the balancing of its freedom, i.e., Justice. In its struggles, the free being expresses, by its oscillations, the formula of its movement; it is this formula that constitutes civilisation and takes the place of providence for us: here is all the mystery. May the day come when all this governmental crew that swarms in the darkness shall disappear.

**Q.**—What is theocracy?

**A.**—A symbolic of the social force.

Among all people, the feeling of this force caused national religion to emerge, under the influence of which domestic religions, little by little, disappeared. Everywhere, the god was this collective force, personified and adored under a mystical name. The religion thus serving as a basis for government and Justice, logic dictated that theology would become the heart of politics, that consequently the Church would take the place of the State, the priesthood that of the noble, and the sovereign pontiff that of the emperor or king. Such is the theocratic idea. A product of Christian spiritualism, its appearance awaited the moment when, all nations meeting under a common law, the things of heaven would gain preponderance over the things of the earth in our souls. But it was the dream of a moment, an attempt aborted as soon as it was conceived, which was to always remain in a theoretical state. The Church, placing the reality of its ideal in heaven, above and apart from the social community, consequently denied the immanence of a force in this community, just as it denied in man the immanence of Justice; and it is this force, of which princes remained only the agents and instruments, that gave the Church its exclusionary status.

**Q.**—What improvement did Christianity bring to the government of peoples?

**A.**—None: it did nothing but change the protocol. The ancient noble, patrician, warrior or sheikh asserted his usurpation by virtue of necessity; the noble Christian asserts it in the name of Providence. For the first, nobility was a fact of nature; for, second; it is a fact of grace. But for both of these, royalty supported noble privilege, religion consecrated it. Wherefore the claims of the catholic Church to sovereignty, and its attempt at theocracy, vigorously repressed by the princes, and soon abandoned by the theologians themselves. A transaction intervened: the separation of spiritual and temporal was set up in axiom of public law; a new leaven of discord was thrown among the nations. Half pagan, half Christian, politics carried tyranny in its train; Justice was sacrificed and freedom compromised more than ever.

INSTRUCTION IV

Constitution of Social Power by the Revolution

**Q.**—In what terms has the Revolution expressed itself on the reality of social power?

**A.**—No express declaration exists in this respect. However, as much as the Revolution finds repugnant the ancient mysticism that placed Justice and power in heaven, it also finds insufficient the nominalism that followed it, which tends to make the collective being and the power that is in it, like Justice, words, concepts. There is not a single idea, not a single act of the Revolution that can be explained through this metaphysics. All that it produced, all that it promises, would be a castle in the air and another illusory transcendence if it did not presuppose in society an effectivity of power, consequently a reality of existence that is assimilated to all creation, to all being. In any case, the silence of the Revolution as to the nature of power pertains only to the first two acts of this great drama: aren't we, today, especially since 1848, in the midst of an eruption of revolutionary ideas? And don't science and philosophy join with induction to confirm our thesis?

**Q.**—In the absence of texts, can you give your reasons?

**A.**—Science says to us that any body is a composite the final elements of which no analysis can find, held to one another by an attraction, a force.

What is force? It is, like substance, like the atoms it holds grouped together, a thing inaccessible to the senses, that the intelligence grasps only through its manifestations, as the expression of a relationship.

RELATIONSHIP: here, in the last analysis, is that to which all phenomenality, all reality, all force, all existence is referred. Just as the idea of being encompasses that of force and relation, in the same way that of relation inexorably presupposes force and substance, becoming and being. So that everywhere where the mind grasps a relation, experience discovering nothing else, we must conclude from this relation the presence of a force, and consequently a reality.

The Revolution denies divine right, in other words, the supernatural origin of social power. That means, in theory, that if a being does not have its power to be in itself, it cannot be; in fact, that the power which is detected in society having human relations for expression, its nature is human; consequently that the collective being is not a phantom, an abstraction, but an existence.

Confronted with divine right, the Revolution thus posits the sovereignty of the people, the unity and the indivisibility of the Republic. Meaningless words, fit only to serve as a mask for the most appalling tyranny, and sooner or later contradicted by events, if they do not refer to the higher organisation, formed by the relation of industrial groups, and with the commutative power that results from it.

The Revolution, renewing civil right as well as political right, places in labour, and in labour alone, the justification for property. It denies that property founded on man's arbitrary whim and considered as manifestation of pure ego is legitimate. This is why it abolished ecclesiastical property, which was not founded on work, and why, before the new régime, it turned the priest's benefice into wages.[24] However, what is property, thus balanced by work and legitimated by right? The realisation of individual power. But the social power is composed of all the individual powers: of which it also expresses a subject. The Revolution could not affirm its realism more energetically.

Under the regime of divine right, the law is a commandment: it does not have its principle in man. The Revolution, in the person of Montesquieu, one of its fathers, changes this concept: it defines the law as *the relation of things*,[25] and with stronger reason, as the relation of persons, i.e., of faculties or functions, giving birth to the social being through their co-ordination.

Turning to the matter of government, the Revolution says formally that it must be made up according to the double principle of the *division* of powers and their *balance*. However, what is the division of powers? The same thing as what the economists call division of labour, which is nothing more than a particular aspect of the collective force. As to the balance of powers, a subject otherwise little understood, I need say only that it is the condition of existence for organised beings, for which the absence of balance entails disease and death.

It is useless to recount the more or less regular steady stream of acts accomplished since 1789 under the terms of this revolutionary ontology: administrative centralisation, unification of weights and measurements, the creation of the general ledger, the foundation of the centralised school system, the establishment of the Bank of France, the amalgamation, under our very eyes, of the railroad systems in preparation for their operation by the State and their conversion into a system of workers' associations. All these facts, and many others, testify to the realistic thought that governs our public law. Thanks to all these achievements, France has become a great organism,

---

24   A "benefice," in Catholicism, was a kind of pay assigned to priests for ecclesiastical duties, a system that became subject to serious abuse; the *Constitution civile du clergé* ("Civil Constitution of the Clergy," a law instituted in 1790) supplanted it, making priests effectively government employees. (Translator)

25   Montesquieu, *The Spirit of Laws* (Cincinnati: Clarke, 1873) 1.1: "Laws [...] are the necessary relations derived from the nature of things." (Translator)

whose power of assimilation would sweep the world, were it not corrupted by those who exploit and govern it.

**Q.**—Why, for seventy years, has the application of these ideas made so little progress? Why, instead of the free State, identical and adequate to society itself, have we preserved the feudal, royal, imperial, military, dictatorial State?

**A.**—That is due to two causes, henceforth easy to appreciate: one is that the balance of products and services did not cease to be a *desideratum* of economy; the other, that the appropriation of the collective forces was maintained, even extended, as if by natural right.

From this follows the whole series of inevitable consequences: in the nation, the conservation of the old prejudice in favour of the inequality of conditions and fortunes, formation of a capitalist feudality in the place of the feudality of the nobles, a recrudescence of the ecclesiastical spirit and a return to the practices of divine right; in government, the substitution of a seesaw system for the balance of forces, a concentration leading to despotism, a monstrous development of the military and police forces, the continuation of machiavellian politics, the destruction of Justice by *raison d'État*, and, to conclude, increasingly frequent revolutions.

**Q.**—What is it that you call the seesaw system?

**A.**—The seesaw, also called *doctrine*,[26] is in politics what the theory of Malthus is in economics. Just as the Malthusians claim to establish balance in the population by mechanically blocking the generative function, in the same way the doctrinaires make the balance of power by transpositions of majority, electoral manipulations, corruption, terrorism. The constitutional machine, such as we have seen it function since 1791, with its distinctions of Upper House and Lower Chamber, legislative and executive power, upper classes and middle classes, large and small colleges, responsible ministers and irresponsible royalty, is inevitably a seesaw system.

**Q.**—One could not better explain, in relation to the reality of the social being, the inmost thought of the Revolution. But the Revolution is also freedom, that above all: in this system of balances, what becomes of it?

**A.**—This question brings back to us to that of weighting forces which we have just raised.

Just as several men, by grouping their efforts, produce a force of collectivity, superior in quality and intensity to the sum of their respective forces, in the same way, several labouring groups, placed in a relation of exchange, generate a power of a higher order, which we have specifically considered as being social power.

---

26   A reference to the Doctrinaires. (Editor)

For this social power to act in its plenitude, for it to yield all the fruit that its nature promises, it is necessary that the forces or functions of which it is composed should be in balance. However, this balance cannot be the effect of an arbitrary determination; it must result from the balancing of forces acting on one another with complete freedom and equalising one another. Which presupposes that the balance or proportional mean of each force being known, everyone, individuals and groups, will accept this as the measure of its right and subject himself to it.

Thus public order results from the citizen's reason; thus this social sovereignty, which initially seemed to us to be the resultant of individual and collective forces, presents itself now in the form of an expression of their freedom and their justice, the attributes *par excellence* of the moral being.

This is why the Revolution, abolishing the corporative regime, the privileges of mastery and the entire feudal hierarchy, declared the principle of public right to be the freedom of industry and trade; therefore it raised above all councils of State, above all parliamentary and ministerial deliberations, the freedom of the press, universal control, and proclaimed, by instituting the jury, the jurisdiction of the citizen over any individual and any thing.

Freedom was nothing: it is everything, since order results from its balancing by itself.

**Q.**—If freedom is everything, in what does government consist?

**A.**—For us to form an idea of it, let us look at it from the point of view of the budget, and posit a principle.

The government has the aim of protecting freedom and making sure that Justice is observed. However, by their nature, freedom and Justice tend to be gratuitous: they take care of themselves, so to speak. Just as work, exchange, and credit have only to be defended against the parasites who, under the pretext of protecting and representing them, absorb them.

What does freedom of trade cost? Nothing; perhaps a supplement of expenses for the maintenance of the markets, ports, roads, channels, railroads, moved by the larger multitude of the merchants.

What does freedom of industry cost, the freedom of the press, all freedoms? Again, nothing, if not some measurements of order relating to statistics, improvement and patents, royalties, etc

In two words, the old State, by the anomaly of its position, tends to complicate its mechanisms, which means increasing its expenses indefinitely; the new one, by its liberal nature, tends to reduce them indefinitely: such is the difference between them, expressed in budgetary language.

Thus, to have a government that is free, reasonable, and cheap, it is enough to simply cut off, reduce, or modify all the articles in the current budget that are contrary to the principles here established. That is the whole system: there is nothing else to be concerned with.

**Q.**—Give an outline of the new budget.

**A.**—Let us suppose the Revolution to have been accomplished, peace with the outside world assured by the federation of peoples, stability guaranteed to the interior by the balance of values and services, by the organisation of labour, and by the restoration of the people to ownership of its own collective forces.

*National debt*—Nothing. It would imply a contradiction, in a society where services are balanced, fortunes levelled, credit organised on the principle of reciprocity, to suppose that the State should contract debts, as if this society had at its disposal anything but its means of production and its products. No one can become his own lender, otherwise than by labour. What the old government is unable to do, the new democracy shall do always: it shall provide for its non-recurring expenses [*dépenses extraordinaires*] by a non-recurring effort [*travail extraordinaire*]. Justice demands it, and it will never cost a quarter of what the capitalists demand.

*Pensions*—Nothing. Any individual, whatever category of service to which he may belong, has a life-long duty to work, except in case of disease, infirmity, or mutilation. In this case, his subsistence is regulated by the law of general insurance and carried by the account of his corporation.

*Civil list*[27]—Nothing.

*Senate*—Nothing. The duality of chambers is a product of class distinctions, or, what amounts to the same thing, to the divergence of interests, marked by these two terms: labour and capital. In democracy, these two interests are fused. The senate, an inert body in the empire, would be an insult to the Republic.

*Council of State*—Nothing. The function of the Council of State is absorbed by the legislative Body and the ministers.

*Legislative body,* or assembled representatives: this costs approximately two million today. Let us accept this figure.

Beside the legislative body will be created an office of jurisprudence, a bureau of historical, legal, economic, political, statistical information, to enlighten the representatives in their work. The supreme court of appeal belongs to this office. Expense to be added to the preceding.

Thus, since the national debt, consolidated and lifelong, forming, along with the expenses of war, the police force, the dynasty, and the aristocracy, the most unproductive part of the budget, is approximately 1,000 million to 1,200 million, one can judge, by this economy, what an ordering power there is in freedom and Justice.

*Ministers' service*—The legislative power is not distinguished from the executive power. Representatives of the nation, being deputy chiefs of the various public services, industrial groups, corporations and all territorial districts, are, by this fact, real ministers.

---

27   i.e., the expense of maintaining the royal family (Translator)

These ministers, amongst whom the parliamentary monarchy had such difficulty maintaining agreement, although their number did not exceed seven or eight, now numbering two hundred and fifty or three hundreds, bearing all the titles of their respective and perpetually revocable categories, form, by their meeting, a national convention, the Council of Ministers, a Council of State, a legislature, a sovereign court. As for their agreement, notwithstanding the heat of the deliberations, it is guaranteed by that of the same interests as they represent.

**Q.**—And what guarantees the agreement of interests?
**A.**—As we have already said, their mutual weighting.

**Q.**—Will you pass on to the budget ministries?
**A.**—The expenditure of the ministries is of two species, according to whether they belong to the overheads of the nation, or that they must be brought back to the service of which the minister, or deputy, is the body. In the first case, they must be charged to the budget of the State: such are the expenditure of the legislative Body itself, of the monuments; in the second, they fall to the charge of the territorial groups, corporations and districts: such are the expenditure of the railroads, the budget of the communes, etc.

This distinction having been established, one can proceed to the ruling.

*Justice*—The legal hierarchy reduced to its simplest expression the jury organised for civil as well as for criminal [law], the court expenses are composed: 1$^{st}$, the salary of the judge directing the hearings and applying the law; 2$^{nd}$, that of the bodies of the public ministry, charged to supervise the observation of the laws throughout the country. The first is the responsibility of the communes which choose the judge; the second is carried by the budget of the State.

*Interior*—Joined together, part with the public ministry, which supervises but does not manage; part with the municipalities, part with other ministries.

*Police force*—On the charge of the localities.

*Worship*—Nothing. No more Church, no more temples. Justice is the apotheosis of humanity. The old budget for worship passes to the medical service and state education.

*State education*—Partly to the charge of the localities, partly to the charge of the State.

*Finances*—Joined with the central bank.

*Tax collection*—The creation of public warehouses in the cantons and districts for the regularisation of markets will make it possible to receive everywhere tax or revenue in kind, which means revenue in labour, of all the forms of taxation the cheapest, the least vexatious, that which tends least to inequality of distribution and exaggeration of demands.

It is useless to push these details further. Each can take the pleasure of doing so and judging for himself, by making the critique of the budget, what would become of government in a nation like France if this great principle were applied to it, at once a moral principle, a governmental principle, and a principle of taxation: That Justice and freedom subsist in themselves, that they are essentially free, and that they tend in all their operations to suppress their protectors as well as their enemies.

### INSTRUCTION V
#### Question of the Agenda

**Q.**—What would you do on the day after a revolution?

**A.**—It is useless to repeat it. The principles of the economic and political constitution of society are known: that is enough. It is up to the people, to its representatives, to do what they must, taking account of the circumstances.

From time immemorial, the question of the day after the revolution worried the old parties, whose every thought is to stop the *cataclysm*, as they say, *by taking the side of the fire*. It is to this end that for six years, issues of aristocratic, catholic, dynastic, even republican publications have appeared, whose authors ask nothing better than to pass for enemies of despotism and devoted to freedom. It would be most naïve to take such proclamations for models, and to play at formulating programs. Let the people be penetrated by the meaning and scope of this word, *Justice*, and take it into hand: there is its day after the revolution. As to its execution: the idea having been acquired, execution shall be infallible.

**Q.**—What do you think of dictatorship?

**A.**—What good is it? If the purpose of dictatorship is to found equality by principles and institutions, it is useless: one does not need for that anything other than the 20 districts of Paris supported by the people of the 86 departments, achieving their mandate in three times twenty-four hours. If, on the contrary, the only end of dictatorship is to avenge insults to the party, to rein in the rich and subdue a frivolous multitude, then it is tyranny: we have nothing more to say about it.

Dictatorship has enjoyed popular acclaim at all times; it does so now more than ever. It is the secret dream of some lunatics, the most extreme argument that democracy can provide for the conservation of the imperial mode.

**Q.**—What is your opinion on universal suffrage?

**A.**—As all constitutions have established it since '89, universal suffrage is the strangulation of the public conscience, the suicide of popular sovereignty, the apostasy of the Revolution. Such a system of votes can well, on the occasion, and despite all the precautions taken against it, give a negative vote to power, as did the last Parisian vote (1857): it is unable to produce an idea. To make the vote for all intelligent, moral, democratic, it is necessary, for having organised the balance of services and having ensured, by free discussion, the independence of the votes, to make the citizens vote by categories of functions, in accordance with the principle of the collective force which forms the basis of society and the State.

Q.—What will be the foreign policy?

A.—It is very simple. The Revolution must spread around the world: peoples depend upon one another, as do industrial groups and individuals in the State. As long as its balance has not globally established, the Revolution may be in danger.

Q.—Will the Revolution, presumably made in Paris or Berlin, declare war on the whole world?

A.—The Revolution does not act in the manner of the old governmental, aristocratic or dynastic principles. It is right, balance of forces, equality. It recognises neither cities nor races. It has no conquests to pursue, nations to subjugate, borders to defend, fortresses to build, army to feed, laurels to gather, hegemony to maintain. Its policy toward the outside consists in preaching by example. If it is realised in one place the world shall follow it. The power of its economic institutions, the gratuity of its credit, the brilliance of its thought, are enough for it to convert the universe.

Q.—The old society will not yield without resistance: who are the natural allies of the Revolution?

A.—Any alliance of a people with another people is given by the idea or the interest that dominates it. Is it capital that governs? then we have the English alliance; despotism? then we have the Russian alliance; the dynastic spirit? then we have the Spanish marriages and the wars of succession. The Revolution has for its allies all those who suffer oppression and exploitation: let it appear, and the universe will open its arms.

Q.—What do you think of the European balance of power?

A.—A glorious notion of Henri IV's,[28] of which only the Revolution can give the true formula. It is universal federalism, the supreme guarantee of all freedom and rights, and which must, without soldiers or priests, replace Christian and feudal society.

Q.—Federalism finds little favour in France; couldn't you render your idea in a different way?

---

28  King Henri IV of France (1553–1610) argued that Europe's nations could end their cycle of perpetual warfare by achieving a "balance of power" ("équilibre européen"); at the same time, he had ambitions to construct a more stable order in Europe, a unitary "Christian republic," forerunner of other conceptions of European unity. (Editor)

**A.**—To change the names of things is to compromise with error. No matter what Jacobin prudence says, the true obstacle to despotism is in the federative union. How did the kings of Macedonia become masters of Greece? By being declared heads of the amphictyonie,[29] i.e. in substituting themselves for the confederation of the Hellenic peoples. Why, after the fall of the Roman Empire, did not catholic Europe be reformed into only one State? Because the foremost thought of the invasion was independence, i.e. the negation of unity. Why has Switzerland remained a republic? Because it is, like the United States, a confederation. What was the *Convention* itself? Its name proves it, a federative assembly. What is true of States, is, by equal reason, true of the cities and districts of the same State: federalism is the political form of humanity.

**Q.**—In this federation, where the city is equal to the province, the province equal to the empire, the empire equal to the continent, where all groups are politically equal, what becomes of nationalities?

**A.**—Nationalities will be all the better assured in so far as the federative principle will have received a more complete application. In this respect, one can say that for thirty years, public opinion has gone astray.

The feeling for one's country is like that for the family, for territorial possession, for the industrial corporation, an indestructible element of the conscience of the people. We might even say, if need be, that the concept of homeland [*patrie*] implies that of independence and sovereignty, so that the two terms, State and Nation, are adequate one with the other and can be regarded as synonyms. But it is far from the recognition of nationalities to the idea using them for certain restorations [then it] becomes useless, not to say dangerous.

What is today called the re-establishment of Poland, of Italy, of Hungary, of Ireland, is nothing else, at bottom, than the unitary constitution of vast territories, on the model of the great powers whose centralisation so heavily weighs on the people; it is monarchical imitation to the profit of the democratic ambition; it is not freedom, much less progress. Those who call so loudly for the restoration of these national units have little taste for personal freedoms. Nationalism is the pretext which they use to dodge the economic revolution. They pretend not to see that it is politics that subjugated the nations that they claim today to emancipate. Why, thus, should these nations undergo the same ordeal under the flag of *raison d'État*? Would

---

29  In ancient Greece, an Amphiktyones was association or religious confederation of Greek communities which lived in the vicinity of a sanctuary (religious centre) which they maintained and organised celebrations for. The most important was the Amphictyonic League (Delphic Amphictyony) in which members sent two kinds of representatives to a council that met twice a year. Although primarily religious, the league exercised a political influence through its membership oath. (Editor)

the Revolution amuse itself, like the first Emperor Napoléon, by carving and re-carving the Germanic Confederation, altering political agglomerations, making Poland or Italy unitary? The Revolution, in rendering men equal and free by the balance of forces and of services, precludes these immense agglomerations, the objects of potentates' ambitions, but for the peoples, pledges of an inescapable servitude.

**Q.**—Is there any hope of dislodging the dynastic principle?

**A.**—Certainly, the world up to now did not believe that freedom and dynasty were incompatible things. The old French monarchy, convening the Estates General, engaged the Revolution; the constitution of 1791, imposed by the French National Assembly, the charter of 1814,[30] imposed by the Senate, that of 1830, corrected by the 221,[31] testify to the country's desire to reconcile the monarchical principle with democracy. The nation found in it various advantages: one reconciled, so it seemed, tradition with progress; one satisfied the habits of command, the need for unity; one entreated the danger of presidencies, dictatorships, oligarchies. When, in 1830, Lafayette[32] defined the new order of things as a *monarchy surrounded by republican institutions*, he conceived what analysis has revealed to us, the identity of the political order and the economic order. The true republic consisting in the balance of forces and services, one was pleased to see a young dynasty maintaining this balance and guaranteeing its accuracy. Finally, the example of England, although equality is unknown there, and that of the new constitutional States, give fresh support to this theory.

Undoubtedly, in France, the alliance of the dynastic principle with freedom and equality did not yield the fruit that was expected from it; but this was the fault of governmental fatalism!: the error here was shared by the princes and the nation. Moreover, though the dynastic parties had shown

---

30  The Charter of 1814 created a limited monarchy rather than a fully fledged constitutional monarchy. It was based on a bicameral legislature, a Chamber of Deputies (representing an electorate of 90,000 men) and a Chamber of Peers (nominated by the King). (Editor)

31  When the Chamber of Deputies and Chamber of Peers were recalled in March 1830, the speech of King Charles X at the opening invoked a negative reaction from many deputies. On 18 March, 221 deputies (a majority of 30) voted that the King's ministers should have the backing of the Chambers. The King's authoritarian response to this eventually provoked the 1830 revolution. (Editor)

32  Marie-Joseph Paul Yves Roch Gilbert du Motier, Marquis de La Fayette (or Lafayette) (1757–1834) was a French aristocrat and military officer. He was a general in the American Revolutionary War. and a leader of the Garde Nationale during the French Revolution. In the 1830 revolution, Lafayette established a committee as interim government, refused to become dictator and agreed to offer the crown to Louis-Phillipe. (Editor)

themselves unfavourable to the Revolution since 1848, the force of things brings it back; and as France, whatever its fortunes, always liked to give itself a Premier, to mark its unity by a symbol, it would be exaggeration to deny the possibility of a dynastic restoration. How we have heard the republicans say: "He shall be my prince who shall raise the flag of freedom and equality!" And they are neither the least pure nor the least intelligent; it is true that they do not aspire to dictatorship.

However, it should be recognised that if the dynastic principle can still play some minor part, it is only as an instrument of transition from the political regime to the economic regime. As of now, one could not deny that it is considerably diminished. The constitutional system, the condition *sine qua non* of modern royalty, destroyed the prestige of monarchy. The crowned head of State is no longer a true king; he is a mediator between parties. What need will there be of one when balance in the State will come of its own accord by virtue of the very fact of the balance of economic forces? The kings themselves are no longer taken seriously: they are no longer the personification of their people. The posterity of kings may return, we know in advance under what conditions, the royalty never. It is no longer even a myth: *Non datur regnum aut imperium in œconomia.*[33]

**Q.**—And of the parliamentary system what do you forecast?

**A.**—In spite of its preceding ambiguities, the seesawing that so long dishonoured it pertained to purely economic causes, its reappearance is inevitable. The Parliament has become a form of French thought: it will survive all the dynasties. The economic revolution, by constituting social power according to true principles, will perhaps modify parliamentary manners; it will not repeal the institution. Languages and the geniuses of languages vary; eloquence clothes itself in forms more or less happy: the word is as irremovable as the thought.

**Q.**—What was, until now, the greatest act of the Revolution?

**A.**—It was neither the Tennis Court Oath, nor August 4th, nor the Constitution of '91, nor the jury, nor January 21, nor the Republican calendar, nor the system of weights and measures, nor the Great Book of the Public Debt:[34] it was the decree of the Convention of November 10, 1793, insti-

---

33  "Neither rule nor sovereignty is given in economy." (Editor)

34  A list of accomplishments of the French Revolution. The Tennis Court Oath (June 20th, 1789) marked the willingness of the newly formed National Assembly to defy the King's soldiers, and its meeting of August 4th signalled the end of the feudal system. 1791 saw the drafting of France's first written constitution, instituting jury trials. January 21st was the date in 1793 when the King was executed. The International (metric) system of weights and measures was instituted on August 1st, 1793, and the Revolutionary calendar on November 23rd. The Great Book of the Public

tuting the worship of Reason. This decree issued in the *senatus-consultum* of February 17ᵗʰ, 1810 which, by joining the Papal States to the Empire, tore up the pact of Charlemagne for all of Europe.[35]

**Q.**—What will be the greatest act of the Revolution in the future?

**A.**—The demonetisation of silver, the last idol of the Absolute.

**Q.**—The Republic once having been organised according to principles of economy and right, do you believe the State secure against all agitation, corruption and catastrophe?

**A.**—Undoubtedly, since, thanks to universal balance, it is impossible for a single living soul to appropriate, by violence or by rhetoric, the labour of any [other], the credit and the force of all, the pretext, the cause, and the means lacking for an 18ᵗʰ Brumaire, a December 2ⁿᵈ, the political edifice can no longer deviate from its upright position: it is firmly seated, it has conquered what it lacked before, stability.

**Q.**—Humanity is, above all, passionate! How shall it live when it no longer has either a prince to lead it to war, nor priests to assist it in piety, nor great men to maintain it in admiration, nor the corrupt nor the poor to excite its sensibilities, nor prostitutes to appease its lust, nor wandering minstrels to make it laugh with their cacophonies and platitudes?

**A.**—It shall do what Genesis says, what the philosopher Martin in [Voltaire's] *Candide* recommends: it shall cultivate its garden. The tilling of the soil, formerly the role of the slave, becomes the first among arts as it is first among industries, man's life shall pass in the calm of the senses and the serenity of the spirit.

**Q.**—When shall this Utopia be realised?

**A.**—As soon as the idea is popularised.

**Q.**—But how to popularise the idea if the bourgeoisie remains hostile; if the people, made stupid by servitude, full of prejudices and bad instincts, remain sunken in indifference; if the pulpit, the academy, the press, calumniate you;

---

Debt (*Grand livre de la dette publique*), a single ledger consolidating and rationalising the government's finances, was inaugurated on August 24ᵗʰ, 1793. (Editor)

35   The *senatus-consultum* of February 17ᵗʰ, 1810 declared, on the grounds that Napoléon Bonaparte was heir to Charlemagne, who had formally given the Papal States to Pope Leo III in the first place (in 781), these lands belonged to the French Empire, not the Pope. This land grab, Proudhon suggests, abrogated the longstanding relations of mutual support between Church and State epitomised by Charlemagne's rescue of Leo and Leo's coronation of Charlemagne as Holy Roman Emperor (in 800). (Editor)

if the courts prevail; if power silences you? For the nation to become revolutionary, it would have to have been revolutionised already. Shouldn't we conclude from it, with the old democrats, that the Revolution must start with the government?

**A.**—Such is, indeed, the circle in which progress seems to turn and which today serves the purely political reformers as a pretext: "First, make the Revolution," they say, "after which everything else will be cleared up." As if the Revolution itself could be made without ideas! But let us be reassured: just as the lack of ideas dooms the most beautiful parties, the war on ideas only serves to postpone the Revolution. Don't you see already that the mode of authority, inequality, predestination, eternal salvation and *raison d'État*, becomes every day, for the affluent classes whose conscience and reason it torments, even more unbearable than it is for the plebeians whose stomachs it makes cry out? From whence we will conclude that what is most certain is to keep to the word of the royal jester: *What would you do, my lord, if, when you said yes, everyone else said no?*[36] To midwife this *No* from the multitude is the task of all good citizens and men of spirit.

**Q.**—Do you concede that insurrection is the first among rights, the holiest of duties?

**A.**—I concede nothing: I say that it is absurd to place a guarantee which is always lacking at the moment when it is claimed in a political constitution. When the ideas are raised, the paving stones will lift themselves, unless the government does not have enough good sense not to await them.

**Q.**—What of tyranny and tyrannicide?

**A.**—We will speak of it elsewhere: it is not a matter for the catechism.

**Q.**—But what! if so many threatened interests, so many offended convictions, so many kindled hatreds finally had the courage to resolutely will what they will, i.e., the extinction of revolutionary thought, couldn't it come about that right would be definitively overcome by force?

**A.**—Yes, if!... But this *if* is an impossible condition. For that, it would be necessary to stop the movement of the human spirit. You can find, whenever you like, four rascals willing to act in concert for the purpose of market speculation; I defy you to form an assembly that decrees theft. In the same way you can, by laws concerning the press, forbid such and such a discussion: you will never decree lies.

Against all the forces of the reaction, against its metaphysics, its Machiavellianism, its religion, its courts, its soldiers, the sheer protest that it carries with it would suffice as a last resort. The same humanity produced, at various

36  Words supposedly spoken to King Philip II of Spain (1527–98) by his court jester. (Editor)

times, religious conscience and free conscience. Was it not the emigration that brought back freedom in 1814? All the same, if we fail at our task, the conservatives of today would be the revolutionaries of tomorrow. But let us not be reduced to this; the idea makes its way in the world, and the right of sanction and revenge does not appear close to perishing from among men.

# LETTER TO MILLIET

My dear former colleague,[1]

I HAVE RECEIVED YOUR TWO LETTERS, THE FIRST DATED SOME MONTHS AGO, the second of the 29ᵗʰ October, which M. Dentu[2] was so kind as to forward to me.

I had put the first aside in order to reply at a convenient time on the subject of both family matters, in which respect it is superfluous to remark that we are in complete agreement, and of the background of my ideas, with which you are only acquainted in a very erroneous and imperfect way. What has happened to me recently shows you that the agitation of my life is still far from settling down; this will suffice as an excuse for my over-long delay. So I will immediately come to your last letter.

I see from your congratulations that my last brochure on Italian unity was unexpected by you; accustomed as you are to conservative thinking and consequently to encountering the democratic crowds along your way, you were far from supposing that a man situated on the extremist frontiers of revolutionary thought would suddenly declare his opposition to the idea of Mazzini and the political tendencies of *Le Siècle*, *La Presse* and others.[3] You would have been of a completely different opinion regarding my person if you had followed the development of my thought for twenty years and if you had grasped the overall·structure and coherence of it. Apart from the political, strategic and religious questions which prohibit the French emperor

---

1    Étienne Milliet, editor of the *Journal de l'Ain*, was a co-worker of Proudhon's from his earlier days as an employee of the Gauthier printing press. (Editor)

2    One of the publishers of Proudhon's books. (Editor)

3    Giuseppe Mazzini (1805–1872) was a leader of the Italian national-liberation movement, an advocate of Italy's unification. *Le Siècle* and *La Presse* were rival moderate and conservative newspapers. (Editor)

from acceding to the wishes of the Italians, there are for me considerations of political economy, international law, progress and liberty which are unsuspected by our ignorant democracy but have been the objects of my study for twenty-five years now.

So much for the most recent question. The situation is the same with all the others; and some day you will be astounded, after all you have heard said and assumed yourself about my opinions, to learn that I am one of the greatest proponents of order, one of the most moderate progressives and one of the least utopian and most practical reformers in existence. All the mystery of my publications consists in my view that we must on no account flinch from any of the conclusions of critical thought, wherever they may lead us, if we wish to make advances in the science of social affairs, for if a part of the truth may sometimes horrify us the whole truth will reassure and delight us. If I may cite one example of this method: I would like to point out to you that if I began in 1840 with *anarchy*, which was the logical conclusion of my critique of the governmental idea, then I finished with *federation*, the necessary basis of right among the European peoples and, later, of the organisation of all States. In all of this it is easy to see that *logic*, *right* and *liberty* have been the dominant factors; thus, as public order rests directly on the liberty and the conscience of the citizen, *anarchy*, being the absence of all constraints—of police, authority, magistracy, regulations, etc—is found to be the correlative of the highest social virtue and following from that the ideal of human government. We are not there yet, no doubt, and centuries will pass before this ideal is attained; but our LAW is to march in this direction, to approach this goal unceasingly; once again, it is for this reason that I support the principle of federation. My thought has been reproached for agreeing with that of the Empire and the episcopacy; but this congruence is of a purely material nature, totally circumstantial—and in any case, far from complaining about it I congratulate myself on it. I am not of the hypocrite sort who will strike out at people who, guided by principles diametrically opposed to mine, accidentally turn up on my terrain. I regard it as more tasteful, more wisely done and politically saner to offer them a hospitable hand.

In a few days you will read the response I am preparing to the jeremiads of the press, as you suggest and as Dentu came to exhort me to do. You will see there that the babble of so-called democratic opinion leaves me just as cold today as it did in 1848. I know where I'm going, while my unfortunate co-religionists are clueless. To say democracy is to say coterie and intrigue; this is true at all times, today more than ever. To break up those coteries and unmask the intrigues is the hardest task of a sincere democrat.

I write to you amongst the chaos of moving house; my two daughters, one twelve years old and the other nine, are ill; their mother is exhausted and I am distracted. No books, my papers are stuffed into trunks; I eat on a stool; on my right is the heating engineer, on my left the carpenter. This house moving has now been going on for a month. It would be enough to bewilder a more resilient man than me.

My dear old colleague, no more than you have I forgotten our life in the printer's workshop thirty-two or even thirty-five years ago; and when I think back to that distant time I cannot help thinking that if the origins of our present social dissolution already existed, at least the contagion was still far from having caused such ravages, and that yesterday's generation was better than today's. We lived more simply, more morally; there was less ambitious speculation and parasitism; in general, existence was easier, healthier and better. With *one hundred francs* a month, which was what I ended up earning in 1834, I was able to offer my family an affluent existence, while today I need three or four times as much! ...How can one not regret [the passing of] such a comfortable age and life-style? If all the signs did not show me that society has entered into a crisis of regeneration, which will be long and perhaps terrible, I would believe in the irrevocable decadence and imminent end of civilisation. But we will come out of it, one must believe that, precisely because our contemporaries are more dissolute and less intelligent than we were. The movement of history is accomplished in oscillations, and it depends on us to mitigate their severity. Let us work on self-improvement and right-thinking; let us endeavour to be frugal and avoid idleness. By doing that we will mitigate the trials we must undergo and be reborn superior to our fathers.

I am writing to you, dear Monsieur Milliet, my old printing shop boss, in all friendship and untrammelled openness of heart. Treat me in the same way and do not let these friendly confidences, not meant for publication, wander into your journal's *copy*. I am sick of publicity; what I need is the fortifying joys of intimate friendship. We will talk journalism and politics another time; for today I wish only to shake your hand.

Yours with all my heart.

P-J PROUDHON

*1863*
*Translation by Nathalie Colibert (First Part) and Ian Harvey*
*(Conclusion)*

# THE FEDERATIVE PRINCIPLE
## AND THE NECESSITY OF RECONSTITUTING THE PARTY OF THE REVOLUTION

## FIRST PART
### ON THE PRINCIPLE OF FEDERATION

### CHAPTER VI
#### Posing Of The Political Problem: Principle Of The Solution

IF THE READER HAS FOLLOWED WITH SOME DILIGENCE THE PREVIOUS EXPOSI-
tion, human society must appear to him like a fantastic creation, full of
surprises and mysteries. We shall briefly recall the different terms:

a.  Political order rests on two related, opposed and irreducible prin-
    ciples: Authority and Liberty.

b.  Two contrary regimes in parallel are deduced from these two princi-
    ples: the authoritarian or absolutist regime, and the liberal regime.[1]

c.  The forms of these two regimes also differ amongst themselves,
    incompatible and irreconcilable in their natures; we have defined
    them in two words: Indivisibility and Separation.

---

1   In Chapter II, Proudhon defines the "Regime of Authority" as monarchy/patriarchy
    ("Government of all by one") and panarchy/communism ("Government of all by
    all"). The "Regime of Liberty" referred to democracy ("Government of all by each")
    and an-archy/self-government ("Government of each by each"). (Editor)

d. Now, reason points out all theory must go according to its principle, all existence according to its law: logic is the requirement of life and of thought. But it is exactly the opposite that expresses itself in politics: neither authority nor liberty can constitute itself apart, give rise to a system that would exclusively be proper to each one; far from it; they are condemned in their respective institutions to borrow from each other in a perpetual and mutual way.[2]

e. The consequence is that loyalty to principles exists only as an ideal in politics, practice having to be subject to all sorts of compromises, the government limits itself, in the final analysis, despite the best will and all the virtue of the world, to an equivocal hybrid creation to a crowding of regimes [*une promiscuité de régimes*] that strict logic renounces, and in front of which good faith recoils. Not a single government escapes this contradiction.

f. Conclusion: the arbitrary inevitably entering into politics, corruption soon becomes the soul of power and society is trained, without rest nor mercy, on the endless slope of revolutions.

That is where the world is. It is neither the consequence of satanical spite nor of a failing of our nature, nor of a providential condemnation, nor a passing fancy of fortune nor of fate stopping: that is how things are. It is down to us to get the most we can out of this odd situation.

Let us consider that for over eight thousand years—historical records go no further—all types of government, all social and political combinations have been successively tried, abandoned, resumed, modified, travestied, exhausted, and that failure has continuously rewarded the reformers' zeal and misled the people's hope. Always the flag of liberty was used to shelter despotism, always the privileged classes have surrounded themselves with, in the very interest of their privileges, egalitarian and liberal institutions; always parties have lied about their program, and always indifference replaced faith, corruption of the civic spirit, states have perished by the development of the ideas on which they were founded. The most vigorous and the most intelligent races wore themselves out in this work: history is full of accounts of their struggles. Sometimes a series of triumphs created illusions in the strength of the State, making one believe the constitution to be excellent, the government wise, when neither existed. But with peace arising, the vices of the system emerged for all to see and the people were simply having a rest in civil war from the fatigue of external war. Thus humanity went from

---

2   In Chapter I, Proudhon argues that all social organisations (or governments, to use his term) involve the balancing of authority by liberty, or vice versa. In Chapter V, he argues that all existing governments either involved the subordination of authority to liberty, or vice versa. (Editor)

revolution to revolution: the most famous nations, the ones that have lasted longest, have supported themselves in no other way. Among all known governments there is not a single one that, if it were condemned to subsist by its own virtue, would live as long as a man could. Strange fact, heads of States and their ministers are of all men those who believe least that the system they represent would last; until science comes, it is the masses' faith that supports governments. The Greeks and Romans, who bequeathed us their institutions with their examples, having reached the most interesting time of their evolution, bury themselves in their despair; and modern society seems to have reached in its turn to a time of anxiety. Do not trust agitators who shout the words *Liberty, Equality, Nationality*: they know nothing; they are dead men who claim they can resurrect the dead. The public listens to them for a while, as it would to buffoons and charlatans; then it moves on, devoid of reason and with a sorry conscience.

A sure sign that our dissolution is near and that a new era is going to open is that the confusion of language and ideas has reached the point that anybody can declare himself as much as he likes to be republican, monarchist, democrat, bourgeois, conservative, distributionist, liberal and all of these at once, without the fear that someone will prove him to be lying or mistaken. The princes and barons of the First Empire had experimented with *sans-culottism*. The bourgeoisie of 1814, gorged with the nation's goods, the only thing that it had understood from the institutions of '89 was [that they were] liberal, even revolutionary; 1830 remade it conservative; 1849 made it reactionary, catholic and more than ever monarchist. The February republicans are currently serving Victor-Emmanuel's monarchy[3] whilst the June socialists declared themselves[4] unitarist [*unitaires*]. Some of Ledru-Rollin's former friends join the Empire [considering it] as the veritable *revolutionary* expression and the most *paternal* form of government; others, it is true, call them traitors, but fly into rage against federalism. It is systematic mess, organised confusion, continuous apostasy, universal treason.

We must know if society can get to something regular, equitable and permanent, that satisfies reason and conscience or if we are condemned for eternity to this Ixion wheel.[5] Is the problem insoluble?...Could you be a bit more patient, reader; and if I do not get you out of this mess in a short while,

---

3   Victor Emmanuel II (Vittorio Emmanuele, 1820–78) became King of Italy in 1861. (Editor)

4   A reference to the February Revolution 1848 and the workers revolt of June 1848 against the new Republican government. Thus "February" refers to the Liberal and Republican tendency within French politics and "June" to the radical, militant socialist tendency. (Editor)

5   In Greek mythology, Ixion was king of the Lapiths. Brought to Olympus by Zeus, Ixion fell in love with Hera, Zeus' wife, and as punishment Zeus ordered him bound to a fiery wheel that was always spinning across the heavens. (Editor)

you will have the right to say that logic is wrong, progress is an illusion and liberty an utopia. Would you please reason with me for a few more minutes, although in such a matter, to reason is to expose yourself to self-deception and to waste your efforts as well as your reason.

1. First, you will notice that both principles, Authority and Liberty, origin of all evil, show themselves in history in a chronological and logical succession. Authority, like family, like the father, *genitor,* is the first to appear; it has initiative, it is assertion. Questioning Liberty [*La Liberté raisonneuse*] comes afterwards: it is criticism, protest, determination. The fact of this succession results from the very definition of ideas and the nature of things and the whole of history testifies to it. There, no inversion is possible, nor the least trace of the arbitrary.

2. Another observation (by no means any less important), it is that the authoritarian regime, paternal and monarchist, moves further away from its ideal as the family, tribe or city becomes more numerous and as the State grows in population and in territory: so that the more authority spreads, the more it becomes intolerable, hence the concessions that it is obliged to make to Liberty. Conversely, the regime of liberty comes near to its ideal and multiplies its chances of success as the State grows greater in population and in its area, [as] relationships multiply and science gains ground. Firstly, it is a constitution which is called for from all sides; later it will be decentralisation. Wait again and you will see emerge the idea of federation. So that we can say of Liberty and Authority what John the Baptist said of himself and Jesus: *Illam oportet crescere, hanc autem minui.*[6]

This double motion, one of regression, the other of progress, resolves itself in an unique phenomenon, also results from the definition of principles, their relative position and their roles: here again not a single ambiguity is possible, not the slightest place for the arbitrary. The fact is obviously objective and of mathematical certainty; it is what we will call a LAW.

3. The consequence of this law, which we can call necessary, is in itself necessary: it is that the principle of authority seeming to be the first, being used as the material or subject for the elaboration of Liberty, reason and right, is little by little subordinated to the juridical, rational and liberal principle; the head of State first immune, irresponsible, absolute, like the father in the family, becomes responsible to reason, first subject of law, finally a simple agent, instrument or servant of Liberty itself.

This third suggestion is as certain as the first two, safe from all ambiguity and contradiction and highly vouched for by history. In the perpetual struggle of both principles, the French Revolution, as well as the Reformation, looks like a crucial period. It marks the time when, in the political order, Liberty officially supplants Authority, just as the Reformation had

---

6    A slight misquotation of the Latin Bible (John 3:30): "illum oportet crescere me autem minui" ("He must increase: but I must decrease"). (Editor)

marked the moment when, in religious order, free examination prevailed over faith. Since Luther, belief has everywhere become questioning [*raisonneuse*]; orthodoxy as well as heresy pretended to lead man to faith using reason, Saint Paul's precept, *rationabile sit obsequium vestrum*, that your obedience be reasoned, has been widely commented upon and put into practice. Rome started to discuss like Geneva[7]; religion tends to show itself as science; submission to the Church surrounded itself with so many conditions and reservations that, except for the difference of articles of faith, there was no more difference between a Christian and a non-believer. They are not of the same opinion, that is all: besides, thought, reason, consciousness behave the same in both. Likewise, since the French Revolution, respect towards authority has weakened; deference to orders of the prince has become conditional; one expected reciprocities from the monarch, guarantees; the political constitution changed, the most fervent royalists, like the [King] John-Lackland barons, wanted to have deeds and MM. Berreyer, de Falloux, de Montalembert,[8] etc., can claim to be as liberal as our democrats. Chateaubriand, the Restoration bard, bragged of being a philosopher and a republican; it was by a pure act of his free will that he made himself an advocate of the altar and of the throne. We know what became of the violent Catholicism of Lamennais.[9]

Thus, while authority, from day to day more precarious, collapses, right becomes more precise, and liberty, always precarious, becomes nevertheless more real and stronger. Absolutism does its best to resist, but is on its way out; it seems that the REPUBLIC, always fought against, held in contempt, betrayed, banished, is getting nearer every day. What advantage are we going to take of this essential fact for the constitution of government?[10]

---

7    Following the excommunication of Martin Luther and condemnation of the Reformation by the Pope, Geneva became the unofficial capital of the Protestant movement. This was because leading Protestant writer John Calvin lived there. (Editor)

8    Three distinguished Catholic political leaders who opposed Napoléon III. (Editor)

9    Felicité Robert de Lamennais (1782–1854) was a French priest who travelled from extreme right to extreme left. Initially arguing for a religious revival and active clerical organisation, by 1848 his plan for a Constitution was rejected as being too radical. That year saw him start the newspapers *Le Peuple Constituant* and *La Révolution Démocratique et Sociale*, both of which espoused radical socialist revolution as well as being named president of the *Société de la Solidarité Républicaine*. Lamennais's political journey illustrates Proudhon's argument that political positions could be highly flexible. (Editor)

10   Use of the word "government" should not be automatically taken to mean that Proudhon had rejected anarchism. In chapter II, he had discussed anarchy as a *form* of government, even using the expression "gouvernement anarchique" (anarchic government). He seems to be somewhat confusingly using the words "government" and "state" for all forms of social organisation. (Editor)

CHAPTER VII

Extrication Of The Idea Of Federation

Since, in theory and in history, Authority and Liberty follow one another as by a kind of polarisation;

That the first declines imperceptibly and withdraws whilst the second grows and reveals itself;

That a kind of subordination results from this double movement in accordance of which Authority takes up more and more the cause of Liberty [*au droit de la Liberté*];

Since, in other words, the liberal or contractual regime from day to day gets the upper hand over the authoritarian regime, it is to the idea of contract that we must attach ourselves to as a dominant idea of politics.

First, what do we mean by *contract*?

The contract, says the civil code art. 1101, is a convention by which one or several person(s) binds themselves towards one or several others to do or not to do something.

*Art*. 1102. It is *bilateral* or *synallagmatic* when the contracting parties bind themselves to one another in a mutual way.

*Art. 1103*. It is *unilateral* when one or several person(s) are bound to one or several others, without any commitment in return.

*Art. 1104*. It is *commutative* when each of the parties commits itself to give or do a thing which is considered the equivalent of what is given or is done for it. When the equivalent consists of a gain or of a loss for each of the parties, following an uncertain event, the contract is *risky*.

*Art*. 1105. The contract of *charity* is one in which one of the parties gives to the other a completely gratuitous benefit.

*Art. 1106*. The *onerous* contract is one that subjects each one of the parties to give or do something.

*Art. 1371*. We call *quasi-contracts* the voluntary acts of man, from which results some commitment towards a third party and sometimes a reciprocal commitment of both parties.

To these distinctions and definitions of the Code, related to the form and condition of the contract, I will add a last one, concerning their subject:

According to the nature of things we deal with or the object we offer each other, the contracts are *domestic*, *civil*, *commercial* or *political*.

It is this last type of contract, the political contract, that we are going to deal with.

The idea of contract is not entirely foreign to the monarchical regime, no more than it is to fatherhood and the family. However, according to what we have said about the principles of liberty and authority and their role in the formation of governments, one understands that these principles do not intervene in the same way in the making of the political contract; that therefore the obligation which binds the monarch to his subjects, a spontaneous obligation, unwritten, resulting from the clannishness and quality of the people, is a *unilateral* obligation, since in accordance with the principle of obedience, the subject is obliged more towards the prince than vice versa. The theory of divine right expressly says that the monarch is responsible only to God. It can even happen that the contract of the prince to the subject degenerates into a contract of pure charity, when by inertia or by idolising the citizens, the prince is requested to take hold of authority and to take care of his subjects, [considered] incapable of governing and defending themselves, like a shepherd and flock. It is much worse when the principle of heredity is accepted. A plotter like the duke of Orleans, later Louis XII, a parricide like Louis XI, an adulteress like Mary-Stuart, retain, despite their crimes, their potential right to the crown. Birth making them inviolable, one can say that a quasi-contract exists between them and the subjects faithful to the prince they have to follow. In short, by the mere fact that authority is preponderant in the monarchical system, the contract is not equal.

The political contract only acquires all its dignity and morality provided that 1) it is *synallagmatic* and *commutative*; 2) it is contained, as to its object, in certain limits: two conditions that one supposed to exist under the democratic regime, but that, here again, are most often only a fiction. Can one say that in a representative and centralised democracy, in a constitutional monarchy based on restricted suffrage, all the more so in a communist republic, such as Plato's, the political contract that binds the citizen to the State is equal and reciprocal? Can one say that this contract, which takes away from the citizens half or two thirds of their sovereignty and quarter of their product, be contained in fair limits? It would be more true to say, what experience confirms too often, that the contract, in all these systems, is outrageous, *onerous*, since it is for a more or less considerable part without compensation; and *risky*, since the promised advantage, already insufficient, is not even assured.

So that the political contract fulfils the synallagmatic and commutative condition that suggests the idea of democracy; so that, contained within wise limits, it remains advantageous and practical to all, the citizen by entering the association must: 1) have as much to receive from the State as he gives up to it; 2) keep all his liberty, his sovereignty and his initiative, minus what is related to the special objects for which the contract is formed and for which one asks for the guarantee of the State. Thus settled and understood, the political contract is what I call *federation*.

Federation, from the Latin *foèdus*, genitive *foederis*, i.e. pact, contract, treaty, convention, alliance, etc., is a convention by which one or several heads of family, one or several communes or States, unite with each other in a mutual and equal way, for one or more specific tasks, whose responsibility specially and exclusively falls to the delegates of the federation.[11]

Let us go back to the definition.

What makes the nature and the essence of the federative contract, and what I draw the reader's attention to, is that in this system, the contracting parties, heads of families, communes, cantons, provinces or States, not only unite synallagmatically and commutatively with each other, they individually reserve for themselves, by forming the pact, more rights, liberty, authority, property, than they give up.

This is not the case, for example, in the universal society of goods and earnings, authorised by the civil Code, in other words community [*communauté*], picture in miniature of [all] absolute States. The one who commits oneself to such an association, especially if it is permanent, is surrounded by constraints, subjected to more burdens than one keeps [in] initiative. But that is also what makes this contract rare, and what in all times made the cenobital life unbearable.[12] Any commitment, even a synallagmatic and commutative one, that, demands from the associates all their efforts, leaves nothing to their independence and sacrifices them entirely to the association, is an excessive commitment, one which is equally repugnant to the citizen and to the man.

According to these principles, the contract of federation, having as an objective, in general terms, to guarantee the confederated States their sovereignty, their territory, their citizen's liberty; to settle their disagreements; to provide, by general measures, everything of interest to the common prosperity and security, this contract, I am saying, despite the size of the interests committed, is basically limited. The Authority in charge of its execution can never get the upper hand over its constituents, I mean that the federal allocation [of tasks] can never exceed in number and in reality the communal or provincial ones,

---

11   In J-J Rousseau's theory, which is the one of Robespierre and the Jacobins, the social contract is a lawyer's fiction, hypothesised [*imaginée*] to provide an alternative to divine right, paternal authority or social necessity for the formation of the State and relations between the government and individuals. This theory, borrowed from the Calvinists, was in 1764 progress, since it had as a goal to bring back to a law of reason that what had been considered until then as belonging to the law of nature and religion. In the federative system, the social contract is more than a fiction, it is a positive, effective pact which has really been proposed, discussed, voted, adopted and which is regularly modified according to the will of the contractors. Between the federative contract and Rousseau's and '93, there is the whole distance from reality to hypothesis.

12   A reference to cenobitic monasticism, a monastic tradition that stresses community life. The life of prayer and communal living in the monastery was one of rigorous schedules and self-sacrifice. (Editor)

likewise these cannot exceed the rights and prerogatives of man and citizen. If it were different, the commune would be a community [*communauté*]; the federation would become again a centralised monarchy, the federal authority, instead of the mere agent [*mandataire*] and subordinate function that it should be, would be regarded as dominating, instead of being limited to a special service, it would tend to embrace all activity and all initiative; the confederated States would be converted into prefectures, intendancies,[13] branches or local governments. The political body thus transformed could be called a republic, democracy or anything you like but it would no longer be a State constituted in the fullness of its autonomies, it would no longer be a confederation. The same thing would take place, even more so, if, by a false sense of economic efficiency, by deference or by some other cause, the communes, cantons or confederated States put one of themselves in charge of the administration and the others the government. The federative republic would become unitary; it would be on the road to despotism.[14]

---

13 An area associated with a supplies or estate office. (Editor)

14 The Helvetic Confederation comprises twenty-five sovereign states (nineteen cantons and six demi-cantons), for a population of two million and four hundred thousand inhabitants. It is therefore governed by twenty-five charters or constitutions similar to our ones of 1791, 1793, 1795, 1799, 1814, 1830, 1848, 1852, in addition to a federal constitution that we do not have in France. The spirit of this constitution, true to the above principles, results from the following articles:

"Art. 2. The confederation aims to insure the homeland's independence against the outside, to maintain tranquillity and order within, to protect the liberty and the rights of the confederated, and to increase their common prosperity.

"Art. 3. The cantons are sovereign as much as their sovereignty is not limited by federal sovereignty, and as such, they exert all their rights which are not delegated to the federal power.

"Art. 5. The confederation guarantees to the cantons their territory, their sovereignty within the limits set by Art. 3, their constitutions, the people's liberty and rights, the citizens' constitutional rights, as well as the rights and attributes that the people has conferred to the authorities."

Thus a confederation is not precisely a State: it is a group of sovereign and independent States, united by a mutual guarantee pact. A federal constitution is not what we understand in France as a charter or a constitution, and neither is it the summary of the public law of the country: it is the pact that contains the conditions of the league, i.e., the reciprocal rights and obligations of the States. What we call a federative Authority, finally is not a government; it is an agency created by the States, for the common running of some services that each State gives up and that become in this way federal attributes.

In Switzerland, the federal Authority comprises a deliberating Assembly elected by the people from twenty-two cantons, and an executive Council made up of seven members nominated by the Assembly. The members of the Assembly and of the

To sum up, the federative system is the opposite of administrative and governmental hierarchy or centralisation by which one distinguished, *ex oequo*, imperial democracies, constitutional monarchies and unitary republics. Its fundamental, characteristic, law is as follows: In the federation, the attributes of the central authority become specialised and limited, decrease in number, in immediacy, and, if I dare to say, in intensity as the Confederation grows by the addition of new [member] States. In centralised governments on the contrary, the attributes of the supreme power increase, expand and immediately draw into the domain of the prince the affairs of provinces, communes, corporations and individuals, in direct proportion to the territorial area and to the size of the population. Hence under this crushing [weight] all liberty, not only communal and provincial but also individual and national, disappears.

One consequence of this fact, by which I will end this chapter, is that since the unitary system is the opposite of the federative system, a confederation between big monarchies, all the more so between imperial democracies, is an impossible thing. States like France, Austria, England, Russia, Prussia, can make alliances or commercial treaties amongst themselves; they are reluctant to federate, firstly because their [organising] principle is against it and would put them in opposition to the federal pact; because, secondly, they would have to give up some of their sovereignty, and to recognise above them, at least for some cases, a referee. Their nature is to command, not to compromise or to obey. The Princes who, in 1813 were supported by the insurrection of the masses, were fighting for the liberties of Europe against Napoléon, and who later formed the Holy-Alliance,[15] were not confederated: the absolutism of their power forbade them to take that title. They were, as in '92, allied; history will not give them any other name. It is not the same for the Germanic Confederation presently in the middle being reformed, whose character of liberty and nationality threatens to erase one day the dynasties that hinder it.[16]

---

federal Council are nominated for three years; the federal constitution being able to be revised at all times, their attributes are, like their members, changeable. So that the federal Power is, in all the strength of the term, an agent placed under the control of his principals and whose power changes as they wish.

15  The Holy Alliance was a coalition of Russia, Austria and Prussia created in 1815 at the behest of Tsar Alexander I of Russia. Ostensibly created to instil the Christian values of charity and peace in European political life, in practice it was a bastion against revolutionary influence (especially from France). It was opposed to democracy, revolution, and secularism. All European nations joined, except for Great Britain, the Papal States and the Ottoman Empire. (Editor)

16  The federative public law raises several difficult questions. For example, can a State with slaves belong to a confederation? It seems not, no more than an absolutist State: the enslaving of one part of the nation is the very negation of the federative principle. In this respect, the Southern States of the United States would be even more justified to ask for separation since the Northern States do not intend to grant, at

## CHAPTER VIII
### Progressive Constitution
History and analysis, theory and empiricism, have led us, through the agitations of Liberty and Power, to the idea of political contract.

---

least for quite some time, the emancipated Blacks their political rights. However we see that Washington, Madison and the other founders of the Union did not agree; they admitted States with slaves into the federal pact. It is also true that we now see this unnatural pact tearing itself apart, and the Southern States, to maintain their exploitation, tend towards an unitarist constitution, whilst the Northern ones, to maintain the union, decree the deportation of the slaves [to Africa, e.g., the colony of Liberia].

The Swiss federal constitution, as reformed in 1848, decided in favour of equality; its fourth article says: "All the Swiss are equal before the law. In Switzerland there are no subjects, nor privileges of place, birth, people or families." From the promulgation of this article, which purged Switzerland of all aristocratic elements, dates the true Helvetic federal constitution.

In case of opposition between interests, can the confederated majority oppose the separatist minority [by invoking] the indissolubility of the pact? The *Sonderbund* answered this question in the negative against the Helvetic majority; today, in America, the Southern Confederacy does so against the Northern Union. For my part, I believe that separation is completely right, if it is about a matter of cantonal sovereignty left outside the federal pact. Thus, it has not been demonstrated to me that the Swiss majority drew its right against the *Sonderbund* from the pact: the proof is that in 1848 the federal constitution was reformed precisely with a view to the dispute which had led to the formation of the *Sonderbund*. But it may happen, by considerations *de commodo et incommodo* [of advantage and disadvantage], that the split compromises the liberty of the States: in this case the question is solved by the right of war, which means that the most significant part, the one whose ruin would lead to the greatest damage, must defeat the weakest one. That is what took place in Switzerland and could also happen in the United States, if, in the United States like in Switzerland, it were not only about an interpretation or a better application of the principles of the pact, like progressively raising the Black peoples' condition to the level of the Whites. Unfortunately M. Lincoln's message leaves no doubt on the matter. The North cares no more than the South about a true emancipation, which renders the difficulty insoluble even by war and threatens to destroy the confederation.

In a monarchy, *all justice comes from the king*: in a confederation, it comes, for each State, exclusively from its citizens. The institution of a federal high court would therefore be, in principle, a dispensation to the pact. It would be likewise for a final court of appeal, since, each State being sovereign and legislative, laws are not uniform. However, as federal interest and federal affairs exist; as offences and crimes against the confederation can be committed, there are, for these special cases, federal tribunals and a federal justice.

Implementing this idea straightaway and trying to give an account of it, we recognised that the social contract *par excellence* was a contract of federation, that we have defined in these terms: *A synallagmatic and commutative contract, for one or several determined objects, but whose essential condition is that the contracting parties always keep for themselves a greater amount of sovereignty and action than they give up.*

This is just the opposite of what happened in the old systems, monarchist, democratic and constitutional, where, by force of circumstances and the driving of principles, individuals and groups are supposed to abdicate their whole sovereignty into the hands of an imposed or elected authority, and yet keep less rights, keep less guarantees and initiative, than the burdens and duties that fall on them.

This definition of the contract of federation is a huge step [forward], one which is going to give us the solution we have longed for.

The political problem, as we said in the first Chapter, reduced to its simplest expression consists in finding the balance between two opposite elements, Authority and Liberty. Any false balance is immediately translated into disorder and ruin for the State, into oppression and misery for the citizens. In other words, anomalies or disruptions of the social order result from the antagonism of its principles; they will disappear when the principles are co-ordinated in such a way that they will no longer be able to do harm.

To balance the two forces is to submit them to a *law* which, by keeping them at bay from one another, gets them to come to an agreement. What shall provide us with this new element, superior to Authority and Liberty, and render it by their mutual consent the dominant characteristic of the system?—The contract, whose terms make RIGHT and [which] imposes itself equally on the two rival powers.[17]

---

17   There are three ways to conceive of law, according to the viewpoint of the moral being and the position he puts himself, as a *believer*, as a *philosopher* and as a *citizen*.

The law is the *command* given to man in the name of God by a competent authority: this is the definition of theology and divine right.

The law is *the expression of the relations* of things: this is the definition of the philosopher, given by Montesquieu.

The law is the *statute of arbitration* of the human will (*Justice in the Revolution and in the Church*, 8th study): this is the theory of contract and of federation.

Truth being one, although many-sided, these three definitions merge into each other and must be regarded as basically identical. But the social systems they generate are not the same: in the first, man declares himself subject of the law and of its author or representative; in the second, he recognises himself as an integral part of a vast organism; in the third, he makes the law his and frees himself from all authority, fate and domination. The first formula is the one of a religious man, the second of a pantheist; the third of a republican. The last alone is compatible with liberty.

But in a concrete and lively nature, such as society, Right cannot be reduced to a purely abstract notion, an indefinite aspiration of conscience, which would be to drag us back into fictions and myths. It is necessary, to establish society, to pose not simply an idea but a juridical act, to form a true contract. The men of '89 sensed it, when they gave France a Constitution, and all the Powers that followed them felt the same. Unfortunately, if the will was good, the enlightenment was insufficient; until now the notary has failed to draw up the contract. We know what the spirit of it must be: let us try now to draft its terms.

All the articles of a constitution can be reduced to a single article, the one that concerns the role and the competence of this great civil servant which has State as its name. Our national assemblies have dealt over and over again with the division and separation of powers, i.e., of the State's faculties of action; as for the jurisdiction of the State itself, its size, its object, one can see that nobody was very worried about it. One thought about *sharing*, as was naively said by a minister in 1848; as for the thing to be shared, it generally appeared that the more there would be of it, the more beautiful the feast would be. And yet the definition of the role of the State is a matter of life or death for liberty, collective and individual.

The contract of federation, whose essence is to always reserve more to the citizens than to the State, more to the municipal and provincial authorities than to the central authority, is the only thing that can put us on the path to truth.

In a free society, the role of the State or Government is *par excellence* a role of legislation, of institution, of creation, of inauguration, of installation; its role as executive should be the minimum possible. In this respect, the name of *executive power*, by which we designate one of the aspects of the sovereign power, has oddly contributed to distorting ideas. The State is not an entrepreneur of public services, which would be to compare it to the companies that undertake the works of a city for a fixed price. The State, whether it enacts, acts or supervises, is the generator and the supreme director of the activity; if it sometimes gets [directly] involved, it is by way of first demonstration, to give impetus and set an example. The creation carried out, the installation or inauguration having been made, the State withdraws, relinquishing the operation of the new service to local authorities and citizens.

It is the State that sets the weights and measures, that gives the units, the value and the divisions of monies. The examples provided, the first issue finished, the manufacturing of gold, silver and copper coin ceases to be a public function, a job for the State, a ministerial attribute; it is an industry left to towns, and there is nothing that would prevent it, just like the manufacturing of scales, weighting-machines, barrels and bottles, from being entirely free. The best market is the only law here. What is needed, in France, for gold and silver currency to be reputable of honest worth? A tenth of alloy and nine tenth of base metal. I want an inspector to watch and supervise the manufacturing: the role of the State goes no further.

What I say about money, I repeat for a host of services, improperly left in the hands of the government: roads, canals, tobacco,[18] posts, telegraphs, railways, etc. I understand, I admit, I call for the intervention of the State, when necessary, in all these great creations of public utility; I do not see the need to leave them in its hands once they have been delivered to the public. Such a concentration, according to me, constitutes a real excess of prerogatives. I asked in 1848 for State intervention in the founding of national banks, institutions of credit, of savings, of insurance, as with the railways: never has it crossed my mind that the State, having accomplished its work of creation, should forever remain a banker, an insurer, a transporter, etc. Indeed, I do not believe in the possibility of organising the education of the people without a great effort from the central authority, but I remain no less a partisan of the freedom of teaching,[19] as I am of all liberties.[20] I want the school to be as completely separated from the State as from the Church. If there is a *Cour des comptes*,[21] formed as a statistics office to gather, check and generalise all data, all transactions, all financial deals across the Republic, that is fine. But why should all the expenditures and takings go through the hands of a treasurer, unique collector or paymaster, ministry of State, when the State, by the nature of its function, must have only little or no service to render, and so little or no expenditures?[22]... Is it also really necessary that tribunals be dependent on the central authority? To dispense justice has been

---

18 The sale of tobacco was a state monopoly. (Editor)

19 While the phrase "freedom of teaching" (*liberté de l'enseignement*), in the context of French political debates, was associated with opposition to government-run, lay education, Proudhon distinguishes elsewhere between "freedom of teaching" and "freedom of worship" (*liberté des cultes*). In an 1850 article for *La Voix du Peuple*, for instance, he insists that "freedom of worship is [...] merely a negative freedom; it is the contrary of freedom of teaching" (*Mélanges* 3.145). (Editor)

20 According to the 1848 Swiss federal constitution, *the confederation has the right to create a Swiss University*. This idea was vigorously fought against as detrimental to the sovereignty of the cantons, and it seemed to me it was good policy. I ignore whether the project has been pursued.

21 The *Cour des comptes* (Court of Auditors) is a quasi-judicial body of the French government charged with conducting financial and legislative audits of most public institutions and some private institutions. Its three duties are to conduct financial audits of accounts, conduct good governance audits and provide information and advice to the French Parliament and Administration. It verifies the good form of accounting and the proper handling of public money and is essentially a cross between a court of exchequer, comptroller general's office, and auditor general's office. (Editor)

22 In Switzerland, there exists a federal budget, administered by the federal Council, but which only concerns the matters of the Confederation, and has nothing in common with the budget of the cantons and towns.

the highest attribute of the prince, I know it: but this attribute is a leftover of divine right; it would not be claimed by a constitutional king, with less reason by the head of an empire established on universal suffrage. Since the idea of Right, becoming human again, gets, as such, preponderance in the political system, the independence of the magistracy would be the necessary consequence of it. It is distasteful that Justice be considered as an attribute of central or federal authority; it can only be a delegation carried out by citizens to municipal authority, at the most provincial. Justice is the attribute of man that no *raison d'État* must deprive him of.—I do not even except the service of war from this rule: militias, armouries, fortresses, [should] go into the hands of federal authorities only in cases of war and for the special purpose of war; apart from that, soldiers and armaments remain in the hands of local authorities.[23]

In a regularly organised society, all must be in continuous growth, science, industry, work, wealth, public health; liberty and morality must go at the same pace. There, movement, life does not stop for a minute. The main organ of this movement, the State, is always in action, because it continually has new needs to satisfy, new issues to solve. If its function of prime driving force and of high director is ceaseless, its works, on the other hand, do not repeat themselves. It is the highest expression of progress. But, what happens when, as we see it almost everywhere, as we almost always have seen it, it dwells on the services that it created itself and gives in to the temptation of monopolising? From founder, it makes itself worker; it no longer is the spirit of the collectivity, who creates it, directs it and enriches it, without imposing on it any trouble: it becomes a vast anonymous company, with six hundred thousand employees and with six hundred thousand soldiers, organised to do everything, and who, instead of helping the nation, instead of serving the citizens and the communes, dispossesses and pressurises them. Soon, corruption, embezzlement, slackening enter this system; busy supporting itself, increasing its prerogatives, multiplying its services and enlarging its budget, Power loses sight of its true role, falls into autocracy and failure to act, the social body suffers, and the nation, against historical law, starts to decline.

Did we not point out, in Chapter VI, that in the evolution of States, Authority and Liberty are in a chronological and logical succession; that, moreover, the first is in continuous decline, the second is in accession, that the Government, expression of authority, is imperceptibly made subordinate by its representatives or organs of liberty, namely: the central Power by the deputies of the departments or provinces; the provincial authority by the delegates of the communes, and the municipal authority by the inhabitants; thus liberty aspires to make itself preponderant, authority to become servant

---

23  Swiss federal Constitution, Art. 13: "The Confederation has not got the right to maintain permanent armies." I give this article to our unitarist republican to meditate upon.

to liberty, and the contractual principle to substitute itself everywhere, in public affairs, for the authoritarian principle?

If these facts are true, the consequence cannot be doubted: it is that, according to the nature of things and the play of principles, Authority retreats and Liberty replaces it, but in a way that both follow each other without ever hurting one another, the constitution of society is essentially progressive, which means more and more liberal, and that this fate can only be fulfilled in a system where governmental hierarchy, instead of being put at its summit, is established right at its base, I mean in the federative system.

The whole constitutional science is there: I summarise it in three proposals:

1. Form groups of average size, each sovereign, and unite them by a pact of federation;

2. Organise in each federated State government according to law of separation of organs; I mean: separate everything in the power that can be separated, define everything that can be defined, distribute between different organs or civil servants everything that can be separated and defined; leave nothing undivided; surround the public administration by all conditions of publicity and control;

3. Instead of absorbing the federated States or provincial and municipal authorities into a central authority, reduce its attributes to a simple rule of general initiative, mutual guarantee and supervision, whose decrees receive their execution only on the approval [*visa*] of the confederated governments and by agents under their orders, like, in a constitutional monarchy, every order emanating from the king must, to be implemented, be countersigned by a minister.

Most certainly, the separation of powers, such as it was practised under the 1830 Charter, is a beautiful institution and of a high level, but which is puerile to restrict to the members of a cabinet. It is not between seven or eight elected people, emerging from a parliamentary majority and criticised by an opposing minority, that the government of a country must be shared, it is between the provinces and the communes: otherwise political life is abandoned in the peripheries for the centre, and stagnation overcomes the nation which has become hydrocephalic.[24]

The federative system is applicable to all nations and eras, since humanity is progressive in all generations and all races, and the politics of federation, which is *par excellence* the politics of progress, consists in calling each population, at any given time, to follow a regime of decreasing

---

24  Hydrocephalus, also known as Water on the Brain, is a medical condition in which sufferers have an abnormal accumulation of cerebrospinal fluid in the cavities of the brain. This may cause increased pressure inside the skull and progressive enlargement of the head, convulsion, and mental disability. It can also cause death. (Editor)

authority and centralisation, corresponding to their state of consciousness and morals.

## CHAPTER X
### Political Idealism: Efficiency Of The Federal Guarantee

An observation to be made in general on moral and political sciences is that the difficulty of their problem comes above all from the figurative way basic reason designed their elements. In the popular imagination politics, as well as morals, is a mythology. There all becomes fiction, symbol, mystery, idol. And it is this idealism which, adopted with confidence by philosophers as an expression of reality, causes them so much embarrassment later.

The People, in the vagueness of its thought, sees itself as a gigantic and mysterious being, and everything in its language seems to keep it thinking of its indivisible unity. It is called the People, the Nation, i.e. the Multitude, the Mass; it is the true Sovereign, the Lawmaker, the Power, the Ruler, the Homeland, the State; it has its Conventions, its Ballot, its Conferences, its Demonstrations, its Pronouncements, its Plebiscites, its Direct Legislation, sometimes its Judgements and its Executions, its Oracles, its Voice, like thunder, the grand voice of God. It feels as vast, irresistible, tremendous as it loathes divisions, scissions, minorities. Its ideal, its most delectable dream, is unity, identity, uniformity, concentration; it curses as injurious to its Majesty all that would divide its will, break up its mass, create in it diversity, plurality, divergence.

All mythology presupposes idols, and the People never lacks them. Like the Israelites in the desert, it improvises gods when nobody cares to give it any; it has its incarnations, its messiah, its messengers sent by God [*Dieudonnés*]. It is the celebrated military leader,[25] it is the glorious king, conquering and magnificent, like to the sun, or even the revolutionary tribune: Clovis, Charlemagne, Louis XIV, Lafayette, Mirabeau, Danton, Marat, Robespierre, Napoléon, Victor-Emmanuel, Garibaldi. How many, to get on the pedestal, are only waiting for a change of opinion, a passing fancy of fortune! For these idols, most of them also empty of ideas, as devoid of conscience as itself, the People is zealous and jealous; it does not suffer itself to be disputed, to be contradicted, above all to be haggled with over power. Do not touch its anointed ones or it will treat you as sacrilegious.

Full of its myths, and considering itself as a mainly undivided collectivity, how would the People understand in one leap the relationship of the citizen to society? How, under its inspiration, would the men of State who represent it produce the true conceptions of government? Wherever universal suffrage reigns in its naivety, one can predict in advance that everything will be done in the sense of indivisibility. Since the People are the collectivity that holds

---

25  "Le chef de guerre élevé sur le pavois" is literally "the warlord raised on the shield." (Translator)

all authority and all right, universal suffrage, to be sincere in its expression, will have to be itself undivided, i.e. elections will have to be carried out by the list system: there even were in 1848 some unitarists who were asking for a single list for the 86 departments. From this undivided ballot sprung up an undivided assembly, deliberating and legislating like a single man. In the case of a division in the vote, it is the majority that represents, without any reduction, national unity. From this majority will emerge in its turn an undivided Government which, taking its powers from the indivisible Nation, is appointed to collectively and jointly govern and manage without [regard for] local feelings or parochial interests. This is how centralisation, imperialism, communism, the absolutist system,—all these words are synonyms,—ensue from popular idealism; that is how in the social pact, conceived after the manner of the Jacobins and Rousseau, the citizens resign their sovereignty, and how the commune, [and] above the commune the department and the province, are absorbed into the central authority, becoming mere agencies under the immediate direction of the ministry.

The consequences will not take long to be felt: the citizen and commune being deprived of all dignity, the invasions of the State increase, and the cost to the taxpayers grows proportionally. It is no longer the government that is made for the people, it is the people that is made for the government. Power invades everything, seizes everything, claims everything, in perpetuity, forever, for good: War and the Navy, Administration, Justice, Police, Public Education, Public works and repairs; Banks, Stock Exchange, Credit, Insurance, Assistance, Savings, Charity; Forests, Canals, Rivers; Religions, Finances, Customs, Commerce, Agriculture, Industry, Transportation. On the whole lot, a tremendous Tax, which strips from the nation a quarter of its gross product. The only thing the citizen has to do is to carry out his little task in his little corner, getting his little salary, raising his little family, and leaving anything else to the government's Providence.

Faced with this predisposition of minds, in the midst of powers hostile to the Revolution, what was the thought of the founders of '89, [being] sincere friends of liberty? Not daring to break the body of the State, they had to concern themselves above all with two things: 1st, to contain Power, always ready to usurp; 2nd, to contain the people, always ready to be led by its tribunes and to replace the morals of legality by the ones of omnipotence.

Until now, indeed, the authors of constitutions—Sieyès, Mirabeau, the 1814 Senate, the 1830 Chamber, the 1848 Assembly—believed, not without reason, that the major point of the political system was to contain the central Power, while leaving it with the greatest freedom of action and the greatest force. To reach this goal, what were we doing? Firstly, as it was said, we were dividing Power into ministerial categories; then we were dividing legislative authority between royalty and the Chambers, with the prince's choice of ministers subject to the majority vote of the later. Finally taxation was voted on yearly by the Chamber, which seized this opportunity to review the government's acts.

However, whilst one was organising the negotiating of the Chambers against the ministers, one was balancing the royal prerogative by the representatives' initiative, the authority of the crown by the sovereignty of the nation, whilst one was matching words with words, fictions with fictions, one was giving the government, without any reserve, without any other counterbalance than a vain faculty of criticism, the prerogative of a huge administration; one was putting in its hands all the forces of the country; one was suppressing, for more safety, local liberties; one was destroying *parochialism*; one was creating, finally a formidable, overwhelming, power to which one was giving oneself the pleasure of waging a war of epigrams, as if reality were sensitive to personalities. Well, what happened? The opposition ended up being considered right by the people: ministries fell one after the other; one dynasty was overthrown, then a second, empire replaced republic, and the centralising anonymous despotism grew, [while] liberty declined. Such has been our progress since the victory of the Jacobins over the Girondists. This was the inevitable result of an artificial system, where metaphysical sovereignty and the right to criticise were put on one side, and all the realities of national domain, all the powers of action of a great people, on the other.

In the federative system, such anxieties would not exist. The central authority, initiator rather than executor, only has a quite restricted part of the public administration, the one concerning federal services; it is placed in the hands of the States, absolute masters of themselves, and having for everything that concerns them the most complete, legislative, executive and judicial authority. The central power is all the better since [it is] subordinate and entrusted to an Assembly formed of delegates of the States, members themselves, quite often, of their respective governments, and who, by this reason, exert over the federal assembly's acts supervision all the more jealous and severe.

The difficulties faced by the publicist in containing the masses were no less great; the means employed by them all too illusory, and the outcome just as unfortunate.

The people are also one of the powers of the State, the one whose explosions are the most terrible. This power needs a counterweight: democracy itself is forced to acknowledge it, since it is the absence of this counterweight which, delivering people to the most dangerous incitements, leaving the State exposed to the most incredible insurrections, has twice brought down the republic in France.

One thought to find the counterweight to the masses' action in two institutions, one very costly for the country and full of dangers, the [other] one no less dangerous, [and] particularly painful to the public conscience: they are, 1st, the permanent army, [and] 2nd, restrictions on the right to vote. Since 1848, universal suffrage has become the law of the State: the fear of democratic unrest having grown in proportion, one had no choice but to also augment the army, to give more support to military action [*de donner plus de nerf à l'action militaire*]. So that, to protect oneself from popular rebellion, one is obliged to, in the system of the founders of '89, increase the strength of Power at the very time one takes on the other hand precautions against it. So that, the day Power and the People hold out their hands to each other, all that scaffolding will collapse. Strange system where the People cannot exert sovereignty without the risk of breaking the government, nor the government exercise its prerogative without marching into absolutism!

The federative system puts a stop to the agitation of the masses, to all the ambitions and incitements of demagogy: it is the end of the regime of the public square, of the triumphs of tribunes, of the absorption [of public life] by capital cities. What is the point if Paris, within its walls, has revolutions if Lyons, Marseilles, Toulouse, Bordeaux, Nantes, Rouen, Lille, Strasbourg, Dijon, etc., if departments, masters of themselves, do not follow? Paris will have wasted its time... The federation thus becomes the salvation of the people: because it saves it, by division, from the tyranny of its leaders and from its own madness.

The 1848 Constitution, on one hand, removed the command of the army from the President of the republic, on the other hand had tried to avert this double danger of usurpation by the central Power and revolt by the people. But the 1848 Constitution did not say what progress consisted of, under what conditions it could be carried out. In the system it had founded, distinction of classes, bourgeoisie and people, still remained: we saw it during the discussion on the right of work and the law of 31st May restricting universal suffrage. The unitary prejudice was stronger than ever; Paris giving the tone, the idea, the will to the departments, it was easy to see that, in case of a conflict between the President and the Assembly, the people would follow its elected leader rather than its representatives. Events confirmed these predictions. The day of 2nd December showed what purely legal guarantees are worth against a Power that united popular favour with administrative strength, and that also has its own right. But if, for example, at the same time as the republican Constitution of 1848, municipal and departmental organisation had been made and implemented; if the provinces had learnt to live a proper life again; if they had had their share of the executive power, if the inert multitude of the 2nd December had been something in the State beyond mere voters, the *coup d'état* would have been impossible. The battlefield being limited to [the area] between the Elysee palace[26] and the Palais-Bourbon,[27] the hue and cry of the executive power would have enthused at the very most only the garrison of Paris and the personnel of the ministries.[28]

---

26   Official residence of the French president. (Translator)

27   Seat of French National Assembly. (Translator)

28   Some imagined that, had it not been for the vote of 24th November 1851, which the President won against the right-wing and ensured the success of the *coup d'État*, the republic would have been saved. There has been a great deal of railing, on this

[...]

The idea of Federation is certainly the highest to which the political genius has risen until now. It exceeds by far the French constitutions promulgated for seventy years in spite of the Revolution, and whose short duration honours our country so little. It solves all the difficulties that the accord of Liberty and Authority raises. With it, we do not have to be afraid of sinking in governmental antinomies; of seeing the plebes *emancipating* themselves by proclaiming a perpetual dictatorship, the bourgeoisie manifesting its *liberalism* by pushing centralisation to excess, the public spirit corrupting itself in this debauchery of licentiousness copulating with despotism, power coming back constantly into the hands of an *intriguer*, as Robespierre would call them, and the revolution, in the words of Danton, *always remaining with the most villainous*. Eternal reason is at last vindicated, scepticism defeated. One will no longer blame human misfortune on the failings of Nature, the irony of Providence, or the contradiction of the Mind; the opposition of principles finally appears as the condition of universal balance.

## CHAPTER XI
### Economic Ratification: Agricultural-Industrial Federation

Not everything has been explained yet. However irreproachable the federal constitution may be in its logic, in the guarantees that it offers in its practice, it can only last as long as it does not encounter constant causes of dissolution in public economy. In other words, political right must have the buttress of economic right. If the production and distribution of wealth is left to chance; if the federative order only serves to protect capitalist and mercantile anarchy; if, by the effect of that false anarchy, Society is divided in two classes, one of owners-capitalists-entrepreneurs, the other of wage-earning proletarians; one rich, the other poor; then the political structure will always be unstable. The working class, the most numerous and poorest class, will end up by seeing it only as a deception; the workers will unite against the bourgeois, who for their part will unite against the workers; and we will see the confederation degenerate, if the people is the strongest, into an unitary democracy, if the bourgeoisie triumphs, into a constitutional monarchy.

---

occasion, against the members of the Mountain who had not declared themselves against the right. But it is obvious, according to the law of political contradictions (see above, chapters VI and VII) and in view of the facts, that if the President had been defeated, the people having abstained, the bourgeois principle prevailing, the unitary republic would have transformed itself without the least difficulty into a constitutional monarchy, and the country would not return to the *status quo* of 1848, but to a regime perhaps even harsher than that of the 2nd December, since a government of at least equal strength would have been joined by the decisive supremacy of the middle-class and the already half established restriction on universal suffrage, the deserved disgrace of the masses.

It is in anticipation of the possibility of a social war, as was said in the previous chapter, that strong governments were formed, the object of admiration by publicists who think that confederations are unable to preserve Power from the aggression of the masses; that is, activities of the government against the rights of the nation. For, once again, make no mistake about it: all power is established, all citadels built, all armies organised against the internal at least as much as the external threat. If the mission of the State is to make itself absolute master of society, and the fate of the people is to serve as a tool for its activities, we have to recognise that the federative system cannot be compared with the unitary system. There, neither the central power because of its dependence, nor the multitude by its division, can one act more than the other against public liberty. The Swiss, after their victories over Charles-the-Bold,[29] were for a long time the first military power of Europe. But, because they formed a confederation, capable of defending itself against external threats but proving inept at conquest and *coups d'État*, they remained a peaceful republic, the most harmless and the least ambitious of States. The German Confederation also had, under the name of Empire, its centuries of glory; but, because the imperial power lacked fixedness and centre, the Confederation was torn to pieces, dismantled, and nationality jeopardised. The Netherlands Confederation vanished in its turn after contact with centralised powers: there is no need to mention the Italian Confederation. Yes, indeed, if civilisation, if the economy of societies had to maintain the ancient *statu quo*, imperial unity would be better for people than federation.

But everything tells that times have changed, and that the revolution of interests must follow, as a legitimate consequence, the revolution of ideas. The twentieth century will open the era of federations,[30] or humanity will

---

29    Charles-le Téméraire (1433–77) was the last Valois Duke of Burgundy and one of the wealthiest and most powerful nobles in Europe. He marched against the Swiss and at Grandson in 1476 he met the confederate army, suffering a shameful defeat. Raising another army, he again invaded Switzerland and was again defeated. He died in an attempt to retake Nancy, when his troops, decimated by severe cold, fought the joint forces of the Lorraines and the Swiss. (Editor)

30    I wrote somewhere (*De la Justice dans la Révolution et dans l'Eglise*, fourth study, Belgian edition, note), that the year 1814 had opened the era of constitutions in Europe. The habit of [automatically] contradicting made people ridicule [*huer*] this proposal, people who wrongly mixing their daily ramblings, history and politics, affairs and intrigues, are even unaware of the chronology of their century. But that is not what interests me now. The era of constitutions, very real and perfectly named, has its comparison in the Actiac [or Actian] era named by Augustus, after his victory over Anthony in Actium, and which started in the year 30 BC. These two eras, the *Actian* era and the era of constitutions have in common the fact they showed a general renewal in politics, political economy, public right, liberty and general

begin another thousand years of purgatory. The real problem to solve is not actually the political problem, it is the economic problem. My friends and I suggested continuing the work of the February Revolution by this last solution. The Democracy was in power; the provisional government only had to act to succeed; had the revolution been carried out in the sphere of work and wealth, one would not have had any trouble to implement it afterwards in government. Centralisation, which would have had to be broken later, had momentarily been a great help. Besides, nobody at that time, except perhaps the one who writes these lines and who has declared himself an *anarchist* since 1840, was thinking of attacking unity and calling for federation.

The democratic prejudice decided otherwise. The politics of the old school maintained, and still maintain today, that the correct procedure, for a social revolution, was to start with government, and to deal afterwards, at leisure, with work and property. The Democracy declined to accept responsibility after having supplanted the bourgeoisie and chased away the prince, and so what had to happen happened. The Empire has imposed silence upon those speakers without plans; the economic revolution was carried out in the opposite direction to the aspirations of 1848, and liberty has been compromised.

One suspects that I am not going to present the whole of the economic science of federation and list everything that ought to be done as regards this. I am simply saying that the federative government, before reforming the political order, must in addition implement a series of reforms in the economic domain: here are a few words on what these reforms consist of.

Just as from a political standpoint, two or more independent States confederate to jointly guarantee their territorial integrity or for the protection of their liberties; just as from an economic standpoint, one can federate for a mutual protection of commerce and industry, what we call a *customs union*; one can federate for the construction and maintenance of communication routes, roads, canals, railways, for the organisation of credit and insurance, etc. The aim of these particular federations is to shield the citizens of the contracting State from bankocratic and capitalist exploitation as much from the inside as from the outside; they form by their ensemble, in opposition to the prevailing financial feudalism of today, what I will call an *agricultural-industrial federation*.

---

sociability. Both of them inaugurated a period of peace, both testified to the awareness that contemporaries had of the general revolution which took place, and of the will of national leaders to contribute to it. However, the Actian era, dishonoured by imperial orgy, has sunk into oblivion; it has been erased completely by the Christian era, which marked, in a far more imposing, moral and popular manner, the same renewal. It will be the same for the so-called constitutional era: it will disappear in its turn before the social and federative era whose profound and popular idea must repeal the bourgeois and *moderate* idea of 1814.

I will not go into detail on this topic. The public, that for fifteen years has been following my works, knows what I mean. Financial and industrial feudalism has for its aim to establish, by monopolisation of public services, by privilege of education, the extreme division of labour, interest on capital, inequalities in taxation, etc., the political decay of the masses, economic serfdom or wage-labour, in a word, the inequality of conditions and fortunes. The agricultural-industrial federation, on the contrary, tends to approximate equality more and more by the organisation, at the lowest price and not in the hands of the State; of all public services; by mutual credit and insurance, by the balancing out of taxes, by guaranteeing work and education, by a combination of work to allow each worker to evolve from a mere labourer to a skilled worker or even an artist, and from a wage-earner to their own master.

Such a revolution would not be the work of a bourgeois monarchy nor of a unitary democracy; it will be the result of a federation. It does not come under the *unilateral* or *charity* contract nor by *charity* institutions; it is an exclusive feature of the synallagmatic and commutative contract.[31]

Considered in itself, the idea of an industrial federation acting as a complement to and ratification of the political federation receives the most

---

31   A simple calculation will show this. The average education given to both sexes, in a free State, can not embrace a period of less than 10 to 12 years, which consists of about the fifth of the total population, i.e., in France, seven and a half million individuals, boys and girls, out of thirty eight million inhabitants. In countries where marriages produce lots of children, like America, this proportion is greater still. Therefore they are seven and a half million individuals of both sexes to whom it is a question of giving, to a reasonable extent, which would definitely have nothing aristocratic [about it], literary, scientific, moral and professional education. Now, what is the number of individuals that go to secondary and higher schools in France? One hundred and twenty seven thousand four hundred and seventy four, according to M. Guillard's statistics. All the others, seven million three hundred and seventy thousand five hundred and twenty five in number, are doomed to never go beyond primary school. But they all have to go there: recruitment committees notice each year a growing number of illiterates. Where would our rulers be, I am asking, if they had to solve the problem of giving an average education to seven million three hundred and seventy thousand five hundred and twenty five individuals, in addition to the one hundred and twenty seven thousand four hundred and seventy four who already are in schools? What use, here, the unilateral pact of a bourgeois monarchy, and the charity contract of a paternal Empire, and the Church's charitable foundations, and Malthus's precautionary advice, and the hopes of free-trade? All the Committees of Public Safety, with their revolutionary strength, would fail. Such a goal can only be reached through a combination of apprenticeship and schooling that would make of each pupil a producer: that which assumes a universal federation. I do not know any fact more overwhelming for the old politics than this one.

striking confirmation by the principles of economics. It is the implementation on the highest scale of the principles of mutuality, of division of labour and of economic solidarity, that the will of people will have transformed into laws of the State.

That labour remains free; that power, more deadly to work than community [*communauté*] itself, refrains from touching it: that would be a fine idea. But industries are sisters; they are parts of the same body;[32] one cannot suffer without the others suffering because of it. I wish that they federate then, not to absorb one another and merge, but to mutually guarantee the conditions of prosperity that are common to them all and on which none can claim a monopoly. By forming such a pact, they will not infringe their liberty; they will only give it more certainty and strength. They will be like the powers of the State, or the organs of an animal, whose separation is precisely what makes it powerful and harmonious.

Thus, wonderful thing, zoology, political economy and politics are all in agreement: first, that the most perfect animal, the one best served by its organs, and consequently the most active, the most intelligent, the best formed for dominance, is the one whose faculties and limbs are the most specialised, separated out, co-ordinated; second, that the most productive society, the richest, the best insured against over-development [of wealth] and pauperism, is the one in which work is the most divided, competition the most whole, exchange the most honest, distribution the most regular, salaries the fairest, property [ownership] the most equal, all industries guaranteeing one another; third, finally, the freest and most moral government is the one where powers are the best divided, administration the best distributed, independence of groups the most respected, the provincial, cantonal, and municipal authorities the best served by central authority; it is, in a word, the federative government.

Thus, just as the monarchic or authoritarian principle has for its first consequence the assimilation or integration of the groups associated with it, in other words, administrative centralisation, what we could even call the community [*communauté*] of the political household; for its second consequence, the indivisibility of power, in other words absolutism; for its third consequence, rural and industrial feudalism; likewise the federative principle, liberal *par excellence*, has for its first consequence the administrative independence of the assembled localities; for its second consequence the separation of power in each sovereign State; [and] for its third consequence the agricultural-industrial federation.

In a republic set up on such foundations, one can say that liberty is raised to its third power, authority reduced to its cubic root. The former, indeed, grows with the State, in other words multiplies itself along with the

---

32   The phrase "elles sont des démembrements les unes des autres" literally means "they are dismemberments from each other." (Translator)

federations; the later, subordinate from level to level [in the social organisation], is only found whole within the family where it is tempered by both conjugal and paternal love.

No doubt knowledge of these great laws could only be acquired by a long and painful experience; perhaps also before reaching liberty, our species needed to run the gauntlet of servitude. To each age its idea, to each era its institutions.

Now the time has come. The whole of Europe is calling vociferously for peace and disarmament. And as if the glory of such a great deed had been reserved for us, it is towards France that hopes are directed, it is from our nation that we await the signal for universal bliss.

Princes and kings, to take them literally, are relics from bygone times: already we have *constitutionalised* [them]; the day approaches when there will only be federal presidents. Then, that will be done with aristocracies, democracies and all the *kracies*, gangrene of all nations, scarecrows of liberty. Does this democracy, which considers itself liberal and which knows only how to curse federalism and socialism, as did its fathers in '93, have a single idea about liberty?... But the ordeal must have an end. And now we are starting to think about the federal pact; it is not to overrate, I assume, the stupor of the present generation, to anticipate that the cataclysm that will overcome it will bring the return of justice.

For my part, whose speech has been muffled by certain of the press, sometimes by a calculated silence, sometimes by misrepresentation and insults, I can throw this challenge to my opponents:

All my economic ideas, elaborated for twenty-five years, can be summarised in these three words: *Agricultural-Industrial Federation*;

All my political views are reduced to a similar formula: *Political Federation* or *Decentralisation*;

And as I do not make my ideas an instrument of a party nor a means of personal ambition, all my current and future hopes are expressed by this third term, consequence of the other two: *Progressive Federation*.

I challenge anyone to make a clearer profession of faith, of a greater scope and at the same time of a greater moderation, I go further: I challenge all friends of liberty and right to reject it.

# CONCLUSION

THE FRENCH PEOPLE are demoralised because they need an idea. They lack understanding of the time and situation and only retain pride in an initiative, the principle and goal of which have escaped them. None of the political systems they have tried have completely met their expectations, and they cannot imagine any others.

Legitimism barely arouses a feeling of pity in the masses or one of regret for the July Monarchy. What does it matter whether the two monarchies, finally reconciled, merge or not? They still have and can only have one meaning for the country: constitutional monarchy. However, we know this constitutional monarchy. We have seen it at work and can render our verdict on it: a transitional edifice that managed to last a century, from which better things could have been expected, but that destroyed itself by its own construction. The constitutional monarchy is finished: the proof is that today we no longer have what would be needed to re-establish it and, if by some impossibility we managed to rebuild it, it would only fall again due to its own powerlessness.

In fact, the constitutional monarchy is the reign of the bourgeoisie, government by the Third Estate. However, there no longer is a bourgeoisie; there is not even anyone to form one. The bourgeoisie was essentially a feudal creation just as the clergy and nobility, the first two orders, were. It had no meaning and could only find one through the presence of the first two. The bourgeoisie, like its predecessors, was stuck a blow in 1789; the establishment of the constitutional monarchy was the instrument of their mutual transformation. In the place of this bourgeois parliamentary and censitary monarchy,[33] which absorbed the two superior orders and shone for a moment on their ruins, we have democratic equality and its legitimate manifestation, universal suffrage. Try to remake the bourgeoisie with that!

Let us add that, if the constitutional monarchy returned to the world, it would succumb under the weight of the task. Would it reimburse the debt? With what? Would it reduce taxes? But increasing taxes is in keeping with the very essence of unitary government, and we would also have the costs of reinstalling the system as an extraordinary expenditure. Would it decrease the [size of the] army? Then what force would it use as a counterweight to democracy? Would it attempt a liquidation? But it would only impede liquidation. Would it produce freedom of the press, association and assembly? No, no, no! The way in which the bourgeois press has exercised the privilege of publication the empire retained for it for the past 10 years also proves that it does not love truth and freedom and that the repressive regime organised in 1835 against social democracy and developed in 1848 and 1852 would inevitably oppose it with violence. Would the restored constitutional monarchy try, as it did in 1849, to limit the right to vote? If so, it would be a declaration of war against the working classes and therefore the prelude to a revolution. If not, February 1848 foretells its fate. Once again, sooner or later, it will die of a revolution. Reflect for five minutes, and you will remain convinced that the constitutional monarchy, placed between two revolutionary destinies, belongs in the history books and that its restoration in France would be an anomaly.

---

33  Censitary [*censitaire*] refers to voting based on census and in which only those whose taxation exceeds a certain threshold can vote. That is, suffrage is limited to the propertied classes. (Editor)

The empire exists, asserting itself with the authority of possession and the masses. But who does not see that the empire, achieving its third manifestation in 1852, is worked upon in turn by the unknown force that incessantly modifies all things and pushes institutions and societies toward unknown goals far beyond the predictions of human beings? The empire, insofar as it acts according to its own nature, tends toward contractual forms. Napoléon I, returned from Elba, was forced to swear by the principles of 1789 and modify the imperial system in the parliamentary sense; Napoléon III already modified the 1852 Constitution more than once in the same way. While containing the press, he allowed it more latitude than his imperial predecessor had; while moderating the podium, because there were not enough harangues from the legislative body, he invited the Senate to speak. What do these concessions mean except that an essential idea in the country soars above monarchic and Napoléonic ideas, the idea of a free pact, imagined and granted by what, oh princes? By FREEDOM... In the long sequence of history, all states appear before us like more or less brilliant transitions: the empire is also a transition. I can say it without offending: the empire of the Napoléons is in total metamorphosis.

We have another unexplored idea suddenly affirmed by Napoléon III as the high priest of Jerusalem affirmed the mystery of redemption at the end of Tiberius' reign: FEDERATION.

Up until now, Federalism has only evoked ideas of decay in people's minds: it was reserved for our time to think of it as a political system.

a. The groups that comprise the confederation, which we name "the state," would be states themselves, self-governing, self-judging and self-administering in complete sovereignty according to their own laws;

b. The confederation's purpose would be to rally those groups to a pact of mutual guarantee;

c. In each of the federated states, the government would be organised according to the principle of the separation of powers: equality before the law and universal suffrage form its basis:

That is the whole system. In the Confederation, the units that form the political body are not individuals, citizens or subjects but groups provided *a priori* by nature, the average size of which does not exceed that of a population of a territory of a few hundred square leagues. These groups are small states themselves, democratically organised under federal protection, and their units are the heads of families or citizens.

Thus constituted, the Federation alone would resolve, in theory and practice, the problem of the agreement between Freedom and Authority and give each its fair measure, true jurisdiction and all its initiative. Therefore, it alone would guarantee order, justice, stability and peace, with inviolable respect for the citizen and the state.

First of all, the federal Power, which is the central power here, the organ of the greater collectivity, could no longer absorb the individual, corporate and local liberties that came before it because they brought the federation into being, and they alone support it; furthermore, due to the manner in which they constituted it and by virtue of it, those liberties would remain superior to it.[34] Therefore, no more risk of upheaval: political unrest could only result in a change of personnel, not a change of system. You could make the press, podium, association and assembly free and eliminate all political police: the state would have no reason to mistrust the citizens, and neither would the citizens have any reason to mistrust the state. Usurpation by the state would be impossible: insurrection by the citizens would be powerless and purposeless. Right would be the linchpin of all interests and become the *raison d'État*; truth would be the essence of the press and the daily bread of opinion.

There would be nothing to fear from religious propaganda, clerical agitation, mysticism or sectarianism. Churches would be free in their opinions and faith: the pact would guarantee them freedom, having nothing to dread from their achieving it. The Confederation would surround them, and freedom would balance them: [even] if all the citizens were united in the same faith, burning with the same zeal, their faith could not be turned against their rights nor [could] their fervour prevail over their freedom. If France were federalised, all the Catholic resurgence we see would instantly fall away. Furthermore, the revolutionary spirit would invade the church, which would be happy to have its freedom and would confess that it has nothing better to offer the people.

With the Federation, you could provide higher education to all the people and be free from the ignorance of the masses, an impossible or even contradictory thing in the unitary system.

The Federation alone could satisfy the needs and rights of the working classes, resolve the problem of the agreement between labour and capital, association, taxes, credit, property, wages, etc. Experience has demonstrated that the law of charity, the precept of benevolence and all the philanthropic institutions are dramatically powerless here. Therefore, the recourse to justice remains, which is sovereign in both political economy and government; the synallagamatic and commutative contract remains. However, what does

---

34  The central or federal power's relationship with the local or federated powers is expressed by the distribution of the budget. In Switzerland, the federal budget is barely one-third of the total contributions the Swiss dedicate to their political life; the other two-thirds remain in the hands of local authorities. In France, on the contrary, the central power possesses nearly all of the country's resources; it governs receipts and expenditures; also, it is responsible for administering, by committee, the large cities, such as Paris, the municipalities thereby becoming purely nominal; central power is also the depository of commune funds, and it oversees employment.

justice tell us, command us, as expressed by the contract? Replacing the principle of monopoly with the principle of mutualism in all cases in which it is a matter of industrial guarantee, credit, insurance and public service: an easy thing under a federalist regime but repugnant to unitary governments. Thus, a reduction and balancing of taxes cannot be obtained from a power with a heavy tax burden because, in order to reduce and equalise them, it would be necessary to start by decentralising them. Public debt will never be liquidated and will always increase rapidly under both a unitary republic and a bourgeois monarchy; thus, the external market, which should bring the nation increased wealth, is cancelled out by the restriction of the internal market caused by the enormity of taxes;[35] thus, values, prices, and wages will never be regularised in an antagonistic environment in which speculation, commerce and trade, the bank and usury increasingly override labour. Finally, workers' association will remain a utopia as long as government does not understand that it must not perform public services itself or convert them into corporations but entrust them by term lease at a fixed rate to companies of united and responsible workers. No more power interfering in labour and business, no more incentives to commerce and industry, no more charters, concessions, lending or borrowing, commissions, industrial or dividend shares, no more speculation: from what system could you expect such reforms if not the federalist system?

Federalism would fully satisfy the bourgeoisie's democratic aspirations and conservative sentiments, two elements that have been irreconcilable everywhere until now: and how is this true? Precisely through this political-economic guaranteeism, the highest expression of federalism. France, returned to its law, which is based on property of medium size, which is honest mediocrity, increasingly approximate levels of wealth, equality; France returned to

---

35   In an average year, France produces 30 to 35 hectolitres of wine. That quantity, along with cider and beer, would not much surpass the consumption of the country's 38 million residents if everyone could go to Corinth [a reference to Horace's famous dictum: *non licet omnibus adire Corinthum*, "Not everyone can go to Corinth," i.e., not everyone can live a life of ease], that is, if everyone could drink their share of wine, beer or cider. Therefore, what good is it to look for a market outside the country when we already have one here? But worse, when the domestic market is closed in some way by state taxes, transportation costs, tolls, etc., then it has been believed that another market should be obtained abroad, but the foreign market only buys expensive wines, not ordinary ones, which it is not much interested in or which it finds too expensive: therefore, producers still have their merchandise but no domestic or foreign buyers. The department of Gironde had counted on the trade treaty with England to sell its wines; large quantities were shipped to London, but remained unsold on the docks. If you look, you will see that this defect, once indicated, is in keeping with a series of causes that all stem from one cause: the unitary system (see my *Théorie de l'Impôt*, volume 1, 1861).

its genius and morals, constituted as a union of mutually-guaranteed sovereignties, would have nothing to fear from the communist flood or monarchic invasions. The multitude, powerless from now on to crush civil liberties with its mass, would also be powerless to seize or confiscate property. Even better, it would become the strongest barrier to the feudalism of land and capital toward which unitary power inevitably tends. While city-dwellers only value property for the income it provides them, the peasants who cultivate it value it above all for itself: that is why property will never find a more complete and better guarantee than when, through continuous and well-arranged division, it approaches equality, federation. No more bourgeoisie and no more democracy but only citizens, as we demanded in 1848: is this not final word of the revolution? Where else can we find the realisation of that ideal if not in federalism? Certainly, and regardless what was said in 1793, nothing is less aristocratic and less *ancien régime* than Federation, but it must be admitted that nothing could be less vulgar.

Under a federal authority, the politics of a great people would be as simple as its destiny: domestically, to make room for freedom, to provide work and well-being to all, to cultivate intelligence and strengthen conscience; internationally, to set an example. A federated people would be a people organised for peace; what would they do with armies? All military service would be reduced to police service, civil service and guards for the armouries and forts. There would be no need for alliances or trade agreements: common law would suffice amongst free nations. In business, there would be freedom of exchange except with regard to the withholding of taxes and income tax in some cases debated in the federal council. For individuals, while waiting for the country's entry [into the Federation], there would be freedom of movement and residence except with due respect for each country's laws.

This is the federalist idea and its consequences. Furthermore, the transition can be as painless as one could want. Despotism is difficult to construct and dangerous to conserve; it is always easy, useful and legal to return to freedom.

The French nation is perfectly ready for this reform. Long-accustomed to hindrances of all kinds and heavy burdens, it is not very demanding. It will wait 10 years for the completion of the building as long as one floor is erected each year. Tradition is not opposed to it: strip the former monarchy of its caste distinctions and feudal rights and France, with its provincial states, customary laws and bourgeoisie, is no more than a vast confederation with the king of France as its federal president. The revolutionary struggle gave us centralisation. Under that regime, equality was sustained, at least in mores, but freedom was gradually eroded. From the geographic point of view, the country is just as well-suited: its overall territory is perfectly assembled and demarcated, with a marvellous fitness for unity, as we have seen all too well, and it is also very suitable for federation due to its drainage basins, which empty into three seas. It is up to the provinces to be the first to make their voices heard. Paris, a capital that would become a federal city, would have nothing to lose in the transformation. On the contrary, it would discover a new and better existence. The force of absorption it exerts on the provinces impedes it, if I dare say so: less burdened, less apoplectic, Paris would be freer and would earn and produce more. The provinces' wealth and activity would ensure a market for its products superior to any in the Americas, and it would recover in real business all that it would lose to decreased parasitism. The fortune of its inhabitants and their security would no longer be intermittent.

Whatever power is responsible for France's destiny, I dare say that there is no longer any other policy for it to follow, no other salvation or idea. Therefore, it should give the signal to the European federations that it is going to adopt federalism's example and model. Its glory will be so great that it will crown all glories.

*Passy, August 20<sup>th</sup>, 1864*
*Translation by Ian Harvey*

# LETTER TO M. X.

Sir,

I HAVE RECEIVED SEVEN VOLUMES OF YOUR GIGANTIC DICTIONARY THROUGH our mutual friend, M. D.; I already had the first volume. I cannot wish enough success for your publication, and I admire M. L.'s courage and dedication to science and how he did not retreat in the face of such an undertaking. Since my convalescence, I have come across some of your articles, and I am increasingly astonished by the enormous mass of material you assemble in your columns. I would be delighted to hear that you found funding for its installments; that would prove to me once again that our nation is not dead. A people who read, who are interested in science and seek it in all its forms, have not resigned themselves.

I read the two articles that you recommended to me, "Abstention" and "Anarchy," and I thank you for the way in which you wrote about me in them. I only regret not having been able to explain myself when you were writing them. On "Abstention," I would have said something more positive and decisive to you than what I found in the dictionary. As for "Anarchy," its writing seems to me to be better and more exact. I wanted, with that word, to demarcate the extreme term of political progress. Anarchy is, if I may express myself in this way, a kind of government or constitution in which the public and private conscience, formed by the development of science and law, suffices by itself to maintain order and guarantee all liberties, in which, therefore, the principle of authority, police institutions, preventive or repressive measures, bureaucracy, taxes, etc., are reduced to their most simplest expression and, even more, in which monarchic forms and high centralisation disappear, replaced by federative institutions and communal mores. When political life and domestic existence are identified, when social and individual interests are united and balanced through the solution of economic problems, it will be obvious that all limitations will have disappeared and that we will have complete freedom or anarchy. Social law will be fulfilled of its own accord, without supervision or command but through universal spontaneity.

When you come to the articles, "God" and "Property," I would appreciate it if you let me know. You will see with a few explanatory words that there is more than paradox in the affirmations, "God is evil" and "Property is theft," which I hold in the literal sense without thinking of making faith in God a crime or of abolishing property.

Sincerely,

P-J PROUDHON

*1865*
*Translation by Paul Sharkey ("To Some Workers" and Second Part:*
*Chapter XV) and John Duda (Second Part: Chapter IV, Chapter VIII,*
*Chapter XIII and Third Part: Chapter IV)*

# THE POLITICAL CAPACITY OF THE WORKING CLASSES

## TO SOME WORKERS FROM PARIS
### AND ROUEN WHO HAD SOUGHT HIS VIEWS OF THE ELECTIONS

December 1864

Citizens and friends,

THIS ESSAY HAS BEEN INSPIRED BY YOURSELVES; IT BELONGS TO YOU.

Ten months ago you asked me what my thoughts were regarding the electoral Manifesto issued by sixty workers from the [department of the] Seine. You were primarily interested in knowing whether, having cast a negative vote in the 1863 elections, you should abide by that line or whether, in the light of circumstances, it was legitimate for you to throw your votes and your influence behind the candidacy of a comrade deserving of your sympathy.

As to the thinking behind the Manifesto, my opinion could scarcely have been in doubt and, in acknowledging receipt of your letters, I told you so frankly. Certainly, I was delighted at this awakening of Socialism; and who but I in the whole of France would have had more right to rejoice at it?… Moreover, I was in agreement with you and with the Sixty that the working class is not represented and that it is entitled to be: how could I possibly have thought otherwise? Today as in 1848, would not worker representation, if such a thing were possible, amount to, in political and economic terms, a formal affirmation of socialism?

But I made no bones about there being, in my view, a huge gulf between this and participation in elections, which would have signed away, along with its democratic conscience, its principles and its future... And let me add that that reservation, which you welcomed to a man, has since been confirmed by experience.

Where is the French Democracy, once so proud and pure, which, on the reassurances of a few ambitious men, suddenly imagined that it was about to stride from victory to victory on the basis of a false pledge? What gains have we made? By what brand new and mighty idea has our politics distinguished itself? Eighteen months on, what success has flagged up the forcefulness of our advocates and rewarded their palaver? Have we not been witness to their perpetual defeats and shortcomings? Gulled by their hollow parliamentarism, have we not seen them, on nearly every issue, routed by the Government's speakers? And quite recently, when hauled before the courts on charges of unwarranted association and assembly and required to explain themselves to the Country and to the Powers that be, have they not been confounded by the very legality into which they invited us and as whose spokesmen they posed? What pathetic scheming! Such an even more pathetic defence! I will leave it to you to judge ... Finally, after all the noisy debates, are we in a position to deny that, at bottom, our representatives have no other ideas, tendencies or policies to offer than the Government's policies, tendencies and ideas?

So, thanks to them, the game is up for the young democracy just as it is for the elderly liberalism to which they would hitch it: the world is beginning to slip away from them both. Truth, it is said, and righteousness and liberty, are no more on their side than on any other.

The issue, then, is to disclose to the world, on the basis of authentic testimony, the thinking, the true thinking of modern folk: to legitimise their reforming aspirations and entitlement to sovereignty. Universal suffrage, fact or fiction? Once again, the preoccupation has been with restricting it and the fact is that very few, outside of the labouring classes, take it seriously.

The point is to show the labour Democracy which, for want of sufficient self-awareness and an inadequate appreciation of its Idea, has lent the backing of its votes to names that do not represent it, on what conditions a party ventures into political life; how, in a nation, the upper class having lost its grasp on and leadership of the movement, it falls to the lower class to pick up the baton and how a people incapable of self-regeneration by means of such an orderly succession is doomed to perish. The issue, dare I say it?, is to get it through to the French plebes that if, in 1869, it sets its sights on winning yet another battle on behalf of its masters, like the one it won for them in 1863–64, its emancipation may be postponed by a half a century.

For—do not doubt this, my friends—protests registered in the form of blank ballot papers are badly misunderstood and not welcomed, but still cause the public some unease and the political world everywhere has started to engage in: this declaration of utter incompatibility between an outmoded system and our most cherished aspirations: this stoic *veto*, finally, which we pronounced upon presumptuous candidacies, was nothing less than a heralding of a new order of things, our self-possession as the party of righteousness and freedom, a solemn registration of our entry into political life and, if I may make so bold, a signalling to the old world of its imminent and inevitable downfall...

I had undertaken, citizens, to explain myself to you on these matters; I have now honoured that promise. Do not judge this essay by its extent, which I might have reduced to forty pages; you will find herein but one idea, the IDEA of the new Democracy. But I thought it useful to present that Idea through a series of examples, so that friend and foe may know once and for all what it is that we seek and with whom they are dealing.

Receive, citizens and friends, my fraternal greetings,

P-J PROUDHON

# SECOND PART

# DEVELOPMENT OF THE WORKER IDEA:
## CREATION OF ECONOMIC RIGHT

### CHAPTER IV
### 2. The Mutualist System, Or, On the Manifesto—Spontaneity of the Idea of Mutuality in the Modern Masses—Definition

WHAT IS IMPORTANT to bring out in popular movements is their perfect spontaneity. Do the people obey an excitation or a suggestion from outside, or do they instead listen to a natural inspiration, intuition, or conception? In the study of revolutions, this is something that one could not be too careful in determining. Without a doubt the ideas that have agitated the masses in all epochs have bloomed previously in the brain of some thinker; in fact, when it comes to ideas, opinions, beliefs, errors, priority never is with the multitude, and it is far from being otherwise today. Priority, in all acts of the mind, belongs to individuality; the relationship between the terms indicates this. But it is hardly the case that every thought which seizes the individual will later on seize hold of the population; among the ideas which do lead to this, it is even less the case that they are always just and useful; and we say precisely that that which is important above all to the philosophical historian is to observe how the people attach themselves to certain ideas more than others, how they generalise them, develop them in their own manner, making from them institutions and customs which they follow traditionally, until they fall in the hands of legislators and *justiciers*,[1] who make of them in their turn articles of law and rules for the tribunals.

Thus, what is true of the idea of community is true of that of mutuality; it is as old as the social condition. Every now and then, some speculative types have glimpsed its organic power and revolutionary scope; never, until 1848, had it assumed the importance and affected the role that it appeared really to be on the verge of playing. Hence, it had lagged well behind the communist idea, which, after having thrown a rather grand radiance in antiquity and in the Middle Ages, thanks to the eloquence of sophists, the fanaticism of sectarians and the power of convents, seemed in our time to be on the verge of taking on a new force.

The principle of mutuality had been explained for the first time, with a certain philosophical hauteur and a reforming intention, in that famous maxim that all the sages have repeated, and that our Constitutions of Year II and Year III, following their example, placed in the *Declaration des droits et des devoirs de l'homme et du citoyen*:

"Do not do to others that which you would not want done to you;

"Always do to others the good which you would like to receive"

This principle, so to speak double-edged, admired from age to age and never contradicted, inscribed, said the author of the Constitution of Year III, *by nature in all of our hearts*, presupposes, first, that the subject to whom this injunction is addressed is free; and second, that he can distinguish between good and evil, in other words, that he possesses justice within himself. Two things, I mean, Liberty and Justice, that take us very far beyond the idea of authority, [whether] collective or of divine right, on which, as we will see, the system of Luxembourg depends.

Until the present this beautiful maxim has not been for the peoples, according to the language of the moralist theologians, anything but a bit of *advice* [*conseil*]. By virtue of the importance which it is accorded today and the manner in which the working classes demand that it be applied, it is becoming a PRECEPT, taking on a decidedly obligatory character, in a word, acquiring the *force of law*.

Let us observe first off the progress accomplished in this regard in the working classes. I can read in the Manifesto of the Sixty:

"Universal suffrage has been given to us for the most part politically; but it still remains for us to emancipate ourselves socially. The liberty that

---

1    A dispenser of justice or righter of wrongs. Historically, a *justicier* was an instrument of the judicial powers. They had the power to judge all affairs, civil or penal, and could administer capital punishment. (Editor)

the Third-Estate knew how to acquire with such vigour must extend itself in France to all citizens. Equal political rights necessarily imply equal social rights."

Let us note this method of reasoning: "Without social equality, political equality is nothing but an empty word; universal suffrage a contradiction." One leaves aside syllogistic reasoning and proceeds by assimilation: Political equality = social equality. This turn of mind [*espirit*] is new; moreover it suggests, as a first principle, individual liberty.

"The bourgeoisie, our older sister in emancipation, had to absorb the nobility and destroy unjust privileges in '89. It is now up to us not to destroy the rights which the middle classes *justly* enjoy, but to acquire for ourselves the same liberty of action."

And a little further on:

"If only they would not accuse us of dreaming of agrarian laws, chimerical equality, that puts each on the bed of Procrustes; division [of wealth], maximum [prices], excessive taxation, etc. No, it is time to be finished with these calumnies propagated by our enemies and adopted by the ignorant.— *Liberty, credit, solidarity*, these are our dreams."

It concludes with these words:

"The day where they (our dreams) are realised, there will no longer be bourgeois, nor proletarians, nor bosses, nor workers."

All this writing is a bit dodgy. No one stripped the nobility of their wealth in 1789; the confiscations came later, as an act of war.[2] One contented oneself with abolishing certain privileges incompatible with right and freedom, and that the nobility had unjustly arrogated to themselves, this abolition had determined its absorption. Now, it goes without saying that the proletariat did not ask beyond this to deprive the bourgeoisie of their acquired goods, nor of any the rights which it enjoyed *justly*; one only wanted to realise, under the perfectly juridical and legal names of *liberty of labour, credit, solidarity*, certain reforms of which would result in the abolition of—what?—the rights, privileges, and so forth that the bourgeoisie enjoyed *exclusively*; by this method to make it such that there would neither be *bourgeois* nor *proletarians* anymore, i.e., to absorb it into itself.

In two words: as the bourgeoisie did to the nobility during the Revolution of 1789, thus will be done to it by the proletariat in the new revolution, and since in 1789 there had been no injustice committed, in the new revolution, which has taken its *older sister* as a model, there will not be any committed either.

That said, the Manifesto develops its thought with a growing energy.

"We are not represented, we who refuse to believe that poverty is a divine institution. Charity, a Christian virtue, has radically proved and

2    The expression Proudhon uses here, "*fait de guerre*," does not mean the incident that starts a war (an *acte de guerre*) so much as a glorious military exploit. (Translator)

acknowledged its impotency as a social institution. In the time of the sovereignty of the people, of universal suffrage, it can no longer be only a private virtue... We do not want to be *clients*[3] or recipients of charity; we want to become EQUALS. We refuse hand-outs, we want justice."

What do you say about this declaration? As you yourselves have done, our bourgeois elders, thus we wish to do. Is that clear enough?

"Enlightened by experience, we do not hate men; we wish to change things"

This is as decisive as it is radical. And the allegedly democratic Opposition pursued previous campaigns under a similar profession of faith!

Thus the Sixty, by their dialectic as by their ideas, leaves behind the old routine of communist and bourgeoisie. They want neither exclusive privileges nor exclusive rights; they have abandoned this materialist equality which places man on a Procrustean bed; they affirm the *liberty of labour*, condemned by the Luxembourg Commission in the inquiry into piecework [*le travail à la tâche*]; they accept *competition* [*concurrence*], even though this is equally condemned by the Luxembourg Commission, they proclaim at the same time *solidarity* and *responsibility*; they want no more clientèles,[4] no more hierarchies. What they want is equality and dignity, unceasing agent of social and economic equalisation; they reject *handouts* and all the institutions of *charity*; in its place, they demand JUSTICE.

The majority among them are members of *mutual credit* societies, of *mutual* aid societies, of which they tell us that *thirty five function, without fanfare,* in the capital; directors of industrial societies, in which communism has been banned and which are founded on the principle of *participation*, recognised by the Code, and on that of mutuality.

From the point of view of the courts, the same workers demand *chambers of workers* and *chambers of entrepreneurs* [*chambres patronales*], complementing each other, controlling each other and balancing each other; *executive syndicates* and *tribunals* [*prud'hommies*]; in short, a total *reorganisation of industry, under the jurisdiction of those who compose it.*[5]

In all of this, they say, universal suffrage is their *supreme rule*. One of the first and most powerful effects shall be, according to them, to reconstitute, according to new relations, natural groups of labour, that is to say, *workers' corporations.*—This word *corporations* is one of those most frequently used to accuse these workers; we are not afraid of it. Do not judge based on words, look at the things themselves, as we do.

This is sufficient, it seems to me, to demonstrate that the mutualist idea has penetrated, in a new and original fashion, the working classes; that they

---

3    Not in the sense of a modern customer, but in the sense of the patron/client relationship in Roman law. (Translator)

4    Again, in the Roman sense of a body of clients legally and economically bound to a patron. (Translator)

5    Response to an article in *Siecle*, March 14th, 1864, by four workers.

have appropriated it; that they have more or less deepened it; that they apply it with reflection, that they have anticipated its development, in a word, that they have made of it their new faith and their new religion. Nothing is more authentic than this movement, which remains weak at the moment, but which is destined to absorb not only a nobility of several hundred thousand souls, but a bourgeoisie reckoned in the millions, and to regenerate the entirety of Christian society.

Let us look now at the idea itself.

The French word *mutuel, mutualité, mutuation*,[6] which has for a synonym *reciprocal, reciprocity*, comes from the Latin *mutuum*, which signifies a loan (for consumption), and in a larger sense, exchange. One knows that in the loan for consumption the object loaned is consumed by the borrower, who for this returns only the equivalent, whether of the same nature, or in a totally different form. Suppose that the lender becomes in his turn a borrower, you will have a mutual loan, therefore an exchange; such is the logical link which has given the same name to two different operations. Nothing is more elementary than this notion: also I will not insist any further on the logical and grammatical side. What is interesting to us is to know how, under this idea of mutuality, reciprocity, exchange, JUSTICE, substituted for those of authority, community [*communauté*], or charity, one comes to construct, in politics and in political economy, a system of relations which tends to do nothing less than to change the social order from top to bottom.

In what capacity, first, and under what influence has the idea of mutuality seized hold of these minds?

We have seen previously how the school of Luxembourg understands the relationship of man and citizen vis-à-vis society and the State: according to it, this relationship is one of subordination. Authoritarian and communist organisation follows from this.

To this governmental conception is now opposed that of the partisans of individual liberty, according to whom society must be considered, not as a hierarchy of functions and faculties, but as a system of equilibrations between free forces, in which each is assured the enjoyment of the same rights on the condition of fulfilling the same duties, obtaining the same advantages in exchange for the same services, a system therefore essentially egalitarian and liberal, which excludes all recognition of wealth, rank, and class. Now, see how these anti-authoritarians, or liberals, reason and conclude.

They maintain that, since human nature is the highest expression in the Universe, not to mention the incarnation of universal Justice, man and citizen derives his rights directly from the dignity of his nature, even as later on he will derive his well-being directly from his personal labour and the good usage of his faculties, in consideration of the free exercise of his talents and virtues. They say therefore that the State is nothing but the result of the free

---

6    As in "mutual," "mutuality" and so forth. (Translator)

union formed between subjects who are equal, independent, and all upholding justice; that thus it stands for nothing but their combined freedoms
and interests; that any disagreement between Power and this or that citizen
reduces itself into a debate between citizens; that, as a consequence, there is
no other prerogative in society but that of freedom, and no other supremacy
than that of Right. Authority and charity, they say, have had their time; in
their place we want justice.

From these premises, radically contrary to those of Luxembourg, they
conclude in favour of an organisation of the mutualist principle on a much
larger scale.—Service for service, they say, product for product, loan for loan,
insurance for insurance, credit for credit, security for security, guaranty for
guaranty, etc. : such is the law. It is the ancient *lex talionis; an eye for an eye, a
tooth for a tooth, a life for a life,* but in a completely inverted manner, translated
from criminal law and the atrocious practices of *vendetta* into economic law,
the products of labour and services rendered in free fraternity. From this all
the institutions of mutualism: mutual insurance, mutual credit, mutual aid,
mutual education, reciprocal guarantees of job opportunities and markets, of
exchange, of labour, of the good quality and fair pricing of goods, etc. This
is what mutualism intends to create, with the help of certain institutions, a
principle of the State, a law of the State, I even would say a sort of religion of
the State, the practice of which is as easy for citizens as it is beneficial to them;
one which requires neither police, nor repression, nor constraints, and cannot,
under any conditions, for anyone, become a cause of deception and ruin.

Here, the worker is not a serf of the State, engulfed in a communitarian
ocean; he is a free man, truly sovereign, acting under his own initiative and his
own personal responsibility; certain to obtain for his products and services a fair
and sufficiently remunerative price, and sure to encounter among his fellow-citizens, for all the objects he consumes, honesty and the most perfect guarantees.
Likewise, the State, the Government, is no longer sovereign; here, authority is
not at all the antithesis of liberty: State, government, power, authority, etc. are
expressions serving to designate liberty itself from another perspective; general
formulas, borrowed from an old language, by which one designates, in certain
cases, the sum, the union, the identity and solidarity of particular interests.

Consequently there is no longer any cause to ask, as in the bourgeois system or
in that of Luxembourg, if the State, the Government, or the community should
dominate the individual, or rather if it should be subordinated to him; if the prince
is more than the citizen, or the citizen more than the prince; if authority takes
precedence over freedom, or if it is its *servant*: all these questions are pure nonsense.
Government, authority, State, community, and corporations, classes, companies,
cities, families, citizens, in two words, groups and individuals, moral persons and
real persons, all are equal before the law, which alone, sometimes by this agency,
sometimes by this ministry, rules, judges, and governs: *Despots ho nomos.*[7]

---

7   A Greek phrase: roughly, "The law is lord." Possibly a slight misquotation of

Whoever stands for mutuality pictures the distribution of land, division of properties, independence of labour, separation of industries, specialisation of functions, individual and collective responsibility depending on whether the work is done by individuals or groups; reduction to the minimum of general fees, suppression of parasitism and poverty.—Whoever stands for community [*communauté*], on the other hand, is calling for hierarchy, indivision, centralisation, a multiplicity of jurisdictions, complication of state apparatuses, subordination of wills, waste of forces, development of unproductive functions, indefinite growth of general fees, and consequently the creation of parasitism and the advance of poverty.

### CHAPTER VIII
### Application of the Principle of Mutuality to Labour and to Wages—Of True Commerce and Agiotage

BEFORE THE REVOLUTION of '89, society and government, both constituted on the principle of authority, had the form of a hierarchy. The Church itself, despite the sentiments of democratic equality with which the Gospels are peppered, had given its sanction to this ranking by conditions and fortunes, outside of which one conceives only nothingness. In the priesthood as in the State, in the economic order as in the political order, a law reigned unquestioned that ends up being taken for the expression of justice itself, a law of universal subordination. Not a protest was heard, as the law seemed rational, divine even; and despite this no one was happy. The discontent was general: the worker and the peasant, their wages reduced to the minimum, complained of the hard-heartedness of the bourgeoisie, the nobility or the priesthood; the bourgeois in their turn, despite their legal privileges, their monopolies, complained about the taxes, about the infringements of their colleagues, about the judges and the clergymen; the nobles bankrupted themselves, and once they had sold or pledged their goods, were left with no means of support besides the prince and their own prostitution. Each was looking, begging for an improvement in his bad fortune: increases in wages and salaries, growth in profits; one would clamour for the reduction of his farm rent while the other would find even this insufficient; those who cried the loudest were the best provided for, abbots who received benefices and taxes [*bénéficiaires et traitants*].[8] In brief, the situation was intolerable: it finished with the revolution.

---

Herodotus' *Histories* 7.104.4, describing the Lacedaemonians: "They are free, yet not wholly free: law [*nomos*] is their master [*despotēs*], whom they fear much more than your men fear you." (Editor)

8   In pre-Revolutionary France, the "benefice" was a kind of pay assigned to priests for ecclesiastical duties, and *traites* were customs duties and taxes collected from the public on behalf of the royal Treasury by persons designated as *traitants*, who received a share of the income. (Editor)

Since '89 society has made an immense 180–degree turn, and the situation does not seem to have improved. More than ever the world demands to be well-housed, well-clothed, well-fed, and to work less. The workers band together and strike for a reduction in the length of the work day and an increase in salaries; the bosses, obligated, it would seem, to give in from this side, search for economies of production at the expense of the quality of the products; even the parasites complain that their sinecures are not sufficient to keep them alive.

In order to assure the decrease in the hours of labour to which they aspire before everything, to maintain the high level of their wages and perpetuate an agreeable *status quo*, the workers are not content to merely organise themselves into coalitions against the entrepreneurs; they organise themselves in certain places against competition from foreign workers, to whom they forbid entry into their cities; they co-ordinate resistance against the use of machines, put themselves on guard against the admission of new apprentices, keep watch on the bosses, intimidating and constraining them by an occult and irresistible policing.

On their side the bosses are hardly to be outdone by the workers: this is the struggle of capital against wages, a struggle in which victory is assured not to the biggest battalions but to the fattest wallets. Which will resist unemployment the longest, the strongbox of the master or the stomach of the worker? As I write these lines, the war is so active in certain parts of Great Britain, that one fears that free trade, imagined to be the triumph of English capitalism, of the great English industries, will turn against England, the people, the organisation, and the equipment of which do not have the flexibility that distinguishes them here in France.[9]

It is necessary however to leave all this suffering behind, to find the remedy for this distress; what does science say? (And I'm speaking here of official science.) Nothing: it keeps harping on its eternal law of *supply* and *demand*; a lying law, in the terms in which it is posed, an immoral law, suitable only for ensuring the victory of the strong over the weak, of those who have over those who have not.

And mutuality, which we have availed ourselves of already in order to reform insurance and to make a happy correction to the law of *supply* and *demand*, can it really have nothing to offer in this situation as well? How do we apply it to the question of labour and wages?

In wooded countries, when at the onset of winter it is time to cut wood for the season, the peasants assemble themselves: everyone together goes to the forest; some fell the trees, others bundle up the firewood, the shooks,[10]

---

9   Sadly, Proudhon makes the all too common mistake of equating England with Britain and *vice versa* here. (Editor)

10   A shook (*merrain*) is a bundle of wood to be used for a purpose other than firewood. (Translator)

etc. the children and the women collect the shavings: then, the bundles having been made, they draw lots. This is labour in common; it is an example of association, if you like: this is not what we demand by these words: application of mutuality to labour and wages.

A village has been destroyed by fire; everyone dedicated themselves to warding off disaster: saving some furniture, some food, some livestock, some tools. The first thing to do is to rebuild the houses. The villagers reunite anew; they share in the difficult labour; some digging new foundations, others taking care of the construction, others dealing with the carpentry, the finish work, etc. Everyone puts their hands to the work, the labour advances right before their very eyes, and soon each family has recovered its house, larger and more embellished. Each having worked for each other, and all for everyone, the assistance having been reciprocal, one discovers in the work a certain character of mutuality. But this mutualism could only appear on one condition, namely the joining of all efforts, and the fusion, for a time, of all interests, of a sort that here we still have more of a temporary association than a mutuality.

In order for there to be a perfect mutuality, it is therefore necessary that each producer, in committing to a certain involvement with the others, who, for their part, commit themselves in the same manner with respect to the first, retains his full and complete independence of action, all his freedom of behaviour, all his individuality of operation: mutuality, according to its etymology, being more consistent with the exchange of services and products than with the unification of forces and the community of labour.

The unification of forces, just like the separation of industries, is a powerful economic instrument; and the same can be said, in certain cases, of association or community. But nowhere in all of this is mutuality to be found, nothing here is able to resolve the problem of free labour and just wages: and it is with this problem, the special application of mutuality, that we are concerned with at this moment.

To arrive at this goal, we have to take a rather long route, and put more than one idea into play.

1. Since 1789, France has become a democracy. All are equal before the law (civil, political, and economic). The ancient hierarchy has been levelled; the principle of authority has evaporated before the declaration of rights and of universal suffrage. We all possess the right to own property, the right to form business enterprises, the right to compete; most recently we have been given the right to form unions and to strike.[11] This acquisition of new rights, which formerly could have passed for rebellion; this democratic

---

11  The *loi Le Chapelier*, enacted in 1791, banning the old workers' guilds or "corporations" (see the Glossary entry for "corporations") as a threat to the integrity of the State, was repealed in 1864, but trade unions in the full sense were only legalized by the *loi Waldeck-Rousseau* of 1884. (Editor)

progress is a first step towards a mutualist constitution for the nation. No more exceptions made for certain people; no more privileges of race or class; no more prejudices of rank; in the end, nothing that would oppose itself to the free transactions between each and every citizen, all now become equal. The equality of persons is the first condition of the levelling of fortunes, which will only result from mutuality, that is to say, from liberty itself.

But it is nonetheless clear that this grand political equation does not also give us the answer to the riddle: what is the relationship between the right to vote, for example, and the determination of just wages? Between equality before the law, and the equilibrium of services and products?

2. One of the first ideas to be conceived by the democratised France was that of setting prices [*tarification*]. The laws of the *maximum*[12] were essentially revolutionary. The instinct of the people wanted it thus, and this instinct has its eminently juridical and judicial side. I asked this for the first time a long time ago, and never have I obtained a response: What is the just price of a pair of shoes? How much is a wheelwright's day worth? A stone cutter's? A blacksmith's? A cooper's? A dressmaker's? A brewer's? A clerk's? A musician's? A dancer's? A digger's? A manual worker's? Since it is evident that if we knew this, the question of wages and salaries would be decided: nothing would be easier than to enact justice, and in enacting justice we would have security and well-being for all. How, by the same reason, should we account for the time of the doctor, the notary, the judge, the professor, the general, the priest? How much for a prince, an artist, a virtuoso? How much is it just that the bourgeois, supposing that there would be bourgeois, would earn over the worker? How much to grant him for his mastery?

*Supply* and *demand*, the economist of the English school, the disciple of Adam Smith, Ricardo, and Malthus, responds imperturbably. Isn't this stupidity irritating? All jobs must yield something to at least keep those who perform them alive; otherwise they would be abandoned, and rightly so. Therefore, for wages, and consequently for labour, a first limit, a *minimum*, below which we cannot go. It is neither supply nor demand that pertains here: it is necessary to be able *to live while working*, as the workers of Lyon said in 1834.[13] If this *minimum* can be improved upon, so much the better: let us not envy the worker the good that he procures for himself through work. But in a society where the industries are recognised as parts of the same body, where the price of each thing exerts a constant influence on the prices of everything else, it is clear that amelioration by raising the amount of this minimum will not go very far. Each resists the ambition of

---

12  The Maximum Price Laws of 1793. (Translator)

13  A reference to the revolt by workers in Lyon On February 14, 1834 which saw them occupying the heights of Lyon. As in a revolt three years previously, they proclaimed "Vivre libre en travaillant ou mourir en combattant!" ("Live free working or die fighting!"). Both revolts were repressed. (Editor)

his neighbours, since the elevation of their wages will necessarily translate itself, no matter how much good will towards all we might have, into a loss for ourselves. Our question returns in this form, and it seems to me to be perfectly reasonable: having found the minimum of expenses necessary for the worker to live, to suppose that the norm of wages could be similarly determined, i.e., to find the conditions for an increase in general well-being in our social environment.

Let us therefore leave aside maximums, price controls, regulations, and the whole apparatus of 1793. For us, this is not what is important. The revolution, in democratising us, has launched us on the paths of industrial democracy. This is a first and very great step to have taken. A second idea arose from it, that of a determination of labour and wages. A long time ago, this idea would have been a scandal; today it appears as nothing but logical and legitimate: we will retain it.

3. In order to equitably value the day of a worker, it is necessary to know of what it is composed, what quantities enter into the formation of the price, if there are not to be found there foreign elements, non-values.

In other words, what is it that we understand ourselves to buy and that we must faithfully remunerate in a worker's day of labour, or, to generalise our thought, of anyone who renders us a service?

That for which we must pay those from whom we ask a service, the only thing that we understand ourselves to acquire, is the service itself, nothing more, nothing less.

But in practice this is hardly what happens: there is a multitude of circumstances where we pay something extra on top of the value of the product of the service asked for, according to the rank, birth, illustriousness, titles, honours, dignities, renown, etc. of the functionary. Thus a counsellor of the imperial court is appointed at 4,000 fr., while the president has 15,000. A chief of a ministry division is taxed at 15,000 fr.; the minister gets 100,000. The incumbents of rural parishes have been paid for several years now at 800 fr., and add to that 50 fr. unofficially; the bishops receive at least 20,000 fr. A lead player in the Théâtre-Français or the Opera claims a fixed salary of 100,000 fr. per year, and I don't know how much on top of that; stand-ins will get 500 fr. per month. The reason for these differences? It is all a matter of dignity, title, rank; a matter of something metaphysical and ideal, which, being beyond such venal considerations, could never be paid for...

While we might exaggerate the revenue of some by holding too high an opinion of their functions and their persons, a far greater number see their salaries and nourishment reduced to almost nothing by the contempt in which their services are held and the state of indignity in which they are systematically kept. One is the counter-part of the other. Aristocracy presupposes servitude: there we have opulence, and here as a consequence we have privations. For ages, the right to his own product has been denied to the slave: so that in this regard he is practically the same as a feudal serf, from

736  Pierre-Joseph Proudhon

whom the seigneur took up to five days of work per week, leaving the serf but one day to secure his weekly sustenance, since of course Sundays were sacred. The concession made to the worker of the right to dispose of his own work and the products of that work dates back to 1789. And should we imagine that today there is no longer any servile work? I do not mean that there is absolutely unpaid labour: no one would dare impose such a thing; but rather whether there is work for which the payment is below that which is absolutely necessarily required, simple respect for humanity? Those who have some doubts in this matter have but to open Pierre Vinçard's book.[14] Our factories, our workshops, our factories, our cities and our countrysides are filled with people who live on less than 60 centimes a day; some of these, they say, do not even have 25. The description of these miseries shames humanity: it reveals the profound bad faith of our epoch.

You are going to say to me that all of this is just a matter of fortunate or unfortunate exceptions; that nations love to honour themselves in raising high the civil list and the emoluments of their princes, judges, great functionaries and illustrious talents, which it is hardly reasonable to equate with the vulgarity of workers and labourers.

But descend the social ladder, from the summit which I have brought you to on down, and you will see to your surprise that all professions of men judge themselves identically. The doctor and the lawyer, the cobbler and the milliner, charge according to the vogue they enjoy; there are even people who put a price on their probity, such as the chef who, for a higher wage, promises to not make *the handle of the basket dance*.[15] What is the man who does not hold himself in just a little more esteem than his compatriots, and does not imagine himself to be doing you an honour by working in order that you can pay him? In all fixing of wages, when it is the producer who does this, there are always two parts, that of the personage, *nominor qui leo*[16], and that of the worker. There are in France one hundred surgeons who would not have been embarrassed to remove the ball from Garibaldi's foot[17]: but it was necessary to find an illustrious person to operate on such an illustrious victim; Garibaldi in this was made to seem ten times more heroic and M. Nélaton[18] ten times more skilled. Each had their publicity: thus the economic world.

Since therefore we are in a democracy, that we all enjoy the same rights; that the law accords to us all equal preference and consideration, I conclude that, when we engage in business, all question of precedence should be

---

14  Probably *L'Histoire du travail et des travailleurs* (1845). (Editor)

15  *faire danser l'anse du panier*: to skim off the top when shopping for one's master. (Translator)

16  A reference to one of Aesop's fables: "because my name is lion." (Translator)

17  Garibaldi was shot in the foot during his 1862 expedition against Rome. (Translator)

18  A famous French surgeon. (Translator)

jettisoned, and that in reciprocally setting a price for our services, we should take into account only the innermost value of the work to be done.

Utility is worth utility; .

Function is worth function;

Service pays for service;

The work day balances the work day,

And everything produced shall be paid for by the product which will have cost the same amount of trouble and expenses.

If, in such a transaction, there had been a favour to be accorded, this would not be due to brilliant, agreeable, honorific functions the likes of which the whole world seeks to carry out; this favour should be accorded, as Fourier had said, to the taxing labours which shock our sensitivity and are repugnant to our pride. A rich person has a fancy to take me on as a valet: "All work is honourable," I will say to myself; "there are only dishonourable men. The attentions that are to be given to the person are more than useful labours, they are acts of charity, which place the person rendering them below the person receiving them. Therefore, as I do not intend to be humiliated, I will place a condition on my service: that is that the man who wishes to have me as a domestic servant will pay me half of his revenue. Otherwise, we will no longer be in a relationship of fraternity, equality, and mutuality: I will have to say even that we have left behind justice and morality as well. We are no longer democrats, we are a society of servants and aristocrats."

But, you will say to me, it is not true that the function, as I have said to you, equals function, that service pays for service, and that the work day of anyone is worth as much as the work day of someone else. On this point the universal conscience protests; it declares that our mutuality will be iniquity. It is necessary, therefore, whether wanted or not, to hold ourselves to the law of supply and demand, tempered, in its ferocity and untruth, by education and philanthropy.

I would agree with this, I admit, except that here one is asking me to suppose that the workers, public functionaries, scientists, merchants, labourers, peasants, in a word that all those who labour, produce, and make useful works, are to one another as animals of different genera, animals of unequal species, between which one cannot establish a comparison. What is the dignity of a beast compared to that of a man, and what common measure can there be between servitude on the one hand and nobility and free action on the other?...This is how the theoreticians of inequality reason. To their eyes, there is more distance between this man and that man, than there is between this man and that horse. They conclude that not only are the products of human labour incommensurable quantities; men themselves are, as they have written, unequal in dignity, divided in rights, and all that is done to try and level the situation is to go against the will of nature. Here, they say, in this inequality of people themselves, is the principle behind the inequality of ranks, conditions, and fortunes.

To those, because of class interest and conceit in the system, hate the truth, can always be taken in by empty words. Pascal, looking for a philosophy of history, conceived humanity as a single individual which could not die, accumulating in itself all knowledge and realising successively all ideas and all progress. It is thus that Pascal represented to himself the unity and identity of our species, and then elevated this identity into the highest thought on the development of civilisation, government of Providence, the solidarity of States and races. The same conception is applied to political economy. Society is considered as a giant with a million arms, which carries out all industries, simultaneously produces all wealth. A single consciousness, a single thought, a single will animates it; and within the interlocking gears of its labours is revealed the unity and identity of its person. Whatever it takes on, it always remains itself, as admirable, as dignified in the execution of the smallest details as in the most marvellous combinations. In all the circumstances of its life, this prodigious being is equal to itself, and one can say that each of its actions, each of its moments compensates the others.

You insist, and you say: When we accord to each individual of which society is composed the same moral dignity, they are nevertheless, from the point of view of their abilities, unequal to each other, and this suffices to ruin democracy, the laws of which we purport to submit them to.

Without doubt individuals, who are the organs of society, are unequal in abilities, even if they are equal in dignity. What must we conclude from this? A single thing: while we are sure as to what makes us all equal, we have to take, as much as we can, the measure of our inequalities.

Thus, apart from the human personality, which we declare inviolable, the moral being and the facts of conscience set aside, we have to study the man of action, or the worker, in his means and his products. Now, at first glance we discover this important fact: that is, if the human faculties of one subject and another are unequal, these greater or lesser differences do not go to infinity: they remain within passably restrained limits. Just as in physics we can achieve neither absolute heat or absolute cold and our measures of temperature oscillate here and there in small deviations around a mean we improperly call zero; it is similarly impossible to assign a negative or positive limit for intelligence or strength, either in men and in animals, or in the Creator and the world. All that we can do, with regard to the mind for example, is to mark the degrees, necessarily arbitrary, below or above a conventional fixed point that we call *common sense*; again, for strength, we settle on a metric unit, for instance the power of a horse, and then count how many of these units and fractions of this unit of force each of us is capable of.

As in the measurement of temperature, we will have therefore, for intelligence and strength, *extremes* and an *average*. The average is the point where the greatest number of subjects are to be found; those who approach the extremes are more rare. I had just said that the difference between these extremes was very small: in fact, a man who within himself has the strength of two or three men is a Hercules; a man with the *intelligence of four* would be a demi-god. To these limits imposed on the development of human faculties are added the conditions of life and nature. The *maximum* duration of existence is between 70 and 80 years, inside of which one has to allow for a period of infancy, of education, of retirement and decrepitude. For everyone the day has just 24 hours, of which, depending on the particular circumstances, only somewhere between 9 to 18 hours can be given to work. Likewise, each week has a day of rest; and while the year has 365 days, one can barely count on 300 of these being given over to work. We see that if the industrial faculties are unequal, this inequality does not prevent the ensemble from being sensibly approximated: it is like a harvest in which all the ears of corn are unequal, but which nevertheless capable of being treated like a level plain, extended to the horizon.

These considerations taken into account, we are able to define the work day: this is, in all industries and professions, the services that can be provided or the value that can be produced by a man of average strength, intelligence, and age, knowing well his state and his diverse parts, for a given duration, this being ten, twelve, or fourteen hours for those situations where the work can be appraised by the day; or a week, a month, a season, or a year for those which demand a long period of time.

For the child, the woman, the old man, the sick man or the man of weak complexion, all not generally able to attain the average of the able-bodied man, the work day will only be a fraction of the official, normal, legal day which is taken as the unit of labour. I would say as much of the fragmented workday, in which the purely mechanical service, demanding not so much intelligence as routine, cannot be compared to a real industrial work day.

On the other hand and reciprocally, the superior worker, who conceives, executes more rapidly, gets more and better quality work done than another; all the more reason that those who, owing to this superiority of execution bring together the genius of direction and the power of command, those surpassing the common measure, will receive a greater salary: he will be able to earn one and a half, two, three days of work and beyond. Thus the rights of strength, of talent, of character even, as well as those of labour, are mixed: if justice is no respecter of persons, it will no longer be mistaken about any capacity.

Well! I would say that nothing is more easy than to settle all these scores, balance all these values, to make right out of all these inequalities; as easy as paying a sum of 100 francs, with coins of forty, twenty, ten, and five in gold; with coins of five, two, one, one-half, and one-quarter in silver, and with coins of ten, five, two and one centimes in copper. All of these quantities being fractions of the others, they can represent each other, complement each other, pay for and make up for each other: this is a speculation of the most simple arithmetic.

But in order for this liquidation to operate, it is necessary, I repeat, to have the co-operation of good faith in the appreciation of labour, services, and products; it is necessary that the labouring society comes to this degree of industrial and economic morality: that all submit themselves to the justice which will be done to them, without regard for the pretensions of vanity and personality, without any consideration for titles, ranks, precedence, honorific distinctions, celebrity, in a word the value of opinion. Only the utility of the product, the quality, the labour and the expenses it required, should here enter into the account.

This calculation, I affirm and repeat, is eminently practical: and our duty is to hold ourselves to it with all our strength: it would exclude fraud, surcharges, charlatanism, sinecurism, exploitation, oppression; but, it must be said, it cannot be treated like a domestic affair, a family virtue, an act of private morality. The evaluation of work, the measure of values, endlessly renewed and repeated, is the fundamental problem of society, a problem that the social will and the power of the collectivity can alone resolve. In this regard, it is still very much necessary that I say that neither science, nor power, nor the Church has fulfilled their mission. What am I saying? The incommensurability of products has been raised up into a dogma, mutuality declared a utopia, inequality exaggerated, in order to perpetuate, along with a generalised absence of solidarity, the distress of the masses and the lie of the revolution.

Now it is up to the workers' democracy to take up this question. What it pronounces, and, under the pressure of its opinion, it will be equally necessary for the State, organ of society, to enact. That if the workers' democracy, satisfied to agitate in its workshops, to pester the bourgeois and to distinguish itself in futile elections, remains indifferent about the principles of political economy, which are those of the revolution, it is necessary that it be known, that it is lying about its duty, and it will be pilloried one day in front of posterity.

The question of labour and wages brings us to that of commerce and agiotage, with which we conclude this chapter.

Among almost every people commerce has been held in distrust and denigration. The patrician or noble who engages in commerce demeans himself. All commercial operations have been forbidden to the clergy, and it made an immense scandal, in the 17th century, when the speculations and benefices of the Jesuits were revealed. Amongst other traffics, the Reverend Fathers secured for themselves the monopoly over cinchona.[19]—From where comes this condemnation, as old as civilisation, which neither our modern customs nor our economic maxims has made up for? From the dishonesty which at all times has appeared inherent in trade, and which moralists, theologians and men of State have been desperate to purge. The *Punic* or *Carthaginian faith* was noted for its infamy in antiquity. But what was this Punic faith?

---

19   Cinchona, a plant derivative also known as Peruvian Bark or Jesuit's Bark, is the source of quinine, the vital ingredient in medicine used to treat malaria. (Editor)

The same faith as the Greeks, the Attic faith, the Corinthian faith, the faith of Marseille, the Judaic faith; the same finally as the Roman faith itself: this was the commercial faith.

In order for commerce to be honest and without reproach, it would be necessary that, independently of the mutual evaluation of services and products of which we have spoken in the previous article, transport, distribution, and exchange of goods take place in the least expensive way and to the greatest advantage of everyone. For this to be the case, it would be necessary that in each country all producers, traders, shippers, brokers, and consumers, reciprocally informed and duly guaranteed about everything that concerns the provenances, raw materials, existences, qualities, weights, cost prices, shipping expenses, handling costs, etc., would additionally commit themselves (those who are supplying and those who are receiving an agreed upon quantity) to determined prices and conditions. Statistics should therefore be perpetually published on the state of the harvests, the workforce, wages, risks and accidents, abundances and shortages of labour, the consequences of demand, the movement of markets, etc., etc.

Let us suppose, for example, that with the most detailed and exact calculations, pursued over a series of years, it results that the median cost of wheat, in an average year, was 18 francs per hectolitre, the retail price varied between 19 and 20 francs, giving to the worker a net profit of 5.3 to 10 percent. If the harvest is bad, such that there was a deficit of a tenth, the price should be increased by a proportional quantity, on the one hand so that the worker is not alone in loss, on the other so that the public does not suffer an exorbitant increase: this is rather better than letting them perish due to scarcity. In good political economy, no more than in good justice, one cannot allow general distress to become a source of fortunes for a few speculators. If there is an abundance of wheat, on the contrary, the price should be lowered by an analogous proportion, so that on the one hand the price of cereals, in lowering itself, does not become for the worker a cause of deficit, as we have seen enough times, and so that on the other the public profits from this good fortune, either for the current year, or for the years to follow; the unconsumed surplus needing to be put into storage. In the two cases, one sees how production and consumption, in mutually guaranteeing each other, at a fair price, one the investment and one the purchase of wheat, would be regularised; how abundance and scarcity, in being distributed across the mass of the population, by the means of mercurial intelligence and good economic policy, no longer have as consequences for anyone either the exaggeration of profit or the excess of deficit; this is one of the most beautiful and fecund results of mutuality.

But it is evident that such a precious institution could only be the act of the general will, and it is precisely against this will that the liberals of political economy, under the pretext of governmentalism, arise. Rather than put a stop to organised extortion, an unassailable extortion, invulnerable to philosophic protestation and private justice, they prefer to assist with the bacchanalia[20] of mercantilism: is perfection therefore to be seen in this world, and isn't liberty fecund enough to pay for their orgies?

The Stock Exchange, the tribunals and the markets ring with complaints against speculation [*agiotage*]. Now, what is agiotage in itself? An apologist for the agiotage business, as good a logician as a man of an intelligence, said to us quite recently: it is the art, in a society given over to anarchic mercantilism, of foreseeing the oscillations in values, and thereby profiting from sales or purchases made in accordance with the increases or decreases in these values. What, he said, in this kind of operation (which, we must recognise, demands a high level of skill, consummate prudence, a multitude of knowledges), makes it immoral? ... In fact, the environment being what it is, the skill of the agiotage trader is as honourable as those of heroes; I shall not be the first to throw a stone at him. On the other hand it must be admitted that if, in a society that is in a state of war, speculation is in no way incriminating, it is nonetheless essentially unproductive. The person who is enriched by *differences* has no right to the recognition or respect of his fellow men. If he has neither cheated nor stolen from anyone—I speak here of the outstanding speculator [*agioteur*], who makes no use in his speculations of anything but his divinatory genius, employing neither fraud nor falsehood—he can also not flatter himself with having been the creator of anything with the least utility. Conscience would prefer it a thousand times better that he had directed his talents towards some entirely different career, leaving prices to follow their natural course, without coming to impose an extra charge on circulation that the public could definitively do without. Why this skimming off the top, parallel to the toll[21] which was imposed at the gates of towns, and which does not have as this did the excuse of raising money to pay for the expenses of the city? Such is the motive which in all times has pronounced agiotage odious, to economists as well as moralists and men of State. A just motive, since it is founded on the universal conscience, whose judgements are absolute and enduring, very different in this respect from our tardy and transitory legislation.

Those who, in testifying to their devotion to the social and political *status quo*, feign a measure of severity regarding speculators, therefore would do well to show themselves to be more consistent and not to stop themselves halfway through. In the current state of Society, commerce, given over to the most complete anarchy, without direction, without information, without points of reference and without principles, is essentially speculation; it could

20  The bacchanalia were wild and mystic festivals of the Roman god Bacchus. It has since come to describe any form of drunken revelry. (Editor)

21  The *octroi* (from the Old French word *octroyer* meaning to grant, to authorise) was a local tax collected on various articles brought into a district for consumption. (Editor)

not be anything else. Therefore, it is necessary to condemn everything, or permit everything, or reform everything. This is what I am going to make understood in a few words.

Is it not just that the private individual who takes on at his own risk and peril a vast commercial operation, from which the public is called to profit, should be honestly remunerated in the resale of his merchandise? The principle is entirely just: the difficulty is in rendering its application other than reprehensible. In fact, all profit realised in business, if it is not exclusively due to speculation, is more or less infected with speculation: its impossible to separate it out. In an environment characterised by a lack of solidarity, deprived of assurances, each works for himself, no one for others. Legitimate profit cannot be distinguished from that made in speculation. The whole world endeavours to carry off the greatest profit: the trader and the industrialist engage in speculation, as does the scientist, the poet, and even the actor, the musician, and the dancer, as do the doctor, the celebrity and the courtesan, all as much as any other; it is really only wage-earners, workers, manual labourers, or public functionaries who do not engage in speculation, because they are paid according to their appointment or at a fixed salary or wage.

Let us agree then: whoever was the first, separating in his thought speculation from exchange, the chance element from the cumulative element, the profit based in speculation from that based in trade, to leave the realities of commerce to others and to content himself with speculation on fluctuations, he not only drew the consequence of the state of war, egoism, and general bad faith within which we all live; he also established himself, if I dare say it, at the expense of the public, as the censor of transactions, in laying bare, by *fictitious* operations, the spirit of inequity which presides over *real* operations. It is up to us to profit from this lesson, since we can regard such an enterprise as prohibiting the games of the Stock Market and the futures markets by mere police measures to be as unrealisable and nearly as abusive as agiotage itself.

Mutualism proposes to cure this leprosy, not by enveloping it in a network of penalties that will not necessarily be judicious and will almost always be applied in vain; not at all by hindering the freedom of commerce, the worst of all remedies: but by treating commerce as assurance, I would say by enclosing it in all public guarantees, and thereby restoring it to mutuality. The partisans of mutuality know as well as anybody else the law of *supply* and *demand*; they would not dare to contravene it. Detailed statistics, frequently recalculated; precise information on needs and supplies, an honest decomposition of the retail price; planning for all eventualities; fixing between producers, traders, and consumers, after amiable discussion, a *maximum* and *minimum* rate of profit, according to the difficulties and the risks; the organisation of regulatory associations: these are pretty much all the measures by which they would dream of disciplining the market. Let the degree of freedom be as great as one likes, they say; but let what is still more important than freedom, sincerity and reciprocity, guide us all. This being observed, let the customers be as diligent and honest as possible. Such is their motto; can one believe that after several years of this reform, our mercantile customs would not be entirely changed, to the great benefit of public happiness?

### CHAPTER XIII
#### On Association, Within Mutuality

I have believed it necessary to consecrate a special chapter to this question, which holds a very large place in the preoccupations of the workers, and over which still reigns a profound obscurity. As do their comrades from [the] Luxembourg [Commission], the authors of the Manifesto, advocate for *association*, considering it to be a powerful means of order, morality, wealth, and progress. But neither the former nor the latter have yet to know how to recognise it; they invoke its name pell-mell with that of mutuality, many times confounding it with community [*communauté*]; no one, outside of the civil and business Codes (which furthermore the workers concern themselves very little with), has known how to disentangle the useful or dangerous characteristics of this idea; above all, no one has recognised the modifications that it is destined to receive in the mutualist regime.

I will try, as much as I can, to shine a bit of light on this interesting subject, and, in the interest of the workers' societies which are developing everywhere and in which a crowd of political notabilities are taking the keenest interest, to fill in this important lacuna with a few words.

I call *economic forces* certain methods of action, the effect of which is to multiply the power of labour far beyond what it would be, if it had been left entirely to individual liberty.

Thus, what we call the Division of labour or the separation of industries is an economic force: it has been proven a thousand times since A. Smith, that a given number of workers will return four, ten, twenty times more work, if this work is partitioned between them in a systematic fashion, than they would have had if they each worked separately, each performing all the same tasks, without agreement and without combining their efforts.

For the same reason, or rather for the inverse reason, that which I was one of the first to name, the *force of the collectivity*, is also an economic force: it is equally proven that a given number of workers will execute with ease and in a small amount of time a task which would be impossible for these same workers, if, instead of grouping their efforts, they purported to act individually.

The application of machines to industry is also an economic force: this requires no demonstration. In bestowing upon man a greater productivity, labour becomes more useful, the product greater: the accumulation of wealth that results attests to the presence of an economic force.

Competition is an economic force, by virtue of the excitement that it induces in the worker;

Association is another, by virtue of the confidence and the security that it inspires in the worker;

Exchange, finally, credit, gold and silver monies, property itself, which no scruple prevents me from naming here, are, at least in anticipation, economic forces.

But of all the economic forces, the greatest, the most sacred, that which, in the combinations of labour, unites all the conceptions of the mind and the justifications of conscience, is mutuality, in which one can say that all the others come to be combined.

Through mutuality, the other economic forces enter into right; they become, so to speak, integral parts of the right of man and of producer: without this they remain indifferent to the good (or bad) of society; they have nothing obligatory about them; they offer no moral character by themselves. We are familiar with the excesses (not to mention the massacres) of the Division of Labour and of the use of machines;—the frenzies of competition, the frauds of business, the despoliations of credit, the prostitutions of money, the tyranny of property. All of this critique has for a long time been exhausted; and, under the current Democracy, it would be a waste of time to insist on it here. We are preaching to the converted. Only mutuality, which holds at the same time intelligence and conscience; the synallagmatic pact, so long neglected, but which secretly inspires all workers, obligates man at the same time that it makes his work fruitful; only mutuality is unassailable and invincible: since mutuality, in human society and in the universe, is at once right and might.

Certainly association, viewed in a good light, is sweet and fraternal: God forbid that I should dishonour it in the eyes of the people!... But association, by itself, and without a thought for the right which rules over it, is nevertheless an accidental link based on a pure physiological and selfish sentiment; a free contract, terminable at will; a limited grouping, of which one can always say that the members, being associated only for their own benefit, are associated against the whole world: this, moreover, is how it has been understood by the legislator: he could not have understood it in any other way.

What is the goal, for example, of our great capitalist associations, organised according to the spirit of mercantile and industrial feudalism? To monopolise production, exchange, and profits; to this end, to group the most diverse specialists under the same management, to centralise trades, to agglomerate functions; in a word, to leave no place for small industry, to kill small scale commerce, by this, to transform the most numerous and the most interesting part of the bourgeoisie into wage-workers: all this for the profit of the so-called organisers, founders, directors, administrators, councillors and shareholders of these gigantic speculations. Numerous examples of this unfair war made by the big capitalists on the small can be seen in Paris: It is useless to cite them. There has been talk of a centralised bookstore which would be financed by M. Péreire and would replace the majority of current bookstores: It is a new method of ruling over the press and ideas. There is hardly a society of men of letters that, jealous of the profits of bookstores, does not dream of making themselves editors of all the works published by living authors. This mania for invasive conquest, no longer has any limits: an unequivocal sign of the poverty of the spirit. I knew of a printing establishment which combined, along with typesetting and printing, which one can hardly separate, retail and wholesale bookselling, paper-making, the casting of letters, the manufacture of presses, engraving, binding, woodworking, etc. There were plans to create a school for apprentices and a small academy there. This monstrous establishment quickly collapsed due to waste, parasitism, oversupply, general expenses, the emergence of competition, the growing disproportion between expenses and receipts. Industrial feudalism has the same tendencies; it will meet the same end.

What about the workers' associations following the Luxembourg system? What is their goal? To supplant, through coalitions of workers subsidised by the Government, the capitalist associations, in other words, to make war upon industry and free commerce, through the centralisation of business, the agglomeration of workers, and the superiority of capitals. In place of the one or two hundred thousand businesses which exist in Paris, there would only be about a hundred great associations, representing the diverse branches of industry and commerce, into which the population of workers would be regimented and enslaved by the *raison d'État* of fraternity, just as at this moment it tends to be by the *raison d'État* of capital. Would we here have won liberty, the happiness of the public, civilisation? Never. We would have exchanged our old chains for new ones, and, what is sadder still, and which shows the sterility of the legislators, entrepreneurs, and reformers, the social idea would not have advanced one step; we would always continue to be subject to the same arbitrary despotism, not to mention the same economic fatalism.

At this first and quick glance, the same holds as much for the communist associations, which anyway remain at the project stage, as it does for general partnerships, mixed liability companies, and publicly traded companies, such as have been conceived within mercantile anarchy and are pursued, with the sanction of the legislator and the protection of the Government, by the new feudalism. The result: that the former as much as the latter have been founded on private interests and with an eye towards selfish goals; that nothing in them indicates a single thought of reform, any superior view of civilisation, nor the least concern for the progress and destiny of humanity; on the contrary, acting, like individuals, in an anarchic fashion, they can always be considered merely as small churches organised against the largest one, in the centre and at the expense of which they live.

The general characteristics of these associations, as recorded by the Code, show their narrowness of spirit and the limits of their impact. They are composed by a determinate number of people, to the exclusion of all others; these persons naturally are designated by their names, professions, residences, qualities; everyone furnishes a contribution to the capital of the enterprise; the society is formed for a special goal and an exclusive interest, and for a limited duration. Nothing in all of this corresponds to the great hopes that the workers' Democracy had placed in the idea of the association: by what right does it flatter itself that it will produce results any more human than those we have seen? The association is a thing that defines itself, and the essential characteristic of which is its particularity. Could one make it such that this were not the case, [placing] everyone alongside each other, separate and distinct, [with] an association of carpenters, of masons, of lamp-sellers, one of tailors, of boot-makers, etc., etc.? Wouldn't this be to follow the option suggested by those who see these associations founded one upon the other, forming one single and equivalent general association? We can boldly refuse to let the workers' Democracy land itself in a similar mess; that is, we can refuse to allow, not just the workers, but their counsellors, the Academy of Moral and Political Sciences, the legislative corps, the School of Law, *en masse*, to propose a formula for association that would unify two heterogeneous groups, such as the masons and the cabinetmakers, [so] confusing their actions and their interests. Therefore, if the associations are distinct, inevitably they will also be rivals; their interests will diverge; there will be contradictions and hostilities. You will never escape this.

But, you say to me, don't we have the principle of mutuality to bring accord to our associations and make them live together in peace without dissolving them [into one another]?...

Excellent! See here how mutuality appears as *Deus ex machinâ*. Let us know therefore what it teaches us; and, to start, let us note that mutuality is not the same thing as association, and that as a friend of liberty as much as that of the group, it shows itself equally remote from all fantasy and all intolerance.

A little while ago we spoke of the *division of labour*. A consequence of this economic force is that as much as it engenders specialities it creates sources of independence, which implies the separation of enterprises, precisely the opposite of that sought by the instigators of communist associations as well as by the founders of capitalist associations. Combined then with the law of natural grouping of populations by regions, cantons, communes, and streets, the division of labour arrives at this decisive consequence: that not only is each industrial speciality called upon to develop itself and to act in full and complete independence, under the conditions of mutuality, responsibility, and security which form the general condition of society; but also that it is the manufacturers which, in their respective localities, each individually represent a speciality of labour: in principle these manufacturers should remain free. The division of labour, freedom, competition, political and social equality, the dignity of man and citizen, permits no subordination. The Sixty say in their Manifesto that they no longer want *clients*: this is only the counterpart of that. It is always the same idea, it is the same thing.

It follows from this that the principle of mutuality inasmuch as it concerns association, is not to associate men except insofar as it is required by the exigencies of production; the low prices for products, the demands of consumption, the security of the producers themselves, requires it, there where it is possible neither for the public to bind itself to a particular industry, nor for it to assume responsibility for and run the risks of enterprises alone. Thus conceived, it is no longer the dream of a system, the calculation of ambition, the spirit of a faction, or a vain sentimentality that unites subjects; it is inevitable, in the nature of things, and this is why in associating in this way they obey only the inevitable, which can conserve, even within the association, their liberty.

This side of the mutualist idea, following from the general principles posited by the Manifesto of the Sixty, is naturally intended to reconcile the keenest sympathies of the petit bourgeois, small manufacturers and small shopkeepers with the new democracy.

What about in large-scale manufacture, extraction, metallurgy, the maritime industries? It is clear that there is a place for association here: no one contests this. Again, what about one of the great concerns that have the character of a public service, such as railways, credit establishments, ports? I have proved elsewhere that the law of mutuality is such that these services are delivered to the public at a price that covers operating expenses and maintenance, while excluding all capitalist profit. In this case again it is obvious that the guarantee of good execution and a good price can be given neither by monopolistic companies, nor by communities patronised by the State, building the concern in the name of the State and on behalf of the State. This guarantee can only come from free co-operators,[22] engaged on the one hand towards the public, by the mutualist contract, and on the other with each other by the ordinary contract of association.

Now, is it a question of these thousands of trades and businesses which exist in such great numbers in the cities and the countryside? There, I no longer see the necessity or utility of association. I see it all the less inasmuch as the fruit one promises will be acquired by the ensemble of mutualist guarantees, mutual assurances, mutual credit, the organising of markets [*police des marchés*], etc., etc. I will it say again: in the case of which we are speaking, given these guarantees, there is more security for the public in dealing with a single entrepreneur, rather than with a company.

Who does not see, for example, that the *raison d'être* of the small shop is in the need that large companies find to establish on all sides, for the convenience of their clients, stores and local offices, in a word, branches? Now, in a regime of mutuality, we are all clients of one another, subordinates of one another, servants of one another. This is what our *Solidarity* consists of,

---

22  *Sociétaires,* members of a co-operative society or a mutual insurance company, as opposed to shareholders. (Editor)

this solidarity that the authors of the Manifesto affirm along with the *Right to Work*, with the *Freedom of Labour*, with the *Mutuality of credit*, etc. What an inconvenience, therefore, would these authors find in the fact that the same man who, in a system of feudalism such as that of the great capitalist companies or those of the communities of Luxembourg, would be condemned to remain a waged subordinate,[23] an ordinary wage-worker, becomes in the system of mutuality where agiotage is no longer anything but a word, a free shopkeeper? The mission of the shopkeeper is not only to buy and sell, from the exclusive point of view of private interest; they must also elevate themselves alongside the social order of which they form a part. Before everything, the shopkeeper is a distributor of products, and he must be an expert in the qualities, manufacture, provenance, and value of these products. It is necessary that he keeps the consumers of his district up to date on prices, new articles, the risks of price increases, the probabilities of price drops. This is a continual work, which demands intelligence, zeal, honesty, and which, I repeat, in the new conditions we establish with mutualism, requires nothing of the rather suspect security offered by the great association. A general reform of morals according to principles is sufficient here for the security of the public. I ask myself therefore why this economic individuality should disappear? What forces us to meddle with it? Let us organise rights and let the shopkeepers be. The favour of the shoppers will go to the most diligent and the most upstanding.

There therefore, if I am not mistaken, must be found the elements of the alliance, highly affirmed and defended by the authors of the Manifesto, between the industrial and commercial petit bourgeois and the working classes.

"Without us," they say with a profound sense of the truth, "the bourgeoisie can rest on nothing solid; without their agreement our emancipation can be delayed for a long time indeed. Let us unify for a common goal, the triumph of true democracy."

Let us repeat following their example: It is not a question here of defending acquired positions; it is simply a matter of, by the reduction of the interest on capital and the rent on lodgings, the ease and insignificance of discount rates, the elimination of parasitism, the extirpation of speculation, the regulation of warehouses and markets, the diminution of the price of transport, the equilibrium of values, the superior instruction given to the working classes, the definitive preponderance of labour over capital, the correct measure of esteem accorded to talent and function, it is a matter, I say, of restoring to labour and to probity that which has been unduly taken from them by capitalist prelibation;[24] of augmenting the general well-being in assuring [the means of] life; of preventing financial ruin and bankruptcy by the certitude

---

23  A *succursaliste à gage*: literally a branch manager, someone hired to manage a part of a company they do not own or control. (Editor)

24  Offering of the first fruits. (Editor)

of transactions; of stopping the expropriation characteristic of exorbitant fortunes without any real or legitimate foundation, in a word, of putting an end to all those anomalies and perturbations which sound critique has for a very long time indicated as the chronic causes of poverty and the proletariat.

But what good is it to fight over words and to waste time on useless discussions? One thing is certain: that the people, no matter what else one says about them, have faith in Association, that they affirm, urge, and herald it, and that however it is really nothing other than the deed of partnership [*le contrat de société*] defined by our laws. Let us conclude, therefore, that in order to remain faithful simultaneously to the data of science and the aspirations of the people, Association, whose formula contemporary innovators have searched for, as if the legislator would have nothing to say about it, but which none of them have managed to define; that Fourier, the artist, mystic, and prophet, called HARMONY, and which he proclaimed would need to be proceeded by a period of Guaranteeism; this famous Association which must embrace the whole of Society, and nevertheless preserve all the rights of individual and corporate freedom; which can consequently be neither the community or universal society of goods and profits, recognised by the Civil code, practised in the middle ages in the countryside, generalised by the Moravian sect,[25] identified with the political constitution, or the State, and regimented in different manners by Plato, Campanella, Morus, Owen, Cabet, etc.; nor the Societies of commerce, general, limited, undisclosed partnerships or joint-stock companies; let us conclude, I say, that Association, which the workers' Democracy persists in invoking as the end of all servitude and the superior form of civilisation, who does not see that it is and could not be anything other than MUTUALITY? Mutuality, indeed, whose lineaments we have tried to trace, is it not the social contract par excellence, simultaneously political and economic, synallagmatic and commutative, which embraces at once, in such simple terms, the individual and the family, the corporation and the city, sale and purchase, credit, insurance, labour, instruction and property; all professions, all transactions, all services, all securities; which, in its very regenerative scope, excludes all egoism, all parasitism, all arbitrary power, all agiotage, all dissolution? Do we not have here, truly, the mysterious association dreamed of by the utopians, unknown to the philosophers and the jurisconsults, and which we will define in two words, contract of mutuation or of mutuality?[26]

---

25  The Moravian Church is a Protestant church which began in late 14th century Bohemia (the modern Czech Republic). Its official name is "Unity of the Brethren" and it places a high premium on Christian unity, personal piety, missions and music. During its 18th revival, its supporters created settlements which emphasised a form of communal living in which personal property was still held but simplicity of lifestyle and generosity with wealth were considered important spiritual attributes. (Editor)

26  The honourable citizens who in recent times have taken under their patronage the development of workers' societies, representatives of the People, journalists, bankers,

Let us glance back one more time on this new pact, such as it presents itself today in sketches which are rough and imperfect (but full of hope), that presents us here and there with the workers' Democracy, and let us note its essential characteristics. However restricted it may appear, in the beginning, in its personnel, specialised in its objects, limited in its duration, open to modification and cancellation in its import, there exists in the mutualist association,—we can from now on give it this name,—a power of development which tends with an irresistible force to assimilate and incorporate all that surrounds it, to remake in its image the State and the Humanity which surrounds it. This power of development belongs to the mutualist association because of its high morality and the economic fecundity of its principle.

Note first of all that in virtue of the principle which characterises it, the ranks of the Association are open to whomever, having recognised the spirit and the goal, asks to join; exclusion is contrary to it, and the more it grows in number the more advantages it gains. From the point of view of personnel,

---

lawyers, men of letters, industrialists, etc. recognise, I hope, that in preferring the term MUTUALITY, *Mutualism,* etc. as a general formula of the economic Revolution, over that of *association,* I am hardly acting out of a vain motive for personal glory, but on the contrary in the interest of scientific exactitude. First, the word association is too specific and too vague; it lacks precision; it appeals less to intelligence than to sentiment; it does not have the character of universality required in similar circumstances. Notwithstanding, as one of the writers of *The Association* has said, that there now exists among workers three types of societies, between which one must find the link, societies of *production, consumer* societies, and *credit* societies; there are also others, of *aid, insurance, education,* of *reading,* of *temperance,* of *singing,* etc. Add to this the societies defined by the Code: *Civil* and *commercial* societies, *universal societies of goods and profits,* or *communities; general partnerships, limited partnerships,* and *joint-stock companies.* All of these hardly resemble each other, and the first thing which has to be done by a writer who would like to write a treatise on association is to find a principle by means of which he can bring together into a single formula these innumerable associations, a principle which consequently will be superior to that of association itself.

But this is not all: it is obvious that three quarters, if not four fifths of a nation like ours, proprietors, farmers, small industrialists, men of letters, artists, public functionaries, etc. can never be considered as being in [a] company; however, unless we declare them outside of reform, outside of revolution, it is necessary to admit that the word *company, association,* does not fulfil the goal of science; it is necessary to find another that, with simplicity and nerve, attains the universality of a principle. Finally, we have observed that in the new Democracy the political principle must be identical with and adequate to the economic principle; now, this principle has for a long time been named and defined; this is the federative principle, synonymous with mutuality or reciprocal security, which has nothing in common with the principle of association.

the mutualist association is therefore by nature unlimited, which is the opposite of all other associations.

It is the same with its object. A mutualist association can have for a special object the operation of an industry. By virtue of the principle of mutuality, however, it tends to involve in its system of guarantees first those industries it is in an immediate relation with, then the more distant ones. Again, in this connection the mutualist association is unlimited, with an indefinite power of agglomeration.

Should I speak of its duration? It may be that mutualist associates, not having succeeded in an enterprise, inasmuch as this was defined, specified, particularly staffed, and delimited, might find it convenient to break these specific agreements. It is no less true that, as their society was founded above all on an idea of right and the economic application of that idea, it will hold in perpetuity, as we have just seen it has held universally. The day when the working masses have acquired the clear notion of the principle that agitates them in this moment, when this notion has penetrated their consciousness, when they have professed it completely, all abrogation of the regime they will have instituted will become impossible: it would be a contradiction. Mutuality, or the mutualist society, is Justice and one cannot go backward in matters of justice anymore than one can in matters of religion. Has the world, having become monotheistic by the preaching of the Gospel, ever dreamed of returning to the cult of gods? Could France, when the Russians have abolished serfdom in their country, return to a feudal system? It will be the same with the new reform. The contract of mutuality is irrevocable by its nature, as much in the small association as in the largest. Purely material and external causes can cause societies of this species, inasmuch as they have a special object, to be terminated; in themselves, and in their fundamental disposition, they tend to create a new order of things and are no longer terminable. Men, after having made between themselves a pact of probity, loyalty, security, and honour, cannot say to themselves in breaking this pact: We had been mistaken; now we are going to become rogues and liars again, and from this we will profit more!...

Finally, its last characteristic: the contribution of capital is no longer indispensable in the mutualist society; it is sufficient, to become an associate, to keep to the mutual faith in all transactions.

In summary, according to the existing legislation, a company is a contract formed between a determinate number of persons, designated by their names, professions, and qualities (*Code civil*, article 1832), with the aim of a particular benefit to be shared between the associates (*ibid.*). Each associate has to contribute money, or other goods, or his industry (article 1833). It is made for a determined period of time (article 1865).

The mutualist association is conceived in an altogether different spirit. It admits, insofar as it is mutualist, everyone in the world, and tends towards universality;—it is formed not directly with the aim of profit, but of security;—one is required to contribute neither money nor other valuables, or even one's industry; the only condition demanded is to be faithful to the mutualist pact;—once formed, its nature is to generalise itself and to have no end.

The communist association, as an instrument of revolution and a governmental formula, also tends to universality and perpetuity; but it leaves nothing belonging to those associated, not their money, nor their other goods, nor their labour, nor their liberty: this is what makes it forever impossible.

Nothing will prevent the generations that have once been transformed by mutualist law from continuing to form, as at present, particular associations having for their object the development of an industrial speciality or the pursuit of an enterprise for an honest profit. But these associations (which can even retain their current designations), subject in their dealing with one another and with the public to the duty of mutuality, imbued with the new spirit, can no longer be compared to their analogues at the current time. They will have lost their egoistical and subversive character while retaining the particular advantages which bestow upon them their economic power. These will be like many particular churches inside a universal Church, able to reproduce it themselves, if it were possible that it had suddenly died out.

—I had very much wanted here to give the mutualist and federative theory of property, the critique of [property] which I published twenty-five years ago.[27] The size of the subject obliges me to return to this important study at another time.

—I will speak in the third part of this volume of free trade, of the liberty of coalition and of several other questions of political economy, which cannot be resolved except by the principle of mutuality.

CHAPTER XV
Objections Against Mutualist Policy. Answer. Primary Cause Of
The Fall Of States—Relation Of The Political And Economic
Functions In The New Democracy

But let us not get lost in digressions. It falls to us to explain what unity and order signify in a mutualist democracy; and here there is a much more grave objection that our adversaries will be sure to raise.

Let us, we will be told, step outside of theories and sentiments: every State requires an authority, a spirit of discipline and obedience, without which no society can survive. The Government requires a force capable of cowing all resistance and subjecting all opinion to the general will. One can argue as much as one may like about the nature, origin and forms of that power: that is not the issue. The real, the only point is that strenuous steps should be taken to establish it. No human will could command the will of another

---

27   See *What is Property?*, *Letter to M. Blanqui*; *Warning to Proprietors*, Paris, 1840, 1841 and 1842, and *Economic Contradictions*, volume II.

man, says de Bonald, and he concludes that what is needed is a higher institution, a divine right. According to J.-J Rousseau, on the other hand, public authority is a collective made up of every individual citizen's surrender of a morsel of his freedom and fortune for the sake of the general interest: such is democratic revolutionary right. No matter what system one espouses, one comes always to this conclusion, that the soul of political society is authority and that its sanction is force.

Moreover, this is how States were constituted down through the ages and it is the way that they are governed, the way they live. Or are we to believe that it is through some act of free affiliation that the masses formed themselves into a phalanx and, under the aegis of a leader, established powerful units, to which the labours of revolutions add so little? No, these agglomerations have been the handiwork of force in the service of necessity. Are we to believe that it was willingly, as the result of some mysterious persuasion, some conviction of indeterminable provenance that these masses let themselves be led like a herd, by a strange notion that takes possession of them and the secret of which no one can fathom? Again, no: this trend towards centralisation to which everyone resigns himself, even should he grumble, is also the effect of necessity, served by force. It is absurd to rebel against these great laws, as if we might alter them and build another life for ourselves on different principles.

What, then, is mutualism's intention and what are the consequences of that doctrine in terms of Government? It is to found an order of things wherein the principle of sovereignty of the people, of man and of the citizen would be implemented to the letter: where every member of the State, retaining his independence and continuing to act as sovereign, would be self-governing, whilst a higher authority would concern itself solely with collective matters; where, as a consequence, there would be certain common matters but no centralisation: and, to take things to their conclusion, a State the acknowledged sovereign parts of which would be free to quit the group and withdraw from the compact, at will. For there is no disguising it: if it is to be logical and true to its principle, the federation has to take things to these extremes. Otherwise it is merely an illusion, boastfulness, a lie.

But it is obvious that this right of secession which, in principle, should be enjoyed by every confederated State, is a paradox: it has never been realised and the practices of confederations refute it. Who does not know that at the time of the First Medean war Greece almost perished, betrayed by her federal freedom? The Athenians and the Spartans stood alone against the great king: the others had refused to stir. After the Persians had been defeated, civil war erupted between the Greeks in order to put an end to this nonsensical constitution: and the Macedonian carried off the honours and the benefit of this.—In 1846 when the Swiss Confederation stood on the brink of dissolution due to the secession of the Catholic cantons (the *Sonderbund*), the majority had no hesitation in resorting to force of arms in order to call back the secessionists. Although the claim has been made, it was not on the basis of any federal law, which was positively opposed to it. How could thirteen Protestant cantons, all of them sovereign, have proved to eleven Catholic cantons, themselves every bit as sovereign, that under the compact they were entitled to hold them inside a union of which they no longer wished to be part? The very term "federation" is a prohibition against any such intention. The Swiss majority acted on the right of national preservation: it took the view that Switzerland, placed between two great unitary states, could not, without great peril, countenance a new and more or less hostile federation, and in surrendering to necessity and basing its rights upon the argument of might, it affirmed the primacy of the unity principle, on behalf of and under the aegis of a supposed confederation.—At the time of writing and certainly with much less grounds than the Swiss liberals of 1846, in that American freedom is not in jeopardy, the Northern United States is also bent upon holding the Southern States inside the Union, calling them traitors and re-bels, no more and no less than if the former Union were a monarchy and Mr Lincoln an emperor. It is plain, however, that a choice has to be made: either the word confederation has a meaning on the basis of which the founding fa-thers of the Union meant to distinguish it from every other political system: in which case, the slavery issue aside, the war waged by the North on the South is unjust: or else, under the appearances of a confederation and just waiting for the right time, what was secretly being pursued was the forma-tion of a great empire: in which case the Americans will be well-advised to banish the words political freedom, republic, democracy, confederation and even Union from their hustings in future. On the far side of the Atlantic they have already begun to deny States' rights, meaning the federal principle, an unambiguous indication of a forthcoming change to the Union. Odder still, European democracy applauds this handiwork, as if it were not an abdica-tion of its principle and the ruination of its hopes.

To sum up: a social revolution along the lines of mutuality is a chimera, because, in this society, political organisation would have to be the corollary of economic organisation and that corollary, which it is accepted would have to be a federative State, is, if one thinks about it, itself an impossibility. In fact, confederations have never been anything other than provisional, States in the process of formation; theoretically, they are nonsenses. So mutuality, by positing federalism as its last word, is ruling itself out: it is nothing.

Such is the crucial argument that we must answer. But first I must put the historic record straight.

Adversaries of federalism benevolently take it for granted that centralisa-tion boasts all of the advantages that they deny federation: that the former enjoys the same vigour as the latter is unlikely; in short, as long as the latter is bereft of logic and force, we are assured that these can be found in the former and that this lies at the root of the huge difference in their fortunes to date. So, if I am to leave nothing out, I should balance out the two positions, counter criticism of the federative principle with criticism of the unitary principle: show that, yes, ever since the dawn of society, confederations have played only a seemingly secondary role; yes, thanks to the mismatch between their institutions, they have not withstood the test of lengthy existence; whereas it appears even to be impossible for them to rely upon the truth of their principle, heavily centralised States, on the other hand, have most times been nothing more than wholesale banditry, organised tyrannies, the chief merit of which has been that for the past thirty centuries, they have dragged the corpses of nations through the mud, as if Providence's aim had been to punish them with centuries of torture for their federal fantasies.

So I should point out that history in its entirety is nothing but a succession of integrations and disintegrations; that pluralities of federations are forever being replaced by amalgamations and those amalgamations by break-ups; that Alexander's empire, established in Europe and Asia, soon gave way to division among his generals, a veritable return to nationalities, as we would put it today; that this nationalist trend gave way to the greater unity of Rome, supplanted in the 5th century by the Germanic and Italian federations; that we have recently seen the Austrian Empire switch from absolutism to federalism, whereas Italy switched from federation to kingdom; that, whilst the First Empire, with its one hundred and thirty two departments, its great fiefdoms and its alliances, proved unable to sustain European confederation, the much more centralised Second Empire, although less extensive than its predecessor, was imbued with a spirit of freedom that was very differently imperious in provincial and communal collectivites than in individuals themselves. This is something which I should have liked to pursue further and which I shall content myself here with quoting from memory.

This, then, is the puzzle that we have to solve: it relates equally to centralisation and to federation *per se*.

1. Why is it that unitary states, be they monarchist, aristocratic or republican, are forever disintegrating?

2. And at the same time what is it that leads federations to tend to evolve towards unity?

This is what we must tackle first, before we offer any opinion on the comparative value of centralised and confederated States. And this is precisely the answer I mean to provide, in accordance with the principles set out in the previous chapter, namely, that Truth and Right are the only foundations of order, the absence of which renders all centralisation voracious and all federation hypocrisy:

What made States, unitary and federated alike, prey to disintegration and ruin, is that, in the case of the former, society is bereft of any sort of political and economic guarantee; and, in the case of the others, no matter how perfectly constituted Authority may be thought to be, society itself has thus far been underpinned only by political guarantees, never economic ones.

Neither in Switzerland nor in the United States do we discover an organised mutuality: now, without a battery of mutualist institutions, without economic right, the political format remains impotent, government is always precarious—a whited sepulchre, as Saint Paul would have it.

What then must be done in order to preserve confederations from decomposition, while upholding a principle thus defined: The right of every component town, territory, province and populace, in short, every State, to join the confederation and to quit it, at will?

Note that no such facility was ever offered to free men; no such problem was ever mooted by any publicist. De Bonald and Jean-Jacques, the divine right man and the demagogue, are as one in declaring, after the manner of Christ, that any kingdom divided against itself shall perish. But Christ was speaking in a spiritual sense; and our authors are out and out materialists, supporters of authority and make their stand on a basis of slavery.

What must be done in order to render confederation indestructible is at last to furnish it with the sanction for which it is still waiting, by proclaiming economic Right as the basis of the right of federation and all political order.

It is here above all that we ought to look to the revolution that is going to be carried out in the social system, simply because of the mutualism, a few instances of which we have previously identified for the reader. Already we have seen that the mutuality principle, carried over from private dealings into the collective, relies upon a battery of institutions that one can readily anticipate will grow. To refresh our memory, we shall review only the most salient of these.

### A. Economic functions

1. CHARITABLE purposes and personal assistance, a transition from the charitable injunction of Christ and the system of justice introduced by the Revolution; an assistance agency, medical service, homes, crèches, sanatoriums, penitentiaries, etc. All of which, of course, is pretty much already in existence, but what is missing is the new spirit which is the only thing that can render it effective, banishing parasitism, hypocrisy, begging and profligacy.
2. INSURANCE, against flood, fire, navigational and rail mishaps, epizooty,[28] hail, disease, old age and death.
3. LOANS, commerce and discount; banks, bourses, etc.
4. Public TRANSPORT services by rail, canal, river and seaways.— Such services pose no threat to private enterprises, serving indeed to regulate and complement them.
5. WAREHOUSING, docks, market and price listing services. The object being to ensure steady optimum distribution of produce

---

28  A disease affecting many animals at the same time; an epidemic amongst animals. (Editor)

to the benefit of both producers and consumers. Spelling the end for commodity speculation, hoarders, cartels and speculation on futures.

6. A service handling STATISTICS, advertising and bulletins setting prices and determining values. Social agencies serving as regulators of retail trade.

7. WORKERS COMPANIES for the carrying out of paving, refor- estation, land clearance, road- and path-building and irrigation works.

8. WORKERS COMPANIES for bridge, aqueduct, dam, port, tun- nel construction and for erecting public monuments, etc.

9. WORKERS COMPANIES operating mines, water services and forestry.

10. WORKERS COMPANIES servicing ports, rail stations, markets, warehousing, shops, etc.

11. CONSTRUCTION COMPANY servicing the construction, maintenance and leasing of homes and cheap housing in towns.

12. PUBLIC EDUCATION along scientific and vocational lines.

13. PROPERTY, overhauling the laws of property title, formation, distribution, means of transference, etc. Reform and consolidation of the *allodial* system.[29]

14. TAXATION...

*Remarks*—1.—Hitherto, the institutions or functions which we have chosen to designate as *economic* have been an *afterthought* in society. We do not invent them, nor do we conjure them up out of some arbitrary whim; we merely identify them in accordance with a principle as simple as it is peremp- tory. Indeed it has been shown that in a number of circumstances individual initiative is powerless to achieve what is derived effortlessly and at consider- ably lesser expense from co-operation by all. Where-so-ever private efforts do not avail, it is only fair, by right and by duty that collective effort, mutuality, be deployed. It is absurd to sacrifice public wealth or happiness to some impotent freedom. Therein lies the principle, the goal and the underlying motivation behind economic institutions. Everything that can be performed by an individual, consistent with the laws of fairness, will therefore be left to the individual; anything that is beyond the powers of one person will fall under the responsibility of the collective.

2. I classify agencies handling *Charity*, *Public Education* and *Taxation* un- der the heading of economic functions or institutions. The nature of things points to the reason for this classification. The eradication of poverty and the relief of human wretchedness have, down through the ages, been regarded as the hardest nuts for science to crack. Like idleness in the worker, social

---

29  See *Theory of Property*, chapter IX. (Editor)

wretchedness goes to the very heart of production and has a direct bearing upon public happiness. So a science, a precise policy is required if this entire class of agency is to be removed from the purview and influence of the powers that be.—The same should hold true for Taxation. In this regard, the Revolution of '89 and all of the Constitutions emanating from it have set out the true principles, determining that taxation demanded by Government needed the assent of the nation, and that the general councils and municipalities should determine how the burden should be shared. The Prince does not bear his own costs: it is the country that bears the costs of its proxy: from which it follows that what we today call the Finance Ministry does not at all fall within the remit of the Authorities.—As for public education, which is merely the extrapolation of domestic education, its economic function has to be acknowledged, lest it be reconverted into a function of religion and the family *per se* be denied.

3. Articles 4, 7, 8, 9, 10 and 11 of the list above show the importance accorded in the New Democracy to workers' associations which are deemed to constitute economic agencies and mutual institutions. Their object is not just to service the interests of the worker, but also to furnish an answer to the legitimate will of society, namely, to remove the railways and mines from the monopolies of joint stock companies—publicly useful constructions from the biased adjudications and whim of State engineers—water resources and forests from the depredations of State property, etc. Such workers companies, established in accordance with the precepts of the Civil and Commercial Code and subject to laws of competition, as stated in the Manifesto, and answerable for their performance, are also tied to society which uses them to meet its mutualist obligations so as to ensure that their services are made accessible at the best possible price.

Added to this list of economic functions, there is a further, complementary series described as *political*. Like the preceding series, these may vary in terms of numbers and definition: but there can be no mistaking their character.

### B. Political functions

15. The ELECTORAL BODY, or universal suffrage.
16. The LEGISLATIVE AUTHORITY.
17. The EXECUTIVE AUTHORITY: Administration.
18. The " " : Police, Courts.
19. The " " : Religion.
20. The " " : Warfare.

The ministries of Agriculture, Trade, Public Education, Public Works and Finance have been revamped and amalgamated into economic functions.

*Remarks:*—1. These functions are described as political to distinguish them from the foregoing so-called economic ones, because their responsibility extends beyond persons and goods, production, consumption, education, work, credit and property, to the collective State, the social Body as a whole in its dealings both with the outside world and with itself.

2. These same functions, moreover, are subordinated to the others and might be described as sub-functions because, for all their majestic apparatus, they play a much less vital role than economic functions. Before legislating, administering, building palaces, temples, and waging war, society works, labours, navigates, exchange and exploits soil and seas. Before kings are consecrated and dynasties instituted, the people lays the foundations of the family, contracting marriages, building towns and establishing property and inheritance. In principle, these are political functions still mixed in with economic ones: in fact, nothing within the specialisation of government and the State is alien to the public economy. That widespread belief, focusing upon the governmental agency, then appears to confer a sort of birthright upon it, is down to the impact of an historical illusion to which we are now immune, now that we have retraced the whole genealogy of society and put everything in its proper place. Between economic functions and political functions there is a relationship analogous to that which physiology suggests obtains between the functions of organic life and the functions of the life of relations; it is through the former that the animal manifests itself to the outside world and fulfils its mission among creatures; but it is through the latter that it exists and, to tell the truth, everything that it does in exercise of its freedom of action is merely a more or less reasoned *conclusum* of its underlying potential.

3. Thus, under the democratic constitution, insofar we can judge from its most salient ideas and most authentic aspirations, the political and the economic are one and the same, a sole and single system based upon a single principle, mutuality. As we have seen, through a sequence of mutualist dealings, the great economic institutions step forward one after another to form this vast humanitarian organism which, previously, there was nothing to convey; similarly, the machinery of government itself is, by dint of some unfathomable fictional convention, imagined as being for the good of the republic and is as quickly withdrawn as posited, but this time on the basis of a genuine contract wherein the sovereignty of the contracting parties, instead of being gobbled up by some central majesty that is both personal and mystical, represents a positive guarantee of the freedom of States, communes and individuals.

Thus, no longer do we have the abstraction of people's sovereignty as in the '93 Constitution and the others that followed it, and in Rousseau's *Social Contract*. Instead it becomes an effective sovereignty of the labouring masses which rule and govern initially at beneficent meetings, chambers of commerce, crafts and trades bodies, and workers companies; in the stock exchanges, the markets, the academies, the schools, agricultural fairs and finally election meetings, parliamentary assemblies and councils of State, national guards and even the churches and temples. It is still universally the same *collective force* that is brought forth in the name of and by virtue of the principle of mutuality: the final affirmation of the rights of Man and the Citizen.

I declare here and now that the labouring masses are actually, positively and effectively sovereign: how could they not be when the economic organism—labour, capital, property and assets—belongs to them entirely: as utter masters of the organic functions, how could they not be all the more emphatically masters of the functions of relations? Subservience to the productive might of what was hitherto, to the exclusion of anything else, the Government, the Powers that be, the State, is blown apart by the way in which the political organism is made up:

a. An ELECTORAL BODY, spontaneously coming together, laying down policy on operations and reviewing and sanctioning its own acts;

b. A delegation, LEGISLATIVE BODY or Council of State, appointed by the federal groups and susceptible to re-election;[30]

c. An *executive commission* selected by the people's representatives from among their own number, and liable to recall;

d. Finally, a chairman for that commission, appointed by it and liable to recall.

Tell me, is this not the system of the old society turned on its head; a system in which the country is decidedly all; where what once was described as the head of State, the sovereign, autocrat, monarch, despot, king, emperor, tsar, khan, sultan, majesty, highness, etc., etc., surfaces once and for all as a gentleman, the first among his fellow-citizens, perhaps, in terms of honorific distinction, but definitely the least dangerous of all public officials? You may brag this time that the issue of political guarantee, the issue of making the government subservient to the country, and the prince to the sovereign, is done and dusted. Never again will you see usurpation or coup d'état; and the authorities revolting against the people, authority and the bourgeoisie in coalition against the plebes becomes impossible.

4. Taking all of this as read, I turn again to the issue of unity raised earlier; under federative law, how can the State retain its stability? How might a

---

30  If the confederated states are equals, one to another, one single assembly suffices; if they are of unequal significance, balance can be restored by establishing two Houses or Councils for the purposes of federal representation; one the members of which have been appointed, in equal numbers, by the states, regardless of their population size and area; the other where the deputies are appointed by the states themselves in accordance with their significance (cf. the Swiss federal constitution, wherein the duality of Parliament means something quite different than it does in the constitutions of France and England.)

system that enshrines as its underlying thought the right of secession enjoyed by every federated component, then act coherently and maintain itself?

To be honest, that question went unanswered as long as confederated States had no basis in economic rights and the law of mutuality: divergent interests sooner or later were fated to lead to damaging splits and unity under monarchy to replace republican error. Now everything is different: the economic order is founded upon entirely different factors: the ethos of the States is no longer what it was; in terms of the truth of its principle, the confederation is indissoluble. Democracy, once so hostile to all thoughts of schism, especially in France, has nothing to fear.

None of the sources of division between men, cities, corporations and individuals obtains among mutualist groups: not sovereign power, not political coalition, not dynastic rights, nor civil list, honours, pensions, capitalist exploitation, dogmatism, sectarian mentality, party rivalry, racial prejudice or rivalry between corporations, towns or provinces. There may be differences of opinion, belief, interests, mores, industries, cultures, etc. But these differences are the very basis and the object of mutualism: so they cannot, ever, degenerate into Church intolerance, papal supremacy, overbearing locality or city, industrial or agricultural preponderance. Conflicts are impossible: one would have to destroy the mutuality before they could resurface.[31]

From where would the rebellion come? On what pretext would discontent rely?—In a mutualist confederation, the citizen gives up none of his freedom, as Rousseau requires him to do for the governance of his republic! Public authority lies in the hands of the citizen: he himself yields it and profits from it: if he has a grievance, it is that neither he nor anyone else

---

31 A little known but highly interesting fact will make this truth plain. In certain places in the Doubs department, in the Montbéliard *arrondissement* where the population is one half Catholic and one half Protestant, it is not unusual for the same building to be used, turn and turn about, at different times, for both faiths and this without the slightest annoyance on either side. Obviously these folk have had to come to some arrangement: for the purposes of their respective worship, they have had to agree on mutual tolerance; and mutuality rules out all thought of conflict. In these villages it is unheard of for anyone to switch from one religion to the other; and it is equally unheard of for any believer to have carried out any act of aggression, any act of zealotry. For some yeas now, the Archbishop of Besançon has been planting disunity and building separate churches for his flock. A genuine friend of peace and humanity might simply have suggested making the house of God larger and more ornate; he would have realised that this chapel-church was the finest monument erected by the hands of men to Christian charity. Which is not how the archbishop sees it. As long as it is up to him, he will pit religion against religion, church against church, graveyard against graveyard. And come the last judgement, Christ will merely have to pass sentence and the sifting of the faithful from the unbelievers will be accomplished.

can any longer usurp it and stake a claim to exclusive enjoyment of it. There are no more hostages to fortune to be given: the State asks nothing of him by way of taxation beyond what is strictly required for the public services which, being essentially reproductive, when fairly distributed, makes a trade out of an imposition.[32] Now, trade amounts to an increase in wealth:[33] so, from that angle too, there need be no fear of disintegration. Might the confederates scatter in the face of a civil or foreign war? But in a confederation founded upon economic Right and the law of mutuality, there could be only one source of civil warfare—religion. Now, setting to one side the fact that the spiritual counts for very little once other interests are reconciled and mutually assured, who can fail to see that the corollary of mutuality is mutual tolerance: which rules out the likelihood of such conflict? As for foreign aggression, from where might that spring? The confederation, which acknowledges that every one of its confederated States enjoys a right of secession, is scarcely likely to want to bully the foreigner. The idea of conquest is incompatible with its very principle. So there can be only one foreseeable possibility of war emanating from without, namely, the possibility of a war for principle: should the surrounding States, hugely exploitative and hugely centralised, determine that the existence of a mutualist confederation cannot be reconciled with their own principle, just as, in '92 the Brunswick manifesto declared that the French Revolution was incompatible with the principles governing other States! To which my response is that the outlawing of a confederation rooted in economic right and the law of mutuality would be the very thing that could happen, in that it would incite federative, mutualist republican sentiment to put paid once and for all with the world of monopoly and bring about the victory of Labour Democracy right around the world ..

But need we labour this point further?

The principle of mutuality, as it moves into the terrain of law-making and mores, and gives rise to economic right, comprehensively overhauls civil law, commercial and administrative law, public law and common law. Or rather, in the working out of that over-riding and underlying category of law, economic Right, the principle of mutuality gives rise to unity of juridical science: better than ever before, it highlights the fact that law is one and the same, that there is a uniformity to all its prescriptions, all its maxims and corollaries, all its laws and variations upon the same law.

The old right, which the science of the old jurisconsults had sub-divided into as many specialised branches as it had different objects, was broadly characterised by a negativity in all its ramifications: by the fact that it thwarted rather than enabled; that it prevented conflicts rather than creating guarantees; repressed a range of acts of violence and fraud rather than offering

---

32   See *Théorie sur l'Impôt* by P-J Proudhon, Paris, Dentu, 1861.
33   See *Manuel du spéculateur à la Bourse*, introduction, by the above named, Paris 1857.

protection against violence and fraud and for the creation of wealth and the common weal.

The new right, by contrast, is essentially *positive*. Its object is to afford, with certainty and comprehensiveness, everything that the old right merely allowed to proceed, pending the freedom to do so, but without concern for guarantees or the means so to do, without so much as a hint of approval or disapproval. Henceforth under the new right, defaulting upon a guarantee and [violating] social solidarity; persisting upon the practices of mercantile anarchy, dissembling, monopolising, speculating, is regarded as every bit as reprehensible as any of the swindling, confidence tricks, deceptions and armed robberies with which law has hitherto been almost exclusively concerned. In matters relating to insurance, supply and demand, price-setting and valuation, bona fide business, credit, transport services, etc.,—in short, what we have described as economic institutions or functions—we have expounded sufficiently upon the positive nature of the new Right, the new obligations flowing from it and the freedom and wealth that spring from it and we need not repeat ourselves.

So how could a group of workers, having belonged to a mutualist federation, turn its back on the positive, material, palpable and recognisable benefits which it bestows? How could it opt instead for a return to the former nothingness, the traditional pauperism, the absence of solidarity and lack of morality? Once having tasted economic order, might they wish to become an exploiter aristocracy and revert to universal wretchedness just for the sordid satisfaction of the few? How, I ask, once the hearts of men have tasted right, could they come out against right and stand exposed to the world as a gang of thieves and pirates?

Once mutualist economic reform is proclaimed anywhere on earth, confederations become necessities everywhere. For them to exist the federating States need not be all contiguous, clustered together as if in a belt, as we see France, Italy and Spain. Federation can exist between States that are separate, disconnected and remote from one another: they need simply declare their desire to marry their interests and offer one another reciprocal assurances in accordance with the principles of economic Right and mutuality. Once established, the federation is not susceptible to disintegration: because, let me reiterate, one does not renege upon a pact, a profession of faith like the mutualist profession of faith, like the federative pact.

As we have stated already, the principle of mutuality in matters political as well as in matters economic is therefore most assuredly the sturdiest and subtlest bond that can be forged between men.

No system of government, no community or association, no religion, no pledge has the power to bring men into such close intimacy while guaranteeing them such freedom.

We are taken to task for encouraging individualism and tearing down ideals with this elaboration upon right. Slander! Where else could the potential of the collective bring forth such great things? Where could souls feel more in tune with one another? Everywhere else one finds sectional materialism, hypocritical association and the weighty chains of the State. Here alone do we feel true fraternity in a setting of justice. It seeps into us and inspires us: and nobody can complain that it bullies him, imposes a yoke upon him or places the slightest burden upon him. This is love in all its truth and all its candour: love which is perfect only insofar as it has espoused the motto of (I nearly said commerce) mutuality: giving and giving again.

# THIRD PART

# POLITICAL INCOMPATIBILITIES—
## CONCLUSION

### CHAPTER IV
### On Municipal Liberty: That This Liberty, Essentially Federalist and Incompatible with the Unitary System, Can Neither Be Demanded By the Opposition Nor Granted By the Imperial Government

ONE OF THE questions on which the Opposition flatters itself the most in receiving the approval of the Country and getting the better of Power, is that of municipal liberties. It is the Parisian population, above all, which the opposition deputies, in their zeal for the independence of communes, like to court, without any care for their oath and their own convictions, or indeed even for logic or facts. For the past twelve years the city of Paris has been administered by an imperial commission: has this been an improvement? Has it been a turn for the worse? One can support either position. But whether the city of Paris has gained or lost—it misses its municipal counsellors: what an occasion for representatives to work on their popularity!

The question of municipal liberties is one of the most complicated and vast: it touches essentially on the federal system; I would gladly say that it is the entirety of federation. Also I do not think I have a need to profess my adhesion to such a reform, which I have pronounced myself in favour of for a long time and in many circumstances. What I propose to do today is to show, by some decisive observations, the extent to which those who, by the spirit of opposition or by some other cause entirely, make the most noise about municipal liberties, and who nevertheless remain attached to the system of unitarist centralisation, are in contradiction with themselves; what a triumph they are preparing for their adversaries, and what a deception for the country!

I say therefore that municipal liberty is by nature incompatible with governmental unity, which has been the goal and definition of all our successive constitutions. I add that this incompatibility is greater still in Paris, due to its status as capital, than in any other city in France.

Let us make this proposition still more explicit, if that is possible. As has been said earlier (2$^{nd}$ part, Chapter IX), two principles are taken into account in the bourgeois world, as that accomplished by the Revolution, as the two pillars of society and state: these are, on the one hand, the principle of political centralisation, and on the other, that of economic lack of solidarity, in other words mercantile and industrial anarchy, which serving as a counterweight to the former leads necessarily to the feudalism of capital. Now, according to the laws of historic evolution which direct all governments, these two principles must in time produce their consequences, and since municipal liberty poses an obstacle for them, it results that municipal life must, as the weakest, progressively subordinate itself to the action of the centre; and if the superior authority, the central Power, has established its seat in a city, this city in becoming the capital must lose its municipal character, to a greater extent and more quickly than any other city.

Such is the proposition, self-evident to anyone who can comprehend the terms of which it is composed, that I oppose to the Parisian municipalists, and that reduces their claims to nothing.

For those of my readers who do not have the habit of grasping in one stroke all that a formula contains, I believe it necessary to bring to their attention certain facts which will make the matter at hand completely palpable.

I. *Decadence of municipal liberties.*—The unity of France is the authentic product of our history. It begins with the Roman conquest, continues under those of the Franks; then, disrupted, or rather transformed by the feudal system, it begins again, with the accession of the Capetian dynasty,[34] by the action of the kings. National unity, as we see it today, being formed therefore by successive annexations, one conceives that the provinces and communes being progressively engulfed had to, for a certain period of time, conserve their customs, franchises, etc. But little by little royal administration and jurisdiction prevail. After Richelieu,[35] the government of the provinces, entrusted to intendants, the Prince's men, returns exclusively to the Crown, and becomes a little more uniform. The reformers of '89, taking up again the work of the monarchy, erect this regime of unity into the doctrine of the State, to the prolonged cheers of all the people until this day.

---

34   The Capetian dynasty refers to the line of French kings tracing itself to Hugh Capet (ca. 939–996). (Editor)

35   Armand Jean du Plessis de Richelieu, Cardinal-Duc de Richelieu, (1585–1642) was a French clergyman, noble, and statesman. He became Secretary of State in 1616, becoming a cardinal in 1622 and King Louis XIII's chief minister in 1624. He aimed to consolidate royal power and crush domestic factions. By restraining the power of the nobility, he transformed France into a centralised state. (Editor)

However, the communes still conserved some remainders of life for a long time after the consummation of this grand unification. The province, ill-defined, extensive, had for generations been ground down and absorbed, a fate which the commune, with its local spirit, with its density of life, still resisted. It was directly impacted by the Constitutions of Year I and Year II, which made the administration of municipalities a mere subdivision of the central administration, then by the institution of the *prefects*, on February 17th, 1800, which replaced the *central commissars* of the Republic, and assisted by the *council of the prefecture*. One can say that the harm done in this period was irreparable. Fifteen years later, at the fall of the Empire, the commune had had its day, and it was in vain that liberalism would try to revive it.

I said earlier (2nd part, chapter XII), how the bourgeoisie, horrified by the exorbitance of the central power and of the example given by Napoléon the First, has tried to subjugate the Government by giving it a triple counterweight: 1st, the constitutional system, representative and parliamentary; 2nd, a municipal and departmental organisation; 3rd, economic anarchy. It is about the second of these counterweights, a renewal of the ancient communes, that I now propose to say a few words.

A great deal of effort was put, under the reign of Louis-Philippe, into this *Municipal and Departmental Organisation*; this was, like the *Crédit foncier*[36] and so many other things, one of the mirages of the bourgeois rule. This was discussed under the Restoration; Napoléon the First himself appeared to be interested in it; it was talked about more than ever during the reign of his heir. The people of the *juste-milieu*, always the most numerous and least intelligent in our country, are those who insisted on this point with the most force. It seemed to them that in restoring to the commune a certain initiative, the result would be a stable equilibrium with the central power; that they would thus remove from centralisation that which made it atrocious, above all that they would escape from federalism, which was as odious to them in 1864 as it was (but for different reasons) to the patriots of '93. These brave men readily admired Swiss and American liberty; they regaled us about it in their books; they made it serve as a mirror to disgrace our adorations; but for nothing in the world would they touch this beautiful unity [in France] which, according to them, was responsible for our glory, and which the nations, they assured us, envied us for. From the heights of their academic self-importance, they treated as exaggerations the writers who, mindful of logic and history, faithful to pure notions of right and liberty, did not believe at all in political resurrections, and tired of eclecticism, wanted to free themselves once and for all from doctrinaire jugglings.

---

36  *Crédit Foncier de France* is a national mortgage bank. It was formed by Napoléon III in an attempt to modernise the medieval French banking system and expand French investment outside Europe. It had a monopoly on mortgages and initially made loans to communes. (Editor)

M. Édouard LABOULAYE[37] is one of these soggy geniuses, very capable of grasping the truth and showing it to others, but for whom wisdom consists in cutting short principles by means of impossible conciliations; who asks for nothing better than to impose *limits* on the State, but on the condition that one also permits it to impose these on liberty; who would be happy to trim the nails on the first so long as the wings are clipped on the second; with whom reason, finally, trembling before all this majestic and powerful synthesis, is happy to paddle around in amphigory.[38] M. Laboulaye, whom the Democracy nearly named as its representative in place of M. Thiers, is a part of a group of men who, while proclaiming against imperial autocracy the so-called guarantees of the 14th of July, have given themselves the mission of refuting the aspirations of socialism and federalism. It was he who wrote this beautiful thought, that I for a moment had the idea of taking for an epigraph: "When political life is concentrated in a tribune, the country splits itself in two, Opposition and Government." Well! That M. Laboulaye and his friends, so zealous for the municipal franchises, deign to respond to a question, just one.

The commune is by essence, like man, like the family, like every individual and collective which is intelligent, moral, and free, a sovereign being. In this quality the commune has the right to govern itself, to administer itself, to impose its own taxes, to dispose of its properties and revenues, to create schools for its youth, to install professors in these schools, to police itself, to have its own gendarmes and civic guard, to name its judges, to have its own newspapers, assemblies, special societies, warehouses, its own bank, etc. The commune, consequently, makes arrests, creates ordinances: what prevents it from going all the way to making its own laws? It has its church, its religion, its freely chosen clergy, even its ritual and saints; it discusses publicly, in its newspapers and circles, everything that happens inside and around it, which touches on its interests and agitates its opinion. This is what a commune is: since this is collective life, political life. Now, life is one, whole, indivisible; it repels every hindrance, knows no limit but itself; all external coercion is antipathetic to it, and, if it cannot overcome it, mortal to it. That M. Laboulaye and his political co-religionists say to us therefore how they intend to bring together this communal life with their unitary reservations; how they will escape from conflicts; how they think to maintain side by side the local franchise with central prerogative, to restrain the former and stop the latter; to affirm at the same time, and in the same system, the independence of the

---

37  Édouard René Lefèbvre de Laboulaye (1811–1883) was a French jurist, poet, and author. He is best known for suggesting the giving of the Statue of Liberty to the USA (and its lesser known twins in France) as a representation of liberty, a symbol for ideas suppressed by Napoléon III. (Editor)

38  *Amphigourie*, a piece of nonsensical writing in verse or, less commonly, prose. (Editor)

parts and the authority of the Whole? Let them make themselves clear so that we may know and judge them.

There is no middle term: the commune will be sovereign or a subsidiary, all or nothing. Favour it as much as you like; from the instant when it no longer falls under its own law, when it must recognise a higher law, when the larger unit of which it is a part is declared its superior, and not the expression of its federal relationships, it is inevitable that one day or another that the commune will find itself in contradiction with this larger State, and that conflict will break out. Now, since there will be conflict, logic and force would dictate that it would be the central Power which prevails, and this without discussion, without judgement, without negotiation, any debate between superior and subordinate being scandalous and inadmissible. Therefore we always come back, after a period of agitation more or less long, to the negation of parochialism, to absorption by the centre, to autocracy. The idea of a *limitation of the State by the groups within it*, effected at the point where the principle of the subordination and centralisation of these very groups themselves reigns, is incoherent at best and a contradiction at worst. There are no limits on the State besides those which it voluntarily imposes on itself, abandoning to municipal and individual initiative certain things with which it for the moment cannot be bothered. But when the day comes when it believes that it must reclaim, as a part of its domain, the things that it had earlier put aside (and this day will arrive sooner or later, since the development of the State is indefinite), not only will the State win its case before the courts, it will be logically correct in its claims.

Because one claims to be liberal, and because it is so daring to speak of limits on the State, all the while allowing its suzerainty, one still speaks of what will be the limit of individual, corporate, regional, and social liberty, the limit of all liberties. Let one explain, since one believes oneself to be a philosopher, what it is to be a limited, dominated, liberty, kept in custody; a liberty to which one has said, while chaining it to the stake: You will graze just over here, you will not go very far! ...

The facts have confirmed all of this critique. During the 36 years of the parliamentary regime which followed the fall of the first Empire, municipal and departmental liberties did not cease to wane, without even the governments taking the trouble to attack them. The movement accomplished this for itself, by the nature of the unitary principle alone. Finally, after a series of invasions, of which the details would be superfluous, the commune was definitively subjugated to the State by the law of May 5th, 1855, which gave to the Emperor, or to prefects, his *missi dominici*, the right to name mayors and their adjuncts. By the law of May 5th, 1855 the commune therefore became that which since 1789, 1793, and 1795 the logic of unity had decided it would be, a mere subsidiary of the central authority.

I say that the result was inevitable, that in it one can see nothing but the product of public reason turning down the path of the monarchy and of unity;

that which the imperial Government had done in 1855 was the consequence, imposed by events, of everything that had previously been done by its predecessors; and that to oppose this necessary development as a means of opposition while also declaring oneself a partisan of unity is one of two things: an act of ignorance or one of bad faith. The municipal regime, such as it still existed under Louis-Phillipe, while singularly demeaned, constituted, in regard to the prefecture, a double government, *imperium in imperio*;[39] unless one only said that it was the prefecture which held a position duplicated by that of the commune and province; which comes to exactly the same thing.

In creating the law of May 5th, 1855 the government of Napoléon III had done nothing else but to put a stop to history, to exercise its right, and, dare I say it, fulfil its imperial mandate. This is the monarchical, unified, and centralised destiny of France that is being pursued: it is not that of a semi-dynastic, constitutional, bourgeois, unitary, and duly deputised Opposition, nor of its texts of protest and reproach.

II. *Paris: capital and municipality.*—As for the city of Paris, and that of Lyon, whose municipal counsellors are named by the Emperor, in other words, transformed into commissions, while everywhere else citizens participate in the administration of their localities through the election of their councils, there is even less room to blame the Government. The two capitals of the Empire are treated, I would not say according to their merits, which one could take for malicious irony, but as befits their dignity being what they are. Paris cannot at the same time enjoy the honours of being the capital and the prerogatives, however weak, which are left to the municipalities. One is incompatible with the other; it is necessary to make a choice.

Paris is the seat of the Government, the ministries, the imperial family, the Court, the Senate, the legislative Body, the Council of State, the Court of Appeal, and the provincial aristocracy themselves and their vast households. It is to Paris that all the ambassadors of foreign powers go, and it is to Paris that all the travellers flock, sometimes as many as 100,000 or 150,000, speculators, scientists and artists, from all over the world. It is the heart and the head of the State, surrounded by 15 fortresses and forty-five kilometres of ramparts, guarded by a garrison which is a quarter of the effective army of the country, which must be defended and preserved no matter what. Obviously, all of this exceeds by far the attributions of a municipality, and the whole Country would rise up, if, by the fact of a municipal constitution, Paris were to become so to speak the equal of the Empire; if the *Hôtel-de-ville* were to claim itself as rivalling the Luxembourg Palace, the Bourbon Palace and the Tuileries; if a municipal order could countermand an imperial decree; if, in case of invasion, the Parisian national guard, capitulating to the victorious foreigners, purported to compel, by the influence of its example, the army at the front to throw down its arms.

---

39  "a state within a state." (Editor)

It is in the capital that are found the academies, the institutions of higher education, even the schools of mining; the great theatres are there, as the great financial and industrial companies have their headquarters there. It is there that the export business has its principal establishments. It is the Bank and the Stock Market of Paris which constitute, evaluate, and liquidate all the great enterprises, operations, loans, etc. of France and of the world. All of this, you have to admit, has nothing to do with the municipal level.

To leave these things to the discretion of a municipality would be to abdicate [responsibilty]. To try to separate the affairs of the municipality from those of the capital would be to try to make an impossible division; in any case, [it would be] to create a perpetual conflict between the municipality and the Government, between the Empire and the capital. Separate, then, in the embellishments of Paris, what it owes to its own resources from those which comes to it from the budget of the state; separate, in the development of this immense capital, what is correctly attributed to the activity, industry, and influence of its inhabitants from that which belongs to the superior influence of the Government and the Country! For better or for worse, it is necessary that the mayors be nothing but the subordinates of the Prefecture. The competition of the *Hôtel-de-ville*, from '89 to '95, struck some severe blows against the monarchy; it hardly did less damage to the Revolution, and I am astonished that the partisans of unity, such as M. Picard, contemplate resuscitating such a power. No, as long as Paris remains what politics and history has made it, the seat of our national agglomeration; as long as, capital of the French Empire (or Monarchy, or Republic—whatever name you choose), it aspires to the even higher title, of metropolis of civilisation, Paris will not belong to itself. For such a possession of itself would be a veritable usurpation; even if the Government would consent to it the departments would never allow it. Paris has an existence apart: like the Rome of the emperors, it cannot be administered except by imperial magistrates.

What I say is so true and follows so much from the nature of things that, even in a confederated France, under a regime that one may regard as the ideal of independence, the first act would be to return to the communes the plenitude of their autonomy and to the provinces their sovereignty, Paris, no longer an imperial city but becoming a federal city, could not combine the attributions of its two natures, and would have to furnish guarantees to the provinces, admitting federal authority over parts of its administration and government. Without this Paris, thanks to its powerful attraction, to the incalculable influence which would give it its double quality of the most powerful of the confederated States and the capital of the Confederation, would again soon become king of the Republic, to the domination of which the provinces would never manage to escape from except by, like the Swiss, making the federal authority nomadic, and assigning as its seat, sometimes Rouen or Nantes, sometimes Lyons, Toulouse, or Dijon, and Paris, only once every ten years. And there is no stronger reason why Paris, administrative centre of the Empire, could not aspire to an autonomy which would be for the Empire the division of sovereignty, or else even an abdication!

Moreover, examine the physiognomy of the capital, study its psychology, and you will recognise, if you do so in good faith, that Paris marched in unison with the Country and the Government. The more it has come into its glory, the more it has lost of its individuality and its character, the more its population, incessantly renewed by the departments and by foreigners, moves away from nativity.[40] Out of the 1,700,000 inhabitants who compose the population of the department of the Seine, how many are true Parisians? No more than 15 percent: all the rest have come from elsewhere. Out of the eleven representatives that the city of Paris sent to the legislative Body, I do not believe that there are four of the Parisian race. As for the opinions of these representatives, which we might generously suppose to be the opinion of the city of Paris, what can we think of them? Who will tell me the opinions of Paris? Is it that of the 153,000 electors of the Opposition? How then have they named subjects as disparate as MM. Thiers, Guérolt, Havin, J. Favre, E. Ollivier, J. Simon, Garnier-Pagès, Darimon, Pelletan? And what became, on the one hand the 82,000 votes given to the government, and on the other the 90,000 which were abstentions?... What to say about the 400,000 souls out of the total of 1,700,000 who are not represented? Is it by the newspapers that we will know the Parisian opinion? But they contradict each other as much as the representatives, and for anyone who has seen up close their various dens, all respect collapses instantly. Paris is a world: that means that one must not seek in it any one individuality, nor one faith, one opinion, one will; it is a plurality of forces, of thoughts, of elements, in chaotic agitation. Paris, considered as a free city, an independent commune, a collective individuality, a singularity, has had its day. In order for it to become again such a thing, it would be necessary for it to start, conscientiously and resolutely, a movement in the opposite direction; for it to set down, along with its mural crown,[41] the crown of capital city, and to fly the flag of the federation. If this is the signal that M. Picard intended to give, claiming in the name of the city of Paris the reestablishment of municipal liberties, fine. We can applaud his efforts. In the contrary case, M. Picard is completely misled, and M. Billaut is right to tell him that the Government will never relinquish the administration of the capital.

For my part, I will end by declaring: I believe, as an axiom of my reason, as a general thesis, that all evolution of a finite being must have an end, that this end is the beginning of another being; in particular, that the

---

40   Autochthony (*autochthonie*) the state of being aboriginal or native to a particular area. (Editor)

41   A mural crown (*couroune murale*) is one whose florets had the shape of a crenellated wall and was given to who first entered a besieged city. It is used in heraldry to denote a crown modelled after the walls of a castle. (Editor)

development of French unity, beginning almost 2,000 years ago, is nearing its end; that our centralising process no longer has anything to engulf, Power nothing more to absorb, the tax office nothing more to squeeze; that, moreover, the old spirit of the communes is dead, long dead, witness Paris, and that the simulacrum of municipal institutions, which have been deluding us since the proclamation of the famous one and indivisible Republic, has had its day. I believe that we are separated from pure political and economic communism only by the thickness of the constitution,—I mean by a sheet of paper. And since, as I say, nations cannot die nor can civilisation regress, I remain convinced, in the depths of my soul, that the moment approaches when, after a last crisis, a movement in the opposite direction, heeding the call of new principles, will begin. Then and only then will we recover our liberties. I communicate this opinion, which certainly is not only my own, by the means of the press, to the public, to the workers' Democracy, of which I have only deduced the basic principles at this time. I do not know what the Democracy will make of my warnings; but it will agree with me at least on one thing: that is with such thoughts in our hearts (on the conditions of municipal liberty, and on political centralisation), we, my friends and I, have only to send a representative to the legislative Body, and there were we know in advance that, if he stays true to his mandate, he can only cause a scandal; if, on the contrary, he obeys his oath [of office], he will become a traitor to his political religion and his friends.

# APPENDIX: THE THEORY OF PROPERTY

*"If I ever find myself a proprietor, may God and men, the poor especially, forgive me for it!"*

PROUDHON'S *Théorie de la propriété* WAS POSTHUMOUSLY PUBLISHED from an unfinished manuscript in the year of his death by his friends. It was started in 1860/1 but, significantly, Proudhon never completed it, preferring to write and publish other works (such as *The Federative Principle*). Given that he completed *The Political Capacity of the Working Classes* on his death-bed, the question remains as how important this work is in terms of the overall evolution of his ideas. This is why this extract is in an appendix.

What becomes clear from this work is that there is no significant change in Proudhon's perspective on property and possession. The usual themes of his work are there, such as the land as common property, workers' associations and the absolutist nature of property. His apparent new found support for "property" is not for capitalist private property. Rather, it is for property which combines ownership and use. As such, rather than a conversion away from his previous ideas this work represented more a slight shift in his position. The vision expounded is the familiar Proudhonian one of an artisan, peasant and workers co-operative based economy.

# CHAPTER IX
## SUMMARY

THE DEVELOPMENTS THAT I have given to my theory of property can be summed up in a few pages.

A first thing to observe is that, under the generic name of *property,* the apologists for that institution have confused, either through ignorance or through artifice, all manners of possession: communal system, emphyteusis, usufruct, feudal and allodial systems;[1] they have reasoned about capital as if it were income, of fungible property as if it were immovable property. We have done justice to that confusion.

*Possession,* indivisible, untransferable, inalienable, pertains to the sovereign, prince, government, or collectivity, of which the tenant is more or less the dependent, bondman or vassal. The Germans, before the invasion, the barbarians of the Middle Ages, knew only it; it is the principle of all the Slavic race, applied at this moment by the Emperor Alexander to sixty million peasants. That possession implies in it the various rights of use, habitation, cultivation, pasture, hunting, and fishing—all the natural rights that Brissot[2] called property *according to nature;* it is to a possession of that sort, but which I had not defined, that I referred in my first *Memoir* and in my *Contradictions.* That form of possession is a great step in civilisation; it is better in practice than the absolute domain of the Romans, reproduced in our anarchic property, which is killing itself with fiscal crises and its own excesses. It is certain that the economist can require nothing more: there the worker is rewarded, his fruits guaranteed; all that belongs legitimately to him is protected. The theory of possession, principle of civilisation of the Slavic societies, is the most honourable of that race: it redeems the tardiness of its development and makes the crime of the Polish nobility inexpiable.

But is that the last word of civilisation, and of right as well? I do not think so; one can conceive something more; the sovereignty of man is not entirely satisfied; [its] liberty and vitality are not great enough.

Simple or allodial property—divisible and alienable—is the absolute domain of the holder over something, "the right of use and of abuse," known initially as the *quiritary* law; "within the limits of the law," the collective

---

1   In Roman law, an *emphyteusis* was a long-term or perpetual lease that carried the obligation to improve the property, while *usufruct,* from the Latin phrase *usus et fructus* ("use and enjoyment"), refers to a right to use the non-consumable property of another (e.g., to farm another's land, keeping the harvest but retaining no title to the land); an *allodium,* in medieval law, was land owned as a freehold, independently of any obligation to serve a lord—i.e., an exception to the *feudal* system of land tenure. (Editor)

2   Jacques-Pierre Brissot (1754–1893), also known as de Warville, a leader of the Girondist faction during the French Revolution. (Editor)

consciousness adds later. Property is Roman; I find it clearly articulated only in Italy; and yet its formation is slow.

The justification of the domain of property has always been the despair of jurists, economists, and philosophers. The principle of appropriation is that *every product of labour,*—such as a bow, some arrows, a plough, a rake, a house,—*belongs by right to whoever has created it.* Man does not create matter; he only shapes it. Nevertheless, although he did not create the wood from which he fashions a bow, a bed, a table, some chairs, or a bucket, it is the practice that the material follows the form, and that property in labour implies property in materials. It is presupposed that this material is offered to all, that no one is excluded, and that each may appropriate it.

Does the theory that the form carries the content apply to cultivated land? It is well-proven that the producer has a right to his product, the settler to the fruits that he has created. It is proven as well that one has a right to limit one's consumption, accumulate a capital, and do with it whatever one likes. But the land question cannot be answered in this manner; it is a new fact which exceeds the limit of the right of the producer. That producer did not create the soil, [which is] common to all. It is proven that he who has readied, furnished, cleaned up and cleared the soil has a right to remuneration, to compensation; it will be demonstrated that this compensation must consist, not in a monetary sum, but in the privilege of planting the cleared soil during a given time. Let us go all the way: it will be proven that each year of culture, involving improvement, entails for the cultivator the right to a fresh compensation. Very well! The property is not perpetual. Farm leases of nine, twelve, or thirty years can take all of that into account with regard to the farmer, with respect to whom the proprietor represents the public domain. The land tenure of the Slavic commune also takes into account the sharecropper; the law is satisfied, labour compensated: there is no property. The Roman law and the Civil Code have perfectly distinguished all of these things: rights of use, usufruct, habitation, exploitation, possession. How do the economists pretend to confuse these with the right of property? What are we to make of M. Thiers' paeans to of the bucolic and all the stupid declamations of the coterie?

Social economy, like right, knows no domain, and exists entirely outside of property: concept of value, wages, labour, product, exchange, circulation, rent, sale and purchase, currency, tax, credit, theory of population, monopoly, patents, rights of authors, insurance, public service, association, etc. The relations of family and city have no more need of property; domain may be reserved to the commune, or to the State; rent then becomes tax; the cultivator becomes possessor; it is better than tenant farming, better than sharecropping; liberty and individuality enjoy the same guarantees.

It must be well understood: humanity itself is not even proprietor of the earth: how could a nation, how could a private individual, say that it is sovereign over the portion that is its due? Humanity has not created the soil: man and the earth have been created for one another and come under a higher authority. We have received the earth in tenancy and usufruct; it has been given to us to be possessed, exploited by us jointly and individually, under our collective and personal responsibility. We become the cultivator, the possessor, by enjoying, not arbitrarily, but according to *rules* that consciousness and reason discover, and for an end which goes beyond our pleasure: these *rules* and this *end* exclude all absolutism on our part, and refer terrestrial domain to a higher authority than ours. Man, said one of our bishops one day, is the *foreman of the globe.* These words have been highly praised. Well, it does not express anything but what I have just said, that property is superior to humanity, superhuman, and that every attribution of that sort, to us poor creatures, is usurpation.

All of our arguments in favour of property, that is, of an eminent sovereignty over things, only succeed in demonstrating possession, usufruct, usage, the right to live and to work, nothing more.

We must always come to the conclusion that property is a *true legal fiction;* only it could be that the fiction is grounded in such a way that we must regard it as legitimate. Otherwise, we do not depart from the realm of the possessory, and all of our argumentation is sophistic and in bad faith. It may be possible that this fiction, which appalls us because we do not see the sense in it, is so sublime, so splendid, so lofty in its justice, that none of our most real, most positive, most immanent rights approach it, and they themselves only subsist by means of that keystone, a true fiction.

The principle of property—ultra-legal, extra-juridical, anti-economic, superhuman—is nonetheless a spontaneous product of the collective Being and of society, and it falls to us to search in it for, if not a complete justification, at least an explanation.

The right of property is absolute, *jus utendi et abutendi,* the right of use and abuse. It opposes itself to another absolute, government, which begins by imposing on its antagonist the restriction, *quatenùs juris ratio patitur,* "within the limits of the law." From the reason of the law to *raison d'État* is only a step: we are in constant danger of usurpation and despotism. The justification of property, which we have vainly sought in its origins—first occupancy, usucapion,[3] conquest, appropriation by labour,—we find in its *ends:* it is essentially political. Where domain belongs to the collectivity, senate, aristocracy, prince or emperor, there is only feudalism, vassalage, hierarchy and subordination; no liberty, consequently, nor autonomy. It is to break the bonds of collective sovereignty, so exorbitant, so formidable, that the domain of property has been raised against it, true sign of the sovereignty of the citizen; it is to break those bonds that this domain has been assigned to the individual, the State retaining only the parts deemed indivisible and

---

3   In Roman law, *usucapion* is a mode of ownership established by continuous occupation or possession. (Editor)

common: waterways, lakes, ponds, roads, public places, waste lands, uncultivated mountains, forests, deserts, and all that which cannot be appropriated.
It is in order to increase the ease of transport and circulation that the earth
has been rendered liquid, alienable, divisible, after having been rendered hereditary. Allodial property is a division of sovereignty: on that account it
is particularly odious to power and democracy. It is odious first because of
its omnipotence; it is the adversary of autocracy, as liberty is the enemy of
authority; it does not please the democrats, who are all on fire for unity, centralisation, and absolutism. The people are cheerful when they look to make
war against the proprietors. And yet *allodium* is the basis of the republic.

[...]

Every institution of property supposes either: 1) an equal distribution of
land amongst the holders; or 2) an equivalent in favour of those who possess
none of the soil. But this is a pure assumption: the equality of property is
not at all an initial fact; it is in the ends of the institution, not in its origins.
We have remarked first of all that property, because it is abusive, absolutist,
and based in egoism, must inevitably tend to restrict itself, to compete with
itself, and, as a consequence, to balance [itself]. Its tendency is to equality of
conditions and fortunes. Exactly because it is absolute, it dismisses any idea
of absorption. Let us weigh this well.

Property is not measured by merit, as it is neither wages, nor reward, nor
decoration, nor honorific title; it is not measured by the power of the individual,
since labour, production, credit and exchange do not require it at all. It is a free
gift, accorded to man, with a view to protecting him against the attacks of poverty and the incursions of his fellows. It is the breastplate of his personality and
equality, independent of differences in talent, genius, strength, industry, etc.

[...]

Under the communist or governmentalist regime, it is necessary for the
police and authority to guarantee the weak against the strong; sadly, the police and authority, as long as they have existed, have only ever functioned for
the profit of the strong, for whom they have magnified the means of usurpation. Property—absolute, uncontrollable—protects itself. It is the defensive
weapon of the citizen, his shield; labour is his sword.

Here is why it is suitable for all: the young ward as much as the mature
adult, the black as the white, the straggler as the precocious, the ignorant as
the learned, the artisan as the functionary, the worker as the entrepreneur,
the farmer as the bourgeois and the noble. Here is why the Church prefers
it to wages; and, for the same reason, why the papacy requires, in its turn,
sovereignty. All the bishops, in the Middle Ages, were sovereign; all, until
1789, were proprietors; the pope alone remained as a relic.

The equilibrium of property still requires some political and economic
guarantees. *Property—State*, such are the two poles of society. The theory
of property is the companion piece to the theory of the justification, by the
sacraments, of fallen man.

The guarantees of property against itself are:
1. Mutual and free credit.
2. Taxes
3. Warehouses, docks, markets. [...]
4. Mutual insurance and balance of commerce.
5. Public, universal and equal instruction.
6. Industrial and agricultural association.
7. Organisation of public services: canals, railroads, roads, ports, mail, telegraphs, draining, irrigation.

The guarantees of property against the State are:
1. Separation and distribution of powers.
2. Equality before the law.
3. Jury, judge of fact and judge of law.
4. Liberty of the press.
5. Public monitoring.
6. Federal organisation.
7. Communal and provincial organisation

The State is composed: 1) of the federation of proprietors, grouped by districts, departments, and provinces; 2) of the industrial associations, small worker republics; 3) of public services (at cost-price); 4) of artisans and free merchants. Normally, the number of industrial workers, artisans, and merchants is determined by those of the proprietors of land. Every country must live by its own production; as a consequence, industrial production must be equal to the excess of subsistences not consumed by the proprietors.

There are exceptions to that rule: in England, for example, industrial production exceeded that proportion, thanks to foreign exchange. It is a temporary anomaly; otherwise certain races should be doomed to an eternal subordination [*subalternisation*]. Moreover, there exist exceptional products in demand everywhere: those from fishing, for example, and those from mineral exploitation. Measured over the entire globe, however, the proportion is as I say: the amount of subsistences is the regulator; consequently, agriculture is the essential and predominant industry.

In constituting property in land, the legislator wanted one thing: that the earth would not be in the hands of the State, dangerous communism or governmentalism, but in the hands of all. The tendency is, as a consequence, we are constantly told, toward the balance of property, and subsequently to that of conditions and fortunes.

It is thus that, by the rules of industrial association, which sooner or later, with the aid of better legislation, will include large industrial bodies, each worker has his hand on a portion of *capital*.

It is thus that, due to the law of the diffusion of labour, and the impact of taxes, everyone must pay his more or less equal part of the public expenses.

It is thus that, by the true organisation of universal suffrage, every citizen has a hand in government; and thus also that, by the organisation of credit, every citizen has a hand in circulation, and finds himself at once general partner and silent partner, banker and discounter before the public.

It is thus that, by enlistment, each citizen takes part in defence; by education, takes part in philosophy and science.

It is thus, finally, that, by the right of free examination and of free publicity each citizen has a hand in all the ideas and all the ideals which can be produced.

Humanity proceeds by approximations:

1st The approximation of the equality of faculties through education, the division of labour, and the development of aptitudes;

2nd The approximation of the equality of fortunes through industrial and commercial freedom.

3rd The approximation of the equality of taxes;

4th The approximation of the equality of property;

5th The approximation of *an-archy;*

6th The approximation of *non-religion,* or non-mysticism;

7th Indefinite progress in the science, law, liberty, honour, justice.

It is proof that fate does not govern society; that geometry and arithmetic proportions do not regulate its movements, as in mineralogy or chemistry; that there is a life, a soul, a liberty which escapes from the precise, fixed measures governing matter. *Materialism,* in that which touches society, is absurd.

Thus, on this great question, our critique remains at base the same, and our conclusions are always the same: we want equality, more and more fully approximated, of conditions and fortunes, as we want, more and more, the equalisation of responsibilities. We reject, along with governmentalism, communism in all its forms; we want the definition of official functions and individual functions; of public services and of free services. There is only one thing new for us in our thesis: it is that that same property, the contradictory and abusive principle of which has raised our disapproval, we today accept entirely, along with its equally contradictory qualification: *Dominium est jus utendi et abutendi re suâ, quatenus juris ratio patitur.*[4] We have understood finally that the opposition of two absolutes—one of which, alone, would be unpardonably reprehensive, and both of which, together, would be rejected, if they worked separately—is the very cornerstone of social economy and public right: but it falls to us to govern it and to make it act according to the laws of logic.

What would the apologists for property do? The economists of the school of Say and Malthus?

For them, property was a sacrament which remained alone and by itself, prior and superior to the reason of the State, independent of the State, which they would humble beyond all measure.

---

4   "Ownership is the right to use and abuse of one's own thing, as far as compatible with the logic of the law." (Editor)

They would desire then property independent of law, as they want competition independent of law; freedom of import and export independent of law; industrial sponsorship, the Stock Exchange, the Bank, wage-labour, tenant farming, independent of law.—That is, in their theories of property, of competition, of concurrence, and of credit, not content to declare an unlimited liberty, a limitless initiative, *which we also desire,* they disregard the interests of the collectivity, which are the law; not understanding that political economy is composed of two fundamental parts: the description of economic forces and phenomena apart from law, and their regularisation by law.

Who would dare to say that the equilibration of property, as I understand it, is its very destruction? What! Will it no longer be property, since the farmer will share in the rent and the surplus value; because the rights of the third who have built or planted will be established and recognised; because property in the soil will no longer necessarily mean property in that which is above or beneath it; because the lesser, in case of bankruptcy, will come with the other creditors to a division of the assets, without privilege; because between legitimate holders there will be equality, not hierarchy; because instead of seeing in property only enjoyment and rent, the holder will find in it the guarantee of his independence and dignity; because instead of being a ridiculous character, a M. Prudhomme or M. Jourdain[5], the proprietor will be a dignified citizen, conscious of his duties as well as his rights, the sentry of liberty against despotism and usurpation?

I have developed the considerations which make property intelligible, rational, legitimate, and without which it remains usurping and odious.

And yet, even in these conditions, it presents something egoistic which is always unpleasant to me. My reason—being egalitarian, anti-governmental, and the enemy of ferocity and the abuse of force—can accept, the dependence on property as a shield, a place of safety for the weak: my heart will never be in it. For myself, I do not need that concession, either to earn my bread, or to fulfil my civic duties, or for my happiness. I do not need to encounter it in others to aid them in their weakness and respect their rights. I feel enough energy of conscience, enough intellectual force, to sustain all of my relations in a dignified manner; and if the majority of my fellow citizens resembled me, what would we have to do with that institution? Where would be the risk of tyranny, or the risk of ruin from competition and free exchange? Where would be the peril to the child, the orphan and the worker?

---

5   Monsieur Prudhomme, created by Henry Monnier, was a caricature of the 19th century bourgeois. Plump, foolish, conformist and sententious, he was called by Honoré de Balzac "l'illustre type des bourgeois de Paris" (the very image of the Parisian bourgeoisie). Monsieur Jourdain is the main character of Moliere's comedy *Le Bourgeois Gentilhomme* (*The Bourgeois Gentleman*), which satirises attempts at social climbing and the bourgeois personality. The idiotic Jourdain is a rich merchant who wants to buy his way into the aristocracy. (Editor)

Where would be the need for pride, ambition, and avarice, which can satisfy itself only by immense appropriation?

A small, rented house, a garden to use, largely suffices for me: my profession not being the cultivation of the soil, the vine, or the meadow, I have no need to make a park, or a vast inheritance. And when I would be a ploughman or winemaker, Slavic possession will suffice for me: the share falling due to each head of household in each commune. I cannot abide the insolence of the man who, his feet on ground he holds only by a free cession, forbids you passage, prevents you from picking a blueberry in his field or from passing along the path.

When I see all these fences around Paris, which block the view of the country and the enjoyment of the soil by the poor pedestrian, I feel a violent irritation. I ask myself whether the property which surrounds in this way each house is not instead expropriation, expulsion from the land. *Private Property!* I sometimes meet that phrase written in large letters at the entrance of an open passage, like a sentinel forbidding me to pass. I swear that my dignity as a man bristles with disgust. Oh! In this I remain of the religion of Christ, which recommends detachment, preaches modesty, simplicity of spirit and poverty of heart. Away with the old patrician, merciless and greedy; away with the insolent baron, the avaricious bourgeois, and the hardened peasant, *durus arator.* That world is odious to me. I cannot love it nor look at it. If I ever find myself a proprietor, may God and men, the poor especially, forgive me for it!

Translation by Mitch Abidor ("Declaration to the French People" and "International Workers' Association: Federal Council of Parisian Sections") and Paul Sharkey ("On the Organisation of the Commune," "Paris Today Is Free..." and "On the Production of Goods During the Commune").

# APPENDIX: THE PARIS COMMUNE

*"The Parisian gentlemen had their heads full of the emptiest Proudhonist phrases. They babble about science and know nothing... Proudhon did enormous mischief... he himself is only a petty-bourgeois utopian... the workers, particularly those of Paris, who as workers in luxury trades are strongly attached, without knowing it, to the old rubbish. Ignorant, vain, presumptuous, talkative, blusteringly arrogant, they were on the point of spoiling everything... I shall... rap them on the knuckles..."*
—Karl Marx, 9th October 1866

*"The direct antithesis to the Empire was the Commune... the commune was to be the political form of even the smallest country hamlet... each delegate to be at any time revocable and bound by the mandat impératif (formal instructions) of his constituents... The very existence of the Commune involved, as a matter of course, local municipal liberty... the political form at last discovered under which to work out the economical emancipation of labour... the Commune intended to abolish that class property which makes the labour of the many the wealth of the few... It wanted to make individual property a truth by transforming the means of production, land, capital, now chiefly the means of enslaving and exploiting labour, into mere instruments of free and associated labour... Working men's Paris, with its Commune, will be for ever celebrated as the glorious harbinger of a new society..."*
—Karl Marx, 30th March 1871

# INTERNATIONAL WORKERS' ASSOCIATION

## FEDERAL COUNCIL OF PARISIAN SECTIONS

WORKERS:

A LONG TRAIN of reverses, a catastrophe that would necessarily seem to bring about the complete ruin of our country; such is the balance sheet of the situation created for France by the governments that have dominated it.

Have we lost the qualities needed to raise us up from this degradation? Have we degenerated to the point that we resignedly submit to the hypocritical despotism of those who delivered us to the foreigner and that we only have no energy except that needed to render our ruin irremediable through civil war?

Recent events have demonstrated the might of the people of Paris; we are convinced that a fraternal accord will soon demonstrate their wisdom.

The principle of authority is powerless to re-establish order in the streets, to put the shop floors back to work, and this powerlessness is its negation.

The lack of solidarity has created general ruin and engendered social war. It is from freedom, equality and solidarity that we must ask for the assurance of order on new foundations and for the recognition of labour, which is its primordial condition.

WORKERS:

The Communal Revolution affirms its principles and casts aside all future causes of conflict. Can you hesitate to give it your definitive sanction?

The independence of the Commune is the guarantee of the contract whose clauses, freely debated, will bring an end to class antagonism and will assure social equality.

We have demanded the emancipation of the workers, and the Communal delegation is the guarantee of this, for it shall furnish each citizen with the means of defending his rights and effectively controlling the acts of its representatives charged with the managing of its interests and determining the progressive applications of social reforms.

The autonomy of each commune removes any oppressive character from its demands and affirms the republic in its highest expression.

WORKERS:

We have fought and we have learned to suffer for our egalitarian principles; we cannot retreat now that we can assist in laying the first stone of the social edifice.

What have we asked for?

The organisation of credit, exchange, and association in order to assure the worker the full value of his labour;

Free, secular, and integral education;

The right to meet and to form associations; the absolute freedom of the press and of the citizen;

The municipal organisation of police services, armed forces, hygiene, statistics, etc.;

We were the dupes of those who governed us; we allowed ourselves to be caught up in their game while they alternately caressed us and repressed the factions whose antagonisms assured their existence.

Today the people of Paris sees things clearly and refuses the role of a child guided by a preceptor, and at the municipal elections—the product of a movement of which it is itself the author—it will remember that the principle that presides over the organisation of a group or an association is the same as that which should govern all of society, and just as it rejects any administrator or president imposed by an external power, it will also reject any mayor or prefect imposed by a government foreign to its aspirations.

It will affirm its superior right to a vote of the Assembly to remain master of its city and to constitute as it sees fit its municipal representation, without imposing it on others.

We are convinced that on Sunday March 26 the people of Paris will vote for the Commune.

—*The Delegates present at the session of the night of March 23rd, 1871*
*Federal Council of Parisian Sections of the International Association*

# ON THE ORGANISATION OF THE COMMUNE

*Manifesto of the "Committee of the 20 Arrondissements"*

The commune is the basic building block of every political state.

It should be autonomous, that is to say, self-governing and self-administering [...] The autonomy of the commune guarantees the citizen's freedom, the city's order and, through the effect of reciprocity, boosts the strength, markets and resources of every single one of the federated communes by making them the beneficiaries of the efforts of them all.

Implicit in this are the widest freedom of speech, of the written word, of assembly and association; respect for the individual and his thoughts free from trespass by the sovereignty of universal suffrage as he remains at all times his own master, free to invoke and relentlessly demonstrate the accountability of underpinning the principle of election of all officials and magistrates who are thus subject at all times to recall under the imperative mandate, which is to say, that the powers and mission of the mandatory is specific and limited [...]

Citizens, you are the masters of your destiny; with your support behind them, the representatives you have just chosen will repair the disasters caused by the outgoing authorities. Industry in jeopardy, work suspended, commercial transactions paralysed, all are to be given a vigorous boost. This very day we have had the long-awaited decision on rents and tomorrow it will be the turn of payments due.

All public services restored and streamlined.

The National Guard, once the city's only armed force, reorganised without delay. These are our first steps.

For the triumph of the Republic to be copper-fastened, all that the people's elected representatives ask is the reassurance of your trust. As for them, they will do their duty.

March 1871

# PARIS TODAY IS FREE AND IN POSSESSION OF HERSELF AND THE PROVINCES ARE IN SLAVERY

ONCE A FEDERATED France comes to understand Paris, Europe will be saved.

Today, my appeal goes out to the artists and I call upon their brains, their feelings, their gratitude. Paris has nurtured them like a mother and given them their genius. In the present hour, every effort of the artists (and there is a debt of honour at stake here) should be geared towards the reconstitution of her morale and the restoration of the arts which are her treasure. As a result, the museums must be reopened as a matter of urgency and serious thought given to a forthcoming exhibition; so let everybody, starting here and now, set to work and the artists of friendly nations will answer our call.

Vengeance has been wrought and genius must have is day, for the real Prussians were not the ones who initially attacked us. By causing us to perish of hunger, they have helped us regain our moral life and elevated every single individual to the dignity of a human being.

Ah, Paris, the mighty city of Paris, has just shaken off the dust of all vassalage. The most heartless Prussians, the exploiters of the poor, were in Versailles. Her revolution is all the more equitable in that it springs from the people. Its apostles are workers, her Christ has been Proudhon.

For the past eighteen hundred years, men of heart have faced death with a sigh, but the heroic people of Paris will defeat Versailles's bamboozlers and torturers, man will have the run of himself, federation will be understood and Paris will have a lion's share of a glory unprecedented in history.

And now I say it again: let everyone set to work selflessly. This is a duty we all owe to our soldier brethren, these heroes who face death for us. They have right on their side. The criminals have set their courage aside for the blessed cause.

Yes, with the genius of everyone given free rein, Paris will double her importance and the international European city will be in a position to offer the arts, industry, commerce and intercourse of all sorts and visitors from around the globe an imperishable order. A pledge given by her citizens, one that cannot be broken by the monstrous ambitions of monstrous claimants.

Our era is about to begin and by a strange coincidence next Sunday is Easter Day! Will our resurrection come on that day?

So long to the old world and its diplomacy!

Gustave Courbet
*Journal Officiel*
April 5th, 1871

# DECLARATION

To the French people:

In the painful and terrible conflict that again threatens Paris with the horrors of a siege and bombardment; that causes French blood to flow, sparing neither our brothers, our wives nor our children; crushed beneath cannonballs and rifle shot, it is necessary that public opinion not be divided, that the national conscience be clear.

Paris and the entire nation must know the nature, the reason, and the goal of the revolution that is being carried out. Finally, it is only just that the responsibility for the deaths, the suffering, and the misfortunes of which we are the victims fall on those who, after having betrayed France and delivered Paris to the foreigners, pursue with a blind and cruel obstinacy the ruin of the great city in order to bury, in the disaster of the republic and liberty, the dual testimony to their treason and their crime.

The Commune has the obligation to affirm and determine the aspirations and wishes of the populace of Paris, to define the character of the movement of March 18th, misunderstood, unknown and slandered by the politicians seated at Versailles.

Once again, Paris works and suffers for all of France, for whom it prepares, through its combats and sacrifices, the intellectual, moral, administrative and economic regeneration, its glory and prosperity.

What does it ask for?

The recognition and consolidation of the Republic, the only form of government compatible with the rights of the people and the normal and free development of society.

The absolute autonomy of the Commune extended to all localities in France and assuring to each one its full rights, and to every Frenchman the full exercise of his faculties and abilities as man, citizen and producer.

The only limit to the autonomy of the Commune should be the equal right to autonomy for all communes adhering to the contract, whose association shall insure French unity.

The inherent rights of the Commune are:

The vote on communal budgets, receipts and expenses; the fixing and distribution of taxes; the direction of public services; the organisation of its magistracy, internal police and education; the administration of goods belonging to the Commune.

The choice by election or competition of magistrates and communal functionaries of all orders, as well as the permanent right of control and revocation.

The absolute guarantee of individual freedom and freedom of conscience.

The permanent intervention of citizens in communal affairs by the free manifestation of their ideas, the free defence of their interests, with guarantees given for these manifestations by the Commune, which alone is charged with overseeing and assuring the free and fair exercise of the right to assemble and publish.

The organisation of urban defence and the National Guard, which elects its chiefs and alone watches over the maintenance of order in the city.

Paris wants nothing else as a local guarantee, on condition, of course, of finding in the great central administration—the delegation of federated Communes—the realisation and the practice of the same principles.

But as an element of its autonomy, and profiting by its freedom of action, within its borders it reserves to itself the right to operate the administrative and economic reforms called for by the populace as it wills; to create the institutions needed to develop and spread instruction, production, exchange and credit; to universalise power and property in keeping with the needs of the moment, the wishes of those concerned and the facts furnished by experience.

Our enemies are fooling themselves or are fooling the country when they accuse Paris of wanting to impose its will or its supremacy over the rest of the nation and to pretend to a dictatorship, which would be a veritable attack on the independence and sovereignty of other communes.

They are fooling themselves or are fooling the country when they accuse Paris of pursuing the destruction of that French unity constituted by the Revolution to the acclaim of our fathers, who hastened to the *Fete de la Fédération* from all corners of the old France.

Unity, as it has been imposed on us until today by the Empire, the monarchy or parliamentarism is nothing but unintelligent, arbitrary or onerous centralisation.

Political unity, as Paris wants it, is the voluntary association of all local initiatives, the spontaneous and free concourse of all individual energies in view of a common goal: the well-being, the freedom and the security of all.

The communal revolution, begun by popular initiative on March 18, begins a new era of experimental, positive, scientific politics.

It is the end of the old governmental and clerical world, of militarism and bureaucracy, of exploitation, speculation, monopolies and privileges to which the proletariat owe their servitude and the Fatherland its misfortunes and disasters.

Let this beloved and great country—fooled by lies and calumnies—be reassured! The fight between Paris and Versailles is one of those that cannot

Appendix: The Paris Commune  791

be ended through illusory compromises. The end cannot be in doubt. Victory, pursued with an indomitable energy by the National Guard, will go to the idea and to right.

We call on France.

Apprised that Paris in arms possesses as much calm as bravery, that it supports order with as much energy as enthusiasm, that it sacrifices itself with as much reason as energy, that it only armed itself in devotion to the liberty and glory of all: let France cease this bloody conflict.

It is up to France to disarm Versailles through the solemn manifestation of its irresistible will.

Called upon to benefit by our conquests, let it declare itself in solidarity with our efforts. Let it be our ally in this combat that can only end in the triumph of the communal idea or the ruin of Paris.

As for us, citizens of Paris, our mission is the accomplishing of the modern Revolution, the largest and must fecund of all those which have illuminated history.

It is our obligation to fight and to win.

The Paris Commune
*Journal Officiel*
April 20th, 1871

# PROPOSAL ON THE PRODUCTION OF GOODS

By DECISION OF the Paris Commune:[1]

All the big workshops of the monopolists, their equipment, machinery, raw materials, agencies, premises, etc. are to be commandeered after an inventory has been made with an eye to compensation at a later date.

Said workshops are to be temporarily ceded to such workers' associations as may make application and the assets of the Commune are to be transferred to said workers' associations through the opening of a line of credit for those associations. The *Louvre Workshops* which churned out armaments were one instance of such requisitioning. The leaders of the workers' council, the workshop heads, team leaders, etc., were chosen by the workers of each section and could be stood down at any moment.

Pierre Vésinier
May, 4th 1871

---

1    This was proposed by a member of the International and Commune but never formally agreed or implemented; nonetheless, it gives an indication of what was aimed for. (Editor)

# GLOSSARY
## OF TERMS, PEOPLE, AND EVENTS

CERTAIN TERMS, PEOPLE AND EVENTS CONTINUALLY APPEAR IN PROUDHON'S work. Rather than footnote each occurrence, information on them is summarised here. As with many French writers he refers to revolutionary events by date (i.e., '89 for the start of the Great French Revolution and so on). He also refers to Year I, Year II, and so on, which are from the French Revolutionary calendar that began on September 22$^{nd}$, 1792, the date of the official abolition of the monarchy and the nobility.

# TERMS

**Agiotage:** This refers to stock exchange business, especially stock-jobbing (i.e., dealing in stocks and shares). It includes speculative dealing in stock exchange securities or foreign exchange. It can also mean any form of speculation on goods and prices.

**Agrarian Law:** Laws passed for the redistribution of property in land (*loi agraire*). It usually referred to the breaking up of estates into parcels of land owned and worked by individuals. In *Confessions d'un Révolutionnaire*, Proudhon cautions that land reform of this kind can easily become a mere populist tactic in the hands of politicians, a route to dictatorship rather than equality.

**Assignats:** Notes issued as paper currency in France (1789–96) by the revolutionary government and secured by confiscated lands. They were usually blamed for the hyperinflation during the revolutionary period as there was little control over how many were printed.

**Collective force:** This is Proudhon's term for the way in which individuals' combined action can produce something greater than their mere sum. This concept entails:

1.  a critique of wage labour. In *What Is Property?*, Proudhon points out that while the labour of one person would be incapable of single-handedly raising a granite obelisk even in two hundred days, two hundred labourers are able to raise it in a single day. As the employer pays nothing for this extra labour-power produced by collective activity and co-operation, workers are exploited by capital;

2.  a theory of "collective reason" for which the results of combined intellectual labour, no less than combined manual labour, can exceed the sum of the parts (anticipating certain theories of the social construction of knowledge—e.g., educator Paolo Freire's);

3.  a theory of political power as deriving from cooperative action or "social power" (reminiscent of Étienne de la Boétie's, and anticipating those of Hannah Arendt and Michel Foucault);

4.  a concept of "collective being" that radically distinguishes Proudhon's philosophy from any liberal or neoliberal conception (where a Margaret Thatcher could say that there is no such thing as society, only individuals, Proudhon contends that it is social relations that give individuals their reality, that freedom itself is a social relationship);

5.  an explanation of the paradoxical relationship between freedom and determinism (while every being is determined by the forces that converge to constitute it, the "resultant" of these forces cannot be simply predicted from their origin—it is what postpositivist philosophers of science term an "emergent" property of the ensemble); and finally,

6.  a theory of alienation or fetishism as the mistaking of effects for causes—e.g., taking money, which only has value by the force of collective agreement, for the source of value, or taking the leader, who only has power by the force of collective obedience, for the source of power.

**Commune:** A commune is the lowest level of administrative division in the French Republic. It can be a city of 2 million inhabitants (such as Paris); a town of 10,000; or just a 10–person hamlet. It appeared in the 12th century from Medieval Latin *communia*, which means a gathering of people sharing a common life (from Latin *communis*, things held in common).

**Commutative:** A *commutative* contract is one in which what is done, given or promised by one party is considered as equivalent to what is done, given or promised by the other. Proudhon rejects the "distributive" conception of justice (for which someone in authority—a judge, a boss, a sovereign, a God—decides what each person deserves) in favour of "commutative justice." See *synallagmatic*.

**Community:** Proudhon usually termed the various schemes of authoritarian socialism he opposed "community" (*la communauté*). He had in mind radicals like Henri de Saint-Simon, Charles Fourier, Robert Owen, Louis Blanc and Pierre Leroux who thought of socialism as being organised around highly regulated (and usually hierarchical) communities.

**Corporation:** This was the term used in France to describe the producer organisations of Medieval times. Like a Guild in Britain, these gathered together craftsmen of the same profession and regulated it locally and nationally. They were abolished during the French Revolution as the new regime proclaimed that no intermediate body could interpose itself between the citizen and the state (the same law was used to ban trade unions and journeymen associations). The term was used by socialists in 19th century France to describe organisations of worker-run co-operatives. Proudhon (particularly after 1848) usually used it in this sense, namely a federation of co-operatives in a given industry. It should not be confused with modern corporations (i.e., stock issuing companies) which Proudhon opposed as being basically identical to state-communist associations.

**Department:** A department (*département*) is a French administrative division roughly analogous to a Scottish region, a United States county or an English district. In other words, an intermediary organisation between the commune and region, a sub-region.

**Deputies:** Deputies (*députés*) are elected representatives, such as Members of Parliament, National Assembly or Senate.

**Doctrinaire:** The Doctrinaires were a small group of French Royalists who hoped to reconcile the Monarchy with the French Revolution during the Bourbon Restoration (1814–1830). As is often the case, their name was given to them in derision and by an enemy. Liberal royalists, they were in favour of a constitutional monarchy but with an extremely limited suffrage based on property restrictions. Such a system was implemented after the defeat of Napoleon Bonaparte, with the new King presiding over a Chamber of Peers and a Chamber of deputies elected by around 100,000 wealthy Frenchmen.

**Eclecticism:** The philosophy of "Eclecticism" espoused by Victor Cousin (1792–1867), which held that truth was to be found not in any one school of thought but "scattered here and there in all systems" (Cousin, in George Ripley, ed. and trans., *Philosophical Miscellanies* [Boston: Hilliard, Gray, and Co., 1838], 102), was a frequent target of Proudhon's criticism.

796 Pierre-Joseph Proudhon

**Force majeure:** *Force majeure* ("superior force") is a common clause in contracts which essentially frees both parties from liability or obligation when an extraordinary event or circumstance beyond their control occurs.

**Garnisaire:** *Garnisaires* (literally garrisons) were (sometimes *ad hoc*) soldiers billeted on households to force them to pay their dues to the state.

**Girondist:** The Girondists were a moderate republican political faction during the French Revolution, so called because the most prominent exponents of their point of view in the Legislative Assembly and the National Convention were deputies from the Gironde. Accused of federalism by the Jacobins and repressed during the Terror.

**Guaranteeism:** For Proudhon, *Garantisme* denoted a comprehensive system of social guarantees which conferring on citizens a series of economic rights and protections based on associations of joint interest and reciprocal guarantees. In short, the economy would be regulated by the producers and their organisations. The term originally referred to a system of association advocated by utopian socialist Charles Fourier which aimed to seek protection against socio-economic risk. In Fourier's scheme, Guaranteeism (or semi-association) was the sixth order of society, a transitional stage before eventually reaching *Harmony*, the final stage of human evolution.

**Hôtel de Ville:** Town Hall.

**Increase:** This is Benjamin Tucker's usual translation of *aubaine*, a French word without an exact equivalent in English, which can mean something like "a stroke of good fortune" (a "bargain," a "windfall"), but which Proudhon uses to designate all forms of unearned income, as he explains in *What Is Property?*: e.g., profit, interest, rent, usury. In short, this term stands for an entire theory of what Marx would call the appropriation of surplus value—that without which property itself could not exist.

**Jacobin:** During the Great French Revolution, a Jacobin was a member of the revolutionary Jacobin Club (1789–1794) and stood for a centralised national republic. Since then it refers to supporters of a centralised Republic, with power concentrated in the national government, at the expense of local or regional governments.

*Journal des Débats*: An influential conservative newspaper.

**Juste-milieu:** "the happy medium" or "middle way." Politically this meant establishing middle-class rule, striking a balance between tradition and revolution and creating a regime safe from the extremes of revolution and reaction. It was the official ideology of the July Monarchy, as expressed in Louis-Philippe's statement of January 1831: "We will attempt to remain in a *juste milieu* [happy medium], in an equal distance from the excesses of popular power and the abuses of royal power."

**The Luxembourg Commission:** Established by a decree of the provisional government of the Second Republic on February 28, 1848, this was an official commission of inquiry into the conditions of French workers in response to the radical upheavals of that year, convened at the Palais de Luxembourg and headed by Louis Blanc. Proudhon often referred to this as the "system of Luxembourg" or "Luxembourg system," opposing it as a form of centralised state socialism.

**Manifesto of Sixty:** This landmark publication of the French labour movement was published in *L'Opinion Nationale* on February 17th, 1864. It was written chiefly by Henri Tolain, a self-proclaimed follower of Proudhon. It called upon workers to bring about their own social liberation and to seek representation in the National Assembly by standing working class candidates in elections. Proudhon wrote *The Political Capacity of the Working Classes* to explore the implications of this work.

*Le Moniteur:* The official gazette of the French Government.

**The Mountain:** The radical Republicans of the Great French and 1848 Revolutions. The most radical part of the National Convention during the Great French Revolution who earned the nickname "the Mountain" (*la Montagne*) because its members occupied the highest rows of seats in the building. Members of this faction where often called "Montagnards."

*Le National:* *Le National* (1830–1851) was a prominent centrist republican journal associated with Thiers and Cavaignac.

**National Workshops:** A French government programme created by the February Revolution of 1848 which was based on Louis Blanc's scheme for state-funded and (initially) state-run producer co-operatives, as described in his book, *L'Organisation du Travail* (1839).

**Phalanstery:** A phalanstery (*phalanstère*) was a self-contained structure which housed a co-operative community. It was developed in the early 1800s by Charles Fourier and based on the idea of a phalanx, this self-contained community was to consist of 1,600 people living under one-roof and working together for mutual benefit. A member's quality of life would vary with their work, talent and amount invested ("capital"). Everyone would be expected to work while a spirit of competition would exist in the shape of emulation. The term comes from the Latin *phalang-* (phalanx) and French *-stère* (as in *monastère*, or monastery).

**Prefect:** A prefect (*préfet*) represents the national government at the local level, i.e., the state's representative in a department or region. Prefects are appointed by a decree of the government, serve at its discretion and can be replaced by it.

**Prefecture:** A prefect's office, department, or area of control is called a prefecture, in short the area over which a civil servant has authority.

***La Presse****: La Presse* was a conservative newspaper.

**The Prince:** A term used by Jean-Jacques Rousseau in *The Social Contract*. The Prince referred to the government, considered to be an intermediate body set up between the subjects and the Sovereign charged with the execution of the laws and the maintenance of liberty, both civil and political. While the members of this could be called magistrates or kings (i.e., the actual governors charged with enforcing the general will), the body as a whole was referred to by the term Prince.

**Raison d'État:** A French expression that can sometimes be translated as "the national interest" or "reasons of State." It refers to the reasons used to justify or rationalise acting in ways which override all other considerations of a legal or ethical kind. It was first used when Secretary of State Cardinal Richelieu justified France's intervention in the Thirty Years' War, despite its Catholicism, on the Protestant side in 1635 to block the increasing power of the Holy Roman Empire.

**Salariat:** A term Proudhon used frequently. It refers to a class of workers who are paid wages by employers (i.e., wage labour). This term was translated, at times, by Benjamin Tucker as "wages" and "wage-receiver" while John Beverly Robinson translated it as "the wage system." This should not, however, be confused with payment by labour (distribution by deed, not need), as subsequent anarchists like Peter Kropotkin used the term "wage system" to describe. A more accurate translation would be "wage labour" or "wage worker" (depending on the context) as the etymology of the word a combination of *sal*aire (salary, from Latin *salarium*) plus *-ariat* (as in *prolétariat*).

**The Sonderbund:** The Sonderbund (German for "separate alliance") was created in 1845 as a league of seven Conservative cantons in Switzerland after the Radical Party gained support in the majority of cantons and took measures against the Catholic Church. This provoked the Sonderbund civil war of 1847, after which the new constitution ended the almost-complete independence of the cantons and transformed Switzerland into a federal state.

**Synallagmatic:** A synallagmatic contract is a bilateral or reciprocal one in which both parties provide consideration and have mutual rights and obligations. Its name is derived from the Ancient Greek *synallagma,* meaning mutual agreement. In *On Justice,* Proudhon flatly states: "Justice is synallagmatic." See *commutative.*

**Third Estate:** In traditional French political parlance, the "Third Estate" refers to the bourgeoisie who had triumphed over the aristocracy (the "First Estate") and clergy (the "Second Estate") in the French Revolution.

**Tribune:** This was a title shared by 10 elected officials in the Roman Republic. Tribunes had the power to convene the Plebeian Council, to act as its president as well as summoning the Senate and laying proposals before it. In other words, it refers to someone who voices the demands of the people (which is why some modern politicians have been called "tribunes of the people").

**Unitarists/Unitary:** Unitarists (*unitaires*) was the term Proudhon used to describe those who were aiming to create a regime that was centralised, indivisible and constituted into a homogeneous unit (*unitaire*).

**Workers' Company:** Proudhon's preferred term for a worker-managed association (or co-operative). These associations would be collectively run by their members, with all positions democratically elected. This would, he argued, end the exploitation and oppression of capitalism.

# PEOPLE

**François-Noël BABEUF** (1760–1797) known as Gracchus Babeuf, was a French political agitator and journalist during the Great French Revolution. He was executed for his role in the *Conspiracy of the Equals.* This aimed an armed uprising of the masses against the bourgeois regime of the Directory to establish a revolutionary dictatorship as a transitional stage to "pure democracy" and "egalitarian communism."

**Claude Frédéric BASTIAT** (1801–1850) was a French classical liberal and political economist. One of the most prominent advocates of *laissez-faire* capitalism of Proudhon's time. His main works were *Economic Harmonies* and *Economic Sophisms.*

**Armand Sigismond Auguste BARBÈS** (1809–70) was a French revolutionary who formed a republican secret society, the *Société des Saisons*, with Louis-Auguste Blanqui in 1838. The failure of a *coup d'état* in 1839 led to an estrangement with Blanqui which had a deeply divisive effect on the extreme left during the revolution of 1848.

**Camille Hyacinthe Odilon BARROT** (1791–1873) was a French politician and Prime Minister of France between 20 December 1848 and 31 October 1849. He was dismissed when Louis Napoleon replaced his legislative advisers with a personal cabinet.

**Louis Jean Joseph Charles BLANC** (1811–1882) was a French politician, historian and reformist state socialist. Most famous for his work *L'Organisation du travail* ("The Organisation of Labour") which advocated state-funded and (initially) state-run producer co-operatives which would compete capitalism away and then abolish competition. In the Revolution of 1848 Louis Blanc became a member of the provisional government and it was on his motion that the government undertook "to guarantee the existence of the workers by work" and the national workshops. He was appointed to preside over the government labour commission (*Commission du Gouvernement pour les travailleurs*) established at the Palais de Luxembourg to inquire into and report on the labour question.

**Jérôme-Adolphe BLANQUI** (1798–1854), brother of Louis Auguste Blanqui, was a leading French economist and disciple of Jean-Baptiste Say. Though he advocated government action for the protection of the working class, he remained a liberal in the tradition of Adam Smith and Say. He was appointed to review Proudhon's first memoir on property that had been submitted to the Academy of Besançon. Though it opposed Proudhon's views, the review shielded him from prosecution and Proudhon responded to it in his second memoir on property.

**Louis Auguste BLANQUI** (1805–1881) was a noted French socialist revolutionary. He organised numerous conspiracies to overthrow the regime and thought that the revolution had to be carried out by a small group. This would establish a temporary dictatorship which would create the new social order after which power would be handed to the people. Blanqui's uncompromising politics and regular insurrections ensured that he spent half his life in prison.

**Louis-Napoléon BONAPARTE** (1808–1873) was the first President of the French Republic and the last monarch of France. Nephew of Napoleon Bonaparte, he was elected President of the Second Republic in December 1848. He organised a coup on 2nd December 1851 and disbanded the National

Assembly. This was overwhelming approved in a plebiscite and exactly one year later another plebiscite confirmed the creation of the Second Empire and his ascension to the throne as Napoleon III. He ruled as Emperor of the French until September 1870, when he was captured in the Franco-Prussian War.

**Étienne CABET** (1788–1856) was a French philosopher and utopian socialist, founder of the Icarian movement. Influenced by Robert Owen, in 1840 he wrote the *Travels in Icaria* which depicted a utopia in which an elected government controlled all economic activity and supervised social affairs (Icaria is the name of this fictional utopian country). He led a group of emigrants to found such a society in the United States.

**Louis-Eugène CAVAIGNAC** (1802–57) was a French general who was given full powers by the National Assembly to crush the June Days revolt provoked by the closing of the National Workshops. This made him France's de facto head of state and dictator. After crushing the rebel workers, killing some 1,500 of them, he laid down his dictatorial powers but continued to preside over the Executive Committee until the election of a regular president of the republic. He was expected to win the Presidential election of 10th December 1848, but lost massively to Louis-Napoleon.

**Michel CHEVALIER** (1806–1879), Professor of Political Economy at the Collège de France, was initially a Saint-Simonian, but later became an enthusiast of free trade and a frequent contributor to the conservative *Journal des Débats*.

**Victor Prosper CONSIDÉRANT** (1808–1893) was a French utopian Socialist and disciple of Fourier. He edited the journals *Le Phalanstère, La Phalange,* and *La Démocratie Pacifique*. He defined the notion of the "right to work" which was so important to French socialists in the 1848 Revolutions.

**Pierre-Charles-François DUPIN** (1784–1873) was a French mathematician and economist who gradually turned to politics. Charles X gave him the title of baron in 1824 but he sided with the Liberals and took his seat in the Left of the Chamber. Under the July Monarchy, he sat with the Centre before siding with the Right in the Second Republic. He rallied to the Second Empire and was appointed senator by Napoleon III.

**Frédéric-Alfred-Pierre, comte de FALLOUX** (1811–86) was a French politician and author, famous for having given his name to two laws on education which favoured private Catholic teaching. The *Loi Falloux* (15 March 1850) organised primary and secondary education and it provided that the clergy and members of ecclesiastical orders could be teachers without the need for qualifications. Primary schools were put under the management of the priests (*curés*).

**Léonard Joseph Léon FAUCHER** (1803–54) was a French politician and economist. He helped to organise the Bordeaux association for free-trade propaganda. After the revolution of 1848 he entered the Constituent Assembly where he opposed many social reforms (the limiting the hours of work, the creation of the national relief works in Paris, the abolition of the death penalty, amongst others). Under the presidency of Louis Napoleon he became minister of public works, and then minister of the interior. He was compelled to resign office in May 1849 but by 1851 he was again minister of the interior, until Napoleon declared his intention of restoring universal suffrage.

**François Marie Charles FOURIER** (1772–1837) was one of the leading Utopian socialists of the early nineteenth century. He advocated highly regulated co-operative communities called *Phalanstères* (his descriptions of these included detailed timetables which included the times members would rise and go to bed). Unusually for his time, he was an advocate of women's equality. Proudhon admitted to being captivated by his ideas for a short period before writing *What is Property?*

**Antoine Eugene de GENOUDE** (1792–1849) was a French priest and publicist. His political program was based on combining hereditary Royalty with universal suffrage.

**Émile de GIRARDIN** (1802–81) was a journalist, publicist and politician. He was editor of the conservative newspaper *La Presse* in 1848 and sometimes showed progressive attitudes (he generally supported the radical Jacobins in the National Assembly). At first he supported the Second Republic, but after the rising of June 1848 he declared his support for Louis Napoleon as President, only to become one of his most violent opponents.

**François Pierre Guillaume GUIZOT** (1787–1874) was a dominant figure in French politics prior to the Revolution of 1848. He was one of the leaders of the liberal opposition to the government of Charles X. After 1830, he took service with the "citizen king" Louis-Philippe, eventually becoming Prime Minister in 1847. He opposed expansion of the franchise, unswervingly restricting suffrage to a mere 200,000 wealthy men. His banning of political meetings in January 1848 was the catalyst for the February Revolution which saw the establishment of the Second Republic. He is known for saying "Not to be a republican at twenty is proof of want of heart; to be one at thirty is proof of want of head'" and considered that "The spirit of revolution, the spirit of insurrection, is a spirit radically opposed to liberty."

**King JOHN** (1166–1216) was King of England and reigned from 1199 to 1216. He gained the epithet "Lack-land" (*Sans-Terre*) because, as his father's youngest son, he did not inherit land out of his family's holdings, and because, as King, he lost significant territory to the King of France. He acquiesced under pressure from the barons to the Magna Carta which limited the power of the Monarch.

**Alphonse Marie Louis de Prat de LAMARTINE** (1790–1869) was a French writer, poet and politician. He was briefly in charge of government during the February Revolution of 1848 and was Minister of Foreign Affairs until 11 May. He was then a member of the Executive Commission, the political body which served as France's joint Head of State. He worked to abolish slavery and the death penalty and supported the right to work and the National Workshops. He was an unsuccessful Presidential candidate in the 10 December 1848 elections, subsequently retiring from politics.

**John LAW** (1671–1729) was a Scottish economist who believed that money was only a means of exchange that did not constitute wealth in itself and that national wealth depended on trade. He originally sought to create a land bank that would issue notes to borrowers against the security provided by land. While in exile in France, he meet the Regant Phillippe, Duc D'Orléans and was provided with a royal edict in 1716 to establish a bank in France; this became a publicly chartered company, the Banque Royale. It collapsed in 1720 after speculating on swamp land in Louisiana, bringing the French economy down with it.

**Alexandre Auguste LEDRU-ROLLIN** (1807–74) was a French Republican politician who was minister of the interior in the Provisional Government of 1848. During the crisis of May 15 he sided with the party of order against the working class, although he stood as a socialist candidate during that year's Presidential election. He opposed President Louis Napoleon and went into exile in London.

**Pierre LEROUX** (1797–1871) was a French philosopher and follower of Saint-Simon who, in an 1834 essay entitled "Individualism and Socialism," introduced the term "socialism" into French political discourse. The son of an artisan, he helped found *Le Globe*, the official organ of the Saint-Simonian community of which he was a prominent member. After the outbreak of the revolution of 1848 he was elected to the Constituent Assembly, and in 1849 to the Legislative Assembly.

**LOUIS-PHILIPPE I** (1773–1850) became King of the French after the July Revolution of 1830. The elected Chamber of Deputies proclaimed Louis-Philippe as the new French king, displacing the senior branch of the

House of Bourbon. He ruled until 1848 in what was known as the July Monarchy. He was termed the Citizen King and was overthrown by the February Revolution.

**Thomas Robert MALTHUS** (1766–1834) was a Reverend who wrote on political economy. He is best known for *An Essay on the Principle of Population* which blamed poverty on overpopulation rather than an unjust social system. Much hated in working class circles as his arguments were invoked against social change and even moderate welfare reforms.

**Charles-Louis de Secondat, baron de La Brède et de MONTESQUIEU** (1689–1755) was a French political thinker of the Era of the Enlightenment. He is famous for his articulation of the theory of separation of powers within a state. He also argued for a *"confederate republic"* to ensure the ideal scale of government required for political liberty (i.e., security against abuse of power).

**Robert OWEN** (1771–1858) was a Welsh utopian socialist who was originally a successful businessman and philanthropist. In his textile factory in New Lanark, Scotland, he used his profits to improve the lives of his employees by introducing shorter working hours, schools for children and renovated housing. From that, he became one of the founders of socialism and the co-operative movement. He aimed to abolish capitalism by means of model communities and set one up called New Harmony in Indiana, USA.

**Jean-Jacques ROUSSEAU** (1712–78) was an extremely influential social theorist whose ideas on democracy predominated in radical circles before, during and after the Great French Revolution of 1789. Key works are *The Social Contract* and *Discourse on the Origin and Basis of Inequality Among Men*. The influence of Rousseau can be seen in Proudhon's work, both from the terminology used and by the fact that he returned to criticise Rousseau time and time again.

**Claude Henri de Rouvroy, comte de SAINT-SIMON** (1760–1825), usually referred to as Henri de Saint-Simon, was one of the leading Utopian socialists of the early nineteenth century. He advocated a form of state capitalism, wherein industrial chiefs would control society as the men who are fitted to organise society for productive labour are entitled to rule it. Class conflict is not present in his work.

**Jean-Baptiste SAY** (1767–1832) was a businessman and the leading French *laissez-faire* economist of his time. He expounded classical liberal views in favour of free competition and free trade and in 1831 he was made professor of political economy at the College de France. He originated Say's law, which is often quoted as "supply creates its own demand."

**Charles Maurice de TALLEYRAND-PÉRIGORD** (1754–1838) was a French diplomat who worked with the regime of Louis XVI, through the French Revolution and then under Napoleon I, Louis XVIII, Charles X, and Louis-Philippe. During the French Revolution, Talleyrand supported the revolutionary cause, then he was instrumental in the 1799 *coup d'état* of 18 Brumaire, and soon after he was made Foreign Minister by Napoleon. After Napoleon, he was one of the key agents of the restoration of the House of Bourbon. After 1830, he became ambassador to Britain where he strove to reinforce the legitimacy of Louis-Philippe's regime. Said of himself: "Regimes may fall and fail, but I do not."

**Louis-Adolphe THIERS** (1797–1877) was a French politician. In his early days, he was well known in Liberal society and was one of the animators of the 1830 revolution. One of the Radical supporters of Louis-Philippe, he become his prime minister. Elected in 1848 to the Constituent Assembly, Thiers was a leader of the right-wing liberals and bitterly opposed the socialists. He suppressed the Paris Commune of 1871.

# EVENTS

**14ᵗʰ July 1789:** The day when the Bastille, a medieval fortress and prison in Paris, was stormed. It represented royal authority in the centre of Paris and its fall was the turning point of the French Revolution. It subsequently became an icon of the French Republic and is a public holiday in France. It is usually called Bastille Day in English.

**10ᵗʰ August 1792:** When tens of thousands besieged the Tuileries palace in Paris. This insurrection, which had the backing of the insurrectionary Paris Commune and its sections, forced the royal family to shelter with the Legislative Assembly. It was the effective end of the French Monarchy. Its formal end came six weeks later, as one of the first acts of business of the new Convention.

**The Eighteenth of Brumaire:** Date of the Napoleonic *coup d'état* of 9ᵗʰ November 1799. According to the revolutionary French Republican calendar this date was 18 Brumaire, Year VIII of the Republic.

**July Revolution:** In 1830 Charles X's attempt to enforce repressive ordinances touched off a mass rebellion (July 27–30). It marked the shift from one constitutional monarchy, the Bourbon Restoration, to another, the July Monarchy with the ascent of Charles' cousin Louis-Philippe, the Duc d'Orléan, on August 9ᵗʰ. It involved a limited substitution of the principle of popular sovereignty for hereditary right. Supporters of the Bourbon line were called "Legitimists," and supporters of Louis-Philippe "Orleanists."

**February Revolution:** The monarchy collapsed on the 24$^{th}$ February 1848 leading to the creation of the Provisional Government in Paris which included state socialist Louis Blanc and worker Albert (the *nom de guerre* of Alexandre Martin). It immediately issued decrees guaranteeing the means of subsistence of the worker by labour, labour for all citizens, the right of association, and the creation of national workshops. The 25$^{th}$ saw groups of workers return to the *Hôtel de Ville* carrying the red flag. An attempt to make this the flag of the new republic failed. Also referred to by Proudhon as 24$^{th}$ February.

**17$^{th}$ March 1848:** Date of a republican march of 150–200,000 calling for the withdrawal of the remaining regular troops from Paris and postponement of the planned elections for the National Guard and Constituent Assembly to allow more time for campaigning. While some radical republicans may have been planning to use this march as the base for an insurrection to purge the Provisional Government of conservatives, nothing came of it. It did gain some concessions from the government as well as frightening the bourgeoisie into seeking action against the working class threat.

**16$^{th}$ April 1848:** Date of a workers march from the Champ de Mars to the *Hôtel de Ville* in Paris which, it was claimed by reactionaries, was planning to seize the town hall and proclaim a communist government. It was met by the mobilisation of 50,000 National Guards.

**15$^{th}$ May 1848:** Date of workers march of between 10 and 20 thousand demanding intervention in Poland and the creation of a Ministry of Labour and Progress. When a delegation of 25 demonstrators was allowed in to petition the Constituent Assembly, thousands flooded into the galleries and the assembly hall. A call was then raised to take the *Hôtel de Ville*. This 'insurrection' was used by the government as the pretext it needed to curtail working class activities, freedoms and organisations.

**23$^{rd}$ June 1848:** Date of French workers' revolt after the closure of the National Workshops created by the Second Republic to give work to the unemployed. The revolt was crushed by the 26$^{th}$ June by General Louis Eugène Cavaignac, with 1,500 killed and 15,000 political prisoners subsequently deported to Algeria. Cavaignac was then named head of the executive power. This marked the end of the hopes of a "Democratic and Social Republic" and the victory of the bourgeoisie over the working class.

**10$^{th}$ December 1848:** Date of the first, and last, Presidential election of the Second Republic. The 1848 election saw the surprise victory of

Louis-Napoléon Bonaparte with 74% of the vote (Louis-Eugène Cavaignac was considered certain to win). His victory was due to the votes of the rural population.

**29th January 1849:** The election of Louis- Napoléon as President was seen as a victory for conservative principles and the make up of his first government reinforced this. Republican officials were purged at all levels and a campaign against the National Assembly was conducted. This climaxed on the 29th of January, 1848, when the assembly voted for its own dissolution and so a new general election.

**13th May 1849:** The date of the elections held after the dissolution of the National Assembly. The Conservatives used the campaign to stress a message that the social order was established by God as wealth was the reward for ability and hard work. The left got nearly 35% of the votes cast, with the Assembly having around 75 moderate Republicans, 500 Conservatives and 180 radical republicans and socialists.

**13th June 1849:** After the President of the Republic, Louis-Napoléon, sent troops to overthrow the Roman Republic of 1849, the remaining Republicans tried to impeach him and his ministers. The Conservative Majority rejected this defence of its own constitutional power and the left-Republicans stormed out. They called a peaceful demonstration on June 13th to protest the Roman expedition but it was dispersed by troops. Some resistance was organised by the more resolute parts of the Mountain at the *Conservatoire des Arts et Métiers* but this failed to gain support. The government used this to declare a state of siege, ban the clubs and further shackle the press. The jails were filled with radical Republicans and socialists.

**31st May 1850:** When the complementary elections to the National Assembly in March and April 1850 resulted in an unexpected victory for the left, the alarmed conservative majority passed an electoral law to restrict universal male suffrage. To register to vote, proof of three years' domicile from the record of direct taxes for the canton or commune had to be provided. This disenfranchised around three million working class men (for example, 62% of the electorate in Paris and 51% in the Nord).

**24th November 1851:** The date when the National Assembly approved the direct election of the President (rather than election by the assembly). This followed on from Louis- Napoléon's year long campaign to change the Constitution so he could stand for re-election for President. When the vote on 17th November failed to achieve the required two-thirds majority, his plans for a *coup d'état* were finalised.

**2ⁿᵈ December 1851:** The date of *coup d'état* staged by Louis-Napoléon Bonaparte. He dissolved the Chamber which he claimed was taking the power he held by virtue of being the directly elected President, re-established universal suffrage, had all the party leaders arrested, and summoned a new assembly to prolong his term of office for ten years. The limited resistance was crushed by a state of siege. A plebiscite on December 20th overwhelmingly ratified the *coup d'état* while another, a year later, similarly ratified the creation of the Second Empire. The plebiscites confirming Louis-Napoléon in power disillusioned Proudhon considerably and his faith in the people fell to its lowest level. This is reflected in his subsequent concerns that a centralised democracy made the people susceptible to supporting demagogues like Louis-Napoléon.

# INDEX

744–753, 745. *See also* workers' co-operatives
and monopoly, 213–215
as mythic obligation, 556
communist, 753
mutualist, 751–753
of commercial interests, 202,
220–221, 244
the Association, 287–288
*aubaine*, 122, 161, 291, 796. *See
also droit d'aubaine*
Austria, 329, 331
authoritarian regime, 692
authority, 88, 205, 223–225, 278,
282–283, 396–397, 428, 429,
446, 482, 589, 597–598,
689–690, 692–694, 703–704.
*See also* power
balanced with liberty, 700
identity with property, 505–506
necessarily entangled with liberty,
690
*autogestion ouvrière*, 3
Avrich, Paul, 40

# B

Babeuf, François-Noël, 131, 147, 299,
554, 799
Bacon, Francis, 623
Bakunin, Michael, 1, 2, 23, 34,
38–39, 40, 41, 42, 43–44,
46–47, 49, 50–51, 54
balance of power (European), 677
Bank of Exchange, 17, 55, 285,
287–290, 290, 292, 296
Bank of France, 285, 340, 341, 393,
514, 525–528, 536–538, 657
Bank of the People, 13, 16, 17, 57,
383–392, 388–389, 389–393,
460, 527, 606
Council of Oversight, 386–387
General Assembly, 387–388
General Syndicate of Production
and Consumption, 385
Barbès, Armand Sigismond Auguste,
409, 411, 456, 800
Barrot, Camille Hyacinthe Odilon,
205, 404, 426, 449, 454, 455,
458, 460, 461, 462, 800
Bastiat, Claude Frédéric, 14, 58, 68,
69, 504, 509–511, 515, 799
Bastide, Jules, 423

Bauchart, Quentin, 423
beauty, 643
*bénéfice d'escompte*, 291
de Béranger, Pierre Jean, 273
Berry, David, 20
bigotry, 35–36
bill of exchange, 284–286. *See
also* money, paper
binding mandate [*mandat impératif*], 41. *See also* imperative
mandate
Bineau, Jean-Martial, 418, 419, 420
Blanc, Louis Jean Joseph Charles, 6,
13, 17, 18, 20–22, 27, 58,
146, 147, 204–206, 215–217,
295–297, 299, 301, 303, 304,
307, 312, 396, 398, 399, 402,
411, 430, 449, 456, 471, 480,
481–482, 482, 484, 486–487,
490–491, 499, 554, 555,
556–557, 581, 795, 797, 800
Blanqui, Jérôme-Adolphe, 34, 54,
72, 126, 139–157, 162, 194,
198, 254, 409, 411, 445, 456,
548, 800
Blanqui, Louis Auguste, 800
de la Boëtie, Étienne, 794
de Bonald, Louis Gabriel Ambroise,
203, 753–754, 757
Bonaparte, Louis-Napoléon, 368–369,
424, 449, 451, 454, 456–457,
457, 458–459, 461, 462, 473,
484, 572, 662, 663, 716, 770,
800, 808
Bonaparte, Napoléon, 57, 58, 88,
244, 259, 309, 310, 398, 406,
663, 716, 767, 805
Bonaparte, Napoléon (emperor's
nephew), 369
Bonaparte, Pierre-Napoléon, 369
Bonifacius VIII, 429
Bonjean, Louis Bernard, 422
bookselling, 745–746
bourgeoisie, 274–275, 503, 610–611,
617–618, 681–682, 715, 718,
719, 727, 749, 782
Boyer, Adolphe, 204
Brissot, Jacques-Pierre, 776
British Labour Party, 22
Buchanan, David, 120–121
Bugeaud, Thomas Robert, 369
Buret, Eugene, 548–549

Dunoyer, M., 186–187, 199–201,
203, 243–244, 504
Dupin, Pierre-Charles-François, 416,
801
Duprat, Pascal, 422

# E

eclecticism, 136, 142, 438, 472, 634,
767, 795
economic forces, 546, 744–745
economics
as discipline. *See* political economy
relation to politics, 660
*Edinburgh Review*, 188
education, 378, 445–446, 593–594,
702, 712, 759
free, 435
Edwards, Stewart, 62
Ehrenberg, John, 10, 17, 55, 57, 80
Eighteenth of Brumaire, 226
election of positions, 441–443
electoral politics, 370–372, 380,
425–426, 474, 573, 724–725
Ellerman, David, 32, 33
eminent domain, 581
emphyteusis, 532
empire, 716
Engels, Friedrich, 3, 9, 10, 18–19, 32,
40, 43, 67, 165–166
entertainment
free/state sponsored, 311
equality, 89, 92, 94, 117, 119, 127,
128–129, 136, 138, 140, 148,
164, 236, 348, 557, 580
commerce as a cause of, 140
of income, 512–513
equilibrium, 139, 180, 191, 203, 217,
232, 237, 428, 431, 464, 512,
513, 531, 546, 553, 598, 729,
779
Ewerbeck, Hermann, 165–166
exchange, 290–292, 729
contractual nature of, 563
exchange value, 175–176, 530, 538
exploitation, 8–10, 66–68, 73, 76–77,
117, 132, 211–212, 253–254,
373, 375, 378, 389, 400, 430,
445, 448, 476, 488, 496,
503–504, 506, 524, 534–535,
586, 596, 610, 677, 711. *See
also* surplus value

# F

Falloux, Frédéric-Alfred-Pierre, comte
de, 417, 419, 449, 454, 458,
460, 801
family, 203, 379, 661–662
farm-rent. *See* ground-rent, rent
Faucher, Léonard Joseph Léon,
210–211, 356, 398, 449, 454,
457–458, 460, 461, 461–462,
466–467, 802
Faure, Sébastien, 1
federalism, 37, 40, 43, 47, 677–678.
*See also* federation
federation, 5, 28–30, 686, 694–698,
701, 707, 708, 709, 716–720,
754–756, 761, 765, 788
agricultural-industrial, 711–714
and separation, 704
composition and decomposition of,
756–757
economic, 709
futility of insurrection, 717
feminism, 45, 48, 496
feudalism
industrial, 609–610
von Feuerbach, Ludwig Andreas,
165–166
Fichte, Johann Gottlieb, 627, 639,
646
First International. *See* International
Workingmen's Association
Flocon, Ferdinand, 312, 419, 426
force, 128, 140, 164, 227, 253, 524,
579, 670. *See also* violence
force majeure, 241, 340, 796
foreign policy, 677
French, 329–333
foreign trade, 377, 521–522, 718
customs, 444–445
postrevolutionary, 588
Foucault, Michel, 794
Fourier, François Marie Charles, 20,
53–54 118, 152, 154, 155,
161, 217, 264, 268, 290, 399,
554, 581, 737, 750, 795, 796,
797, 802
de Franc, Meynard, 459
Franco-Prussian war, 65
fraternity, 301, 580
free credit, 4–5, 348, 389, 500, 514,
516, 520–521, 526, 527,
534–535, 537, 540–541, 606

## Support AK Press!

AK Press is one of the world's largest and most productive anarchist publishing houses. We're entirely worker-run and

democratically managed. We operate without a corporate structure—no boss, no managers, no bullshit. We publish close to twenty books every year, and distribute thousands of other titles published by other like-minded independent presses from around the globe.

The Friends of AK program is a way that you can directly contribute to the continued existence of AK Press, and ensure that we're able to keep publishing great books just like this one! Friends pay a minimum of $25 per month, for a minimum three month period, into our publishing account. In return, Friends automatically receive (for the duration of their membership), as they appear, one free copy of every new AK Press title. They're also entitled to a 20% discount on everything featured in the AK Press Distribution catalog and on the website, on any and every order. You or your organization can even sponsor an entire book if you should so choose!

There's great stuff in the works—so sign up now to become a Friend of AK Press, and let the presses roll!

Won't you be our friend? Email friendsofak@akpress.org for more info, or visit the Friends of AK Press website: http://www.akpress.org/programs/friendsofak